WITHDRAWN

SECOND EDITION

FORENSIC MENTAL HEALTH ASSESSMENT

A Casebook

EDITED BY

KIRK HEILBRUN, DAVID DeMATTEO,
STEPHANIE BROOKS HOLLIDAY,
AND CASEY LaDUKE

OXFORD
UNIVERSITY PRESS

OXFORD
UNIVERSITY PRESS

Oxford University Press is a department of the University of
Oxford. It furthers the University's objective of excellence in research,
scholarship, and education by publishing worldwide.

Oxford   New York
Auckland   Cape Town   Dar es Salaam   Hong Kong   Karachi
Kuala Lumpur   Madrid   Melbourne   Mexico City   Nairobi
New Delhi   Shanghai   Taipei   Toronto

With offices in
Argentina   Austria   Brazil   Chile   Czech Republic   France   Greece
Guatemala   Hungary   Italy   Japan   Poland   Portugal   Singapore
South Korea   Switzerland   Thailand   Turkey   Ukraine   Vietnam

Oxford is a registered trademark of Oxford University Press
in the UK and certain other countries.

Published in the United States of America by
Oxford University Press
198 Madison Avenue, New York, NY 10016

Library of Congress Cataloging-in-Publication Data
Forensic mental health assessment : a casebook. — Second edition / edited by Kirk Heilbrun,
David DeMatteo, Stephanie Brooks Holliday, and Casey LaDuke.
pages cm
Includes bibliographical references and index.
ISBN 978-0-19-994155-1
1. Forensic psychology—Case studies.   2. Mentally ill offenders—Case studies.
3. Forensic psychiatry—Case studies.   I. Heilbrun, Kirk, editor of compilation.   II. DeMatteo, David, 1972–
editor of compilation.   III. Holliday, Stephanie Brooks, editor of compilation.
IV. LaDuke, Casey, editor of compilation.
RA1148.F553 2014
614'.15—dc23
2014001777

1 3 5 7 9 8 6 4 2
Printed in the United States of America
on acid-free paper

The views expressed in this book are those of the authors and do not reflect the official policy or position
of the Department of Veterans Affairs or the US Government.

To Don Bersoff—colleague, mentor, and friend—a giant in American law-psychology
Kirk Heilbrun, David DeMatteo

To my family, Linda, Justin, Lauren, and Jimmy; and husband, Mike, for all
their support
Stephanie Brooks Holliday

To LWC, who is remembered every day
Casey LaDuke

CONTENTS

PREFACE

The second edition of any book is always a balancing act. We wanted to make sure that the field and the literature had advanced sufficiently from the 2002 original to justify a revision. On the other hand, we did not want to wait so long that the original framework and content were no longer relevant. When our Oxford editor, Sarah Harrington, raised the possibility of a second edition about two years ago, it seemed like time to consider it. The original set of forensic mental health assessment (FMHA) principles had been expanded but was still largely intact. There had been significant advances in some areas (e.g., risk and threat assessment; appraisal of response style), although relatively little change in others (e.g., evaluation of mental state at the time of the offense). The empirical literature in many relevant areas was robust, featuring important changes that included additional specialized measures developed to strengthen these evaluations. Updates in ethical guidelines and practice standards were available, and Oxford had published a 19-volume series, "Best Practices in Forensic Mental Health Assessment," premised on the idea that best practices could now be identified. So the time seemed right.

There are a number of individuals who deserve particular thanks for their contributions to this second edition. We are very grateful to every professional who agreed to provide a report (sometimes two) in their respective areas of specialization. (In lieu of a report, Stan Brodsky provided commentary on an existing report that is sure to be of interest to those considering how such a report has implications for expert testimony.) Some also contributed a "teaching point"—a short answer to a very specific question involving the principle, the report, or some issue associated with either. Thanks to all of you for your excellent forensic case reports, which we hope will serve for the field as a model of how such reports should be written. Thanks as well for your timeliness, your dedication, and for the example you set for the entire field.

Our Oxford University Press editor Sarah Harrington has been a genuine pleasure to work with on this and other projects. Andrea Zekus, assistant editor at Oxford, did an outstanding job in the latter stages of this project as well. Randy Otto's suggestion about allowing contributors to interject comments on their work resulted in an interesting additional feature for some of these reports. We are very appreciative to each of you.

Kirk is grateful to his wife, Patty Griffin, and daughter, Anna Heilbrun and her fiancé, Christopher Catizone, for their love and support—as well as to his and Patty's large, extended families for all that they do. Dave thanks his wife, Christina, for her support and patience, his children, Emma and Jake, for providing much-needed perspective, and his parents, Nicky and Julie, for their continuing support. Stephanie would like to sincerely thank her parents, Justin and Linda, as well as her sister, Lauren, and brother, Jimmy, for their unconditional support and confidence in her. She is also extremely grateful for the unwavering encouragement of her husband, Mike. Casey thanks his parents, David and Laurie, and his sister, Lauren, for their sacrifices and support. He also thanks his grandparents, Lauren and Ann

Choate, whose consideration and care are the examples to which he aspires. Both Stephanie and Casey are also grateful to Kirk and Dave for their support and guidance.

Kirk Heilbrun
Dave DeMatteo
Casey LaDuke
Philadelphia, PA

Stephanie Brooks Holliday
Washington, D.C.

August, 2013

ABOUT THE EDITORS

Kirk Heilbrun, PhD, is a professor in the Department of Psychology, Drexel University, and co-director of the Pennsylvania Mental Health and Justice Center of Excellence. He received his doctorate in clinical psychology in 1980 from the University of Texas at Austin, and completed postdoctoral fellowship training from 1981–1982 in psychology and criminal justice at Florida State University. His current research focuses on juvenile and adult offenders, legal decision-making, forensic evaluation associated with such decision-making, and diversion. He is the author of a number of articles on forensic assessment, violence risk assessment and risk communication, and the treatment of mentally disordered offenders, and has published eight books in this area. His practice interests also center around forensic assessment, and he directs a clinic within the Drexel Department of Psychology in this area. He is board-certified in clinical psychology and in forensic psychology by the American Board of Professional Psychology, and has previously served as president of both the American Psychology-Law Society/APA Division 41, and the American Board of Forensic Psychology. He received the 2004 Distinguished Contributions to Forensic Psychology award and the 2008 Beth Clark Distinguished Service Contribution Award from the American Academy of Forensic Psychology.

David DeMatteo, JD, PhD, is an associate professor of psychology and law at Drexel University, where he is director of the JD/PhD program in law and psychology. He received his JD in 2001 from Villanova Law School and his PhD in clinical psychology in 2002 from MCP Hahnemann University. His research interests include psychopathy, forensic mental health assessment, drug policy, and diversion, and he has published numerous articles and book chapters and several books in these and related areas. His research has been funded by several state and national agencies. He is licensed as a psychologist in Pennsylvania, where he provides forensic assessment and consultation services. He was chair of the American Psychological Association's Committee on Legal Issues in 2011, and he is a Fellow of the American Psychological Association.

Stephanie Brooks Holliday, PhD, is currently a postdoctoral fellow with the War Related Illness and Injury Study Center (WRIISC) at the Washington, D.C., VA Medical Center. She completed her predoctoral internship at the Washington, D.C., VA Medical Center, and received her doctorate in clinical psychology in 2013 from Drexel University. Her current research interests are focused on adult offenders, risk assessment, interventions for risk reduction, justice-involved veterans, and neuropsychological functioning in veteran populations. Her practice interests are focused on forensic assessment and neuropsychological assessment. In addition to membership in the American Psychology-Law Society/APA Division 41 and the Criminal Justice Section of APA Division 18 (Psychologists in Public Service), she has served as a member-at-large for the Graduate Student Committee of the Society for the Psychological Study of Social Issues (SPSSI).

Casey LaDuke, MS, is currently a doctoral candidate in the Department of Psychology at Drexel University, with concentrations in forensic psychology and clinical neuropsychology. He received his BA in psychology from the University of Rochester in 2009, and completed his MS in psychology at Drexel University in 2011. His current interests include forensic mental health assessment (particularly violence risk assessment), psychopathy, the diversion of individuals with serious mental illness from the justice system, and the application of clinical neuropsychology in the forensic context. While at Drexel he has worked with the Philadelphia Department of Behavioral Health and the Pennsylvania Mental Health and Justice Center of Excellence, and has completed clinical practica within neuropsychological, forensic, and correctional settings. He is an elected member of the student section committee of the American Psychology-Law Society (APA Div. 41), where he will be serving as chair-elect (2013–2014) and chair (2014–2015).

CONTRIBUTORS

Chad Brinkley, PhD, ABPP, is a clinical psychologist at the United States Medical Center for Federal Prisoners in Springfield, Missouri. He provides inpatient treatment for inmates with severe mental illness and civil commitment cases. He is board-certified in forensic psychology and does a variety of forensic work, including risk assessments, competency evaluations, mental state at the time of the offense evaluations, and competency restoration treatment.

Stanley L. Brodsky, PhD, is a professor in the Department of Psychology at the University of Alabama. He coordinate the psychology-law PhD concentration in clinical psychology and he directs the Witness Research Lab at the university. His areas of specialization are expert witness testimony, forensic assessment, and psychotherapy with involuntary clients.

Ashley Kirk Burgett, PhD, is currently a staff psychologist at the Federal Medical Center in Lexington, Kentucky. Her interests include the evaluation and treatment of the mentally ill in a psycholegal context.

Mary Alice Conroy, PhD, is a professor and director of clinical training for the Clinical Psychology Doctoral Program at Sam Houston State University. She is a diplomate in forensic psychology, past president of the American Academy of Forensic Psychology, and maintains an active practice conducting both adult and juvenile evaluations for the criminal courts.

Dewey G. Cornell, PhD, is a forensic clinical psychologist who holds the Bunker Chair in the Curry School of Education at the University of Virginia. His work is concerned with school climate and safety, youth violence prevention, and threat assessment.

Mark D. Cunningham, PhD, ABPP, is a board-certified clinical and forensic psychologist whose practice in capital sentencing is national in scope. His professional contributions and scholarship have been recognized with the 2012 National Register of Health Service Psychologists A. M. Wellner, PhD Distinguished Career Award and the 2006 American Psychological Association Award for Distinguished Contributions to Research in Public Policy.

Eric Y. Drogin, JD, PhD, ABPP, is a forensic psychologist and attorney currently serving on the faculty of the Harvard Medical School, in the Program in Psychiatry and Law, and with the Forensic Psychiatry Service, Department of Psychiatry, Beth Israel Deaconess Medical Center. He also teaches on the faculty of the Harvard Longwood Psychiatry Residency Training Program. Dr. Drogin's forensic practice focuses on expert witness testimony and trial consultation in criminal and civil matters.

Joel A. Dvoskin, PhD, ABPP (Forensic), is a clinical and forensic psychologist in Tucson, Arizona, affiliated with the University of Arizona College of Medicine and the Threat Assessment Group. He provides expert testimony, consultation, training, and mediation services to criminal justice and mental health agencies, and workplace and campus violence prevention programs to corporations, colleges, and universities.

Eric B. Elbogen, PhD, is an associate professor in the forensic psychiatry program at the

University of North Carolina–Chapel Hill School of Medicine and clinical psychologist at the Durham Veterans Affairs Medical Center. His clinical work and empirical research at the intersection of psychiatry and law concern military veterans, violence risk assessment, and criminal justice involvement.

Jacey Erickson, Esq. is a criminal defense attorney and a doctoral student in clinical psychology (forensic concentration) at Drexel University. Her research interests include risk assessment, female offenders, and offender re-entry.

William (Bill) Foote, PhD, ABPP, is a forensic psychologist in private practice in Albuquerque, New Mexico, since 1979. He is a past president of the American Psychology-Law Society, and the American Board of Forensic Psychology.

Richard Frederick, PhD, is in private practice in Springfield, Missouri. He conducts a wide range of forensic psychological evaluations and consults to others on assessment issues in forensic settings.

I. Bruce Frumkin, PhD, ABPP, is board-certified forensic psychologist and Director of Forensic and Clinical Psychology Associates, P.A., with offices in Miami and Chicago. He has conducted approximately 700 "competency to waive *Miranda* rights" and "alleged false/coerced confession" evaluations throughout the country, has published research in the areas of *Miranda* waiver and interrogative suggestibility, and has presented extensively to both lawyer and psychology groups.

Alan M. Goldstein, PhD, board-certified in forensic psychology—ABPP, is Professor Emeritus at the John Jay College of Criminal Justice and is in independent practice in White Plains, New York. He specializes in cases involving false confessions, *Miranda* waivers, fitness for trial, insanity and related defenses; and sentencing, including capital and post-conviction relief cases, and has published in these areas as well.

Jonathan W. Gould, PhD, is a forensic psychologist in private practice specializing in consulting with attorneys on child custody and related family law issues. He has written extensively on application of forensic methods and procedures to child custody assessment, alienation dynamics, domestic violence, role boundary and related ethical issues, and relocation assessment.

Stephen D. Hart, PhD, is a founding Director of ProActive ReSolutions Inc., where he heads the Threat Assessment Stream. He is a professor of psychology and a member of the Mental Health, Law, and Policy Institute at Simon Fraser University in Canada, and is also a visiting professor in the faculty of psychology at the University of Bergen in Norway. His work focuses on clinical-forensic assessment in criminal, civil, and workplace settings, and especially on the assessment of violence risk and psychopathic personality disorder.

Samuel Hawes, PhD, is a National Institute of Mental Health (NIMH) postdoctoral Fellow at Western Psychiatric Institute and Clinic, University of Pittsburgh Medical Center. His work focuses on the etiology and development of callous-unemotional (CU) features and antisocial behaviors as well as their relationship with maladaptive outcomes such as violence and aggression.

Kathleen Kemp, PhD, is a staff psychologist with Rhode Island Hospital's Department of Child and Adolescent Psychiatry and Bradley/Hasbro Children's Research Center. She specializes in forensic mental health evaluations with adolescents in the juvenile justice system. Her clinical research focuses on developmental factors impacting youths' mental health, substance use, and juvenile justice trajectories, as well as the translation of evidence-based practice to the juvenile justice population.

H. D. Kirkpatrick, PhD, is a licensed psychologist in private practice in Charlotte, North Carolina. He holds a diploma in forensic psychology from the American Board of Professional Psychology. He is the author of two fictional psychological thrillers.

Kathryn Kuehnle, PhD, is an assistant professor in the Department of Mental Health Law and Policy at the University of South Florida and maintains a private forensic practice specializing in child custody evaluations, consultation, and expert witness testimony, with particular sub-specializations in allegations of child sexual abuse, adult sexual assault, and intimate-partner violence. She is the author of four books and author or co-author of 18 book chapters pertaining to issues of child sexual abuse and child custody

Terrance J. Kukor, PhD, is the director of forensic services at Netcare Access in Columbus, Ohio. He is an adjunct faculty member in the

Department of Psychology at Drexel and Miami (Ohio) Universities, and in the Department of Psychiatry at the Ohio State University. His professional interests involve criminal forensic evaluation of adults and juveniles, suicide and violence risk assessment, and forensic animal-maltreatment evaluations.

Craig R. Lareau, JD, PhD, ABPP, is the director of forensic training for the Postdoctoral Fellowship Program at Patton State Hospital in southern California. He is an attorney and a diplomate in forensic psychology, is past president of the California Psychological Association, and is a workshop leader for the American Academy of Forensic Psychology. He maintains an active private practice conducting evaluations of adult defendants for the criminal courts and evaluations of plaintiffs in personal injury and disability matters.

Paul Montalbano, PhD, ABPP (Forensic), is a board-certified forensic psychologist and deputy chief of the forensic psychology postdoctoral fellowship at Walter Reed National Military Center. He provides expert forensic consultation, testimony, and training and is in independent practice in Washington, D.C.

Douglas Mossman, MD, is a professor of clinical psychiatry and the program director for the Forensic Psychiatry Fellowship at the University of Cincinnati College of Medicine. He has authored more than 150 publications on legal and ethical issues, medical decision-making, violence prediction, statistics, and psychiatric treatment. He received the American Psychiatric Association's 2008 Manfred S. Guttmacher Award for outstanding contributions to the literature on forensic psychiatry. His recent scholarly projects investigate predictions of violence, malingering measures, civil commitment, and novel mathematical approaches to assessing test accuracy.

David F. Mrad, PhD, ABPP, is board-certified in forensic psychology. After working for the Federal Bureau of Prisons, he is now the director of clinical training at Forest Institute in Springfield, Missouri. His clinical practice involves criminal forensic evaluations and violence risk assessments.

Daniel Murrie, PhD, is the director of psychology at the Institute of Law, Psychiatry, and Public Policy, and an associate professor in the Department of Psychiatry and Neurobehavioral Sciences in the University of Virginia Medical School. As a clinician, he performs a variety of forensic evaluations. As a researcher, his work addresses reliability and quality control in forensic mental health evaluations.

J. Gregory Olley, PhD, is a psychologist specializing in developmental disabilities in the Carolina Institute for Developmental Disabilities and Clinical Professor in the Department of Allied Health Sciences at the University of North Carolina at Chapel Hill. His interests include community services for individuals with developmental disabilities and people with intellectual disabilities in the criminal justice system.

Randy K. Otto, PhD, ABPP (Clinical Psychology and Forensic Psychology), is a faculty member at the University of South Florida and adjunct professor at Stetson University College of Law. He also maintains a practice limited to forensic psychological evaluation.

Ira K. Packer, PhD, ABPP (Forensic), is a clinical professor of psychiatry at the University of Massachusetts Medical School, where he directs the Forensic Psychology Postdoctoral Fellowship. His publications include *Evaluation of Criminal Responsibility* (Oxford University Press, 2009) and *Specialty Competencies in Forensic Psychology* (Oxford University Press, 2011, with Thomas Grisso).

Lindsey Peterson, MS, is a JD/PhD student in the law and psychology program at Drexel University. She received her master's degree in clinical psychology from Drexel University. Her interests include forensic assessment, false confessions, serious mental illness, and the intersection between law and psychology.

Lisa Drago Piechowski, PhD, ABPP, is a board-certified forensic psychologist specializing in civil litigation. She is an associate professor of clinical psychology at the American School of Professional Psychology in Washington, D.C., and maintains a private practice in Chevy Chase, Maryland. She is the author of *Evaluation of Workplace Disability* in the "Best Practices in Forensic Mental Health Assessment" series.

Phillip J. Resnick, MD, is a professor of psychiatry at Case Western Reserve University School of Medicine and director of forensic psychiatry at University Hospital's Case Medical Center.

Richard Rogers, PhD, ABPP, a Regents Professor at the University of North Texas, has authored several forensic assessment measures widely used in forensic practice. They include the Structured Interview of Reported Symptoms-2 (SIRS-2), the Evaluation of Competency to Stand Trial—Revised (ECST-R), and the Standardized Assessment of *Miranda* Abilities (SAMA). Dr. Rogers is only the third psychologist in APA history to receive Distinguished Professional Contribution awards in both Applied Research (2008) and Public Policy (2011).

Karen L. Salekin, PhD, is a clinical forensic psychologist and an associate professor at the University of Alabama. Dr. Salekin's research interests fall in the broad areas of intellectual disability and the legal system.

Jay P. Singh, PhD, Associate Professor (II) at Molde University College in Norway. His primary research interests include violence risk assessment, forensic epidemiology, and statistical methodology.

Heidi Strohmaier, MS, is a doctoral student in clinical psychology (forensic concentration) at Drexel University. She completed her undergraduate training at the University of Wisconsin-Madison, and then earned her master's degree in psychology from Drexel University. Her research interests include psychopathy, diversion, and reentry.

Kelly A. Watt, PhD, works as a threat assessment specialist at ProActive ReSolutions, Inc., and is a member of the Mental Health, Law, and Policy Institute at Simon Fraser University in Canada. Her work focuses on conducting assessments, providing training, and developing strategies for workplaces related to preventing, assessing, and managing workplace violence.

Robert M. Wettstein, MD, is a clinical and forensic psychiatrist, and clinical professor of psychiatry at the University of Pittsburgh School of Medicine. He is a past president of the American Academy of Psychiatry and the Law.

Amy L. Wevodau is a doctoral candidate in clinical psychology at Sam Houston State University. Her research interests include legal decision-making in laypersons, victim impact statements, and forensic assessment issues. Her clinical interests include forensic assessment and risk mitigation. Amy is currently completing her predoctoral work at the University of Massachusetts Medical School/Worcester Recovery Center and Hospital in Worcester, Massachusetts.

Philip H. Witt, PhD, ABPP, is a forensic psychologist in full-time private practice through Associates in Psychological Services, P.A. in Somerville, New Jersey. He specializes broadly in risk assessment and more specifically in sex offender evaluation. He is the coauthor of *Evaluation of Sexually Violent Predators* (Oxford, 2008).

Patricia A. Zapf, PhD, is a professor in the Department of Psychology at John Jay College of Criminal Justice, the City University of New York. She has conducted over 2,500 forensic evaluations in both the United States and Canada and has published eight books and over 85 articles and chapters on forensic mental health assessment. Professor Zapf travels throughout the United States and internationally to train legal and mental health professionals on best practices in forensic evaluation.

FORENSIC MENTAL HEALTH ASSESSMENT

1

Introduction and Overview

More than a decade ago, in the first edition of this book, we began with the observation that the field of forensic mental health assessment had grown significantly and developed in important ways during the preceding twenty years. This growth has continued, shaped by comparable influences in the domains of research and practice, the legal and health care systems, and the staggering expansion in communications technology. The terms "best practice" and "evidence-based practice" are now used routinely. Interest in applying scientific evidence to the practice of forensic psychology and forensic psychiatry has grown as well.

"Forensic mental health assessment" (FMHA) is now a well-accepted phrase describing the process by which certain mental health professionals (psychologists, psychiatrists, and social workers) conduct evaluations for the courts and/or at the request of attorneys. Such evaluations are intended to facilitate better-informed legal decision-making, or assist attorneys by performing evaluations that (depending on their outcome) may be useful for the attorney in representing a client. Part of the appeal of a single term such as FMHA lies in its capacity to convey the *common* aspects of this process—shared by all those who conduct forensic evaluations, regardless of discipline. The range of questions posed to the *forensic clinician* (our generic term for the psychiatrist, psychologist, or social worker who conducts an FMHA) has historically encompassed civil, criminal, and family law. More recently, there have been other domains that have become identified as more mainstream aspects of FMHA. Risk-needs assessment and post-September 11th evaluations conducted in military contexts are two examples; both receive attention in this second edition.

There are various indicators of the development of the forensic field. Professional organizations, such as the American Psychology-Law Society and the American Academy of Psychiatry and Law, have grown steadily since their establishment. A number of journals publish empirical, theoretical, and practice material relevant to FMHA; examples include *Behavioral Sciences and the Law, Criminal Justice and Behavior, Journal of the American Academy of Psychiatry and Law,* and *Law and Human Behavior.* There are increasing opportunities for training for individuals in the specialty areas of forensic psychiatry and forensic psychology (Bersoff et al., 1997; Vant Zelfde & Otto, 1997; see also the entire issue of *Behavioral Sciences and the Law,* Volume 8, 1990).

One particularly useful way to gauge the status and development of the forensic mental health professions is to consider the books that have been written in this area during the last twenty years. Important books in forensic mental health assessment have included *Psychological Evaluations for the Courts* (Melton, Petrila, Poythress, & Slobogin, 2007, updating the 1997 second edition), the *Handbook of Forensic Psychology* (Weiner & Hess, 2006, updating Hess & Weiner, 1999), *Handbook of Psychology, Volume 11: Forensic Psychology* (Goldstein, 2003), the 19-volume "Best Practices in Forensic Mental Health Assessment" series from Oxford, *Evaluating Competencies: Forensic Assessments and Instruments* (Grisso, 2003, updating the 1986 first edition), *Forensic Evaluation of Juveniles* (Grisso, 1998a), *Assessing Competence to Consent to Treatment: A Guide for Physicians and Other Health Professionals* (Grisso & Appelbaum, 1998), *Principles of Forensic Mental Health Assessment* (Heilbrun, 2001), *The Clinical Assessment of Malingering and Deception* (Rogers, 2008a, updating the 1997 second edition), *Violence and Mental Disorder: Developments in Risk Assessment* (Monahan & Steadman, 1994), *Handbook of Violence Risk Assessment* (Otto & Douglas, 2010), and *Violent Offenders: Appraising and Managing Risk* (Quinsey, Harris, Rice, & Cormier, 2006, updating the 1998 second edition).

There are four important sources of authority in FMHA that appear in these various works. These sources are *law* (relevant statutes, case law, and

administrative code affecting standards and procedure), *ethics* (professional codes guiding the practitioner's conduct in FMHA), *science* (theory and
empirical evidence relevant to the questions being
addressed), and *standards of practice* (professional
literature offering guidelines for good practice in
the area). These books also share another common
feature. Consistently, they either focus on one area
relevant to FMHA (e.g., competence to stand trial,
malingering, violence risk assessment), or discuss
several areas but treat them distinctly. This is a
useful approach to describing FMHA, as there are
numerous important distinctions between different kinds of forensic evaluations.

However, there has been less attention to the
shared features of different kinds of FMHA. Is
forensic assessment an activity that should be
considered a collection of numerous different
evaluations, defined by legal question, or are there
common principles that apply to FMHA of different kinds? This question has apparently been
addressed in three books: Melton et al. (2007),
Heilbrun (2001), and Heilbrun, Grisso, and
Goldstein (2009). In the first, this question was
discussed in a single chapter, and the authors identified certain principles that would apply to the
kinds of FMHA being described in the remainder
of their book. However, the second and third books
involved a somewhat different approach; much of
each was devoted to identifying and describing
broad principles of FMHA, and describing their
support from sources of authority in law, ethics,
science, and standard of practice.

DERIVING PRINCIPLES
OF FORENSIC MENTAL
HEALTH ASSESSMENT

Melton et al. (2007) included a chapter in which
they describe recommended procedures in FMHA
that are relevant to psychological testing. They
began by distinguishing between "therapeutic
assessment" (conducted for diagnostic and/or
treatment-planning purposes) and "forensic assessment." They described differences in:

a. scope (forensic assessment being
   narrower),
b. importance of the client's perspective (less
   in forensic assessment),
c. voluntariness (more limited in forensic
   assessment),

d. autonomy (likewise more limited in
   forensic assessment),
e. threats to validity (greater risk of
   conscious, intentional distortion of
   self-report in forensic assessment), and
f. pace and setting (brisker in forensic
   assessment due to externally imposed time
   constraints).

The distinction between therapeutic and forensic
assessment is not itself a principle of FMHA, but
provides an important perspective for considering how principles of forensic assessment, distinct
from other kinds of mental health assessment, can
be identified.

The "recommended procedures" in forensic
assessment that apply to psychological testing were
next described by Melton et al. (2007), as follows.
First, testing should be relevant to the specific legal
inquiry, with tests selected because they will help
measure behavior or capacities that are related to
the legal question before the court. Second, test
results should be treated as hypotheses to be verified
through other sources, including collateral records
and third-party interviews. Third, such collateral
approaches should be emphasized more strongly
than present-state psychological testing in evaluations calling for reconstruction of an individual's
thinking, feeling, and behavior at an earlier time.
Fourth, tests selected should be *face valid*—they
should *appear* accurate in measuring the indicated
capacities, as well as *being* accurate. Fifth, specific
kinds of tests and measures—forensic assessment
instruments (FAIs; Grisso, 1986), developed particularly to measure the capacities related to a given
legal question—are preferable to conventional
psychological tests, but only if certain criteria are
satisfied for these FAIs. Such criteria include clear
directions for administration, objective scoring
criteria, quantification of the level or degree of performance, research on reliability and validity, and
documentation in a manual. Finally, Melton et al.
suggested that response style should be considered,
particularly the potential for exaggeration or fabrication of symptoms of mental illness or cognitive
impairment.

The principles of FMHA described by Heilbrun
(2001) were described in more detail, as they were
the entire focus of the book. Based on a review of
the literature, each principle was described; discussed in terms of the support (or lack thereof)

provided by applicable law, ethics, science, and standards of practice; and classified as either *established* or *emerging*. It is these principles that were applied in the first edition of this casebook (Heilbrun, Marczyk, & DeMatteo, 2002). These principles were expanded and later slightly revised (Heilbrun et al., 2009) and will be applied in the present book. Each of these revised 38 principles will now be described briefly.

THE PRINCIPLES OF FORENSIC MENTAL HEALTH ASSESSMENT

Be aware of the important differences between clinical and forensic domains. Mental health professionals providing clinical services are engaged in activities that are distinctly different from forensic services in some important respects (see Heilbrun, 2001). It is important to be aware of these differences, as such awareness can be used to guide the conceptualization, planning, selection of sources, interpretation of findings, and communication of results for clinical versus forensic assessment.

Obtain appropriate education, training, and experience in forensic specialization. Forensic psychology and forensic psychiatry are now recognized specialties within those respective disciplines. Becoming a forensic specialist involves distinctive education and training that supplements the foundational work in psychology and psychiatry, respectively. Those who seek forensic specialization should use available formal training (if predoctoral) as well as continuing education and supervised experience to achieve a sufficient level of expertise.

Be familiar with the relevant legal, ethical, scientific, and practice literatures in FMHA. As part of the establishment of forensic specialization, the disciplines have developed scientific and practice literatures devoted to various aspects of FMHA. Specialized forensic ethical guidelines have been developed in both psychiatry and psychology. The process of FMHA is guided by the applicable statutes and case law that define the parameters of different kinds of FMHA. It is important to be familiar with the sources of authority in all four of these areas, as they are instrumental in shaping best practice in this area.

Be guided by honesty and striving for impartiality, disclosing limitations and support for one's opinions. Impartiality and honesty are key aspects of conducting FMHA. This involves a balanced and accurate description of findings, which serve to both support opinions and outline limitations. Allowing findings rather than other influences to guide opinions is fundamental—which means that alternative sources of influence must be recognized and controlled. This leads to the next principle.

Control potential evaluator bias through monitoring case selection, continuing education, and consultation with colleagues. There are various sources of evaluator bias in FMHA. These include financial considerations, personal beliefs, and conflicts of interest. It is important to recognize these various influences and to control them through practices such as annual case reviews, continuing education, and consultation with colleagues. Bias control should be treated as an essential part of forensic practice.

Be familiar with specific aspects of the legal system, especially communication, discovery, deposition, and testimony. Those conducting FMHA and sometimes testifying as a part of such evaluations provide an important service to the legal system. But it is a service offered by professionals to a different system. As an "invited guest" in the legal system, the forensic clinician should become reasonably familiar with the aspects of legal proceedings that are most relevant to interacting with attorneys, identifying the parameters of the evaluation, and communicating the results in forms that include reports, depositions, and testimony in a hearing or trial. Well-informed participants are likely to provide better FMHA services.

Do not become adversarial, but present and defend your opinions effectively. Striking a balance between vigorous and effective presentation of one's opinions while avoiding overreaction to challenge or becoming adversarial is difficult at times. Working with the strong foundation provided by good FMHA is helpful, but the forensic clinician should be prepared to use both substantive and stylistic approaches to the effective and credible presentation of findings.

Identify relevant forensic issues. This principle concerns one of the most basic aspects of FMHA: the relevant capacities and behaviors that are to be evaluated as part of the assessment. It distinguishes between the legal question, which is the ultimate matter to be decided by the court, and the relevant forensic issues, which are the capacities and abilities that are included within the legal question. For example, the legal question in a matter of a defendant's competence to stand trial is whether the individual should be adjudicated competent; the forensic issues involve that defendant's capacities to understand his or her charges and the broader adversarial nature of the legal system, assist counsel in his own defense through communicating with the lawyer, behaving appropriately during a hearing or trial, testifying (if necessary) as part of the defense, and considering options for plea in a rational way and making a decision regarding plea while incorporating the advice of counsel into this decision. This principle was considered to be *established*.

Accept referrals only within area of expertise. This principle begins with the widely-accepted professional tenet that mental health professionals should have sufficient expertise, gained through training and/or experience, to deliver a service well before they decide to provide the service. The principle goes on to address the nature of "expertise." It is concluded that "expertise" in the forensic context has two components: (1) clinical and didactic training and experience with the kind of individual(s) being evaluated, and (2) previous application of this expertise in a forensic context. The principle was classified as *established*.

Decline the referral when evaluator impartiality is unlikely. In roles in which a forensic clinician provides an evaluation and possibly testimony, the impartiality of the clinician is important. This principle identifies influences that can diminish such impartiality, and underscores the importance of declining to accept a case when there is something about the clinician's personal beliefs or the circumstances of the case that could unduly interfere with the attempt to remain impartial throughout that particular evaluation. It cites four possible roles for the forensic clinician in the course of a forensic assessment: (a) court-appointed, (b) defense/prosecution/plaintiff's expert, (c) consultant, and (d) fact witness. This principle does not keep forensic clinicians from vigorously defending appropriate conclusions when challenged; it concerns influences that would unfairly skew data interpretation and conclusions. The principle was seen as *established* when the forensic clinician is either court-appointed or a defense/prosecution/plaintiff's expert, but *neither established nor emerging* for a consultant.

Clarify the evaluator's role with the attorney. This principle addresses the problem of multiple roles and the potentially harmful impact of playing more than a single role in a given FMHA case. It uses the roles described in the previous principle. The role of fact witness is recommended whenever there has been a prior professional treatment relationship with an individual being evaluated. This principle emphasizes that it is typically "cleanest" to play only one role among the first three possibilities in a given case. The principle was described as *emerging*.

Clarify financial arrangements. The importance of describing, in advance, the rate or total amount of billing for services is described in this principle, as well as the way in which the fee will be collected. There are some circumstances, such as performing publicly funded evaluations of criminal defendants, in which the payment for services is specified by the jurisdiction, and there is nothing to be clarified. The principle becomes more important when this is not the case, however. It was classified as *established*.

Obtain appropriate authorization. There are two different forms of authorization that can be obtained in FMHA: (a) a court order, and (b) the permission of attorney and client. The form of authorization that is needed depends on the role being played by the forensic clinician, with the court-ordered role associated with the need for a signed order from the court, and the "expert for the attorney" role requiring the consent of both the attorney and the client. This affects whether the forensic clinician delivers a "notification of purpose" to the individual being evaluated, informing her of the relevant nature, purpose, procedures, and limits on confidentiality, but not asking for consent; or whether the evaluator provides such a notification followed by a request for informed consent. This principle was considered *established*.

Avoid playing the dual roles of therapist and forensic evaluator. Expanding on the description of FMHA roles given in several prior principles, this principle concludes that playing the roles of therapist and forensic evaluator with the same individual creates significant problems and is consistently to be avoided. This principle was classified as *established*.

Determine the particular role to be played within forensic assessment if the referral is accepted. The selection of one's role within the case, when made in the beginning and retained throughout the case, can prevent problems of various kinds from interfering with the forensic clinician's impartiality, and ensure that the expectations of the attorney and the forensic clinician are comparable. There is discussion of a possible exception to the "single role" maxim, involving moving from a role requiring impartiality (e.g., defense expert expected to testify) to a role in which impartiality is not needed (e.g., consultant) *if it is clear from the results of the evaluation that the attorney would not ask for a report or testimony*. However, moving in the opposite direction—from the consultant's role that does not require impartiality to the testifying expert's role that does—would be far more difficult. This principle was considered to be *emerging*.

Select the most appropriate model to guide data gathering, interpretation, and communication. Two broad models of FMHA are discussed: those of Morse (1978) and Grisso (1986). The use of a model can be conceptually valuable in understanding the larger process of FMHA, and more specifically useful in an individual case in formulating an assessment plan. This was considered to be an *emerging* principle.

Use multiple sources of information for each area being assessed. This is a very important principle in FMHA. Because of the circumstances under which FMHA is typically conducted, involving some incentive for the individual being evaluated to distort self-report and psychological testing data, it is important to use multiple sources (including collateral records and interviews) to assess the consistency of information across these sources. Agreement across sources makes it more likely that the agreed-upon information is accurate, while inconsistency across sources means that there is inaccuracy in at least one source of information. This principle was classified as *established*.

Use relevance and reliability (validity) as guides for seeking information and selecting data sources. There are two criteria in evidence law that are frequently cited for the admission of expert testimony. The first is its relevance to the question(s) before the court; the second is reliability (which, when used in the law, means both *psychometric reliability* and *validity*). This principle concerns the use of both criteria when the forensic clinician is deciding which sources of information to use, particularly in selecting third parties to interview and psychological tests to administer. This principle appeared to be *established*.

Obtain relevant historical information. It is virtually always necessary to obtain historical information regarding the individual being evaluated in FMHA, and this historical information is often more extensive than what is needed in a therapeutic evaluation. However, this principle also emphasizes the varying extensiveness of historical information needed in different kinds of FMHA. Some evaluations need a reasonably focused history to provide a context for the evaluation (competence to stand trial, for example), while others require much more breadth (e.g., capital sentencing). This principle appeared to be *established*.

Assess clinical characteristics in relevant, reliable, and valid ways. This principle emphasized the importance of assessing clinical characteristics consistent with at least one model discussed earlier. The choice of which "clinical characteristics" to assess, and how, is facilitated by the use of the "relevant and reliable" test described earlier. The discussion included the "clinical versus actuarial" debate that has been seen in the literature for nearly half a century, and considered how evidence from this debate might be applied toward FMHA. The principle was classified as *established*.

Assess legally relevant behavior. This principle focuses directly on capacities and behavior that are related to the legal question. The criteria of relevance and reliability are applied to determine how to assess these capacities; in some areas, the forensic clinician has the option of using a well-validated forensic assessment instrument. The principle appeared to be *established*.

Ensure that conditions for evaluation are quiet, private, and distraction-free. FMHA can be conducted in a variety of environments, some of which are far from ideal. Particularly in settings that emphasize security and may have a limited capacity for mental health evaluation, the forensic clinician may sometimes find that conditions can potentially compromise the validity of the evaluation because they are noisy, allow sensitive material to be overheard, or present other distractions as well. This principle discusses the balance between reasonable evaluation conditions and other influences (e.g., security, time constraints), and addresses the question of when environmental conditions are sufficiently poor to require the forensic clinician to seek to improve them—and how much. This principle was described as *established*.

Provide appropriate notification of purpose and/ or obtain appropriate authorization before beginning. Whether the forensic clinician provides notification of purpose or obtains informed consent before beginning FMHA depends on the role that is being played and the nature of the associated authorization that was obtained, both of which were discussed in previous principles. Those who are performing a court-ordered evaluation, and have obtained the necessary court order, must provide the individual being evaluated with basic information regarding the nature and purpose of the evaluation, who authorized it, and the associated limits on confidentiality, including how it might be used. In this circumstance, however, participation in such an evaluation is not voluntary, and it would be inappropriate to seek informed consent. By contrast, when a defense or plaintiff's attorney asks a forensic clinician to conduct an evaluation of that attorney's client, the evaluation *is* voluntary, and informed consent should be obtained before proceeding. This principle was classified as *established*.

Determine whether the individual understands the purpose of the evaluation and associated limits on confidentiality. To be meaningful, a notification of purpose or a notification accompanied by a request for informed consent must be understood by the individual being evaluated. This principle describes how the evaluator can assess whether the information was understood, and how the evaluator might proceed if it appears that the information was *not* well understood. The principle was described as *established*.

Use third party information in assessing response style. One of the more important aspects of FMHA is the systematic assessment of response style of the individual being evaluated, particularly the deliberate over-reporting or under-reporting of relevant deficits or symptoms. This principle considers the use of records and collateral informants in establishing a history from multiple sources, and determining whether self-reported information is consistent with other sources and more likely to be accurate. This principle was classified as *established*.

Use testing when indicated in assessing response style. There is an additional approach to assessing response style: through psychological testing and the use of specialized measures developed to assess malingering or defensiveness of mental disorder or cognitive impairment. This principle addresses the application of psychological tests and specialized measures for this purpose, describing the available research on the tests and measures that allow them

to be used in this way. The principle was classified as *emerging* but now appears *established*.

Use case-specific (idiographic) evidence in assessing clinical condition, functional abilities, and causal connection. This principle describes the first of three ways that science can be applied in FMHA. It involves obtaining information that is specific to the circumstances of the case and present functioning of the individual, and making comparisons to that individual's capacities and functioning at other times. The assessment of malingering, for example, should draw upon information about whether the individual has ever been diagnosed with a mental disorder or cognitive impairment in the past, and (if so) what symptoms the individual presented at that time. This principle is very much consistent with the legal goal of individualized justice, and is described as *established*.

Use nomothetic evidence in assessing clinical condition, functional abilities, and causal connection. The second way science can be applied to FMHA is through the use of empirical data applicable to populations similar to that of the individual being evaluated, and through forensic tools that have been developed and validated on similar populations. When forensic capacities are assessed using norm-referenced tools, the evaluator and the decision-maker can consider how similar such measured capacities are to those in "known groups" (such as those who are adjudicated incompetent to stand trial vs. those who are in jail but for whom the issue of trial competence has never been raised). This principle is particularly important for the goal of applying empirical evidence toward informing legal decision-making, and appeared to be *established*.

Use scientific reasoning in assessing causal connection between clinical condition and functional abilities. When the results of one source of information, such as an interview or psychological testing, are considered as "hypotheses to be verified" through further information obtained from multiple sources, then the FMHA is proceeding somewhat like a scientific study. Furthermore, when hypotheses are accepted or rejected depending upon how well they account for the most information with the simplest explanation, another important aspect of science is being used. This aspect involves conceptualizing and reasoning rather than data collection, but is as important as the actual data collection itself. This principle was described as *established*.

Carefully consider whether to answer the ultimate legal question directly. This principle was revised from the earlier version ("Do not answer the ultimate legal question directly"). In part this change reflects a decade's continued maturation of FMHA. As it has become clearer that thoroughness, relevance, and the transparent relationship between data and conclusions are at the heart of good FMHA practice, one of the major justifications for avoiding ultimate issue conclusions—avoiding a conclusion without any apparent foundation, at the end of a brief report with limited information—is no longer as important. But other considerations that drove the controversy on this topic for over three decades remain. Some argue that many judges and attorneys expect the forensic clinician to offer an ultimate opinion, and this practice is almost always permitted under applicable evidentiary law. Others reply that the preferable practice in FMHA is to focus on forensic capacities that are relevant to the ultimate legal question, while avoiding the ultimate legal conclusions that have moral, political, and community-value components that are outside the forensic clinician's expertise. This principles appears to be *established.*

Describe findings and limits so that they need change little under cross examination. The essence of this principle is that FMHA findings need to be described carefully and thoroughly, supported by multiple sources, and have appropriate limitations explicitly acknowledged. When this is done, the forensic clinician can expect that the results of findings conveyed during cross-examination will not change significantly. In effect, the evaluator has anticipated the potential objections, weaknesses, and alternative explanations for his findings, and subjected the data analysis and reasoning to careful scrutiny *in light of these weaknesses.* This principle was classified as *established.*

Attribute information to sources. One of the most important differences between therapeutic and forensic assessment is the nature of the documentation required. Forensic assessment, by definition, is part of a legal proceeding with an adversarial component. It is crucial to have information carefully attributed by source, both for the evaluator's judgment about what information is consistent across multiple sources *and* for the opposing attorney or the judge to identify what information came from which sources. This principle was considered to be *established.*

Use plain language; avoid technical jargon. Many of those who use FMHA are either legally trained

(judges and attorneys) or typically without training in either the behavioral sciences or the law (jurors). It is important, therefore, to avoid the use of technical jargon as much as possible, or to define technical terms if their use cannot be avoided. This principle is most often applied to report writing, but is applicable as well to expert testimony given in depositions, hearings, and trials. This principle was described as *established.*

Write report in sections, according to model and procedures. It is possible to write the report documenting the FMHA in a way that facilitates the application of various principles described earlier. The different report sections recommended by Heilbrun and colleagues (2009) include

Referral (with identifying information concerning the individual, his or her characteristics, the nature of the evaluation, and by whom it was requested or ordered);

Procedures (the times and dates of the evaluations, the various tests or procedures conducted, the different records reviewed, and the third-party interviews conducted, as well as documentation of the notification of purpose or informed consent and the degree to which the information was apparently understood);

Relevant History (containing information from multiple sources describing areas important to the evaluation);

Current Clinical Condition (broadly considered to include appearance, mood, behavior, sensorium, intellectual functioning, thought, and personality);

Forensic Capacities (varying according to the nature of the legal questions); and

Conclusions and Recommendations (addressed toward the relevant capacities rather than the ultimate legal questions).

This principle was classified as *established.*

Base testimony on the results of the properly performed FMHA. There should be a strong relationship between the procedures and findings documented in the report, and the expert testimony that is provided based on this evaluation. Almost the entire substantive basis for expert testimony should be documented in the evaluation, allowing the presenting attorney to use the expert's findings more clearly and effectively, the opposing attorney to prepare to challenge them, the judge to under-stand them, and the expert to communicate them. This principle was considered *established*.

Prepare. Effective expert testimony is facilitated by preparation. In addition to familiarity with the contents of the report and supporting documents, the forensic clinician should seek to talk with retaining attorney prior to testimony. Such a conversation can include a review of important report findings, a plan for a mutually agreeable approach to direct examination, and the anticipation of challenges that may arise upon cross-examination. This principle appears to be *established*.

Communicate effectively. This principle covers two aspects of expert testimony: substance and style. The substantive part of expert testimony is addressed by most of the preceding principles, while the stylistic aspect concerns how the expert presents, dresses, speaks, and otherwise behaves to make their testimony more understandable and credible. It is important that both substance and style be strong for expert testimony to be maximally effective. While substantively strong but stylistically weak testimony may have less impact than it should, it is testimony that is substantively weak but stylistically impressive that should be recognized and accorded little influence if the forensic mental health professions are to contribute meaningfully to better-informed legal decision-making. This principle appears *established*.

Control the message. An effective cross-examination is designed to weaken the credibility of the expert, and elicit alternatives to the opinions presented on direct examination. Even well-conducted FMHA presented by an experienced forensic clinician is subject to this kind of influence. But substantive mastery and stylistic effectiveness can be used to assert and emphasize important points in response to cross-examination, allowing the forensic clinician to regain control that is lost at times on cross-examination. This principle appears to be *established*.

THE NEED FOR
A REVISED CASEBOOK

The field has evolved in the decade since the publication of the first casebook (Heilbrun et al., 2002). The principles have been revised. More specialized measures have been developed, and psychological tests have been updated. The effective use of risk assessment and threat assessment has expanded.

The application of FMHA to military populations has become more visible. A series describing "best practices in forensic mental health assessment" has been published. It is timely to consider, as we did a decade ago, how these principles apply to various kinds of FMHA reports.

In addition, the original reasons for developing a casebook in this area still apply. First, the principles described in this chapter, if they are to be meaningful, must be applicable to most FMHA reports. We have used such reports to illustrate how such principles can be applied. Second, it is helpful to see how expert forensic clinicians conduct such assessments. By using case reports contributed by such experts, this book can answer questions about how experts collect information, interpret the results, and communicate their conclusions. It is also helpful to discuss how the evaluator might have proceeded differently at various points in the evaluation. Third, there are questions concerning these cases and the application of these principles that are discussed at the end of each case in the form of a "teaching point." These questions highlight a variety of perspectives on FMHA and provide a good opportunity for considering some of the detailed procedures involved in FMHA.

APPLYING PRINCIPLES
TO FMHA CASES

To combine the principles, cases, and teaching points as we did, we took several steps (just as we did in the first casebook). We assumed that any of the 38 principles described by Heilbrun et al. (2009) should apply to any of the cases in this book. However, some principles do not lend themselves to illustration through case reports—particularly those reflecting more general FMHA background. So the reports in this book do not demonstrate the application of all of the revised principles, but only those that can be discussed by using case reports. We did not use principles related to expert testimony in the original casebook. In the present revision, however, we used a contributed report that was then analyzed by Stanley L. Brodsky for its implications regarding expert testimony.

We divided the topics into chapters, according to legal question and balanced across criminal, civil, and juvenile areas. Special topics of interest (e.g., military FMHA, threat and risk assessment, response style) were addressed in separate chapters. We sought FMHA case report contributions from colleagues in the field who were known for their expertise in that particular topic. Each principle that could be illustrated with a case was discussed at least once. Teaching points were constructed by identifying specific, contemporary FMHA questions. All FMHA cases in the revised casebook are new contributions.

Contributors were asked to use genuine case material, but also to modify it in consideration of the ethical and legal limits on the use of such material publication. We considered these concerns as described in the next section.

CAUTIONS IN USING CASE MATERIAL

Genuine case material illustrates the richness and complexity of FMHA, as well as its problems and limits. Observing how such problems arise in specific cases, the approaches taken by the forensic clinicians in assessing particular capacities under these circumstances, and the style of communicating the results in a report can all be particularly valuable.

However, there are concerns about the privacy of the individual being evaluated in using such case material. There is not the same ethical expectation of confidentiality or legal right to privilege for individuals evaluated in FMHA as there is in therapy, but this difference arises from the distinctly different purposes of these two activities. A therapy client can reasonably expect that material from treatment will remain private, unless it falls under exceptions provided by law (e.g., physical or sexual abuse of a child, or the threat of serious harm to an identifiable third party in some jurisdictions). By contrast, an individual who undergoes FMHA should be notified at the beginning of the evaluation about its purpose and associated limits of confidentiality. In some cases, the FMHA results will be communicated in a report, expert testimony, or both in a hearing or trial that could be open to the public and covered by the media.

Although the individual being evaluated in FMHA should have been informed about how such information might be used, it would be quite unusual to have this individual, his or her attorney, or the presiding judge notified that the material might be used in publication, or to have obtained the consent of appropriate individuals for such use in publication. Furthermore, it may be that using an FMHA report in publication would exceed

what is in the "public domain," as the report itself (although introduced into evidence) may not have been accessible to the media.

In light of these concerns, there is no undisguised genuine case material used in this book. We asked the contributors to take two steps before we used these cases in the book. First, we have asked that the reports be *sanitized*, with all potentially identifying information of those involved in the litigation changed to prevent the identification of the case. Second, we asked that the case be combined with elements of another case—a process we called *hybridizing*—to ensure that even sanitized cases could not possibly be identified. We asked that contributors attempt to preserve important data and reasoning from the case, but avoid including anything that might increase the risk of case identification. Therefore, we can say with confidence that the cases included in this book preserve some important data and reasoning of genuine FMHA cases, but do not describe undisguised genuine cases.

HOW TO USE THIS BOOK

There are five levels on which this casebook can be read. First, those interested in considering how broad principles might be applied to FMHA cases can focus on the principle described in the beginning of each case. Second, the reader might attend to a particular approach to applying the principle that is discussed in the teaching point. Third, the question of how the case is evaluated may be considered—how the assessment is structured, how the information is analyzed, the reasoning that leads from results to conclusions, and how the entire FMHA is communicated. Fourth, any reader interested in observing the particular style of a given contributor can read the case(s) provided by that contributor. Cases can also be considered according to the particular kind of FMHA being performed (civil vs. criminal/juvenile, conventional vs. high profile, child/adolescent vs. adult, or by particular legal question). Finally, any reader interested in the backgrounds of the respective individuals being evaluated in these reports could go directly to the cases represented, and read the book as a collection of cases involving those who become involved in litigation, and are evaluated as part of such legal proceedings.

2

Miranda Waiver Capacity

The capacity of adult defendants to waive their *Miranda* rights (*Miranda v. Arizona*, 1966) is the focus of the case reports in this chapter. The requirement that all individuals detained by law enforcement officials be "Mirandized" prior to interrogation—that is, informed that they have the right to remain silent, that anything they say can be used against them in court, that they have the right to counsel, and that an attorney will be provided at no cost if they cannot afford one—is quite familiar to the American general public. However, not all individuals being interrogated by law enforcement personnel understand and appreciate these rights. An evaluation may thus be requested to assess whether an individual who was interrogated possessed the "knowing, voluntary, and intelligent" capacities to waive *Miranda* rights when facing criminal interrogation. Importantly, *Miranda* evaluations conducted by forensic clinicians usually are conducted to inform a legal decision regarding whether the individual had the requisite capacities at the time of the *Miranda* warning and interrogation—and therefore whether their statements during the interrogation can be used as evidence against them.

The principle to be applied to the first case concerns the value of nomothetic data, derived from groups and applied through general laws, to forensic assessment. The teaching point in this case will address the value of forensic assessment instruments (FAIs) (Grisso, 1986, 2003) that have been developed and validated for a specific kind of forensic assessment. This will serve to highlight one of the important differences between the methodology of behavioral science and that of law: while science emphasizes nomothetic approaches, the law is inclined toward idiographic procedures, focused on understanding a particular individual or event. The principle associated with the second case in this chapter—use case-specific, idiographic evidence in forensic assessment—addresses how the

forensic assessment process can also be improved through the use of information that is specific to the case at hand. The teaching point for the second case will include a discussion of some of the limits on the applicability of FAIs.

CASE ONE
PRINCIPLE: USE NOMOTHETIC EVIDENCE IN ASSESSING CLINICAL CONDITION, FUNCTIONAL ABILITIES, AND CAUSAL CONNECTION (*PRINCIPLE 28*)

This principle concerns the value of applying scientific data gathered with groups to the assessment of domains that are relevant in FMHA. Over the past several decades, researchers have gathered scientific data in several areas that are particularly applicable to FMHA. First, studies provide data on the reliability and validity of various psychological measures used in FMHA, such as psychological tests, structured interviews, and specialized tools. Second, scientific data provide an estimate of the base rates of relevant behavior (e.g., crime and violence) and the outcomes (e.g., legal decisions on child custody). Such data can be used by evaluators to make empirically grounded judgments regarding the relationship between capacities, behavior, and legal status. Finally, the use of measures with known reliability and validity, with the incorporation of empirically derived base rates, can allow the forensic clinician to generate hypotheses that could help answer questions arising in the case being evaluated.

Support for the application of nomothetic data to FMHA can be found in several sources of authority. The *Ethical Principles of Psychologists and Code of Conduct* (APA *Ethics Code*; American Psychological Association, 2010a) contains several relevant sections. The APA *Ethics Code* emphasizes the value of scientifically derived knowledge, both indirectly ("Psychologists base the opinions contained in their recommendations, reports, and diagnostic or evaluative statements, including forensic testimony, on information and techniques sufficient to substantiate their findings"; Standard 9.01) and directly ("Psychologists' work is based upon established scientific and professional knowledge of the discipline"; Standard 2.04). The APA *Ethics Code* also emphasizes the importance of research on the applications of various tests or instruments (Standard 9.05), and notes that the selection, administration, and interpretation of psychological assessments should be guided by research on the appropriateness and usefulness of the assessment (Standard 9.02a) and on the validity and reliability of the assessment specific to the population being tested (Standard 9.02b). Additional support for this principle can be found in the *Specialty Guidelines for Forensic Psychology* (APA *Specialty Guidelines*; American Psychological Association, 2013b), which states that "Forensic practitioners seek to provide opinions and testimony that are sufficiently based upon adequate scientific foundation, and reliable and valid principles and methods that have been applied appropriately to the facts of the case" (Guideline 2.05). The *Specialty Guidelines* also emphasizes that forensic practitioners use assessment procedures "in light of the research on or evidence of their usefulness and proper application" and "whose validity and reliability have been established for use with members of the population assessed" (Guideline 10.02). Generally, ethical guidelines applicable to psychologists support the importance of current scientific information in FMHA and applying such information to the selection of methods and procedures that are used in these assessments.

Legal support for the use of nomothetic data in FMHA can be found in several important cases. In *Daubert v. Merrell Dow Pharmaceuticals* (1993), the United States Supreme Court held that the *Federal Rules of Evidence* are applicable to scientific testimony. In its analysis, the Court's opinion included dicta that offered criteria that could be used at the trial court level to decide whether the "reasoning or methodology underlying the testimony is scientifically valid" (p. 592) and immediately applicable. These criteria include whether the basis for the opinion has been scientifically tested, whether the theory or technique has been subjected to

peer review and publication, the known or potential error rate, and its level of general acceptance. Furthermore, the United States Supreme Court in *Kumho Tire Co. v. Carmichael* (1999) held that a *Daubert*-like analysis may also be applied to evaluating experts who testify on the basis of technical or other specialized knowledge rather than scientific expertise—which are the types of knowledge mentioned in Federal Rule of Evidence 702—regarding a matter before the court.

Accuracy is important in FMHA, so the forensic clinician should be able to describe the degree of empirical scientific support that has been demonstrated for a particular FMHA procedure (Melton, Petrila, Poythress, & Slobogin, 2007; Packer & Grisso, 2011). Accordingly, a forensic practitioner should consider procedures that have an established empirical base. Heilbrun (1992) offered guidelines on the use of psychological tests in FMHA that underscore the importance of such empirical support. Relevant guidelines include the following:

(a) The test is commercially available and has a manual documenting its psychometric properties;

(b) Tests with a reliability coefficient of less than .80 would require explicit justification explaining why they are used;

(c) The test's relevance to the legal issue or an underlying psychological construct should be supported by validation research;

(d) Objective tests and actuarial data combinations are preferable when there are appropriate outcome data and a "formula" exists.

The present case report provides a good example of the application of this principle. The purpose of the evaluation was to assess the individual's ability to make a knowing, intelligent, and voluntary waiver of his *Miranda* rights following his arrest. In particular, however, the evaluation focused on the "voluntary" aspect of these criteria. (One might assume that the referral request specified that the forensic clinician focus on this area in particular, or that "knowing" and "intelligent" had been evaluated at another time and were not deficient.) The forensic clinician employed several different psychological tools that have an established empirical base. Consequently, the evaluator could describe the degree of empirical support for each of these

FMHA procedures if this question were to arise during testimony.

The tests administered in the present evaluation included a standard intelligence test (Wechsler Adult Intelligence Scale, 4th edition; WAIS-IV) and part of a test of basic academic abilities (Wide Range Achievement Test, 4th edition; WRAT-4). Consistent with this principle, the WAIS-IV and the WRAT-4 have established levels of reliability and validity. The reliability and validity of the WAIS-IV are firmly established in the field (see Wechsler, 2008). Similarly, the WRAT-4 has been extensively validated (see Wilkinson & Robertson, 2006). The use of these tests therefore appears to be consistent with the guidelines suggested by Heilbrun (1992) regarding the selection and use of psychological tests in FMHA.

Another important aspect of the psychological tests used in the present case concerns their relationship to psychological constructs that are relevant to the forensic issues being addressed. Tests of intelligence (WAIS-IV) and basic skills in reading (WRAT-4) have clear relevance to the capacity for making a knowing, intelligent, and voluntary waiver of one's *Miranda* rights, particularly in their measurement of the individual's ability to read and comprehend written material and understand oral material.

The forensic clinician also administered a specialized measure that is useful in appraising an individual's proneness to be influenced by others. Specifically, the evaluator administered the Gudjonsson Suggestibility Scales 1 (GSS 1). Because this measure has an established empirical base, the evaluator was able to compare the defendant's scores on these tests with the data obtained as part of the test validation process.

Psychological Evaluation	
Name: Gus Armstrong	Judge: Frank Davis
	Date of Evaluation:
Birth date: 8/7/85 (25 years)	6/11/11
Education: 10th grade	Date of Report: 6/14/11
Race: Caucasian	Gender: Male

REASON FOR REFERRAL

Mr. Armstrong was referred for a psychological evaluation by Mr. Craig Peters, who is Mr. Armstrong's defense attorney. Mr. Armstrong is appearing before the Honorable Judge Davis of the Circuit Criminal Court, Buffalo, New York, on charges of second degree murder in connection with an offense in which Mr. Armstrong allegedly killed his girlfriend's six-week-old infant by shaking him. The purpose of the evaluation, as a consultation to Mr. Peters, was to assess Mr. Armstrong's psychological functioning as it pertained to the voluntariness and validity of his confession to law enforcement.

PROCEDURES ADMINISTERED

Clinical Interview, Word Reading Subtest of the Wide Range Achievement Test-4 (WRAT-4), Gudjonsson Suggestibility Scales 1 (GSS 1), 16 Personality Factor Test (16 PF), Wechsler Adult Intelligence Scale-IV (WAIS-IV), Minnesota Multiphasic Personality Inventory-2 (MMPI-2), Validity Indicator Profile-Nonverbal (VIP), Rey 15 Item Memory Test (Rey), Word Recognition Test (WRT).

BACKGROUND INFORMATION

Background information about the case was obtained by speaking to Mr. Peters. In addition, the following materials were reviewed:

(a) The State's Synopsis and Background of the Accused,
(b) Report of Post Mortem Examination from Dr. Rey,
(c) Neuropathic Examination of the Brain by Dr. Sachs,
(d) Report from Dr. Hill,
(e) Report from Dr. Leeper,
(f) Reply from Dr. Leeper's report from Dr. Rey and from Dr. Leeper,
(g) DVDs and transcripts of Mr. Armstrong's police interviews from November 17, 2006, and June 26, 2007,
(h) Audio recording of Mr. Armstrong taken at the time of his arrest, prior to his formal interrogation of June 26, 2007,
(i) Various witness statements,
(j) Case notes from Children and Family Services, and
(k) Various reports and notes from law enforcement personnel involved in the case.

Mr. Armstrong was seen at an interview room at a local psychologist's office in Buffalo, New York, on June 11, 2011, for a total of approximately eight hours, approximately two and a half hours of which consisted of self-administered testing time. He was informed that the results of the evaluation were not confidential and would be given to his lawyer to assist in planning for his case.

Mr. Armstrong was a fair historian in that he provided a somewhat detailed description of his life. At times he had problems providing an accurate chronology of various events. Even though he was able to describe in general terms what transpired in his interactions with law enforcement, his memory for those events, particularly the 2007 interrogation, was patchy.

Family/Social History

Mr. Armstrong said he was born in Buffalo and has essentially lived there his entire life except when, at age 13, he and his family moved to Jamestown for a year prior to moving back to Buffalo. He said his parents married when he was four years of age but were together for only three to six months before separating. He said he then did not see his biological father until a visit at age 14 and again at age 18. He said that they now speak often on the phone and his father visits him several times monthly. His mother has been with his stepfather for the past 19 years. He perceives his stepfather as a "father figure." His mother, father, and stepfather all do factory work.

According to Mr. Armstrong, he grew up in an environment he did not perceive as dangerous. He never stayed with groups of kids that caused trouble. He enjoyed playing sports, video games, and building model cars. He said he always had a lot of friends.

Mr. Armstrong described never really having lived independently in his life. He either has always lived with his parents, sometimes with his girlfriend living with him there, or has lived with a girlfriend and her parents. He described a series of relationships in which he and the girlfriend eventually broke up because of infidelity on his partner's part. He said that, beginning in March 2010, he has been involved in another relationship, although he and this girlfriend do not live together. Currently Mr. Armstrong resides at his mother's house. He said he is on "house arrest" and is unable to leave the home except when in the custody of his mother or stepfather.

School and Employment History

Mr. Armstrong said that in school he was an "average" student. He said he was held back and repeated kindergarten because he had tubes in his ears and could not hear well. Beginning in the fourth or fifth grade, he was placed in special education classes because he needed help in reading and writing. Special education classes ended in the sixth grade. He said that children would pick on him (he did not know why) beginning in the fifth grade but that this stopped by the seventh grade when he began defending himself. He said that beginning in the ninth grade, he attended University Hill, which was described as a "trade school." He attended that school up until part of the eleventh grade, at which time, at age 18, he dropped out of school to go to work and earn money to support his newborn son.

Mr. Armstrong has had a somewhat sporadic work history. Most of his jobs were obtained through a "temp" service, although his mother arranged for him, at age 18, to get his first job, working at the same factory where she worked. Mr. Armstrong said he has mainly worked in factories, but for a year prior to his arrest, he has worked in sanitation at Watson Foods, cleaning up floors and the machinery.

Medical/Mental Health History

Mr. Armstrong stated he took medication for seizures for two years beginning at age 11 or 12. He described having several of what were likely *grand mal* seizures. He said he stopped taking the medication per his physician's instructions once it was felt he no longer needed it. Mr. Armstrong said he has broken his wrists several times: once when he fell off a zip cord when he was ten years old and again at age 11 or 12 when he jumped off a swing. He also said that just prior to his arrest for the second-degree murder charge, he had gotten into an argument with a girlfriend and out of anger, hit his hand against a tree, breaking bones in his right hand.

Mr. Armstrong stated that besides having had the seizures, he has never been knocked unconscious or passed out. He said that at age 15 or 16 he was hit in the head with a soda bottle and required three stitches. This happened when he tried to intervene in an incident in which a male was beating up his female cousin.

Mr. Armstrong denied ever receiving mental health counseling or psychotherapy.

Substance Abuse History

Mr. Armstrong said he began smoking marijuana at age 15 or 16. He said that up until his arrest, he was smoking five or six "joints" at a time, once a week. He said that he tried Ecstasy, hashish, and "acid" one time each, approximately six years ago. He denied any other illegal drug usage and he denied ever inhaling glue, gasoline, or other solvents. He said that he began drinking alcohol at age 15, drinking approximately four beers or shots of alcohol at one time. He did this a total of three times at that age and did not use alcohol again until age 19. According to him, he generally would have one or two beers at a time on a weekend night, although on a number of occasions, he might have the equivalent of five or six drinks. He emphasized that since his arrest, he has not used any drugs or had any alcohol to drink.

Arrest History

Mr. Armstrong said that at age 22 he paid a fine for public intoxication. He has had no other arrests except his June 27, 2007, arrest for second-degree murder. He said that at one point he had an additional charge for sexual assault, but that charge was later dropped. Following his arrest, he spent six months in jail prior to bonding out.

BEHAVIORAL OBSERVATIONS

Mr. Armstrong presented as a white male of approximately average height and weight, who came to the session neatly groomed and casually dressed. He appeared a bit older than his age and looked quite different from his appearance during his interrogation some four years earlier. Since that time he gained some weight. He had no difficulty establishing rapport. He was friendly and cooperative and appeared to give his best effort on the psychological testing. Mr. Armstrong's motor activity was within normal limits. Throughout the session he made slight chewing motions with his jaw. It is not known whether this was from nervousness or whether he had some dental problems. His speech was clear, coherent, and relevant. He did not have loose associations. He spoke slowly and, although he answered questions asked, did not often volunteer information.

Mr. Armstrong's affect was appropriate to the content of his speech. Apart from some slight situational anxiety, he did not come across as overtly anxious or depressed. Behaviorally, he came across as concrete in his reasoning and overall, was limited in his verbal skills. His judgment and common

sense were fair at best. It must be noted that Mr. Armstrong was extremely concerned about insuring he did not do anything to violate the conditions of his release. For example, he did not want to be left alone in the interview room for even a minute since he said he was required to be either in the custody of his mother or with Dr. Frumkin at all times.

Mr. Armstrong's reality testing was within normal limits. He denied ever experiencing any auditory, visual, tactile, or olfactory hallucinations. He did not exhibit any delusional, paranoid, or grandiose thinking. Mr. Armstrong denied ever having had any suicidal or homicidal thoughts or attempts and denied ever engaging in self-mutilation.

TEST RESULTS

On the WAIS-IV, Mr. Armstrong obtained a Verbal Comprehension Index of 80 (lower 9%), a Perceptual Reasoning Index of 69 (lower 2%), a Working Memory Index of 74 (lower 4%), and a Processing Speed Index of 76 (lower 5%). His Full Scale IQ score was 70 (lower 2%), placing him at the Extremely Low to Borderline range of intellectual functioning. There is a 95% chance that his true Full Scale IQ score is between 67 and 75.

These test results show that although Mr. Armstrong's relative strengths are in the verbal realm, he is still Borderline to Low Average compared to others his age. Ninety-one percent of those his age obtain higher verbal comprehension scores. He showed major deficiencies in his nonverbal reasoning, visual-spatial integration, and motor coordination, as well as in his ability to mentally manipulate information in his short-term memory (working memory). One of his problems is that he just does not process information very quickly or efficiently. Test results show he is a cognitively impaired individual, particularly in the nonverbal realm.

Mr. Armstrong was given a number of tests to rule out exaggeration of cognitive and memory deficits. Test results (VIP, Rey, WRT) show no evidence he was attempting to feign intellectual problems, although, not unlike many of low intelligence, results show he was unable to sustain his attention for difficult tasks and often either made careless errors or gave up without exerting maximum effort.

The MMPI-2 could not be interpreted because Mr. Armstrong had a tendency to deny common human frailties to which most people would readily admit. This artificially lowered any possible elevations in the clinical and other scales.

Somewhat surprisingly, on the 16 PF (which is not oriented toward assessment of psychopathology as is the case with the MMPI-2, but rather more normal aspects of personality), Mr. Armstrong did just the opposite. He presented an overly negative picture of himself, showing poor self-esteem and a low sense of well-being. In that the 16 PF was administered a number of hours before the MMPI-2 was administered, it is felt that as the session progressed, Mr. Armstrong was more invested in presenting himself in a favorable or overly favorable light. The 16 PF was able to be interpreted and it showed that he is the type of person who follows his own urges to an extreme, is an anxious sort of person, and is someone who does not have good reasoning skills. He is no more accommodating or deferential than others, but will have difficulties managing novel or confrontational social situations. He is an energetic, unconventional, socially timid person, who has a tough, unsentimental approach to life.

The GSS was designed to help identify people who were particularly susceptible to giving erroneous accounts of events when subjected to questioning. This is accomplished by measuring their tendency to giving in to misleading or leading questions as well as their tendency to shift to different responses when pressured. Mr. Armstrong was read a narrative paragraph containing 40 facts. After the story was read, he was asked to verbally recall what he remembered about the story. After a 50-minute delay, he was again asked to verbally recall what he remembered about the story. Mr. Armstrong was then asked 20 questions about the story, 15 of which were misleading or leading questions. He yielded 12 times to these 15 questions. The average Yield score for adults in the general population is 4.6. His scores are at the 97% range compared to other adults. After Mr. Armstrong answered the questions, he was informed in a firm voice that he made a number of errors, that the questions were to be repeated, and that he needed to be more accurate. Mr. Armstrong shifted his answers, right or wrong, to a different response, 15 times to the 20 questions. The average Shift score is 2.9. His score falls within the 99% range compared to adults in the general population. His Total Suggestibility Score, which is the sum of the Yield and Shift scores, is 27. The average score is 7.5. His Total Suggestibility Score falls within the upper 99% range.

FORENSIC CONSIDERATIONS

I do not believe it is appropriate for forensic psychologists to offer an opinion on whether a confession was voluntary or false. Nevertheless, mental health professionals can provide the trier of fact with relevant psychological data that assist in a determination of the voluntariness and validity of a confession.

Mr. Armstrong is at higher risk compared to others for providing false or less than accurate statements to law enforcement. He is particularly susceptible to the tactics the police used in extracting a confession from him on June 26, 2007. This is based on the following factors.

1. Mr. Armstrong is someone who functions at the Extremely Low to Borderline range of intelligence. Although he does not meet criteria for mental retardation, his Full Scale IQ score of 70 is at the lower 2% compared to others his age. His verbal comprehension abilities, which are more relevant to one's interaction with law enforcement, are at the lower 9% range. Research is clear in showing a correlation between low intelligence and interrogative suggestibility (the extent to which an individual comes to accept information communicated during formal questioning as true).

2. On the GSS, Mr. Armstrong's tendency to give in to leading questions and to shift to a different response under pressure was extreme. He is a highly suggestible individual who is going to be at much greater risk than the average person of providing erroneous accounts of events when police provide misleading or false information or pressure him to change his answers. Although he is no more submissive than anyone else, his low intelligence and overall personality style would make it very difficult for him to effectively manage confrontational and novel situations. He does not have the intellectual resources available to him to easily resist police demands, particularly over an extended period of time.

3. In addition, Mr. Armstrong told police he wished he had the Tylenol 3 he had been taking for pain in his broken hand. He was wearing a cast during the interrogation. It was not until he had provided a confession

that he was able to access the Tylenol 3 his mother brought from home (this is not to imply the police made it a condition that to receive the pain medication he must confess, just that since he was in pain, the pain itself would have added to the difficulty of resisting police demands).

Mr. Armstrong told me during the clinical interview that he usually takes two Tylenol 3 tablets, per prescription instructions, but he may have inadvertently taken double that dosage, forgetting he had taken the medication earlier. Although he told law enforcement that he last took the pills "yesterday," he told me that this was not at all true. He had taken the pills several hours before the questioning. He told me that his sister observed him taking two of the pills and he may have taken two more by mistake. He said that the pain pills made him feel "really messed up, got me to feel like I smoked something and got really high." The DVDs showed Mr. Armstrong presenting much differently in the 2007 interrogation than he had in 2006 (and differently from my interview with him). During the June 26, 2007, interrogation, he was very quiet, was often almost inaudible in his speech, and had flat affect (little emotional responsivity). He appeared t as if in a daze. This is consistent with someone being under the effects of a lot of pain medication. Although his behavioral presentation could also be consistent with severe depression, he looked more groggy than anything. In that he told law enforcement he took the Tylenol 3 "yesterday," if in fact he took the pills just prior to being picked up by law enforcement, this might be relevant information in evaluating the reliability of his statements.

4. Throughout the interrogation, Mr. Armstrong told police that he was told by his lawyer not to speak with them and, as a result, felt uncomfortable speaking with them. Law enforcement used a number of interrogation tactics designed to break down Mr. Armstrong's resistance (which was probably already somewhat broken down by the medication he was taking). The seriousness of the crime he was accused of was minimized by his being told numerous times that he was not like the type of bad person who robs a convenience store and ends up shooting the clerk. The crime was minimized by law enforcement, emphasizing that it was "spur of the moment," a "momentary lapse of judgment." He was told that there was a difference between him and someone who does not "take responsibility" or "who can stand up and say, I made a mistake."

During the June 26, 2007, interrogation, Mr. Armstrong was accused of lying during the police questioning on November 17, 2006. He was told to "stand up and be a man." He was lied to and told that they had evidence that the baby died of shaking. He was told that if he did not provide an explanation, people would think that "Gus is a psycho child killer." He was even told by one of the officers that many years ago the officer himself was only a knock on the door away from potentially shaking his baby and causing injury. This implied that almost every male was at risk of killing an infant by shaking.

Mr. Armstrong told me that at some point during the interrogation, he began to believe that perhaps he did shake the child to death because the police told him they had evidence he did it. Otherwise, what else could have accounted for the child's death? He said he began to incorporate the police version of the offense into his own version and began to doubt his own memory for what transpired when he was with the infant. If Mr. Armstrong's confession is false, the confession is of the coerced-internalized false confession type, although there are also elements of a coerced-compliant false confession. This is because, if the confession was false, Mr. Armstrong would have partly confessed to escape the negative effects of the interrogation and for him to be presented in a better light.

When Mr. Armstrong finally admitted to shaking Jerry, he was inconsistent in describing the force of the shaking, both in his demonstrations of the shaking with a doll supplied by the officers, as well in his verbal descriptions of the shaking (how many times he shook the infant and how long the shaking lasted). Toward the end of the interrogation, in summarizing what happened to the infant, Mr. Armstrong said, "…I shook him not realizing what

I was doing. So it wasn't for a long period of time but I guess long enough that it happened to him." Although this can be interpreted as a confession of guilt, it is also a somewhat ambiguous statement. Mr. Armstrong could be saying he did not know what he did at the time, but he must have killed his child because law enforcement had evidence he did so, but that he "stopped when I realized what I was doing."

As far as the voluntariness of this confession, although the police did not outright threaten Mr. Armstrong or make promises, they certainly implied he would be viewed differently than someone who intentionally goes and kills someone. Someone of Mr. Armstrong's limited intelligence would be even more likely to believe this would result in less punishment than someone more intellectually adept.

Mr. Armstrong was questioned off and on for over four hours. This excludes the time prior to his being videotaped (such as the time period of his arrest and the drive to the police station). Mr. Armstrong was either in pain from his hand and did not have access to his pain medication, or, more likely, was "high" from taking the pain medication. Mr. Armstrong said he believed it was a combination of both, that he felt "high" but had a little pain. Nevertheless, Mr. Armstrong was questioned over an extended period of time despite his stating that he was told by his lawyer that he should not talk to the police. Mr. Armstrong, compared to others, is much more susceptible to the police tactics that were used than the average person.

SUMMARY

Mr. Armstrong was 21 years old at the time of the interrogation. He functions at the lower 2% range of intelligence compared to others his age. He is an extremely suggestible individual who is going to be misled by law enforcement and is going to change his responses to questions substantially more often than the average person. At the time of the interrogation in June 2007, he was likely under the effects of a narcotic pain medication. These factors, in combination with the tactics that were used by law enforcement in extracting a confession, place Mr. Armstrong at greater risk than the average person of giving a false or partially false confession. These factors and others described above also have relevancy in assessing the voluntariness of his confession.

Thank you for the opportunity to assist the court with this case. If I can provide any additional information, please let me know.

Respectfully,
I. Bruce Frumkin, Ph.D., ABPP
Clinical Psychologist
Diplomate in Forensic Psychology
American Board of Professional Psychology

TEACHING POINT:
WHAT IS THE VALUE OF SPECIALIZED FORENSIC ASSESSMENT INSTRUMENTS IN FORENSIC MENTAL HEALTH ASSESSMENT?
(contributed by I. Bruce Frumkin)

Psychologists have been increasingly retained to assist the courts in cases in which the voluntariness or validity of a confession is disputed. The ultimate issue of the validity of a defendant's confession, or whether in fact it was involuntarily elicited, is beyond the scope of a forensic psychologist's work. These are either legal determinations to be made by the court based on whether the police exceeded legally permissible means to extract a confession, or are in the domain of a jury, evaluating all the evidence to determine whether a defendant in fact committed the offense. Psychologists can provide the trier of fact with data concerning a defendant's psychological vulnerabilities and the interaction with interrogation tactics used by law enforcement. This provides useful information regarding an individual's risk of providing less than accurate or false statements during the interrogation. In addition to the psychologist having a familiarity with the literature regarding types of interrogation tactics employed to extract confessions from those who are believed guilty (e.g., Reid Technique), the psychologist should also be aware of the various reasons individuals may falsely confess to crimes (e.g., Voluntary False Confessions, Coerced-Compliant False Confessions, Coerced-Internalized False Confessions).

There is a body of research describing psychological factors related to susceptibility to giving a false confession. Such factors include, but are not limited to, low intelligence, anxiety, poor memory, compliance, interrogative suggestibility, and sleep deprivation. The Gudjonsson Suggestibility Scales (GSS) is a specialized FAI developed to help assess interrogative suggestibility. It is an objective psychological test that can provide valuable data regarding an individual's susceptibility to yielding to leading questions and to shifting to different responses under pressure. Although the test administration does not recreate precisely what transpires during a police interrogation, as long as law enforcement misleads the suspect and/or pressures him or her, the test results have relevancy.

One can compare a defendant's scores on the GSS with various populations (e.g., general, forensic, juvenile) in the United Kingdom and in Iceland. Frumkin et al. (2012) provided a large forensic U.S. sample to be used as additional bases for comparisons. Nevertheless, this test is often misused by psychologists. Because of the standard error of measurement, test scores under the 85th percentile should not be considered elevated. A high score does not equal an involuntary confession or a false confession but rather points to a heightened risk of producing one, assuming the police were misleading or pressuring the suspect. In addition, someone may be highly suggestible, commit a crime, confess to that crime, and later retract the confession. The GSS results become useful, as well as other test and empirical data, in providing information to the jury so they can better decide how much weight to give a confession, or to a judge to decide whether the police took advantage of a vulnerable individual in a legally impermissible fashion. The psychologist should not place undue emphasis on the GSS scores, but rather use this measure as part of a comprehensive assessment. Like other FAIs, the information gleaned from the GSS is functionally based and is generally relevant to what a suspect encounters when interrogated by law enforcement.

CASE TWO
PRINCIPLE: USE CASE-SPECIFIC (IDIOGRAPHIC) EVIDENCE IN ASSESSING CLINICAL CONDITION, FUNCTIONAL ABILITIES, AND CAUSAL CONNECTION (PRINCIPLE 27)

There are many important sources of scientific and empirical evidence that can be used to provide relevant information to a variety of legal decision-makers. Although reliable and valid empirical evidence is important in FMHA, such evidence should be used in conjunction with scientific *reasoning*. Such reasoning is particularly important when using an idiographic approach, specifically by employing case-specific information and interpreting it using scientific reasoning (comparable to the "single case study" design).

Idiographic information is particularly important in assessing relevant domains in FMHA for two reasons. First, an idiographic approach can contribute significantly to the overall accuracy of the FMHA, and accurate information is critical to hypothesis development, testing, and verification. Second, the use of idiographic data enhances the face validity and relevance of the FMHA because of its specificity and applicability to the particular case, which makes the FMHA more credible to legal decision-makers. In addition to enhancing face validity (a particularly important concern in FMHA; see, e.g., Grisso, 1986, 2003), the use of idiographic data is important because standards of practice and ethics authorities strongly suggest that FMHA should be based on information and techniques that are sufficient to support the conclusions reached in FMHA (Standards 2.04, 9.01, and 9.06 of the APA *Ethics Code*; Guidelines 9.01 and 10.02 of the APA *Specialty Guidelines*) and that take into account the specific characteristics of the individual being assessed (Standards 9.02c and 9.06 of the APA *Ethics Code*; Guidelines 2.08, 10.02, and 10.03 of the APA *Specialty Guidelines*). Typically, this is accomplished through direct contact with the individual(s) being assessed and the gathering of case-specific information for hypothesis formation and testing.

There is also a strong legal justification for using an idiographic approach in FMHA: the enhanced relevance that results from including idiographic data is directly applicable to the admissibility of expert evidence under *Daubert, Kumho*, and the *Federal Rules of Evidence* (see above) such that FMHA based on nomothetic data without idiographic information would be more likely to be ruled inadmissible by the court (see, e.g., *Lawlor v. Commonwealth*, 2013). The incorporation of idiographic information within FMHA has also been cited as a best practice within FMHA in the professional literature (Grisso, 1986, 2003; Heilbrun, Grisso, & Goldstein, 2009; Melton et al., 2007; Packer & Grisso, 2011).

The present case provides a good example of the use of idiographic evidence in hypothesis formation and testing. This defendant was evaluated to provide his attorney with information relevant to his competence to waive *Miranda* rights. The case provides an example of the relationship between formally measured intellectual functioning and specific competencies. The idiographic data, obtained through a collateral interview and review of case-relevant documents, were applied toward describing actual and potential functioning in a variety of domains relevant to the competence to waive *Miranda* rights.

Miranda warnings are designed to protect a defendant's right against self-incrimination under the Fifth Amendment. Under *Miranda*, a defendant enjoys the protections of several rights (the right to remain silent, the right to an attorney, and the right to have an attorney provided if the defendant cannot afford one) and must also show an awareness of the consequences of waiving these rights (e.g., the knowledge that any statements made can be used against him or her in a court of law). A defendant must be able to waive *Miranda* rights in a "knowing, voluntary, and intelligent" manner. Accordingly, the FMHA must consider the specific capacities relevant to a knowing, intelligent, and voluntary waiver. Furthermore, the primary focus is often on the capacities for a knowing and intelligent waiver, as a number of courts have held that the kind of coercion that would typically be evaluated by a mental health professional (e.g., presenting an individual with "hard choices," implying that a sentence will be more severe if the defendant does not waive *Miranda* rights) does not rise to the level of making a waiver "involuntary" in this context (see, e.g., *Miller v. State*, 1986; *Rhode Island v. Innis*, 1980; *United States v. Velasquez*, 1989).

The FMHA is primarily concerned with the capacities involved in making such a waiver. The clinical symptoms and cognitive deficits that could limit such capacities—either temporarily (e.g., acute intoxication) or more permanently (e.g., severe mental retardation)—are also relevant for this kind of assessment. As with other legal questions, the presence of such clinical or cognitive deficits might be described as a "necessary but not sufficient" basis for a legal decision-maker to conclude that a waiver was not competently made. The relationship between the clinical or cognitive deficits and the specific relevant capacity must be established. An idiographic approach to this assessment issue would have the evaluator seek to determine what the defendant understood about his or her *Miranda* rights at the time of the confession, how the defendant reasoned in waiving these rights, and whether these capacities for understanding and reasoning were more impaired at the time of the waiver than they are currently.

In the present case, the process of assessing the relevant capacities could not begin with a detailed interview with the defendant. Mr. Lopez was not a good reporter, as a result of many of the deficits described in the evaluation. At times it was necessary for the evaluator to repeat information to him. At other times, his responses consisted of repeating what he had been told, in a rote fashion. Fortunately, Dr. Goldstein was able to obtain review fairly extensive records. These included mental health and educational history (with prior testing relevant to his current cognitive functioning), as well as child protective services and offense-relevant documents. The collateral information was supplemented by an interview with Mr. Lopez's brother.

ALAN M. GOLDSTEIN, PhD, PC
13 Arden Drive
Hartsdale, New York 10563
(914) 693-7760
alanmg@optonline.net
Licensed Psychologist in NY, CT, and IA
PRIVILEGED AND CONFIDENTIAL
FORENSIC PSYCHOLOGICAL EVALUATION

Defendant: Paul Lopez   Dates Evaluated: 03/11/08
D.O.B.:   06/19/92   04/13/09
Age: 17 years   Ind. No.:   00291/2007
Date of
Report: 06/29/09

Paul Lopez was referred by his attorney, Hillary Miller. I was informed by Ms. Miller that when Mr. Lopez was age 15, he was arrested, along with a co-defendant, and charged with a number of crimes, including rape in the first degree and criminal possession of a weapon. She reported that Mr. Lopez has a documented history of lead poisoning and has been in Special Education classes throughout his school career.

Ms. Miller asked that I evaluate Mr. Lopez regarding his ability to understand and appreciate his *Miranda* rights. This report focuses on that issue.

The opinions presented in this report are based upon multiple sources of information, consistent with the standard of practice in the field of forensic mental health assessment. I interviewed Mr. Lopez twice at the Candlewood Juvenile Center in Brooklyn. During those sessions, I obtained a personal history from him and questioned him regarding the circumstances associated with the administration of his *Miranda* rights. Mr. Lopez was seen for a total of approximately seven hours.

In addition to my interviews with Mr. Lopez, I administered a battery of tests to him, instruments that are commonly used in the fields of clinical and forensic psychology. The following instruments were administered:

Wechsler Adult Intelligence Scale–III
(WAIS-III)
Wide Range Achievement Test–4 (WRAT-4)
Assessing Understanding and Appreciation of
Miranda Rights
Test of Memory Malingering (TOMM)

Because of Mr. Lopez's low level of reading, it was not possible to administer standardized objective personality tests to him.

I have examined copies of the following documents provided to me by Ms. Miller:

- Criminal Complaint
- Interview Report—Criminal Justice Agency (7/21/07)
- Indictment No. 3487/07
- People's Voluntary Disclosure Form and Bill of Particulars (7/23/07)
- Signed *Miranda* Warning Form (7/12/07)
- Functional Assessment Report (10/12/07; 12/16/07)
- Baffin Valley Community Service Center Termination Summary (2/18/04, 6/28/05)
  - Intake Psychiatric Assessment (7/27/04)
  - Intake Psychosocial Assessment (1/09/04)
- Pediatric Clinic record
- Sherman Hospital record (6/17/92)
- New York City Board of Education records (covering only 2002 and 2004)
- Office of Children and Family Services— Child Protective Services records
  - Intake Report—Donna Lopez
  - CPS Investigation Conclusion (7/13/06)
- CPS Investigation Summary (7/25/06)
- Progress Notes (various dates)
- Printed Statements (7/12/07: 11:18 p.m. and 11:55 p.m.)
- Candlewood Juvenile Center records

I reviewed a CD of the recorded portion of Mr. Lopez's interrogation commencing on 7/12/07 at 6:40 p.m.

I also interviewed Mr. Lopez's brother, Michael Lopez, by telephone for about 30 minutes on 5/30/09.

BRIEF SUMMARY OF RECORDS REVIEWED

According to the Criminal Complaint, on or about 7/10/07, at approximately 1:19 a.m., Mr. Lopez, along with a co-defendant, committed acts that resulted in four charges, including rape in the first degree, first degree burglary in the second degree, robbery in the second degree, and sexual abuse in the first degree. Indictment (00291/07) charges Mr. Lopez with four counts of rape in the first degree, one count of kidnapping in the second degree, burglary in the second degree, and sexual assault in the first degree. He is also charged with two counts of robbery in the second degree.

The People's Voluntary Disclosure Form indicates that Mr. Lopez was arrested on 7/12/07 at approximately 9:45 a.m. It reports that he offered two statements on that date. Although one of his statements was recorded, this document indicates that there was "a technical malfunction and the first of approximately nine minutes of this statement were not recorded."

Mr. Lopez signed a copy of the *Miranda* waiver form at approximately 11:30 a.m. on 7/12/07. Next to each statement, he printed the word "Yes" and printed his initials. His brother, Michael, also wrote "Yes," initialed each of the statements, and signed his name on the bottom of this form.

The two statements offered by Mr. Lopez are printed. There are a number of errors with punctuation and grammar noted in the statements, but very few spelling errors. One statement, of 21 lines, took Mr. Lopez 40 minutes to print. Contrasted with the spelling in his printed statements, a note printed on a page with a photograph (12:15 p.m.) reads, "I dot no whim," most likely meaning, "I don't know him."

Mr. Lopez's New York City Board of Education records are markedly incomplete. The records provided to me cover only the periods of 2002 and 2004. According to an Individual Education Plan (IEP) prepared on 11/29/02, Mr. Lopez was identified as a special education student, classified as Learning Disabled. In this report, his reading was described as "limited," as were his spelling and written expression. This evaluation notes that Mr. Lopez had been retained twice up to that time in his school career. It is reported that he has a history of lead poisoning, accompanied by significant delays in his reading comprehension and other skills. On November 2002, when Mr. Lopez was ten years of age, he was administered the Woodcock Johnson–Revised, a measure of academic skills. His reading comprehension fell toward the beginning of the first-grade level. Listening comprehension was equal to that of the average child in the middle of kindergarten. Mr. Lopez's writing skills, measured at age ten, were equal to that of the average child starting the first grade. At that time, Mr. Lopez was in the third grade at Public School [PS] 87.

The Initial Social History prepared in 2002 reports that Mr. Lopez was required to repeat the second grade. In addition, when he was tested in 2002, he was repeating the third grade for the second time. This document reports that when Mr. Lopez was age four, he was diagnosed with lead poisoning. A psychological evaluation conducted on 10/26/02 indicated that, although no intelligence testing was done, it was believed that Mr. Lopez's IQ fell within the Low Average range. A more formal educational evaluation, conducted as part of the IEP (10/30/02), reported very limited listening comprehension. Problems were noted in his expressive vocabulary. His ability in this regard was equal to that of the average child in the middle of kindergarten. Other scores ranged from those equal to students toward the end of kindergarten up to those starting the first grade.

In 2004, a new IEP was prepared (11/13/04). This document reports that Mr. Lopez was "severely deficient in reading fluency, spelling and writing." The Woodcock-Johnson II was administered as part of this review on 10/25/04. Mr. Lopez's reading and writing skills fell at the first grade level. It was noted that Mr. Lopez, then age 12, demonstrated a range of behavioral problems, including aggression and a low frustration tolerance. The report indicates the presence of a possible organic condition.

A psychological evaluation was conducted (10/23/04). This report indicated the presence of severe academic difficulties, along with problems involving lack of attention, impulsivity, and physical aggression. He was described as "defiant." The Wechsler Intelligence Scale for Children–IV was administered at that time. His full scale or overall IQ fell within the Intellectually Deficient category. Delays in vocabulary and a lack of understanding regarding social rules were reported. His performance IQ was reportedly equal to that of the average child who is six years and three months of age.

Mr. Lopez was seen at the Baffin Valley Community Services Center. The psychosocial assessment conducted at this facility (1/9/04) indicated the presence of a learning disability. It was noted that Mr. Lopez had problems focusing while in school. He was receiving two medications, Risperdal and Adderall. According to the intake psychiatric assessment (7/27/04), Mr. Lopez had severe difficulties learning in school. He was described as coherent, but labile and restless.

A record from the Pediatric Clinic indicated that lead had been found in Mr. Lopez's blood at a normal level when tested in 2000. However, according to this report, prior tests had indicated higher concentrations of lead. Mr. Lopez was diagnosed with attention deficit hyperactivity disorder. Treatment at the Baffin Valley Center was terminated because, according to these records, Ms. Donna Lopez did not want treatment for her son, "only special educational services."

Child Protective Service records indicate that his mother, Donna, had educationally neglected her child. Charges against her were substantiated (7/18/06). The case worker visited Paul Lopez's school and interviewed the assistant principal (7/22/06). At that time, Mr. Lopez was age 14 and was in the sixth grade in a special education program. His counselor reported that Mr. Lopez "doesn't follow instructions well and is unable to complete task [sic]." The counselor reported behavioral problems. Mr. Lopez's teacher indicated that her student demonstrated "behavior problems" and, despite the fact that he was in a special education class, was "very below [sic] in grades." The principal of the school recommended that Mr. Lopez needed "to be sent to a juvenile detention center."

Maia Brookes, Ph.D., of the New York State Office of Mental Retardation and Developmental Disabilities, evaluated Mr. Lopez in October and December 2007. In her report, Dr. Brookes noted,

"Paul had a history of lead exposure about the age of two and one-half. This lead exposure lasted for at least seven years."

Dr. Brookes administered the WISC-IV. On that instrument, Mr. Lopez obtained a full scale IQ of 68, a score that would be surpassed by 98% of the population. His verbal comprehension composite score would be exceeded by 96% of the population. His working memory composite score would be surpassed by 99% of the population. His perceptional reasoning composite score fell within the borderline range. Dr. Brookes reported that differences between Mr. Lopez's scores "are indications of brain damage."

On a task that evaluates verbal comprehension and auditory attention, Mr. Lopez's performance was found to be "severely impaired (0.1 percentile)." His performance on two tests that measure sensory-motor functioning was found to fall within normal limits. Similarly, on a task that evaluates social perception, Mr. Lopez's performance also fell within the norm. Mr. Lopez was administered a measure used to assess attention. His scores on this instrument were found to fall within the normal range as well. On measures of learning and memory, Mr. Lopez's immediate memory for verbal information was found to be impaired, as were other measures of memory, with the exception of visual working memory. On measures of higher cognitive skills, executive functioning, Dr. Brookes reported, "Paul's verbal concept formation functioning deviated from what would have been expected.... [H]owever,... [his] planning ability was in the superior range of functioning...."

In summarizing the data, Dr. Brookes indicated that an evaluation of Paul Lopez's neurological functioning indicated:

> Impairments of auditory attention, verbal comprehension, immediate and delayed memory for semantic and syntax context, associative and verbal learning and immediate and delayed retrieval for visuospatial material. These severe deficiencies, observed in association with normal to above normal functioning in other neuro-cognitive domains and interpreted in the context of this patient's history, are indicative of pediatric brain injury.

Dr. Brookes noted Mr. Lopez's documented history of lead poisoning. She concluded, "the presence of an established neurotoxin at this early age causes significant damage." She opined, "Brain damage of this type is permanent; recovery cannot be expected. The brain symptoms implicated in these functions continue to develop late into the teen years."

Dr. Brookes noted that, at least in part, Mr. Lopez's problems with impulse control and his lack of social judgment were consequences of his exposure to lead at an early age. She concluded, "It is clear from Paul's results that he is classical brain damaged [sic]. He has a severe language learning deficit. His brain damage from the lead has even caused him to function in the mildly mentally retarded range." Dr. Brookes noted some areas of strength that Mr. Lopez demonstrated. However, in light of his deficits, she indicated the need for "educational aides to assist him in learning." She stated, "He cannot read. He cannot function in the classroom. Paul must be given intensive reading therapy, and intensive auditory training in order for him to learn how to compensate for the brain damage caused by the lead poisoning."

Paul was admitted to the Brooklyn Juvenile Center on 7/13/07 and transferred to Candlewood Juvenile Center on 7/16/07. These records note, "Paul continues to display very needy behavior and is receiving support of counseling by all staff to help redirect his maturation process." At Candlewood, it was reported (2/5/08) that Mr. Lopez followed staff directives, although "he can be somewhat needy." He continued to attend school while at Candlewood. One report card (10/12/07) indicated that he received grades of 70 in reading, writing, and math. He received 75 in physical education and art, and a 65 in music. His average was 70.83%. It was noted that Mr. Lopez had "progressed in both behavior and his school work." Another report card (11/5/08) indicated that Mr. Lopez had "come a long way." He received grades of 65 in reading, writing, and career character. He received 70s in law and ethics and in math, and a 75 in physical education. Notes from both report cards indicated a lack of classroom participation.

While he was at Candlewood, a number of medical forms were completed by staff. A Mental Health Discharge Planning Referral form (8/3/07) indicated Mr. Lopez's "history of psy. meds... [and] poor decision-making." In general, however, no mental health problems were noted. Requests for medical attention appear to have been made through forms submitted by staff. There were a number of printed complaints written in the "first person." These complaints tended to be grammatically correct and words were spelled correctly. It is noted, however, that on some of these forms, the printing appears to be different, and other notes, printed in the same manner, were clearly written by professional staff.

SUMMARY OF INTERVIEW WITH MICHAEL LOPEZ, BROTHER

Prior to the start of my interview with Mr. Michael Lopez (5/30/09), I explained the nature and the purpose of my call to him. I informed him that any information he provided me would be included in my report if it were relevant. Michael Lopez had no difficulty in understanding this information, and this interview was conducted with his informed consent. (He was 18 at the time of this interview and thus able to give informed consent.) Michael informed me that he completed the eleventh grade at Neighborhood High School in Queens. He works as a set designer and explained that for the last several years he has traveled and was not home with his brother all of the time.

According to Michael, his brother has been in special education classes "all his life, mostly." He explained that his brother is classified as "learning disabled. He can't focus in school. He's 17 with, like, a ten-year-old's mind. He can't catch things." When asked about his younger brother's reading, Michael explained, "I'd say it's like a first grader. [His spelling] is kind of bad, too." When asked what books his brother reads, Michael explained, "I don't think he can really read."

Michael reported that he and his brother were asleep at his mother's home when the police arrived, "looking for Paul. He was handcuffed, and they took him to the precinct with me, and they started the interrogation of him." Michael stated that the police had asked him to accompany his brother. He reported that the police did not tell them why Paul Lopez was being brought to the precinct. He recalled that the police told them that they would explain "when we got there."

According to Michael Lopez, speaking to interrogators, "I said I would not want him to speak - I was around 17 - till my mom comes, and if she said he'd speak, it's up to her. I knew this from school." According to Mr. Lopez, interrogators "explained it

didn't matter if my mom was there or not and that they'd interrogate him if I'm in the room or not." Michael Lopez told me that he was present during part of one of the two evaluation sessions conducted by interrogators.

Michael Lopez recalled that interrogation began in a downstairs room. His brother was "handcuffed to a pole or a chair and they started interrogating him." He stated that he did not interrupt the interrogation "because they didn't ask me anything." He also stated that he did not advise his brother whether or not he should speak "because before we were in the room, they started speaking to him first, and they were speaking while they were walking inside. They were playing their thing that 'only you'll find out what happened if and when we speak'."

When asked if he was present when his brother was given his *Miranda* rights, Mr. Michael Lopez explained, "I'm not sure because he doesn't know how to read and he's not going to know how it is." Again, I asked whether he was present when the rights were read. He stated, "They gave him a paper and I remember telling them he doesn't know how to read, that he doesn't comprehend things well in his mind. [I told] one of the police officers." When asked whether this dialogue had been recorded, Michael Lopez stated, "Oh no. That happened in the second office when we were separated. There were two interrogations."

Michael Lopez recalled countersigning the rights form. He explained, "I don't remember. I don't think they read it and they only said 'Sign here'." When asked whether he had read the form, Michael Lopez stated, "I'm not sure. I was young and a little terrified, and I didn't know what was going on. I don't remember signing it." He recalled seeing his brother sign "Yes" after each warning. Michael Lopez explained that he, Michael, did not read these statements "because they were telling me what to write and what to do. [I signed it] because they told me to." When asked whether his brother read the form aloud, Michael Lopez stated, "Paul doesn't know how to read."

Michael Lopez recalled that the written statement was made "when we were still downstairs. I don't think that was taped." He stated, "Once we were downstairs, they're interrogating him the first time and then they went upstairs and they separated us from the room and told me to go to another room. I was there from one-half to one hour at the most and then we were back together. He did have something that I read. I know he doesn't know how to write." Michael Lopez reported that when he entered the second interrogation room, "I asked Paul, 'Who helped you write the letter?' and he said, 'One of the officers'. One was white and there was a Hispanic officer, and he said, 'the Hispanic officer helped me write the letter'. I think it was Officer Feldman, I think." According to Michael Lopez, "Paul told me he said it, and he [the officer] was going to write it down and let Paul copy it.... Paul said he first spoke to the guy and the guy wrote it down and he copied it."

Michael Lopez recalled that he was not present for part of the interview that was conducted "upstairs. I walked in and I saw them asking questions and I kept quiet."

Michael Lopez reported that his brother was interrogated by a female. "She was asking him in a manner that he doesn't understand, and I told her he has a disability and you need to repeat questions and get him to understand what they're saying. They told me it doesn't matter. If he answers, he will understand. But, he doesn't know what it means." Michael Lopez believed that this interaction was not taped "because I spoke and they stepped me outside the room. I spoke to her outside the room. We were inside the room and they were asking questions, and I see he doesn't understand the words, and I started speaking to her in the room, and one of the officers stopped me and said, 'Come this way' and the officer took me out and she came out."

When asked whether that interaction had been taped, Michael Lopez stated, "I saw the machine, but it was through a glass door. I saw a red light through the glass, it wasn't that much of a mirror." He believed, "It happened just as I got to the room. I was not even in the room one minute because I heard and knew Paul didn't know what they were telling him.

EVALUATION OF PAUL LOPEZ

Prior to the start of my initial evaluation, I explained to Mr. Lopez, using simple language, the nature and purpose of my assessment. At times, it was necessary to repeat the information that I had given him in order for Mr. Lopez to understand what he had been told. At other times, Mr. Lopez merely repeated, by rote, what I had just told him. With repeated explanation, he provided a somewhat simplistic understanding of the fact that what he told me would not be confidential, and he understood the nature and purpose of my assessment.

When seen for the second time, on 4/13/09, Mr. Lopez acknowledged that he recognized me, but he could provide no other information about who I was, what my role had been in his case, or what we had talked about the year before. It was necessary to present information regarding the limits of confidentiality and the nature and purpose of this reevaluation to him several times, using simpler language each time. Mr. Lopez was eventually able to provide concrete, but adequate informed consent.

Brief History

Mr. Lopez reported that he was born in Sherman Hospital but does not know the circumstances of his birth. He believes that at the time he was born, his parents were married. However, he stated, "I haven't seen my father in a long time." He reported that his father was deported to the Dominican Republic and then to Haiti when Mr. Lopez was age five or six.

Mr. Lopez lives with his mother, Donna. He described his mother in positive terms, explaining, "She asks if I want to talk to her. If I have problems, I can talk to her." He reported that he was raised by his mother and his maternal grandmother. When asked his maternal grandmother's name, Mr. Lopez stated, "I didn't call her by name. I got to ask my mom that [her name]." Mr. Lopez reported that he has an older brother, Michael, four years older than he. His younger brother, John, is two years younger than Mr. Lopez. His younger brother, according to Mr. Lopez, is in regular classes. Although Michael did not graduate from high school, Mr. Lopez reported, "He's always smart and always with girls and stuff."

Mr. Lopez said that he had not been physically abused by his mother or anyone else in his life. Similarly, he told me that no one had ever sexually abused him. When asked whether he had been touched inappropriately by teachers, friends of his brothers, priests, etc., Mr. Lopez stated, "I've been baptized." According to Mr. Lopez, he attended public school from pre-kindergarten through the fifth grade. He believes that he was held back in the sixth grade, despite records that indicate he was retained in both the second and third grades.

He denied being placed in special education classes in the early grades. However, when questioned further, Mr. Lopez became silent. He then reported that he began to have problems because "I was eating lead when I was little, in my room, in my closet. It was paint." When asked what lead poisoning means, Mr. Lopez explained, "It's like paint inside me. It messes up my thinking, my thinking, and it don't keep me focused."

According to Mr. Lopez, he attended PS 89 starting in the fifth grade. He recalled being in special education classes with two teachers. "I didn't pay attention in class and my mom had to come to meetings and they said I needed a lot of help." Mr. Lopez believes he was suspended twice while in PS 89 "for not paying attention, for being in the halls, and for leaving school."

Mr. Lopez reported that he next attended PS 96 for grades seven and eight. He then noted, "I repeated the sixth grade at PS 96." He recalled receiving medication from the psychiatrist. "I took a pill, Seroquel, to calm down. I was very active and I fell asleep the whole time." Mr. Lopez reported that at the time of his arrest, he was in the ninth grade. "I was supposed to be in the tenth." He reported attending school while held at Candlewood House, and "They helped me read, write, and draw and stuff—sketch."

Mr. Lopez explained that he has never been employed. He stated that this was his first arrest. When asked about reading books, Mr. Lopez stated, "I can't read some books. I read some magazines—dirt bike magazines." He identified the current president of the United States as "George Washington," and the president before him as "His father." He enjoys watching "Disney Channel and cartoons." When asked who was running for president in March 2008, Mr. Lopez stated, "I forgot his name. He's Indian and has short hair. Did you hear about a guy, a mayor, who got caught? They say he was using prostitution. I've seen it in the papers and on TV."

Appreciation and Understanding of *Miranda* Rights

On 3/11/08, I questioned Mr. Lopez regarding his recollection of the events leading up to and including his waiver of his rights. He reported that the police arrived at his house at approximately 8:00 or 9:00 a.m. His older brother, Michael, Michael's girlfriend, and his younger brother were home at the time.

Mr. Lopez recalled that he was accompanied to the precinct by his older brother. "The super called my mom." Prior to leaving his home, he reported that the police informed him, "They had a warrant, papers, and said, 'You need to go downtown with us'." Mr. Lopez understood that a warrant is a document "to come and get you at the house or wherever you are, anywhere else." He reported that he was told to get dressed, and "The cops held the door opened while I was getting dressed. They put the cuffs on after I was dressed, in the hallway." He explained that after the handcuffs were placed on him, he was told, "I had to go to the precinct and they will explain what happened."

When asked what the police were supposed to say to him when he was cuffed, Mr. Lopez spontaneously replied, "You have the right to remain silent. Whatever you say will be used against you at all times." Mr. Lopez could recall no other rights spontaneously. Mr. Lopez believed that he was administered his rights, "I guess in the hallway. I don't remember."

Mr. Lopez reported that he and his brother did not speak to one another while in the police car. According to Mr. Lopez, he intended to tell his brother what had happened before he spoke to the police. Mr. Lopez informed me that at the precinct, he and his brother were "placed in an empty room with glass," and he told his brother what happened.

In a somewhat confusing manner (it was difficult to establish a meaningful sequence of events), Mr. Lopez explained that a detective and two police officers "started to talk and asked if I wanted to drink or eat." He recalled that his brother was "in and out [of the room] buying food. It was hours, and the guy showed up with a tape recorder. My brother saw the tape recorder." He recalled being placed in a room with his brother and the police "came with stuff and they were going to do listening things, a tape." When asked specifically, Mr. Lopez recalled that he had spoken to the police before the recording device was placed in the room, "When I first got there."

Mr. Lopez believed that he arrived at the precinct at approximately 10:00 a.m. and was alone from 10:00 a.m. to 1:00 p.m., "till my mother came. She got there at 12:00. She was crying, asking what happened." It was impossible to establish when his mother actually arrived at the precinct based on the information provided to me by Mr. Lopez. He then reported that he was never given his rights, contradicting information he had provided me at the start of the interview. He then appeared to explain that his brother was in the interview room with him from 10:00 a.m. to 1:00 p.m. When asked whether he could tell time, Mr. Lopez indicated that he was able to do so.

According to Mr. Lopez, at approximately 11:00 a.m., he was brought to another room. "There were two detectives and me and my brother was there, too." At that time, Mr. Lopez believed that he was told that he had done "something I wasn't suppose to do." He denied being given his rights in that room while in his brother's presence. When asked whether he was given "a sheet of paper with rights on them," Mr. Lopez explained, "I think so when I was with my brother." He then explained, "I think this was before [his brother entered the room]." He could not recall having the rights read to him, and when asked whether he read them, he stated, "No. I can't read."

When asked what rights were printed on the form, Mr. Lopez shrugged. When I inquired what the rights should say, he replied, "to remain silent and everything I say will be used against you at all times," his version of the rights he provided to me earlier in the session.

Mr. Lopez then defined the right to remain silent: "that I can't talk to them or something or I can't speak." When asked when he could speak, Mr. Lopez explained, "When they ask me to."

When asked to explain his spontaneous version of the incriminating nature of his statements, Mr. Lopez stated, "What I did. What I did for the crime." When asked what "at all times" meant, Mr. Lopez explained, "Anything I did. It's in court." When asked directly, Mr. Lopez recognized that his statement could be used to "hurt" him rather than to "help" him.

I then showed Mr. Lopez a copy of his signed *Miranda* waiver. I asked him to read it, but he replied, "I can't read." He acknowledged that he wrote the word "Yes" after each statement. When I asked him to read the first right, Mr. Lopez hesitated and stumbled after the first word, "You." I then read him the rights on the form.

His explanation of "the right to remain silent and to refuse to answer questions" was "If they ask me questions, I just answer it." He further stated that "to remain silent" means "That I can't talk till when they ask me to." When asked if he

could decide not to talk, Mr. Lopez replied in the affirmative: "by staying quiet till they ask me something."

I read the second right, "anything you say…" to Mr. Lopez. He explained, "what I did will be used against me in court—to try to keep me in."

With regard to "the right to consult an attorney before speaking to the police and to have an attorney present during any questioning now or in the future," Mr. Lopez did not spontaneously recall this right. When it was read to him, Mr. Lopez explained, "I got to have a lawyer before I talk to the cops." When asked what would happen if he did not have an attorney, Mr. Lopez explained, "then I tell them what I was supposed to tell the lawyer." Mr. Lopez could not define the word "consult" and his definition of an "attorney" was "someone who tries to keep you in."

When "If you can't afford an attorney, one will be provided for you without cost," was read to him, Mr. Lopez stated, "I don't know. It's bail or something or a paid lawyer or something." I re-read this right, and Mr. Lopez stated, "I don't know." He defined the word "afford" as, "You mean to pay, like afford to pay my bail." When I had previously asked Mr. Lopez his rights, he did not spontaneously recall this right.

When I read, "If you do not have an attorney available, you have the right to remain silent until you have had an opportunity to consult with one," Mr. Lopez initially stated, "I don't know." I re-read the right, and Mr. Lopez added, "till the judge asks me something? I stay quiet and the judge asks them if I spoke. [He will ask me] what did I do?" When asked to define "available," Mr. Lopez replied, "If you are on a basketball team, I could jump in." He defined the word "opportunity" as "a chance or something." When previously asked, he did not spontaneously recall this right.

I read, "Now that I have advised you of your rights, are you willing to answer questions?" to Mr. Lopez. He explained that this warning meant "that if they ask me something, I've got to answer it."

I questioned Mr. Lopez about his understanding and appreciation of his rights when I again evaluated him on 4/13/09. I asked him to spontaneously recall the rights he should have been provided. He replied, "I don't know. The right to remain silent. Anything we [sic] say they will use against you in a court of law. That's all I remember." When I pushed him for additional rights, Mr. Lopez was unable to spontaneously recall any additional warnings. At one point during this second session, he explained that the police were supposed to say, "to call my mom."

Mr. Lopez reported that his "big brother" was with him for part of the interrogation, and, according to Mr. Lopez, Michael Lopez told him, "Sit and tell them everything that happened." He recalled that he had done so, and when asked to explain why, Mr. Lopez stated, "Because I didn't know if I needed a lawyer or not." When asked whether he now knows whether he needed an attorney, Mr. Lopez stated, "Not to speak without a lawyer or your mother there."

Mr. Lopez explained that he followed his older brother's advice "because he's my big brother. He's in school, Neighborhood High School." He denied that he was frightened of his older brother or that his brother had threatened him. Mr. Lopez believed that he had been given helpful advice by his brother before: "not to go outside, you'll get in trouble. Don't get home late."

When asked to spontaneously define the right to remain silent, Mr. Lopez explained that this right meant "not to talk." He believed that he could talk "when they say you can talk."

When asked to spontaneously ask to define the right involving "anything you say," Mr. Lopez stated, "anything, everything, any evidence." He acknowledged, "I could be accused of the crime." He explained that the prosecutor may "bring it up at trial."

According to Mr. Lopez, he had developed a better understanding of this right because, while held at Candlewood Juvenile Center, "They give us a class in law." When asked what he had been taught, he recalled, "the right to remain silent." He stated that he had been taught, "It can be used against you in a court of law." Mr. Lopez did not recall other rights he had been taught. He stated his teacher's name was "Ms. Grayler." Mr. Lopez also explained that he had been taught to "call your mother and try to get a lawyer. Call your mom and tell her to get a lawyer." When asked if he had been taught what to do if his mother did not have money for an attorney, Mr. Lopez explained, "You get Legal Aid. She told me that. There's a paid lawyer before a Legal Aid lawyer." Mr. Lopez told me that he was taught that if he were arrested, "not to talk to the police." He claimed that his teacher had explained, "You don't have to talk to them."

When asked what he would have to do if he were told by the police that he must speak, Mr. Lopez explained, "I'll wait till a grownup comes." When asked what he would do if the police suggested that it might help him if he spoke, he replied, "If they told me—my grownups—I'd talk." When I asked him what he would do if the police were nice to him and he trusted them, Mr. Lopez replied, "I wouldn't know what to do." When I asked him what he would do if a judge told him to explain what had happened regarding the crime, Mr. Lopez explained, "I'd tell him what happened. I'd have to." When asked what would happen if a judge learned that he had refused to speak to the police, Mr. Lopez informed me, "I don't know." When asked whether the result would be good or bad, he stated, "Good, I guess?" However, he was unable to elaborate, stating, "I was guessing."

According to Mr. Lopez, he would be able to obtain an attorney "when my mom calls." He believed that he would first see his attorney "in court." When asked directly whether he could have an attorney when the police were asking him questions, he stated "Yes." When asked to explain, Mr. Lopez stated, "No. You can't. I already started talking…I don't think so."

When asked what he would now do if he were to be arrested, Mr. Lopez explained, "I wouldn't talk…because I'd tell my lawyer before I tell them [the police]." He stated that he had acquired this information "from the law book from Ms. Grayler." Mr. Lopez believed that Ms. Grayler "used to be a prosecutor." He recalled that, during his class, the students would ask Ms. Grayler questions. They watched movies and television shows, including *Law and Order*. He reported that his teacher had never asked him specific questions about his interactions with the police. Mr. Lopez recalled that this class was offered "around Christmas, every fifth period for a month."

Observations of Behavior

During his first interview with me, Mr. Lopez responded in a very hesitating manner. He found it difficult to provide basic information regarding his personal history. At times, he misunderstood questions. Answers were often brief and required follow-up questions for Mr. Lopez to be thoroughly understood. He appeared to be somewhat withdrawn and mildly depressed. No evidence of an underlying thought disorder or an active psychotic process was found. Mr. Lopez tended to respond in a passive manner, providing little in the way of spontaneous information.

When seen approximately one year later, Mr. Lopez continued to respond in a slow manner. He demonstrated little in the way of facial expression. At times, he stared, and he appeared to be "tuning out." Problems with attention were noted, and it was necessary to refocus him from time to time. (See Comment A, below).

When standardized tests were administered, Mr. Lopez seemed to enjoy the attention given to him. On the WRAT-4, he responded in a plodding manner. He erased some of his responses to the spelling subtest. On a subtest that involves mathematical computation, Mr. Lopez counted on his fingers at times. On the WAIS-III, Mr. Lopez returned to an item and corrected his answer spontaneously. He approached testing with a level of enthusiasm that was not seen at any other time.

Results of Testing

Mr. Lopez was administered the WAIS-III, an objective, standardized measure of intelligence. On this instrument, he obtained a full scale IQ of 72. This score falls within the borderline range of intelligence. It would be surpassed by 97% of the population.

The WAIS-III consists of two major sections, one that taps verbal abilities associated with intelligence, and the second, which measures nonverbal skills associated with intellectual functioning. His verbal IQ of 69 falls within the extremely low range; 98% of the population would have obtained a score higher than did Mr. Lopez. His non-verbal or performance IQ of 80 falls at the bottom of the low average range; 91% of the population would have obtained a score exceeding that of Mr. Lopez.

COMMENT A

It is important to consider the interval of time that has passed between the initial administration of the *Miranda* rights by the police and the time when you first evaluate the defendant. Specifically, what may have intervened during that period of time that might have increased the defendant's understanding of the warnings?

For example, I evaluated a 14-year-old who, according to her lawyer, did not grasp *any* of her *Miranda* warnings. However, when I saw her two months after she had been administered her rights, she provided almost perfect explanations of each right. When I discussed this apparent contradiction with her lawyer, the lawyer explained, somewhat sheepishly, that he had provided his client with a full explanation of each right in an effort to discourage her from discussing her case with anyone at the juvenile detention facility, and the reasons why she should remain silent, and what might happen with the information she revealed. Therefore the defendant had been "contaminated" by this information and no opinion could be reached as to her comprehension of her *Miranda* rights at the time they were administered.

In many cases, juveniles and adults report that they did not know or understand their rights when they were provided, but that they have now learned them from other inmates during their incarceration. For many of these inmates, despite their claim that they now have acquired an understanding of their *Miranda* rights, further evaluation frequently demonstrated otherwise. That is, their understanding continued to remain incomplete, incorrect, or inadequate. An adult defendant who had appealed his conviction successfully after ten years of incarceration was granted a new trial on grounds having nothing to do with *Miranda* comprehension. His newly appointed lawyer had questions about his client's ability to have understood his rights when they were given to him over a decade ago. Although the defendant responded to all questions in a focused, appropriate way and had a WAIS-III Full Scale IQ of 88, he reported that he did not grasp *any* of his *Miranda* warnings. He performed poorly on the *Miranda* instruments and during that part of the interview when asked about each right. Having served more than ten years in prison and having been informed by his lawyer that I was going assess his understanding of his rights, it strained credibility that, in over ten years, while discussing legal issues with inmates, he had learned nothing about any of his rights.

Mr. Lopez's Verbal Comprehension Index score of 72 falls at the 3rd percentile. His Working Memory Index score of 61 falls below the 1st percentile. His score on the Processing Speed Index, 69, falls at the 2nd percentile. His highest Index score of 91 was obtained on the Perceptual Organization Index. This score falls at the 27th percentile.

Mr. Lopez function at a significantly lower level on verbal abilities tapped by the WAIS-III than he does on the nonverbal subtests. Significant intellectual deficits were noted on all of the verbal skills measured by the WAIS-III. His ability to concentrate and focus attention, his short-term memory, his vocabulary, and his mathematical abilities fall at or below the second percentile. That is, 98% of the population would have obtained a score higher than did Mr. Lopez on the subtests. His ability to think abstractly and his common sense or judgment would be surpassed by 91% of the population. Mr. Lopez's general range of knowledge, the kind acquired from school and independent experience, would be surpassed by 95% of the population.

Mr. Lopez's scores on the nonverbal subtests are more heterogeneous. His performance on three Performance subtests reflects significant intellectual deficits, while three other subtest scores fall at or close to the average range. Mr. Lopez's ability to acquire new perceptual learning, his ability to make use of subtle cues in order to establish cause-and-effect relationships, and his ability to concentrate on a perceptual task, would be surpassed by 95% to 98% of the general population. On a task requiring perceptual orientation skills, his score would be surpassed by 75% of the population. As measured by the WAIS-III, Mr. Lopez's ability to discriminate the essential from the unessential and to reason through a perceptual task were found to be his strongest intellectual skills. His scores on theses subtests would be exceeded by 63% of the population.

Mr. Lopez was administered the WRAT-4. Severe impairments are found in his fundamental academic skills. Although Mr. Lopez was 16 years of age when tested, his strongest skill, his ability to perform mathematical computations, was equal to that of the average student in the second month of the third grade. His performance would be surpassed by 98% of the population. His ability to read words was equal to that of the average student in the fourth month of the first grade and would be surpassed by 997 people

out of 1,000. His performance on the Sentence Comprehension Subtest was equal to that of the average student in the sixth month of kindergarten: 999 people out of 1,000 would have performed better on this subtest than did Mr. Lopez. His ability to spell words was consistent with these scores. Specifically, his spelling was equal to that of the average first-grade student in the seventh month of that grade and would be surpassed by 99% of the population.

At the cornerstone of any forensic evaluation is the assessment of the defendant's response style: that is, the degree to which a defendant's responses may have been shaded or affected by secondary gain. The issue of response style, or "malingering," is addressed in numerous ways. I administered the TOMM, a test that evaluates malingered cognitive disturbance associated with memory loss. On this test, Mr. Lopez's performance indicated that he responded in a genuine manner to this instrument. This level of performance strongly suggests that Mr. Lopez's responses to similar tests, including the WAIS-III and the WRAT-4, are a valid reflection of his actual skills. In addition, Mr. Lopez's performance on the WAIS-III and the WRAT-4 is consistent with levels of intellectual and academic performance noted in the records I have reviewed. His scores on the tests administered by me are also consistent with the testing done by Dr. Brookes on 10/10/07 and 12/6/07.

Assessing Understanding and Appreciation of Miranda Rights was administered to check for consistency of responses given Mr. Lopez's specific age and measured IQ. When evaluated at age 15, Mr. Lopez's scores on the various sections that comprise this instrument were consistent with both his age and his full scale IQ as measured by the WAIS-III. As a measure of consistency, it is noteworthy that the content of his responses to questions regarding his right to remain silent were similar to those given during the interviews. For example, with regard to his paraphrasing of this right, Mr. Lopez stated, "I don't have to write something. I don't have to write and have to be quiet until they tell me to."

Mr. Lopez has a long history of being a special education student, classified at various times as "emotionally disturbed" and "learning disabled." Severe problems had been noted in his academic performance while he was in special education classes. In addition, Mr. Lopez's presentation during both interviews was consistent with the scores he obtained on objective testing. Michael Lopez, the defendant's brother, confirmed Paul Lopez's history of special education and his severe reading and writing deficits.

OPINION

Based upon this assessment, the following opinions are offered, to a reasonable degree of psychological certainty:

Mr. Lopez's overall level of intellectual functioning, as measured by the WAIS-III, falls within the borderline range of intelligence. He obtained a full scale IQ of 72. His scores on all of the verbal subtests reflect significant impairments. Mr. Lopez's verbal IQ of 69 falls at the upper limit of the extremely low range of intelligence. He did significantly better on the nonverbal or performance section of the WAIS-III. Mr. Lopez obtained an IQ of 80 on this section, a score falling at the lower limit of the low average range.

Significant impairments are noted in his vocabulary, his general range of knowledge, his overall judgment, his attention span, and his ability to think abstractly. Suspects, in part, rely upon these skills to understand and to make informed, reasoned decisions regarding the waiver of their Miranda rights. Mr. Lopez's noted deficits in these abilities would severely impair his ability to make a knowing, intelligent waiver of his rights.

Mr. Lopez has severe impairments in his basic academic skills, consistent with the records I reviewed. His ability to read words, his spelling, and his sentence comprehension fall at levels that would be obtained by students in the sixth month of kindergarten up to the seventh month of the first grade. His strongest ability, his skill at being able to perform mathematical computations, is equal to that of the average student in the second month of the third grade. Mr. Lopez's ability to read words and to understand the meaning of sentences was found to be severely impaired. These noted deficits would severely impair his ability to make a knowing, intelligent waiver of his Miranda rights.

Mr. Lopez's performance on the TOMM, a test of malingering, indicates that he did not make a conscious effort to present himself as more intellectually limited than the clinical picture warrants. In addition, his responses during the interview to questions regarding his understanding and appreciation of his rights are consistent with those given by other 15-year-olds with IQs in the 71 to 80 range. Furthermore, his school records reflect the presence of classifications of both emotional disturbance and learning disability with accompanying severe problems in reading and writing. His presentation during both interviews is also consistent with the difficulty Mr. Lopez demonstrated when asked to explain the meaning of his Miranda rights.

Mr. Lopez was unable to read aloud the Miranda warnings that appear on the form he signed. His inability to read these statements is consistent with my review of his school records, the information provided to me by his brother, and his scores on the WRAT-4. When these rights were read to him, his inability to define some of the words that appear on this form is also consistent with the sources of data that I considered.

During both interviews, Mr. Lopez could spontaneously recall only two elements of his Miranda rights: his right to remain silent and the use of any statement that he provided in court. Mr. Lopez was able to correctly explain the concept that what he said might be used against him in court. He recognized that any statement he provided would be used to "hurt" him in court. When I read this right to him, Mr. Lopez again demonstrated his understanding and appreciation of this aspect of his Miranda right: "used against me in court to try to keep me in."

When asked to explain his right to remain silent, Mr. Lopez's comprehension was severely impaired. He explained that this right meant "that I can't talk to them or something or I can't speak… [until] they ask me to." When this right was read to him, Mr. Lopez provided a similar response: "If they ask me questions, I just answer it." He elaborated that he cannot speak until "when they ask me to." When asked specifically if he could decide not to talk, Mr. Lopez explained that he could make such a decision "by staying quiet till they ask me something." When asked to explain his right to remain silent one year later, having reported that he had attended a class at the Candlewood Juvenile Center that focused on Constitutional rights related to police interrogations, Mr. Lopez provided a the following explanation: that it was okay "to not talk [until] when they say you can talk."

When his right to consult an attorney was read to him, Mr. Lopez again demonstrated an inability to understand his right to remain silent. He stated, "I've got to have a lawyer before I talk to the cops." When asked what would happen if he did not have an attorney, Mr. Lopez stated, "Then I'd tell them what I'm suppose to tell a lawyer." With regard to the fifth right on the form that he signed, "the right to remain silent until you have had the opportunity to consult with one [an attorney]," Mr. Lopez again demonstrated a lack of comprehension of his right to remain silent. He explained that he could remain silent, "till the judge asks me something. I stay quiet and the judge asks them if I spoke. [He will ask me] what did I do?"

Consistent with the above information, Mr. Lopez explained that the statement on the form, "Now that I have advised you of your rights, are you willing to answer questions?" means "If they ask me something, I've got to answer it."

Mr. Lopez's comprehension of his right to have an attorney appointed for him was imperfect, at best. Although he was able to correctly define the word *afford*, he explained this right by stating: "I don't know. Bail or something or a paid lawyer or something." When the statement was read to him a second time, Mr. Lopez replied, "I don't know [what it means]."

Based upon my evaluation, it is my opinion to a reasonable degree of psychological certainty that because of the intellectual and cognitive limitations noted in this report, confirmed by a number of sources of independent data, Mr. Lopez's ability to understand and appreciate his right to remain silent when interrogated by police on 7/11/07 was severely impaired.

Alan M. Goldstein, PhD, ABPP
Board Certified in Forensic Psychology

TEACHING POINT:
WHAT ARE THE LIMITS OF SPECIALIZED FORENSIC ASSESSMENT INSTRUMENTS?
(contributed by Alan M. Goldstein)

In evaluating Mr. Lopez's functional ability to make a knowing, intelligent, and voluntary waiver of his *Miranda* rights, both nomothetic and ideographic data were used. Nomothetic information is based on scientific data, and relies on norms similar to the characteristics of the individual being assessed. Typically, nomothetic information draws upon psychological tests and forensic assessment instruments (Heilbrun et al., 2009). Forensic assessment instruments have been developed to provide information of direct relevance to the legal question being addressed.

On the other hand, idiographic information describes the individual's level of functioning, not only at the time of the *Miranda* rights waiver, but at times previous to his or her legal involvement. Idiographic information is often used to explain the reasons that underlie that person's lack of legal capacity. Furthermore, idiographic information may shed some light on the genuineness of the examinee's provided history, any problems in meeting the legal capacity required by the law, and, in general, may be of value in addressing the issue of exaggeration and response style.

In this case, nomothetic information was derived from the WAIS-III and the WRAT-4. In New York State, the specialized FAI "Understanding and Appreciating *Miranda* Rights" has, at times, been ruled inadmissible as it relates to a defendant's ability to provide a knowing and intelligent waiver of rights. I use this instrument to compare a defendant's understanding and appreciation of his rights to those with similar IQs and at similar age levels. As such, it provides a check on consistency of response when compared to others of similar age and intelligence—and such testimony has neither been questioned nor barred. A newly released edition of this instrument, "*Miranda* Rights Comprehension Instruments" (Goldstein, Zelle, & Grisso, 2012; see also Goldstein et al., 2011), addresses the *Daubert* criteria, increasing the likelihood that this instrument will survive evidentiary challenges in court. A similar instrument has been developed by Rogers and his colleagues (Rogers, Sewell, Drogin, & Fiduccia, 2013).

In this case, I reviewed various sources of idiographic information. I interviewed Mr. Lopez regarding his background and history, comparing the information that he provided with information contained in the records that I reviewed. I questioned him in detail regarding his understanding and appreciation of each *Miranda* right that he had been shown by interrogators. I reviewed legal records related to his case and his school history. I reviewed Mr. Lopez's medical records and interviewed his brother to obtain an overall picture of Mr. Lopez's functioning. In addition, I listened to a CD of Mr. Lopez's interrogation. What I learned through these sources of idiographic evidence was integrated with the nomothetic data I had collected to form my opinion. Without such idiographic information, the evaluation would be insufficiently individualized—one of the highest priorities of the legal system.

3

Competence to Stand Trial

This chapter focuses on the legal question of competence to stand trial. This form of competence (which has also been called *adjudicative competence* [Bonnie, 1992] in recognition of the reality that most criminal cases are disposed of through plea negotiation rather than trial) broadly requires that a defendant be able to understand the legal process both rationally and factually, and be able to assist counsel in her own defense. As this is a common legal question in FMHA, it will be discussed using three cases. The principle for the first case report addresses the importance of using testing in assessing response style, and the teaching point will discuss integrating different sources of response style data. The second case report will illustrate the principle of using a model for FMHA. Such a model can be applied not only toward structuring how the evaluation is conceptualized and the sources of information that are selected, but also how the report is structured; this utilization is the focus of the teaching point for this case. The final case report in this chapter illustrates the principle of attributing information to sources. This is one of the most fundamental principles of FMHA, and it is used in the teaching point to describe how to separate and integrate data from different sources in analyzing, reasoning about, and communicating FMHA results.

CASE ONE
PRINCIPLE: USE TESTING WHEN INDICATED IN ASSESSING RESPONSE STYLE (*PRINCIPLE 26*)

This principle addresses the value of using psychological and specialized testing to assess response style in FMHA. "Response style" is an important consideration in FMHA; it refers to the exaggeration, minimization, or accurate reporting of symptoms of mental or emotional disorder. When an individual exaggerates (or fabricates) symptoms, or when symptoms that are genuinely experienced are minimized or denied, then self-report is less useful and must be de-emphasized accordingly. The assessment of response style in FMHA is particularly important because of the incentives that exist in forensic contexts, and the perception by judges and attorneys that self-reported information may therefore be inaccurate. The importance of considering response style is also acknowledged in the *Specialty Guidelines for Forensic Psychology* (APA *Specialty Guidelines*; American Psychological Association, 2013b): "Forensic practitioners consider and seek to make known that forensic examination results can be affected by factors unique to, or differentially present in, forensic contexts including response style, voluntariness of participation, and situational stress associated with involvement in forensic or legal matters" (Guideline 10.02).

Rogers (2008c) has described response style as having several distinct forms. He identified two primary categories of response style: *overstated pathology* and *simulated adjustment*. Within the category of overstated pathology, he outlined three more specific types of response style:

(1) *Malingering,* involving a conscious fabrication or gross exaggeration of psychological and/or physical symptoms, understandable in light of the individual's circumstances or motivated by an external gain, but not attributable merely to the desire to assume the patient role (as in factitious disorder);

(2) *Factitious presentations,* which includes symptoms that are intentionally fabricated due to a motivation to assume the patient role; and

(3) *Feigning,* which describes the intentional fabrication of symptoms without inferring a particular motivation.

Within the category of *simulated adjustment*, three response styles have been identified:

(1) *Defensiveness*, or the intentional minimization of psychological or physical symptoms;

(2) *Social desirability*, which describes the tendency of individuals to portray themselves in a positive manner; and

(3) *Impression management*, which involves conscious efforts of an individual to manage others' perceptions of himself or herself.

In addition to the specific subtypes of these categories of response style, Rogers (2008c) identified three other forms of clinically relevant response styles:

(1) *Irrelevant responding*, involving the failure to become engaged in the evaluation, providing responses not necessarily relevant to questions;

(2) *Random responding*, in which responses are selected randomly; and

(3) *Hybrid responding*, by which respondents employ more than one of the previously described response styles in their approach to a given situation.

It is also important to highlight a *reliable/honest* response style, in which a genuine attempt is made to be accurate, and factual inaccuracies result from poor understanding or misperception (Rogers, 1984, 1997).

Otto (2012) identified seven of these response styles as particularly relevant in the context of FMHA. Although he uses slightly different terms, these include: (1) symptom feigning, (2) guardedness/disavowal (or defensiveness), (3) false presentation of positive traits, (3) irrelevant random responding, (4) random responding, (5) honest/candid responding, and (6) hybrid responding. He suggests that "the modal response style in forensic examinations is probably a hybrid one" (Otto, 2012, p. 367).

Forensic evaluators face challenges in the assessment of response style. In addition to deliberate attempts to exaggerate or minimize pathology or deficits, an individual's cognitive abilities or psychopathology may impact response style (Otto, 2012). Moreover, examinees may not necessarily adopt the same response style throughout an assessment. Rogers and Bender (2003) also provide a caution regarding the variability in base rates of malingering and other response styles, noting that "[e]ven within the same setting, rates are likely to vary markedly based on referral issues" (p. 112). Accordingly, it is important for evaluators to be aware of the different types of response style and the potential for an examinee's approach to change during the course of the evaluation, and to carefully select methods of measuring an examinee's response style.

Response style can be assessed through the use of some traditional psychological tests and interviews, and by specialized measures that have been specifically designed and developed for this purpose. These tests rely on a variety of strategies that are designed to detect malingering or defensive responding. For instance, Rogers (2008b, p. 22) described the most common strategies for the detection of malingered mental disorders, which can be categorized as *unlikely presentations* and *amplified presentations* approaches. Although the detection of defensive response styles in the evaluation of mental disorders is relatively less developed, Rogers (2008b) identified four relatively strong detection strategies, including *spurious patterns of simulated adjustment* and *denial of patient characteristics* (p. 27). (For a more comprehensive discussion, see Rogers, 2008b.)

With respect to traditional psychological tests, it is important to note that relatively few include any measure of response style, despite the importance of self-report in such tests and the related assumption that the individual being tested is not deliberately distorting his or her own experience. However, some multi-scale personality inventories, such as the Minnesota Multiphasic Personality Inventory, 2nd edition (MMPI-2) and the Millon Clinical Multiaxial Inventory–III (MCMI-III), include scales designed to assess malingering and defensiveness. In discussing such tests, it is important to consider both the consistency and the accuracy of responding, which encompass under-reporting and over-reporting. We will describe evidence on item response consistency and the accuracy of responding for the MMPI-2, the Personality Assessment Inventory (PAI), and the MCMI-III. Although the scope of the following discussion will be limited, a more detailed discussion is available in recent chapters by Greene (2012) and Sellbom and Bagby (2012).

Greene (2012) provided a framework for determining the validity of an MMPI-2 profile. After assessing for omissions, he recommended that clinicians evaluate response consistency. He described several methods of assessing response consistency, including a visual inspection for obvious patterns (e.g., TFTFTF, TTFTTF; T = True, F = False) and observing elevation of the F scale. In addition, response inconsistency on the MMPI-2 can be detected through an examination of the Variable Response Inconsistency Scale (VRIN) and the True Response Inconsistency Scale (TRIN), although additional research is needed to provide information regarding the optimal cut-off score for VRIN. With respect to the accuracy of item endorsement, the MMPI-2 contains several scales that are relevant to under-reporting or over-endorsement of psychopathological symptoms, including the infrequency scales, F-K Index (or Gough Dissimulation Index), obvious and subtle subscales, Lie (L) scale, and Correction (K scale). The results of several studies, in which participants were provided with detailed information on the nature of the psychopathology to be faked, suggest that the MMPI-2 validity scales are reasonably effective in distinguishing genuine mental disorders characterized by severe psychopathology, such as schizophrenia, from simulated disorders (Rogers, Bagby, & Chakraborty, 1993; for additional detail, see Greene, 2012). Other research, however, suggests that the MMPI-2 validity scales are less effective in distinguishing between genuine but less severe disorders and faking (Lamb, Berry, Wetter, & Baer, 1994; Wetter, Baer, Berry, Robinson, & Sumpter, 1993), and that individuals who receive coaching about the validity scales may be able to feign effectively without detection. Green (2012) emphasizes that clinicians should have an understanding of the scales and cut scores that are appropriate for a given setting and population, and an appreciation of the base rates of malingering and defensiveness.

Sellbom and Bagby (2012) note that response consistency on the MCMI-III is assessed through a three-item Validity Index that contains non-bizarre items endorsed by less than 0.01% of individuals from clinical populations. The endorsement of one such item suggests caution in the interpretation of the results, while the endorsement of two items indicates an invalid profile (Millon, 1994); however, they also caution about the lack of validation

research for this scale (Sellbom & Greene, 2012). Although some validity scales have effectively identified college students who were instructed to malinger (e.g., the Debasement Scale [Scale Z] and Disclosure Scale [Scale X]; Bagby, Gillis, Toner, & Goldberg, 1991), Sellbom and Bagby (2012) highlight the error rates and limited classification accuracy of these scales. They suggest that substantially more research is needed before using this measure in forensic settings.

The PAI has several response style indices. Designed to detect random responding, the Infrequency (INF) scale has been shown to effectively discriminate random profiles from responses provided by normal and clinical samples (Morey, 1991). In addition, scales designed to detect defensiveness (Positive Impression Management [PIM], Defensiveness Index [DEF], Cashel's Discriminant Function [CDF]) have been found to have good classification accuracy, although they may be susceptible to coaching (Sellbom & Bagby, 2012). The scales designed to assess malingering include the Negative Impression Management (NIM), Malingering Index (MAL), and Rogers Discriminant Function (RDF). Some research has found that MAL and NIM have moderately strong and strong associations, respectively, with other measures of malingering; however, based on studies of classification accuracy, Sellbom and Bagby (2012) suggest that these scales be used as screens and that additional evidence be sought before forming conclusions regarding response style.

There are also specialized instruments that are designed to assess response style. For instance, the SIRS-2 (Rogers et al., 2011) is a 172-item structured interview that was developed specifically for assessing the feigning of psychopathology. Based on the responses to these items, a test-taker is classified into one of four categories: feigning, genuine, indeterminate, and disengagement. This test represents an update from the original SIRS (Rogers, 1992), and introduced "more stringent criteria for classifying feigning" (Green, Rosenfeld, & Befli, 2013). The SIRS and SIRS-2 cannot detect a malingerer who falsely reports a single symptom and fails to respond meaningfully to a number of questions. In addition, the SIRS provides limited information regarding the "partial malingerer"—the individual who experiences genuine symptoms, but who also selectively reports, exaggerates, or fabricates some symptoms, depending on the circumstances.

Although some concerns still exist about the sensitivity of the measure, false-positive rates, and the need for additional validation studies (Green et al., 2013; Rubenzer, 2010), this test should be one part of a comprehensive evaluation that incorporates multiple measures of response style, such as the validity scales of personality assessments. Indeed, the limitations of the SIRS and SIRS-2 with respect to single-symptom false reporting and failure to otherwise engage simply underscore the limits that would apply to any measure of this kind—and underscore the importance of collecting different kinds of information (behavioral observation and historical data from multiple sources) and using them in conjunction with a validated specialized measure.

Another example of a specialized measure is the Miller-Forensic Assessment of Symptoms Test (MFAST; Miller, 2001), which was designed as a screening instrument in the assessment of response style. The test consists of 25 questions that are based on seven strategies of malingering detection, including rare combinations and reported versus observed symptoms. A cut score of six on this scale has been found to maximize classification accuracy, and the test has been validated among hospitalized individuals found incompetent to proceed with trial, clinical participants applying for disability, and correctional inmates (Guy & Miller, 2004; Miller, 2001, 2005). Although intended as a screen, this measure may serve as an initial assessment of response style, and scores may be used to determine if additional testing is warranted (Guy & Miller, 2004).

This principle appears to be well supported by ethical, empirical, and standard- of practice authorities. It is important, however, that forensic practitioners select the few tests that meet the appropriate criteria for relevance and empirical support. Toward this end, Heilbrun (1992) offered guidelines that include the explicit assessment of response style through the use of tests that have demonstrated empirical support for this application, such as the MMPI-2. There are also several interview strategies that can help the forensic practitioner in assessing response style. For example, asking specific and detailed questions, recording the responses, and asking the questions again later in the evaluation can help the forensic practitioner assess consistency. Finally, when assessing an individual's response style, it is important for the forensic practitioner to employ multiple measures (Rogers & Bender, 2003). The use of multiple measures, such as psychological tests, structured interviews, and collateral information, provides additional support for conclusions regarding the individual's response style.

The present report illustrates the application of this principle in the context of a court-ordered evaluation of competence to stand trial. Because the referral question involved the question of the defendant's competence to stand trial in a very serious case with a complex clinical presentation and a question of malingering, the forensic clinician selected multiple measures in each of three areas (clinical, competence to stand trial, and response style). It is noteworthy that the measures selected are clearly among the strongest available in these domains. But what is equally noteworthy is that several of the measures (the PAI, the Evaluation of Competency to Stand Trial – Revised [ECST-R]) provide response style data in addition to information on clinical functioning (the PAI) and competency-related capacities (the ECST-R), while another measure (the SIRS-2) provides response style data primarily. As such, the evaluator had multiple sources of testing data to draw on in addressing the response style conclusion; in addition, he noted that the defendant's approach during the interview seemed consistent with the attempt to minimize rather than exaggerate psychopathology. However, the defendant also described some unusual symptoms that might (in the absence of much data to the contrary) have inclined an evaluator to conclude that the defendant was exaggerating. The complexity of this case is striking. The value of the multiple tests employed makes an important contribution to the overall thoroughness with which the evaluator is able to address this complexity.

April 12, 2011
Samuel Bass
Judge 66th District Court
Oklahoma County District Court
320 Robert S. Kerr
Oklahoma City, Oklahoma 73102
Re: State of Oklahoma v. Janet S. Smith
Cause No.: #__ and #__

Dear Judge Bass:

At your request, I conducted a competency to stand trial evaluation on Janet S. Smith. Ms. Smith faces the charges of capital murder and attempted capital murder. This report is organized into three major sections that cover the description of the evaluation, clinical findings, and competency-related abilities.

DESCRIPTION OF EVALUATION

The evaluation consisted of an extensive review of relevant clinical and legal records as they pertain to Ms. Smith. In addition, I conducted a comprehensive assessment of Ms. Smith focusing on current diagnoses, response styles including malingering, and data relevant to competency to stand trial. This evaluation did not include a neuropsychological assessment, which is beyond my areas of expertise; however, I did not observe any significant deficits in cognitive functioning that would affect her ability to stand trial.

Review of Relevant Documents

In preparation of this competency report, I reviewed the following legal and clinical documents:

1. Court order and letter requesting this competency evaluation
2. Criminal indictments of Ms. Smith for Capital Murder (#___) and Attempted Capital Murder (#___) on or about June 5, 2010
3. Competency report by Dr. Charline Alpha, Jr., dated August 10, 2010
4. Psychiatric evaluation by Stephen L. Beta, M.D., January 28, 2011, and his progress notes
5. Post-arrest mental health records from Mental Health Services of Southern Oklahoma, Ardmore, Oklahoma
6. Protective and Sealing Orders for the release of medical records pertaining to Ms. Smith
7. Application for emergency apprehension and detention after suicide attempt on May 21, 2010, and other records from De Paul Center
8. Extensive records from Oklahoma City County Mental Health Services from 2000 to 2010
9. Extensive records from the Family Diagnostic Medical Center in Oklahoma City

10. Records pertaining to Ms. Smith's civil divorce proceedings
11. Unofficial college transcript from Oklahoma City Community College.

Notification

Prior to the evaluation, Ms. Smith was advised that my evaluation was non-confidential and that I would be submitting a forensic report to the court. She was also informed that there was a possibility that I might be called to testify in her case, although that was not planned at the current time. In addition, my role as a disinterested expert was explained. Ms. Smith clearly understood this advisement regarding non-confidentiality and my status as a disinterested expert. She expressed her willingness to proceed with the evaluation. These notifications were repeated before my second consultation with Ms. Smith. As before, she understood and agreed to participate.

Details About the Evaluation

Ms. Smith was evaluated on two occasions at Oklahoma City County Jail in a quiet, multipurpose room that serves as a library and video connection for court proceedings. On March 26, her evaluation consisted of a morning (9:05 a.m. to 1:00 p.m.) and afternoon (1:30 to 5:20 p.m.) session for a total of approximately 7 hours and 35 minutes. On April 6, her evaluation was approximately 3 hours and 25 minutes in duration (8:35 a.m. to 12:00 noon).

Assessment Methods

In addition to clinical interviews, Ms. Smith was administered standardized measures for evaluating (a) diagnosis and impairment, (b) malingering and other response styles, and (c) competency-related abilities.

1. The *Schedule of Affective Disorders and Schizophrenia* (SADS; Endicott & Spitzer, 1978) is used to evaluate the presence and severity of mood, psychotic, and other Axis I symptoms. It has excellent reliability and validity.
2. *Structured Interview for DSM-IV Personality* (SIDP-IV; Pfohl et al., 1997) is a semi-structured interview for evaluating Axis II disorders and prominent traits. It is superior to other Axis II measures because its items are less transparent.

3. The *Personality Assessment Inventory* (PAI; Morey, 2007) is a multiscale inventory for evaluating patterns of psychopathology and response styles, such as feigning. Its reliability and validity are generally considered superior to the MMPI-2.

4. The *Structured Interview of Reported Symptoms-2* (SIRS-2; Rogers et al., 2010) is a well-validated measure of feigning and related response styles; and the SIRS is considered by many experts to be the gold standard for the assessment of malingered mental disorders.

5. The *MacArthur Competency Assessment Test–Criminal Adjudication* (MacCAT-CA; Poythress et al., 1999) is a semi-structured interview for assessing competency to stand trial. The MacCAT-CA asks the defendant to address questions based both on his or her own case, and a hypothetical case. One part requires the defendant to be able to follow and integrate case-relevant information.

6. *Evaluation of Competency to Stand Trial–Revised* (ECST-R; Rogers et al., 2004) is a second-generation measure of factual and rational abilities as applied to fitness to proceed. In addition, the ECST-R includes separate screens for feigning and feigned incompetency.

In addition, the Psychiatric Disorders Screening Questionnaire (PDSQ) was used to screen for common Axis I disorders. Finally, relevant components of the Dissociative Disorders Interview Schedule (DDIS) were used to structure inquiries regarding dissociative disorders.

Clinical Findings

Extensive records from Oklahoma City County Mental Health Services have consistently documented her major depression and borderline personality disorder. Treatment has focused on her depression, often described as "mild" and "recurrent," rather than her borderline personality disorder. It is my understanding that some county Mental Health Mental Retardation (MHMR) centers in Oklahoma are mandated to provide treatment for only a circumscribed range of Axis I disorders (e.g., mood and psychotic disorders); therefore, the apparent lack of attention to her

borderline personality disorder may be in response to an administrative mandate.

Based on the current assessment of Axis I and Axis II disorders, the principal diagnosis for Ms. Smith is borderline personality disorder. She also warrants the diagnosis of obsessive-compulsive personality disorder and antisocial personality disorder. As established by history, she continues to warrant the diagnosis of major depression, which is effectively managed by antidepressant medication.

Borderline Personality Disorder

Borderline personality disorder represents a pervasive pattern of instability in relationships, affect, and behaviors. While able to manage under normal stressors (e.g., her good academic achievement), Ms. Smith experiences an acute exacerbation of symptoms when under severe stress (e.g., perceived or actual abandonment). Because of the dramatic changes in her life in the last nine months, this assessment focused on the most recent five years before her arrest. It was assessed by the SIDP-IV and a clinical interview with corroborative data from the PAI and Borderline section of the DDIS.[1] Her borderline personality disorder is characterized by the following:

1. *Intense and unstable interpersonal relationship.* Ms. Smith describes her relationship with her husband as representing extremes from being great to intensely bad. According to her account, the relationship was often in flux representing these extremes.

2. *Affective instability.* Her moods frequently shift, with the changes in moods being severe. Ms. Smith believes that medication has reduced the severity and frequency of these mood shifts. However, she still describes herself as being irritable.

3. *Transient, stress-related dissociative symptoms.* Ms. Smith experienced "black-outs" for several hours when she and her husband were having conflicts. While not overtly paranoid, she became distrustful of him at these times.

4. *Intense, inappropriate anger.* Ms. Smith acknowledged that she could easily become

---

[1] Although a collateral interview (e.g., with a spouse) is sometimes conducted, it was not deemed appropriate under the current circumstances.

irritated and angry. When she did not "shut down," she would sometimes throw and break things, or punch her husband. She also described spanking her girls when she became angry. Dr. Alpha's evaluation documents frequent physical altercations.

5. *Frantic efforts to avoid abandonment.* Ms. Smith related how she would plead with her husband not to leave when they were experiencing conflict. According to her account, she faked suicide in May of 2010 to keep her husband from leaving. With advice from a friend, Peggy, she reportedly staged the suicide but had no intent to die. As she reported, the suicide letters were "just putting on a show" and that she did not desire to die. She apparently enlisted Peggy's help in staging the suicide.

6. *Unstable sense of self-image.* Ms. Smith devoted considerable efforts to "being what everyone wanted (her) to be." Regarding her identity, she disclosed her thoughts that she was "never anyone." Prior to her arrest, she often wondered if she was evil.

Regarding other borderline criteria, it appears that Ms. Smith did not often experience emptiness in her life. Beyond the faked suicide attempt (see #5), there is no clear evidence of suicide gestures being associated with her borderline personality disorder prior to her arrest. However, a progress note (8/11/09) by Thomas Gamma described a suicide gesture last August. While sometimes impulsive, her behaviors were not generally self-damaging.

As a caveat, mental health professionals sometime stigmatize the symptoms of borderline personality disorders as simply "willful acts;" this phenomenon is described as *iatrogenic stigmatization*. It is important to recognize that patients with borderline personality disorders do not want to experience their internal chaos and intense instability that often typify their day-to-day functioning.

Other Personality Disorders

As previously noted, Ms. Smith is also diagnosed with obsessive-compulsive personality disorder and antisocial personality disorder. Regarding the former, she is often preoccupied with lists and schedules (e.g., she carries multiple lists with her). In addition, she evidences other characteristics of obsessive-compulsive personality disorder,

including perfectionism, reluctance to delegate, a general rigidity, and stubbornness. She describes these characteristics as being a "control freak."

Her diagnosis of antisocial personality disorder is characterized by the failure to conform to social norms, deceitfulness, irresponsibility, and a rationalizing of some of her past misconduct. Both this diagnosis and her obsessive-compulsive personality disorder appear to have minimal relevance to her competency to stand trial.

Major Depression

Ms. Smith has a longstanding diagnosis of major depression, which has been treated with antidepressant medications. Mental health records for the last five years describe her major depression as in the mild to moderate range and being generally well controlled by medication. For example, she was administered the Quick Inventory of Depressive Symptomatology—Self Report (QIDS-SR) repeatedly in 2007 and 2008 as part of her treatment documentation. Her reported symptoms in 2008 tended to be few, with mild severity (i.e., her QIDS-SR scores typically range from 1 to 8 out of a possible score of 27).

The SADS is an extensive, semi-structured interview that was used to evaluate her major depression, as well as other Axis I disorders. Ms. Smith continues to warrant the diagnosis of major depression. Focusing on early February and recent weeks, her depressive symptoms appear to have remained relatively stable. With the assistance of medication, her current symptoms include the following: (1) mild but predominantly depressed mood, (2) fluctuating but generally mild insomnia, (3) recurrent thoughts about death but no specific suicidal ideation. I observed no difficulties with concentration, loss of energy, diminished interests, or feelings of worthlessness. Consistent with her past history, her major depression appears to be well managed with antidepressant medication.

Other Axis I issues will be considered in a subsequent section of this report. Before their review, it is important to consider response styles.

Malingering and Other Response Styles

For any forensic evaluation that involves far-reaching consequences, it is essential to consider whether malingering or other response styles are affecting the assessment and its conclusions. *Malingering* is defined as the fabrication or gross exaggeration of psychological or physical symptoms to meet some external goal. Importantly, malingering is situationally based and may emerge at different times. It is assessed by using multiple methods and multiple strategies. It is my conclusion that Ms. Smith is *not malingering at the present time.* This conclusion is based on the current findings:

1. The PAI has several well-validated feigning scales. Ms. Smith's scores of 4 on the NIM scale and 0 on the Malingering Index fall clearly in the expected range for genuine patients.
2. The SIRS-2 is widely regarded as the best validated measure for feigned mental disorders. Ms. Smith had no scales in either the probable or definite range. Instead, her SIRS-2 profile had five scales in the indeterminate range and three scales in the genuine range. Based on the decision rules, there is a high probability that Ms. Smith was not feigning on the SIRS-2.
3. In clinical interviews, she attempts to impress the evaluator with her ability to think clearly with minimal impairment from her symptomatology. This current presentation is inconsistent with malingering.

As described, Ms. Smith's faked suicide attempt in 2010 represents a circumscribed effort at malingering. By her own account, she took an "overdose" and generated suicide notes falsely claiming that she was killing herself because she had nothing left to live for. As she apparently discussed with a friend, the external goal was to stop her husband from leaving her.

Ms. Smith acknowledges that she has been deceptive in the past and is relatively good at "putting things over on" others. According to Ms. Smith, her "successful" deceptions apparently include deceiving her husband as described previously, and her claimed welfare status. Ms. Smith disclosed that she had hidden psychotic-like symptoms from healthcare providers since last summer until her January evaluation with Dr. Beta. However, it is not clear whether her deceptions involved (1) hiding these symptoms, (2) falsely claiming these symptoms, or (3) some combination of hiding and claiming symptoms. Reports from last summer and fall (Dr. Alpha, 8/10/09; Mr. Gamma, 8/11/09, 9/15/09, 10/27/09) produced no evidence of psychotic symptoms.

Atypical Presentation of Psychotic Symptoms

Ms. Smith claims very atypical psychotic symptoms that are not generally observed in patients with psychotic or other Axis I disorders. She reported the following:

1. Dawn, her deceased daughter, visits her regularly several times per week. She reports that they sing together for hours—songs include Broadway hits, camp songs, and popular chart songs. She also reported that they played with a "puzzle box." Besides auditory and visual hallucinations, she described olfactory hallucinations with Dawn smelling like a "wet dog," the outdoors, and flowers.
2. Reportedly, her mother ("Mom") "pops" in to see her more than once each week. Mom was described as "torturing" Ms. Smith and making her feel like a POW. Ms. Smith also reported tactile hallucinations from Mom: "It goes through me like an electrical current" that feels hot and burns. According to her account, Mom gives her commands, like exercising for four hours a day, which she cannot resist because of the threat of pain. Ms. Smith reported olfactory hallucinations of Mom smelling like cigarettes.
3. Bizarre visual distortions in which the print on the page would become larger as she read it. She described this phenomenon as similar to Disney animations.

In his progress note of January 27, 2011, Dr. Beta documented that Ms. Smith had related that she heard "voices in her head since [she was] a child" and that she sees the Devil in her mother-in-law. However, no psychotic symptoms were reported to Mr. Gamma on January 26, 2011, the day before Dr. Beta's visit. Two weeks later, Mr. Gamma (2/9/10) reported that Ms. Smith "endorses audio, visual, and tactile hallucinations." Moreover, no psychotic symptoms were noted on the next visit (3/25/10). Yet on the next day, she reported extensive psychotic symptoms in my evaluation (see above description). Her atypical presentation plus these documented inconsistencies question the credibility of her reported psychotic symptoms.

Memory Loss and Possible Dissociative Symptoms

Progress notes by Thomas Gamma documented Ms. Smith's memory lapses soon after the alleged offenses. On 6/9/09, he reported that she did not recall being arrested and wanted to be released so she could care for her two babies. A similar memory loss regarding the time of her arrest was reported to Dr. Alpha. Amnestic episodes were reported: (1) waking up in bed without remembering (2004 or 2005), (2) 7- or 8-week period (May, 2007), and (3) the time from completing her exams at Oklahoma City Community College in the spring of 2009 until finding herself in jail with a video arraignment. Dr. Childer's report raised the possibility that her most recent amnesia was being feigned. Subsequent reports in 2010 and 2011 by Mr. Gamma did not comment on any memory difficulties.

In my evaluation of Ms. Smith, she does report having blackouts in which she would "miss a few days." However, her descriptions of each day as being similar make it difficult to establish "missed" days. During my evaluation on March 26, 2011, of 7 hours and 35 minutes, no lapses were observed; she remained well focused and attentive throughout the entire period. For April 6, no lapses were observed. On the contrary, she evidenced above-average ability to focus and respond relevantly.

Regarding the reported memory lapses, several issues deserve consideration:

1. Persons with borderline personality disorders sometimes experience brief, stress-related dissociative symptoms—typically of some minutes in duration. It is quite possible that Ms. Smith has had such brief experiences but has elaborated on them.
2. Persons subjected to extended periods of isolation may be vulnerable to having experiences of "lost time" because they have limited reference points for gauging time-related experiences. It is my understanding that Ms. Smith spends most of each day alone in her cell. Obviously, jail security is a very high priority; nonetheless, Ms. Smith's further involvement in jail-based activities may be helpful.
3. Ms. Smith's description of memory lapses is not typical of dissociative amnesia. She reported isolated periods of lost time that did not appear to have precipitant events. Her longer memory loss in the summer of 2002 was following a motor vehicle accident.

Although an extended inpatient evaluation would be ideal for the assessment of dissociative identity disorder, I found no clinical data to support this diagnosis. When questioned about indirect indicators (e.g., changes in handwriting, missing possessions, possessions that she did not recognize), she categorically denied them. While she has been recognized by some persons that she did not recall—probably individuals she went to school with —she has not experienced meeting individuals claiming to have a relationship with her. In addition, her periods of "missing time" appear to be isolated except for the months after her incarceration. It is my opinion that her current accounts are better explained by extended isolation than a dissociative diagnosis. When asked directly about other personalities or identities, Ms. Smith responded with disbelief at these questions and denied ever having any such experiences.

COMPETENCY-RELATED ABILITIES

As requested, I addressed Ms. Smith's competency to stand trial based on Article ___ of the Oklahoma Code of Criminal Procedure. As outlined in your court order, Section 1 provides the criteria for competency as lacking: (1) sufficient present ability to consult with his/her lawyer with a reasonable degree of rational understanding; or (2) a rational as well as factual understanding of the proceedings against him/her. I will address each prong separately.

Consult with Counsel

During an initial phone conversation with Mr. Howell, the lead defense counsel, I mentioned the possibility of observing his or Mr. Williams's (the co-counsel) interactions with Ms. Smith. He expressed a preference that I conduct the evaluation independently, which is completely understandable in light of attorney–client privilege. My conclusions regarding Ms. Smith's ability to consult with counsel are based on (1) the quality of her interactions with me on court-related issues, (2) her reports on her interactions and relationship with her defense attorneys, and (3) data from standardized competency measures.

Ms. Smith described an adequate working relationship with her attorneys. She expressed considerable frustrations that they provided her with information only on a "need to know" basis. She expressed a preference for Mr. Howell and related several times that Mr. Williams treated her in a "condescending" manner. Ms. Smith also expressed some distrust of her attorneys. When explored further, the distrust centered on whether they would (1) follow through on what they had promised (e.g., bringing her copies of her letters) and (2) comply with requests (e.g., contact her mother). Therefore, the distrust does not appear to be based on paranoid thinking.

Data from the MacCAT-CA and ECST-R also address her capacity to consult with her attorneys:

1. On the Appreciation scale of the MacCAT-CA, Ms. Smith received almost a perfect score (11 of 12), indicating minimal to no impairment in her ability to think about her case and relate these thoughts to her attorneys.
2. The Consult-with-Counsel scale of the ECST-R focuses directly on her ability to communicate with counsel, express expectations, and resolve differences. Her score of 60T is at the threshold of moderate impairment—this category is typically associated with competent defendants. As noted in the clinical interviews, her suspicions and distrust are the key factors in her score of 60T. She expressed concerns that her attorneys are not working diligently on her case.

Taking into account her distrust and related concerns, it is my opinion that Ms. Smith clearly has the capacity to consult with her counsel. She is able to easily articulate her ideas about the case and relate these ideas to her defense attorneys. She is also able to rationally consider alternatives.

Factual and Rational Understanding of the Proceedings

With respect to factual understanding, Ms. Smith is aware of the charges against her and has a sufficient understanding of the court personnel (e.g., the role of the judge and prosecutor) and the trial process. On both the MacCAT-CA and ECST-R, no significant evidence of deficits was observed, with nearly perfect scores.

On the issue of rational understanding, Ms. Smith is able to think clearly about her case and consider different alternatives. When it comes to decisions (e.g., whether to testify), she mentions seeking the advice of "Mom". As noted in the earlier section, "Atypical Presentation of Psychotic Symptoms," the description of "Mom" is not credible as a hallucination. Although it is quite possible that Ms. Smith does have some perceptual disturbances, it is very unlikely that she has sustained hallucinations. Therefore, it is my opinion that any disordered perceptions would have a negligible effect on her rational abilities.

Data from the MacCAT-CA and ECST-R support this conclusion:

1. The MacCAT-CA addresses Ms. Smith's ability to reason about a hypothetical case. Her score (15 of 16) places her in the category of "minimal to no impairment."
2. The ECST-R addresses her ability to reason about her own case. Her score of 53T places her in the expected range for competent defendants.

Ms. Smith does engage in wishful thinking (i.e., hoping that the trial will never take place). However, she realizes that it will occur and believes she is capable of going ahead with her trial. When asked directly about being found incompetent, she stated very assertively that this is not her desire and that she is able to do (what is needed). Her only reservation is her fears about remaining composed at trial because of the publicity and trial-related stresses. In my opinion, these fears probably reflect a realistic appraisal of her pending circumstances.

SUMMARY AND CONCLUSIONS

Ms. Smith's principal diagnosis is borderline personality disorder, which was diagnosed in 2000 and is part of her hospitalization record in May 2010 (see DePaul Discharge Summary, 5/26/09). Her borderline personality disorder is characterized by acute instability in relationships, affect, and behaviors. In the volumes of clinical notes, I found no record of any treatment being provided for her borderline personality disorder. As previously noted, this serious omission is likely to be due to an administrative mandate.

Ms. Smith has a well-documented diagnosis of major depression, which appears to respond well to antidepressants and supportive counseling. She also warrants the diagnosis of obsessive compulsive personality disorder and antisocial personality disorder. Finally, the available clinical data do not support the diagnosis of a dissociative disorder.

It is my opinion that Ms. Smith is not malingering at the current time. However, malingering is a situational response based on an appraisal of circumstances. Therefore, malingering in the future cannot be ruled out. Presently, Ms. Smith describes some very atypical psychotic symptoms that are generally not observed in genuine patients. However, her psychotic presentation does not appear to be motivated by an external goal, which is a necessary requirement for the classification of malingering.

Competency to stand trial is a legal determination. However, the clinical-forensic data provide strong and consistent findings that Ms. Smith probably has sufficient abilities for consulting with counsel and a factual as well as rational understanding the proceedings against her.

In closing, I appreciate the opportunity to consult on this diagnostically complex case. Please do not hesitate to contact me if I can be of further assistance.

Sincerely,
Richard Rogers, Ph.D., ABPP
Diplomate in Forensic Psychology
Cc. Michal Change, District Attorney
Cc. Russell Howell, defense attorney
Cc. Phil Williams, defense attorney

exaggerating or fabricating symptoms of psychopathology. Second, the administration of the PAI and the SIRS-2 yielded results that were consistent with genuine effort rather than malingering. Third, the document review provided information that was consistent with at least one episode of malingering historically (the suicide gesture motivated by the desire to keep her husband from leaving, according to Ms. Smith's description of this event during the present evaluation) but not with present attempts to exaggerate or fabricate symptoms.

Information from these three sources thus provided a multi-sourced depiction of an individual who was not (as the evaluator concluded) presently attempting to malinger. However, there were other observations of symptoms reported by Ms. Smith that would be difficult to explain as conventional symptoms. Ms. Smith provided several atypical symptoms of psychosis, including bizarre visual distortions of printed material, being visited regularly by her dead daughter, and being tortured by her mother. It is tempting for an evaluator to deemphasize or even dismiss such observations in the face of strong evidence such as that described in the previous paragraph. This would be a mistake. Dr. Rogers' evaluation instead describes these atypical symptoms and offers possible explanations that incorporate her genuine symptoms and her current circumstances (isolation in her jail cell). This illustrates the reality that evaluators are seeking a good deal of information from multiple sources so they can draw conclusions that are supported by the bulk of the evidence—but also provides a good example of the constant presence of some information in all evaluations that is not consistent with the conclusions finally reached by the evaluator.

TEACHING POINT:
INTEGRATING DIFFERENT SOURCES OF RESPONSE STYLE DATA

This complex case called for the evaluator to address three major domains: diagnosis, response style, and competence to stand trial. The report provides a good illustration of how information from multiple sources can be integrated in describing response style. First, the evaluator observed that Ms. Smith's approach to the interview was to attempt to impress him with her ability to think clearly, with minimal impairment—quite different from what one would expect from a defendant

CASE TWO
PRINCIPLE: SELECT THE MOST APPROPRIATE MODEL TO GUIDE IN DATA GATHERING, INTERPRETATION, AND COMMUNICATION (*PRINCIPLE 16*)

This principle addresses the selection and use of a forensic assessment model to help guide the forensic clinician in gathering and interpreting data, reasoning about results and conclusions, and communicating the entire assessment. A model for

FMHA is applicable to several areas of the forensic assessment process. Specifically, a model is relevant to the selection of data sources, the identification of specific legal issues, and the determination of the relationship between clinical symptoms and functional legal deficits. Additionally, a model can also serve to clarify communication and reasoning.

Over many years, and even since the publication of the first edition of this casebook more than a decade ago, there has been little discussion in the literature about the use of a model in forensic evaluations. Ethical authorities continue to offer no explicit guidance around this principle, and apparently only two *general* models continue to exist: one developed in the context of civil commitment (Morse, 1978), and the other constructed to describe different criminal and civil competencies (Grisso, 1986, 2003). Some models have also been developed for more specific kinds of FMHA (e.g., American Psychological Association, 2010b; Bonnie, 1992), but are not necessarily broadly applicable.

Morse's (1978) model is premised on the observation that mental health laws generally focus on three broad questions: (1) the existence of a mental disorder; (2) the functional abilities related to the tasks that are part of the relevant legal question; and (3) the strength of the causal connection between the first and the second areas. Morse's model thus describes the implications for data-gathering in FMHA, specifically the need to begin with data about mental health symptoms or intellectual deficits. The model also stresses the importance of capabilities that are relevant to the elements of the legal test. In addition, Morse's model addresses the forensic clinician's reasoning, as the clinician must describe the degree of causal connection between the individual's clinical characteristics and their functional abilities and deficits. Finally, Morse's model facilitates the clinician's task of communicating the results of the evaluation, as it describes the essence of what is being assessed in FMHA. Using this model helps the clinician describe data and reasoning in a more straightforward fashion, whether in a written report or oral testimony.

The other general model of forensic evaluations, developed by Tom Grisso, consists of six components that are shared by all types of legal competencies: *functional, contextual, causal, interactive, judgmental,* and *dispositional* (1986), subsequently reduced to five characteristics (eliminating *contextual* as a separate component by integrating it into *functional*; 2003). These models have both common and unique components. In both models, three elements can be recognized: mental disorder, functional abilities, and the causal connection between the two. Clearly, these three elements should be included in any model used in forensic assessment. Conversely, one element proposed in Grisso's (2003) model—interaction—is not found in Morse's model; it addresses whether the individual's abilities satisfy the demands imposed on the individual by the situation. This element should also be considered for inclusion while selecting a model to guide FMHA.

The use of a model may ultimately assist the forensic clinician in performing a higher-quality evaluation. Certain criteria—such as those offered by Petrella and Poythress (1983)—serve as a basis for judgment in this regard. Specifically, Petrella and Poythress (1983) note the following criteria for high-quality evaluations: (1) use of proper legal criteria, (2) a clearly stated ultimate opinion,[2] (3) provision of an adequate basis for the opinion, (4) clinical characterization of the defendant, (5) a well-balanced use of psychiatric jargon vs. plain language, (6) information needed to assist the court, and (7) overall quality. By including all or most of these elements, forensic practitioners can ensure that their evaluations are relevant, comprehensive, and useful.

The present report illustrates the application of this principle in the context of a court-ordered evaluation of competence to stand trial. The evaluator evaluates the competence of the defendant (Mr. J. C.) by using a model-consistent approach that combines key features of both the Morse and Grisso models.

The evaluator's discussion of Mr. C's competence to stand trial is organized around the three elements that are shared by the Morse and Grisso models of forensic assessment. Specifically, the clinician addresses Mr. C's mental condition (in the section entitled "Clinical Assessment"), his relevant functional legal capacities (in the "Forensic Assessment" section), and the relationship between

---

[2] Although these criteria represent a well-accepted set of standards for forensic practice, it should be noted that there is continuing controversy over whether a clinician should offer an "ultimate opinion" (see Chapter 12, this volume, for a more detailed discussion).

his symptoms and functional capacities. These are components that can be found in the models of forensic assessment described by Morse and Grisso. Each of these three will be addressed in the context of the current evaluation.

Regarding Mr. C's mental condition, the evaluator observed that the defendant had a lengthy history of being diagnosed with a severe mental illness (paranoid schizophrenia) as well as a history of favorable response to the administration of psychotropic medication. She further observed that he presented with active symptoms of this disorder at the time of the evaluation. These symptoms included paranoid delusions encompassing his attorney, which would make it very difficult for Mr. C to work with his attorney in his own defense.

More detailed evaluations of the relevant capacities for competence to stand trial are described in the next section ("Forensic Assessment"). In this case, it was clearly difficult to obtain information about how much Mr. C may have understood regarding his charges, the adversarial nature of the legal system, his possibilities for plea, and other factual information because of his disorganization, tangentiality, and suspiciousness. Accordingly, there was less information about some of the particular capacities important in trial competence than there would have been if Mr. C had been better able to communicate. But the evaluator does offer several illustrations that causally relate Mr. C's deficits in competency-related capacities with his symptoms. For example, she notes that it was "extremely difficult to communicate with Mr. C as he was unable to stay on topic and was tangential and paranoid." Later, she indicates "Mr. C holds numerous paranoid and irrational beliefs about his attorney being part of the Narcotics Task Force, which compromises Mr. C's ability to trust and relate to his attorney."

We do learn about two important contextual considerations in this case: Mr. C is not hospitalized, and he is not taking medication to which he has responded favorably in the past. But why is there little information about the Grisso model's *interactive* component? This is probably because it is difficult to imagine any attorney or legal proceedings that would allow this defendant to meaningfully understand and assist in his present condition. The heart of the interactive component—that a defendant might be considered competent under one set of circumstances but not another—does not apply here because the clinical and functional-legal

deficits are so significant. This might well change, however, if Mr. C were hospitalized, treated, and returned to court with a recommendation that his competence appeared to have been restored. Some attorneys more than others have an inclination and a personal style to work with a defendant such as Mr. C, perhaps by structuring their interactions and "coaching" him. Some judges are inclined toward more flexibility in proceeding with a defendant such as Mr. C; others are not. A report from the hospital concluding that Mr. C appeared ready to return to court for disposition of charges might make recommendations about steps that could be taken with Mr. C to enhance the meaningfulness of his participation in his own defense. Such a report would be addressing Grisso's interactive component.

Patricia A. Zapf, PhD
Forensic & Clinical Psychology

Name: J. C.
Date of Birth: 01/01/1949
SSN: xxx-xx-xxxx
Case No(s): CC2010-xxx
Date of Evaluation: 02/02/12
FORENSIC EVALUATION REPORT
Date of Report: 02/05/2012

REFERRAL INFORMATION

Mr. J. C., a 63-year-old African-American male, was ordered to undergo an outpatient evaluation of his competency to stand trial by the Honorable J. E., __ Circuit Court Judge, _____ County, _____ State, on August 30, 2011. Mr. C. was evaluated with respect to his competency to stand trial on February 2, 2012. Mr. C. is charged with possession of cocaine.

NOTIFICATION

Prior to beginning the evaluation, Mr. C. was informed of the nature and purpose of the evaluation and the limited confidentiality of the information to be obtained. He was told that the results would be submitted to the court in the form of a written report and that copies of this report would be made available to his attorney and the District Attorney. He was also informed that these results might be used in court proceedings, in the form of either the written report or testimony by the examiner. He was further informed that the information obtained might be used to help the court reach a decision regarding his competency to stand trial, but that none of the information would be used as evidence against him concerning the charge itself. Mr. C. indicated that he understood the information provided in the notification, and he signed the notification of rights form indicating his awareness of the limited confidentiality and/or willingness to participate in the evaluation.

SUMMARY OF ALLEGED OFFENSE

It is alleged that on March 3, 2010, at approximately 2130 hours, Mr. J. C. was found in possession of 14.4 grams of crack cocaine. Mr. C. was subsequently arrested and charged with possession of cocaine.

DATA SOURCES

Data sources that were reviewed for the purposes of this evaluation include the following:

- State Uniform Incident/Crime Report
- Treatment records from Mental Health Center dated 10/11/1995 through 8/27/2010 (with a note that further records date back to 1976)
- Interview with the defendant on 02/02/2012
- Fitness Interview Test–Revised (FIT-R)

BACKGROUND INFORMATION

It was extremely difficult to obtain a background and history from Mr. C. The information detailed below was obtained mainly through Mr. C.'s mental health records.

Mr. C. is apparently an only child who was born in _____ State and lived here all his life. He reported that his mother died when he was a young child and that his father raised him. He indicated that his father died in 2001 from a drug overdose. According to a review of records, Mr. C. got along "well" with his father and has denied any physical, sexual, or emotional abuse. Mr. C. lived at home until the age of 38, at which time he moved out on his own. During the period of time that Mr. C. has "lived on his own," he has moved back home for chunks of time as he has been unable to hold a job and has been hospitalized for psychiatric problems multiple times.

Mr. C. reported in past mental health records that he graduated City High School but that he was "passed along" by his teachers, who thought of him as a "behavior problem." He indicated that he had "a few" friends at school and reported being suspended "once or twice."

Mr. C. reported that he has never been married, that he has no children, has never been in a long-term relationship, and that he has never served in the military. He indicated that he has worked on an inconsistent basis, mainly as a brick mason for a friend of his.

Mr. C. reported that he first started using alcohol at the age of 16 and that he began using cocaine and "crank" approximately 16 years ago. Mr. C. reported a lengthy history of "nerve problems" and has been hospitalized numerous times since 1976.

CLINICAL ASSESSMENT

Mr. J. C., a 63-year-old single African American man, was interviewed on February 2, 2012, at my office at XXX. Mr. C. is tall and has a slight build. He was dressed in green pants and a green shirt with a blue nylon jacket that he kept on throughout the interview. He smelled strongly of smoke. He had short, dark hair that was graying at the temples and a full beard, which was also graying. He was missing several of his front teeth and had the habit of sucking his lip through the hole left by his missing teeth. Mr. C.'s left leg was amputated just above the knee and he wore a prosthetic.

Mr. C. appeared to be cooperative with the evaluation, although he was extremely difficult to communicate with, as he was tangential (often veered off-topic and moved randomly from topic-to-topic), paranoid (holding beliefs not based in reality), and religiously preoccupied. His cognitive functioning appeared to be generally intact as he was able to perform a number of operations in different areas; however, he had to be directed to stay on task. He demonstrated appropriate immediate, recent, and remote memory skills and appeared to be able to concentrate well enough to recall lengthy strings of numbers.

Mr. C. appeared to have an adequately developed fund of information, as evidenced by his ability to answer elementary general knowledge questions. He was able to demonstrate some abstract reasoning ability, although he then became perseverative (visiting the same theme over and over again) and religiously preoccupied in his responses. For example, he was able to indicate the similarities between an apple and an orange (stating that both were fruit), but then replied "they're lords, Christ" to queries regarding the similarities between a bird and a tree, a table and a chair, and a poem and a statue. Mr. C. was able to correctly answer social judgment questions and was oriented to person, place, time, and situation.

Mr. C. presented with expansive affect (irritable, easily annoyed and provoked to anger) throughout the interview and continuously spoke even when cut off. He evidenced flight of ideas (moving from one topic to the next at a quick rate) and loose associations between topics (having little logical connection between topics). His speech was somewhat pressured and his affect was labile (abnormal with sudden, rapid shifts in mood). He would raise his voice to shouting level when speaking about the "so-called police."

He denied any suicidal or homicidal ideation or intent. He acknowledged auditory and visual hallucinations (hearing and seeing things that are not present), but I was unable to make sense of the form or content of these hallucinations. He appears to hold a delusional belief system surrounding the people in his neighborhood and the narcotics police. He reported that his "neighborhood has been flooded with whores, whoremongers, bitches, and bastards by the Narcs" and that he has been "anointed and sent to clean it up." His thought style and speech productivity appeared to be excessive and tangential. He maintained appropriate eye contact with the interviewer but exhibited an excessive level of motor activity.

Treatment records from Mental Health Center indicate that Mr. C. has a lengthy history of treatment dating back to 1976. He has been diagnosed with paranoid schizophrenia, and his behavior at the time of interview appeared to be consistent with this diagnosis. He has been prescribed numerous psychotropic medications in the past but treatment records indicate that he has not seen the psychiatrist for medication since October 2010. He indicated that he has not renewed his prescriptions, as he likes the way he is now. He admitted to smoking approximately 1 gram of cocaine per week and stated that these "black market medications" (which include cocaine, coffee, and chewing tobacco) worked best for him. Mr. C. does not appear to have any insight into his mental disorder.

Treatment records indicate that when Mr. C. is compliant with his medication regime his psychotic symptoms are held in check, and he is able to communicate in a meaningful way. This indicates to me that if he were to be treated and placed on a regime of psychotropic medications, with which he was compliant, there is a good chance that his symptoms would again be held in check.

FORENSIC ASSESSMENT

Mr. J. C. was evaluated with respect to his competency to stand trial.

The Fitness Interview Test (revised edition) (FIT-R; Roesch, Zapf, & Eaves, 2006) was used to structure the evaluation of competency to stand trial. This instrument provides a guide to 16 areas of inquiry relevant to competency to stand trial, tapping into such competence-related abilities as the defendant's ability to understand the nature and object of the proceedings, understand the possible consequences of the proceedings, and communicate with and aid counsel.

Competency to Stand Trial

Rule 1.1 of the State Rules of Criminal Procedure states that "a defendant is mentally incompetent to stand trial or to be sentenced for an offense if that defendant lacks sufficient present ability to assist in his or her defense by consulting with counsel with a reasonable degree of rational understanding of the facts and the legal proceedings against the defendant." Mr. C. was evaluated with respect to his ability (a) to rationally understand the facts of the case (including the nature and object of the proceedings), (b) to appreciate the personal importance of the legal proceedings against him, and (c) to assist and communicate with counsel in his defense.

Mr. C. was able to give a brief but jumbled account of the circumstances surrounding his arrest; however, his version was punctuated by paranoid beliefs about the people in his neighborhood and the Narcotics Task Force. He was unable to give the name of his charge and reported that "Christ, God" was his attorney, but that Mr. S (his attorney) was "His mouthpiece." All of his responses to queries about the roles of different individuals (i.e., judge, defense attorney, DA) in the legal process were religiously preoccupied. For example, when asked what the role of the judge was, he replied, "He is a communist, I am a defender of faith; I save the judge, I was anointed and can do no wrong; it is a conspiracy of the world government." He was unable to rationally discuss any of the important aspects of his case or his defense. It was extremely difficult to communicate with Mr. C. as he was unable to stay on topic and was tangential and paranoid.

Mr. C. appears to hold numerous paranoid and irrational beliefs about his attorney being a part of the Narcotics Task Force, which compromises Mr. C's ability to trust and relate to his attorney. In addition, Mr. C's understanding of the legal system and the legal process appears to be religiously preoccupied, which compromises Mr. C's ability to understand the true nature of the proceedings and his ability to appreciate his role as a defendant.

SUMMARY AND RECOMMENDATIONS

In summary, Mr. C. is a 63-year-old African American male who appears to meet criteria for diagnoses of schizophrenia, paranoid type; and cocaine dependence.

Mr. C. indicated that he is not currently taking any psychotropic medications and displays limited insight into his mental illness. He currently appears to be experiencing a number of symptoms of formal thought disorder and, as a result, is unable to communicate in a meaningful way. He is unable, at present, to appreciate the personal importance of the proceedings against him and, in fact, denies that there should be any proceedings at all.

I will outline the statutorily required information should the court find Mr. C. incompetent to proceed.

(i)   The defendant has a number of cognitive deficits that appear to be the result of a thought disorder—schizophrenia, paranoid type, chronic. In addition, he appears to hold a number of delusional (paranoid) beliefs that are also the result of the thought disorder.

(ii) The aforementioned condition can be treated, and has successfully been treated in this defendant in the past, through a regime of psychotropic medications.

(iii) The most appropriate form of treatment is psychotropic medication and close monitoring of his mental state, and the most appropriate place of treatment appears to be an inpatient forensic setting such as Secure Medical Center. A possible treatment alternative would be a setting wherein Mr. C. could be treated and monitored closely as his history indicates that he often is non-compliant with prescribed psychotropic medications and that he self-medicates with illegal substances.

(iv) It is likely that the defendant will regain competency if he is compliant with the treatment and medication regime. The duration of treatment will most likely not exceed three months if the defendant is compliant, as his past history indicates good response to psychotropic medications within a two-month period.

(v)   Secure Medical Center appears to be the most appropriate facility for treatment. If the court determines that outpatient treatment is a viable option, this will need to occur at a facility where the professionals are able to closely monitor the defendant for treatment compliance.

As a forensic psychologist, I recognize that the determination of a defendant's competency to stand trial is ultimately a matter for the court to decide. Therefore, the opinions rendered above are of an advisory nature only. I will be happy to provide the court with any further information, records, or testimony that it may require.
Respectfully submitted,
Patricia A. Zapf, PhD
Licensed Psychologist
Certified Forensic Examiner

TEACHING POINT:
HOW CAN YOU USE A MODEL TO STRUCTURE THE WAY YOU WRITE THE REPORT?

(contributed by Patricia A. Zapf)
Grisso (2003) provided a framework for the assessment of any legal competence. His model begins with a focus on an individual's functional abilities, behaviors, or capacities. He defined functional abilities as "that which an individual can do or accomplish, as well as...the knowledge, understanding, or beliefs that may be necessary for the accomplishment" (Grisso, 2003; pp. 23–24).

A functional assessment dictates that CST cannot simply be assessed in the abstract, independently of contextual factors, particularly for cases in which a finding of incompetence is possible. If a defendant does not have a mental disorder or intellectual deficit, the demands of the defendant's particular legal situation may not be relevant. For defendants who do meet the mental condition prerequisite, an evaluation of contextual factors should always take place. This is the essence of a functional approach to assessing competence, which posits that the abilities required by the defendant in his or her specific case should be taken into account when assessing competence. The open-textured, context-dependent nature of the construct of CST was summarized by Golding & Roesch (1988):

> Mere presence of severe disturbance (a psychopathological criterion) is only a threshold issue—it must be further demonstrated that such severe disturbance in *this* defendant, facing *these* charges, *in light of existing* evidence, anticipating the substantial effort of a *particular* attorney with a *relationship of known characteristics*, results in the defendant being unable to rationally assist the attorney or to comprehend the nature of the proceedings and their likely outcome. (p. 79, italics in original)

The importance of a person–context interaction has been highlighted by Grisso (2003), who defined "a functional assessment" in the following manner:

> A decision about legal competence is in part a statement about *congruency or incongruency between (a) the extent of a person's functional ability and (b) the degree of performance demand that is made by the specific instance of the context in that case.* Thus an interaction between individual ability and situational demand, not an absolute level of ability, is of special significance for competency decisions. (pp. 32–33, italics in original)

Skeem and Golding (1998) suggest a three-step procedure for establishing a link between psychopathology and impairment of legal abilities:

> One might (a) carefully consider the nature and content of the defendant's primary

symptoms, (b) consider how these symptoms might relate conceptually to the defendant's specific psycholegal impairments, then (c) assess, as directly as possible, whether there is actually a relationship between the symptom and the CST impairment. (p. 364)

Zapf and Roesch (2009) identified the following four-step approach to guide the functional evaluation of competence, which can be used to structure the presentation of relevant information in a competency evaluation report, either explicitly or implicitly:

> (1) Learn about what is required of the defendant during the legal proceedings. (2) Assess the defendant's abilities in the context of specific case demands. (3) Consider the relationship between the defendant's symptoms and functional deficits. (4) Specify how the required psycholegal abilities are impaired by the functional deficits. (p. 43)

CASE THREE
PRINCIPLE: ATTRIBUTE INFORMATION TO SOURCES
(*PRINCIPLE 32*)

The communication of the results of FMHA is an important step in the forensic assessment process. Whether such communication is written or oral, the value and influence of FMHA is affected by the way the results are conveyed. The attribution of information to sources is one of the most important elements of the effective communication of FMHA results. In FMHA, it is important to assess the consistency of factual information derived from multiple sources of information. Furthermore, because legal consumers are understandably interested in the sources of such information, it is essential that the forensic clinician cite any sources that provide the basis for the information, impressions, and reasoning presented to the court.

Although this principle is not directly addressed by either of the two major ethics codes for psychology and psychiatry—the *Ethical Principles of Psychologists and Code of Conduct* (American Psychological Association, 2010a) and the *Principles of Medical Ethics with Annotations Especially*

Applicable to Psychiatry (American Psychiatric Association, 2013b), respectively—the specialized forensic guidelines for both psychology and psychiatry contain applicable language. The *Specialty Guidelines for Forensic Psychology* (APA *Specialty Guidelines*; American Psychological Association, 2013b) emphasizes the importance of detailed documentation in FMHA: "Forensic practitioners are encouraged to recognize the importance of documenting all data they consider with enough detail and quality to allow for reasonable judicial scrutiny and adequate discovery by all parties" (Guideline 10.06, p. 16). More directly, the APA *Specialty Guidelines* emphasizes that "Forensic practitioners are encouraged to disclose all sources of information obtained in the course of their professional services, and to identify the source of each piece of information that was considered and relied upon in formulating a particular conclusion, opinion, or other professional product." (Standard 11.03)

The *Ethical Guidelines for the Practice of Forensic Psychiatry* (American Academy of Psychiatry and the Law, 2005) also addresses the issue of attribution:

> Psychiatrists practicing in a forensic role enhance the honesty and objectivity of their work by basing their forensic opinions, forensic reports and forensic testimony on all available data. They communicate the honesty of their work, efforts to attain objectivity, and the soundness of their clinical opinion, by distinguishing, to the extent possible, between verified and unverified information as well as among clinical "facts," "inferences," and "impressions." (p. 3)

The distinction between "verified and unverified information" cannot reasonably be made without an indication of the sources of the information.

No legal authority relevant to this principle could be located, and there is also relatively little in the standard of practice literature regarding this principle. One empirical study by Lander and Heilbrun (2009) found a significant relationship between attributing sources and a report's rated usefulness by forensic mental health experts from both the legal and the clinical fields. It is thus reasonable to consider the attribution of information to sources to be a key element of a well-written report, particularly when the report contains conflicting information obtained from different sources. When this occurs, it is important that the forensic clinician clearly indicate the respective sources of the conflicting information.

The present report is a good illustration of this principle. It describes the results of an evaluation of the defendant whose competence to stand trial is at issue. The defendant had a significant history of previous hospitalization and adjudication as incompetent to stand trial. There was a question of whether his current presentation reflected valid cognitive limitations resulting from dementia, head injury, or both—or whether such deficits were substantially exaggerated. Through a review of his history, the administration of a specialized measure of memory, collateral interviews, and observation of an undercover surveillance DVD, the evaluators concluded that the deficits were exaggerated—and that no meaningful conclusions could be drawn regarding his competence to stand trial.

Throughout the report, the evaluators repeatedly refer to the source(s) of the information being presented. Such attribution helps the court evaluate the relevance and reliability of the information. It also helps the attorney presenting this evaluation do so more effectively, and it provides the opposing attorney with a fair opportunity to challenge these findings. Relevance and reliability, two of the cornerstones of evidence law, could not be assessed as readily without attribution of information to sources.

FORENSIC EVALUATION
COMPETENCE TO STAND TRIAL

Name of Defendant: County: Small
Michael John

Cause #:   Date of
                            Evaluation: 06/03/10

Date of Birth: 00/00/1960   Date of Report:
                            06/23/10

SPECIFIC ISSUES REFERRED FOR EVALUATION

Mr. John is a 50-year-old Caucasian male currently residing in Rural City. He was court-ordered for a psychological evaluation to determine his competency to stand trial, secondary to a charge of possession of controlled substance with intent to deliver.

DISCLOSURES

Prior to beginning the interview, the purpose of the evaluation, procedures involved, and limits of confidentiality were explained to him. He indicated that he understood the disclosure and was given the opportunity to ask questions.

PROCEDURES, TECHNIQUES, TESTS, AND COLLATERAL INFORMATION REVIEWED

RECORDS REVIEWED

Court Order for Incompetency Examination, Dated	05/18/2010
Incident/Offense Report for Charge of Possession of Controlled Substance with Intent to Deliver	02/20/2009
Search and Arrest Warrant	02/19/2009
Records from Archer Psychiatric Hospital	03/04/2008
Records from Archer Psychiatric Hospital	03/05/2008
Letter from Superintendent, Archer Psychiatric Hospital, and Physician's Certificate of Medical Examination	02/13/2008
Competency Evaluation, Dr. Joe, M.D.	04/18/2007
Prior Order of Finding of Incompetence, Cause #	03/06/2008
Release from Custody Orders	04/09/2008
Current Indictment, Cause #	02/25/2010
Record of Current Complaint for Each of Three Counts	02/11/2009
	02/18/2009
	02/19/2009
Order of Incompetency to Stand Trial	06/01/2007
Indictment Cause No.	07/20/2006
Incident/Offense Report for Theft Charge	02/01/2006
Department of Public Safety Motor Vehicle Theft Service Investigative Report	02/13/2006
Prison Managed Care Mental Health Evaluation	06/30/2006
Probation Revocation Judgment for Cause #	06/14/2006
Competency Evaluation, Dr. Kyle, PhD	03/30/2004
Order of Examination Regarding Incompetency	03/04/2004
Motion Suggesting Incompetency and Request for Examination	02/03/2004
Indictment in Cause No.	10/21/2003
Order Dismissing Cause No.	10/20/2000
Order Dismissing Cause No.	10/20/2000
Progress Report from North State Hospital	10/06/2000
Competency Testimony of Dr. Kyle, PhD	07/19/2000
Indictment in Cause No.	09/22/1999
Order Dismissing Cause No.	08/02/1988
Indictment Cause No.	12/08/1987
Order Dismissing Cause No.	08/02/1988
Indictment Cause No.	12/08/1987
Psychological Report of Dr. Kyle, PhD	01/10/1988

COLLATERAL INTERVIEWS*

Interview with Kim Lewis, daughter	06/03/2010
Telephone interview with Jenny Jones, daughter	06/04/2010
Telephone interview with Judy James, ex-wife	06/04/2010

PSYCHOLOGICAL TESTING

Test of Memory Malingering	06/03/2010

DVDs VIEWED

Undercover video surveillance with confidential informant	02/11/2009
	02/18/2009

*Several attempts were made to contact the defendant's brother, Jim Bob; however, he did not return the telephone calls.

CLINICAL OBSERVATIONS AND FINDINGS

Mental Status

At the time of the evaluation, Mr. John was dressed in blue jeans, a white T-shirt and a hat. His clothes appeared to have several stains and his hands were unclean. While his hygiene was minimally adequate, his overall appearance and grooming were rather unkempt. His eye contact was inconsistent as he spent a good deal of time looking around at his surroundings, primarily during the beginning of the evaluation. Also, during much of the initial portion of the evaluation, Mr. John appeared to continually mumble to himself. Rapport was established slowly, as the defendant was hesitant to talk at the outset. However, as the evaluation proceeded he did engage in dialogue.

Mr. John appeared to evidence tremendous difficulty recalling dates and events. He was unable to provide a precise timeline for either recent or remote events. He stated he was unable to recall his date of birth, his father's name, or who he lived with when growing up. His expressive speech capabilities appeared extremely limited during the evaluation. His articulation was poor, and he presented with severe word-finding difficulties. A number of times during the interview he simulated actions such as raking leaves or cutting limbs when he demonstrated difficulties with word finding. He consistently referred to himself in the third person as "Mr. John." Additionally, the defendant's motor functioning appeared impaired. He ambulated with a stooped gait, and his manual dexterity seemed significantly compromised.

The defendant's affect was relatively flat throughout the interview. He said he was not depressed and reported no suicidal ideation, either past or current. There was no evidence of a psychotic thought process. He denied having hallucinations, and there was no indication of bizarre or delusional thinking.

Background Information

As Mr. John appeared to evidence problems with memory recall, the information he provided regarding his background information often lacked detail. A number of historical records as well as collateral interviews were available to provide additional information regarding the defendant's background.

Mr. John's daughter, Kim Lewis, reported that he was born in City, Illinois, but moved to Rural City at a young age and has lived there since. Mr. John reported that he could not recall ever having attended school, but records from a previous evaluation by Dr. Kyle indicate a ninth-grade education as well as a GED.

The defendant reported having one brother and two sisters. He also indicated he had two daughters, Kim and Jenny, and one son, Billy. His daughter Kim Lewis stated that he also has two additional sons. Although records are unclear, it appears Mr. John has been married three times. According to records from Archer State Hospital, Mr. John spent much of the 1970s and 1980s in prison.

The defendant reportedly worked in the logging industry until 1986, but there is no indication of when this employment began. Mr. John reported that he currently works in the yard raking leaves and taking out the trash. His daughter, Ms. Lewis, reported that Mr. John is supervised 24 hours a day and is unable to complete anything more complex than menial chores without assistance.

The defendant's daughter reported that she has been Mr. John's primary caretaker for the past seven years. Prior to this time, she said, he lived with his brother. Ms. Lewis said her father is able to carry out some basic activities of daily living such as bathing himself; however, he is unable to shave, cook, use a microwave, or care for his own finances.

Medical and Mental Health History

Members of Mr. John's family have reported a head injury that occurred while he was logging in December of 1986. This has also been reported by a number of evaluators. It is said he was hit by a log at work. However, when interviewed for the current evaluation, Judy James, his wife at the time, could only recall one accident related to his work as a logger. Specifically, she said at some point he was involved in an accident while driving a logging truck, but sustained no injuries. No records of medical evaluation secondary to the alleged injury were available.

It is further reported that Mr. John sustained a second head injury some time in 1988 when he was allegedly beaten by staff at the Small County Jail. Family report significant changes in the defendant after this injury. However, no records of medical evaluation or treatment are available. Ms. James reported an incident at the jail some time in 1988 where her then-husband briefly barricaded the family in a visiting area, saying he needed to protect them from outside forces who were trying to kill them. Symptoms described appeared to most closely resemble a psychotic episode, whether drug-related or otherwise. The episode as recounted would be totally inconsistent with his current presentation.

Mr. John's first evaluation to assess competence to stand trial occurred on 11/10/1988. At the time of this evaluation, Mr. John was living with his wife, Judy James, and his two daughters, Kim and Jenny. The report from this evaluation by Dr. Kyle refers to the 1986 head injury and states that a CT scan found "suggestions of expanded ventricles which could have signified a developing neurological problem," but Mr. John failed to seek a recommended follow-up CT scan. Additionally, this report indicated Mr. John had reported memory deficits since 1981, as well as a long history of methamphetamine and marijuana abuse. Dr. Kyle indicated Mr. John possibly suffered an amphetamine-induced psychosis around this time. Dr. Kyle reported no active psychotic symptoms at the time of his evaluation; rather, he opined the defendant was not competent due to a dementia of unknown etiology. He described Mr. John's verbalizations as "infantile and concrete" and his mental status as "moderately confused and disoriented." Following a judicial finding of incompetence, the defendant was reportedly committed first to Archer State Hospital and subsequently to Bigger State Hospital for lengthy periods of time. According to information received by Dr. Kyle, he showed no significant improvement during these hospitalizations.

Mr. John was again opined to be incompetent to stand trial on 6/14/00 by the same evaluator. Dr. Kyle determined Mr. John was suffering from "severe dementia" after interviewing Mr. John along with his brother. This report indicated Mr. John to be incapable of managing his finances, that he lived off Social Security insurance benefits, and his brother reported he was unable to even "keep up with his own cigarettes." The findings of this evaluation appear to rely primarily on the accounts of Mr. John and his brother.

Mr. John was committed to North State Hospital from 7/24/00 to 10/06/00, where he was opined to be incompetent and not likely to be restored to competence. This was the defendant's third admission to this facility. The progress report submitted to the court during this admission indicated Mr. John reported he had been framed by the police. However, Mr. John was described as "uncooperative" in answering the interviewer's questions and used "emotional displays to dominate the interview." This report indicated Mr. John would act as though he did not understand the interviewer's questions; however, the evaluator indicated he believed Mr. John was exaggerating his lack of understanding. His speech was again characterized as "infantile." The evaluator stated, "I think he is capable of much more than he is willing to admit." The evaluating psychiatrist at North State Hospital acknowledged reports of two significant head injuries, but noted that "assessments done since that time have not indicated that he had a significant neurologic insult." However, those tests are not specifically described. While Mr. John's psychological testing during this hospital stay were reported to be indicative of someone with profound limitations, it was also reported these scores appeared to be inconsistent with unit behavior. The evaluator raised concerns about these testing results and reported a tendency for Mr. John to exaggerate and/or fabricate symptoms. Final diagnoses included adjustment disorder, substance abuse, personality change due to encephalopathy secondary to chronic use of drugs and trauma to his head, malingering, and borderline intellectual functioning. No psychotic symptomatology was noted. Following his stay at North State Hospital, he was admitted to another state psychiatric hospital for an undetermined length of time.

The defendant was assessed for competence to stand trial again on 03/30/04 by Dr. Kyle. This evaluation indicated Mr. John may suffer from dementia due to injury or drug abuse. It also reported, according to the defendant's brother, that the defendant requires constant supervision and is unable to manage his money. However, the evaluator also noted interviewing the local Chief of Police and the Assistant District Attorney, who provided a very different picture of Mr. John's behavior. It is unclear why the evaluator assumed the accuracy of reports by family members, but completely discounted those of other secondary sources. Dr. Kyle suggested that activities such as driving a car, engaging in grocery store transactions, and discussing parenting with a Child Protective Services (CPS) worker could simply be "examples of over-learned behavior." However, these examples would exceed what is generally accepted as over-learned behavior.

On January 21, 2005, Mr. John was ordered to community supervision for the offense of evading detention on August 21, 2003. However, on June 13, 2006, his community supervision was revoked. At that time he was deemed competent by the court. Although psychometric testing was not clinically indicated, the defendant was referred to a Mentally Retarded Offender Program (MROP). Prior to transfer to the MROP, he was seen briefly for evaluation at one of the prison system's psychiatric units, where no psychotic symptoms were noted.

Mr. John was evaluated by Dr. Joe on 4/18/2007. This evaluation consisted of an interview with the defendant as well as a conversation with his attorney. An examination of the report for this evaluation indicates a diagnosis of dementia not otherwise specified, and a conclusion that he was incompetent to proceed. No new evidence was apparently uncovered.

In 2007–2008, Mr. John was hospitalized at Archer Psychiatric State Hospital (APSH) for approximately six months following a finding of incompetence to stand trial. The defendant received a neuropsychological evaluation at APSH on 2/11/08. This evaluation indicated the defendant appeared aphasic, and his testing scores demonstrated severe deficits. The evaluator opined that his deficits meant he would be unable to communicate verbally except on a very fundamental level, unable to understand complex speech, unable to perform calculations, and would have severe memory difficulties. No formal testing for the possibility of malingering was recorded. These records indicate malingering was not suspected because his test results were consistently poor. However, as Mr. John received scores of almost 0 during both testing administrations, it appears there was not sufficient variability to rule out malingering. At APSH, Mr. John received a primary diagnosis of cognitive disorder not otherwise specified.

Psychological Test Results

While the issue of malingering has been raised previously in regard to Mr. John's competence, this is the first evaluation to use formal psychological testing to specifically address this question. Mr. John was administered the Test of Memory Malingering (TOMM). Mr. John was very hesitant to begin the testing process and required a break during this procedure. During this break he smoked a cigarette and reported to his daughter that he wanted to go home. The TOMM is a 50-item recognition test designed to help discriminate between bona fide memory impairments and testing results that do not reflect actual capabilities. On this test the individual is shown 50 items and then is presented with two pictures, one of which was previously presented to the individual, while the other was not. Therefore, through choosing responses completely at random, an individual would be expected to get approximately 50% of the responses correct. Individuals with traumatic brain injuries have been demonstrated to achieve average scores of 45, 49, and 49 on trials 1–3 of this measure. The test manual indicates that any time a score below chance occurs, the possibility of malingering should be examined. The manual reports that any score below 45 on trial 2 should indicate the possibility of malingering, and any score below 18 implies the individual intentionally picked the incorrect answer. The defendant received scores well below chance on his first (16), second (18), and third (19) trials. Indeed, the chance of scoring this low if one were choosing answers at random approximates 3 in 10,000. These results provide evidence that Mr. John appears to be exaggerating the severity of his symptoms.

Review of DVDs from Undercover Video Surveillance

In an effort to obtain some behavioral sample of the defendant's typical behavior that was not simply the account of a possibly biased informant, the evaluators requested copies of the DVDs made of any undercover operation involving the defendant in February of 2009. The two DVDs were very short—only several minutes in length; however, Mr. John's appearance, mannerisms, verbalizations, and overall presentation were in stark contrast to the behaviors presented throughout the current evaluation or observations described by evaluators at North State Hospital, Archer Psychiatric State Hospital, or by Dr. Kyle. His posture, motor dexterity, and speech patterns appeared very normal. There was no indication he was seeking guidance from his daughter, Kim, or anyone else during the interchange. Mr. John was able to recall the informant by name and indicate they had been carrying out interactions for "a long time." Also, he was able to calculate how much money he was currently owed by the informant. His conversation could in no way be characterized as "infantile."

Case Formulation

Despite his current denial, Mr. John has a well-documented history of both marijuana and methamphetamine abuse. In fact, at times he has reportedly displayed the symptoms of an amphetamine-induced psychotic episode. However, those symptoms have been absent during formal evaluations of Mr. John's competence. There is no evidence that he is currently experiencing such phenomena.

Over the years, there has been considerable evidence that the defendant suffers from a deteriorating neurological condition secondary to two severe head injuries. Both of his daughters have consistently reported that he was hit in the head in a logging accident while at work and was later severely beaten by staff in a jail facility. Subsequent psychiatric records from APSH indicate that Mr. John's family reported that, after this accident, "his personality changed, and they describe him as becoming child-like and impulsive." Once again, records report discrepancies between accounts of family members and other informants (i.e., the defendant's former wife). Since that time, various evaluators have reported symptoms consistent with severe traumatic brain injury. This has included evaluators who had the benefit of long-term inpatient observations on which to base their findings.

During the current evaluation, the defendant presented with classic symptoms of aphasia, severely impaired memory, and extreme reticence about any interaction in which he did not have his daughter at hand for support and clarification. His motor functioning was significantly impaired, and he had extreme difficulty attempting to write his name. He appeared unable to recall even the most over-learned information (e.g., his date of birth, his father's name, two of his children, and where and with whom he was raised). His behavior and conversation, while waiting in the lobby as well as during the interview, could consistently be described as "infantile."

However, interviews, records, and psychological testing demonstrate a number of inconsistencies. Mr. John has been found incompetent to stand trial on several occasions and his family reports he is unable to carry out anything more than the most basic activities of daily living. In contrast, past evaluators have noted several reports from other sources suggesting Mr. John may be exaggerating the extent of his deficits for secondary gain. It is unclear why credence was given to family informants, but not to others. Additionally, Mr. John was found to be competent according to records dated on 6/13/06. In examining descriptions of his presentation given by evaluators over the preceding eight years, as well as his presentation during the current evaluation, it is difficult to see how any attorney or court of law could have deemed him competent if he presented consistently.

Records indicate the defendant's deficits were generally attributed to traumatic brain injuries Mr. John suffered on two separate occasions. Due to the apparent severity of these deficits, it would be expected for the defendant to have an extensive medical history stemming from these incidents. However, neither Mr. John, his two daughters, his ex-wife (to whom he was married at the time of the reported injuries), nor subsequent medical records identify any substantial time spent in the hospital as a result of the reported traumatic brain injuries. The records indicate this information regarding the head injuries was obtained through interviews with Mr. John and his family. Mr. John's daughters, Ms. Lewis and Ms. Jones, both indicated their mother (Judy James) reported that Mr. John suffered a head injury during a logging incident when they were children. However, during a telephone interview with Ms. James, she reported she could recall no logging accident in which her husband received a head injury. She specifically recalled an accident he had while driving a truck at work, but said there was no injury to her husband from that event.

While questions regarding the potential of malingering have long been raised regarding this defendant, there have been no formal attempts to evaluate malingering with psychological assessments until this current evaluation. Psychological testing performed during this evaluation strongly suggests that the defendant was intentionally choosing the incorrect answers in order to present himself in an overtly impaired manner.

Finally, a review of the DVDs recorded in February of 2009 indicates a stark contrast to the presentation Mr. John made during the current evaluation. While these videos are only a few minutes in length, Mr. John's deficits appeared to be absent. His expressive speech is appreciably improved, there is no evident receptive speech problem, his memory appears intact, and the motor dexterity in his hands appears much improved. Unlike during the current evaluation, there was no indication he was seeking guidance from his daughter at any time during the videotape interactions. This would strongly indicate dissimulation on the part of the defendant.

Suspicions expressed by evaluators over approximately the past 20 years, inconsistencies from the defendant's records, current psychological test results, and the wide contrast between Mr. John's presentation for evaluators and his appearance on law enforcement DVDs, lead to the conclusion that the defendant is seriously exaggerating his cognitive deficits. This does not establish that there are no deficits, only that what is presented to mental health evaluators is not a valid representation of Mr. John's abilities.

DIAGNOSES

Axis I:	305.20	Cannabis Abuse
	305.70	Amphetamine Abuse
	V65.2	Malingering
Axis II:	V799.9	Deferred

OPINION ON COMPETENCE TO STAND TRIAL

Given Michael John's behavior during the current forensic evaluation, it was impossible to conduct a clinically valid evaluation of his competence-related abilities. It can only be said that the evaluation provides no evidence that he would not be competent to proceed to trial.

Samuel Hawes,
MA 06/23/2010

Student Clinician
Mary Alice Conroy, PhD, ABPP
Board Certified in Forensic Psychology

TEACHING POINT:
SEPARATING AND INTEGRATING DATA FROM DIFFERENT SOURCES THROUGH SOURCE ATTRIBUTION IN ANALYZING, REASONING ABOUT, AND COMMUNICATING FMHA RESULTS

One of the important challenges in communicating the results of FMHA involves providing a clear description of the information that forms the basis for subsequent reasoning and conclusions. The credibility of some of the information collected in the course of an evaluation is unclear. How much weight should be placed on a single record indicating that the defendant was once evaluated for mental health purposes but not diagnosed or treated? On the report of any employer who stated that the defendant worked for him for a year and was unremarkable in his interactions with others? On the results of a specialized measure indicating that the defendant is probably malingering?

These are questions that the evaluator must answer in the report. Hopefully, the answers are informed by available scientific data, as in the case of a psychological test or specialized measure. But there is still considerable discretion that the forensic clinician exercises in deciding what to emphasize more heavily, less heavily, or hardly at all.

The transition from raw data—psychological test results, interview, collateral interviews, and records—to reasoning can be difficult for the reader to follow. It would be virtually impossible, however, without clearly attributing each individual piece of information to its source. The preceding report almost always informs the reader what information has been obtained and from where. This allows the reader to follow the evaluators' reasoning more closely when they describe how the information has been collected and what it means. This also means that the report can be more readily challenged on cross-examination—consistent with the APA *Specialty Guidelines'* urging that forensic evaluations be prepared to facilitate such cross-examination, with the ultimate goal of better informing the court's decision.

4

Criminal Responsibility

The mental state of adult defendants at the time of the offense—and the related impact on criminal responsibility—is the focus of the three reports in this chapter. The first case report addresses the principle of being familiar with the legal, ethical, scientific, and practice literature pertaining to the legal question being assessed. An updated teaching point describes sources of particularly relevant information from the literature. The second principle to be addressed is that of attributing information to sources. The teaching point discusses two styles of attribution—line-by-line and more general paragraph attribution—that are often used in FMHA. Finally, the principle of declining a referral for FMHA when impartiality is unlikely is the focus of the final case report in this chapter. Maintaining impartiality is important in all cases, but it can be particularly difficult in high-visibility evaluations. This will be addressed in the teaching point.

CASE ONE
PRINCIPLE: BE FAMILIAR WITH THE RELEVANT LEGAL, ETHICAL, SCIENTIFIC, AND PRACTICE LITERATURES PERTAINING TO FMHA (PRINCIPLE 3)

FMHA as a practice has developed greatly since the mid-twentieth century (see Heilbrun, Grisso, & Goldstein, 2009, and Otto & Heilbrun, 2002, for a review of this history), but not all practitioners involved in FMHA are trained as forensic specialists per se. Some forensic clinicians did not receive formal doctoral or postdoctoral professional training in the methods of FMHA, the ethics relevant to forensic involvement, or the laws that govern forensic practice. The methods utilized by forensic evaluators, and the quality of their work, vary widely (see, e.g., Christy, Douglas, Otto, & Petrila,

2004; Cunningham & Reidy, 2001; Tolman & Mullendore, 2003). Given that FMHA can have an important impact on the lives of those evaluated and on the criminal justice system as a whole, and considering the emphasis of the *Ethical Principles of Psychologists and Code of Conduct* (APA *Ethics Code*; American Psychological Association, 2010a) that experts practice within their areas of competence, there is a strong need for establishing best practices in FMHA. Best practices promote competence in the field, convey the collective knowledge of the field regarding methods and decision-making in FMHA, and can enhance legal decision-making by better informing judges and juries tasked with rendering verdicts in complicated cases. In FMHA, best practice standards can be derived from sources of authority in law, empirical science, ethics, and professional practice (Heilbrun et al., 2009).

Law contributes to the practice of FMHA in several significant ways. Legal statutes, standards, and case law define who can act as an expert in the criminal justice system (Federal Rule of Evidence [FRE] 702; *Jenkins v. United States*, 1962), the admissibility of the evidence offered by these experts (*Daubert v. Merrell Dow Pharmaceuticals*, 1993; FRE 702; *Frye v. United States*, 1923; *General Electric Co. v. Joiner*, 1997; *Kumho Tire Co. v. Carmichael*, 1999), and the threshold for offering an expert opinion. Relevant law can also help define the focus of the evaluation and set limits on the testimony of forensic evaluators; for example, on the use of third party information (FRE 703; see also Otto, Slobogin, & Greenberg, 2006) and ultimate issue testimony (FRE 704(b); see also Goldstein, Morse, & Shapiro, 2003). Finally, the law can affect FMHA by regulating its practice through licensing laws, specialty certification requirements and training, and restrictions on jurisdictional practice (see Heilbrun et al., 2009).

Heilbrun and colleagues (2009) also point to the empirical literature from the behavioral and medical sciences as an important contributor to best practice in FMHA. Beyond providing the conceptual and empirical grounds for FMHA, this literature helps promote accurate observation, measurement, and interpretation of relevant behaviors for legal decision-making. Similarly, authoritative sources for professional ethics—such as the American Psychological Association, American Psychiatric Association, American Psychology-Law Society, American Academy of Psychiatry and the Law, and various other professional groups—provide ethics guidance that mental health experts can consider in their forensic practice. Many of the guidelines and standards provided by these groups are discussed throughout this volume regarding specific principles of FMHA. They include both broad concepts such as competence, confidentiality, and privacy, and more specific guidance on assessment, record keeping, fees, public statements, and the like. These sources of professional ethics indirectly affect the regulation of FMHA by defining the process of adjudicating ethical violations (which can result in referrals to state licensing bodies) and by establishing the requirements of expertise in a field. In addition, some states (e.g., Pennsylvania) have incorporated the APA *Ethics Code* into their state licensing laws, giving legal stature to the ethical standards.

Finally, professional organizations such as the American Psychology-Law Society (APA Division 41), the American Academy of Forensic Psychology, and the American Academy of Psychiatry and the Law have published extensively on the practice of FMHA. The literature promulgated by these professional practice authorities—and by established specialized forensic training centers—provides forensic evaluators with resources on graduate and postgraduate training in forensic psychology, practice guidelines for forensic sub-specialties (e.g., *Guidelines for Child Custody Evaluations in Family Law Proceedings*; APA, 2010b), continuing education opportunities, and board certification. Many of these organizations have also been integral to the development, refinement, and understanding of the various legal, empirical, and ethical authorities mentioned above.

Effective practice within FMHA therefore requires an understanding of the relevant legal, empirical, ethical, and professional literatures, and each of these sources of authority makes an important contribution to the process and content

of FMHA (Heilbrun et al., 2009; Melton, Petrila, Poythress, & Slobogin, 2007; Packer & Grisso, 2011). The APA *Ethics Code* notes that psychologists practice "only within the boundaries of their competence, based on their education, training, supervised experience, consultation, study, or professional experience" (Standard 2.01[a]), continually work to maintain their competence (Standard 2.03), and base their clinical judgments "upon established scientific and professional knowledge of the discipline" (Standard 2.04). Furthermore, psychologists should also base their selection, administration, scoring, and interpretation of particular assessments within an evaluation on the relevant scientific and professional literature (Standards 9.01, 9.02, and 9.06). These standards therefore emphasize that psychologists should keep abreast of all relevant and contemporary literature within their area of practice.

The APA *Ethics Code* emphasizes the importance of competence within the context of forensic practice, particularly regarding legal sources of authority: "When assuming forensic roles, psychologists are or become reasonably familiar with the judicial or administrative rules governing their roles" (Standard 2.01[f]). The *Specialty Guidelines for Forensic Psychology* (APA *Specialty Guidelines*; American Psychological Association, 2013b) supports the importance of acquiring and maintaining competence in forensic practice (Guidelines 2.01 and 2.02, respectively) and basing assessment methods on the scientific and professional literature (Guideline 10.02). Furthermore, the APA *Specialty Guidelines* notes the importance of developing a comprehensive understanding of the legal system and relevant legal sources of authority (Guideline 2.04) and the scientific foundation for their opinions and testimony (2.05). This principle is also generally supported by the *Principles of Medical Ethics with Annotations Especially Applicable to Psychiatry* (Sections 3 and 5; American Psychiatric Association, 2013b), and less directly by the *Ethics Guidelines for the Practice of Forensic Psychiatry* (Guideline V, Qualifications; AAPL *Ethics Guidelines*; American Academy of Psychiatry and the Law [AAPL], 2005).

The present evaluation illustrates how the forensic clinician is informed by sources of authority in different areas. The legal question is clearly described in the first paragraph: whether the defendant "had the cognitive ability to formulate the requisite intent to premeditate and deliberate the offense." There are a number of instances throughout the report in which it is clear that Dr. Wettstein, who is medically trained, is able to integrate evidence from medical science in areas such as the description of the victim's wounds, the defendant's medical disorders, the interaction between chemicals in his body at the time of the offense, and the interaction between medical and mental health symptoms in the defendant. This evaluation is also quite consistent with the AAPL *Ethics Guidelines*. The tone reflects honesty and striving for impartiality, as seen in his integration of multiple sources of information and his transparent attempt to give fair consideration to various possible explanations. Finally, it is also apparent that there is a good deal of practice literature and experience supporting the evaluation. One of the clearest examples involves his description of the effects of alcohol on the human brain and behavior. This description is scientifically sound, but also clear and well informed by experience with individuals involved in offending while intoxicated.

Robert M. Wettstein, MD
401 Shady Avenue, Suite B-103
Pittsburgh, PA 15206

----

(412) 661-0300 (tel)
(412) 661-0333 (fax)
April 12, 2013

Morris Jensen, Esquire
Assistant Public Defender
Office of the Public Defender
Philadelphia County Courthouse
102 North Main Street
Conshohocken, PA
REF: *Commonwealth v. Jed Baxter*
Philadelphia County Court of Common Pleas
DOB: 7/12/70
Dear Mr. Jensen:

At your request, I performed a pretrial psychiatric evaluation of Jed Baxter, a 41-year-old, married white male with regard to homicide charges based upon an alleged incident of June 11, 2012, in Philadelphia, Pennsylvania. The purpose of the evaluation was to evaluate his cognitive status at the time of the alleged offense, specifically whether he had the cognitive ability to formulate the requisite intent to premeditate and deliberate the offense. The evaluation consisted of the following document reviews and interviews:

1. Affidavit of Probable Cause and Police Criminal Complaint in this matter.
2. Philadelphia County Detective Bureau police investigation reports in this matter.
3. Autopsy report of the victim with toxicology.
4. Toxicology for the defendant obtained by blood testing on June 11, 2012, 11:00 p.m.
5. Transcript of the preliminary hearing held in this matter on August 19, 2012.
6. Outpatient medical records from the Veterans Affairs Medical Center, Temple, Texas, 2010–2011.
7. Psychiatric interview with the defendant at the Philadelphia County Prison on November 24, 2012 (2.75 hours).
8. Telephone interview with Paula Baxter, defendant's wife, on November 26, 2012.
9. Telephone interview with Anna Baxter, defendant's mother, on December 7, 2012.
10. Telephone interview with Susan Baxter, defendant's sister, on January 10, 2013.

PRESENTING PROBLEM FROM DOCUMENTS

According to available documents, a 65-year-old white male was killed by a single gunshot wound to the back as he sat at the bar at Big Boy's Place in Philadelphia, Pennsylvania, on June 11, 2012, at approximately 6:50 p.m. The autopsy report of the victim indicates that he stood at five feet six inches tall, and weighed approximately 170 pounds. The bullet entered his left lower back, transected his spinal cord, and fractured his thoracic vertebrae, later causing laceration of his lungs and bilateral hemothorax. Toxicology for the victim was positive for alcohol and caffeine. Of note on the autopsy was severe atherosclerosis of the aorta with a large aneurysm of the distal abdominal segment of the aorta.

The defendant, then a 40-year-old married white male, was immediately tackled by two men who had been present at the bar and witnessed the shooting, which occurred with an assault rifle. Interviews with witnesses revealed that the defendant had entered the bar a few minutes earlier, drank some of one beer, sat at the bar, and became upset because the volume on the television was momentarily too loud. The defendant reportedly approached the victim, had a brief conversation about that, sarcastically apologized to the victim, and left the bar to go outside. Witnesses observed that the defendant was stumbling and bumped into the wall as he exited the bar and then reentered with his assault rifle. The defendant had brief words with the victim before shooting him in the back, according to witnesses. Two other witnesses tackled him, and the firearm discharged again without injuring anyone. Others at the restaurant/bar observed that the defendant was intoxicated. The police located a handgun in the defendant's pickup truck parked in the bar parking lot.

The police reports indicate that, after they arrived at the scene, the defendant confessed to the shooting and further elaborated that he had been angry at his stepdaughter, Elizabeth, and her boyfriend, for having taken $1300 from his checking account within the previous days or weeks because they were heroin addicts. He explained that he had been looking for them and had wanted to shoot them rather than the victim. He stated that he was supposed to be taking prescription medications but was not, in fact, taking them. He asked the police to shoot him because of what he had done. His blood was drawn at 11:00 p.m. that evening and was positive for ethanol with a blood alcohol concentration of 0.107% in addition to caffeine, nicotine, marijuana, and citalopram (Celexa). The extrapolated blood alcohol concentration for the defendant at the time of the alleged offense would have been 0.17% to 0.22% according to available data.

Other interviews revealed that the defendant had visited several other bars in Philadelphia County earlier that day. He had consumed alcohol at Barry's Bar in Montgomery, Blue's on South Street, and Chester Beach Bar. A statement from the bartender from the last bar indicated that he had been at her bar from 5:00 p.m. to 5:45 p.m. on that day and had consumed one or two drinks.

PRESENTING PROBLEM FROM DEFENDANT

In the psychiatric interview, the defendant reported that he had started drinking alcohol in the morning of June 11, 2012, at home when he drank several beers. He had no specific work plans that day, and at the time was living with his stepdaughter, Elizabeth, and his wife in Philadelphia County. His wife had already left their home for work. He stated that he did not eat any food that day, to his

recall. He left his home and drove to Barry's Bar in Somerset where he arrived before lunch. He sat at the bar for several hours and could not recall his alcohol consumption there. He had no plans for the day, and did not talk to his wife throughout the day.

He recalled that he left Barry's Bar and then traveled to South Street, where he spent time at Blue's Bar. He may have preferred that bar to the earlier one because it was smaller or quieter, but his recall for the events there was similarly minimal. Throughout the day, he consumed straight shots of Wild Turkey with occasional Coors Light beers. He left Blue's Bar and traveled to Chester Beach Bar but he could not recall even being there.

The defendant had minimal recall for being at Big Boy's Bar in South Street, and had never been there before. He could not recall how long he was there, what he did there, or how much alcohol he consumed there. He did not recall the victim, or the shooting. He recalled being thrown on the floor by two witnesses who restrained him after the shooting. He could not recall any conversation with the victim. He could not recall the bar itself, and reentering or stumbling as he did so. He had a brownout rather than a blackout for his conversations with the police after the shooting, with some minimal recollection of talking to the police while he was sitting in the police car. He was able to recall the blood test at the hospital at 11:00 p.m. that night. He indicated that he had consumed marijuana on the previous day, but not on the day of the offense, to his recollection.

The defendant explained that he knew that he had been angry about his stepdaughter's having taken money from the marital bank account, but could not recall having or verbalizing homicide ideation with regard to her. He could not recall whether the amount of alcohol he consumed on the day of the shooting differed from what it had been previously.

MEDICAL HISTORY

The defendant indicated that he has had several life-threatening medical problems. The defendant's mother told me that he had congenital heart valve disease, but he told me that he developed endocarditis, possibly from intravenous cocaine use, and required an aortic valve replacement. The first procedure occurred at Philadelphia General Hospital in approximately 1992 with a mechanical valve. He has been prescribed and intermittently taking blood thinner in the form of Coumadin since then. In 2002, that valve had to be replaced with a larger one, in Miami, Florida. However, he developed complications from that second surgery, and several months later, underwent a third procedure at the Carter Clinic in early 2004. No medical records are available concerning these procedures. He stated that he has not had cardiac symptoms or failure since then. However, he has felt as though he is "living on borrowed time, which mentally screwed me up."

Other medical problems include polycythemia vera which is a disorder resulting in excessive red blood cell production. He was hospitalized at least on one occasion for this because of enlargement of his spleen. He has regularly required blood removal, even bimonthly, in recent years at the Veterans Affairs Medical Centers. This disorder had its onset in his twenties.

The defendant stated that he contracted hepatitis C in Florida, possibly from a prostitute. He has never been jaundiced nor had other hepatitis C symptoms to his knowledge. He has not received hepatitis C treatment, which is problematic given his cardiac valve and Coumadin history. He has also had gout for the last ten years, which affects his feet. His last medical hospitalization occurred in Texas in 2009 for polycythemia. Other surgeries include a tonsillectomy when he was a child.

On April 26, 2012, the defendant went to his medical clinic at the Veterans Affairs Medical Center in Temple, Texas, where he reported depressive symptoms. The clinic records indicate that he reported depressed mood, low motivation, irritability, and impatience. He had recently been laid off from work and was moving from another part of Texas. He denied suicide and homicide ideas. He agreed to their recommendation to start antidepressant medication. He told me that his wife had previously recommended mental health treatment, which he had refused. Celexa 20 mg was instituted by the clinic, and later increased to 40 mg a day during his present incarceration. He has also been given Vistaril while in custody to address his "tension." His wife reported that he has had episodic periods of low mood with loss of energy, activity, and socialization. These last from days to months at a time. He reported that he had developed depressive symptoms after each of his three cardiac surgeries because of his prolonged incapacitation and loss of income. There is no history

of manic symptoms. There is also no history of psychotic symptoms except during alcohol withdrawal when he has experienced visual hallucinations. He denied suicide attempts, suicide threats, suicide preoccupation, or self-injurious behavior whether sober or intoxicated.

SUBSTANCE ABUSE HISTORY

In the psychiatric interview, the defendant described a long history of excessive use and abuse of alcohol beginning as an early teenager. The defendant's mother confirmed his report in this regard when I interviewed her. He stated that he became alcohol dependent by age 15, when he drank alcohol regularly with an older man friend. He characterized his alcohol use in the United States Army as problematic, and it prompted his "other than honorable" discharge from the Army, before the completion of his enlistment.

The defendant characterized himself as a binge alcoholic who drank excessively, often on weekends for 24 to 36 hours at a stretch. Occasionally, he went to work intoxicated with alcohol. On weekends, he drank from the morning through the night and then overnight into the next day. He developed alcohol tolerance and could drink a case of beer a day or a fifth of whiskey a day. He lost control of his alcohol use during his consumption. He had hangovers and blackouts, alcohol tolerance, alcohol withdrawal, was unable to reduce his alcohol use, and spent considerable time and resources consuming alcohol. He knew that he had an alcohol problem and that his hepatitis C further risked the health of his liver. He stated that he did not deny that he had been an alcoholic over the years, but had been unable to control his use.

The defendant reported that he had at least three driving under the influence (DUI) arrests, after which he was referred for Alcoholics Anonymous (AA) intervention, but did not pursue other substance abuse intervention or treatment. He had two arrests for DUI in Philadelphia County about 20 years ago, and a third in 2011 before the alleged offense. I have not seen documentation concerning these arrests. He also had been cited for public intoxication in Pennsylvania. He denied arrests for fighting while intoxicated, but was involved in physical incidents while intoxicated, mostly at a bar. He consumed alcohol mostly at bars with his wife but sometimes at home. During periods of severe intoxication with subsequent blackouts, he had fistfights, occasional domestic violence against his wife, nausea and vomiting, and made threats to kill others. He had never had alcohol withdrawal seizures or delirium tremens but developed alcohol-withdrawal visual hallucinations. He reported that he was more impulsive and nasty when intoxicated, but his wife indicated that he was often pleasant while intoxicated. He stated that he has consumed alcohol at least two days a week for the last ten years. His present sobriety while in custody is his longest period of sobriety since age 16. His medical records from the Veterans Affairs Medical Center in Texas showed no elevations of his liver function tests in 2010 and 2011, and document occasional binge use of alcohol.

Beyond his alcohol dependence, the defendant acknowledged a history of street-drug use. In the 1980s, he took LSD on innumerable occasions, up to 100 doses in total. He used cocaine powder, intravenous cocaine, and crack cocaine. He denied use of heroin or other intravenous substances. He smoked marijuana on a daily basis for at least the last ten years, several times a day, as long as it was available, even at work. In Texas, he used synthetic marijuana, referred to as "space," which he found more intoxicating than regular marijuana, though it made him irritable. Overall, however, his drug of choice has always been alcohol. He has also been tobacco-dependent.

The defendant denied contact with mental health or substance abuse professionals prior to this evaluation.

FAMILY HISTORY FROM DEFENDANT

The defendant was the older of two children born to his parents in an intact family. He was born in Nashville, Tennessee, where his father's family originated. When he was eight, in 1978, the defendant and his family moved to Erie, Pennsylvania, so that his father could sell coal mine equipment. His father was regularly employed as a salesman in one capacity or another. His father also had a federal firearms sales license. His father suddenly died in 2003 at age 59, after a heart attack, and previously had cardiac bypass surgery. His father frequently traveled out of town during the week, and was absent from the family. However, his parents were never separated. There is no history of domestic violence or infidelity. His mother has

been regularly employed in a clerical capacity and is now retired, at age 66.

The defendant's 39-year-old sister is remarried with two children and lives in Texas. She is a high school graduate and works as a housekeeper in a hospital. They are reportedly close.

There is some extended-family history of alcoholism, including a paternal great uncle and a maternal first cousin, both of whom died from alcoholic cirrhosis. The defendant reported that his father drank a lot but primarily at home and developed alcohol tolerance from frequent alcohol use; however, the defendant's mother denied that her husband abused alcohol. The defendant reported that his father's father had been arrested for a DUI. The defendant's mother never drank much alcohol. There is no other history of psychiatric illness or treatment in the family, according to the defendant and his mother.

The defendant met his wife in Pennsylvania. She is now 63 years old and is 22 years older than he; they married in Florida on December 31, 1997. She was married twice before and has three children. She was always employed throughout their marriage, and has had two DUI arrests herself. He recalled that they separated briefly in 2004 and 2009 due to marital conflict, and they have not participated in marital counseling. Domestic violence has occurred between them. He characterized himself and his wife as "professional gypsies" because they have moved frequently to secure his employment.

FAMILY HISTORY FROM FAMILY MEMBERS

The defendant's mother recounted the defendant's marriage to his wife as highly problematic, with financial dependence upon the defendant, and multiple marital separations. His mother reported that the defendant's wife financially exploited the defendant, and diverted needed marital income and assets to her own children and grandchildren, all of which distressed the defendant. This included providing the defendant's stepdaughter, Elizabeth, with funds for her and her boyfriend to purchase heroin or other illicit drugs, which they had used for many years, with resulting criminal prosecutions but little if any incarceration. In addition, the defendant's wife had several criminal arrests due to her reported manipulative and scheming behavior against others, including defrauding

Unemployment Compensation. The defendant's mother indicated that the defendant was indeed angered and outraged by his stepdaughter's having removed $1300 or so from the marital bank account in the weeks or so before the alleged offense, with his wife complicit in this event. His mother alleged that his wife and stepdaughter had "ruined his life" and were a trigger to the alleged homicide.

The defendant's sister confirmed the defendant's mother's account of the defendant's marital problems. She described the defendant and his wife as abnormally attached and dependent upon each other, with each unable to separate from the other for emotional (i.e., mutually low self-esteem) and financial reasons. The defendant had left his wife several times and lived with his sister, but his wife then went to retrieve him, even after she became aware that he was continually unfaithful to her. The defendant did not excessively consume alcohol, or show alcohol-related violence or other misconduct, when he was living with his sister. During those intervals, he was a hard worker and did not miss work due to alcohol use or its consequences. At times, the defendant told his sister that he was "tired" of supporting his stepdaughter. He talked of divorcing his wife but did not follow through with this idea, much to his sister's displeasure. His sister opined that the defendant's life-threatening medical problems made him feel inadequate, despondent, and worthless, such that he thought that no other woman would accept him. Even to the present time, the defendant maintains his love and devotion to his wife, despite her reported contribution to his long-standing alcoholism, and the instant offense.

WORK AND SCHOOL HISTORY

The defendant graduated from Washington High School in 1988. Shortly thereafter, he enlisted in the United States Army, where he remained for three years. He was stationed in South Korea for a year and a half and never saw combat. He was given an "other than honorable discharge" because of his alcoholism and frequent absences without leave (AWOLs). In the service, he was a heavy-equipment diesel mechanic. He was prescribed Antabuse for his alcoholism but that was unsuccessful. He denied that he was prosecuted while in the service.

After leaving the Army, he has been employed intermittently in various construction jobs in Pennsylvania, Florida, Louisiana, and Texas. He frequently moved to locate employment as a carpenter. No documents are presently available concerning his work history. For periods of time, he received unemployment compensation, but never applied for Social Security or private disability income.

MENTAL STATUS EXAMINATION

The defendant was initially informed of the nature, purpose, and non-confidentiality of the evaluation process and agreed to and understood this. At the time of the interview, he stated that he was taking the following prescription medications while at Philadelphia County Prison: Celexa 40 mg daily for depression, Vistaril 75 mg twice daily for anxiety, Coumadin (blood thinner) 6 mg daily, and colchicine for gout daily.

The defendant appeared as a neatly groomed, healthy, overweight white male approximately his stated age. He had a shaved head and was clean-shaven except for a neatly trimmed mustache. He stated that he stood at five feet, eleven inches tall and weighed over 200 pounds. Tattoos were visible on both upper arms and his chest. He wore a wedding ring and shook my hand at the outset of the interview. There was no tobacco, alcohol, or body odor present.

The defendant's speech was conversational, appropriate, and coherent. There was no pressure of speech, flight of ideas, loose associations, or excessive irrelevancies. There were no signs or symptoms of psychosis such as hallucinations, delusions, thought disorder, or bizarre behavior. His mood was even throughout the interview without significant sadness, tearfulness, agitation, restlessness, irritability, mood lability, euphoria, or overt anger. He had a full emotional expression and occasionally smiled or laughed. He denied suicide ideation, intentions, plans, or impulses. He presented in a matter-of-fact and resigned manner about the prosecution, and likely future incarceration.

No formal written cognitive testing was conducted, but he was alert and oriented in all respects. There were no deficits in attention or concentration, but his memory for dates of previous events in his life was very poor, and he guessed at these. He did not even know his mother's age. He appeared to function at an estimated average level of intellectual capacity and verbal skill and was not psychologically minded or insightful. He maintained direct eye contact with me in the interview. There were no abnormal, involuntary movements, mannerisms, gestures, or tics.

DIAGNOSIS

According to the *Diagnostic and Statistical Manual* (DSM-IV), published by the American Psychiatric Association, the defendant can be diagnosed at the time of the alleged offense as follows:

Axis I 1. Alcohol intoxication.
2. Alcohol dependence disorder.
3. Depressive disorder not otherwise specified.
4. Marijuana abuse or dependence disorder.
5. Hallucinogen abuse disorder in sustained full remission.
6. Cocaine abuse or dependence disorder in sustained full remission.

Axis II Personality assessment and diagnosis deferred; low self-esteem, and dependent personality traits.

Axis III Current medical problems include polycythemia vera; hepatitis C untreated; gout; tobacco dependence; history of endocarditis and aortic valve replacement.

Axis IV Stressors include work; financial; family; relocations.

CONCLUSIONS

This 41-year-old married white male was charged with the criminal homicide of a stranger whom he had just met at a bar early Monday evening, June 11, 2012, in South Street. He had not visited that bar before, did not know the victim or other people at the bar, and had arrived at the bar shortly before the alleged offense. He had been consuming alcohol throughout the day, beginning at home in the morning, at several other bars in the afternoon, and had not consumed food. His extrapolated blood alcohol level at the time of the alleged offense was two to three times the legal limit for driving. Other relevant behavioral indications of his intoxication include the observations of others that he was obviously intoxicated with alcohol at the time. He was seen to be stumbling when he exited the bar and reentered it immediately prior to the shooting. It is notable that the defendant shot the victim in the back, while the victim sat at the bar, rather than in the head or in the chest. They had had minimal interaction verbally, momentarily before the shooting. More than a dozen other people were present at the bar at the time. The defendant used an assault rifle rather than his handgun, which he also had in his pickup truck. He apologized sarcastically to the victim minutes before shooting him. The defendant had no loud confrontation with the victim and was otherwise restrained in his demeanor.

The available behavioral and biochemical data indicate that, at the time of the alleged offense, the defendant was intoxicated with alcohol. Marijuana was found in his blood, but he did not use marijuana or other substances that day, though he had used marijuana on the previous day. It is unlikely that he was technically intoxicated with marijuana at the time of the alleged offense, or that it had any adverse consequences upon him at that time.

In general, and in the defendant's case, alcohol is disinhibiting, distorts one's perceptions of environmental stimuli (i.e., misinterpretation and oversimplification), and clouds one's thinking (i.e., impaired informational processing; difficulty performing more than one attention task at a time). Intoxicated individuals perceive the world and the persons they are interacting with in an oversimplified manner. There may be overt use of over-learned, stereotypical beliefs about persons, situations, and occurrences. The intoxicated individual's behavior is primarily determined by the here and now (i.e., situational factors) rather than other considerations such as moral or legal rules, or future consequential issues. Alcohol intoxication limits an individual's ability to use subtle or peripheral cues and to interpret complex situations. Therefore, a victim can readily provoke an intoxicated person by innocuous words; similarly, when a victim provokes an intoxicated person, the drinker is at an especially increased risk for violence. The defendant's alcohol intoxication obviously triggered the alleged offense. The defendant's wife informed me, for instance, that he was known to misinterpret what other people said to him when he was intoxicated with alcohol.

Based upon the reported facts of this case, and the absence of previous violence to strangers, it is unlikely that the alleged offense would have occurred if he had been sober at the time. We have no information that the defendant had made advance plans to kill the victim before arriving at the bar that evening, and the offense was not instrumental (i.e., achieving another, tangible, purpose). The defendant reported that he regularly kept firearms in his vehicle, and there is no reason to believe that he specifically placed the weapons in the vehicle to drive to the bar to kill the victim.

Complicating the present assessment is the defendant's reported loss of memory for the alleged offense or even being in the bar, except after he was restrained by the eyewitnesses. It is significant that the defendant shot the victim in the back rather than in the head in that the defendant was known to be a skilled and experienced marksman with weapons. A second shot was heard, but it is unclear if the defendant fired that deliberately or it occurred accidentally in the context of his being restrained. The defendant did not originally enter the bar with a firearm or plans to kill this victim, though he had earlier expressed his intention to kill his stepdaughter because she had stolen money from him and his wife, which she reported had been repaid before the alleged homicide. We have no information indicating that the defendant thought that his stepdaughter was to be found at that bar then.

It is well known that intense alcohol intoxication disrupts cognitive functions such as attention, concentration, memory, judgment, and executive function (i.e. problem solving, seeking alternatives, planning future action, organizing one's behavior). Severe alcohol intoxication disrupts an individual's ability to premeditate and deliberate even in the absence of other or severe psychiatric disorders such as psychosis or mania.

Though alcohol intoxication impaired the defendant's ability to premeditate and deliberate the alleged offense, there is no basis to conclude that the defendant, at the time of the alleged offense, completely lacked the requisite cognitive abilities to premeditate and deliberate the alleged offense. He was obviously not comatose at the time. He had some cognitive function and knew the purpose of a firearm, the location of his firearms in his parked vehicle, how to use his firearm, and that he was firing a weapon, even though his cognitive processes to premeditate and deliberate were partly disrupted by his alcohol intoxication.

The defendant's dense amnesia regarding the alleged offense complicates the assessment of his mental state at that time. He has had previous, perhaps frequent, alcohol blackouts. Beyond that history of memory impairment for periods of intoxication, it is common for homicide defendants to assert that they have partial or dense amnesia for the alleged offense, though there is always the possibility of falsification of such memory through malingering of cognitive impairment. Amnesia for homicidal behavior is not unusual, particularly in emotionally charged situations such as a violent confrontation between a defendant and victim like this one.

Just after the defendant was detained by the police, he expressed a wish that they should kill him, upon his realization that he had killed the victim. This verbalization reflects cognitive function, including a realization of the impact of his behavior at the time that he spoke to the police.

Other than the alcohol intoxication, I do not identify symptoms of a major mental disorder at the time of the alleged offense such as schizophrenia, bipolar disorder, major depression, panic disorder, or dementia. He had developed mild depressive symptoms in April 2011 after his job loss, and was supposed to be taking antidepressant medication at the time of the homicide, but was apparently not doing so. Nevertheless, the available data do not justify an opinion that his mild depressive symptoms, to the extent that they may have been present, were of such severity that they significantly impaired or obviated his ability to premeditate or deliberate the alleged offense. He was not experiencing manic or psychotic symptoms at the time of the alleged offense.

LIMITATIONS

All forensic mental health evaluations and opinions are derived from the available data. The quality, accuracy, and quantity of the data in part determine the validity of the resulting forensic opinion. The present evaluation was based upon document review, one psychiatric interview with the defendant, and three collateral telephone interviews with family. The defendant had minimal recall of the crime scene. Military and occupational records are not available. No psychological or medical testing was requested or obtained, given its likely lack of usefulness in this evaluation. All opinions are subject to change upon receipt of additional information.

All opinions are offered to a reasonable degree of psychiatric certainty. Thank you for the opportunity to consult with you in this matter. Please do not hesitate to contact me with any questions about this report.

Sincerely,

Robert M. Wettstein, M.D.
Board Certified in Psychiatry
and Forensic Psychiatry

TEACHING POINT:
SOURCES OF PARTICULARLY RELEVANT INFORMATION FROM THE LITERATURE

The dramatic growth in the literature in forensic psychiatry and forensic psychology over the last decade means that it has become more difficult to isolate important contributions to the literature. It is a much more crowded field!

But there are certain books, journals, and standards or guidelines that continue to be very important. Forensic clinicians will continue to find that journals such as *Law and Human Behavior, Behavioral Sciences and the Law, Criminal Justice and Behavior,* the *International Journal of Forensic Mental Health,* and the *Journal of the American Academy of Psychiatry and the Law* provide valuable scientific and practice-relevant information. Major integrative works on forensic assessment (e.g., Goldstein, 2007; Melton et al., 2007) are very important. The book series describing best practices in forensic assessment published by Oxford can offer guidance according to particular topics within FMHA. The various ethics codes, both general and specific, that have been discussed throughout this book should be well known to the psychiatrist or psychologist doing this work.

But perhaps the most valuable suggestion for relevant sources of information is to stay involved with national and regional professional groups in these areas. Organizations such as the American Psychology-Law Society and the American Academy of Psychiatry and the Law in the United States provide regular conferences, updated interpretation of existing standards, new data bearing upon this work, and the opportunity to use experienced colleagues as a sounding board and source of additional information. Organizations such as the European Association of Psychology and Law; the Australia/New Zealand Association of Psychiatry, Psychology, and Law; and the International Association of Forensic Mental Health Services do likewise. Valuable continuing professional education is offered in a workshop series a number of times each year by the American Academy of Forensic Psychology. Those who would become and remain skilled forensic practitioners would do well to remain active participants in such groups.

CASE TWO
PRINCIPLE: ATTRIBUTE INFORMATION TO SOURCES
(PRINCIPLE 32)

As this principle is discussed in detail in Chapter 3 (this volume) we will proceed directly to the case report. This case, focusing on the defendant's mental state at the time of the offense, includes a wide range of sources of information. The defendant himself was interviewed and tested using the PAI. Collateral interviews were conducted with his mother and work supervisor. The evaluators also reviewed medical records, mental health records (including previous mental health evaluations), educational records, and legally relevant records. In addition, they reviewed letters written by the defendant to his mother and sister.

The range of these sources is impressive, but not atypical, for this kind of evaluation. With the exception of the letters written by the defendant, many of the sources of information included in this evaluation should also been seen in evaluations conducted by others. The diversity of sources is a strength—but it also presents a challenge. It is important to identify the particular source(s) of any given fact, so the evaluator must carefully attribute content to source. This can be seen throughout the report that follows.

Mr. Wood
Public Defender
City of Fairfax
123 4th Street
Fairfax, VA 45678

RE: *COMMONWEALTH V. JONATHAN APPLE*

Dear Mr. Wood:

Pursuant to your request, and to the court order dated December 21, 2010, we have completed an evaluation of Jonathan Apple's mental state at the time of his alleged offense, pursuant to Virginia Code Section 19.2-169.5. As you know, Mr. Apple is a 22-year-old man who stands charged with *Second Degree Murder,* in violation of Virginia Code Section 18.2-32, and *Use of a Firearm in Commission of a Felony,* in violation of Virginia Code Section 18.2-53.1.

We met with Mr. Apple on March 2, 2011, for approximately seven hours in the forensic clinic of the Institute of Law, Psychiatry, and Public Policy (ILPPP) at the University of Virginia. At the beginning of the evaluation, we informed Mr. Apple about the nature, scope, and purpose of the evaluation, including the relevant limits of confidentiality and privilege. We explained that a copy of the ensuing report will be sent to defense counsel, and that defense counsel may, in turn, submit copies to the Commonwealth Attorney and the judge in the event that counsel raises an insanity defense. Mr. Apple conveyed a reasonable understanding of these arrangements, and he agreed to participate in the evaluation. At various points during the interview, we reviewed the scope of the evaluation and limits to confidentiality, and Mr. Apple appeared to maintain a reasonable appreciation of each.

SOURCES
OF INFORMATION

During the evaluation, Mr. Apple participated in a clinical interview and completed the Personality Assessment Inventory (PAI), a self-report measure of personality and psychopathology.

In addition, we relied on the following sources of information:

1. Collateral telephone interview with Mr. Apple's mother, Ms. Jane Mother, on March 3, 2011, approximately one hour in length.
2. Collateral telephone interview with Mr. Apple's work supervisor, Mr. R, and Human Resources representative, Ms. L, on March 4, 2011, approximately two hours in length.
3. Discharge Summary from Heartland Psychiatric Center, signed by Charles D, M.D., dated September 26, 1996.
4. Admission Notes from the Residential Treatment Center, signed by Robert L, M.D., dated October 20, 1996.

5. History and Physical Examination from the Residential Treatment Center, signed by Chris G, M.D., dated October 20, 1996.
6. Copy of Report Card from the Residential Treatment Center, signed by Mr. W, M.A., Education Coordinator, and Ms. R, teacher, dated School Year 1996–1997.
7. Education Discharge Summary from the Residential Treatment Center, signed by Joseph D, Casework Assistant, and Vince P, L.C.S.W., dated November 26, 1996.
8. Summary of Therapeutic Therapist Contacts sessions, conducted by David D, M.S.W., dated April 7, 1989, to May 19, 1997.
9. Autistic Diagnostic Observation Schedule, conducted by Bruce S, dated May 19, 1997.
10. Neuropsychological Report from Fairfax City Public Schools, prepared by Nancy C, Ph.D., dated July 15, 1997, and July 27, 1997.
11. Copy of Behavioral Intervention Plan, Fairfax City Public Schools, authored by Mr. B, dated January 23, 2000.
12. Copy of Individualized Education Program (IEP) meeting results from Fairfax City Public Schools, signed by Dr. R, Principal, and Ms. Mother, mother, dated March 22, 2001.
13. Copy of State of Georgia Department of Mental Health and Developmental Disabilities Discharge Summary, dated June 10, 2003.
14. Copy of Evaluation Notes, conducted by John P, M.D., of Urgent Psychiatric Care, P.L.L.C., dated March 25, 2008, to August 19, 2008, and February 25, 2010.
15. Copy of letters written by Jonathan Apple to Jackie P, sister, and Jane Mother, mother, undated (found at scene of apparent suicide attempt).
16. Copy of screen shots from Jonathan Apple's Facebook page, 27 pages in length, dated from June 9, 2009, to June 1, 2010.
17. Warrants for Jonathan Apple's arrest, signed by T.E.B., arresting officer, dated July 5, 2010.
18. Copy of Commonwealth of Virginia Department of Health, Office of the Chief Medical Examiner Report of Investigation, dated July 22, 2010.

In addition to the sources listed above, we have requested from the Commonwealth's Attorney additional records further detailing the police investigation and account of the offense. At the time of this writing, we have not yet received such records.

RELEVANT BACKGROUND INFORMATION

Family, Developmental, and Social History

Mr. Apple was born on July 12, 1988, to Ms. Jane Mother and Mr. Michael Apple in San Francisco, California. According to Ms. Mother, both of his parents spent most of their careers in government service. Thus, Mr. Apple's family moved to Washington, D.C., shortly after he was born. His parents subsequently divorced when Mr. Apple was a young child. His father relocated to Georgia, while his mother maintained custody of Mr. Apple and resided in Fairfax, Virginia, Ms. Mother stated. Mr. Apple reported living with his mother during the school year but that he eventually spent some summers living with his father and stepfamily. Ms. Mother later remarried, and the couple produced a daughter seven years younger than Mr. Apple. Records noted that Ms. Mother and her second husband were separated by the time Mr. Apple was eight years old, though Ms. Mother was unable to recall the exact dates of their marriage, separation, or divorce.

Regarding developmental history, medical records indicate that Mr. Apple was born full-term as the result of a normal pregnancy. He met all developmental milestones within a reasonable timeframe. Ms. Mother reported that when Mr. Apple was around age three, she "realized something wasn't quite right." Records and Ms. Mother characterized Mr. Apple as impulsive and hyperactive from an early age. Both reported that he first received outpatient psychiatric services around age four. Around then, Mr. Apple ate cat food and reported "hearing cartoon and angel voices" that interfered with his thoughts, according to collateral records and to recent reports from his mother. Mr. Apple was psychiatrically hospitalized for the first time at age four and then hospitalized twice around age eight. (See *Mental Health History* in this report for further details).

Records indicate that when Mr. Apple was around age eight, his father, Mr. Michael Apple, moved back into the home to help take care of him. Michael Apple lived nearby, and assisted the family

in Virginia for approximately three years before returning to Georgia.

Regarding childhood trauma, there have been no accounts of Mr. Apple experiencing physical abuse, or witnessing violence in the home. However, there have been accounts of sexual abuse. Collateral records and Ms. Mother indicated that Mr. Apple reported at age 11 that he had experienced sexual abuse from ages 6 to 10 by a slightly older male peer when the two were left in the same after-school babysitting arrangement. Ms. Mother reported that Mr. Apple tended to be dismissive of the abuse, and he was reluctant to discuss it. Thus, the alleged abuse never came to the attention of authorities.

Socially, Mr. Apple has had chronic difficulties, all collateral sources indicated. Ms. Mother noted that Mr. Apple always struggled to develop friendships. Likewise, records report that as a child, Mr. Apple was more interested in parallel play than group play, and he was often absorbed in fantasy play to the exclusion of other children. During interview, Mr. Apple acknowledged his struggle to develop social relationships as a child, but he emphasized a strong desire to do so. Middle school records characterized Mr. Apple as socially immature. Formal evaluations from school explained that his daily living skills (e.g., dressing and feeding himself) were age-appropriate, but teacher notes from middle school also indicated that he appeared unconcerned about personal hygiene, and awkward around most of his peers. However, during interview, Mr. Apple reported that middle school was also the period when he developed what he considered his two most significant friendships: Mr. Tom (who eventually became the victim in the alleged offense) and Ms. Kelly, a girl of similar age.

Mr. Apple fondly recalled meeting both Mr. Tom and Ms. Kelly at middle school. With Mr. Tom, Mr. Apple reportedly developed a close friendship, spending time together playing video games and visiting each other's homes. Ms. Mother recalled that Mr. Tom eventually referred to her as "Mom" and to Mr. Apple as "bro," indicating a close relationship. Ms. Mother described the childhood relationship between the two boys as generally positive, although she also recalled arguments and occasional physical fights, usually related to Ms. Kelly.

Regarding Ms. Kelly, Mr. Apple reported developing a sexual relationship beginning at age 12.

Mr. Apple and Ms. Kelly engaged in sexual behavior daily, according to his report, and often skipped class to walk into the woods near school together. Mr. Apple described their relationship as "madly obsessed with each other…[they] did what we wanted to and didn't care about the consequences." Neither collateral records nor Ms. Mother provided information on the exact nature or extent of this relationship. But Ms. Mother did report that she grew increasingly concerned about the relationship, and noted that it was a source of constant conflict between her and Mr. Apple.

Thus, at age 14, Mr. Apple's parents arranged for him to move away from Virginia, to live with his father and stepfamily in Georgia. According to Ms. Mother, they arranged the move due to unexpected financial problems, conflict between Mr. Apple and Ms. Mother, and a goal of separating Mr. Apple from Ms. Kelly. Mr. Apple remained in Georgia for the remainder of his adolescence. At age 14, he was sentenced for the attempted sexual assault of his stepsister (see *Criminal History* in this report for details) and remained in the Georgia juvenile justice system until age 19, returning to his mother in Virginia thereafter.

Mr. Apple stated that he had no contact with either Mr. Tom or Ms. Kelly between ages 14 and 19 (while he was in the Georgia juvenile justice facility). But almost immediately after his return to Virginia, he searched for them via the Internet and reestablished relationships with both Mr. Tom and Ms. Kelly.

Regarding Mr. Apple's adult relationship with Ms. Kelly, the two spent time together, including some sexual and romantic contact, according to Mr. Apple. But ultimately, their relationship never developed in the manner Mr. Apple had hoped it would. During interview, Mr. Apple conveyed significant disappointment that they did not resume a romantic relationship. He described considerable frustration with Ms. Kelly because, in his view, she seemed to maintain romantic relationships with other men, whom he considered harmful to her.

Regarding his renewed relationship with Mr. Tom, the pair continued to vacillate between friendship and conflict. Ms. Mother described the relationship between Mr. Apple and Mr. Tom as tumultuous, ranging from close and affectionate friendship to outright conflict. She explained that the men were particularly good at de-escalating each other if one was agitated and one was calm;

however, if both young men were agitated, she reported they had difficulty "backing down," so the conflict would often escalate to the point of a physical fight or physical separation.

Education and Employment History

Mr. Apple's educational history was complicated by a variety of emotional and behavioral problems. Collateral records stated that Mr. Apple was expelled from at least three daycares due to "primitive and dangerous behavior." At age seven (1996), Mr. Apple attended what he called "*special*, special education" classes due to his disruptive behaviors. Consistent with his account, records described unusually intensive intervention and monitoring for Mr. Apple. For example, they indicated that Mr. Apple rode a school bus as the only student on the bus and, even then, was strapped into his seat with a harness and accompanied by an aide. School records from 2000 described Mr. Apple as academically weak and socially immature. The records also stated that he was frequently distracted and inattentive.

School records from seventh grade stated that Mr. Apple often attempted to avoid reading and written work through distraction—which teachers described as "loud vocalizations with unusual noises"—fidgeting, or singing. However, teacher observations also emphasized that Mr. Apple demonstrated the ability to pay attention when he was interested in a topic.

Mr. Apple's high school education occurred exclusively in juvenile justice facilities, when he was incarcerated in Georgia. Unfortunately, few collateral records were available to describe his academic or social functioning during these years. The available records indicate adequate grades (i.e., Bs and Cs) and successful completion of the curriculum, but these records did not provide accounts of his behavior or any psychiatric symptoms. Mr. Apple reported graduating from high school while incarcerated in Riverview Youth Development Center in LaFayette, Georgia.

Criminal History

Mr. Apple's first contact with the justice system involved an arrest in Georgia in 2003, at age 14, approximately four months after he began living with his father. According to the Georgia Department of Mental Health records, Mr. Apple was charged with the sexual assault of his stepsister.

During our interview, Mr. Apple reported that he received an indeterminate sentence and remained incarcerated from ages 14 to 19. According to his report, he was bullied during the first two years of his incarceration before he grew physically larger. He acknowledged physical altercations "once in a blue moon," which he defined as every couple of months. During the last 10 months of his sentence, he reported transitioning to a group home facility and obtaining employment at a local restaurant.[1]

According to all available records, and his self-report, Mr. Apple has no other known criminal history between the time of his Georgia offense and his current arrest.

Medical History

Collateral records suggested that Mr. Apple was generally in good health throughout his childhood. Likewise, Mr. Apple and Ms. Mother both reported he has no history of serious accidents, illnesses, or hospitalizations.

Mental Health History

Ms. Mother and collateral records indicated that Mr. Apple began psychiatric treatment at age four. Around this time, Ms. Mother first realized that "something wasn't quite right," she reported during interview. Based on her son's hyperactivity and frequent mood changes, she sought psychiatric services. Records described Mr. Apple's behavior as "unpredictable and aggressive." Ms. Mother reported that Mr. Apple was initially diagnosed with attention-deficit/hyperactivity disorder (ADHD), mixed type. But over the course of his childhood, he received multiple diagnoses including: pervasive developmental disorder, schizotypal personality disorder, and bipolar disorder.

Records indicated that Mr. Apple's first hospitalization was in January 1993 at age four (though the exact length of hospitalization was not documented). Ms. Mother stated that he was first hospitalized after making bizarre statements and acting "strangely." Ms. Mother recalled that, shortly before his first hospitalization, he reported hearing both

"cartoon voices" and "angel voices" that intruded on his thoughts and kept him from sleeping. However, during interviews, both she and Mr. Apple emphasized that the voices did not command Mr. Apple and he did not consider them distressing (only distracting). Additionally, Ms. Mother also recalled that Mr. Apple made bizarre statements, such as spontaneously telling parents who arrived at his daycare that the babysitter was poisoning the cat. Ms. Mother explained that, throughout these incidents, she and clinicians struggled to determine whether Mr. Apple's behaviors were more attributable to a rich fantasy life or to psychiatric illness. Eventually, Mr. Apple attended a partial hospitalization program beginning in November 1993 (age five), according to collateral records.

From ages four to seven Mr. Apple also received psychiatric treatment, including psychiatric medication, from an outpatient psychiatrist, Dr. D. In a memo to Mr. Apple's school, dated August 9, 1996, Dr. D listed Mr. Apple's diagnoses (at age seven) as bipolar disorder, mixed type with psychotic features, and attention-deficit hyperactivity disorder, severe.

At age eight (September 1996), Mr. Apple was hospitalized for a second time after allegedly attempting to choke his babysitter's four-year-old son and her cat. A Heartland Psychiatric Discharge Summary linked Mr. Apple's behavior to multiple changes in his routine, including a new school and a new babysitter. The discharge summary also noted that Mr. Apple made suicidal statements and placed a string around his neck in an apparent suicidal gesture. He was hospitalized for approximately two weeks. His diagnoses at discharge were bipolar disorder not otherwise specified (NOS), ADHD, and pervasive developmental disorder NOS. Records noted that Mr. Apple was treated with a variety of psychiatric medications, including Depakote (a mood stabilizer), Zyprexa (an antipsychotic), Vistaril (a sedative), and Dexedrine (a psychostimulant for ADHD).

The following month, October 1996, Mr. Apple was admitted to the Residential Treatment Center following the recommendation for long-term residential care from staff during his Heartland Psychiatric Center hospitalization. Records indicated that Mr. Apple resided at the Residential Treatment Center until February 1997 (approximately three and a half months). Records reported that Mr. Apple tended to become obsessed with fantasy play, pretending to be a dinosaur or a Komodo

---

[1] Despite several requests to the Georgia facilities in which Mr. Apple was incarcerated, we have not yet received the records that would provide a more detailed account of his stay. Thus, at the time of this writing, there are no formal collateral records to shed light on some aspects of Mr. Apple's juvenile incarceration.

dragon. The resulting psychological evaluation by Dr. S (September 1996) linked these behaviors to an inability to "deal with strong emotions such as anger or jealousy." Although a discharge summary was not available, an admission summary identified Mr. Apple's diagnoses as "Pervasive Developmental Disorder NOS, Rule Out[2] Asperger's Disorder, ADHD, and Rule Out Bipolar Disorder with Psychotic Features." Further evaluation by Dr. S (May 1997) specifically addressing Asperger's disorder, noted that while Mr. Apple displayed many of the behaviors consistent with Asperger's (i.e., he avoided eye contact, had specialized interests, and little apparent emotional connection to others), he also demonstrated the ability to engage in these same behaviors (e.g., appropriate eye contact and social connection with others) when a topic was of interest to him. Dr. S concluded "these behaviors are more the result of lack of interest or oppositional behavior, than lack of neurodevelopmental skill."

No additional psychiatric records were available from 1996–2003 until Mr. Apple's admission to the State of Georgia Department of Mental Health inpatient facility (March to June 2003), following his arrest. A discharge summary noted that Mr. Apple's previous diagnoses included bipolar disorder and ADHD, with current psychiatric medications Adderall (for ADHD) and Abilify (a mood stabilizer/antipsychotic). Records noted that his father stopped Mr. Apple's psychiatric medications when he moved to Georgia a few months prior to the arrest. Intake records described Mr. Apple as demonstrating "disorganized thoughts and bizarre behavior patterns, including odd facial grimaces." Staff members noted these symptoms were consistent with psychosis and subsequently prescribed Seroquel (an antipsychotic medication). According to the Georgia discharge summary, Mr. Apple "lost contact with reality and lived in a fantasy world at times." The report explained that Mr. Apple struggled with adapting to the changes and demands of adolescence partially related to his consistent immaturity and poor social skills. A psychosexual evaluation (May 2003) by Dr. B described Mr. Apple as "sexually driven and sexually preoccupied," noting

early and frequent sexual activity on an almost daily basis from ages 12 to 14.

Mr. Apple's most recent contact with the mental health system—his only contact as an adult—occurred in February 2010, when he sought counseling from his Employee Assistance Program, and was referred to a psychiatrist. According to records of their first meeting, the psychiatrist, Dr. P, listed Mr. Apple's symptoms as "no motivation or pleasure, depression (recent, severe), able to work at moderate capacity." Dr. P diagnosed Mr. Apple with bipolar disorder, but reported he observed no evidence of psychotic features. Dr. P prescribed an antidepressant medication (Wellbutrin) and an antipsychotic/mood stabilizing medication (Risperdal). After Dr. P met with Mr. Apple the following month (March 2010), a brief note stated, "[Mr. Apple] reports complete reduction of depression and residual mania." As a result, Dr. P continued his psychiatric medication of Wellbutrin at the same dosage and Risperdal at a slightly increased dose (1 mg increased to 2 mg). However, during the current interview, Mr. Apple reported that he stopped taking this medication in the weeks preceding his offense.

Substance Abuse History

Mr. Apple denied any history of illicit drug use but acknowledged that his social circle was actively involved in drug abuse. He denied a history of alcohol abuse or dependence stating that he consumed alcohol on special occasions only, beginning at age 19. He recalled being intoxicated approximately seven times in his life and reported no history of memory loss or blackouts. Nothing in the collateral records or collateral interviews suggested substance abuse beyond what Mr. Apple reported. Likewise, we could find no evidence to suggest Mr. Apple was abusing substances around the time of the alleged offense.

CURRENT CLINICAL STATUS
Interview

Mr. Apple arrived for the interview escorted by two sheriff's deputies, dressed in standard prison attire, and shackled at the hands and feet. He was appropriately groomed with closely cropped hair and glasses. He initially sat quietly, but responded appropriately during the disclosure process. He demonstrated a thorough understanding of the purpose of the interview.

Mr. Apple was oriented to person, place, and time. His speech was normal in rate and tone,

[2] "Rule Out" is a designation clinicians use when they are considering a diagnosis but there is insufficient evidence to either formally assign the diagnosis or to dismiss the diagnosis completely.

though his volume was somewhat soft. His statements were coherent, and did not suggest grossly disorganized thinking or a formal thought disorder characteristic of psychiatric illness. However, his eye contact was variable, sometimes staring at his hands and sometimes making unusually intense eye contact. His emotional expression generally remained neutral throughout the interview. His mood appeared to brighten briefly only when discussing the pizza he would receive for lunch.

He denied auditory or visual hallucinations (i.e., false sensory experiences that involve hearing or seeing things that other people do not). Likewise, he did not appear to be responding to hallucinations or other internal experiences. However, he reported an extensive fantasy life that involved themes related to science fiction and superhero-like powers. For example, he reported fantasies that he was telekinetic (i.e., he could move objects with his mind) and reported that he even practiced focusing on objects and attempting to move them. He reported spending several hours per day thinking about these various fantasies. However, he was quick to realize that his fantasies were incongruent with reality. He described a strong *wish* for these superpowers to be real, along with a clear recognition that they were not.

Regarding mood, Mr. Apple endorsed current symptoms of depression including excess sleep, feelings of sadness and emptiness, lack of enjoyment in daily activities, and thoughts of suicide. He explained that he receives Risperdal but the medication does not reduce his depressive symptoms, so he recently requested additional antidepressant medication. He stated that sleep is the only relief he receives from depression, so he attempts to sleep as many hours as possible. When queried about the severity of his depressive symptoms, he stated that his depressed mood is not currently as "deep and drastic" as it had been in the past, but it is more pervasive, or consistent.

Mr. Apple also endorsed a history of elevated, highly energized mood, perhaps consistent with mania. When asked to describe his symptoms, he reported sometimes feeling on top of the world, "running around, and exercising." When asked what other people noticed about his manic behavior, he stated others observed him pacing the room, "making airplane noises," and talking to himself. He did not endorse symptoms typically associated with mania such as initiating ambitious projects or a reduced need for sleep. There was no indication that symptoms he identified as manic created social, occupational, or interpersonal problems. He denied any current manic symptoms. Regarding anxiety and worry, he relayed several worries that are common and reasonable among defendants facing serious charges. He reportedly spends some time thinking about these worries, but does not consider them excessive.

Interpersonally, Mr. Apple appeared somewhat cautious and detached. Initially, his responses to questions were brief. But with repeated encouragement, his responses became more detailed. He was generally cooperative with the interview and responded to all questions asked. Despite his apparent initial cooperation, when we resumed the interview following a lunch break, Mr. Apple offered that he had not been truthful earlier in the interview, when describing his adolescent years. He then provided an alternate account that was more accurate, though not entirely accurate as compared to collateral records.

Psychological Testing

No psychological test can reliably identify a defendant's mental state at the time of a past offense. Nevertheless, psychological testing is sometimes appropriate in sanity evaluations because a systematic assessment of current symptoms may help shed light on long-term psychological conditions or personality patterns.

Mr. Apple completed the Personality Assessment Inventory (PAI), a 344-item, self-report psychological inventory used in a variety of clinical and forensic contexts. The PAI has well-designed validity scales to gauge response styles that are overly positive (e.g., denying all shortcomings or struggles) or overly negative (e.g., exaggerating or feigning psychological symptoms). In Mr. Apple's case, these validity scales suggest he was not overly defensive about personal shortcomings, nor did he appear to exaggerate or embellish symptoms. Overall, he produced a PAI profile that test guidelines consider valid and interpretable, and that appeared congruent with his clinical presentation during interview.

Mr. Apple's profile included clinically significant elevations on three separate scales measuring paranoia (i.e., unusual suspicion or distrust of others), depression, and borderline features (i.e., symptoms associated with borderline personality disorder). Regarding paranoia, Mr. Apple endorsed hypervigilance (i.e., scanning for threats in his surroundings), persecution (i.e., suspecting others mean him harm), and resentment (i.e., brooding about how others treat him), which is consistent with his clinical presentation. Some of these symptoms are common among prison inmates or men facing criminal charges, but Mr. Apple appears even more sensitive to interpersonal slights and potential rejection, according to his accounts of past relationships. As evident in both his PAI responses and his verbal self-report, this sensitivity has sometimes led him to withdraw from others, and sometimes led him to express anger at others.

Regarding depression, Mr. Apple's responses suggested that he has recurrent thoughts of worthlessness, hopelessness, and personal failure. He endorsed other items consistent with depression, including feelings of sadness, loss of interest in normal activities, and loss of pleasure in activities he previously enjoyed. He also endorsed items suggesting that he continues to have suicidal ideation, although he denied any current plans to commit suicide.

Mr. Apple's responses also suggested a lack of close and supportive interpersonal relationships, and a tendency towards intense and volatile relationships. His responses conveyed that he consistently fears abandonment and rejection by those around him, but that he also struggles with understanding the subtleties of close relationships. His lack of close relationships may serve to foster further feelings of inadequacy and detachment. Indeed, his responses on the PAI appeared quite congruent with his self-reports of feeling rejected when relationships did not develop as he had hoped.

Finally on the PAI, Mr. Apple denied any drug use and reported minimal alcohol use, although he endorsed that alcohol may have created problems in the past.

MENTAL STATE AT THE TIME OF THE ALLEGED OFFENSE

Official Account of Events (Based on Incident Reports from the Fairfax Police Department)

In a brief letter from the Office of the Commonwealth's Attorney, prosecutor John Davidson described the alleged offense as follows:

> The physical evidence shows that Mr. Apple shot his roommate, Mr. Tom, twice, with both shots at close range. The first shot was to the chest. The second shot, from above, struck the back of the head, while the victim lay face-down on the ground. The victim was unarmed.

According to untitled police records, Mr. Apple participated in an interview with Detective E, of the Fairfax Police Department. In this context, Mr. Apple stated to police:

> It was an accident. I didn't set out to do it. [Mr. Tom] was stealing from me, my iPhone. So we were fighting about that. He ended up pulling a gun and we fought over it. It all happened fast, but it was an accident. Shooting him was an accident.

Detective E also interviewed Ms. G, registered nurse, who was on duty in the intensive care unit when Mr. Apple first arrived to the hospital. Ms. G reported that when Mr. Apple was admitted for emergency care, he was alert and talking. According to Detective E's report, Mr. Apple told Ms. G:

> ...he had killed his best friend. He further stated he would rather die than to deal with the consequences. He stated to nurse G, "I'm not an idiot, I know what happens to me next." He told her several times that he had killed his best friend while in Fairfax. He also asked her, "How was I supposed to live with myself after that?"

Defendant's Account of Events

During our recent interview, Mr. Apple explained that, in the month prior to the offense, he experienced increasing depression and isolation. Mr. Apple reported that his friend, Ms. Kelly, moved away in June 2010. He emphasized feeling hurt, rejected, and "totally abandoned" because she "left him alone," rather than leaving her abusive boyfriend and uniting with Mr. Apple, as he had hoped. By his account, Mr. Apple handled this perceived rejection by becoming more isolated from peers at work. He continued to have little, if any, social network outside of work. Mr. Apple explained that he spent most of his free time—up to 8 hours per weekday—on the Internet frequenting Facebook, sites devoted to science fiction and horror fantasy, and sites devoted to pornography. He also described listening to music and watching movies that he characterized as aggressive, nihilistic, and violent. He mentioned that, in retrospect, his heavy consumption of this type of media "probably didn't help my depression any," but he also emphasized that he had little motivation to do anything else, and that he found some solace—or at least distraction—in this heavy media consumption.

Mr. Apple reported that about two weeks prior to the alleged offense, his friend, Mr. Tom, asked to move in with Mr. Apple due to financial difficulties. Mr. Apple agreed and encouraged Mr. Tom to move into his existing apartment with plans to lease a larger two-bedroom apartment. Mr. Apple recalled that he was happy at the prospect of spending more time with his friend ("Things were finally gonna be all right!" he emphasized), and he quickly developed a plan to help Mr. Tom obtain his GED and find employment. Mr. Apple also reported that he began planning a variety of activities and purchases for the two to share. However, Mr. Apple reported that he became quickly disappointed when Mr. Tom moved into the home and—rather than spending time with Mr. Apple—spent most of his time visiting a girlfriend who lived in Washington, D.C. He described over a week of increasing frustration and irritability at home because Mr. Tom was usually absent.

Mr. Apple reported that on the day prior to the alleged offense, Mr. Tom left their home with Mr. Apple's cell phone, so that he could listen to music while traveling to visit his girlfriend. Mr. Apple expressed that he was angry with Mr. Tom for taking his phone without permission. When Mr. Tom returned later that evening, Mr. Apple requested his phone back but otherwise did not speak with or confront Mr. Tom, he reported. According to Mr. Apple, he planned to have a calm conversation with Mr. Tom the following day to help resolve the situation. He reported that, when Mr. Tom woke up around 1:00 p.m. the following day, he told Mr. Tom that he "need[ed] to talk to [him] about something." Mr. Apple reportedly expressed his frustration with Mr. Tom for borrowing the phone without asking. Mr. Apple reported that the conversation escalated into an argument in which each accused the other of annoying roommate behaviors (e.g., poor housekeeping, using computer inappropriately), and then escalated into "all out yelling and screaming." Mr. Apple stated that Mr. Tom ultimately declared he was moving out, and told Mr. Apple "Forget you. Stop clinging on me and get yourself a [expletive] life."

Mr. Apple reported that, upon hearing Mr. Tom reject him and plan to leave, he then "snapped." While Mr. Tom walked to his bedroom and began packing his belongings, Mr. Apple walked to his own closet where he found and removed his handgun, he reported. Mr. Apple stated that he then walked down the hallway to the laundry room, and as Mr. Tom exited the laundry room, he shot Mr. Tom twice (once in the chest, while he was standing, then once in the head, while he lay on the ground). Mr. Apple reported there was no physical contact before the shooting; he speculated that Mr. Tom may have been inclined to strike him before he was shot, but Mr. Apple shot Mr. Tom before he could do so. Mr. Apple openly acknowledged that his account during our interview differed from his earlier report to the police that Mr. Tom had first drawn a handgun. Mr. Apple stated he cannot recall any of his specific thoughts while walking to retrieve the gun or while walking to Mr. Tom and shooting him. He did emphasize feeling "betrayed" by Mr. Tom and indicated that he "wanted to take him out with me." However, he tended to have only brief and vague responses to further questions about his thoughts and emotions around the time of the shooting.

Other Account of the Events

Ms. Mother, Mr. Apple's mother, stated that approximately 18 months prior to the alleged offense, Mr. Apple and Mr. Tom lived together for about one month. She reported that the men had a fight in which Mr. Tom drew a gun to threaten Mr. Apple, so Mr. Apple returned home to live with his mother. As Mr. Apple successfully completed mechanics school and obtained full-time employment, he moved into his own apartment closer to his work in Fairfax. Not surprisingly, contact between Mr. Apple and his mother became less consistent once he moved into his own apartment. She noted that she had phone conversations with Mr. Apple as rarely as once per month or as often as once per day, depending on whether Mr. Apple was having difficulties or feeling discouraged. Ms. Mother stated that Mr. Apple began working 12 to 14-hour days, six days per week. She suspected—but could not confirm—that he stopped taking his psychiatric medications during this time.

Ms. Mother indicated that at some point (she was unsure of the exact timeframe) Mr. Apple expressed concerns about his performance at work and his level of distress. She remembered that Mr. Apple called her stating, "Nobody wants me around there [the workplace] anymore." After speaking with her about how to seek help, Mr. Apple wrote a letter to his employer requesting help, she reported.

During our collateral interviews with his employer, one supervisor reported that Mr. Apple *did* request counseling, so they referred him to the Employee Assistance Program. Nevertheless, another supervisor noted that Mr. Apple's performance was "steady" with "no more problems than anybody else." Mr. R, his direct supervisor, indicated that Mr. Apple required support and guidance to develop his mechanical skills, but neither his job performance nor his behavior was ever problematic enough to require formal action. In short, supervisors perceived Mr. Apple as somewhat discouraged and interpersonally "oversensitive," but maintained that Mr. Apple was not in danger of losing his job.

According to Ms. Mother, Mr. Apple had reported, a few weeks prior to the offense, that Mr. Tom contacted him about moving back to the Fairfax area and living together. His mother stated that Mr. Apple was "almost giddy" that Mr. Tom was going to return to the area. Ms. Mother expressed concerns about the two living together, given the past volatility in their relationship. She noted that Mr. Apple had, historically, sometimes described Mr. Tom in glowing terms, and other times described him quite critically. Thus, she perceived the relationship as erratic and potentially volatile.

Around this time, Mr. Apple likely had periods of low sleep, his mother recalled, because she received late-night calls from him when he was upset. She was unsure when Mr. Tom moved into the apartment or how long he lived there prior to the shooting. Ms. Mother stated that she had been away in Los Angeles during the week prior to the shooting and returned home on the morning of the shooting. She recalled a couple of conversations with Mr. Apple the week prior to the incident, and recalled that he came across "okay," but also recalled that she worried because he was so optimistic about the living arrangement with Mr. Tom.

On the day of the shooting, she first heard from Mr. Apple in the early afternoon when he called her, requesting she pick him up. She noted that such a request was unusual, and he came across as "really agitated" but he refused to explain exactly why. She reported that she took Mr. Apple to a restaurant, and spent several hours attempting to calm him down. She recognized that Mr. Apple was extremely upset, but he never explained why, and she "didn't want to push him" to discuss more than he was comfortable with. She reported that she eventually drove him to stay in a hotel room by himself, because he had requested to stay at a hotel rather than return to his apartment. She reported that, at the time, she assumed this was due to a conflict with Mr. Tom, but she did not inquire further. Mr. Apple appeared to calm down, she stated, but after she left, Mr. Apple continued to call Ms. Mother periodically until late into the evening, when she fell asleep. She remembered waking up the next morning and attempting to call Mr. Apple without success. She drove to the hotel, where she saw through his room window that he was lying motionless on a bed. At her request, hotel staff contacted police to open the door of the hotel room and found Mr. Apple unconscious from an apparent suicide attempt. Subsequent hospital records, consistent with Mr. Apple's account during our interview, indicated that he had attempted suicide by consuming a full bottle of over-the-counter sleep medication, and cutting his wrists (the lacerations reportedly required stitches, but were not life-threatening).

Diagnostic Impressions

In the Commonwealth of Virginia, a defendant must manifest a "mental disease or defect" as a threshold condition necessary to further consider the possibility of legal insanity. Mr. Apple has a long and well-documented history of mental health diagnoses during childhood (see *Mental Health History*, earlier in this report), although documentation of mental health symptoms since age 14 has been sparse. In February 2010, Dr. P, a psychiatrist, described Mr. Apple's symptoms as "no motivation or pleasure, depression (recent, severe), able to work at minimal capacity, preoccupied, but not at all psychotic...." Dr. P diagnosed Mr. Apple with the *Diagnostic and Statistical Manual-Fourth*

Edition-Text Revision (DSM-IV-TR),[3] code of "296.63," which is Bipolar I, most recent episode mixed, severe, without psychotic features.[4] The diagnostic specification "without psychotic features" indicates that Mr. Apple did not report, nor did Dr. P believe, that he was experiencing psychotic symptoms, such as auditory or visual hallucinations (hearing or seeing things other people do not hear or see) or experiencing delusions (fixed false beliefs not based in reality).

Dr. P prescribed an antidepressant medication and an antipsychotic/mood stabilizing medication. After Dr. P met with Mr. Apple the following month (March 2010), a brief note stated, "[Mr. Apple] reports complete reduction of depression and residual mania." As a result, Dr. P continued his psychiatric medication of Wellbutrin at the same dosage and Risperdal at a slightly increased dose (1 mg increased to 2 mg). Mr. Apple reported that he stopped taking his psychiatric medications prior to the alleged offense but was unclear of the exact timeframe when he stopped. Between March and July 2010, there are no additional collateral mental health records indicating whether Mr. Apple experienced a return of psychiatric symptoms.

Based on Mr. Apple's self-report regarding the time period leading up to the alleged offense, he experienced several symptoms consistent with a major depressive episode, apparently due to the perceived rejection by Ms. Kelly. He also reported feeling isolated at work, not spending time with coworkers beyond his job responsibilities. Around this time, Mr. Apple also reportedly believed that his job was in jeopardy (though his supervisors reported he was not at risk of losing his job). When not at work, Mr. Apple reportedly isolated himself at home with the Internet, movies, and music,

---

[3] Diagnostic criteria are drawn from the *Diagnostic and Statistical Manual-Fourth Edition-Text Revision* (DSM-IV-TR), published by the American Psychiatric Association. The DSM-IV-TR is the primary professional text documenting psychiatric or mental health disorders. It lists and describes psychiatric diagnoses, and details the criteria necessary to warrant each diagnosis, in order to facilitate clear, uniform definitions by professionals in varied research and practice contexts.

[4] Bipolar I Disorder, most recent episode mixed diagnosis requires an individual to experience discrete periods of major depression and mania for at least one week that significantly impair social and/or occupational functioning.

which he stated provided a brief distraction from his depressed feelings. Finally, Mr. Apple apparently discontinued his psychiatric medication around this time, which probably exacerbated the symptoms of depression.

In addition to symptoms of this major depressive episode, Mr. Apple also had many symptoms of borderline personality disorder, which is characterized by an unstable identity, rapidly shifting emotions, and a fear of abandonment, all of which lead to a pattern of volatile relationships. Despite an unusual degree of fantasy and preoccupation with idiosyncratic beliefs, we could find no appreciable evidence of psychosis. His unusual beliefs and fantasies are probably better attributable to long-term aspects of his personality and coping style (perhaps consistent with schizoptypal personality traits or his borderline personality traits).

Conclusions Regarding Mental State at the Time of the Offenses

Overall, there is substantial evidence that Mr. Apple has had long-term psychiatric and emotional problems, dating back to early childhood. There is also considerable evidence that these problems, *in a general sense*, played a significant role in his offense. Specifically, Mr. Apple appears to have been quite depressed, and increasingly distressed about what he perceived to be failure at work and the loss of one of his only two significant relationships (i.e., when Ms. Kelly moved away from the area). Mr. Apple was optimistic about his renewed relationship with Mr. Tom, but Mr. Tom began to leave, thereby ending Mr. Apple's only other significant friendship, and many of his hopes for the future. Mr. Apple— consistent with many symptoms of borderline personality disorder, and more so than would other people in similar situations—reacted to this perceived rejection with severe distress and intense emotions.

However, it is our opinion that *Mr. Apple's psychiatric and emotional problems do not fit the narrow, formal criteria for insanity.* In the Commonwealth of Virginia, an individual must manifest a "mental disease or defect" as a threshold condition necessary to further consider the possibility of legal insanity. Usually, this mental disease or defect is so severe that it involves active *psychosis*, which typically manifests in hallucinations, delusions, or other altered perceptions of reality. We could not find evidence that either of Mr. Apple's psychiatric illnesses (i.e., major depressive disorder or border-line personality disorder) resulted in the grossly disturbed behavior, or altered perceptions of real-ity, typical of psychosis. Indeed, Mr. Apple himself frankly denied experiencing any psychotic symp-toms at the time of the offense.

Other aspects of the legal sanity standard in Virginia address whether the defendant: (a) was able to distinguish right from wrong, (b) under-stood the nature, character, and consequences of his act, and (c) was able to resist the impulse to commit the offense. Of course, these additional aspects of the standard are essentially irrelevant if the defendant does not meet the threshold condi-tion of a serious mental illness, but we address them here for the sake of thoroughness.

Regarding *a*, there is little doubt that Mr. Apple understood shooting Mr. Tom to be legally and morally wrong. Indeed, his statements to police and to the emergency nurse, as well as his own attempted suicide, all suggest he recognized (and lamented) the wrongfulness of his behavior.

Regarding *b*, the same evidence indicates that Mr. Apple understood the nature, character, and consequences of shooting Mr. Tom. Mr. Apple reported that he shot Mr. Tom under the influ-ence of intense emotions, but Mr. Apple made no claims, at any point, that he did not understand the nature or consequences of his behavior. Indeed, he described recognizing and lamenting, imme-diately after the shooting, that he had ended his friend's life.

Regarding *c*, Mr. Apple did report that he shot Mr. Tom impulsively, and under the influence of intense emotions. However, we could find no evi-dence to indicate that Mr. Apple *could not* resist the impulse to act as he did.[5] The actual offense involved a series of steps (i.e., leaving the con-flict, retrieving a gun, returning to Mr. Tom) that Mr. Apple reportedly completed under heightened emotion and with little analysis; but we could find no reason to believe he was *unable* to stop during this series of steps.

Thus, although *the ultimate decision regard-ing legal sanity is for the court*, we could not find

sufficient evidence to opine that Mr. Apple met the criteria for legal insanity under Virginia law.

CONCLUSION

Mr. Apple is facing charges for the shooting of a friend, with whom he had a long and tumultu-ous relationship. Mr. Apple has a lengthy history of psychiatric and emotional problems, involving significant depression as well as significant per-sonality pathology. Both of these left him feeling unusually depressed, panicked, and rejected upon learning that his friend was leaving him. Thus, his offense certainly occurred in the context of intense emotional distress. However, he did not manifest psychosis, a state of severe psychiatric illness most typically associated with cases of legal insanity, nor did his offense behaviors appear to meet—in our opinion—the other narrow criteria necessary for raising an insanity defense in Virginia.

The opinions above reflect the information available to us at the time of this writing (that is, the sources listed earlier in this report), and may be subject to modification if additional information becomes available. Please do not hesitate to con-tact us should you have any questions. We can be reached at 434-924-8308.

Sincerely,
Kathleen Kemp, PhD
Forensic Psychology Postdoctoral Fellow
Institute of Law, Psychiatry, and Public Policy

Daniel Murrie, PhD
Director of Psychology,
Institute of Law, Psychiatry, and Public Policy
Associate Professor of Psychiatry and
Neurobehavioral Sciences
University of Virginia School

TEACHING POINT:
LINE-BY-LINE VERSUS
PARAGRAPH-LEVEL ATTRIBUTION
(contributed by Daniel Murrie)

Sanity evaluations, perhaps even more so than other forensic evaluations, require integrating many data sources, some of which may provide contradictory accounts of historical events. Even when the data are not contradictory, readers may perceive and weigh data differently, depending on

---

[5] Generally, an "irresistible impulse" is extremely unusual, even in cases that involve serious mental illness, and occurs among only a few defendants in manic, or psychotic, conditions.

the source from which it comes. So it is crucial to explicitly and specifically attribute each data point to its source. When providing general information that is congruent across all sources, it may be sufficient to use attributions like, "all school records indicated…" or "all collateral sources reported…." But in the many instances when data are available from only one source, we must identify that source explicitly, even if every sentence of a paragraph is based on a different source.

Line-by-line source attribution is a crucial part of showing our work and laying the foundation for reasonable, defensible forensic opinions. The evaluation process should be transparent, in the sense that readers can see the information we considered and review the ways we combined, weighed, and interpreted this information to reach a final conclusion. Attributing each piece of data to its source ensures that we are not misrepresenting our inferences as historical facts, and it allows the reader to gauge the credibility of every piece of information. Although line-by-line source attribution may feel a bit cumbersome, and lengthen the report, doing so is a crucial first step in walking the reader through our evaluation process. After all, we write forensic reports not expecting the reader to trust our opinions "because we say so," but rather to provide the detailed basis for readers to consider our process and opinions and reach their own conclusions. Line-by-line source attribution is a detailed, transparent procedure that helps the readers do just that.

CASE THREE
PRINCIPLE: DECLINE THE REFERRAL WHEN EVALUATOR IMPARTIALITY IS UNLIKELY (*PRINCIPLE 10*)

This principle addresses the nature and value of evaluator impartiality in FMHA, emphasizing the importance of declining to perform a forensic assessment when impartiality is needed but cannot be achieved. In this context, "impartiality" refers to the evaluator's freedom from significant interference due to bias. Such bias can result from characteristics or beliefs of the evaluator (e.g., categorical opposition to capital punishment) or from situational factors that may influence an evaluator in the direction of a given finding (e.g., a preexisting personal or professional relationship with the litigant).

There are several ways to assess an evaluator's potential impartiality. One test involves the following two-part question, which is structured around the dichotomous outcomes (A and B) of most legal decisions: (1) What would be the effect on me if the outcome of the case were A?; and (2) What would be the effect on me if the outcome of the case were B? Any substantial imbalance in the answers to these two questions suggests that impartiality may be unlikely in the given case (Heilbrun, 2001).

A second test of impartiality uses a fraction termed the "Contrary Quotient" (Colbach, 1981). In the Contrary Quotient, the numerator represents the number of times the evaluator has reached an opinion unfavorable to the referring source, and the denominator is the total number of times an opinion has been requested, yielding a percentage estimate. This ratio is one measure of how well a forensic clinician has managed the pressures that can be exerted by a referring source. However, the ratio can be difficult to interpret without knowing the "true rate" at which an evaluator *should* have reached a contrary finding. In light of this problem, it is preferable whenever possible to integrate both the Contrary Quotient *and* any information regarding available base rates. This two-part test of impartiality can be described as (1) a reasonable balance between favorable and unfavorable results rendered to referring sources, and (2) reasonable consistency with the available base rates.

There are several distinct roles that can be assumed in FMHA, although one role per case is strongly preferred. The value of impartiality varies with each role. In the role of evaluator, impartiality is very important, whether the clinician is court-appointed or performing the evaluation at the request of the defense, prosecution, or plaintiff. Impartiality is also highly valued when the mental health professional assumes the role of a scientist. In this role, the clinician addresses questions that may be answered by the relevant scientific literature, without reference to the characteristics of the specific defendant or litigant. Another possible role that can be played by a mental health professional is that of consultant. As a consultant, the primary purpose of the expert's role is to assist the attorney rather than present information to the court. As such, impartiality is less important and probably not required.[6] A final possible role for a mental health professional is that of fact witness. A fact witness can generally testify regarding direct observations only, and he or she cannot offer an opinion or conclusion in the same manner that an expert witness can. If the clinician finds that impartiality is impossible in a particular case and testimony cannot be avoided, one option in some cases involves testifying as a fact witness, thereby avoiding any problems stemming directly from the clinician's lack of impartiality.

Support for this principle can be found in several sources of authority. Ethical guidelines applicable to forensic clinicians address impartiality in several ways. The APA *Ethics Code* considers the importance of impartiality in several ways: refraining from professional activities when personal problems prevent the practitioner from providing adequate services (Standard 2.06a); highlighting the problems of dual-role and other multiple relationships (Standard 3.05); and avoiding professional activities where the practitioner may experience significant conflicts of interest (Standard 3.06). The APA *Specialty Guidelines* addresses this principle more directly: "When offering expert opinion to be relied upon by a decision maker…forensic practitioners strive for accuracy, impartiality, fairness, and independence. Forensic practitioners recognize the adversarial nature of the legal system and strive to treat all participants and weigh all data, opinions, and rival hypotheses impartially" (Guideline 1.02).

The APA *Specialty Guidelines* also emphasizes the particular difficulties that arise from significant conflicts of interest (Guideline 1.03) and multiple relationships, both generally (Guideline 4.02) and specific to therapeutic-forensic role conflicts (Guideline 4.02.01); expert testimony by therapeutic practitioners (Guideline 4.02.02); and providing forensic therapeutic services (Guideline 4.02.03). Forensic practitioners are advised to avoid these situations whenever possible, and to take reasonable and appropriate steps to manage these conflicts when they arise in FMHA.

Additional support from this principle comes from the field of psychiatry. The *Principles of Medical Ethics with Annotations Especially Applicable for Psychiatry* (American Psychiatric Association, 2013b) addresses this principle only in discussing conflicts of interest (Section 8). The AAPL *Ethics Guidelines* emphasizes:

> Psychiatrists practicing in a forensic role enhance the honesty and objectivity of their work by basing their forensic opinions, forensic reports and forensic testimony on all available data. They communicate the honesty of their work, efforts to attain objectivity, and the soundness of their clinical opinion, by distinguishing, to the extent possible, between verified and unverified information as well as among clinical "facts," "inferences," and "impressions." (p. 3)

Furthermore, the AAPL *Ethics Guidelines* notes that psychiatrists should not distort their testimony based on the retaining party, base their evaluations and testimony on contingency fees, or enter into dual relationships with their clients: "Treating psychiatrists should therefore generally avoid acting as an expert witness for their patients or performing evaluations of their patients for legal purposes" (p. 3).

In addition to finding support in the relevant ethical guidelines, this principle is supported by standards of practice. Dual-role relationships, and the potential loss of impartiality that may result, are not conducive to high-quality forensic assessments. It is difficult or impossible for a forensic clinician to perform an evaluation if the clinician has preexisting inclinations as a result of a dual-role relationship. Therefore, a clinician should avoid performing a forensic assessment in a particular case if the clinician is providing (or has provided) therapeutic services to the individual (see, e.g., APA, 2013b, 4.02.01).

The present case provides an illustration of the kind of case that could make impartiality in conducting one's evaluation and communicating the results a difficult proposition. A woman who is a patient in a secure hospital is alleged to have assaulted a staff member. Many forensic clinicians have spent time working in secure inpatient settings; many more have at least some experience in conducting evaluations in secure mental health

---

[6] Although impartiality may not be required when the clinician assumes the role of consultant, it is still valuable. When assisting an attorney, a consultant is most helpful when he or she maintains a balanced viewpoint. This can help to assist the attorney in anticipating the arguments and challenges that may be raised by opposing counsel.

units. Threats and physical aggression toward mental health professionals in such settings are certainly part of the awareness of anyone who has been professionally involved in working a staff position. Some have strong feelings about this, even if they have not personally been assaulted, and such feelings could interfere with a fair collection and synthesis of relevant information. Even though the present case is not "high visibility" in some respects, it also involves the kind of circumstances that are comparably challenging to efforts to remain impartial in conducting the evaluation.

CRIMINAL RESPONSIBILITY EVALUATION

Identifying Information

This is the second State Hospital (SH) admission for Susan Smith, a 28-year-old Caucasian female (d.o.b. 3/12/82). She was admitted to SH on 5/12/10 from the District Court with an order for evaluation of competency to stand trial and criminal responsibility pursuant to the provisions of M.G.L. c. 123, §15(b). She is charged with assault and battery stemming from events that occurred on May 4, 2010. It is alleged that on that date, while a patient at State Hospital, she assaulted a social worker.

Legal Criteria for Determining Criminal Responsibility

In Commonwealth of Massachusetts Courts, a defendant is found not criminally responsible for conduct if, at the time of such conduct, as a result of mental disease or defect, he lacked substantial capacity either to appreciate the criminality [wrongfulness] of his conduct, or to conform his conduct to the requirements of law (*Commonwealth v. McHoul*, 1967).

Sources of Information

This evaluation is based on:

1. Clinical interviews with Ms. Doe at State Hospital on May 25 and June 5, 2010, lasting a total of three hours;
2. Review of current medical chart at State Hospital;
3. Review of records from previous admission to State Hospital in September, 2009;
4. Review of records of admission to County Acute Hospital on April 20, 2008, July 18, 2008, and July 6, 2009;
5. Telephone interview with Mary Jones, LICSW, the alleged victim, on May 22, 2010;
6. Interview with Harry Stone, M.D., Ms. Doe's treating psychiatrist, on May 25, 2010
7. Review of Ms. Smith's Criminal Record information.
8. Review of the police report dated May 4, 2010.

Warning on Limits of Confidentiality and Privilege

At the beginning of the first interview, I informed Ms. Smith that I am a psychologist and would be evaluating her for the purpose of preparing a report to the court regarding the issue of criminal responsibility as well as her need for treatment, including psychiatric hospitalization. I explained that information she provided and my observations would not be held confidentially but would be included in a written report, which would be sent to the court, which could share it with her lawyer and the prosecuting attorney. I also informed her that I might be called to testify in court. Ms. Smith indicated her understanding of this warning by paraphrasing it ["You're a psychologist and what I tell you is not secret, it is for the judge and the lawyers to see if I was mentally ill and if I need to be in the hospital"]. At the beginning of the second interview I repeated this explanation and Ms. Smith indicated that she still understood the parameters of the evaluation. In my opinion, she understood the purpose of the evaluation, the limits of confidentiality, and my role.

I provided similar information to the collateral informants with whom I spoke.

Relevant History

Historical information was obtained from Ms. Smith and corroborated by review of information available in her psychiatric records. The information Ms. Smith provided to me regarding her history was consistent with these records.

Family and Developmental History

Ms. Smith is the only child born to her parents, who were not married and never lived together. She was raised for the first four years of her life by her mother, but was removed from her mother's custody by the State when she was four years old due to her mother neglecting her care. Her mother was addicted to crack and often forgot to feed Ms. Smith, who was described as "an emaciated, four-year-old girl, wearing filthy clothes" when she was removed from the home. Permanent custody was awarded to Ms. Smith's maternal grandmother, who raised her through adolescence. Her mother lived with her sporadically, and, until she was 16 years old, she thought that her biological mother was really her sister. She has never met her father. There are no reports of any physical or sexual abuse. However, Ms. Smith did report observing her mother's boyfriend frequently hit her mother, including once breaking her nose (when Ms. Smith was 12 years old). Ms. Smith's grandmother (who passed away from cancer five years ago) has reported (contained in the medical records) that Ms. Smith was a difficult child, growing up, often "having tantrums" when she did not get her way.

Educational History

Ms. Smith performed poorly in school, and had to repeat the third grade. She was not placed in special education classes, and continued in school until she was 16 (tenth grade) when she dropped out. She reported that she did not like school, found it boring, and also did not get along well with some of the other students. She was involved in a number of fights with other girls, which resulted in suspensions from school for one to three days at a time, but none of these fights involved weapons or resulted in any criminal involvement. Ms. Smith reported that she did not have any "boyfriends" in school, but did have sexual relationships with several different boys and, at age 16, became pregnant and dropped out of school. She gave birth to a baby girl, whom she gave up for adoption (and has had no contact with since). Ms. Smith reports that she has often regretted this decision, and becomes sad when wondering what happened to her daughter.

Substance Use History

Ms. Smith reported that she drank some beer and wine in high school, but not to excess, and occasionally used marijuana. She denied using any other substances. However, at the age of 19, she began drinking much more heavily, becoming intoxicated several nights a week (approximately a six-pack of beer per night). She was charged with driving under the influence in 2004, and given a suspended sentence after completing an outpatient alcohol treatment program. She has experienced several other periods in which she drank more heavily, and attended detoxification programs twice, once in 2006 and once in 2008 (discussed below in the context of her criminal history).

Employment History

Ms. Smith has a sporadic work history. She has worked for a housekeeping service (cleaning houses), but was fired after frequent fights with some of her co-workers. She explained that she felt her co-workers were slacking off, leaving her to do most of the work, and she didn't like it. She would complain about this, but nothing was done, and eventually she was involved in a fight with one of the other women, bloodying her nose. At that point, she was terminated from the job. This occurred in 2006, and she has not worked steadily since.

Criminal History

A review of Ms. Smith's criminal record (CORI) reveals that in addition to the DUI charge in 2004 (which was dismissed), she has been arrested three other times. In November, 2005, she was charged with malicious destruction of property, for smashing a neighbor's windshield. Ms. Smith reported that she was angry because the neighbor owed her $50 and would not pay up. She was found guilty of this charge, given probation, and fined. On May 12, 2006 she was charged with threat to commit a crime. In this instance, she verbally threatened to kill her grandmother, who was trying to get her to stop drinking. This charge was dismissed after she completed a 30-day detoxification program. On February 12, 2006, she was arraigned for assault and battery (A&B) on a police officer. This charge stemmed from an incident in which she was a passenger in a car that was stopped by the police. When the policeman asked her to get out of the car, she became agitated and punched the officer in the face. At her arraignment she was released on pretrial surety on condition that she complete a 30-day detoxification program. However, she left the program after three weeks, with another client, as the two of them went to a bar to drink. She was returned to court, eventually convicted of the A&B on the police officer, and given a two-year sentence. She was released after a year on parole.

Mental Health History

Ms. Smith's first psychiatric hospitalization occurred on April 20, 2008 (at age 26). Her grandmother, with whom she was living, noticed that Ms. Smith was staying up late at night, playing music loudly, and was becoming more irritable. She would often scream at the neighbors for no apparent reason. At one point, she became extremely agitated, claiming that there was poison gas in the house, and she disrobed and ran naked through the streets. She was taken to City Hospital Emergency Room, where she was admitted to the acute psychiatry unit. Upon admission, she was described as "manic, hypersexual, speaking rapidly" and reportedly would stay up late at night, singing loudly. She was diagnosed with bipolar disorder, most recent episode manic, and treated with Lithium. Over the course of her 10-day hospitalization, her mood improved, although she was still described as "hypomanic" (that is, her mood and energy level were still elevated, but not as severely as in a manic episode).

Ms. Smith returned home to live with her grandmother. Over the next few months, there were several incidents in which the police were called because she was screaming at a neighbor in her building, claiming that this woman was making too much noise and disturbing her, but none of these incidents resulted in any criminal charges. Although her grandmother attempted to get her to take her medication, she refused, and decided to move out of the house, ending up in a homeless shelter. On July 18, 2008, she was again psychiatrically hospitalized at City Hospital. This admission was precipitated by an episode in the shelter in which she accused all the men of wanting to have sex with her, claiming that she was the Virgin Mary and that the shelter would be burned to the ground. She remained in the hospital for a month, was diagnosed with bipolar disorder with psychotic features, and treated with Zyprexa (an antipsychotic medication) and Depakote (for mood stabilization). During this hospitalization, she continued to describe paranoid beliefs about the shelter, but her mood stabilized. She was discharged to live with her grandmother.

Ms. Smith lived with her grandmother for approximately 10 months. She saw her outpatient psychiatrist, Dr. Miller, on a monthly basis, and he documented that her acute paranoid and mood symptoms remained in remission. However, in June, 2009, she moved in with a boyfriend and the two of them drank alcohol regularly (she reported that they drank daily). She stopped seeing her psychiatrist, discontinued her medications, and began acting erratically in the community. She stayed up late at night, playing music loudly. When the neighbors complained about the noise, she accused them of wanting to have sex with her. In July, 2009, in the context of a heated argument with a male neighbor, she grabbed a knife and threatened to stab him. Police were called and she was taken to City Hospital, where she was admitted on an emergency basis. Ms. Smith was again diagnosed with bipolar disorder with psychotic features. She refused to accept any medications, and was committed pursuant to §§7&8 (along with an order for involuntary administration of antipsychotic medications pursuant to §8B) and transferred to State Hospital in September, 2009.

Over the next seven months, her mental status stabilized, and progress notes indicated no evidence of paranoid thinking. However, she would become agitated with minimal provocation (e.g., being told she had to wait to use the shower, or another patient trying to change the TV channel) and require a quiet room or Ativan (an anti-anxiety medication) to calm down. In April, 2010, the hospital was considering discharging Ms. Smith to independent living. However, she was then involved in an altercation with another patient, and the discharge was put on hold. Shortly thereafter, the current alleged offense occurred and Ms. Smith was charged with assault and battery.

Ms. Smith reported no history of head injuries, nor does she suffer from any medical condition that would be expected to affect her mental status.

Mental Status and Current Psychological Functioning

Ms. Smith is a 28-year-old woman who looks approximately her stated age. She was dressed appropriately with good hygiene. At several points, she got up from her seat to pace, but was then able to return to complete the interview. Her speech was slightly accelerated, particularly when a sensitive topic (such as the alleged offense) was raised, but she was able to communicate in a coherent manner. On a brief screening instrument of attention, concentration, and memory (the Mini-Mental Status Examination), she scored 29 out of 30, which does not suggest acute cognitive impairment. She was able to remember three simple words after a 5-minute delay, and her memory for recent and remote events appeared intact. She experienced some difficulty interpreting proverbs: for example, stating that she did not know what was meant by "People who live in glass houses should not throw stones" or "Every cloud has a silver lining." However, she responded to the proverb "Don't cry over spilled milk" by saying, "That means, don't worry your head about little things that go wrong, it's not worth it." For the most part, she was able to attend to the questions asked and concentrate on the issue at hand. However, on occasion, as she became more anxious, she became momentarily distracted and asked for the question to be repeated, at which time she responded appropriately. Based on her history as well as her level of vocabulary, it appears that she is likely of below-average intelligence, but there were no indications to suggest significant intellectual limitations.

Ms. Smith reported no current or previous experiences of hallucinations (hearing or seeing things that are not there). She acknowledged that in the past she has experienced delusions (rigidly held beliefs that are impervious to reason) such as believing that she was the Virgin Mary and that people were plotting against her. She indicated that she does not entertain these thoughts currently. However, she stated that she feels that her treatment team (psychiatrist, social worker, and nurse) is unfairly keeping her in the hospital, blaming her for an incident which she claims was really the fault of another patient (discussed below). She described her mood as "fine" and stated that she does not feel depressed or elated. Her observed mood was one of slight irritability, but, other than her pacing when stressed, she did not display unusual movements or excessive energy. She reported that her appetite and energy level are "okay" and that she typically sleeps about six hours a night, without waking in the middle. She denied any suicidal or assaultive thoughts or intentions.

Ms. Smith is currently prescribed Zyprexa (10 mg a day) and Depakote (750 mg a day), and she reports that she takes the medications daily (this is confirmed by the hospital record). She acknowledges that she has a mental disorder ("I'm bipolar") and that the medications help keep her calm.

Official Version of the Alleged Offense

Sgt. Michael Stoner of the City Police wrote in a report dated May 4, 2010, that police received a complaint from Mary Jones (a social worker at State Hospital) that she had been assaulted on that day by patient Susan Smith and she wanted to press charges. Ms. Jones gave a statement in which she stated that she and Dr. Stone, a psychiatrist, had told Ms. Smith earlier in the day that she would be remaining at the hospital for at least a few more months. Later that day, when Ms. Jones was walking by the dayroom, Ms. Smith jumped her from behind, threw her to the ground, and began punching her in the face. Several other staff responded, pulling Ms. Smith away. Officer Stoner noticed that Ms. Jones had a "black eye and abrasions about her face, with visible stitches on her chin."

Information from State Hospital Records

The progress notes for the period before and after the alleged offense were reviewed. According to these notes, Ms. Smith had been described over the month prior to the alleged offense as psychiatrically stable. For example, her treating psychiatrist, Dr. Stone, noted on April 28, 2010, "Mood stable, no evidence of paranoid symptoms," and a nursing note by Gail Small, R.N., on April 30, 2010, stated, "Ms. Smith is following ward routine and interacting well with nursing staff." The progress notes, though, do describe an incident on April 15, 2010, in which Ms. Smith and another female patient were involved in an altercation. According to these notes, the other patient had been newly admitted and was described as "intrusive, with poor boundaries, having to be told repeatedly not to enter other patients' rooms." On April 15, this patient entered Ms. Smith's room and attempted to remove a book from the room. When Ms. Smith returned to her room, she told the other patient to put it back and leave. When the patient refused, Ms. Smith grabbed the book, slapped the patient about the head and shoulders, and punched her in the stomach. Staff intervened and spoke with both patients. According to a note by Mary Jones, LICSW, "Ms. Smith stated that patient…had made her angry by trying to take her book and so she hit her to 'teach her not to do it again.' Ms. Smith was not remorseful and stated that patient…was to blame for coming into her room and taking her book."

On May 3, 2010, the following was documented by Dr. Stone:

Treatment team meeting today regarding disposition of Ms. Smith. Based on her recent incident with Patient _____, and her history of conflicts with neighbors when she was living in the community, discharge plans are being placed on hold. Treatment will focus on helping Ms. Smith deal with frustrations from other patients, without resorting to violence.

A note entered by Mary Jones, LICSW, on May 4, 2010, notes:

> Dr. Stone and I spoke with Susan Smith about the treatment team's decision to delay her discharge and focus on anger management. She reacted angrily, stating that we were not being fair and that it was really Patient X's fault for coming into her room. She turned to Dr. Stone and told him that it was really up to him and he could discharge her if he really wanted to. I agreed to come back tomorrow to discuss this further with her.

Information from Mary Jones, LICSW

On May 22, 2010, I spoke by phone with Ms. Jones, the alleged victim. She informed me that she had not returned to work since the alleged assault, and is waiting for her face to completely heal. She reported that she has been Ms. Smith's social worker since Ms. Smith was admitted to State Hospital in September. She described Ms. Smith as "manic and paranoid" when first admitted to the hospital, but stated that she had improved considerably over the past six months. She also stated that she and Ms. Smith usually have a good relationship, although Ms. Smith can get "testy" at times when she does not get what she wants (like having to wait to go outside, for example). She confirmed that earlier on the day of the alleged assault, she and Dr. Stone had informed Ms. Smith of the decision to delay her discharge. This meeting took place in Dr. Stone's office on the unit, and Ms. Smith was angry, but appeared to be in control. I asked if Ms. Smith had appeared agitated or made any other statements, to which Ms. Jones responded that she only told Dr. Stone that he could discharge her, but made this statement as a plea, not as a threat.

Information from Harry Stone, M.D.

On May 25, I spoke with Dr. Stone, Ms. Smith's treating psychiatrist. He confirmed that Ms. Smith had shown improvement over the course of her hospitalization but would sometimes become annoyed

and frustrated if she did not get her own way. Staff were typically able to intervene before the situation escalated. He confirmed that the treatment team had decided to delay Ms. Smith's discharge due to the incident with the other patient; he stated that although the other patient had provoked the incident, in light of Ms. Smith's history, he thought that it was important to work with her on developing better management strategies for dealing with such frustrations. He stated that he realized that she was angry with him when she left his office on May 4, and seemed to be agreeable to Ms. Jones' offer to talk with her more about it the next day. He noted no change in her mental status in the days prior to the alleged assault. He also stated that the hospital neither encourages nor dissuades staff from pressing charges in such a situation, and the decision was up to Ms. Jones.

Dr. Stone also reported that after the incident, he ordered Ms. Smith to be restrained, and she went to the restraint room without incident. She remained in restraints for an hour, but was then released since she had calmed down. He asked her at that time why she had assaulted Ms. Jones, and she said, "I was just pissed." She also stated, "I figured I'd have to do some time in restraints, but I'm okay now." Since that time, there have been no other incidents with Ms. Smith, although she is monitored more closely.

Defendant's Version of Alleged Offense

Ms. Smith expressed frustration at being charged with assault and battery, claiming that "she [Ms. Jones] is making a big deal of it, so she can go on IA [Industrial Accident leave] and collect money." She acknowledged that she did hit Ms. Jones, but claimed that her injuries were not that severe. Ms. Smith was asked about the preceding incident with Patient X, at which point she became animated and said, "That bitch came into my room, she was trying to take the book I was reading, I just needed to show her that she can't do that, I didn't really hurt her." She stated that this had happened a couple weeks earlier than the alleged offense and she thought that it was over and done with. She stated that she was looking forward to leaving the hospital and having more freedom, and was surprised and angry when she was told that she could not leave.

Ms. Smith was asked to describe her perspective on the meeting with Dr. Stone and Ms. Jones. She stated that Dr. Stone did most of the talking, telling her that the treatment team decided that she couldn't leave because of what happened. She stated that she was angry, but controlled herself and told him that she knew that since he was the psychiatrist it was up to him, and he could discharge her. However, she said, he told her that he did not think she was ready for living in the community, at which point Ms. Jones offered to follow up with her the next day. She described herself as feeling angry and frustrated at that time. She was asked if she had any thoughts of harming either Dr. Stone or Ms. Jones at that time, and she responded, "Well, I thought of picking up one of the books in his office and throwing it at him, but I figured then he'd just put me in restraints, so I just left." She was also asked if she was particularly angry with Ms. Jones at that point, which she denied.

Ms. Smith reported that she went back to her room and felt frustrated. She wanted to go outside to the yard, but it was not yard time, so she just went into the TV room to watch a show. She did not remember what she was watching. A while later, she noticed Ms. Jones walking by to leave the unit, and "I just became angry, thinking, how come she can leave and I can't?" She stated that she could not really describe her thoughts at that time, but felt frustrated and needed to "take it out on someone." She denied maintaining any paranoid thoughts about Ms. Jones (that is, she did not think that Ms. Jones had deliberately delayed her discharge or that Ms. Jones was the person primarily responsible). She reported that she had planned to just knock Ms. Jones down, but once she fell to the ground, "I became enraged, and kept hitting her." When asked to explain this furthermore, she stated, "When I get that angry, it's hard to stop." She remembers someone pulling her off of Ms. Jones, and stated that she did not resist at that point, and agreed to go to restraints. While in restraints, she realized that she was in trouble, but did not think that Ms. Jones was hurt that badly.

Ms. Smith did not describe any distorted beliefs about Ms. Jones and did not claim that she thought the behavior was justified, stating that she knew she would get in trouble, but did not think they would press criminal charges against her. She stated, "They were going to keep me in the hospital anyway; so what if I had to spend a few hours in restraints?" She was asked if she thought that she would have attacked Ms. Jones if there were other staff around at that time, to which she responded,

"No, because I knew they could stop me, but I saw that she was not looking at me, so I figured I could knock her down before she knew what hit her."

Clinical Opinion Regarding Criminal Responsibility

Ms. Smith has a long, documented history of a mental illness, with a diagnosis of bipolar disorder. During periods of acute exacerbation, she has experiences of elevated mood and distortions of reality, including paranoid thinking. She was committed to State Psychiatric Hospital for treatment at the time of the alleged offense and had been there for approximately six months. The sources of information are consistent in establishing that Ms. Smith's mental status had improved over the course of her hospitalization and that she had not been manifesting acute symptoms of her disorder in the weeks prior to the alleged offense. Indeed, she had shown significant enough improvement to the point that she was being considered for discharge. The discharge was delayed because she assaulted another patient (about two weeks prior to the alleged offense). However, all accounts of that incident, including Ms. Smith's, indicate that the assault did not occur in the context of acute symptoms, but rather in reaction to the other patient intruding into Ms. Smith's room and taking her property.

Regarding the specific alleged offense, neither Ms. Smith nor any of the other sources of information (clinical treatment team members) indicate that she was experiencing acute symptoms at that time. She was not distorting reality, but acted out of anger and frustration. She acknowledges now, and close in time to the alleged offense (when speaking with Dr. Stone while in restraints), that she knew that it was wrong to assault Ms. Jones. For example, she told Dr. Stone, just shortly afterwards, "I was just pissed…I figured I'd have to do some time in restraints, but I'm okay now." She clearly stated to this evaluator that she knew she could get in trouble, she just did not expect someone to press criminal charges. She did not report any distorted beliefs to suggest that she thought the behavior was justified. Thus, based on all the data, it does not appear that Ms. Smith's ability to appreciate the wrongfulness of assaulting Ms. Jones was impaired.

Regarding her capacity to conform her conduct, the data do not indicate that she was experiencing acute symptoms of a mental illness that may have impaired her ability to control her behavior.

Although she has been diagnosed with bipolar disorder, which, in an acute phase (and, particularly when accompanied by psychotic features) can impact an individual's ability to exert controls over her behavior, the data available do not indicate that she was experiencing such symptoms at, or near, the time of the alleged offense. She has clearly stated that she acted out of anger. She did say that once she knocked Ms. Smith down she became "enraged" and that "when I get that angry, it's hard to stop." Although this suggests that she experienced herself as having limited control once she began the alleged assault, as noted above, any impairments in control were not attributable to a mental illness, but rather to feelings of anger provoked by a realistic frustration (not being allowed to leave the hospital). Furthermore, based on her own account, at the time she initiated the alleged assault, she made conscious choices about her behavior, and considered the consequences. Thus, the available data do not suggest that her ability to control her behavior was substantially impaired by symptoms of mental illness.

Respectfully submitted,
Ira K. Packer, PhD, ABPP (Forensic)

TEACHING POINT:
REMAINING IMPARTIAL IN HIGH VISIBILITY CASES

There are several common influences that can interfere with a forensic clinician's capacity to remain impartial—by which we mean allowing the data and parsimonious reasoning to lead to one's conclusions, rather than having such conclusions affected by extraneous considerations. Such potentially biasing influences include knowing any of the parties involved, perceiving that much more is to be gained by the forensic clinician by reaching one conclusion rather than another, personal values and moral beliefs, and personal history (perhaps involving the experience of something similar to that occurring in the case).

These influences can be intensified in high-visibility cases due to the level of exposure and scrutiny of the forensic clinician's evaluation. Interacting with media can be valuable in some contexts, but it is almost invariably wise to avoid offering any comment whatsoever about an ongoing case. Refraining from any such additional involvement allows the forensic clinician some level of control over the intensity of exposure in a high-visibility case.

The present evaluation provides an example of a different kind of high-visibility case. Although the facts suggest that there is not likely to be much media attention or public scrutiny involved in this case, the forensic clinician must confront a different kind of visibility: the attention of fellow mental health professionals, patient advocates, family members, and hospital administrators. All of these individuals may play important roles in the professional life of a forensic clinician. As such, it is certainly possible that a forensic clinician might decline to be involved in any case like this occurring in the area in which he or she lives and works. (Consider the influences mentioned in the first paragraph of this teaching point. As the forensic clinician experiences more of them, it becomes decreasingly likely that impartiality will be feasible.) When such a case is not declined, however, it should reflect a decision made after careful consideration—and with the awareness that maintaining one's impartiality may be a challenge throughout the case.

5

Sexual Offending Risk Evaluation

This chapter concerns the evaluation of sexual offenders, particularly for the purpose of legal decision-making that incorporates risk assessment. Laws in some states and the federal jurisdiction permit the government to impose additional post-release conditions for individuals classified as "sexually violent predators" (also referred to as "sexually dangerous persons"), including stricter reporting requirements and even involuntary commitment to a secure facility (*Kansas v. Hendricks*, 1997). The principle applied to this case involves providing appropriate notification of purpose and obtaining appropriate authorization before beginning an evaluation, with the teaching point being used to further describe how to obtain informed consent in such evaluations.

CASE ONE
PRINCIPLE: PROVIDE APPROPRIATE NOTIFICATION OF PURPOSE AND OBTAIN APPROPRIATE AUTHORIZATION BEFORE BEGINNING (*PRINCIPLE 23*)

Providing information to the individual being examined is ethically indicated in any psychological assessment, but when these evaluations occur in the context of legal proceedings, notification of purpose and informed consent may also be legally required. The source of the authorization to perform the evaluation determines whether the individual being evaluated should be provided with relevant information, or whether the provision of relevant information should also be accompanied by obtaining informed consent. When the evaluation is court-ordered, the individual being assessed does not have a legal right to refuse to participate. In these circumstances, providing the individual with a notification of purpose is appropriate. However, if the referral source is the individual's

attorney, then the individual has a right to decline to undergo the evaluation, and the forensic clinician must obtain the informed consent of the individual being assessed.

Regardless of the source of the referral, the nature of the information provided to the individual being evaluated is comparable. Generally an evaluator should identify herself and describe the nature and purpose of the evaluation, who requested/authorized the evaluation, and the associated limits of confidentiality (including how the individual's information might be used in the legal proceedings that generated the referral). The evaluator should also inform the individual being evaluated that the evaluation is not part of a treatment relationship. Informed consent is required when the mental health practitioner is retained by the individual's attorney, and the evaluator should not proceed with the evaluation without first obtaining informed consent. The process of obtaining informed consent (besides being required in some contexts) also serves to establish rapport and facilitate effective information gathering, as it does in other clinical assessment contexts. Therefore, though not legally required, receiving the assent of the individual being assessed under court order may also promote informed participation, help establish rapport, and facilitate the gathering of relevant and accurate information.

There is substantial ethical support for this principle. The *Ethical Principles of Psychologists and Code of Conduct* (APA *Ethics Code*; American Psychological Association, 2010a) highlights as a guiding principle respect for the privacy, confidentiality, and self-determination of individuals receiving psychological services (Principle E). Furthermore, the APA *Ethics Code* emphasizes the integral role of informed consent generally and specifically to psychological assessment (Standards 3.10 and 9.03, respectively), and highlights specific caveats for individuals legally incapable of providing informed consent (Standards 3.10(b) and 9.03(b)), when services are court-ordered or otherwise legally mandated (Standards 3.10(c) and 9.03(a)), and when the focus of the evaluation is to assess decision-making capacity (Standard 9.03(a)). The *Specialty Guidelines for Forensic Psychology* (APA *Specialty Guidelines*; American Psychological Association, 2013b) provides a comprehensive set of guidelines for informed consent, notification, and assent, reasoning that "substantial rights, liberties, and properties are often at risk in forensic matters" and that "the methods and procedures of forensic practitioners are complex and may not be accurately anticipated by the recipients of forensic services" (Guideline 6). The APA *Specialty Guidelines* identifies several important "recipients of forensic services" for whom notification and informed consent is important, including individuals who seek to retain a forensic practitioner (Guideline 6.02); several groups of individuals being evaluated, including those under legal mandate (Guideline 6.03.02) and those who are not (6.03.01); individuals being evaluated who lack the capacity to provide informed consent (Guideline 6.03.03), or individuals not represented by legal counsel (Guideline 6.03.04); and collateral sources (Guideline 6.04). Finally, the importance of respect for individuals' right to privacy and informed consent is also specified in *Principles of Medical Ethics with Annotations Especially Applicable to Psychiatry* (Section 4.10; American Psychiatric Association, 2013b) and *Ethics Guidelines for the Practice of Forensic Psychiatry* (Guideline III; American Academy of Psychiatry and the Law, 2005).

Relevant legal authority regarding this principle involves the rights to confidentiality and privilege. Debates among legal professionals about these rights center on the defendant's right to protect disclosure of confidential (and potentially incriminating) information in the context of a forensic evaluation, and the prosecution's right to obtain a fair verdict (Packer & Grisso, 2011; see also *United States v. Alvarez*, 1975; *United States ex rel. Edney v. Smith*, 1976). Because restrictions on confidentiality and privilege are determined differently by different jurisdictions, forensic evaluators should clarify the rules of their jurisdiction and provide appropriate notification before beginning the evaluation (e.g., *Estelle v. Smith*, 1981). This need is further supported by the professional literature, which, in addition to noting the ethical and legal importance of informed consent, also emphasizes the beneficial influence of proper notification on rapport-building and obtaining information that is both relevant and useful within an FMHA (Melton, Petrila, Poythress, & Slobogin, 2007; Packer & Grisso, 2011).

Classification as a sexually violent predator is generally based on whether the individual has a conviction for a sexually violent offense, evidence of a "mental abnormality" or personality disorder, and evidence that the individual would be likely to re-offend unless additional measures are taken (*Kansas v. Hendricks*, 1997; see also *Adam Walsh Child Protection and Safety Act*, 2006). The following case report was part of an assessment of an individual convicted of a sexual offense. The evaluation referral came from the attorney, so Mr. Brown had a legal and ethical right to decline to participate. Accordingly, the evaluator obtained his informed consent rather than providing him only with a notification of purpose.

PSYCHOLOGICAL REPORT

Name: Jacob Brown
Age: 59 years
Date of Examination: 5/5/12
Examiner: Philip H. Witt, Ph.D.

REASON FOR REFERRAL

Mr. Brown was referred for a psychological evaluation by his attorney, James Smith, Esq., in the context of his challenging a proposed moderate risk, tier 2 Megan's Law classification by the Somerset County Prosecutor's Office.

SOURCES OF INFORMATION

(1) Individual interview of Jacob Brown
(2) Review of:
  • Pre-sentence Investigation report
  • Adult Diagnostic and Treatment Center report
  • Indictment
  • Judgment of conviction
  • Letter from David White, PhD, dated March 19, 2011
  • RRAS scored by the Somerset County Prosecutor's Office on November 14, 2011

INTRODUCTORY COMMENTS

Philip H. Witt, PhD

In 1994, after the rape and murder of seven-year-old Megan Kanaka by an individual who had been previously convicted of a sexual offense, New Jersey's legislature passed a registration and community notification law (termed "Megan's Law," N.J. Stat. Ann. § 2C:7-6). The following year, New Jersey's Attorney General appointed a task force to develop a measure to objectively assess sexual offender risk, so the level of community notification could be tailored to the level of risk presented to the community. Since 1995, the measure that was developed—the Registrant Risk Assessment Scale (RRAS) (Ferguson, Eidelson, & Witt, 1998; Witt & Barone, 2004; Witt, DelRusso, Oppenheim, & Ferguson, 1997)—has been used to classify New Jersey offenders convicted of specific sexual offenses with regard to risk level. Those determined to be at low risk are required to register with the police. Those appraised at moderate risk, in addition to registering with police, also have their names and personal information posted on a searchable New Jersey State Police website. Schools and daycare centers within a certain radius of their worksites or residences are also notified. Those determined to be high risk, in addition to the preceding conditions, are the subjects of door-to-door notification of all who live within a certain radius of the offender's residence.

Due to the increasingly stringent conditions resulting from higher levels of assessed risk, offenders who are appraised as tier two (moderate risk) frequently hope to be placed in tier one (low risk), and those in tier three (high risk) would prefer to be classified as tier two. Registrants are allowed to challenge their tier classification, requesting a judicial hearing and retaining their own experts to assess risk and testify as needed at the hearings.

One hotly contested area involves child pornography cases. Prosecutors in New Jersey typically score the victim characteristics (e.g., age of victim, whether penetration occurred) as if the individual who downloaded and viewed child pornography had actually had a contact offense with the victim. This results in most child pornography offenders being appraised as moderate risk (tier two). This finding conflicts with the research literature on child pornography offenders indicating that, absent a significant antisocial history, child pornography offenders have extremely low rates of further sex-offending after being arrested (see, e.g., Eke & Seto, 2008; Endrass et al., 2009; Lee et al., 2012; Seto, 2008; Witt, 2010).

Until recently, the case law in New Jersey has generally been antithetical to challenges in child pornography cases. Basically, the courts' reasoning is this: the scale is the scale; if the points add up to tier two, then the registrant is tier two. However, on July 26, 2012, the New Jersey Appellate Division in *In the Matter of Registrant PB* (slip decision) ruled otherwise. The Court in *PB* ruled that the possession and viewing of child pornography, as egregious as it might be, is not at the same level of severity as actually producing child pornography. Therefore, victim characteristics should not be scored on the RRAS as if the viewer of the child pornography were actually committing those acts. As the Court stated (2012, pp. 9–10):

> We reject the notion that the RRAS "high risk" standard of "penetration" in criterion 2, "degree of contact," is satisfied by a showing that a registrant merely possessed depictions of penetrative sexual activity with children, without any concomitant indication that he played a role in the penetrative activity either as a participant or a producer.... [U]nder the very terms of Megan's Law alone, the accused must have engaged in some kind of participation in penetrative activity before he or she can be deemed to be responsible for it on any level. [citations omitted]

The present evaluation was conducted prior to the *PB* decision. The evaluator proposed two solutions, one of which (not scoring victim characteristics) is similar to the conclusion reached by the Appellate Division in *PB*.

(3) Telephone interview of Susan Brown (wife).
(4) Telephone consultation with David White, PhD.
(5) Psychological assessment instruments:
—Personality Assessment Inventory (PAI)
The PAI is a 344-item objective person-ality test designed to assess 4 validity indicators, 11 clinical scales, 5 treatment consideration scales, and 2 interpersonal style scales, as well as a number of more specific subscales.
—Registrant Risk Assessment Scale
The RRAS is an instrument developed by the New Jersey Attorney General's Office to evaluate and place sex offenders in risk tiers. It evaluates the seriousness of the offense, characteristics of the offender, characteristics of the offense, and commu-nity support.
—Stable-2007
The Stable-2007 was developed to assess change in intermediate-risk status, assess treatment needs, and help predict recidi-vism in sexual offenders. The Stable-2007 consists of 13 items and produces esti-mates of the relatively stable (but change-able in the long term) personal factors of presence or absence of significant social influences, capacity for relationship stabil-ity, emotional identification with children, hostility toward women, general social rejection, lack of concern for others, impul-sivity, poor problem-solving skills, negative emotionality, sex drive and preoccupation, sex as coping, deviant sexual preference, and cooperation with supervision. The sampling period is within the prior year.
—Acute-2007
The Acute-2007 was developed to assess change in short-term risk status and help predict recidivism in sexual offenders. The Acute-2007 consists of seven items, including opportunities for victim access, hostility, sexual preoccupation, rejection of supervision, emotional collapse, collapse of social supports, and substance abuse. The sampling period is the present time.

BACKGROUND

The records indicate that on August 31, 2009, a cyber tip was given to the Somerset County Prosecutor's Office Computer Crimes Unit, indicating that an individual later identified as Mr. Brown had uploaded suspected child pornogra-phy to the Photobucket website. When Mr. Brown was interviewed by the investigators, he acknowl-edged that a forensic evaluation of his computer would "reveal dozens of images of boys and girls under the age of 16 naked and/or engaged in sex-ual acts." He eventually pled guilty to one count of third-degree endangering the welfare of the child.

On April 11, 2011, after entering a guilty plea but prior to sentencing, Mr. Brown was examined at the Adult Diagnostic and Treatment Center. Regarding his offense, the ADTC report states:

> According to further reports by Mr. Brown, he used the Internet for several years and had access to adult pornography on the Internet from 2006 onwards. He stated that approxi-mately two or three years ago, in 2008, he first accessed child pornography. He stated that he went into a chat room called "MIRC" on mul-tiple occasions, where he read and watched people asking questions, and listed a link for child pornography. Mr. Brown stated, "I accessed pornography and looked for a youth-ful image and was amazed at what I found. I found children, all kinds, sitting on a beach, parks, in nudist colonies." He stated that he found these images online and was interested in the youthful image. The girls were between 13 and 16, and some younger, both boys and girls. Mr. Brown revealed that some of these minor children were engaged in sexual acts with each other, but some were involved with adults. Between 2007 and 2008, Mr. Brown stated that for at least two years he accessed child pornography two or three times a month, for at least an hour. He said, "This is so unusual. It was interesting and I was sucked into that world." He acknowledged that on occasion in his office in the evening, he would masturbate to this pornography. He said, "This is so atypi-cal of my life. I am a conservative, financially responsible person." When Mr. Brown was asked why the behavior occurred, he said, "I'm not sure. I was not molested or raped. I had a curiosity in a younger female body." Mr. Brown stated that he knew his behavior was illegal, but said, "I didn't believe it was hurting someone. I didn't tell anyone." He said that he did not

believe his behavior was "this serious." He said, "It's not that I couldn't stop myself, but I didn't because it was interesting and I was distracted." Mr. Brown denied that he would have engaged in actual behavior with a young adolescent or child as was depicted in the child pornography. In fact, he said he had not met any person with whom he has chatted online.

A therapy progress report by Dr. David White dated March 19, 2011 states, in part:

> …Mr. Brown has been a cooperative and hard-working psychotherapy patient. Much of our time has been spent dealing with the particulars of his offense, and I believe that Mr. Brown is genuinely reflective and thoughtful regarding his involvement with pornography.…I believe that Mr. Brown's prognosis is excellent and consider his likelihood for re-offense to be extremely low. In part, this is based on Mr. Brown's long history of responsible adult behavior, as well as his never having been involved in the actual pursuit or engagement of sexual behavior with children. In the time that I have worked with Mr. Brown, I can unequivocally state that there have been no indications of aggressiveness or predatory behavior. Furthermore, there are no indications that Mr. Brown has now, or has ever, had any inclination toward actual sexual involvement with a child.

TELEPHONE INTERVIEW OF SUSAN BROWN

Mrs. Brown corroborated her husband's account regarding his adjustment during the past few years. She indicated that he is adjusting as well as the circumstances allow. He and his wife spend considerable time together, watching TV, shopping, and visiting friends and family. He remains close to various family members. She indicated that they are getting along well and enjoying each other's company, although she wishes that her husband could continue to practice as a pharmacist as he did in the past.

TELEPHONE CONSULTATION WITH DAVID WHITE, PHD

Dr. White confirmed the impressions that he expressed in his written report of March 2011. Dr. White indicated that Mr. Brown is doing well in treatment. Dr. White sees Mr. Brown as cooperative, responsible, and fully engaged in treatment. He sees Mr. Brown as someone who presents a low risk to the community.

INTERVIEW OF JACOB BROWN

Mr. Brown presented as a thin, balding white male who appeared his stated age. He was notified about the purpose and possible uses of the evaluation, including the limits on confidentiality, and consented to participate. He was oriented to time, place, and person. His thought processes, as assessed through the interview, were relevant and coherent. There were no signs of hallucinations or delusional thinking, or of suicidal thoughts or intent. In summary, there was no evidence of a thought disorder.

Throughout the interview, Mr. Brown was verbal, open, and cooperative. He answered all questions and provided information spontaneously, of his own accord. His demeanor was serious, appropriate to the nature of the interview. His affect was restrained. His eye contact, voice modulation, and social skills in general were good. He presented as an intelligent, articulate man.

Mr. Brown's history is well documented in the records, so in the interest of concision, I will not reiterate here. Rather, I will focus this interview section on issues relevant to scoring him on appropriate risk-assessment scales.

Mr. Brown corroborated the history recounted in the records. He has never had prior contact with the legal system, sexual or otherwise. He does not use illicit drugs or abuse alcohol. He has had only two sexual partners in his life, his wife and one prior girlfriend during his teens. He acknowledged significant sexual problems in his marriage; he and his wife have not had sexual activity in perhaps a decade. Prior to his arrest, he had developed a pattern of masturbating a few times per week to Internet pornography. He acknowledged that some of the pornography he viewed was of underage individuals. He indicated that his primary interest, however, was in legal-age, youthful and athletic-appearing girls, but in the process of searching for those types, he came across underage pornography and became intrigued with this "taboo" material. Currently, he is not permitted any access to the Internet. He still masturbates a few times per week to fantasies of athletic-appearing young women in their late teens or early twenties.

Mr. Brown previously owned a pharmacy, but after his arrest in 2009, he sold his pharmacy. He has retained his pharmacist's license and works a bit through a pharmacist friend. However, he is primarily retired. He spends his days visiting friends and family with his wife, tending to a few investment properties he owns, reading, watching TV, and shopping with his wife. He indicated that he and his wife are getting along well together and enjoying the amount of time they spend together. He reported a good relationship with his supervising parole officer, who has allowed him to travel to Arizona.[1] He noted that when he was working, prior to selling his business, he would sometimes work 60 or 70 hours per week. He was not only involved in running his pharmacy, but was active in the community as well, serving as president of the local Chamber of Commerce.

Mr. Brown reported that he has been in psychotherapy with Dr. David White for the past few years. He feels grateful to Dr. White, who he indicated has helped him remain emotionally stable through an admittedly stressful time in his life. He noted that the one area in his life that remains troublesome is his lack of a sexual relationship with his wife, and he hopes to soon address this in his therapy. He indicated that the only reason he has not addressed this problem already is that there always appears to be some crisis he needs to deal with, such as (originally) his sentencing and (currently) his proposed tiering.

PSYCHOLOGICAL TEST RESULTS

Examination of the validity scale pattern on Mr. Brown's PAI indicates that he presented himself in a slightly socially desirable manner on this test, minimizing faults, flaws, and problems. In fairness to Mr. Brown, such a socially desirable response style is common among individuals taking this test under similar forensic circumstances, when naturally most persons wish to put their best foot forward. Moreover, in Mr. Brown's case, this socially desirable tendency on the test is not particularly extreme. His clinical scales were entirely within normal limits. There are no indications of

significant psychopathology. On the scales assessing interpersonal style, he presents as a confident, assertive man who is well bonded to others. Otherwise, his test profile is unremarkable.

RISK ASSESSMENT

When the Somerset County Prosecutor's Office scored Mr. Brown on the RRAS, he received a score of 72 points, placing him toward the upper end of this instrument's moderate risk range (37 to 73 points). My scoring on this instrument would be different. The main difference is that I would not score victim characteristics. I have previously taken the position that the manner in which the RRAS was scored by the prosecutor's office—that being to score victim characteristics as if these were contact victims—is inaccurate. In a previous report, for example, I stated the following (with the name of the individual redacted):

> The primary question is how the facts in Mr. [X]'s case conform to the RRAS scoring. I served on the New Jersey Attorney General's Office task force that developed the RRAS in 1995. At that time, Internet sex crimes were quite rare. In the various task force meetings that occurred in developing the RRAS, I do not recall a single discussion or mention of how one should score "victims" of Internet sex crimes. In fact, I do not recall the word "Internet" coming up at all during our discussions in developing the RRAS. The question simply never occurred to any of us at the time, given that most of us on the task force had never seen an Internet offender at that time. Although I cannot speak for the entire task force, my own opinion is that unless the individual charged with an Internet sex crime actually created the child pornography, and therefore had direct victims, I would not score the various RRAS criteria concerning victim characteristics on the RRAS. (I testified a few years ago in a hearing before Judge Mahon in Hunterdon County, and he agreed with this reasoning, reaching a decision that the individual in that case should be scored low-risk and that the victim characteristic criteria on the RRAS should not be scored; I realize, of course, that Judge Mahon's unpublished decision is not necessarily binding on other courts.)

---

[1] I have attempted to contact his parole officer, Officer Jenkins, but so far have not been able to do so; his phone is not answered, and the message indicates that his voice mailbox has not yet been set up. Should I learn anything from Officer Jenkins that changes my opinion, I will issue an addendum to this report.

My position remains the same. To score victim characteristics as if Mr. Brown had contact victims results in an inaccurate, falsely inflated assessment of his risk to the community. The reality is that he does not present a moderate risk to the community, as his RRAS would indicate if victim characteristics were scored as above. As the RRAS manual itself states, the purpose of the scale is to assess the likelihood that an individual offender will recidivate, so if the scale is being scored in a manner that gives an inaccurate assessment of that likelihood, that incorrect scoring should be corrected. Rather, as an Internet offender who viewed child pornography with no history of other offenses, sexual or otherwise, Mr. Brown's risk of a re-offense of any kind is quite low, so any accurate risk assessment should reflect that low risk. In fact, when I scored his RRAS by omitting victim characteristics, I give Mr. Brown a score of 13 points, or low risk, obviously quite different from a score of 72 points.

A second solution is possible. Under this alternative, individuals convicted of downloading child pornography could have their points scored on the RRAS as if these were contact victims, typically resulting in their point totals' being within tier two. But then they could be treated as low-risk tier one offenders for the purpose of New Jersey's community registration and notification law. This procedure would amount to carving out an exception for child pornography offenders analogous to that made for incest offenders. That is, for incest offenders, even though their RRAS points typically fall within tier two, moderate risk, unless complicating factors are present (such as a significant antisocial history), incest offenders are treated as low-risk, tier one—in accord with what the literature shows regarding the risk of such persons. By creating a similar exception for child pornography offenders, the accuracy of the RRAS would be maintained, given that the literature shows that child pornography offenders—absent an antisocial history—present an extremely low risk of recidivism.[2]

Furthermore, a risk assessment with Mr. Brown presents difficulties in that most sex-offender risk-assessment scales have been developed and standardized on individuals who have had contact offenses with actual victims. Such is not the case with Mr. Brown, whose illegal sexual behavior was limited to downloading child pornography over the Internet. In fact, one of the major sex-offender risk-assessment scales, the Static-99, specifically excludes individuals such as Mr. Brown, indicating that individuals whose offenses have been limited to downloading child pornography cannot be scored on that instrument.

However, both common sense and the research literature indicate that, all else being equal, an individual whose life is well managed presents less risk than an individual whose life is in disarray. Therefore, to assess Mr. Brown's current and recent adjustment, I am scoring him on two structured instruments that focus entirely on those areas, the Stable-2007 and Acute-2007.

I first scored Mr. Brown on the Stable-2007 to obtain an assessment of relatively enduring (but changeable through effort and treatment) personal characteristics. On the Stable-2007, Mr. Brown receives a score of one point, placing him in this instrument's low-risk range (0 to 3 points). During the sampling period of the past year, he did not associate with negative social influences; held no hostility towards women; was not generally isolated and rejected by others; did not have a callous, exploitive lifestyle; was not impulsive or showing poor problem-solving skills; was not substantially depressed or hostile; was not sexually deviant or sexually preoccupied; and has been cooperating fully with supervision. His one point is the result of the lack of sexual intimacy in his marriage.

I then scored Mr. Brown on the Acute-2007, which was developed to assess change in short-term risk status. On the Acute-2007, Mr. Brown received a score of zero points, placing him in the low-risk/ low-priority range for both sexual and violent recidivism, and similarly in the low-risk/priority range for general recidivism.

INTEGRATION OF FINDINGS AND RECOMMENDATIONS

Mr. Brown is 59-year-old man who has pled guilty to one count of third degree endangering the welfare of a child, a charge that resulted from his

---

[2] See Lee, A. F., Li, N.-C., Lamade, R., Schuler, A., & Prentky, R. A. (2012, April 16), Predicting hands-on child sexual offenses among possessors of Internet child pornography, *Psychology, Public Policy, and Law*. Advance online publication. doi:10.1037/a0027517.

possessing child pornography. He has no other criminal history, sexual or otherwise.

Internet sex cases are difficult in that there is little empirical research on the characteristics that such men possess. There are, however, a few generally agreed-upon principles in assessing such men, and I will attempt to apply those principles in Mr. Brown's case.

First, the illegal Internet activity could be a reflection of a broadly antisocial personality and lifestyle in which the individual violates a variety of societal norms and laws. If this were the case, one would expect to see the usual indicators of an antisocial personality disorder, such as prior criminal offenses (including nonsexual offenses), substance abuse, and both job and relationship instability. There is no evidence that such is the case with Mr. Brown. He has had no prior contact with the criminal justice system. There are no indications of a broadly antisocial lifestyle or of a callous, exploitive personality. In fact, to the contrary, his life has been one of productivity, achievement, and stability. He has been married to the same woman for well over three decades. Prior to his arrest, after which he sold his business, he ran a pharmacy for over two decades. He contributed to the community, serving as president of the Chamber of Commerce and helping to start an educational foundation in his town.

Second, the illegal Internet activity could be a reflection of a preferential pedophilic sexual preference. If this were the case, the individual's risk to the public would be elevated. If this explanation were to apply, one would expect to see significant evidence of preferential interest in sexual activity with minors, including perhaps an extensive collection of child pornography (to the exclusion of adult pornography). In more extreme cases, other behavioral indicators of sexual interest in minors would be present, such as attempts to contact minors over the Internet or otherwise for sexual activity. This possibility is the most difficult to assess, given that it relies heavily on the defendant's self-report. Given present information, I do not see evidence that Mr. Brown's present Internet offense is preferential. Although admittedly he reportedly had a significant quantity of child pornography, there are no indications or allegations that he has ever tried to contact minors for sexual activity. Moreover, by his account, the sexual stimuli he viewed on the Internet were not limited to child pornography, but included a wide range of legal pornography as well. His sexual relationships with others consist apparently of his wife and one prior age-appropriate girlfriend during his teens. There are no indications of sexual behavior with minors.

Third, the illegal sexual Internet behavior could be a reflection of experimentation and exploration on the Internet of various fantasies that the individual would not enact with a real victim. The assumed (although illusory) anonymity and ease of access of the Internet might cause an individual to explore areas that he would otherwise not pursue. The Internet is a highly accessible and affordable medium that provides its users with a sense of anonymity, which in turn can lessen social risk and allow people to engage in highly disinhibited sexual behavior. The phenomenon of engaging in behavior that may not otherwise have been engaged in but for the Internet, and may have contributed to Mr. Brown's present offense, has been termed the "online disinhibition effect."[3] Although the concept of disinhibition might lead one to believe that because Mr. Brown's thinking and behavior were disinhibited, the "true" aspects of his personality were allowed to emerge, this is not necessarily the case. Rather, it is more accurate to understand human behavior as multidimensional, and thus one dimension of Mr. Brown was revealed within a particular situational context.

In short, considering the context in which behavior occurs is necessary and essential to understanding the behavior. If experimentation were the motivator, one would expect that child pornography would be only one part of a broader interest in pornography, much of which focuses on adults, and such is the case with Mr. Brown. In addition, one would expect an absence of indicators of attempts to solicit sexual activity with minors, and there are no indications that Mr. Brown has had or attempted to have sex with any minors. The prognosis in cases like this would be the most favorable,

---

[3] Suler, J. (2004), The online disinhibition effect, *CyberPsychology & Behavior*, 7(3), 321–326.

given the more limited nature of any sexual focus on minors. Given present information, Mr. Brown's case appears to fit this pattern of experimentation and exploration.

Moreover, what research is available on child pornography offenders indicates that the offenders whose only offense is the one child pornography arrest have low rates of recidivism, especially for future hands-on sex offenses. Not surprisingly, the group of child pornography offenders for whom recidivism rates are high are those with significant antisocial histories,[4] and such is not the case with Mr. Brown, who has had no prior contact with the criminal justice system, sexual or otherwise. Consequently, Mr. Brown is a member of a population—that being men who have possessed Internet child pornography but who have no other offenses—that presents a low risk to the community.

Consequently, all factors taken together, Mr. Brown is clearly a low-risk individual, and any scoring of the RRAS, if accurate, should reflect this low risk. It is my opinion that Mr. Brown would be most appropriately treated as a low-risk, tier 1 individual.

Philip H. Witt, PhD
Diplomate in Forensic Psychology, ABPP
Date: 5/5/12

---

[4] See, for example, Eke, A. W., & Seto, M. C. (2008), Examining the criminal history and recidivism of registered child pornography offenders, Presented at the Association for the Treatment of Sexual Offenders convention, October 2008, Atlanta, Georgia; Endrass, J., Urbaniok, F., Hammermeister, L. C., Benz, C., Elbert, T., Laubacher, A., & Rossegger, A. (2009), The consumption of Internet child pornography and violent and sex offending, *BMC Psychiatry*, 9, 43–67. Downloaded from http://www.biomedcentral.com/content/pdf/1471-244x-9-43.pdf on 7/17/09; Seto, M. (2008), *Pedophilia and sexual offending against children*. Washington, D.C.: American Psychological Association; Witt, P. H. (2010), Assessment of risk in child pornography cases, *Sex Offender Law Report*, 11(1), pp. 1, 4, 13–15; and especially Lee, A. F., Li, N.-C., Lamade, R., Schuler, A., & Prentky, R. A. (2012, April 16), Predicting hands-on child sexual offenses among possessors of Internet child pornography, *Psychology, Public Policy, and Law*, Advance online publication. doi:10.1037/a0027517.

TEACHING POINT:
OBTAINING INFORMED CONSENT IN SEXUALLY VIOLENT PREDATOR CASES

The process of obtaining informed consent in a particular kind of forensic evaluation begins with the question of whether informed consent is needed. If the evaluation is requested by the defendant's attorney, then the defendant has a legal and ethical right to refuse to participate. Hence, informed consent must be obtained in such cases. By contrast, if the evaluation has been ordered by the court, then the defendant has no legal right to refuse participation, and receives a "notification of purpose" rather than request for informed consent. The appropriate ethical response under such circumstances is to investigate the reasons for the refusal, attempt to rectify them if possible, and inform the defendant that the evaluation may need to be conducted and the report written even without the defendant's participation.

Next there is the question of whether the elements of informed consent may need to be adapted or modified in sexually violent predator evaluations. (The informational elements of "notification of purpose" and "informed consent" are comparable—the difference involves whether the defendant is asked whether he or she agrees to participate, in the latter circumstance, after receiving the information.) These elements are as follows:

- Who is the evaluator (name, title, discipline)
- Nature of the authorization (whether court-ordered or attorney-requested)
- Purpose(s) for which the evaluation is being conducted (related to the legal questions it may be used to inform)
- Uses of the evaluation (that are possible, as when the defendant's attorney has the discretion to use the findings, or are definite, as when the report will be submitted to certain parties and entered into evidence following its completion)
- Limits on confidentiality (usually best addressed by describing the uses and the way information may be disseminated if the findings are used in a hearing or trial)
- Possible expert testimony (noted as an additional element for clarity, although it is

important to both the uses and the limits on confidentiality)

- Forensic evaluation, not treatment, is being provided by the evaluator.

When the evaluator provides this information, and subsequently clarifies that the defendant has understood it by asking it to be described back, there does not appear to be any need to include additional elements in the notification. Certainly the specific information to be provided under many of these elements varies according to the legal question and applicable evidentiary law. Given the serious consequences that can result from the findings of a sexually violent predator evaluation, it is important that the evaluator provide clear and accurate information to those undergoing such evaluations.

6

Federal Sentencing

This chapter includes two case reports on federal sentencing. FMHA for federal sentencing is guided by the criteria provided in Chapter 5 of the *Federal Sentencing Guidelines Manual*, discussed in more detail later in this chapter. However, in some cases an attorney may request a broader evaluation of factors that influence risk and treatment/rehabilitation needs generally. This kind of referral is demonstrated in the first case, whose principle emphasizes the need to describe evaluation findings in terms of their strengths and weaknesses—and in the consistency of their support—so that they will need to change little under cross-examination. Related to this principle, the teaching point underscores several important considerations in the communication of findings in FMHA to accurately reflect the evaluator's confidence in them. The principle associated with the second case in this chapter discusses the use of scientific reasoning in FMHA, specifically the importance of hypothesis formulation and testing, falsifiability, parsimony in interpretation, awareness of the limits on accuracy, and the applicability of nomothetic research to FMHA. The associated teaching point addresses the role of risk-needs assessment in federal sentencing evaluations, a good example of how broader information about risk and treatment needs may be relevant to this type of evaluation.

CASE ONE
PRINCIPLE: DESCRIBE FINDINGS SO THAT THEY NEED CHANGE LITTLE UNDER CROSS-EXAMINATION
(PRINCIPLE 31)

This principle focuses on how the results of FMHA reports and testimony are communicated. Because many forensic issues involve complex questions, it can be useful to describe data in terms of their strengths and weaknesses. Accordingly, this discussion focuses on communicating the limitations and accuracy of the data and reasoning used in FMHA. There are numerous factors that can influence the accuracy of FMHA, including the unavailability of relevant information, the use of psychological tests that have limited reliability or validity, and the response style of the individual being evaluated. When there are questions that do not have clear and consistently supported answers, the forensic clinician must clarify the limits of knowledge in a written report or during testimony.

The presentation of FMHA findings is always subject to challenge, typically in cross-examination. One effective way to cope with such a challenge involves anticipating the weak or inconsistent aspects of data and reasoning—and incorporating this characterization into the communication of findings. By "challenging" her own findings, appropriately characterizing their strength and consistency, and giving fair consideration to alternative explanations, the forensic clinician can contribute to a reasonable consideration of both sides in an adversarial context. Results that are communicated in this way will need to change little under cross-examination, as the important data and reasoning consistent with an "alternative hypothesis" have been identified and considered.

Ethical guidance suggests that the forensic clinician should clarify the limits of knowledge in an evaluation or testimony. Generally, the *Ethical Principles of Psychologists and Code of Conduct* (APA *Ethics Code*; American Psychological Association, 2010a) states that:

[P]sychologists take into account the purpose of the assessment as well as the various test factors, test-taking abilities, and other characteristics of the person being assessed, such as situational, personal, linguistic, and cultural differences, that might affect psychologists' judgments or reduce the accuracy of their interpretations. They indicate any significant limitations of their interpretations. (Standard 9.06)

This is further emphasized in the *Specialty Guidelines for Forensic Psychology* (APA *Specialty Guidelines*; American Psychological Assocation, 2013b), which states, "Forensic practitioners strive to identify any significant strengths and limitations of their procedures and interpretations" (Guideline 10.03). The APA *Specialty Guidelines* provides additional guidance on the importance of clarifying limits, and the first consideration is the need to test plausible rival hypotheses: "When performing examinations, treatment, consultation, educational activities, or scholarly investigations, forensic practitioners seek to maintain integrity by examining the issue or problem at hand from all reasonable perspectives and seek information that will differentially test plausible rival hypotheses" (Guideline 9.01).

Ethical guidance is also provided for specific limitations likely to occur in the context of FMHA. The APA *Ethics Code*, for example, addresses the circumstance in which a personal examination cannot be conducted:

When, despite reasonable efforts, such an examination is not practical, psychologists document the efforts they made and the result of those efforts, clarify the probable impact of their limited information on the reliability and validity of their opinions, and appropriately limit the nature and extent of their conclusions or recommendations. (Standard 9.01(b))

This is consistent with Guideline 9.03 of the APA *Specialty Guidelines*. The APA *Specialty Guidelines* also addresses the use of third party information that cannot be corroborated ("When relying upon data that have not been corroborated, forensic practitioners seek to make known the uncorroborated status of the data, any associated strengths and limitations, and the reasons for relying upon the data"; Guideline 9.02) and the use of third party information when an examination of the individual is not required: "When conducting a record review or providing consultation or supervision that does not warrant an individual examination, forensic practitioners seek to identify the

sources of information on which they are basing their opinions and recommendations, including any substantial limitations to their opinions and recommendations" (Guideline 9.03).

Further guidance is provided regarding the importance of describing any limitations in the selection of assessment instruments: "Forensic practitioners use assessment instruments whose validity and reliability have been established for use with members of the population assessed. When such validity and reliability have not been established, forensic practitioners consider and describe the strengths and limitations of their findings" (Guideline 10.02). Finally, the APA *Specialty Guidelines* provide general guidance about the importance of clarity and accuracy in the communication of information: "Forensic practitioners make reasonable efforts to ensure that the products of their services, as well as their own public statements and professional reports and testimony are communicated in ways that promote understanding and avoid deception" (Guideline 11.01).

The *Ethical Guidelines for the Practice of Forensic Psychiatry* (AAPL *Ethical Guidelines*; American Academy of Psychiatry and the Law, 2005) provides similar guidance on this issue. There is a broad emphasis on the importance of honesty and striving for objectivity: "[Psychiatrists] communicate the honesty of their work, efforts to attain objectivity, and the soundness of their clinical opinion, by distinguishing, to the extent possible, between verified and unverified information as well as among clinical 'facts,' 'inferences,' and 'impressions'" (Honesty and Striving for Objectivity, paragraphs 2–3). Also emphasized is the need to clarify limits when personal contact with the individual is not possible:

For certain evaluations (such as record reviews for malpractice cases) a personal examination is not required. In all other forensic evaluations, if, after appropriate effort, it is not feasible to conduct a personal examination, an opinion may nonetheless be rendered on the basis of other information. Under these circumstances, it is the responsibility of psychiatrists to make earnest efforts to ensure that their statements, opinions and any reports or testimony based on those opinions, clearly state that there was no personal examination and note any resulting limitations to their opinions. (Honesty and Striving for Objectivity, para. 4)

Legal evidentiary standards under both *Frye* (1923) and *Daubert* (1993) also provide guidance on this issue. Under *Frye*, the trial court considers whether the procedures used to obtain scientific evidence are generally accepted in the field to which it belongs. The issue of whether procedures are generally accepted depends in part on empirical questions, such as their degree of recognition and use by mental health professionals. Because the answers to such questions are usually not known, we often use criteria that *should* apply to the question of general acceptance: the technique's purpose and availability; the population for which it is used; and its available documentation on administration, scoring, reliability, and validity. Each of these is relevant to the limits of the technique, which should be clarified in communicating FMHA findings. Using this reasoning, the *Frye* standard supports the principle that the forensic clinician must clarify the limits of his data, reasoning, and conclusions.

The support for this principle under *Daubert* is even clearer. When the court may consider questions such as whether the technique is testable, whether it has been tested, and the "error rate," there is the explicit expectation that available scientific studies will be applied toward evaluating the admissibility of the technique—and that the absence of such research will be regarded as limiting. This is consistent with the clarification of limits on data and reasoning in FMHA.

The present case provides an example of how the results of FMHA reports and testimony should be communicated in a federal sentencing evaluation. The first step in effective communication that would change little upon cross-examination is an understanding of the forensic issues and relevant legal questions. Krauss and Goldstein (2006) reviewed federal sentencing guidelines that "explicitly recognize a number of grounds for downward and upward departures concerning which forensic mental health professionals may offer expert testimony" (p. 368), including diminished capacity (§ 5K2.13), aberrant behavior (§ 5K2.20), coercion and duress (§ 5K2.12), inadequacy of the Criminal History Category (§ 4A1.3b), downward departures and extreme psychological injury (§ 5K2.3), and inadequacy of the Criminal History Category for upward departures (§ 4A1.3a). They note that

it is most likely that forensic clinicians will provide evaluations relevant to downward departures.

In the present case, the defendant, James Stallworth, is undergoing evaluation at the request of his attorney related to sentencing on federal charges of false statements and fraudulent use of an identification document. The defendant has entered a guilty plea, so the evaluation is requested to provide information relevant to a possible downward departure in sentence. There were several aspects of the defendant's history that prompted this referral. Mr. Stallworth has had numerous convictions as an adult, including offenses for trafficking in cocaine and for possession of marijuana. Other collateral documents that at times he has been diagnosed with obsessive compulsive disorder, attention-deficit/hyperactivity disorder, and bipolar disorder, and that he has a reported history of two concussions. Such a history raises the possibility that Mr. Stallworth experiences a mental or emotional disorder that co-occurs with substance abuse.

This report does *not* reflect information on the 5K2 criteria of understanding wrongfulness or conforming conduct to the requirements of the law. This can happen for two reasons. First, a referring attorney may not make this a focus of the evaluation—possibly because the attorney has no reason to believe that the defendant's understanding or capacity to conform were particularly problematic—but may determine that a broader appraisal of risk and treatment/rehabilitation needs would be helpful. Second, the attorney may initially request both a specific appraisal of the 5K2 factors (understanding wrongfulness and conforming conduct) and a broader evaluation of risk and needs, and subsequently modify this request if informed that the evaluation does not show that the defendant had noteworthy problems with understanding or conforming but still has certain risk- and need-relevant information that might be helpful.

Whether the forensic clinician is willing to evaluate these different aspects of federal sentencing and provide a report on only some of them, as requested by the retaining attorney, should be discussed at the time of the initial referral. It should be noted that this is not ethically or professionally problematic if the forensic clinician chooses to do so; retaining attorneys are entitled to ask for the evaluation of multiple issues, not all of which they will decide to have included in the final report if the finding on a particular issue is not helpful. This should be contrasted with an attorney's request to change or delete factual or interpretive material on a particular issue,[1] which is usually problematic. It should also be contrasted with the parameters of court-ordered evaluations, which involve conveying the information to the court and both attorneys (unless otherwise specified in the court order). For this kind of evaluation, the forensic clinician responds to the court order rather than the defense attorney's request in structuring the evaluation.

The effective communication of FMHA reasoning and conclusions is directly related to the quality and accuracy of the data gathered for the evaluation, and the reliability and validity of results can be strengthened through the use of multiple sources of information. In this case, the evaluation used information from each of three domains: interview; testing; and third party information, including both a collateral interview and records from the arrest and the pre-sentence investigation. Information from these domains was integrated, and the conclusions reached reflected the extent to which the multiple sources seemed to converge in pointing to a given outcome. The evaluators clarified the limits on data and reasoning, and presented them in a way that should withstand adversarial challenge because they are obtained by integrating good information from multiple sources.

Forensic Evaluation
March 5, 2011
Re: James Stallworth

REFERRAL
INFORMATION

James Stallworth is a 48-year-old Caucasian male (D.O.B: 6/12/1962) who is charged with two

---

[1] Comment from the contributor: Forensic clinicians will sometimes receive requests from retaining attorneys to change what has been written in a report. My policy is that I will correct anything that is (a) mistaken (after confirming the error), (b) prejudicial to the defendant on another matter (such as quoting a juvenile in a transfer evaluation to indicate that he had owned or carried a gun, when that individual has an open case involving weapon possession—a modification might involve rewriting to capture the "weapon" aspect without specifically conveying what weapon, or when), or (c) likely to be interpreted in a way that I did not intend. Beyond that, however, I will not change what has been written in a report.

counts of false statements in violation of 18 U.S.C. § 1001, and one count of fraudulent use of an identification document in violation of 18 U.S.C. § 1028(a)(4). A request for a mental health evaluation to provide the defense with information relevant to sentencing, pursuant to U.S.S.G. Section 5K2.13 (18 U.S.C.), was made by his court-appointed attorney (Sally M. Lygon, Esq.).[2]

PROCEDURES

Mr. Stallworth was evaluated at the Federal Correctional Institute [FCI]-Allentown in Allentown, Pennsylvania, for a total of 4 hours on January 31, 2011, during which time testing was conducted. He was also interviewed at the FCI-Allentown on February 14, 2011, for approximately one hour. Testing measures included a standard screening instrument for symptoms of mental and emotional disorder experienced both currently and at the time of the offense (the Brief Symptom Inventory, or BSI), a standard objective measure of risks and needs information relevant to offender treatment planning and assigning levels of freedom and supervision (the Level of Service/Case Management Inventory, or LS/CMI), a standard measure of adult

---

[2] Comment from the contributor (on addressing the criteria described in Section 5K2.13): Before the U.S. Supreme Court considered the question in *United States v. Booker* (2005), the Federal Sentencing Guidelines were considered mandatory in their application to federal sentencing decisions. In effect, this meant that federal sentencing evaluations conducted by mental health professionals prior to this decision focused on the questions set forth in Section 5K2: whether the defendant's "significantly reduced mental capacity" meant that the defendant, although convicted, had significantly impaired ability to (1) understand the wrongfulness of the behavior comprising the offense or to exercise the power of reason; or (2) control the behavior that the defendant knows is wrongful. In the *Booker* decision, the Court held that the Guidelines were advisory but not mandatory. This meant that defense attorneys could request evaluations that were more broadly focused, incorporating questions of the defendant's risk for future offending, criminogenic needs, and other needs. In this respect, federal sentencing evaluations came to resemble capital sentencing evaluations more closely, with aspects of the defendant's history (family, educational, medical, mental health, vocational) important and admissible. The present evaluation resembles many "post-*Booker*" reports in that the attorney did not request opinions about the capacities to understand wrongfulness or conform conduct; rather, the request was for the more broadly focused evaluation.

psychopathology and personality functioning (the Minnesota Multiphasic Personality Inventory, 2nd edition, or MMPI-2), and a standard test of current functioning in relevant academic areas (the Wide Range Achievement Test, 4th edition, or WRAT-4).

Interviews were also conducted with Cloris Samuels, Mr. Stallworth's friend, on 2/2/11 (45 minutes) and 2/4/11 (15 minutes).

The following documents, obtained from Ms. Lygon, were also reviewed as part of the evaluation:

(1) Camberwell Police Department Arrest Report (dated 7/29/1994);
(2) Camberwell Police Department Complaint Report (dated 5/5/2010);
(3) Department of Homeland Security ICE Report of Investigation (dated 5/21/2010); and
(4) Pre-sentence Investigation Report (dated 2/10/11).

Prior to the beginning of the evaluation, Mr. Stallworth was notified about the purpose of the evaluation and the associated limits of confidentiality. Mr. Stallworth appeared to understand the basic purpose of the evaluation, reporting back his understanding that he would be evaluated and that a written report would be submitted to his attorney. Mr. Stallworth understood that his attorney determined whether the report would be introduced in any legal context, and that testimony could be provided based on the information contained in this report if his attorney requested it. Mr. Stallworth further understood that if the report were used in his hearing, copies of the report would be provided to opposing counsel and to the court. The collateral interviewee also understood the purpose of the evaluation and associated limits of confidentiality, and agreed to be interviewed.

RELEVANT HISTORY

Historical information was obtained from the collateral sources described above as well as from Mr. Stallworth. Whenever possible, we have assessed the consistency of self-report information with that obtained from collateral sources. If additional information is obtained prior to Mr. Stallworth's hearing, a supplemental report will be filed.

Family History

According to the Pre-sentence Report, Mr. Stallworth was born in Newark, New Jersey. He reported that his family moved once, when he was one year old, before moving to the house where he still resides. He indicated that his mother already had one son and three daughters when she married his father. After his parents married, he said, they had himself and one daughter, Jane Stallworth.

Mr. Stallworth reported that his parents were married until he was 9 years old, when they separated and his father moved out of the house. He added that they formally divorced two years later, when he was 11 years old. He described his parent's break-up as "tumultuous." From the ages of 9 to 15 years old, he said, he lived with his mother and one of his half-sisters. He also recounted that, during that period, one of his neighbors was also going through a divorce, and that the woman and her three daughters moved in with his family for about one year. Mr. Stallworth described some troubles during the time that he lived with his mother. He said that his mother "has a rage problem." Mr. Stallworth recalled being punished in unusual ways by his mother, such as having pepper put on his tongue if he cursed. According to the Pre-sentence Report, his mother also made him "cut the lawn with scissors" when he was 12 years old. He also said that "if we did something wrong, we'd get beat." He also recalled that his mother "threw me out at 13 [years old]" because he was "drinking too much milk." He indicated that his mother starting "throwing [my] clothes out the window" and then "kick[ed] me out." According to Mr. Stallworth, he then went to live with his sister and her boyfriend before being allowed to return to his house. When Mr. Stallworth was 15 years old, he reported, his mother moved out and his father moved back in. During his senior year of high school, Mr. Stallworth noted, one of his sisters and her boyfriend broke into their house and robbed them.

According to Mr. Stallworth, his father "drank his whole life" until he had bypass surgery in 1989. He stated that he "never really had a relationship" with his father until his father's surgery. Mr. Stallworth said that he "came home, took care of him [his father], and that's when we developed a relationship." According to the Pre-sentence Report, Mr. Stallworth's father passed away in June 2000. With respect to his relationship with his mother, Mr. Stallworth said that he and his mother still have not resolved their problems, such as his feelings of abandonment.

According to Mr. Stallworth and the Pre-sentence Report, two of his half siblings have passed away: Joseph Sanders, who died of a heroin overdose in 1998; and Barbara Sanders, who Mr. Stallworth said died of complications from heroin in 2008. Both sources indicate that two of his half-siblings—Ann and Elizabeth Sanders—are still living. Mrs. Samuels indicated that she believes Ann is currently incarcerated. Mrs. Samuels said that she believes Mr. Stallworth "has a good relationship with Ann." She added, "I would say there's a closeness, there's a bond between them, but I think he knows she's got problems and he can't have a relationship [with her]." She also noted that Mr. Stallworth's mother is raising his sister Jane's children, though she did now know where Jane is or what she is doing.

Currently, Mr. Stallworth reported having some relationship with his mother and siblings. He said that from the year 1999 on, he "spent the summer with my family." During the rest of the year, though, he said that he typically would only see his family on Christmas. He noted that he and his siblings "don't have a calling relationship," and their primary contact was on these family vacations. Mrs. Samuels described Mr. Stallworth's family as "very dysfunctional," and said that although he has "isolated himself from them," she "know[s] they love each other."

Educational History

Mr. Stallworth reported that he was a B and C student from kindergarten through high school. He said that he attended one elementary school, where his attendance was regular and he had no behavioral problems. He noted that he was in extra reading classes in second grade due to some form of learning disorder, and was in speech classes because he "didn't enunciate" well enough. He reported attending one middle school, where he recounted missing 30 days in a row "around the time my parents were separated." During these 30 days, he said that he went to friends' houses and "smoked weed." He added that he was suspended for missing this much school. In high school, he described his attendance as regular, and though he said he was in one fight, which he described as an argument that led to a physical altercation, he had had no suspensions.

Mr. Stallworth said that he attended the University of South Florida for one year and then completed approximately 90 credits at the University of Delaware. He added that this is about equivalent to three years of classes. According to the Pre-sentence Report, he was at the University of Delaware from 1981 to 1984. Mr. Stallworth said that he "didn't mind" his classes in college, and that he "liked intellectual challenges." He reported maintaining a 3.0 grade point average through college. He also noted that he was arrested for selling cocaine while in school. In 1991, Mr. Stallworth said, he decided to go back to school at Bennett College. At this point, he said that he was "trying to start over" and that he "didn't want to be a criminal," so he decided to change his name to Sanford Norris. However, he reported, "a couple months later I got hit by a car" and did not return to school after his recovery. In addition, the Pre-sentence Report indicates that Mr. Stallworth attended the Camden campus of Rutgers University in 2000.

Substance Abuse

Mr. Stallworth reported some history of substance abuse. He said that he used marijuana during college and for some time after college, though he hasn't used it in several years. He also said that he tried Quaaludes and LSD five or six times in college, and used cocaine for five months in college. The Pre-sentence Report described prior use of LSD and mescaline. Mrs. Samuels said that Mr. Stallworth smoked marijuana when she first met him about 23 years ago. However, she reported that she does not believe he currently uses any drugs.

With regard to alcohol use, Mr. Stallworth reported that he had an alcohol problem in college. Also, according to Mr. Stallworth and the Pre-sentence Report, he was charged with a DUI in June 2002 in Harrisburg, Pennsylvania, and a second DUI in December 2002 in Avalon, New Jersey. Currently, he said, he "doesn't drink much." More specifically, he described drinking on weekends and sometimes on a daily basis. According to Mr. Stallworth and the Pre-sentence Report, he typically will have 8 to 10 beers or vodka in a sitting. Mrs. Samuels was asked if she knows whether Mr. Stallworth ever used drugs or alcohol, and she said that he used to "binge drink" with his friend Sam, but that he "stopped [drinking] altogether" when Sam moved out in 2003. When asked about this, Mr. Stallworth said that he did stop drinking for some time, but that he "started again in 2006 when working for Habitat for Humanity." He indicated that he started drinking again after being hit by a car, an accident in which he reported losing part of one of his fingers.

The Pre-sentence Report also noted that Mr. Stallworth reported attending Alcoholics Anonymous meetings in 2001 as a condition of probation.

Social History

Mr. Stallworth reported that, in his free time, he enjoys downloading music and movies from the Internet, reading, and playing chess. He added that he enjoys exercise, and lately has been interested in weightlifting and bicycling. He also said that he has been involved in volunteer work at a church, including putting together bags to help feed the homeless. According to Mrs. Samuels, Mr. Stallworth also enjoys shopping and "likes to try to get free deals." For instance, she said he collects Marlboro Miles to redeem for free merchandise. The Pre-sentence Report indicated that when Mr. Stallworth's home was searched, promotional merchandise from companies including Marlboro, Newport, and Camel was found.

Mrs. Samuels described Mr. Stallworth as having "a lot of friends." She said that he especially receives attention from women, and that "girls especially really want to get to know him." She noted, though, that "he doesn't put such a priority on that, and sometimes he seems almost annoyed by that. When he's out with his friends, he'd rather just be out with his friends." She added that when he used to drink, he used to welcome the advances of other women, but he is "really not that interested in that" anymore. She also described Mr. Stallworth as having maintained "some close friendships," and said he has had some male friends. For instance, in college, she reported that "he was in a little clique and it was a certain group of people he was close with." However, she was unsure why he had not stayed in contact with some friends from past periods of his life. According to Mr. Stallworth, most of his friends have not been involved in legal issues. He reported that he had one friend who was involved in the criminal justice system, but that the offense had occurred "more than 15 years ago."

Mr. Stallworth stated that he is single and "satisfied" with that status. He noted, though, that he regretted that he was "not emotionally mature enough" when he was younger to "tell girls I loved them." He said that he has never been married, and his longest relationship lasted for two years.

Employment

Mr. Stallworth reported that he has been working since he was 12 years old. At that age, he said, he worked over a summer as part of a program for underprivileged kids. In high school, he reported having a summer job at the Fairview Mall, which he described as his longest period of employment. Mr. Stallworth described working at the university cafeteria during college, as a bartender in Camden, and as a waiter and busboy over the summers. He also noted that he sold cocaine and Quaaludes at the university as a way to earn money.

As an adult, Mr. Stallworth said, he has held several jobs. These include working as a waiter, a cook, and in construction. He said, "I call myself 'king of the misers'—I don't need a lot to get by." According to the Pre-sentence Report, Mr. Stallworth worked for a restaurant as a waiter in 2001, was a telephone re-interviewer for the 2000 Census, and also held positions as a waiter, cook, and gas station attendant during the 1990s. The Pre-sentence Report also indicated that Mr. Stallworth worked for Habitat for Humanity in Camden for a year in 2007. The Department of Homeland Security ICE Report of Investigation, though, indicated that Mr. Stallworth "was only employed for a short period of time and may have only made it through his training process" at Habitat for Humanity. Mr. Stallworth reported that he entered the training program, but that he "got hit by another car" and "didn't finish the [training] program." According to the Homeland Security ICE Report of Investigation, Mr. Stallworth used to "sell music CDs made to order" for $3–$5, and this appears to have been a way to make extra money. During 2009, Mr. Stallworth reported being employed for approximately three months by a catering company.

Mrs. Samuels said that Mr. Stallworth typically finds jobs "that are easy to get," such as jobs that "hire just somebody who walks in." She noted that he has worked at movie theaters, a restaurant, a company that made sandwiches for senior citizen centers, Census 2000, and the mall. When asked if she knew why Mr. Stallworth tends to take jobs that are "easy" to find or temporary, she said she did not. She added that if she did have some idea why, she "might be able to answer a question of why he's not stable." She also described a conversation she had with Mr. Stallworth's father when Mr. Stallworth was previously incarcerated. She said that his father found several uncashed paychecks from "all of the jobs he had worked prior to him going to jail."

Medical and Psychiatric History

Mr. Stallworth reported some notable medical history. He said that he had a seizure when he was two years old, and that he was diagnosed with a heart disorder, which he characterized as an "electrical" disorder. According to the Pre-sentence Report, this is a "syndrome of pre-excitation of ventricles of the heart," and Mr. Stallworth was told to take aspirin for the condition. He also reported being diagnosed with a heart valve problem. The Pre-sentence Report indicated that Mr. Stallworth was hospitalized for this condition in 1998. The report also noted that he had stomach surgery in 2007 or 2008.

Mr. Stallworth said that he had a heart scan in 2009, which revealed that the left side of his heart is enlarged. As a result of this abnormality, he said, he gets "pains in my heart and I pass out" when he lies on his back. In March 2010, he reported, he was diagnosed with asthma, and prescribed a steroidal inhaler "which really seemed to work well." He said this diagnosis was made in response to a chronic cough that he has experienced for the past 10 years. He reported that he would "cough anytime I leaned forward, anytime I eat anything dry," and that he is sometimes left "gasping for breath." He also described chronic difficulty in staying asleep. He said that he tends to sleep for 3½ to 4 hours before waking up each night. To cope with this, he said, he usually functions on that amount of sleep until he becomes "really exhausted" and is able to sleep for six hours straight.

In addition, Mr. Stallworth indicated that he has had two concussions in the past. He described the first one as taking place in 1993, and said that he was "hit in the head," but that he mostly recalled "waking up in the hospital." The second concussion was incurred in 1995, he said, during a "fight with a bunch of people over alcohol."

With respect to his psychiatric history, Mr. Stallworth reported being hospitalized while he was in college. He said that, at the time, he was not eating well and his diet consisted mainly of "Suzy Qs [prepackaged pastries], cans of tuna, and macaroni and cheese." He said he had been away from school, and when he returned, a "guy at a frat was giving me a hard time." At this time, he reported, he "had a mental breakdown." According to Mr. Stallworth and the Pre-sentence Report, this took place in 1984. He described being initially hospitalized in Maxwell Hospital, where he was diagnosed as "manic-depressive," and then was transferred to Johnston-Chambers Hospital. The Pre-sentence Report, though, stated that he was transferred to Southern Psychiatric Hospital and was "treated for several weeks." Mr. Stallworth added that he committed himself voluntarily, and then checked himself out of the program when he felt he was ready. The Pre-sentence Report indicated that Mr. Stallworth was prescribed Lithium after this hospitalization, and took it until 1985. When asked about this, Mr. Stallworth said he "never took" his medications because he "didn't like the side effects." However, he noted that the Lithium "might have slowed down" his mania. Two years after this hospitalization, he described experiencing mania again, but said that he did not take any medications. During the summer of 1988 and following his father's death in 2000, Mr. Stallworth said, he experienced depression, for which he also did not take medication. He noted that he is not aware of any family history of mental disorders.

Offense History

According to Mr. Stallworth and the Pre-sentence Report, Mr. Stallworth does not have any juvenile adjudications. With respect to adult offenses, Mr. Stallworth described a substantial arrest history, indicating that he had been arrested for trafficking cocaine, resisting arrest, trespassing, possession of marijuana, burglary, theft, DUIs, and shoplifting. According to the Pre-sentence Report, Mr. Stallworth has had approximately 15 convictions, 6 charges for which the disposition was unknown, and 12 charges that were dismissed. In addition to the charges that Mr. Stallworth indicated, the Pre-sentence Report noted convictions for making false report, disorderly person, "bail jumping," and resisting arrest. Mr. Stallworth is also a registered Step 2 sexual offender, according to the Camberwell Police Report. Though the Camberwell Police Department Arrest Report indicates that he was initially charged with criminal sexual assault and sexual contact, Mr. Stallworth and the Pre-sentence Report noted that this charge was downgraded to Endangering the Welfare of

Children. The Pre-sentence Report indicates that he was sentenced to three years in prison for this offense.

CURRENT CLINICAL CONDITION

Mr. Stallworth presented as a 48-year-old Caucasian male of medium build who appeared his stated age. He was dressed in FCI garb and appeared well-groomed. He was polite and cooperative throughout the evaluation session. During the first interview, his speech was clear and relevant, though often circumstantial. During the second interview, his speech was rambling and tangential, and he largely focused on the early 1980s when asked about his history and background. It was difficult to get him to describe more recent aspects of his life.

Mr. Stallworth reported a history of two concussions. He indicated that the first was in 1993, when he was "hit in the head" and "woke up in the hospital." The second concussion, he said, was incurred in 1995 during a "fight involving alcohol." He indicated that English is his primary language. He denied any auditory or motor problems, and noted that he needs glasses for distance vision. He said he has one scar on one of his arms from when he put his hand through a window when he was younger, and said he has no tattoos or piercings.

Mr. Stallworth's mood throughout the evaluation was calm. He reported no problems with attention or concentration, and worked consistently on all tasks during the evaluation. It would appear, therefore, that the present evaluation provides a valid reflection of his current functioning.

Mr. Stallworth's basic academic skills, as measured by the WRAT-4, were largely consistent with what would be expected of an adult who attended college. Mr. Stallworth ranked in the 77th percentile on Word Reading (grade equivalent > 13th grade), the 95th percentile on Sentence Comprehension (grade equivalent > 13th grade), and the 81st percentile on Math Computation (grade equivalent > 13th grade). On Spelling, he scored in a relatively lower percentile (34th percentile), but this is still equivalent to the 11.6th grade.

Mr. Stallworth did not report experiencing any perceptual disturbances at the time of the evaluation, and there was no evidence of bizarre ideas, delusions, or other thought disturbances. Mr. Stallworth's responses on the MMPI-2 yielded a valid profile (Welsh Code: 31"2'4+−758 0/69: KLF/). His pattern of responses indicates that he responded in an open and cooperative manner. Mr. Stallworth's profile had high-point clinical scale scores on the Hysteria scale (T = 89) and Hypochondriasis scale (T = 86). This pattern is rare, occurring in 1.8% of the normative sample of men. Also, a high-point clinical scale score on the Hysteria scale occurs in 12.1% of the normative sample of men, though only 3.8% of the normative men had a T-score of 65 or above. However, this pattern occurs in a larger proportion of state and federal prisoners (5.1% and 11.3%, respectively), though a T-score of 65 or more was relatively rare in these populations as well (3.3% and 7.5%, respectively). Mr. Stallworth's pattern of responses indicates that he may take advantage of others in interpersonal relationships, though he may tend to meet and talk with others easily. This is somewhat consistent with Mrs. Samuels's report that Mr. Stallworth has had "a lot of friends, people will just approach him all the time and talk to him." This pattern of responses also suggests that Mr. Stallworth has some proneness to addiction, and that he acknowledged alcohol and drug use. He endorsed some specific items related to his substance use, such as "I have a drug or alcohol problem" and "I have used alcohol excessively." This is consistent with Mr. Stallworth's report that he has a history of both alcohol and drug use. He reported having a drug problem in college, and also described two driving while intoxicated (DWI) arrests in the more recent past. In addition, he said, he began using marijuana in college and continued using it after leaving school. He described using Quaaludes and LSD five to six times in college, and using cocaine for a five-month period of time. His pattern of responses also suggests that Mr. Stallworth is experiencing somatic complaints and symptoms and may have a high concern with illness. This is consistent with his description of his medical history, which includes diagnoses of heart-related problems and asthma. He also described experiencing coughing fits, having pains in his chest that cause him to pass out if he lies on his back, and at times feeling as though he is gasping for breath. His scores also suggest that he may use somatization as a defense mechanism, and that he has some histrionic characteristics. In addition, the pattern of elevations on the content scales indicates that Mr. Stallworth may be preoccupied with his physical health, may feel as if he is not in good health, and may have poor coping skills.

His pattern of elevations on the content scales also indicates that he may have difficulty making decisions, may have some obsessive-compulsive symptoms, and can be ruminative and have trouble with change. This is consistent with the report of Mr. Stallworth and Mrs. Samuels. For instance, Mr. Stallworth described himself as "not being able to make decisions" in the time leading up to the offense. Mrs. Samuels stated that when faced with a decision, Mr. Stallworth will "go on for hours, days, months, procrastinating [and] not making a decision." She also said that when decisions require too many details or steps, "he can't organize them in his mind and decide what to do." She noted that, at times, making decisions that result in change is "all very enormous to him, it paralyzes him." Finally, individuals with this pattern of responses frequently have personality disorders with co-occurring substance use. Individuals with this personality style may have some difficulty in treatment due to their tendency toward somatization and the long-standing presence of their personality problems.

Mr. Stallworth also completed two versions of the structured inventory of symptoms of mental and emotional disorders, the Brief Symptom Inventory (BSI). The first concerns his present functioning. Compared to non-patient adult males, Mr. Stallworth's scores were significantly elevated (i.e., greater than two standard deviations above the mean) on four of the nine scales (Somatization, Obsessive-Compulsive, Depression, and Anxiety). In addition, Mr. Stallworth's positive symptom distress index was significantly elevated. This indicates that, in general, he appears to be distressed in multiple areas.

Of the 53 items on the BSI, Mr. Stallworth reported being "extremely" distressed on four items, including pains in his heart or chest, trouble getting his breath, feeling hopeless about the future, and trouble concentrating. He reported being "quite a bit" distressed on three items, including trouble falling asleep, hot or cold spells, and spells of terror or panic. When asked to elaborate on these symptoms, his attributed many of them to his health problems. For instance, he said that a cardiac MRI conducted in January of 2009 revealed that the left side of his heart is enlarged. Accordingly, he said that when he lies on his back, he gets "pains in my heart" and passes out. He said this issue has been present for about a year. He also said that he has had trouble sleeping for 10 to 15 years, and that although he can fall asleep, he has difficulty staying asleep. He said that he will sleep for "3½ hours, then wake up." Mr. Stallworth also described being diagnosed with asthma in March, which results in coughing fits. He said that he uses a steroidal inhaler, which seems to work well. However, when he starts coughing, he reported that he sometimes feels that he is gasping for breath, which makes him feel like he will have a panic attack. He also described some of his symptoms as related to his "current situation," including having a criminal record and being unable to obtain a job. For instance, in terms of concentration, he said "I used to read for hours and hours, and now I can't sit still." He indicated that he is experiencing "depression about my situation."

In addition, Mr. Stallworth was asked to complete the BSI for the period of time leading up to his offense. Compared to non-patient adult males, Mr. Stallworth's scores were significantly elevated on three of the nine scales (Somatization, Obsessive-Compulsive, and Anxiety). His global severity index and positive symptom distress index were significantly elevated. This indicates that, in general, he was experiencing distress across multiple areas.

Of the 53 items on the BSI, Mr. Stallworth reported being "extremely" distressed on two items. These included pains in the heart or chest, and feeling hopeless about the future. In addition, he reported being "quite a bit" distressed on nine items. These included feeling fearful, feeling that he was watched or talked about by others, trouble falling asleep, difficulty making decisions, trouble getting his breath, hot or cold spells, feeling tense or keyed up, spells of terror or panic, and having the idea that something is wrong with his mind. He attributed several of these symptoms to the "anxiety of not being able to get a job." For instance, though he said he experienced pains in his chest due to his medical condition, he also said that it may have been partially due to "a little anxiety because I was having trouble finding a job and my savings were going down to nothing." Similarly, he noted that he felt fearful, tense, and hopeless because of his difficulty finding a job, and reported that it was interfering with his sleep. Mr. Stallworth also cited his medical issues as the cause of some of his symptoms, particularly his frequent coughing. For instance, he said that it resulted in trouble catching his breath, and that "I would cough for a good minute sometimes...I'd get lightheaded and dizzy and had a heat spell." Finally, he indicated that some of his experiences were due to "obsessive-compulsive" tendencies he had developed. For instance, he said that he became obsessive about downloading music and movies on his computer, stating, "I started downloading every single album made by every group in every genre...I derived a lot of pleasure from this." He added that his friend told him that he seemed to have obsessive-compulsive disorder. According to Mr. Stallworth, this obsession resulted in difficulties in making decisions, ranging from how to organize his media collection to how he could stop the behavior. He said this habit also led him to feel like something may be wrong with his mind, as he "realiz[ed] this had taken over my life."

On the LS/CMI, Mr. Stallworth scored in the high risk/need category. Approximately 58.5% of prison inmates and 78.9% of community offenders scored lower than Mr. Stallworth on the LS/CMI. The LS/CMI has eight domains; each domain may reflect a particular problem for that individual. Mr. Stallworth rated in the high risk/need category in two areas, education/employment and family/marital. Mr. Stallworth described a strained relationship with his parents. For the majority of his life, he said, he "never had a relationship with my father." He did say that their relationship improved shortly before his father died. He described his mother as having a "rage problem," and indicated that she was very strict when he was growing up, including throwing him out of the house at one point. He added that he "still hasn't resolved those issues with my mom," such as feelings of abandonment. With regard to his siblings, Mr. Stallworth said that he will typically "only talk to them when I see them." He also noted that his sisters are "in and out of jail due to heroin," which makes communication difficult. He said that all of his siblings "have been addicted to heroin and been incarcerated for it." Mr. Stallworth's history also reveals deficits in the area of employment. He described several jobs that he held, though many were temporary or short-term. For instance, he said he held various jobs in college, such as working at the cafeteria and as a bartender. He noted that his longest-held job was when he worked at the mall in high school. The short-term nature of most of his jobs was also described by Mrs. Samuels, who said

Mr. Stallworth has held jobs at places such as a restaurant, a gas station, and movie theaters. Leading up to the instant offense, Mr. Stallworth was working for the 2010 Census. However, according to the Department of Homeland Security ICE Report of Investigation, his job had been terminated after he was recognized as a registered sex offender and reported to his supervisor, at which point the Census also realized Mr. Stallworth's legal name and the name he used on his employment application were discrepant.

TREATMENT NEEDS AND AMENABILITY

Throughout the interview, Mr. Stallworth described some potential indicators of mental disorders, some of which were corroborated by the collateral sources. For instance, Mr. Stallworth and Mrs. Samuels described Mr. Stallworth as having some obsessive compulsive tendencies. Both parties described how Mr. Stallworth would become obsessive about downloading music from the Internet. According to Mrs. Samuels, Mr. Stallworth wouldn't be able to leave the house because he was only interested in "download[ing] all the music in the world," though he "doesn't listen to it, he just downloads it all." Mr. Stallworth and Mrs. Samuels said that these obsessive compulsive tendencies have resulted in an inability to make decisions. According to Mr. Stallworth, he was having difficulty making decisions about organizing his music and movie collection, and realized that "this had taken over my life." He also described how he would look for patterns in the music and movies he would download, recording details such as the date and television stations on which shows aired. Mrs. Samuels described an instance in which Mr. Stallworth "lost a house" because he spent too much time deliberating about details such as whether he should rent the house and how he should advertise the property. She said that when there are "so many steps, he can't organize them in his mind and decide what to do." She described this as a "really strange mental thing," and said that she believed some of his issues have resulted from his "inability to make a decision." It seems that Mr. Stallworth would benefit from further mental health evaluation to determine if he does have symptoms of obsessive compulsive disorder or obsessive compulsive personality disorder, or some other anxiety or similar disorder. If so, Mr. Stallworth would benefit from treatment, including psychotherapy. This could also focus on his decision-making deficits.

Mr. Stallworth also indicated that he experienced a "mental breakdown" in the 1980s. He said that he was diagnosed with bipolar disorder, and the Pre-sentence Report indicated that he reported taking Lithium after this hospitalization. He also reported experiencing periods of mania and depression in the late 1980s, and depression following his father's death in 2000. Questions regarding attention-deficit/hyperactivity disorder were asked during the evaluation, and Mr. Stallworth endorsed a number of items related to inattention and impulsivity. For instance, he noted that he often fails to give close attention to details, often does not follow through on instructions, and is often easily distracted by extraneous stimuli. He also indicated that he often blurts out answers before questions have been completed, has difficulty awaiting his turn, and often interrupts others. Though it is not clear if these symptoms were present before seven years or whether he also experiences symptoms of hyperactivity, he said that these symptoms do impair his functioning in multiple settings. Mr. Stallworth would benefit from a more formal mental health screening to determine if these disorders, or any other mental disorders, are present, and identify treatment needs.

In addition, it seems that many of Mr. Stallworth's difficulties have been related to his lack of stable employment. He stated that in 2000, he was hit by a car and awarded a $13,000 settlement. He said that he "lived off that" as much as possible. For instance, he reported having a roommate "to cover living expenses." For food, he said, "I would go to a soup kitchen or eat out of a trash can." Mrs. Samuels described Mr. Stallworth as "cheap," although she also said, "I don't think money motivates him." She said that when he does work, she thinks his "primary focus" is the make enough money to "pay the [property] taxes" on his residence. Although Mr. Stallworth described himself as the "king of the misers" and said that he is like Thoreau in that he "can live on very little," it seems that his unemployment has caused him some stress. For instance, leading up to the time of the offense, Mr. Stallworth described a great deal of anxiety related to his unemployment. He said he was feeling fearful "because I wasn't able to find a job," and thought that some of the pain in his heart and chest may have been due

to "anxiety because I was having trouble finding a job and my savings were going down to nothing." He also described difficulty sleeping because of his unemployment, and because he felt he did not have "many qualifications to get a job," such as a college degree or other skills. He reported that his trouble finding a job was resulting in trouble catching his breath, hopelessness about the future, and feeling tense. It was at this time, he said, that he realized he might be able to work for the Census again and applied for a position. His employment history over the past several decades suggests that Mr. Stallworth has tended to hold temporary or short-term jobs. Accordingly, it seems that Mr. Stallworth would benefit from employment services that would help connect him to a long-term, full-time, stable job. Having a stable and full-time job would help ensure Mr. Stallworth has a steady source of income and is able to pay for property taxes and other life expenses. It may also help to occupy his free time.

Finally, Mr. Stallworth seems to have generalized deficits in his coping and problem-solving style. Mrs. Samuels stated that she believes that Mr. Stallworth "kind of got stuck in that phase of adolescence in a way, and there's a part of him that just hasn't moved on from that." More specifically, she said, the "part [of him] that has to deal with life skills and handle grown-up problems" has not been well-developed. Also, Mr. Stallworth described significant health-related problems, and his BSI results suggest that these symptoms are distressing on a regular basis. His MMPI-2 results are indicative of an individual who experiences significant physical health concerns, and may have a poor coping style for dealing with these concerns. Though Mr. Stallworth would benefit from ongoing medical monitoring and treatment for his conditions, it seems that he would also benefit from coping skills and problem-solving training to help him better deal with his physical concerns and other stressful situations.

CONCLUSIONS

In the opinion of the undersigned, based on all of the above, Mr. Stallworth:

1. has a history of symptoms consistent with ADHD, and would benefit from formal screening and treatment, if appropriate;
2. has a history of diagnosis of bipolar disorder, and has symptoms potentially consistent

with an anxiety disorder or obsessive compulsive personality disorder, and would benefit from formal screening and treatment, if appropriate;

3. would benefit from employment services that may help connect him with steady employment to help him to pay his living expenses and avoid future offenses related to his lack of employment;

4. has deficits in his problem-solving, coping, and decision-making skills, and would benefit from skills training in each of these areas.

Thank you for the opportunity to evaluate Mr. Stallworth.

Kirk Heilbrun, PhD
Consulting Psychologist

Stephanie Brooks Holliday, BS
Drexel University Graduate Student

TEACHING POINT:
COMMUNICATING FINDINGS TO ACCURATELY REFLECT THEIR STRENGTH AND THE EVALUATOR'S CONFIDENCE IN THEM

There are several important considerations in communicating findings. First, findings that are presented as strong and confidence-inspiring should actually be that. Data collected using detailed and relevant interviews, psychological tests and specialized measures that are reliable and valid for the purpose of forensic evaluation, collateral interviews with knowledgeable third parties, and records that are as complete as possible will inspire such confidence. It is not always possible to obtain information of this quality and diversity, but the forensic clinician should make reasonable efforts to do so. In addition, it is important to attribute data to its source so that the reader can easily identify its origins—and perhaps make an independent judgment about the credibility of that source.

The next consideration is how the information is interpreted and communicated. Hyperbolic language suggesting conclusions that go beyond the data is to be avoided. Indeed, the forensic clinician might be well served by qualifying conclusions that are less well-supported than needed, identifying them as less clear and noting the limitations that

apply. Evaluators should be parsimonious in how they reach conclusions, applying explanations that account for data in the simplest and most straightforward way. Evaluators should also challenge their own data and interpretations in the process of combining the information, so that cross-examination usually does not involve alternatives that have not been considered.

Evaluations conducted and communicated in this fashion will include some findings in which the forensic clinician can have great confidence, and others in which there is some confidence but the picture is less clear. The key to conveying this information with confidence in testimony involves, among other things, how it is written in the report. Thorough, multisourced, careful evaluations using validated measures and interpreting the findings parsimoniously and in light of possible alternative explanations are more likely to yield conclusions that are relatively unchanged in cross-examination.

CASE TWO
PRINCIPLE: USE SCIENTIFIC REASONING IN ASSESSING THE CAUSAL CONNECTION BETWEEN CLINICAL CONDITION AND FUNCTIONAL ABILITIES
(*PRINCIPLE 29*)

This principle describes the importance of using scientific reasoning in FMHA. Several aspects of scientific reasoning are particularly relevant to this principle, including hypothesis formulation and testing, falsifiability, parsimony in interpretation, and awareness of the limits on accuracy. These in turn affect the applicability of nomothetic research to the immediate case. In any FMHA, there may be several competing explanations for the clinical symptoms or personality characteristics, deficits in relevant legal capacities, and causal relationships between the two. An important goal in FMHA is to test these competing "hypotheses" to determine which is best supported by the available data. For such hypothesis testing to be meaningful, however, the hypotheses must be evaluated in a way that allows them to be fairly tested, and rejected when they are not supported.

Sources of ethics authority in psychology provide direct support for the application of several kinds of scientific reasoning in FMHA, including hypothesis testing, the application (and misapplication) of psychological assessment procedures, and the parsimonious interpretation of psychological test results. The APA *Ethics Code* contains several sections relevant to this principle. Appropriate operationalization depends, to some extent, on selecting procedures that have been developed for a purpose comparable to the purpose of the evaluation: "Psychologists administer, adapt, score, interpret, or use assessment techniques, interviews, tests, or instruments in a manner and for purposes that are appropriate in light of the research on or evidence of the usefulness and proper application of the technique" (Standard 9.02(a)). Furthermore, selecting inappropriate procedures can adversely affect the successful operationalization of variables: "Psychologists do not base their assessment or intervention decisions or recommendations on data or test results that are outdated for the current purposes....Psychologists do not base such decisions or recommendations on tests and measures that are obsolete and not useful for the current purpose" (Standards 9.08(a) and 9.08(b)). This error would limit both the overall accuracy of the findings and the extent to which nomothetic results would be applicable.

The APA *Ethics Code* also addresses the importance of personal contact with the individual being evaluated: "Except as noted...psychologists provide opinions of the psychological characteristics of individuals only after they have conducted an examination of the individuals adequate to support their statements or conclusions" (Standard 9.01(b)). In this context, personal contact is important because it can facilitate hypothesis formulation and testing. When personal contact is not possible, hypothesis testing is considerably more difficult, as the evaluator cannot observe the reaction of the individual to specific questions or procedures:

> When, despite reasonable efforts, such an examination is not practical, psychologists document the efforts they made and the result of those efforts, clarify the probable impact of their limited information on the reliability and validity of their opinions, and appropriately limit the nature and extent of their conclusions or recommendations. (Standard 9.01(b))

Finally, the APA *Ethics Code* addresses the interpretation of assessment results in two ways. The first involves the applicability of validation research for a test or procedure used with an individual:

> Psychologists administer, adapt, score, interpret, or use assessment techniques, interviews, tests, or instruments in a manner and for purposes that are appropriate in light of the research on or evidence of the usefulness and proper application of these techniques....Psychologists use assessment instruments whose validity and reliability have been established for use with members of the population tested. When such validity or reliability has not been established, psychologists describe the strengths and limitations of test results and interpretation. (Standard 9.02(a) and 9.02(b))

Second, the APA *Ethics Code* addresses the interpretation of FMHA test results. When interpreting assessment results, including automated interpretations: "[P]sychologists take into account the purpose of the assessment as well as the various test factors, test-taking abilities, and other characteristics of the person being assessed, such as situational, personal, linguistic, and cultural differences, that might affect psychologists' judgments or reduce the accuracy of their interpretations" (Standard 9.06).

Support for the use of scientific reasoning in FMHA, particularly hypothesis testing, can also be found in the ethical guidelines for both forensic psychology and psychiatry. The APA *Specialty Guidelines* (2013b) emphasizes the value of hypothesis testing in the following way:

> Forensic practitioners strive to utilize appropriate methods and procedures in their work. When performing examinations, treatment, consultation, educational activities, or scholarly investigations, forensic practitioners seek to maintain integrity by examining the issue or problem at hand from all reasonable perspectives and seek information that will differentially test plausible rival hypotheses. (Guideline 9.01)

Similarly, the AAPL *Ethical Guidelines* indirectly supports hypothesis testing by emphasizing the distinction between "verified" and "unverified" information, and distinguishing "among clinical 'facts,' 'inferences,' and 'impressions'" (Honesty and Striving for Objectivity, paragraph 3).

Legal support can also be found for this principle. Both the United States Supreme Court's decision in *Daubert* (1993) and the *Federal Rules of Evidence* underscore the importance of reasoning in cases involving scientific evidence.[3] In *Daubert*, the Supreme Court, in dicta, used the phrase "reasoning or methodology" in outlining the criteria that might be used to determine the scientific validity of the evidence. The *Daubert* opinion also suggested that the Supreme Court took a broad view of "science," with both data and reasoning considered as expert evidence. Furthermore, Rule 703 of the *Federal Rules of Evidence* also provides for some role for reasoning in FMHA: "An expert may base an opinion on facts or data in the case that the expert has been made aware of or personally observed." The nature of this reasoning is elaborated further by the definition of "expert" provided in Rule 702, as follows: "A witness who is qualified as an expert by knowledge, skill, experience, training, or education may testify in the form of an opinion or otherwise."

There is relatively little empirical evidence regarding the role of scientific reasoning in FMHA. However, one study involving forensic psychologists and psychiatrists examined the perceived desirability of various elements of FMHA, including elements that are clearly relevant to reasoning (Borum & Grisso, 1996). In rating the value of providing a "mental illness rationale" describing how the examiner reached an opinion about the presence or absence and degree of mental illness, the majority of responding psychologists and psychiatrists rated this rationale as either essential or recommended. Other elements of FMHA relevant to reasoning were also strongly endorsed, with more than 75% of responding psychiatrists and psychologists rating each as either essential or recommended.

A more recent study examined weaknesses in forensic reports that were submitted by psychologists applying for board certification in forensic psychology, but not accepted (Grisso, 2010). The most frequent issue—identified in 56% of the reports—was the reporting of "[m]ajor interpretations or opinions... without sufficiently explaining their basis in data or logic" (p. 110). Also among the most common weaknesses was the inclusion of data unrelated to the referral (31% of reports) and the absence of alternative hypotheses or explanations (30% of reports). Similarly, Wettstein (2005) listed several common issues in his review of the research regarding the quality of forensic reports, including failure to support clinical diagnoses, psychopathology not linked to expert opinions, psychological test results not linked to expert opinions, inadequate support and explanations for expert opinions, and failure to state limitations of methods and opinions.

Heilbrun (1992) stressed the importance of reasoning in FMHA—particularly in the context of hypothesis formulation, testing, and test interpretation—and compared the process of FMHA to a scientific experiment:

> Following the formulation of falsifiable hypotheses, the verification process can proceed much as it would in a scientific experiment. Does the defendant exhibit behavior consistent with the presence of the hypothesized psychological characteristic? (A researcher might call this construct validity.) Does the defendant show the absence of behaviors that are not consistent with the presence of the hypothesized construct? (We could analogize this to discriminant validity.) The remaining task is then to offer conclusions in terms that reflect the consistency of support for the hypothesis that was framed in psychological rather than legal terms (e.g., psychosis, cognitive awareness and volition rather than insanity). (p. 269)

Use of multiple sources of information, including psychological testing and third party data, is also an important part of this process (Heilbrun, 1992; Heilbrun, Warren, & Picarello, 2003). In addition to increasing the confidence in the results of a forensic assessment, approaching the process scientifically can reduce the potential for

---

[3] Because the United States Supreme Court has also decided that expert evidence that is "technical" or "other specialized knowledge" may be scrutinized in the same way as "scientific" evidence under *Daubert* (see *Kumho Tire Co. v. Carmichael*, 1999), it is clear that *Daubert* may be applied to FMHA *regardless* of whether the latter is considered to be scientific, technical, or other specialized knowledge.

bias and increase the objectivity of an assessment (Weissman & DeBow, 2003).

The present report provides a good illustration of this principle. The evaluation was conducted to determine the individual's risk to others and treatment needs and amenability in the context of a specialized sentencing evaluation. In it, the evaluator demonstrates the applicability of scientific reasoning in the operationalization of variables (through the selection of appropriate and relevant testing procedures), hypothesis formulation and testing, parsimonious interpretation, and an awareness of the limits on accuracy. The evaluator also selected psychological tests that were relevant to the purpose of the evaluation. For example, because risk and needs are an important aspect of the evaluation of a defendant's functioning, the evaluator used the Level of Service Inventory-Revised (LSI-R). Since this evaluation (unlike Case One in this chapter) did discuss the applicability of the 5K2 factors (understanding wrongfulness and conforming one's conduct), the evaluator administered a BSI that was completed to describe the defendant's mental and emotional functioning around the time of the offense.

One of the clearest illustrations of the applicability of scientific reasoning in this case involves the use of parsimony in considering the defendant's motivation for the offense. Mr. Smith described a significant substance-use problem that included smoking marijuana and drinking on the day of the offense. This may have affected his reasoning and decision-making somewhat, but the evaluator makes it clear (through careful reconstruction of the events of that day) that Mr. Smith nonetheless did some fairly careful planning for the offense. His larger motivation for the robbery appeared to be monetary—always one of the simplest possible explanations for property crimes, and one that seemed to parsimoniously account for much of his thinking and behavior in the present case.

Forensic Evaluation
July 23, 2008
Re: Joseph Smith, Jr.
Criminal No. 01-123

REFERRAL

Joseph Smith, Jr., is a 22-year-old African-American male (DOB: xx-xx-xx) who pleaded guilty on July 12, 2007, to one count of conspiracy to commit Hobbs

Act robbery, in violation of 18 U.S.C. § 1951(a) and 18 U.S.C. § 2, and one count of using and carrying a firearm during a crime of violence, in violation of 18 U.S.C. § 924(c). A request for a mental health evaluation to provide the defense with information relevant to sentencing, pursuant to U.S.S.G. § 5K2.13 (18 U.S.C.), was made by Mr. Smith's attorney.

PROCEDURES

Mr. Smith was evaluated for approximately 4.75 hours on June 30, 2008, at Drexel University. In addition to a clinical and psychosocial interview, Mr. Smith was administered a standard screening instrument for symptoms of mental and emotional disorder experienced both currently and at the time of the offense (the Brief Symptom Inventory [BSI]), a standard test of current functioning in relevant academic areas (the Wide Range Achievement Test, 3rd edition [WRAT-3]), a comprehensive objective assessment of offender risks and needs relevant to levels of supervision and treatment (the Level of Service Inventory-Revised [LSI-R]), a standard measure of overall intellectual functioning (the Wechsler Abbreviated Scale of Intelligence [WASI]), and a standard objective measure of mental and emotional functioning (the Minnesota Multiphasic Personality Inventory, 2nd edition [MMPI-2]). Two collateral interviews were conducted. Mr. Smith's mother, Ms. Joann Smith, was interviewed for approximately 45 minutes (via telephone on 7/8/08) regarding Mr. Smith's past and current functioning. Mr. Smith's previous girlfriend and the mother of his daughter, Ms. Natalie Jones, was interviewed for approximately 20 minutes (via telephone on 7/8/08) regarding Mr. Smith's past and current functioning.

The following documents, obtained from Mr. Smith's attorney, were reviewed as part of this evaluation:

(1) Superseding Indictment (filed November 28, 2006);
(2) Guilty Plea Agreement (dated March 19, 2007); and
(3) Pre-sentence Investigation Report (dated August 27, 2007).

Prior to the evaluation, Mr. Smith was notified about the purpose of the evaluation and the associated limits on confidentiality. He appeared to understand the basic purpose of the evaluation, reporting back his understanding that he would be evaluated and that a written report would be submitted to his attorney. He further understood that the report could be used in his sentencing hearing, and, if it were, copies would be provided to the prosecution and court. Similar notifications of purpose were provided to Ms. Smith and Ms. Jones before the collateral interviews.

RELEVANT HISTORY

Historical information was obtained from the collateral sources described above as well as from Mr. Smith himself. Although Mr. Smith presented as a reliable historian, the consistency of the factual information provided by Mr. Smith was assessed through the use of multiple collateral sources whenever possible. If additional collateral information that materially changes the results of this evaluation is obtained prior to Mr. Smith's sentencing date, a supplemental report will be filed.

Family History

Joseph Smith, Jr., reported that he was born on xx-xx-xx, in Philadelphia, Pennsylvania, to Ms. Joann Smith and Mr. Joseph Smith, Sr. Mr. Smith reported being the youngest of nine siblings, who include one older sister, three older maternal half-siblings (two sisters and one brother), and four older paternal half-siblings (three sisters and one brother). Mr. Smith reported that all of his half-siblings are from his parents' prior marriages. He reported that his mother used several illicit substances while she was pregnant with him, which resulted in his being born two months premature and physically dependent on drugs. Mr. Smith's mother, Ms. Joann Smith, confirmed this information. Mr. Smith reported being raised by his mother and father for a brief period of time following his birth, and then being raised by his older sister (Ms. Anna Scott; age 37) while his mother was dependent on drugs. Mr. Smith reported that he was raised by his older sister until age seven, when his mother "cleaned herself up" and began caring for Mr. Smith and some of his siblings. Mr. Smith reported that his father died from liver cancer when Mr. Smith was age four. He reported that his family changed residences on three occasions when he was between the ages of 6 and 10. Mr. Smith reported that he has lived with his mother and several siblings in North Philadelphia since he entered fourth grade.

Mr. Smith described his childhood as "alright," but described having limited food and no electricity on several occasions. Ms. Smith reported being employed as an assistant teacher at a daycare center for 10 years. Ms. Smith reported that she and Mr. Smith began attending church on a regular basis in 1991, and she described having a close relationship with their pastor. When asked about a history of abuse, Mr. Smith reported that his mother administered "whoopings," but was not physically abusive. He denied any other abuse (psychological, sexual). When asked about neglect, Mr. Smith reported that his mother would occasionally leave him and his siblings with friends of the family "for days or weeks" when she was abusing drugs. Ms. Smith similarly reported that she "wasn't around much" when she was abusing drugs, and she confirmed that she has not used any drugs since Mr. Smith was age six.

Mr. Smith reported that he has never been married, but has one daughter, Sally Smith (age one). He reported that he and his daughter's mother, Ms. Natalie Jones, were in a relationship for two years before Sally was born, but ended their relationship immediately after Sally's birth because they "didn't see eye to eye." Ms. Jones reported that their relationship ended because Mr. Smith "changed...he was moody." Mr. Smith reported that Sally lives with Ms. Jones, and that he takes care of Sally (at his mother's house, where he currently lives) from Friday through Sunday. Mr. Smith reported that he and Ms. Jones have a civil relationship, but occasionally argue. Ms. Jones reported that she is planning to attend the police academy starting in August 2008.

Educational History

Mr. Smith reported that he graduated from Peterson Vocational High School in 2004. He reported attending the following schools: Apple Elementary School for Kindergarten through fourth grade, Skipper Elementary School for fifth grade, Watts Junior High School for sixth through eighth grades, and Peterson Vocational High School for ninth through twelfth grades. Mr. Smith described his academic performance as "good." He described earning "As and Bs" when he "applied myself," but acknowledged that he would "get off track real fast...I tried to be the class clown." He described occasionally receiving failing grades for some courses, particularly in high school, but noted that he never repeated a grade. Ms. Smith described Joseph as an "A student" who was occasionally on the "honor roll." Mr. Smith reported that he attended school every day, but "was late almost every single day." He attributed his chronic tardiness to "not being a morning person." Mr. Smith reported receiving the "worst behavior grades" and being suspended "15 to 20 times" for various infractions, including "fighting, talking back to teachers, not respecting authority figures...not going to detention." He reported that his detentions began in elementary school and his suspensions began in middle school. He denied ever being expelled from a school. Ms. Smith reported that Mr. Smith began displaying "erratic behavior" in tenth or eleventh grade, which she attributed to the negative effects of drug use and his peer group. Mr. Smith's official academic records were not available at the time this report was written.

Medical and Psychiatric History

As noted, Mr. Smith reported that he was born two months premature and drug-dependent due to his mother's abuse of drugs while she was pregnant. According to Ms. Smith, Mr. Smith sustained two broken legs at age six months when he was "accidentally dropped" by someone. Mr. Smith reported being struck by cars "five or six times" while playing basketball, but denied sustaining any serious injuries. He denied any history of serious illnesses or hospitalizations. He denied any significant family medical history.

Mr. Smith denied experiencing any mental health problems, being diagnosed with a mental health disorder, or receiving counseling or medications for mental health symptoms. He did not report experiencing any significant symptoms of a mood or anxiety disorder during the present evaluation, including any changes in his mood, appetite, or sleep. Mr. Smith denied any history of suicidal ideation or attempts. When asked about a family history of mental health problems, Mr. Smith reported that his maternal grandfather had Alzheimer's dementia. Ms. Smith reported that Mr. Smith has been "self-mutilating his feet" for the past three years. When questioned further, she reported that Mr. Smith "digs holes" on the bottoms of his feet with "any instrument...like a nail-clipper." Ms. Jones also reported that Mr. Smith "likes to dig in sores and pick off scabs" on his feet and other parts of his body.

Substance Abuse History

Mr. Smith reported heavy use of multiple drugs and alcohol, both historically and currently. He reported experimenting with marijuana at age 15, and then using it on a daily basis starting in eleventh grade. He reported smoking "15 blunts" per day for approximately four years, adding that a "light day" of marijuana use consisted of "7 to 8 blunts." Mr. Smith reported that he started using Xanax, Seroquel, and Percocet in 2004, and he acknowledged that he still uses those substances. He also reported that he recently began using PCP ("angel dust") with his marijuana. Mr. Smith also reported heavy use of alcohol. He stated that he began using alcohol on a regular basis when he was age 14, and he acknowledged using alcohol on a daily basis for the past two years. He reported that he drinks "anything," including vodka, beer, and cognac.

In terms of current use, Mr. Smith reported that he uses multiple drugs and alcohol on a daily basis. He reported abstaining from marijuana for approximately 15 months when he was under house arrest for the current offense, but resuming daily use of marijuana approximately three months ago. He described experiencing symptoms of withdrawal ("runny nose, watery eyes") after he discontinued using marijuana and pills while on house arrest. He reported smoking 15 blunts per day, noting that he most recently smoked marijuana two days before the current evaluation; he noted that he abstained from smoking marijuana for two days before the evaluation because he wanted to be able to participate meaningfully in the evaluation and because he has "the flu." In addition to using marijuana at the present time, Mr. Smith reported that he still uses Xanax, Seroquel, Percocet, and PCP on a regular basis. Finally, Mr. Smith reported using alcohol on a daily basis for the past two years, but abstaining from drinking alcohol for the two days preceding this evaluation for the same reasons he abstained from marijuana. Mr. Smith denied ever receiving treatment for his drug or alcohol use. Although he denied having a problem with drugs or alcohol, he acknowledged that he "could use some help" to reduce his use of those substances.

Social History

Mr. Smith reported having six close friends and several "associates." He described his current friends as "not a negative influence," adding that he and his friends enjoy playing basketball and "chilling." He denied ever being part of a gang. Mr. Smith reported that he has been involved in 15 physical altercations over "arguments, playing basketball, and money." Ms. Smith described Mr. Smith's friends as a negative influence on him because they introduced him to drugs and influence him in making "bad decisions."

Occupational History

Mr. Smith reported a lengthy history of employment beginning at age 15. He reported working at a summer camp, a McDonald's restaurant, a grocery store, and a cleaning company. Although Mr. Smith initially denied ever being fired from a job, he later reported that he was fired from the cleaning company due to poor attendance. Mr. Smith reported that he was most recently employed at XYZ Corp., which makes plastic cups, for 14 months. He reported that he ended his employment at XYZ six weeks ago in anticipation of being taken into custody for the current offense. Mr. Smith reported that he obtained money during the previous six weeks by working side jobs, such as "construction and cutting grass." Mr. Smith reported that his occupational goal is to become an "entrepreneur," own a construction company, and support a family.

Offense History

Mr. Smith reported being arrested three times, including the current offense. He reported that his first arrest occurred at age 18 when he was charged with carrying a firearm without a license; he stated that the case was eventually "thrown out." Mr. Smith reported that his arrest for the current offense at age 19 was his second arrest. Finally, he reported that his third arrest occurred at age 20 when he was charged with "a high-speed chase…reckless endangerment," and he reported being found "not guilty" of those offenses. He denied any history of juvenile arrests. Mr. Smith's official arrest history was not available at the time this report was written. Mr. Smith was also asked about the role of drugs and alcohol vis-à-vis his criminal activity. He reported being "under the influence" of drugs and/or alcohol during the commission of all three offenses that led to arrests. He also reported "never thinking rational" when he is using drugs.

CURRENT CLINICAL CONDITION

Mr. Smith presented as an African-American male of average height and medium build who appeared his stated age. He failed to show for the initial date of the evaluation (6/26), reportedly due to a scheduling conflict related to his daughter, which led to the evaluation being rescheduled for June 30, 2008. Mr. Smith arrived over one hour early for the evaluation. He was casually dressed and well-groomed. Mr. Smith reported having eight tattoos: his name ("Walt") on his right arm, the initials "FR" (for Fern Rock) on his right arm, the phrase "Thug Now, Chill Later" on his right arm, a tombstone in memory of his father on his left arm, boxing gloves on his left arm, his daughter's name on his neck, the name of his daughter's mother on his neck, and his mother's name on his chest. He was cooperative and polite throughout the evaluation. His speech was clear, coherent, and relevant. He appeared to give reasonable effort to the tasks involved. Mr. Smith's capacity for attention and concentration appeared adequate, and he was able to focus reasonably well on a series of tasks during the four-hour-and-fifteen-minute evaluation without becoming visibly distracted or fatigued. Therefore, it appears that this evaluation provides a reasonably good estimate of Mr. Smith's current functioning.

Mr. Smith's mood throughout the evaluation was largely subdued and neutral, but he showed appropriate emotional variability. He was correctly oriented to time, place, and person. He did not report experiencing any perceptual disturbances (auditory or visual hallucinations) or delusions (bizarre ideas with no possible basis in reality) during the present evaluation, and his train of thought was clear and logical.

Wide Range Achievement Test, 3rd ed. (WRAT-3)

On a test of his basic academic skills, Mr. Smith displayed deficits in two of the three areas measured (as reflected by his grade equivalency scores): Reading (high school equivalent), Spelling (grade 5 equivalent), and Arithmetic (grade 6 equivalent). These results suggest that his spelling and arithmetic skills are under-developed (compared to others his age), and both areas should be considered in need of remediation.

Wechsler Abbreviated Scale of Intelligence (WASI)

Mr. Smith's intellectual functioning was formally measured with the WASI. Mr. Smith obtained a Full Scale IQ score of 90, which places him within the Average range of intellectual functioning and at the 25th percentile relative to others his age (meaning that he obtained an IQ score equal to or higher than 25% of similarly aged individuals). Given the measurement error on the WASI, there is a 95% likelihood that his Full Scale IQ score is between 86 and 94 (Average range). His Verbal IQ score was 92 (30th percentile) and his Performance IQ score was 90 (25th percentile); his Verbal and Performance IQ scores fall within the Average range of functioning.

Brief Symptom Inventory (BSI)

Mr. Smith completed two versions of a structured inventory of symptoms of mental and emotional disorders, one concerning his present functioning (discussed here) and the second describing his thoughts and feelings around the time of the incident (February 2006) for which he is currently facing sentencing (discussed later). He reported being "quite a bit" or "extremely" bothered by 5 of the 53 items on the BSI. Those items were "feeling nervousness or shakiness inside" (due to his present legal situation), "feeling lonely even when he is with people" (because "people are not going through what I'm going through"), "feeling blue" (because he anticipates that he will be taken into custody in the near future and will not be able to spend time with his family), "feeling no interest in things" ("like sex," due to anxiety about his current legal situation), and "feelings of guilt" (because he committed the current offense and will not be able to spend time with his daughter once he is sentenced to prison).

Level of Service Inventory-Revised (LSI-R)

On the LSI-R, Mr. Smith scored in the low/moderate risk/needs category (raw score = 23). A score within this range is associated with a 31% chance of recidivism (defined as re-incarceration within one year of release from incarceration) among individuals who are returned to the community following a period of incarceration. In addition, approximately 41% of prison inmates scored lower than Mr. Smith on the LSI-R. Mr. Smith endorsed problems in the following areas assessed by the LSI-R: Employment (because he is not employed at the present time), Family/Marital (due to reported discord with the mother of his daughter), Companions (because several members of his peer group have engaged in criminal behavior), and Alcohol/Drug Problem (due to his heavy use of drugs and alcohol historically and currently).

Minnesota Multiphasic Personality Inventory, 2nd ed. (MMPI-2)

Mr. Smith was administered the MMPI-2 to measure his current personality functioning. Each item was read to him to facilitate appropriate item comprehension. Although Mr. Smith attempted to present himself in a favorable light by minimizing any problems he might have been experiencing, the resulting MMPI-2 profile (Welsh Code: 4'8+6-71392/0# KL-/F:) was marginally valid. It is possible, however, that the resulting profile underestimates any problems he may be experiencing. Mr. Smith's MMPI-2 profile suggests that he may behave unpredictably and engage in impulsive and antisocial behaviors; his MMPI-2 profile reveals a pattern of disinhibition associated with risk-taking and impulsive behaviors. He obtained an elevated score on the MMPI-2 Addiction Acknowledgement Scale, which suggests that he openly acknowledged having a substance-use problem (although he denied having a substance-use problem during the clinical interview portion of this evaluation). His profile also suggests that he may abuse licit drugs, which is consistent with his self-reported abuse of Xanax, Seroquel, and Percocet.

TREATMENT NEEDS AND AMENABILITY

There are three areas in which Mr. Smith has treatment/rehabilitation needs, which, if addressed, should serve to reduce his risk for future antisocial behavior. These areas are: (1) treatment for substance abuse; (2) skills-based training in impulse control and decision-making; and (3) the development of a more pro-social social support network.

First, Mr. Smith would benefit from substance abuse treatment. He described heavy use of multiple drugs and alcohol, both historically and currently. He reported daily use of marijuana beginning in eleventh grade and lasting four years, noting that he smoked 15 blunts per day during that time. He reported that he began abusing Xanax, Seroquel, and Percocet in 2004, and recently began using

PCP. In addition, Mr. Smith reported that he began using alcohol on a regular basis at age 14. When asked about his current use of drugs and alcohol, Mr. Smith reported that he has been smoking marijuana on daily basis for the past three months, using prescription pills on a regular basis, and drinking alcohol on a daily basis for the past two years. As such, Mr. Smith would benefit from substance-abuse treatment. Treatment in this area may be particularly important because Mr. Smith reported being under the influence of drugs and/or alcohol during all of his previous offenses. Furthermore, both he and Ms. Smith acknowledged that his drug use leads to irrational thinking. Ms. Smith stated that Mr. Smith's use of drugs "clogged his decision-making [and] clouded him from seeing the consequences of his actions." Given the length and severity of Mr. Smith's use of drugs and alcohol, and his family history of substance use, any intervention should include a relapse prevention component. If Mr. Smith is able to avoid further drug use, his risk of engaging in future antisocial behavior should be reduced.

Second, Mr. Smith would benefit from skills-based training in impulse control and decision-making. He acknowledged a long history of acting impulsively and making poor decisions. He reported that all of his arrests have resulted from a combination of substance use, "not thinking," and "making bad decisions." He acknowledged that he often does not consider the consequences of his actions, which has further contributed to his poor decision-making. Furthermore, Ms. Smith describing Mr. Smith as having "an inability to make good decisions." As such, Mr. Smith would benefit from skills-based training designed to help him reduce his impulsiveness and make better decisions. His rehabilitation should include exposure to interventions designed to improve his ability to recognize and avoid "high-risk" situations that have historically resulted in criminal activity. Training in these areas is directly relevant to Mr. Smith's risk for future anti-social behavior, and participating in such interventions should decrease his risk for future offending.

Finally, Mr. Smith would benefit from developing a more pro-social social support network. Although Mr. Smith maintained that his present friends are a "good influence" on him, he acknowledged using drugs and engaging in criminal activity with his friends. Moreover, Ms. Smith reported that Mr. Smith's friends are a negative influence on him because they influence him to make "bad decisions." As such, Mr. Smith would benefit from distancing himself from negative peers and developing more positive, pro-social peer relationships. If Mr. Smith can develop positive, pro-social peer relationships, his risk for antisocial behavior should be significantly reduced.

SENTENCING CONSIDERATIONS

Pursuant to *United States v. Booker* (2005), the information contained in the previous sections may be relevant, and the information contained in this section is relevant but advisory, in the matter of Mr. Smith's sentencing.

U.S.S.G. section 5K2.13 (18 U.S.C.) provides:

> A downward departure may be warranted if (1) the defendant committed the offense while suffering from a significantly reduced mental capacity; and (2) the significantly reduced mental capacity contributed substantially to the commission of the offense. Similarly, if a departure is warranted under this policy statement, the extent of the departure should reflect the extent to which the reduced mental capacity contributed to the commission of the offense. However, the court may not depart below the applicable guideline range if (1) the significantly reduced mental capacity was caused by the voluntary use of drugs or other intoxicants; (2) the fact and circumstances of the defendant's offense indicate a need to protect the public because the offense involved actual violence or a serious threat of violence; (3) the defendant's criminal history indicates a need to incarcerate the defendant to protect the public; or (4) the defendant has been convicted of an offense under Chapter 71, 109A, 110, or 117, of Title 18, United States Code.

A. Violence of Offense, Need to Protect the Public, and Nature of Prior Convictions

Whether Mr. Smith's current offense involved actual violence or a serious threat of violence, whether his criminal history indicates a need to incarcerate him to protect the public, and whether he has been convicted of an offense under Chapter 71, 109A, 110, or 117, of Title 18, United States Code, are questions of law and, therefore, cannot be appropriately addressed by this forensic mental health evaluation.

B. Significantly Reduced Mental Capacity Not Resulting from the Voluntary Use of Drugs or Other Intoxicants

Mr. Smith reported that he had been smoking marijuana and drinking alcohol on the day of the offense, and he described himself as "drunk" and "under the influence" at the time of the offense. Specifically, Mr. Smith reported smoking several blunts while in the car immediately before the offense took place. He also reported that he and his friends consumed "two fifths" of vodka (i.e., 750 mL/bottle) several hours before the offense. This pattern of use is consistent with information provided by Mr. Smith regarding his use of drugs and alcohol at that point in his life.

According to the Application Note of § 5K2.13, "significantly reduced mental capacity" means the defendant, although convicted, has significantly impaired ability to:

(1) Understand the wrongfulness of the behavior comprising the offense or to exercise the power of reason; or

(2) Control the behavior that the defendant knows is wrongful.

MENTAL STATE AT THE TIME OF THE OFFENSE

Mr. Smith was able to provide a detailed and coherent description of the current offense and the events leading up to the current offense. He reported that the offense took place on February 2, 2006, when he was age 19. According to Mr. Smith, at the time of the offense, he was living with his mother in North Philadelphia, no longer in school (because he graduated from Peterson Vocational High School in 2004), and had recently been fired from a cleaning job. He reported that his daughter was born several months before the offense. He also reported that one of his friends had recently been shot and killed by drug dealers. As previously noted, Mr. Smith reported that he was smoking marijuana and using alcohol on a daily basis at this point in his life, and he was also abusing Xanax, Seroquel, and Percocet.

Mr. Smith reported that he woke up at 11:30 a.m. on the day of the offense. He did not recall any particular activities, but reported that he and his friends were using drugs and drinking alcohol. According to Mr. Smith, he and his co-defendants developed a plan to rob the XYZ store several days before the offense took place. He reported being confident that they would not be apprehended for the offense because he and the other co-defendants had previously worked at this XYZ store and were familiar with the location of the money and security system. In particular, Mr. Smith stated that he knew that the security cameras in the XYZ store did not record material, despite posted warnings to the contrary.

Mr. Smith reported that the offense took place at 10:50 p.m. on February 2, 2006. He reported that they entered the XYZ store shortly before the store closed at 11:00 p.m. because they knew the money would be transferred to the office. Mr. Smith reported that he was dressed in black pants, black jacket, black gloves, and a black hat, adding that he pulled his hat down low to obscure his appearance. He acknowledged carrying a .25 caliber handgun when he entered the store. Mr. Smith reported that he and the co-defendants staggered their entrances into the store because they were concerned they would arouse suspicion if they all entered the store at the same time. Mr. Smith reported that there were two employees and one manager in the store, but no customers. He stated that he remained at the front of the store, one co-defendant went to the back of the store, and the other co-defendant went into the office with the store manager to get money.

According to Mr. Smith, after one employee ran out of the store, he told his co-defendants to exit the store because he suspected the employee would alert the police. Mr. Smith reported that he and one co-defendant left the store, but that the other co-defendant was in the back office trying to get money from the store manager. According to Mr. Smith, the whole incident lasted 2–3 minutes. Mr. Smith reported that the employee who left the store flagged down a passing police patrol car, and the police officers immediately pulled their guns and demanded that Mr. Smith and his co-defendant surrender. Mr. Smith stated his co-defendant immediately surrendered, but that he ran from the police, threw his gun in a sewer, and was caught by the police approximately 90 seconds after he fled. Mr. Smith reported that he subsequently vomited while in the back of the police car due to the amount of alcohol he had consumed that day.

To assess Mr. Smith's mental and emotional functioning around the time of the offense, he was asked to complete another Brief Symptoms Inventory (BSI) for the time period immediately surrounding February 2, 2006. He reported being "extremely bothered" by one of the 53 items: difficulty making decisions (noting he has "always had trouble making decisions"). He reported being "a little bit" bothered by two of the 53 items: nervousness or shakiness inside (due to the recent birth of his daughter), and feeling blue (due to the recent death of his friend).

When Mr. Smith was asked about his state of mind around the time of the offense, he described himself as "a little depressed" over the recent death of his friend and the recent termination of his employment. He also described himself as "desperate" because he needed "fast money," which he reportedly planned to use to buy drugs, support his daughter, and make a financial donation to the grandmother of his deceased friend. As previously noted, Mr. Smith also reported that he was "drunk" (from alcohol) and "under the influence" (of marijuana) at the time of the offense, and he acknowledged "not thinking rationally" due to his substance use.

Ms. Smith reported that she did not notice any significant changes in Mr. Smith's behavior immediately before the offense took place. She reported that he "didn't want to go to church as much [and] didn't do as much around the house," but she did not describe any notable changes in his psychological functioning. According to Ms. Smith, the biggest contributing influence was "him and his friends making bad decisions." She reported that Mr. Smith "couldn't say 'no' [to his friends] and didn't want to be labeled a chump."

There is no reason to believe Mr. Smith suffered from an inability to understand the wrongfulness of his behavior or to control behavior that he knew was wrongful around the time of the offense. Although Mr. Smith may have been "a little depressed" over recent events (i.e., death of his friend and losing his job), there is no indication that any aspect of his mental and emotional functioning impaired his capacity to understand the wrongfulness of his behavior or conform his behaviors to the requirements of the law. Based on Mr. Smith's self-report, it appears that the primary influence on his behavior was his need for money, which he planned to use to buy drugs, support his daughter, and donate money to the grandmother of his deceased friend. Although his desire to obtain money appears to be the overriding impetus for the current offense, his heavy drug and alcohol use,

lack of impulse control, and tendency to make poor decisions (which are personality characteristics supported by Mr. Smith's self-report, his MMPI-2 profile, and information obtained from Ms. Smith) were likely to have influenced his behavior, and it is possible that these factors affected his ability to exercise the power of reason.

CONCLUSION

In the opinion of the undersigned, based on all of the above:

(1) There is nothing to suggest that Mr. Smith's ability to understand the wrongfulness of his behavior was impaired at the time of the offense, although his heavy use of drugs and alcohol, desire for money, poor impulse control, and poor decision-making skills may have affected his ability to exercise the power of reason;

(2) There is nothing to suggest that Mr. Smith's ability to control behavior that he knew was wrongful was impaired at the time of the alleged offense;

(3) Mr. Smith has treatment/rehabilitation needs in the areas of substance abuse, impulse control and decision-making, and his social support network.

Thank you for the opportunity to evaluate Joseph Smith, Jr.

David DeMatteo, JD, PhD
Consulting Psychologist

TEACHING POINT:
RISK-NEED ASSESSMENT IN SENTENCING

After the United States Supreme Court's decision in *United States v. Booker* (2005), which held that the Federal Sentencing Guidelines were advisory but not mandatory, referral questions from defense attorneys in the context of federal sentencing evaluations could be much broader. Rather than limiting the scope of the sentencing evaluation to the 5K2 criteria of the defendant's abilities to understand the wrongfulness of his or her behavior and control behavior the defendant knows is wrong, post-*Booker* sentencing evaluations could broadly assess a criminal offender's risk for future offending and criminogenic needs across multiple domains. As such, measures that assess offender risks and needs have obvious relevance in sentencing evaluations.

There is a variety of risk-needs measures for adults, but the Level of Service (LS) measures—including the Level of Service Invention–Revised (LSI-R) and Level of Service/Case Management Inventory (LS/CMI)—are among the most widely used. The risk-need component of the LS measures is actuarially based to predict general recidivism (using the "Central 8" risk factors), and the LS/CMI also facilitates the development of an appropriate treatment/rehabilitation plan (based on the Risk-Need-Responsivity model; Andrews & Bonta, 1998). In the context of a sentencing evaluation, in which a court may often consider factors relating to the defendant's recidivism risk and treatment/rehabilitation needs, the use of a risk-needs measure such as the LS/CMI provides useful information to the decision-maker. The information used to arrive at the General Risk/Need score (which forms the basis for the recidivism estimate on the LS measures) and other items on the LS/CMI allow for consideration of various aspects of the defendant's history, and the identification of dynamic risk factors provides important targets for intervention with the goal of reducing the likelihood of re-offending.

7

Capital Sentencing

This chapter contains two case reports on criminal sentencing. Although FMHA on criminal sentencing may be conducted for a variety of charges (see Chapter 6, this volume, for examples of a federal criminal sentencing evaluation), both reports in this chapter are capital sentencing evaluations. Such evaluations are among the most detailed and demanding assessments performed by forensic practitioners. The principle applied to the first case involves the importance of utilizing multiple sources of information in FMHA, particularly given the accidental or purposeful inaccuracy or bias of single pieces of information in cases as complex as capital sentencing. This complexity can also mean that evaluators can easily become overwhelmed with information in these cases, so the teaching point for this principle focuses on maximizing the efficiency of data collection—using the economic concept of the "point of diminishing returns"—to help determine when enough information has been collected. The principle regarding the importance of history is applied to the second case, reflecting the particular relevance of historical information on defendants undergoing capital sentencing evaluations. The teaching point addresses the accuracy of different sources of third-party information that contribute to the development of an appropriately comprehensive history in this kind of FMHA.

relevant to the legal questions in FMHA, and the importance of using information from more than one source. These sources typically include the formal evaluation conducted by the forensic clinician; conversations with individuals who know the individual being evaluated, such as family members, friends, and current and former treatment providers; and collateral documents obtained through discovery or specifically requested by the forensic evaluator. During the evaluation and report-writing phases of FMHA, forensic clinicians are encouraged to identify important gaps in the information provided and actively seek information to better inform these areas (Heilbrun, Grisso, & Goldstein, 2009).

The use of multiple sources of information in FMHA is important for several reasons. First, multiple measures enhance accuracy in measuring a given trait, symptom, or behavior by reducing the error that can be associated with a single source of information. Second, multiple measures allow the evaluator to test rival hypotheses of behavior that may have been generated, in part, by observations stemming from one or more of the measures. Independently obtained information on a second measure about the same construct can be used to support (or refute) hypotheses that may have been generated by the results of the first measure. Finally, multiple measures allow the forensic clinician to assess the consistency of data across sources and attempt to corroborate particularly important data before reaching conclusions that are being considered in the course of performing a FMHA.

Support from this principle come from several sources of authority. The *Ethical Principles of Psychologists and Code of Conduct* (APA *Ethics Code*; American Psychological Association, 2010a) notes that psychologists base their opinions resulting from assessment, including their forensic testimony, "on information and techniques sufficient to substantiate their findings," and "only after they

CASE ONE
PRINCIPLE: USE MULTIPLE SOURCES OF INFORMATION FOR EACH AREA BEING ASSESSED. REVIEW THE AVAILABLE BACKGROUND INFORMATION AND ACTIVELY SEEK IMPORTANT MISSING ELEMENTS.
(*PRINCIPLE 17*)

This principle concerns the sources of information to be used in assessing the forensic issues that are have conducted an examination of the individuals adequate to support their statements or conclusions" (Standard 9.01). This should include a thorough review of all records that may better inform their interpretation of the data available and their ultimate opinions and judgments. The *Specialty Guidelines for Forensic Psychology* (APA *Specialty Guidelines*; American Psychological Association, 2013b) addresses this principle directly by emphasizing that forensic practitioners "seek to maintain integrity by examining the issue or problem at hand from all reasonable perspectives and seek information that will differentially test plausible rival hypotheses" (Guideline 9.01). The APA *Specialty Guidelines* further state that:

> Forensic practitioners ordinarily avoid relying solely on one source of data, and corroborate important data whenever feasible. When relying upon data that have not been corroborated, forensic practitioners seek to make known the uncorroborated status of the data, any associated strengths and limitations, and the reasons for relying upon the data. (Guideline 9.02)

Finally, although the *Principles of Medical Ethics with Annotations Especially Applicable for Psychiatry* (ApA *Principles of Medical Ethics with Annotations*; American Psychiatric Association, 2013b) does not address this principle, the *Ethics Guidelines for the Practice of Forensic Psychiatry* (AAPL *Ethics Guidelines*; American Academy of Psychiatry and the Law, 2005) indicates that psychiatrists undertaking forensic roles "enhance the honesty and objectivity of their work by basing their forensic opinions, forensic reports and forensic testimony on all available data" (p. 3).

Legal sources of authority generally indicate that legal opinions should be based on relevant comprehensive methods, with some important caveats. Specifically, the Federal Rules of Evidence require that an expert opinion to be based "on sufficient facts or data" (FRE 702), further indicating that "An expert may base an opinion on facts or data in the case that the expert has been made aware of or personally observed" (FRE 703). Thus, the evaluator's opinion may be based on information from a variety of sources, each of which can differentially influence the admissibility of this evidence in the eyes of the law:

If experts in the particular field would reasonably rely on those kinds of facts or data in forming an opinion on the subject, they need not be admissible for the opinion to be admitted. But if the facts or data would otherwise be inadmissible, the proponent of the opinion may disclose them to the jury only if their probative value in helping the jury evaluate the opinion substantially outweighs their prejudicial effect. (FRE 703)

Although experts are not required to testify individually to each underlying fact or datum used to formulate their expert opinion, they must be prepared to do so if requested (i.e., during cross-examination; FRE 705). This is particularly relevant in the use of third party information, which the law may consider as "hearsay." The inclusion of collateral information in FMHA is considered to be common practice—the type of information that experts "reasonably rely on" in reaching opinions—but recent case law (*People v. Goldstein*, 2005) suggests that forensic practitioners should be prepared to explain the rationale behind their use of collateral information as part of their forensic testimony (see Chapter 10, this volume, for a discussion of incorporating third party information into evaluation of response style).

The professional literature clearly supports basing forensic opinions on multiple sources of information as an established aspect of FMHA (Melton, Petrila, Poythress, & Slobogin, 2007). In *Specialty Competencies in Forensic Psychology* (Packer & Grisso, 2011), the authors note that it is rare to have forensic practitioners base their opinions solely on clinical interviews with the individuals being evaluated. Furthermore, they emphasize standardized measurement, collateral records, and collateral informants as important additional sources of information in FMHA: "The practice of obtaining information from this variety of sources is fairly standard practice across areas of forensic assessment" (p. 77). Although they also address the admissibility of collateral information in FMHA, it is to suggest that this practice is largely supported by the field—and that recent restrictive case law (e.g., *People v. Goldstein*, 2005) should not deter the forensic practitioners from seeking collateral information from a variety of sources.

The present case provides an illustration of the importance of obtaining and incorporating multiple sources of information. The forensic clinician in this case was retained at the request of defense counsel regarding mitigation of the death penalty. The defendant, Mr. Dawkins, was preparing for trial on two counts of murder. Capital cases provide perhaps the broadest focus for the forensic clinician conducting FMHA: not only are there enumerated aggravating and mitigating circumstances in capital jurisdictions, but there is often a "catch-all" mitigator describing any other aspect of the defendant's life (not specified in earlier mitigating factors) that might be relevant. With such a broad focus, there are far fewer limitations imposed by relevance than is usually seen in FMHA.

In such cases, there should be a great deal of historical and offense-related information obtained. This comes both from records and collateral interviews. If there is a mitigation specialist also working on the case (for defense referrals), then the forensic clinician has another extremely valuable source of historical information to consider. In the present case, there were several collaterals interviewed and numerous records reviewed. In addition, there were psychological tests, a specialized risk-need measure (i.e., the LSI-R), and two clinical interviews administered. These different sources of information offer a basis for considering information from multiple sources as part of this evaluation.

Forensic Evaluation
October 9, 2008
Re: David Dawkins
PP#: 123456

REFERRAL INFORMATION

David Dawkins is a 49-year-old African American male (D.O.B.: 11/1/58) who is charged with two counts of murder, carrying firearms in public street/place, possession of instruments of a crime, and carrying firearms without a license. Mr. Dawkins's attorney (Darnell Baker, Esq.) requested a mental health evaluation to provide the defense with information, pursuant to 42 Pa. C.S.A. § 9711(e), relevant to capital sentencing.

PROCEDURES

Mr. Dawkins was evaluated for a total of approximately five hours on September 7, 2007, and two and a half hours on September 12, 2007, at the City Jail. In addition to a clinical interview, Mr. Dawkins was administered a standard screening instrument for symptoms of mental and emotional disorder experienced both currently and at the time of the offense (the Brief Symptom Inventory, or BSI), a standard objective measure of risks and needs information relevant to offender treatment planning and assigning levels of freedom and supervision (the Level of Service Inventory–Revised, or LSI-R), a standard test of current functioning in relevant academic areas (the Wide Range Achievement Test, 4th edition, or WRAT-4), a measure of overall intellectual functioning (the Wechsler Adult Intelligence Scale—3rd edition, or WAIS-III), and a standard measure of adult psychopathology and personality functioning (the Minnesota Multiphasic Personality Inventory, 2nd edition, or MMPI-2).

Collateral interviews were conducted with Mr. Dawkins's wife, Anna Jeffers, his daughter, Mary Jackson, and his former employer, Deanna Simmons. Anna Jeffers was interviewed for approximately forty minutes on October 7, 2007. Mary Jackson was interviewed for approximately thirty minutes and Deanna Simmons was interviewed for approximately twenty minutes on September 18, 2007. Efforts were made to contact Mr. Dawkins's long-time friend, James Peters, twice on September 18, 2007. Contact was made with James Peters on the morning of October 5, 2007. He was unable to be interviewed at that time, but agreed to be interviewed that evening at 7:00 p.m. However, he did not answer the phone at 7:00 p.m. on October 5, 2007, or at 7:30 p.m., when another attempt was made to contact him.

The following documents, obtained from Mr. Baker's office, were reviewed as part of the evaluation:

(1) County pre-sentence and mental health reports (illegible) (dated 4/26/79)
(2) State parole records (dated 8/17/88 to 4/28/08)
(3) Prison Report of Psychological Evaluation (dated 5/10/96)
(4) Prison psychological evaluation for parole (dated 5/21/97)
(5) Prison social services records (dated 6/17/98 to 9/18/08)
(6) Pennsylvania Department of Corrections Classification Summary (dated 6/18/01)

(7) Prison State Parole Psychological Evaluation (dated 6/22/01)

(8) Criminal history record (dated 7/12/01)

(9) Report of Psychological Evaluation (dated 9/20/01)

(10) Parolee risk assessments (dated 1/18/02 to 5/28/04)

(11) Witness statement from Witness 1 (dated 1/18/06)

(12) Witness statement from Witness 2 (dated 1/18/06)

(13) Witness statement from Witness 3 (dated 1/18/06)

(14) Witness statement from Witness 4 (dated 1/18/06)

(15) Witness statement from Witness 5 (dated 1/18/06)

(16) Witness statement from Witness 6 (dated 1/18/06)

(17) Witness statement from Witness 7 (dated 1/18/06)

(18) Statement from Officer 1 (dated 1/18/06)

(19) Statement from Officer 2 (dated 1/20/06)

(20) Statement from Officer 3 (dated 1/18/06)

(21) Statement from Officer 4 (dated 1/18/06)

(22) Autopsy report of Max Charles (dated 1/18/06)

(23) Autopsy report of Norris Jenkins (dated 1/18/06)

(24) Property receipts of property taken from crime scene (dated 1/18/06)

(25) Policy Activity Sheets (dated 1/18/06 to 11/07/06)

(26) Crime Scene Log (dated 1/18/06)

(27) Crime Scene Investigation Report (dated 1/18/06)

(28) Crime scene photographs (dated 1/18/06)

(29) Incident Report (dated 1/18/06)

(30) Investigation Report (dated 1/18/06)

(31) Search Warrant (dated 1/18/06)

(32) Affidavit of Probable Cause (dated 1/18/06)

(33) Arrest Warrant (dated 1/18/06)

(34) Attempt to Apprehend log (dated 1/19/06)

(35) Property receipts of property taken from Medical Examiner's Office (dated 1/19/06)

(36) Wanted poster (dated 1/19/06)

(37) Request cancellation of bolo alert on Chevrolet van (dated 4/28/06)

(38) Arrest Warrant (dated 11/07/06)

(39) Arrest Biographical Information Report (dated 11/07/06)

(40) Arrest Transport Report (dated 11/07/06)

(41) County criminal docket (dated 11/8/06 to 4/24/08)

(42) County prison health records (dated 11/9/06 to 9/11/08)

(43) Department of Education GED transcript (dated 12/14/06)

(44) Court records (dated 2/12/88 to 5/11/07)

(45) Prison records (dated 11/8/06 to 9/15/08, and undated)

(46) Court History (dated 6/4/07)

(47) Ballistics reports (dated 7/28/08 and 7/29/08)

(48) Preliminary hearing transcript (dated 5/16/07)

(49) Mitigation report, Joanne Morris, MA (dated 10/1/08)

(50) Life history statement, David Dawkins (undated)

(51) School records

Prior to the evaluation, Mr. Dawkins was notified about its purpose and the associated limits of confidentiality. He appeared to understand the purpose, reporting back his understanding that he would be evaluated and that a written report would be submitted to his attorney. He further understood that the report could be used in the sentencing hearing, and, if it were, copies would be provided to the prosecution and the court. In addition, Anna Jeffers, Mary Jackson, and Deanna Simmons were also notified of the purpose of the evaluation and agreed to be interviewed.

RELEVANT HISTORY

Historical information was obtained from the collateral sources described earlier, as well as from Mr. Dawkins himself. Whenever possible, we have assessed the consistency of self-reported information with that obtained from collateral sources. If additional information is obtained prior to Mr. Dawkins's hearing, a supplemental report will be filed.

Family History

Mr. Dawkins was born in Baltimore, and he resided there until he was two, when he moved to live with an aunt and uncle in Norristown. Mr. Dawkins's life history statement indicated that he lived with his aunt and uncle for approximately two years before his mother and siblings moved to Norristown. According to his wife, Anna Jeffers, Mr. Dawkins's family moved to Norristown when he was between the ages of four and six. Mr. Dawkins reported in his life history statement that when his mother moved to Norristown he had some difficulty adjusting to the idea that his aunt was not his mother. According to Mr. Dawkins, he is the youngest of five children. However, his wife and his daughter both reported that he is the youngest of seven children. Ms. Jeffers stated that Mr. Dawkins's oldest two sisters have a different father than the rest of the children in the family. According to Ms. Jeffers, Mr. Dawkins's mother left her oldest two daughters in Baltimore with their father when she moved with Mr. Dawkins's father and the other children to Norristown. Ms. Jeffers reported that Mr. Dawkins's mother did not have contact with her oldest two children for many years after she left them in Baltimore. She noted that Mr. Dawkins told her that his mother used to cry about leaving her children behind.

Mr. Dawkins reported that he was raised by his parents until the age of 10, when his parents separated. In his life history statement, Mr. Dawkins reported that his father moved to Norristown when Mr. Dawkins was approximately 10 years old. Mr. Dawkins noted that his mother and father argued verbally, but not physically. Ms. Jeffers stated that Mr. Dawkins's father "just left" Ms. Dawkins and the children; after he left them he had contact with Mr. Dawkins "whenever he came around." Regarding Mr. Dawkins's reaction to his father's departure, Ms. Jeffers stated, "I think he took it hard, being the youngest in the family." In his life history statement, Mr. Dawkins reported that he did not "remember feeling one way or another" about his father leaving because "we lived without him before." Both Mr. Dawkins and Ms. Jeffers reported that Mr. Dawkins's mother began drinking after Mr. Dawkins's father left the home. Ms. Jeffers stated that his mother "drank a lot," and Mr. Dawkins reported that his mother would drink after work and then go to sleep. About Mr. Dawkins's mother's drinking, Ms. Jeffers noted, "It started when the dad left, but when he got older, it got heavier and heavier and heavier...then she lost her job, it got heavier." Ms. Jeffers stated that Mr. Dawkins's brother also drank "a lot."

According to Mr. Dawkins, he grew up in a "strict household...I couldn't venture off the block." He added that he "came home from school, cleaned, (and) did school work." He indicated that since he is the youngest, he "had four people to watch (him)." Deanna Simmons, Mr. Dawkins's former employer, stated that from what Mr. Dawkins told her, "his mother was strict...she didn't throw no punches." Mr. Dawkins noted that his mother was the disciplinarian, and she used her "hands, (a) belt, (and a) broom" to discipline him. However, he added, his father never hit him or his siblings. Mr. Dawkins admitted that the way he was disciplined by his mother would probably be considered physical abuse by today's standards. His wife also stated that physical abuse "may have been possible" since his mom "worked a lot and the older kids watched him a lot." Both Mr. Dawkins and Ms. Jeffers stated that Mr. Dawkins had not suffered from any sexual abuse. Mr. Dawkins's school records from 1976, when he was in tenth grade, note "general family conditions are extremely disoriented...parents separated and other siblings have severe problems."

Mr. Dawkins stated that he got along well with his sisters when he was growing up, but he fought with his brother, who is three years older, "all the time." Mr. Dawkins reported that his youngest sister "has some damage from LSD," and she began receiving treatment at the age of 17. Ms. Jeffers and Mr. Dawkins's daughter, Mary Jackson, both stated that Mr. Dawkins's sister suffers from paranoid schizophrenia. During his state parole psychological evaluation in June 2001, Mr. Dawkins also reported that his sister was diagnosed with paranoid schizophrenia. Ms. Jeffers added that Mr. Dawkins was a teenager when his sister first started showing signs of mental illness and had to be involuntarily admitted into a psychiatric hospital. She reported that this "really got to him." Although the family did not have contact with the two oldest siblings for many years after they were left in Baltimore, Ms. Jeffers reported that the family later regained contact with the oldest siblings when Mr. Dawkins was in his thirties. While Ms. Jeffers at first stated that Mr. Dawkins has "no contact" with his siblings, who all live in Norristown, she later noted that they see his brother "when he pops up." Regarding the sister who suffers from schizophrenia, Ms. Jeffers stated, "We see her when she sees us. We know she doesn't like pop-up visits." According to Ms. Jeffers, one of Mr. Dawkins's sisters is deceased, and another of his sisters moved—Mr. Dawkins never received her new address to keep in contact with her. Mr. Dawkins reported that he does not have much contact with his extended family (aunts, uncles, cousins).

Mr. Dawkins characterized his relationship with his mother as "good." He noted that he usually listened to what his mother had to say because "usually she was right." Mr. Dawkins's daughter noted that he was "the baby" of the family and that she "heard stories about him being spoiled, being a momma's boy." She added that she thought he tried to "fight the image (of being a momma's boy) by being rough on the street." Ms. Simmons reported that Mr. Dawkins had a "loving mother" and he "talked about his mother a lot." Ms. Simmons added, "He talked about how good she was and she raised him by herself." Mr. Dawkins reported that his mother died in February of 1997 and his father died in February 1990. Mr. Dawkins's daughter, Ms. Jackson, noted that Mr. Dawkins was incarcerated when his mother died. She noted, "I know that he was really close to his mother and the fact that she passed away when he was incarcerated really weighed on him."

Ms. Simmons, Mr. Dawkins's former employer, reported that he had told her in the past that he was from a bad neighborhood. Mr. Dawkins stated that the high school he attended, Jefferson City High, was "not good," as there was often fighting and "a lot of gang activity." In his life history statement, Mr. Dawkins reported that while in high school he was not involved in a gang but his brother was, and this meant Mr. Dawkins was "fair game." Mr. Dawkins reported that his high school was located in the opposing gang's neighborhood; he subsequently avoided going to school, which contributed to his failure to complete high school. Ms. Jeffers and Ms. Jackson both reported that Mr. Dawkins was stabbed when he was a teenager. In addition, Ms. Jeffers described a frightening incident that Mr. Dawkins encountered in the neighborhood that she believes affected Mr. Dawkins. She reported that when she and Mr. Dawkins were teenagers, they were sitting in the playground one day when "the police came to the playground and arrested every young black kid in the neighborhood for something that happened...they kind of beat up on those boys ridiculously (and) he was one who got beat up." She stated that she could not recall his injuries precisely, but they left the playground and

found his mother immediately after this occurred. Ms. Jeffers reported that Mr. Dawkins's mother was "really upset" and she took him to the hospital. Regarding this event, Ms. Jeffers stated, "That was a really bad, nasty encounter. It was teenagers just playing in the playground and the police showed up with guns and said 'freeze'...it was crazy for a child." She stated that the police arrested the children on the playground "because something happened blocks away."

Mr. Dawkins noted that he has a common law marriage with Ms. Jeffers. He reported that they have been together since he was 14; she recalled that they have been together since they were both 15. Ms. Jeffers reported that she grew up in the same neighborhood as Mr. Dawkins. Mr. Dawkins indicated in his life history statement that Ms. Jeffers played a role in Mr. Dawkins's decision to enroll in the Youth Corps program, through which he obtained employment after he ceased attending school. Together, Mr. Dawkins and Ms. Jeffers have four children (two daughters and two sons), according to Mr. Dawkins. Their daughter, Ms. Jackson, stated regarding her parents, "You can tell they were friends for a long time," but "they weren't very affectionate around us kids." Mr. Dawkins stated that his sons are 31 and 22 and his daughters are 28 and 23. Mr. Dawkins reported that both sons are presently incarcerated, the older for gun possession and the younger for drug possession. Ms. Jeffers reported that she and Mr. Dawkins have three grandchildren, ages 9, 6, and 5. Ms. Jackson, however, stated that he has four grandchildren, ages 8, 6, 5, and 1. Ms. Jeffers and Ms. Simmons both noted that Mr. Dawkins cares deeply about his grandchildren. Ms. Jeffers reported that Mr. Dawkins is a "softy" for the grandkids. She stated that he often told his children to bring the grandchildren over so he could take care of them. She reported that he liked to take the grandchildren to the movies. Ms. Jackson noted, "At least once a month he would take the grandchildren to Chuck E. Cheese's or just ride around with them and play with them." In addition, Ms. Simmons stated, Mr. Dawkins talks about his grandchildren "a lot and he talks about his kids, too." She added, "He used to talk about them coming over and spending the night...he missed out on his kids, so he used to talk about them a lot." Ms. Simmons also noted, "I could tell he really loved his grandkids."

Regarding her relationship with her father, Ms. Jackson stated, "When he was around he was very playful with us." She noted that he "spent lots of weekends hanging out with us and things." She added, "He wasn't really affectionate...but he wasn't cold, either." Ms. Jackson stated, "It seems like he had a really hard time expressing his emotions, but he tried to show it." She noted that her father spent "quite a bit of time in and out of prison" when she was growing up, although she never knew why he was incarcerated. She reported that when her father was incarcerated, her mother would visit him every week and she would take the children to visit him every month. Regarding Mr. Dawkins's criminal behavior, Ms. Jackson stated, "Whatever he did on the street, he kept from his family...there was nothing going on in our home...we were really sheltered from whatever was happening." Ms. Jeffers reported that when Mr. Dawkins was employed, he supported his children. Regarding Mr. Dawkins's parenting, Ms. Jeffers stated, "My children never been punished by him a day in their life. He was a softy towards punishing them or correcting them." She added, "They knew they could always count on him or depend on him for things."

Educational History

According to Mr. Dawkins's school records, he did not attend any kindergarten or preschool classes prior to entering first grade at the age of five. Mr. Dawkins stated that he attended one school from first grade to eighth grade. He noted that his attendance was "good" during these grades, as he lived across the street from the school. He reported that his behavior was "great," but added that he was suspended once or twice for fighting. Mr. Dawkins reported his performance was "excellent" and he had a B average. He denied repeating any grades, being placed in special education classes, or having an Individualized Educational Plan. Ms. Jeffers reported that her husband was "really good" when he was in elementary school, but she noted, "He really changed...grew life experiences when his mother started drinking."

Mr. Dawkins's first report card from first grade reflects that he received Cs, Ds, and Es in most of his classes, although he received Bs in handwriting. His teacher noted on the report card, "David is friendly and enjoys working with the other children, but he must learn to be quiet during work time. He needs help at home in every area...please come to school Tuesday evening to see how you can help him." All of his report cards from first

grade request assistance from his mother in teaching Mr. Dawkins. For instance, his third-quarter report card stated, "He needs more reading practice at home...please get him a homework book, and come to see me so we can talk about his playful behavior at home." His final report card also requests more parental involvement in his education, as it states, "Please help him at home so he can make a good start in the fall." Mr. Dawkins's final report card reports that he was absent from school three times in first grade.

According to his school records, Mr. Dawkins received Bs and Cs in second grade. His report card notes that his mother had been working with him at home, as it stated, "David has improved with the help you have given at home. Thank you for this most needed and valued assistance." According to his school records, he missed two days of school in second grade.

Mr. Dawkins's school records indicate that throughout elementary school he exhibited disruptive classroom behavior, although his records also reflect that Mr. Dawkins had potential to do well in school. According to his school records, he received Bs and Cs in all of his third-grade classes. His teacher reported on his report card that "he works well but lacks self-control," but noted that he was a hard worker. His report card from fourth grade states, "David can do good work when he shows self control in class." According to his fourth-grade report card, he received Bs, Cs, and one D in his classes. Mr. Dawkins's IQ was measured at 109 in fourth grade, according to his school records. In fifth grade, Mr. Dawkins's teacher also noted that his classroom behavior needed improvement; however, his second report card noted that he had done a "remarkable job improving his behavior in the classroom." Mr. Dawkins's report card from fifth grade indicates that he received Bs and Cs in most of his classes, although he received As in Art, Spelling, and Music. His school records note that he did not miss any days of school in the fifth grade.

According to Mr. Dawkins's sixth-grade report card, he received Bs in Arithmetic, Art, Health Education, Language Arts, Physical Education, Science, and Social Studies; he received Cs in Reading, Written Expression, Spelling, Handwriting, and Music; and he received Ds in citizenship practices and work habits. His teacher noted in his sixth-grade report card that Mr. Dawkins had a "very immature attitude" and "is capable of more than he produces." His attendance, however, was excellent, as he missed two days of school out of 184 school days. Mr. Dawkins's report card from seventh grade also notes that he missed two days of school. According to his school records from seventh grade, he received Bs in Art, Health Education, Mathematics, and Science; received Cs in English, French, Music, Physical Education, and Shop Class; and received Es in Reading and Social Studies. His report card for the first quarter notes that Mr. Dawkins needed to improve his work habits, as he "has the ability to do much better work." His final report card indicates that Mr. Dawkins's work "improved in most areas."

According to Mr. Dawkins's school records, he had no unexcused absences during the 1971–1972 school year, when he was in eighth grade. He received the following "end of year" grades in eighth grade: a C in Art, an E in English, a D in French, a D in Health Education, a C in Mathematics, a C in Music, a C in Physical Education, a D in Reading, a E in Science, an A in Shop and a B in History. Mr. Dawkins's grades appeared to decline as the school year progressed, as his grades fell by one grade level in three of the aforementioned classes from the mid-year report to the end of the year report, according to his school records. His school records reflect that Mr. Dawkins's scores on the Iowa Tests of Basic Skills were in the Low Average range for Reading; in the Average range for Vocabulary, Total Language, and Composite; and in the High Average range for Total Work-Study and Total Arithmetic. His eighth-grade report card notes, "David has a lot of talent in art. However, he does not work at achieving."

Mr. Dawkins attended high school at Jefferson High School. He reported that his grades were "excellent" in ninth grade, but he began having problems in tenth grade. Ms. Jeffers also noted that Mr. Dawkins received "good grades…especially if it was a subject he liked." Mr. Dawkins's school records reflect that he did receive good grades in ninth grade, as he received an 80 in English, a 75 in Social Studies, a 92 in Math, a 90 in Music, an 80 in "Shop—electric," a 90 in Physical Education, and a 90 in Health Education. According to his school records, he was present 179 days, was absent 8 days, and was late 41 days.

Mr. Dawkins's school records reflect that he was enrolled in tenth grade at Jefferson High School during the 1973–1974 school year. Regarding high school, Mr. Dawkins stated that it was "not conducive to my health." He reported that there was a lot of gang activity at the school and there were tensions between students from different parts of town. He reported that he was involved in the fighting, and that his attendance was "sporadic." However, Ms. Jeffers reported that he went to school every day. Mr. Dawkins's school records for the 1973–1974 school year (tenth grade) indicate that he was suspended three times. There were no school records from the 1973–1974 school year regarding his grades. There are school records indicating that Mr. Dawkins was again enrolled in tenth grade at Jefferson High for the 1974–1975 school year. It appears based on his school records that he only attended school from September to November of the 1974–1975 school year, and his grades were poor, as he received Es in English, Social Studies, and Science, and he received a D in Math.

Mr. Dawkins reported that he was placed in Jackson Alternative School because of his fighting behavior and was required to repeat tenth grade because of his sporadic attendance. According to Mr. Dawkins, he was expelled from Jackson in tenth grade for "fighting the teacher." However, he stated, "If I would have went, I would have passed." He also reported, "I was always good at math." Mr. Dawkins's school records indicate that he was enrolled in tenth-grade classes in Jackson Academy's "disruptive pupil program" from September 1975 to January 1976. According to the school records, he exhibited "constant disruptive behavior" at Jackson and "was observed…causing disruptions when he should have been with the Jackson group." While at Jackson, his school records indicate that he attended counseling and met with a social worker to address his behavioral problems. However, the school records report that in February 1976, Mr. Dawkins "led [an] attack on a teacher" at Jackson Academy. He was subsequently transferred to the George Washington Disciplinary School in April of 1976, according to his school records. There are no records regarding his performance at George Washington Disciplinary School.

Ms. Jeffers reported that Mr. Dawkins did not graduate from high school, but obtained his GED when he was incarcerated. The Department of Education official transcript indicated that Mr. Dawkins withdrew from school in 1976, that his last grade completed was the ninth grade, and that he successfully tested for his GED in September

1980. Mr. Dawkins, Ms. Jeffers, and Ms. Jackson all reported that Mr. Dawkins took electrician classes when he was incarcerated. The Prison psychological evaluation report (dated 5/10/96) indicated Mr. Dawkins had been enrolled in the Electronics School program since 1991, and that Mr. Dawkins was a "teacher's aide" in the program at the time of the report. Ms. Jackson noted about her father, "He's very intelligent and very perceptive."

Employment History

Mr. Dawkins stated that his first job was at Norristown General Hospital, where he worked in the mailroom. He stated that he worked for the Youth Corps for one year and for ACME for three years. In his life history statement, Mr. Dawkins reported that he was put on probation at this job after he was caught "not ringing up items" so that he could take the money paid for the items. He reported that he stopped taking money but was later fired when he accidentally missed scanning an item. According to Mr. Dawkins, he also worked as a parking lot attendant for three years, as a supervisor for after-school and summer workers for the City of Norristown for one year, and as a laborer for one year. In his life history statement, Mr. Dawkins indicated that he lost his job at the parking lot after leaving with patrons' cars during his shift (12:00 p.m. to 8:00 a.m.) in order to attend parties and clubs. He indicated that he was fired when a car went missing and he was viewed as a car thief. Mr. Dawkins reported that he was unable to retain his job with Norristown after he was incarcerated in 1985. In his life history statement, Mr. Dawkins reported that he was let go from his job as a laborer because the electrical technician he worked under would drink and not "make it to work," resulting in the company firing both Mr. Dawkins and the technician. State parole records for Mr. Dawkins also indicate inconsistent employment. Based on Mr. Dawkins's chronology of jobs, he has not had stable employment since 1979, when he was first incarcerated. He reported that he was incarcerated from 1979–1982, 1985–1987, and 1989–1998. According to Mr. Dawkins, he worked for maintenance and electrical while he was incarcerated. He stated that since 1998, he has been self-employed, doing carpentry and remodeling homes. He added, "I do a lot of subcontracting." About his job, he reported, "I love my job—I'm real good at it." He noted that he had "a lot of customers" and "worked

5–7 days a week." Mr. Dawkins reported that he is currently employed in the kitchen of the City Jail.

Ms. Jeffers reported that Mr. Dawkins has "been steadily employed in the time he's not incarcerated." Ms. Jackson also noted that he has been "employed regularly" in the past few years. Ms. Jackson reported that in addition to doing carpentry or electrical jobs with his construction company, Mr. Dawkins "also did jobs outside of that to establish his own clientele." Ms. Jackson added, "His goal was to become a certified electrician and maintain his own business."

Ms. Simmons stated that she hired Mr. Dawkins to complete several remodeling projects at her home. She reported that he was working for her at the time he was arrested. Ms. Simmons indicated that she was pleased with the work that Mr. Dawkins had done in her home. She noted that if there were things Mr. Dawkins knew he could not do, "he wouldn't just slop it together, he would let me know that there were things he couldn't do." She added, "He would say he wouldn't even take on the plumbing job because it wouldn't work right." Ms. Simmons reported that Mr. Dawkins helped her when she was in need. According to Ms. Simmons, after her son was shot, she "didn't have much money" and Mr. Dawkins installed a floor, bathtub, and door in her bathroom for less than $300. She reported that sometimes Mr. Dawkins would tell her, "I'll do the job and you can pay me when you get the money." Ms. Simmons stated that Mr. Dawkins was proud of his job. Not only was she happy with the work that he was doing, but she reported that her husband was "very happy" with the job that Mr. Dawkins did when he fixed their door.

Records from the Social Security Administration indicate that in the period from January 2003 to December 2007, Mr. Dawkins reported earnings in 2003 and 2004. He reported earning $1,862.00 in 2003 at ABC Management Company and $532.63 in 2004 at Jamestown Hospital.

Medical and Psychiatric History

Mr. Dawkins reported no present health problems, and he stated that he is not presently taking any type of medication. However, he reported that he was shot in August of 1987. According to Mr. Dawkins, the injury required surgery. As a result of the surgery, Mr. Dawkins stated, he has a large scar that extends from below his belt to his sternum. He also reported that the little finger on his left hand is "deformed" because of a "bone infection." In addition, Ms. Jeffers and Ms. Jackson reported that Mr. Dawkins was stabbed multiple times in the abdomen and chest area when he was a teenager. Ms. Jeffers stated that Mr. Dawkins was hospitalized for approximately 10 days after the stabbing.

When asked about his history of mental health treatment, Mr. Dawkins reported that he received drug counseling while he was incarcerated in the past. He also reported that he went to Father James for drug treatment in 2004. Mr. Dawkins's school records indicate that he underwent psychological examinations in 1968 and 1969, but do not indicate why the examinations were necessary or what the examinations revealed.

Substance Abuse History

Mr. Dawkins reported that he has used alcohol, cocaine, and marijuana. He stated that he drank "too much on the weekends," which he said was "a case of beer a weekend." When asked if he ever had a drug problem, he stated, "well, no...yes." He reported that he used cocaine once every three weeks in the year prior to his incarceration. When asked if he currently has an alcohol problem, he stated, "Right before I came here it was a problem." He added, "It's all I wanted to do." He reported that his wife complains about his drinking. Mr. Dawkins said, "I don't make too good of decisions when drinking or using drugs." When asked to elaborate, he stated that he would oversleep for work because he had a hangover. In his life history statement, Mr. Dawkins cited his drinking and nightlife as the cause of poor consequences numerous times. For example, he indicated that he missed scanning an item at his job because he had been up late the night before, and that he developed a plan to steal money from parking lot patrons while drinking with a friend. He also noted that when he was younger his drinking would cause him to get into fights. The mitigation report indicates Mr. Dawkins has been in treatment for alcohol and substance use twice while incarcerated and once while on parole. Ms. Morris also concluded in the mitigation report that Mr. Dawkins's involvement with the legal system is closely tied to his drug and alcohol use. Ms. Morris noted that while incarcerated and abstaining from substance abuse, Mr. Dawkins proves to be "a non-violent, well-mannered individual with a strong work ethic and pleasant demeanor."

Ms. Jeffers stated that Mr. Dawkins has problems with drugs and alcohol. However, she reported that he knew that she "didn't like or approve of it" so he "tried to hide it." She stated that she did not know when he began using drugs, or what drugs he uses, but she suspects drug use because of his attitude and because his personality changed. Ms. Jeffers reported that he did not drink alcohol or do drugs in the home, but he drank beer "if he was watching a fight or a football game." She noted that he would never do drugs in front of his wife or his children. She stated that there were times where Mr. Dawkins would leave and not come home for a day. She added, "That's when I know he's doing something...I can hear it in his voice." Ms. Jeffers stated that she believes "there might be times when he tried to get clean—there are times when things are going good." According to her, when Mr. Dawkins "feels bad about something he's done," like feeling "bad about being drunk, he'll go home and stay in his room for three weeks." Ms. Jeffers stated that there were times when she would tell her husband, "If you can't do it by yourself, you need to get help." However, she reported that he would respond by telling her that he was all right. She said that Mr. Dawkins never admitted to her that he used drugs, but she stated, "I could tell, I could see he was fighting his own battle."

When Ms. Jackson was asked if her father has ever used drugs or alcohol, she responded "I never saw it (and) he never told me...I suspected it because of some of the behaviors, (but) I don't know." Then she stated, "It could have just been anything now that I'm thinking about it...I'm still unclear." Ms. Jackson noted that there were times when her father was hanging around people that he normally did not hang around, and she knew that some of these people were drug users. When she was asked whether Mr. Dawkins was using alcohol or drugs prior to his incarceration, she stated, "I'm sure he was consuming quite a bit of alcohol before he was arrested." She added, "He didn't drink alcohol, like 'live it up,' but more to calm down."

Social History

When asked about his interests and hobbies, Mr. Dawkins stated, "I love the gym." He stated that he lifts weights five days a week, both when he is living in the community and when he is incarcerated. In addition, he reported that he enjoys playing football, and he plays basketball every Sunday.

Mr. Dawkins also reported that he belongs to the Norristown Community Organization, which is a neighborhood organization that attempts to clean up the neighborhood. He stated that he also belongs to the YMCA and he still has a membership at a local fitness club. He reported that he has "a lot of associates," and they get together to watch fights and football games. When asked if he has positive friends (friends without criminal involvement), he stated that in the past 10 years, his good friends have been friends with no criminal involvement. However, he added that he also has friends who are involved in offending.

Regarding Mr. Dawkins's friends, Ms. Jeffers stated that she does not know all of them, but she knew the friends that "came past the house and the ones from his childhood." She stated that she approved of "some of them," but, "a few of them weren't doing anything with their lives, but for the most part, most of them were alright people, I guess." When asked if she knew how Mr. Dawkins and his friends spent their time together, she replied, "No." She added, "They would probably just go out—probably went out to the bar or the club." She reported that she did not mind that he went out to the bar or club with his friends. Ms. Jeffers reported that Mr. Dawkins likes to play pool and go to the movies. She stated that she and her husband went to the movies together "now and then" but added, "Basically, if we went out together, we might go out to the bar, but he'll have me home by 10:00 p.m." She noted that she and Mr. Dawkins also used to go visit family and friends together.

About Mr. Dawkins's leisure activities, Ms. Jackson stated, "Him and my mom always had Friday night movie dates at least a couple times a month." She reported that her father loves music and likes to read. In addition, she stated, "I know he likes beer and he likes to eat…of course, there's football Sundays at home (and) occasionally he would go out with friends." Ms. Jackson noted that Mr. Dawkins has a few friends, but "There's not a large group of friends…he has a select group of people that he communicates with and that's usually it."

Ms. Simmons, Mr. Dawkins's former employer, reported that she met Mr. Dawkins at the gym in 1999. She stated that he trained her and some other people at the gym. About this, she stated, "He was good at the gym, he had a crowd in the gym that he was training…and he didn't charge us a penny."

She reported that there were other men in the gym that charged for training, but she noted that Mr. Dawkins "said if we were serious about working out, he wouldn't charge us." She stated that Mr. Dawkins is "very serious" about working out, and she added, "He had us working really hard in the gym." In addition to enjoying working in the gym, Ms. Simmons reported that Mr. Dawkins "loves putting houses together," and he loves football. She stated that he used to talk about playing football. She reported that she met some of Mr. Dawkins's friends at the gym. When asked if she knew how they usually spend their time together, she stated, "I know he used to be at the gym all the time."

Offense and Incarceration History

Mr. Dawkins's reports and his criminal record reflect the following history of criminal involvement. He stated that he was first arrested at the age of 13 for auto theft. He reported that he was incarcerated from 1979–1982 for robbery, and from 1989–1998 for aggravated assault and robbery. In addition, he was convicted of conspiracy and reported that he was incarcerated from 1985–1987 for those charges. His court history documents that he has been convicted of burglary (1978); theft and unlawful taking (1979); robbery and criminal conspiracy (1979); criminal conspiracy (1985); recklessly endangering another person and simple assault (1987); aggravated assault, simple assault, and carrying firearms in a public place (1989); and possession of the instrument of a crime and robbery (1989).

Mr. Dawkins's prison records indicate he has been involved in only one altercation during his current incarceration. The records state that Mr. Dawkins ended the altercation upon the direction of a correction officer and returned to his unit when requested to do so. Prison social services records indicate Mr. Dawkins has "adjust[ed] well" to his current incarceration, is "affable," and "works hard." The state parole psychological evaluation (dated 6/22/01) indicates Mr. Dawkins was involved in two altercations during a previous incarceration: he received misconducts for assault or fighting in 1992, and an assault in 1994 during which he beat another inmate with a "sock filled with batteries." However, the report summarizing the evaluation (dated 9/20/01) was "positive in terms of institutional adjustment" and determined "it does not appear [Mr. Dawkins] will be a management problem if he is awarded an advanced status." The summary report assigned Mr. Dawkins a "Stability Rating" of "A." Similarly, the psychological evaluation for parole conducted at prison (dated 5/21/97) determined Mr. Dawkins had "maintained a satisfactory adjustment since [the 5/10/96] review." A Department of Corrections classification summary (dated 6/21/01) indicated that Mr. Dawkins had an assault charge more than 6 months prior, had no disciplinary reports in the past 12 months, had no known escape history, was active and partially compliant in programs, demonstrated average work performance, and also had above-average housing performance, resulting in a custody level classification of 2. Ms. Morris, in the mitigation report, noted that Mr. Dawkins demonstrates "[e]xtremely positive adjustment to prison and success in highly structured environments," and is a "hard working, mature inmate." Ms. Morris also noted that Mr. Dawkins is an "older inmate whose propensity for violence decreases over time."

State parole records indicate that while on parole, Mr. Dawkins was cooperative and complied in reporting to his parole office, obtaining employment, and submitting to drug testing. Parolee risk assessments (dated 1/18/02 to 5/28/04) indicate Mr. Dawkins required medium to maximum supervision. However, state parole records indicate Mr. Dawkins violated parole on at least three occasions. Mr. Dawkins was arrested for driving under the influence on 3/26/00, and found not guilty of the charge on 4/3/01. State parole records indicate Mr. Dawkins submitted drug tests positive for cocaine in April of 2003, March of 2004, and April of 2005, and was committed to the Norristown Hall Program in 2005 for the parole violation. State parole records indicate Mr. Dawkins admitted to using cocaine in March 2004 and entered the ABC program as directed by his parole officer. State parole records also indicate Mr. Dawkins was cited for owning or possessing a firearm in July of 2004 when U.S. marshals entered his residence in an attempt to locate another individual. The U.S. marshals found a gun during their search of the residence. The mitigation report indicated Mr. Dawkins did not know the gun was in his house, as it belonged to his son. State parole records also indicate Mr. Dawkins was declared delinquent on 1/13/06 after not reporting to his parole officer.

CURRENT CLINICAL CONDITION

Mr. Dawkins is a 49-year-old African American male of average height who appeared his stated age. He displayed a muscular build, good posture, and normal eye contact. He wore institutional garb, and he was adequately groomed during the evaluations on September 7, 2007, and September 12, 2007. He brought glasses to the evaluation, which he used for the testing portions of the evaluation. Mr. Dawkins reported that he has a scar that extends from below his belt to under his diaphragm from surgery on a gunshot wound in August 1987. In addition, he reported that part of the bone in his left little finger has been removed, leaving the finger slightly deformed. He attributes this injury to a "cumulative effect" of injuring his finger playing football and basketball and a bone infection. He stated that his left ear was pierced, but it has been closed up for years. Mr. Dawkins has a tattoo of "A-N-D" on his right upper arm. He stated that the "A" stands for his wife's initial, the "N" means "and" and the "D" is his initial. He also reported having a tattoo of a Chinese symbol meaning "long life" on his left upper arm. He was very polite and cooperative throughout the evaluation sessions. In addition, his mood appeared positive and his affect was appropriate. His speech was clear and coherent, and he responded openly and with relevance when questioned. He also appeared to give reasonable effort to the tasks involved, despite the duration of the evaluation and his report that he had not eaten anything the day of testing. His capacity for attention and concentration appeared adequate. He was able to focus reasonably well on a series of tasks throughout the five-hour evaluation on September 7, 2007, and the two-and-a-half-hour evaluation on September 12, 2007, without becoming visibly distracted. Therefore, it would appear that this evaluation provides a reasonably good estimate of Mr. Dawkins's current functioning.

Mr. Dawkins's basic academic skills, as measured by the WRAT-4, showed a marked deficit in one of four areas: Word Reading (grade equivalent = 11.6), Spelling (grade equivalent = 7.2), Math Computation (grade equivalent = 11.2), and Sentence Comprehension (grade equivalent = >12.9). On a measure of overall intellectual functioning (the WAIS-III), Mr. Dawkins was measured as performing in the Average range (Full

Scale IQ = 95), placing him in the 37th percentile relative to others his age. He was also measured in the Average range for both verbal tasks (VIQ = 93) and performance tasks (PIQ = 97), placing him in the 32nd and 42nd percentiles, respectively, relative to others his age. Although Mr. Dawkins appears to have a significant deficit in his spelling skills, he appears to be of average intellectual functioning.

Mr. Dawkins was presented two versions of a structured inventory of symptoms of mental and emotional disorders, the Brief Symptom Inventory (BSI), one concerning his present functioning (discussed here) and the second describing his thoughts and feelings around the time of the offenses with which he is currently charged. However, Mr. Dawkins stated that he could not report how he was feeling at the time of the offense—he could only report how he was feeling when he was arrested and told of the murders. Therefore, he only completed the BSI concerning his present functioning. On the BSI, Mr. Dawkins reported currently being "extremely" distressed on one of the 53 items. He reported that he was extremely distressed with having to check and double-check what he does. When asked to elaborate on this, he stated that he has to make sure he does things correctly so he does not get into trouble with prison staff. He reported being "moderately" distressed by getting into frequent arguments. Mr. Dawkins's scores on the nine scales (somatization, obsessive-compulsive, interpersonal sensitivity, depression, anxiety, hostility, phobic anxiety, paranoid ideation, and psychoticism) were first compared to non-patient adult males. None of the scales was significantly elevated (i.e., greater than two standard deviations above the mean).

Mr. Dawkins completed the MMPI-2 in approximately two hours, and he appeared to remain focused throughout the entire test. The personality profile generated is likely to be a valid indication of his present personality functioning. However, the results indicate that Mr. Dawkins approached the items in a defensive and overly cautious manner, and he may have been evasive and unwilling to admit many personal faults. Mr. Dawkins's profile (Welsh Code 4'''+18-37259/60: K-LF/) is often seen in individuals who are described as immature, impulsive, and hedonistic, and frequently rebel against authority. These results are consistent with the results of the psychological evaluation conducted in 1996, which described Mr. Dawkins

as "impulsive" and "impatient" and tending to "not consider the consequences of his actions." Mr. Dawkins's profile is seen in 9.1% of normative men, but found in 36.8% of men in a state prison and 21.5% of men in a federal prison. His score indicates that he may have drug or alcohol problems, as many individuals with this profile develop severe addictive problems. Furthermore, over 24% of men in substance abuse treatment programs have this pattern. This profile indicates that Mr. Dawkins may appear charming and may make a good first impression, but may also be perceived as superficial and untrustworthy in the longer term. These results are consistent with the state parole psychological evaluation conducted in 2001, which indicated Mr. Dawkins may be "egocentric, more concerned with 'image' than substance, and lacking in personal insight." The profile also suggests that he is outgoing and sociable and has a strong need to be around others, but has more difficulty forming stable, warm relationships. However, it should be noted that Mr. Dawkins has been in a relationship with his wife for over 30 years. Many individuals with this profile have marital problems that require counseling because of the individual's behavior, although this has not been reported for Mr. Dawkins. Such individuals also frequently have a history of offending and other antisocial behavior that is significant.

On the LSI-R, Mr. Dawkins showed particular deficits in the domains of Criminal History, Educational/Employment, Financial, Family/Marital, Accommodation, Leisure/Recreation, Companions, Alcohol/Drug Problem, Emotional/Personal, and Attitudes/Orientation. Specifically, Mr. Dawkins's responses indicate that he has a significant history of prior offenses and convictions (seven prior adult convictions and one juvenile conviction). Mr. Dawkins also reported concerns about financial matters, housing problems (including living in an unsafe areas with frequent drug and gang activity), and marital difficulties. Although he indicated that he has some positive friends who are not involved in criminal activities, he acknowledged that some of his friends have been involved in crime. Additionally, Mr. Dawkins reported a substance abuse problem, including using crack and binge drinking. He admitted that he had a problem with alcohol at the time of the arrest, and added, "It's all I wanted to do." Mr. Dawkins showed mixed evidence in the Attitudes/Orientation domain. On one hand, he expressed attitudes reflecting the absence of distress related to being arrested or the impact of his behavior on others. On the other hand, he also reported that he would like to live a life without crime, believes that education is "extremely important," and thinks having a job "is everything." The LSI-R was also completed in March of 2004 and November of 2005 by Mr. Dawkins's parole officers. The reports concluded that Mr. Dawkins fell within the high–medium risk/needs classification. The reports indicate that Criminal History, Education/Employment, Family/Marital, Leisure/Recreation, Companions, and Alcohol/Drug Problem were problematic areas for Mr. Dawkins.

SENTENCING CONSIDERATIONS

According to 42 Pa. C.S.A. § 9711(a)(2), any evidence relating to mitigating circumstances can be presented at the sentencing hearing. The following factors, as enumerated in 42 Pa. C.S.A. § 9711(e), can be considered as mitigating factors:

(1) The defendant has no significant history of prior criminal convictions.
(2) The defendant was under the influence of extreme mental or emotional disturbance.
(3) The capacity of the defendant to appreciate the criminality of his conduct or to conform his conduct to the requirements of law was substantially impaired.
(4) The age of the defendant at the time of the crime.
(5) The defendant acted under extreme duress, although not such duress as to constitute a defense to prosecution... or acted under the substantial domination of another person.
(6) The victim was a participant in the defendant's homicidal conduct or consented to the homicidal acts.
(7) The defendant's participation in the homicidal act was relatively minor.
(8) Any other evidence of mitigation concerning the character and record of the defendant and the circumstances of his offense.

The mitigating factors that can be addressed through forensic mental health assessment are factors 2, 3, 5, and 8. Mr. Dawkins did not report any circumstances relevant to factors 2, 3, or 5; however, information related to factor 8 is discussed in this section.

When asked about the circumstances surrounding the offense for which he is currently charged, Mr. Dawkins stated that he was "somewhere else" at the time of the offense. Mr. Dawkins stated that he did not know the younger victim, Norris Jenkins. However, he reported that he knows "Old Head," the other victim. He stated that Old Head (Max Charles), "is a plumber (and) also a crackhead," and Mr. Dawkins noted that he "used to use him as cheap labor." He added, "Old Head never did anything to me in my life." Mr. Dawkins denied involvement in the crime.

(8) Any other evidence of mitigation concerning the character and record of the defendant and the circumstances of his offense.

Mr. Dawkins has faced a number of difficulties throughout his life, as his father left his home when he was only 10 years old, leaving his mother to care for five children on her own. As a result of his father's absence, Mr. Dawkins's mother was forced to work long hours, leaving Mr. Dawkins in the care of his older siblings. Mr. Dawkins and Ms. Jeffers both reported that Mr. Dawkins's mother began drinking after his father left the home, and according to Ms. Jeffers, her drinking became increasingly worse. In addition, Mr. Dawkins's mother reportedly beat him with her hands, a belt, and a broom. Mr. Dawkins also was raised in a rough neighborhood and attended a school with significant gang activity. Mr. Dawkins suffers from a significant substance abuse problem with cocaine and alcohol, and he may have been prone to this problem because of his family history of alcohol problems (both his mother and brother drank excessively). His wife believes that he attempts to quit using drugs and alcohol for periods of time but ultimately ends up relapsing. She noted that he feels guilty after he has relapsed, or drunk too much, and stays in his room for weeks at a time. It appears that he is aware of the problems that his substance abuse causes but is unable to stop using substances on his own. Mr. Dawkins has received treatment in the past but would benefit from further substance abuse treatment.

Mr. Dawkins has important strengths, as he has several people in his life for whom he appears to care very much, including his wife, his children, and his grandchildren. He has maintained regular contact with his wife and daughter, and he was active in his grandchildren's lives. Mr. Dawkins is also a relatively intelligent and sociable man. He reported that he has had several jobs while he has been incarcerated. Prison social service records indicate Mr. Dawkins has maintained employment during his current incarceration. Furthermore, he received training to be an electrician while he was incarcerated, which he utilized after his release to start his own business. Mr. Dawkins also received his GED while he was incarcerated. In addition, Mr. Dawkins's prison records indicate he has been involved in only one altercation during his current incarceration. The records state that Mr. Dawkins ended the altercation upon the direction of a correction officer and returned to his unit when requested to do so. Based on his achievements while he was incarcerated, and the reports of his former employer, Mr. Dawkins appears to be a hard worker who would be a relatively low risk for disciplinary problems if incarcerated in prison.

CONCLUSIONS

In the opinion of the undersigned, based on all of the above:

(1) Mr. Dawkins's considerations relevant to mitigation include significant substance abuse problems, his problems in his early family life, his mother's drinking problem, and his father's absence from the home. He also has positive influences in his life and reports an attachment to his children and grandchildren. He is relatively intelligent, reports that he values work, and appears at low risk for disciplinary problems if incarcerated in prison following disposition of charges. These factors can be seen as strengths, and they are consistent with a favorable response to treatment in a structured, secure prison environment.

Thank you for the opportunity to evaluate David Dawkins.

Kirk Heilbrun, Ph.D.
Consulting Psychologist

Jacey Erickson, B.A.
Clinical Psychology
Graduate Student

TEACHING POINT:
HOW MUCH IS ENOUGH?
DIMINISHING RETURNS FROM
INFORMATION SOURCES

How much information is enough? How many sources of information should be considered? When is it time to stop collecting information from multiple sources? The collection of data from multiple sources can be time consuming. It is important to recognize that there are diminishing returns from the numerous sources of information that might be used in this process. The following suggestions may help identify when we have reached this "point of diminishing returns."

First, the evaluator should identify an appropriate investigation strategy. As part of this strategy, the evaluator should identify the key domains and constructs that are most relevant to the forensic issues being assessed. In this case, psychological testing, clinical and structured interviews, and collateral documents were used to gather historical information and assess a broad range of domains and constructs. Each source provided valuable information on Mr. Dawkins' functioning across a variety of domains, and also identified important questions to be asked in collateral telephone interviews.

Second, it is useful to focus on the domains that are the most relevant to the forensic issues, or most unclear, rather than spending time on domains that are only tangentially related or non-contributory to the forensic issues. For example, in this case Mr. Dawkins denied any participation in the alleged offense, making it virtually impossible to meaningfully evaluate his mental state at the time of the offense. It would not have been useful, therefore, to gather direct and collateral information about his thinking and feeling around this time, as his denial of culpability would make it impossible to relate any symptoms to offending behavior.

Finally, the evaluator should discontinue the investigation of a domain or construct after a number of data sources have yielded comparable information. For example, in this case, Mr. Dawkins' sister was described by the defendant during the present evaluation as suffering from "LSD damage." However, two collaterals (and the defendant himself, on a prior occasion) reported that she had been diagnosed with paranoid schizophrenia.

Given this, it does not seem necessary to obtain further information about his sister's mental health before reporting that she has been diagnosed with paranoid schizophrenia.

CASE TWO
PRINCIPLE: OBTAIN RELEVANT HISTORICAL INFORMATION
(PRINCIPLE 19)

This principle concerns both what constitutes "relevant" historical information and how to obtain such information in a particular case. In forensic assessment, the range of potentially relevant domains is much greater than in therapeutic assessment. For example, when conducting FMHA, in addition to gathering historical information about the social, medical, mental health, and family functioning of the individual being evaluated, it may be important to obtain further information about the individual's criminal, military, school, sexual, or vocational histories, depending on the nature of the evaluation.

Historical information is particularly important for several reasons. These include the value of behavior, the importance of the person's response style, and the accuracy of self-reported factual information, as well as characteristics, symptoms, and the obvious need for information about the relevant thoughts, feelings, and behavior of the individual at a certain time when a reconstructive evaluation is being conducted. In addition, accurate historical information can strengthen the basis for predicting future outcomes (e.g., violent behavior, treatment response) that are part of certain FMHAs.

There is reasonably strong support for the importance of history in FMHA from ethical, legal, empirical, and standard-of-practice sources of authority. In general, ethics sources of authority emphasize that the person's history is an integral part of mental health evaluation within accepted clinical and scientific standards. For example, the APA *Ethics Code* indirectly addresses the importance of historical information as follows: "Psychologists' work is based upon established scientific and professional knowledge of the discipline" (Standard 2.04; see also Standard 9.01a). The APA *Ethics Code* emphasizes that practitioners should be able to substantiate the

interpretations and opinions of their assessments based on all available information (Standards 9.06, and 9.01a, respectively). Furthermore, the APA *Specialty Guidelines* indirectly supports this principle by noting that practitioners should consider relevant individual and cultural differences in their assessment (Guidelines 2.08 and 10.03), investigate the relevant legal question from "all reasonable perspectives and seek information that will differentially test plausible rival hypotheses" (Guideline 9.01), and use multiple sources of information to corroborate important data (Guideline 9.02). However, the APA *Specialty Guidelines* also suggests that practitioners limit discussion of historical information "that does not bear directly upon the legal purpose of the examination or consultation" and avoid including information "that is irrelevant and that does not provide a substantial basis of support for their opinions, except when required by law" (Guideline 11.04; see also Guideline 2.04). Neither the ApA *Principles of Medical Ethics with Annotations* nor the AAPL *Ethical Guidelines* address this principle.

Legal support for this principle can be found in several sources. Generally, relevant legal standards emphasize the application of history to various legal questions. The still-relevant *Criminal Justice Mental Health Standards* (American Bar Association, 1989), which is currently undergoing revision, indicates that the contents of a written report should include the "clinical findings and opinions on each matter referred for evaluation" as well as the "sources of information and... factual basis for the evaluator's clinical findings and opinions" (p. 109). Although the *Criminal Justice Mental Health Standards* does not indicate specifically that historical information must be obtained, it can be reasonably inferred that it is important to describe an individual's history in adequate detail when information from the individual's history serves as either a source of information or a factual basis for "clinical findings and opinions."

Case law provides some additional support for the importance of relevant historical information, particularly in cases in which the forensic issues are broad or when the legal decision can have very serious consequences for the individual being evaluated. For example, in capital cases, the defense is entitled to psychiatric assistance to provide mitigating evidence (if applicable) at sentencing, and to counter prosecution evidence of future dangerousness (see *Ake v. Oklahoma*, 1985). History is relevant to assessing both future dangerousness and adjustment to incarceration, which are included among aggravating and mitigating criteria for capital sentencing in many jurisdictions (see DeMatteo, Murrie, Anumba, & Keesler, 2011).

The application of history to FMHA may also be valuable in establishing a pattern of behavior that can serve as a context for the forensic issues being assessed, and for using historical information to suggest and test hypotheses. The importance of history in establishing a pattern of behavior, including serving as a source of information about the probability of certain types of future behavior, is particularly apparent when addressing forensic issues that involve prediction. Making and testing hypotheses regarding forensic issues can be facilitated when a detailed history is obtained, as the likelihood that a given hypothesis may account for relevant legal behavior (e.g., "He shot a stranger because he experienced command auditory hallucinations instructing him to do so") may depend on both previous experience (e.g., the prior frequency of experienced command hallucinations) and behavior (e.g., the prior frequency of compliance with such command hallucinations).

Although historical information is part of virtually every form of mental health assessment (whether therapeutic or forensic) the scope of the needed information varies according to the type of evaluation being conducted. When the forensic issue is narrow and focuses primarily on the individual's present state, there is less history that is relevant; when the forensic issue is broader, or if potentially serious consequences may result, then the breadth of the relevant history may expand accordingly.

The present report provides an example of the application of this principle. It focuses primarily on the presentation of relevant historical information. The forensic clinician consulted numerous sources of information in an effort to obtain as much historical information regarding the defendant as possible. In doing so, he was able to offer a very comprehensive picture of the defendant's history. This historical information was presented partly to establish a description of behavioral propensities that could serve as a context for the forensic issue(s) being addressed. For example, one consideration in capital sentencing in Texas, where Dr. Cunningham is based, is whether the defendant is likely to engage in future dangerous behavior.

Accordingly, that is one consideration in this report. But since the report's findings would not be heard unless the defendant had been convicted of murder and facing a sentence of either life without parole or death, the proper context for the appraisal of future violence risk is prison, not the community.

PSYCHOLOGICAL EVALUATION: CAPITAL SENTENCING
05/29/13
Albert Jones, Esq.
Office of the Public Defender
100 Main Street
Metropolis, State

Re: *State vs. John Wilson*, Capital sentencing evaluation of mitigation and violence risk assessment for prison

Dear Mr. Jones:

Thank you for providing me the opportunity to evaluate your client, Mr. John Wilson, regarding capital sentencing determinations, including mitigation and violence risk assessment for prison. In providing this evaluation, I have interviewed Mr. Wilson at length, as well as his father, mother, three siblings, paternal grandmother, four uncles, two aunts, three aunts-by-marriage, ex-wife, two childhood friends, three teachers, and a childhood neighbor. I have reviewed educational, social service, employment, medical, mental health, correctional records, and instant offense records. I have also reviewed records detailing the criminal adjudications/incarcerations of family members. My findings and opinions may be revised by additional information that is made known to me.

Interviews Conducted
[Name, relationship, duration, date, and mode of interviews detailed]

Records Reviewed
[Voluminous records detailed]
At the outset of my interview of him, Mr. Wilson was informed that though I was appointed as an agent of the defense, my findings and opinions might not prove favorable to him. He was additionally advised that should I be called by the defense to

testify, and/or my report was released to the State, and/or I was made available by the defense to the State for interview, any information I had learned from him or any other source regarding him may be disclosed. Consistent with your instructions, I did not inquire of Mr. Wilson regarding the instant offense or any prior unadjudicated conduct involving serious violence. This limitation had little if any effect on my findings and opinions regarding adverse developmental factors in his background and/or his likelihood of serious violence if confined for life in the State Department of Corrections. Though I have no independent knowledge, for purposes of this evaluation, I am considering that Mr. Wilson is guilty as charged.

Conceptual Considerations Regarding Background Factors and Rationale for Evaluation Methodology and Focus

Moral culpability is a concept at the heart of mitigation (*Burger v. Kemp*, 1987), citing *Woodson v. North Carolina* (1976) (see also other SCOTUS decisions, e.g., *Coker v. Georgia*, 1977; *Lockett v. Ohio*, 1978; *California v. Brown*, 1987; *Wilson v. Lynaugh*, 1988; *Penry v. Lynaugh*, 1989; *South Carolina v. Gathers*, 1989; *Payne v. Tennessee*, 1991; *Graham v. Collins*, 1993; *Penry v. Johnson*, 2001; *Atkins v. Virginia*, 2002; *Wiggins v. Smith*, 2003; *Roper v. Simmons*, 2005; *Abdul-Kabir v. Quarterman*, 2007). An understanding of the concept of moral culpability is critical to the jury's or court's consideration of the nexus between the mitigating factors presented to the jury and the capital offense (see Cunningham, 2010). To explain, the concept of moral culpability acknowledges an elementary psychological reality: we do not all arrive at our choices out of equivalent raw material. It follows that the degree of "blameworthiness" of an individual for criminal or even murderous conduct may vary, depending on what factors and experiences shaped, influenced, or compromised that choice. The relationship of developmental damage and other impairing factors to the exercise of choice, and subsequently to moral culpability, is illustrated in the graphic models (Figures 7.1 and 7.2) below. As the damage and impairing factors (e.g., neglect, abuse, psychological disorder, corrupting socialization, substance dependency/intoxication, etc.) increase, choice is exercised on an increasing slope, and moral culpability is correspondingly reduced.

The greater the damaging or impairing factors, the steeper the angle or slope on which the

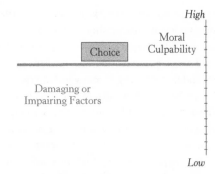

FIGURE 7.1: The relationship of developmental damage or other impairing factors, choice, and moral culpability.

choices are made; and thus the lower the level of moral culpability. This concept of moral culpability is central to the rationale of *Wiggins v. Smith*, *Atkins v. Virginia*, and *Roper v. Simmons*—i.e., background factors, mental retardation, and/or youthfulness all have an impact on the level of moral culpability of a capital defendant, and the associated death-eligibility and death-worthiness of that defendant. The formative or limiting impact from any source of developmental damage or impairment is relevant in the weighing of moral culpability. An appraisal of moral culpability involves an examination of the degree to which the background and circumstances of the defendant influenced, predisposed, or diminished the defendant's moral sensibilities and the exercise of volition or free will. Stated more plainly, how steep was the angle from which his choices were made?

In considering the nexus between damaging developmental factors and adverse outcomes in adulthood, everyone need not totally succumb to adverse developmental exposures in order for a "toxic" effect to be implicated. Correspondingly, all similarly situated persons need not commit acts of criminal violence or suffer adverse life outcomes in

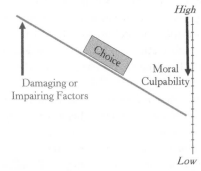

FIGURE 7.2: The influence of developmental damage or other impairing factors on choice and moral culpability.

order to demonstrate a relationship between background and outcome. The analysis of risk, vulnerabilities, and protective factors in the etiology of criminal violence and other adverse life outcomes is quite similar to explanations of why some individuals contract cancer and others do not (i.e., carcinogen exposure, predisposing factors, and protective factors). All of the children growing up in a neighborhood built on top of a toxic waste dump do not get cancer—rather, these children as a group experience a markedly increased incidence of cancer compared to children in more benign settings. Similarly, only 20% of heavy smokers eventually suffer from lung cancer—yet the role of this exposure in these cancers is well-established. A history of adverse developmental experiences does not invariably result in a criminally violent or markedly impaired adult outcome—only a much increased likelihood of it.

An extensive body of research confirms the critical role that developmental experience has on the likelihood of delinquency and/or substance abuse in adolescence, and criminality and criminal violence and substance dependence in adulthood. This literature identifies that cumulative "risk" and "protective" factors account for much of the differences in who does or does not end up engaging in chronic delinquency, criminality, and criminal violence. Specific to Mr. Wilson, there are a number of adverse developmental and life trajectory factors that singly and collectively increased the likelihood of his having teen and adult outcomes that were marred by substance dependence, relationship dysfunction, and/or criminally violent outcomes. These factors also formed the trajectory leading to his capitally charged conduct. These scholarly and case-specific perspectives are critically important if Mr. Wilson's sentencing jury is to have knowledge of the adverse factors in his background, and an informed mechanism to weigh them.

The U.S. Department of Justice has embraced the nexus between developmental factors and criminal outcomes in its own research findings and resultant prevention efforts. More specifically, research on factors associated with an increased risk of chronic delinquency and serious violence in the community has been conducted and synthesized under the sponsorship of the U.S. Department of Justice (DOJ) as part of their increasing commitment to violence-prevention programs. Consistent with long-accepted explanations (e.g., Masten & Garmezy, 1985), DOJ-sponsored reviews have concluded that risk of violent criminal outcome is a function of the interaction or balancing of risk and protective factors (Howell, 1995).

Findings Regarding Background Factors

A 1995 study published by the U.S. Department of Justice identified the risk and protective factors for delinquency and criminal violence (those present in Mr. Wilson's background designated by check marks, "±" reflects partial or probable presence):

RISK FACTORS

Conception to age 6:
- ✓ Perinatal difficulties

Minor physical abnormalities
- ± Brain damage
- ✓ Family history of criminal behavior and substance abuse
- ✓ Family management problems
- ✓ Family conflict
- ✓ Parental attitudes favorable toward, and parental involvement in, crime and substance abuse

Age 6 through adolescence:
- ✓ Extreme economic deprivation
- ✓ Community disorganization and low neighborhood attachment

Transitions and mobility
- ✓ Availability of firearms
- ✓ Media portrayals of violence
- ✓ Family management problems
- ✓ Family conflict
- ✓ Parental attitudes favorable toward, and parental involvement in, crime and substance abuse
- ✓ Early and persistent antisocial behavior
- ✓ Academic failure
- ✓ Lack of commitment to school
- ✓ Alienation and rebelliousness
- ✓ Association with peers who engage in delinquency and violence
- ✓ Favorable attitudes towards delinquent and violent behaviors
- ✓ Constitutional factors (e.g., low intelligence, hyperactivity, attention-deficit disorders)

PROTECTIVE FACTORS

Individual characteristics:
    Female gender
    Intelligence
    Positive social orientation
    Resilient temperament

Social bonding to positive role models:
    ± Family members
    Teachers
    Coaches
    Youth leaders
    Friends

Healthy beliefs and clear standards for behavior, including those that promote nonviolence and abstinence from drugs.

EFFECTIVE EARLY INTERVENTIONS

Mr. Wilson's background reflected a paucity of the 40 developmental assets specified from large-scale research by the Search Institute. The concentration of these assets has been found to be associated with both problematic outcomes (when fewer are present) and adaptive outcomes (when more are present).

Hawkins et al. (2000), in research sponsored by the DOJ, identified a number of developmental arenas and associated specific factors that have a cumulative effect on the risk for delinquency and violence. Numbers in parentheses reflect odds ratios regarding the impact of that single factor on the likelihood of delinquency and violence. Such adverse developmental factors in the background of Mr. Wilson include (designated by checkmarks):

RISK FACTORS

Individual factors:
    ✓ Hyperactivity, concentration problems, restlessness, and risk taking (x 2–5)
    ✓ Aggressiveness (x 1.5–6)
    Early initiation of violent behavior (x 6)
    ✓ Involvement in other forms of antisocial behavior
    ✓ Beliefs and attitudes favorable to deviant or antisocial behavior

Family factors:
    ✓ Parental criminality (x 1–3.8)
    ✓ Child maltreatment
    ✓ Poor family management practices (x 2)

✓ Low levels of parental involvement
✓ Poor family bonding and family conflict
    Residential mobility (±)
✓ Parental attitudes favorable to substance abuse and violence (x 2)
✓ Parent–child separation

School factors:
    ± Academic failure
    ✓ Low bonding to school
    ✓ Truancy and dropping out of school
    Frequent school transitions
    ✓ High delinquency rate schools

Peer-related factors:
    ✓ Delinquent siblings
    ✓ Delinquent peers
    Gang membership (x 3–4)

Community and neighborhood factors:
    ✓ Poverty (x 2)
    ✓ Community disorganization (crime, drug-selling, gangs, poor housing)
    ✓ Availability of drugs and firearms
    ✓ Neighborhood adults involved in crime
    ✓ Exposure to violence and racial prejudice

Situational Factors

Other DOJ-sponsored longitudinal studies detail the effects of child maltreatment (e.g., Widom, 2000; Kelley, Thornberry, & Smith, 1997); the effects of family disruption (e.g., Thornberry et al., 1999) and the cumulative effects of hostility, observed violence, and personal violent victimization within the family (e.g., Thornberry, 1994) on criminal outcome and violence rates. Important research on the risks associated with various developmental factors has also been published in the peer-reviewed literature apart from the sponsorship of DOJ, with empirical findings illuminating adverse outcomes associated with adverse circumstances and developmental risks such as those experienced by Mr. Wilson. Mr. Wilson's developmental history demonstrates a heavy concentration of the risk factors, and only limited presence of the protective factors identified in the above studies. The adverse factors, as well as others that will be detailed in the section that follows, acted to singularly and collectively increase the likelihood of psychological and social maladjustment, substance abuse and dependence, morality deficits, poor impulse control, poor judgment, criminal activity, and violent criminal offending.

Another lens for establishing a nexus between Mr. Wilson's background and his criminal conduct, including the capital offense, arises from clinical perspectives and application of other research and scholarship. Analysis of Mr. Wilson's background in light of these perspectives and research finds 25 toxic formative influences and compromising factors (supplementing and elaborating on the risk factors for delinquency and criminal violence detailed by the 1995 and 2000 reports from the U.S. Department of Justice), each with malignant implications for Mr. Wilson's life trajectory culminating in drug dependence and associated criminal activity, including the capital conduct. Each of these factors can be illustrated in anecdotal detail from interviews and records, with research findings illustrating the relationship of each factor to adverse outcomes and/or criminal violence.

Neuro-developmental:

1. Potential prenatal exposure to alcohol and/or illicit drugs
2. Premature birth
3. Attention-deficit hyperactivity disorder
4. Learning problems in school
5. Head injury with loss of consciousness
6. Inhalant abuse
7. Hereditary predisposition to psychological disorder and personality pathology
8. Hereditary predisposition for alcohol and drug abuse/dependence

Parenting and family:

9. Trans-generational family dysfunction and distress
10. Inadequate parental bonding
11. Functional maternal abandonment in early childhood
12. Parental neglect
13. Parental alcohol and drug abuse
14. Physical abuse by sequential stepfathers
15. Chaotic household
16. Corruptive extended family
17. Emotional and supervisory neglect in household of paternal grandmother
18. Ejection from mother's household as a teen

Community:

19. Low-income neighborhood
20. Prescription drug epidemic

Disturbed trajectory:

21. Teen-onset alcohol and drug abuse
22. Criminal activity from late teens
23. Prescription drug dependence
24. Spiraling deterioration in life status
25. Intoxication at the time of the offense.

CONCEPTUAL CONSIDERATIONS REGARDING POTENTIAL FOR A POSITIVE ADJUSTMENT TO PRISON (POSITIVE PRISONER EVIDENCE)

The potential for Mr. Wilson to adjust without serious violence to the State Department of Corrections (DOC) under a life sentence may be relevant as a mitigating factor (i.e., positive prisoner evidence, see *Skipper v. South Carolina*). Additionally, evidence that Mr. Wilson is likely to have a positive adjustment to a life sentence in the DOC would tend to rebut any implicit, if erroneous, future risk implications of personal characteristics, offense features, or other factors that may be asserted or implied by the State (see Sandys, Pruss, & Walsh, 2009) in characterizations of the defendant and/or in alleging a statutory aggravating factor (i.e., there is a probability that the defendant would commit criminal acts of violence that would constitute a continuing threat to society).

Capital Juror Concern with Future Violence

Research studies involving both actual capital jurors and mock capital jurors demonstrate that these jurors are concerned with the potential for future violence by a capital offender regardless of whether this is overtly alleged at trial (Blume, Garvey, & Johnson, 2001; Sandys et al., 2009). Though they represent illusory correlations that are without predictive value in the assessment of the risk of prison violence (see Cunningham, 2006; Cunningham & Reidy, 1999, 2002; Cunningham, Sorensen, & Reidy, 2009; Edens et al., 2005), capital juries are prone to make inferences regarding future violence risk based on the perceived remorse, the perceived viciousness of the offense, and perceived personality pathology (Sandys et al., 2009).

Prison Violence

Analysis of a defendant's past behavior pattern (in a similar setting) and the application of group statistical data are the two approaches that are most reliable in assessing the likelihood of violent behavior in a prison context. Regarding the application of group statistical data, it should be noted that any scientifically informed individualization in the medical and mental health sciences in diagnosis, therapeutics, or prognosis (i.e., risk) is, by necessity, based on group statistical data. Group statistical data need not be specific to a particular corrections department to have application to the inmates within that prison system. Because of numerous common features between corrections departments and offender populations, as well as replication of findings from studies in a variety of jurisdictions, these data generalize widely. For similar reasons, well-replicated data on risk factors for heart disease or cancer collected from samples in various states generalize to other states within the United States.

Behavior pattern analysis that is specific to the context is critically important because prison represents a fundamentally different context from the community—and prison violence does not predictably follow from pre-confinement violence or the capital offense of conviction.

FINDINGS REGARDING POTENTIAL FOR A POSITIVE ADJUSTMENT TO PRISON

With these two approaches in mind, there are numerous factors that can be analyzed regarding Mr. Wilson's likelihood of adjusting to a capital life term in the DOC without serious violence. These factors each reflect characteristics for particularizing the assessment to Mr. Wilson. Again, these either address a mitigating factor or illuminate the risk-implication of factors intuitively employed by the jury and/or implied as having risk implications by the State. These perspectives include the following:

1. A number of factors are present that would be associated with a reduced risk of prison violence for Mr. Wilson relative to broader categories of "inmates" or "capital offenders."
   a. *Behavior pattern in custody:* For approximately 27 months, Mr. Wilson has been confined in the county jail. During this tenure, Mr. Wilson has had no disciplinary tickets. Mr. Wilson was previously confined in the county main jail. At age 19 he was confined for two periods of three months each at minimum security in the South facility, without disciplinary incident. At age 20, he was confined at minimum security for three months in the North facility, and subsequently for six months at minimum security in the North facility. These confinements were also without disciplinary infractions. This pattern of compliant and nonviolent adjustment to jail confinement predicts a continuing compliant and nonviolent adjustment to DOC.
   b. *Age:* Mr. Wilson is 35 years old (D.O.B. 12/05/77). Age is one of the most powerful predictors for prison misconduct, including among capital offenders sentenced to life without parole (LWOP) terms (Cunningham, Reidy, & Sorensen, 2008), with aging inmates having progressively *lower* rates of misconduct (Bench & Allen, 2003; Hirschi & Gottfredson, 1989; Haun, 2007; Kuanliang, Sorensen, & Cunningham, 2008) and assaultive misconduct (Cunningham, Reidy, & Sorensen, 2008; Cunningham & Sorensen, 2006a, 2006b, 2007a, 2007b; Cunningham, Sorensen, & Reidy, 2005; Haun, 2007; Kuanliang et al., 2008; Sorensen & Pilgrim, 2000). Thus, holding other factors constant, Mr. Wilson, at age 35, presents a markedly lower risk of violence in prison compared to inmates in their teens, twenties, or early thirties. The inverse relationship between age and prison misconduct or violence holds even when the offender committed his crimes/murders in the community at an older age. As this is a continuous rather than dichotomous factor, his risk would be somewhat greater than that of inmates in their forties or older.
   c. *Continuing contact with community members:* Mr. Wilson has maintained relationships with family members during pretrial custody. These visitors

and/or phone contacts have included his ex-wife, mother, and children. He also corresponds with his father and paternal grandmother. To the extent that such relationships continue after he enters DOC, as is expected, the pro-social influence of these and the associated incentive to maintain good conduct so as to facilitate visitation and telephone access would contribute to better inmate adjustment.

  d. *Correctional appraisal:* While awaiting trial on the current charge, Mr. Wilson has been double-celled and has had access to a common dayroom with approximately 30 other inmates, eight hours daily. Correctional staff walk among the unshackled inmates in this dayroom. This classification, in full knowledge of his charges, reflects the determination of corrections professionals that Mr. Wilson is not an imminent risk to staff or other inmates.

2. A single factor, i.e., robbery/burglary in the capital offense, is present that may serve to modestly increase Mr. Wilson's risk of committing serious prison violence (relative to the very low base rate).

3. Group data demonstrate that the seriousness of the offense of conviction is not a good indicator of prison misconduct or violence. This is the conclusion of multiple studies, including a recent large-scale comparison of the disciplinary misconduct and institutional assaults by murderers with those by other prison inmates (Sorensen & Cunningham, 2010).

4. There are other individualizing factors that can be specified in forecasting Mr. Wilson's likelihood of serious violence in DOC.

  a. *Convicted murderer:* A recent large-scale study demonstrates that convicted first-degree murderers have low rates of serious assault in prison, and that these rates are consistent with those of inmates convicted of other offenses (Sorensen & Cunningham, 2010). A homicide conviction was also not predictive of violence in another state corrections department (Reidy, Sorensen, & Cunningham, 2012).

  b. *Convicted capital murderer:* Multiple group statistical studies indicate that the majority of individuals convicted of capital murder are not cited for serious violent misconduct in prison. These studies include retrospective examinations of the records of former death-sentenced inmates in Arizona (Sorensen & Cunningham, 2009) and Texas (Cunningham, Sorensen, Vigen, & Woods, 2011a; Cunningham, Sorenson, Vigen, & Woods, 2011b; Marquart, Ekland-Olsen, & Sorensen, 1989), federal capital offenders serving life sentences in the Bureau of Prisons (Cunningham, Reidy, & Sorensen, 2008), mainstreamed death-sentenced inmates in Missouri (Cunningham, Reidy, & Sorensen, 2005), and aggravated murderers sentenced to death or serving life sentences in Oregon (Reidy, Sorensen, & Cunningham, 2013). Similarly, group statistical data point to capital offenders' representing better institutional assault risks than inmates serving shorter sentences.

  c. *Long-term inmate or LWOP:* An 11-year comparative study of life-without-parole (LWOP) inmates and parole-eligible inmates in a high-security prison demonstrated that LWOP inmates were half as likely to be involved in assaultive misconduct (Cunningham, Sorensen, & Reidy, 2005). In another large-scale study, LWOP inmates were not a disproportionate risk of prison violence compared to inmates serving lengthy (10+ year) sentences (Cunningham & Sorensen, 2006b).

5. Several actuarial models are available to provide perspectives regarding both likelihood of assaultive misconduct and comparative risk. In applying these studies, it is important to note that lifetime risk is *not* a multiple of the time period specified in the study. Inmates who exhibit violence in prison tend to do so early in their sentences.

  a. Applying group statistical data from a large-scale ($N = 6,390$) study (Sorensen & Pilgrim, 2000) of assaultive conduct by convicted murderers in state prison, a convicted murderer would have the following probabilities of serious institutional violence across a capital life term: 16% any serious assault, 1% aggravated assault on staff, and 0.2% homicide of an inmate.

b. Utilizing data on 13,341 inmates entering state prison (Cunningham & Sorensen, 2006a), inmates sharing predictive characteristics with Mr. Wilson were in the best 20% (i.e., 80% of inmates are more likely to be involved in assaultive misconduct in the first year of confinement). In the risk group corresponding to Mr. Wilson's characteristics, 4.5% engaged in assaultive misconduct and 95.5% did not.

c. Utilizing a study of capital offenders in state corrections custody (Cunningham & Sorensen, 2007a), inmates sharing risk correlates with Mr. Wilson were in the middle of three risk groups, with 10.9% engaging in assaults and 1.8% in serious assaults during prison tenures that averaged 2.37 years.

d. Utilizing a study of 110 capital offenders averaging over 18 years in state corrections custody (Cunningham, Sorensen, Vigen, & Woods, 2011a), inmates sharing characteristics with Mr. Wilson were in the middle of three risk groups, with 4.3% engaging in serious assaults.

6. The above analyses support a conclusion that there is a very low likelihood that Mr. Wilson would perpetrate serious violence confined for life in the State Department of Corrections. As the severity of the projected violence increases, the likelihood that Mr. Wilson would perpetrate this level of violence becomes increasingly remote.

7. As risk of violence is always a function of context, the above estimates of the risk of serious violence could be markedly reduced by ultra-secure confinement. Should DOC determine that Mr. Wilson is disproportionately likely to perpetrate serious institutional violence, there are mechanisms to confine him under heightened security procedures that involve single-celling, application of restraints with any movement, solitary or small-group recreation, and other

security measures. Under such conditions, any opportunity to engage in serious violence is substantially reduced.

It is anticipated that my testimony regarding Mr. Wilson's history and associated implications, as well as risk assessment findings, will be accompanied and illustrated by numerous digital demonstrative exhibits.

Please advise me if I may provide additional information or perspective. Thank you for your consideration.

Respectfully,
Mark D. Cunningham, Ph.D., ABPP

TEACHING POINT:
EVALUATING THE ACCURACY OF DIFFERENT SOURCES OF THIRD PARTY INFORMATION

The accuracy of third party information—records and collateral interviews—is an important aspect of FMHA. Since the review of such information does not lend itself to quantitatively based judgment, however, the traditional scientific domains of reliability and validity are not directly applicable. Rather, the forensic clinician must consider criteria that are theoretically and conceptually related to accuracy, and then make a judgment about the accuracy of a given source in consideration of such criteria.

There are several considerations that might be applied to the question of the accuracy of third party information:

- The first is *bias/motivation*. To what extent does the collateral interviewee or document author have an interest in the outcome of the case? This might apply to family members and friends on one end of the spectrum, and victims and their families on the other end. (It is not always accurate to assume that family members are inclined toward less punitive outcomes and victims toward more punitive results. Asking "How would you like this to turn out?" at the end of a collateral interview can help gauge the motivation of the person being interviewed.)
- The second consideration is the interviewee's or document's *familiarity* with the person

being evaluated. Are the observations based on a very limited opportunity, gathered over a period of years involving regular contact, or something intermediate? How recently was the defendant observed?

- Next consider the *time spent* in composing the document or responding to the evaluator's interview questions. More knowledge is likely to be elicited with a longer interview— although an interviewee with limited familiarity with the defendant may, because of such limitations, only need to be evaluated for a short time.
- Related to the previous point is the *level of detail* provided. Detailed responses to specific questions are one indicator of greater knowledge.

- In addition, the *uniqueness and consistency* of the contribution are important. Third party information that provides data that are unusual or even not addressed at all by other sources can be quite valuable, but cannot be judged by its consistency with other evaluation sources—a useful indicator of potential accuracy.
- Finally, there is the question of whether the information conveys *only observations* or *both observations and judgment*. For the most part, the preferable strategy is to use third party information as a source of observations, but refrain from adopting judgments made in documents or interviews. Such judgments are to be made by the forensic clinician.

8

Capital Sentencing, *Atkins*-Type Evaluations

The focus of the previous chapter was on capital sentencing evaluations. The present chapter contains two case reports that demonstrate a particular type of capital sentencing evaluation: *Atkins*-type evaluations. In the case of *Atkins v. Virginia* (2002), the United States Supreme Court effectively prohibited the execution of individuals with mental retardation by deciding that doing so violated the Eighth Amendment ban on cruel and unusual punishment. Because the assessment of mental retardation (now called *intellectual disability*) is essential to these cases, it has been noted that such evaluations "are more properly viewed as a clinical assessment in a forensic context" (Cunningham, 2010, p. 171). Given the potential consequences of an *Atkins*-type capital sentencing evaluation, it is especially important to ensure assessment procedures are conducted in a competent, reliable, and valid manner.

The principle associated with the first case emphasizes the importance of practicing within the scope of one's expertise and areas of competence, with a teaching point that specifically addresses the types of expertise necessary to conduct *Atkins* evaluations. The second case presented highlights the importance of considering relevance and reliability when gathering information for an FMHA, and the associated teaching point addresses how relevance and reliability guide the selection of particular assessment measures.

CASE ONE
PRINCIPLE: ACCEPT REFERRALS ONLY WITHIN AREA OF EXPERTISE (*PRINCIPLE 9*)

This principle concerns the importance of the forensic clinician's having sufficient expertise and experience to perform a given FMHA competently. Because FMHAs are conducted for a wide range of individuals in legal contexts, the clinician must consider a variety of individual factors pertaining to the evaluee, such as age, racial, and ethnic background; disorders in mental, emotional, cognitive, and developmental functioning; substance use disorders; physical problems; and the impact of incarceration. Given these diverse influences, it is important that the clinician have sufficient training and experience with specific populations of which the individual being evaluated is a member. It is also important to have training and experience in forensic areas, including knowledge of relevant law and procedures, an awareness of the differences between forensic and clinical psychology and psychiatry, and a working knowledge of the techniques and tools that are applicable in such evaluations.

Support for performing FMHA only within one's area of expertise can be found in several sources of authority. In psychology, the *Ethical Principles of Psychologists and Code of Conduct* (APA *Ethics Code*; American Psychological Association, 2010a) directly emphasizes the importance of professional competence:

> Psychologists provide services, teach, and conduct research with populations and in areas only within the boundaries of their competence, based on their education, training, supervised experience, consultation, study, or professional experience....Where scientific or professional knowledge in the discipline of psychology establishes that an understanding of factors associated with age, gender, gender identity, race, ethnicity, culture, national origin, religion, sexual orientation, disability, language, or socioeconomic status is essential for effective implementation of their services or research, psychologists have or obtain the training, experience, consultation, or supervision necessary to ensure the competence of their services, or they make appropriate referrals. (Standard 2.01(a))

Of import it is further noted that, "Psychologists undertake ongoing efforts to develop and maintain their competence" (Standard 2.03).

The *Specialty Guidelines for Forensic Psychology* (APA *Specialty Guidelines*; American Psychological Association, 2013b) elaborate on competence for forensic practice:

When determining one's competence to provide services in a particular matter, forensic practitioners may consider a variety of factors including the relative complexity and specialized nature of the service, relevant training and experience, the preparation and study that they are able to devote to the matter, and the opportunity for consultation with a professional of established competence in the subject matter in question. (Guideline 2.01)

Furthermore, the APA *Specialty Guidelines* note that there is a responsibility for a fundamental and reasonable level of knowledge and understanding of the legal and professional standards that govern experts in legal proceedings, as well as an obligation to:

adequately and accurately inform all recipients of their services (e.g., attorneys, tribunals) about relevant aspects of the nature and extent of their experience, training, credentials, and qualifications, and how they were obtained. (Guideline 2.03)

A similar position can be found in the *Principles of Medical Ethics with Annotations Especially Applicable to Psychiatry* (American Psychiatric Association, 2013b), where it is noted that a "psychiatrist who regularly practices outside his or her area of professional competence should be considered unethical" (Section 2.3). Furthermore, the *Ethical Guidelines for the Practice of Forensic Psychiatry* (American Academy of Psychiatry and the Law, 2005) notes that, "[e]xpertise in the practice of forensic psychiatry should be claimed only in areas of actual knowledge, skills, training, and experience" ("Qualifications," paragraph 1). Clearly, these ethical standards define the boundaries of competence by knowledge, skill, experience, and education/training, and provide no exceptions to the need for competence in an area of practice.

Legal support for accepting referrals only within an area of expertise can be found in Rule 702 of the *Federal Rules of Evidence*, under which an expert can offer evidence in scientific, technical, or other areas of specialized knowledge. Further, the prospective expert must have acquired special knowledge, skill, experience, training, or education that would allow that individual to address the issues within their areas of expertise that are before the court.

The question of when a forensic clinician is sufficiently "expert" to perform a forensic assessment has also been addressed by the American Bar Association's *Criminal Justice Mental Health Standards* (1989). Under Standard 7-3.10, no professional should be appointed by the court to evaluate a person's mental condition unless his qualifications include:

(a) sufficient professional education and sufficient clinical training and experience to establish the clinical knowledge required for the specific type(s) of evaluation(s) being conducted; and (b) sufficient forensic knowledge, gained through specialized training or an acceptable substitute therefor, necessary for understanding the relevant legal matter(s) and for satisfying the specific purpose(s) for which the evaluation is being ordered. (p. 130)

Regarding minimum professional education and clinical training requirements for evaluators and expert witnesses, the *Standards* notes that "necessary" and "desirable" education and training requirements differ according to the subject matter of the evaluation and the specific legal issue. For example, it is suggested that an evaluation concerning a person's present mental competence could be conducted by a variety of mental health providers at different levels of training. However, for an evaluation concerning a person's mental condition at the time of an alleged offense, or a person's future mental condition or behavior when these issues arise as part of a sentencing proceeding or special commitment proceeding, the *Standards* suggests that the clinician should be a psychiatrist or a doctoral-level psychologist.

Heilbrun (1995) proposed a two-step process for conceptualizing and evaluating the question of expertise in the context of forensic assessment based on the above sources of authority: the first step is determining whether the clinician has *substantive expertise* with a given population; the second involves whether this expertise has been *applied in forensic contexts*. Substantive expertise involves formal training and experience (both supervised and independent) with a given population. The second step involves demonstrating how one's specialization, formal training, supervised experience, advanced certification, and related professional activities can be demonstrated in *forensic* applications. Pertinent questions include the extent to which the clinician has applied substantive expertise with a particular population to issues arising in the course of litigation, and how often the clinician has applied this expertise in the course of litigation.

There is clear agreement within the ethical standards of psychology and psychiatry about the importance of providing services only within areas of competence. In addition, some sources of legal authority provide definitions of "expertise" in the forensic context, stressing the importance of education, training, and experience in the practice of FMHA. The available professional literature in the area of standard of practice strongly supports the principle of providing services only in areas of competence, including a delineation of levels of training and competence in both substantive areas and forensic applications (Bersoff et al., 1997; DeMatteo, Marczyk, Krauss, & Burl, 2009; Heilbrun, 1995).

The present case report provides a good example of the application of this principle. Specifically, this case involves the evaluation of Mr. Jackson to assess the possibility that he has an intellectual disability, in the context of an *Atkins* decision in a potentially capital case. As suggested in *Criminal Justice Mental Health Standards* (1989), the forensic clinician in this case is a doctoral-level psychologist. In addition to having relevant education, training, and experience in FMHA, it is important that the clinician conducting an *Atkins* evaluation understand the applicable law that defines mental retardation in the jurisdiction in which the evaluation is taking place (see, e.g., DeMatteo, Marczyk, & Pich, 2007) and have training and experience in the assessment and diagnosis of mental retardation, as is true of the clinician conducting the present evaluation (see, e.g., DeMatteo, Murrie, Anumba, & Keesler, 2011). The report reflects awareness of the criteria for determining the presence of mental retardation, and the evaluator also showed an awareness of good forensic practice by using a variety of data sources, including psychological testing, clinical interview, collateral interviews, and collateral document review. Many of these data sources are specifically selected because of their relevance to intellectual and adaptive functioning.

Psychological Evaluation
Jackson, Samuel   Date of Birth: March 14, 1983
Date of Report: October 26, 2010 Age: 27
Re: People v. Samuel Jackson, Case No. YA069803

This evaluation took place at the request of Mr. Jackson's attorneys in order to address the question of whether the defendant had intellectual disability (a.k.a. mental retardation) in childhood and at the time of the crime of which he is accused.

SOURCES OF INFORMATION

- School records from Los Angeles Unified School District
- California Department of Corrections academic records
- California Department of Corrections physician's orders
- California Department of Corrections medical records
- California Department of Corrections mental health records
- Report of neuropsychological evaluation by Andrew Rogers, Ph.D.
- Sheriff's Department report of murder of A.V. Able, 9/20/2007
- Interview of Samuel Jackson, Jr., at County Jail, 7/9/10
- Interview with Kareem Metta, former substance abuse counselor to Mr. Jackson, at MLK Community Center, 7/10/10
- Interview with Shavon Adams, aunt of Mr. Jackson, at home of Candace Davis, 7/10/10
- Interview with Barbara Blue, cousin of Mr. Jackson, at home of Candace Davis, 7/10/10
- Interview with Georgia Ann Sanders, half-sister of Mr. Jackson, at home of Candace Davis, 7/10/10

- Interview with Susan Taber, great-aunt of Mr. Jackson, at her home in Modesto, California, 7/11/10
- Interview with Al Norris, Jr., husband of Susan Taber, at their home in Modesto, California, 7/11/10
- Interview with Randall Bolles, friend of Mr. Jackson and fiancé of Georgia Ann Sanders, at their home, 7/12/10
- Interview with Carl Bolles, father of Lamar Bolles, at his home, 7/12/10
- Interview with Denise Gonzalez, former neighbor of Mr. Jackson and his parents, at her home in South Central Los Angeles, 7/6/10
- Interview with Jack Jones, former teacher of Mr. Jackson, at his home, 7/6/10
- Interview with Donna Jackson, aunt of Mr. Jackson, at home of Candace Davis, Anderson, California 7/7/10
- Interview with Douglas Jackson, husband of Patty Jackson, at home of Candace Davis, Anderson, California 7/7/10
- Interview with Candace Davis, mother of Mr. Jackson, at her home, Anderson, California, 7/7/10
- Interview with Vincent Adams, stepfather of Mr. Jackson, at his and Ms. Davis's home, Anderson, California, 7/7/10
- Interview with Edward Jones, younger half-brother of Mr. Jackson, at his mother's home where he lives, Anderson, California, 7/7/10
- Interview with Joseph Griffin, cousin of Mr. Jackson, at California State Prison, 7/8/10
- Interview with Samuel Jackson, Sr., father of Mr. Jackson, at a restaurant, 7/9/10
- Interview with Bernice Sanders, step-grandmother of Mr. Jackson, at her home, 7/10/10
- Interview with Elaine Kennedy, godmother of Samuel Jackson, and Alan Moon, grandparents of Samuel Jackson's friend Barry North, at their home, 7/11/10
- Transcript of County Sheriff's detectives' interrogation of Samuel Jackson, 10/25/07
- Video of interrogation of Samuel Jackson 10/25/07
- 1999 sample of Samuel Jackson's handwriting at age 16 when asked to write two things he liked about himself

CRITERIA FOR INTELLECTUAL DISABILITY DIAGNOSIS

California Penal Code §1376 and all contemporary definitions of intellectual disability (a.k.a. mental retardation) refer to three required elements for a diagnosis. These are "significantly subaverage general intellectual functioning existing concurrently with deficits in adaptive behavior and manifested before the age of 18."

Authoritative sources on the diagnosis of intellectual disability include publications by the American Psychiatric Association (2000) and the American Association on Intellectual and Developmental Disabilities (2010, 2012; formerly American Association on Mental Retardation). The information gathered in the determination of intellectual disability for Mr. Jackson has relied on these authoritative sources, which are referenced below.[1]

DEVELOPMENTAL HISTORY

Since the early grades, Mr. Jackson has had significant problems in learning that have been documented by school records. He was provided with Special Education services for students with learning disabilities. In addition to his learning problems, he had behavior problems in school and dropped out in the eleventh grade. Mr. Jackson has a history of thyroid disease from childhood. He had two seizures as a preschooler. In December 1996 (age 13), a car hit Mr. Jackson, resulting in loss of consciousness. He has a very limited job history. Dr. Rogers's report states that Mr. Jackson "briefly worked for a church stacking and stapling papers. He also briefly worked as a painter for his cousin's father."

---

[1] American Association on Intellectual and Developmental Disabilities (2010). *Intellectual disability: Definition, classification, and systems of supports* (11th ed.). Washington, DC: Author.

American Association on Intellectual and Developmental Disabilities (2012). *User's guide: Intellectual disability: Definition, classification and systems of supports – 11th edition.* Washington, DC: Author.

American Psychiatric Association (2000). *Diagnostic and statistical manual of mental disorders* (4th ed., text revision). Washington, DC: Author.

Mr. Jackson was raised by his mother and had limited contact with his father, who has experienced mental illness and has been homeless and a drug user for much of his adult life. Mr. Jackson has six siblings or half-siblings. He has not been married and has had few female relationships. He has no children. He has been incarcerated twice before his current charge.

EDUCATION HISTORY

Mr. Jackson attended public school in the Los Angeles Unified School District. His school records indicate grades of mostly C, D, and F in Special Education classes. My interview with Al Jones, who taught Mr. Jackson in the ninth grade, was helpful in clarifying information in school records.

School records indicate that in the third grade, Mr. Jackson was referred to Special Education and placed in a day program. School records indicate poor academic and social skills. Teacher comments in both fourth and fifth grades indicated "does not get along well with peers." A note in fifth grade stated "unable to read." In seventh and eighth grades, he received Ds and an F in PE, but in ninth grade he received an A in basketball. At age 13 at Lincoln Middle School, a teacher commented, "He makes friends very easily." In middle school, Mr. Jackson received Special Education services in the Resource Specialist Program, but by ninth grade at Adams High School he was back in the Special Day Class, which was a more restrictive placement in which all of his classmates were students in Special Education.

Mr. Jones taught Mr. Jackson social science in the ninth grade at Adams High School during the 1998–1999 school year. Mr. Jackson was served in the Special Day Class (SDC), which Mr. Jones described as a lower-level part of Special Education. In this program, students move from class to class, but they are all in Special Education classes. Mr. Jackson received an F in Mr. Jones's class, although it was a Special Education curriculum and graded with lower expectations than a regular class.

I asked Mr. Jones whether the curriculum that Mr. Jackson received was any different than one that a student with mental retardation would receive. Mr. Jones replied that it was not and that it was quite plausible that Mr. Jackson had mental retardation, Although he received services in the Learning Disability classification. Mr. Jones reported that the curriculum was individualized to follow the student's Individualized Education Program (IEP). The program of instruction that Mr. Jones described had an emphasis on structure and clear expectations. Student progress was charted every day, and clear consequences were enforced. Mr. Jones noted that this method of instruction was the same that a student with mental retardation would receive. He recalled that Mr. Jackson was responsive to rewards usually used for younger students. He "liked gimmick rewards—stickers, gum."

When asked about a teacher comment in the school records indicating that Samuel made friends easily, Mr. Jones said that such teacher comments were not always a true picture, because they were made in the context of the lower expectations of Special Education. Mr. Jones did not recall that Samuel was a behavior problem in his class, although other teachers had a problem with him. Mr. Jones said that when other kids would "show out," Samuel would try to show off for others.

I asked about Mr. Jackson's communication skills, and Mr. Jones said that he "didn't let you know when he needed help. He had a hard time explaining stuff." Mr. Jones said that he would "go over things two, three, four times, and he'd understand at the time but wouldn't retain it." Mr. Jones said that his class required reading and understanding and that Samuel "definitely couldn't read well." Mr. Jones said that Samuel was enthusiastic about the class at first but couldn't stick with it. When I asked about the absences on Mr. Jackson's record, Mr. Jones said, "Why do you want to be somewhere where you're failing all the time?"

Mr. Jackson's records indicated only one good grade. He received an A in basketball. Mr. Jones explained that the class was adapted physical education (PE), and the grade "was probably given to him," because he was on or trying out for the Freshman/Sophomore basketball team. Despite this grade, Mr. Jackson was academically ineligible to play basketball.

With regard to Mr. Jackson's emotional adjustment, Mr. Jones reported that some "days his energy was good, and days it was bad." He said that Mr. Jackson might have been using marijuana at the time, because he was "up and down a lot."

Mr. Jackson's IEP dated 5/31/96 (age 13) cited the following scores from the Kaufman Test of Educational Achievement. Standard scores below 70 indicate significant impairment congruent with a diagnosis of mental retardation.

	Standard Score	Grade Equivalent
Mathematics Application	66	2.4
Reading Decoding	61	1.8
Spelling	64	2.3
Reading Comprehension	66	2.3
Mathematics Computation	76	5.1
Overall Composite Scores		
Reading	62	2.0
Mathematics	67	3.7
TOTAL BATTERY	62	2.7

Samuel's Special Education teacher, Peter Brown, described these scores as "in the extremely low range." The IEP suggested that Samuel would benefit from instruction in a more restrictive placement. Mr. Jackson's IEP dated 8/12/97 (age 14) also reported scores from the Kaufman Test of Educational Achievement (KTEA) indicating the following grade equivalents, which are even lower than those of the previous year.

Reading decoding	1.9	Math computation	3.9 ("with help")
Spelling	1.1	Math application	2.7
Reading comprehension	1.8		

The same IEP cited scores from April 1997 testing indicating pre-primer level in reading and spelling. Math grade level on the Brigance Comprehensive Inventory of Basic Skills was 1.2.

An Individualized Transition Plan dated 4/28/98 (age 15) stated, "Samuel will enroll at a ROP (Regional Occupational Program) Center when he is 16 yrs old." Mr. Jones clarified that ROP is a vocational program. Mr. Jackson left school in the eleventh grade when he was incarcerated and never returned to public school.

With regard to the question of the proper Special Education classification for Mr. Jackson, it is useful to consider the following quote from Peter Mitchell, psychologist for the Los Angeles Unified School District (LAUSD) on 4/24/98 regarding Samuel Jackson. Mr. Mitchell apparently provided this information in support of a classification of "learning disability." I have added the information in brackets in order to clarify the acronyms that Mr. Mitchell used.

#2 No IQ tests given based on Los Angeles Unified School District Board of Education policy. Alternative means of assessment included adaptive behavior analysis, test interpretation, teacher-guardian input, school records, and professional judgment. The Woodcock Language Battery-R[evised] test was used as part of this evaluation and indicated general ability to be in the low average range. The Auditory Processing subtest of the TAPS-U [Test of Auditory Processing Skills] placed this student in the low average range.

#3 Academically, the WRAT-3 [Wide Range Achievement Test] shows: reading (word recognition\decoding) to be at grade level 2. A sight vocabulary approach was used, with a standard score of 59; Spelling (written encoding) GE [Grade Equivalent] of 1 and St. [Standard] Score of 60. Manuscript writing was used. Arithmetic (number computations) GE of 5 and St. Score of 80. The four basic math processes were used. Does not know how to do fractions.

#4 Social\emotional status based on the Burk's [Burks] Behavior Rating Scales demonstrates problems with sense of persecution. In addition, teacher and other school staff input shows generally marginal behavior.

#5 This student is not bilingual...General expressive language is below average based on the Woodcock Language Battery-R. The TAPS-U [Test of Auditory Processing Skills] test for rote memory and ability to concentrate shows delayed ability.

#6 Visual motor integration based on the Beery Visual Motor integration test demonstrates poor ability. TVPS [Test of Visual Perceptual Skills] (Upper Level—R) visual discrimination was poor, visual memory was in the below average range.

#7 A significant gap does exist between academic achievement and general ability. A learning disability is indicated for Samuel based on delays in the psychological processes of attention-visual-auditory processing. These discrepancies are not the result of environmental, cultural, or economic disadvantages. These discrepancies cannot be corrected through other regular or categorical services with the regular instructional program.

As a basis for a classification of learning disability, this justification has many problems. A learning disability was regarded as a condition in which a student has average intellectual ability but a significant learning problem in one or a small number of academic areas. Mr. Mitchell concluded that Samuel had a discrepancy between achievement and general ability. Yet he reported no test of general ability. He noted that there was no IQ test administered and no other measure of general intellectual ability. Furthermore, test results (and grades) showed that Samuel was performing at very low levels in every area tested. Although one of the means of assessment was said to be "adaptive behavior analysis," no information on adaptive behavior was presented. Thus, Mr. Mitchell offered no reasonable evidence for a diagnosis of learning disability. Samuel's academic performance was poor across all academic areas and every test that Mr. Mitchell administered. Therefore, the information was more compatible with a diagnosis of mental retardation. However, pursuant to school district policy, no IQ test was administered, and no IQ score was available to sustain such a diagnosis. This distinction between the academic performance of a student with mental retardation versus a learning disability is discussed more fully by several authors (e.g., Baroff, 1999).

POST–PUBLIC SCHOOL TESTING

While at Juvenile Hall School, Mr. Jackson was administered the STAR Math test twice.

	Grade Equivalent	Percentile
2/15/2001	2.3	1
4/05/2001	3.8	2

While at State Prison on 1/10/2006, Mr. Jackson completed the Test of Adult Basic Education and achieved the following grade equivalents.

Reading	5.0
Math	4.5
Language	3.4
Total	4.2
Spelling	4.8

In summary, Mr. Jackson has an extensive record of academic achievement testing over many years and has consistently shown significantly impaired academic skills across all areas. His impairment is not limited to one or two areas, as would be expected for a person with a learning disability.

PREVIOUS PSYCHOLOGICAL EVALUATIONS RELATED TO MENTAL RETARDATION

Although no IQ score is available from his childhood, Mr. Jackson participated in a neuropsychological evaluation administered by Andrew Rogers, Ph.D., on December 29, 2008. Dr. Rogers administered tests to determine whether Mr. Jackson put forth good effort and concluded that Mr. Jackson did give satisfactory effort in his test performance. On the Wechsler Adult Intelligence Scale, 3rd edition (WAIS-III), Mr. Jackson achieved a full scale IQ of 66, which indicates significantly impaired intelligence, in the range of mental retardation.

Dr. Rogers administered the Wide Range Achievement Test (3rd edition), on which Mr. Jackson achieved a fourth-grade reading level, second-grade spelling level, and sixth-grade arithmetic level. These low scores are congruent with earlier education testing described in the previous two headings.

Dr. Rogers administered several other neuropsychological tests, which are not tests used to diagnose mental retardation; however, these tests generally showed severely impaired neurocognitive functioning. Dr. Rogers described these areas of impairment as "learning and memory, executive function, academic ability, and speed of cognitive processing." In addition, Dr. Rogers reported that Mr. Jackson showed "symptoms of depression,

---

COMMENT

Although the report of the earlier psychological evaluation indicated that there was no evidence that the defendant did not "put forth good effort," it should be noted that the instruments often used to identify poor effort or malingering of low intellectual functioning are lacking in evidence for their validity (Heilbronner, 2009; Hurley & Deal, 2006; Salekin & Doane, 2009). Note also that the report gives the full scale IQ, because that is the criterion for demonstrating significant impairment in intelligence. Although other scores may be available, they are not necessary and may be distracting from the main evidence for the diagnosis.

including history of suicide attempt, along with indications of psychotic symptomatology, predominate." All of these problems were noted to predate Mr. Jackson's current incarceration.

ASSESSMENT OF ADAPTIVE BEHAVIOR

All current and widely accepted definitions of intellectual disability (or mental retardation) require, in addition to significant impairment in intelligence, evidence of significant limitations in adaptive behavior. Although there is no single test of adaptive behavior (such as there is for intelligence), impairment can be documented by drawing on several sources of information regarding the individual's typical functioning in community settings. Information may come, for example, from people who know the individual well, from records of testing, or records from reliable sources before the time of incarceration.

It is important to emphasize several aspects of adaptive behavior (American Association on Intellectual and Developmental Disabilities, 2007; American Association on Mental Retardation, 2002; American Psychiatric Association, 2000). First, adaptive functioning is the person's actual performance, not estimates of his potential or achievement that might have occurred under other circumstances. Second, it is typical behavior, not isolated successes or failures. Third, it is one's performance in one's community, not performance in prison or in therapeutic treatment settings. Fourth, assessment of adaptive behavior deficits focuses on deficits. People with mild mental retardation typically have strengths or areas of adequate behavior in addition to their adaptive deficits. Identifying areas in which an individual performs adequately does not rule out intellectual disability. As noted by the American Psychiatric Association (2000), there are no exclusion criteria for the diagnosis of mental retardation (intellectual disability). Fifth, the definition of intellectual disability does not require that a cause be identified for impairments in intelligence or adaptive behavior. The diagnosis can be made regardless of the cause of the impairment, although there must be reasonable evidence that the impairment originated before age 18. There are hundreds of identified causes of intellectual disability, but the cause for any individual is often not known. This is particularly true for individuals with IQs in the 60s who usually do not have

a medical syndrome that is known and do not have an obviously different appearance or manner.

The definitions of mental retardation (intellectual disability) cited in the *Atkins v. Virginia* decision in 2002 were those of the American Psychiatric Association (2000) and the American Association on Mental Retardation (AAMR, 1992). These definitions require evidence of impairment in 2 of 10 specified areas of adaptive functioning. The AAMR definitions of these 10 areas are provided in this report in italics. The AAMR definition also recognizes measures of overall functioning, and such scores are reported where they are available. More recently, the American Association on Mental Retardation (2002) changed its name to the American Association on Intellectual and Developmental Disabilities (AAIDD, 2010) and revised its criteria for significant impairment in adaptive behavior to require significant impairment in one of three broad areas (*conceptual, social,* or *practical*) or significant impairment in an overall measure of adaptive functioning. Both criteria for determining deficits in adaptive behavior (1992 and 2010) will be considered here.

Interview with Mr. Jackson

I met with Mr. Jackson on 7/9/2010 at the county jail. He appeared in an orange jail jumpsuit with shaved head and a mustache. He was cooperative and answered all questions. He accurately named his parents and siblings. He described a strained relationship with his father, who "barely came around." Mr. Jackson reported that his father seemed to appear only when he was there to discipline his son. Mr. Jackson reported that "He'd try to discipline, so I didn't want him to come around no more." His version of discipline was to "whop me." Mr. Jackson reported that his mother took care of him his whole life, and [with reference to his father], "he didn't do nothing." Mr. Jackson named the other men with whom his mother had relationships and said that he "looked up to them more than my father."

With regard to social relationships growing up, Mr. Jackson said that he had good relationships with his cousins who were close in age. He mentioned that his best friend, Barry North, died earlier this year. He was shot coming out of his house by someone who was being chased. Mr. Jackson guessed that it was something gang-related, but emphasized that Mr. North had never been involved with gangs and was just in the wrong place at the wrong time.

Mr. Jackson described his close relationship with Barry North and activities that they did together since elementary school. More information that confirmed Mr. Jackson's description was provided in other interviews described later in this report. Mr. Jackson also cited his half-sister Georgia's boyfriend, Lamar Bolles, as a friend, and noted "other cats weren't friends."

When I asked for clarification of this latter point, Mr. Jackson said that other people tried to bully him and tried to get him to fight, but he didn't want to fight. He described himself as "not violent." When I asked him about gang involvement, he denied such involvement. He said that he had been recruited for gangs and that he sometimes got into fights, because he wore a rival gang's colors, but he did that unknowingly and was never in any gang. He said that even in prison there are gangs, but he tries to stay out of it.

When I asked more about his relationship with his mother, Mr. Jackson said that she wanted him to get a job and pay his share of expenses when he came home from prison in 2007. He said that he was on General Relief but "didn't have enough money to do nothing." He noted that there was conflict with his mother around his paying bills. During the time in September and October 2007 when Mr. Jackson was last out of prison, he said that he smoked weed a lot but denied doing other drugs. He said that everything went bad during that time, including conflict with his mother.

On the topic of his health, Mr. Jackson reported being hit by a car in 1996. He said that he fell and hit his nose on a rusty nail when he was about 10 years old. He said that he had hyperthyroidism and sweated a lot. He said that he used to be on medication for this condition but was not any longer, because the prison said he did not need it.

COMMENT

The literature on intellectual disability has for many years emphasized vulnerability to exploitation and the naiveté of people with intellectual disability who can be easily taken advantage of. Barry North provided a stable influence, but upon his death, Mr. Jackson fell under the influence of people involved in criminal activities.

When asked about mental health issues, Mr. Jackson reported that he has heard voices for many years and talks back to the voices. He said that because of the voices, he has tried to commit suicide three times. Currently he reported trying to keep busy to avoid the voices that tell him that he doesn't deserve to live anymore. As a result, he said, he is depressed. He reported that he couldn't read, so he tries to stay busy with other things, including talking back to the voices. He said that he no longer has the patience that he once had, and he "is at the breaking point now." He reported that it is helpful to talk to his mother and that he is unable to sleep and is awake up for two or three days.

When asked about his education history, Mr. Jackson was able to name several schools that he attended. He reported that he did not do well in school, and that by junior high, he "ditched a lot," because he didn't like his classes. He acknowledged that he could not do the work in school and that his way of hiding his difficulties was to be the class clown and to ditch school. He reported playing basketball in school and that his coach made him go to class. Nevertheless, he didn't do well. He said that he was put in Special Education, but even then, the work was too hard. He noted that he could not read but was better at math. While at Jackson School, he said, he did play basketball and lost only one game.

There are no suitable standardized tests of adaptive behavior for a person who is incarcerated because of the restricted opportunities in such a setting. An alternative is to test one's knowledge of adaptive behavior, but such tests are poorly correlated with actual performance. Therefore, I gave Mr. Jackson a few tasks that he could do in this restricted setting in order to get a sample of his practical and functional academic skills.

I showed Mr. Jackson a map of the world, which he was able to identify. He was able to identify the United States, Europe, and Africa by reading initial letters, but he could not find continents or countries on the map when asked. When asked to read South America, he mistook it for Los Angeles. He identified the map of the United States as a map of the world. He did not have a strategy for finding things on the map and searched randomly until he found a word that he thought matched. He could not point to the directions west, south, or north. He identified a map of California as "Continent." He was able to find Los Angeles on the California map but when asked to find Sacramento, he looked in the Los Angeles area and then gave up. On a map of Los Angeles County, he also had no strategies but could find some familiar names by randomly searching.

When given a phone book and asked to find a dentist named Adams, he paged through randomly and was unsuccessful. He did not appear to understand that a telephone book is organized by categories that are alphabetized. When asked to measure with a ruler, he used the metric side of the ruler and was not able to measure accurately. Mr. Jackson reported that he did not drive.

Finally, I asked Mr. Jackson to write a letter to someone he knew. I asked him to take his time and to write the best letter that he could. He wrote a letter that was about one-half page long to his mother. I asked my colleague, Ann Barrows, to assess the letter's academic level. Ms. Barrows is the head of the Education Section at the State Institute for Developmental Disabilities. She is an experienced teacher and currently is working on a federally funded research project on children's writing. Ms. Barrows indicated that Mr. Jackson's letter was at the late second- or early third-grade level. She noted that it had simplistic language, no punctuation, run-on sentences, and irregular letter formation.

In summary, Mr. Jackson was cooperative in his interview with me. The information that he provided was congruent with earlier information indicating very low academic skills and application of those skills to everyday tasks. He did not demonstrate overt signs of mental illness. His communication skills were concrete.

Adaptive Behavior Findings

The most recent standards for diagnosis of mental retardation/intellectual disability (AAIDD, 2010, 2012; AAMR, 2002) recommend collection of information from as many sources as may have valid information. They also recommend the use of an adaptive behavior scale when there is an informant available who can provide the information necessary to complete such a scale. Adaptive behavior scales are standardized instruments that yield scores that can be compared to the performance of the general population. Such scales use ratings by individuals who know well the individual to be rated. In Mr. Jackson's case, four of the 20 people whom I interviewed met the criteria set forth by Olley and Cox (2008) for an appropriate rater. Those criteria for an informant for the Adaptive Behavior Assessment System, 2nd edition

(ABAS-II; Harrison & Oakland, 2003) are stated as follows:

> The scale should be completed only by informants who have known the defendant well, preferably during childhood and adolescence. The person administering the scale should spend some time getting acquainted with the informant before deciding whether this person can provide suitable information. For example, the examiner should establish the nature of the relationship between the defendant and the informant. Are they related? How long have they known each other? In what capacity have they known each other (e.g., relative, friend, neighbor, former teacher, employer, coach, Scout leader)? Some informants may have known the defendant's functioning well in one setting and be able to provide useful anecdotes yet not know enough to complete all sections of the ABAS-II. If the focus of adaptive behavior is work, the informant may be a former employer or co-worker. He or she may provide useful information by completing only the Work adaptive skill area. If the focus of adaptive behavior is school, the informant may be one or more educators with whom the ABAS-II's Teacher Form would be used. If the focus of adaptive behavior is home, the informant may be a parent, siblings, other relative, or close neighbor.... Before administering the ABAS-II, discuss with the informant the importance of providing complete, honest, unbiased information." (pp. 388–389)

The following information is drawn from several sources and included administration of the Adaptive Behavior Assessment System (2nd edition) to four people who knew Mr. Jackson well before his current incarceration. The other individuals whom I interviewed provided useful interview information, which I have indicated in the following sections. Thus, my conclusions regarding Mr. Jackson's adaptive functioning are drawn from several sources, including documents, ratings on the ABAS-II, and interview information. A more complete description of the use of the ABAS-II for retrospective assessment and related information on the assessment of adaptive functioning can be found in Olley and Cox (2008).

The four people who completed the ABAS-II were Candace Davis (Mr. Jackson's mother), Georgia Sanders (Mr. Jackson's half-sister), Patty Edwards Jackson (Mr. Jackson's aunt), and Lamar Bolles (Mr. Jackson's friend since childhood). Their ratings were based on the most recent time at which they were able to rate Mr. Jackson's community functioning. Scaled Scores in each of the 10 areas of adaptive functioning have a mean of 10 and standard deviation of 3. The range of possible Scaled Scores is 1–19. Therefore, a scaled score of 4 or lower represents a significant impairment in adaptive functioning. The ABAS-II Also yields a composite score, the General Adaptive Composite (GAC).

Information on adaptive behavior is presented below in each of the 10 categories of adaptive behavior, with the definition of each category (American Association on Mental Retardation, 1992).

1. *Communication*: Skills include the ability to comprehend and express information through symbolic behaviors (e.g., spoken word, written word/orthography, graphic symbols, sign. Skills include the ability to comprehend and express information through symbolic behaviors (e.g., language, manually coded English) or non-symbolic behaviors (e.g., facial expression, body movement, touch, gesture). Specific examples include the ability to comprehend and/or receive a request, an emotion, a greeting, a comment, a protest, or rejection. Higher-level skills of communication (e.g., writing a letter) would also relate to functional academics.

ABAS-II scaled scores in the area of Communication were as follows:

Ms. Davis	7
Ms. Jackson	6
Mr. Bolles	7
Ms. Sanders	3

Mr. Kareem Metta knew Mr. Jackson as a neighbor since Mr. Jackson was six or seven years old. He also was Mr. Jackson's court-ordered drug counselor when Samuel was 17. Mr. Metta described Mr. Jackson as a quiet kid who used simple language and did not elaborate. Mr. Metta noted that Mr. Jackson appeared to have a limited understanding when he talked to him about his legal situation.

Mr. Jackson's step-aunt, Karen Adams, knew him best in the time before his first incarceration. She described Mr. Jackson at that time as slow to respond and with poor understanding. She said that she "would have to change the way I talked to him—like break it down like you would for a young child. He wouldn't understand." She said that he tried hard to explain what he didn't understand but just didn't have the words. Ms. Adams said that she had a special and close relationship with Mr. Jackson and that he would go to her for support. However, she said that even at the present time, in phone conversations, she has to break down the things that she tells him and explain the meaning of words. She also pointed out that she read the transcript of Mr. Jackson's interrogation by detectives, "and I know he didn't understand none of that."

Vincent Adams said that he had to explain things to Samuel over and over. Even Samuel's younger half-brother, Edward Jones, said that Samuel was "slower than everybody else," and he had to explain things to him. For example, he said that if you sent "Pookie" (Samuel) to the store, he'd probably forget and bring the wrong item. Mr. Jackson's great aunt, Susan Taber, said, "You'd have to tell him and tell him again." She said he had poor attention and problems understanding. Her husband, Wayne Norris, however, said that Samuel always did what Mr. Norris told him to do, and he did not notice communication problems.

Mr. Jackson's half-sister, Georgia Sanders, who is five years younger, said that her conversations with him were always simple and that he could talk about basketball but not other things. She said that her phone conversations with him now are similar. He asks her what she said, and she has to simplify her language for him to understand.

Mr. Jackson's aunt, Patty Jackson, lived with him or nearby from the time that he was three to 15. She said, "If he tried to tell a story, it wouldn't be clear. He couldn't explain himself. He couldn't get the words. He couldn't think." Ms. Jackson's husband, Douglas Jackson, independently reported similar information. He found that it was sometimes hard to understand what Samuel meant and he had to ask him to repeat himself.

The available information regarding the adaptive behavior area of communication is mixed. Only one of four informants on the ABAS-II rated

Mr. Jackson's communication to be significantly impaired. However, anecdotes from nearly all people I interviewed described significant communication problems. Mr. Jackson's communication was adequate for the concrete communications of his everyday life but at the level of a child.

2. *Self-Care*: skills involved in toileting, eating, dressing, hygiene, and grooming.

ABAS-II scaled scores in the area of Self-Care were as follows:

Ms. Davis	8
Ms. Jackson	1
Mr. Bolles	3
Ms. Sanders	6

Mr. Jackson's aunt, Patty Edwards Jackson, said that Samuel would just put on any old clothes and didn't care how he dressed. Others would comment on his clothes, and then arguments started. Mr. Bolles noted that Mr. Jackson had poor hygiene.

Information on the adaptive behavior area of self-care is mixed. Two of four informants on the ABAS-II rated his self-care as significantly impaired, and comments by people who knew him noted that he dressed poorly and required reminding to present himself appropriately.

3. *Home-Living*: skills related to functioning within a home, which include clothing care, housekeeping, property maintenance, food preparation and cooking, planning and budgeting for shopping, home safety, and daily scheduling. Related skills include orientation and behavior in the home and nearby neighborhood, communication of choices and needs, social interaction, and application of functional academics in the home.

ABAS-II scaled scores in the area of Home Living were as follows:

Ms. Davis	7
Ms. Jackson	1
Mr. Bolles	4
Ms. Sanders	4

Ms. Taber said that when Samuel lived with her, he needed reminding, but he did the things around that house that she asked. Georgia Sanders reported that Mr. Jackson never did anything around the house before he went to prison but that he helped out some when he got out in 2007.

Mr. Bolles gave several examples of Mr. Jackson's difficulties with home tasks. "Like he wouldn't do it right. Sandy taught him to separate colors when washing clothes at age 14, but he still messed it up. First, she would tell him, and he'd say yeah but still do it the same way. Then she'd show him how to do it and still get the same result. In his eyes, I don't think he saw that he did it wrong. He did it continuously." And: "He burned a pot of water—trying to cook hot dogs. Nearly caught the house on fire. He was about 15 years old. It was just water—said he was going to put hot dogs in—I don't know if he just forgot. Smoke alarms went off." And: "Once he took a blue freezer pack. He opened the blue pack and put it in soda. Little stuff like that."

"Cleaning up—He just didn't know how. We used to have to wash the dishes. Everybody would do it, but he'd throw plates and forks away. I don't know why. I think he just couldn't do it." Mr. Bolles said that things that were easy for him were difficult for Mr. Jackson. "Even his brother [nine years younger] was doing things better than Pookie. "We made easy, basic foods. Others could do it, (but) not Pookie."

Lamar Bolles said that Mr. Jackson never talked about getting his own place and just talked about moving in with Mr. Bolles and his fiancée (Mr. Jackson's half-sister, Georgia Sanders). When I asked if Mr. Jackson would have been able to live independently, Mr. Bolles said, "No. He would need supervision."

In the adaptive behavior area of home living, Mr. Jackson never had the responsibility for maintaining a home and required reminding to carry out the simplest home tasks. Although the ratings on the ABAS-II are mixed, anecdotal reports strongly indicate a significant deficit in Home Living.

4. *Social*: skills related to social exchanges with other individuals, including initiating, interacting, and terminating interaction with others; receiving and responding to pertinent situational cues; recognizing feelings; providing positive and negative feedback; regulating one's own behavior; being aware of peers and peer acceptance; gauging the amount and type of interaction with others;

assisting others; forming and fostering of friendships and love; coping with demands from others; making choices; sharing; understanding honesty and fairness; controlling impulses; conforming conduct to laws; obeying rules and laws; and displaying appropriate socio-sexual behavior.

ABAS-II scaled scores in the area of Social were as follows:

Ms. Davis	7
Ms. Jackson	1
Mr. Bolles	3
Ms. Sanders	4

Mr. Jackson's Aunt Patty Jackson reported that in childhood, "He stayed by himself all the time." She said that she could recall three friends. "Nobody else got along with Pookie." Like most of the people I interviewed, Ms. Jackson commented on Mr. Jackson's poor judgment in choosing friends. In addition, she felt that he had an attitude that led to conflict with others. In her words, "Social was the big issue."

Mr. Kareem Metta noted that Mr. Jackson had very bad judgment about the company that he kept. Mr. Metta described them as "incorrigibles" and "street kids" and that Mr. Jackson was easily "maneuvered" by them. Mr. Metta described Mr. Jackson as "gullible," "easy to follow others," and "definitely a follower or neutral but surely not a leader." He said that Mr. Jackson "based on his actions, didn't seem to understand common sense. Didn't grasp what he was dealing with." Although he said Mr. Jackson was happy, smiling, and joking, he found this demeanor to be inappropriate to the situation. Other than the street kids that Mr. Metta described, he said that Mr. Jackson "stayed around his family" and was "passive" and "in his own world, detached from everyone else."

Ms. Karen Adams reported that Mr. Jackson's friends made fun of him and that he would run to her. She said that even when he was living with his mother in 2007, he was afraid to go anywhere by himself. She said that his concern went beyond any real danger. He was so nervous about being out that he would wash his clothes in the sink, rather than go to a laundromat. Ms. Adams described Mr. Jackson as "always alone"; "he shied away"; "not trusting." She described him as a follower within the family

and definitely not a leader. Douglas Jackson also reported that Samuel didn't hang out outside of the family and "stayed to himself."

Elaine Kennedy and Alan Moon (grandparents who raised Barry North) reported that Samuel and Barry North were friends from childhood and that they played and rode bikes together and never got into any trouble. Barry North was the only friend who was consistently mentioned by people I interviewed.

Susan Taber reported that Samuel played well with her children, but "he used to get on people's nerves, because his laughing and joking went way beyond when it should be over, and adults would have to tell him to leave it alone. He didn't know when to stop." She and her husband independently reported that Samuel had poor judgment about friends and wanted to be part of the crowd. She said that when the kids got in trouble, everyone ran, and he was the one who got caught. She said that they took advantage of him. When asked for an example, she said, "If they did stuff, they would say, 'I'll tell Sandy you did it if you don't give me candy.'"

Several people I interviewed remembered Mr. Jackson's having one girlfriend at some time, although no one could remember a name, and no one could remember his having a girlfriend for long. Lamar Bolles knew Mr. Jackson well during their adolescence and said that he liked girls, but girls didn't like him, and he doubted that Mr. Jackson was sexually active. Mr. Bolles felt that Mr. Jackson had poor skills in approaching others.

Mr. Bolles reported that when he was young, Mr. Jackson was known as the kid who wasn't as smart. Kids would try to take advantage of him. So-called friends would take advantage, but he'd let them do it. For example, he was talked into robbing a Hispanic guy, and those who did it with him blamed him. If they wanted to fight someone, they'd have Pookie (Samuel) do it, and he'd do it just to fit in. His mother reported similar information. She said that every time something happened, his friends would blame him. She said that they took advantage of him.

Georgia Sanders said that she thought her brother wanted to have friends, but most other people didn't like him, partly because of the childish way he acted. Mr. Bolles said that Mr. Jackson had few friends and fought with all of them except Barry North. Mr. Bolles said that Samuel did not have the skills to work out conflicts to avoid fights, so there was fighting almost every day in high school.

Ms. Blue (cousin) noted that in September 2007, Mr. Jackson stayed around his mother's apartment and didn't go out. She remembered that Mr. Jackson expressed upset to her that young kids in the family were "bad-mouthing" him and that they should be showing him more respect, because he was an adult. He didn't know how to handle the situation, and Ms. Blue told him that he should talk to the kids' parents. She was struck by the fact that he could not work out this simple social problem.

Reports by people who knew Mr. Jackson throughout his life reported his social difficulties as a significant problem. The available evidence indicates that Social is an area of significant impairment of adaptive functioning.

5. *Community Use*: skills related to the appropriate use of community resources, including traveling in the community; grocery and general shopping at stores and markets; purchasing or obtaining services from other community businesses (e.g., gas stations, repair shops, doctors' and dentists' offices); attending church or synagogue; using public transportation and public facilities, such as schools, libraries, parks and recreational areas, and streets and sidewalks; attending theaters; and visiting other cultural places and events. Related skills include behavior in the community, communication of choices and needs, social interaction, and the application of functional academics.

ABAS-II scaled scores in the area of Community Use were as follows:

Ms. Davis	5
Ms. Jackson	7
Mr. Bolles	5
Ms. Sanders	3

Mr. Kareem Metta reported that Mr. Jackson knew his immediate neighborhood and rode a bike to get around. However, Ms. Adams noted that she never knew Mr. Jackson to leave without someone he trusted with him. "If he wanted to go somewhere, he'd go to someone he trusted. He wouldn't walk." She said that he would have gotten lost. Susan Taber also noted that when Samuel lived with her in Rialto, he always took someone with him when he went out.

Lamar Bolles said that when Mr. Jackson got out of prison in 2007, Mr. Bolles drove him everywhere (e.g., to his parole officer). Ms. Blue noted that Mr. Jackson didn't feel comfortable in the neighborhood (in 2007) and "stayed to himself." "He wasn't one for getting out."

Mr. Jackson participated in a very narrow range of community life; however, the available evidence for a significant impairment is mixed.

6. *Self-Direction*: skills related to making choices; learning and following a schedule; initiating activities appropriate to the setting, conditions, schedule, and personal interests; completing necessary or required tasks; seeking assistance when needed; resolving problems confronted in familiar and novel situations; and demonstrating appropriate assertiveness and self-advocacy skills.

ABAS-II scaled scores in the area of Self-Direction were as follows:

Ms. Davis	7
Ms. Jackson	1
Mr. Bolles	4
Ms. Sanders	3

Mr. Kareem Metta reported that Mr. Jackson did not think through his actions or learn from his mistakes. He said that he questioned Mr. Jackson a lot about what he wanted to do. He just shrugged his shoulders when asked about his dreams or goals and said, "I don't have any."

Lamar Bolles also said that Mr. Jackson never talked about the future. He said that if he won the lottery, Mr. Jackson would just spend all of the money. Bernice Sanders said that she never heard Mr. Jackson talk about what he wanted to do with his life. Georgia Sanders said that Mr. Jackson only talked about today and not about the future. She said that he did talk about getting a job, although he did not follow through.

Interviews consistently described Mr. Jackson as a follower and one who did not show good judgment in a wide variety of life decisions. The available evidence supports a significant impairment in the adaptive behavior area of Self-Direction.

7. *Health and Safety*: skills related to maintenance of one's health in terms of eating;

illness identification, treatment, and prevention; basic first aid; sexuality; physical fitness; basic safety considerations (e.g., following rules and laws, using seat belts, crossing streets, interacting with strangers, seeking assistance); regular physical and dental check-ups; and personal habits. Related skills include protecting oneself from criminal behavior, using appropriate behavior in the community, communicating choices and needs, participating in social interactions, and applying functional academics.

ABAS-II scaled scores in the area of Health and Safety were as follows:

Ms. Davis	7
Ms. Jackson	1
Mr. Bolles	4
Ms. Sanders	4

Georgia Sanders said that Mr. Jackson did not have good judgment, but she could not remember his doing dangerous things. Mr. Jackson lived most of his life with his mother or in prison, so he had little opportunity to demonstrate his judgment regarding Health and Safety. Although three of the four scores on the ABAS-II show significant impairment, the evidence from all sources regarding a significant impairment is mixed and insufficient to draw a conclusion.

8. *Functional Academics*: cognitive abilities and skills related to learning at school that also have direct application in one's life (e.g., writing; reading; using basic practical math concepts, basic science as it relates to awareness of the physical environment and one's health and sexuality; geography; and social studies). It is important to note that the focus of this skill area is not on grade-level academic achievement but, rather, on the acquisition of academic skills that are functional in terms of independent living.

ABAS-II scaled scores in the area of Functional Academics were as follows:

Ms. Davis	5
Ms. Jackson	3
Mr. Bolles	3
Ms. Sanders	3

Mr. Jackson's academic difficulties in school and very low scores on academic achievement tests have been described earlier. His sister, Georgia, reported that she exchanged letters with Samuel while he was in prison, and the letters that he wrote were like those of a younger person. She said that when she wrote to him, she would print her letters, because he couldn't read cursive. She said that she would write as simply as she could so that he could understand her letters. She said that he was not able to complete a job application. Mr. Jackson never had a credit card or a bank account, nor did he manage a budget. He never filed an income tax return. He did not have a driver's license. He could make simple purchases.

In an interview, Mr. Jackson's mother, Candace Davis, acknowledged few significant difficulties in other areas, but she did describe Samuel's academic limitations and the ways that they limited his everyday functioning.

As noted earlier, Mr. Jackson wrote a letter during my interview with him, and the letter was written at a third-grade level. When Mr. Jackson was 16 years old and incarcerated, he was asked to complete the sentence, "Two things I like about myself are...." I gave Mr. Jackson's written response to this request to my colleague Ms. Donna Barrows for her evaluation. Ms. Barrows indicated that the writing sample was at approximately the third-grade level. She found some relative strengths in sentence formulation (4/5 intact, capitalization, and ending punctuation). However, there were many deficits in grammar, spelling, semantics, illogical and non-sequential ideation, and lack of a cohesive and organized paragraph. Furthermore, Mr. Jackson misunderstood the request to write two things that he liked about himself and wrote two things that he would like. The things that he indicated that he would like were to get out of jail (misspelled) and be become a basketball player. This paragraph indicated not only deficits in functional academics, but deficits in comprehending the reality of his situation.

With the exception of Ms. Davis's slightly higher rating on the ABAS-II, information about Mr. Jackson's academic skills is very consistent in school records, academic achievement testing (e.g., Kaufman Test of Educational Achievement, Test of Adult Basic Education), anecdotes provided to me in interviews, and the letters and other applied academic skills that he demonstrated in my evaluation of him.

Evidence from many sources and throughout Mr. Jackson's life consistently points to a significant impairment in the adaptive behavior area of Functional Academics.

9. *Leisure*: the development of a variety of leisure and recreational interests (i.e., self-entertainment and interactional) that reflect personal preferences and choices and, if the activity will be conducted in public, age and cultural norms. Skills include choosing and self-initiating interests, using and enjoying home and community leisure and recreational activities alone and with others, playing socially with others, taking turns, terminating or refusing leisure or recreational activities, extending one's duration of participation, and expanding one's repertoire of interests, awareness, and skills. Related skills include behaving appropriately in the leisure and recreation setting, communicating choices and needs, participating in social interaction, applying functional academics, and exhibiting mobility skills.

ABAS-II scaled scores in the area of Leisure were as follows:

Ms. Davis	6
Ms. Jackson	2
Mr. Bolles	4
Ms. Sanders	4

Mr. Jackson's interest in basketball was the only commonly mentioned leisure theme in my interviews. Bernice Sanders said that she never saw him engage in any other leisure activity. Wayne Norris reported helping Mr. Jackson with his basketball shooting form. Although Mr. Jackson reported to me that he played on his school team, others I interviewed said that he did not. Mr. Norris said that he did not play, and Mr. Jones and Mr. Bolles reported that Mr. Jackson was academically ineligible. Mr. Bolles reported playing neighborhood basketball with Mr. Jackson. Neither he nor Ms. Sanders thought that Mr. Jackson played on the school team. Mr. Bolles said, "Pookie played basketball, and that's the only thing he could do good." He did ride bikes with other children, and his stepfather, Vincent Adams, reportedly took him fishing.

Mr. Bolles also reported that Mr. Jackson and several other boys used to play video games, and everyone would win an equal number of times except Samuel. "He didn't know how to play well and wouldn't ask. He'd just walk away or quit."

Mr. Jackson did have a consistent interest in playing and talking about basketball, but apparently he had no other consistent interest and did not use his leisure time to do more than hang around the house. He did not initiate leisure interests or explore available community leisure opportunities. With the exception of his mother's rating, the ABAS-II ratings for Leisure are significantly low. The available evidence indicates a significant impairment in the adaptive behavior area of Leisure.

10. *Work*: skills related to holding a part- or full-time job or jobs in the community in terms of specific job skills, appropriate social behavior, and related work skills (e.g., completion of tasks; awareness of schedules, ability to seek assistance, take criticism, and improve skills; money management, financial resources allocation, and the application of other functional academic skills; and skills related to going to and from work, preparation for work, management of oneself while at work, and interaction with coworkers).

Because of Mr. Jackson's lack of work experience, the Work area of the ABAS-II was not rated. Mr. Jackson had a very limited work history, due in part to the amount of time that he spent in prison. When Samuel was last out of prison in 2007, Lamar Bolles said that he talked to him about getting a job; Mr. Jackson agreed but wouldn't do it. Mr. Bolles took him to job interviews, but Mr. Jackson never followed through. Georgia Sanders reported that their mother took Mr. Jackson to fill out job applications, because he could not read or complete them.

Dr. Rogers's report noted that by Mr. Jackson's report, "At the age of 15–16 he briefly worked for a church stacking and stapling papers. He also briefly worked as a painter for his cousin's father." California State Prison records indicate that at age 18, Mr. Jackson reported having done "odd jobs," but there is no documented history. At age 19, his Department of Corrections record notes "satisfactory work performance" in prison with no mention of the nature of his work. Prison records indicate that on 12/12/2002, Mr. Jackson requested "an assignment in Vocational Masonry." Prison records of 12/18/2003 indicate that he had recently begun working in "Culinary" but that there were no records of his work performance.

Mr. Jackson's mother, Candace Davis, said that he had never had a job. When Samuel got out of prison in 2007, she pushed him to get a job, but he thought he didn't have to listen, because he was an adult. She took him to a temporary agency to look for a job and took him to apply for General Relief. She said that he became angry with her for these demands and mostly hung around the house.

Mr. Jackson's extremely limited job history, work in unskilled tasks, and lack of job initiative or job-seeking skills indicate a significant deficit in the adaptive behavior area of Work.

Summary of Adaptive Behavior Information

In addition to the scaled scores for each of the 10 areas of adaptive functioning noted above, the ABAS-II yields a General Adaptive Composite and Composite Standard Scores in the three areas of adaptive functioning that are used in the 2002 and 2010 definitions of the American Association on Intellectual and Developmental Disabilities. These standard scores have a mean of 100 and standard deviation of 15 in the general population. Therefore, a Standard Score of 70 or below would indicate significantly impaired adaptive functioning. The AAIDD criteria for impaired functioning is a score of 70 or below in one of the three areas of Conceptual, Social, or Practical, or a score of 70 or below on the General Adaptive Composite. These scores have a 95% confidence interval of 3, indicating that the obtained score could vary from the hypothetical "true" score by plus or minus three points. Scores are as follows for the four raters:

In summary, Mr. Jackson's mother, Ms. Davis, rated his adaptive functioning consistently higher than the other raters; however, her General Adaptive Composite score of 72 is very close (within the 95% confidence interval of the test) to the customary cutoff score of 70. The other three raters found Mr. Jackson to have significant deficits in all three areas of functioning and in the General Adaptive Composite.

Composite	Composite Standard Scores for Ms. Davis, Ms. Jackson, Mr. Bolles, and Ms. Sanders	Percentile Ranks for Ratings by Ms. Davis, Ms. Jackson, Mr. Bolles, and Ms. Sanders
General Adaptive Composite	72, 54, 60, 59	3, 0.1, 0.4, 0.3
Conceptual	81, 63, 70, 61	10, 1, 2, 0.5
Social	81, 58, 66, 68	10, 0.3, 1, 2
Practical	82, 48, 67, 69	12, <0.1, 1, 2

Note: The General Adaptive Composite score is based on all items in the scale; however, it is not the mean of the Conceptual, Social, and Practical standard scores. In this case, the GAC is generally lower than the Conceptual, Social, or Practical scores, because it is based on the probability of obtaining scores that far from the mean of the general population.

These scores meet the criteria of the American Association on Intellectual and Developmental Disabilities for significant impairment in adaptive functioning.

RELATED INFORMATION

Ms. Adams, Lamar Bolles, and Georgia Sanders each independently mentioned that Mr. Jackson did not seem to have grown up any during his late teens and early twenties when he was in prison. Ms. Adams said, "He was just the same when he returned." Mr. Bolles said that Mr. Jackson did not mature in prison and "still had the mind of a 17-year-old." Mr. Bolles thought that Mr. Jackson "still wanted to be a child. At 24, instead of looking for a job, he was hanging with his brother's friends who were 16." Mr. Bolles said, "I tried to show him what grownups do, but he still had the mentality of a kid."

Ms. Sanders provided a similar picture. She said that although she was his younger sister, she felt that he was much less mature than she. She gave examples of how childish he was. He would hit people and run and laugh, "like a little boy who wanted attention." She said, "I don't think he was capable of being an adult." Although she was reporting on his behavior at age 24, she said that he has always acted younger. She remembered always telling him to "act your age." Mr. Jackson's mother independently reported similar concerns. She said that when he got out of prison in 2007, "he seemed stuck in a child's mind" and didn't take stuff seriously as an adult. She expressed concern that something had happened to him in prison that he wouldn't talk about.

Bernice Sanders said, "He didn't grow up." She added, "When I saw him as he got older, he was still the same. His mind hadn't fully developed."

My interview with Mr. Jackson's father, Samuel Jackson, Sr., yielded little new information. I met him at an outdoor restaurant near an area under a highway where he slept with several other homeless people. He was dressed in very dirty clothes and was difficult to understand. In short, he acknowledged that he had not been much of a father to his son and blamed the school system and others for his son's problems. He acknowledged his son's academic deficiencies and pointed out times that he had tried to help with homework and other things, but his son showed no interest. With regard to Mr. Jackson's learning problems, he said, "Things didn't register very well." He also said, "He'll acknowledge something, then go do the opposite. It makes you wonder." He added, "I don't think he ever really understood. Some days he could talk you into believing he knew what he was doing."

SUMMARY

The diagnosis of intellectual disability requires significant impairment in intelligence and adaptive functioning that originated in childhood. With regard to the first component of the definition, Mr. Jackson was not administered an intelligence test in childhood, although he has an IQ score of 66 from an appropriate test administered in 2008. Mr. Jackson's general level of impairment in school, his low scores on standardized tests of academic achievement, and difficulty with demands related to intelligence makes it likely that he would have scored at the level of intellectual disability if he had been administered an IQ test in childhood.

With regard to the second component—deficits in adaptive behavior—evidence from many sources is consistent in documenting significant impairment from childhood through the time of the crime for which Mr. Jackson is accused. The information that I gathered from records and from face-to-face interviews with 20 people who knew Mr. Jackson at various times throughout his life showed that he met the criteria of impairment in at least 2 of 10 areas of adaptive behavior (Home Living, Social, Functional Academics, Leisure, and Work). Ratings by 3 of 4 raters also showed significant impairment in overall functioning and in all three areas of adaptive behavior noted in the most recent standards of the American Association on Intellectual and Developmental Disabilities (Conceptual, Social, and Practical). There were no areas of adaptive behavior strength that I could document.

In my judgment, these impairments in intelligence and adaptive functioning originated before age 18. Based on the information provided in this report, it is my opinion that Mr. Jackson meets the diagnostic criteria for intellectual disability.

J. Gregory Olley, Ph.D.
Psychologist

TEACHING POINT:
GAUGING THE TRAINING AND EXPERIENCE IN FORENSIC AND MENTAL HEALTH AREAS NEEDED FOR THIS KIND OF EVALUATION

There are two kinds of expertise that are needed to conduct *Atkins* evaluations. First, the forensic clinician must have experience with the particular population she is evaluating. In this instance, that means having been trained and supervised, having conducted research (or at least being very familiar with the research in the area), and having had clinical experience with individuals with mild intellectual disability. The second needed area of expertise is forensic—taking the training and experience with individuals with intellectual disability and applying it in a forensic context. This need not be limited to *Atkins* evaluations, which are of relatively recent vintage. Forensic questions arise involving individuals with intellectual disability in other contexts, including juvenile commitment, adult sentencing, competence to stand trial, and mental state at the time of the offense. Prominent questions in civil law include guardianship, as well as habilitation-related questions involving housing and work. A very good understanding of such individuals from a research, clinical, and forensic perspective is needed to conduct an evaluation for the high stakes that are involved in *Atkins* decisions.

CASE TWO
PRINCIPLE: USE RELEVANCE AND RELIABILITY (VALIDITY) AS GUIDES FOR SEEKING INFORMATION AND SELECTING DATA SOURCES (*PRINCIPLE 18*)

This principle concerns how obtaining information and selecting different sources of such information in FMHA should be guided by their relevance to the forensic issues and the legally defined "reliability" (that is, both reliability and validity as understood in behavioral science research) of the different sources. FMHA can involve a number of potential sources of information. To the extent that any such source is inaccurate, it cannot increase the overall accuracy of the evaluation; most likely, it will decrease overall accuracy, particularly if given too much weight. The forensic clinician must therefore be selective about the data sources that are used in the FMHA. Relevance and reliability, two important components of evidence law, can serve as useful guides for determining which sources of information should be considered.

Relevance can be established by describing the logical basis for a connection between a mental health construct (e.g., severe mental illness) and the relevant forensic issues (e.g., capacities to consider information in a knowing and intelligent way). It can also be described by citing empirical evidence about the strength of the relationship between these constructs in clinical research.

The concept of legal reliability can also be applied to FMHA through the legal constructs found under the *Federal Rule of Evidence 702* and *Daubert v. Merrell Dow Pharmaceuticals*, (1993). One particular criterion for "reliability," a term used by the U.S. Supreme Court in *Daubert* to connote both scientific reliability and validity, involves the "error rate" of the measure. To obtain an "error rate," there must be existing research with a "correct" outcome against which the accuracy of a particular measure can be calibrated. Given the difficulty in operationalizing such a "true" outcome in legal settings, such data are rarely available.

Sources of ethics authority address the issue of validity and relevance in a number of ways. The APA *Ethics Code* notes that psychological test construction should incorporate "current scientific or professional knowledge for test design, standardization, validation, reduction or elimination of bias, and recommendations for use" (Standard 9.05). Furthermore, other aspects of the testing should be considered when interpreting test results:

> When interpreting assessment results...psychologists take into account the purpose of the assessment as well as the various test factors, test-taking abilities, and other characteristics of the person being assessed, such as situational, personal, linguistic, and cultural differences, that might affect psychologists' judgments or reduce the accuracy of their interpretations. (Standard 9.06)

The APA *Specialty Guidelines* addresses the issue of legal reliability by stressing the importance of forming "opinions and testimony that are sufficiently based upon adequate scientific foundation, and reliable and valid principles and methods that have been applied appropriately to the facts of the case" (Guideline 2.05). More specific to conducting forensic assessments, the APA *Specialty Guidelines* state, "Forensic practitioners use assessment procedures in the manner and for the purposes that are appropriate in light of the research on or evidence of their usefulness and proper application" (Guideline 10.02). Regarding "relevance," it is noted that, "Forensic practitioners avoid offering information that is irrelevant and that does not provide a substantial basis of support for their opinions, except when required by law" (Guideline 11.04). This language underscores the importance of relevance in both the selection and the communication stages of the evaluation process: the forensic clinician should select approaches and tests whose results allow communication of data relevant to the forensic issues underlying the evaluation's legal question.

Consistent with these sources of ethical authority and FRE 702, the U.S. Supreme Court emphasized in *Daubert v. Merrell Dow Pharmaceuticals* (1993) the importance of relevance and reliability as criteria for acceptance of scientific evidence in federal jurisdictions. The Court in *Daubert* considered Rule 702 in terms of relevance—there must be "a valid scientific connection to the pertinent inquiry as a precondition to admissibility" (p. 592)—and reliability, in that the expert's assertion must be based on scientific evidence and "supported by the appropriate validation"

(p. 592). The focus is on the evaluation of particular methods or measures, which may allow a court to go beyond the general acceptance of a method to consider its scientific base (Thames, 1994).

The present case report provides an example of the application of relevance and reliability to the selection of data sources in the context of another *Atkins* evaluation. The importance of selecting relevant and reliable data sources is especially salient in the context of this type of evaluation. As noted by Cunningham (2010), "These are virtually the only assessments where a clinical diagnosis is wholly dispositive of a psycholegal issue" (p. 171). Certainly the stakes are high. However, there are some aspects of this type of evaluation that make it particularly challenging: variability in how states define "mental retardation"; psychometric considerations in selecting relevant tests and interpreting their results; and debate over the appropriateness of adjustment procedures, such as adjusting for the Flynn Effect (discussed later in this chapter) and practice effects (see, e.g., DeMatteo et al., 2011; Macvaugh & Cunningham, 2009; Olley, 2009). Given these challenges and the implications of an *Atkins* evaluation, the importance of selecting relevant and reliable sources of data is substantial.

Relevance in the FMHA context can be established both qualitatively and quantitatively. Qualitatively, relevance to the forensic issue can be established by describing the logical, theoretical, or empirical relationship between the mental health construct and the relevant forensic issues. States vary in their definitions of "mental retardation," with some utilizing the criteria outlined by the DSM-IV-TR (American Psychiatric Association, 2000), American Association on Mental Retardation (AAMR, 2002; now the American Association on Intellectual and Developmental Disabilities [AAIDD], 2010, 2012), or American Psychological Association (Jacobson & Mulick, 1996). (See the review completed by DeMatteo and colleagues [2007] for a detailed description of the definitions used in each state jurisdiction.) Although different in some ways, each of these standards outlines specific criteria in three domains: (1) impairment in intellectual functioning, (2) impairment in adaptive functioning, and (3) onset prior to adulthood (Bonnie & Gustafson, 2007; DeMatteo et al., 2007). Others use a definition that differs in some way (e.g., identifying a specific IQ level as the only necessary element; identifying the importance of a given domain, but

not providing a specific definition) (DeMatteo et al., 2007). However, as recommended by Macvaugh and Cunningham (2009), "Regardless of the definition…used to diagnose mental retardation in death penalty cases, evaluators should address all three of the clinical components of the widely accepted definitions in the field" (p. 143). Furthermore, they advise that, "because of the high stakes nature of these cases, it is essential that forensic assessment practices are consistent with standards of professional practice and psychological testing" (p. 143). Given the recent publication of the DSM-5 (APA, 2013a) and the changes made to the diagnostic criteria defining intellectual disability (which reflect an update in terminology, as DSM-IV-TR utilized the term "mental retardation"), this guidance is especially important. The diagnostic criteria no longer include an IQ score cutoff, a decision made to emphasize that these scores should not be "overemphasized as the defining factor of a person's overall ability, without adequately considering functioning levels" (American Psychiatric Association, 2013c). It is emphasized that this is an especially important consideration in forensic contexts (APA, 2013c).

To assess impairment in intellectual functioning, the selection and administration of a standardized intelligence measure is essential (Bonnie, 2004). There are particular intelligence tests that are considered "generally accepted" (Bonnie & Gustafson, 2007; Macvaugh & Cunningham, 2009); the WAIS-IV used in the current case is among those tests. However, there are other important considerations in the interpretation of such tests. For instance, the Flynn Effect describes the process by which the average IQ score for the population increases over time (Cunningham & Tassé, 2010). Accordingly, as the number of years since the normative data were collected for a test increases, an individual's IQ score does not reflect his or her actual level of intellectual functioning in the same way that such a score would have previously. Some have recommended against adjustments for the Flynn Effect (Hagan, Drogin, & Guilmette, 2008), and there have been instances in which the court has rejected the use of such adjustments (e.g., *Green v. Johnson*, 2008; *Neal v. Texas*, 2008). However, others have reviewed the scientific evidence for Flynn Effect adjustments, and concluded that although the practice of adjusting IQ scores may not yet be generally accepted, there is significant scientific evidence and peer-reviewed support for this practice (see Cunningham & Tassé, 2010), as well as sufficient legal precedent (Bonnie & Gustafson, 2007). Accordingly, some recommend that both obtained and adjusted IQ scores be reported (Cunningham & Tassé, 2010; Macvaugh & Cunningham, 2009).

Other psychometric considerations are also important to consider when describing the results of intellectual assessments. The *standard error of measurement* (SEM), for example, "provides an estimate of the amount of error in a person's observed test score…[it] is simply another way of expressing the reliability of a test" (Macvaugh & Cunningham, 2009, p. 146). As such, an individual's IQ score is better interpreted "as existing within the range of error for the test instrument" (p. 146). For instance, if an individual obtains a full scale IQ of 70 on the WAIS-IV, there is a 95% chance that their true score falls within the range of 66–74. Moreover, *practice effects* can result when an offender is tested multiple times with the same test in close succession, which is possible when both defense and prosecution retain experts to evaluate the defendant (Bonnie & Gustafson, 2007; DeMatteo et al., 2011; Macvaugh & Cunningham, 2009). Each of these considerations is important because of its potential effect on the validity of IQ scores.

Relevance and reliability are also important considerations when evaluating adaptive functioning. It is recommended that a standardized measure be administered as part of the assessment of adaptive functioning (Bonnie, 2004). However, evaluating adaptive functioning should also involve collateral interviews with individuals familiar with the evaluee (e.g., family members, employers), and it is important to consider potential bias in the accounts of collateral sources (Macvaugh & Cunningham, 2009). For this reason, the accuracy of collateral interviewing can be improved by conducting several collateral interviews with multiple sources—and by determining what information is reported consistently across interviews.

Much of this is clearly illustrated in the present case report. In addition to conducting multiple psychosocial interviews and psychological testing with the evaluee, Mr. Novak, Dr. Salekin conducted a total of 15 collateral interviews as part of her evaluation. These interviews ranged from very lengthy (with family members with substantial knowledge of the defendant) to fairly brief (those with much more limited opportunity to see him). The range and diversity of such interviews yielded a great deal of information that could be compared across observers, and when interpreted along with the formal interviews and assessment of Mr. Novak, enhanced the reliability and validity of the final report.

Expert Report of Karen Salekin, Ph.D.

Defendant: Novak, David
D.O.B.: 05/15/1988
Age: 22 years, 1 month
Race/Gender: Caucasian/Male
Date of Report: 04/17/12

EVALUATION PROCEDURES

Clinical Interview and Test Administration
Mr. David Novak: In-person: Interview
    //** (4 hours, 45 minutes)
In-person: Interview & Testing
    //** (1 hour, 22 minutes)
In-person: Testing
    //** (2 hours, 40 minutes)

Collateral Sources[2]
(See Table 1)

Review of Records[3]
Academic: Empire City Schools (Limited Documentation; Grades 7–9 Only)
Medical/Psychiatric
- East Louisiana Medical Center (diverse documents totaling ~215 pages)
- Eddie's Drug Company
- Empire Catholic Hospital
- Empire Regional Medical Center
- St. Elias Medical Center

---

[2] This writer requested contact information from Mr. Duvall for Dr. Ross Dennit, a physician who informed Mr. Duvall that he was instrumental to David's commitment at the East Louisiana Medical Center. Dr. Dennit stated that he has no recollection of the event and no files could be found. Based on this information from Mr. Duvall, this writer was not in contact with Dr. Dennit.

[3] Attorney Carl Duvall requested records from the Centrage Medical Center and was told that all records for Mr. Novak were destroyed five years after his last contact with the center. Therefore, no records were available. Ms. Emma Duvall spoke with Margaret Novak and requested that she get birth records for David. Ms. Novak informed Ms. Duvall that they were no longer available because, in accordance with hospital policy, these records were destroyed 10 years after his birth.

TABLE 8.1. COLLATERAL SOURCES

	Name	Relation to David	Interview	Date	Length of Time
1	Stephanie Novak	Sister	In person	**/**/**	3 hours, 15 minutes
2	Rose Novak	Sister	In person	**/**/**	3 hours, 11 minutes
3	Steven Novak	Brother	In person	**/**/**	2 hours, 14 minutes
4	Margaret Novak	Mother	In person	**/**/**	5 hours, 5 minutes
5	Officer M. Thompson	Correctional Officer at Lexington County Jail	In person	**/**/**	15 minutes
6	Officer K. Evans	Correctional Officer at Lexington County Jail	In person	**/**/**	30 minutes
7	Officer J. West	Correctional Officer at Lexington County Jail	In person	**/**/**	7 minutes
8	Officer W. Bonner	Correctional Officer at Lexington County Jail	In person	**/**/**	25 minutes
9	Officer J. Stein	Correctional Officer at Lexington County Jail	In person	**/**/**	18 minutes
10	Officer M. Varner	Correctional Officer at Lexington County Jail	In person	**/**/**	40 minutes
11	Sgt. Eric Morton	Correctional Officer at Lexington County Jail	In person	**/**/**	16 minutes
12	Ann Pratt	First-grade teacher	In person	**/**/**	10 minutes
13	Madeline Stephens	Supervisor at Emmerson's Restaurant	In person	**/**/**	13 minutes
14	Wes Stills	Employer: Willington-Stills Salon	In person	**/**/**	40 minutes
15	Catherine Holmes	GED teacher at Standifer Academy	Telephone	**/**/**	30 minutes

Legal

- Adult Disability Application with supporting documents (e.g., Disability Determination Evaluation conducted by Dr. William G. Cormier dated **/**/**; parts of application completed by Rose Novak)
- Juvenile Court records (e.g., history of involvement in juvenile court; order denying youthful offender status for the current case; Louisiana Uniform Arrest Reports)
- Motions for current case
- Records from the Lexington County Jail up to **/**/** (diverse documents including but not limited to, visits to the Centrage Medical Center, incident reports, inmate requests)
- Crime scene report (**/**/**) and other documents relaying the history of the case, including statements made by witnesses and co-defendants
- Acknowledgement of Rights forms signed by David Novak and co-defendants
- Empire Police Department—Serious Incident/Arrest Activity Report (**/**/**)
- Various documents not applicable to this evaluation (e.g., ambulance response, crime scene photos, evidence receipt, drawings of crime scene, warrant of arrest)
- Letter to attorney Carl Duvall from David Novak (not dated)

Psychological Testing/ Procedures—David Novak

- The Wechsler Adult Intelligence Scale—4th Edition (**/**/**)
- The Woodcock-Johnson Test of Achievement—3rd Edition (**/**/**)

Psychological Testing/Procedures— Collateral Sources

Scales of Independent Behavior- Revised (SIB-R):

1. Scored and used for comparison to norm sample
   a. Ms. Margaret Novak—completed for Mr. David Novak in relation to her

perception of his adaptive skills at the age of 20 years (age at the time of the crime).

b. Mr. Steven Novak—completed for Mr. David Novak in relation to his perception of his adaptive skills at the age of 16 years (developmental period).

c. Ms. Stephanie Novak—completed for Mr. David Novak in relation to her perception of his adaptive skills at the age of 16 years (developmental period).

d. Ms. Rose Novak—completed for Mr. David Novak in relation to her perception of his adaptive skills at the age of 16 years (developmental period).

Submitted To
The Honorable Ethan Picard
Lexington County Circuit Court

Prepared by
Karen Salekin, Ph.D., Psychologist
License #1148

The information contained in this Evaluation Report is confidential. It is intended only for use of the presiding judge, authorized court personnel, the parties' counsel, and retained experts except upon Court Order or request of other authorized court personnel

REASON FOR REFERRAL

David Novak is a 22-year-old Caucasian male who was referred to this examiner for an evaluation of intellectual disability in the context of a criminal matter for which he is charged with capital murder. This charge is in relation to his alleged involvement in the drive-by shooting and death of Matthew LeBlanc. The request for evaluation was put forth by Mr. Carl Duvall, of Duvall and LeBlue, P.C., counsel for the defendant. At the time of writing, David resides at the Lexington County Jail (Empire, Louisiana) where he has been since the date of his arrest (**/**/**).

NOTIFICATION

Prior to speaking with David and all third-party informants, a notice of the limitations of confidentiality was presented to them. Specifically, all individuals

were informed that the information obtained during discussions with this examiner (by telephone or in person) would not be held in confidence and that any or all of this information could be presented to the Court in written or oral format (i.e., via a report that would be submitted to the Court or via testimony). All individuals were informed that they had the right to refuse to participate in the evaluation, and if they chose to participate, they had the right to end the discussion at any time. In addition, all individuals were informed that they had a right to refuse to answer any question that was posed to them. All the individuals contacted stated that they understood this information and agreed to participate.

INTELLECTUAL DISABILITY: AN OVERVIEW[4]

Over the years, intellectual disability (ID) has been defined in many ways, but the consistent theme is that ID is a problem of learning. People with ID learn more slowly and with a lesser degree of complexity than do the majority of the population (Everington & Olley, 2008). Two of the most commonly used definitions of intellectual disability are put forth by the American Association on Intellectual and Developmental Disabilities (formerly known as the American Association on Mental Retardation, AAMR) and the American Psychiatric Association (APA). These definitions are provided in the paragraphs below:

American Association on Intellectual and Developmental Disabilities (AAIDD, 2010)

According to the AAIDD, *intellectual disability* is defined as "disability characterized by significant limitations both in intellectual functioning and in adaptive behavior as expressed in conceptual, social, and practical adaptive skills. This disability originates before the age of 18" (AAIDD, 2010, p. 1). The following five assumptions are essential to the application of this definition:

1. Limitations in present functioning must be considered within the context of community

---

[4] Some of the following information was excerpted directly from Salekin, K. L., & Olley, J. G. (2008), Intellectual disability, in *Encyclopedia of Forensic Science*, Indianapolis, IN: Wiley Publications. Some of this information can be found in other reports written for hearings in which the diagnosis of intellectual disability was at issue.

environments typical of the individual's age peers and culture.

2. Valid assessment considers cultural and linguistic diversity as well as differences in communication, sensory, motor, and behavioral factors.

3. Within an individual, limitations often coexist with strengths.

4. An important purpose of describing limitations is to develop a profile of needed supports.

5. With appropriate personalized supports over a sustained period, the life functioning of the person with intellectual disability generally will improve (AAIDD, 2010, p. 1).

With regard to the measurement of intellectual functioning, the AAIDD states that the person must obtain an intelligence quotient (IQ) "that is approximately two standard deviations below the mean, considering the standard error of measurement for the specific assessment instruments used and the instrument's strengths and limitations" (AAIDD, 2010, p. 27). Similarly, for the diagnosis of intellectual disability, significant limitations in adaptive behavior should be established through the use of standardized measures that are normed on the general population; included in that sample should be people with and without disabilities. On these standardized measures, significant limitations in adaptive behavior are defined as performance that is at least two standard deviations below the mean of either (a) one of the following three types of adaptive behavior: conceptual, social, or practical; or (b) an overall score on a standardized measure of conceptual, social, and practical skills (AAIDD, 2010, p. 27). Furthermore, the assessment should relate to an individual's typical performance during daily routines and changing circumstances, not to maximum performance (AAIDD, 2010, p. 45).

American Psychiatric Association (APA, 2000)

Similar to the definition put forth by AAIDD, the American Psychiatric Association conceptualizes intellectual disability as a disability characterized by deficits in both intellectual functioning and adaptive behavior that are present before the age of 18 years. Specifically, the diagnosis of intellectual disability is made if the following criteria are met:

A. Significantly sub-average intellectual functioning; an intelligence quotient (IQ) of approximately 70 or below on an individually administered IQ test (for infants, a clinical judgment of significantly sub-average intellectual functioning).

B. Concurrent deficits or impairments in present adaptive functioning (i.e., the person's effectiveness in meeting the standards expected for his or her age by his or her cultural group) in at least two of the following areas: communication, self-care, home living, social/interpersonal skills, use of community resources, self-direction, functional academic skills, work, leisure, and health and safety.

C. The onset is before age 18 years. (APA, 2000, p. 49)

A feature of the diagnosis that was dropped by AAIDD in 2002, but maintained by the APA, is severity of impairment. Specifically, according to the APA, intellectual disability falls along a continuum of four levels of severity that are tied to measured IQ: (1) Mild; (2) Moderate; (3) Severe; and (4) Profound. The diagnosis of Intellectual Disability, Severity Unspecified may be applied when there is strong evidence to support the diagnosis, but the individual cannot be tested using a standardized measure of intelligence. The following paragraphs provide summary data on the intelligence quotients associated with each level and some of the abilities and disabilities typical for each sub-group.

Levels of Intellectual Disability[5]
(1) Mild Intellectual Disability

Approximately 85% of the individuals with intellectual disability are classified in the mild category and have IQ scores within the interval of 50–55 to 70–75 (2 to 3 standard deviations below the population mean). These individuals may show some delays in the development of their motor, speech, social, and/or cognitive skills, but often are not identified as having intellectual disability until they begin school. Given appropriate educational support, individuals with mild intellectual disability

---

[5] See, for example, APA, 2000; Baroff, 1999; Beirne-Thompson, Patton, & Ittenbach, 1994; Hickson, Blackman, & Reis, 1995; Reschly, Myers, & Hartel, 2002.

can learn to read and write and can become gainfully employed (see, e.g., APA, 2000, p. 43; and Heber & Dever, 1970). Once out of school, individuals with IQ scores at the high end of the mild intellectual disability range often blend into the general population; they have friends, marry, and have children, and need assistance only during periods of personal or economic stress (APA, 2000; Baroff, 1999). "With appropriate supports, individuals with mild intellectual disability can usually live successfully in the community, either independently or in supervised settings" (APA, 2000, p. 43).

(2) Moderate Intellectual Disability

Individuals classified as having moderate intellectual disability typically have IQs within the interval of 35–40 to 50–55 (3 to 4 standard deviations below the mean) and comprise approximately 10% of individuals diagnosed with intellectual disability. Individuals with moderate intellectual disability usually show significant delays in motor and language skills early in childhood and are often identified as having intellectual disability before beginning their formal education. Many individuals within this category can learn to read and write simple words and sentences, and with training, can work in unskilled or semiskilled jobs. These individuals will always require some level of assistance and supervision.

(3) Severe Intellectual Disability

Approximately 2% to 4% of individuals diagnosed with intellectual disability fall within the category of severe intellectual disability and have IQ scores within the interval of 20–25 to 35–40. Significant delays in the acquisition of motor and language skills areas are evident early during infancy, and physical abnormalities are typical. Individuals with severe intellectual disability may learn some basic self-help skills and typically develop some useful speech by late adolescence. Individuals with severe intellectual disability will never be able to function independently and will always require close supervision.

(4) Profound Intellectual Disability

Individuals within the category of profound intellectual disability have IQ scores that fall below the interval of 20–25 (> 5 standard deviations below the mean), and they comprise approximately 1% to 2 % of individuals diagnosed with intellectual disability. These individuals are usually identified at birth, often because of physical abnormalities, which may preclude their ability to walk or talk. Up to 40% of the individuals with profound intellectual disability are bedfast or semi-ambulatory (O'Grady & Talkington, 1977), while all are unable to care for their own needs and require lifelong care.

IMPORTANT CORRELATES OF INTELLECTUAL DISABILITY

In addition to the more visible deficits in adaptive functioning (e.g., limited success in school), intellectual disability can result in less obvious deficits, such as poor self-confidence, impaired social functioning, impaired moral reasoning, and personal failures (Baroff, 1999; Keyes et al., 1998, p. 531). Certain characteristics, such as poor memory, poor transference and generalization skills, poor judgment, and a tendency to acquiesce to those in authority, are related to the adaptive functioning of individuals with intellectual disability and are common within this population (Everington & Keyes, 1999). Individuals with intellectual disability often develop compensatory behaviors or appearances to offset their deficits in social and intellectual functioning. These compensatory behaviors result in a less obvious or even hidden disability, thereby hindering the accuracy with which one can identify the degree of impairment. These compensatory behaviors are particularly problematic for individuals who fall within the mild range, as they can be misclassified as falling outside of the range of intellectual disability (Keyes et al., 1998).

It is common for individuals with mild intellectual disability to be active participants in their communities, and as a result, they are vulnerable to exploitation by others. As the degree of intellectual disability is more severe, the need for support and supervision becomes greater. People with moderate or severe intellectual disability are more likely to require constant or nearly constant supervision. As a result of this high level of supervision, they are less likely to be exploited in the community or to become involved in criminal activity. The small percentage of people with intellectual disability who commit criminal acts are predominantly those with mild ID, rather than moderate or severe.

In contrast to individuals with mild intellectual disability, individuals with more severe degrees of impairment are likely to have an identifiable medical or environmental cause for their impairment (e.g., Down syndrome, fetal alcohol syndrome) and to need specialized medical care. These individuals are also more likely to have serious behavior problems that require professional services. Problems of aggression, self-injury, self-stimulation, property destruction, and other disruptive behavior can limit an individual's opportunity for integrated community living. These problem behaviors are sometimes associated with mental illnesses that coexist with intellectual disability (Fletcher, Loschen, Stavrakaki, & First, 2007).

With regard to support, it is typical for individuals with mild intellectual disability to receive informal help from family members, neighbors, and employers, rather than from provider agencies. In fact, the majority of individuals with intellectual disability, at all levels of functioning, reside with their parents or other family members throughout their lives. Residential care is typically reserved for more impaired individuals (Lakin, Prouty & Coucouvanis, 2007). Within the mild range of intellectual disability, few people require a legal guardian, many marry and have meaningful social relationships, and it is quite likely that they have, or have had, gainful employment in jobs that require limited decision-making, judgment, and skill. People with mild intellectual disability typically have basic functional academic skills and do not have physical disabilities that would limit their work opportunities. They may, however, require more supervision than the average worker.

Etiology

Like many disabilities, intellectual disability does not have a single identifiable etiological factor. As described in the AAIDD manual (2010), the etiology of intellectual disability is conceptualized as multifactorial and is composed of four broad categories of risk factors: (1) biomedical, (2) social, (3) behavioral, and (4) educational (AAIDD, 2010, p. 61, Table 6.1). These four factors do not function in isolation, but instead interact across the life of the individual and across generations (AAMR, 2002). In fact, in each category there exist many distinct factors that can cause deficits in intellectual functioning. For instance, chromosomal disorders (e.g., Down syndrome), maternal illness, birth injury, and traumatic brain injury are all factors found in the biomedical domain. In the social domain are

risk factors such as poverty, domestic violence, lack of adequate stimulation, and institutionalization. Maternal drug and alcohol use, parental smoking, parental rejection of the caretaking role, and social deprivation are examples of behavioral risk factors. Finally, parental intellectual ability, lack of preparation for parenthood, inadequate education services, and inadequate family support have been identified as educational risk factors.

In their review of epidemiological studies on the etiology of intellectual disability, McLaren and Bryson (1987) found that as many as 50% of the population of individuals diagnosed with intellectual disability had more than one causal risk factor. It is important to note that the presence of any one risk factor, or perhaps even a combination of many risk factors, does not mean that an individual has, or will have, intellectual disability. Similarly, the absence of an identifiable risk factor or etiology does not mean that an individual does not, or will not, have intellectual disability. Ultimately, the diagnosis of intellectual disability requires observable impairments in functional abilities, regardless of etiology, and as previously stated, in about half of cases of intellectual disability, the etiology is not known (McDermitt et al., 2008).

ASSESSMENT OF INTELLECTUAL DISABILITY

Intelligence

Like many theoretical constructs, the construct of *intelligence* has been defined many ways, and depending on the purpose, such definitions can come in the form of single paragraphs, brief manuscripts, or detailed books. For the purpose of this evaluation, the construct of intelligence will be presented in a succinct manner with citations to more comprehensive treatises.

Intelligence is a general mental ability. It includes reasoning, planning, solving problems, thinking abstractly, comprehending complex ideas, learning quickly, and learning from experience (Gottfredson, 1997). As reflected in this definition, intelligence is not merely book learning, a narrow academic skill, or test-taking smarts. Rather, it reflects a broader and deeper capacity for comprehending our surroundings—catching on, making sense of things, or figuring out what to do. Thus, the concept of intelligence represents an attempt to clarify, organize, and explain the fact that individuals differ in their ability to understand complex ideas, to adapt effectively to their environments, to learn from experience, to engage in various forms of reasoning, and to overcome obstacles by thinking and communicating (Neisser et al., 1996). (AAIDD, 2010, p. 15)

As is clear from the definitions of intellectual disability previously presented, an individual's level of intellectual functioning must be established before a diagnosis can be made. To do this, an individual must be administered a standardized measure of intellectual ability that provides an intelligence quotient. While there are many tests of intelligence, the most commonly used, individually administered, and well-standardized tests, are the Wechsler Adult Intelligence Scale (currently in the fourth edition, WAIS-IV; Wechsler, 2008), the Wechsler Intelligence Scale for Children (currently in the fourth edition, WISC- IV; Wechsler, 2003), and the Stanford-Binet Intelligence Scale (currently in the fifth edition, SB5; Roid, 2003). For diagnostic purposes, the most important index, regardless of the test, is the overall or full scale IQ.

As previously noted, both the AAIDD and the APA require an IQ of approximately 70 or below for a diagnosis of intellectual disability. A score of 70 places an individual two standard deviations below the mean of the general population at the time the test was normed. As noted by the AAIDD,

> the intent of this definition is not to specify a hard and fast cutoff point/score for meeting the significant limitations in intellectual functioning criterion of ID. Rather, one needs to use clinical judgment in interpreting the obtained score in reference to the test's standard error of measurement, the assessment instrument's strengths and limitations, and other factors such as practice effects, fatigue effects, and age of norms used. (AAIDD, 2010, p. 35)

Measurement Error

Similar to other forms of testing, intelligence testing can be affected by a variety of events that can result in over- or underestimates of an individual's measured intelligence. These events are known as *measurement errors* and originate from many sources. In general, these sources fall into two broad categories: (1) random variation that originates from the person during testing, and (2) random variation that originates outside of the person being tested. Factors internal to the person that may affect testing are many and varied, but include such things as fatigue, motivation, ability to understand instructions, emotional state, ability to attend, and the like. Room conditions (e.g., temperature, noise, lighting), time of day, unexpected interruptions, general level of comfort (e.g., softness of chair, comfort of clothing, presence or absence of shackles), and errors in test administration (e.g., administration, scoring) are a few examples of sources of error external to the individual. Regardless of the origin of measurement error, the presence of these factors may result in an IQ score that is not a precise measure of a person's true ability.

With the knowledge that error affects scores, it is standard practice to interpret the obtained IQ within a confidence interval that is created by doing two things: (1) adding the standard error of measurement (SEM) to the obtained score, and (2) subtracting the SEM from the obtained score. For intelligence testing, it is customary to add and subtract 5 points for measurement error. Thus, if a person obtained an IQ of 70, the range within which a person's "true score" (the score that would exist under perfect test conditions) would fall is between 65 and 75. The application of the SEM protects against an overreliance on a single score that is known to contain error. Interpretation using SEM is recognized and recommended by the American Psychological Association, the American Education Research Association (AERA), and the National Council on Measurement in Education (NCME); these three organizations develop standards of practice for educational and psychological testing.

One source of measurement error that deserves a more detailed explanation is known as the Flynn Effect and is error that is related to the use of outdated norms for scoring and interpreting IQ scores (see for example, Flynn, 1984, 1987, 1999, 2000). James Flynn, a New Zealand political scientist, has studied the gradual rise in measured IQ scores for decades, and his research has found that with each passing year there is an average increase in IQ of 0.33 points, ultimately resulting in an increase of approximately 3 points per decade. The American Psychological Association Dictionary of Psychology (2006) defines the Flynn Effect as:

> the gradual rise of IQ level that has been observed since the time when records of IQs first were kept. Although the average IQ remains 100, due to periodic re-norming of IQ tests, raw scores have been rising. These increases have been roughly 9 points per generation (i.e., 30 years). The gains have been unequally distributed across the different abilities, with fluid abilities showing substantially greater gains than crystallized abilities. [James Flynn (1934—), New Zealand philosopher who first documented its occurrence]. (p. 382)

A controversial issue is whether IQ scores should be adjusted in accordance with the calculated rise in scores. The method for correction is quite simple and is as follows: First count the years from publication to testing,[6] multiply this number by 0.33, and subtract this number from the obtained IQ. For example, if a person obtained a score of 76 in 2011 on a test published in 2005, the resulting score would be 74 (0.33 x 6 = 1.98; 76 − 1.98 = 74.02). At the time of writing, adjusting for the Flynn Effect is not done by all practicing clinicians, but it is recommended by many scholars and supported by the AAIDD (see AAIDD, 2010, p. 37).

Adaptive Behavior

Adaptive behavior refers to skills that are exhibited by people that allow them to function in their everyday lives. As previously noted, the AAIDD and the APA have different categorizations of adaptive deficits, but the two organizations do not differ with regard to the meaning behind the construct. In fact, the AAIDD (as delineated in AAMR, 2002) created a table that depicts the similarity between their 1992 definition (which is the same as APA, 2000, which was in place at the time of this evaluation) and their 2002 definition (which is the same as AAIDD, 2010, which was in place at the time of this evaluation).[7]

Domains AAIDD (2002 & 2010)	Skill Areas AAIDD (2002 & 2010)	Skill Areas, AAIDD (1992) and APA (2000)
Conceptual	• Language • Reading • Money concepts • Self-direction	• Communication • Functional academics • Self-direction • Health and safety
Social	• Interpersonal • Responsibility • Self-esteem • Gullibility • Naiveté • Follows rules • Obeys laws • Avoids victimization	• Social skills • Leisure
Practical	• Activities of daily living • Occupational skills • Maintains safe environments	• Self-care • Home living • Community use • Health and safety • Work

As noted by the AAMR (2002), the change from 10 independent skill areas of adaptive behavior to three broad domains was due to the gradual realization that the 10 skill areas did not represent unique constructs. According to the AAIDD, research has shown that there has been "an emerging consensus that the structure of adaptive behavior consists of the following three factor clusters: (a) Cognitive Communication and Academic Skills (i.e., conceptual skills), (b) Social Competence Skills (i.e., social skills), and (c) Independent Living Skills (i.e., practical skills) (AAMR, 2002, p. 41).

As previously mentioned, for the diagnosis of intellectual disability, the AAIDD definition requires the following:

> significant limitations in adaptive behavior should be established through the use of standardized test measures normed on the general population, including people with disabilities and people without disabilities. On these standardized measures, significant limitations in adaptive behavior are operationally defined as performance that is at least two

---

[6] James Flynn argues that the date should begin at the beginning of the norming cycle, which is typically two years prior to the date of publication.

[7] AAMR, 2002, p. 82.

standard deviations below the mean on either (a) one of the following three types of adaptive behavior: conceptual, social, or practical, or (b) an overall score on a standardized measure of conceptual, social, and practical skills. The assessment instrument's standard error or measurement must be considered when interpreting the individual's obtained scores. (AAIDD, 2010, p. 43)

Like the AAIDD, the APA recommends the use of standardized measures in the assessment of adaptive behavior. That said, it is well recognized that in some instances quantitative analysis of functional abilities is either inappropriate, or does not provide enough information to make a determination. In addition to standardized, quantitative measures, both the AAIDD and the APA state that the final determination of intellectual disability should be based on multiple sources of information and clinical judgment (see, e.g., AAIDD, 2010, pp. 100–102; and APA, 2000, p. 42).

There exist numerous scales of adaptive behavior that can be used for the purposes of diagnosis, classification, and planning for supports; no single measure is best for all three. Examples of adaptive functioning scales commonly used in the assessment of intellectual disability include the Scales of Independent Behavior–Revised Full Scale (SIB-R; Bruininks, Woodcock, Weatherman, & Hill, 1996), the Adaptive Behavior Assessment System–Second Edition (ABAS-II; Harrison & Oakland, 2003), and the Vineland Adaptive Behavior Scales–Second Edition (VABS-II; Sparrow, Balla, & Cicchetti, 2005). It is important to note that, regardless of the measure chosen, the utility of the information obtained is limited by the quality of the information provided by the rater (AAIDD, 2010).

THE EVALUATION OF MR. DAVID NOVAK

Background Information

David Novak is the second child born to the union of Mr. Marcus Simon and Ms. Margaret Novak. Mr. Simon and Ms. Novak were never married and,

according to Ms. Novak, separated when David was approximately one year of age. The termination of their relationship occurred after approximately eight years and was secondary to Ms. Novak's becoming intolerant of Mr. Simon's substance abuse/dependence and the problems associated with these disorders. In addition to his one biological sister (Rose Novak), David was raised with his three half-siblings (Chris, Steven, and Stephanie Novak), all of whom are older then he and Rose. From the age of approximately nine years, David was raised in the presence of Mr. Jonathon Bernard, his mother's boyfriend.

Early Developmental Period

There appears to be some consensus that David was born approximately two weeks late, that he was abnormally dark in color, and had yellow sclera making the background of his eyes appear discolored. Information obtained from David's mother indicates that his prenatal development was not compromised, as she did not drink alcohol, use illicit drugs, take medications that were not prescribed, or drink caffeine in excess (she drank two small cups/day) during her pregnancy. When asked about head injuries during childhood (documented or not), Ms. Novak stated that she does not recall David's having had a head injury, but upon further query she reported that he fell out of his bed "maybe five times" when he was between 7 and 10 months of age. She also stated that at the age of two or three years, David was taken to the hospital for treatment of a fever (102 degrees); she does not recall if he was admitted, but she believes that he was.

Records and statements by Steven and Rose Novak indicate that the defendant had significant problems with enuresis that lasted until he was approximately 10 years of age. For example, according to Rose, her brother would urinate

---

The following historical information should be considered a *summary* of personal data pertaining to David's upbringing and life experiences. Information provided in this section was obtained from statements made by the

defendant, third-party informants, and review of records. This examiner looked at the totality of information provided by all three sources and commented on consistencies and inconsistencies in data. Of import, there was remarkable consistency of information with regard to adaptive behavior, intellectual ability, and behavioral problems.

Records for David's birth and prenatal period were requested but not located; therefore, statements regarding his prenatal development and birth are based on the reports of collateral sources.

on himself at school and at times would urinate while walking through the home. With respect to the latter behavior, David was reported to have told her that he was trying to get to the bathroom but was unable to do so. David was also known to urinate while sleeping, and though unclear, it appears that there may have been times when urinating in his bed occurred because he did not want to get up to go to the bathroom. Though not much is known to this examiner regarding David's treatment for the disorder, records from East Louisiana Medical Center indicate that he had a positive response to pharmaceutical treatment when he was 10 years of age. Treatment for the disorder occurred during his inpatient psychiatric hospitalization (see below for details). Nothing else is known to this examiner about this problem.

Education
Data Obtained from Statements from Collateral Sources

Ms. Ann Pratt:

Ms. Ann Pratt, David's first-grade teacher, was interviewed for a period of 11 minutes, during which time she relayed the information that she could recall from her time with him. Ms. Pratt stated that she did not remember details but could comment on a few areas of his functioning. She noted that he was a talented gymnast, and because of this, she recommended that he participate in a gymnastics program put on by the local university. Ms. Pratt is aware that he was accepted into the program, but she lost contact with the family and does not know anything more about this opportunity. When asked about his functioning within the school, she stated that she could not remember if David failed kindergarten or the first grade, but it was her recollection that she taught him during his second attempt at the first grade. She noted that school was a struggle for him both academically and socially. Ms. Pratt mentioned that she often put David's desk beside hers and noted that this seating arrangement was secondary to behavior problems triggered by negative peer interactions. According to Ms. Pratt, David "had a temper," and he became upset when people looked at him "the wrong way." She also recalled that he sometimes bullied other children, but she could not provide details. Though she could not provide details regarding grades, she remembered that he tried hard to succeed, but still earned average to below-average grades. In her opinion, David was a frustrated child who was unlikely to have success in academia, and she surmised that this would be due to his lack of stamina and/or perseverance.

Statements by Members of the Novak Family Interviewed for This Evaluation:

David's mother and all siblings recalled that David had difficulty in school from an early age and was placed in speech classes from kindergarten to approximately the fifth grade.[8] According to Ms. Novak (Margaret), David failed more than one grade, and she believes that he failed the first and third grade. Records show that he was also held back in the seventh (see below for details). With regard to grades, Ms. Novak stated that David showed a consistent pattern of low academic functioning, and the data obtained from the city schools show this to be true. As evident in the school records, David skipped the eighth grade. Though David stated that he did not know why this occurred, it is the opinion of his mother that this was due to "social promotion" that was occurring within the school system. With regard to social promotion, Ms. Novak opined that David was accelerated due to his age; David was 16 years old during his second year of the seventh grade, while the typical age of a student in the seventh grade is 12 or 13. Of note, all of David's family members stated that he was teased by children, because it was clear that he couldn't learn at the level required to succeed in his classes.

The notion of social promotion was also put forth by David's siblings, as well as his GED teacher, Ms. Holmes (see below for more details). In fact, according to his brother and sisters, David's inability to learn and understand was so pronounced that he could not even complete his homework assignments. Based on all accounts, David tried to complete the assignments, but did not have the ability to do so. Eventually he would become frustrated and, in response, one of the siblings would complete it for him. Though it is impossible to know how much this intervention

---

[8] Records were not available regarding these grades; therefore, the length of time in speech therapy is an estimate based on his mother's recollection.

helped to raise his grades, it is very likely that it did, so the grades obtained by David are likely to be somewhat artificially inflated. According to David's mother, there was only one time when he was evaluated for special education, and that occurred when he was attending Pritchard Primary School. The only information she could provide regarding this evaluation was that the results did not indicate that he needed to be in the special education program.

Ms. Holmes of Standifer Academy (and Supporting Data from Records)

At the age of approximately 16 years, David was enrolled at the Standifer Academy, a nontraditional school that offered vocational training and access to alternative teaching models. According to David, his mother withdrew him from the traditional public school system when he was in the ninth grade and placed him at the academy where he could obtain his GED. Information obtained in David's disability application indicates that he failed the GED test in August of **** and planned to retake the exam a month later. There were no notations regarding a second attempt at the GED, but David and members of his family stated that he did not complete the program.

According to Ms. Holmes, David was "a very troubled child—teenager actually." It was her opinion that he suffered with some form of psychiatric illness and was in need psychiatric treatment. When asked what led her to believe that he needed treatment, she replied, his "lack of response to people, the way he looked and acted. Something was wrong." She stated that David did not want to be in school, and that at times he just sat at his desk, nonresponsive, and appeared "comatose." Upon further query she remarked that she did not consider David to be totally incapable of thinking, but instead that he "just didn't think." Though Ms. Holmes is not 100% confident, she thinks that it is possible that David could have done the work, but showed no initiative to do so. Records from this program were requested, but according to Mr. Duvall, these records could not be located and may have been destroyed. Therefore, information regarding documented grades, behaviors, and the like could not be obtained.

Data Obtained from Records

A. Information regarding the ninth grade:
1. Title of Page: Empire High School: Official Withdrawal Form, Guidance Department, Empire, Louisiana
   Official Date: **/**/**
   Grade: 9
   Reason for Withdrawal: No explanation regarding the withdrawal.
2. Scholarship Record: Empire High School; Grade 9; **-** school year

Course	SEM	SEM	FIN	—	SEM	SEM	FIN	—
English	57	62	59	F				
English					23	3	13	F
Algebra 1	39	30	39	F				
Algebra 1					65	40	45	F
Biology	36	70	65	D				
History and Geography					32	0	11	F
Life					0	50	50	F
Int. Mason	75	75	75	C				

Total Credits: 2:00
GPA: Standard: [not present on form]; Weighted: 0.215; Unweighted: 0.298
Rank: 300/300

B. Information regarding the seventh grade:
1. Page title: Scholarship Record Grades 7–8
   Grade 7: school year **–**
   School: Empire Middle School

Course	Grade	Grade
Lang. Arts	42	58
Algebra 1 7	47	53
Science	64	69
Social Studies	64	64
Creative Writing	66	66
Career Planning	70	70
P.E.	72	81

Notices of Suspension

1. Title of Page: Empire City Schools, Empire, Louisiana Notice of Suspension
   Date: **/**/**
   Age: 16
   Grade: 7
   Suspended for 10 days and can return to school on 03/21/06 accompanied by parent at 8:00 a.m. No school listed on the form.

YEAR	GRADE	DAYS ON ROLL	DAYS PRESENT	DAYS ABSENT	DAYS UNEX. ABSENCE	TIMES TARDY	WITHDRAWAL
-	7	177	126	21	03	17	
-	7	89	62	26	06	02	1/13/06 (code W11)
-	8[9]	88	72	16	08	00	
-	9	180	140	40	140 (as written on document)	4	

Reason: "Fighting, aggravated battery, failure to follow instruction, defiance at School Board Employee."

2. Title of Page: Empire City Schools, Empire, Louisiana: Notice of Suspension
Date: **/**/ **
Age: 15
Grade: 7
Form letter addressed to Margaret Novak notifying her of David's suspension from Glen Oaks Alternative School for 10 days. Form letter says: He/She may return to school on **/**/ ** accompanied by parent at 8:00 a.m. Glen Oaks Alternative School.
   Reason: "Intentionally assaulting another student by kicking them."

3. Title of Page: Empire City Schools, Empire, Louisiana: Notice of Suspension
Date: **/**/ **
Age: 15
Grade: 7
Form letter addressed to Margaret Novak notifying her of David's suspension from Glen Oaks Alternative School for 10 days. The form letter says: "He/She may return to school on Expulsion."
Reason listed: "Gang related fight. Recommended expulsion." No dates in areas designed to have parent bring David back to school.

---

[9] Interpretation of data regarding David's enrollment in the eighth grade is impossible. According to multiple sources, he did not attend the eighth grade. However, the fact that the same academic year is listed for both the seventh and eighth grades, this examiner surmises that it is possible that he was in the seventh grade for the first semester and the eighth grade for the second. Once again, the records do not contain sufficient information.

Criminal History

Prior to the current charge of capital murder (**/**/ **), available information indicates that David's criminal history is limited to his involvement in the juvenile justice system, with the following documented charges.

Date	Charge	Finding/ Disposition
// ** (15 years old)	Destruction of Property	Informal Adjustment
// ** (17 years old)	Disorderly Conduct	Probation
// ** (17 years old)	Theft of Property—3rd Degree	Dismissed
// ** (20 years old)	Capital Murder	Pending

Of note, David and many collateral sources reported that David stole things more often than he was caught, and was also involved in street fighting. The exception to the latter was his mother, who stated that David did not engage in intentional acts of violence.

Employment History

The following history of employment is created on the basis of statements made to this examiner by David, Margaret Novak (mother), Madeline Stephens (employer), Wesley Stills (employer), and data obtained in David's application for disability. Of interest, the work history section for David's application for disability was completed by his sister, Rose Novak, on **/**/ **.

Based on available information, David has had limited involvement in the area of employment. At the time of his arrest, he had had two salaried jobs and one job in which he was paid cash on an informal basis. As evident from the table above, David did not succeed in his places of employment, and

Employer/Job title	Responsibilities	Approx. length of employment	Reason for leaving
Willington-Stills Salon (paid for helping, but not on salary)	Sweeping floors; cleaning spills; taking out garbage; other custodial or helper tasks.	Off and on for a while; varied over time; came in whenever he wanted to work.	David stated that he didn't know why he didn't go back.
Emmerson's Restaurant/ Unspecified job title	Cooking; maintaining a clean station; taking food orders Disability records said "clean up lobby and wash dishes."	1 month (as per disability records)	Fired.
City of Empire/laborer	Landscaping (manual labor) and a member of the "Clean-up Crew" (picked up trash in the community).	2 months, 3 hours/day	Not in records.

none of the tasks required of him were complex or required a high level of understanding or skill.

Emmerson's Restaurant

Discussion with Ms. Madeline Stephens, David's supervisor at a local Emmerson's Restaurant, indicated that Dave had significant problems in both carrying out the tasks of his job and in following rules of the establishment. She recalled that with David worked at Emmerson's Restaurant sometime in ****, and estimated that he worked there for a period of approximately two months. She stated that she knows David well, but her knowledge is limited to the context of working at Emmerson's restaurant.

Ms. Stephens stated that David did not function well in his position at Emmerson's and had difficulty performing virtually all tasks required. Based on her report, this was the first time that David worked at a restaurant, and she viewed his position as too complicated for him to handle. She explained that his job involved taking special orders such as "double cheese, no pickles" and this was simply not something that he could do. Upon realizing that he could not function in the assigned role (i.e., taking orders over an intercom), Ms. Stephens moved David to the grill, a position that she stated most people can do independently. Unlike others, however, David was not able to function independently, and in response, she and other managers made sure that there was always someone there to assist him. Ms. Stephens noted that David could clean his area "okay," but added that even mopping was difficult for him. It was her opinion that David attempted the tasks required of each job, but they were too complex for him to understand, and this would lead to him to become

frustrated. She noted that his frustration stemmed from his awareness that he was unable to do the task.

With regard to responsibility, Ms. Stephens noted that there were two primary areas of concern for David: timeliness and following instructions. With regard to the first, Ms. Stephens stated that it was typical for David to arrive late to work, sometimes hours late. To illustrate the problem, Ms. Stephens stated that on more than one occasion David would come in two hours late for his shift and had no understanding that this might jeopardize his employment. It was her opinion that David "thought it was fine because it was okay to come in after he got out of bed." She further opined that this is an atypical view of employment and was certain that other employees knew that arriving late for a shift was unacceptable.

The second area of concern was his inability to understand that he could not eat while on shift, despite having been told this rule multiple times. According to Ms. Stephens, David had no understanding that eating while working was not permitted and this behavior was grounds for dismissal. David had been warned numerous times about this behavior and was ultimately fired when he engaged in this activity in front of a manager. When caught eating on the job, his response to authority was reported to have been, "But I was hungry." Once again, it was the opinion of Ms. Stephens that David tried to function in his various roles at Emmerson's, but he simply did not understand how to do the tasks and/or would forget what he had learned.

Willington-Stills Salon

Though David was not formally employed at Willington-Stills Salon, he frequented this establishment and participated in tasks for which he was paid. According to both the defendant and Mr. Wesley Stills (owner of the salon), the jobs carried out by David were simple and involved a variety of menial tasks such as sweeping, cleaning, and taking out the garbage; his estimated earnings were between $40 and $60 each day that he worked.

When asked about David's ability to complete his tasks, Mr. Stills stated that he did not have any problems with David, but volunteered that he would not trust David to function independently. He further stated that he did not believe that David could make good, quality decisions in a work environment, but the tasks at the salon were within his capabilities. Moreover, the job did not entail set hours or the requirement that David must work a certain number of days per week. Instead, David functioned on his own schedule and showed up whenever he wanted to work. Mr. Stills stated that this worked well for both of them. It worked well for David because he had difficulty following schedules, and it worked well for Mr. Stills because David did not carry out duties that were essential to the running of the business.

City of Empire

Little is known to this examiner about David's involvement with the city of Empire, Louisiana. According to his mother, David "cut grass" for the city and was able to carry out this task without a problem. She noted that his employment was temporary as it was part of a summer program for kids. The job required that he begin work at 6:00 a.m. and end at 11:00 a.m. each day; transportation was provided by the city. Statements from David support this brief description of his role at the City of Empire. Records of his employment and contact information for his employer were requested, but neither was able to be located.

ADAPTIVE BEHAVIOR/ INDEPENDENT LIVING SKILLS

Statements Made by David Novak (Defendant)

According to David, he was born and raised in the company of his family members and never

moved out of the family home. He depended on his family members for the majority of his needs and, until the age of 18, he did not participate in household chores. According to David, at the age of 18 years he cut the grass, washed dishes, put laundry in the wash bin, and "helped with the babies." In the latter category, he stated that he would "watch them," change their clothes, and put on diapers. He also stated that he was allowed to babysit the children on his own, a statement that was directly refuted by the mother of the children (his sister). When asked about home repairs, he indicated that he did not participate in those types of tasks.

When asked about relationships among family members and level of conflict in the home, David stated that everyone was close with each other and that there were few problems in the home (e.g., they "eat, talk and have fun" together). He did not volunteer information regarding conflict between him and his family members secondary to his negative and dangerous behavior (see below for details), but during discussion of discipline (frequency, type, and reason) he alluded to having problems in these areas,[10] but did not elaborate.[11]

Discussions with David indicated that he does not believe that he had the ability to live independently. He noted that one of the reasons for this belief is his awareness that he can't cook. He noted that he has the ability to make things such as toast, grits, and sausages, but added that he cannot make a meal. David went on to discuss mobility and informed this writer that just prior to his arrest, his brother Steven had given him a truck (a statement that was refuted by family members), and when asked about how well he cared for it, he said, "Pretty good." Upon further questioning it was revealed that the truck was not his. He was allowed to drive the vehicle and was able to fill it with gas; all other tasks related to the truck were left to his brother. Another area in which David's self-report suggested problems in independent functioning related to money. According to David he has never

---

Note: This section does not include a comprehensive review of David's functioning in the employment or academic domains; see previous sections for details on these areas of functioning.

---

[10] This information falls within the domain of practical skills (AAIDD) and under the skill area of Health and Safety (APA).

[11] During this discussion, David frequently mumbled, looked down, and appeared very uncomfortable answering these questions.

had a checking or savings account and he has no understanding of the concept of a credit card. He knows that it can be used to purchase items, but is unclear about what else is involved. David stated that he does have the ability to pay for items using cash, but admitted that he doesn't count change and has become aware that, on more than one occasion, he was overcharged for items.

David did not state or allude to problems in the area of social functioning. He stated that he had only a few friends as a child, but had "a whole lot of 'em" between the ages of 13–20. David stated that his friends "were cool people" and noted that he would go out with them and shoot basketball, play football, and just hang around. He stated that his mother knew his friends and she thought that they were "alright." According to David, he has been a member of the gang known as "Crip." He stated that his family was unaware of his involvement and that only his cousin, Ethan, knew anything about it. He indicated that he has been in the gang for three years, and is at the "first level," rank "30." There is no indication from any other source that David was affiliated with a gang. During a conversation with David, he stated that the reason that wanted to be around gang members was so that he could "be like them," but when pressed to elaborate, he could not state why he wanted to be like them ("I don't remember"). David also stated that he has had many sexual relationships with girls and listed the names of four girls whom he stated he had dated (not necessarily had sex with). His mother reported that he had one sexual relationship with a girl who she described as similar to David in that she viewed her to be "slow."

Statements Made by Collateral Sources (In-Person and via Record Review)

Ms. Katelyn Dumont (Cousin; Information Culled from Records)

Ms. Dumont's report of David's functional ability was obtained from records from the Social Security Administration that were found within the defendant's application for disability (title of section: "Function Report—Adult Third Party, **/**/**"). Ms. Dumont's information suggests that, in her opinion, David demonstrated deficits in practical, social, and conceptual domains of functioning. She indicated that he was able to

attend to some of his personal care needs (i.e., dress—"okay"; bathe—"okay; feed self—"okay"; use toilet—"okay"), but not others (i.e., care for hair—"not okay"; shave—"not okay").[12] In an open-ended section on this form, she noted that he needed reminders for "keeping himself up and getting his shoes" and that he needed help with caring for his medical needs (the example was a failure to remember to take his medications— a task that, for this reason, had been taken over by David's mother and sister). In response to questions about meal preparation, Ms. Dumont reported that David did not prepare meals and had not done so in the past. She was questioned about her opinion as to why he did not prepare meals and stated, "He can't, he might set the house on fire." She noted that at that time David engaged in some menial work around the home (e.g., "he tries to keep the yard clean sometimes"), but nothing that required skill or a need for follow-through.

With regard to getting around in the community, Ms. Dumont stated that David was not able to drive and that, while he was allowed to go out alone, his family tried to "keep an eye on him." Ms. Dumont's responses to the section entitled "Money" suggested that David did not function well in this domain. She reported that he was unable pay bills, could not handle a savings account, and was unable to use a checkbook. She elaborated by stating that he was not responsible enough to handle these tasks. Based on the questions and responses on the form, it appears that David spent time with his family and attended church and the community centers with members of his family. There was no direct mention of David's having had friends, but in the section that evaluates an individual's ability to function within the social realm, the notations indicate that he had problems getting along with people; she wrote, "He would fight sometimes." On this form there is a section where there is a series of checkboxes regarding "Information About Abilities," and on this form she checked a few boxes related to problems with physical capabilities (e.g., lifting, bending, and hearing) and six areas of functioning unrelated to physical impairments in which he had

---

[12] These answers were obtained from check boxes on the form, not statements made by Ms. Dumont.

problems (i.e., memory, completing tasks, concentration, understanding, following instructions, and getting along with others). Included in this section was a statement in which she remarked that David was very good at following simple instructions, but not very good at following instructions presented verbally.

Ms. Stephanie Novak (Sister; In-Person Interview)

When queried about his functioning within the practical realm, Stephanie's responses indicated that her brother was able to engage in basic home and self-care, but he could not manage money nor live independently. He did not have a bank account and was typically not allowed to make purchases on his own. When asked about the reason behind this decision, Stephanie stated that David could not be trusted with money because he would either lose it, spend it on things that he did not need, or be conned out of it in a game of dice. She noted that David had the ability to cook simple foods, but did not have the ability to cook a complete meal. She also noted that there were times when he had problems cooking items that required heating. According to Stephanie, her brother's attention span was very limited, and instead of attending to the stove, he would become distracted and walk away. She stated that his distractibility was a problem that impacted all areas of his life, and this was just one of the reasons that she did not allow him to care for her children. She did, however, allow him to do things such as make their breakfast, help them get dressed, and play with them.

With regard to other areas of functioning within the practical realm, Stephanie reported that David demonstrated some abilities to assist with chores. He was noted to have swept the floors, cleaned bathrooms, tidied his room, and attended to outdoor chores such as mowing the lawn. When asked about his ability to drive a car or navigate in a city, Ms. Novak stated that he began driving at the age of 18 years. She noted that he did not drive before this because he did not have access to a vehicle. However, based on her responses, David would probably not have had the ability to navigate the streets independently, because he could not even call a taxi—and when placed in a taxi, he could not he tell the driver where he needed to be taken. In fact, according to Ms. Novak, there were times

when David could not inform his family members of his location, and because of this they had to find alternative ways to locate him so that they could pick him up.

When asked about issues that pertain to safety, Stephanie noted that David would often walk too far into the street and would not move out of the way of traffic in a timely manner. Though she was unsure, she surmised that he either didn't understand the danger and/or could not estimate the speed with which cars were approaching. She further noted that he played with guns and threw rocks in an alligator pond. According to Stephanie, David threw the rocks into the water with the goal of seeing the alligator, and he did so in a location where, had the alligator been roused, he could have easily been attacked.

Information provided by Stephanie pertaining to friendships and involvement in outside activities suggested that David exhibited problems within the social domain of functioning. She noted that her brother had significant problem with anger and, when not given his way, would "behave like a child having a temper tantrum." She stated that he would begin by crying and would then go outside, talk to himself, and hit himself on the chest with his fists. Within his peer group, she noted that he was always a follower (i.e., "most definitely a follower") and as such, in order to be accepted, he would be led to do things other people might not do (e.g., engage in fights for his friends; steal to give property to others). In her opinion, David's behavior was guided by peer pressure and it was her belief that he would do anything in order to be a part of a group. Of note, she stated that his peer group had always been much younger than he and consisted of individuals who were often in trouble within the legal system. At the time of his arrest (age 20 years), his primary peer group was noted to be composed of adolescents between the ages of 13 and 15 years. Stephanie was clear in stating her belief that, though David thought these were true friendships, the reality was that they were not. She stated that these were predatory relationships in which his peers took advantage of him by taking his money, accepting gifts from him, and getting him to do things that they themselves would not do. In essence, it was her opinion that he bought his "friendships," and it wasn't until he was arrested on the current charge that he realized that he had never really had friends.

According to Stephanie, upon his arrest, all of the people that he thought were his friends disappeared from his life.

With regard to communication, Stephanie commented that her brother was often silent for long periods of time (e.g., entire days) and generally only spoke when asked questions. She noted that he did not initiate conversations, and his responses to questions were generally short and without detail. She said that there were times he would sit alone for hours, and when asked what he was thinking, he would be completely nonresponsive or would state that he was not thinking of anything. She added that David had significant problems in attention and comprehension and that these problems were noticeable to others. For example, she noted that he would often ask the same question over and over again, "even within three minutes." She noted that he "didn't understand and we would explain and explain things, and then he would get so frustrated that he would give up."

Ms. Rose Novak (Sister)

Many of the statements provided by Rose Novak were similar or identical to those provided by Stephanie Novak (see above); their statements demonstrated remarkable consistency with regard to strengths and weaknesses in areas of adaptive behavior.

When asked about her brother's ability to attend to practical needs, such as attending to personal needs and home living, she indicated that David could only attend to basic tasks such as cooking simple foods (e.g., eggs, sausages), getting dressed, and the like and added that he did not have the ability to live on his own. When asked to elaborate, she stated that it is partly due to his self-injurious behavior (e.g., suicide attempts; banging his head against walls), and partly due to a lack of knowledge and ability (i.e. "He doesn't know how to do the things he needs to do to live independently—he needs a lot of help doing things that are required when you live by yourself.") For example, Rose stated that David did not have the ability to shop for groceries because he could not handle money or food stamps. She further noted that his short-term memory was so poor that it wasn't worth having him attempt the task. Rose stated that problems with short-term memory were evident in other realms of his life, as evidenced by the frequent need to remind him to attend to his assigned tasks.

With regard to managing money, Rose stated that her brother did not have a bank account, and it wasn't until he was 16 or 17 years of age that he was allowed to have any money on his person. When asked why he was not allowed to carry money, she stated that he would either spend it on items that he didn't need or give the money to his friends. According to Rose, David's friends would trick him out of his money by asking him to buy them something with the promise of paying him later. She noted that David was very gullible and truly believed that they would pay him back, but they never did. With regard to working with cash, she noted that her brother could count bills, but was less adept at managing change. Rose commented that her brother had the ability to go to the bank and cash checks (e.g., a paycheck), but did not do this task independently, as he was always accompanied by a family member. She also noted that David never filled out a work application by himself; a family member was required to be there because his reading skills were generally low, as was his comprehension.

Like her sister's, Rose's description of David suggested that he displayed significant deficits in social functioning. She viewed his peer group to be predatory and noted that these individuals took advantage of David's gullibility and his desire to fit in. She referred to David as a follower and commented that he "never had it in his mind to do what he wanted to do. He'd do whatever other people wanted him to do, even if it got him in trouble. He has always been a follower—he never did anything on his own." She further stated that his peers would trick him into doing things, and he could not foresee the consequences. Rose also stated that there were times when David would do things because his friends would threaten to beat him up or kick him out of the group if he didn't (e.g., steal clothing and shoes for them; steal his mother's car and take it for a joyride). When asked about gambling, she noted that David would shoot dice, but would lose each the time he played. Apparently his ineptness at the game was known to others, and people would take advantage of this by gambling with him, knowing that he would lose. Rose stated that David and his family would sometimes play cards together, but despite multiple attempts to teach him the rules, David never really caught on.

During a discussion related to dangerous behavior, Rose spoke about her brother's interest in the alligator pond. Like her sister, she considered her brother's activities at the pond to be a significant safety risk and one that he simply did not understand: "He'd go behind the fence at the alligator pond and throw rocks—when asked why he would say 'I'm just throwing rocks.' I'd go try to pull him out and he'd fall out kicking and screaming." Rose believed that he just wanted to see the alligator, and despite repeated attempts to convince him that this was dangerous, he continued to do it on a daily basis.

Steven Novak (Brother)

Steven Novak is approximately six years older than David and was in the military for three years when David was between 12 and 15 years of age. Therefore, one-to-one contact with David did not occur during these years. Prior to his departure to the military and after his return, Steven was frequently in contact with his brother and, because of this, he was able to comment on many areas of his brother's functioning in the distant and recent past.

Statements regarding David's ability to attend to self-care and the daily tasks of home living were similar to those provided by his sisters. He viewed his brother as unable to live independently, but noted that he did have the ability to carry out simple tasks. For example, he noted that David "could cook a hot dog or boil an egg," but added that he did not trust him to be alone around the stove. According to Steven, David was not aware of dangers associated with cooking, and because of this, allowing him to use the stove was always a risk. To illustrate the problem, Steven stated that David enjoyed eating fried bologna and cooked this on the stove. However, on many occasions he would stand there and watch it burn without realizing what was happening. When asked about his beliefs regarding David's ability to wash clothes, pay bills, or manage money, Steven stated with confidence that he did not believe that his brother could handle any of these tasks.

Steven was clear in stating that he did not believe that David had the same level of intellect as his same-aged peers. He noted that David failed multiple grades in school and commented that, even at this point in his life, he cannot read very well—"he can barely read *Green Eggs and Ham* now—if at all." Though he never spoke with David's teachers, Steven reported that he did not believe that David had the ability to learn at the same level as other children. He reported that, despite David's trying to learn, he simply could not catch on. In fact, Steven stated, what other people may construe as "learning" may be better conceptualized as memorization.

Throughout the discussion with Steven, it was clear that he did not believe that David had the ability to understand the rules that were required to carry out tasks that were even remotely complicated. For example, Mr. Novak stated that his brother did not comprehend rules of games, and despite having been observed using PlayStation, he never figured out the rules of the games to the degree that he could succeed. Steven also commented that David could not play dominos and that he did not grasp the rules of card games. In short, Steven stated that if something required a higher than basic level of thinking and understanding, David would not be able to do it. When asked about communicating with his brother, he stated that "you have to slow it down for him and keep it very simple for him to understand." Like Stephanie, Steven noted that repetition of information was common, but did not always lead to improved understanding.

Similar to the others, Steven reported significant problems in the social domain. He described his brother to be a follower who was easily influenced by others and a person who would believe anything that people say ("I think you can probably convince David of anything—even things that are ridiculous. Tell him a lie and stick to it and he'll believe it"). Steven commented that David was taken advantage of by his peers, and that he would protect them if they asked him to or if he felt that they were being disrespected. Steven added that David not only fought in order to fit it in, but that he would also hit people for no reason. Despite Steven's trying to explain to him that this was not appropriate behavior, David did not understand—"he treated it like a game." He further noted that David's friends took advantage of him by having him steal clothes for them. Steven attributed David's decision to participate in this behavior as being partly related to a desire to please others, but more to the complete lack of understanding that these behaviors were not in his best interests.

Ms. Margaret Novak (Mother)

Similar to other members of the Novak family, Ms. Novak did not view her son to be capable of living independently. The majority of information provided by Ms. Novak related to behavior problems, scholastic problems, and mental health issues. She clearly stated that David did not participate in many household tasks and that she viewed him as incapable of doing so. Based on her statements, much of her focus while raising her son was on keeping him safe and within her view.

As mentioned, David's mother reported significant problems in relation to safety. She stated that David was virtually oblivious to dangers that would be obvious to others, and that his behavior would not change regardless of how often the dangers were explained to him. Like other members of her family, Ms. Novak talked about his frequent trips to the alligator pond and the dangers thereof, but also provided information regarding his lack of understanding of road safety. Specifically,

> he'd get on that four wheeler and I told him not to—he didn't have a helmet and in the City of Empire you had to. He'd be on the street and was supposed to be on the sidewalk and he wouldn't stop for stop signs. Just go straight across the street without stopping— just straight across with arms out." When asked if he said anything while doing this she responded, "look, I'm ridin', Ma, I'm ridin'."[13]

Ms. Novak stated that she talked to her son about the seriousness of this activity and the fact that this behavior could result in his death, but he would just say and do the same thing over and over again. She also reported that her son drove 100 mph on Highway 23 in a Chevy Suburban (SUV) and had no understanding that this was dangerous: (1) he didn't understand that it was dangerous to drive 100 mph in general, (2) that 100 mph in a Suburban is particularly dangerous; and (3) that he should not be driving without a license. With regard to the latter, Ms. Novak stated that David never had a driver's license because he could not pass the written part of the test; she did not know if he could pass the driving component because he had to pass the written one to move forward to the next step. When asked if she would trust him enough to drive her grandchildren in the car she remarked, "No, no. He can't drive by himself safely. Like a kid

he's playful and does not concentrate." She further noted that even if an adult was in the car with him, the adult would have to closely supervise to ensure that he was following the rules of driving, such as stopping for red lights, stopping at stop signs, and not speeding.

Questions pertaining to David's functioning in the social domain indicated that there were problems, and that they were evident in both peer-to-peer interactions as well as non-peer contacts (e.g., teachers, store clerks, strangers). Like others, Ms. Novak stated that her son was teased, and she noted that this would make him very angry. During his younger years (5–12 years of age), David spent time with his cousins and brothers and did not have friends who came to the house or stopped to talk. She noted that David had difficulty interacting with kids in an age-appropriate manner and stated that he behaved more like a child of three years when he was actually eight. Based on her statements, this perception of his mental age relates to his playing roughly with children and the fact that he had temper tantrums when he did not get his way. Ms. Novak recalled that it wasn't until her son was approximately 16 years of age that he made friends, and she identified them as "a bad crowd." When asked to elaborate, she stated that she might not say "bad," but noted that these kids were the type that acted like they owned the street, would cuss, and would not allow people to walk by. When asked if she perceived David to be a follower or a leader, she stated that he was a follower and would do anything that his peers asked him to do.

Contrary to the statements of others, David's mother stated that David was not the type of person to engage in physical fights and added that people would have to really push him to make him respond aggressively. As previously mentioned, she noted that he had "temper tantrums" and described them as being quite dramatic and aggressive (e.g., running, kicking, screaming, and throwing), but remained adamant that violence toward others was not part of his personality. Based on reports in records and by other collateral sources, this belief is inaccurate, but it may reflect her experiences with David.

Wes Stills (Prior Employer; Refer to "Employment" Section for More Information)

Statements by Mr. Wes Stills indicate that he also perceived David to have difficulties within the

---

[13] Ms. Novak estimated that David was 15 or 16 years of age at this time.

social domain. Mr. Novak, who has known David since he was a young child, referred to the defendant as a follower and expressed concern regarding the ease with which he is influenced by his peers. For example, according to Mr. Stills, David might be heading to the store to purchase something to drink, but on the way back from the store he might bump into some friends who were going to steal food, and he'd stop what he was doing and go with his friends. He further noted that he believed that due to his gullibility and naiveté David would be particularly vulnerable to peers (especially those who are older) and is at risk for victimization within a correctional facility.

In addition to being easily influenced by others, Mr. Stills stated, David lacked foresight and because of this, it was easy for him to make bad decisions. He further explained that while David may eventually recognize that something was a bad idea, this insight would only happen after the decision was implemented and he was faced with the ramifications. Mr. Stills made it clear that he believed that David knew "right from wrong," but also noted that David's cognitive abilities were not the same as others'. He described David in the following manner: "He ain't the fastest fella, but he ain't the slowest either."

Social Security Disability Application

Within the disability determination records (see below for more details) completed around the time David was 19 years of age, the following comment was made: "ADLs[14]—cares for personal needs, does not cook or do chores, cannot handle money, socializes with family, does not have friends, goes to church and community center."

DAVID NOVAK'S HISTORY OF PSYCHOLOGICAL/ PSYCHIATRIC EVALUATION[15]

Outpatient Treatment

Though records were not available regarding treatment that occurred on an outpatient basis, notations in records obtained from the East Louisiana

Medical Center (ELMC; see below for details) indicated that David received outpatient psychiatric treatment with Dr. James Broussard. This treatment was confirmed by Dr. Broussard (via David's attorney), but he could not locate any records of treatment, nor could he recall details of treatment. Dr. Broussard did recall that he was integral to having James hospitalized at East Louisiana Medical Center and that David's therapist, whose name he could not remember, concurred with this decision. Records from ELMC indicate that Dr. Broussard had been treating David with an antidepressant medication (Imipramine, 25 mg, frequency unreadable) and an antipsychotic medication (Mellaril, 10 mg, once in the evening); there was no information regarding the disorder for which he was being treated, nor the date that outpatient treatment was initiated.

According to Ms. Margaret Novak, David's pharmacological treatment ended abruptly when he was approximately 15 years of age. The cessation in treatment was not due to his lack of need for treatment, but instead to the fact that Ms. Novak had no way of transporting him to the medical center. She reported that while on medication, he "did not act badly--he would generally just eat and sleep." When asked if she believed that David needed to take the prescribed medication, she stated that she did, and added that without the medication he would have "outbursts" and his personality would be "mean." With regard to outbursts and having a mean temperament, statements by all family members suggested that David exhibited severe behavioral problems that began early in his childhood and continued until the time of arrest on the current charge. For example, David had a long history of animal cruelty (e.g., fed chicks to dogs; killed cats and chicks and put them on the grill; threw bricks at animals; spray painted cats), destruction of property (e.g., kicked down a door; punched holes in walls; smashed household items), threatening and dangerous behavior (e.g., threatened to harm family members; set his brother's pillow on fire when his brother was using it), and demonstrated an inability or refusal to follow directions. Of note, Margaret Novak indicated that her typical response to his negative behaviors was to hit him. When asked to elaborate, she estimated that she used corporal punishment "probably 2–3 times per day, 4–5 times per week. Maybe four times per day—he was always doing something." As an example, she

---

[14] ADL refers to Activities of Daily Living.

[15] All sources of data were reviewed for information regarding possible substance use by David Novak. Substance use problems were denied by David and other members of his family, and data in records support this notion. As such, there will not be a review of this information in the report.

reported that David would be "hollering, running and jumping through the house and out of control. I'd hit him a couple of times with the belt to see if it would calm him down, but it only helped for a minute." She also reported that she believed that David purposefully misbehaved and that he understood why he was being punished—"When I hit him he knew why I did it, and he knew I was right to do it."

Hospitalizations

Available records indicate that David's only psychiatric hospitalization occurred at the East Louisiana Medical Center (admit date **/**/**) when he was nine years of age. As previously mentioned, the referral for inpatient hospitalization was made by Dr. James Broussard, via the emergency room, and based on the content of various notes in the record, the hospitalization was related to concerns regarding psychotic processing (i.e., hearing voices from a baby chick named Eric; talking to his brother when his brother was not in the room) and recent violence toward animals (e.g., spray painted two kittens which ultimately caused their death; fed chicks to dogs; buried his pet chick, Eric, alive) and humans (i.e., set his brother's pillow on fire while he was using it). There were other statements in the record that depict violence at school, as well as in the community (e.g., destruction of property; fire-setting; lying; oppositional behavior).

During one of his initial evaluations at the ELMC, his affect was described to be "flat" and mood as "mild confusion." His thought processes were noted to be "most logical and coherent in his history, his thought content is most significant for endorsement of psychotic symptoms, in addition to most conduct disorder symptoms with a theme of no appreciation for the destructiveness and dangerousness of his behavior." Abstraction was noted to be minimal, concentration fair, and he counted using his fingers, even for simple arithmetic. Judgment was noted to be "extremely poor, placing himself and others at risk for harm and even death."

Records regarding discharge diagnosis were virtually unreadable, but review of readable text indicates that David was released one week after admission with the diagnosis of "psychotic disorder." Recommendations upon discharge were noted to be group therapy, individual therapy, and treatment with Zyprexa, an antipsychotic medication (2.5 mg, once in the evening). Of import to the current evaluation, reference to low intelligence and a learning disability were present in the documents, and a recommendation for psychological assessment on an outpatient basis was made.

Social Security Disability

Available records and discussions with family members indicates that David was placed on disability status at the age of nine following his discharge from the East Louisiana Medical Center (see above) and received financial support from this agency until February, ****. According to an undated document entitled "Explanation of Determination" that was directed to claimants Margaret and David Novak, the rules of disability had changed, and David needed to be reevaluated to see if he met the new childhood criteria or, if over the age of 18, if he met the adult criteria. Since David was over the age of 18 years, it appears that he would have had to meet the standards set forth for adults.

Though the exact date is unknown, information obtained from records suggests that a reevaluation of disability status was initiated sometime during that same year, at which time David would have been 18 or 19 years of age. The reason for reapplication was noted to be the following: "Mental problems; violent; suicidal; learning disability." There was no documentation regarding who initiated the reapplication or any information regarding the sources of information present in the application. However, based on the wording of the information (i.e., David was always referenced in the third person) it appears that the information was unlikely to have originated from David. The date that the above-listed problems began to interfere with functioning was noted to be **/**/**, at which time David was eight years of age.

Sometime during spring **** (date not known to this examiner, but estimated to be approximately five months after his reapplication), David received word from the Social Security Administration that his application for disability had been denied. Review of the "Psychiatric Review Technique" document, signed by Adrian Edmonds, M.D. (**/**/**), indicated that there was "insufficient evidence" to support a medical disposition. The only piece of data provided within this 14-page document related to mental health issues was within the "Consultant Notes" section (p. 13) in which three scores from an intelligence test were provided (i.e., Full Scale Intelligence Quotient = 57; Verbal Intelligence Quotient = 61;

Performance Intelligence Quotient = 60) and references to ADLs were made (see prior section titled, "Adaptive Behavior/Independent Living Skills" for more details). The final disposition by Dr. Edmonds was reflected with a simple "x" when he chose the option of "Insufficient evidence" under the subtitle "Medical Disposition." Of importance to this evaluation was the presence of notations in the records indicating that the SSA was having difficulty receiving and/or locating records to support or refute the claims made for services.

Mental Health Status and Treatment at the Lexington County Jail

Information provided to this examiner regarding psychiatric treatment at the Lexington County Jail indicates that between December **, ****, and January **, ****, David was treated with Xanax (1 mg, once per day). On January ** his treatment regime was changed to Prozac (20 mg once per day in the morning) and Zyprexa (10 mg in the evening) and then on or about March *, ****, his prescription was changed to Prozac (40 mg once per day in the morning) and Seroquel (200 mg once per day in the evening). Information regarding the reason for treatment between December **** and January **, ****, is not known to this examiner, nor is the rationale for changing medications in March of ****. This examiner was provided information regarding the evaluation and need for treatment as of January **, **** (see below for details), but all other information is absent from the records provided to this examiner.

On January **, ****, David was evaluated by Dr. Derek Brennon, a psychiatrist at the Centrage Medical Center for Mental Health, the mental health center that provides services to the jail. Dr. Brennon met with David for 30 minutes and conducted an evaluation at the request from the Court, secondary to his attempted suicide on January **, ****. Notes written on a Lexington County Jail incident report indicate that at 2:43 in the afternoon, David was observed to have had a bedsheet tied around his neck and the bars on one of the tiers, and was going to jump off the tier in an attempt to kill himself. Discussion with David regarding this attempt produced a confusing picture, but the information gathered suggests that he was hearing voices telling him he was going to die and that he should kill himself. These voices were coupled with somatic symptoms related to heart

pain and palpitations. David met with this examiner approximately two months after he attempted to kill himself. At that time, he mentioned that he had been receiving treatment with "a blue and white pill" (these were two different pills), but stated that he didn't know the names of the medications or for what he was being treated.

Based on the two-page progress note written by Dr. Brennon, David was evaluated solely via in-person self-report, without review of prior mental health records or contact with collateral sources (though it is likely that the doctor spoke to officers and reviewed the incident report related to David's attempted suicide). Dr. Brennon's presentation of David's mental status at the time of the evaluation was brief and did not cover many details relevant to the assessment of intellectual disability. He noted that David's hygiene was slightly deficient (i.e., "Mr. Novak was slightly malodorous at time of evaluation") and in response to a question regarding hallucinations,[16] David was reported to have said, "Something be telling me I'm going to die, it's in my head." Dr. Brennon stated that David's thoughts were coherent without signs of thought intrusion. During the brief meeting, David was reported to have denied current thoughts of harming himself or others.

In the end, Dr. Brennon determined that David met criteria for "Depressive Disorder NOS with somatic preoccupation, without psychosis." He also remarked that he "suspected" that David's intellectual ability fell in the borderline to low average range of intelligence. The progress note produced by Dr. Brennon lacked detail regarding how he came up with his diagnostic impression, though once again, it appears that all of his statements are based on the 30-minute in-person interview and not on testing or review of his well-documented psychiatric history. Dr. Brennon prescribed Fluoxetine (20 mg qam #30 X2; an antidepressant that is commonly known as Prozac) and Zyprexa (10 mg hs, samples given, #30 X2 written). Zyprexa is an atypical antipsychotic that is used in the treatment of psychotic disorders, as well as other psychiatric

---

[16] A distortion in a person's perception of reality, typically accompanied by a powerful sense of that the distortion reflects reality. Hallucinations present via the senses and therefore can be visual, auditory, olfactory, gustatory, or tactile.

illnesses, including mood disorders. The recommendation was to remain on suicide watch for one more day with a follow-up appointment in two months.

Other

As previously noted, statements regarding animal cruelty, self-harm, auditory hallucinations, aggressive behavior, and dangerous behavior were supported by information obtained in records and by statements made by David and all family members who were interviewed for the purpose of this evaluation. Quotes provided from the interview with David's sister Rose provide an illustration of the extent to which David displayed odd and dangerous behavior:

"We were living in a trailer park and he had a panic attack—we had animals all over the trailer park and there were chickens and there were chicks and then they were gone. And we looked for them and we found them on the grill spray-painted black and there were four chicks and one kitten" (examiner query). "He said that they were his friends and he wanted them to sleep with him" and when she asked him again, he stated that he "did not know why he had done it."

(Examiner query regarding panic attacks): "He had them when people fussed at him, he'd be crying and yelling and would close the door and bang his head against the wall. He would also punch the wall, and me and my momma and sister would have to get him and hold him down." (Examiner query regarding frequency): "This was not every day, but it was not uncommon that he would lose control and break things. He'd also get up in the middle of the night and come to you and he'd stand over you and watch you and then he'd walk through the house and go outside sometimes—it was scary. He'd stand over and watch you." (Examiner query regarding her statement, if any, made to David at these times): "I would just say, David, go back to bed—what are you doing?" She then stated that her brother "would get knives and glass and try to stick himself. One time I walked in and saw him trying to break a glass with his hands. I was scared of him, because I never knew what he was going to do; always hurting animals and stuff." When asked about other instances of animal cruelty, Rose stated that David would throw things at animals, run after chickens, throw bricks at dogs and any of the animals—"goats, cows, and the tall bird."

Information provided by Rose and Margaret Novak indicates that David had experienced periods of time in which he expressed the desire to kill himself. These thoughts were at times linked to auditory hallucinations in which he heard voices telling him to kill himself. David attempted suicide at least once prior to his most recent attempt at the Lexington County Jail. Specifically, David hanged himself from a door frame with a belt. According to Rose, they reached David in time, but it was a close call in that he was observed to be "frothing at the mouth." Details regarding this incident were also relayed to this examiner by Margaret Novak, who noted that this attempt was related to her having threatened to spank David because he stole a plastic cup from the home of his aunt (estimated value, 25 cents). David's mother noted that they had to kick in the door and cut him down to save his life. She stated that she called the ambulance, and the paramedics provided onsite evaluation and recommended that David be taken to the hospital. For reasons unknown to Ms. Novak, the paramedics were not permitted to transport David to the hospital and, due to her lack of transportation, David was never taken. According to Ms. Novak, the police were also at her home, and they, too, would not provide transportation.

PRIOR ASSESSMENTS OF COGNITIVE FUNCTIONING

A. *Assessment of Cognitive Functioning—Prior to 18 years of age.*

None known to have been conducted.

B. *Assessment of Cognitive Functioning—Post 18 years of age.*

Within David's reevaluation for disability benefits that occurred when he was between the ages of 18 and 19 years, there is a brief notion that Dr. Fredericks completed the Wechsler Adult Intelligence Scale–3rd edition (WAIS-III) with David. On this document the three primary index scores were reported, and they were as follows:

Full Scale Intelligence Quotient = 57

Verbal Intelligence Quotient = 61

Performance Intelligence Quotient = 60

This brief notation was followed by the statement, "He did not put forth adequate effort."

Also included in the SSA documents was a three-page Disability Determination Evaluation that was written by Dr. Thomas Cormier, Ph.D., who is a licensed psychologist. Within this document, Dr. Fredericks provided data on the WAIS-III (raw scores and scaled scores) but did not provide any details regarding what led him to believe that David did not put forth adequate effort. He did, however, make the statement that it was his opinion that David's "ability to understand, carry out, to remember instructions, and to respond appropriately to supervision, co-workers, work pressures in a work setting appear intact for level of intellectual functioning." Support for this statement was not provided by Dr. Fredericks, and review of the background information section of the report provided no indication as to how Dr. Fredericks came to this conclusion (e.g., there is no information regarding questions pertaining to any aspect of work, including David's response to supervision, ability understand and follow through with instructions, or handle pressure). Looking to his one-paragraph summary of David's mental status at the time of the meeting, it appears that there were no noticeable signs of cognitive, behavioral, or emotional problems. It is important to note, however, that Dr. Fredericks did not provide anything to support his interpretation and therefore statements such as "Judgment, insight, and decision-making abilities appear intact" cannot be directly evaluated. Based on this writer's knowledge of mental status evaluations within the context of this type of assessment, it is possible that Dr. Fredericks conducted a cursory mental status evaluation that would not provide adequate insight into areas of mental status important to this evaluation (e.g., decision-making, concentration, attention, judgment). This is unclear, however, because there are insufficient details in the report.

Despite coming to the conclusion that David did not evidence disability sufficient to warrant assistance, Dr. Fredericks made two statements that suggested that he viewed his evaluation to be incomplete. Specifically, he stated that he believed that school records should be reviewed to help determine his level of cognitive functioning, and that he wanted to speak with David's mother to gain additional information. There is no indication that Dr. Fredericks reviewed school records before coming to his conclusion, or that he spoke with Ms. Novak. In fact, there is no indication that Dr. Fredericks even attempted to speak with Ms. Novak, other than asking David not to leave the building without bringing his mother to him. On that day, David did not follow through with this instruction, but instead left the building without bringing in his mother.

It appears that the data that Dr. Fredericks used to support his decision regarding need for continued support (i.e., David would not be awarded funds) were based on his interaction with the defendant (length of contact not noted on the report) and documents included in the disability file (documents reviewed were not listed). Of note, the interview data reported in this evaluation were obtained from David and, based on knowledge obtained for the purpose of this evaluation, were at times absent, wrong, or limited in detail. For example, Dr. Fredericks was operating under the belief that David had no history of hospitalizations, no history of psychiatric issues, and completed the tenth grade, all of which are incorrect. David was noted to be unable to relay information as to why or how long he had been on disability, did not know anything about his family medical history, could only state that he left school because his "probation officer said I was too bad," and despite stating that he had a probation officer, David denied any history of involvement in the legal system. Of note, though not stated in the text of his report, Dr. Fredericks overtly acknowledged his suspicion that David may meet criteria for mild mental retardation. This acknowledgement is found in the section of his report titled, "Initial Diagnostic Impression: DSM IV" in which he deferred a diagnosis on Axis I (meaning that he did not have an opinion on the presence or absence of major mental illnesses such as schizophrenia, anxiety disorders, depression and the like) and put a rule-out diagnosis on Axis II for mild mental retardation (meaning that he needed to investigate the possibility that David met criteria for mild mental retardation because there is information to support the possibility that he does). There is no statement regarding whether or not the initial impressions put forth by Dr. Fredericks were supported or not by the data he collected for this evaluation.

FAMILY HISTORY OF MENTAL HEALTH PROBLEMS AND TREATMENT

Though records were not available for review, statements made by Margaret Novak indicate that three individuals on her side of the family exhibit signs of mental health problems. According to Ms. Novak, her brother Adrian Novak (age ~50) is on disability for physical ailments, and she described him to be "slow." It is unclear whether the term "slow" related to intellectual ability, physical disability, or both, but she noted that he walked slowly with his head facing down. Adrian Novak is reported to be receiving treatment at the East Louisiana Medical Center. In addition to her brother Adrian, she reported that her sister, Elizabeth Leroy (age ~55 or 56) is also on disability and is similar in status to her brother, "like she has lost her mind." Though Ms. Novak did not know if her sister is currently receiving treatment, her sister also used to go to the East Louisiana Medical Center. Ms. Novak stated that her niece Michelle Leroy (daughter of Elizabeth Leroy) also received mental health treatment, but could not elaborate.

Of note, in the treatment records of David (East Louisiana Medical Center), there is a reference to his having a 17-year-old brother who is "mentally retarded." This information was not relayed to this examiner by any member of the Novak family and was not present in other documents provided for review by this examiner. In fact, according to Ms. Novak, with the exception of David, all of her children attended college, which, if true, means the above-mentioned statement is inaccurate.

FUNCTIONING WITHIN LEXINGTON COUNTY JAIL

Information in this section was obtained from documents obtained from the Lexington County Jail and discussions with correctional officers who currently work with David. Consistent across all informants was that David is a quiet and well-behaved inmate who is respectful toward others. There is no indication that he has been a behavioral problem since his arrival at the facility, and in general, it appears that David stays to himself or interacts with only a few inmates at a time. None of the collateral sources stated that they have witnessed or heard of incidences in which David was observed to be acting strangely.

Of the six officers interviewed, only Officer Thompson stated that he believed that he knew David well and perceived him to be without significant problems (i.e., "All I know is that he is normal. Doesn't act off like some others back

there—doesn't beat on the glass").[17] He described David to be "real laid back" and, with the exception of not speaking unless spoken to, he speaks no differently than other inmates. Officer Thompson has observed the defendant playing dominos and watching TV, and offered that he had never seen him read, but added that this doesn't mean that he cannot read. When asked if it is easy to function within the Lexington County Jail, Officer Thompson stated that he believed that it was and noted that the officers look out for the inmates. When asked about what happened on the typical day, he stated that a day involves "getting up and not doing too much—play dominos." Officer Thompson indicated that he has daily contact with David, but that they do not talk for long periods of time (i.e., "I speak to him and he speaks back"). He offered that his rating of knowledge of David would be "7 or 8" out of 10.

In contrast to Officer Thompson, Sergeant Eric Morton, Officer Stein, and Officer Varner provided statements that suggested that David is not a typical inmate in relation to many issues relevant to the assessment of adaptive behavior. The following paragraphs provide the reader with statements from each of these officers.

Sergeant Morton

In the opinion of Sgt. Morton, David "is a follower, not a leader." He noted that the defendant "looks like he is just waiting on someone to take his hand and lead him. He is the kind of guy who would be talked into stealing something. If you told him to go up the stairs and jump off, he probably would." When asked why he believed this to be the case, he noted, "You can tell by looking at him." In his role as a correctional officer, Sgt. Morton has contact with David 4–5 times per day when he is on shift and in the unit. His other role is observation off the unit from an observation room.

Officer Stein

In the opinion of Officer Stein, David appears to be "a little slow—doesn't really understand." She

---

[17] Officers West and Bonner provided limited information regarding David. The information that they did provide was not detailed, as both of them noted that their contact with him was limited. In general, however, both officers viewed David to be compliant, quiet, and typical of other inmates. Neither reported anything that would indicate above-average functioning within the facility.

noted that her conversations with the defendant are very short and generally limited to "yes" and "no" responses.[18] When clarifying her statements, Officer Stein noted that she doesn't perceive him to be "crazy or stupid—just slow." The reference to "slow" was with regard to "slow at picking up on stuff." Based on her statements, Officer Stein is not in frequent contact with David, but instead sees him infrequently when he has "visits with attorneys, sick call, or anytime."

Officer Varner

Of the six officers interviewed, Officer Varner provided the most information regarding David's functioning in the facility. Over the course of the 30-minute interview, it became clear that Officer Varner perceived David to be very different from other inmates. He stated that David lacked common sense, was "not smart enough to take care of himself," and did not understand things in a way that most people would. He further explained that David tries to hide the fact that he doesn't know certain things and this becomes apparent when he is asked open-ended questions. In essence, David will generally respond to questions with "yes–no" answers or provide an answer to a multiple-choice question, but when required to provide details or further explain his response, it becomes clear that he is not familiar with the topic and/or doesn't understand what is being asked of him.

Officer Varner referred to David as "a little slow" and stated that David is one of the top five inmates in need of safety. He further noted that David behaves in a childlike manner and that he needs to be cared for within the facility (e.g., "you have to nurture him"). During discussion of David's ability to function within the facility, Officer Varner volunteered that he does not view the defendant to be "streetwise" and when asked to elaborate he provided the following explanation:

> He probably doesn't understand the rules in the street—he wouldn't understand and get in trouble. He wouldn't realize that the guys in C block were going to jump on him and he should have known. Doesn't pick up on

things—he should have known. And the fire alarm that just went off could have been done purposely to distract the officers, but he'd never know that. He is very slow to catch on.

Officer Varner also noted that he finds David to be different from others in relation to social functioning. He indicated that the defendant does not seem to have general knowledge similar to other people his age and noted that there are times when he asks questions that are inappropriate to the situation. For example, Officer Varner stated that during a fight on the unit, David approached the officers and asked them when the food trays were going to be delivered. He also reflected on David's honesty and noted that David is a truthful person, but added that this characteristic does not originate out of a sense of morality, but instead is a reflection of David's lack of understanding that there are times when it might be a good idea to stretch the truth.

THE CURRENT EVALUATION: MENTAL STATUS AND RESULTS OF TESTING

Observations/Mental Status

David Novak was evaluated for a total of approximately nine hours, over a period of three days. Prior to beginning each meeting, this examiner informed David of the limits of confidentiality and informed him that he could end the process of evaluation at any time. On all three occasions, David agreed to participate in the evaluation, and termination was the decision of the examiner. Records provided from the Lexington County Jail indicate that David was not receiving psychiatric treatment during the first two days of interviewing and testing (intelligence testing was completed at this time), but was taking an antidepressant (Prozac) and an antipsychotic (Seroquel) at the time of the third meeting (achievement testing was completed at this time).

With regard to basic mental status, David presented similarly on all three occasions. Though he was oriented to time, place, and person, there were signs of impairment in various areas of cognitive functioning. For example, he demonstrated some impairment in recent memory, showed limited ability to attend, and questions had to be put in simple language and asked slowly with a frequent need for repetition. David showed a limited range of emotion, spoke slowly, and did not initiate conversation

---

[18] This statement was supported by other correctional staff, who noted that he was very quiet and generally only spoke when spoken to.

Wechsler Adult Intelligence Scale- IV	Standard Score (Composite)	Percentile Rank	95% Confidence Interval	Qualitative Description
Full and Index Scores				
Full Scale IQ	67	1	64–72	Extremely Low
Verbal Comprehension Index	63	1	59–70	Extremely Low
Perceptual Reasoning Index	73	4	68–81	Borderline
Working Memory Index	71	3	66–80	Borderline
Processing Speed Index	84	14	77–94	Low Average
General Ability Index	65	1	61–71	Extremely Low

Note: A standard score of 100 is considered average, with most individuals scoring between 85 and 115.

with this examiner. The majority of questions put forth to David were answered in a "yes-no-I don't know" format (via words or nodding) or in short sentences with little to no detail. His ability to understand directions, such as "count backward by three," was noticeably impaired, and there was evidence throughout the evaluation that repetition of instructions, accompanied by an explanation, did not always lead to improved understanding.

David reported that he had been having difficulty sleeping and that, similar to when he was living in the community, he had been hearing voices telling him that he should kill himself. On the first day of the evaluation, he reported that he had been seeing "little white things" for a couple of months, but could not elaborate further. There were no signs of ongoing psychotic processing during the evaluation, and David denied interference related to such symptoms. His mental status, while impaired, was not impaired to the degree that it invalidated the test results. Based on the totality of the information gathered for this evaluation, David's mental status during the current evaluation was typical and reflective of what it was like in the community.

Results of Psychological Tests/Procedures
Wechsler Adult Intelligence Scale–4th Edition (WAIS-IV)

The WAIS-IV is an intelligence test that is composed of ten core subtests and five supplemental subtests. In addition to individual subtest scale scores, the WAIS-IV provides four index scores: Verbal Comprehension, Perceptual Reasoning, Working Memory, and Processing Speed, and a full scale IQ score. The test was standardized on 2,200 people who ranged in age from 16 to 90, and the sample closely matched U.S. population figures on major demographic variables. Full scale and index scores have a mean of 100 and a standard deviation of 15,

Wechsler Adult Intelligence Scale—IV	Raw Score	Scaled Score	Percentile Rank
Verbal Comprehension Subtest Scores			
Similarities	10	3	1
Vocabulary	7	3	1
Information	4	5	5
Comprehension	10	4	2
Perceptual Reasoning Subtest Scores			
Block Design	20	5	5
Matrix Reasoning	8	4	2
Visual Puzzles	11	7	16
Figure Weights	7	5	5
Picture Completion	5	4	2
Working Memory Subtest Scores			
Digit Span	19	5	5
Arithmetic	7	5	5
Letter-Number Sequencing	17	8	25
Processing Speed Index Scores			
Symbol Search	27	8	25
Coding	50	6	9
Cancellation	30	7	16

Note: A subtest scaled score of 10 is considered to be average, with most individuals scoring between 8 and 12.

while individual subtest scale scores have a mean of 10 and a standard deviation of 3.

Woodcock-Johnson Tests of Achievement— 3rd Edition (WJ-III)

The following information was obtained from the Examiner's Manual for the Woodcock-Johnson III (WJ-III, 2001). The WJ-III is a comprehensive set of norm-referenced tests for the measurement of academic achievement. Normative data are based on a national sample of over 8,000 individuals ranging in age from 2 to over 90 years. The demographic and community characteristics closely matched the general U.S. population's. The tests in the Standard Battery combine to form 10 cluster scores, including a Total Achievement score. Cluster interpretation results in higher validity because the score comprises more than one broad component of a broad ability and thus serves as the best interpretation. The use of audio equipment was not allowed, so the tests that required this equipment were administered verbally by this examiner (as per WJ-III protocol).

CLUSTER/Test	Age Equivalent	Relative Proficiency Index	Standard Score (68% Band)	Grade Equivalent
Oral Language (Ext.)	8–4	29/90	64 (61–67)	3.0
Oral Expression	8–11	36/90	66 (61–70)	3.6
Listening Comp.	8–0	23/90	69 (66–72)	2.6
Broad Reading	8–9	5/90	63 (61–66)	3.4
Basic Reading	8–6	2/90	62 (60–64)	3.1
Reading Comprehension	7–8	3/90	60 (58–63)	2.3
Broad Math	8–3	4/90	49 (46–52)	2.9
Math Calc. Skills	8–4	10/90	45 (40–50)	3.0
Math Reasoning	8–1	1/90	57 (54–60)	2.7
Broad Written Lang.	8–3	10/90	51 (47–55)	2.9
Basic Writing Skills	8–4	4/90	61 (58–64)	3.0
Written Expression	8–1	15/90	57 (52–61)	2.7
Academic Skills	8–5	1/90	49 (46–52)	3.1
Academic Knowledge	7–1	1/90	58 (55–62)	1.8
Total Achievement	8–5	6/90	55 (53–56)	3.1

Form A—Tests	Age Equivalent	Relative Proficiency Index	Standard Score (68% Band)	Grade Equivalent
Letter-Word Recognition	8–8	0/90	65 (63–68)	3.3
Reading Fluency	11–7	39/90	80 (77–83)	6.2
Story Recall	11–3	86/90	91 (80–103)	5.8
Understanding Directions	8–7	52/90	76 (71–81)	3.3
Calculation	7–11	1/90	48 (42–54)	2.6
Math Fluency	9–10	48/90	61 (59–64)	4.5
Spelling	8–6	5/90	65 (61–69)	3.1
Writing Fluency	9–7	26/90	69 (63–75)	4.2
Passage Comprehension	7–11	9/90	67 (63–71)	2.6
Applied Problems	8–1	1/90	62 (58–66)	2.8
Writing Samples	7–4	8/90	51 (45–57)	2.0
Story Recall—Delayed	6–0	76/90	68 (53–83)	K.7
Word Attack	8–1	9/90	74 (71–77)	2.8
Picture Vocabulary	8–3	5/90	69 (66–73)	3.0
Oral Comprehension	7–7	7/90	69 (65–73)	2.2
Editing	8–2	4/90	65 (61–69)	2.8
Reading Vocabulary	7–4	1/90	62 (59–64)	2.1
Quantitative Concepts	8–0	2/90	54 (49–59)	2.7
Academic Knowledge	7–1	1/90	58 (55–62)	1.8
Spelling of Sounds	5–7	1/90	31 (24–38)	K.3
Sound Awareness	7–3	12/90	59 (55–63)	2.0
Punctuation and Capitalization	7–5	2/90	43 (36–51)	2.1

As is evident from the results depicted above, David shows broad-based deficits in achievement as measured by the WJ-III. All Cluster Scores fell in the age range of 7.1 years to 8.11 years (lowest score obtained on Academic Knowledge). Grade equivalents on the Cluster Scores ranged from first to third grade and from kindergarten to the sixth grade on the subtests.

Scales of Independent Behavior–Revised (SIB-R)

The following information was obtained from the SIB-R Comprehensive Manual (1996). "The SIB-R is a comprehensive measure of adaptive and problem behaviors. It is primarily a measure of functional independence and adaptive functioning in school, home, employment, and community settings. These functions are evaluated using objective assessment procedures that allow users to compare one individual to others" and has been normed on individuals "from early infancy to mature adult levels (80 years and older)." "The SIB-R Full Scale is a broad measure of adaptive behavior composed of 14 subscales organized into four adaptive behavior clusters (Motor, Social Interaction and Communication, Personal Living, and Community Living)." Cluster Score interpretation provides the primary and substantial basis for normative interpretations as it minimizes the danger inherent in "generalizing from a single narrow measure of behavior to a broad, multifaceted ability."

The SIB-R is intended for administration to informants who have extensive knowledge of the person of interest (preferably a parent or caretaker), over a long period of time, and preferably in multiple settings. While there is no requirement regarding recency of contact between the person of interest and the rater for the SIB-R, it is safe to assume that information obtained from individuals who have been in recent contact with the person of interest would produce more valid results. Furthermore, the SIB-R is used to assess an individual's current level of functioning, rather than that of the past. Test-retest reliabilities have been documented for a maximum of four weeks.

Due to David's incarceration, there is no way to assess his current adaptive behavior in a community setting. Moreover, in order to assess his functioning prior to the age of 18 years, adaptive behavior measures must be administered retrospectively. That is, administration of the SIB-R must be for time periods in the distant past. As such, the SIB-R was given to Ms. Rose Novak, Ms. Stephanie Novak, and Mr. Steven Novak for their recollections of David when he was 16 years old. The goal of these retrospective evaluations was to obtain quantitative information related to the respondent's memories of David's abilities prior to the age of 18 (Prong 3 of the diagnostic criteria requires onset during the developmental period). A SIB-R for the age of 20 was given to Ms. Margaret Novak. The purpose of this rating form was to assess her memory of her perception of his abilities at the time of the crime.

A word of caution is required regarding this unorthodox administration of the SIB-R. As already stated, the scores obtained from the measure are being used as a means to objectively evaluate the rater's memory for specific abilities related to overall adaptive functioning. The examiner is well aware of the problems related to memory of life events and the absence of studies determining the validity of this type of administration. Therefore, the scores obtained from the following SIB-R protocols are not intended to reflect true scores, but instead the raters' memory of their perceptions of David a number of years prior to the date of assessment. On a positive note, prior contact for all raters was in the recent past, with each of them having had contact with the defendant in the days or weeks prior to the time of the crime.

As is evident in the following tables, all of David's family members provided ratings that indicate that he is less able than his similar-aged peers to function independently on a day-to-day basis. As a reminder, these perceptions were in relation to when he was 16 and 20 years of age. Though there was some discrepancy in level of impairment across raters, there was a high level of consistency on the most robust index, the Broad Independence score.

The Broad Independence score is calculated by averaging the scores produced on the four subscales and as such is equally weighted for each area of functioning. All raters produced scores on the Broad Independence scale that were two standard deviations below the mean (all of which were well below the cut-score for ID), but the areas of strength and weakness varied between raters. Looking at consistency across raters, it appears that Steven and Margaret Novak viewed him as similarly impaired

SIB-R Scores for David Novak at Age 16 Years

CLUSTER/ Subscale	Age Equivalent	Percentile Rank	Standard Score	Relative Mastery Index[19]	Skill with Age-Level Tasks
1. SIB-R COMPLETED BY MS. ROSE NOVAK (SISTER)					
BROAD INDEPENDENCE	8–6	0.1	50	39/90	Limited
MOTOR SKILLS	6–8	0.1	46	27/90	Limited to very limited
Gross-Motor (raw score = 50/57)	7–5				Limited
Fine-Motor (raw score = 51/57)	5–9				Very limited
SOCIAL/COMM.	7–0	0.1	55	27/90	Limited to very limited
Social Interaction (raw score = 29/54)	7–1				Limited
Language Comp. (raw score = 24/54)	5–8				Very limited
Language Expr. (raw score = 39/60)	9–9				Limited
PERSONAL LIVING	11–4	4	74	58/90	Limited
Eating (raw score = 35/57)	9–9				Limited to very limited
Toileting (raw score = 50/51)	8–6				Limited
Dressing (raw score = 38/54)	13–9				Limited to age-appropriate
Self-Care (raw score = 28/48)	10–10				Limited
Domestic Skills (raw score = 7/54)	14–7				Age-appropriate
COMMUNITY LIVING	9–6	0.4	61	42/90	Limited
Time & Punctuality (raw score = 36/57)	7–6				Very limited
Money & Value (raw score = 20/60)	10–3				Limited
Work Skills (raw score = 19/60)	9–1				Limited
Home–Community (raw score = 27/54)	12–2				Limited to age-appropriate

across all Clusters with skill levels ranging from "limited" to "very limited to negligible" (this being the lowest in the range). Stephanie and Rose Novak

[19] Relative Mastery Index allows examiners to make predictive statements about the individual's expected quality of performance on tasks similar to the ones evaluated on the SIB-R (see p. 58 of SIB-R Comprehensive Manual).

produced scores that were similar to one another with skill levels ranging from "age appropriate" (one subscale for each rater) to "limited to very limited." With the exception of two Cluster scores (Personal Living for Rose and Motor Skills for Stephanie), all standard scores fell at least one standard deviation below the mean, with virtually all scores produced by Margaret and Steven at two standard deviations below the mean.

CLUSTER/ Subscale	Age Equivalent	Percentile Rank	Standard Score	Relative Mastery Index	Skill with Age-Level Tasks
BROAD INDEPENDENCE	9–0	0.1	54	45/90	Limited
MOTOR SKILLS	10–3	4	74	66/90	Limited
Gross-Motor	13–4				Age-appropriate
(raw score = 50/57)					
Fine-Motor	8–4				Limited to very limited
(raw score = 51/57)					
SOCIAL/COMM.	6–3	0.1	49	19/90	Limited to very limited
Social Interaction	7–1				Limited
(raw score = 29/54)					
Language Comp.	5–3				Very limited
(raw score = 24/54)					
Language Expr.	6–5				Very limited
(raw score = 39/60)					
PERSONAL LIVING	9–6	1	63	39/90	Limited
Eating	8–2				Very limited
(raw score = 35/57)					
Toileting	7–10				Limited
(raw score = 50/51)					
Dressing	12–4				Limited
(raw score = 38/54)					
Self-Care	10–2				Limited
(raw score = 28/48)					
Domestic Skills	11–7				Limited
(raw score = 7/54)					
COMMUNITY LIVING	10–7	2	68	53/90	Limited
Time & Punctuality	8–1				Limited to very limited
(raw score = 36/57)					
Money & Value	11–0				Limited
(raw score = 20/60)					
Work Skills	11–8				Limited
(raw score = 19/60)					
Home– Community	13–0				Limited to age-appropriate
(raw score = 27/54)					

CLUSTER/ Subscale	Age Equivalent	Percentile Rank	Standard Score	Relative Mastery Index	Skill with Age-Level Tasks
BROAD INDEPENDENCE	7–5	.01	40	27/90	Limited to very limited
MOTOR SKILLS	6–10	0.1	48	29/90	Limited to very limited
Gross-Motor	8–5				Limited
(raw score = 46/57)					
Fine-Motor	5–5				Very limited
(raw score = 37/57)					

(continued)

CLUSTER/ Subscale	Age Equivalent	Percentile Rank	Standard Score	Relative Mastery Index	Skill with Age-Level Tasks
SOCIAL/COMM	6–1	0.1	47	18/90	Very limited
Social Interaction (raw score = 28/54)	4–0				Very limited
Language Comp. (raw score = 22/54)	5–8				Very limited
Language Expr. (raw score = 34/60)	8–7				Limited to very limited to negligible
PERSONAL LIVING	8–3	0.1	55	27/90	Limited to very limited
Eating (raw score = 24/57)	4–7				Very limited to negligible
Toileting (raw score = 45/51)	7–5				Limited
Dressing (raw score = 40/54)	8–4				Limited to very limited
Self-Care (raw score = 35/48)	11–4				Limited
Domestic Skills (raw score = 26/54)	11–7				Limited
COMMUNITY LIVING	8–8	0.1	54	32–90	Limited to very limited
Time & Punctuality (raw score = 33/57)	7–10				Limited to very limited
Money & Value (raw score = 20/60)	8–9				Limited to very limited
Work Skills (raw score = 21/60)	7–2				Limited to very limited
Home–Community (raw score = 27/54)	12–5				Limited

SIB-R Scores for David Novak at Age 20 Years

4. SIB-R COMPLETED BY MS. MARGARET NOVAK (MOTHER)					
CLUSTER/ Subscale	Age Equivalent	Percentile Rank	Standard Score	Relative Mastery Index	Skill with Age-Level Tasks
BROAD INDEPENDENCE	8–1	0.1	35	23/90	Limited to very limited
MOTOR SKILLS	7–1	0.1	48	29/90	Limited to very limited
Gross-Motor (raw score = 50/57)	8–2				Limited
Fine-Motor (raw score = 51/57)	6–0				Very limited
SOCIAL/COMM.	5–11	0.1	36	11/90	Very limited
Social Interaction (raw score = 29/54)	6–3				Limited to very limited
Language Comp. (raw score = 24/54)	6–6				Very limited

(continued)

4. (CONTINUED)

CLUSTER/ Subscale	Age Equivalent	Percentile Rank	Standard Score	Relative Mastery Index	Skill with Age-Level Tasks
Language Expr. (raw score = 39/60)	5–8				Limited to very limited
PERSONAL LIVING	9–3	0.2	56	25/90	Limited to very limited
Eating (raw score = 35/57)	8–2				Very limited
Toileting (raw score = 50/51)	10–6				Limited to age-appropriate
Dressing (raw score = 38/54)	8–4				Very limited
Self-Care (raw score = 28/48)	9–7				Limited to very limited
Domestic Skills (raw score = 7/54)	11–7				Limited
COMMUNITY LIVING	10–0	0.2	56	34/90	Limited
Time & Punctuality (raw score = 36/57)	8–6				Limited to very limited
Money & Value (raw score = 20/60)	10–3				Limited to very limited
Work Skills (raw score = 19/60)	8–9				Limited to very limited
Home– Community (raw score = 27/54)	12–5				Limited

SUMMARY AND CONCLUSIONS

In the opinion of the examiner, Mr. David Novak meets criteria for intellectual disability as delineated in both the DSM-IV: TR (APA, 2000) and the AAIDD manual (AAIDD, 2010). Given the level of detail provided in the text of this report, this next section will briefly cover the three prongs required for the diagnosis of intellectual disability as put forth by the AAIDD and the APA. The reader is encouraged consult the text if there are questions related to the basis for the opinions put forth by this examiner.

Prong 1: Significantly Sub-Average Intellectual Functioning
Definition

According to the AAIDD, in order to qualify for the diagnosis of intellectual disability, the person must obtain an intelligence quotient (IQ) "that is approximately two standard deviations below the mean, considering the standard error of measurement for the specific assessment instruments used and the instrument's strengths and limitations" (AAIDD, 2010, p. 27).

According to the APA, significantly sub-average intellectual functioning is indicated by an IQ of approximately 70 or below on an individually administered IQ test (for infants, a clinical judgment of significantly sub-average intellectual functioning is used) (APA, 2000, p. 49).

David Novak

On both occasions that David was tested, he received a full scale intelligence quotient below 70, which is two standard deviations below the mean. Specifically, he obtained a score of 57 in **** and a score of 67 in **** (the current evaluation). Though the results of the **** (older) score must be looked at within the context of insufficient effort, it is the opinion of this examiner that the obtained score from that evaluation is reflective of the range within which David's ability lies, namely within the range of mild intellectual disability. Indeed, less than optimal effort at the time of testing would have artificially reduced his scores, but in light of the totality of information obtained for this evaluation, it is considered extremely unlikely that with adequate effort, David's score would have fallen outside of the range required for the diagnosis of intellectual disability (i.e., above 70).

The opinion regarding the presence of subaverage intellectual functioning is supported by information obtained from records and statements of multiple collateral sources regarding important areas of cognitive ability. For example, there is ample evidence to support deficits in decision-making, reasoning, memory, knowledge, and comprehension, all of which are relevant to intellectual ability. Unfortunately, as with many individuals, formal testing of intellectual ability was not carried out during the developmental period, or if it was, it was not available for review.

Prong 2: Significant Limitations in Adaptive Behavior
Definition

According to the AAIDD, for the diagnosis of intellectual disability, significant limitations in adaptive behavior should be established through the use of standardized measures that are normed on the general population; included in that sample should be people with and without disabilities. On these standardized measures, significant limitations in adaptive behavior are defined as performance that is at least two standard deviations below the mean of either (a) one of the following three types of adaptive behavior: conceptual, social, or practical, or (b) an overall score on a standardized measure of conceptual, social, and practical skills (AAIDD, 2010, p. 27). Furthermore, the assessment should relate to an individual's typical performance during daily routines and changing circumstances, not to his maximum performance (AAIDD, 2010, p. 45).

According to the APA, in order to meet the criteria for intellectual disability, there must be evidence of impairment in present adaptive functioning (i.e., the person's effectiveness in meeting the standards expected for his or her age by his or her cultural group) in at least two of the following areas: communication, self-care, home living, social/interpersonal skills, use of community resources,

self-direction, functional academic skills, work, leisure, and health and safety (APA, 2000, p. 49).

With regard to deficits in adaptive behavior, it is the opinion of this examiner that David demonstrated significant deficits across all domains of functioning—conceptual, social and practical—as per the AAIDD. When looking at deficits in the 10 skill areas delineated by the APA, it is the opinion of this examiner that David demonstrated significant deficits in nine of the 10, the exception being self-care. These deficits were present during the developmental period and at the time of the crime. While this examiner suspects that David has the ability to take care of basic needs such as showering, brushing his teeth, dressing, and the like, and is reported to have done so in the community setting, it is doubtful that he would continue to produce the behaviors necessary to maintain adequate level of care if he lived independently. However, available information was not sufficient to be able to make this determination, so the level of impairment in this skill area is not considered significant enough to meet the requirement for intellectual disability.

The following table, presented previously, delineates some of the abilities relevant to each

Domains, AAIDD (2002 & 2010)	Skill areas, AAIDD (2002 & 2010)	Skill areas, AAIDD (1992) & APA (2000)
Conceptual	• Language • Reading • Money concepts • Self-direction	• Communication • Functional academics • Self-direction • Health & safety
Social	• Interpersonal • Responsibility • Self-esteem • Gullibility • Naiveté • Follows rules • Obeys laws • Avoids victimization	• Social skills • Leisure
Practical	• Activities of daily living • Occupational skills • Maintains safe environments	• Self-care • Home living • Community use • Health & safety • Work

domain and serves as a guide on which to base the opinions of this examiner. Once again, the reader is referred to the information provided in the body of this report for more details.

Prong 3: Onset During the Developmental Period
Definition

AAIDD: This disability originates before the age of 18

APA: The onset is before age 18 years.

Based on the totality of the information, both sub-average intellectual ability and deficits in adaptive behavior were present prior to the age of 18 years and existed at the time of the crime when David was 20 years of age.

In closing, based on all available information, it is the opinion of this examiner that David Novak currently meets the diagnostic criteria for mild intellectual disability, and did so prior to the age of 18 years, as well as at the time of the crime for which he is charged.

Respectfully Submitted,
Karen L. Salekin, Ph.D.
Psychologist
Louisiana License #****

TEACHING POINT:
SELECTING TOOLS FOR USE IN FMHA

The criteria of relevance and reliability applied to the selection of psychological tests and specialized measures will always considerably reduce the number of such measures appropriate for use in FMHA. Evaluators should be prepared to provide an explanation of how each selected measure provides useful additional information—and how such information is relevant to the clinical condition, forensic issues, and causal connection.

In the present case, there is an interesting juxtaposition of considerations. The defendant has charges that could become capital, which would imply a very broad range of considerations (and, accordingly, a broader range of possible measures). However, the question before the court at this stage of the proceedings is whether the defendant is intellectually disabled—and, under *Atkins*, therefore exempt from the death penalty. The present evaluation was conducted solely for that purpose. Consequently, the measures selected were those directly relevant to the diagnosis of intellectual disability, and not to the broader range of questions that would have applied to a defendant (without an *Atkins* exception) at the sentencing stage of a capital case.

9

Competence for Execution

The report in this chapter describes an evaluation of competence for execution. These evaluations have been guided by *Ford v. Wainwright* (1986) and *Panetti v. Quarterman* (2007), although the statutorily defined criteria may differ by state. The principle illustrated by this case describes the importance of identifying relevant forensic issues as they apply to both the broad and the specific aspects of the legal question in a given case. The teaching point provides guidance on the identification of assessment targets when legal standards are broad or non-specific.

CASE ONE
PRINCIPLE: IDENTIFY RELEVANT FORENSIC ISSUES (*PRINCIPLE 8*)

This principle discusses the importance of identifying the relevant forensic issues in a case. "Forensic issues" encompass functional abilities, capacities, and skills that are relevant to a broader legal question. Some of these legal questions addressed in FMHA (e.g., sanity at the time of the offense) are well defined by statute or case law, making it reasonably straightforward to identify the associated forensic issues. Unfortunately, other legal questions are poorly defined by statute and case law, making it difficult for the forensic clinician to identify the relevant forensic issues. When the forensic issues are unclear or vaguely defined, the forensic clinician must clarify them to the extent possible. Some potential sources of guidance for the forensic clinician include the legal and behavioral sciences literature, and consultation with the referring attorney or the legal decision-maker in a court-ordered evaluation.

This principle is addressed only indirectly in the *Ethical Principles of Psychologists and Code of Conduct* (American Psychological Association, 2010a): "When assuming forensic roles, psychologists

are or become reasonably familiar with the judicial or administrative rules governing their roles" (Standard 2.01(f)). An evaluator's ability to adequately identify the relevant questions to be decided by the trier of fact naturally extends from an understanding of her role within the trial process.

More specifically, the *Specialty Guidelines for Forensic Psychology* (APA *Specialty Guidelines*; American Psychological Association, 2013b) describe the importance of identifying and focusing on the relevant psycholegal constructs (i.e., forensic issues) when conducting FMHA. According to the APA *Specialty Guidelines*:

> Forensic examiners seek to assist the trier of fact to understand evidence or determine a fact in issue, and they provide information that is more relevant to the psycholegal issue. In reports and testimony, forensic practitioners typically provide information about examinees' functional abilities, capacities, knowledge, and beliefs, and address their opinions and recommendations to the identified psycholegal issues. (Guideline 10.01)

Additionally, the APA *Specialty Guidelines* describe the importance of the forensic clinician having "a fundamental and reasonable level of knowledge and understanding of the legal…standards, laws, rules, and precedents that govern their participation in legal proceedings and that guide the impact of their services on service recipients" (Guideline 2.04). Similarly, the APA *Specialty Guidelines* indicate that forensic psychologists should "inform examinees about the nature and purpose of the examination…[which] may include the purpose, nature, and anticipated use of the examination" (Guideline 6.03), presumably including a notification of the forensic issues being evaluated.

Legal sources of authority indirectly support the importance of identifying relevant forensic issues. Some case law suggests that the evidentiary principle of relevance is consistent with identifying the forensic issues of a given case. For example, in *United States v. Green* (1977), the United States Court of Appeals for the Sixth Circuit adopted four criteria for reviewing trial court decisions involving expert testimony, including that the expert testimony had to concern the "proper subject" of the issue at hand. This appears to be consistent with the idea that the proper identification of forensic issues might directly affect the admissibility of expert testimony. The U.S. Supreme Court's holding in *Dusky v. United States* (1960) is also indirectly relevant to this principle. In *Dusky*, the Court addressed the issue of competence to stand trial and adopted a functional standard, requiring that an individual have sufficient present ability to consult with counsel with a reasonable degree of rational understanding, as well as a rational *and* factual understanding of the proceedings.

Identification of the relevant legal question and related forensic issues is an essential first step in a properly performed FMHA. Although this would seem to be straightforward, there have been many criticisms of forensic assessment suggesting that insufficiency, irrelevance, and ignorance—including failure to clearly identify the forensic issues—are common problems in FMHA (Grisso, 1986, 2003). It is important that the forensic clinician identify relevant forensic issues and capacities, as the failure to do so can substantially compromise the accuracy, relevance, credibility, and effectiveness of the FMHA.

It can be challenging to identify the relevant forensic issues for a particular type of evaluation when there are ambiguities in the legal standards or variability in the way that courts consider an offender's functional abilities associated with such an evaluation. This applies to competence for execution (CFE) in a few jurisdictions. According to Zapf (2009), "Thirty of the 38 states with capital punishment statutes have provided a standard or test for CFE, either through statutory definition (19 states) or state case law (11 states)" (p. 273). Furthermore, "the ability to understand the nature of the punishment being imposed and the ability to understand the reasons why it is being imposed" have been established as the criteria for determining competence for execution in some states, and this is taken directly from the language used in the decision for *Ford v. Wainwright* (1986; ref. in

Zapf, 2009, p. 273). This standard, known as the "one-prong" test, is relatively narrow and serves as the established test in the majority of states with capital punishment statutes. Following the U.S. Supreme Court's decision it *Panetti v. Quarterman* (2007), it became essential for forensic evaluators to appraise whether the individual had both a factual and a rational understanding of the death penalty. However, the Supreme Court did not define a particular standard, instead remanding the issue to the lower court. The remaining states have identified a two-prong standard that is similar to the standard for evaluating competence to stand trial set forth *Dusky v. United States* (1960), involving the abilities to understand and to assist counsel.

Given the variability among states and the recent changes in the interpretation of the "understanding" prong, some have recommended that evaluators conceptualize the relevant forensic issues broadly, thereby providing more information for the court to use as it sees fit (Zapf, 2009; Zapf, Boccaccini, & Brodsky, 2003). According to Zapf (2009):

> In light of this ambiguity and evolving standard, a broadly focused evaluation of factual and rational understanding is recommended in CFE assessments. Whether this includes ability to assist, even in those jurisdictions where this is not an aspect of the current statute, is a complex consideration. (p. 292)

She then concludes that, given the recommendations of professional organizations such as the American Bar Association, American Psychological Association, American Psychiatric Association, and National Association of Mental Illness, as well as the "evolving nature of the intersection between mental illness and the death penalty, a case can be made for more rather than less information" (p. 292).

In this report, Dr. Zapf provides an evaluation of Mr. J. C., a 63-year-old African American male who has been on death row in Texas for 33 years. The relevant legal standard in Texas for competence for execution is identified early in the section of the report describing the abilities relevant to this competence. The identification of the standard includes the forensic issues of understanding (a) that execution is forthcoming and imminent, and (b) the reason he or she is being executed.

Explicitly identifying the relevant forensic issue in this manner provides several benefits. First, by identifying the relevant forensic issue the evaluator effectively avoids any confusion regarding the purpose of the evaluation. Second, identifying the relevant forensic issue enables the evaluator to conduct an evaluation that is focused and relevant (Grisso, 1986, 2003). Specifically, by identifying and targeting the relevant forensic issues the evaluator in this case avoids offering information that would be irrelevant to the issue being addressed. Finally, identifying the relevant forensic issue helps the evaluator structure the content of the evaluation; the evaluator selected psychological tests and a specialized checklist that provide information relevant to competence for execution.

Patricia A. Zapf, Ph.D.
Forensic & Clinical Psychology
Name: J. C.
Date of Birth: 1/1/1949
SSN: xxx-xx-xxxx
Case No(s): CC2010-xxx
Dates of Evaluation: 2/2/12, 2/3/12, 2/5/12
FORENSIC EVALUATION REPORT
Date of Report: 2/5/2012

REFERRAL INFORMATION

Mr. J. C., a 63-year-old African-American male, was referred by his defense counsel for an evaluation of his competency to be executed. Mr. C. was convicted in 1979 of three counts of first-degree murder and was sentenced to death. He has been on death row in Texas for the last 33 years. An execution date has been set for March 5, 2012, for Mr. C. Defense counsel for Mr. C. indicated that she has serious concern regarding Mr. C.'s current mental state and believes that Mr. C. is not competent to undergo his sentence of death. Mr. C. was evaluated with respect to his competency for execution on February 2nd, 3rd, and 5th, 2012.

NOTIFICATION

Prior to beginning the evaluation, Mr. C. was informed of the nature and purpose of the evaluation and the limited confidentiality of the information to be obtained. He was told that the results would be provided to his defense counsel in the form of an oral report and that a written report might also be provided upon the request of his defense counsel. He was also informed that these results might be used in court proceedings, in the form of either the written report or testimony by the examiner, and to assist the court in reaching a determination regarding his competency to be executed. Mr. C. indicated that he understood the information provided in the notification, and he signed the notification of rights form indicating his awareness of the limited confidentiality and willingness to participate in the evaluation.

DATA SOURCES

Data sources that were reviewed for the purposes of this evaluation include the following:

- Secure Mental Health Facility (Texas) medical records dated from 1965 through 2001
- Treatment records from Mental Health Center dated 10/11/1969 through 12/10/2011
- Texas Correctional Facility Mental Health Records dated from 1979 through 1/30/2012
- Texas Correctional Facility Medical Records dated from 1979 through 1/30/2012
- Texas Juvenile Correctional Facility Mental Health records dated from 1/5/1962 through 12/31/1969
- Texas Juvenile Correctional Facility Medical records dated from 1/5/1962 through 12/31/1969
- Texas Death Row Medical records dated 1/1/1999 through 12/31/2011
- Texas Death Row Mental Health records dated 1/1/1999 through 12/31/2011
- Texas State Forensic Facility mental health records from admissions in 1969, 1971, 1974, and 1979
- Competency Evaluation Report by Dr. A. A. dated March 12, 1979
- Competency Evaluation Report by Dr. B. B. dated May 15, 1981
- Competency to Waive Appeals Evaluation Report by Dr. C. C. dated July 12, 1999
- Insanity Evaluation Report by Dr. D. D. dated March 10, 1979
- Interview with Correctional Supervision E. E. on 2/4/2012

- Interview with the Defendant on 2/2/2012, 2/3/2012, and 2/5/2012

TEST DATA

- The Structured Interview of Reported Symptoms, 2nd edition (SIRS-2) was administered on 2/5/12
- The Test of Malingered Memory (TOMM) was administered on 2/5/2012
- Checklist for Evaluations of Competency for Execution

BACKGROUND INFORMATION

Mr. C. is a 63-year-old African American male who received a sentence of death in 1979 and who has been living on Texas's death row for the last 33 years. The Texas governor signed his warrant of execution on January 1, 2012, setting a date of execution for March 5, 2012.

Mr. C. reported that he was an only child who was born in Texas, where he has resided all his life. He reported that his mother died when he was a young child, after which time he was raised by his paternal grandmother. He indicated that he had limited contact with his father throughout his life until 2001, when his father died of a drug overdose. His paternal grandmother informed Mr. C. of his father's death while she was visiting Mr. C. on death row. Since that time, Mr. C. has cut off all contact with his family, as he does not "want to hurt them further when I die." According to a review of records, Mr. C. had very limited contact with his father while growing up, as his father was a "career criminal" and served most of his life in prison. Records indicate, and Mr. C. confirms, that he lived with his paternal grandmother from the age of two until he was sent to Juvenile Corrections in 1962 at the age of 13. Mr. C. reported that he "got into trouble a lot" when he was growing up and that he has been in and out of correctional facilities "most of" his life. Indeed, a review of records appears to indicate that Mr. C. has been incarcerated from the age of 13 until the present, with only brief stints living back in the community when he was 20 years of age and again at 24 years of age. Records also indicate that Mr. C. has been hospitalized numerous times from the age of 19 to the present, mainly with a diagnosis of schizophrenia, paranoid type.

Mr. C. reported that he has never been married, that he has no children, has never been in a long-term relationship, and that he has never served in the military. He indicated that he worked for a "fast food joint" when he was 20 years old but was fired for stealing food after "about 3 months." He reported that he held one other job, also at a fast food restaurant, when he was 24 years of age but that he was then hospitalized "for mental problems" and never returned to the community.

Mr. C. reported that he first started using alcohol at the age of nine and that he began using cocaine and "crank" at the age of 12. Mr. C. reported that he has had problems with drugs and alcohol all his life and that he would "drink or smoke anything I could get my hands on." Records indicate that Mr. C. has a lengthy history of mental illness and drug dependence and has been hospitalized numerous times since 1965. Records also indicate that Mr. C. has been found incompetent to stand trial at least three times (in 1969, 1971, and 1973), has been found not guilty by reason of insanity twice (in 1973 and 1978), and has been adjudicated as incompetent to waive appeals and incompetent to proceed at least four times during his most recent incarceration (which has been for a period of 33 years).

Records indicate that at least 33 different psychiatrists and psychologists have diagnosed Mr. C. with paranoid schizophrenia throughout the course of his lifetime, with the first diagnosis appearing to have been around the age of 19 and then continuously since that time. By all accounts, Mr. C. has a lengthy (over 40 years) history of paranoid ideation and psychosis, including hallucinations and delusions, severe mood disturbance, and impaired judgment and insight.

CLINICAL ASSESSMENT

Mr. J. C., a 63-year-old single African American man, was interviewed on February 2, 3, and 5 in 2012 in an interview room on Texas's death row. Mr. C. is tall and has a slight build. He was dressed in standard orange prison gear and wore shackles and leg irons. He had short, dark hair that was graying at the temples and a full beard, which was also graying. He wore glasses and had a small prison tattoo of an anchor on his left inner wrist.

Mr. C. appeared to be cooperative with the evaluation. He was, at times, difficult to communicate with, as he was tangential (often veered off-topic and randomly from topic to topic), paranoid (holding beliefs not based in reality), and religiously preoccupied. His cognitive functioning appeared to be generally intact as he was able to perform a number of operations in different areas; however, he had to be directed to stay on task. He demonstrated appropriate immediate, recent, and remote memory skills and appeared to be able to concentrate well enough to recall lengthy strings of numbers.

Mr. C. appeared to have an adequately developed fund of information, as evidenced by his ability to answer elementary general-knowledge questions. He was able to demonstrate some abstract reasoning ability, although he then became perseverative (visiting the same theme over and over again) and religiously preoccupied in his responses. For example, he was able to indicate the similarities between an apple and an orange (stating that both were fruit), but then veered off topic and became religiously preoccupied when asked about the similarities between a bird and a tree, a table and a chair, and a poem and a statue. Mr. C. was able to correctly answer social judgment questions and was oriented to person, place, time, and situation.

Mr. C.'s mood was generally depressed, although he denied most of the neurovegetative symptoms of major depression (crying spells, sleep or appetite disturbance). His affect was generally flat or blunted. When asked (and not otherwise) he reported the extensive paranoid delusions as described throughout his mental health records as well as his hearing his (deceased) father's voice and, at times, God's voice. At various times he stated that God's voice told him to do things but that, in general, this was comforting to him. He denied any type of command auditory hallucination that instructed him to injure himself or others. He denied any symptoms that would be consistent with an anxiety, post-traumatic dissociative, or obsessive-compulsive disorder. At times he would become very insistent and adamant, especially when reporting his paranoid ideation and his religious grandiosity. Mr. C. was insistent that, despite everything that he reports (see all of the aforementioned mental status and history), he is not mentally ill and neither requires nor wants any medications for mental illness.

Mr. C. appears to have a lengthy history (for more than 40 years) of paranoid schizophrenia and a well-rooted delusional belief system that dates back at least 30 years. Numerous mental health records and evaluations by more than 33 mental health professionals consistently indicate that Mr. C. reports symptoms of a delusional and paranoid psychotic thought process. In addition, Mr. C. appears to have limited insight into his mental health. Records indicate that he has had adverse reactions to various psychotropic medications, and his current physician has recommended that Mr. C. not be medicated because of his sensitivity to these drugs. Records indicate then he has not responded well to any psychotropic or antipsychotic in the past.

The results of the SIRS-2 failed to show any evidence of malingering of psychiatric disturbance or exaggeration of psychiatric symptoms. None of the SIRS-2 Primary Scales fell into the definite or probable malingering categories. In fact, Mr. C.'s reported pattern of symptoms has been remarkably consistent over a more than 40-year history and interviews with more than 33 mental health professionals. The results of the Test of Memory Malingering (TOMM) failed to show any evidence of malingering of cognitive deficit or exaggeration of cognitive difficulties. Mr. C. achieved a perfect score (100% correct) on the second trial. This is consistent with my clinical observations of his putting forth good effort throughout these many hours of testing and interviewing with no evidence of any attempt to deliberately do poorly or to feign inadequate performance.

FORENSIC ASSESSMENT

Mr. J. C. was evaluated with respect to his competency for execution. The Checklist for Evaluations of Competency for Execution (Zapf, Boccaccini, & Brodsky, 2003) was used to structure the evaluation of his competency for execution. This interview provides a guide to four main areas of inquiry relevant to competency for execution: the inmate's understanding of the reasons for punishment, the inmate's understanding of the punishment, the inmate's ability to appreciate and reason in addition to simple factual understanding, and the inmate's ability to assist his attorney.

Competency for Execution

Texas Rules of Criminal Procedures Article 46.05(h) states that a "defendant is incompetent to be executed if the defendant does not understand: (1) that he or she is to be executed and that the execution is imminent; and (2) the reason he or she is being executed."

The application and interpretation of this standard is a matter for the court to decide, although it is relevant to note that the interpretation and application of standards for competency for execution continue to evolve. The United States Supreme Court, in *Ford v. Wainwright* (1986), had the opportunity to provide specific guidelines both for raising and evaluating a claim of incompetency for execution but failed to specify a proper legal test of incompetence in the execution context. Only Justice Powell, in his concurring opinion, addressed the issue of the legal test for competency for execution, stating that the Eighth Amendment "forbids the execution only of those who are unaware of the punishment they are about to suffer and why they are to suffer it" (p. 2608). Further, he concluded that the proper test of competency should be whether defendants can comprehend the nature, pendency, and purpose of their execution. Justice Powell argued that the retributive goal of criminal law is satisfied only when defendants are aware of the connection between their crime and the punishment, and defendants can only prepare for death if they are aware that it is pending shortly. Moreover, Justice Powell asserted that the states were free to adopt "a more expansive view of sanity," which included the "requirement that the defendant be able to assist in his own defense" (p. 2608).

It is important to note that some authors (this evaluator included) have commented on the relatively low standard of competence for execution as set out by the *Ford* decision and the necessity for evaluators to perform comprehensive assessments of all relevant aspects of competency—including those that go above and beyond the standard set out in *Ford* (see, e.g., Zapf, 2008, 2009). The argument is that competence-related abilities such as rational understanding and appreciation (in addition to factual understanding) need to be addressed in the evaluation and discussed in the report to the court so as not to interpret the *Ford* criteria for the court, but rather to describe all relevant aspects of competency so the court can make an informed decision in each case.

Indeed, the issue of how the standard for competency for execution is to be interpreted was the subject of a more recent Supreme Court decision. On June 28, 2007, the United States Supreme Court decided the case of *Panetti v. Quarterman*. This decision, which broadened the legal standard for competency for execution, changed the landscape for evaluations of this legal competency. Rather than ignore the inmate's rational understanding abilities and focus solely on his or her factual understanding abilities, as had been done to this point, the Supreme Court decided that these must be taken into consideration in determining competency for execution.

Thus, this evaluation focused on all the abilities that are relevant to the issue of an inmate's competency. Each of these will be described below, and the evaluator leaves it to the court to decide which abilities are relevant and important considerations in this case.

Factual Understanding

Mr. C. was able to demonstrate an adequate factual understanding of the punishment and the reasons for the punishment. He indicated that he was convicted of multiple counts of first-degree murder for an event that took place more than 30 years ago, and that he received a sentence of death for that crime. Mr. C. did not appear to demonstrate any impairment in his ability to factually understand that he was convicted of murder and sentenced to death for that conviction. Mr. C. also was able to indicate a factual understanding of the meaning of death. He was able to indicate that when someone dies their bodily functions cease and that they no longer have the ability to breathe, think, or live. Mr. C. did not appear to evidence any impairment of his factual ability to understand the meaning of death.

Rational Understanding/Appreciation

As indicated throughout this report and throughout Mr. C.'s more than 40 years of mental health history records, Mr. C. has a longstanding delusional belief system that involves religiously preoccupied content. Mr. C. holds the delusional belief that he will not die because a divine intervention will occur to prohibit his death. Although Mr. C. has the ability to factually understand what it means to die, his appreciation of this (or the application of this factual understanding to his own circumstance) is impaired by his irrational beliefs surrounding his ability to be put to death. Mr. C. does not appear to be able to make the spiritual preparation for death because he holds the longstanding, strong, delusional belief that he is the Son of God and that he will not be put to death. As a result, Mr. C. is unable to understand the personal implication of death.

Ability to Assist

Mr. C. was able to demonstrate the ability to assist his counsel in very basic ways by providing them with information that is relevant to his case and potential appeals *as long as* the information required by his attorneys does not involve his delusionally held belief system surrounding his inability to be put to death as a result of a divine intervention. Mr. C. is able to discuss relevant aspects of his case with his legal team, including a summary of the events that occurred more than 30 years ago, a description of his time in prison, a description of his mental health history (in terms of places that he has been hospitalized and doctors who have evaluated him), and a description of the current legal status of his appeals. However, when the discussions turn to the topic of his death, or rather, his beliefs regarding his death or inability to be put to death, it is difficult, if not impossible, to have a rational conversation with Mr. C. because of the conviction with which he holds these religiously preoccupied delusional beliefs. In this regard, he is unable to assist counsel.

SUMMARY AND RECOMMENDATIONS

In summary, Mr. C. is a 63-year-old African American male who appears to currently meet criteria for diagnoses of schizophrenia, paranoid type, and who has been diagnosed as having this mental disorder by more than 33 mental health professionals over a more than 40 year history.

Mr. C. is not currently taking any psychotropic medications (as per the orders of his prison physician) and displays limited insight into his mental illness. He currently appears to be experiencing a number of symptoms of formal thought disorder and, as a result, has difficulty communicating in a rational manner about his sentence of death and possible appeals. He appears to have the ability to factually understand his conviction and his sentence; however, he is unable to appreciate the personal importance of his sentence of death or rationally understand the personal significance of this sentence. In addition, his ability to assist counsel with appeals or legal proceedings specifically directed at his death sentence is impaired by his longstanding religiously preoccupied delusional belief system.

As a forensic psychologist, I recognize that the determination of a defendant's competency for execution is ultimately a matter for the court to decide.

Therefore, the opinions rendered above are of an advisory nature only. I will be happy to provide the court with any further information, records, or testimony that it may require.

Respectfully submitted,
Patricia A. Zapf, Ph.D.
Licensed Psychologist
Certified Forensic Examiner

TEACHING POINT:
IDENTIFY ASSESSMENT TARGETS WHEN LEGAL STANDARDS ARE BROAD OR NON-SPECIFIC
(contributed by Patricia A. Zapf)

As is especially true in areas that are still emerging or that do not have a strong empirical or legal base, it is important for the forensic evaluator to set out for the court the assessment targets to be taken into consideration. This is especially evident in the case of competency for execution wherein, because of the low base rate for this issue, the standard and the application and interpretation of that standard are still evolving. In this type of situation, it is especially important for the evaluator to resist the urge to interpret the standard for the court. Rather, the evaluator should identify for the court the specific assessment targets and then provide the court with information relevant to each so that the court might make a determination of the ultimate legal issue using its own application and interpretation of the standard. It is appropriate for the evaluator to cite empirical literature or relevant legal or clinical commentary on the issue in the context of the evaluation report. One of the roles of the evaluator is educative; therefore, including relevant educational information with the appropriate references or citations in the evaluation report is well within the professional role of the evaluator.

In the case of competency for execution, the standard set out by the Supreme Court in *Ford v. Wainwright* (1986) is low; in fact, it is arguably lower than that set out for competency to stand trial. If an evaluator were to assume that factual understanding is what the Court was referring to by using the term "understand," he or she would run the risk of making a false-negative error (opining that the inmate was competent to be executed when the inmate may have actually been incompetent).

Interestingly, 21 years after the *Ford* decision, the Supreme Court clarified in *Panetti v. Quarterman* (2007) that "understanding" should be interpreted to mean both factual *and* rational understanding. This highlights the importance of an evaluator not interpreting standards for the court, but rather identifying the assessment targets and then providing relevant information to the court for each of the relevant targets. The court is then free to apply or interpret the standards as it sees fit and to use the evaluator's opinion about each of the assessment targets accordingly.

10

Competence to Consent to Treatment

The single case report in this chapter is on the competence of adults to consent to treatment in a civil context. Evaluations for competence to consent to inpatient treatment arise in circumstances that involve an individual seeking inpatient psychiatric treatment, and may be associated with impaired psychosocial functioning and rational decision-making. Evaluations of competence to consent to treatment are therefore useful in assessing whether the individual appreciates the nature of inpatient treatment, is willing to consent to such treatment, is able to provide such consent voluntarily, and is able to understand the part of treatment associated with hospital discharge.

There are two principles illustrated in this report. The first concerns the use of third party information to assess response style in FMHA, including how a variety of collateral sources of information can be used to assess the accuracy of self-report information provided in an evaluation. The teaching point discusses how to balance the results of psychological testing, self-report, and third party collateral information as it relates to response style. The second principle describes the importance of using plain language rather than technical jargon in conveying findings, with the teaching point elaborating on the communication of complex scientific material to legal and lay audiences.

CASE ONE
PRINCIPLE: USE THIRD PARTY INFORMATION IN ASSESSING RESPONSE STYLE (*PRINCIPLE 25*)

This principle addresses the importance of using third party information in assessing response style. Third party information is important in FMHA for several reasons. First, the use of third party information to assess response style is an

integral part of a comprehensive approach to FMHA and provides valuable collateral information. Second, some measures relevant to FMHA (e.g., the Psychopathy Checklist–Revised, 2nd edition; Hare, 2003) require the forensic clinician to incorporate third party information as part of the assessment and scoring process. Third, the use of collateral and corroborative information increases accuracy in detecting deception (e.g., Conroy & Kwartner, 2006; Rogers, 2008a; Vitacco, 2008). Fourth, third party information can increase the face validity of FMHA and enhance the credibility of the evaluation. Finally, third party information may be helpful in allowing the forensic clinician to clarify a constellation of symptoms and to identify, confirm, and disconfirm the presence of various forms of psychopathology.

The *Ethical Principles of Psychologists and Code of Conduct* (APA *Ethics Code*; American Psychological Association, 2010a) provides the following caution regarding considerations that may reduce the accuracy of assessment:

> When interpreting assessment results…psychologists take into account the purpose of the assessment as well as the various test factors, test-taking abilities, and other characteristics of the person being assessed, such as situational, personal, linguistic, and cultural differences, that might affect psychologists' judgments or reduce the accuracy of their interpretations. They indicate any significant limitations of their interpretations. (Standard 9.06)

This underscores the importance of identifying influences that might reduce the accuracy of observations and the resulting conclusions, such as the individual's response style. The use of third party information to assess response style can thus help gauge the accuracy of testing results and observations. The *Specialty Guidelines for Forensic Psychology* (APA *Specialty Guidelines*; American Psychological Association, 2013b) describes the role of third party information in FMHA by noting that the forensic clinician conducting an evaluation actively seeks information "that will differentially test rival hypotheses" (Guideline 9.01). Common "rival hypotheses" relevant to response style in FMHA involve the possibilities that an individual: (a) experiences a genuine mental disorder and presents these symptoms accurately, (b) experiences a genuine mental disorder but exaggerates or otherwise distorts the experience of symptoms, or (c) presents but does not actually experience the symptoms of a mental disorder. Additionally, the APA *Specialty Guidelines* emphasize that forensic practitioners differentiate between observations, inferences, and conclusions in their reports and testimony, including the information received from collateral sources (Guideline 11.02). The *Ethical Guidelines for the Practice of Forensic Psychiatry* (AAPL *Ethical Guidelines*; American Academy of Psychiatry and the Law, 2005) considers the potential contribution of third party information to both enhancing accuracy and facilitating reasoning:

> Psychiatrists practicing in a forensic role enhance the honesty and objectivity of their work by basing their forensic opinions, forensic reports and forensic testimony on all available data. They communicate the honesty of their work, efforts to attain objectivity, and the soundness of their clinical opinion, by distinguishing, to the extent possible, between verified and unverified information as well as among clinical "facts," "inferences," and "impressions." (p. 3)

Taken as a whole, the APA *Ethics Code* reflects the general importance of accuracy, while both forensic specialty guidelines (i.e., the APA *Specialty Guidelines* and AAPL *Ethical Guidelines*) stress the need for hypothesis testing and distinguishing between facts and inferences. In this regard, they directly support the need to assess response style to improve the overall accuracy of the FMHA, eliminate rival hypotheses, distinguish between facts and inferences, and gauge the accuracy of self-reported symptoms and experiences—all of which can be done better with the inclusion of third party information.

There are competing considerations in the law regarding the use of third party information to assess response style in FMHA. One consideration is the value of providing reliable and relevant information to the decision-maker: when third party information relevant to response style facilitates this, its use in legal contexts is desirable. However, the law can also impose limits on the use of third party information in FMHA. In some jurisdictions third party information might be challenged as hearsay on the grounds that it constitutes out-of-court statements being presented to prove the truth of an in-court statement. Conversely, under Rule 703 of the *Federal Rules of Evidence*, facts or underlying data need not be admissible if they are of a type "reasonably relied on by experts...in forming opinions or inferences upon the subject," and the use of third party information in forming opinions is indeed considered an established practice in FMHA (Heilbrun, Grisso, & Goldstein, 2009). While some states have evidentiary rules similar to Rule 703, others require that expert testimony be based on sources of information that would be independently admissible. In the latter jurisdictions, an entire FMHA could be ruled inadmissible if it relied significantly upon the use of such third party information in supporting its conclusions. This underscores the importance of forensic practitioners knowing the relevant legal literature in their jurisdiction of practice, and applying it correctly within their FMHA.

PRINCIPLE: USE PLAIN LANGUAGE; AVOID TECHNICAL JARGON (*PRINCIPLE 33*)

This principle concerns the importance of communicating the results of FMHA using language that is easily understood by those who are not mental health professionals. FMHA results can be used in a variety of contexts, and many consumers of such information are not formally trained in medicine, mental health, or the behavioral sciences (Grisso, 1998a; Melton, Petrila, Poythress, & Slobogin, 2007). For example, although many legal and criminal justice professionals (e.g., judges, attorneys, administrators, parole officers, case managers) make decisions about individuals with mental disorders on a regular basis, they may have little or no formal training in psychopathology, personality, human development, diagnosis, treatment, or research methodology. Moreover, mental health professionals from different theoretical orientations sometimes attach different meanings to the same terms, further complicating the results of FMHA. Given the nature and implications of the legal decisions of which FMHA is a part, it is important that results be communicated in a way that avoids confusion and promotes better-informed decision-making. The best way to establish this "common language" is to avoid technical jargon and use plain language in communicating results.

One approach to facilitating a shared language is to minimize the use of technical terms that might be misinterpreted by others (Fuhrmann & Zibbell, 2012; Grisso, 2010). When using technical language is essential to conveying accurate information, technical terms should be clearly defined. This allows FMHA consumers to integrate relevant behavioral, scientific, and clinical evidence with minimal distortion and optimal understanding and application.

The APA *Ethics Code* indicates that "psychologists take reasonable steps to ensure that explanations of the results are given to the individual or designated representative" (Standard 9.10). Although this statement focuses on the individual or designated representative, this could apply to the legal representative (e.g., attorney), opposing attorneys, and judges in the context of litigation of which FMHA is a part. Similarly, the APA *Specialty Guidelines* addresses this point: "Forensic practitioners make reasonable efforts to ensure that the products of their services, as well as their own public statements and professional reports and testimony, are communicated in ways that promote understanding and avoid deception" (Guideline 11.01).

Guidelines regarding the use of plain language have also been described in the context of specific types of evaluations. For instance, in discussing child custody evaluations Fuhrmann and Zibbell (2012) note that, in addition to the court and each party's attorney, the "parties to the legal action, (typically the parents)" (p. 181) often have access to the report. As such, they recommend that evaluators select language that is respectful and avoids "unnecessary, irrelevant, or inflammatory claims" (p. 180). This is consistent with recommendations that forensic evaluators carefully select language so as to avoid bias or judgment in their reports (Grisso, 2010), and these guidelines can certainly

be extended to other types of evaluations. Neither the *Principles of Medical Ethics with Annotations Especially Applicable to Psychiatry* (American Psychiatric Association, 2013b) nor the AAPL *Ethical Guidelines* contain guidance directly relevant to this principle.

This principle emphasizes the need for language that is reasonably understandable to the consumer of the evaluation, although the primary "consumers" with FMHA are typically judges and attorneys rather than the individual being assessed. The use of plain language is particularly valuable in the clinical presentation section of the report, as the forensic clinician might be tempted to use technical terms to describe the clinical condition of the individual evaluated.

The following report demonstrates the application of these two principles in a case of adult competence to consent to inpatient treatment. The forensic clinician identified relevant sources of third party information, including available records pertaining to the individual being evaluated ("John"). These records included police reports, hospital and family physician treatment records, and collateral interviews with the individual's mother and treating psychiatrist. By identifying and using a number of third party sources, the clinician not only provided a more detailed and accurate description of John, his capacities, and his needs, but also an assessment of the consistency and accuracy of the information obtained from John. For example, in this case John was noted as being a particularly poor historian, therefore the clinician obtained information from both John and his mother regarding several relevant historical domains to facilitate a more coherent and comprehensive understanding of John's psychosocial development. Obtaining information from multiple sources, including several third party sources, also allowed the clinician to avoid having to rely solely on self-report and increased the "convergent validity" of his conclusions, thereby enhancing the credibility and usefulness of the evaluation. Using collateral sources of information in this manner can also be helpful in determining the response style of the evaluee, such as John's observed exaggeration of mental health symptomatology. The present report also provides good examples of the appropriate use of technical language in FMHA, including definitions and specific examples of technical terms when indicated.

Forensic Evaluation
April 19, 2012
Re: John Smith

REFERRAL

John Smith is a 22-year-old Caucasian male (DOB: x-x-x) who was brought to ABC Hospital by his mother. A request for a mental health evaluation to help determine Mr. Smith's competence to consent to inpatient treatment, pursuant to Section 7203 of the Pennsylvania Mental Health Procedures Act, was requested by legal counsel of ABC Hospital.

PROCEDURES

Mr. Smith was evaluated for approximately 4.5 hours on April 11, 2012, in the Admissions Unit of ABC Hospital. In addition to a psychosocial interview, the following assessment measures were used:

- a standard screening instrument for currently experienced symptoms of mental and emotional disorders (Brief Symptom Inventory [BSI]);
- a structured clinical interview that assesses current and lifetime diagnoses of primary mental health disorders contained in the most recent edition of the American Psychiatric Association's *Diagnostic and Statistical Manual of Mental Disorders* (Structured Clinical Interview for DSM-IV Axis I Disorders–Clinician Version [SCID-I-CV]);
- a standard objective measure of current mental and emotional functioning (Minnesota Multiphasic Personality Inventory, 2nd ed. [MMPI-2]);
- a standard measure of overall intellectual functioning (Wechsler Abbreviated Scale of Intelligence [WASI]);
- two subtests from a standard test of basic academic skills (Wide Range Achievement Test, 4th ed. [WRAT-4]); and
- a structured assessment instrument for competence to consent to treatment (MacArthur Competence Assessment Tool for Treatment [MacCAT-T]).

In addition, interviews regarding Mr. Smith's past and current functioning were conducted with Mr. Smith's mother, Betty Smith (approximately 30 minutes; in person at ABC Hospital on 4/11/12), and Mr. Smith's treating psychiatrist, Dr. James Anderson (approximately 25 minutes; via telephone on 4/13/12). Limited documents were available for review, including the following documents provided by Mr. Smith's mother:

(1) Treatment records from ABC and XYZ hospitals;
(2) Treatment records from Mr. Smith's family physician; and
(3) Police report regarding Mr. Smith's arrest in 2010.

Prior to the evaluation, Mr. Smith was notified about the purpose of the evaluation and associated limits on confidentiality. After minor prompting and repeated explanations, he appeared to understand the basic purpose of the evaluation, reporting back his understanding that he would be evaluated to assess his competence to consent to inpatient treatment.

RELEVANT HISTORY

Historical information was obtained from Mr. Smith and the collateral sources of information identified above. Mr. Smith presented as a relatively poor historian, and he was often unable to construct a coherent timeline of events or provide detailed information regarding his history, so much of the historical information came from Mr. Smith's mother. Whenever possible, the consistency of the factual information provided by Mr. Smith was assessed through the use of multiple sources of information. An amended or supplemental report will be filed if additional information that materially changes the results of this evaluation is obtained.

Family History

Mr. Smith was born on [date], in Mahwah, New Jersey, to John Smith, Sr., and Betty Smith. He reported having one older sister, Shannon Smith (27). Mr. Smith reported that he was raised by his parents in Mahwah until they relocated to Philadelphia when he was age 9. Mr. Smith's mother reported that she and her husband divorced when Mr. Smith was age 13, but that Mr. Smith remained in contact with his father. Ms. Smith reported that her husband was employed as a computer technician. She reported being a "stay-at-home" mom until Mr. Smith was age 15, and then taking on part-time work as a substitute teacher. Mr. Smith reported that his mother is "a good woman who cares," and he described his father as "a good guy...decent guy...who loves me." Ms. Smith reported that her son always lived in the family residence, except for two occasions when he was hospitalized for mental health treatment and one occasion when he "decided to be homeless." Mr. Smith denied any history of physical, sexual, or emotional abuse, but stated that "people have sometimes been mean to me." He also denied any history of neglect. Ms. Smith reported that she suspects her son is sexually active and is concerned that he may not "take necessary precautions" to protect against unwanted pregnancy and sexually transmitted diseases/infections. Mr. Smith reported that he has had "lots of girlfriends," but is not currently in a relationship.

Educational History

Mr. Smith reported attending public schools throughout his education, but he was unable to provide a coherent narrative of his educational background. Ms. Smith described her son's academic performance as "great" until age 16, which is when he began experiencing symptoms of mental health disorders (discussed later). She reported that his "grades went down as his symptoms got worse...and he just fell right off the radar screen." Mr. Smith described himself as "a smart student, but I sometimes acted stupid." Ms. Smith reported that her son was suspended several times later in his schooling, which she attributed to the onset of his mental health problems. Mr. Smith reported that he graduated from AAA High School in 2008, and Ms. Smith confirmed this information. When asked about his educational goals, Mr. Smith reported that he would like to attend college to study business. Mr. Smith's academic records were not available at the time this report was written.

Medical and Psychiatric History

Mr. Smith denied any history of serious illnesses or injuries, but he acknowledged breaking his left wrist while riding a bicycle (at age 13) and spraining his ankle twice. He denied ever receiving stitches, and he denied any history of serious head injuries or loss of consciousness. Ms. Smith reported that Mr. Smith has had asthma since he was born, which he manages with an inhaler.

When asked about the family's medical history, Ms. Smith reported that diabetes runs in the family (father, grandparents).

When asked about his mental health functioning, Mr. Smith reported "everything was normal until I turned 18." Ms. Smith confirmed that her son began experiencing significant mental health symptoms at age 17 or 18. She reported that he experienced frequent auditory hallucinations and occasional outbursts, and she described him as becoming "completely withdrawn from his friends, family...and life." Ms. Smith reported that her son was involuntarily hospitalized at age 20 after he reportedly made suicidal threats while getting arrested. She reported that he spent "about a month or two" in the hospital before being discharged with several medications and an "order for treatment." She reported that he remained on his medications for several months and was "doing pretty well," but eventually discontinued his medications and stopped attending therapy. Ms. Smith reported that her son previously took Risperdal, Seroquel, Lithium, Depakote, and Prozac, but she was unsure of the dosages and was not able to construct a timeline of when he took these medications. Ms. Smith reported that her son was voluntarily hospitalized, at her suggestion, after his mental health decompensated approximately 6 months ago. She reported that he spent approximately 3 weeks in the hospital before he was discharged because they could no longer afford to pay for his care. Ms. Smith reported that her son was again prescribed several medications, which she thinks may have included Risperdal and Prozac, but that he stopped taking the medications shortly after he was discharged. Mr. Smith acknowledged several treatment episodes over the past few years, and he described "struggling with my brain" for the past 4 years. He reported that he discontinued his medication because "it made me worse...or didn't work...or something...but I didn't like taking those pills." He recognized, however, that he is currently in need of treatment, and he expressed a willingness to comply with "whatever treatment they say I need to lead a normal life."

Substance Use History

Mr. Smith reported that he began using marijuana "on weekends" at age 17 or 18 to "help me deal with the things going on in my head." He reported using marijuana twice per week for approximately

6 months. He denied using any other drugs or ever selling drugs. Mr. Smith reported that he also occasionally drank alcohol—"maybe three or two times each week"—when he was using marijuana. Ms. Smith denied first-hand knowledge of her son's drug use, but acknowledged that she "suspected he was using something sometimes."

Social History

Mr. Smith reported having "about 80 friends… until I got sick," by which he was referring to the onset of his mental health symptoms. He reported that they enjoyed watching movies, playing sports, and "hanging out like friends do each day." Ms. Smith reported that her son spent time with a small handful of friends who "did well in school and didn't get in trouble." She reported, however, that Mr. Smith became "withdrawn" and "lost his friends" when he began experiencing mental health symptoms. She also reported that Mr. Smith occasionally goes to public places and "asks random people to be his friend." Mr. Smith denied any history of violence, but reported being "kicked out of school" (suspended) due to a fight. Ms. Smith was unable to recall if her son had been suspended for fighting, but stated, "It wouldn't surprise me because he was acting strange toward the end of high school."

Occupational History

Mr. Smith reported working at a restaurant as a busboy for approximately 7 months when he was age 16. He denied any other formal employment. When asked about his occupational goals, Mr. Smith reported that he wants to "own a business," but he was unable to provide more details about the nature of the business other than stating it would involve computers. He reported that he plans to attend college "once my treatment stuff is worked out." Ms. Smith reported that her son has an interest and some aptitude in working with computers, and that he has talked about opening a "computer consulting" business.

Offense History

Ms. Smith reported that her son was arrested in 2010 at age 20 for disorderly conduct. The police report confirms that he was arrested for disorderly conduct and resisting arrest. According to Ms. Smith, her son was arrested for "accosting people at a Wal-Mart…probably because he wanted

to be friends with them." Ms. Smith reported that the charges were "dropped or withdrawn," but criminal justice records detailing the outcome of Mr. Smith's arrest were not available at the time this report was written.

CURRENT CLINICAL CONDITION

Mr. Smith presented as a Caucasian male of average height and heavy build who appeared somewhat older than his stated age. He was dressed in jeans and a T-shirt, and his appearance was somewhat disheveled (wrinkled clothes, missing button on his jeans). He was initially hesitant to engage in the evaluation, but he eventually was cooperative and polite. His speech was clear, but often tangential. He also asked the questions multiple times. Mr. Smith asked for one break "to call his girlfriend," but then he simply stood by the phone for approximately 5 minutes before returning.

Mr. Smith's mood was somewhat depressed, and he did not show appropriate emotional variability throughout the evaluation. He was correctly oriented to place and person, but he was unsure of the date. Although Mr. Smith and his mother acknowledged that he has a history of experiencing auditory hallucinations, he did not report experiencing any perceptual disturbances (auditory or visual hallucinations) or delusions (bizarre ideas with no possible basis in reality) during the present evaluation.

Wechsler Abbreviated Scale of Intelligence (WASI)

Mr. Smith's intellectual functioning was formally measured with the WASI. He obtained a full scale IQ score of 90, which places him within the Average range of intellectual functioning and at the 25th percentile relative to others his age (meaning that he obtained an IQ score equal to or higher than 25% of similarly aged individuals). Given the measurement error on the WASI, there is a 95% likelihood that his full scale IQ score is between 85 and 95 (Average range). His Verbal IQ score was 80 (9th percentile; Low Average) and his Performance IQ score was 104 (61st percentile; Average).

Wide Range Achievement Test, 4th ed. (WRAT-4)

Mr. Smith performed relatively well on a test of his basic academic skills, as reflected by his grade equivalency scores: Spelling (grade 11.1 equivalent) and Word Reading (grade 11.5 equivalent).

Brief Symptom Inventory (BSI)

Mr. Smith was administered a standard screening instrument for currently experienced symptoms of mental and emotional disorders. He reported being "quite a bit" or "extremely" bothered by 39 of the 53 items on the BSI. Specifically, he reported being "quite a bit" bothered by the following 12 symptoms: trouble remembering things, pains in his heart or chest (when he is "mad at other people" or experiencing anxiety), feeling lonely even when he is with people (because he does not have any friends), feeling blocked in getting things done, his feelings being easily hurt (by people important to him), feeling inferior to others ("because of my head problems"), having to check and double-check what he does (noting he forgets "little stuff...like waking up"), difficulty making decisions ("because I have trouble thinking sometimes"), his mind going blank, spells of terror or panic (noting he imagines "terrorizing people"), feeling nervous when he is left alone, and feelings of guilt ("because I've probably wronged people when not taking my treatment pills").

Mr. Smith reported being "extremely" bothered by the following 27 symptoms on the BSI: nervousness or shakiness inside (because he "let down" his family by "being sick"), feeling others are to blame for most of his troubles ("whoever made me like this"), feeling easily annoyed or irritated, feeling afraid in open spaces or on the streets (noting there is "too much space for danger"), thoughts of ending his life (but noting he never formulated a plan), feeling that most people cannot be trusted ("because people will screw you if you are weak"), being suddenly scared for no reason, temper outbursts he cannot control (noting he sometimes "snaps" if people try to hurt him), feeling lonely (noting he has no friends), feeling blue (noting he feels like he is being "punished for trying"), feeling no interest in things, feeling fearful (noting he fears dying while incarcerated before he can spend time with his children), feeling most people are unfriendly or dislike him, feeling he is watched or talked about by others, having to avoid certain things because they frighten him, numbness or tingling in parts of his body (noting it is sometimes physical but also due to "tenseness from thoughts"), feeling hopeless about the future, trouble concentrating, thoughts of death or dying (noting such thoughts are "now stronger and around more"), having urges to harm someone ("only sometimes"), having urges to break or smash things, feeling very self-conscious when he is with others, feeling uneasy in crowds, never feeling close to another person, feelings of worthlessness, feeling that people will take advantage of him if he lets them, and the idea that something is wrong with his mind ("because my mind is fucked up or something").

Minnesota Multiphasic Personality Inventory–2nd edition (MMPI-2)

Mr. Smith was administered the MMPI-2 to measure his current personality functioning. Although he responded to the items by endorsing a wide variety of rare symptoms, the resulting profile was still valid and likely provides a reasonably good indication of his present mental and emotional functioning. It is possible, however, that Mr. Smith was exaggerating some of his symptoms in an effort to obtain mental health treatment. Individuals with this profile often are experiencing serious mental health symptoms, including psychotic symptoms such as hallucinations. Mr. Smith's MMPI-2 profile suggests that he is also experiencing symptoms of anxiety, depression, and paranoid thinking. He acknowledged the presence of strange thoughts and odd experiences, and he endorsed content suggesting that the presence of interpersonal problems.

Structured Clinical Interview for DSM-IV Axis I Disorders–Clinician Version (SCID-I-CV)

Mr. Smith was evaluated using the SCID-I-CV, which is a structured clinical interview that assesses current and lifetime diagnoses of primary mental health disorders contained in the American Psychiatric Association's *Diagnostic and Statistical Manual of Mental Disorders, 4th ed.* (DSM-IV) and the more recent (2000) text revision of the DSM-IV (DSM-IV-TR). The results of the SCID-I indicate that Mr. Smith currently meets diagnostic criteria for (1) 295.90—Schizophrenia, Undifferentiated Type; and (2) 300.02—Generalized Anxiety Disorder. Although the results of the SCID-I do not indicate the presence of other disorders, records from Mr. Smith's prior hospitalizations indicate that he received a diagnosis of major depressive disorder, recurrent, severe with psychotic features.

COMPETENCE TO CONSENT TO TREATMENT

The relevant provision (§ 7203) of the Pennsylvania Mental Health Procedures Act states:

> Before a person is accepted for voluntary inpatient treatment, an explanation shall be made to him of such treatment, including the types of treatment in which he may be involved, and any restraints or restrictions to which he may be subject, together with a statement of his rights under this act. Consent shall be given in writing upon a form adopted by the department. The consent shall include the following representations: That the person understands his treatment will involve inpatient status; that he is willing to be admitted to a designated facility for the purpose of such examination and treatment; and that he consents to such admission voluntarily, without coercion or duress; and, if applicable, that he has voluntarily agreed to remain in treatment for a specified period of no longer than 72 hours after having given written notice of his intent to withdraw from treatment. The consent shall be part of the person's record.

The results of the current evaluation (interview, MMPI-2, BSI, and SCID-I) indicate that Mr. Smith is experiencing severe mental health symptoms. As previously noted, Mr. Smith currently meets diagnostic criteria for schizophrenia and generalized anxiety disorder, and has a past diagnosis of major depressive disorder, recurrent, severe with psychotic features. Moreover, the results of the MMPI-2 and BSI suggest that he is experiencing significant mental health problems. Although Mr. Smith denied experiencing active psychotic symptoms during the present interview, he acknowledged experiencing such symptoms "a few days ago." However, Mr. Smith's mental health symptoms do not appear to substantially impair his ability to provide informed consent to inpatient treatment.

Mr. Smith was administered the MacArthur Competence Assessment Tool for Treatment (MacCAT-T) to assess his decision-making capacities as they relate to providing informed consent to treatment. The MacCAT-T assesses:

(1) understanding of treatment-related information,

(2) appreciation of the significance of the information for the patient's situation,

(3) reasoning in the process of deciding on treatment, and

(4) expressing a choice about treatment.

Mr. Smith's summary ratings in each of the four areas were in the average range. With respect to section (1), Mr. Smith understood that (a) he would admitted to the hospital and (b) that his treatment would involve a combination of talk therapy and medications. Given his experience with psychotropic medications, Ms. Smith displayed a sufficient understanding of the side effects of such treatment. With respect to section (2), Mr. Smith acknowledged being in need of treatment to "get my head screwed on right again." He recognized that his mental health has deteriorated over the past few months, and he expressed a willingness to receive treatment "that could help me get better again." With respect to section (3), Mr. Smith was able to articulate his reasoning for wanting treatment, and what would likely happen if he did not receive treatment. Specifically, he indicated that he wants treatment "to be better again...like I was doing before," and that he is at risk of further mental health problems, and associated consequences ("like getting arrested again"), if he does not comply with the treatment plan. Finally, with respect to section (4), Mr. Smith expressed a clear choice to receive inpatient treatment with all that such treatment entails. Given Mr. Smith's IQ and reading ability, it is unlikely that he would be confused by the written or verbal information presented to him during the informed consent process. Taken together, these results suggest that Mr. Smith is capable of providing informed consent to inpatient treatment.

Thank you for the opportunity to evaluate John Smith.

David DeMatteo, JD, PhD
Licensed Psychologist

TEACHING POINT:
BALANCING RESULTS FROM INTERVIEW, TESTING, AND THIRD PARTY SOURCES AS THEY RELATE TO RESPONSE STYLE

Examinees in forensic assessment contexts often have reason to present to evaluators in a particular manner, by either denying or minimizing the presence of psychological dysfunction (for example, in a child custody evaluation context) or by exaggerating or feigning symptoms of mental illness (perhaps in an evaluation for competence to stand trial or mental state at the time of the offense). As such, assessing an examinee's response style has obvious importance in FMHA contexts.

Evaluators can look to various sources of data to assess an examinee's response style, including interviews and testing with the examinee and third party information from collateral sources. A key consideration, therefore, is how evaluators can effectively balance results from these various sources of information in drawing conclusions about an examinee's response style. Each data source should perhaps best be viewed as a data point, and the data points should not be viewed in isolation. Examining the independent contribution of each data source, but placing more emphasis on the sum of data across data sources, provides the richest and most defensible view of the examinee's response style. Undue weight should not be placed on any one data source, and evaluators should recognize the limitations associated with each source of data. For example, data obtained from an interview (self-report) should be viewed more cautiously than data obtained from objective testing, and the credibility of the data obtained from collateral sources may differ depending on whether the collateral source is a police report or an interview with the examinee's relative. When assessing an examinee's response style, evaluators are on solid footing if they gather data from multiple sources, recognize the strengths and limitation of various sources of data, and integrate those multiple sources of data in a manner that permits the most parsimonious and defensible assessment of the examinee's response style.

TEACHING POINT:
COMMUNICATING COMPLEX SCIENTIFIC MATERIAL TO LEGAL PROFESSIONALS AND LAY AUDIENCES

An important aspect of conducting a forensic evaluation is ensuring that the results of the evaluation are communicated in a clear and easily understood manner. An evaluation loses value—in terms of assisting an attorney or legal decision-maker to make better-informed decisions—if the consumers of the written report or courtroom testimony are not able to understand what the evaluator did and the results obtained. As noted previously, FMHA reports can be used in several contexts by a variety of professionals, many of whom have no formal training in medical, mental health, or behavioral sciences, so it is important that evaluators strive to ensure that the information they present—both in the written report and courtroom testimony—can be understood by those who do not have formal training in relevant areas.

The field of mental health is full of technical terms for assessment measures, test results, mental health symptoms, diagnosable disorders, psychotropic medications, and treatment modalities, and the meaning of many of these terms may not be readily apparent to those without relevant training or experience. Moreover, some mental health terms may have a different meaning in the popular media or the community at large, which can lead to confusion. For example, terms such as "psychosis," "psychopathic," and "psychopathology" may be confused, and they likely bring certain images to mind among non-trained individuals.

As such, evaluators should attempt to minimize the use of technical terms in their reports and testimony. Even complex scientific information can typically be conveyed with a minimum of jargon, which makes it more accessible to both legal professionals and lay audiences. If using technical terms is necessary, evaluators are advised to define those terms in the report or testimony; a brief explanatory note (even parenthetically) can help ensure that the consumers of the report or testimony are not misunderstanding what the evaluator is trying to convey. Providing examples (of symptoms, disorders, treatments, and the like) is another way to convey the meaning of terms and concepts. The goal of FMHAs is to assist attorneys or legal decision-makers in making better-informed decisions, so communicating the results in a manner that is easily understood by legal professionals and lay audiences is imperative.

11

Testamentary Capacity

The case report in this chapter is an example of an evaluation for testamentary capacity. The issue of testamentary capacity arises when there is some question about whether an individual has sufficient ability to make or alter a valid will. The principle discussed in this case addresses the importance of determining whether the individual being assessed understands the purpose of the evaluation and the associated limits on confidentiality, or, in legal terms, obtaining informed consent. Given that evaluations focusing on testamentary capacity often arise due to concerns about an individual's mental state, obtaining informed consent can be challenging. The accompanying teaching point will discuss oral and written methods of obtaining informed consent, and provide guidance on when each method should be used.

CASE ONE
PRINCIPLE: DETERMINE WHETHER THE INDIVIDUAL UNDERSTANDS THE PURPOSE OF THE EVALUATION AND ASSOCIATED LIMITS ON CONFIDENTIALITY (*PRINCIPLE 24*)

This principle addresses the importance of determining whether the individual being assessed understands the purpose of the evaluation and associated limits on confidentiality. Accurately conveying the purpose of the evaluation and associated limits on confidentiality is the responsibility of the forensic clinician. In addition to identifying the clinician's role in the process, it is an important component of providing notification of purpose and, if necessary, obtaining informed consent for the FMHA. The legal doctrine of informed consent contains three distinct and related elements: disclosure, competency, and voluntariness (Melton, Petrila, Poythress, & Slobogin, 2007). In practice, "informed consent" refers to a person's agreement

to a procedure that is based on a full disclosure of facts needed to make the decision intelligently and with knowledge of the risks and alternatives involved. Informed consent and notification of purpose are particularly important in the FMHA context where serious legal consequences, including loss of liberty, could result from participation in the evaluation. Therefore, the forensic clinician must be certain that the individual being assessed has an accurate understanding of the nature of the evaluation, its purpose(s), associated limits on confidentiality, and possible uses of the evaluation.

The *Ethical Principles of Psychologists and Code of Conduct* (APA *Ethics Code*; American Psychological Association, 2010a) addresses the principle of informed consent for assessment services directly:

> Psychologists obtain informed consent for assessments, evaluations or diagnostic services…except when (1) testing is mandated by law or governmental regulations; (2) informed consent is implied because testing is conducted as a routine educational, institutional, or organizational activity…; or (3) one purpose of the testing is to evaluate decisional capacity. Informed consent includes an explanation of the nature and purpose of the assessment, fees, involvement of third parties, and limits of confidentiality and sufficient opportunity for the client/patient to ask questions and receive answers. (Standard 9.03)

Even when testing is mandated or the examinee may lack the capacity to consent to testing, the APA *Ethics Code* highlights the importance of describing the nature of the testing:

> Psychologists inform persons with questionable capacity to consent or for whom testing is mandated by law or governmental regulations

about the nature and purpose of the proposed assessment services, using language that is reasonably understandable to the person being assessed. (Standard 9.03(b))

These principles are also highlighted in the ethical guidance regarding informed consent more generally:

For persons who are legally incapable of giving informed consent, psychologists nevertheless (1) provide an appropriate explanation, (2) seek the individual's assent, (3) consider such persons' preferences and best interests, and (4) obtain appropriate permission from a legally authorized person, if such substitute consent is permitted or required by law. When consent by a legally authorized person is not permitted or required by law, psychologists take reasonable steps to protect the individual's rights and welfare. (Standard 3.10)

Similarly, the *Specialty Guidelines for Forensic Psychology* (APA *Specialty Guidelines*; American Psychological Association, 2013b) note that:

Forensic practitioners appreciate that the very conditions that precipitate psychological examination of individuals involved in legal proceedings can impair their functioning in a variety of important ways, including their ability to understand and consent to the evaluation process. For examinees adjudicated or presumed by law to lack the capacity to provide informed consent for the anticipated forensic service, the forensic practitioner nevertheless provides an appropriate explanation, seeks the examinee's assent, and obtains appropriate permission from a legally authorized person, as permitted or required by law. (Guideline 6.03.03)

The APA *Specialty Guidelines* also outline the types of information that should be discussed with an examinee, including:

[T]he purpose, nature, and anticipated use of the examination; who will have access to the information; associated limitations on privacy, confidentiality, and privilege, including who is authorized to release or access the information contained in the forensic practitioner's records; the voluntary or involuntary nature of participation, including potential consequences of participation or nonparticipation, if known; and if the cost of the service is the responsibility of the examinee, the anticipated cost. (Guideline 6.03)

The *Principles of Medical Ethics with Annotations Especially Applicable to Psychiatry* (American Psychiatric Association, 2013b) addresses the need for understandable notification indirectly by focusing on the contractual nature of the relationship, and asserts that it is important to determine whether the "explicitly established" provisions of the contractual relationship are understood (Section 2.5). The *Ethical Guidelines for the Practice of Forensic Psychiatry* (AAPL *Ethical Guidelines*; American Academy of Psychiatry and the Law, 2005) also addresses the principle of informed consent:

At the outset of a face-to-face evaluation, notice should be given to the evaluee of the nature and purpose of the evaluation and the limits of its confidentiality. The informed consent of the person undergoing the forensic evaluation should be obtained when necessary and feasible. If the evaluee is not competent to give consent, the evaluator should follow the appropriate laws of the jurisdiction. (Consent section, para. 1)

In addition, the AAPL *Ethical Guidelines* discuss the importance of ensuring that examinees understand the nature of the role of the forensic evaluator: "Psychiatrists have a continuing obligation to be sensitive to the fact that although a warning has been given, the evaluee may develop the belief that there is a treatment relationship" (Confidentiality section, para. 2). This guideline stresses the importance of clarifying the nature of the relationship and the need for ongoing assessment of understanding throughout the FMHA. Finally, the AAPL *Ethical Guidelines* describes the importance of communicating limits to confidentiality, stating that "[s]pecial attention should be paid to the evaluee's understanding of medical confidentiality. A forensic evaluation requires notice to the evaluee and to collateral sources of reasonably anticipated limitations on confidentiality" (Confidentiality section, para. 1).

Although not a source of ethical authority, the *Criminal Justice Mental Health Standards* (American Bar Association, 1989) emphasizes the importance of providing notification of purpose and obtaining informed consent. Standard 7-3.6 notes that, in any evaluation, the mental health professional conducting the evaluation has an independent duty to provide notification of purpose and obtain informed consent. The nature of this notification should include: (1) the purpose of the evaluation; (2) the potential uses of any disclosures made during the evaluation; (3) the conditions under which the prosecutor will have access to information obtained and reports prepared; and (4) the consequences of the defendant's refusal to cooperate in the evaluation.

The present report provides a good illustration of the application of this principle in the context of an evaluation for testamentary capacity. Obtaining appropriate authorization may be somewhat more challenging when conducting evaluations for testamentary capacity because the potential deficits in an individual's decision-making abilities that gave rise to the evaluation may also impair the individual's ability to provide informed consent. Therefore, particular attention should be paid to the sources of ethical guidance that describe the appropriate steps to take when an individual is unable to provide consent. As noted, even in situations in which an individual is unable to provide informed consent, a clear and understandable description of the nature and purpose of the evaluation should be provided, and limits to confidentiality should be discussed.

In the present evaluation, Dr. Drogin notified Mr. Smith about the purpose and confidentiality limitations of the evaluation. After providing a "thorough explanation," he went on to obtain Mr. Smith's informed consent—necessary because this evaluation was requested by the attorney, meaning Mr. Smith had a legal right to decline to participate. The client, Mr. Smith, agreed to participate in this evaluation following a thorough explanation of its purpose and of the confidentiality limitations attending forensic mental health assessment.

John Q. Public, Ph.D.
(contributed by Eric Y. Drogin, J.D., Ph.D.)
Clinical and Forensic Psychologist

123 Main Street
Capital City, East Dakota 98765-4321
May 1, 2012

Willard M. Jones, Esquire
Jones, James, Jonas, & Johnston, PLLC
456 Courthouse Square
Capital City, East Dakota 98765-1234
Re: *Mr. Charles J. Smith*

Dear Attorney Jones:

Pursuant to your request of March 1, 2012, I have conducted a forensic psychological evaluation addressing "the capacity of testator Charles J. Smith to execute a valid will, pursuant to the requirements of EDCS Ch. 23, § 11-C.2." Following is a report containing the results of the requested evaluation.

STATUTORY AND CASE LAW BASES AND DEFINITIONS

According to EDCS Ch. 23, § 11-C.2:

Any will executed in the State of East Dakota shall be deemed invalid if it can be established by preponderance of the proffered evidence that the testator failed at the time of execution, due to mental incapacity, duress, or mistake occasioned by fraud, sufficient contemporaneous awareness of:

(1) the identity of the instrument in question as a will;

(2) the nature and extent of his estate;

(3) a rational plan for disposition of his estate; or

(4) the natural objects of his bounty.

In *Filson v. Wasterby*, 22 E.D. Sup. Ct. 317 (1998), the Supreme Court of East Dakota established that a "rational plan for disposition" is one that "reflects a genuine intent to award, compensate, or otherwise favor devisees as opposed to an expression of spite, caprice, or baseless, random assignment" (p. 333). The Court later clarified in *In re Hammond*, 24 E.D. Sup. Ct. 21 (2000) that "[r]andom assignment [is] most aptly characterized as the distribution of wealth in a fashion that the trier of fact can neither discern nor obtain sufficient explanation thereof" (p. 40).

In *Cranmore v. Bader*, 19 E.D. Ct. App. 45 (1995), the East Dakota Court of Appeals included as examples of "the natural objects of [one's] bounty…first degree relatives, certain long-standing or otherwise well-established social and business acquaintances, and other persons for whom it can be established that a demonstratively [*sic*] close relationship existed" (p. 55).

In *Harper v. Harper*, 23 E.D. Sup. Ct. 69 (1999), the Supreme Court of East Dakota defined "mental incapacity" in this context as "an inability to attain or demonstrate sufficient awareness, which inability is based upon minority, mental retardation, diagnosable psychiatric illness, or otherwise medically determined brain injury" (pp. 72–73).

EVALUATIVE MEASURES EMPLOYED

- Cognitive Capacity Screening Examination (CCS)
- Beck Depression Inventory (BDI-II)
- Beck Hopelessness Scale (BHS)
- Peabody Picture Vocabulary Test (PPVT4)
- Shipley Institute of Living Scale (SILS-2)

In addition to these psychological assessment instruments, Mr. Smith engaged in clinical and forensic psychological interviews. The only persons present in person for these interviews were Mr. Smith and this evaluator. These interviews were documented by digital audiovisual recordings, transcripts of which are appended to this report.[1]

Reviewed supplemental materials consisted in their entirety of the February 12, 2012, report of a general medical examination conducted by Sarah Sloane, M.D.; Mr. Smith's certified combined checking and savings statement dated March 15, 2012, from Capital City Savings and Loan; Mr. Smith's state and federal 2011 income tax returns; and an unsigned "Draft Will and Testament of Charles J. Smith" proffered by Mr. Smith in person and dated in the margins of each page as March 22, 2012. Each of the aforementioned documents is appended to this report.

DESCRIPTION OF EXAMINATIONS AND RESULTS

Mr. Smith was initially examined on April 1, 2012, at his current residence, 29 Knightsbridge Lane in Capital City, East Dakota. Your client agreed to participate in this evaluation subsequent to a thorough explanation of its purpose and of the confidentiality limitations attending forensic assessment. Informed consent documentation is appended to this report.

Presenting as a casually and appropriately attired 62-year-old Caucasian male with good hygiene, Mr. Smith was polite, cooperative, and responsive during the course of this examination. His speech was normal for pace, tone, volume, pressure, content, and articulation. Your client displayed a full range of affect. He was not in any apparent physical distress. Psychomotor functioning was seen as resting within normal limits. No overt indicia of psychosis were noted.

Mr. Smith claimed to have slept for approximately eight of the 24 hours preceding this morning appointment, and stated that he had just finished a full breakfast of pancakes, sausage, and orange juice. No current medications were identified. Your client denied that he was suffering from any headache, pain, nausea, or other acute condition that would interfere with the assessment process. He wore eyeglasses that he maintained were suitable for reading purposes, and asserted with a smile that his hearing was "flawless."

The first assessment measure applied was the CCS. This test enables the examiner to gain an initial understanding of a patient's general cognitive capacity at the screening level. Mr. Smith's perfect score of 30 points on this measure failed to identify any deficits in orientation, concentration, calculation, abstract reasoning, or short-term memory abilities.

BDI-II testing was utilized to screen for the presence of current and recent symptoms of depression. Mr. Smith's raw score of 2 points fell within the normal range of affect for this measure, and the following item endorsement was noted: "I don't have any thoughts of killing myself."

BHS testing addressed Mr. Smith's outlook on future as opposed to current and recent life events. His raw score of 2 points fell within the normal range of affect for this measure as well, identifying a positive view of his general life circumstances.

PPVT4 testing (Form B) was employed to assess Mr. Smith's oral comprehension. The following results were obtained:

Raw Score:	110
Standard Score:	115
Percentile Rank:	84th

---

[1] Please note that transcripts and other appendices included in the original report have been redacted from this volume to save space.

This performance reflected approximately high average spoken word recognition, consistent with impressions formed on the basis of interview contact.

SILS-2 testing constituted a screening measure for general intellectual ability, with the following results:

Vocabulary Standard Score: 111
Abstraction Standard Score: 116
Composite Standard Score: 115

These outcomes reflected approximately high average overall intelligence, with an essentially normal balance of crystallized and abstract reasoning capacities.

During an initial interview conducted in this evaluator's Capital City offices on April 1, 2012, Mr. Smith described himself as having been born into a "typical, all-American family" with a patent lawyer father, a homemaker mother, and two younger sisters. He maintained that his mother used to brag that he always attained developmental milestones (standing upright, walking, talking, and reading) earlier than most children, and recalled his childhood as "frankly, idyllic." Your client correspondingly denied having been exposed as a child to any form of physical, sexual, verbal, or emotional abuse, and further denied any history of excessive alcohol use, recreational drug use, criminal activity, mental health treatment, or notable medical illness.

Mr. Smith recalled that he had attended a competitive-admission preparatory school, after which his choice to attend the University of Alabama ("face it, for the girls") was rather surprising to his friends and family. He indicated that after graduating in just three years with B.A. in Business Administration he had spent about six months "just carousing" before starting with two fellow classmates a local restaurant that within four years had become the well-known "Smitty's Chicken" franchise. Your client indicated that he had retired from that business a multimillionaire at the age of 52, and that "unlike so many of these guys who just crack up after they walk away, I never looked back."

Never married, Mr. Smith claimed that he had considered adopting children at one point, but that he had ultimately abandoned this plan because of "prying, patronizing questions from social workers...I knew they were just doing their job, but I got cold feet." Upon retirement, your client "got serious" about the oboe playing in which he had engaged as a hobby since his sophomore year in high school. He described in detail and with considerable evident pride his eventual attainment of the rank of "second chair" in the oboe section of the Capital City Symphony Orchestra. Your client indicated that he donated all of his earnings from this avocation to local public school music programs, and that much of his spare time was spent curating his collection of "no kidding, over 250,000" classical music and jazz recordings.

During a second interview conducted in counsel's Capital City offices on April 5, 2012, Mr. Smith initially greeted this evaluator evidencing a pronounced full-body tremor, peering quizzically through his glasses and repeatedly asking in a quavering voice, "Mabel, is that you?" He then laughed out loud and exclaimed: "Come on, Doc, I'm just f—ing with you!"

Mr. Smith's attire, hygiene, and interpersonal aspect were similar to those displayed during his prior examination. He claimed to have slept for approximately seven of the 24 hours preceding this morning appointment, and stated that he had recently consumed a full breakfast of cereal, toast, milk, an orange, and orange juice. No current medications were identified. Your client again denied that he was suffering from any headache, pain, nausea, or other acute condition that would interfere with the assessment process. No changes were noted in his hearing or vision.

On this occasion, Mr. Smith recounted—without reading from the document itself—the general scheme outlined in the aforementioned "Draft Will and Testament." He stated, "Look, I like to keep things simple. One third of everything I've got to my remaining sister Helen as executor [sic], one third to the Orchestra, and one third to good ole 'Bama—as if the school really needed the money. I'm not gonna make them name a gym after me or anything; they can do whatever they want with it."

Mr. Smith further explained that both of his parents and his elder sister were deceased, that he had never engaged in a long-term romantic relationship—"Hey, that's why I've got anything to leave anybody at all"—and that his other social relationships were essentially confined to fellow orchestra musicians. He denied that he was involved in any ongoing business relationships or that he maintained any substantial investments, as "it's all in the bank—currently, over fifty-two million . . . not bragging; you asked. Why mess around with money? I'm busy! Okay, my accountant says I'm an idiot." The aforementioned Central City Savings and Loan records identified current accounts amounting to a total of $53,119,895.34.

Concerning the value of his home, its contents, and his one automobile—the 2007 Honda Accord seen parked in his driveway ("Is that eccentric? Whatever!"), Mr. Smith estimated their combined value as "just shy of two million." The combined figure appearing in the aforementioned 2010 tax returns was $2,002,000.09, with a total annual interest income of $2,198,333.45.

When asked why he was in the process of executing a will at this point in his life, Mr. Smith replied: "Look, I'm not getting any younger, and it's kind of a morbid exercise, okay, but it just makes sense." Consistent with the aforementioned medical report that declared him "utterly fit without any identifiable disease process or questionable vital signs," Mr. Smith elaborated,

I feel fine, but a will is just the responsible thing to do at my age. When my father died without a will 20 years ago, his brother—rest in peace—raised holy hell with the rest of the family over some imaginary loan from 30 years earlier. Don't get me wrong . . . I miss my parents and my other sister, but I'm glad I'm at a point in my life when there are just a few people to worry about, and it would've been good, I suppose, to have a kid to leave stuff to, but simple is the way to go.

Mr. Smith adamantly denied that he was in any way being pressured to devise any of his possessions: "My lawyer knows who's in charge . . . and ditto for the accountant. Don't forget, I spent over 30 years as the primary active shareholder and CEO for a national-level franchise, and I know my way around the money game. I just figured it was time. Do I feel creepy even thinking about it? You bet, but there it is. I'm just being responsible." Your client concluded by offering that the present evaluation was actually his own idea: "I know I wouldn't be around to see it, but I can't stand the thought that someone would think there was something wacky about this will. Having you prove the neurons are still firing will take care of that, I hope."

CONCLUSIONS

Mr. Charles J. Smith presents as an individual of approximately high average intelligence, without evidence of acute affective disturbance or neuropsychological dysfunction at the screening level.

Consistent with the requirements of EDCS Ch. 23, § 11-C.2, Mr. Smith displays sufficient awareness of the identity of the instrument he seeks to execute, the nature and extent of his estate, a rational plan for disposition of his estate, and the "natural objects of his bounty."

Please do not hesitate to contact me whenever I may provide any additional information in this regard.

Sincerely,
John Q. Public, Ph.D.
Licensed Psychologist

TEACHING POINT:
ADVANTAGES OF WRITTEN VERSUS SPOKEN NOTIFICATION IN DETERMINING WHETHER THE NOTIFICATION IS UNDERSTOOD

There are several considerations regarding whether the forensic clinician selects a written versus spoken notification. One such consideration involves gauging how well the information provided during the notification is understood. It is ethically important to provide basic information regarding who the evaluator is, who requested the evaluation, how it will be conducted, the purposes for which it may be used, and the limits on confidentiality. It is also useful to remind evaluees that there is no treatment relationship as part of the evaluation, and that a submitted report may result in testimony during a hearing or trial. Oral notification tends to be simpler, as complex material becomes confusing more easily in spoken form. When a written notification is used, the form can be refined, tested through standard software for grade equivalency, and laid out to facilitate comprehension. Appraisal of understanding of written material can be either written (e.g., asking open-ended or multiple choice questions about the meaning of words and concepts) or oral (e.g., asking the evaluee to describe what such words and concepts mean).

Depending on the extent to which the evaluator is seeking measurement of the understanding of notification, then, it seems that written notification holds some advantages. The larger question, however, is whether a failure to understand some or all of the notification in a meaningful way will affect the way the evaluation is subsequently conducted. If the forensic clinician decides that no evaluation can be conducted without meaningful informed consent in attorney-referred cases, then it would make sense to use a written notification accompanied by some measurement of understanding.

However, this would create a problem. Often the same deficits that would interfere with a meaningful understanding of information provided in the informed consent process are the same deficits that triggered the referral for evaluation. Waiting until those deficits were addressed would create a kind of Catch-22 if the evaluation was requested as part of potential action that would, in light of a certain kind of decision by the court, result in such

an intervention being ordered. The alternative is to assume that an attorney who is employed to advocate for his client is an ethically acceptable alternative in providing permission for the evaluation to be conducted. This assumes that the individual is willing to proceed.

The other consideration involves whether documentation in the form of written notification materials is necessary, or whether documentation in the report of the spoken notification and the evaluator's judgment about how well it was understood will suffice. It may be that in some cases that are complex, the attorney and evaluator may agree that written notification and consent are needed. In many cases, however, spoken notification and the evaluator's judgment about the extent to which it appears to have been understood are acceptable.

12

Personal Injury

The two reports in this chapter focus on FMHA in the context of personal injury, which is sometimes referred to as *civil psychological injury*. The much-debated principle associated with the first case in this chapter—whether to answer the ultimate legal question—discusses the importance of considering whether to directly answer the legal question that is before the court. The teaching point for this case provides a more specific discussion on answering ultimate legal questions. The principle involved in the second case addresses the decision to decline a referral for personal injury evaluations when impartiality is unlikely, with a teaching point on situations in which the evaluator may find impartiality too difficult.

CASE ONE

PRINCIPLE: CAREFULLY CONSIDER WHETHER TO ANSWER THE ULTIMATE LEGAL QUESTION. IF ANSWERED, IT SHOULD BE IN THE CONTEXT OF A THOROUGH EVALUATION CLEARLY DESCRIBING DATA AND REASONING, AND WITH THE CLEAR RECOGNITION THAT THIS QUESTION IS IN THE DOMAIN OF THE LEGAL DECISION MAKER (*PRINCIPLE 30*)

This principle discusses the importance of conveying information about the ultimate legal issue in FMHA. The "ultimate legal issue" is the legal question that the court must answer: for example, whether the defendant is liable for a psychological injury suffered by the plaintiff, or whether the criminal defendant is competent to stand trial. In the first edition of this book, this principle asserted a blanket prohibition on answering the ultimate legal question as part of FMHA. It has since been

modified (see Heilbrun, 2001, and cf. Heilbrun, Grisso, & Goldstein, 2009) to reflect certain limited circumstances under which the ultimate legal question could be answered.

There is little ethical guidance in this area. The *Ethical Principles of Psychologists and Code of Conduct* (APA *Ethics Code*; American Psychological Association, 2010a) provides no explicit guidance. The *Specialty Guidelines for Forensic Psychologists* (APA *Specialty Guidelines*; American Psychological Association, 2013b) emphasizes that forensic practitioners distinguish mental health and scientific material from legal facts, opinions, and conclusions (Guideline 2.04), and it suggests that forensic practitioners be prepared to explain "the relationship between their expert opinions and the legal issues and facts of the case at hand" (Guideline 11.02). In discussing the scope of FMHA, the APA *Specialty Guidelines* states:

> Forensic examiners seek to assist the trier of fact to understand evidence or determine a fact in issue, and they provide information that is most relevant to the psycholegal issue. In reports and testimony forensic practitioners typically provide information about examinees' functional abilities, capacities, knowledge, and beliefs, and address their opinions and recommendations to the identified psycholegal issues. (Guideline 10.01)

Neither the *Principles of Medical Ethics with Annotations Especially Applicable to Psychiatry* (American Psychiatric Association, 2013b) nor the *Ethics Guidelines for the Practice of Forensic Psychiatry* (American Academy of Psychiatry and the Law, 2005) address the issue of answering the ultimate legal question in FMHA.

Additional guidance can be found in legal evidentiary standards. Generally, under the common law, conclusions regarding the ultimate legal question were to be made by the trier of fact and not the forensic clinician. The *Federal Rules of Evidence* (FRE) elaborates in two parts. First: "An opinion is not objectionable just because it embraces an ultimate issue" (FRE 704(a)). Second, the FRE notes an important exception in the context of mental status at the time of the offense evaluations: "In a criminal case, an expert witness must not state an opinion about whether the defendant did or did not have a mental state or condition that constitutes an element of the crime charged or of a defense. Those matters are for the trier of fact alone" (FRE 704(b)).

Thus, in federal jurisdictions on the issue of mental status at the time of the offense, forensic evaluators are prohibited from testifying to both the *ultimate* issue (i.e., sanity) and the *penultimate* issue (i.e., whether the defendant meets the criteria for insanity as established by the Insanity Defense Reform Act, 18, U.S.C. Sec. 17, 1984). In some states (e.g., Pennsylvania), experts are not prohibited from offering ultimate issue testimony on any issue. Although FRE 704(b) or its state law equivalents in some jurisdictions specifically bars ultimate issue testimony in mental state at the time of the offense evaluations, ultimate issue conclusions are not necessarily inadmissible in criminal cases involving other types of legal questions and forensic issues. Indeed, forensic mental health experts are allowed to offer ultimate legal opinions in most jurisdictions (Goldstein, Morse, & Shapiro, 2003; see Heilbrun et al., 2009, for a more detailed discussion of this issue). Even when such an opinion is offered, however, it may be used in an advisory fashion—but should never substitute for the court's consideration of the ultimate legal issue (Melton, Petrila, Poythress, & Slobogin, 2007).

Legal guidelines for standards of practice provide some additional guidance. The American Bar Association *Criminal Justice Mental Health Standards* (1989) describes the contents of written reports of mental evaluations relevant to ultimate issue communication: "The evaluator should express an opinion on a specific legal criterion or standard only if the opinion is within the scope of the evaluator's specialized knowledge" (p. 109). On the admissibility of expert testimony concerning a person's mental condition or behavior, the *Standards* indicates:

> Expert testimony, in the form of an opinion
> or otherwise, concerning a person's present

mental competency or mental condition at some time in the past should be admissible whenever the testimony is based on and is within the specialized knowledge of the witness and will assist the trier of fact. However, the expert witness should not express, or be permitted to express, an opinion on any question requiring a conclusion of law or a moral or social value judgment properly reserved to the court or the jury. (p. 117).

Whether a forensic clinician should answer the ultimate legal question directly has been the subject of considerable debate in the professional literature. There is little empirical evidence on the frequency with which verbal or written ultimate opinions are expressed and the impact of such communications, leaving much room for debate on theoretical and applied grounds. Advocates suggest that answering the ultimate legal question is appropriate because many judges and attorneys anticipate that the forensic evaluator will do so as part of the evaluation, and that a ban on addressing the ultimate issue is not supported by empirical evidence (Rogers & Ewing, 1989; Rogers & Shuman, 2000). Others, in contrast, assert that answering the ultimate legal question will inevitably confound relevant clinical and scientific evidence with unrelated and non-clinical/non-scientific societal values (Melton et al., 2007; Morse, 1999). Additionally, some (Tillbrook, Mumley, & Grisso, 2003) have observed that "mental health professionals cannot properly draw conclusions about how much incapacity, dangerousness, etc. is enough to meet the legal standard" (p. 83), and that offering ultimate issue opinions is therefore inappropriate, illogical, and threatening to the integrity of the legal process and the credibility of forensic practitioners.

There is some guidance in the professional literature regarding ultimate issue testimony in specific evaluations. The *Guidelines for Child Custody Evaluations in Family Law Proceedings* (American Psychological Association, 2010b), for example, summarizes the issue by providing the following rationale:

> Psychologists strive to base their recommendations, if any, upon the psychological best interests of the child...Not every child custody evaluation will result in recommendations. Psychologists may conclude that this is

an inappropriate role for a forensic evaluator or that available data are insufficient for this purpose. If a recommendation is provided, the court will expect it to be supportable on the basis of the evaluations conducted. (Guideline 13; p. 866)

Regarding the application of this issue within child custody evaluations, the *Guidelines* continues:

If psychologists choose to make child custody recommendations, these are derived from sound psychological data and address the psychological best interests of the child. When making recommendations, psychologists seek to avoid relying upon personal biases or unsupported beliefs. Recommendations are based upon articulated assumptions, interpretations, and inferences that are consistent with established professional and scientific standards. Although the profession has not reached consensus about whether psychologists should make recommendations to the court about the final child custody determination (i.e., "ultimate opinion" testimony), psychologists seek to remain aware of the arguments on both sides of this issue and are able to articulate the logic of their positions on this issue. (p. 866, included citations removed)

Though much has been written about this debate, the question of whether the forensic clinician directly answers the ultimate legal question remains unresolved. Forensic clinicians should thus weigh the advantages and disadvantages of ultimate legal conclusions, and gauge the impact of each on the FMHA process. If forensic clinicians do offer an opinion regarding the ultimate issue before the court, either on their own or in response to a direct question, these opinions should be made in the context of a thorough evaluation, clearly describing the relevant data and reasoning that went into the opinions, and with the explicit recognition that answering this question is within the domain of the legal decision maker.

The application of this principle in the context of *Atkins*-type evaluations deserves particular comment. In an *Atkins* context, in which a finding of intellectual disability makes the defendant ineligible for the death penalty (*Atkins v. Virginia*, 2002), there is little meaningful distinction between the clinical issue (the presence or absence of intellectual disability) and the legal issue (whether the defendant should be excluded from the death penalty based on the presence of intellectual disability). The diagnostic criteria and functional legal criteria are virtually synonymous. Nevertheless, we recommend that evaluators limit their conclusions to the circumscribed issue of whether the defendant is intellectually disabled, without addressing the legal consequences that flow directly from such a diagnosis.

The present report provides a good illustration of the application of this principle to an evaluation of personal injury in the civil context. As the report indicates, the prosecution retained the forensic clinician in an effort to determine the nature and extent of possible psychological damages for the defendant, Ms. Blake, following an automobile accident. In this case the ultimate legal question was therefore whether the defendant was liable under the applicable elements of tort law, which include duty, a breach of duty, and harm resulting from that breach. Consistent with this principle, the forensic clinician did not answer the ultimate legal question directly: rather, the forensic clinician provided clinical data and conclusions within his area of expertise that should assist the trier of fact in answering the part of the legal question relating to psychological damages resulting from the accident.

Throughout the report, the forensic clinician provided several types of data regarding Ms. Blake's psychosocial development and psychological functioning before, during, and after the accident based on clinical interview, collateral information, and psychological evaluation. This information was then used in support of the forensic clinician's overall *clinical* (as opposed to legal) conclusion regarding the nature and extent of Ms. Blake's psychological dysfunction. At the end of the report, the forensic clinician concluded Ms. Blake suffered several areas of dysfunction: some that predated the automobile accident, and others that were likely the result of it. Despite not answering the ultimate legal question directly, the forensic clinician's clinical conclusion should assist the trier of fact in reaching the broader legal conclusion regarding Ms. Blake's psychological damages.

Personal Injury Psychological Evaluation Report
  Client: Elaine Blake
  Date of Birth: May 18, 1961
  Dates of Evaluation: September 10 and
  September 11, 2012
  Date of Report: September 20, 2012
  Evaluator: Garrett W. Williams, Ph.D.

REFERRAL

Ms. Blake was referred for psychological evaluation by Mr. Mark Smith of the firm Smith, Roberts and Chester, P.C., counsel for Overland Transport. Overland is the defendant in a lawsuit filed by Ms. Blake and her daughter, Alicia. The purpose of this evaluation is to determine psychological damages that Ms. Blake may have experienced in relation to events that occurred on January 28, 2010. At that time, Ms. Blake was the driver of an SUV that was hauling a rental trailer. An 18-wheel truck struck both the SUV and the trailer from behind. The impact caused the trailer to become separated from Ms. Blake's vehicle, and her SUV rolled over into the median of a four-lane highway east of Gallup, New Mexico. Ms. Blake's daughter and a co-plaintiff in this matter, Alicia Morton, was a passenger in the vehicle at the time.

EVALUATIVE PROCEDURES

I met with Ms. Blake initially in the afternoon of September 10, 2012. At that time she was administered the Personality Assessment Inventory. On that same date I conducted a 2 and 3/4 hour clinical interview with her. She returned to my office on September 11, 2012. At that time she met with my testing assistant, Jennifer Martinez, who administered the Wechsler Adult Intelligence Scale-IV; the Wechsler Memory Scale-IV, Trails A and B; the Wide-Range Achievement Test-4; and the TOMM to Ms. Blake. On that same day, Ms. Blake completed the Minnesota Multiphasic Personality Inventory-2. In addition, I met with Ms. Blake again, this time for a 2 and 3/4 hour clinical interview. I have gathered information concerning Ms. Blake from interviews with her daughter, Alicia Morton, and Fred Golden, the man who drives a taxi that she frequently uses in Tampa.

In addition, I have had an opportunity to review a number of documents in relation to this case. These include the following:

- Traffic Accident Reconstruction Report prepared by Robert Fitzgerald.
- Psychological Evaluation Report by Mandy Oliver, Ph.D., dated December 22, 2009.

COMMENT

Collateral interviews are part of current professional standards in both civil and criminal cases. Choice of collaterals in civil suits when the examiner is hired by the defendant are constrained somewhat by the adversarial nature of these evaluations. It is good practice to seek names from the examinee for collaterals, which includes permission from the examinee to conduct the collateral interviews. One problem with this procedure is that the individuals chosen by the plaintiff are likely to be predisposed to provide information favorable to the plaintiff's case. In some cases, it is appropriate for the examiner to ask the counsel for the defendant to provide names for collaterals who can provide information as well. However, the defendant may not be able to provide the names of those who can provide relevant information. Thus, the examiner may be left with names provided by the plaintiff. In this case, one of those names provided by the examinee was her daughter, a co-plaintiff in this auto accident case. I chose to interview her in spite of an expectation that she would provide history that would be biased in favor of the examinee. However, it was evident in this case that one major issue in the case would be a tragedy shared by the co-plaintiffs. In my mind, the examinee's daughter, and co-plaintiff, was one of the best sources of information concerning the impact of that tragedy upon the plaintiff. As in all cases in which the evaluator gathers collateral interview information, it is best to evaluate this information with sensitivity to the bias brought to the information gathered from that source.

- Decision materials related to Ms. Blake's application for Social Security disability dated November 3, 2009. This packet included a number of other medical records, including those from Sacristan Medical Center and Quentin Memorial Clinic.
- Elaine Blake's answers to defendant Overland Transport, Inc.'s First Request for Admissions.
- Plaintiff Elaine Blake's answers to defendant Overland Transport, Inc.'s First Set of Interrogatories.
- Deposition of Elaine Diane Blake, dated August 9, 2012, with exhibits.
- Adult Function Report for Social Security Administration, completed by Elaine Blake on November 16, 2009
- Records of Tampa Community Health Clinic.
- Records of Psychologist Priscilla Gibson, Ph.D.

PLAN OF REPORT

In order to provide the best explication of the results of this evaluation, I will begin by reviewing Ms. Blake's history prior to the February 2, 2010, auto accident. The second part of the report will deal with events that occurred in the course of the accident and its immediate aftermath. I will then cover events that occurred in the period between the auto accident and the time of this evaluation. The report will then turn to results of the current evaluation. I will conclude with a Summary Section, which will deal with issues of recommendations and prognosis.

HISTORY PRIOR TO
AUTO ACCIDENT

Elaine Diane Blake was born on May 18, 1961, in Anaheim, California. Her biological father, Ronald Tennyson, was never part of her life because he was an alcoholic who died at age 49 of alcohol-related complications and cancer. Of him, Ms. Blake says: "He pretty much drank himself to death."

Her mother, Cheryl Matthews, is currently 67 years old. Ms. Blake indicates that her mother served in the United States military and worked most of her life as an office worker. For a time she had her own store in Rochester, New York. Her mother apparently has an alcohol problem because, as Ms. Blake notes, "She has been in AA for 25 or 30 years. We remember a handful of times that we tried to wake her up a couple times and we could not wake her up. She quit by the time we were old enough to know the extent of the problem."

Because her mother was involved in a series of relationships with men, Ms. Blake's sibling lineup is complicated. She is one of six children born to her mother. She has an older brother and sister who were raised by her biological father, whom she never knew until she was an adult. She recalls being raised with two brothers and a sister. She is the second oldest in that sibling line. Of the siblings she was raised with, she believes that none of them has serious mental health problems or drug or alcohol difficulties.

It is her recollection that she began kindergarten in the town of Anaheim, California. She does not recall much of her early childhood, but she does recall going to school with her sister. She completed fourth grade after her family moved to Spokane, Washington, but she recalls, "I was confused about stuff." She believes that she spent part of her childhood at her grandmother's house. She recalls attending Roy Rogers Middle School in Hollywood, California, and she recalls that she enjoyed living there. At that time, her mother was living with George Matthews, a stepfather, who was the third man her mother had been with during the course of her lifetime. He retired from the United States Air Force, and the family moved to Indianapolis, Indiana, where the Matthews extended family resided. There Elaine Blake attended Raceway High School, but she dropped out of school in the tenth grade.

She recalls that her home was one in which there was a great deal of disruption and one in which significant violence occurred. Her parents frequently had physical fights, and she spent a great deal of time at a friend's house just to feel safe.

She recalls that she dropped out of school in the tenth grade because, "I think I had no interest other than to go see my friends. I loved cooking and sewing. I loved music and dance class. My English writing class, I loved that." In those days she occasionally had a drink with her friends when they went out for a bonfire or to the skating rink where "We drank or smoked a little bit of pot."

In spite of the relatively chaotic picture at home, Ms. Blake describes it as a relatively "normal" place. The girls were in the Girl Scouts and Brownies, and her younger brother was in the Cub Scouts and Little League: "Normal stuff."

Before her stepfather George Matthews came on the scene, she recalls her mother being quite physically abusive, and on one occasion at least, her mother attempted to choke her with a belt when she was a very small child. When asked about the impact of those experiences, she says, "I think I've always probably been the quiet one. I have seen things going on that are probably not good. I have just been quiet—don't rock the boat." She eventually decided that the only way to get out of her home was to get married.

Records indicate that she married Fred Clancy on May 28, 1979. She admits, "I only knew him for two months. We got married and about that time I thought this was not a good idea, I got pregnant with Alicia. I thought he was not a bad guy; we could work this out. I wanted Alicia to have a stable home." Alicia was born on February 7, 1980, and her second child, Johnny, was born on April 21, 1982. About a year after Johnny was born, she asked herself, "What am I doing here?" She began to realize that Fred Clancy was into drugs during the time that they were together. She eventually separated from him in 1983 and moved to Spokane, Washington, where her parents lived. She recalls that the breakup with Fred Clancy was not acrimonious: "He drove me out there with my family. I was way too young to be making that decision."

She worked at several jobs when she moved to Spokane, Washington, including working at a grocery store and deli and a short stint at a fish plant, which she recalls as being "gross." She met Phillip Blake after she moved back to Brookings and eventually divorced Fred Clancy on June 8, 1987. She returned to Spokane, Washington, about 1989, and worked at a restaurant while she was there. After two years of living together, she married Phillip Blake on July 18, 1992. Not long after they were married, they began working together to build a business called Blake's Stone, which was engaged in granite fabrication for both commercial and residential settings. They later opened another business out of their home called Take Us for Granite.

In the context of that business, Ms. Blake indicates that she served a number of functions. She was the chief bookkeeper and used computer programs to keep track of the books in the business. She was quite active in day-to-day operations.

Ms. Blake's grandson, Joaquin, was born on January 9, 2000. By all accounts, her grandson was quite dear to her, and she spent a substantial amount of her time helping raise this child. Alicia and Joaquin lived in the Blake home, so Elaine Blake was able to have frequent contact with him and to engage in much of his rearing. In a tragic accident that occurred on March 4, 2004, Joaquin was run over by a customer to their business that was also located in their home. Joaquin had been riding his bike in their driveway and was run over repeatedly by a driver who never saw the child until after the accident. The four-year-old died at the scene.

By all accounts, Ms. Blake had a profound reaction to these tragic events. She recalls that she became very depressed about that time and even thought about killing herself. For a long time she would not even leave the house and would not go to work. As would be expected, everybody else in the family reacted to this terrible event. Her husband Phillip immersed himself in his work. As a family they attempted to deal with the problem by going to a grief counseling group, but they found the tragedy was still too fresh in their minds for them to be able to cope with other people's similar tragedies. Not too much later, Elaine Blake went to a therapist for individual grief counseling at the local hospice and found that to be helpful.

Eventually she went into treatment with Priscilla Gibson, Ph.D., in April 2004, and the records indicate that treatment continued through February of 2007. Even with the treatment, Ms. Blake found that she was not able to function in the office. She recalls, "I would get into the office and someone would ask me how I was doing, and I would fall apart. I would freak out with the different noises in the dock and the back-up buzzer." In her treatment with Dr. Gibson, in addition to dealing with the loss of her grandson, Ms. Blake grappled with her history of abuse and the conflicted relationship with her mother.

At one point, Phillip was focused on buying a new piece of property to which they would relocate their business, and he threw himself into that process. She recalls, "I said, 'I can't do this, I am done.' But he did it anyway." She found she could be at the store as long as she did not have to communicate with anybody. In the course of this post-tragedy period, she resumed smoking and before long was smoking about a pack a day. Over time her smoking has escalated; at the time of the evaluation she smoked about two packs a day.

Following the tragedy she found herself going to Alcoholics Anonymous. She had been attending

Alcoholics Anonymous since about 1990, and she recalls that she stayed sober for the full seventeen years of their marriage, in part because Phillip did not drink. She returned to Alcoholics Anonymous after her grandson's death, and she recalls that she kept going there until 2007. She recalls, "It was a therapeutic thing. I felt like maybe I was an alcoholic." She recalls that she has resumed drinking over the last three years and will occasionally have a drink when she goes out to eat.

In relation to her reaction to her grandson's death, she says, "I think I did not have the coping skills for that." She realized she could not have contact with people at work, and an assistant was hired to help her. The assistant took over many of her responsibilities, and then the company hired a professional bookkeeper to take care of things she once did.

Elaine Blake recalls that over the course of the time after Joaquin's death, she and Phillip grew apart, and she really does not understand what happened to her relationship with her husband. She says, "Even today, I don't have an answer. Phillip was a good father, loving and respectful. There's not a mean thing I could say about him." She recalls that she realized the marriage was over following some events that occurred around the time of Phillip's grandfather's passing, which stimulated painful recollections of her grandson's death. She said, "I went home and I said, 'I want a divorce.'"

In spite of her treatment with Priscilla Gibson, she did not feel as though she could put her thoughts together. She found she often burst out crying. In reaction to this lack of success with these depressive symptoms, Priscilla Gibson suggested that she take an antidepressant medication. Ms. Blake recalls that she received antidepressant medication from her general practitioner, but she did not feel that the medication helped her very much, and the family noticed an actual negative change in her functioning while she was taking the medication.

By mid-2005 she was experiencing a serious sleep disorder and would wake up early in the morning, go out into her yard, and pull weeds, even before the sun rose. She did not think she was eating very normally during that time. Her recollection of it was, "It was the worst time in my life."

She and Phillip separated in 2007, and she moved to Seattle, Washington. About the same time she began a relationship with a man named Rob, whom she had known as a friend for many years before: "We went right into being an item. Everything has not worked out. I was trying to figure out what to do. Trying to communicate with Phillip." In the course of the separation and divorce, Phillip Blake got the stone business and she was to get their house, although she later learned that Phillip had a lien placed on the house related to the business and she was not able to keep the house. Out of the divorce, however, she did get substantial alimony. She was nevertheless forced to declare bankruptcy in 2008, and the last time she worked at the stone business was in April 2007. At that time, she was still quite sensitive in the work place and found that if she heard the forklift moving around, or any sort of big crash, "I would completely flip out."

Ms. Blake never went back to work after April 2007. She had a plan to put a bed-and-breakfast into their home, but because of the problem with the bankruptcy and the lien on the house, that plan came unraveled. Also, by that time, her boyfriend Rob had moved to Tampa, Florida, and had had a heart attack and was in the hospital. She recalls, "I felt like I needed to do something. I was not sure what I was going to do." Rob asked her to come out to Florida. She recalls, "I needed to do something and he needed some caretaking." By the end of 2009, she had made a decision to go to Florida. By that time she was really tired of Phillip and his new girlfriend, and she wanted to start over and to take what she wanted of her belongings and to put the rest in storage. The things she wanted to keep were in the trailer at the time of the accident. It was in the course of this move that the January 28, 2010, accident occurred.

DAY BEFORE ANALYSIS

In order to best understand the impact of the events that occurred on January 28, 2010, it is critical to develop a clear picture of Ms. Blake's status at the time of that accident. In most cases that status must be reconstructed by way of the plaintiff's self-report, collateral reports, and available records. In this case, the available records are extraordinarily helpful, because in the fall of 2009, Ms. Blake entered into a disability evaluation process with the Social Security Administration and completed a number of documents and evaluations in the course of that assessment. These provide a very clear picture of her functioning in the period immediately preceding the January 28, 2010, accident.

In the psychological evaluation by Mandy Oliver, Ph.D., dated December 22, 2009, Dr. Oliver completed a clinical interview and mental status examination, and also reviewed some of Ms. Blake's medical records. On the basis of that evaluation, Dr. Oliver provided a DSM-IV diagnosis of "major depression, chronic, severe, without psychotic features, with melancholic features." She noted that Ms. Blake had been under severe stress at the time, including financial conflicts with her former husband, loss of business, home in foreclosure, loss of grandson, and social isolation. At the time, Dr. Oliver determined that Ms. Blake's level of Global Adaptive Functioning was at 45, which is described in the DSM-IV as a condition with "serious symptoms or any serious impairment in social, occupational or school functioning." At that time, Dr. Oliver provided the following summary.

Elaine can best be described as having severe depression with melancholic features, including excessive guilt, sleep disturbance, marked psychomotor retardation, loss of pleasure in all activities, and a lack of reactivity to things that should be pleasurable. This state of depression has been persistent for several years despite counseling and medication. Additional trauma to her psyche has been dealing with what appears to have been a contentious divorce, and her husband's failure to take responsibility of court-ordered financial obligations. Elaine may benefit from retrying antidepressant medication and counseling now that she is no longer living with her husband, who apparently was critical of her seeking therapeutic support.

As part of the assessment, Dr. Oliver provided a description of Ms. Blake's activities of daily living (ADLs):

Elaine lives in a home in Spokane. Elaine raised her children in this home. This is the home where Joaquin died. Elaine drives and has a car but rarely goes out. Her mother often brings her groceries. Elaine avoids doing errands. Elaine can do personal grooming but often stays in her pajamas during the day. She can sweep, vacuum, do laundry and prepare simple meals. She does not watch television, but works on a computer. Elaine can take and receive telephone calls. Elaine can pay bills and has a checking account. She does not socialize and does not go out to dinner or movies.

In the course of evaluation with Dr. Oliver, Ms. Blake also demonstrated "slowed concentration with adequate persistence and pace."

EVENTS THAT OCCURRED IN THE COURSE OF THE ACCIDENT AND THE IMMEDIATE AFTERMATH

On the night of the accident, Ms. Black and her daughter Alicia were returning to Florida from Washington, and were driving at night in an isolated desert section of the highway near Gallup, New Mexico. Ms. Blake recalls looking in the rearview mirror of her vehicle and seeing headlights. Then, she says,

I remember hearing a big noise. Alicia said, "He hit us!" There was a god-awful "bam!" I remember asking Alicia if her legs were okay. I did not even know I was hanging upside down, I was so worried about her. I would just die if anything happened to her. I remember asking about her legs, and she kept asking, "Mom, are you okay?" I could not see her face, but I could tell that she was so worried about me, I went into automatic mode. I was super calm because I could not freak her out. Then she [Alicia] got out. I don't even know how. I realized she was gone, and then I was trying to get my arm to move. Somehow I got the horn to honk, so she came back. She was hysterical. I told her that I am just fine, I needed her to know I was okay. She said, "I'm going to get help." I can't piece it all together. I remember the motor of the car being on. I was worried that the car would blow up. I just prayed for the car to blow up if she was not in it. I realized she was running around out there and it was dark. I would honk the horn for her to come back. Somewhere in there I got the car to shut off. She was running back and forth. I remember there was a book or something that she slid under my head. I could tell that she was moving my head because something was stabbing me in the head. There was glass in the mud, and it had embedded in my hair.

Ms. Blake recalls that the police officer came and got her out of the car and asked if she was okay, and she said, "Yes." He undid her seatbelt and she recalls dropping rather suddenly, and believes that the police officer must have cut her seat belt. She recalls, "My body was numb from being upside down and having the circulation cut off. And it was freezing cold." The ambulance came, and she and her daughter were taken to Gallup.

The plaintiff was asked about her thoughts during the course of the accident and its immediate aftermath. She recalls, "When I was hanging upside down in the car, I didn't know if my body was so numb and I could not feel, it was scary." She did not indicate that she thought she was going to die in the course of the accident.

She and her daughter spent several days in Gallup in the hospital for much of that time. Her experiences at the hospital were quite unpleasant, and she recalls that someone stole money from her purse while she was there. Once she reported that money had been stolen, she was abruptly discharged from the hospital by the hospital manager. Because their car was destroyed, they had some difficulty getting out of Gallup, but eventually were transported first to Albuquerque, then to Alicia's house in Louisiana.

Ms. Blake recalls that while she was in Louisiana, she was having trouble with her left leg and with her left shoulder, and she found she could not raise her arm. She says, "My back felt like it would shoot pain like it was broken, but I knew it was not." She saw Dr. Chu in Louisiana, and he prescribed "a whole bunch of pills and gave me a couple of injection shots. It was hard to turn my neck. I had a headache that would not go away. Everything hurt—the light, everything. It felt like somebody had gotten a baseball bat and beaten me up."

She recalls that she was in Louisiana until mid-March, and she was having difficulty getting her automobile insurance carrier to provide compensation to them for what was lost in the course of the accident. She eventually made it to Florida in March 2010. She recalls when she got there, "I just needed to not do anything. Not mess with the insurance. It was almost like I just shut down....I ended up feeling like I had a heart attack. Rob took me to the hospital. It felt like my heart was going too fast. It was like if I moved, it just stabbed me. They told me at the hospital, I was having an anxiety attack."

At that time, Ms. Blake recalls that she was experiencing some emotional reactions to the accident. She says, "Bright lights, like headlights, startle me, almost paralyzing, like I had to go into the house. I had nightmares. Alicia screaming. It was always a variation of the accident." She recalls that her sleep was, "Not good. I had trouble staying asleep. Sometimes I would mentally zonk out. I would wake up a few hours later, and then up and down, up and down. I would sleep maybe four hours a night."

Medical records indicate that Ms. Blake sought treatment at the Tampa Beach Community Health Clinic on April 26, 2011. She was evaluated by Dr. Spinoza. The reason for her presenting herself to the mental health clinic was that she had had a car accident. Dr. Spinoza heard her saying, "I had a car accident. That's why I didn't want to come here. This is ridiculous." Dr. Spinoza noted that Ms. Blake was reporting panic attacks triggered by car-related thoughts, including car insurance, rental cars, and seeing cars. He noted that her panic attacks were "basically overwhelming (sweating, nightmares, poor sleep, easily startled, avoidant behavior, difficulty concentrating)."

At the time of this 2011 assessment, Dr. Spinoza had the following clinical impression: "49-year-old white female divorced x2, two grown-up children. Unemployed. Moved to Tampa over a year ago, with history of PTSD and panic, without agoraphobia, after loss of consciousness in motor vehicle accident in 1/2010. Patient seeking help. Motivated, intelligent. Diagnostic impression: PTSD; panic disorder without agoraphobia; rule out depression disorder NOS." At that time, Dr. Spinoza determined that her Global Assessment of Functioning (GAF) score was 55.

She was seen two other times by Dr. Spinoza, in April and June of 2011. In April, Dr. Spinoza noted that her symptoms were reduced and she felt as though she was able to relate better and experienced a lower degree of avoidance related to her post-traumatic stress disorder symptoms. In June, 2011, Dr. Spinoza noted that the medication was working better, and that she had fewer tearful episodes, but was still having difficulty getting into the car, but had stopped taking the bus after several bus accidents. "Rides her bike with mild to moderate anxiety. Hypersensitive to noise. Completes ADL's. Diagnosis: PTSD, slight, fewer episodes, tearfulness; panic, slight, still agoraphobic, able to ride bicycle. GAF: 59."

CURRENT STATUS

Ms. Blake indicates that she has a number of symptoms commonly seen in individuals who have had traumatic experiences. She reports that over the last year especially she has had more encounters with lawyers and other lawsuit-related events that she indicates "keeps everything on the surface." She indicates that she experiences intrusive recollections several times a week, and that she has to stop doing whatever she was doing at the time when the thoughts came to mind. When this occurs at home, she will often go outside and smoke a cigarette. She reports, "I get overwhelmed by it."

She says she occasionally has nightmares, which sometimes include content related directly to the accident. For example she occasionally dreams about her daughter Alicia screaming. She has some emotional reactions to things that remind her of the accident. She says, "Every time I see a semi truck, I ask myself if that is the same size. I'm measuring that. There are trucks everywhere. Even talking about it, my chest is in a knot. Like daily. Every time there's a truck. Sometimes also when I see the trailer rental place."

When she is reminded of the accident, she sometimes experiences physical reactions. She says, "I tense up. I feel a heavy push on my chest. I sweat on my forehead, around the back of my neck." In addition, she reports that she avoids some things related to the accident. As noted above, she avoids driving and tries to avoid going anyplace requiring riding in a car.

She was asked if she was avoiding things that she normally did before the accident. Ms. Blake replied, "Getting in the car at all costs." When asked how she gets around, she said, "I walk. I will ride my bike. Sometimes I physically cannot ride a bike. I take a bus, I take a cab. I have one cab driver I call. He knows he has to drive safe. I trust him. I have to sit in the back seat. I am terrified in a car. The times I have to be in a car I will sit in the back seat, but I try not to pay attention to anything. When we get out of the car, I feel weak and nauseated, almost like you're going to faint, almost claustrophobic. It's been this way since the accident." This avoidance of driving and fearfulness while a passenger in an auto were verified in collateral interviews with her daughter, Alicia, and the driver of the taxi she calls, Fred Golden.

Elaine Blake reports that there are activities that she did prior to the accident that she no longer pursues. She avoids some social activities, even when the neighbors ask her to come down for a barbeque: "I make an excuse not to go." She reports a sense of detachment or estrangement from other people: "If you're at the grocery store, the checker will say 'hi.' I don't want to chit-chat, I don't want to make friends in Tampa." However, she indicates that she spends a substantial period of time with homeless people in the neighborhood, providing food for them from her family. She reports, however, that she does not feel like talking to her family members.

Although she does not report a restricted range of affect or a sense of a foreshortened future, she does report that she has difficulty staying asleep. Once she wakes up, she gets up and then returns to bed, and gets up again. She says, "I would sleep maybe four hours a night."

She reports that she has experienced outbursts of anger in relation to ongoing legal proceedings. In addition, she says that she experiences difficulty focusing on things. She says that before the accident she was always a list-maker, which helped her know what she was going to do. However, she reports, "This is something new. Some days that out-of-left-field thing, I cannot put it together. There are days it is perfectly fine. I can do everything I need to do. I don't ever know when I can do it." She has not reported any sense of hypervigilance that is new since the accident, and reports no changes in her reaction to things that might otherwise startle her.

The history indicates that she was not working before the accident, and she reports that she has not returned to work since the accident. When asked if she thinks she could work, she says, "Sometimes I think yes and sometimes I think no." When asked what would keep her from working, she says, "I think physically I cannot stand or sit too long."

She reports no changes in her alcohol consumption since the accident. She indicates that she does not drink very much, and that the most she has had was a piña colada two months before the evaluation.

Reported Daily Activities

Ms. Blake indicates that she gets up at 7:00 or 8:00 in the morning and will have a cup of coffee. She will then watch the television news. She says, "Then Rob and I will take a walk. We are just a couple of blocks from the park. If we get anything from a grocery store, it is within ten blocks, I will walk. I have a little cart for my groceries, or get a bag or a tote. I fix lunch, and we usually walk and go through the park. We ride our bikes. I try to ride the bike at least every other day." She cooks dinner for both of them and usually will watch television or play dominos at night. For recreation, she and Rob will often go to the beach, which is four blocks away from their house. She says, "Sometimes we will walk up to the beach between two lifeguard shacks. I have to put ice on my back almost every night, which keeps my leg from jumping. Sometimes if I've made a pot of stew I will take some to the park (for homeless people). I will work at the Salvation Army with immigrant children. It feels good to give it back." She enjoys reading and likes to watch college football and car races.

Current Medications

Ms. Blake indicated that she was taking three medications at the time of the evaluation. This medication regime was verified by my review of her medication bottles. This review indicates that she is currently taking Clonazepam, 0.5 mg, one tablet by mouth, twice daily. She has also been prescribed hydrocodone/acetaminophen, one tablet by mouth, twice daily. She has also been prescribed and takes Sertraline, 100 mg, two tablets by mouth in the morning.

Mental Status

At the time of the evaluation, Ms. Blake appeared to be well groomed and her stated age. Her clothing was appropriate for the circumstances. She was oriented as to person, place, time, and situation. Her psychomotor activity would be considered normal. Her behavior was appropriate in the course of the evaluation, and her affect was also generally appropriate but occasionally tearful. Her mood was normal, but appropriately sad with discussion of the loss of her grandchild. Her reasoning is generally intact, and her speech was normal in rate and tone. Her speech showed no evidence of pressure, of poverty, or of incoherence. Her thought processes appeared to be intact and appropriate. She showed no ideas of reference, circumstantiality, or tangentiality. Her judgment approves to be generally intact, and her insight would be considered fair. Her attention was generally focused, although when discussing anxiety-related matters, she became somewhat distracted.

PSYCHOLOGICAL TESTING

Ms. Blake was administered two groups of psychological tests. The first included cognitive testing administered by my testing assistant, Ms. Jennifer Martinez. She showed good effort on a test that measures effort, indicating that this intellectual assessment was an accurate measure of her cognitive functioning, and her scores were not reduced because of lack of effort on her part.

The cognitive battery included the **Wechsler Adult Intelligence Scale-IV**. On this measure, Ms. Blake achieved a full-scale IQ of 81, which places her at the 10th percentile of the general population. Overall, her Verbal Comprehension scores were at 87, the 19th percentile; Perceptual Reasoning at a Scale Score of 90, the 25th percentile; Working Memory at a Scale Score of 83, the 13th percentile; and Processing Speed 76, the 5th percentile.

A comparison of these scores indicates that only two sets of scores fall outside of expected difference range. Her Perceptual Reasoning scores and her Processing Speed scores differed significantly, with her Processing Speed scores significantly lower than would be expected. Also, there was an overall difference between her Full-Scale IQ and the score that would be predicted on the basis of other tests. This suggests that the low Processing Speed scores may have diminished her overall level of functioning.

The **Wechsler Memory Scale-IV** produced a number of scores within an expected and relatively narrow range based upon what was observed in the Wechsler Adult Intelligence Scale-IV. Her Auditory Memory score was at a Scale Score of 87, the 19th percentile; her Visual Memory was at a Scale Score of 89, the 23th percentile; her Visual Working Memory was at a Scale Score of 83, the 13th percentile; her Immediate Memory was at a Scale Score of 87, the 19th percentile; and her Delayed Memory was at a scale score of 84, the 14th percentile. A review of these scores indicates that her memory scores are all within expectable ranges and suggest no evidence of impaired memory function. Ms. Blake's scores on the **Wide-Range Achievement Test-4** were within expectable ranges, with most falling around the 20th percentile, as were her scores on **Trails A and B**.

Overall, the cognitive testing shows relatively low scores on tests reflecting processing speed. Processing speed is often reduced in the context of depressive disorders, and as noted above, Ms. Blake had been diagnosed with a depressive disorder prior to the auto accident of January 2010.

Personality Assessment

Ms. Blake was administered the **Minnesota Multiphasic Personality Inventory-2**. On that instrument, all of her Validity Scales, save one, were within acceptable ranges. The FBS Scale indicates that she may have exaggerated the extent and severity of her physical complaints on the MMPI-2. Indeed, a review of her MMPI-2 profiles indicates elevations on three scales reflecting physical complaints. In addition, she shows elevations on two scales commonly elevated in individuals who experience ruminative thinking and confusion. She showed evidence of depression, low positive emotions, and the experience of unusual psychological experiences. Much of her elevation on the Depression Scale arises from the experience that her body is not working as it should in the sense of mental dullness. She shows a number of somatic complaints and a general sense that she has little energy. Through her responses, Ms. Blake indicates that she is functioning at a lower level than she has in the past and also that she experiences physical symptoms that other people do not experience. She reports health concerns in a number of systems, including gastrointestinal symptoms, neurological symptoms, and overall general health concerns.

On the **Personality Assessment Inventory**, Ms. Blake produced a valid pattern. She had a sole elevation on the Somatoform scale. On this scale, two subscales were elevated, one on the Conversion and the other on the Somatization scale. In addition she showed elevations on the scale reflecting overall physiological activation and anxiety related to post-traumatic stress. She showed a number of physiological symptoms commonly seen in people who are depressed, and had complaints of confused thinking. Overall, the computerized interpretive system of the PAI provided the first diagnostic consideration as DSM-IV, 300.11, Conversion Disorder with a Rule Out of Somatization Disorder.

SUMMARY AND CONCLUSION

The history taken in this evaluation, along with available medical records, indicate that in the period before the January 28, 2010, auto accident, Elaine Blake was coping with a number of ongoing psychological problems. In part, these arose from a complicated history of abuse and neglect in her childhood, and from a very conflicted current relationship with her mother.

However, prior to 2010, for Elaine Blake, the defining event in her life had been the 2004 death of her four-year-old grandson, Joaquin, after he was run over by a car in the driveway of her home. This event reduced this woman from one who was by all reports quite functional in her work life and her life as a mother and grandmother, to one who could no longer function in any of those spheres. Her social withdrawal was so total that she could no longer function in the workplace. She withdrew from her marriage with her husband and diminished her social activities to a quite minimal level.

Her dysfunction was so complete that she applied for Social Security benefits in the fall of 2009, and although she did not qualify for disability benefits at that time, the very thorough investigation of her problems and symptoms provided an unusually detailed benchmark in the period immediately preceding the January 2010 accident. At that time it was clear that Ms. Blake had a number of emotional problems and was diagnosed with major depressive disorder by a psychologist. She was experiencing a number of limitations in daily activities.

Following the 2010 auto accident and her recovery from many of the physical problems from that crash, many of Ms. Blake's emotional complaints continue to be depressive in nature. These symptoms are similar in nature and severity to those reported in the late-2009 Social Security evaluation, and do not appear to have been exacerbated by the 2010 accident. In fact, if her General Adaptive Functioning levels as assessed by evaluating professionals are taken as a metric, she is currently actually functioning better now than she was in 2009.

She reports some post-traumatic symptoms related to the 2010 auto accident, and these conform to a pattern seen in post-traumatic stress disorder. This pattern was assessed by Dr. Spinoza in Tampa and was seen to be relatively mild. I would agree with that assessment.

Part of the post-traumatic picture is often avoidance of people, places, and activities associated with a frightening event. In her case, this avoidance is evident in her inability to return to driving an auto, or to even be comfortable while a passenger when someone else drives. Because she was the driver of the vehicle at the time of the January 2010 accident, a tendency to avoid driving would not be unexpected.

However, this particular avoidance symptom causes some degree of functional impairment. The actual degree of disability imposed by this impairment is mitigated because Ms. Blake is able to do most of the things she wants to do using other means of transport. For many of the activities she does every day, she is able to walk to where she wants to go. She takes a cab, using the same cab driver. She takes the bus. That she experiences this impairment has been verified by her daughter, Alicia. In her deposition, Ms. Blake indicated that she had little interest in getting back into the driver's seat.

Ms. Blake has sought treatment for this avoidance reaction and visited Dr. Spinoza, who diagnosed her condition as PTSD, panic disorder without agoraphobia; rule out depressive disorder, NOS. However, records indicate that she only attended two sessions of this treatment.

In summary, Ms. Blake presents with ongoing symptoms of major depressive disorder that were evident prior to the January 2010 accident. The new symptoms arising from that accident appear to be post-traumatic in nature and relate to functional changes in her desire to drive or to be a passenger in a vehicle.

RECOMMENDATIONS

Ms. Blake would benefit from treatment focused on her post-traumatic symptoms, particularly those related to panic reactions. These kinds of symptoms are readily treatable by available treatment methods, including Eye Movement Desensitization and Reprocessing therapy and cognitive behavior therapy. Although Ms. Blake has attempted treatment, she did not complete the treatment regime. For problems related to the January 2010 accident, Ms. Blake would benefit from return to treatment with a competent therapist, and she should complete this treatment. This treatment should last no more than one year, if she participates actively in it. She may require additional follow-up sessions, which would amount to an additional twenty sessions, for a total of fifty sessions.

Her prognosis, should she complete this treatment, is good. However, given the persistence of her preexisting depressive disorder, even in the midst of ongoing medication, I am concerned that she may not fully recover from the tragedy of her grandson's death some eight years ago. She received over a year of treatment in the period immediately following that tragedy, yet is still showing a complicated bereavement/depressive pattern, indicating a lack of recovery from this loss. She needs additional treatment for this problem and should be evaluated by a psychiatrist or prescribing psychologist in order to determine if she requires changes in her medication regime.

Respectfully submitted,
Garrett W. Williams, Ph.D.
(Contributed by Bill Foote, Ph.D.)

TEACHING POINT:
ANSWERING THE ULTIMATE
LEGAL QUESTION DIRECTLY

Much of the debate about whether the forensic clinician should directly answer the ultimate legal question can be traced to the 1970s and 1980s—a time before the standard of practice in FMHA clearly specified that reports should provide sufficient information to inform the court about relevant, credible information that could usefully inform the legal decision. In this context, answering the ultimate legal question reinforced the perception that psychiatry (and psychology) practiced what Judge David Bazelon called "the ultimate wizardry," providing an answer without a concomitant explanation.

Certainly the context for expectations about FMHA has changed. Throughout this book, there is discussion of the current scientific, ethics, and practice literatures that guide the contemporary approach to FMHA. Conclusions of *any* kind in FMHA should be based on relevant and credible information, with data described and reasoning explained. That is the heart of good forensic mental health assessment.

When this is done, the question of whether the evaluator also answers the ultimate legal question is of less concern. It is appropriate for the forensic clinician to acknowledge that this question differs from other domains addressed in the forensic report or expert testimony. This may be as simple as indicating, "I recognize and respect that this is a question for the court to answer. My clinical opinion is…." The forensic clinician has already provided the evaluation that informs the domains of clinical condition, functional legal capacities, and causal connection. This is available for the court and attorneys to read and consider. Accordingly, the forensic clinician's answer to the ultimate legal question should be understandable in light of the information provided in the report.

Finally, there is the question of whether the ultimate legal question *needs* to be answered by the forensic clinician. In cases in which there are clear, harmful consequences for not doing so (e.g., other evidence from the report or testimony is excluded; the answer triggers a response such as transporting a hospitalized defendant back to the community for trial, so lack of clarity would understandably create problems), the question should be answered. If the expert is asked directly in testimony, then (with appropriate cautionary language) it is still appropriate to answer it. But there are many instances in which courts and attorneys seem satisfied with reports and testimony focusing on clinical and functional-legal criteria—so the default assumption should not be that answering the legal question is necessary. If it is not necessary, and recognizing that there has been an active and ongoing debate within forensic psychiatry and forensic psychology for many years on this question, it seems quite appropriate to refrain from answering the ultimate legal question directly.

CASE TWO
PRINCIPLE: DECLINE THE REFERRAL WHEN EVALUATOR IMPARTIALITY IS UNLIKELY
(PRINCIPLE 10)

This principle is discussed in detail in Chapter 4 (this volume), so we move directly to discussing a case that provides an illustration of the importance of declining a referral when impartiality is unlikely. In this particular case, Dr. Goldstein did not decline the referral, however his discussion in the teaching point that follows describes some of the particular stresses associated with this evaluation. Future referrals for this kind of evaluation would very likely be considered in light of such impact and its associated challenge to remaining impartial.

Alan M. Goldstein, PhD, PC
Board Certified Forensic Psychologist—ABPP
New York, Connecticut, & Iowa Licensed Psychologist
13 Arden Drive
Hartsdale, NY 10530
(914) 693-7760
alanmg@optonline.net

FORENSIC PSYCHOLOGICAL EVALUATION

Plaintiff: Charlie Inuktuq
Dates Evaluated: 9/17/03, 12/14/05, 4/14/06, and 4/18/07
D.O.B.: 12/17/70
Age at Time of Initial Assessment: 32 years
Date of Report: 7/18/08

Charlie Inuktuq was referred by his attorneys. I evaluated Mr. Inuktuq in Hamilton Township on four occasions. He was referred for psychological evaluation because of his claim that Frank James, a teacher at his school, had sexually abused him. Mr. Inuktuq, along with other plaintiffs, is suing the government, claiming that officials were aware of this teacher's history of abuse at the time of his employment, allowed him to remain as a teacher in a number of communities over a ten-year period, and that as a result of this abuse, Mr. Inuktuq has suffered a number of damages. Mr. James has served two prison terms following jury trials for his criminal actions.

Mr. Inuktuq's ability to understand English was minimal. As such, each time I saw him, he was evaluated with the assistance of an interpreter. This person, Imala Toonow, is certified in this territory. She lives in Mr. Inuktuq's community and has a passing acquaintanceship with him. Prior to my first interview with him, Ms. Toonow was aware of his claim of having been sexually abused. Mr. Inuktuq had no objection to my using her as his interpreter.

Prior to the start of each evaluation session, I explained the nature and purpose of this assessment to the plaintiff. I informed Mr. Inuktuq that any relevant information that he provided might be included in my report if his attorneys ask me to submit one. I explained, through his interpreter, that this would not be a confidential assessment if I were to write a report or testify. I informed him that I would make notes based on my questions and his answers to them, and that if I submitted a

COMMENT: USE OF AN INTERPRETER

Although most of the plaintiffs spoke English, several required an interpreter, especially when asked to describe information related to their claim of sexual abuse. I wanted to give the plaintiffs the opportunity to use their full range of vocabulary, in their preferred language, to describe what took place, how they experienced it, and the effects of their abuse on all aspects of their lives. The interpreter was court-certified. However, in this specific case (and in a few others), she lived in the same community as the plaintiff. Obviously, this is far from the ideal situation, especially when people are asked to describe intimate, embarrassing details of sexual abuse that they experienced when they were young children. No other certified interpreter was available. The person who was used recognized the confidential nature of the evaluation and the sensitive nature of the information revealed by the plaintiff. She was aware, from the first group of plaintiffs, that sexual abuse had, in fact, occurred in her community, and that many of the male students between the ages of five and 17 had been victims of this teacher. The ground rules of these assessments were discussed with her in the presence of Mr. Inuktuq. He indicated that he was aware that she had served as the interpreter for some members of the first group of plaintiffs, and the assessment continued. This seemed to be the most reasonable way to proceed.

report, my notes would be provided to the government's attorney if requested.

Mr. Inuktuq was able, with some additional explanations by me, to paraphrase this information. He understood why I was evaluating him, and he recognized the limits of confidentiality should he decide to continue with this assessment. In addition, prior to the start of the initial evaluation session, the interpreter read him the Consent for Evaluation form, and Mr. Inuktuq signed it after paraphrasing the information contained in it. Therefore, sessions were conducted with Mr. Inuktuq's informed consent.

At the start of his second evaluation interview, I reminded Mr. Inuktuq of the limits of confidentiality should he agree to continue to participate. Through the interpreter, Mr. Inuktuq acknowledged that he understood these cautions, so the session continued with his informed consent. Similar information was provided to Mr. Inuktuq, through his interpreter, prior to the start of the other assessment sessions, and his informed consent was again obtained.

EVALUATION PROCEDURES

Mr. Inuktuq was initially interviewed by me on 9/17/03 for approximately three hours in Hamilton Township. During this assessment, I questioned him regarding his background and history, his recollection of the events surrounding and including his claim of sexual abuse, and his perception of the

effects that this abuse may have had on his overall functioning.

I interviewed Mr. Inuktuq for a second time in Hamilton Township for approximately three hours on 12/14/05. I again evaluated him on 4/14/06 and 4/18/07 in Hamilton Township. Those sessions lasted for a total of approximately 90 minutes each. During his final session with me, through his interpreter, I administered the Wechsler Abbreviated Scale of Intelligence (WASI).

I reviewed Mr. Inuktuq's school records from Hamilton Township. I also reviewed copies of his medical records from Baldary Regional Hospital and the Baldary Correctional Centre, both in Iqaluit. Many of these records were incomplete and illegible.

In forming the opinions presented in this report, I have relied on my four interviews with Mr. Inuktuq. The school records, described below, are such that it is not possible to identify all of this examinee's records, and thus, I cannot reasonably rely upon many of the school records that I have reviewed. I have considered the medical records provided to me in forming the opinions presented in this report.

During the course of my assessment sessions with Mr. Inuktuq, he identified school peers in his community whom he recalled being present during his claimed episodes of abuse. A cross-check of interviews I had conducted with them while assessing their respective claims of sexual abuse corroborates that Mr. Inuktuq was present at the locations

---

COMMENT: INTERVIEWS OF THIRD PARTIES

This unusual case presents a number of practical problems and raises several ethical issues in addition to the use of an interpreter who lives in the plaintiff's village. Ideally, a psychologist trained in forensic psychology and familiar with Inuit culture (and someone who speaks Inuktitut) should conduct these assessments. No such individual could be located. I consulted with someone who had conducted over 40 of these cases in the past and received supervision from him for several of the earlier cases. As noted below, records were poorly prepared, incomplete, and replete with errors.

Perhaps the greatest challenge in conducting these evaluations was locating people who might confirm the plaintiffs' information as to what might have occurred. Most cases of child sexual abuse occur out of the sight of witnesses. Young children, especially those in isolated areas of the world, may not be able to understand what has happened to them. Most were threatened if they revealed their abuse to anyone. Therefore, parents, peers, social workers and teachers were not told of their victimization. The only medical professionals in the community were government nurses. Physicians had to be flown in on an as-needed basis or, in emergencies, the patient would be flown out to a city with a hospital—often 90 minutes or more away. As such, pediatricians rarely conducted psychical examinations on the children, and even if they had done so, it would have been unlikely, without direct information from the child, that a report of sexual abuse would have been filed. The Royal Canadian Mounted Police (RCMP) Barracks consisted of three to four officers, none of whom were Inuit. They were viewed almost by everyone as outsiders, and there was little interaction with members of the community. The RCMP were, for the most part, people who arrested members of the community for public drunkenness and spousal abuse. They were not seen as people in whom a child could confide.

The teacher lived in the community and had befriended many of the parents whose children he had abused and was about to abuse. He was seen as a trusted authority figure, a person who would be believed over the allegations of their children. In fact, when one child reported his teacher/neighbor's abuse to his parents, he was punished for lying; his mother smashed his head into the sink, leaving deep scars that are visible today. It is not surprising that there is a dearth of third parties who could corroborate the plaintiff's rendition as to what had occurred. These evaluations required flexibility and reasonable attempts to handle practical and ethical concerns unique to these cases.

---

where he claimed he had been abused. The interviews I did with these plaintiffs only confirmed his presence at the times and places where he reported abuse. Almost never did one child see another child being abused (except for fondling that occurred in the group shower following gym). I have not reviewed other independent sources of information that might corroborate Mr. Inuktuq's background, history, or the events associated with his claim that Frank James had sexually abused him.

BRIEF SUMMARY OF RECORDS REVIEWED

School Records

The Hamilton Township school records are confusing regarding the enrollment and attendance of Mr. Inuktuq at school. The records I was given include the name of "Ottakie Iterlook Inuktuq," or "Charlie Inuktuq," but some have a different birth date from that of the examinee. The parents listed for the "Inuktuq" with one date of birth are "Mary & Kingwaisiaq," and, on a later record, "Bill & Mary"—different names than those given to me by the examinee, who told me that his parents were Peter and Abenyia.

The school records for the Charlie Inuktuq whom I considered are those that include his *correct* date of birth. Those records indicate that he was included on an enrollment register for the "7/8 grade." Students registered in that class ranged from the second to ninth grade levels. This was his first year of formal education.

COMMENT: RECORD REVIEWS

In any forensic assessment, the use of records and third-party information is needed to corroborate information provided by the plaintiff. In these cases, records were frequently missing, illegible, and vague. Class lists were inaccurate and often incomplete. Teacher comments, a frequent source of relevant information, were frequently missing. Even medical records often proved to be incomplete and illegible. Reasonable steps were taken to review these records, and when there were questions of accuracy or significant contradictions that could not be resolved, little to no weight was given to those records.

While conducting this assessment, I also evaluated other plaintiffs regarding their reports of sexual abuse. During the course of each interview, each was questioned, in detail, whether other people were present during their abuse—including the teacher's wife or child, peers, or other teachers. Some recalled that Mr. Inuktuq was in the classroom or in Mr. James's house when they were abused. But none witnessed him being abused by his teacher. Similarly, no one who was present could confirm that these third parties (and plaintiffs) were victims of abuse. As previously noted, Mr. James separated potential victims from one another, herding them to an isolated area of the school, library, gym, or his house. In general, victims never spoke of their abuse to one another or to teachers, parents, siblings (some of whom were also abused by Mr. James), social workers, or nurses at the health center—either at the time of the abuse or at any time thereafter. I was able to confirm this plaintiff's presence at the places and times that he indicated he was abused by reviewing other interviews of victims.

A note written by a seventh-grade teacher, Maya Hilgard, in 1985–1986, when this examinee would have been 15, states that "Charlie...is a bully..., and never comes to school long enough to accomplish anything. He is not well liked by the teachers, or by mature students. He is well below his grade level in every subject." A final note for that year indicates that Mr. Inuktuq had dropped out of school, having attended only sporadically since the middle of his first year at school.

A review of the Charlie Inuktuq with the August date of birth—different from this litigant's birthdate—finds that he was enrolled in the first grade for the 1975–1976 school year. However, the person I examined was insistent that he lived in an outpost and never attended school until he was age 12 or 13, suggesting that if he is correct, this individual's records are those of a different child living in this community. Because of the confusion in the spelling of the names, the dates of birth, and the names of the parents, it was not possible to reasonably rely on many of the school records without further clarification.

Medical Records

According to treatment records from Baldary Regional Hospital (10/21/99), the Royal Canadian Mounted Police (RCMP) brought Mr. Inuktuq to the hospital because of suicide threats he had made to his sister over the telephone. He explained to the treating staff that he had "felt betrayed by his common-law girlfriend while he was in jail. She already was unfaithful to him and slept with other men...feels very hurt by this—felt that if he died he would no longer have to face these feelings." At that time, Mr. Inuktuq was described as angry, initially unwilling to answer questions; he demonstrated little eye contact. The treatment records report that following his "suicide intent," he was discharged with a referral to social services to "follow him up...." These records also indicate two prior hospitalizations for suicide attempts, but provide no additional information.

Another record from Baldary Regional Hospital (no date visible on the case history and progress notes) reports that while Mr. Inuktuq was working in Iqaluit, he complained of abdominal pain and blood in his stool. An Operative Report (8/8/02) indicates that Mr. Inuktuq underwent a colonoscopy. An "unusual lesion" was found, and a biopsy was sent for analysis. A Treatment Record form (12/2/02) reports that Mr. Inuktuq was "booked for proctoscopy." In Mr. Inuktuq's Inmate Medical Discharge Summary from the Baldary

Correctional Centre (12/16/02), it is reported that a colonoscopy was performed and results were negative. Mr. Inuktuq was described as "non-compliant with second set of testing requested." The hospital records note that he was to see a physician on 1/13/03 for repeat testing. An appointment was made with a physician for 2/14/03, related to his "rectal lesions and [for] further testing." The same record notes that on 7/25/04, he did not "show to clinic."

A review of Mr. Inuktuq's more recent medical records reports a number of gastrointestinal problems. On 7/19/05, a call was received from Mr. Inuktuq's mother indicating that her son "was unable to get out of bed and has been vomiting blood." It was noted that Mr. Inuktuq had been seen at the Hamilton Township Health Center three days earlier because of a hangover. She reported that since Mr. Inuktuq's return from the hospital, her son had been vomiting, and she noted that he had been losing weight. Although he was asked to come into the Health Center, his mother indicated to the medical staff that her son "could not walk because he was too weak." He was taken to the Health Center by stretcher. At that time, Mr. Inuktuq was found to be "Very thin and gaunt...." The question of alcohol-induced gastritis was raised.

On 7/15/05, Mr. Inuktuq's girlfriend called the Hamilton Township Health Center. She reported that Mr. Inuktuq was "puking and shaking." It was reported that Mr. Inuktuq was mad at her, and she was advised to leave their home and go to her sister's house, "to feel safe."

PERSONAL HISTORY

The following information was obtained during my first evaluation session with the plaintiff.

Mr. Inuktuq's father died in 1995. Mr. Inuktuq explained that his father, like he, was a carver. He reported that his father's death was related to "something with his lungs. He was injured first." Mr. Inuktuq's mother was approximately age 55 at the time of this initial assessment. Mr. Inuktuq recalled that when he was a child, his mother would "look after me well." When I first saw Mr. Inuktuq, he reported that his mother was experiencing health problems, "usually a shortness of breath." (However, when he was seen in April 2006, his mother remained alive, and Mr. Inuktuq was residing with her.)

Mr. Inuktuq reported that his parents got along well, but also stated that at times they would become involved in physical altercations. He did not believe that this father had ever been arrested for spousal abuse.

Mr. Inuktuq told me that he has four sisters and two brothers. Another brother died in a sledding accident in 1999 or 2000. When asked whether any of his siblings were involved in the Frank James sexual abuse case, Mr. Inuktuq stated, "The deceased one was a victim in the first group [of plaintiffs]."

When asked about his educational background, Mr. Inuktuq provided a somewhat confusing chronology, and it was difficult to comprehend what he was attempting to convey. He first reported that he had left school in the fifth grade, after attempting to return to school. When asked to clarify, Mr. Inuktuq stated, "I dropped out between classes one and two, and I tried to go back at grade five, but I did not." When asked for additional details, Mr. Inuktuq stated, "I don't remember which because of the classes then." (A review of the school records does suggest that "grade" and "class" had different meanings when Mr. Inuktuq attended school. Students in a specific class may have come from a heterogeneous range of grade levels.)

Later in the interview, I asked Mr. Inuktuq to clarify some of the information that he had provided regarding his academic history. He then indicated, "I lived in an outpost camp, so I didn't go to school until I was 12 or 13, and I was put in a higher class. I had never been to school before." When asked how long he had attended school on a formal basis, Mr. Inuktuq replied, "Less than one year." He stated that he is able to read English "a little," and when asked whether he could read his own language, Inuktitut he stated, "kind of. I can't read too much now. I forget some of the 'finals.'" The interpreter was unable to explain why Mr. Inuktuq had referred to "finals" or what he meant when he used this expression.

Mr. Inuktuq reported that he had been a student of Frank James "when he was my teacher. Like when I was tired, I would go back and they would let me skip some grades, and I was put in his class with my two cousins because I was the same age as people in his class."

Mr. Inuktuq recalled that when he was age 13 or 14, he began to inhale a variety of toxic substances, including: "gas, camping fuel, airplane glue, all kinds." At age 15, he began to smoke marijuana and hashish. He denied the use of other substances, but when asked specifically about his use of cocaine, Mr. Inuktuq stated, "three times." He continues to smoke marijuana and hashish, "usually most of the time." When he was asked how these substances affect him, Mr. Inuktuq reported, "I'm stoned most of the time. I take it most of the time because it helps me to cough up phlegm because I smoke cigarettes."

Mr. Inuktuq initially stated that he had been arrested "six or seven times." However, when he described his arrest record, it was clear that he had significantly understated the number of times that he had been arrested. His first arrest, he reported, occurred when he was age 16. At that time, he was charged with breaking and entering. Mr. Inuktuq then stated that he had been arrested "about ten times or more [for breaking and entering]; there were times I didn't go to jail." His longest period of incarceration was approximately eight months. Mr. Inuktuq was also convicted of assaulting family members, "my sister and my girlfriend." He was remanded to the Baldary Correctional Center for that crime. He claimed that he had been convicted for sexual assault in 1994 and that he served six months. According to Mr. Inuktuq, he was intoxicated when the assault and the sexual assault had occurred. He stated that on other occasions, he had been in the "drunk tank" overnight and at times held for periods of up to three nights. Mr. Inuktuq reported that his last arrest, prior to my initial assessment of him, occurred in 2002 for spousal abuse.

Mr. Inuktuq told me that he has held very few jobs during his lifetime. "I worked for a very short time, guarding a building being built." After three weeks, he was laid off. He was then employed in Iqaluit, "as a guard when they were building a building." His last job, in 2000, involved "building a house in Iqaluit."

Mr. Inuktuq reported that he has very little energy. When asked how he spends his days, he responded, "Not doing anything for a while, resting, sleeping, and if I'm rested, I start to carve." When asked how much money he earned as a carver, Mr. Inuktuq was either vague or evasive: "I never keep track, so I can't say, but it's my only income." He stated that there are periods of time when he is unable to work, but he will work "when there's a full moon and I get ache bones [sic]."

When questioned about prior hospitalizations, Mr. Inuktuq stated that when he was incarcerated at the Baldary Correctional Center, an X-ray had been taken, and "They saw a growth and told me I had to have it taken out. But I never went through surgery." When asked for details, Mr. Inuktuq indicated that they had found "a growth in my intestine." (A review of his medical records from Baldary Regional Hospital confirms this information.) He continues to suffer from pains in his lower abdomen, back, and arms. When asked, Mr. Inuktuq reported that he had lost approximately 10 to 15 pounds, most of this weight loss occurring while he was incarcerated.

When asked whether he had noticed any rectal bleeding, Mr. Inuktuq answered in the affirmative. Based upon this information, I advised Mr. Inuktuq to go to the Hamilton Township Health Center with his interpreter. Mr. Inuktuq agreed to do so the next morning, accompanied by his interpreter. I notified his attorney of my concern.

Mr. Inuktuq's medical records indicate that he did follow through and he initially sought medical advice. However, based upon the records I received, it does not appear that he returned for follow-up testing, as recommended. When seen in December 2005 and April 2006, Mr. Inuktuq continued to complain of rectal bleeding and weight loss. He was again very strongly encouraged to visit the Hamilton Township Health Center, and, to my knowledge, he had scheduled an appointment to see a member of their staff shortly after my departure.

Mr. Inuktuq reported two suicide attempts, one in 1991 and the second in 1996. The first time, he attempted to end his life by hanging, "but the rope broke. I guess I was sad, tired of living, thinking about what happened a lot, and worrying." When asked to elaborate, Mr. Inuktuq stated that he worries about "different things, but mostly because I'm tired of life," a theme he spontaneously repeated in April 2006. He elaborated, "I'm unhappy about things in life, what was done to me, and I miss people who you were very close to [sic] who killed themselves." He explained that a cousin, Inuksiaq, had been in the first group of litigants. However, this cousin "had an accidental death. He died of hypothermia. There were just two of them out there [on the ice]. I think he was sniffing and drank liquor."

Mr. Inuktuq again tried suicide five years later. He reported that a cousin "didn't have a happy life because of the things that happened to him with Frank James, like he [James] did to me." This man committed suicide, and approximately one week later, Mr. Inuktuq cut his left wrist. He was discovered semiconscious, lying in the snow, and was taken to the Health Center. That day, he was evacuated by plane to a hospital in Edmonton, where he received medical treatment. He explained through his interpreter that his cousin's death "made me think about everything that was done to me. I couldn't take it any more."

Mr. Inuktuq's medical records from Baldary Regional Hospital also report a prior suicide threat, made to his sister by telephone while he was incarcerated at the Correctional Center in October 1998. At that time, it was reported that Mr. Inuktuq was depressed because his girlfriend had been unfaithful to him.

BEHAVIORAL OBSERVATIONS

Mr. Inuktuq arrived for his initial appointment over two and a half hours late. His appointment was rescheduled for later that evening. Although he appeared for that appointment on time, he was clearly "stoned." Mr. Inuktuq appeared lethargic, his eyes would close during the evaluation, and he maintained virtually no eye contact with me. Answers he provided were extremely brief and sometimes contradictory and confusing. Because of his drug-impaired condition, it was not possible to determine whether his confusion represented an underlying thought disorder, was indicative of an active psychotic process, or was related to the drugs he had used.

For the second session, two years later, Mr. Inuktuq arrived ten minutes early for his appointment. Although he appeared a bit "drowsy," Mr. Inuktuq denied that he had recently smoked marijuana, stating that he had "only used it yesterday." He appeared to be emaciated, greenish-yellow in complexion, and highly lethargic. During the second session, Mr. Inuktuq was severely depressed, sighing throughout the interview and responding in a very slow fashion. Signs of psychomotor retardation were observed during the interview. These included slowing in speech, thinking, and motor behavior.

For his third appointment, Mr. Inuktuq arrived approximately 45 minutes late. Mr. Inuktuq reported to me that he found it hard to sit still. Consistent with information that I had obtained from him three years earlier, he explained, "I'm defecating and bleeding all the time. I'm very worried and afraid if

I'm operated on, it might get worse." Mr. Inuktuq appeared to be physically uncomfortable and severely depressed.

As this session progressed, Mr. Inuktuq expressed suicidal ideation, but denied a specific plan or time that he would act on these feelings. He demonstrated numerous signs of severe clinical depression, including psychomotor retardation and thought blocking. At times, he cried during the session. Mr. Inuktuq refused to accompany his lawyer, his interpreter, or me to the Health Center so that he could be evaluated. Because of his condition, this session was terminated prematurely. I notified the charge nurse at the Health Center of my concerns.

Mr. Inuktuq arrived on time for his rescheduled appointment. He continued to look physically ill and clinically depressed. He presented in a sad manner, demonstrating no facial expression at all. Mr. Inuktuq stated that he had scheduled an appointment at the Health Center for later that week.

SEXUAL ABUSE HISTORY

Mr. Inuktuq recalled that when he started school at age 12 or 13, he had been placed in Frank James's class. He reported that three separate incidents involving sexual victimization had occurred.

During the second interview, Mr. Inuktuq stated that he believes he was 13 years of age when Frank James was his teacher and that he was in grade seven when his teacher sexually abused him. When asked what grade he had completed in school, in a somewhat detached, disorganized manner, Mr. Inuktuq stated, "It was like I went, but I never completed a grade. I dropped out and I tried to go back, but I couldn't because of what happened." This information is consistent with the responses he had given during the first evaluation session over two years earlier and with records I have examined.

Mr. Inuktuq claimed, "The first time, I went to school and I remember he picked me up and put me behind his back. I didn't know a teacher to do that to any student [sic]." He reported that he and Frank James were dressed at that time: "I remember he touched outside my clothing and outside the rectal area and it hurt very much. It was a pain I never felt." When asked how being touched through his clothing could have been so painful, Mr. Inuktuq stated, "It was with his hand. He put it on my shoulders. I was on his back and he was touching me on my butt, through my clothing." He recalled that Mr. James was "feeling around [for] about five minutes." When asked what happened next, Mr. Inuktuq responded blandly, "I walked, looking at math books." Mr. Inuktuq stated, "My cousin was with other guys, someone with the same name as mine."

A second incident reported by Mr. Inuktuq occurred at the school.

> He [James] got mad at me because I was having difficulty with the books. He took me in the corner, and after that, it was about four in the afternoon, he let me work on my books and then he got mad again. I was the last kid to be there, and he wanted me to take off my pants, and I thought he was going to hit me because he was getting mad. He looked like he was mad. He raped me. He put his penis into my ass. My mind fell out of control.

Mr. Inuktuq recalled that he had experienced considerable pain, and "I go unconscious because it was so painful. When he was finished, he prevented me from looking at him. He was wiping himself. I left the building crying, uncomfortable. He told me not to tell anyone." Mr. Inuktuq explained that following his abuse, he did not tell his parents, peers, or others in the community because "I didn't know what it meant. I hurt but didn't know what to think."

A third incident occurred at Frank James's house, according to Mr. Inuktuq. He explained that his teacher would frequently invite children into his house after school or on the weekend to "play videogames and have snacks." At that time, "He touched me again on my butt. I was scared and called a friend to walk over to us and he stopped. I think he was abusing kids at his house."

Mr. Inuktuq reported that approximately two or three weeks after this last incident of alleged sexual victimization, he dropped out of school. He explained that he never returned to school again because "I couldn't go.… [I] was so scared of him and he was being there [sic]."

Mr. Inuktuq stated that following these incidents, "I got real unhappy and really angry at times." He reported that his episodes of depression and anger last "for a whole month." Mr. Inuktuq stated that at times, he dreams of Frank James, and he has experienced nightmares involving his former teacher. Mr. Inuktuq reported that approximately five times a month, he experiences intrusive thoughts and memories of Frank James's abuse of him. At such times, "I get tired and angry and get a short temper."

When asked specifically, Mr. Inuktuq reported, "Sometimes I feel I hear voices out of nowhere." He elaborated, "It's like what we're talking; it usually seems in my head and sometimes outside." Mr. Inuktuq allowed for the possibility that these voices "could be my imagination and I don't actually hear [them]." When asked specifically, Mr. Inuktuq stated that he has experienced visual hallucinations as well. "I've seen a body, like my body, without a face existing. It was when I was incarcerated, so it was 1992 or 2000." These hallucinations have occurred, according to the plaintiff, both when he was on drugs and during periods of sobriety. Mr. Inuktuq stated that he has experienced nightmares, and "I've felt there was something at the end of my bed."

FOLLOW-UP INTERVIEWS

I evaluated Mr. Inuktuq in Hamilton Township for a second time on 12/14/05. Again, because of his obvious language difficulties, he was seen with the assistance of an interpreter.

Mr. Inuktuq is not currently employed. He last worked as a janitor, explaining that he performed this function while an inmate in Baldary Correctional Center. In 2004, he had been convicted of spousal abuse and served eight months in prison. Mr. Inuktuq stated that he had been "unhappy, and I wanted to commit suicide," but he turned his unhappiness on his common-law wife and assaulted her.

At the time of the second assessment, Mr. Inuktuq continued to live with his common-law wife, a relationship he had had for seven years. Following his release from the Baldary Correctional Center, Mr. Inuktuq reported that his relationship with her "has gotten better.…"

Because, during the first interview, Mr. Inuktuq had provided a confusing and detached description of what had occurred when Frank James abused him, he was re-interviewed regarding these details. On the whole, his rendition was consistent with the information he had provided me over two years before. During this second interview, Mr. Inuktuq recalled that he was abused twice, "that I remember.

I was in his class, in the seventh grade and about 13 years old."

On 12/14/05, he reported that during the first incident, Frank James "lifted me up, behind him, and touched me around my bum area and I thought he was just touching me. I never experienced anyone do it to me. It was over my pants, probably. My pants were on. Other students were watching, but he didn't do anything further." Mr. Inuktuq named these students.

Shortly after the first incident, Frank James again allegedly abused Mr. Inuktuq. He reported, "My peers, they were smarter than I was. That time, I tried to go back and work in my math book. I got stuck working and the teacher [James] put me in the corner and got angry. After everyone left, he abused me." Mr. Inuktuq was highly resistant to describing exactly what had occurred. He stated, "like the way he sexually abuses kids." When asked for more details, Mr. Inuktuq stated, "He put his arm around my neck and knocked me out, like putting me to sleep. He pulled my pants halfway down and did it." Again, Mr. Inuktuq had to be encouraged to continue. He stated, "He put in his...It felt like I was waking from a sleep and felt him abusing me. He never said anything." As Mr. Inuktuq reported this episode, his description of his mental state during the time of this abuse appeared to reflect a state of dissociation.

During this follow-up session, Mr. Inuktuq reported that after the second incident, "I got so scared, I couldn't even walk around him. I never tried to go back again. It was my last time there [in the school]." He then spontaneously added that he and other boys had been invited to his teacher's house to play videogames months after the second incident. Mr. Inuktuq recalled that while in the house, his teacher isolated him from his friends. His teacher then "put his hand on my butt." According to Mr. Inuktuq, he was scared that "he would rape me again." He called out to a friend to come into the room, which the friend did. He recalled that his teacher "was very angry, but did stop doing it to me then."

Mr. Inuktuq again reported that he has experienced both auditory and visual hallucinations. Consistent with his very strange demeanor, Mr. Inuktuq stated, "[recently] I was hearing this—the sound of like flying. Also voices and visions. It's like watching a movie and like voices, like echoes and it gets close. I understood, but I can't explain it. You wouldn't understand it." In describing his visual hallucinations, Mr. Inuktuq recalled seeing a faceless man; "I've seen that and different ones when I'm alone."

Mr. Inuktuq was again seen on 4/14/06 and 4/18/07 with the assistance of an interpreter. During both sessions, Mr. Inuktuq was highly depressed and he expressed considerable concern about his mental and physical well being. "I was thinking if there can be any way my life can be helped by somebody. I am very fed up with my life. This year, it seems tougher. I've lost appetite [sic] and thought about friends I used to have here. I was with my brother when he committed suicide."

According to Mr. Inuktuq, he often thinks of suicide "when I'm too tired and I think the government is playing with me—the representatives in our community. Right now, I try not to think about it. I try to stay away from thinking about suicide and when I'm defecating, bleeding all the time. I'm very worried and afraid if I'm operated on, it might get worse." Although Mr. Inuktuq acknowledged that I had recommended to him that he go to the Health Center for a physical examination on at least two prior occasions, he indicated that he had not done so, explaining, "I'm suppose [sic] to go to the health clinic, but most of the time, I don't feel like doing anything."

When seen in April 2007, Mr. Inuktuq explained that he had broken up with his common-law wife a few months earlier. He explained, "I'm living with my mother right now."

Mr. Inuktuq explained that he reported Frank James' alleged sexual abuse of him to his attorney because "I thought I'd have this bad feeling forever, until I'm an old man. I decided I have to bring it forward. An abuse victim says [to me] not to be shy and I came forward." According to Mr. Inuktuq, a cousin, Adamie Nunsiaq, and a person in jail, Tunillie Ashono, and another cousin encouraged him to report these alleged incidents of sexual abuse. Mr. Inuktuq informed me that when he was incarcerated, a guard, Martin Sprung, had encouraged him to continue to discuss details of his abuse.

RESULTS OF TESTING

Because of Mr. Inuktuq's physical health problems and discomfort, his severe depression, and his accompanying suicidal ideation evidenced during his two April 2006 appointments, the Beck Depression Inventory–II was not administered to him. Similarly, because of his distraught

COMMENT: USE OF PSYCHOLOGICAL TESTS

The APA *Ethics Code* makes it clear that tests should be used for their intended purpose and should be appropriate for those evaluated. This is a highly unusual population of plaintiffs—speaking Inuktitut as their first language, raised in a highly isolated community, and with many who had dropped out of school shortly after the abuse had occurred. Tests were used in a highly cautious manner, stating the problems inherent in employing these instruments and describing the limits that must be imposed on test interpretation. Students were required to take courses in English from an early age, and where conditions permitted in most other cases, the WRAT was administered. To obtain an estimate of intellectual functioning in this case, only the Performance section of the WASI was given.

mental state, his poor physical condition, and his very limited knowledge of English, the Wide Range Achievement Test–4 (WRAT-4) was not administered.

Mr. Inuktuq was administered the Performance subtests of the Wechsler Abbreviated Scale of Intelligence (WASI) on 4/18/06. His lack of English language skills made the administration of the Verbal section of this test meaningless. Consistent with his clinically depressed state, he appeared to find it difficult to concentrate and focus his attention. Mr. Inuktuq was quickly overwhelmed by difficult tasks. While he stuck with them, his thinking was highly rigid and concrete. Mr. Inuktuq demonstrated marked psychomotor retardation as well, consistent with his significantly depressed clinical state.

On the non-verbal section of the WASI, Mr. Inuktuq obtained a Performance IQ of 72, a score falling within the Borderline range of intelligence. This score would be surpassed by 97% of the general population. With a 95% degree of certainty, Mr. Inuktuq's actual non-verbal IQ would fall between 67 and 79. This range of scores encompasses the Extreme Low to the Borderline categories.

SUMMARY AND OPINIONS

Mr. Inuktuq reported three separate incidents involving claims that he had been sexually abused by Frank James. At the time of these incidents, Mr. Inuktuq reported that he was approximately 12 or 13 years of age. Two incidents occurred at school and one in Frank James's house.

During the first incident, Mr. Inuktuq recalled that both he and Frank James were dressed.

Despite being dressed, he reported feeling "a pain I never felt… [when he was] touching me on the butt." Despite attempts to clarify exactly what Mr. Inuktuq was attempting to convey, he was unable to provide a clearer description of exactly what had occurred, insisting that both he and his teacher had their clothing on at the time, but that he felt intense pain in the anal area. Two years later, Mr. Inuktuq recalled details of this episode in a similar manner.

The second incident involved anal intercourse. "He raped me. He put his penis into my ass. My mind fell out of control because it hurt [and] I go unconscious because it's so painful." At the end of this episode, his teacher allegedly told Mr. Inuktuq "not to tell anyone."

A third incident of sexual abuse occurred at Frank James' house. At that time, "He touched me again. I called a friend to walk over to us, and he stopped. I think he was abusing kids at his house."

Mr. Inuktuq arrived "stoned" for his initial evaluation session in 2003, rescheduled because he had missed his first appointment. He was lethargic and maintained virtually no eye contact throughout the session. Answers were frequently offered in a confused, contradictory manner. It was unclear at that time whether Mr. Inuktuq had an active thought disorder or whether his thinking was disorganized because of his use of marijuana or hashish. As such, it was difficult to evaluate the accuracy of Mr. Inuktuq's reports of sexual victimization.

When he was interviewed two years later, Mr. Inuktuq reported that he was not high. He claimed that he had not smoked marijuana since the evening before our appointment. Mr. Inuktuq did not appear to be under the influence of alcohol or marijuana when I met with him. Mr. Inuktuq was more focused, and despite his severely depressed state, he provided some additional information about these alleged incidents of sexual abuse.

It is noted that he provided the name of four friends that had been with him when one or more of these incidents occurred. When interviewed by me and others, each of those individuals, in describing their own sexual abuse to the evaluator, reported that Mr. Inuktuq was present with them at the time and place where he had been abused. It is also significant that Mr. Inuktuq readily admitted that on one occasion, when he believed he was about to be anally penetrated by Frank James, he had called a friend to walk over to him, and Mr. James, although angry, ceased his abuse. This friend, Anokie Samiannie, recalled this incident. However, in almost all of the cases evaluated, there were no witnesses to the sexually abusive act. The teacher separated each child from his peers (brought them to an empty classroom, shower room, or isolated room in his house). Therefore, although these collateral interviews confirmed Mr. Inuktuq's presence in a room, none of his peers could verify that they witnessed him being sexual abused.

Because Mr. Inuktuq's initial presentation was difficult to follow and his descriptions of the abuse he reported sometimes lacked a sense of logic, no determination could be made as to the credibility of his self-report after the initial assessment session. During that first session, Mr. Inuktuq admitted to both auditory and visual hallucinations, but, upon closer questioning, Mr. Inuktuq stated that the voices he heard might very well have been his imagination. He did not attempt to "overplay" the role of visual hallucinations in his life, reporting two such instances in a matter-of-fact manner.

During the second assessment session, Mr. Inuktuq reported that he was not under the influence of marijuana. His description of his auditory and visual hallucinations was easier to understand (and consistent with what he had stated in vaguer terms two years earlier). His reported symptoms closely resembled those experienced by psychotic patients. As such, based upon this second session, his report of these symptoms appears to be valid.

During his second evaluation, Mr. Inuktuq provided a somewhat more focused description of what he claimed occurred when Frank James sexually abused him. He claimed three incidents of physical sexual abuse. While his description was consistent with the information he first provided

me more than two years ago, Mr. Inuktuq appeared to be more logical, and he responded to questions about what he recalled in a somewhat more focused manner.

He again explained, during the second session, that his anal area had been fondled through his clothing, but because "other students were watching…he [James] didn't do anything further." Mr. Inuktuq identified these students by name. The second incident involved penile anal penetration. Mr. Inuktuq recalled that Frank James had put a "sleeper hold" on him. He became drowsy or unconscious, and when he awoke, he "felt him abusing me." It is my opinion that Mr. Inuktuq's report of these incidents is credible and reflects his recollections as best as he can report them. In addition, his description of that specific incident suggests that Mr. Inuktuq experienced a dissociative episode at the time of this alleged abuse.

Mr. Inuktuq did not report these incidents of sexual abuse at the time they occurred, in part because of his fear of Frank James. He had been told by his teacher not tell anyone what had happened. He explained that he had dropped out of school because he was frightened of Frank James. His teacher was still at the school, and he could not face him again. In addition, as a 12- or 13-year-old, Mr. Inuktuq accurately perceived his teacher, Frank James, to be a powerful authority figure, and he was clearly intimidated by him. His teacher was one of only two or three Caucasian people he had ever seen in person. Mr. Inuktuq explained that at the time this abuse occurred, he could not fully grasp the nature of the act that was committed against him. He was raised in an isolated outpost, had never heard of "sex abuse," and he was unable to make sense of what had happened. However, he did report feeling embarrassed and that he could not tell others, including family members, what had happened to him. (This was a common factor claimed by other victims in this case, who stated that they were ashamed, that their parents were "friends with the teacher," that they would not be believed, or that they would be ostracized if they spoke publicly of their abuse).

It was only after Mr. Inuktuq was encouraged by two relatives and someone he met while incarcerated at the Baldary Correctional Center that he decided to come forward. In addition, he believed that if he were able to "bring [these memories] forward," he could put "these bad feelings" behind him. In my opinion, Mr. Inuktuq's stated reasons for not reporting these incidents at the time they occurred, as well as his reasons for finally coming forward, are credible.

According to Mr. Inuktuq, he attended school for less than one year. He had lived in an outpost camp, and he first started school when he was age 12 or 13. Because of his age, he was placed in an advanced class, although he had no background to do the academic work that was required of him. During his first year of school, Mr. Inuktuq reported that he was sexually abused by Frank James, his teacher, and because of his fear of him, he did not return to complete the school year. I did not administer achievement testing because of Mr. Inuktuq's highly depressed, suicidal state and his debilitated physical condition when I saw him in April 2006. However, Mr. Inuktuq reported that not only does he have difficulty reading English, but he also encounters problems when required to read in his own language, Inuktitut. On the Performance section of the WASI, Mr. Inuktuq's non-verbal IQ was found to be 72, a score that falls within the Borderline range of intellectual functioning and at the 3rd percentile.

Because Mr. Inuktuq reports that he completed less than one year of formal education, he does not possess even the rudimentary skills that are necessary to obtain and hold a job in his community. Mr. Inuktuq recalled that he has been employed for only two or three short intervals throughout his lifetime. All of these jobs involved low-level activities. Twice, he worked as a guard at construction sites. At another time, Mr. Inuktuq claimed, he was employed as a laborer.

Mr. Inuktuq reported two suicide attempts. One involved hanging himself (the rope broke), and the other involved cutting his wrist (he was found in the snow, semiconscious). He did not attribute these attempts solely to his claim that Frank James had sexually abused him. He also stated, "I was tired of living, thinking about what happened a lot, and worrying." (A report that he intended to commit suicide resulted in his hospitalization at Baldary Regional Hospital as well. Records indicate that this incident was precipitated by problems Mr. Inuktuq had with his girlfriend.)

Mr. Inuktuq claimed that he began to abuse drugs following Frank James's alleged sexual abuse of him. Although he minimized his use of alcohol, Mr. Inuktuq reported candidly that he is "stoned most of the time" (as he was when I first evaluated him in September 2003). He reported a large number of arrests, a number that grew as he was questioned. According to Mr. Inuktuq, he experiences episodes of depression and anger several times a month.

Based upon my evaluation, it is my opinion that Mr. Inuktuq is educationally and vocationally disabled, and this is related to Frank James's sexual abuse of him. Mr. Inuktuq reported severe impairments in his ability to read and write in English. He may also be impaired in his ability to read and write in his own language, but he could not be assessed in this regard by me. He lacks academic preparation that would allow him to pursue a meaningful vocation. This impairment is related to Frank James' sexual abuse of him during Mr. Inuktuq's first attempt at school. Although his measured non-verbal IQ falls within the Borderline range, it is possible that had Mr. Inuktuq continued with his education, he would have been able to develop reading, writing, and mathematical abilities beyond the level that he most likely possesses at the present time (but which were not evaluated by me because of his mental and physical condition).

In addition, throughout the interviews, Mr. Inuktuq demonstrated non-logical thinking. His verbalizations were frequently strange, and it was difficult to follow his thinking, especially during the initial assessment session. At the time of the initial assessment, it was not possible to determine whether his disordered thinking was attributable to his drug use or to an underlying psychosis. However, based upon the second session, it is my opinion that his thinking and the auditory and visual hallucinations which he claims to experience are related to the toxic effects of his early history of inhaling chemicals, his almost daily use of marijuana, and are partially caused by Frank James's sexual abuse of him.

Mr. Inuktuq is in need of an inpatient drug treatment program with long-term follow-up drug treatment care. Drug treatment for Mr. Inuktuq should be a lifelong process. Without such treatment, his addiction and mental deterioration are likely to continue.

Mr. Inuktuq requires long-term individual psychotherapy. In my opinion, he is currently too fragile to be considered a candidate for group psychotherapy. Individual treatment for this man with a major depressive disorder, severe, chronic with psychotic features, will require a long period of treatment. He should also be assessed for the appropriateness of antidepressant and antipsychotic medication. Without appropriate treatment for his mental disorder, Mr. Inuktuq is likely to continue to remain depressed, socially isolated, and withdrawn. Furthermore, in my opinion, he will most likely continue to deteriorate emotionally.

Based upon Mr. Inuktuq's lack of any meaningful formal education and his lack of preparation to pursue an occupation, he is in need of educational therapy and vocational counseling. Educational therapy will, in all likelihood, require a period of years. At this stage in his life, Mr. Inuktuq would best be served by specific vocational training. Vocational training, requiring one to two years, could not begin until Mr. Inuktuq possesses a fundamental understanding of reading in his own language and the ability to perform simple mathematical calculations. Mr. Inuktuq is likely to remain unemployed and unemployable without adequate educational and vocational training.

In addition, Mr. Inuktuq requires a thorough medical workup. Over a period of years, he reported symptoms that include pain and anal bleeding. When seen in April 2006, Mr. Inuktuq told me that these symptoms remain, and his physical appearance has deteriorated still further. I have again implored Mr. Inuktuq to seek medical consultation. Alan M. Goldstein, Ph.D., P.C.
Board Certified Forensic Psychologist
American Board of Forensic Psychology

TEACHING POINT:
DECLINING THE CASE WHEN IMPARTIALITY WOULD BE TOO DIFFICULT
(contributed by Alan M. Goldstein)
This personal injury case is traumatic not only for the plaintiff, but for the evaluator as well. A brief summary of the background of this case is necessary for an understanding of the impact of such cases on the examiner.

Prior to my acceptance of this referral, I had conducted forensic evaluations related to claims of sexual abuse in approximately 30 to 40 cases. Most were criminal cases, and these assessments (for mental state at the time of the offense and

sentencing purposes) were performed at the request of defense attorneys. I then became involved in a series of sexual abuse cases in Canada when my name was given to a law firm representing approximately 50 individuals who were suing the Territory of Nunavut, claiming that they had been damaged by the sexual abuse they had suffered at the hands of a teacher who was employed by the territory. This teacher worked in isolated communities for one or two years and then "moved on" to other communities for the same period of time. He would return to some communities (such as the one in this case) two or three times. Abuse occurred over a 12-year period.

His abuse was reported by a social worker at a community health center when a young adult patient revealed, during the course of therapy, that he had been sexually abused by a teacher. She reported this information to Territory leaders, and the teacher was removed from his position. Prior to this, he had become a principal of the elementary school, changing the system so that he taught only classes of boys. Soon after the report was filed and the teacher left the community, large numbers of men stepped forward to report that they, too, had been victimized by the same teacher. Word of this abuse spread to other communities, and others reported that they had been abused by the same man. Through mental health workers, the group obtained the services of a law firm to represent them in a personal injury suit. A board-certified forensic psychologist, William Foote, Ph.D., ABPP, was hired to conduct assessments. The government all but acknowledged that abuse had occurred (the teacher had been tried and convicted in criminal court on two separate occasions for this abuse). The question was not so much whether these people were victims of abuse. Rather, the assessments focused on three major questions: the nature of the damages, if any; the prognosis for each plaintiff; and what would be required to make each victim whole again.

The original cases were all settled, and financial settlements were paid based on the quantity and the quality of abuse that each victim had suffered. Shortly after the settlement, a second group of possible victims of this teacher's abuse filed claims against the government. Many stated that they had been reluctant to join the first group because they were embarrassed to make public their history of sexual abuse, and they believed that as they were ethnic minorities, no one would believe that a white teacher would have done this to them. Plaintiffs, from a number of communities where this teacher had taught, numbered approximately 60. The government, while questioning that some of these suits might have been "opportunistic," again focused on the nature and extent of damages, the prognosis, and the need for treatment for each plaintiff. Dr. Foote asked me to accompany him to several communities where most of the victims lived to help in conducting these assessments.

The APA *Ethics Code* and the APA *Specialty Guidelines* emphasize the importance of impartiality in conducting any assessment. Forensic psychologists must approach each assessment with an open mind, free of prejudices and biases that may interfere with objectivity.

After the first two "rounds" of assessment, the psychologist who had brought me in to conduct these assessments with him no longer wished to participate. Therefore, I continued with these evaluations alone for four years more. In total, I conducted approximately 50 of these forensic evaluations and submitted reports to the attorneys for almost all of them. Listening to details of sexual abuse from adults who were ages five to 17 at the time of their victimization by a trusted teacher—an adult pedophile—takes a toll on the examiner. I would return home after three or four weeks of assessments in these isolated communities both physically and emotionally exhausted.

Since these evaluations were completed, approximately five years ago, I have turned down referrals from lawyers asking me to conduct assessments of pedophiles and of those who have murdered young children. Such referrals have asked me to focus on the defendant's mental state at the time of the crime, either as a possible defense, or for mitigation of sentence. These defendants did not have a prior mental health history or a documented history of cognitive deficits. As a consequence of the Inuit cases, I did not believe my bias against such defendants would allow me to conduct an impartial assessment either for the prosecution or for the defense. In addition, I have young grandchildren. I have become increasingly sensitive to the victimization of children, such that I have questions as to my ability to conduct these evaluations in an impartial manner. While any person is entitled to have an impartial assessment conducted on their behalf, I believe that my intense experience working on these Inuit cases may have impaired my ability to be objective in performing such assessments.

13

Civil Commitment

This chapter focuses on the impact of forensic assessment on civil commitment decisions. Civil commitment questions can, in some cases, involve committed individuals exercising legitimate legal rights to secure their release, sometimes against medical advice. Therefore, the results of a FMHA in this context can be subject to adversarial scrutiny in the same way as could other kinds of FMHA. Civil commitment as a form of FMHA has received less attention than other evaluations conducted in the course of different kinds of civil and criminal litigation. This has changed some in recent years, as reflected by the excellent summary of this issue from both a clinical and legal perspective that highlights implications for evaluation (see Pinals & Mossman, 2012).

The principle illustrated by the present case addresses the importance of considering both relevance and scientific reliability and validity in seeking information and selecting data sources in forensic assessment. Following the report, the teaching point discusses the strengths and weaknesses of classification systems.

CASE ONE
PRINCIPLE: USE RELEVANCE AND RELIABILITY (VALIDITY) AS GUIDES FOR SEEKING INFORMATION AND SELECTING DATA SOURCES (PRINCIPLE 18)

This principle was discussed previously in Chapter 8 (this volume). The present case report provides an example of the application of relevance and reliability to the selection of data sources in the context of civil commitment. The application of relevance in a FMHA context can be established both qualitatively and quantitatively. Qualitatively, relevance to the forensic issue can be made by describing the logical basis for a connection between the

mental health construct and the relevant forensic issues(s). In this case, the forensic clinicians were asked to assess whether Mr. Lantern met the criteria for civil commitment. There are a few particular mental health constructs and certain historical information that might be relevant to this legal question, with some data sources being more relevant than others when the forensic issues are considered. Since civil commitment criteria basically involve two broad criteria—mental disorder and adaptive functioning (specifically, risk of harm to self or others)—it is important to gather information in these areas directly from the individual, and indirectly from collateral interviewees and records.

Other aspects of civil commitment evaluations both distinguish it from many other kinds of FMHA, and create problems for gathering third party information. Unlike almost all other kinds of FMHA discussed in this book, civil commitment evaluations are often conducted on a time-urgent basis. This means that evaluators often do not have the luxury of gathering extensive records or conducting numerous collateral interviews. Instead, they focus on the identification of symptoms of mental disorder and impairments in adaptive functioning that can be obtained fairly quickly. In the present case, for example, the evaluator interviewed Mr. Lantern, reviewed a description of his recent behavior submitted by a fellow student, and read his records from the county hospital where he had been taken in the course of the events described in the report.

Some of the strength of this report reflects the evaluator's willingness to seek explanation and to provide recommended alternatives to involuntary hospitalization. For example, Dr. Narishkeit concludes that Mr. Lantern does experience both depression and social anxiety. The evaluator further recommends mental health treatment in the community for this individual. But he concludes that neither the level of impairment nor the nature of the intent were such that Mr. Lantern presents a significant threat to harm others or himself. Rather, his symptoms and somewhat impaired adaptive functioning appear to make him an appropriate candidate for voluntary mental health treatment in the community.

Report on Civil Commitment
Contributors: Tadeus Edward Kowalski, M.D.,
and Douglas Mossman, M.D.
November 31, 2012
The Honorable Judith Sheindlin
Gevalt County Courthouse
Sumwerrin, Ohio 49999

Re: Proposed civil commitment of Jack O. Lantern
Dear Judge Judy:

Pursuant to the Court's order, I have conducted a psychiatric evaluation of Jack O. Lantern concerning his possibly being a mentally ill person subject to court-ordered hospitalization. Ohio civil commitment law authorizes involuntary psychiatric hospitalization by court order if an individual:

A. Has a mental illness, defined as "a substantial disorder of thought, mood, perception, orientation, or memory that grossly impairs a person's judgment, behavior, capacity to recognize reality, or ability to meet the ordinary demands of life," and

B. Because of the person's mental illness, he:
1. Represents a substantial risk of physical harm to self as manifested by evidence of threats of, or attempts at, suicide or serious self-inflicted bodily harm;
2. Represents a substantial risk of physical harm to others as manifested by evidence of recent homicidal or other violent behavior, evidence of recent threats that place another in reasonable fear of violent behavior and serious physical harm, or other evidence of present dangerousness;
3. Represents a substantial and immediate risk of serious physical impairment or injury to self as manifested by evidence that the person is unable to provide for and is not providing for the person's basic physical needs because of the person's mental illness, and that appropriate

provision for those needs cannot be made immediately available in the community; or
4. Would benefit from treatment in a hospital for the person's mental illness and is in need of such treatment as manifested by evidence of behavior that creates a grave and imminent risk to substantial rights of others or the person.

SOURCES OF INFORMATION

- A 70-minute interview of Mr. Lantern conducted at Gevalt County Hospital (GCH), November 30, 2012
- All entries to Mr. Lantern's GCH record, November 28–30, 2012
- Affidavit completed by Dolly Parton, November 28, 2012

STATEMENT OF DISCLOSURE

Before I evaluated Mr. Lantern, I explained that the evaluation was not confidential, that he was not my patient, and that I was not acting as his treating physician. I said that I would prepare a report for the Court using the information I obtained from him and that I probably would testify about what he told me at his civil commitment hearing. I also told him that he did not have to answer any of my questions, but if he chose not to, I might ask him his reasons for not answering and disclose his not answering in my report or testimony. To find out whether Mr. Lantern understood what I had said, I asked him to restate what I had explained in his own words. He accurately summarized the information and agreed to speak with me.

AFFIDAVIT

The following comes verbatim from the Affidavit of Dolly Parton, a fellow student of Mr. Lantern:

I got an instant message from Jack last night that said, "I might as well kill myself." When he said that, I got really scared, because he had been acting weird for a couple of weeks. A couple of weeks ago, I went to a party with Jack and some of my friends. Jack came with us because he was roommates with my friends. Jack stayed in the corner the whole time we were at the party, which is kind of weird. After the party, Jack, my roommates, and I went to my dorm room to hang out for a while. Jack sat on my bed and didn't say anything. I just figured he was real quiet, but then he pulled out a screwdriver and started to stab the plaster wall. We were all kind of freaked out, so his roommates took him home.

I didn't see Jack much during the next couple of weeks, but I kept getting texts and Facebook messages from this unknown person who called himself "pumpkin head." I think [the texts and Facebook messages] were from Jack. The messages weren't scary or threatening or anything, but instead they were sad, like he was depressed. I think one of the texts said, "I do not know who I am." I would try to respond positively and tell him we all feel down at times but things will get better. When I responded, I almost always asked if I was talking to Jack, but I never got an answer. I told my dad about the texts and Facebook messages because I did not know what else to do. My dad thought they were from Jack as well and told me to stop responding to him.

A few days ago, I walked out of my dorm room and someone had written on the white erase board next to my door: *"By a name, I know not how to tell thee who I am, My name, dear saint, is hateful to myself, Because it is an enemy to thee, Had I it written, I would tear the word."* I thought this was Jack's because it was similar to the Facebook messages and texts he wrote. I got scared because this meant he had been outside my room, and I wasn't sure if he was stalking me. I called my dad again, who told me to contact the school's residential staff, the residence life administrator on call, and a bunch of other people. My dad also said he was going to contact the police.

The next day campus police told me they had talked with Jack and to let campus police know if Jack attempted to contact me. Yesterday, in one of the classes I have with Jack, he said, "You lowlife barbarians make me so sick to the stomach that I wanna barf all over my new shoes." He then said something about eating babies and everyone burning in hell for mass murder. Then today, I got the text message about his wanting to kill

himself. I am worried about him, and this is why I think he needs to get help.

BACKGROUND
Social and Developmental History
Mr. Lantern was born to married parents in Crudville, Ohio, on April 31, 1990. He has one sibling, an older sister. Mr. Lantern had a heart condition as a child that required surgery. He described an emotionally difficult childhood, stating he had always been a loner who was very quiet and had only a few friends. His unhappiest childhood memories, said Mr. Lantern, were occasions when his parents had visitors at their house. His parents insisted that Mr. Lantern talk with the visitors, and he recalled having sweaty palms, becoming pale, "freezing," and sometimes crying—a humiliating experience for him.

In 1998, when Mr. Lantern was eight years old, he and his family moved to a suburb of Sumwerrin, Ohio. Mr. Lantern described this move as difficult for him, after which he became quieter and more withdrawn. For many years, said Mr. Lantern, he did not like speaking or making eye contact with most other people.

Education
Mr. Lantern said he did well academically in elementary and middle school, but his shyness affected his grades because he did not want to participate in classes. In high school, Mr. Lantern continued to do well academically, having trouble only in classes that required active verbal participation. Because of his difficulty in participating in classroom activities, his parents enrolled him in Special High School, which had educational offerings that included special classes for kids with speech and language problems. In June 2008, he graduated from Special High School having completed the college preparatory program, and the following fall, he enrolled in Gevalt College. Mr. Lantern initially majored in business information technology, but discovered he had a passion for English and switched his major.

Relationships
Mr. Lantern had never been in a dating relationship and did not have any children. Mr. Lantern described his sexual orientation as heterosexual. I asked for his thoughts about never having a girlfriend. Mr. Lantern seemed interested in the idea of a girlfriend, but said, "I'm too shy to approach girls."

Employment

Mr. Lantern never held a job, but he was a full-time student.

Psychiatric History

Mr. Lantern met with a psychiatrist and an art therapist while attending Special High School because "my parents forced me to." Mr. Lantern thought he had been diagnosed with "social anxiety disorder." He denied ever being hospitalized for psychiatric reasons, but did take an antidepressant once. He thought the name was Paxil, but he was not sure. Mr. Lantern said he could not remember whether the medication helped.

Substance Use

Mr. Lantern denied ever using tobacco, alcohol, or illicit drugs.

Legal History

Mr. Lantern denied ever having been arrested.

HOSPITAL COURSE

Doctor Freud admitted Mr. Lantern to GCH under an involuntarily status on the evening of November 28, 2012. Mr. Lantern created no problems for the nursing staff or other patients while at GCH. He stayed in his room and spoke to no one unless spoken to first, but he ate portions of all meals the hospital had served. He slept most of both nights he was hospitalized. He had not taken any medications since being admitted to the hospital.

PSYCHIATRIC INTERVIEW

When I interviewed Mr. Lantern, I asked him several questions about statements in Ms. Parton's affidavit. His responses follow.

- *The plaster-stabbing incident.* Mr. Lantern said he had been trying to impress the girl in the room; he had thought he might look "cool" and "tough" by stabbing the plaster. Mr. Lantern said he had always had a difficult time expressing himself, especially his emotions, but he understood that stabbing the plaster was "not a very smart thing" to do. He commented, "If I could do it again, I would not have done that."
- *The texts and Facebook messages.* Mr. Lantern stated he felt more comfortable expressing himself through texts and Facebook, and those methods of communication allowed him to overcome his fears of talking with girls. Mr. Lantern saw himself as a poor speaker but a good writer, and believed he could communicate his feelings to Ms. Parton through writing.
- *Violent writings and threatening behavior.* Mr. Lantern said he wanted to be a writer and was trying to emulate the authors he read. Mr. Lantern believed he had a better chance of being published if he wrote the same way. Mr. Lantern said some of what he had written was "just a joke," but he acknowledged that others might not have perceived his writing as a joke. Mr. Lantern expressed concern and sorrow for appearing violent and said this was not how he wanted people to see him.
- *The Facebook posting stating "I might as well kill myself."* Mr. Lantern said he was trying to get the attention of the girl on whose Facebook page he posted it. Mr. Lantern denied any thoughts of suicide and said he wrote a portion of *Romeo and Juliet* on Ms. Parton's whiteboard because he thought she would understand he was trying to get her attention. Mr. Lantern commented, "Looking back on it, I guess it was a stupid thing to do."

MENTAL STATUS EXAMINATION

Mr. Lantern was a thin, 22-year-old white man with short dark hair who looked his stated age. He was well groomed and wore hospital attire and glasses. He displayed no abnormal movements during the interview. He was quiet and appeared shy and withdrawn; he made poor eye contact, gazing down most of the time, and only looking up while answering questions. His speech was barely audible, just above the volume of a whisper. His thinking was goal directed, but he hesitated significantly before answering many questions, taking up to thirty seconds before giving an answer.

Mr. Lantern's stated that his mood was "okay." His affect was restricted, with very little change while discussing the events that led to his being in the hospital. He denied having any thoughts of wanting to hurt himself or anyone else. He denied seeing or hearing anything that other people could not perceive. He denied having delusional thoughts such as others' being able to read his mind, or beliefs that others were out to get him or harm him.

Mr. Lantern knew the day of the week, the date, the month, the season, the year, and the reason he was in the hospital. His concentration appeared intact, as evidenced by his ability to spell the word "world" backwards and do serial subtractions from 100 by 7s ("93, 86, 79, 72, 65"). His short-term memory was adequate, as evidenced by his ability to register and repeat five words immediately and after five minutes. Mr. Lantern provided abstracted explanations of the similarities between pairs of items (e.g., *train* and *boat* as "forms of transportation").

OPINION

Mr. Lantern is a 22-year-old white man who was involuntarily admitted to GCH after displaying behavior that caused concern for the safety of others.

Based on my evaluation, it is my opinion to a reasonable degree of medical certainty that Mr. Lantern suffers from a substantial disorder of mood; namely, depressive disorder not otherwise specified. He also has social anxiety disorder. Mr. Lantern's disorder of mood influenced his decisions and actions in recent weeks. When I evaluated him, however, his judgment, behavior, capacity to recognize reality, and ability to meet the ordinary demands of everyday life were not grossly impaired.

It is also my opinion to a reasonable degree of medical certainty that Mr. Lantern's mental illness is not so severe that it causes him to represent a substantial risk of physical harm to himself or to others or that it causes him to be unable to care for himself. Although Mr. Lantern needs mental health care, he would not benefit from further hospitalization. Instead, it is my opinion to a reasonable degree of medical certainty that outpatient mental health treatment is the appropriate and least restrictive form of care for Mr. Lantern.

Very truly yours,
Jonathan Narishkeit, M.D.

TEACHING POINT:
THE STRENGTHS AND WEAKNESSES
OF CLASSIFICATION SYSTEMS

The use of classification systems in FMHA can be discussed in terms of the advantages, but also the significant problems, that such systems may provide. The clearest example is the *Diagnostic and Statistical Manual* (DSM) of the American Psychiatric Association (2013a), now in its fifth edition. DSM-5 provides a conventionally accepted diagnostic classification system that is widely used, particularly in North America, based on behavioral health conditions with differing etiologies, stability, and developmental concomitants. Additionally, the DSM-5 classification system provides clinicians with the additional advantage of considering other influences relevant to their appraisal and diagnosis of individuals.

But consider some of the limitations to directly citing the specific diagnoses, such as those catalogued in the DSM-5, within the FMHA report. First, the various iterations of the DSM were not developed to apply directly to legal proceedings. The warning provided in the initial section of the manual makes this clear. Some of the reasons why this warning is important become clear when diagnoses *are* used in reports. They tend to attract undue attention from judges and attorneys, and convey a precision that can be misleading in a forensic context. It is certainly important to determine, for instance, whether a defendant has a serious mental illness; it may also be important to determine whether a personality disorder is present. Likewise, the particular symptoms or characteristics that are present may be important. But the challenge for the forensic evaluator is to appraise whether clinical characteristics relate to functional legal capacities—and this is a more straightforward task when conducted at the broad-category level (people with severe mental illness are recognized as having some symptoms and characteristics that are meaningfully different from those without such severe mental illness) or the specific-symptom level (people who experience command hallucinations must cope with a challenge to their self-control that is different in this important respect than people without this symptom). But what is the relevant information provided by the specific diagnosis of schizophrenia, for example, that is distinct from the information provided by the diagnosis of bipolar disorder? The conclusion for some is that the disadvantages of citing specific diagnoses outweigh the particular advantages.

In the present case, the evaluator does not rely much on a classification system. Dr. Narishkeit does cite the experience of depression and social anxiety in Mr. Lantern, which is diagnostically relevant information, but does not use either of these categories to overly influence his conclusions. One could certainly imagine the experience of depression and social anxiety as being clinically sufficient, when experienced at a high level of severity, to meet the criteria set forth in civil commitment statutes. But the evaluator provides both clinical information *and* an account of Mr. Lantern's risk of harm toward others and himself, ultimately drawing conclusions that combine the clinical and the functional-legal domains in a way consistent with good FMHA practice.

14

Harassment and Discrimination

The single case report in this chapter concerns workplace harassment and discrimination. Evaluations of harassment and discrimination typically arise when a civil plaintiff makes a claim involving suffering mental or emotional harm that is causally related to their experience in the workplace. This report is used to highlight two principles. The first emphasizes the importance of presenting and defending your opinions effectively, and avoiding becoming adversarial in this context. The teaching point emphasizes the importance of communicating results firmly yet fairly. The second principle illustrated by this case addresses the organization of the FMHA report. Proper organization facilitates the effective communication of findings, and can also be useful when testimony is needed. The second teaching point elaborates on the organizational theme by discussing the sequential communication of forensic mental health results.

CASE ONE
PRINCIPLE: DO NOT BECOME ADVERSARIAL, BUT PRESENT AND DEFEND YOUR OPINIONS EFFECTIVELY (*PRINCIPLE* 7)

The role of a forensic evaluator is that of an impartial and objective assessor tasked with gathering and integrating data to assist an attorney or legal decision-maker. However, it is important to balance the "need for honesty and relative impartiality" (Heilbrun, Grisso, & Goldstein, 2009, p. 139) with the effective communication of one's opinions and conclusions in a given case. Yet it can be challenging for evaluators to avoid being drawn into adversarial battles between opposing attorneys, particularly in cases that are emotionally charged (e.g., child custody and the death penalty). To that end, evaluators are advised to focus on the presentation of their data and opinions, without becoming unduly concerned about the outcome of the case.

There is little ethical support for this principle that is clearly delineated. The *Ethical Principles of Psychologists and Code of Conduct* (American Psychological Association, 2010a) provides only indirect reference to this principle by establishing that psychologists make efforts to prevent the misuse or misinterpretation of their assessment data (Standard 9.04(a)). The *Specialty Guidelines for Forensic Psychology* (APA *Speciality Guidelines*; American Psychological Association, 2013b) emphasizes the importance of expressing conclusions and opinions "in a fair manner" (Guideline 11.01), and indicates that "the role of forensic practitioners is to facilitate understanding of the evidence or dispute" (Guideline 11.01). In addition, the APA *Specialty Guidelines* states:

> Forensic practitioners do not, by either commission or omission, participate in misrepresentation of their evidence, nor do they participate in partisan attempts to avoid, deny, or subvert the presentation of evidence contrary to their own position or opinion...This does not preclude forensic practitioners from forcefully presenting the data and reasoning upon which a conclusion or professional product is based. (Guideline 11.01)

More guidance for this principle is found in the professional literature. As described by Heilbrun and colleagues (2009), "There are both substantive and stylistic contributions to communicating one's meaning effectively" (p. 140). Such stylistic elements of effective communication may include organizing data logically, separating background information and test data from conclusions and opinions, and using clear and neutral language (Grisso, 2010). Substantive considerations include clearly explaining the results of psychological testing or forensic assessment instruments; explicitly describing the connection between data gathered during the evaluation and any opinions and conclusions that are offered; and limiting the discussion to information and opinions relevant to the referral questions, while excluding conclusions that are irrelevant or unrelated to the question at hand (Grisso, 2010; Wettstein, 2005).

When providing testimony during cross-examination, forensic evaluators are most effective when they focus on presenting their findings, reasoning, and conclusions, and avoid getting drawn into argumentative or combative exchanges with the opposing attorney. Brodsky (1999, 2004, 2013) offers numerous substantive and stylistic maxims that represent best practice in expert testimony. Evaluators are strongly encouraged to consult these valuable resources.

The current report illustrates how an evaluator can effectively communicate meaning using both substantive and stylistic means. With regard to substantive considerations, the evaluator relies on multiple sources of information, thoroughly summarizes relevant information, describes the connection between clinical characteristics and the psycholegal constructs, and explicitly considers other sources of causation. By detailing his procedures and reasoning, as well as considering alternative hypotheses, the evaluator strengthens his resulting opinions. There are also many stylistic aspects of this FMHA that help the evaluator effectively communicate his findings. The data are logically organized, and headings and subheadings are used to further highlight each relevant component of the report. The language is clear and neutral. Because earlier proceedings had not yet determined whether the alleged harassment had occurred, this report provides two analyses of damages: one analysis in the event that the finder of fact determines that Ms. Kruger's supervisors did not act in a retaliatory way, and an alternative analysis in the event that the finder of fact determines that she was the recipient of retaliation. In this way, the evaluator is able to effectively communicate his findings, while remaining impartial and objective.

PRINCIPLE
WRITE REPORT IN SECTIONS, ACCORDING TO MODEL AND PROCEDURES (*PRINCIPLE 34*)

This principle addresses the importance of the organization of a FMHA report. Organization is important for two main reasons. First, it facilitates the effective communication of findings, and the relationship between the data, reasoning, and conclusions in the report. This is particularly important in FMHA because the written report is often the only formal mechanism for communicating the results and recommendations of the evaluation. Second, a well-organized report can also be useful when testimony is needed. Presenting the data and reasoning that have already been documented in the report can enhance the effective communication of FMHA results in testimony.

There is little ethical guidance directly relevant to this principle. The APA *Specialty Guidelines* addresses report organization and structure only indirectly: "Forensic practitioners make reasonable efforts to ensure that the products of their services, as well as their own public statements and professional reports and testimony, are communicated in ways that promote understanding and avoid deception" (Guideline 11.01). Similarly, the APA *Specialty Guidelines* briefly identifies some important aspects of a report or testimony, stating:

> [F]orensic practitioners strive to offer a complete statement of all relevant opinions that they formed within the scope of their work on the case, the basis and reasoning underlying the opinions, the salient data or other information that was considered in forming the opinions, and indication of any additional evidence that may be used in support of the opinions to be offered. (Guideline 11.04)

It is also useful to consider the impact of a poorly organized report, as FMHA reports are provided as part of litigation in an adversarial context. A report that is well written and organized can be used to describe data and reasoning clearly, and deliver effective and persuasive testimony; in contrast, a poorly organized report can be used to discredit the forensic clinician (Melton, Petrila, Poythress, & Slobogin, 2007). One effective approach to challenging a poorly organized FMHA report involves asking a number of detailed questions, each of which calls for a very specific answer. Without access to an effectively condensed description of the evaluation, the forensic clinician is left to rely on his memory, search through notes, or offer an "approximate" answer. Contrast this to testimony in which the forensic clinician can refer to a well-organized report, which provides a great deal of information that can be located quickly.

Some flexibility in choosing a report's overall organization is indicated, depending on the nature of the evaluation and the clinician's purpose. At a minimum, however, the professional literature indicates that the following areas should be addressed in the FMHA report: (1) the circumstances of the referral; (2) date(s) and nature of clinical contacts; (3) collateral data sources; (4) relevant personal background information; (5) clinical findings; and (6) psychological-legal formulation (Melton et al., 2007; Rogers & Shuman, 2000). This approach to report writing allows the forensic clinician to describe relevant symptoms or characteristics, functional legal capacities, and the relationship between these two areas. In addition, this kind of structure reveals inconsistencies in findings, and facilitates preparation for testimony.

A model report structure specific to evaluations for workplace discrimination and harassment has also been described by Goodman-Delahunty and Foote (2011). They identified three primary sections: the Preamble, Assessment, and Opinion (p. 190). Within the Preamble, they recommend including details of the referral, procedures followed, and behavioral observations. In the Assessment section, they recommend providing historical information; details of the discrimination or harassment; characteristics of the evaluee before the discrimination, details of the event(s), and any changes that took place afterwards; current features of the individual, including mental health, physical health, and occupational status; interpretations of any psychological testing; and a summary of the data and evaluee functioning. Finally, in the Opinion section, the authors recommend providing the final opinion on the referral question and describing any long-term effects of the discrimination.

The current report provides another strong example of a FMHA report written in sections, using the kind of structure that is consistent with this principle. First, the report makes use of several headings and subheadings, which effectively highlights each relevant aspect of FMHA. In addition, this report clearly describes relevant background, symptoms, and clinical characteristics (e.g., Ms. Kruger's work history and the course of her depressive disorder); acknowledges the legal question (i.e., if Ms. Kruger experienced adverse emotional reactions as a result of workplace discrimination); and clearly describes the relationship between these two areas. By using this structure, the results of this FMHA have been presented in a way that maximizes its usefulness to the legal decision-maker or trier of fact.

Moreover, the structure used in this report is consistent with the guidelines described by Goodman-Delahunty and Foote (2011). The report begins by describing the referral question, evaluative procedures, and relevant behavioral observations. Next, this report thoroughly presents each component of the assessment, including Ms. Kruger's personal history; a "day before analysis," which describes Ms. Kruger's psychological and social functioning prior to the alleged discrimination; and a detailed account of the evaluee's experiences while "on the job," including a description of the alleged discrimination, Ms. Kruger's self-reported reaction to these events, and the consideration of other potential sources of causation. The report also details the aftermath of the alleged events, including mental health and occupational status, and summarizes the results of psychological testing. The report concludes with the evaluator's opinions, including his reasoning with respect to causation, an analysis of damages, a functional assessment, and recommendations/prognosis for Ms. Kruger. Through the use of this report structure, the evaluator's conclusions and recommendations are well supported.

PSYCHOLOGICAL EVALUATION REPORT
(contributed by Bill Foote, Ph.D.)
Client: Patricia Ann Kruger
Examiner: Walter M. Samuels Ph.D.
Date of Birth: January 17, 1958
Dates of Evaluation: February 2, February 3, and February 10, 2013
Date of Report: February 17, 2013

REFERRAL

James Martinez of the firm Martinez, Martin, and Kuzek, P.A., referred Ms. Kruger for psychological evaluation. His firm is counsel for one of the defendants in this case, the New Mexico Department of Highways Engineering Division. The purpose of this evaluation is to ascertain the presence of emotional problems for Ms. Kruger that may be related to events that occurred while she was an employee of the New Mexico Department of Highways Engineering Division. In particular, in earlier proceedings, the court established that Ms. Kruger had been the target of discrimination in her work assignments, based upon her gender. The earlier proceedings left open the question of whether she had experienced retaliation following her legitimate and lawful complaints concerning the discrimination. The purpose of this evaluation is to determine if she experienced adverse emotional reactions from this alleged retaliation.

EVALUATIVE PROCEDURES

Ms. Kruger first came to my office on February 2, 2013. At that time, she met with Ms. Bonnie Freeman, my testing assistant, who administered a battery of cognitive tests. These included the Wechsler Adult Intelligence Scale–IV, the Wechsler Memory Scale–IV, the Wide Range Achievement Test–4, Trails A&B, and the Test of Memory Malingering. On the same day she met with me for a 2.5-hour clinical interview. The next day, February 3, 2013, she returned for the Minnesota Multiphasic Personality Inventory–2, the Personality Assessment Inventory, and the Millon Clinical Multiaxial Inventory–III. On the same date, she met with me for a 2-hour clinical interview. Ms. Kruger returned to my office on February 10, 2013, and completed a 1.5-hour clinical interview. I also have had an opportunity to conduct telephone interviews with five individuals whose names Ms. Kruger provided. These include Jennifer Sanchez, Joyce Harrison, Emilie Halstadt, George Chavez, and Emily Casados. I also had an opportunity to conduct interviews with two individuals who are defendants in this case, James Milton and Arnold Miller. Both of these were conducted in the offices of their counsel, with their counsel present, on February 11, 2013.

In addition, I have reviewed the following documents related to this case, which I received from attorney James Martinez:

1. Complaint
2. Answer to Complaint
3. Defendant's Responses to Plaintiff's First Request for Production
4. Plaintiff's Answers to Defendant's First Set of Interrogatories and Requests for Production (without attachments)

5. Defendant's Responses to Plaintiff's Second Request for Production
6. Plaintiff Patricia Kruger's Personnel File
7. Affidavit of Plaintiff Patricia Kruger (with attachments)
8. Affidavit of Defendant James Milton
9. Affidavit of Defendant Arnold Miller
10. Supplemental Affidavit of Defendant Nolan LeBlanc, Jr.
11. Supplemental (2nd) Affidavit of Defendant Nolan LeBlanc, Jr.
12. Affidavit of Defendant Richard Gonzales
13. Supplemental Affidavit of Defendant Richard Gonzales

I have also reviewed 18 other affidavits from this case, which you will find listed in Appendix I to this report.[1]

INFORMED CONSENT

I met with Ms. Kruger on February 2, 2013, prior to the onset of any testing or evaluative procedures. At that time, I advised her that I was hired by the defendants in the ongoing lawsuit, and we discussed the parameters of confidentiality and the purpose of the evaluation. I advised her that she had the right to terminate the evaluation at any time and that she could call her lawyer at any time during the proceedings. I also advised her that my role was evaluative and not therapeutic, and, if in the course of the proceedings she became upset by any of the procedures, that she should seek counseling from an independent therapist. Ms. Kruger was able to state the essential points of the informed consent in her own words, indicating that she understood all of these issues, and she signed an informed consent on that date.

BEHAVIORAL OBSERVATIONS

Ms. Kruger arrived early or on time for each of the three days of interview and testing. She was appropriately dressed and groomed and related in an open and friendly manner throughout the evaluation. She established rapport easily with both me and my testing assistant, Ms. Freeman, in the course of the cognitive assessment, but became

---

[1] Please note that the appendices included in the original report have been redacted from this volume to save space.

tearful several times during the administration of one of the intellectual assessment tests. In my interviews with her, she maintained her composure except for some instances in the course of the final interview on February 10, 2013, when she became tearful. Ms. Kruger commented that having the interview broken up into three segments made it easier for her.

In the course of my interviews, a Mental Status Examination with Ms. Kruger indicated that she was oriented as to person, place, time and situation. She showed some evidence of tangential and circumstantial thinking when discussing work-related events, but none when discussing other aspects of her life. She reported no history of hallucinations or delusions. However, she reports some experiences that may constitute ideas of reference, depending upon the accuracy of her perception.

PERSONAL HISTORY

Patricia Lee Kruger was born on June 17, 1958, in St. Cloud, Minnesota. Her father, Heinrich Halstadt, is living and is about 80 years old. He has owned a plumbing, heating, and sheet metal business in St. Cloud. Her mother, Emilie Halstadt, is living there with Ms. Kruger's father. She is 81 years old and has not worked substantially outside of the home since she had children. Ms. Kruger is the older of two children. Her sister, Catherine Mullins, lives next to Patricia's mother and father in St. Cloud.

Ms. Kruger reports no history of drug or alcohol problems in her family. Also, she reports that she was never the victim of physical or sexual abuse. Her mother described her as "the perfect child" and she was rarely the recipient of discipline from her parents. This account is substantiated by her sister.

Ms. Kruger says she has been in good health throughout most of her life. She had a tonsillectomy when a junior in high school, and as a child broke her leg climbing a tree. She received a tubal ligation in the early 1980s. She reports she suffers from no chronic illnesses and has had chronic pain problems related only to job-related stress. She reports that she has had an uncomfortable feeling of pressure in her chest and is taking herbal remedies in order to "open up her veins." At the time of the evaluation, she was taking no prescribed medicine, nor had she used alcohol within the previous 24 hours.

Ms. Kruger is a cigarette smoker, and she says that her smoking has increased significantly over the last three years. At the time of the evaluation, she was smoking at least a pack a day. She reports that her current alcohol use fluctuates. She says, "Maybe I might get a bottle of wine every couple of months. It will be a couple of glasses every night until it is done." She says she drinks the wine because, "It is supposed to be healthy for you." Over the last several years she rarely drinks more than several drinks at a sitting and she reports that she does not get drunk. She reports no serious problems with drugs. She takes herbs in order to avoid taking prescription medications.

The plaintiff reports a normal early childhood and states that she had no serious childhood illnesses. She grew up in the town of St. Cloud, Minnesota, which she described as a community of about 50,000 people. Grade school was described as "easy." She said, "I had a very social background." She described junior high school as being normal and that she was just an average student. She attended St. Cloud Senior High School and graduated from there in 1976 with about a B average. She reports no extracurricular activities except for working part-time during her senior year at a local medical clinic. She reports no history of juvenile legal, drug, or alcohol problems. She recalls, "I was a tomboy and I lived in the woods. It was actually a good way to grow up."

Following graduation, she married Mark Kruger, who she says "turned into a jerk." He was a college boyfriend and she married him in 1976. By her recollection, "I was young and foolish, and I had been so protected as a child, I did not realize what the world was like. I made a bad choice." Two children were born to this union. Andrew was born on June 7, 1977, and George was born on December 28, 1978. Her husband was a commercial painter and did sand blasting. She describes him as a "jerk" because he drank heavily, and she considered him an alcoholic. From her recollection, "I was young and thought that love would conquer all. I learned that lesson quite young too." She was married to Mark Kruger for 15 years. One day, she came home unexpectedly from work, and saw him beating her youngest son. She recalls, "I left the next week and left him everything. I moved into town and then I was trying to support my kids, because he would not help me."

It was at this time that she decided to try to go to college. Because she worked and she went to school, it took her a long time to finish. In fact, her older son finished school before she did. She attended the University of Minnesota in Duluth and got a Bachelor of Arts in Engineering in 2000. She says, "It took a long time, but it led to the best event I have ever had in my life. The department knew how hard a struggle it was. When I crossed the stage and got my diploma, about eight of my professors stood up and shook my hand." Altogether it took more than six years for her to get her degree.

After obtaining her degree, she had a "wonderful job" working in engineering research with the university. By that time, her boys were raised and pretty much on their own. She felt that she needed to find a place to live where it was a little warmer than northern Minnesota. She really had no idea where she wanted to live but checked out Alaska, Canada, and Nevada. She was hired by a highway building company in Winnemuka, Minnesota, but took time off to come to New Mexico to visit friends in Santa Fe. On the basis of that visit, she recalls, "I gave my notice, threw my clothes and vacuum cleaner into my truck and I came down and started all over again." She moved to Espanola, New Mexico, in 2001 and put in applications for about 20 jobs. She worked at temporary jobs for a while, but really wanted to work for the state. She sold cars for a short time, but found that sales did not really suit her. After submitting many applications for state employment, she was offered an Engineering Tech II job for the State Department of Highways. The job required her to do stress analyses for highway material in a lab. She worked in that job for three years until she had an opportunity to get a job in her field, civil engineering.

DAY BEFORE ANALYSIS

Ms. Kruger recalls that she began working as a highway engineer in April 2003. Before then, she reports that she had no psychological or psychiatric treatment. She reports that over the course of her adult life, she has never been the recipient of any kind of interpersonal violence and has never been raped or assaulted. She had never been the recipient of medications for sleep or depression. She had an auto accident prior to 2003 when her vehicle was stopped at a stoplight and she was struck from behind. She had no serious or continuing problems from this accident. She had another auto accident in Santa Fe when she was stopped a red light. As a result of this accident, she developed whiplash and underwent some months of physical therapy and

recovered from that condition and suffered no continuing pain or disability from it.

She reports that since her marriage dissolved, she occasionally dated. She enjoyed dating men and going out, although the longest she went out with any one man was only several months, because she had difficulty finding a man who matched her very well. She also spends time with her female friends. She was part of two book groups that met on a monthly basis. She also occasionally went out with her friends for a movie and dinner. She enjoyed inviting people over to her house for meals, and sometimes found herself up late at night in conversation.

She reports that in prior jobs, she was never fired, nor was she ever asked to quit. She says she had never filed any sort of complaint against her co-workers or supervisors in prior positions.

MS. KRUGER'S ACCOUNT OF ON THE JOB EVENTS

When she began work as a highway engineer, Ms. Kruger found that her duties included supervising bridge design and inspection. She supervised highway equipment operators as part of a crew of two or three individuals. Her immediate supervisor was Arnold Miller. She recalls that in her first meeting with him, he said "Women have difficulty working on the road, can't live out of a truck, and they whine when they break a fingernail." Mr. Miller does not share that recollection. She recalls that he was her supervisor for a three-year period.

Ms. Kruger began working in the field and spent a good deal of her time going to sites where contractors for the state were building a bridge or an overpass. She and the crew inspected the ongoing operation, and it was her job to document details of construction to determine if those matched the blueprints provided by the contractor. This was strenuous work, as it required scaling and crawling through bridge structures, and evaluating welded seams, as well as taking core samples of concrete in the structure.

She reports that when she first went to work for this division, one of her supervisors, Jimmie Hernandez, took her out for about two weeks of training, which involved four days of bridge inspection. She recalls that after this training, "whenever Mr. Hernandez showed up on the job, he would just insult me. He would say rude things." He would imply she did not know what she was doing, or she was not fast enough. She recalls, "I was doing a hell of a good job. All my workers would tell you that. It was a male-dominated job. I totally believe that some women seek a male-dominated job who cannot handle it. I also accepted that a woman in a male-dominated position was required to work ten times harder to get the same recognition." It is Ms. Kruger's recollection that early in her tenure on the job, in spite of the fact that she was trained as an engineer, she was the only woman working in her unit and was required to clean the women's bathroom at her offices.

From Ms. Kruger's perspective, her working conditions became progressively more difficult. "They start alienating me. I was not told about meetings that were essential to my job. Usually, Monday mornings you found out where your assignments were. When they decided what the hardest job was to be, they would come out of the meeting and give us the assignment. I would be ridiculed on my evaluations because I was not associating with the management." She asked about why she was not included in the meetings, but she could never get an explanation. Eventually, she went to Mr. Gonzales, who is above Arnold Miller on the chain of command, to tell him what was happening. As time progressed, they were giving her less and less information about her jobs, and she felt like this was "so they could eventually attack me for it." Even after she complained in writing, she was only sporadically included in planning meetings.

After that, she recalls, things got even worse. It was her view that she and her crew were being placed on all the worst jobs. She accepted this because "I was going to show them that I could do it, and meet any challenges they were going to give me. I got respect from my crew because I worked hard."

As time went on, Ms. Kruger felt like "they were setting me up to fail because I was a woman. Like women don't belong here." She felt that her supervisors started making it hard on the men she supervised, and she eventually lost three of the men who worked for her because they were getting so "stressed out." These men, who she recalls were reliable workers and her supporters, were replaced with "troublemakers."

By 2009, she recalls, "They were making it pretty brutal for me. I complained. All I wanted was a little respect. They would attack me for everything. I would hang in there and do a heck of a good thing. I would hang in there and do a heck of a good job." It was her perspective that to add insult to injury someone had written the phrase "f*** you b****" on a bulletin board near her office. A few days later, she found a big tie down, which is structured like a screw, on the bumper of her vehicle. She was asked what that indicated to her and she said, "Screw you." Ms. Kruger says she continued to feel unsafe. She started looking around for the first opening she could find to get out of there.

Ms. Kruger filed a lawsuit for discrimination and reprisal in April 2010. Immediately following that filing, she recalls, "I felt forced to get out of that situation. I took a civil engineering tech job [which was in another division of the state government], desperate to get out." Ironically, her new office was right next door to her former workplace. In her new position, she worked with a supervisor, Michael Vigil. The third-level supervisor above her was still John Tennyson, who had been her third-level supervisor in her prior position as an engineer.

Her current duties involve reviewing plans and blueprints to determine if they meet state regulations. This job demands some of her skills as an engineer, but does not require her to go into the field. When asked about this new position, she says, "I hate the job, but I like the people I work with." However, Ms. Kruger is frustrated because she finds that her duties do not call upon her training and skills as a field engineer.

ANALYSIS OF REACTIONS AND ALTERNATIVE CAUSES DURING THE ALLEGED RETALIATION

Claimant's Description of Reactions

Ms. Kruger says that when the alleged retaliation began, "I took it in stride. I didn't expect a walk in the park, being a girl engineer." When she was first excluded from planning meetings, she started becoming more anxious. She indicates that she had difficulty getting to sleep and often lay awake for two or three hours before she could sleep. She noted that she was eating compulsively to manage her increased anxiety. She observed that she was more anxious when she was back at her home base, in part because it meant being exposed to the men who she believed were trying to hound her out of her job.

She claims she gained about 30 pounds over a one-year interval, which was the most weight she had ever gained over that period of time. However, when questioned in more detail, she indicates that her diet changed during that period because she was on the road and could not cook for herself. Prior to that time, she had managed her weight by controlling what she ate for lunch and dinner. In the field, she started eating more fast food, and her crew inevitably knew the best New Mexican food restaurants in each town.

After she started losing her best men due to what she saw as supervisory interference and reprisal, she started becoming more depressed. She found she tended to cry over little things, and was sad much of the time. She developed more severe sleep problems characterized by early awakening, and difficulty returning to sleep. She reports that during this time she had increasing difficulty getting going in the morning. She had increasing difficulty concentrating on the bookkeeping aspects of her job, especially filling out the time slips and requests for her men, which began to result in problems for them in the form of late paychecks. These problems drew complaints from both her men and supervisors.

Other Sources of Causation

Discussions with Ms. Kruger's supervisors and a review of her personnel file indicate that the quality of her work aroused concern not long after she took over the field crew. No one doubted her technical expertise, and even her harshest critic had to admit that she was very good at determining what needed to be done and directing her men to do it. However, from the onset of that placement, she had difficulty with the paperwork demanded by the job. In her role as field crew leader, she had to fill out requests for materials, equipment, and for specialized assistance. In all these areas, she sometimes forgot to request one or two essential things, which resulted in delays for her crew. In addition, she had difficulty with the personnel administration part of her job, and sometimes did not get her payroll paperwork in on time. In a practical sense, no one else could fill out those forms, and when she failed to complete them, her men were paid late, or got short paychecks because she failed to accurately record the hours that they actually worked.

Concerns about these failures and problems were the topic of a number of the conversations that her supervisors had with her. At first she responded to what her supervisors viewed as serious complaints with appropriate reactions. However, as time went on, she began to attribute their complaints to "retaliation." Her supervisors claim that they made similar interventions with similarly situated male supervisors who had similar problems. When asked about her supervisor's account of the on-the-job problems, Ms. Kruger admits that she did have some difficulty, but the problems were minor and "they blew them out of proportion just to get to me."

In reviewing other sources of causation, Ms. Kruger's relationship status remained the same over this interval; if anything, she dated less than before she took this position. The frequency of contacts with her friends and with eligible males was reduced by her frequent trips out of town, and feeling tired when she was home on weekends. Her financial situation actually improved because she was getting per-diem allowances and was able to save most of her salary, enough to purchase a new car.

Events Which Followed the Alleged Retaliation
Plaintiff's Complaints

After Ms. Kruger moved to her new position, she was still quite fearful of what she viewed as continuing retaliation. Some of these fears diminished after she left her former position, and she got along well with her new supervisors. However, she reports, during this interval she continued to struggle with depression. Her sleep disturbance continued, and she continued to gain weight, putting on an additional 30 pounds. She tried to change her eating habits after she left the former position. She recalls, "I don't eat much during the day. I am up all night. I take a catnap. I will wake up after an hour or so and I will eat ice cream. I will make cake batter and have it in my bed. I will eat cake batter just to appease that urge." She reports that she is not engaged in any purging in relation to these binge episodes, nor does she engage in excessive exercise. She says, "No, I am too tired all the time to exercise."

When asked about symptoms related to depression, she reports that she feels depressed day in and day out. She says, "I try not to make it so much that way. I know what it is to feel truly happy and optimistic, and I am not there." She feels like she has been depressed like this since about 2005.

Sources of Alternative Causation

In the three-year interval between when Ms. Kruger left her former position and when she was evaluated, she has been stable in the same position.

Her financial situation has been stable, as is her intimate relationship status. She has had no severe accidents, and has developed no new medical problems. Her extended family has been well and undemanding, and she has had no change in residence.

Her current supervisors and vocational records indicate that she has had few problems in the new position. She has done well with the paperwork, and she gets along well with her supervisors and co-workers.

Plaintiff's Current Status

Ms. Kruger describes the following sleep habits. She says she goes to bed at 7:00 p.m., watches a little TV and tries to get tired. She says, "I will sleep an hour or an hour and one-half, then I will wake up. Sometimes I cannot sleep at all."

Ms. Kruger recalls that she has markedly diminished interest in many activities almost every day. She says, "I don't even enjoy eating anymore." Although she used to enjoy hiking, getting together with friends, going to plays and to museums, she stopped doing these things about five or six years ago. She spends much of her time playing computer games, which involve hand–eye coordination. She reports she does not read too much anymore, because it requires too much effort. She says, "I am turning into a very dull person."

She reports she has pretty well cut herself off socially. She felt like it was very hard to be sociable when she didn't feel good about herself. She reports that she started feeling bad about herself probably in the year 2007 (about when the retaliatory activity is alleged to have started). This was in response to receiving poor work evaluations. As she recalls, "I took such pride in my job, and they were starting to get really hard on me."

She gets home about 6:00 p.m. and is usually in bed by 7:00. She normally gets up at 5:30 a.m. She feels that she may be sleeping too much, but that she does not have much energy in the course of a day. She says, "I just endure. I just get through."

When asked about her feelings about herself, she says, "I have no self esteem left. I don't feel like I am capable of doing anything right anymore. Before, I could tackle the world. I still enjoy people. They still have not killed that part of it. As far as my life goes, they have destroyed it."

She had aspired to working her way up in the engineering section because that is what she loved to do. Now, she says, "I just kind of find myself lost. I am not sure where I belong anymore." Even now, she feels that she avoids making decisions, and she attributes this difficulty to being "shell shocked" by her former work situation. She reports some preoccupation with ideas about death. She has considered taking pills as a way of committing suicide. She never hoarded pills as a way of developing a "suicide stash." In the current evaluation, she indicates that she currently does not consider suicide as a "solution to my problems."

She reports that she experiences chest pains "all the time." She has been to see a doctor about the chest pains, but her EKG proved normal. She has not received any medications for the chest pains. She is currently going in for stress treatments with an acupuncturist.

She reports a number of frankly paranoid symptoms. She believes she is being followed, but not all the time. She says, "Although I have not seen them [her former supervisors], I am thinking it is very possible that they are following me, but hiding themselves well." She was asked if there were people who wanted to hurt her physically. She said, "I don't know, I think they want to hurt me physically. Some of these people carry guns." She has gone through her house and taken pictures of everything in case someone tries to burn it down. She owns a gun, but states that she is afraid to use it.

The plaintiff reported that she has recently sought out a counselor, Ms. Susan Stockman. She said she had problems with memory loss and thought it would be good to find someone to talk to. She started working with this licensed counselor some two or three months prior to this evaluation.

PSYCHOLOGICAL ASSESSMENT

Cognitive Assessment

A battery of cognitive and personality assessment measures was administered to Ms. Kruger. My testing assistant, Ms. Bonnie Freeman, conducted the cognitive assessment. The battery given to Ms. Kruger produced scales that would allow comparisons between Ms. Kruger's various skills and also comparisons between her skills and those measured in the general population. Ms. Kruger showed no evidence of attempting to do more poorly on these measures than she could actually do. On the Wechsler Adult Intelligence Scale–IV, she received a Verbal Comprehension score of 108, which places her at the 70th percentile. Her Perceptual

Reasoning scaled score is 99, which places her at the 47th percentile compared to individuals in her same age group. Her Working Memory is significantly above average and at a level consistent with her verbal IQ. Her Processing Speed, however, is somewhat lower with the score at an IQ equivalent of about 93. Her Processing Speed scores were significantly lower than her Verbal Comprehension scores and her Working Memory scores. This suggests that overall her ability to deal with the things that require cognitive speed is somewhat slower than might be expected. This may be reflective of psychomotor retardation attendant to depressive illness.

The Wechsler Memory Scale–IV indicates that overall her memory skills are average or above average and show no serious deficits that could be attributable to depression or any other psychological process. Her General and Working Memory scores are, in fact, higher than might be expected based upon her overall IQ.

The WRAT-4 indicates that her reading, writing, and arithmetic skills were all at a level consistent with her overall IQ and reflects well-developed skills in those areas. Her ability to deal with a task requiring active sequencing and flexibility proved to be significantly above average.

Personality Assessment

The personality assessment was conducted using three instruments. The first of those, the Minnesota Multiphasic Personality Inventory–2, proved to be valid. There was no evidence of an attempt on her part to either exaggerate or minimize her emotional difficulties. Ms. Kruger produced a generally elevated profile on this measure. She also showed evidence of depression primarily related to demoralization, and she also showed problems sometimes seen individuals who experienced emotional distress through physical complaints. Overall, this pattern would be one of an individual who is experiencing moderate emotional distress characterized by brooding, resentment, negativism, and an inability to experience satisfaction or pleasure from day-to-day activities. This is a pattern of a person who is irritable, grouchy, stubborn, and often feels angry and is prone to express that anger directly. She experiences her emotions in a very sensitive fashion and more intensely than other people do. This is a pattern of an individual who finds it hard to get going and does not have a lot of hope for her

future. She is like people who find it hard to concentrate, and she feels as though her judgment is not as good as it might have been in the past. Overall, the plaintiff shows a pattern of somatic concerns and depression.

The Personality Assessment Inventory yielded a pattern very similar to that produced in the MMPI-2. This measure also ruled out malingering. On this scale, depression appears to be the most significant component. Ms. Kruger also shows elements of anxiety, somatic concerns, and suspiciousness. On these scales, she reported a level of depression that is unusual even in clinical samples. She reports feeling severely depressed, discouraged, and withdrawn in a pattern not inconsistent with that of a major depressive episode. She also reported experiencing some level of anxiety and tension, which is primarily manifested in physiological or somatic symptoms. She has substantial concerns about physical functioning and health matters. On this scale, it was noted that she feels she is being treated inequitably and believes that there is a concerted effort among others to undermine her interests. Overall, this is a pattern consistent with a post-traumatic stress disorder or major depressive disorder.

SUMMARY AND CONCLUSIONS

Psychological evaluation of Ms. Patricia Kruger was conducted to determine the presence, if any, of emotional problems and disorders that may be related to her experience of working with the New Mexico Department of Highways. In this case, several aspects of her behavior bear initial consideration. First, it is clearly evident that she is experiencing a serious depressive disorder. This is evident not only in her psychological test data—it appeared in both of the measures given to her—but also in the course of symptoms provided by her in the clinical interview. In both of these contexts she currently appears to be experiencing a major depressive disorder characterized by vegetative and cognitive symptoms. All measures of malingering and exaggeration yielded normal results, which indicates that the test data are a valid representation of her current functioning.

Causation

On the basis of the analysis, it is clear that Ms. Kruger developed this depressive disorder during the course of her employment with the Engineering Division. The data indicate that she had high expectations concerning this job, which was the culmination of years of college and hard work. But when she got into the job, the court has already determined that the deliberate actions of her supervisors in controlling the conditions of her employment made the job much more difficult than it was for men working doing the same job. Then, when she complained about what was going on, she claims that the supervisors, or their subordinates, harassed her and made her fearful for her own safety. In reaction to these disappointments and stressors, Ms. Kruger developed a worsening depression that had anxiety components. Eventually, she started to see the world as a more hostile and dangerous place, which caused even more social isolation and loss of previously enjoyable activities. She gained weight, developed an early-awakening sleep disorder, and began to think poorly of herself.

A review of the employment records indicates that the accounting problems did not occur early in her tenure as a supervisor, but appeared after she says the adverse job actions by her supervisors were begun. A review of the documentation of and reports from supervisors about these problems indicates that, while present, they were not serious. A discussion with one of her subordinates indicates that the reported paycheck problems were not that unusual, and many of the workers had experienced similar problems with other supervisors.

The development of a depressive reaction to the losses and stressors that Ms. Kruger experienced would be a reasonable reaction to the changes she experienced. That these problems continued after she left that position would be predictable because she developed a depressive illness, which did not respond to her changed circumstances. A review of all the data does not indicate a reasonable alternative explanation for the development of this illness, as she lacked any prior history of affective disorder, and had no significant family history supportive of a genetic explanation. In addition, the balance of her life did not show any serious losses or emotional setbacks that would give rise to reactive depression.

Analysis of Damages

If the finder of fact determines that the actions of Ms. Kruger's supervisors were appropriate reactions to her performance, then this analysis would apply: Her depression may be due to her perception that she failed in a highly valued part of her life, one for which she had worked many years to prepare herself. Her perspective that this was all part of a plot against her may have been a way of saving face, and accounting for her failure without her being at fault. This construction would have reasonably caused her to become more suspicious of her supervisors' actions, and to perceive them as more prejudicial than they were. Over time, this pattern of attribution could have resulted in her becoming markedly paranoid, assuming that many benign people were out to get her, and that her problems with the New Mexico Department of Highways were not her fault but the fault of those who sought to harm her.

If the finder of fact determines that Ms. Kruger was in fact the recipient of retaliation, then the following analysis of damages would apply: Ms. Kruger entered this situation as a normal individual. Over time, being the target of her supervisors' repeated negative actions ground her down and caused her to lose self-respect. This, in turn, led to a chronic depression characterized by vegetative and cognitive symptoms. The evaluation shows no evidence that she was exaggerating her problems or malingering in any way.

In addition, many of the incidents that occurred on the job that she experienced, particularly the disruptive subordinates who were assigned to her, made her feel as though her workplace was unsafe, and caused her to have fears concerning her personal safety. She has been afraid, for what she feels are good reasons, of being the victim of some sort of physical harm from her former supervisors. This causes her to be on alert for potentially harmful events and to be constantly fearful of injury or harm. In this context, the evidence of her paranoid thinking would follow the maxim "You are not paranoid if they are really out to get you." In other words, she is fearful because people, presumably her former supervisors, have done what they could to make her afraid. Even though the origins of her fearfulness may be valid, the persistence of these reactions is the result of a developing paranoid reaction. While she is not delusional, this reaction is more akin to post-traumatic hypervigilance. However, her suspiciousness has led to serious social isolation.

Her depression persists, although it is unclear why she should still be depressed, since she is now out of the unfavorable job situation. One hypothesis is that Ms. Kruger essentially had all her self-esteem "eggs in one basket": that is, her work. By any metric, she spent most of her time in some sort of work. In addition to a 40-hour-plus workweek for the State of New Mexico, she worked many evenings in other jobs. This left little time for the development of extra-work friendships, hobbies, church or temple attendance, or other connections that form the stuff of a stable, satisfying life. When her job situation changed, and she was no longer in a position in which she wanted to work, she lost all the sources of things valuable to her, and depression would be a natural consequence.

FUNCTIONAL ASSESSMENT
Activities of Daily Living
On the basis of available data, Ms. Kruger is suffering from ongoing depression, which has not yet responded well to treatment. Her self-esteem is diminished relative to how she felt about herself before the incidents on the job. Her depression reduces her energy level, interferes with her initiating new tasks, stifles her optimism, and saps her of pleasure in even the most mundane life activities, including cooking and dining. She has even given up reading. She has a sleep disorder, which leaves her tired much of the time. She has lost her ability to relate to others outside of the most familiar circumstances. Her ability to trust others has diminished from previous levels. Although she had some intimate relationships before these events, she has been unable to place herself in a position to meet men or to date. Her out-of-work activities have diminished, and she does very little other than work. She has become frankly paranoid, and is concerned about her personal safety.

Work-Related Activities
Her work-related activities appear to have been less affected than her personal life. She has thrown herself into her work, and by all reports she is able to function in that position well. However, this position does not satisfy her because it does not fully utilize her skills and education, so that she feels frustrated much of the time. Also, she enjoyed working in the field, and the loss of "hands-on" activities has bothered her.

The cognitive testing pattern suggests that she would have difficulty working quickly. She validates this concern by stating that it takes her longer to get things done in her current job. Paperwork is especially tedious to her and takes her a long time to complete.

Other Life Activities
On the basis of the analysis of her Activities of Daily Living, it is evident that Ms. Kruger does not get much pleasure from her life. Previously enjoyed activities, such as reading, have been abandoned. Her social life has diminished significantly. Overall, her quality of life is less than it was before she went to work for the New Mexico Department of Highways.

RECOMMENDATIONS AND PROGNOSIS
Ms. Kruger is in need of comprehensive treatment for her depression and paranoia. In both cases, cognitive behavior therapy would be efficacious. In addition, she may benefit from a psychiatric assessment that would provide antidepressant medication. She may also benefit from medication focused upon reducing her agitation related to her paranoid thinking. On the basis of her current status, she should receive at least three years of both treatments, which would cost approximately $18,000 total at current fee levels. Although cognitive behavior therapy is a relatively short-term treatment model, it is likely that one of the goals of her work would be to assist her in changing jobs to a position that is more gratifying. Because of the unfortunate events that occurred in the current case, she is likely to have more difficulty beginning and adapting to a new job situation. Extending the treatment to cover this transition process can ease that change.

With proper treatment, it is likely that Ms. Kruger's depression will improve. This should result in an improvement in her activities of daily living and other life areas. Her work performance should also improve with decreased depression. However, her ability to reestablish her ability to trust others, especially in the workplace and in her personal life, may be permanently impaired. It is my experience that individuals who have been caused to distrust their own perceptions often have difficulty trusting others as well. It is my perspective that she will always have difficulty establishing new relationships and functioning effectively in situations requiring close cooperation with others.

Respectfully submitted,
Walter M. Samuels, Ph.D.

TEACHING POINT:
COMMUNICATING FIRMLY
BUT FAIRLY

When retained as evaluators, forensic mental health professionals should strive to be impartial assessors who assist attorneys or legal decision-makers in making better-informed decisions. An important aspect of the forensic evaluator's role—indeed the culmination of the evaluator's work in a particular case—is communicating the results of the evaluation in (typically) a written report and (occasionally) in courtroom testimony. Therefore, evaluators must take great care in terms of *how* they present the results of their work.

There are various aspects to effective communication in forensic contexts, and this teaching point focuses on communicating the results of the evaluation in a firm but fair manner. In a written report, communicating firmly but fairly means that the evaluator should present information, including opinions and conclusions, using clear language that accurately reflects the data and effectively captures the evaluator's reasoning and conclusions. The "firm" aspect of communicating evaluation results means that the evaluator should be clear about his or her opinions and present those opinions with as little ambiguity as possible, and the "fair" aspect means that the evaluator should use circumscribed and cautious language when appropriate, recognize limitations in the data, and address alternative explanations.

The same ideas discussed in relation to written reports apply in the context of courtroom testimony, but the often unpredictable nature of testimony calls for additional considerations. One aspect of communicating evaluation results firmly and fairly in the context of testimony is avoiding "waffling" (see Brodsky, 2013). Waffling occurs when experts discuss topics about which they have incomplete knowledge, or when they give conflicting and contradictory answers (typically during cross-examination). Evaluators should offer testimony about their findings that reflects what is contained the report, which is presumably accurate,

and do so in a manner that reflects their level of confidence in the findings. A related point—relevant to the "fair" aspect of communicating firmly but fairly—is not being afraid to say "I don't know," assuming that there is no reasonable expectation that the evaluator should know the answer. Saying "I don't know" is one way for experts to acknowledge the limitations of the evaluation data and the limits of their knowledge, and it can function to make experts appear more credible in the eyes of the court.

TEACHING POINT:
THE VALUE OF SEQUENTIAL
COMMUNICATION OF FMHA
RESULTS

Previous principles and teaching points in this book have addressed the value of using a model to guide data gathering, interpretation, and communication, and the benefits of writing forensic reports in sections. Among other benefits, using a model and writing a report in sections can help evaluators structure the evaluation data and communicate the findings (opinions, reasoning, conclusions) in a clear and accessible manner.

An important aspect of writing a report in sections is determining the order in which information is presented. As noted previously, the professional literature indicates that, at a minimum, the following areas should be addressed in the FMHA report: (1) circumstances of the referral; (2) date and nature of clinical contacts; (3) collateral data sources; (4) relevant personal background information; (5) clinical findings; and (6) psychological-legal formulation (Melton et al., 2007; Rogers & Shuman, 2000). Presenting the information in this order makes conceptual sense; it would be illogical, for example, to present the psycho-legal formulation before presenting the clinical findings and referral question. Moreover, presenting the information in this order reflects the evaluation process and helps readers follow the evaluator's thinking.

15

Workplace Disability

This chapter will focus on two reports concerning FMHA in the context of workplace disability. The determination of disability in the workplace is a common question within the civil legal context, and may include assertions of psychological injury and resulting damages by the plaintiff that are evaluated through FMHA. The principle applied to the first case concerns assessing legally relevant behavior, and how this information can be used to aid the court in accurate decision-making. The teaching point in the first case will highlight the importance of translating legal criteria into forensic capacities, specifically the relationship between symptoms and disability in capacity to work. The principle for the second case relates to the importance of assessing clinical characteristics—symptoms of disorders of mental, emotional, or cognitive functioning that are recognized in an authoritative source such as the DSM-5 (American Psychiatric Association, 2013a)—in ways that are reliable and valid. The teaching point will address useful approaches to assessing clinical characteristics in FMHA.

CASE ONE
PRINCIPLE: ASSESS LEGALLY RELEVANT BEHAVIOR (*PRINCIPLE 21*)

This principle addresses the importance of gathering information that is directly related to the forensic issues, and more generally relevant to the legal question being addressed by the court. A forensic assessment must obtain information that clearly describes capacities relevant to the forensic issues being assessed (Grisso, 2003). Depending on the nature of the forensic issues and the functioning of the individual being evaluated, information regarding the capacities in question can be obtained from a variety of sources, including clinical interviews, psychological testing, specialized measures, behavioral observation, self-report, collateral interviews, and collateral document review.

Data from these sources are particularly applicable to relevant legal behavior under certain conditions. First, when such data pertain directly to the relevant functional legal capacities, they are more applicable than broader diagnostic or treatment-planning data. Relevant legal behavior in a case involving potential disability in the workplace, for example, would be considerably different from relevant legal behavior when the legal question is guardianship. Second, this kind of approach has the additional advantage of excluding data that are clearly irrelevant to the legal capacities being assessed. Third, a focus on the relevant legal issues allows the evaluator to use both observable behavior and inferred capacities, and to relate each to the forensic issues through reasoning that is explicitly described in the report. Finally, gathering data on legally relevant behavior and capacities contributes to the accuracy and credibility of the evaluation by providing information to the legal decision maker in a manner that is easy to understand and directly applicable to the legal questions.

FMHA should provide data and reasoning that are directly relevant to forensic capacities and also relevant to the legal question. However, the evaluator should remain aware of the distinction between the decision-making role of the court and the informing/recommending functions of the forensic clinician, so that the communication in the report or testimony is not intrusive (see Grisso, 2003). Sufficient data should also be gathered in a way that promotes confidence in its accuracy to yield conclusions that seem reasonable and well-supported.

This principle is only indirectly supported by the *Ethical Principles of Psychologists and Code of Conduct* (APA *Ethics Code*; see Standards 2.04, 9.01, and 9.02; American Psychological Association, 2010a) and the *Ethics Guidelines for the Practice of Forensic Psychiatry* (AAPL *Ethics Guidelines*; Guideline IV; American Academy of Psychiatry and the Law, 2005). The *Specialty Guidelines for Forensic Psychology* (APA *Specialty Guidelines*; American Psychological Association, 2013b) provides more direct support for this principle by emphasizing that forensic practitioners be knowledgeable about the legal system and sources of legal authority (Guideline 2.04), and that they focus on legally relevant factors throughout their evaluation:

> Forensic examiners seek to assist the trier of fact to understand evidence or determine a fact in issue, and they provide information that is most relevant to the psycholegal issue. In reports and testimony, forensic practitioners typically provide information about examinees' functional abilities, capacities, knowledge, and beliefs, and address their opinions and recommendations to the identified psycholegal issues. (Guideline 10.01)

Support for this principle in the legal literature comes from an emphasis on providing expert opinions only after obtaining sufficient information and conducting a thorough evaluation, and for applying the data gathered during this evaluation directly to the facts of the case (*Daubert v. Merrell Dow Pharmaceuticals, Inc.*, 1993; FRE 702; *Kumho Tire Co. v. Carmichael*, 1999). Finally, the professional literature establishes the assessment of legally relevant behavior as a cornerstone of quality FMHA (Heilbrun, Grisso, & Goldstein, 2009; Melton, Petrila, Poythress, & Slobogin, 2007; Packer & Grisso, 2011).

In the present case, the disability-related question is the capacity to work. Mr. Atwell was referred for an independent psychological evaluation (a form of "independent medical evaluation" [IME] sometimes requested by insurance carriers regarding the work capacity of an insured individual). A thorough discussion of the parameters of this kind of evaluation, including relevant law, science, and practice, has recently been provided (Piechowski, 2011).

The evaluation's major purposes are summarized by Dr. Piechowski in the present report in the following manner: "to determine his functional psychological abilities and limitations, the effect any psychologically related impairments have on his work capacity, the nature and efficacy of his treatment, his prognosis, and whether lack of motivation or secondary gain play a role in his prospects for returning to work." In her evaluation of Mr. Atwell's present capacity to work, Dr. Piechowski focuses most directly on his symptoms and their relationship with such capacities, his response to the mental health treatment he is receiving, and whether his presentation involves distorting the nature and severity of his symptoms and incapacities. She does this in several ways.

First, she observes Mr. Atwell carefully throughout the evaluation. Such evaluations involve a demand for sustained attention/concentration over a four-hour period or longer. This alone provides valuable information. To what extent does Mr. Atwell display the patience, focus, and motivation to allow him to answer questions of various kinds over this period of time? To the extent that these demands are comparable in nature and scope to what an individual might do in a typical day at work, the evaluation provides the opportunity to sample the individual's behavior that is relevant to his work capacity.

Next, she administers psychological testing to appraise his cognitive functioning, attention/concentration, symptoms, and response style. Interpreting the results of testing in conjunction with the behavioral observations provided the important observation that Mr. Atwell presented himself, via psychological testing, as far more impaired than he appeared on observation and through direct questioning.

In addition, she obtains a multisourced history through self-report, document review, and collateral interviews. Of particular interest are Mr. Atwell's history of vocational and mental health functioning, as well as the onset of his disability. Her interview with Mr. Atwell includes his account of changes in his functioning, his current daily activities, and his current symptoms. Ultimately, she is led to conclude that Mr. Atwell's self-report describes much poorer functioning than behavioral observation and history would suggest, that this discrepancy has been observed in other IME evaluations, and it is therefore not possible to provide a meaningful answer to questions concerning his genuine present capacities.

This conclusion may create some frustration for any reader seeking an accurate and meaningful appraisal of Mr. Atwell's present functioning and capacities in these areas. Ultimately, however, it is more valuable than anything else that Dr. Piechowski might conclude. She does not go beyond her data. She does not succumb to the temptation to conclude that because someone is inaccurately reporting symptoms and deficits, no such symptoms or deficits exist. Rather, she points out that symptoms, deficits, inaccurate reports, and complex motivation may co-occur—and makes recommendations about obtaining further information that would bring the company closer to an accurate appraisal of Mr. Atwell's capacity to work at present and in the future.

Lisa Drago Piechowski, Ph.D., ABPP
Clinical and Forensic Psychology
Diplomate in Forensic Psychology
American Board of Professional Psychology
155 Sycamore Street
Glastonbury, CT O6033
Phone (860) 659-0732
Fax (860) 659-3713
lpiechphd@gmail.com
Licensed Psychologist in Connecticut,
Massachusetts, New York, and New Jersey

INDEPENDENT PSYCHOLOGICAL EVALUATION

Claimant: Steven Atwell
Policy Number: 55555555
Referred by: New England National
Date of Disability: 5/5/2010
Date of Evaluation: 6/3/2011
Date of Birth: 11/8/1951

REFERRAL

Steven Atwell is a 59-year-old man who was referred for an independent psychological evaluation by Jane Smith of New England National Insurance Company. Mr. Atwell claims to have been disabled since May, 2010, with diagnoses of major depressive disorder and panic attacks. The purpose of this evaluation was to determine his functional psychological abilities and limitations, the effect any psychologically related impairments have on his work capacity, the nature and efficacy of his treatment, his prognosis, and whether lack of motivation or secondary gain play a role in his prospects for returning to work.

Prior to beginning the evaluation, Mr. Atwell was informed of the nature and purpose of this

evaluation and the limits of confidentiality. Specifically, he was informed that the evaluation would consist of a clinical interview, psychological testing, and information from collateral sources. He was informed that I would be creating a written report summarizing the findings of my evaluation that would be forwarded to New England National, and that I did not have the authority to give him feedback, written or oral, about my findings. He was notified that my role was that of an independent examiner and that ultimate determinations regarding his disability benefits would be made by New England National. He was informed that no doctor–patient relationship would be established by this evaluation, and that no treatment would be offered to him. It was explained that his participation was voluntary, but that any failure to participate in or cooperate with this evaluation would be communicated to New England National. Mr. Atwell was given the opportunity to ask any questions he had about the circumstances of the evaluation. He indicated that he understood this information and was willing to participate in the evaluation. He signed a detailed consent form confirming this.

SOURCES OF INFORMATION
- Clinical interview (3.25 hours)
- Psychological testing (3.75 hours):
  - Minnesota Multiphasic Personality Inventory II (MMPI-2)
  - Repeatable Battery for the Assessment of Neuropsychological Status (RBANS)
  - Validity Indicator Profile (VIP)
- Review of records:
  - Claim forms
  - Treatment summary by Alfred French, EdD
  - List of treatment dates by Thomas Holmes, PhD
  - Medical records of Dennis Brockton, MD
  - Medical records of Alex Williams, MD
  - Report of Independent Medical Evaluation by Eric Stewart, PhD, ABPP
- Collateral interview: Alfred French, EdD

INFORMATION OBTAINED FROM RECORDS

History of Disability Claim

Mr. Atwell submitted a claim for disability benefits on July 12, 2010. He listed his occupation as owner of a stationery store, "Atwell's Stationery." Work duties are listed as "book work" and "floor work." He reported he had been

> having trouble with my mental functioning…for years. I can now hardly function with my important duties of my job. I have to often return to my office and sit quietly. I have intense panic attacks at least once a day.…I suffer from chronic depression and dispare [sic].…I have morbid thought and suffer from sleep disturbance. I am always very tired. I have loss of appetite and a great deal of difficulty concentrating on any details with my business.…I have a hard time relating to people.

The Attending Physician's Initial Report was completed by Dr. French. Restrictions and limitations are described as "Cannot concentrate or organize his thoughts. Lack of energy—therefore cannot function at work." According to Dr. French, Mr. Atwell was "nonfunctioning" as of the end of December 2009.

Treatment History

Thomas Holmes, PhD

Dr. Holmes, a psychologist, provided a list of treatment dates indicating he treated Mr. Atwell from October 2002 through March 2006 for a total of 64 sessions of individual psychotherapy. Mr. Atwell's diagnosis is listed as 309.24 (Adjustment Disorder with Anxiety).

Alfred French, EdD

Dr. French, a psychologist, first treated Mr. Atwell in July 2007. The diagnosis was listed as 309.24 (Adjustment Disorder with Anxiety). Over the next nine months, Dr. French saw Mr. Atwell 40 times. His presenting problem was anxiety related to marital discord. Mr. Atwell was seen alone and with his wife. Apparently little progress was made in addressing the marital problems, but Mr. Atwell terminated treatment in April 2008, reporting he was feeling better.

Mr. Atwell returned to treatment in October 2008. He reported he was unable to cope, was having trouble concentrating, and was suffering from insomnia. Marital problems were reported to be worse. The diagnosis continued to be listed as 309.24. Mr. Atwell was seen for 32 sessions over

a fourteen-month period. Marital therapy was attempted again. It was noted that he "became more and more anxious around the house. He was worried that his children would reject him because his wife was so critical. He found that he constantly worried about these things and that they had interfered with his ability to function in his business." Mr. Atwell also complained of shortness of breath, various physical symptoms, having trouble making decisions, and having "morbid thoughts." He was described as having made minimal progress. He terminated treatment against Dr. French's advice in December 2009.

Mr. Atwell returned to treatment on May 19, 2010, complaining of feeling overwhelmed and depressed. The diagnosis was changed to 296.23 (Major Depressive Episode, single episode, severe). "His anxiety at work had interfered to the point where he felt he could no longer function." He was described as suffering debilitating panic attacks. Marital discord was ongoing. He was having panic attacks, difficulty sleeping, and difficulty concentrating. His ability to cope with stress was described as "extremely poor." He was seen twice weekly, May through July 2010; once or twice weekly in August, September, and November 2010; and three times weekly in October and December 2010. Since January 2011, Mr. Atwell has had only eight sessions. He was noted to have suicidal ideation. Dr. French reported he recommended hospitalization, but Mr. Atwell refused to consider this. His wife was apparently angry at him for not being more functional at home. He was trying to close his business. Dr. French noted deterioration in Mr. Atwell's cognitive functioning. No sustained improvement in Mr. Atwell's condition was reported. His prognosis is described as "not good."

Dennis Brockton, MD

Dr. Brockton is Mr. Atwell's primary care physician. On April 7, 2010, Mr. Atwell was seen complaining that he was feeling "a little depressed." Paxil 20 mg was "restarted."

Alex Williams, MD

Dr. Williams, a psychiatrist, first saw Mr. Atwell in December 2010 for complaints of depression and panic. He reported having been in individual and marital therapy with Dr. French for "a couple of years." He reported that Dr. Brockton was prescribing paroxetine (generic Paxil) and alprazolam (generic Xanax). He continued to have panic attacks. His mood was "down." He was having suicidal ideation. He reported that his store had been robbed in 2006 and 2007. This led him to "go into shock." Dr. Williams' diagnoses are listed as Depressive Disorder NOS and Panic Disorder with Agoraphobia. Dr. Williams discontinued alprazolam and started Mr. Atwell on clonazepam (generic Klonopin). Paroxetine was continued. In January 2011, Mr. Atwell complained of being more depressed and anxious. Paroxetine was changed to Sertraline (generic Zoloft).

Mr. Atwell continued to be seen on a monthly basis. In April 2011, Mr. Atwell reported feeling "horrible." Specifically, he complained of being unable to read and of feeling tired, depressed, anxious, and overwhelmed. "No longer involved in his business. Unable to complete tasks at home." When seen in May 2011, Mr. Atwell complained of being extremely anxious and having panic attacks. He was depressed. "Feels stressed by disability carriers."

BEHAVIORAL OBSERVATIONS AND MENTAL STATUS

Mr. Atwell arrived early for this evaluation. He had been transported to my office by a car service arranged by New England National. He is a tall, heavyset man with gray hair. He was casually dressed with fair grooming. Despite the fact that the weather was warm and dry, he wore tall, fleece-lined sheepskin boots. He arrived carrying a plastic bag from a grocery store that contained a banana, a pear, a pile of papers apparently related to his disability claim, and a pair of slippers. Periodically, he would attempt to locate a document in this bag relevant to our discussion, but he was never able to retrieve the document he needed. Eye contact was intermittent. He reported feeling very anxious. He declined to leave the office for the lunch break, stating that he felt "safe" in the office and preferred to eat his fruit in the testing room.

Mr. Atwell was generally responsive to all questions and provided a detailed history. There were no problems with language, concentration, or memory evident during the interview. He told me that he had been through two prior IME's, including one the week before. He had another IME scheduled the following week. Mr. Atwell described how anxious he had felt about the first IME (Dr. Stewart's) and that when Dr. Stewart had refused to tell him

in advance the tests that were to be administered, Mr. Atwell developed homicidal ideation toward Dr. Stewart and feared he would hurt him. He reported that he did ultimately go through with the evaluation and remarked that Dr. Stewart turned out to be very professional and nice.

Mr. Atwell asked me if we were going to do the "500-question test" (i.e. the MMPI-2), stating that he had done so for all the other evaluations. Despite this, when presented with the test, he seemed to have difficulty understanding the instructions. It was explained to him that the test would be administered on the computer rather than by paper and pencil. Although he affirmed that he had no problem using a computer, he appeared to be confused by the relatively simple instructions, which state that the examinee should click the button next to "true" or "false" and then hit "next" to advance to the next question. He spent several minutes studying these instructions and then asked for clarification.

CLINICAL INTERVIEW

The following information was self-reported by Mr. Atwell.

Personal and Family History

Mr. Atwell was born and raised in Spring Valley, New Jersey. His father was a banking executive, so they moved around a lot. The family settled in New Haven, Connecticut, when Mr. Atwell was nine. Based on this experience, Mr. Atwell stated that he always wanted to be part of "a place." This led to his decision to open a stationery store, "Atwell's Stationery," in Stars Hollow, Connecticut, in partnership with his father. About a year and a half later, Mr. Atwell's father died of brain cancer. Mr. Atwell's mother remarried and moved to the Chicago area. She died in 2008. Mr. Atwell has one sister who is two years older. He reported they recently became estranged after an argument.

Mr. Atwell married in his early thirties (he could not remember the exact year). He and his wife have two sons, ages 20 and 22. The older son lives and works in New York City. The younger son attends college in Pennsylvania. Mr. Atwell's wife is an art teacher and also teaches a course at Harbor College. He reported that their marriage is very acrimonious. He described his wife as "volatile" and "violent." She has pulled a knife on him. They have been in marriage counseling for years, but there has been no improvement in their relationship. Mr. Atwell stated he is very sad about this, but feels "committed" to staying with his family.

Mr. Atwell discussed in great detail two romantic relationships that ended unhappily for him. One occurred while he was in college. The second occurred while he was in his thirties. He described feeling devastated and depressed for a long period of time following these break-ups.

Educational History

Mr. Atwell stated that he did well in school despite having what he believes to be dyslexia and attention deficit disorder. He reported that he was able to overcome these potential obstacles due to being very "competitive" and working hard. He attended Ivy College, earning a BA in Economics. During college, he spent his junior year in Brussels, Belgium. He reported this experience had a tremendous impact on him. He stated that he developed the idea of owning a business based on people he knew in Brussels who owned a bookstore. He found their lifestyle to be appealing.

Vocational History

Mr. Atwell started a business with his father the day after he graduated from college. He opened "Atwell's Stationery," a stationery store specializing in fine writing papers, "high-end" pens, and calligraphy supplies. At one point, he owned three stores in various locations. He stated he was very connected to the town of Stars Hollow and was active in local organizations and politics. He was instrumental in preventing a large corporation from building a shopping center in town. He eventually combined his businesses into one store, which apparently closed earlier this year.

According to Mr. Atwell, owning a business with his father changed their relationship in a very positive way. His father ran the "business end," while Mr. Atwell ran the front of the stores and dealt with customers. He described this as a "true partnership." He felt respected by his father. He reported that losing his father was very difficult for him, but he continued to feel connected to his father through the store. He stated he could feel his father's presence there. When he closed the store, he reported that he "walked around the store with his father's picture so that his father could say good bye."

Mr. Atwell reported his store had been twice broken into. In one case, he was convinced that the store had been watched prior to the break in. He reported being extremely unnerved and upset by these events and felt "violated."

In addition to owning his store, Mr. Atwell also has a business called "New England Up Close" in which he provides driving tours of historic sites located in the Stars Hollow area. He reported having to curtail this activity due to fears about having a panic attack.

Psychiatric History

Mr. Atwell stated that he has been in therapy most of his adult life. He reported that he experienced his first episode of depression when he was in his early thirties following the end of a romantic relationship. He stated that the depression went on for years. He sought psychiatric treatment, but it was no help whatsoever. He reported that he couldn't function effectively as a manager at work, but his staff pulled him through.

Mr. Atwell's next bout of depression began about five years ago. He was having problems with his wife and became obsessed with the idea of calling his ex-girlfriend. He again sought therapy, which this time did prove helpful. His depression improved.

The most recent depressive episode began in 2008. His primary care physician (PCP) prescribed Paxil, and Mr. Atwell began treatment with Dr. French. This therapy has included both individual therapy and marital counseling. Currently, he sees Dr. French about every ten days. Previously, he has seen him as often as three times per week. He is now seeing a psychiatrist for medication and is taking clonazepam and sertraline.

Substance Abuse History

Mr. Atwell reported that he has never had problems related to substance abuse. He drinks very little alcohol. He does not use street drugs, nor does he abuse prescription medications.

Disability Onset

According to Mr. Atwell, he experienced a severe panic attack while driving in December 2008. He thought he was having a heart attack. He pulled his car over. He eventually drove home and made an appointment with his doctor. For reasons that are not entirely clear, Mr. Atwell's doctor believed his symptoms were a reaction to something he ate. Mr. Atwell then became obsessed with what he was eating, developing what he described as an eating disorder. He noted that he also has a problem binging on junk food and has vomited after such binges. Mr. Atwell continued to have panic attacks that left him "depressed" and "debilitated." He tried to hide these attacks from his staff and other people. He reported that his wife didn't understand him or provide any support or sympathy. Work felt "safer" than home. He stated he was "confronted" by a business associate who said, "What's going on? You seem disabled." Mr. Atwell thought that if he closed his business, he would feel more "peaceful." He reported that his family was unhappy about this decision. Despite his hopes to the contrary, he has not felt better since closing the business. He stated he has become extremely disorganized and has piles of papers everywhere.

Changes in Functioning

Mr. Atwell reported that he feels more "muddled." He can't think clearly and is disorganized. After a panic attack, he has to lie down for several hours. He can't make decisions. He has become reclusive. He doesn't see friends or go into town. He has suicidal thoughts and had homicidal thoughts about Dr. Stewart. He has angry outbursts. He feels lethargic. He reported that he "knows" he'll never be able to manage a business again. He stated, "I was there every single day. I always had nineteen balls in the air. I can't do that anymore." He stated he can no longer give driving tours due to frequent panic attacks.

Current Daily Activities

Mr. Atwell stated that if he doesn't have to get up for something in the morning that he'll sleep very late. He stays home, watches TV, walks the dog, and goes to the drug store or the supermarket. He is unable to concentrate to read. He usually retires around 10:00 p.m. He falls asleep easily, but wakes up due to having nightmares. He stated he is afraid of getting upset, so he tries to stick to a routine. He reported that he thought he'd be "doing more" after he left work, but this has not been the case.

Current Symptoms

Mr. Atwell reported that he thinks about suicide when he gets upset. He stated that a few months ago he went to the top of a building in Stars Hollow and thought about jumping off. He continues to have regular panic attacks, although none as severe as the attack in December 2008. He is easily upset. He described calling New England National and leaving an angry, threatening message when he received a letter stating he would not receive his full benefit check one month. He binges on junk food. He feels more "threatened." He avoids going out or socializing.

PSYCHOLOGICAL TESTING

Psychological testing was employed to obtain information about Mr. Atwell's current cognitive and emotional functioning. As a part of this, an assessment of Mr. Atwell's response style was made in order to determine if he was making a full effort and being forthright in his responses.

Validity and Response Style

The VIP verbal subtest was utilized to assess his effort and motivation on tasks measuring cognitive functioning. His performance on the verbal subtest is consistent with an invalid response pattern. This suggests he was either attempting to provide incorrect answers or he was responding inconsistently. His performance on the VIP raises questions about the validity of Mr. Atwell's performances on other measures of cognitive functioning.

The MMPI-2 contains numerous validity scales to assess under-reporting or over-reporting of symptoms and other response styles that compromise validity. A scale used to determine the consistency of Mr. Atwell's responses indicated he did not respond randomly (VRIN [Variable Response Inconsistency] = 38T). Two scales designed to detect the underreporting of psychopathology were very low (L [Lie] = 43T, S = 40T), while one (K [Defensiveness] = 45T) was in the normal range. Three scales employed to detect attempts to exaggerate or over-report problems were extremely elevated (F [Infrequency] = 113T, F_B [Infrequency Back] = 120T, FBS [Symptom Validity] = 33). One such scale (F_p [Infrequency Psychopathology] = 63) was in the normal range[1]. These scores, taken together, and considered in light of his low VRIN score, suggest that Mr. Atwell was intentionally exaggerating the severity of his symptoms and was attempting to create an

---

[1] Note that reported scores are T-scores.

extremely pathological picture of himself. The magnitude of this attempt at distortion rendered the clinical scales of the MMPI-2 uninterpretable.

Current Cognitive Functioning

Mr. Atwell was administered a neuropsychological screening battery to obtain an overview of his cognitive functioning in the domains of memory, language, attention, and visuospatial performance. Mr. Atwell performed extremely poorly across the board, with scores in the impaired range in all domains. His performance was inconsistent with his observed presentation during the interview. Scores at this level would typically be found in individuals with advanced dementia. For example, when presented verbally with a list of 10 items to remember, Mr. Atwell was only able to recall three items on the first trial and only four items on each of the subsequent three trials. When later asked to recall items from the list, he was able to recall only one item. In a test of verbal fluency, he was given 60 seconds to name as many fruits or vegetables as he could. He came up with only nine responses. When asked to repeat a series of numbers, he was unable to remember more than three digits.

Current Psychological Functioning

The MMPI-2 was used to assess psychological and emotional functioning. In light of Mr. Atwell's validity scores, the results of the MMPI-2 are considered invalid. He produced an extremely elevated profile with a number of T-scores in excess of 100. After completing the test, he was queried about his responses to some individual items that appeared to be inconsistent with the symptoms he had reported in the interview. For example, he answered "true" to the item "Evil spirits possess me at times." When asked about this, he stated that he felt his father's spirit was with him when he was in the shop. I asked him if he thought his father was "evil" (since he had reported having an extremely close relationship with him). He replied, "No." I then asked him why he had answered this item affirmatively. He stated that he must have been thinking about when his store was robbed. He also answered "true" to the item, "I see things or animals or people around me that others do not see." His explanation for this was that he has felt very close to the spirit of his great grandmother.

COLLATERAL INTERVIEW: DR. FRENCH

I spoke to Dr. French by telephone on May 26, 2011. He has been treating Mr. Atwell for symptoms of anxiety and depression using cognitive behavioral techniques. He reported that despite these efforts, Mr. Atwell's symptoms have not improved. He described Mr. Atwell as "blocked off" from himself. Mr. Atwell often reports suicidal ideation. He stated that he has noted a decline in Mr. Atwell's cognitive functioning recently. For example, he confuses appointment times and reported he had trouble finding Dr. French's office. Dr. French noted that Mr. Atwell's wife is extremely angry and critical. He described their marriage as terrible, but Mr. Atwell declines to leave. I asked Dr. French his opinion about Mr. Atwell's invalid test performance. He reported that he was not surprised that his test results were exaggerated, but he believes Mr. Atwell is legitimately suffering and has valid symptoms of anxiety.

DR. STEWART'S INDEPENDENT MEDICAL EXAMINATION

Subsequent to performing my evaluation of Mr. Atwell, I was provided with a copy of Dr. Stewart's IME. I reviewed this after formulating my opinion about Mr. Atwell's condition and functional capacity. It appears that Mr. Atwell presented in a comparable manner during Dr. Stewart's evaluation, and obtained similar results on psychological testing. The MMPI-2 resulted in an invalid profile due to probable symptom exaggeration. Scores on Dr. Stewart's administration of the MMPI-2 were more exaggerated than those Mr. Atwell produced during this evaluation. Similar scores were obtained on the VIP verbal subtest as well. Dr. Stewart concluded that Mr. Atwell's symptom presentation was not credible and suggested that he be reevaluated in three to six months. This presumably led to the current evaluation.

OPINION

Formulation

Mr. Atwell may have very real symptoms of anxiety and depression. Unfortunately, due to his attempts to exaggerate the severity of his problems and functional impairment, the exact nature of any valid symptoms could not be determined. His performance on cognitive and psychological testing was not credible. Not only were most validity indicators elevated, but his test responses were inconsistent with my direct observations of his behavior, presentation, and functioning. Individuals with the degree of cognitive dysfunction suggested by Mr. Atwell's test performance would be likely to require 24-hour supervision and care. This is clearly inconsistent with Mr. Atwell's known (and acknowledged) functional capacity, which includes activities such as shopping unaccompanied at the drug store and supermarket.

Given his long history of mental health issues, it is likely that Mr. Atwell does manifest some valid symptoms, and it should be noted that symptom exaggeration does not preclude the possibility of valid impairment. However, the extent and impact of such impairment, if present, could not be determined in this evaluation due to Mr. Atwell's invalid performance and his attempts to exaggerate the severity of his symptoms.

Responses to Questions

1. What are Mr. Atwell's functional psychological abilities and limitations?

It is not possible to determine valid functional abilities and limitations due to Mr. Atwell's unreliable and exaggerated performance on testing. This performance also calls into question the credibility of his self-reported symptoms and functional impairment. According to Mr. Atwell, he experiences panic attacks that are debilitating and require him to lie down for several hours. He is fatigued and lethargic. He is disorganized and has trouble remembering things. He experiences frequent suicidal ideation. He has angry outbursts. These symptoms, if valid and if present at the severity Mr. Atwell claims, would probably interfere with his ability to run a business. Unfortunately, the true nature and scope of his symptoms could not be verified in this evaluation.

2. Is the severity and scope of any impairment found sufficient to remove and preclude the option of returning to gainful employment as the owner of a stationery store?

If Mr. Atwell is having panic attacks or a depressive episode, these symptoms are likely to respond, at least partially, to treatment. It is premature to conclude that returning to gainful employment as a result of these symptoms would be permanently precluded.

Cognitive impairment, if related to an organic disease or a form of progressive dementia, might be irreversible and could permanently preclude a return to occupational functioning. However, there is no reliable evidence that Mr. Atwell has such a condition. His performance on cognitive testing was inconsistent with his observed cognitive functioning during the clinical interview and with his own description of his daily activities.

3. If psychological limitations are present, please indicate their potential functional effects on work-related executive abilities (i.e., intellectual, cognitive, organizational, social, and behavioral, etc.) in as much detail as possible.

Dr. French described symptoms of anxiety and depression that he has observed in treating Mr. Atwell. His observations are consistent with Mr. Atwell's report during the clinical interview. The extent to which these symptoms impair Mr. Atwell's functioning, and the potential impact of these symptoms on his work capacity, could not be determined due to Mr. Atwell's invalid test performance and the questionable reliability of his self report.

4. Please summarize the various test scoring and scales for any testing performed.

Test	Score	Interpretation
VIP Verbal	52 (total)	Invalid/ Inconsistent
RBANS (Index Scores)		
Immediate Memory	53	Extremely impaired
Visuospatial/Construction		
Language	64	Severely impaired
Attention	79	Borderline impaired
Delayed Memory	53	Extremely impaired
	48	Extremely impaired
MMPI-2 Validity (T Scores)		
VRIN (inconsistency)		
L (under-reporting)	38	Very consistent
K (under-reporting)	43	Low
S (under-reporting)	45	Normal
F (over-reporting)	40	Low
F_B (over-reporting)	113	Extreme elevation
F_p (over-reporting)	120	Extreme elevation
FBS (over-reporting)	63	Normal
	33 (raw score)	Extreme elevation

MMPI-2 Clinical (T Scores)

Hs		
D	88	Marked elevation
Hy	104	Marked elevation
Pd	89	Marked elevation
Mf	92	Marked elevation
Pa	48	Normal
Pt	108	Marked elevation
Sc	107	Marked elevation
Ma	115	Marked elevation
Si	56	Normal
	82	Marked elevation

5. What forms of mental health treatment, if any, do you currently recommend, and what is your opinion regarding the efficacy and appropriateness of the current pharmacological and therapeutic treatment regimen?

Based on my discussion with Dr. French, he is providing very appropriate and efficacious treatment for Mr. Atwell's reported symptoms of anxiety and depression. Mr. Atwell is likewise receiving psychotropic medication management from a psychiatrist. This combination of cognitive behavioral therapy and medication management usually produces results in terms of at least partial remission of symptoms. To the extent that Mr. Atwell has valid symptoms of anxiety and/or depression, his current treatment would be considered appropriate and it is recommended that he continue in this treatment. To date, Mr. Atwell has reported very little response to treatment. This is not consistent with typical outcomes from such treatment.

6. Does the current treatment regimen have, as one of the goals, attempting to rehabilitate and return Mr. Atwell to gainful employment?

Dr. French indicated that he believes that working in some capacity would be beneficial for Mr. Atwell. This does appear to be an important goal of his treatment.

7. Is Mr. Atwell motivated to return to his usual occupational work? If lack of motivation is a problem, is it attributable to a diagnosed clinical psychiatric condition or illness, or are factors and circumstances of a non-clinical nature mainly responsible?

Mr. Atwell, despite purporting to have loved his work, stated that he will never again be able to manage a business. Having reached this conclusion, Mr. Atwell is not actively attempting to return to work in his usual occupation. There are several explanations for this. First, Mr. Atwell may be experiencing valid symptoms of depression that have diminished his self-confidence and sense of optimism about recovery. Feelings of lethargy and fatigue may contribute to this. Alternatively, Mr. Atwell may have become frustrated with the struggles of business ownership—especially given the difficult economy and the advent of electronic communication that has significantly decreased the demand for fine writing paper and pens. Finally, Mr. Atwell's refusal to consider returning to work may be an outgrowth of his dysfunctional marital relationship. He described his wife as being opposed to his closing the business. Doing so may be an expression of his resentment and anger toward her.

8. Is secondary gain playing a role in perpetuating the current psychiatric status and presentations? Is it undermining Mr. Atwell's ability and/or willingness to return to gainful employment?

The viability of a store selling fine writing papers and pens is questionable, given the current predominance of e-mail and other forms of electronic communication. These factors may compromise Mr. Atwell's ability to return to gainful employment and contribute to his need for alternative sources of income.

9. What is Mr. Atwell's prognosis and conditional timetable to return to work in his occupation on either a part time or full time basis?

Due to Mr. Atwell's exaggerated presentation and invalid test results, his prognosis and the time frame for return to work cannot be determined.

10. Are Mr. Atwell's reported symptoms consistent with test results?

Psychological testing failed to provide support for Mr. Atwell's reported symptoms. Test results were deemed invalid due to Mr. Atwell's apparent attempt to exaggerate the severity of his condition.

Thank you for the opportunity to evaluate this claimant. Please feel free to contact me if you would like additional information or clarification.

Lisa D. Piechowski, PhD, ABPPCT Licensed Psychologist #1993
Board Certified in Forensic Psychology by
The American Board of Professional Psychology

TEACHING POINT:
THE RELATIONSHIP BETWEEN SYMPTOMS AND DISABILITY IN CAPACITY TO WORK

This case is a good illustration of the model of mental health law described by Morse (1978). In his discussion of mental health law, he focused on three components: clinical condition, functional legal capacities, and causal connection. Individuals are typically referred for this kind of disability evaluation (independent psychological examination or independent medical examination) because they have experienced mental health problems or brain dysfunction, and are receiving insurance benefits because they are not able to work. An important question is whether the insured individual continues to be clinically symptomatic—and whether such symptoms in turn impair his or her capacity to work. Accordingly, the evaluator must obtain a good picture of past and current clinical functioning (as well as treatment interventions to improve symptoms) and work-relevant capacities such as attention-concentration, motivation, stamina, and a variety of other important capacities.

In the course of this evaluation, the forensic clinician must focus on whether the insured continues to experience genuine clinical symptoms. If so, there is the further question of whether such symptoms impair his relevant work capacities. This amply illustrates the three components of the Morse model. Beyond these basic questions, there are additional considerations as well. If the insured individual does continue to experience genuine clinical symptoms, are these symptoms being treated appropriately? (It might be, for example, that an insured continues to experience significant depression but is being treated by a family physician prescribing a low dose of antidepressant medication accompanied only by monthly counseling sessions. In this case, one recommendation might involve a more intensive, assertive approach to treatment.) Are the reports of symptoms and impaired work-relevant capacities presented inaccurately as a function of secondary gain? (A different recommendation—for more intensive observation and frequent evaluation—might result from this finding. This is basically the conclusion in this case.) Finally, the evaluator might comment on any other findings that seem relevant to the capacity to work, such as the nature of the job and possible rehabilitative steps to increase the chances of successful resumption of work.

CASE TWO
PRINCIPLE: ASSESS CLINICAL CHARACTERISTICS IN RELEVANT, RELIABLE, AND VALID WAYS
(*PRINCIPLE 20*)

This principle describes the importance of assessing clinical characteristics in ways that are relevant, reliable, and valid. Clinical characteristics are symptoms of disorders of mental, emotional, or cognitive functioning relevant to a specified forensic issue or legal question. Generally, the assessment of clinical characteristics in FMHA is performed through the use of properly validated assessment measures, clinical interviews, and various sources of collateral information. The assessment of clinical characteristics in ways that are relevant, reliable, and valid is important to FMHA on both a broad and narrow level, depending on the context of the evaluation and the forensic issues under consideration. For example, a wide variety of clinical characteristics might be relevant when the forensic issue or the legal standard in question is broad, such as in a capital sentencing mitigation evaluation. Conversely, other forensic issues might lend themselves to a narrow evaluation of clinical characteristics. For example, a Competence to Stand Trial evaluation will typically focus on severe mental illness, neurological dysfunction, and cognitive limitations as they bear on an individual's ability to understand the nature of the charges and assist counsel in mounting an effective defense. Regardless of the approach used, the assessment of clinical characteristics must ultimately be relevant to the forensic issues and legal questions being addressed by the evaluation.

There is substantial ethical support for this principle. The APA *Ethics Code* emphasizes that practitioners' judgments are based on "established scientific and professional knowledge of the discipline" (Principle 2.04, p. 5), and that recommendations made in the context of assessments (including forensic testimony) must be based on "information and techniques sufficient to substantiate their finding" (Principle 9.01). Furthermore, the APA *Ethics Code* notes that assessments should be conducted "in a manner and for purposes that are appropriate in light of the research on or evidence of the usefulness and proper application of the techniques," and that psychologists should only use assessment measures "whose validity and reliability have been established for use with members of the population tested" (Principle 9.02). This clearly refers to the most valid possible assessment of "clinical characteristics," noting that it is important to determine not only what areas will be assessed, but the measures used to assess these areas and the psychometric properties of these measures. Finally, the APA *Ethics Code* emphasizes that steps must be taken to explicitly identify and discuss the limitations encountered when evaluators use assessment measures whose validity and reliability have not been established (Standard 9.02b), or when characteristics of the evaluation or evaluee raise questions about the validity and reliability of an assessment's interpretation (Standard 9.06).

The APA *Specialty Guidelines* addresses the assessment of clinical characteristics by emphasizing the importance of forensic practitioners basing their opinions and testimony on properly applied and scientifically valid principles and methods (Guidelines 2.05, 9.01, and 10.02), as well as the individual and cultural differences of those they assess (Guidelines 2.08 and 10.03). The APA *Specialty Guidelines* also notes the importance of personal contact with the individual being evaluated:

> Forensic practitioners recognize their obligations to only provide written or oral evidence about the psychological characteristics of particular individuals when they have sufficient information or data to form an adequate foundation for those opinions or to substantiate their findings.... When it is not possible or feasible to examine individuals about whom they are offering an opinion, forensic practitioners strive to make clear the impact of such limitations on the reliability and validity of their professional products, opinions, or testimony. (Guideline 9.03)

Without such contact, there is no opportunity to observe the individual's presentation, behavior, form of communication, capacity for attention and concentration, response to stress, and reaction to the evaluator, all of which are important to the accurate assessment of clinical characteristics. There is also no opportunity for direct questions that would yield responses about relevant clinical characteristics that cannot be observed (e.g., thoughts, fantasies) and are therefore difficult or impossible to infer through the behavioral observations offered by others. Accordingly, without personal contact, there is less face validity to the evaluation. Importantly, the APA *Specialty Guidelines* suggests that experts carefully consider the clinical judgments they give in the context of forensic evaluations: "Forensic practitioners are encouraged to consider the problems that may arise by using a clinical diagnosis in some forensic contexts, and consider and qualify their opinions and testimony appropriately" (Guideline 10.01).

The *Principles of Medical Ethics with Annotations Especially Applicable to Psychiatry* (American Psychiatric Association, 2013b) does not provide material that is relevant to this issue. The AAPL *Ethics Guidelines* (2005) indicates that forensic psychiatrists must apply "clinical data to legal criteria" (p. 3) and "communicate the honesty of their work, efforts to attain objectivity, and the soundness of their *clinical* opinion, by distinguishing, to the extent possible, between verified and unverified information as well as among *clinical* 'facts,' 'inferences,' and 'impressions'" (p. 3; italics added for emphasis). It should be noted that there is some explicit contrast between the "hypothesis testing" approach to achieving reliability advocated by the AAPL *Ethics Guidelines* and the "actuarial measures" approach that is apparent in the APA *Ethics Code*, whereas the APA *Specialty Guidelines* explicitly endorses both as approaches to improving the validity of evaluations.

Legal guidance stresses the importance of the relationship between clinical characteristics and functional capacities. Rule 401 of the *Federal Rules of Evidence*, for example, states that evidence is relevant if "(a) it has any tendency to make a fact more or less probable than it would be without the evidence; and (b) the fact is of consequence in determining the action." Further, Rule 402 mandates that evidence that is not relevant under Rule 401 is not admissible. Accordingly, the assessment of clinical characteristics in a reliable and valid way is very important for accurate and effective FMHA. In risk assessment, for example, the professional literature generally underscores the advisability of using actuarial or structured professional judgment approaches whenever possible, and avoiding unstructured clinical judgment (Heilbrun, et al., 2009; Melton et al., 2007; Packer & Grisso, 2011).

The present report provides an example of assessing clinical characteristics in the context of workplace disability. Dr. Sadoff uses several approaches that should be part of almost any FMHA. First, he conducts a lengthy interview (in this case, three hours). As part of this interview, he performs a mental status examination. He seeks a history focusing on medical, mental health, and professional (vocational) domains. He reviews relevant records, including those associated with current psychiatric treatment, previous hospital and rehabilitation records, accident and police reports, and insurance policy records. Finally, in his reasoning, he relates the currently experienced mental health symptoms (as well as physical symptoms) with work-related incapacities whenever appropriate.

March 3, 2011
William J. Jones, Esquire
c/o Jones and Smith
4500 Market Street
Philadelphia, PA 19149
RE: Dr. Elliot Sherman

Dear Mr. Jones:

INTRODUCTION

Pursuant to your request, I examined your client, a 50-year-old (birthday; January 1, 1961), divorced white male, for approximately three hours, on February 28, 2011. Dr. Sherman was told that I am a psychiatrist requested by your office to conduct this examination with respect to the litigation in which he is involved. He was told that I would be taking notes during the examination and preparing a report that I would send to you. Further, he was told that I would not be treating him and there could be no traditional doctor–patient confidentiality. Dr. Sherman understood the directions and agreed to be examined.

DESCRIPTION AND MENTAL STATUS EXAMINATION

Dr. Sherman is a man of average height, about 5' 9", who weighs approximately 150 pounds, and appears his stated age. He presents with a knee brace, walking with a cane, due to his spinal injury with sciatic nerve inflammation. He states that he was sent for a psychiatric examination because his lawyer believes he has a severe disability that keeps him from working in his designated profession of orthopedic surgery. He has become extremely angry and paranoid because his claim for disability was rejected by his insurance company. Dr. Sherman presents his difficulties in a clear and relevant manner, without evidence of psychotic thought disorder, hallucinations, or delusions. He is well oriented, and his memory is not impaired. He does admit to having had periods of depression and anxiety, and stated that he had been treated previously with medication and has been hospitalized on two occasions for his depression since the insurance company had rejected his claim for disability.

SUMMARY OF THE ISSUES

Dr. Sherman states that he bought a disability policy through his County Medical Society, as did a number of his colleagues. He said the policy reads, very clearly, that if he is disabled from practicing in his specific profession, which is orthopedic surgery, that he is entitled to receive $10,000/month disability payments. He said the insurance company did not read the policy in the same manner as he did. He said the insurance company has told him that since he is able to work conducting medical examinations, that he is not totally disabled even though he is not able to perform surgery as he used to before his injury. He argues that practicing in his profession as an orthopedic surgeon requires him to perform surgery as well as conduct medical examinations of patients with orthopedic problems. He is not working totally in his profession and has lost a great deal of income because he has not been able to operate. He states he used to be able to work several days a week in the operating room and had conducted 10-hour procedures while standing at the operating room table. He states he cannot stand for more than a few minutes at a time and has great difficulty walking at the present time. He can only see one or two patients a day, two days a week, Monday and Thursday, so that he has two or three days between the days that he works.

PROFESSIONAL HISTORY

Dr. Sherman states that he attended Jackson Medical School in Ohio, graduating in 1988, receiving his undergraduate degree from Monahan University in Indiana in 1983. He states he did well in college, achieving a 3.0 grade-point average, but had some difficulty in medical school, especially in the psychiatry rotation. He took his orthopedic surgery residency at the Special Hospital for Surgery in Los Angeles, California, completing his training in 1995. He joined an orthopedic group in Philadelphia following his completion of his residency training. He worked for several years with the Diamond Orthopedic Group in Bryn Mawr, Pennsylvania. He then went out on his own, in a solo practice, in the year 2007. He had been practicing for about two years when he developed a severe spinal injury in a motor vehicle accident. He was not charged with any violation from the accident, as the car behind him had crashed into him and the driver was found liable for the accident in court. Dr. Sherman has been treated for his spinal injury, which left him partially paralyzed, for several months, until he was treated effectively with physical rehabilitation, and is now able to walk with a cane, but also with pain in his back and in his right leg. He has not been in the operating room since the day of his accident and only returned to the medical examination of patients in June, 2010.

Past personal history reveals that Dr. Sherman was born and raised in the Philadelphia area, the younger of two, having an older brother who is currently an attorney working in Center City Philadelphia. His parents are both deceased, his father having died of coronary artery disease in 2005, at the age of 78, and his mother having died of complications of breast cancer in 2006, at the age of 73. He states he is close with his brother, who is three years his senior.

Dr. Sherman relates no difficulties in his growth and development as a child and adolescent. He denies any history of physical, emotional, or sexual abuse when growing up.

MEDICAL HISTORY

Dr. Sherman relates that he had the usual childhood diseases and had an operation on his tonsils at age five. He also had a hernia operation at age 24 without any complications or repeat herniation. He has had no other surgery except for the surgery and treatment that he received following the auto accident in 2009. He has had no significant allergies, infections, head injuries, seizures, or blackouts. He has been treated by his family doctor on a regular basis for minor colds, sore throats, and minor injuries.

MARITAL HISTORY

Marital history reveals that Dr. Sherman had been married for 10 years to his wife, Lynda, who divorced him after they had three children together. He was married in 1988, after finishing medical school. His wife was a nurse whom he met during his training. Their children are two girls and a boy, ages 21, 19, and 16. He was upset at the separation and divorce, becoming depressed and requiring psychiatric treatment, with medication and/or hospitalization. He was treated by Dr. Silver as an outpatient for two years after his hospitalization and has not required further treatment until after his motor vehicle accident and injury in 2009. He continues to see his children and to support them. He is currently in a serious relationship with another woman whom he hopes one day to marry.

PSYCHIATRIC HISTORY

Psychiatric history reveals that Dr. Sherman had treatment with Dr. Silver as an outpatient for two years following his separation and divorce. The hospitalization occurred at Lankenau for 10 days, during which time he was given medication for depression.

Following his motor vehicle accident and injury to his back, Dr. Sherman also became depressed and saw Dr. Silver again for several months on a weekly basis. He continues to see Dr. Silver on an as-needed basis. Since he has not been able to work regularly and is not receiving disability payments, he has difficulty affording private psychiatric treatment.

Dr. Sherman denies the use of recreational drugs. He will drink alcohol at night to help relieve his pain and help him sleep. He drinks two cups of coffee in the morning, but not after noon. He has never smoked cigarettes.

Dr. Sherman has difficulty sleeping, requiring the alcohol that he takes at night, usually in the form of a glass of wine. He also takes 5 mg. of Ambien when needed to help him sleep. He has difficulty with his appetite, eating only two meals a day, and has lost about 25 pounds since his injury. He also describes experiencing feelings of anhedonia, i.e., that he is not able to achieve pleasure, which also affects his relationship with his significant other, with whom, at times, he has lack of libido. He states that it helps him to go to work and try to live a more normal life, though he is depressed and has had feelings of self-destruction or suicide in the past. He states that he is not currently actively suicidal and would not harm himself. He has great confidence in his psychiatrist, and states that he will call Dr. Silver before doing anything rash or impulsive.

In addition to my examination of Dr. Sherman, I also reviewed the following records:

1. The psychiatric records of Dr. Silver, who gives him a diagnosis of depressive disorder. He also diagnoses him with anxiety disorder and ascribes his psychiatric condition to the injury that he received at the time of the motor vehicle accident.
2. The records from Lankenau Hospital, which show that he was diagnosed as being depressed and was given Effexor XR for treatment. He was also given Ambien, 5mg. PRN (as needed) for sleep.
3. The records from the motor vehicle accident, with the police reports, revealing the extent of damage to his automobile, which was totaled and not repairable. The records from the hospital where he was taken following the accident also revealed the extent of his physical injury and the requirements for treatment.
4. A copy of the records from the Physical Medicine and Rehabilitation Hospital, where Dr. Sherman went for treatment following his motor vehicle accident. This was Moss Rehab in Philadelphia.
5. A copy of the insurance policy that he had taken out for disability in 2005, when he opened his own office for the practice of orthopedic surgery.

Based on my examination of Dr. Sherman and review of the aforementioned records, the following are my opinions, given with a reasonable degree of medical certainty:

Dr. Elliot Sherman is a 50-year-old man who has been a practicing orthopedic surgeon until he was injured in an automobile accident in 2009, causing him to have a spinal injury requiring rehabilitation that has left him unable to walk normally or to stand for long periods of time. He continues in his physical therapy, and also in his psychotherapy for depression and anxiety following the accident that rendered him unable to work in his profession of orthopedic surgery. He is currently engaged in a legal battle with the insurance company that claims he is able to work in medicine, which is his profession, rather than orthopedic surgery, which he claims is his true profession. It is my opinion, with a reasonable degree of medical certainty, that Dr. Sherman is not able to enter the operating room, stand for long periods of time, and has no emotional stability to handle the surgery that is required in the practice of orthopedic surgery. His depression is such that he has moods of suicide and self-destructive behavior, and he would not be safe in the operating room to operate on a patient. He is aware of that and has voluntarily kept himself from the operating room. He is working two days a week, part-time, examining patients, which he is able to do with some difficulty. He states it takes him several hours longer for each patient than it used to.

I would encourage Dr. Sherman to continue to work as much as he is able, since that is therapeutic for his depression and his mental state. However, he is not able to work at his full profession of orthopedic surgery because of the combined physical and mental disability that he has. Because the condition has lasted well over a year, almost two years now, it is my opinion that the condition is permanent and he will not, in the foreseeable future, be able to resume his specific profession of orthopedic surgery. He is totally and permanently disabled from that profession.

Should further records become available, I would be pleased to review them and prepare an addendum to this report, if necessary. All opinions are given within a reasonable degree of medical certainty.

Yours very sincerely,
Robert L. Sadoff, M.D.

TEACHING POINT:
USEFUL APPROACHES TO ASSESSING CLINICAL CHARACTERISTICS IN FMHA

There are certain differences between how a psychiatrist such as Robert Sadoff assesses clinical characteristics and how a psychologist might. Trained in mental status evaluation and in-depth interviewing, forensic psychiatrists often conduct very lengthy interviews as part of their forensic assessments. Psychologists, by contrast, might be inclined to spend less time in the interview but supplement that by administering certain psychological tests and specialized measures in the course of conducting FMHA.

This case offers a good illustration of how a skilled forensic psychiatrist evaluates clinical characteristics—but also demonstrates approaches that bridge disciplinary differences. The duration of the interview (three hours, in this case) provides the opportunity to obtain self-reported information in numerous domains. It serves other purposes as well. It allows the evaluator to carefully observe the individual being evaluated over a relatively long period of time, requiring attention/concentration and cognitive endurance. It offers the opportunity to return to domains already covered, to see whether the evaluee is being consistent in self-reported information within the interview (but across time). It encompasses both historical information-gathering and mental status examination. When combined with the review of relevant records, it also allows the evaluator to check the consistency of self-reported information against that provided by other sources, and attempt to clarify any inconsistencies.

In some cases, an evaluator might take the information obtained in such a lengthy interview and record review into consideration in seeking additional information through collateral interviews. Often the nature, frequency, and intensity of mental health treatment being provided, and the individual's response to such treatment, are important considerations in workplace disability evaluations. An interview with the treating psychiatrist or psychologist can sometimes yield information that is not readily obtained through a review of treatment records.

16

Guardianship

The case report in this chapter is about the competence of adults to manage their own affairs. Evaluations of this type help courts decide whether a guardian should be appointed to handle the day-to-day affairs of the individual deemed incompetent to do so. Unlike previous chapters, this case report will be described in the context of two principles: (1) awareness of the important differences between clinical and forensic domains; and (2) awareness of the relevant legal, ethical, scientific, and practice literatures pertaining to FMHA. The teaching point for this report highlights important changes to the revised *Specialty Guidelines for Forensic Psychology* (APA *Speciality Guidelines*; American Psychological Association, 2013b).

CASE ONE
PRINCIPLE: BE AWARE OF THE IMPORTANT DIFFERENCES BETWEEN CLINICAL AND FORENSIC DOMAINS (*PRINCIPLE 1*)

PRINCIPLE: BE FAMILIAR WITH THE RELEVANT LEGAL, ETHICAL, SCIENTIFIC, AND PRACTICE LITERATURES PERTAINING TO FMHA (*PRINCIPLE 3*)

The importance of familiarity with the relevant literatures (*Principle 3*) was discussed previously in Chapter 4 (this volume), so we turn our focus here to the important differences between the clinical and forensic domains in FMHA (*Principle 1*). Several important differences have been noted between practicing within therapeutic versus forensic evaluation domains. Specifically, Heilbrun (2001) highlighted several differences between therapeutic and forensic evaluations, including the

purpose of the evaluation, the relationship between the examiner and the examinee, assumptions and content of the notification of purpose, who is serving as the client, the nature of the standard being observed, relevant sources of data, assumptions regarding the response style of the examinee, the importance of clarifying one's reasoning and the limits of knowledge, the length and comprehensiveness of the written report, and the expectation of giving court testimony. These differences have been supported and further developed in subsequent literature (see, e.g., DeMatteo et al., 2011; Melton, Petrila, Poythress, & Slobogin, 2007; Packer & Grisso, 2011) (Table 16.1).

The importance of recognizing and understanding the differing roles of practice in clinical and forensic domains is broadly supported by the relevant literature. The *Ethical Principles of Psychologists and Code of Conduct* (APA *Ethics Code*; American Psychological Association, 2010a) discusses this principle in terms of boundaries of competence (Standard 2.01), specifically noting that "[w]hen assuming forensic roles, psychologists are or become reasonably familiar with the judicial or administrative rules governing their roles" (Standard 2.01(f)). Furthermore, the APA *Ethics Code* also emphasizes the importance of basing assessment recommendations in forensic testimony on information and methods sufficient to support their findings (Standard 9.01(a)), including using assessments with established psychometric properties for the members of the populations tested (i.e., forensic populations; Standard 9.02(b)). When interpreting the data collected during an assessment, the APA *Ethics Code* notes that psychologists should consider important factors such as "the purpose of the assessment" and the "situational" characteristics of the individual being evaluated (Standard 9.06).

The APA *Specialty Guidelines* was developed in light of the important differences between forensic

TABLE 16.1. FORENSIC VERSUS THERAPEUTIC ROLES

	Forensic Examiner	Therapeutic Clinician
Purpose of Evaluation	• Assist a legal decision-maker, typically a judge, to make a more informed decision; mental health needs are explored only to extent they are relevant to the legal issue	• Assist in diagnosis and treatment planning for mental health disorders
Nature of Standard(s) Considered	• Medical (psychological, psychiatric) • Legal	• Medical (psychological, psychiatric)
Identity of the Client, or for Whom Services Are Rendered	• The client is the party who requested the evaluation (e.g., attorney, court, employer, insurer)	• The client and the examinee/patient are the same
Relationship Between the Professional and Examinee	• Objective or quasi-objective	• Therapeutic alliance is cultivated • Clinician assumes the traditional "helping" role
Voluntariness of the Evaluation	• Evaluations may be compelled by courts, employers, insurers, or at the behest of legal counsel, with no option for the examinee to decline	• Relationship typically initiated by patient, who is free to terminate at will • Length, course, and goals of treatment, or assessment aims, may be partly directed by patient
Confidentiality	• Not limited to examiner–examinee; varies as a function of the client (e.g., attorney, court, employer, insurer) and purpose of the evaluation	• Typically limited to the clinician–patient relationship unless disclosure obligations arise
Requirement of Obtaining Informed Consent	• Examinee must be informed of who requested the evaluation, the purpose of the evaluation, how the results will be used, and limits on confidentiality • Formal and explicit consent (for voluntary participation) or notification of purpose (for involuntary participation) are necessary	• Consent is implied by patient's having sought out the clinician; obtaining informed consent is recommended
Response Style of the Examinee	• Because of potential for secondary gain and possible non-voluntary nature of the evaluation, there is an expectation that the examinee may conceal or distort information • No presumption of reliable and truthful responses; collateral data should be utilized	• Because the evaluation is typically voluntary, clinician presumes client responses are honest
Data Collection	• Emphasis is placed on the accuracy of the information obtained • Corroboration of information via collateral documents or third party sources is expected	• Emphasis is placed on the patient's experiences, beliefs, feelings, and perceptions of self and environment • Third party or collateral sources of information may be helpful, but may not be necessary
Sources of Information	• Self-report • Psychological testing • Behavioral assessment • Medical procedures • Observations by others • Relevant documents • Collateral interviews	• Self-report • Psychological testing • Behavioral assessment • Medical procedures

(continued)

TABLE 16.1. CONTINUED

	Forensic Examiner	Therapeutic Clinician
Setting	• Settings can vary (e.g., private office, correctional setting with limited privacy)	• Typically an office with privacy
Pace	• Deadlines are imposed by the legal process; less time is available for rapport-building, and single-session evaluations are common	• Therapist and patient can often work collaboratively to negotiate frequency and duration of treatment, and nature of intervention and treatment goals
Written Report	• Customary to write a lengthy and detailed report that focuses on functional legal capacities relevant to the legal issue being addressed • Expected that the report will be entered into evidence in the legal proceeding • Follow conventions/standards in the field of forensic psychology	• If a report is written, it may be brief and conclusory, and it focuses on the mental health or clinical functioning of the examinee • No expectation that anyone other than the therapist or client will see the report
Expected Outcome of the Assessment	• Testimony should be anticipated as a possible follow-up to the evaluation and report	• Testimony is unlikely and, although it may be acceptable in some limited instances, it is discouraged by ethical and best-practice guidelines

This table combines material from DeMatteo et al. (2011), Heilbrun (2001), and Melton et al. (2007).
A portion of this table is reprinted from Heilbrun, K. (2001), *Principles of forensic mental health assessment*, Table 1.2, p. 9, New York: Kluwer Academic/Plenum Press; with kind permission from Springer Science+Business Media B.V.

and "more traditional practice areas" (Introduction, p. 7), and it explicitly highlights how these differences impact forensic practice in regards to competence (Guidelines 2.01, 2.04, 2.05); professional relationships and role conflicts within therapeutic and forensic practice (Guideline 4.02); communication with various forensic examinees (Guideline 6.03) and collateral sources of information (Guideline 6.04); and the focus, selection, and use of assessment procedures (Guidelines 10.01 and 10.02, respectively). The *Ethics Guidelines for the Practice of Forensic Psychiatry* (American Academy of Psychiatry and the Law, 2005) was also established with specialty practice within the forensic context as a guide, and incorporate important differences between traditional and forensic psychiatric practice in discussing confidentiality (Guideline II), consent (Guideline III), honesty and objectivity (Guideline IV), and qualifications (Guideline V).

In this case, the evaluation is clearly consistent with the description of the role of the forensic examiner described in Table 16.1. It was conceptualized as FMHA from the time it was requested by the evaluee's court-appointed guardian. The standard being considered is guardianship—particularly the capacity to exercise rights that had previously been removed as part of the guardianship decision. The client in such a case is the requesting guardian rather than the individual being evaluated. Although the evaluator is polite and respectful, there is no "therapeutic alliance" cultivated, and the evaluator is quite clear about the purpose of the evaluation and its associated limits on confidentiality if the evaluation becomes part of litigation. In the present case, the evaluation was voluntary, but a similar evaluation might be ordered by the court as part of litigation on this issue. The issue of informed consent was addressed through a notification of the purposes of the evaluation and obtaining the agreement of Ms. Lembeck and her guardian, Ms. Mancini, to participate. Response style was considered. Multiple sources of information were used, so that the evaluator could cross-check their consistency. These sources included self-report, psychological testing, document review, and collateral interview. The evaluation was conducted in a single session. The report was lengthy, as is typical of the reports in this book, and could easily be used as the basis of testimony if it were required. In short, this case report well illustrates the distinctive aspects of the forensic evaluation role and report.

An awareness of the relevant law, science, ethics, and practice literatures is likewise clear from this report. In particular, the recently revised APA *Specialty Guidelines for Forensic Psychology* applies in some important respects (discussed afterwards in the teaching point).

FORENSIC PSYCHOLOGICAL EVALUATION
Name: Maureen Lembeck
Date of Evaluation: 8/29/09
Age: 69
Date of Report: 9/16/09
Date of Birth: 5/12/40
Marital Status: Widowed
Education: MA, Education
Occupation: Schoolteacher (retired)

IDENTIFYING INFORMATION/ REFERRAL QUESTION/ NOTIFICATION

Susan Mancini, court-appointed guardian for Maureen Lembeck, requested that this writer assess Ms. Lembeck's capacity to exercise rights that had previously been removed, restricted, or transferred via a guardianshpip that was in place at the time of the evaluation.

Ms. Lembeck was tested and interviewed in the Orlando-area assisted living facility where she currently resides—Highlands Outlook. Additional contact with Ms. Lembeck was made in response to a brief phone interview she initiated. Prior to initiating the evaluation, its nature and purpose were explained to Ms. Lembeck and Ms. Mancini. Both offered a basic understanding of this notification and agreed to participate in the evaluation.

SOURCES OF INFORMATION

The following sources of information were considered in conducting this evaluation:

- Clinical interview with Maureen Lembeck (8/29/09, 3.00 hours).
- Telephone interview with Maureen Lembeck (10/06/09, 0.75 hour).
- Cognistat (8/29/09).
- Wechsler Abbreviated Scale of Intelligence (8/29/09).
- Independent Living Scales (8/29/09).
- Interview with Gale Lembeck, the examinee's son (8/29/09, 0.5 hour).
- Telephone interview with Gale Lembeck (10/06/09, 0.25 hour).
- Telephone interview with Stephen Lembeck, the examinee's son (9/25/09, 1.00 hour).
- Telephone interview with the examinee's daughter-in-law, Helen Mound (9/25/09, 0.25 hour).
- Telephone interview with Steve Grey, examinee's money manager (10/02/09, 0.25 hour).
- Telephone interview with Craig Peden, the examinee's attending physician (8/26/09, 0.33 hour).
- Guardianship evaluations completed by Ann Harvey, LCSW, James Mangum, MD, and Scott Grady, MD (8/29/09).
- April 2009 neuropsychological evaluation completed by Peter Morgan (8/28/09).
- Case manager's assessment and report completed by Suzanne Pesche, RN (8/29/09).

BEHAVIORAL OBSERVATIONS AND CURRENT CLINICAL FUNCTIONING

Maureen Lembeck is a 69-year-old white female who appears somewhat younger than her stated age. She greeted this examiner appropriately and introduced herself immediately prior to beginning the evaluation. Ms. Lembeck was casually and appropriately dressed, wearing a plaid shirt, white pants, and shoes.

Ms. Lembeck displayed a range of emotions during the face-to-face interview, and her expressed emotion was always appropriate to and consistent with the content of her speech. She spoke clearly but demonstrated some difficulties with word-finding during the interview (i.e., she struggled to select a word that she was searching for as she spoke), which is probably a product of her October 2008 stroke. She also displayed what appeared to be some slight slurring of speech during a phone conversation she initiated approximately four weeks later.

Ms. Lembeck demonstrated significant limitations with her memory during both contacts. For example, she frequently repeated herself during her phone interview with little apparent awareness, and she could not remember her phone number, physician's name, medications' names, when federal tax returns are due, or the name of the college she attended when queried about such during the clinical interview. She did use some aids, however, to manage these problems (i.e., she ultimately referred to a list she had in her possession, which included her physician's name and medications she took).

Whereas Ms. Lembeck, during both contacts, expressed considerable concern about and distrust of her older son—Stephen Lembeck—she consistently voiced trust and confidence in her younger son—Gale Lembeck. Ms. Lembeck expressed concerns that Stephen Lembeck had previously mismanaged her financial assets to his own benefit, contrary to the account offered by her money manager, Steve Grey, who was interviewed by phone (also see below).

During both interviews, Ms. Lembeck's responses to questions were somewhat circumstantial and tangential. That is, she sometimes offered overly detailed information and went on to talk about irrelevant and unrelated issues. For example, when asked about her educational history during the clinical interview, Ms. Lembeck was unable to identify the college from which she graduated, and then quickly went on to talk about her teaching career and an episode in which she used a telescope to facilitate instruction of her students. The examinee exhibited a greater tendency towards tangential and circumstantial thinking during an unscheduled phone interview. Her responses to a fair number of questions were irrelevant and off-point, and her attention frequently had to be redirected to the topic at hand (e.g., in response to a question about whether Stephen Lembeck had mismanaged any of her financial assets, she replied that, when younger, he was involved with a number of friends who were responsible for "blowing up buildings during the Korean War" (her son was a toddler during the Korean War—she presumably meant the Viet Nam War), and indicated that, shortly thereafter, "he put on his minister's outfit."

Ms. Lembeck was administered the Cognistat. Her performance on this screening tool indicated no gross problems with orientation, expressive or receptive language, or abstract reasoning. Moderate impairment, however, in attention/concentration, judgment, and short-term memory was indicated.

Ms. Lembeck was also administered three subtests of the Wechsler Abbreviated Scale of Intelligence. Her performance on this measure indicated that she was functioning in the average range of intelligence (which is lower than expected given her educational history) and she demonstrated similar verbal and nonverbal, visual motor abilities. Her performance on this measure is consistent with her performance on a similar measure of intelligence administered by Dr. Morgan in April 2009 (see below for more detail).

RELEVANT HISTORY

Note: Unless otherwise indicated, all information in this section was provided by the examinee.

Family and Social History

Ms. Lembeck reported that she was an only child who was born in Nebraska, but moved a number of times during her childhood because of her father's vocation as a salesman. Ms. Lembeck indicated that her mother was employed as a teacher, and she described a generally positive upbringing, with no history of abuse, neglect, or exploitation. Ms. Lembeck explained that she met her husband when she was 24 and married him two years later, after which she ended her career as a teacher and focused on raising their two sons. Ms. Lembeck described her marriage in positive terms and indicated that she remained happily married to her husband until his death in 2002.

Gale Lembeck described his mother as a loving and concerned parent who was intellectually gifted. He stated that his parents had a positive relationship over the course of their 33-year marriage, which ended when his father died in 2002. Mr. Lembeck estimated that his parents had established at least a part-time residence in Florida approximately 35 years prior.

Consistent with the reports of both sons, Ms. Lembeck stated that, prior to her October 2008 stroke, she was living independently in two different residences—one in Minnesota (during the summer) and one in Florida (during the winter). She reported, however, that she declared her residency in Florida because of tax advantages this provided.

Prior to her October 2008 stroke, reported Gale Lembeck, his mother was living independently and spent most of the year in Florida and summering in her Minnesota home. Mr. Lembeck described his mother as having a well-developed support system in Winter Haven, Florida, and engaging in a variety of recreational activities, including attending the theater, volunteering at a shell museum, socializing with friends, participating in book clubs, and being involved in her condominium association. Mr. Lembeck explained that, after his mother's stroke, she was briefly hospitalized, after which she spent approximately four months at two different rehabilitation programs prior to entering the assisted-living facility in which she has resided since January 2009. Mr. Lembeck reported having regular contact with his mother, particularly since she had moved from Winter Haven to Orlando.

Stephen Lembeck indicated that, prior to his mother's stroke, he spoke with her on a monthly basis and saw her a few times per year—primarily during the summers when she was living in Minnesota, where he resides. Mr. Lembeck indicated that he always enjoyed a good relationship with his mother until shortly after her October stroke, at which point she began to make false claims about him (e.g., that he had a history of treatment for bipolar disorder) and accused him of stealing from her financial accounts. Although Mr. Lembeck acknowledged that his mother's investment accounts had diminished in value in the preceding year (which he attributed to the general stock market decline), he specifically denied mismanaging her funds in any way, and this claim was corroborated in a separate interview with Steve Grey—the examinee's financial advisor. Since the spring of this year, reported Mr. Lembeck, his mother has refused to speak to him and letters and gifts he sent have gone unacknowledged.

Attempts to gain collateral information from significant others revealed considerable family discord. In their separate interviews with this writer, Gale Lembeck and Stephen Lembeck made cross-allegations and questioned each others' motives as they related to the welfare of their mother. For example, Gale Lembeck reported that his brother had an arrest history, had little involvement with their mother historically, admitted to having no feelings generally or for his mother specifically, and could use his charm and intelligence to manipulate others. Stephen Lembeck reported that his brother was a "con man" who had defrauded insurers, had taken steps to alienate their mother from him subsequent to her stroke (when their mother previously had concerns about him [Gale]), had persuaded Ms. Lembeck to spend money inappropriately on his children, and was someone who was capable of using his charm and wit to manipulate others.

Educational History and Employment History

Ms. Lembeck described a history of academic achievement and reported no history of learning disabilities, emotional problems, or behavioral problems that resulted in suspensions or expulsions, or placement in special education programming. She stated that, upon graduating from high school, she attended colleges in Wyoming and Iowa—the names of which she could not remember. Stephen Lembeck reported that his mother attended the University of South Dakota (not Wyoming) for two years before enrolling at and obtaining bachelor's and master's degrees from Grinnell College in Iowa.

Ms. Lembeck indicated that she worked for two years before marrying and retired shortly thereafter in order to focus on her marital relationship and two sons.

Legal History

Ms. Lembeck reported no history of contact with the criminal justice system.

In a report summarizing his March 2009 guardianship evaluation, psychiatrist James Mangum described Ms. Lembeck as in need of a plenary guardianship because of impaired capacity to make decisions regarding all referenced rights. Dr. Mangum, however, described Ms. Lembeck as capable of returning home if she were provided appropriate supportive care surrounding such issues as taking medicine and making healthcare decisions. Dr. Mangum recommended reexamination of Ms. Lembeck within six months to assess her cognitive functioning and abilities, and to inform a decision regarding possible restoration of at least some rights.

In a March 2009 report summarizing her guardianship evaluation, social worker Anne Harvey wrote that Ms. Lembeck was in need of a plenary guardianship because of limitations in all legally relevant areas. Ms. Harvey described Ms. Lembeck as alert, cooperative, friendly, and oriented to time, place, and person, but "concrete" in her thinking, "communicating in a fragmented way," often unable to answer questions appropriately, and demonstrating possible paranoia regarding the cause of her October 2008 stroke—suggesting that she had been poisoned by a neighbor. Ms. Harvey also described the examinee's memory as impaired as evidenced by the fact that she was unable to identify the current or past president, the names of her treating physicians, the name of her bank, or words that were presented to her earlier during the interview. Finally, Ms. Harvey described the examinee as having "grandiose thoughts" about her capacity to live and manage her finances independently.

In his March 2009 guardianship evaluation of Ms. Lembeck, psychiatrist Scott Grady offered diagnoses of "vascular dementia...suspected degenerative dementia...early Alzheimer's." He described the examinee as capable of engaging in self-care skills without supervision and demonstrating remarkable progress since suffering a cerebrovascular accident, but showing limitations with respect to making rational and self-interested financial and healthcare decisions. Dr. Grady recommended that a limited guardianship be instituted and that Ms. Lembeck retain the rights to vote, and to make decisions about her travel, residence, and social environment.

Gale Lembeck indicated that, although there was no current litigation surrounding the guardianship of his mother, there was the potential for such because of differences of opinion between him and his older brother about what was in their mother's best interests. Mr. Lembeck indicated that his brother had initiated the guardianship proceedings and requested, at that time, to be appointed plenary guardian. While Gale Lembeck described his perception that the guardianship was unnecessary because his mother was capable of expressing and protecting her interests, Stephen Lembeck stated that his mother was in need of a guardian—although he acknowledged that he had had no contact with her since the spring of 2009. Stephen Lembeck further indicated his belief that a professional guardian should remain in place due to concerns he had about his brother's motivations as well as the acrimony between the two of them. Gale Lembeck also reported that his mother had requested that he be trustee for her, which represented a change of the existing trust and was a source of tension between him and his brother. Steve Grey—Ms. Lembeck's money manager—opined that Stephen Lembeck had managed his mother's account in a responsible manner, and that she had always expressed considerable trust in him (Stephen Lembeck) prior to her October 2008 stroke.

Medical History, Psychiatric History, and Substance Use History

When asked about her history of alcohol use, Ms. Lembeck responded, "Rarely...hardly ever," and indicated that she might take one serving of alcohol every six months. She reported no history of heavier drinking and no history of alcohol-related problems or difficulties. She reported no history of illegal drug use. Her son, Gale Lembeck, also reported that his mother rarely drank and did not use illegal drugs.

With the exception of isolated migraine headaches, Ms. Lembeck described herself as healthy and having an uncomplicated medical history until her October 2008 stroke. This was corroborated in a phone call with her attending physician, Dr. Peden. Ms. Lembeck reported participating in regular checkups with her physician prior to and after her stroke, and she identified her current physician to be Dr. Peden—after referencing a notebook she had in her possession. Although Dr. Peden acknowledged that his patient had shown considerable improvement during the preceding year, he expressed concern about her current functioning as it affected her abilities to make informed medical decisions and live independently. Dr. Peden stated that Ms. Lembeck's impaired memory compromised her ability to manage her medications and keep medical appointments, and indicated that this had been an ongoing issue for the staff at the assisted living facility where she resided. More specifically, Dr. Peden indicated that, because the staff's attempts to make Ms. Lembeck more responsible for managing her medications and appointments with him and other physicians were unsuccessful, they had returned to managing these matters for her. Dr. Peden also noted that the examinee was largely noninvolved when discussing treatment issues with him and typically responded with "Whatever you think is best—you're the doctor," despite his efforts to engage her in decision-making.

Gale Lembeck described his mother as exhibiting generally good health until her 2008 stroke, with the exception of an isolated period shortly after the death of his father, when she experienced migraine headaches. Mr. Lembeck reported that he was his mother's healthcare surrogate and indicated that there had been some tension between himself and Ms. Lembeck's guardian regarding healthcare decision-making as a result. Stephen Lembeck reported that he suspected that his mother had experienced some concerns about her health prior to her stroke, as evidenced by her purchase of a long-term healthcare insurance policy.

In a January 2009 case manager's report, nurse Suzanne Pesche reported that Ms. Lembeck resided at Highlands Outlook Assisted Living Facility and participated in speech therapy. Ms. Pesche described Ms. Lembeck as pleasant and sociable, but as having some difficulty with word-finding. She noted that Ms. Lembeck was generally cooperative with staff and participated in rehabilitation and treatment services appropriately. Ms. Pesche described Ms. Lembeck as frustrated and concerned about the conflict between her two sons, capable of expressing her opinions and needs adequately, and having the "capacity to make decisions regarding her life."

In a report summarizing his April 2009 neuropsychological evaluation of the examinee, psychologist Peter Morgan wrote that neuropsychological testing revealed "profound impairment of language, language based reasoning, decision making, and judgment." Dr. Morgan opined that Ms. Lembeck lacked the capacity to make decisions about power of attorney, healthcare surrogates, or trustees because of her impaired reasoning ability and "somewhat paranoid and convoluted thinking" involving her oldest son. He also indicated that Ms. Lembeck continued to display significant limitations that impaired her capacity to make informed and rational decisions around the specific rights referenced in Florida Statute 744, including marrying, voting, applying for government benefits, operating a motor vehicle, traveling, seeking employment, contracting, participating in litigation, gifting, and making decisions about residence, social environment, and health care. In contrast, Dr. Morgan described Ms. Lembeck as having the ability to execute a will. Dr. Morgan opined that Ms. Lembeck was "in need of significant supervision, the nature of which is best determined by a home health visit by a registered nurse or other healthcare professionals that are trained to make this determination. The level of care that she receives at the ALF [assisted-living facility], which, I believe, is supplemented with other caregivers, seems appropriate." Dr. Morgan noted that, although Ms. Lembeck expressed clear preferences with respect to who should manage her affairs, there was a lack of logical process underlying these stated preferences. He predicted ongoing improvement in her functioning and offered a "guarded" prognosis for "significant recovery."

In an August 2009 case-manager assessment, Ms. Pesche described Ms. Lembeck as oriented to time, place, and person, but showing some ongoing difficulties with memory that she managed reasonably well—thereby demonstrating good insight and problem solving. She noted that Ms. Lembeck expressed a strong preference to return to her Winter Haven condominium as soon as possible.

EXAMINEE'S CURRENT FUNCTIONING AND ADJUSTMENT

Ms. Lembeck described an adequate adjustment in the assisted-living facility in which she currently resides but described herself as feeling "awfully lazy." She indicated that she participated in the facility's recreational activities, exercised, went shopping, cared for her cat, and met regularly with one son—Gale—who lived nearby.

When asked to describe a typical day, Ms. Lembeck reported that she participated in a daily "coffee clutch" each morning, ate lunch at noon, and participated in an exercise class and bingo program. She also reported traveling to her son's home on a regular basis, and shopping and running errands with him as well. She described herself as "pretty busy" most of the day and identified her biggest challenges to be problems with word-finding and remembering names.

DIAGNOSTIC IMPRESSION

Axis I: Vascular Dementia (possible paranoid delusions)

Axis II: No Diagnosis

Axis III: Deferred

EXAMINEE'S CAPACITY TO EXERCISE LEGAL RIGHTS AT ISSUE

Ms. Lembeck was administered the Independent Living Scales (ILS), which provide normative data regarding a person's capacity to engage in important, everyday tasks that are part of independent living (e.g., managing one's money and household, ensuring one's health and safety, traveling, interacting with others). When tested with the ILS, Ms. Lembeck clearly demonstrated some capacity with respect to these independent living skills (e.g., she was oriented to time, place, and person [i.e., she correctly reported when, where, and who she was], she identified sources of personal income, she correctly counted change, she correctly described the functions of a will and insurance policy, she indicated how she might use public transportation, she described strategies for ensuring her safety at home, she offered a strategy for managing medications).

However, Ms. Lembeck's overall performance on the ILS indicated that she, when compared to same age peers, had significant deficits with respect to memory functioning (e.g., she provided an inaccurate personal phone number, she could not remember an important appointment time she was instructed to remember, she could not remember a shopping list she was instructed to remember), managing money and finances (e.g., she could not report when federal taxes were due, she made errors when directed to write a check and calculate money differences, she could not balance a checkbook, she could not voice a strategy to avoid being taken advantage of by others financially), and managing home and transportation needs (e.g., she could not identify how to call the operator on a phone, she did not appreciate that fluctuations in her home's temperature might reflect a malfunction in the heating/cooling system). She showed lesser deficits, however, with respect to ensuring her health and safety (e.g., she offered incomplete strategies for what to do if she smelled gas in her home or suffered a bad cut).

Ms. Lembeck made clear her desire to return to her Winter Haven condominium. She estimated that, while most residents of this condominium resided there seasonally, there were between 12 and 14 persons who lived there year-round and were able and willing to assist and support her as necessary. Ms. Lembeck stated her belief that she was capable of living independently and saw herself as being entitled to restoration of all of the rights referenced in Florida Statute 744.

When asked about issues surrounding marriage, Ms. Lembeck responded that she would not marry "because if I get married, I do not have access to the trust for the kids." This statement was consistent with information provided by her guardian and money manager, Steve Grey. She went on to explain that marriage had the potential to threaten her financial stability and that, although she might seek to socialize with others—including men—she had no intention of marrying because of the financial and legal ramifications. This explanation and description on Ms. Lembeck's part demonstrated

rational and informed decision-making with respect to this right, but concerns about her judgment as it affects contracting (see below) raise questions about her ability to exercise this right.

Surrounding issues regarding voting, Ms. Lembeck expressed concern that political candidates often did not represent their true motivations and interests when campaigning. She identified the current president (Obama) by name but reported having no memory for his major opponent. When provided with the name of the president's opponent (McCain), Ms. Lembeck indicated that she could not offer anything about him or his personal or political history. When asked if she would be willing to sell her vote, Ms. Lembeck responded, "No way...that's a criminal thing." She went on to state that she could not vote in Orlando because she was not a resident, but rather, would have to vote in Winter Haven—her official residence. When asked how she might vote in a Winter Haven election if she was not living there on election day, Ms. Lembeck responded that she could travel to the polls or direct someone to get her "the invoice." Further inquiry revealed that Ms. Lembeck was referring to an absentee ballot. The above is considered to reflect general capacity in this area.

Ms. Lembeck was asked whether she was entitled to or received any government benefits, broadly conceived. She initially reported that she did not receive nor was she entitled to such benefits. When asked whether she received Social Security benefits, however, Ms. Lembeck responded affirmatively, and she also acknowledged receiving Medicare benefits, which she supplemented with private insurance—which was consistent with information in her medical record. When asked what she might do if her Social Security check stopped being deposited into her bank account, Ms. Lembeck responded that she would "call my son." Further inquiry revealed that Ms. Lembeck could not identify the agency to which she would need to direct such an inquiry. This lack of understanding and appreciation on Ms. Lembeck's part raises some concerns regarding her capacity to seek and access government benefits.

Ms. Lembeck indicated that her driver's license had been revoked, but offered her belief that she was fully capable of driving, which, she stated, would require taking a test. Ms. Lembeck saw herself as having no physical limitations or impairments that affected her ability to drive. Although this writer observed no obvious physical impairments that might limit Ms. Lembeck's capacity to drive, problems with memory and judgment raise some questions about her potential for becoming confused or disoriented when driving.

Ms. Lembeck described herself as capable of traveling independently and in need of no assistance, but limitations in her capacities relevant to travelling independently (e.g., judgment, problem solving, memory) raise questions about her abilities in this sphere. For example, when asked what she would do if she were traveling and had a flat tire on the side of the highway, Ms. Lembeck responded that she would "wait for the police to come and investigate." When asked how she would ensure that she had a hotel room in a city to which she was traveling, Ms. Lembeck responded, "I guess keep going to hotels until you find one that has a room," with no reference to or apparent appreciation of the concept of making a reservation.

When asked about seeking and maintaining employment, Ms. Lembeck indicated little desire for such. However, she did indicate that—before her stroke—she was a volunteer docent at a Winter Haven museum for three to four hours per week. Ms. Lembeck expressed no interest in working provided that she had adequate funds on which to live. No significant impairment with respect to making decisions in this sphere was observed.

With respect to the issues of contracting for services, Ms. Lembeck expressed her belief that she was capable of doing this. When asked how she might go about finding a vendor or service person to contract with, she replied she would seek the advice and input of other people who might have some experience. With respect to reviewing and considering a specific contract, Ms. Lembeck indicated she would probably rely on an attorney for review and consultation. This reflected no significant impairments with respect to this sphere, but given more general concerns about the examinee's judgment, vulnerability to manipulation, memory and problem solving, the court could consider capping an amount of money that Ms. Lembeck might be able to commit at one time (e.g., $200).

Ms. Lembeck expressed confidence in her ability to make decisions surrounding litigation. She acknowledged, however, that involvement in litigation was always a financial challenge and indicated that she would avoid litigation whenever possible. It was at this point in the interview that Ms. Lembeck described some of the legal matters surrounding her current guardianship and the tensions between her two sons. Given more general concerns about judgment, memory, vulnerability to manipulation, and problem solving, however, significant concerns remain with respect to her capacity to make decisions in connection with litigation.

With respect to passing property on to others, Ms. Lembeck indicated that she had executed a will subsequent to her husband's death. She reported that she was unsure, however, of what her most recent will directed and indicated that she did not have a copy of such. Ms. Lembeck voiced her desire to remove her older son—Stephen—as trustee and replace him with her younger son—Gale—because she did not believe she could trust Stephen. Ms Lembeck's description of these concerns was contradicted by the account offered by her money manager—Mr. Grey—who stated that she had historically placed her trust in Stephen and had had concerns about Gale. When asked about this apparent discrepancy, Ms. Lembeck responded, "Oh, Mr. Grey is confused—or maybe Stephen has gotten to him." When asked about the significance of a will, Ms. Lembeck responded that this document distributed a person's assets upon death and directed what would otherwise occur. Although Ms. Lembeck demonstrated a basic understanding of the nature and purpose of a will, concerns about her vulnerability to manipulation and that her current appraisal of her potential beneficiaries is impacted by some paranoid thinking raise questions about her capacity to make such decisions in her interest at this time.

Although Ms. Lembeck described herself as capable of making medical decisions and managing healthcare issues, she demonstrated some limitations in this area. Upon referring to a notebook she has with her, Ms. Lembeck identified her treating physician by name and correctly reported that she took medicine to thin her blood, manage her heartbeat, and neutralize stomach acid. As noted above, however, Dr. Peden expressed concern that Ms. Lembeck's memory limited her ability to manage her medications and keep medical appointments, and associated cognitive impairments limited her capacity to engage in rational and self-interested decision making with respect to medical interventions. When asked about these issues, Ms. Lembeck responded that her memory problems were "normal" for someone her age, that staff had "blown up" the significance of her problems surrounding managing medications and keeping doctors' appointments, and her reluctance to discuss medical treatment issues with Dr. Peden was because, "He's the doctor and knows best—how am I to understand this stuff? No one does."

Ms. Lembeck portrayed herself as fully capable of managing her money and estate. When asked about regular and recurring expenses, Ms. Lembeck identified property taxes, a monthly condominium fee, and power bills for her Minnesota residence (she noted that water and electricity were provided by way of her monthly condominium fees in Florida). When asked about recurring sources of income that were available to her, Ms. Lembeck correctly identified a Social Security check—the value of which she estimated to be $800; a small teacher's retirement, which she estimated to be approximately $900 monthly; and interest on the trust that was established in her name—all of which was corroborated in an interview with Gale Lembeck. Ms. Lembeck estimated the value of her holdings with Smith Barney to be approximately $750,000 in 2008 (which was corroborated by Mr. Grey), but complained that she had not been provided access to her financial documents and expressed concern that her older son—Stephen—mismanaged her assets for his own advantage. Ms. Lembeck stated—during both contacts with this writer—that she held "insured stocks," which, if they failed, were guaranteed by the government. Ms. Lembeck, during the clinical interview, insisted that "insured stocks" were not savings accounts or related mechanisms (e.g., Certificates of Deposit), and she described them as a "great deal" because these holdings were protected and one could not lose any principal invested. This claim, not surprisingly, was contradicted by Mr. Grey during his phone interview. More specifically, he indicated that no such investments existed, and he reported that Ms. Lembeck's assets included Certificates of Deposit, gold, "blue chip" stocks that typically paid dividends, and money market accounts. When asked to identify other assets, Ms. Lembeck estimated the value of her Winter Haven condominium to be approximately $75,000 and her Minnesota lake home to be approximately $100,000. Gale Lembeck estimated the current value of these homes, conservatively, to be $350,000 and $500,000. Ms. Lembeck reported having two vehicles—one in Florida and one in Minnesota. While she described the value of the six- or seven-year-old Buick in Minnesota to be approximately $1,000, she estimated the value of her three-year-old Honda to be between $30,000 and $40,000. Problems with judgment and memory described above raise concerns about Ms. Lembeck's capacity to manage money and related assets at this time.

SUMMARY AND RECOMMENDATIONS

Susan Mancini, court-appointed guardian for Maureen Lembeck, requested that this writer assess her client's capacity to exercise rights that had previously been removed, restricted, or transferred via an existing guardianship. Ms. Lembeck was tested and interviewed in the Orlando assisted living facility where she has resided since January of this year.

A little less than a year ago, Ms. Lembeck suffered a stroke that resulted in significant language, memory, and other cognitive deficits, but she has shown a gradual improvement in functioning and adjustment in the ensuing 12 months. She continues to demonstrate, however, deficits in memory functioning and judgment that raise concerns about her ability to exercise important rights and protect her interests, along with possible paranoid thinking regarding the motivations of one of her sons.

Decisions regarding the revocation, restriction, or transfer of rights are ultimately legal ones that are to be decided by the legal decision maker. It is the opinion of this writer that Ms. Lembeck only shows adequate capacity to exercise rights and make decisions about voting and (limited) contracting (i.e., for smaller amounts of money). As detailed above, Ms. Lembeck continues to demonstrate deficits in memory functioning and judgment, along with possible paranoia and vulnerability to influence by others that raise serious concerns about her ability to exercise other important rights including the rights to marry, have a driver's license, contract, seek and retain employment, seek government benefits, litigate, manage finances, make healthcare decisions, make decisions about her living and social environments, and dispose of property. As such, restoration of these rights is not recommended at this time.

Thank you for this evaluation opportunity. If you have any questions about this evaluation, please do not hesitate to contact me.

Randy K. Otto, Ph.D.
Licensed Psychologist
Board Certified in Forensic Psychology
Board Certified in Clinical Psychology
American Board of Professional Psychology

TEACHING POINT:
GUARDIANSHIP AND THE REVISED
SPECIALTY GUIDELINES FOR
FORENSIC PSYCHOLOGY
(contributed by Randy K. Otto)

Guardianship/conservatorship evaluations are among the most challenging forensic psychological evaluations to conduct, given the diverse rights and capacities that are referenced in the laws of many states.

The APA *Specialty Guidelines* recommends that examiners carefully consider use of assessment tools. Measures of emotional, behavioral, and cognitive functioning (such as the measures of intelligence and cognitive functioning that were employed in this evaluation) provide the examiner with little information about an examinee's capacity to exercise specific rights such as making healthcare decisions, managing finances, deciding place of residence, applying for government benefits, or gifting assets. They can, however, prove of assistance in identifying emotional, behavioral, or cognitive impairments that are responsible for limitations that may exist in the person's ability to exercise these rights. In contrast, conducting focused inquiries and employing forensic assessment instruments (i.e., instruments designed to assess specific psycholegal abilities) such as Independent Living Scales can provide more relevant information regarding specific impairments in the capacities that are at issue in legal proceedings.

The APA *Specialty Guidelines* advises psychologists to consider multiple sources of information when conducting forensic evaluations. The case above highlights the potential value of this approach. Review of reports summarizing previously conducted evaluations of the examinee; interviews with informed third parties, including the examinee's sons, financial advisor, and treating physician; and data gathered via interview and psychological testing each provided information relevant to understanding the examinee and her current functioning, abilities, and limitations.

The APA *Specialty Guidelines* recommends that forensic psychologists affirmatively disclose the factual bases for their expert opinions. This is so that the legal decision maker can fully understand the rationale underlying opinions that the examining psychologist offers, and make informed judgments about their weight and legitimacy accordingly. This report demonstrates the value of such transparency, insofar as it provides the legal decision maker with a rich description of what the examinee can and cannot do, and the underlying basis for the opinions and recommendations that are offered.

17

Child Custody

The two reports in this chapter are assessments of child custody. Requests for child custody evaluations typically come from the court, or from attorneys representing one of the divorcing parties. Even under the latter circumstances, however, the evaluator may be court-appointed in some jurisdictions. In the first case, the principle being applied addresses the importance of determining the particular role to be played if the referral is accepted. This principle focuses on the implications of assuming simultaneous professional roles, such as therapist and evaluator, in the context of FMHA. The teaching point addresses the question of whether a professional can play more than one of these roles in a single case. The principle associated with the second case addresses the importance of using multiple sources of information to test rival hypotheses and improve the accuracy of the evaluation. The teaching point then discusses in more detail the role of the forensic clinician in collecting third party information.

CASE ONE
PRINCIPLE: DETERMINE THE PARTICULAR ROLE TO BE PLAYED IF THE REFERRAL IS ACCEPTED
(PRINCIPLE 15)

Forensic evaluators are often confronted with the "dual role relationship" issue in their practice. A dual role relationship in the FMHA context is one in which two roles are assumed by a mental health professional in the same case. This might arise under a variety of circumstances, and the dual role relationship can be the result of a combination of various roles played by a mental health professional. For example, a dual role could result when a professional role is combined with a personal or vocational role, or when two professional roles are combined (e.g., treating therapist and forensic

evaluator). This discussion will focus on simultaneous professional roles from different contexts, such as therapist and evaluator, in FMHA.

Assuming dual roles is frequently a source of complaints to ethics committees and licensure boards for both psychiatrists and psychologists (Bersoff, 2008), and is particularly challenging in the context of custody evaluations (Pickar, 2007). Various sources of ethics guidance and authority discourage dual role relationships. According to the *Ethical Principles of Psychologists and Code of Conduct* (American Psychological Association, 2010a), it is the responsibility of the professional to avoid relationships that "could reasonably be expected to impair the psychologist's objectivity, competence, or effectiveness in performing his or her functions as a psychologist, or otherwise risks exploitation or harm to the person with whom the professional relationship exists" (Standard 3.05). When it is not possible to avoid serving in multiple roles, the *Specialty Guidelines for Forensic Psychology* (APA *Specialty Guidelines*; American Psychological Association, 2013b) states that professionals should "consider the risks and benefits to all parties and to the legal system or entity likely to be impacted, the possibility of separating each service widely in time, seeking judicial review and direction, and consulting with knowledgeable colleagues" (Guideline 4.02.01). For instance, if a professional is in the position of "providing both forensic and therapeutic services," he is encouraged to "seek to minimize the potential negative effects of this circumstance" (Guideline 4.02.01).

The potential for dual role relationships is particularly salient in emotionally charged child custody evaluations. Generally, psychologists avoid conducting a child custody evaluation when their impartiality might be compromised; a typical example is when the psychologist has previously served as a therapist for the child or his or her immediate family (APA, 2010b). This caveat also applies to mental health professionals who find themselves in the role of a fact witness for the courts. Under some circumstances, a court may require a psychologist to testify as a fact witness regarding information to which the psychologist was privy in the course of a professional relationship with a client. Preferably, however, the psychologist should decline the role of expert witness and avoid giving a professional opinion regarding custody and visitation when that psychologist has previously served as a therapist (APA, 2010b). The *Ethics Guidelines for the Practice of Forensic Psychiatry* (American Academy of Psychiatry and the Law, 2005) notes that treating psychiatrists should also avoid dual role relationships:

> Forensic evaluations usually require interviewing corroborative sources, exposing information to public scrutiny, or subjecting evaluees and the treatment itself to potentially damaging cross-examination. The forensic evaluation and the credibility of the practitioner may also be undermined by conflicts inherent in the differing clinical and forensic roles. Treating psychiatrists should therefore generally avoid acting as an expert witness for their patients or performing evaluations of their patients for legal purposes. (Honesty and Striving for Objectivity, para. 7)

In addition to ethical considerations, standards of practice discourage dual role relationships. Some commentators have advocated a strict separation of roles (Greenberg & Shuman, 2007; Heilbrun, 1995), even to the extent of barring treating mental health professionals from the courtroom in cases in which they have treated one of the litigants (Shuman, Greenberg, Heilbrun, & Foote, 1998). Similarly, other commentators emphasize the importance of functioning within a single role from the outset of a custody evaluation (Emery & Rogers, 1990), recommend that dual roles be avoided even following the completion of an evaluation (Stahl, 2011), and support the view that custody evaluators should be unknown to the respective parties to avoid ethics complaints in custody cases (Glassman, 1998). Despite the limited legal and empirical support against the dual role relationship, current ethics guidelines and professional standards of practice strongly discourage the dual role relationship (Heilbrun, Grisso, & Goldstein, 2009).

There are also numerous practical reasons for avoiding dual role relationships. First, selecting and maintaining a single role makes the clinician's participation safer, in the sense that this role becomes the only basis for participation in the evaluation. Focusing on a single role also encourages forensic clinicians to think clearly about which role they will choose, and to avoid being drawn into forensic participation with clients for whom the role was not initially selected. Multiple roles can potentially create complications and make matters more complex. There is also an associated enhanced risk of client dissatisfaction, in some cases leading to ethics complaints and malpractice litigation against clinicians involved in dual roles. Clinicians should be exceedingly cautious under circumstances that might result in dual role participation, and avoid assuming more than one role in a single case whenever possible.

In the present evaluation, the evaluator was careful to clarify her role as part of the notification of purpose. Moreover, this information was provided in writing to ensure that the nature of her role was clear to all parties involved. The evaluator also performed collateral interviews with the mother's former therapist and the couple's former marital therapist, which provided her with extensive information about the parents while still maintaining an impartial stance.

8/25/11
PARENTAL ACCESS EVALUATION
Clark v. Clark # XXXXXX

BACKGROUND

This matter was referred for a forensic parenting evaluation by court order of 3/31/11. At issue is the residential schedule for the parties' daughter, Emma (DOB 4/10/10).

INFORMED CONSENT

In written documents, the following information was provided to the parties: the evaluator's role, the nature of the forensic examination process, that the examination was not therapy, and that forensic evaluations are not confidential and not covered by therapist–patient privilege. It was also explained to the parties that when considering the interviews, psychometric testing, and collateral information, and when formulating opinions in this matter, the focus is to generate legally relevant hypotheses and provide information to the court. The parties have indicated that they understood and agreed to the above by signing the necessary consent form. Collateral sources were also informed prior to obtaining any information that that their information would not be confidential.

Readers of this report should be aware that, given the extensive amount of information provided by both parties, this report is likely to contain some inaccurate and/or contradictory information. The information presented here is to inform the reader of the data reported to the examiner, not to assert its truthfulness or accuracy. Presentation of any statement in this report does not necessarily mean that the statement is factual or that each statement presented was accorded equal weight by the evaluator.

PROCEDURES

As part of this evaluation, the following interviews were conducted:

6/28/11 Mary Clark	1.25 hours
7/5/11 Ed Clark	2.0 hours
7/7/11 Mary, Emma—home visit	1.0 hour
7/12/11 Ed, Emma—home visit	1.0 hour
7/14/11 Ed Clark	2.0 hours
7/19/11 Mary Clark	1.25 hours

Both parties were administered a PAI and an MMPI-2 and both completed a Parenting History Survey and a Social-Psychological History Questionnaire. Relevant affidavits and written documents submitted by the parties were reviewed. In addition, the following collateral contacts were made:

Edith Bunt—Mary's former therapist
Lisa Brown—did marital therapy with these parties
Eileen Smith—visitation supervisor
Wendy Conroy—nanny
Katie Rogers—friend of both parents
Jessica Swift—former friend of Mary's
Heidi—scheduler at Indaba

SOCIAL HISTORIES
Mary

Mary gave the following information regarding her background: She was born in Illinois and grew up primarily in Madison, Illinois, with a brother three years older and a brother three years younger. Her father was an accountant with the telephone company, and her mother was a kindergarten teacher.

Mary described her father as "very warm, not as energetic as my mother. He was very dedicated. We did sports and camping and he didn't bring work home." She described her mother as "a people person. She is very energetic...kind and loving. She was our main caretaker." In talking about the relationship between her parents, Mary stated, "They had a great relationship. They're good friends. They call each other on things and have arguments—it wasn't hidden—but they have a very loving relationship. They put each other first."

When asked about her brothers, Mary stated, "My younger brother and I have always gotten along well. The older brother and I were like oil and vinegar. Everyone thought I was the older one. I was good at sports and he wasn't. But we're close now." Mary stated that both her brothers live in Chicago. Her older brother is a certified public accountant (CPA) and is married with two children. Her younger brother is not married. She reported that she had regular contact with both of them.

With regard to school, Mary stated, "I was definitely an over-achiever. I did well." She felt she had sufficient friends, and added, "I was not in a specific clique so I was lonely when they would have their get-togethers....Not lonely—that was the wrong word....I was always happy and very friendly." Mary graduated in 2001.

After high school, Mary attended the University of Michigan and graduated with a degree in biomedical science in 2005. Next, she attended medical school at Marquette and graduated in 2009. In talking about her work history since graduating, Mary stated that she has been "working here, thirty hours a week at the medical building, and I teach at the medical college." When asked about plans for the future, Mary stated, "I would like to relocate to Illinois. I have a job offer there. It's a good opportunity with benefits. Now I'm an independent contractor."

Mary married for the first time in 2005 "right after college," and noted that her husband was "seven years older. It was short-lived. We had a long-distance relationship while dating and things continued to go in a wrong direction." Mary and her husband separated after a year and a half, and she said, "It was also an abusive relationship. I got an annulment. Josh was very controlling and possessive—a very angry person....There was nothing physical before we were married—it was just us against the world. School was a major issue. Things became increasingly physical as time went on. My main goal was to move on. I just wanted to be out." This marriage ended in August 2007.

Mary is currently living in a two-bedroom apartment in Redmond.

Ed

Ed gave the following information regarding his background: He grew up in Tennessee with a brother three years younger than he. His father "worked his way up through a food service company," and his mother was a public school teacher.

Ed described his father as "a good mentor, good leader, and a good person. He was well respected and consistent....He makes people comfortable. He was very involved and a good example for us— how to live through life...how to be a man...He was always giving us confidence and he led by example....He would always be there for us and was very loving." He described his mother as "very empathetic with a big heart. She would do anything for anybody. She was very kind and very caring." When asked about the relationship between his parents, Ed stated, "They were always on the same page....They went out of their way to make sure they were on the same page and presented a united front." Ed stated that his parents live in Tennessee and he has regular contact with them, both in person and on the phone.

Ed indicated that he and his brother got along "very well. I cast a broad shadow for my brother. He favored athletics and I favored academics." Ed's brother lives in Boulder and does marketing for a biking company. He is not married. In talking about his contact with his brother currently, Ed stated, "He has fallen in love and I'm in a different place. I've been protective of him, so it's difficult right now for me to be the big brother."

With regard to schooling, Ed reported that he did "very well" and had sufficient friends. He thought others would remember him as "a genuine person and nice guy—fun to be around and well respected." He graduated in 2000.

After high school, Ed attended Vanderbilt University and received a degree in business and economics in 2003, graduating a semester early. He worked at Ernst & Young for a year doing "systems analysis" and then entered medical school at

Marquette, graduating in 2009. After graduating, Ed worked in a medical practice for one year and then enrolled in a graduate program through the University of Washington, which began in June 2010. He expects to be finished in May 2013.

Ed married for the first time in 2004. He indicated that he met his first wife while in college, and they were "fast friends. We hung out together....It was my first time being in a serious relationship. We started living together our sophomore year....We became more like roommates." Ed moved to Milwaukee in 2005 and lived with his in-laws. He stated, "After six months, she joined me. In 2006, we were sleeping in different bedrooms....We were officially separated in January 2007 and divorced in August 2007."

Ed is currently living in an apartment on Eastlake in Seattle.

MARITAL HISTORY

These parties met in medical school in August 2005. Ed said, "She said to me, 'We're going to be great friends.' We were....I was a class officer and was organizing events....I was low and blue. It was a tough thing for me. I had made everything work and I couldn't get my marriage to work....Mary was going through a similar thing and it was good to have a friend." Ed stated that he was attracted to Mary by "what a caring, kind person she was. There was never a scorecard....In October 2006, we went camping together and that was the first time we were intimate....We both felt unbelievably guilty over our marriages. I separated and then she separated. As hard as we tried to not just fall into each other, we did. We were inseparable."

Talking about this same time period, Mary stated, "He was president of our class and we had the same group of friends. Ed was also married and I knew things weren't good very early. I moved in with my parents at the separation and we fell into each other because we were going through the same thing....In October 2006, it started to develop and we were dating in the spring 2007....He was my knight in shining armor coming to the rescue. He was caring and good-hearted, I thought at the time. It was when I was vulnerable and low. I was questioning how I so quickly allowed somebody in my life. It moved very quickly." Ed stated, "It was great. We were both doing well in school and it was good socially. It was fun....Both of us graduated....We left our school a better place and the world was our oyster. She was at the top of our class—she has the most brilliant mind I've ever met. I have to work more."

The parties moved in together in the summer of 2008 and became engaged in October. They married in March 2009. Mary stated, "Things were good. Looking back, there were minor things. I should have seen signs. He wanted to have children very much—more than I did. I agreed to have children fairly quickly. Through the pregnancy, things were good. As the birth got closer, he was breaking things. When she was born, it was like flipping a switch. There were a lot of changes.... He applied to several schools, but the University of Washington was his first choice. He got accepted and I started crying. I felt awful. I was nervous about moving across the country with a child." Emma was born in April 2010. Ed stated, "She said, 'I'm ready to have a family,' and I was overjoyed. A big part for me was being a provider for my family. We were so excited.... She had to go off her heart medication and that was a big stressor.... Her pregnancy was very difficult. She was constantly vomiting.... I tried to help her but she was so sick. She lost weight and had to be induced a little early."
Ed went on to say,

> From there, we had a lot thrown at us. It was a big transition.... We moved to Washington when Emma was two months old. I tried to set everything up.... I started my residency program.... She missed her circle of colleagues and we had no childcare. We found a daycare and she really needed that.... She found a job she loved. It was *the* job. She was meeting so many people. She had been blue and sleeping a lot.... I couldn't help her.... She finally got to someone who could help her [medication].... She was happy when she was working.... She was learning a lot and it gave her a lot of pride. She kind of went overboard. She was doing marketing, and her boss was asking her to do a lot without compensating her. I didn't want to say anything because she was doing better.... She wanted to buy the practice but the practitioner became reluctant. She was holding out a carrot. It became a big stress.... It became a contentious relationship. She was having trouble sleeping.... She would twitch or shake.... She would sleep a lot during the day. She did sleep studies and they

gave her a CPAP [continuous positive air pressure device]. She couldn't do it. Debbie [her boss] really weighed on her.... We had been looking for a home, and that was a stressor too. As we got closer to Christmas, neither of us wanted to admit it, but we thought we could do it all.... I assumed we were strong enough—the way we came together wouldn't affect us. We were more insecure than we would admit. I had been killing myself. I was trying to pick her up, clean the house, take care of the dog, take care of Emma. We never would keep score, but the hard part was she would say I wasn't giving enough. I would say, "I'm giving you all I have." There was a lot of negativity.

Mary stated,

> The move out here was very hard. He was now in school and we were used to being together. The main change was when Emma was born. The day I was home from the hospital, he had a friend over and went for a three-and-a-half-hour bike ride. I thought, "That's weird. He's always wanted children." He bought a dog without talking to me.... I felt he fell out of love with me. He told me I was a bad mother, constantly. I was low and I missed my family terribly. I started taking antidepressants and things seemed to improve. He continued in school and it spiraled out of control. There were constant put-downs. It was like he didn't want what he had wanted so badly. I found a nanny.... At Christmas he didn't want me to go home. His parents came out. They knew it wasn't going well.... I told his mother, "I don't think Ed loves me anymore." He hung out with a friend at school.... He ended up not going snowshoeing with her because he knew I wasn't comfortable with that.... In January 2011, he began tracking me.... He was very different from the Ed I had fallen in love with. There had been violent incidents—breaking doors off hinges that I was behind, ripping up paperwork. I wanted to fix it and make it better.... Emma was not growing properly. We were in the hospital two times with her but no cause was found. There was a lot of turmoil in the home. He would not call. I would invite the nanny's son over and he would get

jealous....I said, "Are you tracking me?" and he said "no"....On February 14, I got in a minor accident. It felt like things were falling apart....He became very erratic.

In talking about other difficulties, Mary stated,

> He very much wanted to buy a home. I didn't want to buy a home....My mom wanted to visit and he was extremely upset. Ed held on to Emma and wouldn't leave. I left without Emma....I had a [domestic violence, DV] advocate who was very nervous I hadn't healed from the past. I was doing everything I could do to fix it and help him be the best father I knew he could be. I had a safety plan. I didn't know what to do about Emma. I would put her down, he would come home, and I would leave....I had a continuing education course in Oregon....I told him "I don't think we're good married. Let's stay friends.

Mary described a subsequent incident in which Ed "tried to grab the phone....He was swearing and calling me names....He proceeded to tackle Emma and me. I kicked him with all my might. Emma is freaking out....We slept in separate bedrooms. I don't know the right way to do it. I told him 'I won't do anything with you unless it's in public.'"

Ed discussed events around Christmas by saying,

> My parents were coming and I wanted it to be a pleasant experience. It became a big point of contention....Things started going downhill. I couldn't understand it. I didn't listen. Christmas was particularly tough....There had been times throughout the relationship when she escalated, flooded. It was gone completely during the pregnancy but they started to come back. Honesty was a big thing. She became more dishonest. She got fired. She went in on her day off and copied papers. The owner freaked out and changed the locks. She had the other employees sign that they wouldn't talk to her. We couldn't purchase a house. She lost her friends, she had a young baby, and the lady is threatening litigation. It was happening all at once. I don't think I fully saw it, "We're superhuman." Emma got sick. Her sleep pattern was off and she was crying

and upset. The dog got sick. Mary is telling me I'm not cherishing her enough. It was tough for me to hear.

Ed went on to say that in the aftermath of losing her job, Mary wanted to set up her own business. He said, "It was a logistical nightmare. She was staying out late and on the weekends." Ed stated that he wanted to do something for Valentine's Day and went to Mary's office after she had gone in at 6:00 a.m. He stated,

> Her staff told me she had left at 8:30 a.m.... I did check up on her. I thought she was having an affair....She told me "I wanted you to think I was having an affair. I'm leaving you." It hit me like a ton of bricks. Before, she would say, "I want to be left alone" when she needed a hug. I couldn't believe it....We started talking about custody....She sent an email that said I was violent and cruel. I sent an email to her and to her parents saying, "Don't do this. You can't distort the truth like this." Her mom came into town....The day she said there was emotional abuse, I said, "I don't think so, but if you do, let's see a therapist." She got us in right away. She was well-intentioned but she saw us in her apartment, which was disconcerting to both of us.

Ed indicated that while Mary's mother was in town, she and Emma had moved to a hotel with her. He stated,

> She would bring Emma back....We would hold each other....She didn't want to do things in front of her mother....Her mother left. Around that time, I began to feel that it was not her goal to make the marriage work. I could tell. I felt like I was being set up but I couldn't believe she would do those things....She would go out constantly....come home at 11:00 p.m. and want to be intimate. I'm insecure and hurt....She said I was being emotionally abusive. She would dance on the exercise equipment naked. She wouldn't stop and would say, "You're being withholding." I would pull her into bed and hold her.

Mary indicated the parties separated on February 11. Ed indicated that Mary left the home on March 6 with Emma and he filed a missing persons report shortly thereafter. The next morning, Mary went to Eastside Domestic Violence and discovered that the police had contacted them because of the missing persons report. She stated,

> They asked me "Was there violence?" and I said, "Yes, there was." He said, "I have to report this." I gave a statement.... He evaded service for a week and stole my laptop.... Mom stayed with me. I left a message for him, "I need my laptop back and you need to be served." He went into the police station, was arrested and spent the night in jail.

Mary stated,

> There is continued frustration, but I'm feeling much better and healthier. Emma has grown like a weed. He has not utilized visits because of his schedule, which is completely heartbreaking to me.... I'm stuck. I want to be out of this situation. He was putting gifts in the diaper bag and the police were involved. The next day, there was a 35-page document about how I'm a horrible person.... I want him to be the person he was, if that's possible.

ISSUES

Ed summarized his view of the current situation by stating:

> In all honesty—I have no idea. It baffles me how she can possibly justify what has happened here. The picture she paints of me and our past is very serious—but it simply is not accurate. Almost her entire declaration is simply fiction. Start to finish, I do not know how she expects to stand behind what she has written. She has evaded deposition from that point to this, but ultimately she is going to have to account for what she has written, and I don't understand how she expects to do so. My lawyer wrote me this on Saturday 6/11/11: "With respect to the deposition, Mary is not cooperating at all. she is refusing all dates we have noted either because she is gone or because her attorney is not available. She is refusing June 13, 14, 15, and 16, and is now refusing June 27, and June 30, when she will be required to appear in court.

What I advise you to do is file a motion to compel her deposition on the afternoon of June 30, 2011."

I understand the severity of such claims and that the courts must take them seriously until they have time to investigate. The court system is safeguarding and looking out for the best interests of my wife and daughter— I would want it no other way. At some point, however, the truth has to shine through—love has to win out. I realize every single person who has been a part of this (police, lawyers, commisioners, judges) have to protect their own interests, and any shred of doubt cannot be overlooked, but eventually the truth has to win out.

I am not perfect. I put a lot of stress on our family with going back to school, with the purchase of a home, with not being a provider. When Mary was blue, or later when she was fired and began working tirelessly to start a medical practice, and I was overwhelmed because I was trying to take care of Emma and stay above water at work with my residency, complete my Free Application for Federal Student Aid (FASFA) and our taxes, and I was consumed with the daily details of life that were left to me...the cleaning the house and making the meals, the buying of the groceries, the running of the dog and paying the bills and trying to keep things going, I know I could have tried to do things differently and make Mary feel more cherished and loved in that time. And while there is no excuse for it, from our past, I was insecure and sad and hurt when I thought Mary was having an affair.

The current situation though...even our mutual friends have said Mary told them, "she didn't want this to happen and it was my fault for calling the police." Her lawyer has said the same thing in court. I called her parents, I called my parents, I went to the police and I filed a missing persons out of fear and love. I love my wife, and I love my daughter. My wife wasn't making logical or rational choices (her termination, her car accident, her dishonesty, her infidelity) and I feared that my daughter was being taken from me. I filed for divorce because my lawyer asked Mary two separate times if I could even have visitation and she refused. I was willing to wait...even after what she had done....I wasn't in a rush to get a divorce—I didn't and don't even want a divorce—was willing to let her settle down and figure things out and find a way to dig herself out of the mess she created, but once Emma was put in the middle, my lawyer told me that was the only way I could ensure getting my daughter back in my life. I simply had no choice.

Maybe that is what Mary is trying to say: She was embarrassed by what happened at work and over Christmas and with this other guy, and that her parents and my parents knew, and she had been spending nights and weekends away from Emma and just trying to lose herself in starting a business so she could just take a break from everything (from her husband and her baby and from the loss of her job and from being married, etc.) but once she found out my parents were coming in town and Wendy (our nanny) knew what was going on, she took Emma and never came home. Maybe Mary is trying to say that just like me filing for divorce, that day when the police showed up she feared that she was going to be accused of abandoning Emma (she states this in her declaration) or of withholding Emma from me...and out of fear that Emma would be taken from her, she felt compelled to use claims of abuse as the only tool left at her disposal to maintain 100% custody of our daughter.

Mary summarized her view of the current situation by stating:

Significant change in my husband since Emma was born. While there were control issues and emotional issues from early on in our relationship, the situation escalated substantially upon her birth. Emotional and physical abuse from Ed became a more than normal occurrence in our household. Destruction of my personal property, intimidation, physical assaults, stalking, tracking, breaking into email accounts, constant control and emotional mind games, were just some of the tactics Ed utilized. As time went on and Emma was present to witness more and more of these awful events, she failed to grow and stopped sleeping through the night.

She became ill on several occasions and no tests could explain the illness. Emma actually fell off the growth charts and simply was not gaining proper weight. And then in March of this year, Emma was involved in a physical assault from Ed. I went into protective mode, both for Emma and I myself. I placated Ed as best I could as the exit strategy was devised and protective order obtained. I found the best way I knew how to give safety to my daughter Emma. I initially asked Ed for a "time out." I then obtained a protective order and left the home with Emma. All the while, I was working with the Eastside Domestic Violence Agency to plan the safest exit strategy. In turn, Ed attempted and succeeded to avoid service of the order for almost a week. Ed then sent his lawyer to the courthouse on May 17th and instructed him to serve me with a lengthy divorce/dissolution of marriage. I had no legal representation at this time. As I continued to seek safety for my child and myself, Ed chose to make further poor decisions—removing the guns from the home, taking my personal laptop, involving my workplace, utilizing some type of spyware to obtain my new and personal banking account information as well as its balance, claiming it was a joint account. Ed emptied our savings with major credit card payments to his personal credit card and again claimed it was me that liquidated accounts and removed him from accessing the accounts. I did neither. Ed was charged by the Kirkland Police for a domestic assault that took place on March 6. The police, he involved by attempting to file a missing persons report upon my not being home for an hour during which I did not answer my phone on the evening I picked Emma up and did not go home. The police ended up calling the Eastside, where I had signed a release for my safety. They were able to tell the police I had been utilizing their services and had gone to obtain a protective order. When the order was in effect, I went to the police station and was asked if there had been a recent physical assault, since they would need to report that and it seems there must have been if a protective order was granted. The police took my statement and said they would serve Ed with the protective order. After Ed filed for divorce and he asked for a temporary parenting plan allowing him one weekend a month supervised with Emma by his mother, as well as one dinner a week, he was denied the parenting plan. The judge told him there was a lot of evidence of domestic violence and huge risk factors for myself and Emma which she saw in the discovery, as well as his own declaration. He was granted two supervised visits per week for a maximum of three hours each—court-approved supervisors to be used at each. Ed has chosen to forgo using the max time with Emma on multiple occasions, has continued to change, switch, and alter the schedule every single week, many times at the last minute. Ed and his attorney have made multiple court dates on days they are aware I will be out of town, of which I changed my flights for, and again asked for a continuance at the last minute. He continues to request dates and times he is aware Emma and I will be out of town. This has been and continues to be the absolute hardest time in my entire life. I have received much support from my family and friends. However, they are all back in the Midwest—mainly Illinois. My mom has stayed with Emma and for extended stays, even months at a time, as this whole situation has unfolded. I have traveled back to Illinois as often as I can and will continue to do so. I need the support and help of my entire family and network of friends who have been involved in Emma and my life in a major way, only limited when we moved across the country to enable Ed to take part in a post-graduate residency program—which he is still in. I was and am the only one, between the two of us, with an income, and have supported Ed through school up until March 31st when our assets were requested to be frozen, yet Ed removed ten thousand–plus dollars, until finally there were no funds, and I stopped depositing money. Emma and I now reside in a two-bedroom apartment in Redmond. More recently, on the weekend of June 4 and 5, Ed used Emma's diaper bag to communicate/transport gifts to me during the residential exchanges in violation of the temporary order for protection. I have reported these communications/gifts/violations of the order for protection to the police.

Ed is being criminally prosecuted for his physical assault of me.

I want what is best for my daughter. I do see it as very important to have her father in her life. However, it is up to Ed to better himself in order to be around Emma in the future. It breaks my heart when Ed chooses to not maximize his time with Emma. However, that is his choice. I know I am the better primary parent for Emma and will continue to be the positive influence in her life. I will love her and surround her with loving family and friends. I will work and provide for her and continue to talk to her about her daddy and how she is half him and I love every part of her.

Something is very broken in Ed. His thoughts and declarations are ever changing and even bizarre, and he discusses things that are strange in nature and completely false. He has used the courts to continue to abuse and control me and has even tried to communicate with me via his declarations by going on and on about Emma and their conversations—which are all words he said to me and plans he planned with me, and dates we had, etc. He describes Emma as an "orange on a toothpick" as well as a "little ram." It frightens me when I read his declarations. The fact is that even after a protective order and no-contact order were put in place, Ed has manipulated situations, hacked into my personal bank accounts, violated the orders clearly on multiple occasions. It's hard for me to wrap my head around. It is simply not rational. Ed is making a choice to be in his residency program and put that first over his daughter whom he is only allowed [to see] "six hours a week"—something he has been unable to meet. I want Ed to get better and be a wonderful healthy father for Emma, but until that truly takes place I believe it to be in Emma's best interest to reside with me and have limited supervised contact with Ed.

BEHAVIORAL OBSERVATIONS
Ed

Ed is a 29-year-old Caucasian male of average height and average build. He arrived punctually for appointments dressed in business attire and was well groomed. Paperwork was completed in a timely and competent manner. Ed provided a greater volume of supporting documents than is typical. Some of these submissions were relevant to issues in dispute between the parties, but a greater number were documenting happier times with Emma and Mary through journals and photos, but without direct reference to conflicts in the case.

Ed's cognitive functioning was organized and coherent with no evidence of thought disturbance. Intellectual functioning, though untested, is apt to be substantially above average. Speech was moderately paced with good use of expressive vocabulary and regular use of clichés. Affect was generally appropriate but increasingly depressive, sad, and tearful. In general, Ed presented as deferential and cooperative. Although paperwork indicated careful attention to detail, Ed's narrative often focused on affective issues and a somewhat grandiose, rose-colored presentation of his history with Mary and Emma. He avoided negative statements regarding Mary and verbalized responsibility for some of the difficulties between them. Insight appeared to be variable.

During the home visit, Ed was cheerful and upbeat with Emma. He was completely engaged with her and adept at responding to her verbalizations and signals. Ed shadowed Emma closely, in an anxious effort to intervene if she fell as she careened around his apartment. He was clearly familiar with her likes and dislikes as well as her behavioral patterns and was obviously gratified by her happy responses to him.

Ed is living in a small studio apartment in the Eastlake area of Seattle. The apartment is adequately furnished and appropriately baby-proofed.

Mary

Mary is a 28-year-old Caucasian female of above-average height and slender build. She arrived for her appointments punctually and was stylishly dressed in casual attire and well groomed. Cognitive functioning was organized and coherent with no evidence of thought disorder. Intellectual functioning, though untested, is apt to be substantially above average. Speech was rapid and fluid with good use of vocabulary. Affect was limited and unvarying during the initial interview, but during the second interview, Mary's responses had a noticeably angry and sarcastic tone. Her eye contact was poor during this interview. In general, Mary presented as socially adept and capable but

lacking in self-awareness. Defensiveness and minimization were evident.

During the home visit, Mary interacted with Emma in an exuberant, affectionate manner. She provided opportunities for Emma to work on new skills and responded to her efforts in a positive, elaborative way. When Emma engaged in unwanted behavior, she was adept at moving her away and providing alternatives.

Mary lives in a well-furnished, two-bedroom apartment in Redmond. It was nicely decorated and very well organized and appropriately baby-proofed.

Emma

Emma is an irresistibly cute 15-month-old who was cheerful, active, and easily engaged throughout both home visits. She is developmentally on target with pre-verbal expressions, and her motor skills appear good as she moves from walking to running. Emma was alert and interested in new stimuli and affectionate with both parents. During the home visit at her father's, I asked Ed to move out of sight and then picked Emma up. She immediately looked for him and shook her head firmly.

TEST RESULTS

Psychological test results presented below are only hypotheses and should not be used by the reader of this report in isolation from other information in this matter. The interpretive statements are primarily computer-generated, actuarial predictions based on the results of the tests. Personality test results reflect characteristics of persons who have provided test response patterns that are similar to those of the current individuals. Although the test results are presented in an affirmative manner, they are probabilistic in nature. Furthermore, the reader should interpret these findings cautiously in that it is impossible to tell, from test results alone, if these personality patterns and deficits preexisted the events in question or are the results or sequelae of the events. Therefore the reader should examine the test interpretation for general trends and put limited weight on any one specific statement. In the integration and presentation of the test data, where results were unclear or in conflict, I used my clinical judgment to select the most likely hypotheses for presentation here. The reader's task is to keep in mind the information available regarding these parties and utilize that to test whether these hypotheses are confirmed or disconfirmed.

Mary

Mary produced an MMPI profile that was significantly more defensive than the norm for this context. Individuals with this validity pattern are presenting in an overly favorable manner, either due to a lack of self-awareness, a conscious attempt to minimize flaws, or some combination of these. Clinical scales were not elevated beyond the upper limits of the normal range but are apt to have been suppressed by this approach to the task. Individuals with this particular clinical pattern are apt to be outgoing and socially confident but with some concerns around physical functioning. These individuals tend to develop somatic symptoms when stressed. They are apt to be friendly, but their interpersonal relationships often lack depth. Self-centeredness and difficulties recognizing problems in themselves and others would also be consistent with this profile.

This individual also produced a PAI profile that was somewhat more defensive than the norm for this context, again suggesting difficulties with self-awareness and with acknowledging personal flaws. Clinical scales were not elevated but again are apt to have been suppressed by the defensive stance. Individuals with this profile view themselves as confident and optimistic as well as resilient and adaptive. They tend to be cheerful and positive and prefer to be with others rather than involved in solitary pursuits.

Ed

Ed produced an MMPI profile that was substantially more defensive than the norm for this context. Individuals with this validity pattern are apt to be psychologically unsophisticated and naïve, with a tendency to deny personal shortcomings. Clinical scales were elevated beyond the upper limits of the normal range, suggesting some difficulties in functioning. Individuals with this clinical pattern are apt to be socially skilled and over-controlled. They are used to receiving approval based on their intelligence, appearance, and status, and may stimulate distrust and hostility in others. These individuals tend to believe that they feel things more deeply than others. They are apt to be somewhat self-righteous with a tendency to deny anger and hostility.

This individual produced a PAI profile of questionable validity due to a level of defensiveness that was significantly greater than the norm for this context. Clinical scales were not elevated but are apt to have been suppressed by this approach. Individuals with this profile are apt to have strong needs for affiliation and positive regard from others. They may be described as attention-seeking and their relationships are apt to lack depth.

COLLATERAL CONTACTS

Lisa Brown

Lisa Brown, marital therapist, stated that this couple came to see her initially in February 2011. She saw them together on 2/21, saw Mary alone on 2/22, Ed alone on 2/23, and together on 2/28. She stated

> The presenting problem was that the relationship had seriously deteriorated since Christmas 2010. Both talked about trouble after their daughter was born. They characterized the first year as pretty good, but trust issues had sprung up and insecurities. There was a lot of verbal conflict and some physical.... Each partner reported some emotional abuse and each reported being contacted in a violent way by the other, but without injury. Both reported having been shoved by the other.... In the battery of questions, she endorsed being knocked down, and he endorsed being scratched, hit, and pushed. She admitted throwing a bottle of Jack Daniels, which broke a computer. She said he broke three doors. He admitted that he slammed one and there was a vacuum cleaner behind the other when he opened it.... In one conflict incident, a fight escalated. He was trying to get a piece of paper from her, and he wound up sort of hovering over her and reaching for the paper. There was a bit of a wrestle over that, but I don't think anyone got hurt. He reported her pursuing him, that she hit him and trapped him in a room.... The violence seemed to come from both. I told them that compliance with treatment would be an indicator of whether it was safe for them to be in therapy together. Both said they were willing. I told them there was to be a moratorium on any further physical contact. I was very nervous about this couple. People need to feel safe to tackle issues, and this was a highly reactive couple, she in particular.

Both reported that things escalated very quickly. Both had high scores on physiological issues. There was a ton of Gottman's "four horsemen"—criticism, defensiveness, stonewalling, and contempt. Small things would escalate, it became too heated, and then they couldn't pull out.

Ms. Brown went on to say, "He reported her being physically violent as well. We make a distinction between low-level episodic violence versus characterological violence where there's a perpetrator and it's about power and control. I did not view this couple to be in that category. I would not have invited them into treatment if I had." In talking about the content of the therapy sessions, Ms. Brown stated,

There were insecurity problems and triangles going on for both. She admitted lying to him. She said she was going to work and she met some guy. She said the guy was a medical patient and she met him in a coffee shop. She said it was a friendship. He [Ed] "was full of suspicion" so he tracked her whereabouts through her cell phone. That was real upsetting to her and he apparently broke into her emails. They were initially sharing passwords but eventually didn't. He really was confused about what was going on. Apparently he had a female friend, and there was some sense of insecurity on her part about his motives.

Ms. Brown went on to say,

She talked about having post-partum depression and that he then became critical and abusive verbally and was not attending to her in the same way....He acknowledged that he didn't pay enough attention to her. He talked about an incident in which there was a verbal fight in a restaurant and she kept trying to put food in his mouth and touching him on the head. The only way to get away from her was to go in a different room....She said three doors were broken down. He said, "I did break three doors and I did rip her papers." He acknowledged he said things that were hurtful and acknowledged all as not okay. That's something you don't see usually with perpetrators. He didn't justify.

When asked if Mary had demonstrated the same level of acknowledgement, Ms. Brown said,

I didn't see that. She characterized him as abusive but at the same time she said she was afraid of her first husband but "I'm not afraid of Ed." He described her as volatile and said, "she would chase me around." She got very defensive [about breaking the computer] and said, "I couldn't see the computer." My question was to what extent alcohol was involved. She described their first year as a lot of drinking and a lot of passion. Both said the other acted like a detective and both felt controlled and manipulated. Both became suspicious.

Ms. Brown was asked if parenting had been an issue in the sessions, and she stated, "No. I got the sense that that was one of the strengths in this couple and that they came together around that. No one checked any issue with regard to children." When asked if Mary had conveyed that Ed was not capable of caring for Emma, Ms. Brown responded,

That was not one of the concerns I heard from her....In her individual session, she said, "It's so easy to love initially but as time goes on, it gets harder. It's hard to admit that abuse goes on." That may be a reference to emotional abuse. She said, "The man I married is so different from this." There was something about trauma, in reference to her former marriage....I experienced Ed to be better at regulating emotional affect in sessions but I don't know what they are like when they get home. Both left in a calm state and slightly more hopeful. A couple of days later, I got a text from her out of the blue. She recommended a book for me to read about men and abuse and said I should know more about that. She terminated treatment, and I had no further contact until there was a request for records. I sent a set to her and to Ed as well. There was some way in which she felt I wasn't getting it right. I wasn't seeing her as a victim. I saw them both as having problematic ways of handling conflict and anger. I was planning to refer both of them to anger management if there was not improvement. I was concerned about the baby because of their volatility. Things turned so hostile in such a quick amount of time. He was her bitter enemy and I think it took him aback. He was very concerned about the extreme and steep change in how she cast him in such a villainous way. His demeanor in sessions was willing and rational. He acknowledged that he needed to make changes....It was not clear about the role of alcohol....I made it so clear that they had both reported violence and said, "You can't trap people." I made it very clear that this is a shared problem.

Eileen Smith

Eileen Smith has been supervising Ed's visits with Emma through Indaba. She stated,

Emma is completely adorable and seems very well-adjusted....Both parents show very good skills. Dad is very attentive and engaged. He's very informed on stages [of development]....Ed is very concerned about not making any mistakes....He's very accommodating if Mary needs the schedule to be changed....Ed is very attentive to Emma. I've spent over 80 hours with them and there's nothing that draws a red flag.

When asked about any observations of Mary, Ms. Smith stated,

She seems to be more nervous about the schedule for Mary. She gets very intense if things aren't progressing the way she wants them to. On July 9, Wendy [the nanny] was stuck in traffic and was late. When we finally made arrangements to meet, it was a half hour into the visit. I extended the visit to compensate. She was not upset with me, but it was like she was taking it out on Ed and saying it was Ed's fault. Mary is really good about keeping Emma on a schedule and she thought Ed was being selfish because he knew Emma's schedule. It took a long time to calm her....Emma always comes in tip-top shape and is always happy. She blows kisses to mom and to dad.

Ms. Smith went on to say, "He's ultra-polite....He's finally giving her [Emma] more space and is not right on top of her. We went to the Bite of Seattle and I saw great growth in that he was letting her

go a few steps ahead. She fell right on her face and I thought he would cry, he was so pained."

Ms. Smith was asked about an observation during the home visit in which Ed had prevented Emma from using her hand to eat blueberries. She stated,

Emma comes dressed in beautiful outfits and she's gotten them dirty during the visit. He's frantic and so worried about getting in trouble....I keep a close eye on the diaper bag. I didn't see anything. A book was sent that had an inscription in it—that he had bought. It was after the allegation [that he had been putting things in the diaper bag]. He was very upset by that.

Wendy Conroy

Wendy Conroy was the Clarks' nanny prior to their separation, and she continues to work for Mary. She stated that she met the Clarks "last June or July, and I've been the full-time nanny since last August." Ms. Conroy indicated that she works "forty hours more or less" and went on to say, "Mr. Clark was there when I watched her the first time....He was probably nervous to leave his four-month-old with someone they didn't know and wanted to observe me." When asked if she was aware of difficulties between the parties, Ms. Conroy responded, "Not until after they separated...when Ed told me in February." Ms. Conroy was asked if she had been concerned about either parent prior to that time, and she stated, "No, everything was fine. There was one incident where Ed came to get her and he had alcohol on his breath and there were last minute changes in plans." Ms. Conroy was also asked about any concerns that Ed didn't know how to take care of Emma and she stated, "There were a couple of times. Once he told me to give her Tylenol and it was quite a bit more...it was the wrong dosage....Another time, I was going to give her salmon and asked him if she had had it before. He said 'You should probably ask the boss.' I felt like she [Mary] was the main person." When asked if she had any concerns about Ed's ability to feed, diaper, or bathe Emma, Ms. Conroy answered, "Oh no, not at all."

Ms. Conroy was asked if Mary had talked to her about the possibility of moving, and she said, "No. I've asked her, 'Are you sure you're not moving?'

and she said she wasn't. I think she would tell me. It's my job. I've asked her and she said, 'no.' "

Katie Rogers

Katie Rogers was in medical school with both parties and is married to Ed's best friend. She stated, "We began medical school together in 2005 and were together for four years. There were 80 students in our medical class. We were a pretty close, tight-knit group. I knew both of them very well. We did things socially, were in school together every day. I saw all aspects of their character and personality—all the ups and downs."

When asked if she had any concerns about either party during that time, Dr. Rogers stated,

I definitely had concerns about Mary. I don't think she had the best reputation in the class. She had a really hard time maintaining relationships. There were extreme highs and extreme lows....We were really close friends and I would periodically ask "How are things?" If a subject came up that she didn't want to deal with, she would get angry and defensive. There were irrational emails making accusations—then on the other extreme, she'd be my best friend. Afterwards, she would refuse to discuss her behavior. She can be fun but I couldn't understand her. I thought she was really manipulative.... [She and Ed] were very much in love but it was a dangerous, adventurous love. They were flying by the seat of their pants. I thought they loved each other very much. I thought Ed was protective of her and put her needs first. He was protective of her highs and lows and would make thoughtful and elaborate plans.

Dr. Rogers was asked about Mary's prior marriage, and she stated, "I would ask her about that and she would get really upset. She said she was abused....I never met Josh. She said he would lock her in the bathroom and that was the reason she hadn't been able to call me.... One time I said to her 'You and Ed are both married.' If you challenged her she would get defensive and he would be protective as well."

When asked about Ed, Dr. Rogers stated, "Ed was class president. I think that says a lot about his rapport with the class. All I saw was him being loving and caring. He's appreciative. I can only say I saw excellent things.... I was concerned about how

mad she would get. There were outbursts. I didn't trust her anymore. It's abnormal for me to have the kind of relationship I had with Mary." When asked to elaborate on her statement that Mary had outbursts, Dr. Rogers stated that this occurred

when I asked her about her and Ed's relationship. But there were also little things. If she asked "Do you like my shoes" and I said, "no," she'd be mad for a week. She would scream and yell at me....They never fought. It was more like she would give him the cold shoulder if she was upset....If you ask anyone who knew them they'd say "I've never seen any abusiveness by him." I do think Ed's a wonderful father. There were all these conversations we had about the joys of parenthood—with Mary too.

Heidi

Heidi does scheduling for Indaba, and when asked about any difficulties with this case, she stated,

I've been working at Indaba for a while, and with these families, there are always problems. I felt at times there wasn't communication. She would say she had sent her travel plans to Ed's attorney but then there were be an email from Ed as though he didn't know what it was. I did feel Mary thought he should know....There was a lot of back and forth. They were always cordial but it did take a lot of time....We tried to maintain neutrality.

Jessica Swift

Jessica Swift was a friend of Mary's after she moved to Seattle. She was contacted after Ed provided an email from her indicating that she had terminated her relationship with Mary because of her erratic behavior. She was initially reluctant to provide information for the evaluation out of concern that Mary would retaliate. After deciding to become involved, Dr. Swift stated,

I'm a dentist in a group practice. Mary interviewed at our practice as she was moving here and we really hit it off. We became good friends immediately. I introduced her to Debra Edwards because Mary was looking for a practice and Debra wanted an associate. Deb thought it was a really positive match and talked about how much they liked each other.... In January, my contact with her completely dropped off.... Shortly after, I found out they had had a falling out professionally. I wanted to stay separate from that.... I sent texts to check on Mary. We talked once after sending her a wedding invitation. She asked if she could use the graphics on my wedding invitation for her new business announcements. I told her she should contact the graphic artist who I had paid to do my invitations. Shortly thereafter, Debra called and said I should check Mary's website and there was the design. I talked to the artist and asked if she had contacted him and he said she hadn't and that he was going to pursue it. I sent her a text and said I would like to talk and "I'm worried about you." She came back with a slew of statements attacking my character.... There was nothing that had happened before. This was a completely different person.... I tried to get her to meet with me, but all she would do is attack me. Basically, I said, "Don't contact me anymore" because I felt like it was unsafe. It was so opposite from what I had known. I haven't heard from her since.

Dr. Swift went on to say, "I found out [Mary and Ed] were having marital problems and I touched base with him through a friend.... My husband and I had liked both of them.... He didn't know we'd had a falling out.... I found the texts from her to be so strange.... There was a disagreement over ethics.... She opened up a business across the street from my mentor [Debra Edwards] and you just don't do that."

When asked what the texts from Mary had said, Dr. Swift stated,

> They were saying things like, "Your true colors are showing now, Jess." I had no idea what she was talking about. I was just trying to investigate what had happened with the graphic designer.... She had always been really dynamic and fun.... To this day, I don't know what she thinks I've done. All I said in my texts was "I care about you. Can we talk?" and she would come back with "You were never my friend at all." I had nothing to do with the lawsuit [Debra Edwards].... I was shocked and lost sleep over it. Her behavior

was scaring me and I just thought, "If you can't sit face to face with somebody...."

Dr. Swift clarified that she had met Mary in the summer of 2010. She characterized their relationship by saying, "She came to my bachelorette weekend. We had a very social relationship. There was nothing abnormal about her behavior. We talked about our marriages and we would joke that we were each other's wife." When asked if Mary had discussed any problems in her relationship with Ed, Dr. Swift stated,

> Not at all. In December, I was having my own relationship issues, and she talked about nothing that was a problem. In fact, she was laughing about them doing fun stuff in the car in the parking lot—that they still "had it" in their marriage. She told me she had called his mother to say he had bought too big a Christmas tree. She was joking. She would say that her first marriage was very abusive but she didn't say anything about Ed.

DISCUSSION

These are two very bright individuals who have both been in and out of two very short marriages since 2005. Ed acknowledged that he and Mary became involved with one another prior to separating from their respective spouses, while Mary emphasized abusiveness in her first marriage and omitted her involvement with Ed prior to the separation. The allegations in this case centered largely around Mary's report that Ed was physically and emotionally abusive of her. Having an affair with someone else does not preclude the possibility that domestic violence might also be a factor in ending a marriage. However, there are reasons to be concerned about the validity of Mary's allegations against Ed. These factors are as follows:

(1) Ed provided an email exchange between himself and Mary that he had also forwarded to Mary's parents at the time of the exchange. In this email of February 16, Mary stated to Ed, "Last night when I stayed at home, we began to make progress and speak to each other honestly and openly about improvements we were willing to make and going to counseling etc. And not bringing ugliness like lies, emotional cruelty, or violence into our marriage."

Ed responded, "This is unacceptable. You are not being honest with anyone, including yourself.

You are insinuating that I am being violent and cruel. I have attached your parents on this, because this is completely unacceptable and so far from the truth, and if you honestly believe what you are writing then things have gone way too far, and we need perspective and guidance very badly here." Mary responded to this with a text that asked why he had forwarded the exchange to her parents, and Ed answered, "Because I'm tired of your lies and I'm not going to stand for you insinuating Emma is not safe with me or that I'm being violent or cruel to you." To this, Mary texted in return, "I'm not insinuating that at all, I will tell whoever you want...Jesus."

(2) During this period, Mary and Ed began seeing Lisa Brown for marital therapy. Her statements as a collateral contact to this evaluation as well as her therapy notes indicate that the issue of physical contact was discussed extensively and that both Mary and Ed acknowledged some minor incidents of physical contact, which Ms. Brown did not view as rising to a level of domestic violence on either part. Ms. Brown also noted that during the sessions, "this was a highly reactive couple, she in particular," and "I experienced Ed to be better at regulating emotional affect in sessions but I don't know what they are like when they get home," and finally, "I saw them both as having problematic ways of handling conflict and anger....I made it so clear that they had both reported violence and said, 'You can't trap people.' I made it very clear that this is a shared problem." The incidents that Mary later reported to the police were all discussed in these sessions.

(3) Mary acknowledged during this evaluation that there was no other information to substantiate Ed's having difficulties with anger beyond what was discussed in therapy and outside of her own statements. It is certainly possible to come up with explanations for the lack of substantiation of her claims (i.e., that victims of domestic violence are reluctant to disclose, that perpetrators may behave very differently outside the relationship). Moreover, Ed did acknowledge tracking Mary during the period that their marriage was deteriorating. However, when the data are viewed in their totality, there appears to be considerable substantiation for the hypothesis that the violence that did occur between this couple was mutual, of a low level, and not part of a pattern during the relationship but rather related to an escalation as the relationship deteriorated.

(4) There was information from two individuals who had reportedly been close friends of Mary's about a pattern of abruptly ending close relationships after being confronted with concerns about her behavior. Katie Rogers indicated that she raised concerns with Mary about her relationship with Ed because they were both married and that this precipitated "outbursts. I didn't trust her anymore." She also noted, "If a subject came up that she didn't want to deal with, she would get angry and defensive. There were irrational emails making accusations—then on the other extreme, she'd be my best friend. Afterwards, she would refuse to discuss her behavior. She can be fun but I couldn't understand her. I thought she was really manipulative." Dr. Rogers also noted, "She had a really hard time maintaining relationships. There were extreme highs and extreme lows." Ed noted that Dr. Rogers's husband was his best friend and was going to be best man at his wedding until "Mary had a dramatic 'falling out' with Dennis's wife, Katie, and ultimately Mary refused to invite Katie to our wedding even though Dennis was my absolute best friend (other than Mary). It put Dennis and me in the difficult position—we both had to choose our best friend or our wife."

These statements are strikingly similar to information provided by Dr. Swift, who described Mary as "dynamic and fun" until she raised an issue regarding Mary's having used an artist's work without permission. She went on to say that after having communicated with Mary that she would like to discuss this with her, Mary "came back with a slew of statements attacking my character....There was nothing that had happened before. This was a completely different person....I tried to get her to meet with me, but all she would do is attack me. Basically, I said, 'Don't contact me anymore' because I felt like it was unsafe. It was so opposite from what I had known."

The descriptions of these two individuals regarding Mary's behavior when confronted is corroborative of Ed's descriptions of Mary's personality during the marriage. He described their relationship as being exceptionally romantic, devoted, and fun, but also described incidents in which Mary would behave in ways that were erratic and poorly controlled. He alleged that in the aftermath of Mary's having lost her job after her employer discovered that she had removed contact information from the office, there were disagreements between them regarding a house they were in the process of buying, and that Mary's behavior then changed abruptly. He stated that she was being untruthful about contact with another man and that she was working obsessively to establish her own practice while leaving him with Emma, followed by a precipitous announcement that she wanted a divorce.

(5) Ed also alleged that Mary fabricated allegations regarding domestic violence in her first marriage in order to justify leaving the marriage to be with him, and "she is doing the same thing now." He indicated that she wrote an essay for a scholarship describing having spent "January 28, 2007.... sleeping at Marquette's library" because she was too frightened to go home to her abusive husband. Ed also provided an email from Mary to him dated January 29, 2007, detailing "that we spent less than ten hours together last night and we talked and laughed and listened to music and made love three times." There is no way to ascertain the reality of what went on in Mary's first marriage, and no attempt was made to contact her first husband. However, it is relevant that Ed's first wife provided a declaration for him, and she described him as "incredibly kind, caring, and generous.... Ed never exhibited any form of violent behavior or violent outbursts. I always felt safe with him."

(6) There were instances during this evaluation in which Mary appeared motivated to distort information. Most prominent of these were her written and verbal statements that "Ed has also chosen to cancel as well as not utilize the entire six hours per week and it is heartbreaking," suggesting that Ed was not sufficiently motivated to have a relationship with his daughter. Information from the Indaba scheduler and email exchanges as well as letters between the attorneys made it clear that Ed had made strenuous attempts to see Emma despite Mary's resistance to scheduling make-up time after taking Emma to Illinois on weekends. When Mary was questioned about this, she responded, "Ed only wants to see her from 5:00 on or when she's not napping." She was asked if this didn't "make sense," given that Ed is doing surgery every day until 5:00 p.m. and has limited, supervised contact with Emma, and she responded, "I would take one afternoon off a week [in his situation]."

This was a labor-intensive evaluation that required extensive scrutiny of information—most of which was provided by Ed contradicting information provided by Mary. In the end, the totality of the data provided by each party strongly suggested that Mary is apt to have fabricated or distorted information about the marriage in order to secure primary

custody of Emma, allowing her to return with Emma to Illinois. Ed painstakingly provided information that supported his version of events, and ultimately Mary was not able to counter this information other than through unconvincing denials and references to the literature on domestic violence.

There is a disturbing pattern in the descriptions of Mary's behavior from former friends and Ed, her behavior during this evaluation, together with allegations regarding her having taken information from her employer in order to start a practice of her own. This pattern is of an individual who can be personable, warm, and engaging but also highly defensive, manipulative, deceptive, and volatile. Psychological testing was not helpful in looking at this issue because of the level of defensiveness in Mary's response, but there are sufficient other data to suggest the strong possibility of a personality disorder in this individual. Personality disorders are long-term, firmly entrenched ways of dealing with interpersonal issues. As such, Mary's difficulties are likely to continue to impact the stability of her relationships with others, the behavior she models to her daughter, and eventually her relationship with her daughter.

Ed acknowledged some problematic decision-making during his relationship with Mary. He acknowledged that having an affair with her during his first marriage created difficulties for both himself and Mary throughout their own marriage. He also described breaking one door during a conflict with Mary, ripping up papers having to do with her business, and tracking her via her cell phone. He denied any behavior that would constitute a pattern of domestic violence or emotional abuse, however.

Ed's psychological testing was also defensive and therefore of somewhat limited usefulness. However, two scales were elevated despite the defensiveness. In integrating other data and the data from psychological testing, there was evidence of self-righteousness, significant difficulties recognizing and acknowledging anger in himself and others, and a belief that he feels things more strongly than others.

Throughout this evaluation, it was difficult for Ed to separate data that would be useful within the confines of a parenting evaluation and descriptors that might more appropriately belong to a romance novel. He described his relationship with Mary in expansive, melodramatic ways and provided piles of photos, their notes to one another, and his writings to Emma without much awareness that this would not be helpful in ascertaining the reality of the allegations in this case. This did not appear to be an attempt at subterfuge, but rather evidence of Ed's exceptional difficulty viewing Mary and his relationship with her in an accurate light. Despite considerable evidence to the contrary, and through much of the evaluation, Ed continued to refer to Mary as his "best friend" and to Mary and Emma as "my girls." This might be seen as controlling and possessive, and there are some aspects of Ed's naïve devotion that could easily be felt as smothering or burdensome. However, it would be going well beyond the data to suggest that this was part of a pattern of domestic violence. Ed did acknowledge sending items to Mary in violation of a protection order, apparently in a belief that Mary was sending items to him that carried special significance. While this again underscores Ed's naïve beliefs about Mary and is a concern because it is a violation of a court order, it appears to be an exception to Ed's generally strict adherence to rules and regulations.

Mary alleged during this evaluation that Ed was not capable of caring for Emma. It is apt to be the case that Mary was the primary parent during the few months these parties were together after the birth of their daughter. Mary stayed home after Emma was born and did not have a job immediately after the parties moved to this area in 2010. However, the parties' nanny was clear that Ed was completely capable of executing basic parenting functions prior to the separation. Moreover, information from the visitation supervisor and during the observation for this evaluation indicated that Ed is conscientious, devoted, and adept at dealing with Emma.

Mary has requested permission from the court to move with Emma to Illinois because she feels she has a support system there. In most cases, it is contraindicated to move a child this young to a geographically distant location from one parent because of the need for frequent contact in order to maintain the attachment. Ed is in a residency that will not end for another two years, and he would not be able to travel to see Emma often enough for her to maintain a sense of who he is or his importance in terms of security and attachment. If Mary were allowed to move with Emma, this would have nearly inevitable impact of severely impairing, if not severing, Emma's relationship with Ed.

In this case, there are additional reasons to be concerned about allowing Mary to move with Emma. Research has indicated that the mental health of the primary parent and conflict between the parents are the two most important factors in predicting the well-being of children in the aftermath of divorce. These are also factors that increase the risk to a child with regard to relocating. Children who relocate with one parent who has mental health issues are exposed to an undiluted version of those mental health issues, which generally increases their negative impact. Additionally, when the moving parent has been involved in "gate-keeping" or creating unnecessary conflict with the other parent that has the effect of limiting that parent's contact with the child, this is apt to be exacerbated by a relocation. The information available to this evaluation strongly suggested that Mary has significant mental health issues in the form of a personality disorder and that she was involved in generating unnecessary conflict that has significantly hindered Ed's contact with Emma.

RECOMMENDATIONS

There are substantial difficulties in making recommendations that will effectively deal with all the factors that are likely to impact Emma's well-being. Although Ed is apt to have had a very solid relationship with Emma prior to the separation, Mary is likely to have been somewhat more central to Emma because she stayed home with her during her early months. It is certainly the case that Mary is now the primary parent because of the circumstances of the conflict that has ensued in the aftermath of the separation. It is in Emma's best interests that Ed's time with her be increased immediately, and that their relationship be normalized. Moreover, given concerns about the impact of Mary's difficulties with interpersonal relationships and evidence that she can be substantially manipulative, deceptive, and volatile, there are concerns about leaving Emma in her primary care. Mary's skills in parenting Emma are excellent at this stage in Emma's life. However, Mary will increasingly expose Emma to the interpersonal difficulties in her life and will increasingly model ways of dealing with conflict that are detrimental to Emma. This makes for a difficult equation in terms of weighing the detriment of moving Emma away from the primary parent versus the detriment of being exposed to Mary's difficulties.

Given these considerations, it would seem to be the most conservative and least risky alternative to increase Ed's time with Emma, moving towards an equally shared parenting arrangement. If there is evidence that Mary continues to generate unnecessary conflict or that her behavior is otherwise negatively impacting Emma in significant ways, a further evaluation may be necessary in order to consider limiting her contact with Emma. If the court were to feel that shared parenting is not an option in this case, then the recommendation would be for Ed to be the primary residential parent.

Emma is currently with a nanny full-time, and the parties have substantially the same work hours at this time. If Ed feels that he can work with Mary's nanny without difficulty, then that would be preferable. This would allow Ms. Conroy to transfer Emma between the parties during the week and minimize contact between them.

In moving this case towards shared parenting, it is recommended that Ed immediately have two non-consecutive overnights a week with Emma. One of these nights would be during the week and the other would be on the weekend. Weekend time will presumably need a third party other than Ms. Conroy to effect transfers. This might suggest that, for now, it would be best for Ed to have either Friday night overnight or Sunday night in order to minimize logistical difficulties. For example, if Ed had Emma on Friday night, he would have her after work until Saturday morning at 9:00 a.m. initially. After two Friday night visits of this sort, the transfer time should be moved back to noon. After two more visits, the time could be extended to 3:00 p.m., and with two visits on that schedule, the time could be moved to 5:00 p.m. It is not recommended that Mary be able to take Emma for the weekend while this schedule is being implemented. If Mary needs to travel during Ed's time with Emma, Emma would stay with Ed.

When Emma is two years old, it is recommended that the parties move to a schedule in which Ed has Emma one midweek overnight and every other weekend from Friday to Sunday at 5:00 p.m. After six months on that schedule, it is recommended that the parties move to a schedule in which one parent would have Monday and Tuesday overnight, the other parent Wednesday and Thursday overnight, with weekends alternating. At age seven, it is apt to be appropriate to move to a one-week/one-week schedule.

These parents should adopt the concept of parallel parenting, rather than co-parenting. This is not the optimal parenting pattern for children in the aftermath of divorce, but given the difficulties in this case, there is too much risk in having Emma exposed to direct contact between her parents. High-conflict parents always have the option of working their way towards co-parenting, but the concern is that Ed will assume this can happen and will not sufficiently protect Emma from the outfall if it doesn't.

Both of these parties would benefit from individual therapy. Ed needs to work on looking at himself and others more realistically and understanding the ways in which he does not allow himself to accurately view information that is negative and unpleasant. Mary needs to address the characterological dysfunction that is a pattern in her relationships with others. Specifically, she needs to address her propensity to be highly defensive, volatile, and manipulative in her relationships, and the focus of her therapy is likely to be enhanced by giving her therapist this evaluation.

There is little to be gained from mandating therapy for either party as part of the parenting plan. However, any further evaluation would certainly look at participation in therapy as one factor. It is not recommended that future evaluations or court actions have access to the content of the parties' therapy, since this would certainly result in posturing that would not be therapeutically beneficial.

If these parties cannot move forward without additional conflict, a guardian ad litem (GAL) may need to be assigned to this case in order to monitor and intervene to protect Emma's access to both parents.

Marsha Hedrick, PhD, ABPP
Licensed Psychologist
Diplomate in Forensic Psychology
American Board of Professional Psychology

TEACHING POINT:
CAN ONE EVER PLAY MORE THAN ONE ROLE IN A SINGLE FMHA CASE?

Some of the debate regarding playing more than a single professional role in one case, most often those of therapist and forensic evaluator, has been described earlier in this chapter. The most recent synthesis of that discussion has been offered as part of the Oxford Best Practices in Forensic Assessment Series (see, e.g., Fuhrmann & Zibbell, 2012). For the careful mental health professional—aware that dual role problems in child custody evaluations are one of the most frequent sources of complaints to ethics committees and licensure boards—the prudent answer to this question should be "No."

There are various reasons why the practice of serving as both therapist and forensic evaluator continues, although hopefully at a diminished rate, as of this writing. It may be requested by one of the parties involved in the litigation, the attorney representing this party, or even occasionally by the court. There may be a small number of qualified individuals who would be appropriate to do a child-custody evaluation, and one of those individuals may have served as a treating therapist. The substantive justification for the request may be that the mental health professional "knows" the family and the issues in a way that an outside evaluator would not. None of these seems sufficiently compelling to enter into a second role in which the risk of significant problems is clearly present.

One of the clearest ways to frame the question is to ask how many individuals, if informed at the outset of a therapy relationship that the therapist might subsequently use this information to testify in a legal proceeding against the expressed wishes of that individual regarding child custody, would agree to enter into treatment. Probably very few. When the problem is compounded by the therapist's serving in a dual role *without warning the individual in the beginning that this might occur*, then the client's sense of betrayal is exacerbated. Therapists *and* their clients are best served by avoiding this dual role minefield.

CASE TWO

PRINCIPLE: USE MULTIPLE SOURCES OF INFORMATION FOR EACH AREA BEING ASSESSED (*PRINCIPLE 17*)

This principle concerns the sources of information to be used in assessing the forensic issues that are relevant to the legal questions in FMHA, and the importance of using information from more than one source. The use of multiple sources of information in FMHA is important for several reasons. First, multiple measures enhance accuracy in measuring a given trait, symptom, or behavior by reducing the error associated with a single source. Second, multiple measures allow the evaluator to test rival hypotheses of behavior that may have

been generated, in part, by observations stemming from one or more of the measures. Independently obtained information on a second measure about the same construct can be used to support (or refute) hypotheses that may have been generated by the results of the first measure. Finally, multiple measures allow the forensic clinician to assess the consistency of data across sources and attempt to corroborate particularly important data before reaching conclusions that are being considered in the course of performing a FMHA.

Ethical guidance supports the importance of gathering information from multiple sources. The APA *Specialty Guidelines* states: "Forensic practitioners ordinarily avoid relying solely on one source of data, and corroborate important data whenever feasible" (Guideline 9.02). Practically, the use of multiple sources of information is helpful in gathering information across a variety of domains, a practice that has been supported within the child custody literature. For instance, Gould and Bell (2000) described several sources of information that should be considered as part of a child custody evaluation, including information garnered from a clinical interview; data from self-report measures and psychological testing; data from collateral sources, including interviewees and records; and direct behavioral observations. Furthermore, the Association of Family and Conciliation Courts (2007) has observed that, when conducting a child custody evaluation, "Evaluators shall use multiple data-gathering methods that are diverse as possible and that tap divergent sources of data, thereby facilitating the exploration of alternative plausible hypotheses that are central to the case" (p. 79).

In addition to psychosocial interviews, psychological testing is a frequently used and important aspect of forensic evaluations. However, the use of psychological testing and forensic assessment instruments is somewhat controversial in child custody evaluations (Fuhrmann & Zibbell, 2012). In part, this is due to the psychometric weaknesses of many instruments designed for use in child custody evaluations. There is also some debate about the applicability of psychological test data—for instance, personality testing—to the relevant psycholegal constructs in child custody cases, although research suggests that these types of tests are often used (for more detail, see Fuhrmann & Zibbell, 2012).

In addition to psychological testing and structured clinical interviews, the direct observation of an individual being evaluated is an important source of information. The direct observation of the individual can be considered from two sources. First, collateral interviews may be conducted with those who frequently observe and interact with the individual (e.g., family members, friends, employers, teachers, nurses, aides). In a child custody evaluation, an evaluator seeks information from individuals who have contact with both parents and the child, which may include contact in professional contexts (e.g., physicians, teachers) and personal contexts (e.g., neighbors, coaches; Fuhrmann & Zibbell, 2012). Second, the evaluator may solicit direct observations from those who have observed behavior that is relevant to the referral question. In the context of child custody evaluations, this includes the evaluator's direct observations of parent–child interactions, and may also include a home visit (American Academy of Child and Adolescent Psychiatry, 1997; Association of Family and Conciliation Courts, 2007; Fuhrmann & Zibbell, 2012; Gould & Bell, 2000).

Finally, records in areas such as mental health, medical, criminal, school, vocational, and military functioning are another source of potentially valuable information in FMHA. In the context of a child custody evaluation, evaluators may consider records or documentation from sources such as "schools, health care providers, child care providers, agencies, and other institutions" (APA, 2010b, p. 866); legal documents, such as motions, affidavits, court orders, restraining orders, prior court decisions, and criminal records; and prior reports, including child protective reports and prior custody evaluations (Fuhrmann & Zibbell, 2012). When children have more specialized needs—including medical or education needs—then additional records become important as well.

In the current case, many sources of information were used. These included multiple interviews with each parent, various psychological tests (including specialized parenting measures, and those measuring effort), observations of and interviews with the children, a review of relevant records, and multiple collateral interviews. Each of these sources of information, considered separately, would not have provided a complete or accurate picture of the individuals. For example, in the present case, the self-report of each of the parents regarding the other was often inconsistent with that

other's self-description; accordingly, it was important to obtain interview impressions from others and from the children. Similarly, psychological testing and structured interviews in isolation could have yielded clinical impressions unsupported by historical or factual context. Over-reliance on one or two measures is a potential source of error in FMHA. Only through multiple sources of information can the evaluator create a comprehensive, cross-checked account of the individual's functioning across a range of relevant domains.

Jonathan W. Gould, Ph.D., ABPP
Board Certified in Forensic Psychology
American Board of Professional Psychology
Charlotte Psychotherapy & Consultation Group
417 A South Sharon Amity Road
Charlotte, North Carolina 28211
(704) 364 0452
Charlottepsychotherapy.com
jwgould@aol.com
Facsimile (704) 837 2969
Forensic Psychology Trial Consultation

Forensic Psychological Evaluation
Child Custody Advisory Report
Daniel Waters v. Susan Waters
County File No.: 11 CvD 1234
March 27, 2012

Biological Mother: *Susan Philips*
Date of Birth: May 25, 1973
Age: 39 years old

Biological Father: *Daniel Waters*
Date of Birth: June 10, 1975
Age: 37 years old

Children Born of Marriage:

Randy Michael
Date of Birth: August 31, 2004
Age: 8 years

Michelle Kate
Date of Birth: October 27, 2007
Age: 5 years

Attorney of Record:

Jeffrey Counsel, Esquire
(704) 555-1234

Mary-Anne Attorney, Esquire
(704) 555-4321

REASON FOR REFERRAL

In a Consent Order dated October 6, 2011, The Honorable William Smith ordered that the above-referenced parents and their children undergo a "custody psychological examination/evaluation." The Consent Order indicated that the child custody evaluation shall address the following issues:

1. An extensive analysis of the custodial needs of the minor children;
2. The strengths and weaknesses of each of the parties as to the custody of the minor children;
3. The appropriate testing of the children of the parties for the purposes of custodial care;
4. The propensity of either party for alienating the affections of the minor children from the other party, and for the propensity and desire of either party to control, dominate, and intimidate the other party, and for their propensity to make derogatory remarks about the other party in the presence of the minor children;
5. The propensity of either party to engage in behavior that can have a detrimental effect on the two (2) minor children, and the further propensity of either party to engage in behavior that will serve as a poor role model for the two (2) children;
6. For other such matters that are suitable for such an examination/evaluation regarding the minor children's custody (paragraph 2 of Findings of Fact).

SUMMARY OF FINDINGS

Susan and Daniel have raised two children who have strong and healthy relationships with each parent. The children are thriving at school and are developing healthy relationships in social, school, and community-based activities. The children are able to talk in a positive and loving manner about each parent, and they report enjoying time with each parent.

Susan and Daniel have very different personality styles and somewhat different parenting styles. I would characterize Susan as emotional, passionate, reactive, and dramatic. I would characterize Daniel as cool, detached, and controlled. One might hypothesize that when the relationship was new and without the stress of marital discord, each parent provided a useful complement to the other. Susan would be the emotional spark to Daniel's dispassionate reactions, and Daniel would be the calm, reasoned voice to Susan's passionate reactions. When the relationship became stressed, each parent tended to move toward their individual

---

COMMENT

I encourage evaluators to obtain from the referring attorneys or from the court order a specific list of questions that serve to guide the custody investigation. The questions must be suitable for psychological examination. There are times when attorneys neglect to include relevant questions in their list of areas to investigate. In such cases, it is important for the evaluator to identify additional questions and to seek permission from the court or from the attorneys to broaden the scope of the evaluation to include the new questions. The reader will note that I was not asked to opine on a parenting plan for these children. There is significant discussion in the custody literature about the appropriateness of evaluators' providing the court with opinions about legal (decision making) and/or physical (residential placement) custody. Some jurisdictions expressly forbid custody evaluators to opine on the ultimate issue of custodial placement and decision-making. Other jurisdictions presume that all evaluators will opine on decision-making and custodial placement. It is my recommendation that evaluators ask the attorneys or the court whether such opinions are being invited before evaluators provide such opinions.

strengths without the benefit of the other parent's complementary influence. I found that Susan was perceived as becoming increasingly emotionally reactive, while Daniel was perceived as becoming increasingly dispassionate. Susan's perceived emotional reactivity was viewed by Daniel as Susan being out of control, requiring Daniel to step into a role viewed by Susan as controlling and intrusive. Daniel increasingly was unable to trust Susan, leading Daniel to further question her actions. Susan viewed this increased questioning as Daniel becoming inappropriately intrusive.

As for their parenting styles, both parents have revealed similar values and efforts toward their children's educational achievement, social development, and other relevant developmental dimensions. That is, there is little difference between the parents' values about what is best for their children. The primary tension lies in both parents having difficulty trusting the other parent.

Daniel views Susan's less structured and less organized approach to parenting as an example of her emotional reactivity. Daniel talked about Susan's parenting style as an example of inconsistent (read: irresponsible) parenting. He also views Susan as not supporting the children's relationship with him. Daniel believes that he loves the children more than does Susan and that the children have a stronger attachment with him than they do with Susan.

Susan's view is that Daniel is a "control freak" who is unable to allow the children the freedom to develop in their natural direction. Susan talked about Daniel's parenting style as an example of a controlling and intrusive parenting. Susan views Daniel as not supporting the children's relationship with her. Susan views the children as having a strong and healthy relationship with both parents.

The children behaved well with each parent during my observation time. Susan was observed to engage in less vigilant monitoring of the children's behavior compared to Daniel's monitoring. Both styles of monitoring were appropriate for children. The children responded somewhat differently to each parent, in part due to differences in the parents' monitoring vigilance. Randy and Michelle were observed to ask permission from their father about nearly each change in activity. They waited for a response from their father before engaging in their new activity. When

observed with Susan, the children were more carefree and spontaneous. They tended to ask permission less often when they changed activities compared to their permission-seeking from Daniel. Neither parenting style was determined to be counter to the children's psychological best interests.

In interviews at Susan's and Daniel's home, Randy reported that Susan told Randy about actions taken by Daniel that interfered with Susan's being able to purchase a home. In both interviews, Randy expressed anger at his father and a belief that he (Randy) is unable to trust his father. Randy has adopted Susan's view of the events that led to the loss of the home purchase and has described a view of his father as one who cannot be trusted to take care of his family.

Susan refutes that she told Randy anything about the loss of the home purchase. She insists that she told Randy only that they would have to find another home because they are not allowed to move into the hoped-for home.

The children—with the most reliable information coming from Randy—support Daniel's view that Susan tends to outwardly display her upset and anger in the children's presence. Randy described instances during which his mother would cry in front of him and say negative things about Daniel. Randy did not support Daniel's assertion that the children were exposed to Susan throwing objects. Randy also talked about hearing his parents argue often when they were living together. He indicated that he seldom hears his parents argue now that they live apart, although he is aware that they often argue over the telephone.

Susan's assertion that Daniel is inappropriately controlling and intrusive was not supported by the data from this evaluation. Email documentation revealed Daniel's inquiries to focus on obtaining information about the children. Susan's reactions as revealed through her emails indicated a tendency to overreact to Daniel's inquiries. Daniel's assertion that Susan intentionally keeps school-related information from Daniel was also not supported by the data from this evaluation. During the evaluation process, Daniel reported that he spoke with Randy's teacher and requested information directly from her.

Collateral interviews and written questionnaires revealed that each parent has many advocates. Susan's collaterals described Susan as involved in the daily activities of the children and described Daniel as emotionally and often physically removed from the care of the children. They often described Daniel as socially isolated compared to Susan's socially active approach to others, especially the children.

Daniel's collaterals viewed Daniel as involved in the daily activities of the children and described Susan as self-absorbed and inconsistently involved in the children's activities. Of concern was collateral description of Susan that contained virtually nothing positive to say about her parenting.

One interpretation of the collateral information is that Susan's socially active approach was viewed by Daniel's collaterals as not attending to the children, while Daniel's more socially isolated behaviors were viewed by Susan's collaterals as inattentive or uninvolved.

My concern is that the seeds of an alienation dynamic are being planted in this family. Daniel and his family do not see much value in the type of parenting that Susan brings to the children. Susan's collaterals do not see Daniel's involvement in the children's lives.

Susan reveals too much information and emotions to the children, especially Randy, and that may continue to influence Randy to view his father in a negative light.

Daniel's dismissive attitude toward Susan's positive contribution to the children's lives may also contribute to the children's developing a negative view of their mother.

These parents are in need both of parent coordination and a family therapist. In my judgment, the primary issues that brought about this evaluation reflected the parents' need to continue to fight about their marital issues rather than any substantial parenting concerns. Both parents agreed that the children are doing well in school and all other related activities. Both parents agreed that the children have strong relationships with each parent. Both parents talked about wanting the other parent to have an active role in the children's lives.

At the end of the interview process with each parent, I summarized for Daniel and Susan what I learned from them. Both parents agreed that the children were doing well in school, the children were doing well with the other parent, the children were doing well with their friends, the children were doing well in their physical development, emotional and psychological development, and in their academic development.

Both parents agreed that the biggest obstacle was their inability to communicate with each other. Both cited significant distrust in the other parent's motivation and a belief that the other parent was withholding important information about the children.

At the end of the final, scheduled interview, I also asked each parent to contact me if there was anything else that needed to be discussed. Daniel emailed me the following day and wrote: "I do not feel that our children are getting the same love and attention and bonding that I give them and that's why this 2-2-5 is not working. I think it would be in the childrens [sic] best interest if they were placed with me."[1]

Daniel's concern about the children not receiving the "same love and attention and bonding" from Susan as they receive from him was not supported in the data gathered for this evaluation. The children have strong and healthy relationships with each parent. The children talk about engaging in a variety of activities with each parent and seeking out each parent when they feel distressed—this was more clearly stated by Randy than by four-year-old Michelle.

From a psychological assessment perspective, it is not possible to measure the amount of love and bonding a child has with each parent. Although one might be able to measure parent–child attention through direct observation across multiple activities and circumstances, a child custody evaluation is not structured to gather such data. Parent–child observations tend to be limited to a few hours under similar conditions at each parent's home (when possible) or at the evaluator's office.

My opinion, based upon the collateral data reviewed for this evaluation, my interview data,

---

[1] Daniel's full text written on October 19, 2012: "After I left today I thought about what you asked me—if I was agreeable to the 2-2-5 schedule and if I feel its [sic] working. Please understand that I was hesitant on answering this because I do not want to speak negatively about Susan, as she is my childrens [sic] mother. However, I would like to provide you with a more detailed answer to your question. Please reference the document I provided you today where I addressed your question 'what I would like from the court and why.' I do not feel that our children are getting the same love and attention and bonding that I give them and that's why this 2-2-5 is not working. I think it would be in the childrens [sic] best interest if they were placed with me."

and my observation of parent–child interactions, is that each child has a strong and healthy relationship with each parent.

My opinion, based upon the above information, is that the children are caught in the middle of their parents' conflict. Susan shares too much information with the children and reveals too much about her emotional upset with Daniel and his purported actions. The children are sensitive to these emotionally charged behaviors, and, in the case of Randy, Susan's revealing information and feelings about situations involving Daniel are interfering with his positive view of his father.

Daniel's continual criticisms of Susan and his belief that the children love one parent (Daniel) more than the other parent (Susan) are not in the children's psychological best interests. Daniel must learn to respect the children's strong and healthy relationship with their mother and communicate to the children that he finds value in Susan's parenting.

ANSWERS TO THE COURT'S QUESTIONS

Five specific questions were identified in the Consent Order as defining the scope of my evaluation. Below are my answers to the questions posed by the Order.

1. An extensive analysis of the custodial needs of the minor children.

Data Collected in Present Evaluation Used to Inform Opinion

Data were obtained from several collateral sources, review of medical records, interviews with parents, interviews with children, observation of each parent and children, and psychological testing.

The children are reported by the parents to be doing well. Collateral information supports the view of the children doing well in their respective activities. Neither child is reported to have any significant developmental delays. There are aspects to Michelle's activity level that suggest a need to monitor her over the next few years, but no recommendation for therapy or assessment is offered at this time because of her young age.

Randy's behaviors at school that were identified by Daniel as a source of some concern are, more likely than not, reactions to the significant changes that have occurred in Randy's life over the past two years. Just as I recommended above for Michelle, I would recommend that Randy's behavior be monitored, but that no psychological or psycho-educational intervention is needed at this time.

Research Foundation for Opinion

Current peer-reviewed research argues strongly for children to have relatively equal time with each parent. No definition has been provided in the literature that defines the concept of "relatively equal time." Five-year-old children often need somewhat more frequent access to each parent than do eight-year-old children. The frequency of parent–child contact is related to the quality of their interactions and consistency of contact that leads to strengthening their relationship. Disruptions to frequent parent–child contact may lead to difficulties in developing healthy parent–child relationships that can affect a child's sense of safety, security, and predictability of his or her environment.

Opinion

The current 5-2-2-5 parenting access schedule is serving the children's development well. I would not recommend a change to the access schedule.

2. The strengths and weaknesses of each of the parties as to the custody of the minor children

Data Collected in Present Evaluation Used to Inform Opinion

The mother and father have similar parenting goals and values. Their pre-separation ideas about parenting are similar to their post-separation ideas about parenting goals and values. The conflict focuses mainly on how each parent attends to parenting the children, and the ways in which each parent's parenting style takes different directions when not influenced by the other parent.

Randy reported that his mother talked to him about the loss of the hoped-for home and placed blame for the loss of the home on the father. Randy voiced his anger at his father and his distrust of his father over this incident. Randy also described how his mother has cried in front of him about the difficulties associated with the divorce and her view of the father's behaviors.

Daniel voiced concern that the children were being exposed to negative statements made by

---

COMMENT

A 5-2-2-5 plan is a 14-day parenting plan that rotates every weekend and allows for the same two days per week to be custodial time for one parent. For example, Parent One would have the first weekend in the month followed by Monday and Tuesday. The other parent would have Wednesday and Thursday followed by the next weekend. The advantage of the 5-2-2-5 plan is that the children are with the same parent the same two days of the week, every week. The weekends rotate, but not the weekdays.

Susan about him. Daniel's concerns about the children's exposure to negative statements about him uttered by Susan in the presence of the children were supported.

The children did not talk about their father making negative statements about their mother.

Research Foundation for Opinion

Children's exposure to parental conflict runs counter to their psychological best interests. Children's exposure to one parent's negative statements about the other parent also runs counter to children's psychological best interests.

Children's exposure to one parent's negative statements about the other parent tends to undermine the children's view of the other parent's parental authority, parental competency, and often leads children to take sides in the parents' battle about who is telling the truth about marital and family discord. Such parental influence can result in the children taking sides in the parents' conflict, leading to children aligning themselves with one parent against the other parent. Alignments such as these can lead to children having disrupted relationships with the other parent.

Opinion

Both parents are competent and fit parents. Susan must learn to better control her emotional reactions so that the children are not exposed to her outward expressions of anger, frustration, and/or annoyance with Daniel. Daniel, for his part, needs to learn how to handle communications with Susan in a more productive manner.

Daniel and Susan need to work with a family therapist, with whom they can discuss with Randy their son's emerging view of his father as unsupportive of Susan and therefore as someone whom Randy does not trust. Randy's view has developed, in large part, from exposure to his mother's statements. Susan and

Daniel need to address this concern with Randy in an open and forthright manner. If the parents are able to have such a talk with Randy without the aid of a mental health professional, I would support such a step. It is my belief, however, that the parents are unable to conduct such a discussion together with Randy without one or both parents placing blame.

3. The appropriate testing of the children of the parties for the purposes of custodial care.

No testing of the children was conducted for this evaluation. A battery of psychological tests was administered to each parent. None of the results from the psychological testing conducted on the parents raised any concerns about abnormal or psychopathological functioning.

4. The propensity of either party for alienating the affections of the minor children from the other party, and for the propensity and desire of either party to control, dominate, and intimidate the other party, and for their propensity to make derogatory remarks about the other party in the presence of the minor children.
5. The propensity of either party to engage in behavior that can have a detrimental effect on the two minor children and the further propensity of either party to engage in behavior that will serve as a poor role model for the two children.

Data Collected in Present Evaluation Used to Inform Opinion

Data were obtained from several collateral sources, review of medical records, interviews with parents, interviews with children, observation of each parent and children, and psychological testing.

COMMENT

There are times when two questions can be answered with the same information. In this example, the Consent Order's questions 4 and 5 are very similar. It is often helpful to answer similar questions with one answer in order to create a shorter report. The similarity in questions lies in the general concept of *alienation*. Question 4 asks about alienation in general, and Question 5 asks about specific behaviors that may adversely affect the children. Framing the response to include one answer that addresses the general question about alienation and the specific question about inappropriate behaviors that may have a detrimental effect on the children helps create a more coherent answer.

There are no data to indicate that the children are being alienated by either parent. The children have a strong and healthy relationship with each parent.

Daniel asserted that Susan was making negative statements to the children. Susan asserted that she was not making such statements. Randy described statements made by Susan about Daniel. His statements about what his mother told him about his father were consistent across two interviews that I held with Randy. Although collateral witnesses alleged that each parent was saying negative things about the other parent, none described directly observing either parent making negative statements about the other parent in the presence of the children.

There are no data to support Susan's allegation that Daniel is making negative statements about her in front of the children. However, Daniel's belief—articulated several times during our interviews and in emails—that the children love one parent more than the other and that the children have a stronger bond with him than with Susan may serve to undermine the children's view of their mother as a loving, competent parent. Both parents need to support the children's relationship with the other parent.

Research Foundation for Opinion

There is an increasingly substantial and complex literature on the development of alienation dynamics and the ways in which such alienation may adversely influence children. The most powerful adverse effect of alienation dynamics is the disruption of children's relationship with a parent. Some authors have classified substantiated allegations of alienation as a form of emotional abuse.

Another concern is the effect of one parent's making negative statements about the other parent

in the presence of the children. Negative statements may have their most powerful effects on young children, who tend to be more susceptible to influence.

Opinion

The children are not alienated from either parent. Neither parent is engaged in active attempts to alienate the children. Daniel's view that the children love him more than they love Susan is of concern, although it is not classified in this report as an alienating behavior. It is, in my opinion, a statement of Daniel's disrespect for Susan's role in the children's lives. Daniel's disrespect may serve to undermine the children's view of their mother, which then would be viewed as an alienating dynamic. Daniel needs to find value in Susan's role as the children's parent and communicate that positive value both to Susan and the children. He needs to work on finding a way to be supportive of Susan's positive relationship with the children. More to the point, whether one categorizes this behavior as alienating or not, it is a behavior that does not serve the psychological best interests of the children.

Susan needs to develop greater control over her emotional reactivity, especially when she is around the children. I also believe that she needs to develop greater emotional control over her behavior with Daniel, especially email and phone communications.

Both parents would be well served by working with a therapist. They also would profit from working with a parent coordinator.

UNDERLYING DATA TO SUPPORT OPINIONS

In this section of the report, I provide a summary of information obtained from interviews with each parent, interviews and observations with the children alone and with their parents, interpretation of psychological test data, and a summary of information obtained from collateral interviews.

Interviews with Daniel Waters
Daniel Interview, 110 Minutes, October 9, 2012

I began the interview by apologizing for the unanticipated delay due to my out-of-town commitments on a case and asked what had changed over the four months since we last spoke. Daniel said, "Susan lost her home due to credit [problems]. She is still in the apartment that she has been in. Things have been quiet for the past months. No new concerns except for Michelle's problem sleeping at her mom's. Susan brought this to the pediatrician's attention. This is good. I don't understand why she is having problems sleeping there. She has no problems sleeping at home. She is given melatonin to help her sleep."

[How did you find out that Michelle was taken to the pediatrician?]

"I didn't. I had to call after Susan told me. During bedtime routine one night, Randy mentioned that Michelle did not have to take her sleep medicine. I started asking questions then. It was after May."

[You asked your son questions about what?]

"I asked what Michelle takes at Mommy's? Randy said that she took melatonin. My next question was how often and he said every night. Later, I wrote Susan and kindly asked her, 'Is Michelle taking melatonin and how is it working?' Her response was the doctor recommended that she take it. I told her that I was concerned that Michelle was not having sleeping problems at home [with Daniel]. Susan became defensive as soon as I said Michelle did not have a problem sleeping with me. Conversation ended. I ended it. I know better. When she becomes defensive or angry, I don't know how to proceed from that point with her."

[What could you have done differently that might have reduced her defensiveness?]

"Probably not talk about Michelle not having sleep difficulties at my house. I think about what I am trying to communicate. It also bothers me that she didn't tell me about the appointment and this was a scheduled four-year-old wellness check-up."

[What is your understanding of why you were not informed about her doctor's visit?]

"I don't have an understanding of why I was not informed. I inform her of things of that nature, so I don't know. I don't want to be informed to find something wrong. I want to be kept up to date."

[Are there other areas in which you feel out of the information loop?]

"Yes, Randy's Boy Scouts and Michelle's dance. I only hear about those activities if it falls on my time and I have to bring them to something. I missed Michelle's parent observation night. I wasn't told."

[You know where she has the dance classes?]

"Yes. I do call the dance studio and to see the schedule, and I was told that she no longer dances there. Ultimately, I depend on Susan to keep me informed. Maybe it is wrong for me to expect the same from her. I realize that."

[How have you changed?]

"I call the doctor. I call the dance studio. I do what I have to do to keep myself up to date."

[You have other scheduled wellness visits? How do you know about those?]

"Calling the doctor's office. I took Randy to his. I found out about that by calling the doctor. I informed Susan before and after."

[Susan did not attend?]

"No, she didn't. I believe she was working the night before."

[What was her reaction in response to you taking the child to the wellness visit?]

"She said that I was doing it to look good. Recent dental visits: I have taken him to two during the course of the time we have been separated. I let her know before and after."

[Since we last spoke, describe any concerns you have had about access to your children?]

"What do you mean?"

[Are you seeing the children when you are supposed to be seeing the children?]

"Yes. We have been on a schedule. I have not had any problems getting the children."

[What has that schedule been?]

"Still on 5-2-2-5."

[How do you feel that has been working for the children?]

"First thing is Michelle's sleeping. Why is she having difficulties at Susan's home and not mine? We have had trouble with homework last year with Randy."

[This year?]

"It has been working pretty well. No homework problems to speak of....Another concern is that I don't want my kids to refer to 'Mommy's home' and 'Daddy's home' but to 'my home.' It bothers me. She tells the kids that 'Daddy won't let us move' or 'Daddy makes it where we cannot move.' The information Tom sent you—Susan wrote a letter to my mother indicating that the kids hate me because I won't let Susan move."

[What is positive about how the children have been adjusting to the separation?]

"The kids seem to be adapting to life with me just fine. They are happy to come stay with me."

[How do you know they are happy to stay with you?]

"Had lunch with Randy at school. He walked up to me at school and said, 'Only one more day,' meaning that he would come and be with me for five days....Michelle, last five days I had them, she went to sleep at 8:30 on a school night. She woke up and it was 6:45. She put on her own clothes which I was shocked, her shoes on backwards, tried to put her hair in a ponytail....I was fixing breakfast. She said, 'Thanks for laying my clothes out for me. I wish Mommy would do that for me.' I said that it was okay that Mommy does things different. Sunday evening I met Susan. I had the thermos and Michelle had a picture that she drew. Her house, the dogs, and her room and toys. She is four and the dogs looked like rats. I just think the kids are happy at home."

[What is negative about what has been happening with the children for the past several months?]

"Her sleeping. The homework."

[I thought you said the homework is fine?]

"All of Randy's weekly work comes home with him on Mondays. That means that Susan always gets the homework. I have asked Susan to let me see how he is doing. If she does respond, it is that he is doing fine and I don't have to see it."

[What do you say?]

"Okay."

[Why?]

"I told her that I want to see it, but I won't argue with her. I know he is doing okay, I see his progress reports. I pick my battles, I guess."

[What would you want to the court to do?]

"The reason I am concerned about the children going to Susan's. Randy tells that he goes to his room, closes the door, locks his door and goes into his closet and shuts the door to get peace and quiet. He said that Mommy is fussing always with Michelle. Michelle hits him and is mean to him while he is there. She doesn't do that when they are with me."

[How have you talked with the children about this?]

"I asked questions. I ask why is Mommy fussing at Michelle or at you. He said that he doesn't know. I ask whether Mommy sent you to your room. He says 'no.' He goes in by himself."

[Have you raised this with Susan?]

"No. I don't want to come across as being controlling. She says that it is none of my business what they do there....Michelle is always told not to hit anyone. Randy, I ask him why she hits him, 'Are you guys playing?' He says that she is just mean to him."

[Have you talked to the two children together about this?]

"If I ask Michelle, I ask why she hit him. He will say that Michelle is always mean. Michelle will apologize and hug him. I can't get any clear information out of him. One time she said that I hit Randy because Mommy was mad. That made no sense to me. Recently there was a conversation between me and Randy. He feels left out because Scott, Susan's boyfriend, always plays with Michelle. At church, I am always there. Scott will walk in holding Michelle's hand in church. Susan is next to Scott. Randy is walking behind them."

[Tell me about Scott's role in the life of your children.]

"Scott has dinner with them. He lives in the apartments. He is sometimes there late at night, according to Michelle. He has a son in middle school that plays with Randy sometimes....I shook Scott's hand and introduced myself. It went good. Seems like a nice guy. It does bother me to some degree to see that, but I know that I need to expect that in the future. I try to be as open as I can. If I let it bother me, it makes me unhappy. I try to be positive."

[Are you able to talk to Scott about Randy's feelings about being left out?]

"No, I only see him at church when he comes. My first thoughts were....I looked at the sex offender's registry. I found nothing."

[Is there somebody in your life who the children have had contact with?]

"No. I have many friends but I am not dating one person in particular."

[Daniel talked about a change in Randy's behavior that he has observed.]

"Randy is more shy within himself since we separated. He is more withdrawn. When he first started reading, he would sit and read for an hour. He would take reading over sports. Starting in second grade, he seems to have lost interest as if something is preoccupying his mind. Same thing with sports. At recess time at school, he is sad because no one will come play with him. That has been going on since the start of school. Up until then, he was the kid who would run into a crowd and start playing."

[Have you talked with the school about your observations?]

"Not yet."

[Why not?]

"I am still collecting information about whether this is short or long term. I have a relationship with his teacher and I can talk with her very easily. A friend of mine picks up his daughter. He was there when Susan was picking up Randy. Randy came out crying. The guy called me and said that Randy was upset. Had it been me, I would have reacted differently. I would have turned around and talked with the teacher. When I did ask Randy, he said that no one played with him at recess."

[I asked Daniel why he did not contact the teacher. He said that he still wanted to gather information and he wanted to be better prepared to talk with the teacher since she would ask questions, too.]

"I did call the teacher. I had a classroom meeting with her shortly after that. I got off the subject at that point in time. Other parents were there at the time....Susan's level of anger and resentment affects her ability to go forward in a productive way."

[Anger and resentment toward who?]

"Me. The things that she says in public with them around. Sadly that has not changed for a long time....I have another concern to discuss openly with you. Her attitude toward Randy. She seems like she has pulled away from Randy since the separation. He complains, 'Mommy doesn't play with me.' If he has issues with school, he does not tell Susan on Monday. He waits until he sees me on Wednesday. It may be that Randy loves being with me at my home. I don't know what he says to her at home. I know that he does not want to say things for fear of hurting people's feelings, specifically his mother's feelings."

[What do you think he is not saying to Susan?]

"I am sure he would not say that he would rather be with Daddy or to 'go back home' as he puts it. When we first separated, Susan would tell Randy that he was hurting her feelings, and she would cry in front of him when he would say that he wanted to go back home. I don't know exactly what he said, because he would not tell me. He wanted to talk with me but she would not allow him to call me. I know that he has asked to stay back with Daddy and she won't let him."

[Is Randy able to call you now?]

"They don't call me. I call them."

[When you call them, are you able to reach them?]

"Yes. It is more difficult now that Scott is in their lives. She doesn't pick up. It concerns me that she would make Randy feel that it is his fault. I tell Randy that he can tell me anything and that it would not hurt my feelings.

"Last Christmas, Randy said, 'I want you and Mommy to get back together.' It hurts my feelings that he says that. I explained, 'Mommy and Daddy have things to work out. You need to tell us if you are sad.' I let her know that he said that. Trying to keep her up to speed on how he is feeling. I have never gotten anything from her about how the children are feeling. I think that this is important for parents to keep each other up to date on how the children are feeling. She would not—if the kids wanted to come home, she sure wouldn't tell me."

Daniel Interview, October 19, 2012, One Hour

[I began by asking about the home visit I conducted. I asked how typical was the children's behavior compared to other times in which they are at home and playing.]

"Very typical. They behaved as they normally would. Every chance they get, they play outside. Always looking at their books. Moving them around the house. They bring their books to everywhere in the house. They acted normal as they always do."

[What did the kids say after the visit?]

"Randy was excited that you were writing a story about his life. Michelle asked why you didn't stay for dinner. That is Michelle: bubbly personality."

[Who is she more like?]

"A little bit of both of us, I think. Girls are always more outspoken, ask a lot more questions than boys would."

[*During the home visit, Daniel's brother walked over. I asked Daniel,* Your brother lives down the road?]

"Yes, three houses down. That is my middle brother. Oldest brother is 52. Middle brother is about 45. I was a mistake. Tony and his wife live three houses down and have two kids. They are both in high school."

[Tell me about Randy's strengths and weaknesses.]

"Randy is outgoing and determined. He is always willing to learn new things. Well mannered. He is always interactive with friends and in school. Back to my concern that I mentioned last week, it does not seem that he is as outgoing with his friends as he was. Tends to shy away from group activities. I went to his school and watched him play during recess. He tended to stay by himself. That is not like him. He has been complaining recently that no one wants to play with him. He used to be the leader of the pack, so to speak. Like he feels insecure, possibly."

[What does he feel insecure about?]

"I don't know what caused that (the shyness). I talk to him as much as I can or as much as he will talk to me about it. Randy is also a very serious…he can be a very serious kid in conversations. More serious in trying to understand things than being a class clown. He is definitely not that. He is overall a very sweet little boy."

[Tell me about Michelle's strengths and weaknesses.]

"Very bubbly personality. Loves attention and being in front of people. She loves to talk and be involved in everything she can be involved in. I hope that stays that way."

[Why?]

"From a social standpoint, that is a benefit. Her friends, her social groups. She tries to sing. Loves to dance. Has a real outgoing personality. Very affectionate, too. She will tell you that she loves you 10 times a day.

"That is another difference I saw in Randy. He seems to be less affectionate toward me. It doesn't seem as if we are as close as we were. He doesn't talk to me as much as he used to, whereas before, he would tell me everything without me having to ask. Almost like he is afraid that he will say something wrong."

[Do you have a sense when Randy's change began to occur?]

"During the transition period during the separation."

[Can you be more specific?]

"I noticed the change in him after he told me that his mom cries when he tries to talk with me."

[When was that?]

"Within the first month of the first physical separation. Within that first week, he would tell me that he misses me, how much he wanted to come back home, seemed angry as well. Angry in a way that he had a worse temper."

[What does his temper look like?]

"Before separation when he would get angry, he would talk. He would talk and talk and talk. Since the separation, he has become more physically aggressive during his outbursts. He will throw something. Talk back. Argue with me. I have seen a lot of that. Him and his mother have always argued back and forth. I put fires out always. I can only assume that is happening. He doesn't show any aggression toward other kids. That is where he becomes shy. Thing that bothers me the most is that he is not as open with me.

"When he would do something wrong—not listening in the store and he knows he did wrong, now he runs away. Sometimes he starts crying before I say anything. He asks me if I am mad and if I will spank him in the car. I have done. From that point forward, he was begging me not to be mad at him. He becomes afraid with what is going to happen now if he gets into trouble."

[Any similar changes in Michelle?]

"No. Maybe sleeping. She still sleeps good at home. She cries and whines at night. This separation has disrupted that process according to what Susan says. She has sleep problems at Susan's. At home, she sometimes cries that she wants to sleep in Mommy's bed. Not so much now. I am not seeing that much change in her. Maybe due to her age. She was three when we separated.

"That conversation with Susan was the first phone call I have gotten in which she did not yell at me. There was an assignment due on Friday. The assignment was sent home on Monday and Susan said that she sent the assignment with Randy on Wednesday. I did not get it. I don't understand why she did not get it done Monday or Tuesday.

"Blackhawk (the teacher) did not tell parents at the parent meeting that she would be sending home monthly activity sheets explaining what the students would do and when during the course of the month. Susan gets everything that is sent home on Mondays.

COMMENT

There are times when it may be useful to record your clinical impressions drawn from interview data. In this case, the tone of the father's interview suggested that he was unaware that the mother had ended her relationship with her boyfriend. I was not certain at this time whether this would be important, so I made note of it in my interview notes.

"Susan has been acting very strange."

[Strange how?]

"At the game, she showed up on time and she looked like a zombie. I don't know if there is something on her mind. She goes through these periods of depression. She gets very unhappy, and it can last four to five days. Ends up with her crying for a day before it gets better. I can only assume that maybe that is what is going on. She returned all the clothes that were mine this morning. The kids' clothes and socks. What I bought that were at her house. The phone call, the clothes, last Sunday when she did not talk to the kids, I don't understand it."

[*It is clear from this conversation that Daniel does not know that Susan and Scott stopped seeing each other because Scott did not want to deal with the pressures from the custody dispute.*]

[What have we not talked about that you believe I need to know?]

"I think it would be important to discuss how Susan handles her anger. Clearly, you can see how she handles her anger toward me and the kids. She has hit Randy on top of his head when he doesn't listen. Threatens to hit him again if he doesn't stop crying. She has always had a difficult time keeping her patience. Losing control."

[How does she lose control?]

"Throwing something or running out of the room. How many times I have comforted the kids after she has kicked something, thrown something. I just say that Mommy is okay, she is just tired. Along with that, several years ago, she got angry with Randy. She got mad and picked him up and threatened to put his hand on the burner. She caught herself in the act. Put Randy down and ran out of the room to calm down.

"How she acts around me when we are in public. She says that I am a piece of shit, her favorite word. Probably three, four, or five months ago, she had the kids in the car. It was last Christmas. She was angry over how Christmas visitation worked out. She would not unlock the door so I could see the kids. When she did, I walked around and hugged Randy. Susan said to me in front of the kids that Michelle wasn't even mine."

[What did you do with that comment?]

"I ignored her. I always ignore her when she says those things in front of the kids. I just smile. After I closed the door, she spun her wheels and sped away. She had the kids in the car. My attorney wrote a letter describing that event, and asking her to stop the behavior. Numerous events at church. Three weeks ago at a soccer game, when Michelle's team was getting ready to play and Susan was standing beside me where the benches are."

Daniel, Fourth Interview, November 14, 2012

"Randy seems to be very frustrated and on the edge all the time. Disorganized. I see him having difficulties staying focused, like homework. At school, she sees it also. Perhaps his home life plays into all of this. A feeling of instability."

[What does that mean?]

"He is not where he wants to be, not happy. Overall, I think this is problem—his home life, him going back and forth so much—he is not adapt [*sic*] well to it. Looking at things that he writes and pictures that he draws. Things he says about his mom lead me to believe that this is affecting the way he acts at school."

[What does Randy say about his mom to you?]

"I took time to write this down for you."

[*Daniel provided me with a two-page summary of statements the children are alleged to have said to him.*]

"I brought you Randy's journal."

[*Daniel interpreted picture from journal (#1) that the picture is of Susan looking angry.*

Picture of Daniel, Michelle, and Randy (#2) shows his idea of a family. Unfortunately, for whatever reason, he did not put his mom in the picture because she never got involved with him, never bonded with him, did not have a close relationship with Randy.

Statement that Randy likes to play at home with his dogs (#3). In his mind, my home is his home. He feels more comfortable there. I believe that with him wanting to be home, might make him sad or frustrated. Knowing that he won't be home for the next 5 days.]

[Daniel wrote in "peaceful." I asked him what meaning this had to him.] "I believe he feels there is less fussing, less.... I have a lot more patience with him. I make things flow a lot more smoothly, like discipline. Things at home are quieter. He does not have to close the door for peace like he does at Susan's home. I believe that these pictures and these comments that I wrote for you all go hand and hand. He wants to spend more time at home."

[I asked how Daniel determines whether the children are more comfortable at their family home or with him.]

"Mom doesn't play with him at home. Considering the past years, Susan was never all that involved with Randy, or Michelle for that matter. He is closer to me. He tells me. He does not have that bond with his mom. I can give you an example from this past week. We got to church at the same time. I got the kids out. Susan walks up to the kids. Randy walks to her, waves and walks away. I think that he has a lot of resentment built up to his mom because of the things that Susan says to him about me. With her not bonding with him over the year, it makes her feel distant to him."

[Daniel continues to argue that Susan has a weaker relationship with Randy than he does. We had a discussion about how he continues to use the same problem-solving skills that led to the failure of the marriage—his part at least.]

"This past weekend, Saturday night, me, Randy, and Michelle were sitting on the floor playing Legos. He could not get something to go together. He was getting frustrated. He said out of the blue, he said 'f--- this, I am done with this.' That is his mom's favorite word. She says this in front of the kids. I was floored. I took him to another room and told him never to say the word. It is the worst word. It is a negative term. It does not make you look good. He started crying. I kept asking him, Where did you hear this, where did you hear this? This is where I get confused. He said he heard it from a friend at school. The friend said it to Randy. He said, No wait, I heard it at Mommy's. Caleb said it, Scott's son. He is in middle school. It is almost like he is afraid of telling me."

FORENSIC EVALUATION OF SUSAN WATERS

Susan Interview, May 30, 2012, 100 Minutes
She was asked about her understanding of the reason for the evaluation. She said, "My understanding is to determine what the situation is and who is more suitable, how the custody should be decided. I originally asked for a psychological evaluation in May of last year so that I could get separated. At that time, the judge did not deem it necessary to have an evaluation. His statement was that he saw enough evidence that he could make a decision that day for a temporary situation. Some things happened over the course of a few months and he agreed that a psychological evaluation was necessary."

[What was the initial custody situation last May?]

"It was joint. Equal. He puts on a set schedule, every two weeks it is the same. 5-2-2-5."

[What happened over the months that led to these concerns?]

"I was being constantly harassed. We could not get along with anything related to the children."

[Give me some examples.]

"Biggest example was when my son went back to school. I would have them on Monday. Everything would come home from school on Monday and although the assignments were due Friday, we would go ahead and finish the assignments on Monday and Tuesday, so that when he went to his dad's on Wednesday, everything was done."

[Why not allow your son to do homework at his father's home?]

"He didn't have much. The reason is—I am getting to that. About two weeks into school, assignments were getting lost. I would start receiving texts accusing me of losing the assignments or just not completing them, accusations of not helping him do homework."

[How typical was his behavior during the marriage?]

"As we became more unhappy, this badgering became more constant. There was never actual communication. It was never a face to face. That is the real problem now. There was never a face to face communication."

[Was there ever a time when it was different? Had good face to face conversation?]

"When we dated, we did not live in the same town. I don't think there was ever good communication. He is challenging me on not being honest with the children.

"A lot of our problems started once we had a child. He would stay on the computer for hours at a time. He locked his computer so that I never saw his computer."

[About how many hours per week was he on the computer?]

"Ninety percent. He was always on his computer."

[Does his job require him to be on the computer?]

"Yes. Now, he owns his own business. I don't know if he needs to be on the computer all night long.

"He has a first wife. She and I now speak."

[What is her name?]

"Charlotte Williams. She said that he did the same thing to her regarding the computer. He put a tap on my computer. He had done the same thing to her."

[What do you mean he put a tap on your computer?]

"He could track everything I had done on the computer all day. He would show it to me."

[He did this without your permission?]

"Yes. He put a keystroke program on my computer. Earlier in our marriage, he built computers and he built mine. He put in a secret recipient on my email so that everything I received and sent he received a copy.

"He also tracked my car. Bugs in my car, tracking device, GPS."

[What information can you provide to me that supports your assertion that Daniel was tracking your communications and movements?]

"That was the whole reason that I left the marriage. Throughout the whole marriage, I was not allowed to do anything. I was not allowed to go with girlfriends anywhere. It would be a fight. Constant fighting. He would say that married women should not go out anywhere. I could not leave him home. He had a misconception that if you go out, you are looking for a man. I never went out anywhere. His sister in law—I was very close to her during our marriage—she invited me and her mother to go the beach, he got so very angry—we were in the car discussing this—he got angry that he ran us off the road. We were coming back from the beach with my family. My child—son—was in the car."

[Who witnessed this?]

"No one. My parents were a few miles back. I told my sister-in-law about this. She got to where she saw this stuff going on."

[What is her name?]

"Wendy Waters...."

"Charlotte is scared of Daniel. He told me that he was very possessive and controlling. He threatened to harm her. He came after her where she lived."

[Was there a police report?]

"I am not sure."

[If there is a police report, please provide it to me.]

"Her youngest child and our youngest daughter are in the same daycare. She sees him now."

[What would happen when you would get into arguments?]

"He would come after me when I left the argument. He would pursue me. He punched a hole in the wall beside my head. He repaired three different walls where he put a punch. He gets angry and shakes. He does not physically hurt me.

"Last year, when I asked for divorce, he came after me in the kitchen in front of the kids. With his fists in the air. He said he was waving his hands but they were in a fist. I got up and ran to the garage. He came after me screaming. I had just gotten a new car. He started beating on the car. I wanted to leave and get away from the situation. He started to yank on the seatbelt and tried to stop me from leaving. He ended up backing away and letting me leave. I had been in an abusive relationship in college, and he was yelling that he understood why that I would get beat up again."

[Did anyone observe these events?]

"No....

"I called my sister in law, Wendy. Her husband is the sheriff in Nassau County. I didn't call the police. I came back and moved into the guest room. I asked for a divorce that night."

[What was going on with the children?]

"They were still sitting there eating. The little boy just sat there eating. When I came home, my little boy came running over and asked if I was still angry at Daddy for what he did."

[Kids did not cry? Did not show upset?]

"Not before I left....

"What started the fight was that he got into my computer. He found an email from a Facebook friend asking how I was doing. It was from a male friend. He accused me of having more of a relationship with this person than I did. Any time I had a male friend, he accused me of having more than it was."

[Tell me about Daniel's parenting.]

"He takes care of the kids, more now since he has to. He is asleep all day. I pretty much would care for the babies because he was sleeping during the day. Once my son got old enough to play, Daniel became more involved. He was three or four. I don't recall that he spoke to our child until he was three or four years old...."

"My daughter, he is involved with her care now. It is just different. It is almost like she is too much to handle. My son said that Daddy says that she is high maintenance. I don't think she gets the same care from Daniel. I notice that she is often not bathed when she comes back from Daniel's. My son tells me that she does not get bathed every night the way that he does."

[How have you talked about this with Daniel?]

"He says that it is not true. He tells me that I shouldn't listen to our son. I have given up on trying to talk with Daniel."

[If Daniel is here, what will he tell me about you?]

"He says that I am never there, he is their primary caregiver, and that he does everything. It makes it look like I don't exist. I was only gone from the home three nights a week. I left at 6:30 p.m. They were fed before I would leave. Daniel would be responsible for bathing the children three nights a week. He bathed them...."

"Daniel has been very involved in our son's life over the past three to four years. He signs him up for every sport and he coaches everything. He is involved now. Lately, I have seen the control issue come up in the relationship between my son and Daniel. The past few weeks, my son has been involved in baseball. Last Saturday, my son said that he did not want to go to baseball. My son uses the word 'forces' in describing his father's behavior. Randy is not interested. He sits and plays in the dirt. Daniel tells Randy that he has to play. Daniel is almost hovering. He is controlling Randy's friends."

[Tell me about your children.]

"Randy is seven. He loves to play. He is happy-go-lucky. He takes in strays. He plays with everybody. That is the type of kid he is. He is so smart. One of the top kids in the class. He gets frustrated when he cannot do everything right. He wears his heart on his sleeve. Gets his feeling hurt easily. He is all boy. Wants to get dirty. Play with bugs. Happy little kid."

"Michelle is four. She is messy. She talks to everyone who walks by. She is always the center of attention. She talks to everybody and talks nonstop...like me. She is bubbly. You never see her upset. She wraps people around her finger every time."

[How do brother and sister get along?]

"Pretty good. They play well together. She forgets she is a girl and plays real hard. They seem to be doing very well. I have seen kids go through this and not do well. Our kids seem to be doing very well with all of this. They almost make the transitions fun—they get excited about going to their other house. They make it fun rather than becoming upset about it. I have been surprised at how well they have done."

[What do you want out of this litigation?]

"From the way things have been in the last year, I want them more. Mainly because there are so many issues. It is a constant battle. It is exhausting. Lying about losing homework. He will start telling the teacher....She asked me one day about Daniel being vindictive."

[What did the teacher tell you about concerns about Daniel being vindictive?]

"She said she would keep an eye on the homework issue and asked me if he was a vindictive person. She did not say much more." [*Linda Blackhawk, first-grade teacher at New Hope Elementary school— Randy's teacher.*]

[What does "more" mean to you?]

"I want them through the week. He might have them Wednesday evenings and every other weekend."

[*Susan tells me two incidents in which Randy studied his vocabulary words on Monday and Tuesday, went to his father's home and took the test Friday. He scored a 41 and 70- something. His explanation was that his father does not review the vocabulary words with him during the week. This is the type of concern that Susan has about the children spending more weekday time with their father.*]

"Daniel has accused me of poisoning him with Visine. One day I was on the phone with a friend. Daniel received a lab result that indicated that a Coke bottle had been contaminated with Visine. This test was $700.00. I know that I did not do it. He did."

[You think that he put the Visine in the coke?]

"Yes. He never drank out of the small 15-oz. bottles. He always drinks out of the 64-oz. bottles."

[When did this happen?]

"This happened more than a year ago. He told the judge and the judge asked me. I told him that I did not do it.…

"He has done so many other things."

[What other things has he done?]

"The major invasion of privacy. When we dated, he videotaped our intercourse. He showed it to me. He said it was an accident. When we lived in another home, we had security cameras.…

"Daniel did not understand why this video made without my consent would upset me. When I told him that I was upset, he would tell me it was funny. Then he sent me the video. I deleted it."

Susan Interview, October 23, 2012, One Hour

[Tell me how typical your children's behavior was on the day that I observed them at your home.] "Pretty much a normal day for us. Monday is a busy day. Tuesday is relaxed. We kind of hang out. They are pretty wild like that most of the time. Sometimes it is put on for people there."

[What did you see that was wild?]

"I let them run around. Michelle screams. Her teacher says she has no indoor voice. It doesn't faze me. When people are there, I am conscious of them being wild and rambunctious."

[What did they tell you about my visit at Daniel's house?] "Randy brings up the loss of the house. I haven't mentioned that for a while. I told him that I am not upset about that. He has not brought it up since."

[Do you recall what you told him about losing the house?]

"I told him about needing the papers. That it was what I was waiting on. He knew that I was waiting on the papers. Finally, I just told him that I was waiting on the paperwork. He is eight. He would not understand. I told him that I needed papers that I needed his daddy to sign. He would come back and say that Daddy did not have the papers. He told me that he is not a child. Randy tells me that he wants to hear what is happening. Sometimes I would hear.…

"Yesterday, I spoke with the teacher, Ms. Blackhawk. She told me that she believes that Randy is choosing not to be involved. She had the same episode when he came out crying. He told the teacher that no one was wanting to play with him. He would play in the dirt by himself. She would ask

Randy to ask other boys to play with him. Her son will play with him—he is in another class. Randy is choosing to play by himself. Randy was listening to this."

[Did Randy say anything to explain himself?]

"No. We didn't talk about this.…

"He told me the wrong homework assignment. His teacher said that he knows the assignment, and when asked yesterday, he was able to repeat the assignment. When asked why he does not report to his mother the correct assignment, he said he did not know."

[Daniel has talked about a change in how Randy behaves toward him. What, if anything, have you observed?]

"The only time I have observed Daniel and Randy and the warmth thing is at church. I haven't seen any differences. He hugs his dad. I have not seen any difference out in public. Randy has always been very attached to other kids and he has also been okay playing on his own. He has no problem going between the two. Even at his ball games, he finds one kid to get attached to.…

"Daniel's family is very reserved. His mom and dad would sit in the corner during a party while everyone else was out enjoying themselves. One of his older brothers is very open: Tony. Scott is more reserved."

[Tell more about the children.]

"The children are doing very well. It is going very well. Better than I would have imagined."

[What does it mean?]

"The parenting schedule seems to be doing well. The only concern I have about the schedule is the school stuff. Ms. Blackhawk agreed to start giving Daniel school work on Wednesdays."

[What do you think I need to know more about before we end our interview?]

"Daniel's goal is to stop me from seeing the kids. I feel that he is out to ruin me for the past two years."

[What does "ruin me" mean?] "He says that I am unfit. He would tell lies to the judge. I was the only one who took them. Trying to set me up that I was trying to poison him."

[How has your ability to solve problems with Daniel changed over time?]

"Some of his mindset was in another place at the time. We could sit down and work it out. The mediator was scared of him. He has that manipulative personality."

[What do you mean that the mediator was scared of him?]

"She would come back to our room and say that he was odd, made her feel uncomfortable. February a year ago, Daniel asked me recently about the mediator. Just weird things."

[What is it that you would like the judge to hear from you?]

"I want what is best for them (the children). I want to get along. I want it to be easier to talk with him. I don't want to feel scared to talk with him. I want fairness in the time, especially over the holidays. I need a judge to put into writing the plan. I don't want to miss out on the important things."

[Are things different at all with Daniel since the evaluation began?]

"Yes, ever since he started coming here. He is not good at face-to-face confrontation. He is an email and text guy. He does not deal a lot with people face to face. He is over the phone and computer."

[What do you think I need to look at that I haven't looked at?]

"I can't think of any one area. I think you have done what you are supposed to do.

"There is something that I have been meaning to ask you—is Michelle's hyperactivity. She doesn't slow down. She doesn't go to sleep at night. She was laying in her room wired. Her teachers report the same thing. They cannot get her to lie down. No one can get her to relax. Randy will tell us that she doesn't go to sleep at Daniel's house either."

[Have you talked to your doctor?]

"She told me to give her melatonin before she goes to sleep. I talked to Daniel and he said that he doesn't have any trouble. She is a nonstop talker. She does not stop all day long."

[Is Michelle hyperactive/ADHD?]

"The doctor has never raised this as a concern. She has two cousins on my side where they have ADD. My first cousin has issues in school. He is on medicine. I don't want to judge her, but if it is an issue, I want to know so it doesn't affect her school."

[*I explained that I would offer no opinions on any issue until I finished gathering all the information for the evaluation.*]

[What other difficulties are there between you and Daniel that I need to know about?]

"I don't have a lot of say. He wants to be the decision maker. During the marriage, I made all the medical and school decisions. When I moved out and he became Superdad and took over, but he is not fully aware of everything that went on with [their]

health. He comes in and takes over. He wants to show up but he does not want to financially help."

[What does that mean, that he does not help financially?]

"He had to be told by the lawyers to help with school. He wants to participate fully but not help out financially. He still only pays 30 dollars a week out of $140. He is covering them on health insurance."

[Where else is it not even?]

"School and activities. That is it. That is about all we do."

Susan, Fourth Interview, November 14, 2012, 70 Minutes

[*Susan began the interview talking about her concern from the last interview in which I discussed my view that she tends to be somewhat emotionally reactive in some of her actions toward Daniel.*]

"I am still uneasy about how the process is going; he is still giving me a hard time. Some of the things…you said that you jumped to conclusions. He is always on me. He is constantly texting me. I did not know that he called but it did not show up on my phone. He will take a picture of his call log and send it to me. I don't need a text to show me that you called. It is nit-picky things like that."

[How is that related to parenting?]

"We can't talk. We can't discuss little things like that. Any time family things come up, he calls the lawyer. He doesn't talk to me. You need to be able to talk to me like a co-parent. Don't threaten me. You can't call the lawyer forever."

[Do you turn to the attorney for advice?]

"Frances says that she never hears from me. I always give in. We have arguments about Thanksgiving. He wants the whole entire day. His family doesn't do it on Thanksgiving. It always falls on his weekend. I asked for him to bring them back early. He didn't understand that. He told me that I couldn't have all the time that I asked for."

[*Susan and I discussed how to copy her texts so that she could email them to me.*]

"I still get uneasy about not being honest. We had to go to court over homework last year. He said that I never did the homework."

[*I showed Susan the homework log that I was provided. She said that the homework log was not the original. She said the original was lost.*]

"Randy's teacher sent the books home on Wednesday. They did not do reading on Monday and Tuesday. I did not sign the log because there was no reading on Monday or Tuesday."

[When I speak to the teacher, the teacher will say what about Randy?]

"He is doing well this year."

[*I showed Susan the information I have about the children's schooling. She said that she provided more documents than I have in my possession. I have one page of Randy's 2011–2012 semester. She indicated that she will forward additional documents. At the time of writing this report, Susan never provided the additional information.*]

[*I showed Susan the texts from November 10th. I asked her to explain to me her view of these texts.*]

"The attorneys worked out a schedule. We have not agreed to the schedule. Last year, he would only let me have Christmas Day—a couple of hours on Christmas Day and I had them two hours for dinner on Christmas Eve. It was his weekend. He had them for five days at Christmas. My reaction to the November 10th emails is that he will ask for the whole night to do Santa. That is fine if he would have done the same for me, but he would not. So, I had to pick a whole other weekend that Santa was coming."

[What weekend is that?]

"Last year, it was the weekend before Christmas."

[This year?]

"It has not been finalized. He tells me that he is taking them to Disney. He wants them at 3:00 on Christmas day and I agreed to that. What they told me, the arrangement the lawyers came up with was the 19th until Christmas day at three. Daniel is saying different dates. I told him that I was asking the lawyers about the agreement. He said that he had not agreed to that. He will ask me for favors, and then he does nothing for me. I am willing to work with whatever. This is not about me. It is for them. It is not about me, but I am a Christmas fanatic. I want to be able to get along and work this out."

[*We reviewed the texts that Daniel brought today so that I could understand how Susan reacts to his messages.*]

"He will always get away with what he did. The lies he told about me. All I did was try to be a good mom. He is telling people that I am a horrible mom. I prided myself on being a good mom. Once I wanted a divorce, he comes along and says that I did nothing and he did everything. He never knew what was going on until the morning

of Christmas. Now, I have to defend myself, that I didn't do anything. . . .

"The kids are adjusting well. Things like this get to me. When the trial is over, it will stop. It is all about how they will do better with him than with me. Why would you want to set out and believe that your kids can't be with their mom? I got them to their school. I went to every doctor's visit. The doctor would say that I am doing this fine."

INTERPRETATION OF PSYCHOLOGICAL TEST DATA

Susan and Daniel were administered a battery of psychological tests examining their respective psychological health, which included:

a) Symptom Checklist-90–Revised SCL-90-R
b) Minnesota Multiphasic Personality Inventory–2nd Edition MMPI-2
c) Millon Clinical Multiaxial Inventory–3rd Edition MCMI-III
d) Personality Assessment Inventory PAI
e) Revised NEO Personality Inventory NEO-PI-R
f) State-Trait Anger Expression Inventory STAXI-2
g) Cognitive Distortions Scale CDS
h) Paulhaus Deception Scale PDS
i) Substance Abuse Subtle Screening Inventory SASSI

The information obtained from these psychological tests addresses several psychological dimensions of emotional and mental health functioning. Susan asserted that Daniel was overly controlling and intrusive. She also asserted that Daniel was emotionally abusive toward her. Although Susan did not assert that these alleged behaviors adversely affected the children, she stated that Daniel's alleged behavior affected her ability to effectively parent and co-parent. The data from these psychological tests provide data that may be useful in determining support for Susan's assertions.

Similarly, Daniel asserted that Susan was highly emotionally reactive, impulsive (and therefore irresponsible) and self-focused in ways that adversely affected the children. He also asserted that Susan's rigidly held beliefs about Daniel adversely affected his ability to effectively co-parent with her. The data from these psychological tests provide data that may be useful in determining support for Daniel's assertions.

Results of Daniel's Testing

The results of the validity scales of the psychological tests listed above indicated that Daniel approached the testing with a strong tendency to present himself in a highly favorable light. Although most fathers involved in child custody litigation score highly on these scales, Daniel's scores on the MMPI-2, MCMI III, and PAI were higher than expected from male custody litigants. When a person approaches psychological testing with the intention to present a highly favorable picture of himself, it becomes very difficult for the evaluator to accurately interpret the meaning of the clinical scales of each psychological test. Daniel's scores on the clinical scales are likely to be underestimates of his true functioning at the time of testing.

Within the above-stated limitation, Daniel's psychological test scores suggest a hypothesis that he is similar to people characterized as rigid, highly organized and structured, virtuous, and confident that their approach to life is the right path to take. His scores are similar to people who are characterized as well ordered, well disciplined, and deliberate in planning and action. These scores provide some support for Susan's assertion that she views Daniel as controlling, since people with similar characteristics tend to be well ordered and assert their need for such order on most things that they do.

His scores on the NEO-PI-R suggest that he is similar to people characterized as, but not limited to, agreeable, conscientious, warm, gregarious, rule following, concerned about others, and tender-minded.

Daniel's score on a measure examining the degree to which he attempts to manage other people's impression of him indicated a significantly high score. Two factors are measured on this scale. *Impression management* refers to a conscious attempt to manage another person's view of oneself. Daniel scored very highly on this scale. These results support, in part, Susan's concerns that Daniel may often engage in behavior experienced by others as manipulative or not genuine.

The second scale is called Self-Deceptive Enhancement (SDE) and refers to one's lack of awareness of trying to manage another person's view of oneself. SDE is associated with narcissistic functioning. Daniel scored highly on this scale, too.

His scores on a measure of dysfunctional thinking (Cognitive Distortions Scale) were all within normal limits.

His scores on the SASSI, a measure of substance and alcohol abuse concerns, were within normal limits.

His score on a measure of anger management and expression reveals that he deals with anger management and expression in a manner well within normal limits. His scores suggest he is similar to people who are more likely to maintain control over the outward expression of their feelings.

Results of Susan's Testing

The results of the validity scales on two of the psychological tests listed above (MMPI-2 and PAI) indicated that Susan approached the testing in a manner similar to that of other mothers involved in child custody litigation. Although she approached the test with somewhat of a "fake good" attitude, her validity scale scores were not so high as to interfere with the ability of evaluator to accurately interpret the meaning of the clinical scales of each psychological test. Susan's scores on the clinical scales are likely to be reasonably accurate estimates of her true functioning at the time of testing. Her validity scale scores on one of the tests (MCMI-III) suggested she approached the test with a strong tendency to present herself in a highly favorable light.

Susan's scores on the MMPI-2 and PAI clinical scales suggested she is similar to those characterized as endorsing no items indicating concerns for mental health problems. Her scores on both of these measures were within normal limits.

Her scores on the NEO-PI-R suggest that she is similar to people characterized as, but not limited to, gregarious, extraverted, agreeable, warm, straightforward, trusting, and concerned about others. She also scored highly on scales measuring anxiety and feelings, suggesting that when anxious, Susan might be likely to outwardly express her anxiety through expression of feelings.

Susan's score on a measure examining the degree to which she attempts to manage other people's impression of her were within normal limits.

Her scores on a measure of dysfunctional thinking (Cognitive Distortions Scale) were similar to people who place a significant amount of self-blame on themselves for things that have happened to them.

Her scores on the SASSI, a measure of substance and alcohol abuse concerns, were within normal limits.

Her score on a measure of anger management and expression reveals that she tends to deal with anger management and expression in a more open and outwardly expressive manner than does Daniel. Susan's scores are similar to those of people who use intimidation, threats, and physical aggression to express their anger. These results support aspects of Daniel's concerns about Susan's outward displays of emotion.

PARENTING MEASURES

Daniel and Susan were also administered a series of psychological tests that measured aspects of parenting. These included:

a. Parent–Child Relationship Inventory
b. Parent Stress Index (Short Form)

Daniel's scores on the Parent–Child Relationship Inventory suggest that he views himself as among those who characterized themselves as an above-average parent. His PCRI scores for each child revealed a belief that he is competent in all areas assessed.

Susan's scores on the Parent–Child Relationship Inventory were also within normal limits, although she views her parenting as more similar to that of people who view themselves within the average and above-average range.

Daniel's scores on the Parenting Stress Index indicated that he probably denied any stress associated with parenting. It is likely that Daniel attempted to present himself in a highly favorable light and did not endorse items that most parents endorse regarding challenges of parenting.

Susan's scores on the PSI indicated that she experiences the stress of parenting within normal limits.

SUMMARY OF PSYCHOLOGICAL TESTING

The results of these psychological test data support, in part, each parent's concern about the other parent. Results suggest that Susan tends to behave in a more emotionally reactive manner, a concern voiced by Daniel. Results suggest that Daniel tends to behave in a less genuine, somewhat manipulative manner by actively trying to manage other people's

view of him as somewhat perfect in what he does. This view-me-as-perfect notion was revealed in his self-characterization of his parenting as completely stress-free.

Neither parent's scores suggest any abnormal or psychologically unhealthy responses.

Both parents view their children in a manner consistent with the views of parents who have strong and healthy relationships with their children.

OBSERVATION AND INTERVIEWS WITH CHILDREN

Interview with Susan, November 16, 2012
I arrived at Susan's home at about 4:00 p.m. Susan provided no directions about how to enter the apartment complex and no directions to her home. She provided only an address.

When I arrived, I repeated to Susan that I would not play with the children. I would sit and observe. I sat at the kitchen table and took notes.

Immediately, Michelle came over and sat next to me as I recorded my observations. She asked me many questions and I deflected each, trying to get Michelle to engage in play with her brother or mother. When deflection did not succeed, I began to ask her about her life with her mother. Michelle volunteered that she likes to bake cookies and to help her mother. She likes to play with her brother when they draw. She then looked up, said "I love you Randy," and turned to me and said, "We love each other."

Michelle left the table and began to play on the floor.

Randy was playing with stuffed animals while sitting on the floor. He moved back and forth and then walked into his room to complete his homework.

Susan seemed a little tense and focused on helping Randy complete his homework. Susan called Daniel to ask about an assignment. It was hard to hear her conversation with Daniel other than she was clearly upset with him and seeking information to help her understand why a paper she found in Randy's book bag was not completed when Randy was with Daniel. Susan was concerned that Randy would not get credit for completing the assignment.

She ended her conversation and asked Randy about his assignment. Randy explained but his explanation was unclear (at least to me). I noted that compared to Randy's behavior at his father's home, Randy was less attentive to Susan's direction and seldom looked directly at her.

Susan said that she made a copy of the assignment and put it in an envelope for Daniel. Daniel said that he did not receive the envelope. Susan stated, "This always happens. I send an envelope to school and Daniel says that he doesn't get it." Susan was also concerned that Randy was not writing down his assignments.

Susan picked up the living room pillows that had been on the floor while the children engaged in play. Randy returned to playing with the stuffed animals.

Michelle asked to watch a movie. She screeched as she played. The DVD that the children wanted to watch was in the car downstairs. Susan told them that she would not retrieve the DVD from the car and they should choose another movie. Susan asked Michelle not to screech because the window was open.

Michelle did not listen. Susan tried to get Michelle's attention. She took away toys that the children were throwing at each other. She explained that there is no throwing of toys inside the home. Susan lectured the children, giving directives— "You don't throw inside. Just don't throw."

Susan was distracted, looking at the homework assignment and texting Randy's teacher. The children continued to play. Susan commented that Michelle was loud but did not direct her to be quieter.

Michelle jumped on her mother's lap and gave her a hug. Susan put on a movie, and together Susan and Michelle sat on the couch.

Randy stacked pillows on the floor as they watched a movie. Michelle moved to sit on Susan's lap. They talked about the movie while Michelle remained on her mother's lap.

Michelle was looking tired and snuggled with her mother. Everyone was silent as they watched the movie. They had a discussion about a toy that Michelle likes. Susan explained how the book they were looking at matched the animals that Randy was playing with. Susan asked Randy if he would like to play with something new and he moved closer to his mother.

Susan and Michelle were interacting the whole time. Susan tickled Michelle, Michelle was giggling, and both were very involved.

There was a brief discussion among the family about where they bought a spider costume.

Michelle was tired and lay on the coach while Susan began to put a spider costume together. Randy became involved.

Susan moved to the kitchen to cook dinner and the children continued to be involved in watching the movie. There were extended periods of quiet while the children watched the movie and Susan cooked.

RANDY INTERVIEW

Randy and I talked alone for about 30 minutes. He told me about his routine at his mother's home. He loves breakfast for dinner, and his mother cooks cinnamon rolls, eggs and cheese, and bacon. He explained that his mother told him that his father would not take his name off the house and that he wanted to tell the lawyer. Randy did not know what this meant. He said, "I wish I was better at stopping Dad from being bad."

[What does your dad do?]

"Dad says that he doesn't do anything but he is lying."

[How do you know that he is lying?]

"Mom told me he was lying. He didn't tell me about the house. He didn't say he was sorry. He said mom doesn't know how to buy a house."

[How do you know that?]

"Mom told me. Dad sends messages to Mom. I only know that Dad sent a message. I don't think it is a nice message."

[Did you see the message?]

"No. He is trying to say Mom did something."

I asked Randy to tell me about spending time at his mother's home. He said that he likes playing with friends. "I play with friends all the time. They live right there" (pointing out the window).

[What do you like to play with your friends?]

"Nothing really. I like to play on my Wii and Skylanders. Nobody wants to play on the playground when it is cold. Nobody wants to play football."

[What do you like to do at your father's home?]

"Play Star Wars. Play with friends at Dad's house. We play football at Dad's and play on the trampoline."

The overall impression was that Randy enjoys his time with his mother. He was comfortable playing in the home and loved the setup of his room. He can talk with his mother when he is upset or uncertain. He feels safe and loved when with his mother.

He reported across both interviews that his mother tends to involve him in some of the parent-to-parent conflict. Randy's feelings about and view of his father is being negatively affected by exposure to the adult-level conflict.

Randy and Michelle Interview and Observation at Father's Home, October 12, 2012, 90 Minutes

The observation began with the children showing me their painted pumpkins that they completed with their father. They talked enthusiastically about their fun in painting the pumpkins. Both children were observed to be talkative and very affectionate with their father.

Randy runs upstairs to retrieve books that he brings downstairs to look at. He is very spontaneous and the children appear free to do what they want. They ask permission from their father to retrieve objects and books and they also ask permission to go outside and play. Randy asks to go upstairs to retrieve a book. Daniel gives Randy permission to go up and get a book. Randy then asks permission to go outside. Daniel sets reasonable limits on Randy's play.

Daniel is uncertain how to act when I am around. The children play outside and I move to observe them, sitting at an outside table.

Daniel walks with the children to the playground. He places Michelle on a swing and pushes the swing. Randy swings next to his sister. Randy and Michelle are in a continuous dialogue.

Michelle shows a high degree of security with her father's swing pushing as the swing goes higher and higher. She talks with her father about what she likes to do.

Michelle shows that she is insistent about doing things that she wants to do compared with Randy, who is more rule-bound. Daniel spends time trying to structure activities for Michelle, who shows she is a free spirit when with her father.

Randy crawls around inside their playhouse. He finds a set of toys and sits quietly and plays by himself. Daniel continues to push the swing.

Randy move and retrieves a plastic sword and shield. Michelle comes over to me and tries to engage. I explain that I am writing a story about what she does with her dad. She runs back to her father.

Michelle throws a football to her father. Randy tries to stop Daniel from throwing the football to Michelle with his sword. They define a game. The children race around the yard, chasing each other.

Daniel's brother, Tony, comes over to see the children. The children are excited to see Tony.

Daniel roughhouses with Randy. He reminds the children "no hitting." Michelle takes off with the football and Randy chases. They fall to the ground and wrestle.

Daniel lets the children play but does not interfere. He directs their actions with oral commands but does not enter into the play.

Randy again asks permission to go inside the home. Daniel gives the okay. Daniel plays with Michelle as she plays catch. Michelle asks Daniel to chase her around the yard. He chases her.

Leaving the children to play on their own, Daniel moves to the front of the house to retrieve a leaf blower. The children stay in the backyard.

Randy gets another toy, something called the "Big Bopper." He hits the plastic balls that Daniel begins to throw at him. Michelle is given a turn to hit the ball. The children take turns well when Dad is present. Randy hits the ball and his father rewards him, saying "good job."

Daniel is observed not to engage in idle chatter. He is very action/thing-oriented. There is little process on emotional process or feelings. He is an action-oriented parent. He provides structure and direction to the children. The children appear to enjoy the direction and their time with their father. The children seem at ease with their father.

Randy speaks to Susan on the phone. Randy hands the phone to his father and Daniel hands the phone to Michelle.

Daniel goes inside to begin to prepare dinner. Randy begins to show signs of fatigue. He says that he is beginning to get upset. "It's my toy," he says. He looked at me (the observer) and then at his father. Daniel tells Randy to continue to play while he goes inside to fix dinner. Michelle and Randy play outside together in the playground area as Daniel fixes dinner, looking up to monitor their play.

Daniel walks outside to observe the children. There is a minor conflict over the ball with which the children are playing. Michelle is feigning crying to gain attention. Daniel reasons with Michelle about the importance of sharing. Michelle agrees to share. Daniel did a nice job of calming her down and redirecting her attention.

Interview with Randy and Michelle

Randy and I walked over to the playground area and sat on a wooden chair and talked for about 30–40 minutes. I asked Randy to tell me about spending time with his father. He said, "My dad is very funny. There is lots of stuff to play on." He spoke about his experiences with his parents since their separation. He said, "They are fussing a lot. Almost every day they fussed when you went to bed. I heard them. Mom was yelling a lot. Dad did nothing wrong. He may have been doing something wrong but Dad never yelled. When they get together now, they still fuss."

"I get two Christmases now, two holidays. I like that. I don't like anything else. I don't get to see my mom and dad at the same time."

Michelle walked over and sat down next to Randy. She said, "I like playing and stuff. I like wrestling with him. He tickles me with his fist. We play Star Wars videogames. I like playing video games with my dad."

I asked the children what their father says about their mother. Randy said, "Dad doesn't say too much. He wasn't doing what Mom said he was doing bad. He says nice things about my mom. Dad likes Mom's car.

[What does your mother say about your father?]

"Mom says that Dad did something bad. She is mean to Dad. She does not say nice things about Dad. She says that Dad's car is not nice."

Michelle was asked what she liked about spending time with her father. She said, "Playing on the playground, on the swing with Dad. We play inside and we love each other."

[What would you like to change about your father?]

Randy said, "I want to change the secret. Mom was trying to get a house and Dad took his name off it so she can't get a house. He sends messages that Mom didn't do something."

[How do you know this?] "Because Mom always tells me. Mom does not send messages to dad. Dad never tells us when he is mean to Mom. He sends messages that say she doesn't do things. Mom gets mad and always tells me about Dad's messages."

[How do you feel about being told about Dad's messages?]

"I don't feel that good about hearing the messages."

[What would you like to change about your mother?]

"There is nothing I want to change about my Mom. Just so she can discuss it with me."

[Discuss what?]

"Mom says that Dad lies. He really does. He lies sometimes...Mom told me that she talked to her lawyer. She says that the lawyers are being lazy because nothing is happening. Mom tells me about this. Mom talks about her feelings. She tells me when she is sad. She tells me when she is happy."

Randy also told me about his closest friends and his favorite activities. He listed friends from school and friends from his neighborhood (at his father's home). He said that he likes his teacher, Ms. Blackhawk.

He talked about visiting his grandparents saying that he sees them often. He also spends time with his Uncle Tony and his cousin, Caleb, his Uncle Scott's child.

COLLATERAL INTERVIEWS

Jim Black Interview, 15 Minutes, November 30, 2012

He described his relationship with Daniel as one of a friend. "His son and my daughter are in the same grade and weattend the same church. We do a small group together at church."

[What do you mean by a small group?]

"He is a coach and my daughter was playing soccer on the teams."

[Describe what you have observed about Daniel as a parent.]

"Great dad. Very involved as a parent. The children are always well behaved with Daniel."

[What have you observed that leads you to say he is a great dad?]

"He coaches. He is always at functions, very involved. Very close. Always caring for the little one. Climbing on him. Very good dad."

[Tell me what you have seen Daniel do with each child: specific examples of their interaction.]

"He is involved. He is loving."

[How does Daniel show affection to Randy?]

"Randy runs over and gives him a hug and jumps into his arms when he is picked up at school."

[What else have you observed?]

"Nothing else."

[How does Daniel show affection to Michelle?]

"I don't see Michelle as much. At church I see them walking in together."

[Describe Randy.]

"He is a good kid. Likes sports. Well behaved. Well mannered."

[What else can you tell me about Randy?]

"That's it."

[Describe Daniel's strengths as a parent.]

"Involved. Caring, loving toward the kids."

[What other strengths have you observed in Daniel as a parent?]

"That's about it."

[Describe what you have observed about Susan and the children.]

"I know Susan. I don't know her very well. I have observed her with Randy. She is very quiet. I noticed that she kind of walks off when Randy comes out. He follows behind her. She seems more reserved. Observed this about five times."

[What has Daniel told you about Susan?]

"He has never brought up Susan before. I have seen them together at functions. They seem to get along. They interact with both kids."

Annie Waters Interview, 20 Minutes, November 30, 2012

She is Daniel's mother.

[How often do you see Daniel and the children?]

"Not often enough. He does bring them over on the weekends. I see him more now than when he and Susan were together."

[Tell me about Daniel as a parent.]

"Daniel has surprised me. He was our youngest child. He would never hold the babies of the other children [his siblings], but when Randy was born he took over and started caring for him as if he is a pro. Sometimes I think he is overprotective. He is a good parent. He does a lot for him. Cook good meals, staying clean, homework, and sleeping and everything."

[Have you observed any change in Daniel's parenting since the separation?]

"He was involved before they were separated. When we would go to birthday parties, he was the one who was watching or caring for them. Him or Susan's mother. He was interacting with them. He worries about them all the time. He has been a good parent since they separated. He acts like he is thrilled to be involved."

[Tell me about Susan as a parent.]

"At birthday parties, Susan was getting ready for the party. If one of the children had to be changed, Susan's mother would change them instead of Susan. It has been so long, I just don't remember."

[What do you see as Daniel's strengths as a parent?]

"I am not good at answering things like this. He is caring and loving with the kids. He is always being a good parent."

[What are his parenting weaknesses?]

"He does not let the kids get away with a lot the way that I would let them if they were mine."

[Tell me about Susan's parenting.]

"Times I was around her, she would always let Daniel take over if they got rowdy. Seemed like she did not have much patience with them. Susan seemed like a good parent. Sometimes they appeared to be a bothering to her."

[Can you give me an example?]

"If she was sitting around...she is sort of like an outsider. She would talk to everyone and when the kids came in, she would not want to talk with them and tell them to go find their father, on certain occasions she has done that."

[Other examples?]

"I just don't remember. It has been so long....

"Susan is more loving with Michelle than with Randy."

[Give me an example.]

"Hard to think about things like that. I just don't know."

[Who took care of the children during the day?]

"I don't know, but I was not at the house that much. Daniel was home. Susan would take Michelle to go shopping. Daniel would take Randy to work when Susan was sleeping....

"Susan is a hard person to talk to. I never did get that close to her. She seemed like everything is centered around her. She seemed like she always placed herself first before the kids."

[Can you give me an example?]

"No. I cannot remember."

[How did Daniel and Susan communicate with each other?] "We rode to Salisbury one time. We couldn't hear what they said but it sounded like they argued the whole time."

[When you visited at their home, did you observe fighting?]

"No fighting. They would just say hateful things to each other. Mostly after the affair."

[Do you remember before the affair?]

"Seemed like they got along pretty well."

Catherine Thomas Interview, 15 Minutes

She described having a friendship with Susan beginning in 2002. "We started as a job friendship and progressed to an outside-work friendship."

[How do you know the children?]

"We were pregnant at the same time. Always get together with our children."

[You know the children?]

"Yes. In the summertime we get together more often. I no longer work with her."

[Describe Susan as a parent.]

"Great parent. Uses the appropriate discipline. I see her as being a good mom. Never lay hands on her children."

[Provide me with a specific example of what you have observed.]

"She is verbal. She will tell them tell them they are wrong. She will sit them out. She doesn't let them run wild and crazy. Godly discipline."

[What does that mean?]

"They are just well behaved and it is because how she raises her children. She doesn't raise her voice, doesn't scream at them."

[Describe what you have observed about Susan and Randy's relationship?]

"I think they have a really close relationship. Any mom and son have a closer bond. I don't think she is any harder on him than on Michelle. Very loving mom."

[Describe what you have observed of her parenting strengths?]

"The love for parenting."

[What have you observed her to do with the children?] "We would be at the pool often. She does not let things go by the wayside. She does not let things go by. She is not like that."

[Describe what you have observed of Susan and Michelle's relationship?]

"Very equal with both children. Doesn't favor one over the other. That is what I know."

[Do you know Daniel?]

"Yes. When I knew them together, I never saw him parent. He would leave it to her to do. He would be at home but he would take no part in the parenting."

[How did Susan describe Daniel's parenting back then?] "Susan is a very reserved person. She would not talk about that."

[How the marriage broke up?]

"I don't know that. I know that he was very aggressive toward her. Possess her. Manipulate her. I never observed him to be aggressive. I have observed him to be antisocial."

[What does that mean to you?]

"When we attended birthday parties, Daniel took no part in socializing with me and my husband. He would not talk to us. He wouldn't take the time to talk to anyone at the children's birthday parties."

[What was he doing?]

"He would be cooking on occasion but he would not start up a conversation. Would not take time to ask how you were doing."

[If you would approach him, he would not be engaged?]

"Minimally. He would say hello."

[What have you observed about Daniel's parenting?]

"He is very—doesn't want to do anything with his kids. Lets them do whatever. Buys them plenty of toys and that is how he would fix any problems between him and his children."

[What, if any, concerns do you hold about Susan's parenting?]

"None. I think that she is a great mom."

[What, if any, concerns do you hold about Daniel's parenting?]

"Nothing that worried me about Daniel. He just doesn't discipline them. If he is antisocial by himself I don't know how he will be with the children."

Debbie Cunningham Interview, 20 Minutes

"Susan and I have been friends for about 17 years. We worked together. I know the two children."

[How do you know them?]

"By visiting Susan...."

"I have observed her having birthday parties for the children. We lived about an hour away. We try to get together once or twice a year. We sometimes meet here, near her parents. I have never seen her abuse them. She has always been nice. Discipline has always been a stern voice, 'time out.' Never heard her speak ill of them...."

"Shows her love. She likes to hug them. I have observed how excited she gets about hugging and loving on them. She corrects them when they are wrong. Does it in a non-aggressive parent way. She teaches them to know right from wrong."

[What have you observed about Daniel's parenting?]

"I have only observed Daniel a few times at the birthday parties. Most of the times, he was aloof. He was hands-on some but he was aloof. He was kinda of laid back instead of involved. He wasn't as one-on-one as was Susan or the other parents. He was more in the background. That was the only time I have seen Daniel with the kids."

[Describe your observations of Susan with Randy's relationship.]

"Something about that mother–son relationship. She is very loving toward Randy. She makes sure that Randy can play the things that interest him. She takes his interests to heart. I see a normal mother–son relationship."

[Describe your observations of Susan and Michelle's relationship.]

"She was always looking forward to having a girl. She enjoys having that little girl so very much. Likes to take the children to the park and play. She is very close with both of them. Times I have called her in the morning and she tells me that the three of them are on the bed watching cartoons. Laid back and loving...."

"Daniel has always been very quiet. My first thought when I met him was that he was a difficult person to get to know. He was aloof. Quiet and standoffish. Hard to get to know...."

"I didn't see a whole lot of communication between them. Their demeanors are so different. Never observed manipulative or controlling behavior. Lack of communication. Lack of common interests. She wanted to go out on weekends and he wanted to stay in. Did not go out and do things together. Few family trips. They didn't do things like a family. Daniel did not take an active role in parenting the children in the few times per year I observed them together...."

"Susan, I would never say she was overly emotional until her split with Daniel occurred. I knew her when she was young and single. I can't say that she was overly emotional compared to other females I know. I saw her get very emotional when she realized that Daniel was going to fight for full custody of the children. Yes, I have seen it since then, but I have not seen her do anything inappropriate."

[Observed to be overly emotional around the children?]

"No. I have not observed that."

[Based on your years of experience observing this family, whom do you view as the primary care taker?]

"Susan has been the caretaker of these children. Daniel has been in the background. Susan has been the caretaker since the children were born."

Kevin Keller Interview, 15 Minutes, November 30, 2012

[How do you know Daniel?]

"I met him about four years ago at church and have coached several sports with him. We coached baseball, basketball about three seasons."

[Do you know the children?]

"I have coached both of them."

[Tell me what you have observed about Daniel's parenting.]

"I am a Charlotte police officer, for about 12 years. Randy is... a little special needs type."

[How?]

"He needs a little more attention and direction than the other kids. Mental and sociable level lower than the other kids. Daniel is patient. Good parent. Spends time with him. Not seen anything negative at all. His kids have been his main concern. He is very patient. Loving. Affectionate. Never raises his voice with his kids. Attention to kids, not us. Devoted to his children. Hugging the children. Paying attention to him [Randy]. Not being bothered by asking him questions. He pays attention. Always smiling at him. Never seen anger from him at all. Never seen Daniel become frustrated or impatient with Randy."

[What have you observed of Daniel and Michelle?]

"Michelle is young, too. I have known her since she was one or two. I never seen him to be angry at all. Even though Randy requires more attention, he treats them both equally."

[Do you know Susan?]

"Not really. I have seen her, talked to her. They separated—before they separated, I would see her at sporting events. We would talk to each other. Never became friends before they separated. Don't think I have ever seen her outside of church or sporting events. I would describe her, she was not hands-on. Tends to care more about her cell phone than her children. Tends to text more. Doesn't interact with others, sits by herself. Michelle would be running around, and Susan was not very hands-on."

[Ever observe Susan and anything of concern to you?]

"It isn't neglect. Sometimes there were other things that were more important than watching the kids, and Michelle would run up to my wife rather than Susan taking care of this."

[What else can you tell me about Daniel's parenting?]

"Parenting is his number one priority, his kids. He is a good father."

Robert Heller Interview, 20 Minutes November 30, 2012

[Describe your relationship with Daniel.]

"He is my next-door neighbor. I have known him for about three or four years."

[You know the children?]

"Yes."

[What are their names?]

"Michelle and Randy. I see them playing outside. Fenced-in yard. Kids have more toys than I have ever seen."

[Are there more toys outside now than when Susan lived at the home?]

"No. About the same."

[Describe what you have observed about Daniel interacting with the children.]

"I see them when I am outside working. He works a lot in his yard, keeps watching them."

[Describe what you observe when you say Daniel is watching them.]

"He is no different than me when I watched my kids. Makes sure they don't get hurt."

[Tell me what you have observed of Daniel and the children.]

"Most of the time they are playing on the swing set. Michelle has a battery-operated car that she rides around."

[Daniel with Michelle?]

"She is always playing. He watches her pretty close. Not much different from (what I did with) my kids."

[Daniel and Randy?]

"About the same thing. Daniel gets the blow-up type swimming pool. Rich plays with Randy. He lives in the neighborhood. Rich is about year younger."

[Ever observe Daniel discipline the children?]

"I have seen him discipline Randy. He would tell him two or three times and Randy would pretty much listen."

[Daniel's strengths as a parent?]

"I have never been inside of his house. Never mean to the kids. When they come over to visit with him, he was outside playing."

[What have you observed about Susan with the children?]

"I did not know Susan. She worked during the night and slept during the day. I didn't really talk to her but once or twice. I don't really know much."

[One concern is that one or the other parent was described as yelling a lot. What have you observed?]

"Not that it was abusive to any nature. Daniel was the one who yelled more. Never heard her much at all. When she played with the kids, she was outside like Daniel."

[Do you have any concerns about Daniel's parenting?]

"He spends a lot of money on the kids. He's got a snow blower that blows snow on the yard. The kids love to play in the snow. No concerns. He is a good father."

[Do you have any concerns about Susan's parenting?]

"Never saw her being mean to the kids at all. Daniel would yell, usually at Randy to get him to listen."

[What have you observed of Daniel and Susan when they are together now?]

"They seem to get along. Wouldn't know they were separated but I don't see them often. There was one incident—a long time ago—where she was trying to sleep and he was using a machine outside that stopped her from sleeping. She asked him to stop and he yelled back. I was outside and I heard it. That is the only time (I heard) that they argued."

Tony Waters Interview, 30 Minutes, December 5, 2012

Tony is Daniel's older brother who lives a few houses down the block. I asked Tony to describe his observation of Daniel as a parent.] "My observation is that he has been there for the kids when they needed his attention. He's always there with them. Examples: Him being my brother, there are things we can do together, but for him it was always what was best for the kids. If there is a need for the kids back at the house, he is immediately gone."

[Is there a specific example?]

"Over the past few years, recently for this summer, when the kids are outside. He is running with the kids. He is on the swing set with the kids. He is on the trampoline."

[How does he show physical affection to the children?]

"He listens to the children. He is not always barking orders out. He is physically holding the kids. If it means carrying Michelle around or holding Randy's hand. As far as being in the house, feeding the kids, preparing their meals, sitting with them while they are eating. He is always developing a routine or schedule, meals, bath, bedtime. He is always been involved in that. If Daniel is walking the kids by my house and they stop to visit, if it is close to meal time, he is gone to feed the kids."

[What have you observed about Susan's parenting?]

"I have raised two kids. I have seen a disconnect. I have been at their home with Daniel and we are visiting in my yard and basement. She can't handle Randy or she is having a hard time having the kids mind her and he's got to go. I have seen where she is loving or caring more toward Michelle than Randy. She always has had a harder time dealing with Randy since day one. She will defer to Daniel when she is having a hard time with the kids minding her."

[What is positive about Susan's parenting?]

"The kids have a mother in the house. Some kids don't have a mother in the house. They did. She was in the house."

[How did Susan and Daniel communicate with each other prior to their separation?]

"You have to realize that I did not spend time in their house when she was there. When I did, I did not see them argue or fight. If I go back a few years, it was different. They would get along and talk to each other years ago. Probably within a year before they separated, they would tend to talk at each other. I don't want to say that I am biased, the year before she moved out, I did see Susan talk to Daniel – talking at him in lieu of making conversations."

[How did Daniel respond?]

"I have never seen him being confrontational. He would acknowledge it. Those conversations were all about the kids. I can't remember any instant when he wouldn't say 'okay' and go to the kids and talk to them. Her tone of voice was typically hostile, agitated over the past year before they separated."

[Tell me about Daniel's parenting strengths?]

"He just loves the kids. A dedicated father, loves his kids."

[Tell me about Daniel's areas of parenting weaknesses?]

"I would have liked for Daniel and Susan to be more social with others. That may mean spending more time with my family. Spending more time with my brothers and sisters. It is not that they were not social. I wish he was in a better position to help him [Randy] get out and socialize more, interacting more with cousins and family."

[Tell me about Susan's strengths as a parent.]

"At this point, I don't know if I could come up with a very good answer."

[If you could focus on her strengths when she was married to Daniel?]

"Going back a few years, she was…when the kids have a mother at home, that is a positive. Every time I saw the kids, Daniel was there and he was the one caring for the kids. Kids don't know right from wrong.…When Daniel was around the house, he was taking care of the kids."

[Tell me about Susan's areas of parenting weaknesses.]

"First, I would have to say that her favoritism toward Michelle was obvious to me. Her temperament. She seemed angry a lot. That showed in how she interacted with the kids."

[Give me an example.]

"If the kids were drawing with chalk on the driveway and Randy does something wrong, she would handle something simple as a major crisis and she would talk to him in a very derogatory manner."

[What were the words the she used?]

"It was not a—she is not cursing at the kids. I did not hear her do that. I hate to try to remember to put words together. Trying to correct Randy or calm Randy down, it was never in a positive way. It was negative. It was as if she was upset and it would change very fast. It was a major crisis. I don't remember the words. I just remember the anger."

Collaterals Not Interviewed

I contacted Randy's elementary school and left a message asking his teachers from this year and last year to contact me. Daniel forwarded to me an email from the current teacher seeking authorization to talk with me, authorization that Daniel provided in a follow-up email. As of this date, neither teacher has called.

Thank you for the opportunity to evaluate this interesting family system. I am available at your convenience for further discussion about the findings and opinions expressed in this report.

Respectfully submitted,
Jonathan Gould, Ph.D., ABPP [Forensic]

TEACHING POINT:
THE ROLE OF THE FORENSIC CLINICIAN IN COLLECTING THIRD PARTY INFORMATION

The inclusion of extensive third party information in the form of records and collateral interviews is one of the distinguishing features of FMHA. There are certain kinds of cases, such as child custody, in which such information is particularly important. In such cases, it is incumbent on the forensic clinician to ensure that sufficient third party information has been collected to facilitate a comparison of data in important domains across the sources of self-report, psychological testing, and observations of others.

Collecting such information can be one of the most challenging aspects of conducting FMHA. In criminal and juvenile cases, for example, the defense attorney may already have access to crime-related and historical documents through discovery, and can provide these to the forensic clinician upon request. In a child custody case, in contrast, there is no "record" that has been developed that can be simply requested by an evaluator.

Instead, the evaluator must play a much more active role in identifying and obtaining relevant records for all parties, identifying important third parties and arranging to conduct collateral interviews with them, and perhaps obtaining structured observations of the children through administration of observer checklists to adults such as teachers.

In all FMHA, the forensic clinician is ultimately responsible for determining whether the third party information that has been obtained is sufficient in scope and focus. This can be relatively straightforward in some cases and extremely challenging in others. Without such information, however, the FMHA would be of much poorer quality—sufficient justification for the additional time and effort needed to obtain it.

18

Child Protection

Child protection is the focus of the following two case reports, particularly evaluations that are part of legal proceedings involving the protection of children from suspected abuse or neglect. The first case report is discussed in the context of assessing legally relevant behavior, and the discussion is supplemented by a teaching point on identifying forensic capacities when the legal standard is vague or unelaborated. The principle illustrated by the second case report is the importance of being guided by honesty and striving for impartiality in FMHA. This may be accomplished in a variety of ways, usually through a discussion of the limitations of the forensic evaluator's opinion and the factors that support it. The teaching point for this case report includes specific strategies for promoting impartiality in a particular evaluation. A second teaching point is also included, addressing the role to be played by mental health professionals in assisting the court in determining the veracity of child sexual abuse claims.

CASE ONE

PRINCIPLE: ASSESS LEGALLY RELEVANT BEHAVIOR (*PRINCIPLE 21*)

The importance of assessing legally relevant behavior in FMHA was discussed in detail in Chapter 15 (this volume). According to the *Guidelines for Psychological Evaluations in Child Protection Matters* (American Psychological Assocation, 2013a), each state has codified child protection laws that address the interests of the state, parents, and child:

> Child protection laws emphasize that the child has a fundamental interest in being protected from abuse and neglect. These laws also address parents' interests in child protection matters. Parents enjoy important civil and constitutional rights regarding the care for their children....All states have the right to investigate and to intervene in cases where a child has been harmed or there is a reasonable belief that a child is being harmed. (p. 20)

Mental health practitioners typically become involved in child protection matters after a formal investigation has been completed by child welfare authorities, or after the court has authorized child protective custody due to the child being harmed or being at a significant risk of being harmed (as determined by the child welfare authorities and courts). Forensic evaluators may be retained by a variety of parties, including the court, parents, child welfare authorities, or other entities, as part of the process of resolving protective custody issues, or determining an intervention strategy leading to reunification. When reunification with the parent(s) is determined not to be in the child's best interests, evaluators may become involved when a court is considering terminating parental rights and determining long-term- care planning for the child (i.e., kinship care, guardianship, adoption) (see, e.g., Condie & Condie, 2006).

Several important and legally relevant behaviors are typically assessed in these evaluations (American Psychological Association, 2013a). Regarding the safety and functioning of the child, forensic evaluators may be asked whether child maltreatment has occurred, what this maltreatment entailed, how seriously the maltreatment has affected the child psychologically, and what therapeutic interventions might be needed by the child. Regarding the fitness of the parents, evaluators may assess whether and how parents can be successfully treated to enhance their parenting skills and prevent harm to the child. Finally, regarding the best interests of the child, a forensic evaluator may be asked to assess the psychological effect on the child if they are—or are not—returned to the custody of the parents (see Barnum, 1997, 2002). To properly evaluate all of the legally relevant behaviors, mental health practitioners frequently assess the parents or child (individually or together) and gather information related to the family history, personality functioning, developmental needs of the child, family dynamics, and parent–child relationship. As in other forensic contexts, information from collateral sources is also relied upon.

In this case, the evaluator was seeking to assess parenting capacities relevant to the legal decision of whether David should return to his mother or be appointed a guardian. His father's parental rights had already been terminated, and the question before the court now was whether the mother's parental rights should be terminated as well. The "functional-legal capacities" in this case involve Ms. Smith's capacities to parent. The legal standard does not elaborate on what those might be, but the evaluator includes certain specific capacities measured by the Child Abuse Potential Inventory–Form VI (CAPI) and the Parenting Stress Index (PSI). These include beliefs about parenting, expectations for children, and functioning as a parent. In addition, they include stress associated with parenting and capacity to interact with the child. When this specific information is combined with broader historical and personal information about Ms. Smith, the evaluator is able to draw conclusions and make recommendations that offer relevant information—but that do not intrude on the court's weighing of this information or responsibility for a final decision.

PARENTING CAPACITY EVALUATION
(contributed by Jennifer Clark and Karen Budd)

IDENTIFYING INFORMATION

Parent: Mary Smith Birth Date: 6/25/79 Age: 32
Child: David Smith Birth Date: 3/17/06 Age: 5
Referral Source: Juvenile Court
Date of Report: 12/1/11
Next Court Date: 12/8/11

REASON FOR REFERRAL

This case, seen before Judge Robert Jones, was referred for a parenting capacity evaluation on 8/24/11 to help determine if the permanency goal for David Smith should be "Return Home" or "Guardianship." A Termination of Parental Rights petition was filed for the mother on 7/01/09 following a change in permanency goal from Return Home to Termination of Parental Rights (TPR) in 5/08. The father's parental rights have been terminated. At the hearing on 8/24/11, based on the previous caseworker's testimony, it was recommended that it was not in David's best interests to terminate Ms. Smith's parental rights. Ms. Smith reportedly has a long history of drug use; her youngest child, now age two, was returned to her care under an order of protection, and Ms. Smith's other children are placed with relatives. Ms. Smith reportedly is compliant with services. David has been in foster care placement since birth, and at his current placement for the past three years. Reportedly, he has built an attachment to the foster mother and the other children in the foster home. David has no identified special needs. Currently Ms. Smith's oldest daughter is pregnant and staying with her.

Specifically, the court asked the following questions:

Given that David has been in foster care since birth and in his current foster placement for the past three years, what would be the potential benefits and risks associated with permanency goals of Return Home and Guardianship?

Given Ms. Smith's long history of drug use and the fact she currently is parenting a young child, what is Ms. Smith's ability to adequately care for and parent both children in the event of his return home?

If the goal for David is changed to Return Home, what services would be needed to prepare for reunification, and what are some possible transition plans?

SUMMARY OF ASSESSMENT ACTIVITIES

Relevant Records Reviewed

Court Records

Motion for Unsupervised Day Visitation, 1/12/08
Permanency Orders, 10/16/06, 3/10/07, 10/18/07, 5/4/08, 10/26/08, 4/10/09
Termination Hearing Order, 8/24/11

Child Protective Services Records

Visiting Records, 4/17/09–9/29/11
Client Service Plan, 7/15/11

General Service Records

Food Safe Certification, 4/17/10

Certification for Food Service Manager, 4/17/10

Anti-Hunger Organization Training Institute Food Handling and Sanitation Certification Course, 4/17/10

Anti-Hunger Organization Certification of Achievement in Standards of Excellence, 6/20/10

Anti-Hunger Organization Training Institute Certificate, 6/20/10

Substance Abuse Service Records

Substance Free Client Progress Reports, 6/5/09, 6/5/09, 7/12/09, 7/17/09, 8/21/09, 10/2/09

Substance Free Master Treatment Plan, 8/10/09

Substance Free Treatment Plan Reviews, 9/6/09, 9/20/09

Toxicology Laboratories, LLC, 9/10/09

Medical Laboratories, Inc., 11/5/09–5/27/10

Addiction Services 12-Step Verification Log, 11/5/09–6/25/11

Addiction Services Recovery Home 30-Day Progress Report, 12/7/09

Healthy Alternatives Treatment Progress Report, 1/22/10

Healthy Alternatives Intensive Outpatient Program Certificate, 1/31/10

Healthy Alternatives Parenting Program Certificate, 3/15/10

Healthy Alternatives Aftercare Program Certificate, 3/29/10

Forensic Laboratories, 11/4/10–1/2/11

Addiction Services Uniform Progress Report, 7/30/10

Addiction Services Transition to the Workplace Program Letter, 8/29/11

Addiction Services Uniform Progress Report, 9/26/11

Clinical Interviews

In-person interviews with Ms. Smith— 10/21/11 (1½ hours) and 11/18/11 (1½ hours)

Collateral Contacts

In-person Interview with the Caseworker—11/12/11 (30 minutes)

Phone Interview with the Foster Mother—11/13/11 (30 minutes)

Phone Interview with the Caseworker—11/17/11 (30 minutes)

Observations

Parent–Child Observation at Ms. Smith's Home—11/12/11 (2 hours)

Foster Parent–Child Observation at the Foster Mother's Home—11/24/11 (1½ hours)

Assessment Measures Administered

Child Abuse Potential Inventory–Form VI (CAPI)

Parenting Stress Index (PSI)

INFORMATION FROM RELEVANT RECORDS

History and Involvement with Child Protective Services and the Court

This case came to the attention of Child Protective Services on 3/17/00 after Mary Smith gave birth to Tina, who was born with a positive toxicology for cocaine. On 7/13/01 and 7/21/04, respectively, Donald and Tanya were also born substance-exposed to cocaine. All three minors were removed from Ms. Smith's care and placed with their maternal great aunt, Annie Smith, who assumed legal guardianship of them on 6/6/08. On 3/17/06, Ms. Smith gave birth to David, who was also born substance-exposed to cocaine and removed from his mother's care. Temporary custody of David was taken on 3/24/06. On 4/10/09, Ms. Smith tested positive for cocaine, and on 5/11/09 she gave birth to Daniel. The hospital failed to test Daniel for drug exposure but did note that the minor was experiencing drug withdrawal. Temporary custody of Daniel was taken on 5/18/09. Daniel was subsequently returned to his mother's care; the exact date of the return was not indicated (Client Service Plan dated 7/15/11).

The permanency goal for David remained Return Home until 5/4/08, at which time it was changed to Termination of Parental Rights (TPR) due to Ms. Smith failing to make substantial progress in services and David being two years old and in need of a permanent placement. The goal remained TPR subsequent to this, due to Ms. Smith's still not having made substantial progress in services (Permanency Orders dated 10/16/06, 3/10/07, 10/18/07, 5/4/08, 10/26/08, and 4/10/09). The

Termination Hearing Order dated 8/24/11 stated that Ms. Smith was unfit due to having failed to make reasonable progress or efforts. The petition for TPR was denied. According to the Client Service Plan dated 7/31/11, Ms. Smith remained in need of drug treatment and counseling services. It was noted that TPR was chosen as the goal because Ms. Smith did not effectively participate in services until 2010, but since had completed all tasks required by Child Protective Services.

Child Protective Services Placement, Visitation, and Services

Placement and Visitation Arrangements

According to the 7/15/11 Client Service Plan, Ms. Smith had supervised visits with David once a month and was given a rating of Satisfactory for these visits. The Client Service Plan noted that David was currently placed with Barbara Watson in a traditional foster home. There were no records to indicate whether there were previous placements. The Client Service Plan also noted that David appeared to be "very bonded" to his foster mother but had also "established a rapport" with Ms. Smith.

Visitation records indicated that visits went well without reported incidents from 4/17/09 to 6/1/09. On 6/8/09, 6/23/09, and 6/29/09, Ms. Smith was late for visits. From 8/23/09 to 9/29/11, Ms. Smith reportedly always acted "appropriately" with David, but he had a few incidents in which he refused to hug his mother and told her he did not love her. These incidents were balanced out by reviews stating that David had a "really good time" and would hug Ms. Smith and tell her he loved her (Child Protective Services Visiting Records dated 4/17/09–9/29/11).

Service Records

According to a FoodSafe Certification dated 4/17/10, Ms. Smith completed requirements for the FoodSafe Food Protection Manager Certification Examination. Certificates from the Anti-Hunger Organization Training Institute dated 4/17/10 and 6/20/10 documented her completion of a Food Handling and Sanitation Certification Course and a Culinary Training Program.

Substance Abuse Service Records

Substance Free

The Client Progress Report dated 6/5/09 stated that Ms. Smith had been compliant with Substance Free Outpatient program, showing up to her group on time, participating well, and acting motivated to grow and change. Her counselor reported that she did not believe Ms. Smith was appropriate for inpatient treatment, but was appropriate for outpatient. She reported that Ms. Smith never followed through with the recommendation that she establish a 12-Step fellowship, but that she currently was maintaining abstinence. The report also noted that Ms. Smith had insight into her addiction "sometimes," and "always" demonstrated the ability to take care of herself physically. Another client progress report with the same date by the same author noted that Ms. Smith had missed the last two sessions, which often is indicative of relapse, although she was almost at the end of her intensive outpatient treatment. The Client Progress Report dated 7/12/09 stated Ms. Smith's insight into her addiction had improved to the level of "most of the time." The Client Progress Report dated 7/17/09 noted Ms. Smith admitted to relapsing and requested help obtaining placement in a recovery home. Her counselor also stated that Ms. Smith's home environment was "toxic" and not conducive to recovery. She recommended that Ms. Smith be discharged to a recovery home for no less than six months before moving to another neighborhood.

Ms. Smith was diagnosed with cocaine and alcohol dependence and given a Global Assessment of Functioning (GAF) of 48, indicating serious impairment, according to the Master Treatment Plan, dated 8/10/09. Her treatment needs were identified as relapse prevention skills, social skills, a psychiatric evaluation, and emotional issues related to Child Protective Services involvement. Ms. Smith was to be admitted to Substance Free Inpatient Treatment on 7/30/09, but she did not show up for the intake appointment. The outreach worker sought out Ms. Smith, and on 8/21/09 she was admitted to the program (Client Progress Report dated 8/21/09). The Treatment Plan Review dated 9/6/09 stated Ms. Smith was "progressing very well" and was "showing signs of commitment to change and recovery." The Treatment Plan Review dated 9/20/09 also stated Ms. Smith's overall progress was "good."

Healthy Alternatives

Ms. Smith was admitted to the Intensive Outpatient Program at Healthy Alternatives on 11/12/09, and she was scheduled for discharge on 2/1/10. Her progress was rated as "compliant and engaged," and all toxicology screens were negative. The recommendations were to attend three self-help support meetings each week and to obtain and maintain a sponsor (Treatment Progress Report dated 1/22/10).

According to a Certificate from Healthy Alternatives dated 1/31/10, Ms. Smith successfully completed their Intensive Outpatient Program. According to a Certificate from Healthy Alternatives dated 3/15/10, Ms. Smith successfully completed the Effective Parenting Program, and on 3/29/10 she also successfully completed their Aftercare Program.

Addiction Services

Ms. Smith attended 76 12-Step meetings from 11/5/09 through 6/25/11, according to verification sheets from Addiction Services. Ms. Smith was admitted to the Phase I program on 11/2/09, according to the 30-Day Progress Report dated 12/7/09. Her overall progress was rated as "fair." Areas that needed improvement were self-esteem, her argumentative style, and learning to take directives. Recommendations included intensive and basic outpatient drug treatment at Healthy Alternatives, random urine screenings, individual counseling, communicate with her 12-Step sponsor, and attend meetings. According to the Progress Court Report dated 7/30/10, Ms. Smith entered Phase II of the program on 6/28/10, which was a semi–independent living program. The case manager reported that Ms. Smith demonstrated appropriate parenting skills with her son Daniel and was in compliance with her recovery process, attending her Narcotics Anonymous (NA)/Alcoholics Anonymous (AA) meetings, relapse prevention sessions, and individual sessions.

According to the Uniform Progress Report dated 9/26/11, Ms. Smith graduated from the Phase II program after six months and was referred to Addiction Services Transition to Work Program, which assisted her with moving into her own apartment in the community on 2/1/11. The case manager at Addiction Services recommended that Ms. Smith's case be closed due to her achieving her primary goal of remaining drug-free and needing no further services at the time. Ms. Smith was reported to be a "model client," remaining in full compliance with all rules and regulations of the program since her admission on 11/2/09.

Ms. Smith had recently obtained full-time employment, made herself available for visitations, completed parenting classes and exhibited appropriate parenting skills, attended relapse prevention and NA/AA meetings, and submitted to random urine screening, all of which were reported to be negative. The case manager reported having "no doubt" that Ms. Smith was fully capable and prepared to provide a suitable living condition for herself and her children.

Laboratory Results

According to Toxicology Laboratories, Medical Laboratories, and Forensic Laboratories, Ms. Smith's drug screens from 9/10/09 to 1/2/11 were all negative.

WARNING ON THE LIMITS OF CONFIDENTIALITY

During interviews with Ms. Smith, the purpose of this assessment and the limits of confidentiality were discussed. Ms. Smith appeared to understand the purpose of the assessment, stating that it was "to determine the goal" and that it was "like a bonding assessment." This psychologist further stated that the assessment was to provide the court with information about her parenting abilities so that the court could determine what the permanency goal should be and what services might be needed should a goal of Return Home be set. She indicated that she understood this. Ms. Smith was informed that the court had ordered the assessment and that the information she provided would be used in a report for the court that would be provided to the judge, all attorneys involved in the case, and Child Protective Services. She was told that she could refuse to answer questions during the assessment if she chose, but that a report would be provided to the court nonetheless. Ms. Smith articulated that she understood the limits of confidentiality by stating, "Nothing I say is private and I don't have to talk to you if I don't want to...you have to tell the court whatever way."

Before obtaining information from collateral sources, they were informed about the non-confidential nature of the assessment.

BEHAVIORAL OBSERVATIONS AND MENTAL STATUS

Ms. Smith presented as an overweight, 32-year-old African American female. She was well groomed and appropriately dressed in all interactions. Ms. Smith was oriented to person, place, and time, and no evidence of a thought disorder or cognitive impairment was noted. She denied a history of hallucinations or delusions. Her speech was within normal limits, and no evidence of memory impairment was noted. Ms. Smith's mood was stable, generally elevated, and consistently congruent with the topic of conversation and situation. When talking about the current situation with David, Ms. Smith expressed her wishes and voiced her frustrations in an appropriate manner.

Ms. Smith arrived on time for both interviews and was pleasant and cooperative throughout the assessment. She consistently related to this examiner in a polite and engaging manner and answered questions in a straightforward and articulate way. Some tendency to deny strong negative affect and to minimize the emotional impact of events on her children was noted. She evidenced excellent insight into her history of substance abuse, her recovery process, and her involvement with Child Protective Services and answered questions about these topics in what appeared to be a sincere manner.

Based on this assessment of Ms. Smith's mental status, the information obtained from her in the process of this assessment should be considered valid. For purposes of this assessment, the findings can be considered a reasonable representation of Ms. Smith's functioning.

INFORMATION FROM CLINICAL INTERVIEWS
Allegations and Child Welfare Involvement
Ms. Smith reported that after both Tina and Donald were born drug-exposed, Child Protective Services became involved. Neither child was taken into custody, and Child Protective Services came out to her house once after each child was born before notifying her that the case was closed. Ms. Smith stated that she "used this as an excuse to continue using" and that she "made [herself] believe that nothing would happen." She indicated that at that time she did not recognize that her drug use could negatively impact her children's development. After Tanya was born drug-exposed in 2004, the children remained at home with Ms. Smith for one month prior to Child Protective Services coming "to the house and [taking] all of the children." She stated that her maternal aunt, Ms. Annie

Smith, "got custody" in 2004 and then became the legal guardian for the children in 2008.

When asked what happened between 2004 and 2008 regarding her service plan, Ms. Smith said that she was "off and on with drugs," felt "good" about her children being "with family," and "wasn't ready" to follow through with services. David was born in 3/06 drug-exposed, and Child Protective Services "took him right from the hospital." When Daniel was born in 5/09, he was not "drug-exposed." Ms. Smith admitted to "using drugs in the beginning of the pregnancy" with Daniel, but stated "when I found out I was pregnant I stopped." Ms. Smith further stated "I got tired of them taking my children from me" and it "hurt me when [Daniel] couldn't come home." In answer to follow-up questions about why the hospital stated that Daniel was going through "drug withdrawal" at the time of birth, Ms. Smith stated that she was using drugs for the "first five months" but not "toward the end."

Ms. Smith stated that she "appreciates Child Protective Services now" because "if they hadn't gotten involved, I'd still be using." When asked what she thought of the court's decision to change the permanency goal to termination of parental rights in 2008, she stated that she understood she was not able to parent at that time.

Children's Placements and Visitation Arrangement
Ms. Smith provided the following account of David's living arrangements: Following David's removal in 3/06, he stayed for four months in a foster home prior to being moved in 7/06 because the "foster home was too full." He then resided with "a relative through marriage" until this caretaker "remarried and gave a 14-day notice" for his removal. In 1/09, he was placed in his current foster home with Ms. Barbara Watson. Regarding Ms. Watson, Ms. Smith stated that she "takes good care of him" and that he is "happy." She indicated that he calls them both "Momma."

Ms. Smith reported that she has been consistent with visits with David since he was taken into custody. Once David was moved to Ms. Watson's home, "[Ms. Watson] did visits." Ms. Smith said that visits now take place in her own home, once a month, and that all of her children are included. She reported that David "used to be upset when [the visits] ended" and that he "looks forward to visits." She indicated that during visits he "gets very comfortable, takes off his shoes, and plays with his siblings" and that he is "never cold or disconnected." When asked if there have ever been times that visits have not gone well, Ms. Smith stated that "there have been a few times when he was upset with me, tired of coming and going, trouble with leaving." She described that when he arrives for visits he "always has a glow" on his face.

Regarding her relationship with Ms. Watson, Ms. Smith stated that when she "pursued return home...the foster mother was not happy because she want to adopt" David. She stated, "Me and Barbara always had a good relationship," but sometimes Ms. Watson would "sabotage" visits by not being available when visits were scheduled. When asked to describe her behavior toward Ms. Watson, Ms. Smith said that she would call her and "voice her opinion" and would "tell Barbara she was wrong for not calling back." She denied that her behavior toward Ms. Watson was at any time inappropriate. Ms. Smith stated that she is not angry with Ms. Watson because she is "thankful for what she has given" David.

Ms. Smith stated that her oldest daughter, Tracy, is currently staying with her and that her other three children (Tina, Donald, and Tanya) who live with her aunt stay with her on the weekends. She indicated that her aunt has no concerns about the children's safety when with her. Regarding future plans for her children, Ms. Smith stated that Tracy will stay with her after her baby is born, and that she and her aunt plan for Tina, Donald, and Tanya to return to her (Ms. Smith's) care. She hopes to have all of her children with her as soon as possible.

Ms. Smith was asked to describe the pros and cons of David staying with Ms. Watson. Ms. Smith stated that she could not identify any pros and that her children "all want to come home and all want to have David come home." This examiner asked what she thought the emotional impact would be on David if he were moved from Ms. Watson's home. Ms. Smith stated that she did not "think it would be an impact" and that "he would grow out of that." She stated that the process would have to be a "transition" with movement through the visitation steps and that she would let Ms. Watson and David visit once he came home.

She stated that she has "childcare set up," with the plan for Daniel's babysitter to also serve as childcare for her grandchild and for David should he return home.

When asked what services her family might need to assist in the adjustment were David to come home, Ms. Smith stated that family therapy and individual counseling for her children would be helpful. She stated that none of her children present with any significant problems in need of therapeutic intervention, but that having a place to talk would be helpful because "sometimes kids are not able to talk to their mother." When asked if she thought she would need any individual counseling, she stated "No." When asked what other things would need to be in place for reunification to be successful, Ms. Smith listed "new housing," "continuing with meetings," "talking to her sponsor" and support network, "keep the kids in childcare and school," and maintaining her employment.

Substance Abuse History

Ms. Smith reported that she started using cocaine in 1999, at first using three times a week, and then "reaching" a point of using "every day." She stated that she started selling drugs in 1998 and then, once she started using, "sold drugs to buy drugs." At the time of this assessment (11/11), Ms. Smith reported "being clean" for 27 months.

When asked about triggers to drug use, Ms. Smith stated, "I don't have any triggers now; I've made up my mind that I don't want to use anymore." She further stated, "I got clean for me, not just to get my kids back." She described her triggers in the past as "people, places, and things." Ms. Smith described her old neighborhood and the people there as triggers to drug use, stating that out of her "family building" that was owned by her grandfather, drugs were sold and used by many of her family members. When she "got out of Substance Free" she went to Addiction Services' Recovery Home rather than returning to her "family building." She stated that her "family building" is different now (her uncles still use drugs in the basement, but all selling activity has stopped) and that this is where her aunt, Annie Smith, resides. She does talk to her family members and sometimes spends time there. The triggers she described included her "feeling unsupported" and as if "no one cared about me," having no money, and stressors such as her "bad experience" with Child Protective Services.

Although Ms. Smith was adamant that she would not relapse, she was able to talk about what a plan for her children would be should that situation occur. She stated that she would give the children back to her aunt, "where they will be taken care of."

Service History

Ms. Smith reported a lengthy history of involvement with substance abuse treatment that started in 2004 and included participation in a variety of outpatient and inpatient programs. She stated that not until 2009, when she went to Substance Free for a 60-day outpatient program and a 90-day inpatient program and then participated in a six-month outpatient program at Healthy Alternatives, did she fully engage in the recovery process. In 11/09, Ms. Smith entered the Addiction Services Recovery Home, where she lived until 2011, as she completed Phase 1 and Phase 2 of the program before moving into her own apartment under the program's supervision.

Ms. Smith described that she was going to treatment "for my kids" and that it felt like "life or death." She described herself as initially being "on the pity pot" and that she "felt really guilty." As part of her recovery she realized that she had to "accept and forgive myself." She further stated that she had to realize, "I wasn't responsible for what I did during my addiction because I was under the influence, I wasn't thinking right."

Ms. Smith reported that she currently participates in NA/AA meetings two to three times a week and has weekly one-on-one contact with her sponsor. She stated that she has also completed parenting classes through Healthy Alternatives and currently attends a monthly group that covers "different topics" through Addiction Services.

Current Living Situation

Currently, Ms. Smith lives in a "two-bedroom apartment" with Daniel and Tracy where rent is paid by Addiction Services. She stated that her "lease is up" on 2/1/12. Ms. Smith described her neighborhood as "typical" and as "not safe." She described drug use and selling activity on her block and stated that, because of this, she walks the other way out of her building to avoid the area of activity. Ms. Smith has a housing advocate through Child Protective Services who is helping her locate housing after her current lease is up. She feels "optimistic" about finding something and intends to get a "big enough apartment for all of [her] children." She described wanting to live in a different neighborhood than she does now because of the drug activity and she does now because of the drug activity and stated that, although there are "drugs everywhere," some neighborhoods are not as "infested as others."

When asked about her support network, Ms. Smith indicated that it is "good." She identified her sponsor, her "sponsor sisters" (members of her support group), Annie Smith, her case manager from Addiction Services, and her counselor from Substance Free as making up her support network. Ms. Smith said that her aunt, Annie Smith, was very supportive of her when she was using and assisted her in getting clean.

Personal Background

Ms. Smith grew up in a large city and is the oldest of six siblings, the youngest of whom is six years old. Her mother, Ms. Rebecca Smith, is currently 48 years old and has never been married. Ms. Smith does not know who her father is. Rebecca Smith is currently "not together" with the father of her youngest child. Ms. Smith described her family as "close knit" and stated that they always "ate together" and did things as a family. When asked, she reported no history of physical abuse or sexual abuse. Ms. Smith is the first member of her family to be involved with Child Protective Services; she reported feeling "embarrassed" about this. Ms. Smith described her mother as "nurturing" but not as a good "communicator," as she did not teach her about "the streets, the do's and don'ts, the birds and bees."

Ms. Smith described a pervasive substance abuse history in her family. Her maternal grandmother used drugs in the past, but is currently clean, and her maternal grandfather is an alcoholic. Rebecca Smith began using cocaine once her "kids were grown" and continues to use currently. She further stated that "just about all" of her mother's 12 siblings (including Ms. Smith's aunt, Annie Smith) used drugs and that all of her own siblings currently use drugs. She stated that her aunt has been "clean since 1999." Ms. Smith reported some contact with one of her siblings, but she stated that she does not have ongoing or close relationships with her family members due to their ongoing drug use.

When asked more about her mother's current substance abuse and the impact it has on her parenting of her six-year-old daughter, Ms. Smith stated that her mother is not "out there in the streets" and that she does not "worry about" her mother and the care of her daughter.

Ms. Smith reported no current romantic relationship, as she "wants stability" and is "focused on" herself. Ms. Smith has never been married; she remains in regular contact with the father of Tracy (Randy) and in sporadic contact with Tina's father (Kevin) and Donald's father (Michael). The father of David and Daniel (Darryl) and Ms. Smith "broke up" one year ago after an eight-year relationship due to his "deciding to be with another woman." David has not seen his father in approximately one year. Ms. Smith reported that he sometimes asks about his father and where he is, but said that she is "not sure how to explain" it. She described a pattern of drug use and selling amongst the fathers of her children, but she denied any domestic violence. Two of the fathers have criminal backgrounds, Kevin for murder charges and Darryl for drug-related charges.

Ms. Smith identified herself as a "Christian" and as "spiritual." She stated that her religion provides her with significant support and that "without God, I'd be nothing." Ms. Smith reported attending church weekly with her children.

Ms. Smith stated that because she was pregnant while in high school and because she was "failing" and "cutting class," she "went to an alternative school." She reported dropping out before finishing high school and then getting her GED in 2006 while incarcerated.

Ms. Smith reported having always been employed, with jobs in various restaurants and shops since 1996. Most recently she worked as a driver for a medical company for three months. Ms. Smith indicated that she chose to leave this job to pursue "job training at General Hospital" which ended on 10/31/11. She made this change so that she could have "better pay and full benefits." On 11/10/11, Ms. Smith began working at General Hospital in the housecleaning department in an on-call capacity. She stated that she is not guaranteed full-time work, but that she is confident that she will be able to work enough to pay her bills and support her family.

Ms. Smith stated that she has no current physical or medical problems. She described herself as "healthy" but "overweight." She reported no history of mental health problems for herself and in her family of origin. She did state that she used to be "depressed a lot because of the drugs," but that the depression "lifted" when she stopped using. She described the depression as manifesting in "crying" and feelings of "guilt" about her children, but she denied any other symptoms. When asked if she

ever felt suicidal during that time, she stated she "thought about it while using" but never attempted to follow through because she was "too scared" and did not want to "go to hell." She reported receiving no therapy or counseling beyond what she received for her substance abuse.

Ms. Smith was asked about descriptions by mental health professionals of her as having an "argumentative style" and as needing to "learn to take directives." She admitted that she had problems in both of these areas and that counseling had helped her to "listen more," to be more "open," and to realize that "arguing doesn't get me anywhere."

Regarding criminal history, Ms. Smith was arrested and put on probation in 1998 for selling drugs. She also was arrested in 2003 and 2006 for selling drugs and spent 61 days and one year in jail respectively.

Relationships with Children and Parenting History

Ms. Smith reported having C-section births with all six of her children. She has since "had [her] tubes tied." None of her children were born premature, and she reported having prenatal and postnatal appointments with a doctor for all of her pregnancies. Ms. Smith was 16 when she became pregnant with Tracy and received "support" and "advice" from her mother. When she had Tracy, Tina, and Donald in her care, she "had a lot of support from family." Ms. Smith indicated that Tracy was in her care from birth to age eight, Tina from birth to age four, and Donald from birth to age three. When asked how this time was for her, she said, "I loved being a parent."

Regarding the impact of her drug use on her children, Ms. Smith responded that it led to her children being "placed with my aunt and not with me." When asked how she thinks her drug use impacted her children's functioning, Ms. Smith stated that she sees some poor "attention span and a hard time staying focused" in her children and that this "hurts" her. She stated that she "feels bad" for "putting the kids through this." Ms. Smith "didn't see the impact of the drugs early on" with Tina and Donald, as they were "on target developmentally" and "good babies."

When asked to describe her children, Ms. Smith indicated that Daniel is the most problematic, as he "acts up." She also described him as a "typical two-year-old" and said that she feels "good because he is my first baby that has my attention." Ms. Smith described the children in her aunt's care as "respectful" and not exhibiting any concerning behavioral or emotional difficulties.

Ms. Smith reported "using things [she] learned in therapy and parenting classes" when parenting Daniel. She stated that when he acts up for attention, because "he is a little spoiled," she "ignores" him if he is not in danger and that this is effective. Other forms of discipline Ms. Smith reported using include "saying no" and using "time out." With her older children on the weekends, Ms. Smith reported "taking things away" or putting them "on punishment." Ms. Smith reported that she "used to spank" her children when they were in her care. When asked to elaborate on what a "spank" was, she stated she would give them a "pop on the hand" and demonstrated by slapping one hand with the other. She denied any current use of corporal punishment.

When asked to describe her strengths and weaknesses as a parent, she listed some strengths as that she "talks to them about their problems," is "firm" with them, is "open" about her history, and that she lets "them know how much [she] loves them." For weaknesses, she listed "giving in to them sometimes."

Ms. Smith was also asked to describe the stresses that she experiences and anticipates experiencing as a parent. She said that "when they don't listen," she feels stress. She could not identify any other examples. Ms. Smith stated that she has the support of Public Aid for food stamps and a medical card and that she will receive assistance in living expenses from Subsidized Housing Assistance. When asked what would happen if she were to not be able to get full-time work from General Hospital, Ms. Smith stated, "I think I can pay the bills" and did not report worrying that this would be a problem.

When asked about the impact of drugs on parenting in general, Ms. Smith stated that "some people can parent only to a certain degree while under the influence" and that there might be "some neglect because they are not giving the child undivided attention." She described parenting as a "24-hour-a-day" task. To questions about when a child should not be with a drug-abusing parent, Ms. Smith stated "when totally unmanageable, can't pay bills, buy food...when they let the kids raise themselves." She further admitted, "I wouldn't have been able to parent my kids when using drugs." This examiner clarified that she did

parent her children for four years when using drugs, to which she replied that her using was "manageable" and "only to a certain degree" at that time. She further clarified that losing her children led to an increase in drug use due to her not knowing "how to accept it," and that during that time she could not have parented her children.

INFORMATION FROM COLLATERAL CONTACTS
Sarah Carter—Caseworker

Ms. Carter was asked about David's foster placement with Ms. Watson. She stated that also living in Ms. Watson's home are a one-and-a-half-year-old female foster child and Ms. William's two sons (ages 12 and 15). David gets "a lot of attention" in the foster home and is "very close to the younger girl and calls her his sister." He also calls Ms. Watson's sons his "brothers." She described David's relationship with Ms. Watson as "really good," stating that he is "happy" and that they are "very active together." She described Ms. Watson's discipline and David's behavior as "appropriate." David "does excellent" in kindergarten and is "doing well" in his speech therapy.

Regarding the relationship between Ms. Watson and Ms. Smith, Ms. Carter stated that they "used to have a good relationship" and that the "foster mom did visits for a while." As the case "moved toward termination," Ms. Smith "started acting out a bit...she left some inappropriate messages with the foster mom saying how 'foster mom isn't answering the phone, foster mom is trying to keep David away from her'." Ms. Carter described Ms. Smith's actions as "extremely inappropriate." Ms. Smith and Ms. Watson "cut ties" in August or September of 2011.

Ms. Carter stated that the "loss of either mom would be a loss" for David, but that she is going to recommend to the court a goal of guardianship for him. She stated that the "foster mom is the mom he knows," that his relationship with "Mary is more as a second mom," and that she "sees a stronger relationship and bond with the foster mom." She also indicated that she views David as having a "very strong bond with Daniel" as opposed to Ms. Smith.

Ms. Carter stated that David reports that he wants "to live with both mommies." When asked about his living situation and feelings about both his mother and his foster mother, he often replies, "I don't know" or responds with other statements of ambivalence/confusion.

Following the parent–child observation (described below) on 11/12/11, Ms. Carter indicated that Ms. Smith was more interactive with David during this visit than is typical and that usually David and Daniel spend most of the visit playing together while Ms. Smith talks to the caseworker in the kitchen. She said that typically for the first 30 minutes, David will not speak to Ms. Smith, but that after that he "warms up." She reported that David usually "leaves okay," and that he "sometimes says he wants to stay." When all the children are present at the visits, "Tina interacts the most with David and Daniel" while the other children "watch TV."

Ms. Carter reported that, as of 10/30/11, supervised visits for David increased to two times a month from one time a month.

Barbara Watson—Foster Parent

Regarding David's general functioning, Ms. Watson described him as getting "along with the family" and as performing "very good at school, his teacher says he is 'very smart'." She also said that he can be "very hyper" but that he is "compliant." She stated that he "loves to give hugs and kisses" and "gets along very well with her sons," with whom he "always wants to play." Regarding the 16-month-old foster child in the home, Ms. Watson indicated that David "tries to care for her" and that they play together often and well.

When asked about his response to visitation with Ms. Smith, Ms. Watson stated that David says he "doesn't want to go," "I not like them," and "I'm coming back, aren't I?"

Regarding her interactions with Ms. Smith, Ms. Watson stated that Ms. Smith "gave [me] attitude on the phone." She stated that Ms. Smith will call, and when Ms. Watson is not at home, will accuse her of "keeping David from her." She also stated that Ms. Smith will respond to David's calling Ms. Watson "Momma" with "that aren't your Momma, she Ms. Barbara." Ms. Watson expressed her desire to have David stay with her, stating "I love him, I care about him very much."

RESULTS OF ASSESSMENT MEASURES

Child Abuse Potential Inventory–Form VI (CAPI)

The CAPI is a 160-item self-report measure designed to be used as a screening device to identify characteristics that are often found in or shared with known physical abusers. The measure contains items related to parents' beliefs about parenting, expectations of their children, and personal functioning. The CAPI provides a validity score and factor scores for several aspects of parent functioning (e.g., distress, rigidity, unhappiness) and parent–child relations (e.g., parent–child problems, problems with family members, and problems with others). The measure was designed to be administered and interpreted in conjunction with evaluation data from additional sources such as interviews, case history, and direct observations. Ms. Smith's responses indicated a valid profile with patterns in the nonclinical range, which suggests minimal risk for engaging in physical child abuse.

Parenting Stress Index—(PSI)

The PSI is a 120-item self-report measure that assists in identifying parent–child systems that are under stress and at risk for dysfunctional parenting behavior or behavior problems in the child. The PSI results provide information about whether or not the parent responded in a defensive manner to the items, total stress in the parenting role, child factors contributing to stress, and parent factors contributing to stress. The measure was designed to be administered and interpreted in conjunction with evaluation data from additional sources such as interviews, case history, and direct observations. On the PSI subscales, Ms. Smiths' responses did not yield significantly elevated scores. However, Ms. Smith's scores on the Defensive Responding Scale were slightly elevated, suggesting that she may have responded to the measure with the intention of portraying herself as competent and free of the emotional stresses normally associated with parenting.

OBSERVATIONS
Parent–Child Observation

The parent–child observation took place during the regularly scheduled supervised visit. Every effort was made to minimize the possible interference of an "observer" in the family dynamics. The conclusions here are based upon observations of the parent–child interactions in an artificial situation under time constraints. Nonetheless, several observations can be made.

The initial hour included Ms. Smith, David, Daniel, Ms. Smith's oldest child (Tracy), and the caseworker (Ms. Carter). For the second hour, Ms. Smith's other three children—Tina, Donald, and Tanya—were present. The apartment was a two-bedroom first-floor apartment with a kitchen and living room of fair size. It was observed to be clean. The living room was empty of furniture, which, according to Ms. Smith, was due to her not having items to place in there. This room served as the playroom during the visit. This examiner noticed uncovered power outlets that would be easy for a young child to access. However, overall, the apartment appeared safe and orderly.

David, upon entering the apartment, appeared shy and was very quiet. Ms. Smith, in approaching him, insisted on a hug, and did not cease hugging him when he tried to move away from her. David did not greet his sister, Tracy, who was standing in the kitchen, and she did not greet him either. (Tracy and the caseworker spent the remainder of this hour in the kitchen talking.) Ms. Smith spent the first few minutes asking David questions about his tooth, which had come out. She was observed to be speaking rather loudly and quickly and to have a lot of energy. This appeared to overwhelm David somewhat, as he seemed to want to move away from her, appeared very shy, and did not answer her questions. Ms. Smith did not change her manner of interacting with him in response to these cues.

The visit soon moved into the living room when Ms. Smith removed a large box of toys from the closet. David and Daniel, with the help of Ms. Smith, removed the toys and began playing with them. There were age-appropriate toys for both boys in the box. Of note was that Ms. Smith tended to continuously remove toys from the box and show them to the boys, not allowing them much opportunity to focus on any one item. At other points her focus was more on the toys than on interacting with the boys. She was observed to not attend to the fact that the boys were stepping on and walking through the toys, at times losing their balance.

After one hour, Ms. Smith's aunt, Annie Smith, arrived with Tina, Donald, and Tanya. They were all well dressed and groomed. Upon entering, the siblings did not greet David with any outward displays of happiness or affection. The children soon after went outside to play baseball in the yard (a small fenced-in area). It was slightly chilly outside, and Ms. Smith did not have the children put on their coats. After approximately 10 minutes, she did say that it was cold and they should come in. Ms. Smith was observed to move from the inside to the outside and to not provide consistent supervision for the younger children (David and Daniel). At one point David bumped his head on a railing; he looked to Ms. Smith for a response; however, she did not notice. He rubbed his head for a few moments, did not seek comfort from his mother or siblings, and then moved back to playing.

During this time outside, a neighborhood boy (he appeared to be around 13 years old) entered the yard and said he wanted to play with the children. Ms. Smith did not object, and he came into the yard to play. Ms. Smith did not know his name, or who he was, but said that he had come around during the previous visit and on some weekends to "hang out." At one point she left David and Daniel alone outside with the boy. On a few occasions during the visit, David was observed to look at the boy in a concerned way as if to communicate his confusion about his presence.

Ms. Smith stated that it was time for ice cream and instructed the children to clean up the toys before she served it. She implemented a creative and effective way of getting the children to clean (i.e., saying she would count to 100 and that they needed to get all the toys in the box before she finished). The children were observed to all work together and complete the task.

In David's interactions with Daniel, some aggression from David was observed. For instance on one occasion he pushed his brother, and then looked to both this examiner and Ms. Smith for a reaction. Although Daniel did not react with any outburst, Ms. Smith did not notice the incident.

This examiner observed a tendency for the older children to assist with and play a caretaking/protective role with the younger children. Donald and Tina especially were very thoughtful and nurturing to David and Daniel and helpful to Ms. Smith. Tanya was somewhat hyperactive and stubborn during the visit; this led Ms. Smith to call her "spoiled" to the group. Daniel exhibited age-appropriate two-year-old behaviors (e.g., stubbornness, saying "no," having a brief tantrum when frustrated). Ms. Smith's responses to these behaviors were appropriate and characterized by patience and insight into what he was communicating. In general, all the children were well behaved and exhibited no concerning behavioral problems or clear emotional difficulties. Ms. Smith remained patient and calm throughout the visit and at no point needed to set any significant limits. The children were compliant with her requests and all interacted positively with each other.

When it was time to leave, David indicated with his body language (pouting, crossing his arms, standing still, resisting putting on his coat) that he did not want to leave. He hugged his family members when it was requested that he do so, but remained quiet and nonverbal throughout these interactions.

Overall, Ms. Smith was noted to be patient with her children, calm, and interactive in an appropriate manner (e.g., asking questions, responding to requests, giving reasonable directives). A tendency to not provide consistent supervision and to pay attention to overall events rather than individual children was noted as well. David responded in a compliant manner, at no point displaying any concerning behaviors toward his mother. He was observed to be quiet throughout the visit, rarely initiating conversation with adults or his siblings and answering questions in a soft voice and with short answers.

Foster Parent–Child Observation

Present at the observation were Ms. Watson, her two sons—Jamie and Charles, her foster child—Alice, and David. The observation took place after school hours, and when this examiner arrived the children were having a snack and getting ready to complete homework. Time was spent interacting one-on-one with David and also observing him interact with his foster family in a nonstructured way.

David did not initially remember this examiner, but he introduced himself loudly and with a big smile after his "brothers" introduced themselves. He eagerly showed this examiner how to play a video game and expressed much enjoyment while doing so. He was observed to be somewhat hyperactive, but he was able to be redirected and to calm down with little difficulty. David was very expressive verbally toward this examiner and the members of his foster family. He played cooperatively with all foster siblings and talked easily and openly with his foster mother. He responded well to directives given by Ms. Watson.

When one-on-one with this examiner, David was asked to draw a picture of his family. He quickly became distracted and did not finish. When asked to list "the people in [his] family," David stated,

"Mom, her name starts with a 'B', Jam (Jamie), Charlie (Charles), and Alice." He was then asked who is in his "other family" and he said "none." During this interaction, David became noticeably more fidgety and silly. When asked to list the names of the siblings who live with his mother, he was able to begin to do so. He did not finish, stating in a silly tone, "You know who they are." He was resistant and ultimately unable to engage in any dialogue about visits. This examiner asked David if Daniel used to live in the foster home with him; he said "yes," and then, when asked about why Daniel does not live with him anymore, stated, "He was bad so he had to stay over there." When back with the rest of his foster family, Ms. Watson asked David if he wanted to live "here or with Mary," and David said, "here." He answered in a soft-spoken manner with a nervous look on his face.

During the observation David called Ms. Watson "Mom" and his foster siblings his "brothers and sisters." He eagerly showed this examiner his room, which he shares with Charles. When it came time for this examiner to leave, David responded similarly to how he did when it was time to leave his visit with Ms. Smith (pouting and crossing his arms). However, on this occasion he verbalized his feelings loudly stating that he wanted this examiner to "visit again" and appeared sad when he was told that this would not happen.

CLINICAL SUMMARY REGARDING REFERRAL QUESTIONS

Ms. Smith presents as a woman who has made considerable strides toward improving her life. Related to her history of substance abuse, she has embraced her recovery process, gained a great deal of insight into her triggers and how to maintain her sobriety, created a support network, and begun to understand the negative impact that her drug use had on her children. In addition, she has found much support and strength through her religious beliefs. Related to her involvement with Child Protective Services and parenting abilities, she has accepted responsibility for her involvement with Child Protective Services, improved her parenting skills, made gains toward fostering healthy relationships with her children, and sought out employment training so as to be able to meet her family's needs.

In this assessment process it also became clear that Ms. Smith was invested in presenting herself in a positive light. Related to this was a tendency to deny some of the stresses that she currently experiences as a parent and to minimize the stresses that she will probably experience if she is to parent more children. Furthermore, her minimization of the negative impact that separation from Ms. Watson will have on David, and her poor attention to his cues and needs during visits, are suggestive of a limited understanding of his emotional development and needs. Questions about her judgment when assessing the safety of children and need for supervision were noted as well. This was observed during the parent–child observation (i.e., not providing consistent supervision, allowing an unknown neighborhood boy to be alone with David and Daniel) and came across in Ms. Smith's interview (e.g., not asserting concern for her six-year-old sister who is being cared for by her drug-abusing mother).

A factor in this case that is important to keep in mind is Ms. Smith's expressed intention to have Tracy and her newborn baby remain in her care, as well as her intention to have Tina, Donald, and Tanya return to her care. This is significant given her tendency to minimize the stresses of parenting and, thus, to not necessarily be fully aware of her limitations when under stress.

1. Given David has been in foster care since birth and in his current foster placement for the past three years, what are the potential benefits and risks associated with permanency goals of Return Home and Guardianship?

David clearly has an attachment to his foster mother as his primary caretaker and to his foster siblings as his "brothers and sister." This attachment has formed as a result of his living in that home from ages two to five, significant years for forming early attachments, and that his time there has been characterized by a sense of consistency, security, and nurturance.

Were David to remain with Ms. Watson with a goal of guardianship, his contact with his biological siblings would be likely to continue. Ms. Watson has stated that she is open to allowing David to have as much contact with his biological family as is possible. In the short term, remaining with Ms. Watson would not have as significant a negative emotional impact on David as would moving to his mother's home. This scenario would not entail a disruption in placement for David. However, in the long term, if David maintains an ongoing relationship with his biological mother and siblings, he may experience confusion regarding why he is the only child not in her care (assuming she were to regain custody of all of her other children).

Given that David has been in foster care since birth, he has never known Ms. Smith as a primary caretaker. Furthermore, visitation with his mother has not been at a frequency to support the formation of a secure attachment. It is not clear from records what contact occurred between temporary custody in 2006 and the change in goal to TPR in 2008, although Ms. Smith was actively abusing substances during this time, probably hindering consistency in visitation. Beginning in 2008, Ms. Smith only had visits with David one time a month; this has only recently increased to twice a month. In addition, David has not lived with any of his siblings, beyond Daniel while he was in Ms. Watson's home. David is aware that his biological siblings are his brothers and sisters, but, beyond Daniel, he does not appear to have a strong attachment to them. He appeared to enjoy playing with them during his visit, but did not greet them warmly or appear upset to say goodbye to them. However, it is evident that David does have a connection with Ms. Smith and his siblings and that fostering an attachment to them is possible. Furthermore, Ms. Smith evidences some parenting skills and the insight and intelligence to respond to intervention geared at improving her ability to interact with David in a manner that will foster a healthy and secure attachment.

Were the goal to be changed to Return Home, the loss of Ms. Watson as a primary caretaker and of his foster siblings as his primary "brothers and sister" would be likely to have a significant negative emotional impact on David and could lead to some disruptions in his current functioning (i.e., emotional and behavioral instability). Were he to return home to Ms. Smith, he would probably mourn the loss of his foster mother and siblings and need considerable time to adjust, support to understand what is occurring, and contact with his foster mother and siblings to maintain a relationship.

During this assessment, discrepant reports were made regarding the nature of interactions between Ms. Smith and Ms. Watson, with both women reporting problematic behavior from the other related to visits and caretaking. The caseworker, Ms. Carter, reported that Ms. Smith's behaviors have been "extremely inappropriate" and characterized by anger and accusation. Given Ms. Smith's history of having difficulty in conflicted situations, as well as her desire to portray herself in a positive light to this examiner, it is likely that she is downplaying her own behaviors in her reports. Both women have indicated a willingness to have the other remain involved with David when a decision is made about his permanency, suggesting that this conflict will need to be addressed so that David will indeed be able to maintain a relationship with both women. Furthermore, in addressing this conflict, it will be important to address the issue of both women's attending to David's clear confusion regarding the situation and not asking him to choose where he wants to live. He is unable to understand the complexity of this question, wants to please both "Mommas," and will only become more confused if such questions continue.

2. Given Ms. Smith's long history with drug use and the fact she currently is parenting a young child, what is Ms. Smith's ability to adequately care for and parent both children in the event of David's return home?

Ms. Smith has been clean for 27 months and has made considerable progress in her recovery process. While her risk of relapse appears low, were she to come under a great deal of stress, this could change. Parenting a two-year-old with some challenging behaviors, as well as having a teenage daughter parenting a newborn for the first time, will present Ms. Smith with significant caretaking tasks. Additional risks relate to her tendency to deny some of the stresses that she currently experiences as a parent and to minimize the stresses that she will probably experience if she is to parent more children. Were Ms. Smith to experience increased stressors related to parenting, the risk increases that she may not recognize when to seek help.

Based on this assessment, David will need considerable individualized attention from Ms. Smith so that he can gain an increased sense of comfort in the home and so that a secure attachment can be fostered. The discrepancy in his behaviors in his mother's home and in his foster mother's home suggests that he was not at ease during the visit with Ms. Smith. Furthermore, if David were to be returned home with Tracy, Daniel, and a newborn present, he would be entering a situation in which there is risk of his not getting his individualized emotional needs met, as Ms. Smith will have numerous caretaking tasks. This situation would also increase the risk that a secure attachment to Ms. Smith will not be formed. Were he to return home and Ms. Smith assume guardianship of her other three children in the near future, this would place David at even higher risk of not getting his individualized needs met and put the parent–child attachment process at even higher risk of failure.

3. If the goal for David is changed to Return Home, what services would be needed to prepare for reunification, and what are some possible transition plans?

Were the goal to change to Return Home, it would be vital to proceed slowly and provide considerable support to all parties involved:

a. Increase in visitation to unsupervised time would need to proceed slowly, with attention being given to David's emotional reactions to greater contact and the awareness that he is spending less time in his foster home.

b. Providing a therapist to work with Ms. Smith and David toward developing a healthy and strong attachment would be important. This therapist would assist in monitoring David's reactions to increased contact and help him better understand what is occurring. Focus would also be needed around helping David see Ms. Smith as a supportive figure whom he could seek out for comfort.

c. Furthermore, an individual therapist would be recommended for Ms. Smith to assist her in better understanding and meeting David's emotional needs related to the separation from Ms. Watson and his foster siblings. Ms. Smith will also need some assistance in learning to better read and respond to David's cues and in recognizing safety concerns. This assistance could be provided by an individual therapist or by a parenting coach present during visits.

d. Finally, were the goal to change to Return Home, it would be highly recommended that David and Ms. Smith have ample time to form a secure attachment and connection before plans to return the other children to her care would be considered.

SIGNATURE

Jane Parker, Psy.D.
Licensed Clinical Psychologist
License # 0000000

TEACHING POINT:
IDENTIFYING FORENSIC CAPACITIES WHEN THE LEGAL STANDARD IS VAGUE OR UNELABORATED

The forensic clinician begins any FMHA by identifying the relevant legal standard and associated functional-legal capacities. This may be contained in applicable statutes, case law, or both. In some kinds of cases, the function-legal capacities are described in detail (competence to stand trial is perhaps the best example). In others, however, the legal standard may be less explicit and the associated functional-legal capacities unelaborated. To clarify what kind of circumstance applies in a given case, it can be helpful to cite the applicable legal authority and describe the standard early in the report.

In the instances in which the legal standard provides relatively little guidance, the forensic clinician might consider the following as a useful strategy. Reviewing the literature can identify a number of functional-legal capacities that might reasonably apply if the standard were interpreted broadly. Beginning with such a broad operationalization of the legal standard, the evaluator can use it as a framework for various areas to be addressed in the evaluation. Mindful that the court may interpret the standard more narrowly, however, the evaluator should make every effort to distinguish various functional-legal capacities that *might* apply—and discuss each separately in the report. The court can then more easily exclude criteria that it does not judge to be appropriate in contributing to the decision, or weigh some criteria more heavily than others.

The final aspect of this strategy is to avoid answering the ultimate legal question. Such an answer can be problematic even when given in an evaluation using a clear and detailed standard. When given in cases in which a less detailed standard applies, however, the problems of intruding on the court's decision-making domain are exacerbated.

CASE TWO
PRINCIPLE: BE GUIDED BY HONESTY AND STRIVING FOR IMPARTIALITY, ACTIVELY DISCLOSING THE LIMITATIONS ON, AS WELL AS THE SUPPORT FOR, ONE'S OPINIONS
(PRINCIPLE 4)

This principle is firmly established in the context of FMHA. The *Ethical Principles of Psychologists and Code of Conduct* (APA *Ethics Code*; American Psychological Association, 2010a) addresses honesty and impartiality in several of its overarching principles (Principle C, Integrity; and Principle D, Justice) and in its coverage of multiple relationships (Standard 3.05), conflicts of interest (3.06), and the proper assessment of individuals (Standards 9.01 and 9.02). The APA *Ethics Code* also emphasizes the importance of basing opinions on clearly stated and appropriate information and procedures (Standard 9.01) and discussing the limitations of one's opinion due to characteristics of the individual assessed, the assessment methods, and relevant situational factors (see Standards 9.01(b), 9.02(b), 9.03(c), and 9.06). The importance of objectivity and impartiality is also addressed directly in the *Specialty Guidelines for Forensic Psychology* (APA *Specialty Guidelines*; American Psychological Association, 2013b) in the guidelines covering Integrity (Guideline 1.01) and Impartiality and Fairness (Guideline 1.02), and indirectly in discussions of the basis for opinion and testimony (Guideline 2.05), conflicts of interest (Guideline 1.03), and multiple relationships (Guideline 4.02). Recognizing and presenting the limitations of recommendations and opinions is also discussed in regard to the impact of personal beliefs (Guideline 2.07), assessment methods (Guidelines 9.02, 9.03, and 10.02), and the characteristics of the individuals being assessed (Guideline 10.03).

An emphasis on honesty and impartiality is also made in the *Principles of Medical Ethics with Annotations Especially Applicable to Psychiatry* (American Psychiatric Association, 2013b) both directly (Section 2) and indirectly (Section 8), and the *Ethics Guidelines for the Practice of Forensic Psychiatry* (Guideline IV, Honesty and Striving for Objectivity; American Academy of Psychiatry and the Law, 2005). Finally, and specific to the evaluations discussed in this chapter, the *Guidelines for*

Psychological Evaluations in Child Protection Matters (American Psychological Association, 2013a) notes that during these evaluations, evaluators should strive to maintain an unbiased and impartial approach (Guideline 4); to be aware of their personal biases and address these appropriately (Guideline 6); to avoid multiple relationships, conflicts of interest, and other issues that may impair their objectivity and impartiality (Guideline 7); and to provide both the bases and limitations of their interpretations and recommendations (Guideline 11).

Legal literature addresses this principle indirectly by generally establishing that opinions offered by expert witnesses must be relevant, reliable (i.e., valid), based on scientific methodology, and generally accepted in the field (see generally *Daubert v. Merrell Dow Pharmaceuticals, Inc.*, 1993; FRE 401, 402, 403, 702, 703; *Frye v. United States*, 1923). An expert must also be prepared to testify as to the facts or data underlying his opinion (FRE 705). Scientific methodology is by definition based upon objectivity and impartiality. Furthermore, the professional literature from the field invariably supports honesty, objectivity, and impartiality as core elements of FMHA, and emphasizes recognizing and describing the support for and limitations of all opinions in forensic reports and testimony (Grisso, 1986, 2003; Heilbrun, 2001; Heilbrun, Grisso, & Goldstein, 2009; Melton, Petrila, Poythress, & Slobogin, 2007; Packer & Grisso, 2011).

In the present case, striving for honesty and impartiality is demonstrated throughout the report. But there are two ways in which it is illustrated very clearly. First, the report is very thorough and detailed. It includes extensive information gathered from multiple sources and does not attempt to present it in an argumentative or advocacy-based fashion. It is this "gathering of extensive information and describing all of it before reasoning and conclusions" that clearly demonstrates that the evaluator is being driven by data, not any *a priori* position. Second, the evaluator offers a series of hypotheses near the end of the report and describes the support for each. This is an interesting and valuable way of framing the possible conclusions, and draws upon the information that has been presented in the earlier part of the report. By clearly describing the possible explanations and the observed support for each, the evaluator makes it clear that it is this

support—and not evaluator advocacy or values—that is important in framing the conclusions.

CHILD SEXUAL ABUSE EVALUATION

(contributed by Kathryn Kuehnle and H. D. Kirkpatrick)

MOTHER:	Shelly Carter
D.O.B.:	March 21, 1969
AGE:	40 Yrs
FATHER:	Daniel Nelson
D.O.B.:	October 27, 1967
AGE:	42 Yrs
CHILD:	Quinn Nelson
D.O.B.:	October 1, 2003
AGE:	6 Yrs–4 Mos
CASE NAME:	Carter V. Nelson
CASE NUMBER:	08-DR-000123
COMPLETION OF REPORT:	February 15, 2010

COURT APPOINTMENT AND AGREEMENT FOR SERVICES

The Honorable Marilyn Warner, Circuit Court Judge in the First Judicial Circuit in and for Desoto County, Florida, signed an order on October 20, 2009, appointing Suzanne Parker, Ph.D., as forensic evaluator to perform an evaluation regarding the allegation of child sexual abuse and an allegation of alienation of the child Quinn, in the case of *Carter v. Nelson*. The order reads, in part:

> Suzanne Parker, Ph.D., is hereby appointed by this Court to act as an independent expert, for the purpose of conducting an evaluation of allegations of child sexual abuse. The evaluation will address the probable veracity of the sexual abuse and parental alienation allegations and include a psychosexual evaluation of Respondent. To the extent that Dr. Parker does not feel that she has the requisite expertise to perform any particular test or evaluation that she deems appropriate in this case given the nature of the allegations, she has the authority to designate a qualified third party to handle such tests or evaluation and to rely on such third party's findings and conclusions, so long as she clearly discloses all of the foregoing in her report. The action

is a post-judgment modification to modify time-sharing.

INFORMED CONSENT AND ASSENT

Shelly, Dan, and their attorneys signed Dr. Parker's Agreement for Services, which delineates her court appointment, her expectations for the parties' participation and cooperation, fees for services, and that communication or information provided to Dr. Parker is not privileged or confidential. The child, Quinn, is not of an age to provide legal informed consent; therefore, his formal written consent was not obtained. He was informed that what he told me was not "a secret," and that I did not keep secrets. Prior to interviews with collateral informants, the limits of confidentiality were explained to them. Collaterals were informed that what they said to Dr. Parker was not confidential, was accessible to the attorneys in this case after her written report was provided to them, and could be included in Dr. Parker's report, and that what they told Dr. Parker might be repeated if Dr. Parker were to testify in this matter.

SOURCES OF INFORMATION

Accompanying the report was this declaration: *All contacts, interviews, testing, and documents received from the clients, counsel, personal collateral sources, and professionals during this evaluation have been reviewed and are listed below and may be subpoenaed by the clients' attorneys after the written report has been released to the attorneys and provided in a sealed envelope to the Court.*

Quinn Nelson (age 6 years 4 months)
Interviews
- Observation of Quinn—unable to conduct forensic child sexual abuse substantive interview—brought by maternal aunt (agreed-upon neutral party)—session videotaped 11/7/09 (1 hr)
- Observation and informal psychological assessment of Quinn—brought by mother—session videotaped 11/11/09 (1 hr)
- Observation and informal psychological assessment of Quinn—brought by father and paternal grandmother, court-appointed supervisor—session videotaped 11/18/09 (1 hr)

- Forensic child sexual abuse substantive interview of Quinn—brought by maternal aunt (agreed-upon neutral party)—National Institute of Child Health and Human Development NICHD interview protocol used and session videotaped 12/20/09 (1 hr)

Parent–Child Observations
- Home visit with father and Quinn (paternal grandmother [visitation supervisor] present) 12/1/09 (2 hrs)
- Home visit—mother; mother's live-in boyfriend, David Miller; Josh, David Miller's son; Quinn's half siblings, Maria and Sophia; and Quinn 12/8/09 (2 hrs)
- Father teaching Quinn (paternal grandmother [visitation supervisor], present) 12/13/09 (0.75 hr)
- Mother teaching Quinn 12/18/09 (1 hr)

Questionnaires
- Structured Child Assessment of Relationships in Families (SCARF) 11-18-09

Teacher Questionnaire
- Teacher Report Form—completed by Stacey Greenberg 12/20/09

Daniel K. Nelson (age 41)
Interviews
- Joint interview with Shelly Carter and Dan Nelson 11/5/09 (3 hrs)
- First individual interview with Dan Nelson 11/13/09 (2 hrs)
- Second individual interview with Dan Nelson 1/10/10 (2 hrs)

Observations
- Home visit with father, paternal grandmother, and Quinn 12/2/09 (2 hrs)
- Father teaching Quinn (paternal grandmother, visitation supervisor, present) 12/14/10 (.75 hr)

Testing
- Administration of Minnesota Multiphasic Personality Inventory—2nd Edition (MMPI-2)—11/13/09

Other Testing Requested by Dr. Parker
- Drug and Alcohol Testing (conducted by Drug and Alcohol Testing of America, Inc.)—12/07/09

- Psychosexual Assessment—conducted by Dr. Michael Gates—12/16/09

Forms Completed
- Completion of Parent Forensic Questionnaire
- Completion of the Child Forensic History Questionnaire
- Completion of Child Behavior Checklist for ages 6–18 for Quinn
- Completion of the Child Sexual Abuse Inventory (CSAI)

Shelly A. Carter (Age 38)

Interviews
- Joint interview with Shelly Carter and Dan Nelson 11/5/09 (3 hrs)
- First individual interview with Shelly Carter 11/15/1/09 (2 hrs)
- Second individual interview with Shelly Carter 1/3/10 (2 hrs)

Observations
- Home visit—mother; mother's live-in boyfriend, David Miller; Josh, David Miller's son; Quinn's half siblings Maria and Sophia; and Quinn 12/8/09 (2 hrs)
- Mother teaching Quinn 12/18/09 (1 hr)

Testing
- Administration of Minnesota Multiphasic Personality Inventory–2nd Edition (MMPI-2)—11/15/09

Other Testing
- Drug and Alcohol Testing (conducted by Drug and Alcohol Testing of America, Inc.).—12/02/09

Forms Completed
- Completion of Parent Forensic History Questionnaire (Greenberg Questionnaire, modified with permission)
- Completion of the Child Forensic History Questionnaire
- Completion of Child Behavior Checklist for ages 6–18 for Quinn
- Completion of the Child Sexual Abuse Inventory (CSAI)

David Miller, Shelly's live-in boyfriend

Interviews
- Interview 11/23/09 (2 hrs)

Testing
- Administration of Minnesota Multiphasic Personality Inventory–2nd Edition (MMPI-2)—11/23/09

Observation
- Home visit—mother; mother's live-in boyfriend, David Miller; Josh, David Miller's son; Quinn's half siblings Maria and Sophia; and Quinn 12/8/09 (2 hrs)

Forms Completed
- Completion of the Parent Forensic Questionnaire

Collaterals

Contact with professionals who are familiar with the family members, such as pediatricians, mental health providers, previous evaluators, and child welfare staff, should be attempted. To obtain information from the most important personal collaterals, each parent is requested to provide the names of five family members, friends, and/or acquaintances who will be the most informative. The parents are informed that these personal collateral sources should be able to provide information relevant to the allegations that are the focus of the current evaluation. The parents are also informed that if they have more than five collaterals, they may have these individuals write letters to the evaluator.

Professional Collaterals

Professional Telephone Interviews and Consultations
- Telephone interviews—John Peters, M.D., pediatrician, telephone interview 11/16/09 (0.25 hr), 1/10/10 (0.25 hr); Hope Persons, Sheriff's Office 12/15/09 (0.25 hr); Child Protection Investigator, Grace Dunn 12/15/09 (0.25 hr); Teri Smith, LMHC, Quinn's previous therapist, telephone interview 12/15/09 (0.5 hr); Stanley Shelton, LMHC, previous marriage therapist and Shelly's current therapist 12/15/09 (0.5 hr); Georgia Holder, M.D., Quinn's previous psychiatrist, 12/15/09 (0.5 hr); Stacey Greenberg, Quinn's teacher, 10/20/09 (0.25 hr), 1/10/10 (0.25 hr).

- Telephone consultation—Doug Lewis, Ph.D., vice president of US Drug Testing Labs, Inc., regarding results of drug testing 12/15/09 (0.5 hr); Michael Gates, Ph.D., ABPP, regarding psychosexual evaluation 1/5/10 (0.50 hr)

Personal Collaterals

Personal Collaterals for
Dan Nelson—Letters and E-mails
- None received

Personal Collaterals for Dan Nelson—Interviewed

Dan provided the names of two personal collaterals and reported that these were the only personal collaterals he wanted to involve.

- Interview in person–Jennifer Pauley, Dan's mother, 12/15/09 (2 hrs)
- Unable to reach—Dave Nelson, brother, did not return five voicemail messages

Personal Collaterals for Shelly Carter—Letters and E-mails Received
- Email—Martha Patrick, neighbor and friend 11/18/09

Personal Collaterals for Shelly Carter—Interviewed

Shelly provided the names of five personal collaterals: one of these individuals Shelly identified as a personal friend. When this friend was contacted, she did not want to be involved.

- Interview in person—Maria Carter, daughter 10/23/09 (1 hr); Sophia Carter, daughter 11/11/09 (1 hr); David Miller, live-in boyfriend, interview and evaluation 11/23/2009 (2 hrs)
- Interview by telephone—Margaret Carter, sister 12/15/09 (0.50 hr)

Records Reviewed

All documents received and the names of the individual providing the document are listed below. Documents are listed even when they are duplicates.

Documents Provided by Attorneys

Court Orders/Court Motions
- Court appointment of Wayne Myers, Ph.D., to conduct an evaluation of Child Sexual Abuse—alleged victim Quinn Nelson, 1/6/09
- Notice of filing—with Psychiatric Evaluation Report 3/12/09; with three Investigative Summaries and closure letter attached
- *Ex parte* order—compelling former husband to submit to drug and alcohol testing required by Dr. Suzanne Parker 12/4/09
- Stipulated order—to discontinue child's therapy during evaluation process, 11/1/09; to continue final hearing, 12/4/09

Depositions and Affidavit
- Depositions—Dr. Georgia Holder, psychiatrist, 6/8/08; Dr. John Peters, pediatrician, 6/8/08; Jennifer Pauley, paternal grandmother, 10/28/09; Daniel Nelson, father, 10/28/09

Transcripts of Proceedings
- Family Court Hearings—11/1/07; 4/3/08; 7/21/08; 9/21/08; 10/6/08

Records and Test Results
- Investigative Summaries 10/25/07, 4/19/08, 8/21/08, 10/14/08, 11/5/08, 12/10/08, 5/20/09, 1/11/10
- Dan's DUI charges—1988, 1995, 2000, 2001, 2002, 2006
- Dan's drug tests 2007—2008—Goodwill Industries—In House Substance Abuse Test 11/10/07, 11/19/07, 12/3/07, 12/17/07, 1/7/08, 1/20/08, 2/10/08; Due to allegations, substance abuse tests resumed 5/15/08, 7/6/08, 8/1/08
- Moss Glenn therapy records, 10/06–12/06
- Video of Dan Nelson drinking, 12/21/09
- Polygraph tests mandated by attorneys— Shelly Carter 8/11/08, 1/8/10; Polygraph Test, Dan Nelson 1/8/10

Medical Records for Quinn Nelson
- Childcare Medical Group—John Peters, M.D.
- Toxicology Reports—10/13/08, 12/13/08

Documents Provided by Wayne Myers, Ph.D. (Previous Court-Appointed Evaluator)

- Documents—Psychiatric Evaluation— written report dated March 12, 2009; Former attorney memos regarding communication with Shelly Carter
- Transcripts of:

Deposition of John Peters, M.D.; Deposition of Georgia Holder, M.D., July 21, 2008, proceeding; Excerpt of October 6, 2008, proceeding; April 3, 2008, proceeding; Department of Children and Families (DCF) documents— DCF Investigative Summary 10/25/07, 4/19/08; Investigative Summaries Provided by Shelly Carter to Dr. Myers—DCF Investigative Summary 8/21/08, 10/14/08, 11/5/08, 12/10/08; Police and Sheriff Incident Reports—Desoto County Offense Incident Reports 4/19/08, 12/13/08, 11/12/08; Medical Records and Toxicology Reports for Quinn Nelson 11/05/08, 12/3/08; MMPI-2 raw data and reports and other testing data; Polygraph results for Shelly Carter 8/11/08; Various pleadings, orders and motions; Prescription records of Shelly Carter; Text messages between Shelly Carter and Daniel Nelson; Affidavits—pediatrician John Peters, M.D., psychiatrist Georgia Holder, M.D., mental health therapist Teri Smith; Correspondence and medical records of/from psychiatrist Georgia Holder, M.D; Correspondence from Stanley Shelton, LMHC; Handwritten notes of pediatrician Dr. Peters; Miscellaneous correspondence, notes from Shelly Carter, e-mail correspondence and other documents; Attorney correspondence—May 29, 2008, correspondence from Heath to Morgan; May 30, 2008, correspondence from Morgan to Heath; June 2, 2008, correspondence from Heath to Morgan; June 9, 2008, correspondence from Morgan to Heath; June 12, 2008, correspondence from Heath to Morgan; December 31, 2008, correspondence from Morgan to Gillman; January 13, 2009, correspondence from Morgan to Gillman; July 14, 2009, correspondence from Morgan to Lund.

Documents Provided by Dan Nelson
- Emails to Dr. Parker: 11/24/09, 12/12/09, 12/18/09, 1/22/10; Between parents: 10/19/09, 11/11/09; Between parent and third party

- Desoto County Sheriff's Office Child Protective Investigation—Closure Letter 9/29/08
- Glen Moss therapy records 10/06–12/06 for Dan

Documents Provided by Shelly Carter
- Emails to Dr. Parker: 10/9/09, 10/13/09, 10/14/09, 10/15/09, 10/16/09, 10/17/09, 10/18/09, 11/11/09, 11/13/09, 11/15/09, 11/16/09, 11/20/09, 11/21/09, 11/23/09, 11/29/09, 12/18/09, 12/26/09, 12/28/09, 1/1/10, 1/2/10, 1/8/10, 1/11/10, 1/13/10; Between parents, 11/21/09; Between parent and third party, 11/29/09, 11/8/09; timeline 11/25/09 with copy of documented text message
- Desoto County Court Dockets—Desoto County Traffic Citations for Dan Nelson; Individual Charge Reports for Dan Nelson 6/13/96, 10/27/02, 9/24/06
- Timeline Shelly Carter
- Information printed from the web on Ambien Sex
- Received from Shelly Carter in separate book: Documents—Department of Children and Families (DCF) Investigative Summaries 10/25/07, 4/19/08, 8/21/08, 10/14/08, 11/5/08, 12/10/08; Police and Sheriff Desoto County Incident Reports 4/19/08, 10/14/08, 11/12/08, 12/13/08

Documents Provided by David Miller, Shelly's Live-In Boyfriend
- Emails from David Miller to Dr. Parker 11/27/09 and 12/18/09

ALLEGATIONS OF CHILD SEXUAL ABUSE AND THREATENED HARM

The specific statements that have been reported to the child protection services, police, and/or sheriff's department are important to obtain and review. The chronology of abuse allegations, the number of unfounded reports to child protection, and elaboration of allegations over time should be considered. To the degree possible, an accurate timeline should include all allegations and informal as well as formal interviews. For example, if the child was interviewed by a parent, then interviewed by another relative or family friend before the initial "official" interview, these first two interviews should also be documented in the chronology of interviews. The parent alleging abuse should be asked how the information was discovered prior to the reporting of the information that is contained in each of the reports to Child Protection.

First Allegation

October 25, 2007; Investigative Summary, intake number 2007-11111-01, reads:

> There is ongoing concern for the father's ability to care for Quinn due to his substance abuse. The father was forced to participate in rehabilitation after his third DUI arrest. He is drinking and using drugs again; cocaine is his drug of choice. Quinn is diagnosed with asthma which has quickly developed into pneumonia requiring emergency medical treatment in the past. The father gets hammered [drunk] before Quinn's visits and has to sleep it off. The father lives with the paternal grandmother, but she has health problems.

The report summarized: "No indication of substance misuse. Dad denied using any illegal drugs, drug screen was negative."

First Interview by Child Protection Investigator (CPI)

Alleged victim (AV) did not know about any drug use on Dad's part; Mom also stated that she has suspicions that Dad is using drugs but stated that AV does not know about if Dad is using. Paternal Grandmother stated that Dad is not using any illegal drugs. Dad did admit to being an alcoholic but is receiving treatment for it." This case, Intake Number 2007-11111-01, was closed on November 9, 2007.

Informal Questioning

Prior to the second report to Children Protection, Shelly reported that she questioned Quinn about why he was wetting his bed, not listening to her, and acting badly at home after visits with his father. Quinn responded "because of his father." Shelly asked Quinn if his father told him not to listen to his mother, and Quinn said yes. She asked Quinn where he was sleeping when he was with his father, and Quinn reported he was sleeping with his father. Shelly asked Quinn if his father was touching his

"peeper" (penis), and Quinn responded yes, and upon further inquiry stated that his father touched his "peeper" with his hand. Shelly believes Quinn and reported that Quinn would not lie to her.

Second Allegation

April 19, 2008; Investigative Summary intake number 2008-11111-01,

> Additional information received 4/19/2008. Over the past few weeks, Quinn has been wetting his bed and having behavior problems. It was discovered that on 4/11/2008, the father touched Quinn's penis while he was sleeping in the bed with his father. The father touched Quinn's penis with his hand. It is believed that this is a first-time incident. Quinn has not had contact with the father since the incident. Law enforcement has been notified, but the father has not been arrested.
>
> Quinn has asthma. Quinn is scared and afraid to visit with his father because he yells at [Quinn's] mom. As a result, Quinn is wetting himself and had two accidents. Quinn doesn't talk to anyone when he comes back from his visits with dad. On 1/08, the father got violent and was screaming. Since 10/07, the father used cocaine at least once or twice a week. Since the father was a teenager, he had an alcohol problem. He had four driving under the influences (DUIs). The father drank around Quinn.

This case was closed on May 2, 2008.

> There are no findings of substance misuse. The father admitted to trying cocaine in college but denies any use since getting married and having his son. He and the mother no longer are together. He was offered a drug/alcohol screen but was not willing to take it, stating that he is subjected to random drug tests ordered by the court that began on 11/10/07 in order for him to have contact with his son. The child is too young to know what drugs are and hasn't been alone with the father since these same allegations were addressed in 10/07. There are no findings of sexual abuse. The mother states that the child told her that the father touched him.

Second Interview by Child Protection Investigator (CPI)

The report states

> "The child was interviewed, and he knows what his private parts are and points to his penis. He denies that anyone has seen his private parts or that anyone has ever touched his private parts. He states that he sleeps by himself and no one gets in bed with him. The father also denies ever touching the child as was alleged, stating that the child has not slept in his bed except for when he was a baby and he would sometimes sleep with him and the mother."

Shelly filed an Offense Incident Report at the Desoto County's Sheriff's Office in regards to this incident.

Informal Questioning

Prior to the third allegation, Shelly and her live-in boyfriend, David, questioned Quinn about why he tried to put his finger in Josh's butt (Josh is the son of David and two years older than Quinn). Quinn responded that his father and grandmother do that to him. Quinn said his father told him not to tell. Quinn told his mother he is afraid of his father.

Third Allegation

August 21, 2008, Investigative Summary, intake number 2008-22222-01,

> Grandmother has fibromyalgia. Something is going on with Quinn and it is believed to be Dad and Grandmother in conjunction. There might be sexual abuse going on. Quinn has been doing sexual things. He put his finger in his 8-year-old brother's butt and manipulated his genital area. Dad and Grandmother touched Quinn's 'peeper' [penis]. Quinn is continuing to wet himself at night. The wetting started when he began visitations with Dad. At one time, Dad told Quinn, 'Don't tell anyone what goes on at Dad's or Grandmother's home.' Per court order, Dad will now have supervised visitations with Quinn with Grandmother supervising the visitation.

The case closed on September 23, 2008.

Third Interview by Child Protection Investigator (CPI)

Investigative Summary reads:

> Alleged Victim (AV) was unable to specify the intent of his father's touch to his private[s], nor could AV offer any time frame for the event. This allegation was addressed in a 4/08 report, found with no indicators of abuse. The mother has withheld visits between AV and his father since 4/08 despite the Court ordering the mother in 7/08 to resume visits. Father had a drug screen on 8/1/08, it was negative, as well as almost two months after his last visit with Quinn. There are various motions filed by the parents, which will be handled in Family Court. Dr. Georgia Holder, a psychiatrist, met with Quinn one time, they talked about the poking incident; Quinn reported it never happened again. Dr. Holder also informed CPI that the bedwetting had ceased a while ago. It appears that Quinn poked Josh, son of [his] mother's paramour, in the butt, one time without penetration, according to Josh. This was addressed with Dr. Holder, and according to Josh never occurred again, no indication of threatened harm, as all adults in the family are aware of the incident and keeping their eyes open for any further behaviors.

Informal Questioning

Prior to the fourth report to Child Protection, Shelly and her boyfriend David questioned Quinn when they observed him acting strangely after his return from visiting his father. They asked Quinn if anything happened at his father's house and told Quinn he should not keep secrets from his mother. Quinn reported that his father kissed him on the mouth, and upon further inquiry reported his father kissed him with his tongue. Quinn reported that he is afraid of his father and does not want to visit him.

Fourth Allegation

October 14, 2008. Investigative Summary intake number 2008-33333-01,

> On this past Saturday, the father kissed Quinn with his tongue. This occurred while Quinn was with the father for visitation. It was

unknown if the father received sexual gratification from the incident. There may be a history of that type of incident occurring. In the past, the father touched Quinn's penis. Quinn did not sustain any injuries as a result. The location of where the incident occurred was not known.

Case closed with no findings on December 10, 2008. Summary intake number 2008-33333-01 reads: "There are some negative implications for the safety/permanency of the child based on the findings of maltreatment. The investigation is being closed with no indicators of sexual abuse by the father/Daniel Nelson."

Fourth Interview by Child Protection Investigator (CPI)

Child Protection Team (CPT) exam was negative, and the child has failed to disclose anything to Child Protective Services/law enforcement officer (CPS/LEO) and when making comments stated his mother told him what to say.

Informal Questioning

Prior to the fifth report to Child Protection, when Quinn returned home from a visit with his father, Shelly and Quinn's maternal aunt, Margaret Carter, noticed he was covered in rashes, had trouble breathing, and was sleepy. When asked what happened to him at his father's house, Quinn reported that his father touched his "peeper" and his father put his own "peeper" and his finger in Quinn's butt and it hurt. Upon further questioning, Quinn told his mother and aunt that his father gave him a green, yellow, and blue pill.

Fifth Allegation

November 5, 2008; Investigative Summary intake number 2008-44444-01.

On 11/05/08, the father dropped Quinn off at home, he had bumps and rashes on his arms, legs, and he was having some respiratory problems. Quinn is asthmatic, but hasn't had attacks in the past year. The father gave Quinn some pills. Quinn was taken to the hospital. The toxicology test was negative. The father stated he gave Quinn a vitamin. The grandmother stated that she saw the father give Quinn a vitamin. The father's visitation is supervised by the grandmother.

Additional information to fifth allegation— November 9, 2008, Investigative Summary intake number 2008-44444-01: "On 11/09/08 additional information was provided. Quinn resides with the mother. Quinn visits the father. On 11/5/08 Quinn was in the hospital for unknown oral exposure to pills. The father fed Quinn pills to sedate him. There are concerns of possible sex abuse from the father. It is unknown how. The father may possibly sodomize Quinn. No injuries known to Quinn."

Additional information to fifth allegation— November 12, 2008, Investigative Summary intake number 2008-44444-01: "On 11/12/08, sometime between 1500 and 1900 hours, the father 'put his peeper in Quinn's butt, again, and it hurt.' Quinn went to his visitation with the father at his home located in Desoto County. When he returned to the mother's home, she began getting him ready for a bath. The child's underwear was wet with urine and there was feces in the back."

Additional information to fifth allegation— November 12, 2008, Investigative Summary intake number 2008-44444-01: "The father has penetrated Quinn's anus with his finger. The father gave Quinn a blue and yellow pill so he could sexually abuse Quinn. It is not known what the yellow pill was. The mother said Quinn has been asleep and slept for 24 hours three times. The pills did not cause any health problems for Quinn. On 11/12/08, Quinn did have irritation inside of his anus but the cause is not known."

Additional information to fifth allegation— November 12, 2008, Investigative Summary intake number 2008-44444-01: "On 11/12/2008, Quinn's father penetrated Quinn's anus with his penis. Quinn's father also manipulated and penetrated Quinn's anus with his finger. Quinn's father's parental rights were taken from him months ago due to cocaine and alcohol abuse. Quinn's father gained supervised visitation with him recently. There have been allegations of Quinn's father sexually abusing him in the past in Desoto County."

Fifth Interview by Child Protection Investigator (CPI)

Case closed. Quinn reported his father gives him pills but was unable to describe the pills.

Shelly filed an Offense Incident Report at the Desoto County's Sheriff's Office in regard to this incident on November 12, 2008.

Informal Questioning

Prior to the sixth report to Child Protection, Shelly asked Quinn if his father gave him more pills, and Quinn answered yes. Quinn was crying and telling his mother he does not want to visit his father.

Sixth Allegation

December 10, 2008, Investigative Summary, intake number 2008-55555-01:

> Quinn visits at the father's home. In the past the father has given the child pills that were green, yellow and blue in color. The father has stated that he gives the child "vitamins." The father has been counseled by law enforcement not to give the child any medications "prescribed or over the counter." After returning from the father's home this week, [Quinn] stated that the father gave him another pill to take (incident occurred 12/3/2008). The child was taken to the doctor to determine what medications were in his system. It was determined that he had 4.5 mg/ml of the drug Ambien in his system. The parents are in a heated custody battle.

This report, regarding intake number 2008-55555-01, summarized: "There are strong negative implications for the safety/permanence of the child based on the findings of maltreatment."

Sixth Interview by Child Protection Investigator (CPI)

Case closed on January 9, 2009. Summary intake number 2008-55555-01 reads: "The investigation is being closed with some indicators of substance misuse as the child was actually found to have a positive toxicology for Ambien. Despite the tangible evidence to show the child had an unprescribed substance, which according to his pediatrician could be fatal in children, there is no definitive way to pinpoint where the child acquired the pill or by whom."

Informal Questioning

Prior to the seventh report to Child Protection, Shelly questioned Quinn about what he did at his father's house. Quinn reported that he put his "peeper" in his father's butt and his father liked it. Quinn was hysterical and begging his mother to not make him go to visit his father.

Seventh Allegation

May 20, 2009, Investigative Summary, intake number 2009-11111-01, reads:

> Even though the grandmother is supposed to be supervising the visitation between Quinn and his father, the father continues to sexually abuse Quinn. After returning from his last visit on 5/03/09, it was found out that Quinn put his "peeper" (penis) in his father's butt. The father liked it but, at some point, told him to stop. At the time of the incident, the grandmother was in the bathroom for a long time. Quinn has been experiencing increased enuresis. This is not the first incident where the father's continued sexual abuse of Quinn has happened while the grandmother was supposed to be supervising the visit, including the week prior to the last incident. The sexual abuse history includes the father putting his "peeper" in Quinn's butt.

Seventh Interview by Child Protection Investigator (CPI)

Case closed on July 18, 2009. Investigative Summary, intake number 2009-11111-01, reads:

> There are negative implications for the safety/permanency of the child based on the findings of maltreatment; however, the investigation is being closed with no indicators of threatened harm, inadequate supervision or sexual abuse. The child has made no credible or concrete statement to law enforcement, CPS or CPT to substantiate the allegations of sexual abuse as his statements are confusing. The child appears to be adequately supervised when in his father's care and he does not appear to pose any threat of him to the child. At the time of case closure, the findings remain the same. The Paternal Grandmother is writing a safety plan that she will be present for any/all visits when Alleged Victim visits the father which follows court appointment of supervised caretaker. The case remains open in Desoto County Law Enforcement for final disposition.

Eighth Allegation

January 11, 2010, Investigative Summary, intake number 2010-11111-01, reads: "The mother reported that no one believes her son is abused and her son's life is in danger. The father has told the AV that he will kill him, his sisters, his mother, her boyfriend, and the boyfriend's son." Child was not interviewed by Child Protection Investigator (CPI).

The case was closed January 20, 2010.

RELATIONSHIP OF PARENTS

The parents' perceived chronology and perceived quality of their relationship is important for understanding the current relationship dynamics and the timing of the allegations of child sexual abuse. The discrepancy in information provided by each parent will be further evaluated by corroborative sources of information.

In October 2002, Shelly and Dan were 33 and 35 years old, respectively, when they met at a bar where Dan was performing with a rock band. When Dan and Shelly began dating in November 2002, Shelly was a single mother with two daughters (Maria, age seven, and Sophia, age three) and employed as a secretary at her mother's insurance business. Dan's employment was as an environmental scientist and a member of a band. Shelly reported that she and Dan shared an interest in the environment and her daughters liked Dan, which "cemented her relationship with him." Dan was vague concerning what drew him to Shelly and reported that he and Shelly had a good relationship and great intimacy. Dan moved into Shelly's house in December 2002. Dan said the transition of moving in with Shelly and her children was an adjustment for him because he had never been married before or lived as an adult with children. Dan reported that Shelly's girls were "nice children."

In December 2002, the night before Dan moved in to Shelly's house Dan was arrested and charged for driving under the influence (DUI), found guilty, and had his driver's license revoked for one year. This was Dan's fifth alcohol-related driving offense; however, Shelly reported Dan told her it was his first. Factually, Dan was charged and found guilty of his first DUI in 1988 when he was in college; charged and found not guilty by a jury of his second DUI in June 1995; charged with a third DUI in 2000 that was later dismissed; and charged with a fourth DUI in 2001 that was reduced to reckless driving. In December 2002, Dan was charged and found guilty of his fifth DUI. According to Shelly, the financial aspects of the DUI were stressful. Dan quit his job as an environmental scientist, and

Shelly paid for Dan's fines and the attorney's fees; she also drove Dan to various events where his band was playing. Shelly's salary was primarily supporting Dan. Dan helped provide childcare for Shelly's youngest child, Sophia; Maria was attending first grade. According to Dan, he worked on his drinking problem after he moved in with Shelly, although he did not attend AA or therapy for his substance abuse. In February 2003, Shelly noted that Dan had become very unreliable and would not come home some nights after performing with his band. During this time, the police came to their home and served Dan with a credit card debt notice. Shelly brought him to a bankruptcy attorney, and she made payments on his student loans, as the student loans were not included in the bankruptcy motion. According to Shelly, Dan was approximately six thousand dollars in debt.

Shortly after moving in together, Shelly became pregnant with her third child, Quinn. According to Dan, his relationship with Shelly was good throughout the pregnancy. He was "elated" over having a child. Dan stated that Shelly perceived this time as stressful. Shelly terminated her employment in September 2003, and Shelly's mother assisted Shelly financially. Quinn Nelson was born on October 1, 2003; Quinn's half siblings, Maria and Sophia, were eight and four years old. Dan thought his relationship with Shelly was "wonderful and healthy" after the birth of Quinn; Shelly perceived their relationship "was good." Following Quinn's birth, Dan was a stay-at-home father and caretaker for Quinn and Sophia, and Shelly returned to work full time. Sophia began kindergarten when she was age five and Dan remained Quinn's full-time caretaker.

Following the birth of Quinn, Dan and Shelly married in December 2003, and Dan's drinking escalated to consuming a bottle of wine on a daily basis. Shelly reported that Dan was drinking with his band members and not coming home until early in the morning. Shelly also found illicit drugs that Dan had brought into the family home. According to Shelly, Dan's drinking and drug use interfered in the children's caretaking. On several occasions when Shelly arrived home from work, she would find Dan passed out and Quinn left unsupervised. She stated that when Dan was not drinking during the day, he was hung over from the night before; he became increasingly irritable and detached from the family. Dan reported that at times he was detached and not a "perfect dad." He stated that he would "zone out" sometimes while watching sports games but not because he was inebriated. Dan reported that he never drank to the point that it interfered in his caretaking of the children or brought illicit drugs into the family home, and rarely did things alone with the children due to "Shelly's element of control." According to Dan, both he and Shelly were "drinkers," and Shelly frequently had members of Dan's band over for parties.

On one occasion, Shelly came home to find Dan passed out and Quinn chewing on a plastic bag containing cocaine. Shelly asked Dan to move out after this incident. According to Dan, Shelly kicked him out of her house because she was angry at him for not providing more financial support for the family. Shelly and Dan briefly separated for the duration of several weeks and then reunited. On September 24, 2006, Dan was arrested and charged with his sixth DUI, his license was revoked, and he was ordered to attend therapy for his substance abuse. Shelly asked Dan to move out of the marital home and immediately filed for divorce; Quinn was two years, 11 months old. In January 2007, Dan signed an uncontested divorce agreement. At that time, Dan perceived the divorce agreement to be "fair" because Shelly had assured him that he would be a consistent part of Quinn's life. The agreement granted Shelly sole parental responsibility and Dan visitation every other weekend Saturday morning through Sunday afternoon. From October 2006 through December 2006, Dan attended 12 group and three individual counseling sessions for his substance abuse, as ordered by the court.

In 2007, Shelly and Dan attempted to reunite on two separate occasions. According to Dan, their reunification was unsuccessful because Shelly contacted people he had met when he was in New Orleans and attempted to obtain information about him; Shelly emailed his friends from his email account pretending she was him. Dan did not provide the names of collateral sources to corroborate this allegation. According to Shelly, their reunification was unsuccessful because Dan was involved in online chat rooms when they were attempting to repair their relationship. She reported that he had solicited 20 to 50 females for sex and was soliciting males for sex as well. Shelly did not provide documentation, such as a forensic computer analysis, to corroborate this allegation. Shelly did not find

any solicitation of minors or child pornography on Dan's computer. In May 2007, during their attempt to reunite, they participated in couples' therapy for several sessions.

Three-and-a-half-year-old Quinn began spending the night every other Saturday with Dan at the paternal grandmother's house where Dan was residing. The every–other-weekend visits initially went smoothly, and Quinn did not resist spending time with his father. In June 2007, Dan was frequently traveling to New Orleans to visit his new girlfriend, and his visits with Quinn were becoming sporadic and infrequent.

According to Dan, ten months after the divorce in the summer of 2007, Shelly decided that if they were not living together, then Dan would not be a part of his son's life. At that time, Quinn would have been approximately 3½ years old. Shelly informed Dan he was not allowed to pick up Quinn or remove him from her house, and he would abide by her rules. According to Dan, this controlling gatekeeping behavior by Shelly continued for several months, and then he sought legal advice. According to Shelly, she began to require Dan to visit Quinn at her house after she discovered a text message from a woman demanding money for "the cocaine Dan had stolen from her." Shelly took a video of the text and gave it to Child Protective Services. Dan maintained sporadic visits with Quinn at Shelly's home until the first child protection investigation commenced October 25, 2007, followed by a Family Court Hearing on November 1, 2007. At that hearing, the Court ordered Dan to participate in random drug screens through Goodwill Industries beginning in November 2007, and for Dan and Quinn to resume every-other-weekend visitation with overnights.

In January 2008, Dan and Shelly engaged in a verbal argument in front of all three children. Shelly then terminated Dan's visitation with four-year-old Quinn. When Shelly and Dan returned to Family Court on April 3, 2008, Shelly reported that she felt threatened by Dan during a verbal fight that took place in January 2008. According to Shelly's narrative, Dan was inebriated when he came to visit Quinn and proceeded to call her names such as "cunt" and threatened her as he held Quinn in his arms. The judge ordered Dan to resume random alcohol and drug screens provided by Goodwill Industries and to have Dan's mother present during all child exchanges between the parents.

The week of April 6, 2008, 4½-year-old Quinn had his first visit with his father since January. After the visit, Quinn, in addition to wetting himself, regressed by constantly picking his nose and shoving it in his mouth, biting his nails, hitting, biting other children, whining, and "if the littlest thing happened he would cry and scream hysterically." Shelly further observed "I couldn't be out of his site [*sic*]; he was so afraid of going to the bathroom he had to leave the door open; anytime someone would try to close the door he would completely panic." On April 9, 2008, Shelly took Quinn to his pediatrician, Dr. Peters, who questioned Quinn when Shelly was present. Dr. Peters advised Shelly that Quinn seemed to be very uncomfortable around his father and that Shelly needed to be with Quinn on the supervised visits. Dr. Peters believed Quinn's wetting accidents were caused by an "emotionally traumatic event." That same week, Quinn told his sister he was afraid of his father. On April 10, 2008, Shelly entered Quinn into play therapy to help him disclose possible abuse by his father. On April 11, 2008, Quinn told his mother that he had a "secret" but he would not tell his mother or his therapist his "secret."

The second visitation between Dan and Quinn occurred April 13, 2008, and was supervised by Dan's mother. On April 14, 2008, 4½-year-old Quinn reported he was scared and, when asked why, Quinn stated that his father was going to kill him, his mother, and his sisters. On April 19, 2008, when the maternal aunt drove Quinn home from school, Quinn told his aunt he was "touched" one time by his father when they were playing outside. A child protection report on April 19, 2008, indicated that on the first visit in April 2008, the father touched Quinn's penis while Quinn was sleeping in the bed with his father. On April 19, 2008, visitation between Quinn and his father was again terminated by Shelly. The allegation that Dan had sexually abused Quinn was investigated by Child Protection and closed with no findings. Quinn was interviewed by investigators and denied that anyone has ever touched his penis. He stated to the investigator that he slept by himself at his father's house and no one gets in bed with him. In May 2008, Shelly placed Quinn in therapy with psychiatrist Dr. Georgia Holder. Shelly reported that Quinn continued to make allegations of sexual abuse perpetrated on him by his father but did not disclose these allegations to the psychiatrist. Shelly

continued to block visitations between Quinn and Dan. Shelly and Dan returned to court in July 2008. At that time, Quinn was four years, nine months old. The judge appointed visits to be supervised by Dan's mother every other weekend with no overnights. According to Shelly, after the commencement of visits between Dan and Quinn, Quinn continued to make statements to Shelly about his father sexually abusing him. Shelly terminated the visits between father and son in late August 2008.

At a hearing in September 2008, the presiding judge found that Shelly was an alienating parent. The judge ordered supervised visits between Dan and Quinn to commence. In October 2008, several weeks after visits resumed, Shelly alleged that Dan and his mother were physically and sexually abusing Quinn. Shelly reported: "The regression started immediately once the visits occurred. He would come home from visits extremely sleepy, with wet clothes from his urine, physically attack his siblings, pull his hair, and wet his bed for several nights after visits." Shelly reported, "I just kept my eye on things, I didn't ask any questions then." Shelly had Quinn examined by Dr. Peters, and when an attempt was made to examine Quinn's anus, Quinn began to panic and screamed "not the butt, not the butt" and cover his anus with his hands. A report was made to child protection services and to the Desoto County Sheriff's office on October 14, 2008. According to Shelly, on October 13, 2008, Quinn told her that his father had given him pills and she observed he was very tired and lethargic. Following this disclosure, Shelly took Quinn to the hospital for testing. The toxicology test was negative. On December 10, 2008, an investigation was closed with no indicators of sexual abuse by the father/Daniel Nelson and some indicators of mental injury of the child by the mother.

On December 13, 2008, Quinn again informed his mother that his father had given him pills. Following this disclosure, Shelly took Quinn to the hospital for testing. The toxicology test was positive for Ambien. The attorneys sent their clients for polygraphs to determine whether Dan or Shelly had given Quinn the medication Ambien. Because polygraph results are inadmissible in court, the current child sexual abuse evaluation will not include the polygraph results. Dan denied he has any Ambien medication in his home or had been prescribed Ambien. Shelly admitted that she has a prescription of Ambien in her home but denied giving this drug to Quinn. Shelly again began to withhold visitation between Dan and Quinn from December 2008 to January 2009.

In January 2009, the court ordered make-up visitation for Dan and an evaluation of the sexual abuse allegations to be conducted by Wayne Myers, Ph.D. Shelly was held in contempt of court for discontinuing visitation between father and son. The visitation commencing in February 2009 allowed Dan to visit with Quinn five hours every other Saturday and Sunday with supervision conducted by Dan's mother. At the conclusion of the court-ordered evaluation in March 2009, the evaluator, Dr. Myers, concluded: "There is no compelling evidence to indicate Mr. Nelson or the grandmother sexually, medically, or physically abused Quinn." Shelly did not accept the findings by Dr. Myers and was steadfast in her belief that Quinn was being sexually abused by his father during father–son visitation. Quinn persisted in making statements to his mother that his father was sexually abusing him. In September 2009, the court ordered a second evaluation of the allegations of child sexual abuse after Shelly filed a motion identifying Dr. Myers' credentials as having expertise in child custody evaluations but lacking expertise in evaluating allegations of child sexual abuse. The Court ordered Suzanne Parker, Ph.D., an expert in evaluating allegations of child sexual abuse, to reevaluate the allegations.

PARENT HISTORIES

The history of each parent is important information when assessing allegations of child sexual abuse. The parents' childhood histories must be examined for experiences of child maltreatment and neglect; intimate partner violence; family history of mental illness, drug or alcohol abuse, criminal behavior, or behavior that has flouted societal rules; lack of respect for personal boundaries; visual/verbal exposure to adult sexual acts or nudity; and/or family messages that dehumanize individuals and view them as sexual objects.

Daniel Nelson

Dan was born in Jacksonville, Florida, on October 27, 1967, to parents Jim and Jennifer Nelson. Dan is the younger of two children; his sibling Dave is two-and-a-half years his senior. The family identified their religion as Catholic, but they did not regularly attend church. Jim and Jennifer were well-educated college graduates and employed full time by the state of Florida. Dan's father worked as a social worker with delinquent youth, and his mother worked a desk job.

Relationship with Father

Although Dan described his father as "always around, trusting, and easy to respect," Dan's mother reported that her husband was a chronic alcoholic who entered and failed several treatment programs. Dan reported that he and his father got along exceptionally well during his childhood; his father was his Little League baseball coach for four years, and throughout Dan's childhood he attended the majority of Dan's other music and sporting events. Jennifer noted that Jim was not consistent in his punishments, and Dan became manipulative, whereas Dave fought back. When Dan was a freshman in high school, his father was fired from his job due to his drinking. Jennifer reported she would have left Jim, but was unable to support herself and the boys. Jennifer remained with Jim until his death in 2003.

Relationship with Mother

Dan described his mother as "always around, fragile, timid, and accepting" and stated he and his mother got along better than average during his childhood and adolescent years. Dan did not discuss his worries and problems with either parent. Jennifer reported that Dan did not confide in her, and both boys became increasingly emotionally distant from her and their father. Dan had a very close relationship with his brother, Dave, when they were children. During this evaluation, Dan was residing with his mother, which he has done periodically throughout his adulthood.

Exposure to Adult Sex

Dan perceived his parents' marriage to be unhappy and absent an affectionate or sexual relationship. During his alcoholic rages, Jim would refer to Jennifer as a "whore" and a "cunt" in the presence of the children. Sex was not discussed by Jim or Jennifer, and Dan learned about adult sexual behaviors from his peers. There were adequate physical boundaries in the home. Dan was not exposed to adult nudity by either parent, nor was he exposed to observing sexualized touching between his parents. Dan and his brother shared a bathroom, and there was a lock on this door for privacy. Dan did not engage with his brother or other children in sexual play, and Dan did not experience physical or sexual abuse.

Exposure to Intimate Partner Violence

Jennifer reported that Jim was a chronic alcoholic who was verbally abusive to her and his two sons; Dan and Dave were humiliated and called names such as "pussies" when their father was raging. Jim was not physically abusive to his wife or children and was sexually impotent due to his alcoholism. Jennifer reported that she carried out the primary parenting and used removal of privileges for discipline. Dan and Dave would engage in sibling pushing and hitting when one brother angered the other, but they never physically assaulted each other. When the boys' father would go into alcoholic rages, Jennifer reported she was not protective enough of the boys because she was afraid of her husband. Jennifer perceived Dan to be most affected by his father's emotional abuse, due to Dan's sensitivity. Jennifer did not seek therapy for herself, Dan, or Dave. Jim was not physically hurtful to their family pets, and Dan was very nurturing to their dog and hamsters.

Intimate Relationships as an Adult

Prior to his marriage to Shelly in 2003, Dan was involved in two committed heterosexual relationships. While in college, Dan met his first serious girlfriend, Samantha. They dated exclusively for two years until Dan graduated from college and moved to another city. Dan reported that they were simply too young to commit to one another. Dan casually dated other women until 1998, when Dan, then 31, began dating his first cousin, Michelle. He reported that their relationship lasted three or four years and they loved each other very much. Dan stated that they broke things off because her family was very against their relationship. In October 2002, Dan met Shelly while his band was playing at a bar. In December 2002, Dan moved into Shelly's house, Quinn was born on October 1, 2003, and Dan and Shelly married in December 2003.

Medical and Mental Health

Dan's childhood medical history is unremarkable other than his extended bedwetting into late childhood. He reported being easily upset, anxious, and especially sensitive as a child. According to Dan and his mother, he was not an oppositional child

and did not have behavior problems at home or outside of the home. Dan reported an adult history absent any medical problems and stated that he is currently in good health. He was ordered by the court to enter substance abuse counseling, commencing in October 2006; Dan participated in 12 group and three individual counseling sessions for his substance abuse. In May 2007, after they were legally divorced, Shelly and Dan attended four or five couple's counseling sessions with the same mental health therapist, Stanley Shelton, LMHC, Shelly had seen as an adolescent. Marriage counseling was discontinued when their reunification efforts failed.

Ability to Achieve Goals

At the age of seven, Dan began to show an interest in playing the drums, and his parents encouraged his involvement in music. Over the course of his childhood and adolescence, he and Dave formed several bands together, which their parents encouraged. Dan attended public schools throughout elementary, middle, and high school. He earned average to above average grades. He was not a behavior problem and was involved in various social clubs and music organizations. He discontinued his involvement in sports when he entered high school and focused on his membership in his brother's band. After graduating from high school, Dan attended and graduated from the University of Miami. During college, he was a member of a fraternity and served as the community service chairman for three years. Dan also was in a band during his college years. Upon college graduation, Dan was employed as a staffer at a youth offender program where he worked with juvenile offenders for approximately one and a half years. Dan returned to college and obtained a Master of Arts degree in biology and was then employed as an environmental scientist for almost a decade. In December 2005, Dan lost his driver's license due to a DUI and resigned from his job.

Alcohol and Drug History

Dan first used alcohol at the age of 14 years. He reported partying on the weekends, consuming 3 to 6 drinks per occasion, 2 to 3 times a month. Between the ages of 18 to 21, Dan reported drinking at his fraternity house every night and on the weekends, consuming 2 to 6 beers an evening. In 1988 at age 21, Dan was involved in a car accident that resulted in his arrest and conviction for a DUI. Dan reported drinking 2 to 6 beers per occasion between the ages of 22 and 39 years. In June 1995 at age 28, Dan was charged with a second DUI, hired an attorney, and was found not guilty by a jury. In 2000 at age 33, Dan received a third DUI charge, hired an attorney, and the charge was dismissed. In 2001 at age 34, he was charged with a fourth DUI, hired an attorney, and the charge was reduced to reckless driving. In December 2002 at age 35, Dan was charged and convicted of his fifth DUI, and his driver's license was revoked for one year. In September 2006 at age 38, Dan was charged and convicted with his sixth DUI, his driver's license was revoked for one year, and he was ordered to participate in substance abuse counseling. Dan stated that he consumed the most alcohol between the ages of 35 and 38, which would have been the years he was living with Shelly. During this time, he reported drinking to the point of intoxication. Dan's verbal history of identifying his highest level of alcohol consumption as when he lived with Shelly does not coincide with his DUI history.

Dan's reported history of illicit drug use includes experimentation with marijuana at the age of 15 years when he smoked marijuana at weekend parties with friends. Between the ages of 18 and 21 years, he began using acid (LSD) at the end of each school semester. He reported taking one tab of acid per occasion while at home. Dan began using cocaine at the age of 30 years. According to Dan, he used cocaine recreationally on the weekends and at parties. He stated he used cocaine several times a year, snorting two to four lines per occasion. Dan reported that he has been a recreational drug user and never chronically abused legal or illicit drugs.

During my first individual interview with Dan on November 13, 2009, he reported that he has spent the past year "getting sober" and did not currently drink alcohol or use illicit drugs. He reported that in November and December 2008, he complied with a Family Court order to participate in random drug screens administered by Goodwill Industries. He produced clean drug and alcohol results on 11/10/07, 11/19/07, 12/3/07, and 12/17/07, 1/7/08, 1/20/08, 2/10/08, 5/15/08, 5/20/08, 6/13/08, 6/30/08, 7/6/08, 8/1/08 and did not fail any of the random tests he was asked to complete. He attended group and individual counseling through the Moss Glenn program, involving group sessions once a week and individual sessions once a month from October 2006 to December 2006. At this same November 2009 interview, Dan reported he was also actively involved in Alcoholics Anonymous.

In contrast to Dan's statements during his November 13th interview, on the Forensic Parenting Questionnaire, which he completed in December 2009, Dan wrote that he had consumed alcohol up until December 2009. This apparent discrepancy in Dan's report of alcohol consumption appears to be related to Dan's positive drug and alcohol test results after I requested on December 2, 2009, that Shelly and Dan provide specimens of urine, blood, hair, and fingernails to an alcohol and drug testing facility, Drug and Alcohol Testing of America. On December 2, 2009, Dan refused to comply with the requested testing, and the specimens were not collected until December 7, 2009, following a court order for Dan to submit to the drug and alcohol testing requested for my evaluation. It was not until after Dan received the positive test results that he admitted he had been using drugs and alcohol up until December 2009. He had no explanation why his drug and alcohol urine screens conducted over the past year by the Goodwill Industries facility were clean. Dan has not been arrested or charged with any criminal acts other than for DUI.

On December 7, 2009, after a court order mandating Dan to participate in alcohol and drug testing, Dan provided urine, blood, and hair specimens for analysis by United States Drug Testing Laboratory. Drug testing included a 12-panel drug analysis. The results from urine and hair specimens obtained were positive for cocaine. The drug testing results indicated that Dan's cocaine use was more than an occasional once-every-month usage. The urine test results indicated that Dan used cocaine within a three-day period of the drug testing on December 7, 2009. Hair testing further indicated that Dan has combined his cocaine use with simultaneous alcohol use. The level of cocaine found in Dan's hair and urine specimens indicate that, although Dan most likely does not use cocaine every day, he is a "sub-chronic" user and most likely engages in the use of cocaine multiple times a month.

EtG and EtS results for the urine specimen also indicated that in the past three to five days Dan had ingested a fairly large quantity of alcohol; the significantly elevated levels ruled out unintentional

COMMENT

Alcohol and Drug Testing. Urine samples are useful in detecting current abstinence from consuming alcohol or drugs. However, simply testing for the presence of alcohol in the urine provides a very gross and unreliable estimate of a person's alcohol or drug consumption. It takes the body only one hour to metabolize and excrete one standard alcoholic drink, and diuretics can be used by the specimen provider to increase the amount of urine excreted by sucking out the liquids in the circulatory system. The more sophisticated ethyl glucuronide (EtG) and (ethyl sulfate) EtS urine testing evaluates the urine sample for metabolites that are left in the body after the alcohol has been urinated out. After the body has excreted the alcohol, the metabolites remain in the body for 3 to 5 days and provide information on the level of alcohol consumption during this time period (Goll, Schmitt, Ganbmann & Aderjan, 2002; Wurst, Kempter, Seidl, & Alt, 1999). In contrast to alcohol, testing for drugs using urine specimens has different windows for identification. Blood specimens are also useful in detecting levels of alcohol consumption over the past several weeks. Phosphatidyl ethanol (PEth) is an abnormal phospholipid formed in cell tissues following alcohol exposure. PEth in blood is found primarily in red blood cells. PEth is a mid- to long-term biomarker measurable after consumption of approximately 200 grams of alcohol. An individual consuming 2 to 3 drinks per day for a week will produce a positive result. PEth can be measured for 2 to 3 weeks following the most recent alcohol consumption. Because ethanol stays in the membranes of the red blood cells for approximately 50 days, blood specimens provide information on the level of alcohol consumption a person ingests over a two- to three-week period. Head hair specimens (4 cm) provide a window of drug and alcohol consumption over a 60- to 90-day period, and fingernail specimens over a 9- to 12-month period (Varga, Hansson, Johnson, & Alling, 2000; Varga, Hansson, Lindqvist & Alling, 1998).

exposure to alcohol (e.g., rum cake, cold medicine, hand wipes...). EtG results for hair was positive for alcohol. A positive hair EtG result confirms that Dan participated in binge drinking; incidental exposure is not possible. "Binge drinking" is defined as a large amount of alcohol consumed in one sitting. It takes 4 or more drinks consumed in a short time, in one sitting, 4 or 5 consecutive times, to trigger a positive result on a hair EtG test. This is what establishes the presence of risky drinking behavior.

Alcohol testing was conducted with Dan using a blood specimen. Results for the blood specimen indicated that Dan had consumed large quantities of alcohol over the past two or three weeks prior to testing. Cumulative test results show that Dan had not abstained from substantial cocaine and alcohol consumption as of December 7, 2009.

Psychosexual Evaluation

Psychosexual assessments examine features, characteristics, behaviors, and factors that are associated with individuals' risk for sexually abusing children. Results are not conclusive as to whether an individual did or did not in fact sexually abuse an identified child.

A psychosexual evaluation was conducted in December 2009 by Michael Gates, Ph.D., an expert in conducting evaluations and treatment of sex offenders. Dr. Gates concluded:

The available historical data, factual evidence and clinical examination findings are inconsistent with what one might expect to see in an individual who has resorted to sexual misconduct or sexual abuse of his young, biological son. Mr. Nelson does not appear to have any of the features, characteristics, or behaviors that would put him at risk for this kind of behavior, with the exception of his alcohol and substance abuse. Again, I remind the interested reader that these findings are not determinative as to whether Mr. Nelson did or did not in fact sexually abuse his son, but if there is evidence that leads the court to conclude that such misconduct did occur, then I would consider it to be highly atypical, unexpected and inconsistent with the lifestyle, psychological characteristics, historical behavior and psychosexual adjustment of Daniel Nelson.

Psychological Testing

The psychological test interpretations presented below are hypotheses and should not be considered in isolation from other information in this matter. Personality test results reflect characteristics of persons who have provided test response patterns similar to those of the current individual. Although test results are presented in an affirmative manner, they are probabilistic. The reader should examine the test interpretations for general trends and put limited weight on any one specific statement or set of statements without additional support from an alternative source of data such as information obtained from collateral information.

On November 13, 2009, Dan was administered the MMPI-2. He produced a valid profile. His validity scales' T-scores were as follows[1]:

VRIN	TRIN	F	FB	FP	FBS	L	K	S
42	57T	45	42	41	43	56	60	63

His MMPI-2 clinical scales' T-scores are as follows:

Hs	D	Hy	Pd	Mf	Pa	Pt	Sc	Ma	Si
45	40	52	50	60	65	51	40	51	42

Dan's MMPI-2 data from the profile obtained by Dr. Myers in February 2009 are offered for comparison:

VRIN	TRIN	F	FB	FP	FBS	L	K	S
34	50	39	42	41	53	61	68	72

Hs	D	Hy	Pd	Mf	Pa	Pt	Sc	Ma	Si
51	45	45	48	34	57	45	53	39	42

The MMPI-2 data obtained by Dr. Wayne Myers in early 2009, compared to the more recent MMPI-2 results obtained for the current child sexual abuse evaluation by Dr. Parker, suggest that in February 2009, Dan approached this measure in a more defensive manner than in November 2009. His overall MMPI-2 profile suggests, at the time of the current testing, he was functioning in a stable and well-adjusted manner. His clinical scales T-scores are reasonably congruent with the normative scores for male custody litigants in the Bathurst et al. (1997) and Butcher (1997) studies. Substance abuse assessment data showed that he was successfully hiding/denying an honest reporting of his substance use (past and present).

Because Dan had taken two MMPI-2s within less than a year of each other, Dr. Gates administered the MMPI-2-RF as part of Dan's psychosexual evaluation.

His validity scales' and higher order and restructured clinical scales' T-scores were as follows[2]:

VRIN-r	TRIN-r	F-r	Fp-r	Fs	FBS-r	L-r	K-r
43	57F	47	42	42	51	62	72

EID	THD	BXD	RCd	RC1	RC2	RC3	RC4	RC6	RC7	RC8	RC9
36	48	46	37	42	46	41	39	43	34	47	38

Overall, Dan's validity scales for this measure show some effort at under-reporting. His overall protocol is interpretable. Although his L-r scale supports a hypothesis that he was *not* under-reporting, this hypothesis is offset by his K-r scale, which suggests he presented himself as remarkably well-adjusted. His level of self-reported psychological adjustment suggested by a K-r T-score of 72 is

---

[1]   VRIN = Variable Response Inconsistency; TRIN = True Response Inconsistency; F = Infrequency; FB = Infrequency Back; FP = Infrequency Psychopathology; L = Lie; K = Defensiveness; S = Superlative; Hs = Hypochondriasis; D = Depression; Hy = Hysteria; Pd = Psychopathic Deviate; Mf = Masculinity/Femininity; Pa = Paranoia; Pt = Psychasthenia; Sc = Schizophrenia; Ma = Hypomania; Si = Social Introversion.

---

[2]   VRIN-r = Variable Response Inconsistency; TRIN-r = True Response Inconsistency; F-r = Infrequent Responses; Fp-r = Infrequent Psychopathology Responses; Fs = Infrequenty Somatic Responses; FBS-r = Symptom Validity; L-r = Uncommon Virtues; K-r = Adjustment Validity; EID = Emotional/Internalizing Dysfunction; THD = Thought Dysfunction; BXD = Behavioral/Externalizing Dysfunction; RCd = Demoralization; RC1 = Somatic Complaints; RC2 = Low Positive Emotions; RC3 = Cynicism; RC4 = Antisocial Behavior; RC6 = Ideas of Persecution; RC7 = Dysfunctional Negative Emotions; RC8 = Aberrant Experiences; RC9 = Hypomanic Activation.

rare in the general population. Further, his substance abuse (SUB) scale with a T-score of 41, suggests he was denying or minimizing his past (and possibly present) alcohol and substance abuse.

Shelly Carter

Shelly was born in Arcadia, Florida, on March 21, 1969, to parents Julie and Christopher. She was the youngest of four children. Her sisters, Joan and Trudy, and brother Chris are 9, 6, and 2 years older, respectively. Christopher and Julie completed high school and, following graduation, married. The family identified their religion as Baptist, but they did not attend church. Shelly's mother became a successful business owner, and Shelly's father became a stay-at-home father after the children were born. Christopher and Julie separated and filed for divorce when Shelly was in sixth grade and approximately 11 years old. Christopher and Julie's divorce process was bitter and did not become legally finalized until Shelly was age 14.

Relationship with Father

Shelly's father was the stay-at-home parent and prepared his children for school and maintained their daily routines. Shelly described her father as always being around, open, accepting, and easy to respect. Shelly got along with her father exceptionally well during her childhood. She perceived herself to be a "tomboy" and to be like her father's "second son." Her parents separated, and her father moved into the family beach house when Shelly was 11 years old. Her sisters moved with their father, and Shelly and Chris remained with their mother. Shelly and her brother saw their father infrequently. Her father immediately remarried when his divorce from Julie was legally finalized; Shelly was 14 years old and was not invited to the wedding ceremony. Her oldest sister married when Shelly was 14, and her other sister married when Shelly was 16. As an adult Shelly maintained a distant relationship with her father until his death in 1994 when Shelly was age 25.

Relationship with Mother

Shelly's mother was a businesswoman and worked 60 hours a week outside of the home. Shelly described her mother as being around very little, bold, difficult to confide in, and hard-working. Her relationship with her mother during childhood was average. Following the parents' separation,

Julie increased the hours she worked outside of the home. Shelly's mother did not remarry, but dated a man for several years after the divorce. Her mother did not bring her boyfriend to the house, so Shelly only met him twice. Shelly's relationship with her mother grew in intimacy when Shelly was an adult and had children. She moved in with her mother after she was pregnant with her first child and abandoned by the father of her child. Shelly's mother has emotionally and financially supported Shelly and bought her a house.

Exposure to Adult Sex

Sex was not discussed by Shelly's parents, and she received information on this topic from overhearing her older siblings talk to each other. Her parents were not affectionate with each other and did not make romantic or sexual comments to each other, at least in the presence of their children. Shelly learned about menstruation from observation of her sisters; she did not speak with anyone about her sexual development. Shelly was not exposed to adult nudity by either parent or her brother. Her sisters were uninhibited when nude in the presence of Shelly, but never inappropriately sexual. There were adequate physical boundaries in the home. Shelly and her sisters had their own bathroom, Chris and their parents each had their separate bathroom with locks on the doors for privacy. Shelly did not engage with her sisters or other children in sexual play. Shelly did not experience physical or sexual abuse.

Exposure to Family Violence

During her childhood, Shelly was not exposed to physical, verbal, or emotional abuse between her parents. Her parents disciplined using "time out" or revoking privileges. Her siblings were not violent with her or each other. Occasionally, her sisters and brother would yell, hit, or push each other because of some perceived infraction. Shelly was rarely the target of a sibling's anger. The family pets were well cared for and nurtured by Shelly and her family members. During her childhood, Shelly's family had dogs, cats, and parrots.

Intimate Relationships as an Adult

Twenty-three-year-old Shelly began her first committed relationship, with James. They met at a bar. This relationship endured for approximately two years and produced Shelly's first child, Maria.

During her pregnancy, James abandoned Shelly and moved to Georgia. Twenty-seven-year-old Shelly began her second committed relationship, with Bud. They met at a bar. This relationship produced Shelly's second child, Sophia. The relationship of Bud and Shelly lasted several years; they never married, and they have remained friends. Bud has remained involved in Sophia's life, but he does not have a consistent visitation schedule. Bud and Shelly have made several unsuccessful attempts to reunite. Thirty-three-year-old Shelly met Dan, the father of her third child, Quinn. They met at a bar where his band was performing. In October 2002, Dan moved into Shelly's home; on October 1, 2003, Quinn was born; and in December 2003, Dan and Shelly married. In September 2006, after three years of marriage, they divorced. Shelly reported divorcing Dan due to his substance abuse. Shelly and Dan attempted several unsuccessful reunifications in 2007.

Medical and Mental Health

Shelly's childhood medical history is unremarkable. All three of Shelly's children were delivered by C-section. At age 29, Shelly underwent an appendectomy. In 2004 at age 35, Shelly was diagnosed with diabetes and hypoglycemia. The doctor recommended a healthy diet and weight loss. During the summer of 2007, at age 36, she underwent surgery for the removal of an ovarian cyst. Shelly reported that she is currently in good health. Shelly received individual therapy when she was an adolescent. In May 2007, after they were legally divorced, Shelly and Dan attended couple's counseling with the same mental health therapist, Stanley Shelton, LMHC, Shelly had seen as an adolescent. They attended four or five sessions with the counselor. Shelly has continued to see Mr. Shelton over the past two years. She perceives her therapy has helped her look at herself and take responsibility in her decisions and mistakes. She denied any further mental health history.

Ability to Achieve Goals

Shelly was a good student until the fifth grade, when her parents began to have marital problems. Shelly attended a public school for six months during the sixth grade and then was transferred by her mother to a private school. She attended private school through eleventh grade, transferred to public school for twelfth grade, and then dropped out of high school prior to completing her last year. Shelly worked for her mother's insurance agency briefly after high school before moving to Panama City, Florida. While in Panama City, Shelly maintained employment for two years at a pizza restaurant. In 1989, Shelly returned to Arcadia and began working for her mother's insurance agency where she has been employed as a secretary by her mother for the past two decades. Shelly has never been arrested or charged with a crime.

Alcohol and Drug History

Shelly tried alcohol for the first time at the age of 24. She reported that she went out to dance clubs approximately two or three times a year, having two alcohol-based drinks per occasion. Her drinking has remained the same over the years. On the Forensic Parent History Questionnaire, Shelly wrote that she drinks "two to three times a year, having one to two glasses of wine per occasion." She prefers white zinfandel or Riesling wine. She has never had a problem with alcohol, and her last drink was in July 2009. Shelly denied the use of illicit drugs or abuse of prescription drugs at any time in her life. The alcohol history provided by Shelly is inconsistent with her report of meeting the father of her first child in a bar when she was 20 years old. Discrepancies are also found between her reports of very limited consumption of alcohol, frequenting bars and clubs as her primary social venue, and meeting all her significant relationships at various bars. Dan also stated that Shelly enjoyed partying with his band. Although Shelly may have minimized her alcohol consumption and illicit drug experimentation, Shelly has never been arrested or charged with DUI, and there are no documents or collateral reports that Shelly has ever been treated for substance abuse or that substance use has interfered with her daily functioning.

Alcohol and Drug Testing

For descriptions of alcohol and drug testing, refer to Dan's Alcohol and Drug Testing section.

On December 2, 2009, upon request, Shelly provided urine, blood, and hair specimens for analysis by United States Drug Testing Laboratory. Drug testing included a 12-panel drug analysis. Results from urine and hair specimens were negative for all drugs tested. Alcohol testing was also conducted with Shelly, using urine and blood specimens. The results for the urine specimen indicate that in the past three to five days prior to testing Shelly had not ingested any alcohol and did not attempt to dilute or adulterate her urine specimen. The results for the blood specimen indicate that Shelly had not consumed large quantities of alcohol over the previous two or three weeks.

Psychological Testing

For cautions in personality test interpretation, refer to Dan's Psychological Testing section.

On November 15, 2009, Shelly was administered the MMPI-2. Shelly produced a valid profile with the following validity scales' T-scores:

VRIN	TRIN	F	FB	FP	FBS	L	K	S
42	65T	44	42	41	55	58	63	66

Her MMPI-2 clinical scales' T-scores are as follows:

Hs	D	Hy	Pd	Mf	Pa	Pt	Sc	Ma	Si
56	55	63	66	52	63	51	46	37	46

Shelly's MMPI-2 validity scales T-scores suggest she was slightly defensive, but basically approached this measure in an open and honest way. With the exception of her scale 3 (Hy), 4 (Pd), and 6 (Pa), Shelly's T-scores are reasonably congruent with the normative T-scores for female custody litigants in the Bathurst et al. (1997) and Butcher (1997) studies. Although a T-score of 66 on Pd is not a significantly high score in the overall MMPI-2 normative data, it is relatively high for a female custody litigant. As Graham (2006, p. 74) puts it, scale 4 (Pd) can be conceptualized "as a measure of rebelliousness." The relative elevations on scales 3 (Hy) and 6 (Pa) are also high for female custody litigants, and some possible personality symptoms and behaviors are suggested, such as suspiciousness, moderate tension, anxiety, somatic complaints, and possible deeply seated hostility towards family members. An individual with this type of MMPI-2 profile may exhibit self-centeredness (refer to Dan's Psychological Testing section for the note of caution when interpreting psychological test data.)

Shelly's MMPI-2 data from the Myers' February 2009 evaluation are as follows:

VRIN	TRIN	F	FB	FP	FBS	L	K	S
42	50	48	46	49	51	52	63	66

Hs	D	Hy	Pd	Mf	Pa	Pt	Sc	Ma	Si
59	55	63	58	52	68	51	50	49	32

A comparison of Shelly's two MMPI-2 profiles suggests she was reporting in early 2009 relatively less social and family conflict (Pd) than she reported approximately nine months later, and a relatively high degree of suspiciousness and feeling threatened (Pa). Her validity scales from these two profiles showed she was moderately defensive during both test administrations. Both MMPI-2 profiles suggest some relatively stable personality features of likely self-centeredness and a tendency to somaticize her emotions.

David Miller, Shelly's boyfriend

David is a Caucasian male who moved in with Shelly during the summer of 2007. He grew up in an intact family with four younger siblings. His father was a blue-collar worker, and his mother was a full-time homemaker. His parents are Baptist, and the family attended church every Sunday and Wednesday. His mother and father equally disciplined the children and used spanking with their hand for punishment when the children were young, and removal of privileges when the children were older. David never experienced sexual, physical, or emotional abuse as a child. He was actively involved in baseball from age six through high school. His parents both attended his baseball games. He was an average student and never failed a grade or subject. He was never suspended or expelled from school and was not a delinquent during his juvenile years. He has experienced a close relationship with his father, mother, and siblings during his childhood, adolescence, and adult years. His siblings are married with children and maintain steady blue-collar jobs. David attended electrician school after graduating from high school and has been employed by the same company as an electrician for the past two decades. He married his high school sweetheart and had one child during their marriage. They were married for seven years and share custody of Josh. Their son rotates between their homes on a weekly time-sharing basis. Following his divorce and until he moved in with Shelly, David lived with his parents. David met Shelly at the school their children attend. David and Shelly dated for approximately one month prior to David moving into Shelly's house; they had known each other casually through their children's school activities for one year before dating.

David perceives Shelly to be an outstanding and protective mother. He believes that Quinn has been sexually abused by his father. David reported that he and Shelly are very involved in the lives of the children. David reported that he tries to help out with the children and their schoolwork. While Maria, Sophia, and Josh are self-motivated and independently do their homework, Quinn resists doing his homework. David thinks Shelly should more rigorously monitor and enforce Quinn's completion of homework. Dan reported that Shelly is very "laid back" with her children. David perceives that he and Quinn have a close relationship. He is planning on enrolling Quinn in the same Little League baseball team as Josh.

On November 23, 2009, David was administered the MMPI-2 by Dr. Parker. David produced a valid profile, with the following validity scales' T-scores:

VRIN	TRIN	F	FB	FP	FBS	L	K	S
46	57T	42	46	41	64	52	60	60

David's MMPI-2 clinical scales' T-scores are as follows:

Hs	D	Hy	Pd	Mf	Pa	Pt	Sc	Ma	Si
57	54	65	50	52	53	51	47	56	37

The elevation of scale 3 (Hy) suggests some possible tendency to somaticize his reactions to stress and/or a proneness to needing attention. In light of his history, he may be someone who can be naively optimistic about other people.

CHILD HISTORY AND OBSERVATIONS

The alleged child victim's cognitive, behavioral, social, and emotional functioning is important to evaluate as well as any medical or physical handicaps that may create greater vulnerability for exacerbation of medical problems, educational problems, or exploitation. Observations of the child individually and observations with each parent may assist in understanding the parent–child relationship at the time of the observation, as well as offer a comparison of current interactions vis-à-vis known interactions prior to the sexual abuse allegations. Videotaping of interviews with the child is conducted when there is an allegation

of abuse. Interviews addressing substantive issues should use a structured protocol, such as the National Institute of Child Health and Human Development (NICHD) Investigative Interview Protocol (Lamb, Hershkowitz, Orbach, & Esplin, 2008; Lamb, Orbach, Hershkowitz, Esplin, & Horowitz, 2007), with the alleged victim. All interviews with alleged victims of sexual abuse should be videotaped so that an electronic record can be provided for review by other professionals. Research is robust in showing that interviewers are highly inaccurate in documenting their specific questions and the child's responses to those questions (Ceci & Bruck, 2000).

Quinn—Observations and Interviews of Child

Quinn has curly light brown hair, blue eyes, and freckles. He is tall for his chronological age. He was consistently appropriately dressed for the weather and for a six-year-old boy. Quinn's unstable family environment is documented in the above two sections, "Allegations of Child Sexual Abuse and Threatened Harm" and "Relationship of Parents."

Brief History

His primary caretaker from infancy to toddlerhood was his father. During this period of development, his needs may or may not have been met, due to his primary caretaker's abuse of alcohol. From ages three to six, Quinn's primary caretaker has been his mother. During the past three years, Quinn's relationship with his father has been affected by withholding of father–son visitation, his mother's fear for Quinn's safety with his father, and multiple interviews questioning Quinn about his father's behaviors. Quinn's childhood medical history is unremarkable with the exception of asthma. His educational history indicates that he has successfully adjusted to an educational environment from preschool, at age three, to kindergarten. During his current kindergarten year, Quinn's teacher has voiced concern regarding Quinn's distractibility, incomplete classroom work, and missing homework.

Total Sessions with Quinn

Quinn was interviewed, observed, and evaluated in a number of different settings, including: four times at a county child-advocacy interview center, in order to videotape all interviews and individual sessions; one time at his mother's home with his mother, his sisters, mother's boyfriend, and son of mother's boyfriend; one time at his paternal grandmother's home with his father; and two times at my office for a teaching session conducted by each parent. Quinn was seen eight times altogether, for a total of ten hours.

First Session

Quinn's first session was on November 7, 2009. Initially, Quinn was observed to be a withdrawn and guarded child. At the time of the November session, Quinn had been interviewed by the Child Protection Investigators seven times; twice each by his pediatrician, psychiatrist Dr. Georgia Holder, and the first court-appointed evaluator, Dr. Wayne Myers; and experienced four sessions of play therapy focused on disclosure of abuse. It is unknown how many times he was questioned by his mother, father, or other family friends and relatives regarding the allegations of sexual abuse.

As requested, Quinn was brought to his first session by his maternal aunt, who was the neutral person agreed upon by both parents and was a person familiar to Quinn. Quinn separated from her with some hesitancy and reluctance. This first interview was videotaped. During the 60-minute session, Quinn avoided any conversation about his family and would not make eye contact. He reported he liked to ride his bike, play with army men, and play his videogames. When asked the names of people who live in his house or family activities, he either did not respond or responded "I don't know." Quinn's cognitive functioning was informally assessed to be average or above average. His social and emotional functioning did not appear to be within normative expectation, possibly negatively affected by the instability in relationships with his primary attachment figures. At his first session, Quinn made no disclosures about abuse, and a formal forensic child sexual abuse interview was not attempted.

Second Session

Quinn's mother brought Quinn to his second session. In the waiting room, he appeared to be in a fetal position on his mother's lap and was clinging to her blouse. Quinn refused to separate from his mother. His mother also appeared anxious and was invited into the session with Quinn. During this session, Quinn was not asked substantive questions, and the mother was asked not to question

Quinn, but to be an observer. Quinn again was reticent to answer any questions about his family. He played with plastic army men and participated in art activities. Again, when asked to identify names of family members or family activities, Quinn was nonresponsive or responded, "I don't know." If I probed for seemingly neutral information about his family, he physically withdrew from me and became sullen. After seeing a photo of my dog, he informed me he liked dogs. Quinn appeared to enjoy playing with me but remained guarded throughout the hour. Although he refused to allow his mother to leave the play room, he did not pay attention to her and did not seek her out for comfort. Quinn did not initiate affection, such as hugging, with his mother. On two occasions he reported he had a stomachache. Quinn was not asked any substantive questions during his second interview and made no disclosures about abuse.

Third Session

Quinn's father and paternal grandmother, the visitation supervisor, brought Quinn to his third session. Quinn's behavior was significantly different at this session. In the waiting room he sat on his father's lap and was relaxed and cheerful. He did not appear anxious to separate from his father but wanted his father to come into the interview room so he could show his father my toys. Quinn allowed his father to leave, and Quinn remained with me. He was talkative and reported that his grandmother had gotten a kitten. Quinn was verbally engaged when talking about his activities with his father but remained reluctant to talk about his activities at home with his mother. When questioned about his activities with his mother, David, Josh, Maria, or Sophia, he was silent or would change the subject. However, he reported that he liked his mother's boyfriend, David, and his son, Josh. Quinn reported that his father is a good cook. He has his own bed at this father's house, and he and his father sleep in the same room. Quinn reported that he and he father sleep in their own beds and the only thing that he does not like about sharing a bedroom with his father is that his father snores. Quinn reported that he and his father like to play army, build forts, and ride bikes. Quinn's social skills were observed to be within normative expectations for a 6-year-old boy. He was playful and, at times, silly and attention-seeking. His emotional functioning was very different from his first 2 sessions; he was cheerful and inquisitive. This change in behavior could possibly have been related to Quinn having 2 previous sessions and becoming less anxious with me. However, this explanation does not account for the significantly different interactions I observed between Quinn and each parent. When he returned to the waiting room, Quinn greeted his father with a hug and presented him with artwork he had created during the session. Quinn was not asked any substantive questions during his third interview and made no disclosures about abuse.

Fourth Session

The parents were again asked to agree upon a neutral person to bring Quinn to a fourth interview. This interview was a formal forensic child sexual abuse (CSA) interview. The videotapes of the first three sessions showed that Quinn had not been previously questioned by me regarding the allegations of CSA. The NICHD Interview Protocol was used, and its structured steps were followed. Upon being asked open-ended questions, Quinn reported that his father touched his peeper, and when asked to tell me more about his father touching his peeper, Quinn reported that he knows it happened because his mother told him. Quinn did not remember a time when his father touched his peeper. Quinn disclosed that his father touched his peeper with his hand but did not disclose other sexual abuse such as anal penetration or French kissing allegedly perpetrated by his father, or Quinn touching his father's penis or anus. Quinn reported that he likes to be with his father, and his father and grandmother are nice to him. He noted that his parents don't like each other and his mother does not want him to be with his father. His sisters, David, and David's son Josh think his father is "bad." Quinn reported that he likes David and Josh; they are nice to him. He further reported that no one hurts him and if any one hurt him he would tell his father and David.

Following Quinn's structured interview, he was administered the Structured Child Assessment of Relationships in Families (SCARF; Strachan, Lund & Garcia, 2010). Although more research needs to be conducted on this instrument before relying on the quantitative scores, it provides a potentially non-threatening structured interview format where the child uses colorful stamps to provide his or her response to questions about parents and other family members. The questionnaire

items are organized into four major dimensions with sub-scales within each:

(1) Emotional Security: subscales—security, closeness, and emotional support;
(2) Positive Parenting: subscales—practical caretaking, fostering the child's development, setting clear limits, and expectations and positive reinforcement;
(3) Negative Parenting; and
(4) Co-Parenting: subscales—support and undermining.

Compared to children in the normative group, Quinn endorsed fewer items that indicated a perception of emotional security with his mother. He indicated a perception of positive parenting demonstrated by his mother, but he did not perceive his mother as firm in setting limits. There were several items endorsed by Quinn that suggested negative parenting behaviors exhibited by his mother, including his mother being too busy to pay attention to him, and one item indicating that his mother does not keep promises. Quinn's responses indicated that he has a positive perception of his mother's boyfriend, David, who received moderate endorsement on Positive Parenting items and no item endorsement on Negative Parenting. Quinn's responses to items regarding his father indicated a perception of Positive Parenting demonstrated by his father, with high item endorsement on the subscales Closeness and Emotional Responsiveness, and no endorsement of Negative Parenting items. Quinn did not endorse the red-flag items, such as, "Is there anyone who touches you in a way you don't like?" or "Is there anyone who is nasty?" Quinn had high item endorsement on the Co-Parenting, Undermining subscale, indicating Quinn perceives his parents as lacking a positive co-parenting relationship. Quinn's item endorsement on the SCARF indicates Quinn perceives he lacks emotional security with his mother, father, and David, which leads to a hypothesis that he does not currently have a secure parenting figure. The remainder of the relatives identified by Quinn as family members received moderate or low item endorsement on all scales.

Observation of Father and Son

Quinn was observed interacting at home of his father for two hours, during late afternoon and dinner time, and a second time during a structured teaching activity at my office.

Home Observation

I visited Dan and Quinn at the paternal grandmother's home on December 1, 2009, where I observed the family during a meal and unstructured family time. Dan currently resides with his mother, Jennifer; she is the court-appointed supervisor of father–son visits. The back porch was Quinn's organized play area, and he was playing with his army men when I arrived. The two-bedroom house was clean and well organized. Throughout my visit, Dan was good at setting limits and following through with most of his requests of Quinn. Jennifer appeared distractible and several times left Quinn unsupervised with his father. She had a new kitten, which she let out of the house, became worried about the whereabouts of the kitten, and left Quinn unsupervised to go outside and look for the kitten. Another time, when Quinn was unsupervised, Quinn and his father went bike riding and stopped to build a fort. Jennifer is 70-plus years old, frail, and not athletically inclined, and could not possibly accompany her son and grandson on these activities.

We sat down to a midday meal soon after I arrived. Dan helped his mother set the table for dinner. Quinn asked to sit by his father during dinner. Quinn asked his father why he did not pick him up today. Dan responded, "Because your mom was nice enough to drive you." Dan had cooked the dinner, and Jennifer reported that Dan cooks most of their meals. Dinner was yellow rice, chicken, peas, and black beans, and Dan served Quinn a small serving, appropriate for a six-year-old. Quinn was cheerful and joked with his father while at the dinner table. The television was on throughout the entire visit. It was on a sports channel showing a football game. The grandmother appeared confused and commented several times that it was very unusual they were not eating in front of the television.

After dinner, Dan asked Quinn what he would like to do. Quinn responded that he wanted to play baseball. Dan gathered together a baseball and bat, but Quinn became focused on putting together a puzzle, so Dan stopped gathering the baseball materials and joined Quinn on the floor. After Quinn took the puzzle apart, Dan suggested they put it back together again. Quinn ignored the request and

began playing with his army men. Dan appeared to be patient and allowed Quinn to lead him in their play. Next, Dan and Quinn went outside, and Dan pitched Quinn whiffle balls. Quinn had a plastic bat and hit the ball very well. Dan started throwing overhand pitches, which Quinn could not hit. Dan was sensitive to this and began throwing underhand pitches so that Quinn was successful. Quinn pitched the ball to his father and Dan hit the ball. Quinn chased his father around the bases and giggled while running. Dan was observed to be good at providing instructions on pitching and placement of his feet at an appropriate developmental level.

Quinn asked his father to play Army with him, and they commenced in running around the backyard shooting the "bad guys." Quinn then rode his bike with his father running beside him. Quinn built a fort in the bushes. He and his father played Army men and used the bushes as their fort. Quinn rode his bike back to his grandmother's house. He pretended he was wounded and wanted to his father to fix him and wanted to share his water with his father. Dan was very good at engaging with Quinn in fantasy Army play. When Quinn was tired, he and his father sat on the couch and watched a Disney movie. Dan's physical interactions with Quinn were tender and nurturing; Dan rubbed Quinn's head and brushed hair off his forehead. When Quinn's grandmother joined father and son on the couch, Quinn snuggled up against her. During this visit, I did not observe any fear by Quinn of his father or grandmother. Quinn was happy and playful with his father and enjoyed affection from both his grandmother and father. Dan exhibited sensitivity and appropriate expectations for his six-year-old son. Dan showed the capacity to set limits, engage in playful behaviors, and nurture his son. There was no indication in Dan's interactions with Quinn that he lacked the capacity to have empathy.

Teaching Observation

Dan was observed a second time on December 13, 2009, interacting with Quinn. On this occasion, Dan had been asked to organize a learning activity that involved teaching an academic skill that was age-appropriate for Quinn and was a skill Quinn had not yet mastered. He was instructed that the teaching session was to last for one hour. Dan came well prepared to his teaching session with Quinn at the office. His goals were to increase Quinn's knowledge of the classification system of animals and increase his skill in addition. He brought an animal science book, a grease board, grease pens, and a storybook about a frog for Quinn's lesson. The book on animal classification was very advanced, with photographs and detailed written information about different animals. Quinn wanted to play Army men. Dan brought him three Army men and Quinn gave them to me and told me the Army men were for me. Quinn looked in all the drawers in my office and asked if there were Army men in there. He had his finger up his nose, and Dan told him to stop this behavior. He continued to put his finger in his nose, and Dan asked twice if he needed a tissue. Quinn responded no, but he appeared to need a Kleenex. He continued to pick his nose and put his fingers in his mouth. Dan handed him a Kleenex and asked him to blow his nose.

Dan requested that Quinn sit on the couch with him throughout the teaching task. Once Quinn settled down to sitting on the couch, he stopped picking his nose. Dan showed Quinn pictures and explained the definition of a "mammal." He showed his son a photo of a giraffe and other mammals. Next, he showed him pictures of primates. He helped Quinn connect with the material by using the movie *Madagascar* as an example. He told him that the king in the movie was a primate. Quinn's attention was fully focused on the book. Quinn leaned against his father while Dan explained several different photographs. Dan asked his son questions about the animals. He incorporated humor into his lesson with questions like, "Would polar bears live in Florida?" Next, he explained the prey-and-predator relationship. The book had sections on reptiles, birds, invertebrates, insects, etc. Although the book was very advanced for a six-year-old child, Dan was very good at keeping Quinn's attention and presenting the information at Quinn's developmental level. Quinn appeared content to lean against his father and listen and ask questions. When they were looking at pictures, Quinn cheerfully talked about his experiences with spiders at school and how a boy in his class held a spider in his hand. Quinn asked his father a lot of questions.

After 25 minutes, Dan put away the animal book and introduced a book about frogs and ponds; the reading level in this book was age-appropriate for Quinn's developmental level. Quinn lay on the couch and leaned his head against his father's side as his father read to him. After finishing the frog story, Dan presented Quinn with markers, a grease board, and pictures of concrete objects. Dan put on the board a picture of one umbrella, a plus sign, and a picture of another umbrella and asked Quinn for the answer. Quinn responded with the correct answer. Dan was verbally very reinforcing. Quinn had difficulty writing his numerals, and Dan patiently assisted him in writing numerals such as 5 and 6. Quinn completed a number of problems and then said "I do not want to do any more of these." Dan was responsive to Quinn's request and told Quinn he knew something Quinn would enjoy more. Dan flipped the grease-board book to a page of different shapes. Quinn was observed to be tired after 40 minutes of learning. He put his hands on his chin and pouted. Dan moved on and the pouting only lasted about a minute. Dan had a good balance of moving on to a different task and setting a firm limit that something needed to be tried. Quinn was cooperative, and even when momentarily frustrated, he was not inappropriate. Quinn wrote his numbers from 0 to 15 and Dan responded with "Terrific" and "Fantastic," and Dan then appropriately ended the lessons after 45 minutes rather than an hour. During this second observation of the interaction between father and son, Dan again exhibited an understanding of Quinn's developmental level, and was appropriately playful and nurturing. Dan organized tasks so that Quinn would feel successful, and changed the learning activities throughout the hour so that Quinn would not become bored. The one weakness Dan demonstrated was introducing too many new words and concepts when he presented Quinn with the book on animals. Quinn, again, showed no fear of his father and appeared to enjoy being physically close to his father. When Quinn first entered the evaluation room with his father he exhibited some anxiety that was demonstrated by him picking his nose. This behavior stopped when Quinn sat by his father on the couch and he and his father began to examine the photographs of animals in a book.

Observation of Mother and Son

Quinn was observed interacting at home of his mother for two hours, during late afternoon and dinner time, and a second time during a structured teaching activity at my office.

Home Observation

I visited Shelly's home on December 8, 2009. In June 2008, David Miller and his eight-year-old son Josh moved into Shelly's house. Quinn has lived in this house since he was born. The family has six cats. When I arrived, I was met outside the house by Quinn. I was introduced by Quinn to neighbors Tommy and Greg, sibling Sophia, and David's son, Josh. Quinn showed me his video games and his room, which is next to Sophia's room, on the second floor of the house. His bedroom was appropriately decorated for a young boy. His room held toys organized into bins, several bookshelves with books, and a keyboard and drum. Quinn said that David's son Josh (who lives with Quinn) had cockroaches in his room. The house appeared to have been straightened up but it did not appear very clean. The swimming pool was very dirty. Quinn stated that he swims almost every day. There were superhero toys in bins on the front porch that were full of dead cockroaches and other dead bugs. Josh, David's son, brought their cat Walter to meet me. Quinn's oldest sister, Maria, politely introduced herself to me. Josh and Sophia worked on homework. Sophia reported she was good at English and showed me how she is adept at spelling words. All four children appeared to enjoy and want positive adult attention. Shelly finished cooking dinner while Quinn showed me around the house. When the salad and shepherd's pie were prepared, Maria sat down at the dinner table and began to eat dinner by herself. Sophia then helped herself to dinner while Shelly and David chatted and Quinn and Josh busied themselves with other activities. Josh showed me his other cat, Princess. All the children, one by one, sat at the table and began eating before Shelly and David eventually joined them. Quinn wanted me to sit next to him and asked for iced tea so we could drink the same beverage. Quinn wanted me to have the same salad dressing as him, as well.

During the meal, Shelly and David talked and asked the four children about their day. It was a very relaxed conversation. After dinner, Sophia practiced piano and Josh finished his homework. Quinn played a video game called Army Men Helicopters. Quinn was very social, affectionate, and well-behaved. He talked easily with his siblings, mother, and David. He smiled at me frequently throughout my visit. Each child was very friendly and talkative. Quinn helped Josh and David work on a volcano for a school project. Next, he played with tubs of Nerf dart guns, superhero figurines, Army tanks, helicopters, etc. There were several tubs filled with toys on the screened-in porch. All four children eventually went outside to play. Both David and Shelly gave instructions to all of the children. David asked Quinn and Josh if they wanted to hit some balls. Quinn responded "no" and continued to play with his own toys. Quinn asked his mother to find him different toys several times. Quinn eventually ran to Josh and David and said he wanted to play ball with them. Shelly got Quinn's mitt for him and helped him get his shoes on. Quinn, Sophia, and Josh took turns hitting the ball pitched by David and running the bases. David was very patient with all three children. Quinn appeared to be happy and relaxed with his mother, David, Josh, and his sisters. The four children were social, engaging, and did not appear to be guarded in my presence. David interacted more with the boys compared to Shelly, but Shelly was readily available if Quinn needed her help. During my visit there were no negative comments made by the adults or children in reference to Quinn's biological father.

Teaching Observation

Shelly was observed a second time on December 18, 2009, interacting with Quinn. On this occasion Shelly had been asked to organize a learning activity that involved teaching an academic skill that was age-appropriate for Quinn and was a skill Quinn had not yet mastered. She was instructed that the teaching session was to last for one hour. Shelly came prepared for the teaching task with a plastic bin full of toys, which she never utilized during her teaching. She also brought a math exercise workbook that was already partially completed. Shelly did not appear to have a structured plan for teaching Quinn a new academic skill or working on newly learned skills. Quinn lay on the floor and Shelly sat at a table. Shelly gave Quinn the opportunity to choose his first lesson. Quinn chose math and she gave him the workbook. Shelly chose a page in the workbook and asked Quinn to count objects and write the corresponding number. Quinn turned to pages he had already completed. He then went back to the page he had started and looked at it and said he did not want to do that page either; he reported he had a stomachache. He chose another page and wrote the number 9 for the number of glasses of milk. Quinn flipped to another page where Shelly instructed him to mark the picture that had 8 objects. He incorrectly put an X on the picture of 9 objects; this error reflected carelessness and lack of motivation rather than Quinn's lack of knowledge. Quinn told Shelly he did not want to do that page either and flipped to another one. Shelly then selected three pages from the workbook, tore them out, and placed them on the floor in front of Quinn so he would look at one sheet at a time. Shelly was very focused on Quinn and gave him instructions for each workbook page. Quinn was asked to color in parts of a rocket ship by numbers that identified the color. He had to read numbers 1 through 5 and color the worksheet according to a key at the top of the page. This exercise appeared to be using a skill six-year-old Quinn already had developed, rather than teaching him a new skill or increasing his skill development to a higher level.

Next, Quinn was asked to draw five rowboats in a picture next to a person fishing. Shelly held his hand and helped him make the shape of a rowboat. Quinn was more focused on doing the art than learning the math. He created an elaborate boat rather than five rowboats. Shelly did not pursue the math task, but instead watched him decorate the boat. Quinn was very talkative and asked his mother several questions. Quinn continued to lie on the floor on his stomach while drawing. When Quinn finished his drawing, Shelly gave Quinn a small, numbered keyboard. Shelly called out numbers to Quinn so he could push the corresponding key and make a song. Quinn only played one song on the keyboard and then stated he no longer wanted to do this exercise. Shelly again presented Quinn the workbook and asked him to identify the pages he wanted to complete.

Approximately 50 minutes of the teaching session was Shelly's observation of Quinn coloring objects in the workbook rather than teaching him new information and concepts. Both Shelly and Quinn were relaxed, and Shelly did not set limits on Quinn. Shelly did not demonstrate an organized approach to teaching; it appeared she had grabbed Quinn's used workbook and some toys without much of a plan. The academics that Shelly did present Quinn were skills he had already mastered. Quinn was in charge throughout this one-hour session.

STANDARDIZED QUESTIONNAIRES—DAN AND SHELLY RESPONDENTS

The "Children's Behavior Checklist (CBC) Ages 6 to 18" was administered to Quinn's father and mother in order to obtain their perceptions of Quinn's competencies and problems. Quinn's Total Competence score was in the normal range for parents' ratings of boys aged six to 11, when both Shelly and Dan were the respondents. Both Dan and Shelly also endorsed items that produced elevated Internalizing scores on Quinn, which fell in the Borderline Clinical and Clinical ranges, respectively. These results indicate that Quinn's parents report their son demonstrates problems of an internalizing nature. Quinn's father endorsed items that produced externalizing scores in the average range, and Shelly's endorsement of externalizing items produced scores in the Clinical range. On the DSM-oriented scales, Quinn's scores were in the Borderline Clinical range for somatic problems with Shelly as the respondent. Quinn's scores on the anxiety problems were also in the Borderline Clinical range when Shelly was the respondent and in the Normal range when Dan was the respondent.

The CBC scores indicated that Quinn is most likely to exhibit his stress through physical symptoms, such as headaches and stomachaches, and more likely to show his distress through oppositional or aggressive behaviors when with his mother in contrast to his father.

On the CBC, in reply to the question *What concerns you the most about your child?* Shelly wrote, "He is very sensitive—that he might be confused trying to deal with abuse sexual and emotional from his father." Dan wrote, "How his parents' divorce will affect him and how his mother's alienation of me will harm him." When asked *Please describe the best things about your child,* Shelly wrote, "Loving—sweet disposition—funny—smart—cute kid." Dan wrote, "He is smart, sensitive, and funny."

On the Children's Sexual Behavior Inventory, with Dan as the respondent, Quinn's scale scores were not elevated on the Developmentally Related Sexual Behaviors (DRSB) or Sexual Abuse Specific Items (SASI), in contrast to Quinn's significantly elevated scale scores on the SASI with Shelly as the respondent. This suggests that Shelly observes Quinn exhibiting highly aberrant sexualized behaviors, which are at times exhibited by sexually abused children, while Dan does not observe aberrant sexualized behaviors. Quinn's teacher reported that Quinn does not exhibit sexualized behavior in the classroom or in other settings at school.

COLLATERALS

The personal collateral sources provided to me by Shelly and Dan were limited and did not provide substantial information to assist in supporting or negating the allegations of CSA. The dearth of personal contacts provided to me may have been significant in reflecting the limited intimate friendships experienced by both Shelly and Dan. Collateral professional sources, including child protection investigators, Quinn's pediatrician, and the previous forensic evaluator, Dr. Myer, unanimously reported concerns regarding Shelly's refusal to acknowledge the possibility that Quinn was not the victim of sexual abuse perpetrated by his father and alleged by the ongoing reports to child protection services. Quinn's pediatrician also provided information that indicated during this evaluation that Shelly's description of the pediatrician's recommendations to her regarding Quinn's needing protection from his father were embellishments by Shelley. Written documents, including depositions, documentation of DUIs, and random substance abuse testing, were useful collateral data sources in substantiating Dan's serious long-term problem with abusing alcohol and illegal drugs.

SUMMARY

Quinn was born to Dan and Shelly on October 1, 2003. The childhoods of Dan and Shelly have several positive and negative similarities. Neither Dan nor Shelly was sexually exploited, physically abused, or visually and verbally exposed to adult sexual or sexualized behavior. They were raised in middle-class neighborhoods and were not exposed to violent neighborhoods and community crime. Both were the youngest children in their families and learned information about adult sexual behavior from overhearing their older siblings and receiving information from their peers. They each had early nurturing experiences with at least one parent, had positive experiences with their older siblings, and their histories were absent any delinquent behaviors during their juvenile years. During childhood, both Dan and Shelly experienced potentially traumatizing experiences with their fathers. Dan's father was a chronic alcoholic who was verbally abusive to his children and wife but also could be emotionally nurturing and was actively involved in Dan's sports when he was not inebriated. Dan's mother was nurturing but dependent and unable to protect Dan from his father's alcoholic rages. Shelly's father was a stay-at-home parent and her primary caretaker until she was 11 years old, and he then abandoned Shelly after he and Shelly's mother divorced. Shelly's mother was a successful businesswoman who was emotionally and physically unavailable to Shelly. Dan coped with his father's alcoholism through music and success in school. As an adult, Dan earned bachelor's and master's degrees at major universities. Unlike Dan, Shelly was unable to find positive coping strategies for handling her abandonment by her father. Commencing in sixth grade, Shelly lost her motivation to be successful in school. She eventually dropped out of high school, worked at a pizza restaurant for several years, had her first child out of wedlock in her early twenties, and gave birth to her second child out of wedlock by her mid-twenties.

At the time Dan and Shelly met, they were in their mid- and early 30s, respectively. At that time, Dan played in a band at night and was employed full-time as an environmental scientist. Shelly's mother had bought Shelly a house, and Shelly worked as a secretary for her mother. Dan also was an active alcoholic and had a history of DUIs that were unknown to Shelly. Dan received his fifth DUI the day he moved into Shelly's house. Dan and Shelly moved in together one month after they met, and Shelly gave birth to their son Quinn 10 months later. They married several months after the birth of Quinn. Their marriage was unstable; Dan continued to be an active alcoholic, and Shelly primarily financially supported the family. Dan was a stay-at-home father due to the loss of his driver's license after conviction of his fifth DUI and was Quinn's primary caretaker until he and Shelly separated when Quinn was age two. The divorce and post-divorce were amicable until Dan and Shelly experienced two failed attempts at reunification, and Shelly then moved her current boyfriend and his son into her home. Approximately one year following their divorce, Shelly began restricting Dan's time-sharing with Quinn, and multiple reports that Dan was physically and sexually abusing Quinn began to emerge. Child Protection Services closed eight reported cases of the abuse of Quinn as "Unfounded"; Quinn was interviewed seven times by CPIs during these investigations and was repeatedly questioned by Shelly. The court ordered an evaluation of the allegations of child sexual abuse to be conducted by Dr. Myers, a forensic psychologist. Shelly did not accept Dr. Myers's finding that CSA was unsubstantiated. Following Dr. Myers's evaluation, the court ordered the current evaluation to be conducted.

The interviews with and observations of Quinn suggest that he has an emotionally close relationship with his father and that the allegations by Shelly of Quinn's fear of his father are not substantiated by Quinn's verbal information provided during interviews or observations of his interactions with his father. The multiple investigations, forensic evaluations, and repeated questioning of Quinn have negatively impacted his sense of security and created anxiety and confusion regarding his relationships with his primary attachment figures. Evaluation of Dan did not find features, characteristics, or behaviors that would put him at risk for sexual exploitation of children, with the exception of his alcohol and substance abuse, and it is undetermined whether Shelly's adamant pursuit of positive findings that Quinn is the victim of sexual abuse by his father may or may not be for Quinn's protection. These findings are not determinative as to whether or not Quinn is the victim of sexual abuse by his father, and the ultimate decision must be determined by the Court. The next section provides four hypotheses for the Court's consideration.

HYPOTHESES

The Court will make the ultimate decision regarding whether Quinn was the victim of sexual abuse. Central to an objective analysis of child sexual abuse allegations, the evaluator must consider multiple hypotheses. In this case, five hypotheses were considered. The following hypotheses may aid the Court in its decision-making regarding the sexual abuse allegations.

Hypothesis One

The child is probably not the victim of sexual abuse, but a sincere, hypervigilant parent and/or caretaker inaccurately believes her child is the victim of sexual abuse. The concerned caretaker unintentionally contaminates the child's perspective.

The data reviewed gives the greatest weight to Hypothesis One and Hypothesis Two (the latter is discussed below). Shelly and Dan legally separated in September 2006; Quinn was two years, 11 months old at that time. Following the separation, Quinn did not see Dan on a daily or every-other-day basis, which would make it difficult for a two- or three-year-old child to maintain a secure attachment to a parent figure. In January 2007, Shelly and Dan were legally divorced. In March 2007, Shelly and Dan attempted to reunite, but this was unsuccessful and conflicted, and this couple exposed their young son to some of their conflict. From May to June 2007, according to Shelly, she was picking up Dan for his visits with Quinn because Dan did not have a car. When spending the night with his father at Dan's mother's house, Quinn exhibited problems with separating from his mother. Because of Quinn's young age when his parents separated, and because of the inconsistency in contact with his father when he was three years old, Quinn was at high risk of showing symptoms of anxiety when he was separated from his mother and left with his father. For example, young children may be very anxious when they are first taken to a new daycare facility, but after going every day for a period of time, they develop a feeling of safety.

During the first year after the separation of his parents, Quinn's visits were not stable enough for him to develop a feeling of safety due to his parents' failed attempts at reunification, intense arguments upon repeated separations, and Shelly's interference in Dan and Quinn's time-sharing when she and Dan were not living together. Furthermore, Quinn may have felt Shelly's anxiety about leaving him with Dan, because of her concerns over Dan's drinking and drug use. Shelly may have misinterpreted Quinn's symptoms of anxiety as symptoms of sexual abuse; and therefore began to question Quinn; and through questioning contaminated Quinn's memory.

The first report to Child Protection authorities took place on October 25, 2007, when a report was filed that Dan was using illicit drugs and Quinn was at risk of exposure to illicit drug use by his father. At that time, Dan had lost his driver's license due to a DUI. The Child Protection intake summary reads: "There is ongoing concern for the father's ability to care for Quinn due to his substance abuse. The father was forced to participate in rehabilitation after his third DUI arrest. He is drinking and using drugs again; cocaine is his drug of choice." The case was closed as unfounded, but based on the information collected for this evaluation, there is a high probability Dan was using illicit drugs and alcohol at the time of the first report to Child Protection. At that time, Shelly was legitimately concerned about Quinn's safety due to Dan's alcoholism and drug use.

Six months after the first report to Child Welfare, Quinn reportedly disclosed to his maternal aunt his sexual abuse and identified his father as the perpetrator. Quinn's reported disclosure to his maternal aunt occurred after his aunt had picked Quinn up at school and questioned Quinn about why he was wetting his pants at school. His aunt reported that Quinn told her that he was wetting his pants because his dad touched his penis. The aunt further reported, following this statement by Quinn, she and Quinn had approximately a four-hour conversation about his father touching him, because Quinn only revealed small pieces of information a little at a time. Shelly's sister informed Shelly, and Quinn reportedly told his mother the same information he had disclosed to his aunt. Since Shelly's sister and Shelly are not trained interviewers, the potential for asking Quinn leading questions and obtaining unreliable information is very high.

Quinn's first disclosure of sexual abuse to his aunt, during which five-year-old Quinn gave his aunt the presumed psychological reason that he was wetting his pants, would not be supported by developmental research. At age five, Quinn would not understand that wetting his pants was related to some stressful event in his life. It is therefore likely that Quinn had been asked questions or overheard conversations and been given this idea by some other person prior to his disclosure to his Shelly's sister, or his aunt elicited this cause-and-effect relationship through her questioning. Following Quinn's statement to his aunt, Quinn was interviewed by Child Protection Services on April 19, 2008. Child protection investigators reported no findings of sexual abuse. The report reads: "The mother states that the child told her that the father touched him. The child was interviewed and he knows what his private parts are and points to his penis. He denies that anyone has seen his private parts or that anyone has ever touched his private parts. He states that he sleeps by himself and no one gets in bed with him."

During the next year and a half, Shelly periodically stopped visitation between Dan and Quinn when new allegations of sexual abuse would arise.

Quinn reportedly made new disclosures to his mother. All of the allegations of sexual abuse were deemed "Unfounded" by child protection investigators.

I did not find compelling evidence that Quinn was the victim of sexual abuse by his father. Although Quinn reported to me that his father touched his penis, his behavior and affect did not match the alleged event. When he told me he was touched by his father and I asked where he was touched, he smiled and pointed at his penis. Furthermore, Quinn was observed to show no fear of his father and to enjoy playing and being affectionate with his father, which is not consistent with his allegations to his mother that his father sodomized him. Dan also was evaluated by an expert in the evaluation and treatment of sex offenders.[3] The results of the psychosexual evaluation indicated Dan, other than his alcohol and substance abuse history, did not have characteristics similar to known sex offenders, and did not appear to be a risk for sexual violence. There is, however, compelling evidence that Dan is still actively using drugs and alcohol, which will put Quinn at risk if Dan is allowed unsupervised visits with Quinn. Dan has been deceptive with the Court, Child Protection authorities, this evaluator, and his mother (who is his current supervisor) regarding his continued use of drugs and alcohol. He has somehow managed to produce clean drug and alcohol screens during the random screening conducted by Goodwill Industries.

Hypothesis Two

The child is probably not the victim of sexual abuse, but a parent and/or caretaker is using the allegation of sexual abuse to manipulate the court system during litigation. This hypothesis considers the custody litigation context in which the allegations arise.

This hypothesis has equal weight with Hypothesis One. There are data to indicate that Shelly has interfered repeatedly in the time-sharing between Dan

---

[3] The psychosexual evaluation of Dan included the following: a structured forensic interview, MMPI-2; MMPI-2-RF; Multiphasic Sex Inventory II (MSI-II), Psychosexual Life History (Adult Male Form); PAI, Sexual Violence Risk-20 (SVR-20); Psychopathy Checklist–Screening version; Michigan Alcohol Screening Test (MAST); mental status exam; review of collateral materials; and collateral interviews.

and Quinn. Whether this has been done to manipulate the court or is the result of a frightened mother who has distorted perceptions and misinformation is unknown. Shelly has refused to accept any information from Child Protection authorities or from professionals, such as Dr. Myers, who have determined that Quinn is not the victim of sexual abuse by his father. Although Shelly repeatedly reported statements made to her by her son, multiple professional investigators could not corroborate her accounts. Despite these findings, Shelly put Quinn in therapy at a facility that treats sexually abused children, and Quinn's therapist, Teri Smith, LMHC, supported Shelly's perception that Quinn was the victim of sexual abuse, despite a forensic evaluation by Dr. Myers and multiple, "unfounded" findings by investigations by DCF.

Shelly also alleged that Dan had given Quinn the drugs during his sexual abuse of his son. Quinn was taken to the hospital and given a blood test, the first of which was negative. Shelly reported that the testing was most likely negative because only a urine test was conducted and the drug Ambien does not show up in urine. The second time Shelly took Quinn for drug testing after a visit with his father, the drug Ambien showed up in Quinn's system. Shelly reported that Quinn said his father was giving him pills during his visits. Based on this allegation, the parties' attorneys requested that Shelly and Dan take a polygraph regarding whether Shelly or Dan had given Quinn the drug Ambien.[4] After failing the polygraph test, Shelly acknowledged to the polygrapher that she had the prescription Ambien at her home, but denied giving it to Quinn.

Hypothesis Three
The child is probably a victim of sexual abuse, but due to age or cognitive deficits, does not have the verbal skills to provide a credible description of his abuse.

This hypothesis does not have great weight, given the data reviewed about Quinn. Quinn has the verbal skills to make a credible description.

Hypothesis Four
The child is probably a victim of sexual abuse, but due to fear or misguided loyalty, will not disclose his abuse.

This hypothesis has little weight given the data reviewed, although there is evidence that Quinn's emotionally close relationship with his father may make him vulnerable to misguided loyalty.

Hypothesis Five
The child is probably a victim of sexual abuse and there appear to be credible child disclosures and other factual data to support the finding of sexual abuse.

This hypothesis does not have great weight given the data reviewed.

RECOMMENDATIONS
Although *Carter v. Nelson* has been filed as a modification of custody, the Court requested that this evaluation solely address allegations of CSA. As previously stated, the ultimate decision on Quinn's abuse status is within the purview of the Court and the data presented in this report are to assist in that resolve.

The data contained in this report have identified safety issues, independent of the question of Quinn's sexual victimization, which must also be addressed by the Court. Dan's history of significant alcohol and drug abuse continue to be a serious risk to Quinn's safety and psychological development. Since Dan has not been successful in outpatient therapy and has attempted to mislead evaluators and the Court regarding his alcohol consumption and cocaine use, the Court may need to consider continued supervised father–son time-sharing until substance abuse professionals inform the Court that Dan has successfully completed an inpatient substance abuse program. Shelly's extreme pursuit of the CSA, and (if true) giving Quinn the drug Ambien to prove Dan was drugging their son, suggests psychopathology and also is a risk to Quinn's safety and psychological development. The Court may need to address and require weekly outpatient mental health intervention by a professional with an advanced degree, such as a psychiatrist or clinical psychologist, for Shelly, if Quinn is going to remain in her care.

Signed,
Suzanne Parker, PhD
Licensed Psychologist

---

[4] Polygraph exams were initiated twice by the parties' attorneys during the course of this case. The exams were not initiated by Dr. Parker, nor were the results utilized in her overall evaluation.

TEACHING POINT:
SPECIFIC STRATEGIES FOR PROMOTING IMPARTIALITY IN A PARTICULAR EVALUATION

Conducting evaluations and communicating their findings in an impartial fashion are very important in FMHA. We recommend seven specific steps for promoting and maintaining impartiality in any given case.

First, evaluators should not accept a referral with which they have a conflict of interest, whether personal, professional, or financial. Second, the evaluator should be measured in tone and language in conducting the evaluation and communicating the results (whether in the report or in testimony). Hyperbolic language, unnecessarily critical comments, and an argumentative tone should be avoided. If someone reading the report can anticipate the conclusions by the tone early in the report, then this second recommendation has not been implemented. Third, the report should be clear about the purpose, the standard applied, and the procedures—including how long was spent in each procedure. Fourth, the report should appear thorough and even-handed. The reader should get the sense that the evaluator is being driven toward conclusions by data, rather than having preferred conclusions shape the information that is obtained or described. Fifth, the evaluator should scrupulously avoid premature impressions. This includes offering such impressions to referring attorneys prior to the completion of all necessary work providing the basis for solid conclusions. Even tentative allegiance to a premature conclusion can affect the way subsequent information is gathered and interpreted. Sixth, evaluators should consider alternative explanations to their own conclusions. The Case Two report did this in a formal way borrowed from science: by describing hypotheses and the support for each. Even without such formality, however, the articulation and consideration of alternative explanations provide an important counterweight to accepting a given conclusion too readily. Finally, and related to the previous recommendation, evaluators should rigorously challenge their own findings before submitting a final draft. In addition to fact- and error-checking, this kind of challenge includes questioning the scope and credibility of the information collected, the reasoning by which it is interpreted, and the form and strength of the resulting conclusions.

TEACHING POINT:
MENTAL HEALTH PROFESSIONALS' ROLE IN ASSISTING THE COURT IN DETERMINING THE VERACITY OF ALLEGATIONS OF CHILD SEXUAL ABUSE
(contributed by Kathryn Kuehnle and H. D. Kirkpatrick)

In the adjudicative process there are four major types of judicial proceedings: criminal, civil, administrative, and quasi-criminal (e.g., therapeutic courts) (Melton et al., 2007). States vary in how they organize court divisions of civil judicial proceedings. Various states may hold cases for child custody (i.e., parent responsibility and time-sharing), adoption, and potentially other family matters in "family courts"; child protection matters in "dependency courts"; juvenile delinquency cases in "juvenile courts"; and personal injury or tort proceedings in "general civil courts." Other states may combine child custody and child protection cases in "unified family courts" and handle juvenile delinquency cases in a different court (Kuehnle, Sparta, Kirkpatrick, & Epstein, 2013). In this discussion, we will refer to child custody cases (parenting plan and child access cases) as "family law" matters, child protection cases as "dependency law" matters, and personal injury cases as "tort law" matters.

DEPENDENCY COURT
Mental health (MH) professionals, in most cases, do not conduct formal assessments to assist the court in determining the veracity of allegations of CSA. In initial dependency proceedings, the MH professional is rarely asked to assist the court in assessing the veracity of an allegation of CSA. Such information is most often provided by child protection investigators and child protection teams. Nevertheless, a MH professional, upon a motion by any one of the numerous parties involved in a dependency proceeding, can be appointed to assist the court in addressing the veracity of the CSA. Formal evaluations are conducted by MH professionals to provide treatment recommendations—but not to address the veracity of CSA allegations—following a determination by the court on whether the child is a victim of sexual abuse. MH professionals may also conduct formal evaluations on the needs of the

sexually abused child during a legal proceeding of "termination of parental rights."

In rare cases in dependency court, a court may appoint a MH professional, or the family may privately retain a MH professional, to conduct a formal CSA evaluation. Also, the Guardian *ad litem* or counsel for the child may ask a MH professional to formally assess the allegation of CSA. There may be other unusual circumstances when a MH professional may be retained or appointed to conduct such an assessment. Some of the components of the written report may differ, depending on the identity and relational status of the alleged perpetrator (e.g., biological parent, grandparent, uncle or aunt, adolescent sibling, step-sibling, cousin).

CRIMINAL COURT
MH professionals are not appointed independently to conduct formal assessments to assist the court in determining the veracity of allegations of CSA, although such an appointment may occur in a juvenile criminal court proceeding when the defendant is a child. Under these circumstances, a MH professional may provide forensic services as a trial consultant for the prosecution or the defense. When the child-defendant is indigent and when the child's mental health is a concern, the court-appointed defense counsel may apply to the court to fund a MH consultant to aid defense counsel. Similarly, the prosecution can seek its own MH trial consultant. Private criminal defense attorneys often retain a MH professional. When the defendant is an adult, MH professionals are also frequently retained as trial consultants.

GENERAL CIVIL COURTS (PERSONAL INJURY OR TORT PROCEEDINGS)
In personal injury and tort proceedings, the MH professional is retained by plaintiff's counsel or defense counsel to conduct a formal evaluation to assess the likelihood of injury to the CSA victim that has resulted from the child's sexual victimization experiences. In the majority of cases, the legal finding of sexual victimization of the child has previously been made in another setting (e.g., criminal proceedings), and the MH professional is not retained to focus on the veracity of the sexual abuse allegations. In the minority of CSA personal injury cases, the MH evaluator may be asked to review documents and previous interviews and testify to problems with the reliability of the child's statements, but the MH evaluator is not retained to conduct a formal evaluation with the child regarding the veracity of the allegations of CSA.

FAMILY COURT
MH professionals, in most cases, do conduct formal, independent assessments to assist the court in determining the veracity of allegations of CSA. In family law cases with allegations of child sexual abuse, the MH professional is typically appointed by the court, in response to a motion from either the petitioner or respondent, to conduct a formal evaluation of CSA within a custody/child access evaluation or as a separate, specialized sexual-abuse evaluation. A family court may also appoint an attorney to represent the child; a MH professional may then be appointed, on motion of the child's counsel, to assess CSA. In general, some of the components of the written report may differ, depending on the identity or relational status of the alleged perpetrator (e.g., biological parent, grandparent, uncle or aunt, adolescent sibling, step-sibling, cousin). In *pro se* cases, formal evaluations of CSA are typically not conducted by MH professionals due to the cost, so the veracity of CSA allegations is judged by evidence provided to the court by child protection investigators.

19

Juvenile *Miranda* Waiver Capacity

The two case reports in this chapter focus on the capacities of juvenile defendants to waive their *Miranda* rights (*Miranda v. Arizona*, 1966). For additional discussion of this legal question, see Chapter 2 (this volume). As has been noted elsewhere (Goldstein & Goldstein, 2010), juveniles especially may have "difficulty providing knowing and intelligent waivers of rights" (p. 135). As such, there are particular considerations related to juvenile *Miranda* waiver evaluations (see Otto & Goldstein, 2005). The principle to be applied to the first case concerns the value of nomothetic data, derived from groups and applied to the individual in comparison with the larger group, to FMHA. The teaching point in this case will address the value of specialized forensic assessment instruments (FAIs) (Grisso, 1986) that have been developed and validated for a specific kind of forensic assessment. The second case illustrates the importance of presenting and defending one's opinions effectively, but without becoming adversarial. The associated teaching point addresses the question of whether and how to criticize materials obtained from records in FMHA.

CASE ONE
PRINCIPLE: USE NOMOTHETIC EVIDENCE IN ASSESSING CAUSAL CONNECTION BETWEEN CLINICAL CONDITION AND FUNCTIONAL ABILITIES (*PRINCIPLE 28*)

This principle has been discussed previously in Chapter 2 (this volume), so we will move directly to showing how the present report illustrates the application of this principle. Certain psychological tests may provide information about a juvenile's abilities that are relevant to his capacity to waive *Miranda* rights. These include "traditional tests of intellectual functioning and educational achievement because of their direct relationship to vocabulary, reasoning, and comprehension" (Otto & Goldstein, 2005, pp. 192-93). In addition, neuropsychological or personality testing may be appropriate if there are questions about the effect of a juvenile's cognitive or emotional functioning on his competence to waive these rights.

There are also forensic assessment instruments that have been designed specifically to assess whether a juvenile's waiver was "knowing" and "intelligent." For many years, the seminal *Instruments for Assessing Understanding and Appreciation of Miranda Rights* (Grisso, 1998b) has been recommended as a resource for assessments of *Miranda* waiver capacity (Lally, 2003; Otto & Goldstein, 2005). The four instruments include the Comprehension of Miranda Rights (CMR), designed to assess general understanding of the warnings; the Comprehension of Miranda Rights–Recognition (CMR-R), which assesses a juvenile's ability to "recognize the meaning of each right" (Otto & Goldstein, 2005, p. 194); the Comprehension of Miranda Vocabulary (CMV), which assesses understanding of the vocabulary used in the warnings; and the Function of Rights in Interrogation (FRI), which assesses understanding of the "function of [these rights] in the context of an arrest and interrogation" (p. 194). More recently, *The Miranda Rights Comprehension Instruments* (MCRI; Goldstein, Zelle, & Grisso, 2012) was published and includes an updated version of these instruments. Specifically, the MCRI reflects more recent versions of the warnings and updated juvenile norms, includes the now-common "fifth warning" about the continuing nature of the rights, simplified warning language, minor revisions to clarify scoring criteria, and additional words on the vocabulary measures.

The present case offers a good illustration of using nomothetically based psychological tests and specialized measures to gather relevant information.

Dr. Frumkin administered several psychological tests that measure some aspects of functioning that are relevant to the capacity to waive *Miranda* rights, including the MMPI-A, the WISC-IV, and two sub-tests of the WRAT-4. In addition, he administered several specialized measures that provide information that is even more directly relevant to *Miranda* waiver capacities. These included the Comprehension of *Miranda* Rights (CMR), Comprehension of *Miranda* Rights–Recognition (CMR-R), Function of Rights in Interrogation (FRI), Gudjonsson Suggestibility Scale 1 (GSS 1), and the Gudjonsson Compliance Scale–Forms D and E (GCS). Taken together, the psychological tests and specialized measures yielded nomothetically based empirical support for the measurement of capacities that are specific to this kind of evaluation.

PSYCHOLOGICAL EVALUATION
Name: Nathaniel Doe Case #: 06-XXXX
Birthdate: 6/1/91 (15 years)
Judge: Elliot Snyder
Education: Eighth Grade Date of
Evaluation: 10/25/06
Ethnicity: African-American Date of
Report: 11/9/06
Gender: Male

REASON FOR REFERRAL

Nathaniel Doe was referred for a psychological evaluation by his defense attorney, Mr. Max Brewer. Nathaniel is currently appearing before the Honorable Elliot Snyder of the Juvenile Court of Springfield County, Georgia, on charges of armed robbery of a convenience store. The purpose of the evaluation, as a consultant to Mr. Brewer, was to evaluate Nathaniel's psychological functioning as it pertains to his ability to have made a knowing and intelligent waiver of his *Miranda* rights at the time of the police interrogation, as well as evaluating for psychological factors relevant to the voluntariness of the rights waiver.

PROCEDURES ADMINISTERED

Clinical interview, Minnesota Multiphasic Personality Inventory–Adolescent (MMPI-A), Wechsler Intelligence Scale for Children–Fourth Edition (WISC-IV), Word Reading and Sentence Comprehension subtests of the Wide Range Achievement Test–4 (WRAT-4), Comprehension of Miranda Rights (CMR), Comprehension of Miranda Rights–Recognition (CMR-R), Function of Rights in Interrogation (FRI), Gudjonsson Suggestibility Scale 1 (GSS 1), Gudjonsson Compliance Scale–Forms D and E (GCS).

BACKGROUND INFORMATION

Background information about the case was obtained by speaking to Mr. Brewer and reviewing the following materials: (a) audiotape of Nathaniel's statement, (b) *Miranda* waiver form, (c) Statement Form, (d) Petition for Delinquency, (e) police reports, and (f) various Springfield County intake forms.

Nathaniel was seen individually for a total of 6.75 hours in a room at his attorney's office. Nathaniel's mother, Jeannette Doe, was interviewed alone for one-half hour. She works as a department manager at a local Sears store. Prior to the evaluation, Nathaniel was informed that the results of the assessment were not confidential and would be given to his lawyer to assist him in planning for the case.

Nathaniel was a fair historian as far as relating information about his life. Background data were obtained from both Nathaniel and his mother. At times, the information each one provided was somewhat inconsistent from the other's report.

Nathaniel attends the eighth grade at Valley Middle School. He was born in Chicago. His parents broke up when Ms. Doe was pregnant with him. She and Nathaniel moved to the Atlanta area shortly after his birth. Nathaniel essentially has been raised by his mother. He did live with his maternal grandmother for two years, beginning at age 12 or 13, after Ms. Doe had been arrested for child neglect. After she took the requisite parenting courses, Nathaniel and his three younger siblings went back to live with her. Nathaniel's father lives in Tennessee with Nathaniel's cousin. Nathaniel reported infrequent contact with his father. They do not communicate by telephone, and Nathaniel visits him perhaps once yearly, generally for no more than a day or so.

Nathaniel stated he enjoys riding his bicycle, going to movies, and riding his skateboard. He had been looking for a part-time job prior to his arrest (he has never been employed). Since his arrest, he has been on house arrest. Nathaniel stated he used to have a lot of friends and was rather popular. Many of his friends have since moved away. Thus, Nathaniel describes himself as "the quiet one now."

Nathaniel's school records were unavailable at the time of the preparation of this report. He stated he makes B and C grades, although he failed algebra. According to his mother, he has been making A and B grades and got a D in math. Nathaniel said he had to repeat the fifth grade. His mother said it was the sixth grade. Apparently he was not performing well academically at that time (he had just moved in with his maternal grandmother). Nathaniel said that he currently works hard in school. He is trying out for the basketball team. He hopes to do construction work when he is an adult. Both Nathaniel and his mother state he has not had any behavioral difficulties. Ms. Doe describes him as a "good son." He has not been arrested previously.

Nathaniel's birth and his mother's pregnancy were apparently without complications. Developmental milestones as described were within normal limits. According to Ms. Doe, Nathaniel has always been healthy. He has never been hospitalized. He has not had any seizures or head injuries. He has never had any counseling or mental heath treatment. Nathaniel denied ever using any alcoholic beverages or illegal drugs.

BEHAVIORAL OBSERVATIONS

Nathaniel presented as a soft-spoken, 15-year-old black male of approximately average height and weight. He came to the session neatly groomed, hair in dreadlocks, and casually dressed, sporting a jacket containing numerous sport team insignias. Nathaniel was oriented to person, place, and time. He was one day off about the date. Nathaniel had no difficulty establishing rapport. He smiled appropriately, maintained good eye contact, and appeared to give his best effort on the testing. He tried to answer all questions. Nathaniel's motor activity was within normal limits. His thoughts were clear, coherent, and relevant. He did not have any loose associations. He was very quiet during the session. Often his speech was barely audible.

Nathaniel's affect was within normal limits. His mood was a bit depressed. He frequently appeared to be deep in his own thoughts. During the session, Nathaniel was often concrete in his reasoning and

did not have a particularly sophisticated vocabulary level. His judgment and common sense were fair. His immediate, short-term, and long-term memories were not particularly good. Nathaniel's reality testing was within normal limits. He did not evidence any symptoms indicative of a major mental disorder. He denied ever having had any auditory, visual, tactile, or olfactory hallucinations. He did not exhibit any delusional or paranoid thinking. Nathaniel denied ever having had any suicidal or homicidal ideation.

TEST RESULTS

On the WISC-IV, Nathaniel obtained a Verbal Comprehension Index of 67 (1%), a Perceptual Reasoning Index of 88 (21%), a Working Memory Index of 59 (0.3%), a Processing Speed Index of 88 (21%), and a full scale IQ score of 71 (3%), placing him at the borderline to extremely low range of intellectual functioning for his age group. There is a 90% chance that his true full scale IQ score is between 67 and 77. The disparity between Nathaniel's verbal comprehension skills and working memory (his ability to retain and actively process information in immediate memory) compared to his nonverbal, perceptual reasoning skills and processing speed is clinically and statistically significant. While Nathaniel's nonverbal intelligence is low average to average, his verbal intelligence, including his ability to attend to and process information, is substantially impaired, compared to that of others his age.

Results from the WRAT-4 suggest Nathaniel has a learning disability. While he can read words out loud at grade level (Word Reading Standard Score was 97 [42%]; 8.0 grade equivalent), his ability to comprehend what he reads in sentences is very much reduced (Sentence Comprehension Standard Score was 72 [3%]; 3.5 grade equivalent). This score may well be influenced by his poor memory, concentration, and attention. Although he can read a passage out loud as well as others his age, he does not understand much of what he reads because he forgets what was just read.

MMPI-A results show a remarkably "normal" profile. He had no elevations on any of the validity or clinical scales. Despite Nathaniel's appearing slightly depressed during the evaluation, this was probably due to his ongoing legal difficulties as well as his concern regarding the results of the evaluation. Even though Nathaniel's thinking about his arrest and upcoming court hearing makes him feel sad, overall this is a child without significant emotional or behavioral problems.

FORENSIC CONSIDERATIONS

If he was able to pay attention as his *Miranda* warnings were read, Nathaniel was probably able to make a knowing waiver of his rights at the time of the police questioning. Nevertheless, test results indicate he has difficulty with attention and concentration. In my review of the audiotape of his *Miranda* administration (the rights were read to him, and he was asked to read the rights silently as well), I was unable to determine with any certainty how attentive Nathaniel was while the rights were administered. Even if he was able to make a knowing waiver of his rights, it is doubtful he could have made an intelligent waiver of those rights. There are also several psychological factors that the court may wish to consider in determining the voluntariness of the *Miranda* waiver. The following factors were considered in forming my opinion.

1. Research has shown that juveniles age 14 and 15 with IQs below 80 do not understand *Miranda* warnings as well as same-aged juveniles with higher IQs or as well as older juveniles and adults. Nathaniel's WISC-IV results indicate that approximately 99% of individuals his age have a higher level of verbal intelligence.
2. Nathaniel was capable of spontaneously stating each of the four *Miranda* warnings administered by law enforcement. This does not assess whether or not he understands or appreciates the meanings of each of the warnings, just that he is capable of remembering the wording of the warnings.

Despite low intelligence testing scores, Nathaniel performed surprisingly well on two standardized tests developed by Dr. Thomas Grisso: the CMR and the CMR-R. These tests were designed to help assess *current Miranda* knowledge or understanding. The CMR required him to paraphrase each of the four *Miranda* warnings, while the CMR-R required him to state whether a particular *Miranda* warning meant the same or something different from various comparison statements.

The key issue, though, is what Nathaniel would have understood at the time of the police questioning. Although he was probably under substantially more stress when interrogated than during this assessment, and stress interferes with how well one attends to and processes information, there are no objective data to indicate one way or the other whether he would have understood his warnings, despite the stress. When asked why he did not ask for a lawyer and why he spoke to the police, Nathaniel stated that he believed he did not need a lawyer. According to Nathaniel, he was told he would spend only two days in detention. He felt he could get a lawyer after that if he still needed one.

After the specialized *Miranda* assessment tests were administered (including the FRI as described below), Nathaniel was asked to define the warnings using the actual wording given to him by law enforcement. He appeared to have no difficulty paraphrasing the meaning of each of the four warnings.

3. Despite having the capacity to make a knowing waiver of his rights if he was able to attend to the warnings as they were being read, it is unlikely that Nathaniel could have made an intelligent use of his right to counsel and right to silence. An *intelligent* waiver of rights involves a decision-making capacity, appreciating the significance of waiving the rights, based upon knowledge of the legal system.

The FRI was administered to help assess *current capacity* to intelligently waive the *Miranda* rights. Nathaniel was presented with a series of vignettes. One vignette involved a juvenile being questioned by the police, one involved a juvenile meeting with a lawyer, and a third and fourth involved a juvenile being questioned by police and later appearing in court. Hypothetical questions were asked about these scenarios to assess (a) whether there was an understanding that the police are adversarial, (b) intelligent use of the right to counsel, and (c) intelligent use of the right to silence.

Nathaniel had no problem understanding that the police are adversarial. He had major difficulties with the other two portions of the test, however. When asked about the "main job of the lawyer," Nathaniel replied, "To interrogate with him, see what he knows, see what his facts are with his facts...lawyer helps you out of your situation, to see if he did the crime or not." When Nathaniel was asked what was the lawyer's job if the person were not innocent, he replied, "To persuade him that he'll try his best to get you, for you to be specific with him...try his best to do what he can if he didn't do it." He then indicated that the lawyer does that only if his client is innocent. When Nathaniel was reminded that the question pertained to a client who was not innocent, he replied, "to be a step ahead of that." He was later questioned about what specifically a lawyer would do if he knew his client committed a crime. Nathaniel said, *"Get the boy to try to confess, if they find out he did it, there were witnesses, court will say he wasn't truthful."* Thus, even if Nathaniel understood one has a right to a lawyer, he could not have made an intelligent use of that right. He erroneously believed the defense attorney would try to get his client to confess.

Nathaniel also appeared unable to make an intelligent use of the right to silence. He was presented with a scenario of a boy named Greg who committed a crime. There were no witnesses. Greg elects not to speak to the police about the offense. Nathaniel was asked what would happen in court if the judge finds out Greg did not speak to the police. He responded, "He'll give him a long sentence...(because) Greg did not talk." Thus, even if Nathaniel knew he had a right to remain silent, he could not make an intelligent use of that right. He erroneously believed it would be used against him for invoking his right to silence.

4. Nathaniel's mother was present during the *Miranda* waiver and the subsequent interrogation. Both Nathaniel and his mother had difficulty describing accurately what transpired when they were with the police. Although I have no way of knowing what transpired prior to the police's recording the interview (law enforcement waited until they got a confession before deciding to tape it and then administering *Miranda* a second time), Nathaniel's and his mother's recounting of what transpired differed from each other and differed from what we know from the recording. Nathaniel does not have an independent recollection of chronological specific details of what transpired. This is not surprising, based on what we know about his working memory.

Significantly, Nathaniel is highly suggestible to influence from others and to giving in to misleading information (or what he has interpreted someone as saying). A good example of this is that he truly believes he wrote out his "confession" to law enforcement himself. Nathaniel believes this because, weeks earlier, his attorney showed him the written "Statement Form." He misinterpreted what Mr. Brewer had said to him, thinking that he was told he physically wrote a statement himself prior to the police's preparing one. Nathaniel said, "I know I wrote a statement, my lawyer showed me the statement I wrote." The facts are that the officer wrote a summary of Nathaniel's verbal confession, which he then got Nathaniel to sign.

5. Nathaniel was administered the GSS 1 to help assess his interrogative suggestibility. After being presented with a short story containing 40 facts, Nathaniel *yielded* 10 times to 15 leading questions presented to him about the story. The average Yield score is 4.6. His Yield score of 10 was at the 93% range compared to older juveniles and adults. He was then firmly told he had made errors, that the questions were to be repeated, and he now needed to be more accurate. He subsequently *shifted* 12 times from one response, right or wrong, to a different response. The average Shift score is 2.9. His Shift score of 12 was at the upper 99% range. His Total Suggestibility Score, which is the sum of the Yield and Shift, was 22. The average Total Suggestibility Score is 7.5. Nathaniel scored at the upper 99% range for interrogative suggestibility compared to older juveniles and adults.

The results of these findings mean that Nathaniel is highly susceptible to giving in to leading questions and to changing his responses when pressured to do so. Nathaniel is going to be more easily swayed and misled than the average juvenile. Research has shown that low intelligence is correlated with suggestibility as well as poor memory. We do not know what transpired when Nathaniel was first read his rights. If the police were at all misleading in what they said, or pressured him to cooperate, he is going to be substantially more influenced by this than the average person. This may be relevant for the court to consider when determining the voluntariness of his *Miranda* waiver (or resultant confession). While Nathaniel's mother's presence during the interrogation may be a factor for the court to consider as well, research has clearly shown that the presence of a parent during a rights administration generally increases the probability the juvenile will waive the rights.

6. The GCS was administered to both Nathaniel and his mother. This test contains 20 questions related to compliance. Nathaniel was asked to answer questions about himself. His mother answered the same questions about Nathaniel. Because this test has no validity scales (it is possible for someone to present themselves inaccurately in terms of compliance), it is useful to have a parent also rate the child to check the consistency of the score. The two ratings were almost identical. Nathaniel had a raw score of 13 (the higher the score, the more compliant). When his mother completed the form, the raw score was 14. Using the lower number (Nathaniel's rating of himself), he is at the 83% range for compliance compared to adults and the 90% range of compliance if one compares him to other juveniles. Although this test was administered for this evaluation, it is one that this examiner rarely gives. There are no built-in validity scales with this test. It thus becomes difficult to assess whether the test-taker is purposely, or unconsciously, making himself appear more compliant or less complaint than actually is the case.

SUMMARY

Nathaniel is a 15-year-old whose verbal comprehension skills are at the lower 1% range compared to others his age. He has significant problems with attention, concentration, and processing information in short-term memory. Despite Nathaniel's low verbal abilities, he currently has a fairly good knowledge of his *Miranda* warnings. Assuming he was attending to what was transpiring at the time of the rights' being given, he certainly had the capacity to make a knowing waiver. He said he gave the incriminating statements because he was told he would only be in detention for two days and, if he needed a lawyer, he could get one when he got released. He said he did not believe he really had a

choice but to comply with what the police wanted him to do and say.

Nathaniel would not have been able to make an intelligent waiver of his right to counsel and right to silence at the time of the interrogation. He erroneously believes a defense attorney would try to get a client to confess if he committed a crime. Moreover, he believes a judge will give someone a long sentence if it is learned that the defendant did not speak to the police about what was done that was wrong.

Nathaniel is a highly suggestible individual who is at high risk for giving in to leading information and changing his response when pressured to do so. This may be an important factor for the court to consider when determining the voluntariness of his *Miranda* waiver or resultant confession, particularly if the police used tactics designed to mislead or pressure Nathaniel to cooperate. Although there is no evidence that the police used illegal tactics to extract a confession, Nathaniel is substantially more at risk to giving in to the police tactics than the average person.

Thank you for the opportunity to assist the court with this case. If I can provide any additional information, please let me know.

Respectfully,
I. Bruce Frumkin, Ph.D., ABPP
Clinical Psychologist
Diplomate in Forensic Psychology
American Board of Professional Psychology

TEACHING POINT:
APPLYING GROUP-BASED EVIDENCE SUPPORTING A SPECIALIZED FORENSIC ASSESSMENT MEASURE IN A SINGLE CASE
(contributed by I. Bruce Frumkin)

Forensic evaluations need to be functionally based, integrating clinical data with the legally relevant criteria. In the case of a *Miranda* rights waiver evaluation, it is important that the psychologist be aware how the terms *knowing, intelligent,* and *voluntary* waiver of rights are defined by the courts. These terms, while often inappropriately used interchangeably, have different meanings. A *knowing* waiver pertains to how well the individual understands the warnings in conjunction with how they were administered by law enforcement.

An *intelligent* waiver involves an assessment of the individual's ability to appreciate the significance of the particular right based on the understanding of the legal process. Thus, a juvenile may understand the right to counsel but erroneously believe that an attorney will only defend someone if they are innocent. That person would be unable to make an intelligent use of the right to counsel. Based on case law (e.g., *Colorado v. Connelly*, 1986), a waiver can only be involuntary if there is a showing of police impropriety. Although it is beyond the expertise of forensic psychologists to opine whether police were unduly coercive in obtaining a *Miranda* waiver, useful information can be given to the trier of fact describing psychological characteristics that make the juvenile more vulnerable than the average person in resisting police demands.

The Grisso specialized FAIs (CMR, CMR-R, FRI) provide useful data for the psychologist to incorporate into an overall, comprehensive evaluation. They provide functionally based data directly relevant to the constructs of knowing and intelligent waiver of *Miranda* rights. They provide good behavioral data. The actual responses produced by the defendant when administered the *Miranda*-focused test items can be described verbatim to the court. The responses are also objectively scored. A national panel of judges, lawyers, and legal scholars determined which type of response indicates a *full understanding, partial understanding*, or *no understanding* of a particular warning.

There are limitations in the use of the Grisso tests. They cannot be used to determine what the individual would have understood or appreciated *at the time of the police questioning*. The wording of the warnings also will not correspond to the actual wording of the warnings given by law enforcement in the specific case at hand. The warnings given by the police may be more or less easy to understand than those contained in the Grisso tests. Also, the actual warnings may have been administered by police in a fashion that makes it more difficult for the individual to understand and appreciate the warnings. Other psychological factors can include intoxication or withdrawal from drugs, anxiety, sleep deprivation, pain, or a host of other factors that are unlikely to be present at the time the defendant is being evaluated by the psychologist. Psychologists should be particularly careful not to interpret the test scores without consideration of the standard error of measurement. Also, interpretation of tests

scores needs to consider whether one is using a relative versus absolute understanding and/or appreciation of the rights, and whether the courts would view capacity in a relative or absolute fashion.

Specialized FAIs are often a crucial component to conducting a capacity to waive *Miranda* rights evaluation—but only one part of a comprehensive assessment. As research has shown a correlation between understanding and appreciation of *Miranda* warnings, IQ tests should be administered. A comprehensive clinical interview with a special focus on the juvenile's mental state at the time of the interrogation, as well as more commonly used generic personality tests (e.g., MMPI-A, PAI-A), can provide the psychologist with useful data to help extrapolate the subject's mental state during the interrogation. Psychological tests should also be administered to rule out a subject's minimizing or exaggerating psychological or cognitive conditions impacting his capacity to waive *Miranda* rights. The use of specialized FAIs is a necessary but not sufficient method to evaluate the capacity to waive *Miranda* rights.

CASE TWO
PRINCIPLE: DO NOT BECOME ADVERSARIAL, BUT PRESENT AND DEFEND YOUR OPINIONS EFFECTIVELY (*PRINCIPLE 7*)

This principle has been discussed previously in Chapter 14 (this volume), so we will turn to a discussion of the ways that the present report illustrates the application of this principle. This principle involves a balance between presenting findings in a clear way, and avoiding selectivity, exaggeration, hyperbole, or argumentativeness. Results from testing and observations from interviews and record reviews should be neither minimized nor exaggerated. If there is clear and consistent information from multiple sources on a given point, this supports a conclusion that is comparably strong and clear. When data are less consistent and less clear, then it is important to indicate that as well. Throughout the present report are examples of each kind of finding. Since the report provides the major foundation for subsequent testimony (where there is greater temptation to be drawn into an adversarial exchange), it is particularly important to describe the report findings in a way that is clear with respect to both strengths and limitations—and hopefully reduces the risk of subsequent expert testimony's being affected by the adversarial nature of the hearing or trial.

FORENSIC EVALUATION
January 20, 2013
Re: William Jackson

REFERRAL INFORMATION

William Jackson is a 17-year-old African American male (D.O.B. 4/1/1995) who is currently charged with aggravated assault and firearms violations. He entered an admission to the charges on 2/4/12. The Public Defender's Office in Norristown, Pennsylvania (Stanley Sue, Esq.) requested a mental health evaluation to provide the defense with information, pursuant to Pennsylvania Code, relevant to William's capacities to waive his *Miranda* rights.

PROCEDURES

William was evaluated for approximately three hours on January 8, 2013, at the Montgomery County Jail. In addition to a clinical interview, William was administered a structured screening instrument for adolescent symptoms of mental and emotional disorder (the Massachusetts Youth Screening Inventory–2, or MAYSI-2), a standard objective test of mental and emotional functioning for adolescents (the Minnesota Multiphasic Personality Inventory–Adolescent, or MMPI-A), a measure of *Miranda* rights comprehension (*Miranda* Rights Comprehension Instruments, or MRCI), and a clinical interview for his capacities related to *Miranda* rights waiver. A collateral interview was conducted with William's mother, Susan Jackson. Ms. Jackson was interviewed on January 16, 2013, for approximately 30 minutes.

The following documents, obtained from the Public Defender's office, were reviewed as part of the evaluation:

1) Forensic Evaluation, Community Mental Health Center (David Sanders, Ph.D., dated 5/1/2012),
2) Norristown Police Department Investigation Report (dated 2/4/2012),
3) District of Pennsylvania Secure Court Summary (printed 12/15/2012),
4) Norristown Police Department, Statement of William Jackson (dated 1/31/2012),
5) Norristown Police Department, Biographical Information Report re: William Jackson (dated 1/31/2012),
6) Montgomery County Arrest History (dated 12/12/2012),
7) Montgomery County School Records (2000–2011),
8) Jail Academic Progress Report, School Year 2011–2012 (undated),
9) Jail School Records, School Year 2012–2013 (undated),
10) Honor Roll Certificate, Jail School (dated 4/1/2012),
11) Honor Roll Certificate, Jail School (dated 12/1/2012),
12) Certificate of Achievement in Academics, Jail School (dated 06/1/2012),
13) Certificate of Achievement in Recognition of Outstanding Effort and Behavior in English Class, Jail School (dated 9/20/2012),
14) Certificate of Achievement in Recognition of Outstanding Effort and Behavior in English Class, Jail School (dated 10/10//2012),
15) Certificate of Achievement in Recognition of Outstanding Effort and Behavior in English Class, Jail School (dated 10/25/2012), and
16) Certificate of Accomplishment, Super Student, Jail School (dated 10/1/12).

Prior to the evaluation, William was notified about the purpose of the evaluation and the associated limits of confidentiality. Initially, William required a reminder that the purpose of the evaluation was only for assessment and not for treatment; that the report could be used by his attorney and, if it were, copies would be provided to the prosecution and the court. William was able to report back his understanding that the evaluation was only for assessment and that a written report would be submitted to his attorney. In addition, Ms. Jackson was notified of the purpose of the evaluation and agreed to be interviewed.

RELEVANT HISTORY

Some of the history in this section was obtained from William. His mother, Susan Jackson, also provided historical information during a collateral telephone interview on 1/18/2013. Additional historical information was obtained from the other collateral sources described earlier. Whenever possible, we assessed the consistency of self-reported information with that obtained from collateral sources. If additional information is obtained prior to William's hearing, a supplemental report will be filed.

Medical and Psychiatric History

William reported that he has ADHD. He was unsure when he received this diagnosis and suspected that it was given to him by a teacher. William's mother, Susan Jackson, also reported that William was diagnosed with ADHD. Both William and his mother denied that he has ever taken prescription medication for his ADHD. William reported that he has never taken any prescription medication for mental, emotional, or behavioral problems. However, he said that he uses prescription medications, especially Xanax, recreationally. School records indicate that William was not formally diagnosed with ADHD, although his behavior in school did reflect problems with impulsivity and attention and concentration.

Regarding therapy, William reported that he attended therapy for "anger problems" as a child. According to William, his grandmother took him to Norris Home twice a week for therapy to address behavior problems at school and anger management. He stated that he attended therapy for three years. William denied that he was involved in frequent fighting at school and reported that his anger problems related to his behavior towards teachers, stating, "I used to be snappin' at teachers and stuff. Not fighting. Snappin'." William stated that his behavior problems were limited to the school environment, saying, "It [behavior problems] was only at school, though, not at home." William said that he discontinued therapy when he moved in with his mother after his grandmother's death.

Regarding serious illnesses or injuries, William reported that he had sustained a serious head injury approximately five years before, when he slipped and fell by a pool at a family reunion. He said that he blacked out and woke up in the hospital. William stated that he received staples in his head at the hospital and was discharged later that day. He also reported that he injured his head and neck in 2010 when he hit his head on his sister's knee. He stated

that he did not black out, but his neck hurt for several weeks after the incident. William reported that he still suffers from a limited range of neck movement due to the incident.

When asked about mental or emotional disorder in other family members, William reported that his mother suffers from bipolar disorder. He stated that he was unsure if she had ever received treatment for this condition. According to Dr. Sanders, Ms. Jackson previously denied having any mental health problems. During the current collateral interview with her, Ms. Jackson denied any family history of mental, emotional, or behavior problems.

Educational History

William stated that he is currently in the eleventh grade at school in Montgomery County Jail, where he is incarcerated. He reported that he attended one elementary school and one middle school. William indicated that he attended Lincoln Elementary School. He claimed that he had good grades and good behavior in elementary school. He added that he was suspended "like two times" in elementary school for running the hallways. He said that he was never suspended for fighting in elementary school. William's mother also reported that he was not suspended for fighting in elementary school. She stated that William's behavior problems in elementary school were mostly for "being [the] clown of the class—not fighting." School records reflect a total of five suspensions in elementary school and three in middle school, with two of the five suspensions in elementary school for fighting. Regarding his grades, William reported that he received "Cs and Ds and two As." William stated that he has received special education services since third grade. These statements are largely consistent with school records, which indicate that most of William's grades were Cs and Ds—and that he was tested academically and placed in special education classes in third grade. William was unable to recall whether he had received an IEP. School records indicate that he had an IEP in third, fourth, and fifth grades that addressed his significant problems with reading. His mother reported that William also received speech therapy.

William stated that he attended one middle school. He described having good attendance in middle school, saying, "I was going every day." His mother also reported that William "was always at school." Regarding his behavior, William reported that he was suspended "two or three times" for fighting. He said that his grades were mostly Cs and Ds, and one A. Again, this was largely consistent with school records. William reported that he was involved in an after-school program that provided homework help and activities, such as X-Box and pool. Additionally, William reported that he received academic support from his grandmother, stating, "My grandma was my tutor . . . 'til she died."

William reported that he only attended one high school before his incarceration, Washington School. According to school records, he also attended Martin Luther King High School for a short time in the eleventh grade before transferring back to Washington School. According to Dr. Sanders, William was transferred to Washington for failing to follow classroom rules and being disruptive in class. William reported that his attendance at Washington "was good." He indicated that he was never suspended in high school, but then added, "There wasn't [sic] suspensions at the high school I was at." Regarding his grades at Washington, William stated, "They was [sic] good." School records indicate that William received passing grades that were mostly Ds and Cs. He added, "they [his grades] are better here [Montgomery Jail School] because they tutor me here."

William currently attends the Montgomery Jail School within the county jail. He stated that his academic performance at Montgomery was "good." According to his Montgomery School 2012–2013 records, William has been enrolled there since 9/7/2012. These records indicate that William received As in English 3, Algebra 2, and Biology. He received Bs in Civics/Social Science and Arts/Humanities. William has also received several award certificates at Montgomery, including: Honor Roll (4/10/2012), Certificate of Achievement in Academics (6/14/2012), Certificate of Achievement in Recognition of Outstanding Effort and Behavior in English Class for the Week of September 24th, 2012 (9/28/12), Certificate of Accomplishment as a Super Student (10/2/12), Certificate of Achievement in Recognition of Outstanding Effort and Behavior in English Class for the Week of October 8, 2012 (10/8/2012), Certificate of Achievement in Recognition of Outstanding Effort and Behavior in English Class for the Week of October 22, 2012 (10/29/2012), and Honor Roll (12/5/2012).

Substance Abuse History

William described a history of substance use, including marijuana, prescription pills, and alcohol. William reported that before his incarceration, he smoked more than four "blunts" of marijuana every day. He estimated that he started smoking marijuana when he was about 13 years old. According to Dr. Sanders, William began smoking marijuana at the age of 15. William also reported that he used to take Xanax daily, stating, "I would pop like six a day." Later in the evaluation, William reported that he occasionally drinks alcohol, stating, "I don't drink every day, only special occasions . . . if friends are drinking." He stated that he prefers to drink vodka and juice, and estimated that he started drinking alcohol when he was about 13 years old. His mother reported that she did not know anything about William's drug and alcohol use.

Regarding the family's history of drug use, Dr. Sanders indicated that William's mother has a history of crack cocaine use and that she stopped using drugs around 2006 after the death of her own mother. These records also suggest that William's mother currently uses alcohol and marijuana occasionally. During the present collateral interview with Ms. Jackson, she denied any knowledge of family history of drug or alcohol use.

Offense History

William reported that he has had three juvenile arrests. He said that his first arrest occurred when he was 14 years old. County arrest records indicate that William's first arrest occurred on 8/2/2009 when he was arrested for auto theft. These records reflect that William admitted to the charge, and adjudication was deferred. Additionally, these records indicate that William was given probation for this incident and successfully discharged from probation on 11/20/2009.

Next, according to county arrest records, William was arrested on 12/28/2009 and charged with robbery. The records indicated that this charge was dismissed.

Finally, county arrest records indicate that William was arrested on 11/24/2010 and charged with car theft, unauthorized use of a vehicle, and conspiracy. These records state that William admitted to unauthorized use and was adjudicated delinquent. He was put on probation.

Previous Psychological Testing

William completed several academic and psychological measures as part of a psychological assessment conducted by Dr. Sanders. During this evaluation, William completed a measure of academic achievement, the Woodcock-Johnson (WJ-III). Results from this test suggest that William's reading skills are far below what would be expected for his age (Letter-Word Identification, grade equivalent = 2.0; and Reading Fluency, grade equivalent = 1.5). William's math skills also measured below grade level (Calculation, grade equivalent = 3.5; and Math Fluency, grade equivalent = 4.0).

Additionally, William also completed the Wechsler Adult Intelligence Scale, 4th edition (WAIS-IV) during his evaluation conducted by Dr. Sanders. William's overall level of intellectual functioning was measured in the Borderline range (FSIQ = 74). His performance on the composite indices ranged from extremely low to low average (VCI = 68; PRI = 86; WMI = 83; PSI = 79).

CURRENT CLINICAL CONDITION

William presented as a 17-year-old African American male, about 5 feet 7 inches tall with a medium build, who appeared his stated age. He was dressed in institutional attire and fairly well groomed when seen for evaluation at the Montogomery County Jail, where he is currently placed. William reported that he had no motor, visual, or auditory problems. He stated he had no scars or piercings. He has several tattoos, including three on his face. He had a teardrop under his right eye, which he explained as the sadness he feels regarding his grandmother's death. Additionally, he had a "W" tattoo between his eyebrows. He said that this tattoo was for his name, William. Finally, William had a star tattoo under his left eye. He indicated that this tattoo was for his nephew, stating, "He is going to be a star when he gets older." William also had tattoos on his hands and arms. He had a tattoo of the word "Norris" on his right hand and "town" on his left hand. He also had the number "2" on his right arm and the number "9" on his left arm, which he explained as, "I'm from 29th Street." William also reported that he had his sister's name, "Bianca," tattooed on his chest, and his mother's name, "Susan," tattooed on his stomach.

William's speech was clear, coherent, and relevant during the present interview. He was cooperative and polite. William's mood throughout the evaluation appeared neutral, and his range of emotional expression was appropriate to the interview context. He displayed appropriate eye contact and provided relevant responses to most questions. He appeared to give reasonable effort to the tasks involved throughout the three-hour evaluation session. His capacity for attention and concentration appeared adequate. He was able to focus reasonably well on a series of tasks without becoming visibly distracted. There was no evidence of bizarre thinking. His thought process was clear and goal-directed. William denied any current thoughts of harming himself or others or any past suicide attempts. He was oriented to person, place, and date. Taken together, it appears that this evaluation provides a reasonably good estimate of William's current functioning.

On a structured inventory of symptoms of mental and emotional disorders specifically designed for use with adolescents (MAYSI-2), William endorsed numerous symptoms. Out of a total of 52 items, William endorsed 23 items. Specifically, he reported having lost his temper easily; having problems concentrating or paying attention; having nervous or worried feelings that kept him from doing things he wanted to do; having trouble concentrating; having been easily upset; having done something he wished he hadn't when he was drunk or high; having too many bad moods; having felt lonely too much of the time; having his parents or friends think he drinks too much; having part of his body always hurting him; having gotten in trouble while drunk or high; having a bad feeling that things don't seem real, like he is in a dream; having felt shaky when he is nervous or anxious; having a fast heartbeat when he is nervous or anxious; having felt short of breath when he is nervous or anxious; having clammy hands when he is nervous or anxious; having an upset stomach when he is nervous or anxious; having felt like he doesn't have fun with friends anymore; having felt angry a lot; having felt like he can't do anything right; having gotten frustrated a lot; having had bad headaches; having people talk about him when he is not there; having something very bad or terrifying happen to him; and having bad thoughts or dreams about a scary event that happened to him.

When asked to elaborate on these some of these symptoms, William gave brief responses. Many of his responses were related to his experiences at Montgomery County Jail, behavior problems at school, and substance use. Specifically, he stated that he loses his temper at school when he doesn't "get it." He added, "I start snappin', but I can control it though. I got better at controlling it." William reported that he controls his temper by taking 10 deep breaths. He reported that he learned this technique in therapy. William reported that he has problems concentrating and paying attention, "mostly at school." Additionally, he reported that he has been easily upset when things don't go his way or when he doesn't understand things at school. He reported that he has too many bad moods recently because he wishes he was not in prison and the Correctional Officer's make him mad by telling him what to do. William reported that he feels lonely too much of the time and attributed that to "losing a friend and those close to me, like my grandma." He reported that his mom and friends think that he drinks too much, and that he has gotten in trouble with his mom for drinking. William reported that things do not seem real, like he is in a dream, in prison. He stated that he feels shaky, his heart beats fast, he is short of breath, his hands feel clammy, and his stomach is upset when his is nervous or anxious at court. He added, "I don't let it show, though." William reported that he has felt like he doesn't have fun with his friends because he is in prison. He stated that he has waked up with bad headaches lately, and that, although they don't happen often, they are "real bad" and interfere with his sleep when they do occur. William reported that his grandmother's death was something very bad or terrifying that happened to him. Finally, he stated that he has bad dreams about a shooting that he witnessed when he was younger. He added that he has seen several shootings and has lost one friend to gun violence.

William completed the MMPI-A as part of the current evaluation to measure his current mental and emotional functioning. Given William's low reading level, the MMPI-A statements were read to him. William was cooperative with completing the 478 items on the MMPI-A; however, his moderately elevated F score suggests a tendency to endorse a variety of psychological symptoms and problem behaviors. This may indicate inconsistent responding, a tendency to exaggerate symptoms, or possibly serious psychopathology. William's VRIN and TRIN scores rule out inconsistent responding as accounting for this response pattern. Although William's profile had a moderately elevated F score, his MMPI-A is still valid and interpretable, provided that his F score is taken into consideration.

William's MMPI-A clinical profile contains one of the least frequent high-point profiles in both mental health and alcohol/drug treatment settings. Individuals with such clinical profiles (Welsh Code 2638'14 + 70-5/9: F' +-L/K:) are often described as experiencing symptoms of depression, including sadness, fatigue, crying spells, and self-deprecatory thoughts. They are also described as feeling lonely and pessimistic. Such individuals are often angry at others, who they feel may have harmed them and may be responsible for their difficulties. Some unusual thoughts and experiences were reported, including hallucinations and persecutory ideas, but these were not consistent with William's direct report, observed behavior, or collateral observations. Finally, such profiles are often associated with the development of alcohol or other drug-use problems. He endorsed items suggesting increasing involvement with alcohol and other drugs. He also endorsed items suggesting that he recognizes that his substance use is problematic and he may be aware that others are critical of it. Using alcohol or drugs may be a coping strategy for him.

CAPACITY TO WAIVE MIRANDA RIGHTS

William's comprehension of his *Miranda* rights was evaluated in a number of ways. First, he was asked to spontaneously recall the events leading up to and including his waiver of his rights. He was then asked to explain the meaning each of the rights that he signed on his *Miranda* waiver form. Finally, William was administered a set of instruments commonly used in the field of forensic psychology to assess understanding and appreciation of *Miranda* rights. His performance on these instruments was evaluated using an objective scoring system, and his scores were compared to age- and IQ-based norms.

Recollection of Waiver of Rights

During the present interview, William was questioned about his recollection of the events leading up to and including his waiver of his rights. William stated that, on the day of the arrest, 1/21/2012, he and a friend were sitting on the street on 29th and Jefferson Streets. William reported that an undercover police officer drove by, stopped, and then came back to where he and his friend were sitting. According to William, the police officer attempted to apprehend his friend first. William added that his friend did not initially believe the man was a real cop. William reported that he (William) was then taken to the police station. He stated that the police recognized him from a photograph.

While at the police station, William reported, two officers questioned him. When asked about the questioning, William responded, "He read me my rights, though. Told me if you don't got [sic] a lawyer one will be handed to you and that." William reported that detectives made him promises, stating, "He said he was going to tell the judge, get me switched to juvenile and stuff like that…they was [sic] going to get me five years." William also said that he asked for a lawyer. When asked what happened after he made this request, William replied, "He ain't say nothing." William also stated that he asked for his mother: "I asked for my mom because I know I am a juvenile and she was supposed to be with me."

William reported that he had been drinking, smoking marijuana, and taking prescription pills on the day of his arrest. According to William, he was "lost out of my mind" when the police were questioning him. He said that he took four Xanax throughout the day, starting at 7:00 a.m. He also reported that he had smoked three marijuana blunts with his friends, starting around 2:45 p.m. Additionally, William reported, he was drinking shots and playing drinking card games with friends before the arrest. He indicated that he'd had five shots in the afternoon and little to eat during the day. When asked whether he was "drunk" at the time of his arrest, William responded, "Yes." William reported that the police asked him whether he had been drinking and using drugs. He said that he told them "no" because he did not want his mom to find out. William reported that he was trying to hide his intoxication from the police, but also stated that he was "laughing a lot" at the police station.

Explanation of Rights Signed on the Waiver Form

Next, William was read each of the statements that he signed on the *Miranda* rights waiver form. He was asked to define and explain the meaning of each statement in his own words.

Right to Remain Silent

William defined the right to remain silent by saying "that I don't have to talk if I don't want to. You ain't got to say nothing at all." When asked whether he has to talk if the police want him to, William stated, "No, you ain't got to.…When they say you have the right to remain silent, you ain't gotta talk."

Anything You Say Can Be Used Against You

William's explanation of "Anything you say can and will be used against you in Court" was "they can use any statement in Court…to get me locked up." He later elaborated, "If I tell them something, they can use it…to keep me in here [prison] and hold it against me."

Right to an Attorney

He explained this right—"You have a right to talk to a lawyer of your own choice before we ask you any question, and also to have a lawyer here with you while we ask questions"—as "You get to talk to your lawyer before they ask you questions" and "Your lawyer can be in the room while they ask you questions." He added, "If I got a lawyer, you can't ask me no questions."

Right to Free Counsel

William was asked to explain, "If you can not afford to hire a lawyer, and you want one, we will see that you have a lawyer provided for you, free of charge, before we ask you any questions." William stated that this means, "They would give you a lawyer…a P.D." When asked whether there is a difference between a lawyer and a Public Defender, William responded, "Yeah, the PD is free. He a [sic] real lawyer though." William added, "If I don't have a lawyer they will give me one…the city pays for it."

Right to Discontinue

When asked to explain the statement "If you are willing to give us a statement, you have a right to stop any time you wish," William stated that it meant, "I can stop any time I want. If they questioning me, I ain't gotta talk to them." However, when asked what happens if the police want him to keep talking, William stated, "Gotta keep talking."

Standardized Assessment Measure

As part of the evaluation, William was administered the *Miranda* Rights Comprehension Instruments (MRCI), an objective, standardized assessment tool used as part of an overall approach to assessing an individual's abilities to make a knowing, intelligent waiver of *Miranda* rights. William's responses to the four MRCI instruments were consistent with his answers throughout the interview regarding his understanding and appreciation of his rights.

For example, on the first instrument within the assessment tool (Comprehension of *Miranda* Rights–II), when asked to paraphrase the right to remain silent, William stated, "You ain't gotta talk if you don't want to." He correctly explained that what he told investigators could be "used in court against me" and added, "They got proof that I said it." William believed that his right to an attorney before and during interrogation meant "I ain't have to [*sic*] tell them nothing if I ain't have [*sic*] no lawyer." William's overall score on the Comprehension of *Miranda* Rights–II was a 9 out of 10. In comparison, the average score for 17 year olds with verbal IQs less than 70 in the juvenile justice system is 5.00 (SD = 2.37).

On the Comprehension of *Miranda* Rights–Recognition–II (CMR-R-II) instrument, which involves distinguishing whether statements mean the same as or something different from each of the *Miranda* warning statements, William received a score of 14 out of 15. He demonstrated an incorrect understanding of his right to an attorney if he was unable to afford one. His score of 14 out of 15 is exceeded by only 7.7% of juveniles in the juvenile justice standardization sample. The average score for 17 year olds with verbal IQs less than 70 in the juvenile justice system is 10.33 (SD = 1.03).

The Function of Rights in Interrogation (FRI) measures a defendant's appreciation of his or her rights, the psychological equivalent of the legal ability to make an intelligent waiver of rights. That is, it measures the ability of the defendant to apply each of the rights to interrogation-related situations in an appropriate, focused, realistic manner. There are three subscales within this instrument, which involve appreciating the nature of interrogation, the right to counsel, and the right to silence, respectively. William's FRI total score, the sum of his subscales, was 25 of a 32 possible points. Interpretation of William's FRI score, however, must take into account the discrepancies among his performances on the subscales.

William obtained a score of 9 out of 10 on the Nature of Interrogation scale and appeared to understand the adversarial nature of the interrogation situation. Similarly, with regard to right to counsel, William obtained a score of 9 out of 10. However, regarding his ability to appreciate the right to remain silent and apply it to the interrogation situation, William received a score of 2 out of 10. He believed that if interrogators tell a suspect to talk, "he gotta talk." He later added, "No, he should ask for a lawyer, so the police won't make him talk." Similarly, when asked what should happen if a judge learns that a suspect would not talk to the police, he responded, "The judge would be mad. That's my opinion." Thus, William's appreciation of the nature of this right and his ability to apply it in an interrogation situation in an appropriate manner were significantly impaired.

The final instrument in this assessment tool involves 16 vocabulary words, Comprehension of *Miranda* Vocabulary–II (CMV-II). William received a score of 25 out of 32 on this measure. He demonstrated incomplete understanding of two words (*right* and *statement*) and a lack of understanding of three words (*consult, interrogation,* and *remain*). William's score of 25 out of 32 is in the 89th percentile. The average score for 17 year olds with verbal IQs less than 70 in the juvenile justice system is 15.67 (SD = 6.19). Accordingly, William appears to have an adequate understanding of the vocabulary often employed in *Miranda* warnings.

SUMMARY OF CAPACITY TO WAIVE *MIRANDA* RIGHTS ABILITIES

William generally demonstrated a good understanding and appreciation of the *Miranda* warnings. However, he displayed a limited understanding of the right to remain silent. Specifically, he showed a poor appreciation of the right to remain silent and how it might apply in the interrogation situation. William's responses to questions about the right to silence indicate that he thinks that remaining silent when ordered to answer questions will result in further punishment. However, he also indicated that he thought having a lawyer present would keep the police from forcing him to talk. Additionally, William demonstrated an adequate understanding of the specific vocabulary often used in *Miranda* warnings, although having difficulty understanding of five of the 16 words. Taken together, it would appear that William's ability to understand and appreciate the *Miranda* warnings in order to waive them is generally adequate, but limited regarding his understanding of the right to remain silent.

There are two other considerations with respect to his capacities to waive his rights. First, William described drinking, smoking marijuana, and taking Xanax on the day of his interrogation, adding that this resulted in his being "out of my mind." He did reply "no" when asked by interrogating officers whether he had consumed any such substances. It is not clear whether he exaggerated or fabricated this account, whether he was being accurate but was not affected very much by these substances, or his condition was not detected by interrogating officers but did impair his capacities for exercising a knowing, intelligent, and voluntary waiver of rights. Second, William's previously measured capacity for reading is very poor, although he does better in spoken language. He would probably not have been adequate if he needed to read the waiver, but would have done better if informed of his rights orally.

CONCLUSION

In the opinion of the undersigned, based on all of the above:

William appears to have an adequate understanding and appreciation of the *Miranda* warnings as a whole. He has a more limited understanding of the consequences of invoking the right to remain silent. This limited understanding does not appear to be a matter of low cognitive functioning, as William displayed adequate to good understanding of other aspects of the *Miranda* warnings.

Thank you for the opportunity to evaluate William Jackson.

Kirk Heilbrun, Ph.D.
Consulting Psychologist

Megan Murphy, B.A.
Drexel University
Graduate Student

TEACHING POINT:
WHETHER AND HOW TO CRITICIZE MATERIAL FROM THE RECORDS

This discussion addresses potential criticism of material from records gathered in the course of FMHA. In a consultant's role, by contrast, some of the comments about records provided to attorneys may be different.

Relevance and credibility are two important considerations in deciding whether to comment directly (in the report or in testimony) on a particular record or collateral interview. Third party information is obtained to provide different sources of information in domains that are important in the evaluation. The extent to which a given record or interview is weighed in the FMHA depends both on its relevance and its credibility. Either of these may justify direct comment when describing the record or interview.

When reviewing the reports of professional colleagues, it may also be appropriate to offer some comment on the relevance of their content to the present evaluation. Since the emphasis should be on citing the observations of the other evaluator rather than the conclusions, there may not be much need to comment on credibility. Even when such critical comments are made, however, they should be conveyed in a respectful fashion. For example, a psychologist reviewing the report of another psychologist conducted on the issue of *Miranda* waiver capacity that involved administering several psychological tests that are irrelevant or outdated (e.g., projective drawings) might either (a) note that such tests were administered, comment that they are no longer regarded as within the standard of practice for evaluating justice-involved adolescents, and refrain from describing the test findings; or (b) note that the tests were administered and say nothing about the results.

20

Juvenile Competence to Stand Trial

This chapter focuses on juveniles' competence to stand trial (for further discussion of this legal question, see Chapter 3, this volume). The principle illustrated by the first case addresses the importance of considering both relevance and scientific reliability and validity in considering how to seek information and select data sources in forensic assessment. Following the case report, the teaching point discusses the selection of specialized tools that might be used in evaluating juvenile trial competence. The second case concerns the importance of evaluation conditions that are quiet, private, and distraction-free. The teaching point following the second case will discuss how an evaluator might recognize and respond to inadequate conditions.

CASE ONE

PRINCIPLE: USE RELEVANCE AND RELIABILITY (VALIDITY) AS GUIDES FOR SEEKING INFORMATION AND SELECTING DATA SOURCES (PRINCIPLE 18)

This principle was previously described in Chapter 13 (this volume), so we will move directly to introducing the case report. In this case, the evaluation was done to help inform the decision about the competence to stand trial (CST) of a 17-year-old juvenile. Unfortunately, the evaluator does not have the luxury of including a validated specialized measure of juvenile CST among the tests administered to John. This is discussed further in the teaching point following the report.

However, there are numerous psychological tests and screening measures that are available; these can be employed to help assess the functioning of this individual relative to others his age. Dr. DeMatteo administered the MAYSI, a screening measure for adolescent mental health functioning that can be expanded by having the youth, after completing the measure, give additional information about any item endorsed. This can serve as a useful supplement to the interview and other psychological tests administered.

He also administered the MMPI-A, WRAT-4, and WASI. These are standard, well-validated, and relevant measures of mental, emotional, intellectual, and educational skills functioning. Some of these areas may be directly relevant to trial competence capacities if they reflect very substantial deficits.

FORENSIC EVALUATION
September 13, 2010
Re: John Doe
PP#: 123456

REFERRAL

John Doe is a 17-year-old Portuguese-American male (DOB: xx-xx-xx) who is currently charged with aggravated assault, possession of an instrument of crime, simple assault, and recklessly endangering another person. A request for a mental health evaluation to provide the defense with information relevant to John's competence to stand trial was made by John's attorney.

PROCEDURES

John was evaluated for approximately four hours on September 8, 2010, at Drexel University. In addition to a psychosocial interview, John was administered a structured screening instrument for adolescent symptoms of mental and emotional disorders (the Massachusetts Youth Screening Inventory, second edition [MAYSI-2]), a standard test of current functioning in relevant academic areas (the Wide Range Achievement Test, fourth edition [WRAT-4]), a standard objective test of mental and emotional functioning among adolescents (the Minnesota Multiphasic Personality Inventory–Adolescent [MMPI-A]), and a standard measure of overall intellectual functioning (the Wechsler Abbreviated Scale of Intelligence [WASI]). In addition, John's father, Frank Doe, provided information during the evaluation regarding John's past and current functioning. The following documents, obtained from John's attorney, were reviewed as part of this evaluation:

(1) Psycho-Social Summary (dated 8/13/10);
(2) Criminal Docket, Court of Common Pleas of Philadelphia County;
(3) Court Summary, First Judicial District of Pennsylvania;
(4) Criminal Complaint, Commonwealth of Pennsylvania (Philadelphia County) (dated 6/17/10);
(5) Philadelphia Police Department Arrest Report (dated 6/17/10);
(6) First Judicial District of Pennsylvania, Pretrial Service Division, Investigation Report (dated 6/17/10); and
(7) Records from the School District of Philadelphia.

Prior to the evaluation, John was notified about the purpose of the evaluation and associated limits on confidentiality. He appeared to understand the basic purpose of the evaluation, reporting back his understanding that he would be evaluated and that a written report would be submitted to his attorney. He further understood that the report could be used in his pretrial hearing, and, if it were, copies would be provided to the prosecution and court. A similar notification of purpose was provided to Frank Doe prior to the collateral interview.

RELEVANT HISTORY

Historical information was obtained from John and the collateral sources noted above. The consistency of the information provided by John was assessed through the use of multiple sources whenever possible. An amended report will be filed if additional collateral information that materially changes the results of this evaluation is obtained prior to John's court date.

Family History

John Doe was born on [x/x/x], in Philadelphia, Pennsylvania, to Cindy Doe and Frank Doe. John reported that his parents are married and have a healthy relationship. John's father, Mr. Doe, reported that he and John's mother came to the United States from Argentina about 21 years ago. John reported having two older paternal half-sisters, one older paternal half-brother, and one older maternal half-sister. He reported that his paternal half-siblings live in Argentina, and his maternal half-sister lives in New Jersey. John reported being raised by his parents in West Philadelphia. He reported that he has always lived in Philadelphia, except when his family briefly relocated to Delaware for six months in 2007 in an effort to find work. John reported that his family owns and operates a house-cleaning business, and that all the family members are involved. Mr. Doe reported that business has been declining in recent years, which has led to financial difficulties.

John described his childhood as "average." He described spending time playing sports, doing household chores, playing video games, playing musical instruments, and spending time with "church friends." He reported that his neighborhood is relatively safe, but that a "bad influence" recently moved into the neighborhood. John reported having a "good" relationship with his father. He reported that they spend time together, and he described his father as supportive. John described his mother as his "best friend," and he reported having a "very close" relationship. John reported that his family's involvement in their church is a source of guidance and strength for him. He noted that his father is an elder in the church and his mother is a deacon, and he reported playing drums in a worship group. He denied any history of abuse or neglect. He reported dating, but denied any long-term relationships. He denied having any children.

Educational History

Records from the School District of Philadelphia indicate that John attended kindergarten through third grade at Orange Elementary. He reported beginning fourth grade at Jones Elementary School, but transferring to Jackson Elementary School for the remainder of fourth grade because his family relocated. He reported completing the fifth grade at Jackson and part of sixth grade in Delaware. He reported completing part of the seventh grade at Jackson before transferring to Simmons Middle School for the remainder of seventh and eighth grade. John reported that his parents transferred him to Simmons because it was a "better school." John reported completing ninth and tenth grade at ABC High School, where he is currently in eleventh grade. He reported earning "mostly Bs and Cs," but acknowledged being "lazy." He reported that math is his strongest subject, and that he struggles with social studies. John reported that he attends school every day unless he is sick or has a doctor's appointment. Records from the School District of Philadelphia reflect relatively few unexcused absences, with the exception of academic year 2006–2007 (21 absences). In all other years, John's unexcused absences ranged from a low of one to a high of 10. He acknowledged being suspended once for a uniform violation and once for failing to complete his homework. His academic records confirm two suspensions. John reported that he played baseball and lacrosse in school. He reported that his educational/occupational goal is to graduate from high school and attend college to study civil engineering.

Medical and Psychiatric History

John denied any history of serious illnesses or injuries. He reported breaking his left arm playing basketball at age eight, but denied breaking any other bones. He denied ever receiving stitches. He denied any history of serious head injuries or loss of consciousness, and he denied any hospitalizations. He reported that his mother was successfully treated for bladder cancer in 2004. John described this as very stressful. Mr. Doe indicated that he had to take care of the kids and run the family business by himself while his wife was undergoing treatment for cancer.

John reported receiving counseling for "depression and anger problems" at a mental health clinic beginning at age 15. He reported that a school counselor suggested to his parents that they take him for an evaluation because he was "acting up" in school and occasionally crying. John reported attending weekly counseling sessions for approximately nine months, and then attending sessions less frequently because "I was getting better and didn't need it." He reported taking a psychotropic medication for several months, but both John and his father were unable to recall the name of the medication. He reported discontinuing the medication because of side effects, including fatigue and weight gain. Records from the mental health clinic were not available at the time this report was

written. He denied any history of suicidal ideation or attempts. When asked about his current functioning, John reported being "sad" and having "crying spells." Mr. Doe denied any family history of major mental health problems.

Substance Use History

John denied ever using any drugs or alcohol. He reported that he is able to avoid drug use by "looking for the right friends…and staying away from bad influences." He also reported that his parents taught him "to go the right way." He denied ever selling drugs.

Social History

John reported having 15 friends, including three close friends. He noted that they enjoy playing soccer, playing video games, having sleepovers, and watching movies. John reported that his friends are a good influence on him. He denied any drug use or illegal activity among his friends. He reported being involved in two or three fights, and noted that it takes a lot of provocation for him to fight. He denied ever being part of a gang or carrying a weapon.

Occupational History

John reported that he works in the family cleaning business during the summers. He reported that his responsibilities include cleaning houses by vacuuming, taking out the trash, and general cleaning. He denied any other history of formal employment. As noted, John reported that his occupational goal is to become a civil engineer. He reported that he would initially prefer to work for a city so he can learn the profession before eventually opening his own business.

Offense History

According to John's arrest records, this is his first arrest (adult or juvenile). John denied ever having had contact with the justice system prior to this arrest.

CURRENT CLINICAL CONDITION

John presented as a Portuguese-American male of average height and medium build who appeared his stated age. He was casually dressed and well groomed when evaluated on September 8, 2010, at Drexel University. He arrived to the evaluation

10 minutes early and accompanied by his father. John was cooperative and polite throughout the evaluation. His speech was clear, coherent, and relevant, and he appeared to give reasonable effort to the tasks involved. His capacity for attention and concentration appeared adequate, and he was able to focus reasonably well on a series of tasks during the entire evaluation without becoming visibly distracted or fatigued. Therefore, it appears that this evaluation provides a reasonably good estimate of John's current functioning.

John showed appropriate emotional variability throughout the evaluation. He was correctly oriented to time, place, and person. He did not report experiencing any perceptual disturbances (auditory or visual hallucinations) or delusions (bizarre ideas with no possible basis in reality), and his train of thought was clear and logical.

Wide Range Achievement Test, 4th Ed. (WRAT-4)

John performed relatively well, although a bit unevenly, on a test of his basic academic skills, as reflected by his grade equivalency scores: Word Reading (grade 9.6 equivalent), Sentence Comprehension (grade 6.5 equivalent), Spelling (grade 11.0 equivalent), and Math Computation (grade 5.7 equivalent). His math computation and sentence comprehension skills would benefit from some improvement.

Wechsler Abbreviated Scale of Intelligence (WASI-II)

John's intellectual functioning was formally measured with the WASI. He obtained a full scale IQ score of 93, which places him in the Average range of intellectual functioning and at the 32nd percentile relative to others his age. Given the measurement error on the WASI, there is a 95% probability that his true IQ score falls between 88 and 99. His Verbal IQ score was 87 (19th percentile; Low Average) and his Performance IQ score was 102 (55th percentile; Average).

Massachusetts Youth Screening Inventory, 2nd Ed. (MAYSI-2)

On a structured inventory of currently experienced symptoms of mental and emotional disorders designed for use with adolescents (the MAYSI-2), John endorsed six of the 52 items. Some of the items endorsed by John were having problems concentrating or paying attention, having too many bad moods (noting he was in a bad mood when he was arrested and in court), feeling too tired to have a good time (noting he was too tired to go to the movies with his friends while he was cleaning houses), and having something bad or terrifying happen to him (referring to being arrested and his mother being diagnosed with cancer twice).

Minnesota Multiphasic Personality Inventory-Adolescent (MMPI-A)

John was administered the MMPI-A to measure his current personality functioning. Each item was read to him to ensure appropriate item comprehension. He responded to the items in an open and cooperative manner, thereby producing a valid MMPI-A profile that probably provides a reasonable indication of his current functioning. His clinical scales are within normal limits, which suggests he is well adjusted and not experiencing any significant psychological distress at the present time. This is not consistent with his self-report of being "sad." John's MMPI-A profile suggests that he enjoys spending time with other people, and there is no indication that he has difficulty with social interactions. He endorsed content suggesting the presence of some cynical attitudes and beliefs. He also endorsed content suggesting a desire to succeed in life, which may be an asset to build on during treatment. John's MMPI-A profile does not suggest the presence of any mental or emotional disorder.

COMPETENCE TO STAND TRIAL

John was first questioned about the nature of his charges. He reported that he has been charged with "assault," which is consistent with information contained in his arrest records indicating that John was officially charged with aggravated assault and related offenses. John reported that he was charged with assault because he "hit a kid near my house." He was not sure whether he was charged with a felony or misdemeanor, but acknowledged that it was "serious." At this point, the evaluator explained the difference between a felony and misdemeanor. When John was questioned about the difference between a felony and misdemeanor about 30 minutes later, he stated that a "felony is a more serious charge...for a worse offense."

John was then questioned about the possible penalties that could result from a conviction for his charges. He reported that he is not sure what penalty could result, but that he "would probably have to do some time." When questioned further, John reported that he could only be detained until he is "18 or maybe 21, but not longer than that." Therefore, it appears that John understands that he could be incarcerated if he is convicted, and he appears to understand the distinction between juvenile detention and adult confinement.

John was then asked to describe the respective roles of judge, prosecutor, and defense attorney in the adversarial context. He stated that the judge's job is to "find people guilty." After further questioning, John reported that the judge could also sentence people to "probation" or find them not guilty. John reported that the defense attorney's job is to "see that I get a fair trial [and] make sure the prosecutor is not lying." Finally, John reported that the role of the prosecutor is to "make people think I'm guilty...by saying I did it." John's understanding of the roles of the players in the adversarial context appears to be adequate.

John was also questioned about his relationship with his attorney, Mr. Smith. He reported that he and Mr. Smith get along "all right." When John was asked if he and Mr. Smith understand each other, he replied, "I hope so, because he's my lawyer." When John was asked if he trusts Mr. Smith, he replied, "In a way...[because] he sends me mail and talks good, and I heard he's a good lawyer." John quickly added, however, that he "can't trust nobody [sic]." John reported that he believes Mr. Smith will do a good job defending him because "he is a good lawyer...can't take that away from him."

John was also questioned about appropriate courtroom demeanor. When he was asked how he would behave in court, he replied, "I don't know." Upon further questioning, John reported that he would "just sit down and not talk until Smith tells me to." When John was asked what he would do if a witness made a mistake or lied while testifying, he responded that he would "tell my lawyer or the judge." Finally, when John was asked if he would be able to testify, he responded by saying "Probably so, probably not because I'd be nervous." Upon further questioning, however, John stated that he would be able to testify "if that's what he [Mr. Smith] wants me to do."

John was able to voluntarily identify and explain two possible pleas: "not guilty" and "guilty." John stated that a guilty plea meant "I did it," and that a not guilty plea meant "I'm innocent." He was unable to state what rights are waived by entering a guilty plea. It was explained to John that pleading guilty results in the waiver of the following rights: right to an appeal, right to remain silent, right to jury trial, and right to be represented by an attorney. He was able to recall three of these elements when later questioned. Two other possible pleas, "not guilty by reason of insanity" and "no contest" were described to John. He was unable to explain the meanings of those pleas, at which point the pleas were explained to him. When asked about the meaning of a plea bargain, John stated that it "is a deal to get a better outcome."

Finally, John was asked about his plea preference. When John was asked what plea he would like to enter, he responded, "I guess not guilty, but I need to hear what my lawyer thinks is best." Upon further questioning, John reported that he would take the advice of his attorney, stating, "I'll listen to anything Mr. Smith says."

It would appear, therefore, that John's overall capacity to assist counsel in his own defense is sufficient. He demonstrated an adequate understanding of the adversarial process and his specific situation, and he was able to describe how he would interact with his attorney. There is nothing to indicate that John has deficits that would interfere with his ability to assist counsel.

CONCLUSION

In the opinion of the undersigned, based on all of the above, John appears to have a basic understanding of his current legal situation and a sufficient ability to assist counsel in his own defense.

Thank you for the opportunity to evaluate John Doe.

David DeMatteo, JD, PhD
Licensed Psychologist

TEACHING POINT:
SELECTING A SPECIALIZED MEASURE ON JUVENILE COMPETENCE TO STAND TRIAL

The development of specialized measures that directly assess functional-legal capacities for particular legal issues has been one of the most important advances in FMHA in the last three decades.

Legal questions such as competence to stand trial, capacity to waive *Miranda* rights, and sentencing are now informed by various specialized measures that are legally relevant and scientifically strong.

For other legal questions, however, there is not yet a specialized measure that has been developed and validated. That is the present circumstance for *juvenile* competence to stand trial. At some point, the field may see a juvenile adaptation of a scientifically respectable adult measure such as the MacCAT-CA or the ECST-R. Alternatively, some research team may develop a measure for juveniles from the ground up.

Until that time, the forensic clinician has two choices when evaluating juvenile competence to stand trial. The evaluator may carefully review the applicable law and relevant literature, identifying facets of the *Dusky* standard that are particularly important with juveniles and incorporating those into the evaluation through interview, behavioral observation, and collateral interviews (particularly with the attorney, for example). Alternatively, the evaluator may employ a semi-structured checklist of items developed through careful legal, scientific, and professional review (see, e.g., Grisso, 2013). Either of these alternatives works reasonably well, as may be seen in both Case One and Case Two in this chapter. However, the improved capacity to link case-specific results with the broader scientific data is one of the most important justifications for developing specialized measures. Hopefully, the legal question of juvenile competence to stand trial will benefit from the development of such a measure in the near future.

CASE TWO

PRINCIPLE: ENSURE THAT CONDITIONS FOR EVALUATION ARE QUIET, PRIVATE, AND DISTRACTION-FREE (*PRINCIPLE 22*)

This principle describes the degree of quiet, privacy, and freedom from distraction that are important in FMHA. Providing a private and distraction-free environment initially seems so basic as to be a truism: it is *always* important to ensure that administration conditions are reasonably good in any type of evaluation setting. In a forensic context, however, there may be certain problems that are encountered more frequently than they might be in other kinds of mental health assessment. Individuals undergoing FMHA are evaluated in a variety of settings, ranging from jails, prisons, detention centers, courthouses, and secure hospitals, to outpatient clinics and private offices. When FMHA is performed in criminal or juvenile cases, the defendant is often incarcerated or hospitalized in a secure setting. Forensic clinicians must be careful to respect security needs, but they must also be clear about the minimally acceptable conditions under which the evaluation can be meaningfully performed.

What are appropriate conditions for conducting FMHA? Relatively little attention is paid to this question in the literature, perhaps because it seems so obvious. Ethical and legal literatures generally support that forensic opinions be based on valid and reliable methods (see, e.g., American Academy of Psychiatry and the Law, 2005; American Psychiatric Association, 2013b; American Psychological Association, 2010a, 2013b), which presumably would include quiet and distraction-free assessment environments. Indeed, some manualized measures specifically mention these types of conditions as promoting valid and reliable outcomes. For example, the manual for the Minnesota Multiphasic Personality Inventory–2 (MMPI-2)—one of the most widely used instruments in FMHA—states, "The typical testing situation for administering the MMPI-2 requires adequate space at a table to lay out the test booklet and answer sheet, good lighting, a comfortable chair, and *quiet surroundings free of intrusions and distractions*" (Butcher, Graham, Ben-Porath, Tellegen, & Dahlstrom, 2001, p. 9, italics added for emphasis). There is also a lack of empirical research in support of this principle; except for the influence of environment on performance in psychological testing, the impact of such influences has rarely been studied. Based on research on the influence of assessment conditions on psychological test performance, Anastasi and Urbina (2007) recommend that the evaluator should (1) follow standardized procedures in detail; (2) record unusual testing conditions, however minor; and (3) take testing conditions into account when interpreting test results. They observed that the assessment room should be free from undue noise and distraction, and provide adequate lighting, ventilation, seating, and working space for test takers.

Similar considerations have been stressed for clinical interviewing and mental status examinations (Nurcombe & Gallagher, 1986).

Unfortunately, these ideal conditions are not always feasible in FMHA. The present evaluation is somewhat unusual in this respect. The conditions for evaluation were reasonably good. There is no indication that limited privacy, ambient noise, or significant other distractions created a problem. However, the young man being evaluated was suspicious and agitated. In this instance, it was appropriate to bring a familiar staff member into the room to help calm him so he could continue the evaluation. This is something that is rarely done—usually the need for privacy would mean that clinical or security staff members are asked not to be present—but there are some circumstances in which an exception is appropriate.

The Institute of Law, Psychiatry and Public Policy
School of Medicine and University of Virginia
School of Law
University of Virginia Health System
October 27, 2011
Honorable Charles L. Ricketts III
P.O. Box 1336
First Floor, 6 East Johnson Street
Staunton, VA 24401
Re: Terry S. D.

Dear Judge Ricketts:

In response to a court order issued pursuant to §16.1-356 of the Code of Virginia, I have completed an assessment of Terry S. D. for competency to stand trial (CST). Terry is currently charged with two counts of assault and battery under Virginia Code §18.2-57 based upon events that are alleged to have occurred at Commonwealth Center for Children and Adolescents during two separate admissions of Terry to the facility.

I met with Terry for approximately one hour on October 24, 2011. During the assessment, his mother, Ms. Donna Smith, was in the room with me. Near the end of the assessment, Tara Hummel, a staff person, joined us to further calm the young man and allow the assessment to be completed. Prior to the assessment, the purpose and scope of the assessment was explained to Ms. Smith and Terry, and the limitations of confidentiality were explained to them both. Terry demonstrated a partial understanding of the assessment. He understood the legal nature of the inquiry but was not willing or able to listen to more detail about it, as he was constantly pacing around the room, shrugging, and repeatedly asking me to leave.

In conducting the evaluation I reviewed the following sources of information:

1. Records from the Lynchburg Juvenile and Domestic District Court dated November 3, 2000;
2. Records from Page Memorial Hospital dated April 25, 2007;
3. Records from Virginia Baptist Hospital, Child and Adolescent Psychiatry, dated April 7 through April 25, 2007;
4. Records from the Commonwealth Center for Children and Adolescents dated March 2010 through October 21, 2011;
5. A letter from Linda Royster, Esq., Office of the Public Defender, dated October 5, 2011;
6. A telephone interview with Ms. Smith on October 20, 2011;
7. Pre-screening reports by Valley Community Service Board staff, Faith Purdie, M.A., on October 18, 2011 and Lisa Baker, M.A., on October 25, 2011.

COMMENT

In subsequent sections of the report, the source of factual information is identified with a number in parentheses. For example, rather than saying, "according to the Records from the Commonwealth Center for Children and Adolescents," the evaluator follows the statement with a "[4]" to reference that source from the list above. This has the advantages of brevity and enhanced readability. It has the disadvantage of forcing the evaluator, when testifying, to either memorize the list of sources and their corresponding numbers or refer to a list linking them rather than having the source explicitly described in the text.

Records were requested from Liberty Point Behavioral Healthcare, Grafton Integrated Health System, Northwestern Community Service Board, Child Help, and Paul Lyons, M.D. They were not received by the time that this report was due to the Court. The information that was available, however, was extensive and comprehensive, and there is no reason to believe that any information that was not received would influence my observations concerning Terry's competence to stand trial as summarized below.

IDENTIFYING INFORMATION

Terry Smith is a 14-year-eleven-month-old Caucasian male from Staunton, Virginia. He was transferred under Temporary Detention Order status to the Commonwealth Center for Children and Adolescents from the Shenandoah Valley Juvenile Detention Center on October 18, 2011, after he tried to harm himself by repeatedly banging his head on a toilet and trying to choke himself with stitching that he had removed from his suicide blanket [4]. It was noted at that time that the presenting problems were self-injurious behavior and the report of psychotic symptoms. Terry had been transferred to the Shenandoah Valley Juvenile Detention Center on September 20, 2011, from Commonwealth Center for Children and Adolescents after an alleged incident of violence toward a staff member [4].

According to the pre-screening report dated October 18, 2011, Terry had been doing well in detention until three days before his transfer. He attributed his distress to not being treated well and having been threatened by another peer who said that he was going to sexually assault him [7]. Prior to his hospitalization, Terry had been living with his mother, Donna Smith, who had recently separated from Terry's biological father after an attempt at reconciliation. The separation apparently occurred after Mr. Gooden (Terry's father) pushed Terry and spat on Ms. Smith and possibly threatened her with a BB gun, prompting them to leave the home and take up residence in a hotel.

In a second pre-screening report conducted by Lisa Baker, M.A., on October 25, 2011, she noted that Terry has been accepted at Cumberland Hospital for Children and Adolescents in New Kent, Virginia, and was waiting for approval of Medicaid funding.

FAMILY HISTORY

Terry's biological parents, Donna Smith and Donald Gooden, have been involved with each other for over thirty years but have never married. They separated when Terry was four years old but reconciled in 2009 when Terry returned home after a placement in the Grafton program. Terry is the only child born to the couple, although Mr. Gooden has two grown daughters by two other women (neither of these daughters have any contact with Terry). Records from the Grafton program describe Mr. Gooden as suffering from a psychotic disorder, as having a significant substance abuse problem for which he was in recovery, and as having been diagnosed with cancer from which he might not recover. The records indicate that Mr. Gooden receives a disability pension, and according to the in-home worker is in constant pain and "is a very ill man." Ms. Smith suffers from depression and has not been able to fill her medication prescription for the past two months because of financial difficulties. The family, when together, lives in two-bedroom trailer on a farm in Staunton, Virginia [4].

PSYCHIATRIC HISTORY

Terry was born by Caesarean section, weighing close to ten pounds. According to his mother, there were no complications with the pregnancy or delivery, and all of Terry's early developmental milestones were within normal limits. Ms. Smith stated that she did not think that Terry was hyperactive, but school personnel urged her to get him evaluated when he was in kindergarten and one day was suspended for behavioral problems [4].

Records from Commonwealth Center for Children and Adolescents indicate that Terry was first evaluated at the Kluge Children's Center, where, according to Ms. Smith, he was given a number of different diagnoses, including oppositional defiant disorder [4]. He was later diagnosed with attention-deficit hyperactivity disorder and started on medication. Terry was placed at Childhelp Alice C. Tyler Village when he was nine years old and remained there for eight months because of escalating problems at school [4].

A psychological report prepared by Behavioral Resources PLC dated November 2008 indicates that Terry underwent a psychological assessment in 2006 and was found to have a full scale IQ of 73 (Borderline range). On the testing conducted in 2008, he achieved a full scale IQ of 48 (Extremely

Low range). An evaluation conducted by the Warren County Schools in October of 2009 indicated that Terry's fluency and hearing skills were within normal limits. His articulation skills were determined to be 100% with mild distortions on the "s" and "r" phonetics, which were not educationally significant. His receptive and expressive language skills were determined to be in the Moderate to Severe range of impairment. Terry was described as being able to develop positive, empathetic relationships with peers but also demonstrated disruptive behaviors that included running away, poor cooperation, perseveration on issues, poor social boundaries, impulsiveness, physical aggression, and difficulty following directions. According to his mother, Terry has had four seizures and was diagnosed with cryptogenic epilepsy. He was reported to have an IEP in 2010 that identified the need for day treatment [4].

From April 7 through April 25, 2007, Terry was hospitalized at the Virginia Baptist Hospital following a day of escalating violence toward his family requiring his mother to call the police [3]. At the time of admission, Terry described himself as "sad, mad, and scared." At discharge, he stated that he would try to show his love for his family by "being good, listening and being nice, and talking to Mom" [3].

In July of 2007, Terry was admitted to the Grafton treatment program and remained there for two years until October of 2009 [4]. Terry returned home and was enrolled in the Grafton Day Treatment Program for approximately a year before he was hospitalized at Commonwealth Center for Children and Adolescents on March 2, 2010 [4].

Terry was first admitted to Commonwealth Center for Children and Adolescents on a voluntary status after being seen at the Winchester Hospital Medical Center Emergency Room. He had been brought there by his mother and in-home therapist. Records indicate that there was no school on March 1, 2010, and Ms. Smith took Terry to his neurologist's office for a scheduled visit. While there, Ms. Smith told him that he would have to wait until after his appointment to go to McDonald's for lunch. Terry became agitated and aggressive, used profanity, spat on his mother's face and leg, and punched his in-home therapist. Terry also began to bang his fist on the wall, kicked the door, and tore the cover off the desk. The pre-screener noted that Terry at times seemed to become a different person

with "aggressive and hostile behavior." While waiting at the emergency room, Terry attempted to throw a stool though the window, requiring five people to restrain him while he was given a shot of Ativan. Before contacting the Commonwealth Center for Children and Adolescents, the pre-screener attempted to find a bed for Terry in a private hospital, but none would accept him. Terry remained at Commonwealth Center until March 19, 2010, when he was transferred to the Liberty Point residential program [4].

Terry remained at Liberty Point until February of 2011. While at Liberty Point, Terry was described as struggling at times with aggressive behavior toward staff and peers but doing well academically and participating in family therapy with his mother. He was in special education but reported liking math and science and being on the B honor roll. During his stay, Terry was taken for additional testing concerning his seizure disorder. No evidence of seizure activity was found, and the medical staff suggested that the Depakote that Terry had been taking be discontinued. According to Ms. Smith, following the decrease in Depakote, Terry became increasingly aggressive to staff and residents [4].

At the time of admission to the Commonwealth Center for Children and Adolescents on February 7, 2011, Terry reported that he had been returned to the hospital because he had kicked one staff person in the face and had "broken the nose" of another. Terry could not recall what had prompted his behavior but did not believe that he had been angry with either of the two staff members. The pre-screener report indicates that Terry had told her that "monsters" took over his body and caused him to act in this way. He also reported that he had been hearing voices over the past three days telling him to kill himself and other residents. He said that he had been hearing these voices since he was five years old and that they would tell him to "fight and kill." Terry told staff at the hospital that sometimes he wished he was dead when he gets into trouble, but he denied suicidal ideation or plans [4].

During this hospitalization, Terry was described as being quite needy and demanding and tending to feel that he was not being listened to when he was simply having difficulty waiting or not getting what he wanted. He was also described as often getting into power struggles, although he responded fairly well to clear but gentle limits and emotional support. A report conducted during this hospitalization observed that Terry might suffer from some obscure genetic syndrome that accounted for his significant behavioral disinhibition, mood symptomatology, short stature, seizure history, and syndromic facies (unusual facial features often associated with a genetic disorder). It was determined that Terry would be kept in the hospital despite no further aggressive behavior so that the staff could provide a thoughtful review of prior placements and provide informed recommendations concerning discharge. The records indicate that Ms. Smith wanted Terry to return home. This was considered to be a viable placement if Terry could be provided close psychiatric follow-up, intensive individual and family therapy, specialized school support, mentoring, and involvement in structured, supervised peer-group activities. Terry was discharged on March 26, 2011, with arrangements having been made for in-home therapy by National Counseling Services. A plan had also been identified to offer Ms. Smith support in making application for Social Security Disability Insurance assistance, and a second request had been made to Family Assessment and Planning Team for mentoring services to support Terry [4].

On March 26, 2011, Terry returned home, with services being provided by National Counseling Services and Northwestern Community Services Board [4]. He was described as doing well up until the separation of his parents. This separation had occurred because of a fight between his parents that had become violent. Terry and his mother were residing in a hotel, and he became agitated when his mother would not let him walk from the hotel to the local library.

On April 19, 2011, Terry was seen at Winchester Hospital Emergency Room after he began to fight with his mother and "scared her." He apparently had tried to pull the mirror off the car, tore his mother's necklace off, and put his hands around his own neck saying to her "get me some help." Terry stated that he did not like getting angry, wanted help with his anger, and would be willing to go to the hospital for treatment. Terry remained at the Commonwealth Center for Children and Adolescents until May 9, 2011. During the hospitalization, his lithium and Zoloft were tapered off as neither appeared to be effective, leaving him on Guanfacine, Abilify, and Depakote. He had multiple restrictive interventions, but it was determined that there was no

reason to keep him in the hospital, where his behavior tended to regress, and he was discharged home after several successful family visits [4].

Terry was seen for a pre-screening evaluation on the night of June 22, 2011, at Warren Memorial Hospital Emergency Room after he became aggressive with his mother. After his outburst, Terry became remorseful, asking her to forgive him and begging her to take her back to the hospital. Terry had been receiving in-home services since his last admission, and according to the in-home worker, had been "spiraling" for the past couple of weeks and had also threatened the worker. Ms. Smith had arranged for a second babysitter, after the first one quit after being assaulted by Terry as she was working at a 7-11 convenience store on the night shift. Apparently, they had returned to the home that they shared with Mr. Smith, but Terry refused to stay with his father, saying that he was afraid of him. During the hospitalization, Terry was found to have a decrease in his hemoglobin, and a comprehensive metabolic panel was requested along with a urine screen that was negative and an EKG that was normal. Terry was placed on the older adolescent ward, in part due to his past history of aggression. He experienced only two episodes of aggression and immediately began to ask to go home. He was described as approaching staff with a childlike presentation, asking for hugs and nurturance, but becoming aggressive with hitting, spitting, and chair throwing when he felt that his needs were being frustrated. A discharge meeting was held with all the agencies providing care with efforts being again made to have Terry's treatment needs reviewed by FAPT. Terry was discharged home on July 28, 2011, with a plan for him to begin a half-day alternative program at Breck Alternative School on July 5, 2011 [4].

On July 3, 2011, Terry was taken to the Emergency Room at Warren Memorial Hospital because of what appeared to be a seizure. His Depakote level was increased from 250 mg twice a day to 500 mg. twice a day. On July 5, 2011, Terry was seen by Dr. Goshen and no major problems were noted at that time. Two days later, Terry was reported to have "snapped" with his babysitter and became aggressive with her. He was taken to Warren Memorial Hospital, where he raised his fist at the admitting nurse and spat at her. The next morning, Terry told the staff that his parents did not get along and that his father would spit on his mother [4].

On July 8, 2011, Terry was admitted to the Commonwealth Center for Children and Adolescents for the fifth time. Terry was treated for head lice and underwent a medical examination that was notable for syndromic facies, short stature, wide-set eyes, lower back pain, loss of consciousness at age four, some soft neurological signs, and cryptogenic epilepsy (a disorder characterized by recurrent episodes of brain dysfunction due to sudden, disorderly, and excessive neuron discharge). During the admission, Terry had 14 restrictive interventions deriving from his aggressive behavior toward both peers and staff. A schedule was devised that allowed him to have therapeutic passes only when he had demonstrated no aggression for three days. Terry's last incident of aggression was on July 25, and, at his request and that of his mother, he was discharged home on July 28, 2011. A meeting of various treatment providers was held on July 27, and it was determined that Northwestern Community Services Board would coordinate his outpatient services with in-home services to include family therapy, psychiatric follow-up, and intensive educational services. Further contact with Dr. Lyons was recommended to further assess the use of Depakote, as it was not clear the benefits were sufficient to warrant its continued use [4].

On September 19, 2011, Terry was admitted to the Commonwealth Center for Children and Adolescents for the sixth time, after being taken to Page Memorial Hospital by his parents. He had broken a window, had been making threats of harming himself, and had also begun to make vague threats of harming both parents. Terry became agitated during the pre-screening and told the evaluator that he might do something he would regret. He changed his mind several times during the evaluation as to whether he would be willing to be admitted to the hospital. Based on the assessment, the evaluator ultimately determined that commitment was necessary due to the many risk factors suggesting that "Terry presented as a serious danger to self and others to the extent that severe or remedial injury could result" [4].

At the time of admission, Terry reported having experimented with cigarettes and snuff over the summer, with a toxicology screen conducted at Page Memorial Hospital being positive for barbiturates. He was diagnosed as suffering from the following disorders:

Axis I: Disruptive Behavior Disorder Not Otherwise Specified

Mood Disorder Not Otherwise Specified
Attention-Deficit Hyperactivity Disorder, Combined Type
Pervasive Developmental Disorder Not Otherwise Specified
Phonological Disorder
Axis II: Borderline Intellectual Functioning, Provisional
Axis III: Cryptogenic Epilepsy
Short Stature
Allergies to Biaxin and Lamictal
Axis IV: Stressors: Moderate: Family Conflict, Educational Problems, Legal Problems
Axis V: GAF at Admission, 40.

Terry's past medications have included Adderal, Risperdal, Depakote, Seroquel, Stattera, Abilify, Clonidine, Tenex, and lithium. He is currently being prescribed Abilify 20 mg. each evening, Depakote 500 mg. each morning and evening, Tenex 1.5 mg. each morning and evening, and 1 mg. each day at 2:00 p.m., and Prozac 20 mg each morning.

CLINICAL PRESENTATION

Terry presented as a boy of small stature who appeared much younger that his actual age. He was brought to meet me at the door of the hospital, and despite the obvious nature of our meeting, I spontaneously asked if he were Terry, as I thought I was looking at a ten-year-old boy rather than an almost 15-year-old young man. He was dressed in shorts and a T-shirt and appeared disheveled and poorly kempt. He became quickly agitated, and as soon as we entered the interview room, he began to pace about the room, refusing to sit down, and with profanity thrusting one of his fists into each other and demanding that I leave. At one point while sitting on the floor he quickly reached out to slap my foot and then tried to remove my shoe by pulling on the heel. There was a provocative, controlling, and slightly contemptuous quality to these behaviors, and they gave me the impression that he believed that if he offered enough resistance and was threatening enough in his behavior, he would not have to complete the evaluation. He clearly stated that he wanted to finish with me and be able to go and have a one-to-one visit with this mother. However, for reasons that were largely inexplicable to me, he seemed to experience a sudden change of mind, and jumping up from the floor, he came over to me, wanting to put his head on my shoulder, while telling me that he was sorry. Terry tended to say "I don't know" to anything and everything I asked him—and then when he did begin to respond to my questions, he began to count my questions, saying that I only had a certain number before he quit (answering). Terry suffers from articulation problems, which made it difficult to understand what he said at times, particularly because he speaks very quickly, in short sentences, and with minimal eye contact while moving and repositioning himself constantly. Occasionally, he would peek over at me to see what I was doing. At one point in the evaluation, Terry told me "I'm scared," with no particular context or prompt for this reporting.

Terry demonstrated good memory for past events and was able to recall events that had occurred in the past, even during times when he was very agitated and upset. His judgment, however, was significantly impaired, and he was never able to accept the possibility, as explained to him repeatedly by his mother, that the competency assessment was for his benefit, would not last long, and was best completed to the best of his ability. He did not appear to be experiencing any psychotic symptoms and at no time appeared to be responding to internal stimuli. His intelligence was clearly above the most recent testing that resulted in a full scale IQ of 48 and seemed to be more congruent with the earlier testing that suggested a full scale IQ of 73. At one point, Terry stated that he needed to take time out and wanted to return to his room with his mother. He returned about five minutes later with his favorite staff person, asking that she and his mother join him in the interview. The remainder of the interview was completed with Terry sitting between Ms. Hummel and his mother, and in a contrite but antsy manner, answering the questions that I asked of him. When we were done, he reached out to shake my hand as I had done upon first meeting him.

ASSESSMENT OF COMPETENCY TO STAND TRIAL

There were no indications that Terry understood the purpose or nature of the competency evaluation. He continued throughout the assessment to view it as a noxious event that he should disrupt by threatening behavior, or terminate by his repeated demands. He did become more cooperative at the end of the interview, but this change in behavior appeared to derive from the close presence of two adults he trusted and not from an informed understanding of the significance or impact of the assessment to him. His strained cooperation appeared to derive primarily from this mother's request that he be "good" and his wish not to act up in front of his favorite staff person.

At the beginning of the evaluation, Terry sought to deny any knowledge of the court process or any awareness of his current legal situation. He stated that he did not know the role of the attorney, was not acquainted with or familiar with his defense attorney, Ms. Royster, and did not know what he had done that might have contributed to his move to detention and the current charges against him. To each of these inquires he responded, "I don't know," adding "can you please go," with various profanities intermixed with these demands.

As the evaluation proceeded, Terry began to convey what appeared to be a more accurate portrayal of his current level of understanding. He acknowledged that "yeah, yeah" he did know Ms. Royster and had meet with her on one occasion. When asked about her role or job, Terry said that it was her job to tell him if he had to go to "juvie" [juvenile detention]. He described there being two attorneys in court, one "good' and one "bad." The "good attorney" would try to say that he "didn't do it or didn't mean to do it." In contrast, the "bad attorney" would try to say that he "had done it on purpose." At a later point in the interview, Terry reflected that he knew the answer to my question, but added, "I will tell my attorney but not you!" Asked about the way he might work with his attorney, Terry explained that he would do this by "being good, no fights, no arguments."

Terry indicated that the judge was the person "wearing black." He did not clearly articulate the role of the judge but explained that if he were found not guilty he "could go free." When asked what it meant to plead guilty or not guilty, Terry did not offer any explanation other than asserting forcefully that he was going to plead guilty "because I'm mad." There were no indications that Terry understood the nature of a plea bargain or that there may be legal reasons why he might want to plead not guilty to the charges. He had no understanding of the rights that he would be giving up if he followed his current inclination and pled guilty.

When asked about the nature of a charge, Terry stated that it was what happened when "you act up." He explained that the outcome of a charge could involve being sent to "juvie," "detention" or "get one of those things on my ankle." He told me that he thought he "might have to go to juvie," and would if he had to, although he would prefer to stay in the hospital as it was "more comfortable."

When asked about the type of behavior one should demonstrate in the courtroom, Terry stated that he had "a big heart" and was "going to use it." He added that he was "going to do good" and demonstrated how he was going to act by saying, "yes ma'am, yes sir." When asked if he wanted to testify, Terry said that he did not know and seemed confused by this question, reiterating that he would say, "yes, ma'am and yes, sir."

Near the end of the evaluation, Terry was asked about the circumstances of his arrest from the Commonwealth Center for Children and Adolescents. He stated that a police officer came to the hospital and put him in handcuffs before leading him out of the hospital. He recalled that the police officer asked him how old he was and commented that it was wrong to put such a small 14-year-old in detention. He was asked about whether he had been Mirandized prior to being taken into custody. He was not familiar with this term, but when these rights were articulated to him, he stated that he had not been told these things by the police officer. Asked further what they might mean, Terry did not seem familiar with them and interpreted the right to remain silent as meaning that he was to "not cuss and don't try to get back." His explanation of these rights suggested that he had no understanding of the meaning of the word *right* and was not able to apply the principle to his own situation. He described them as imperatives for curbing his disruptive behavior rather than protections designed to protect certain of his legal rights and interests.

CONCLUSIONS

Terry is a seriously emotionally disturbed young man with cognitive abilities that are most likely in the Borderline Level of intellectual functioning. His deficits in adaptive functioning are significant, and might further warrant a diagnosis of mild mental retardation, which is generally diagnosed at IQ scores three points below those achieved by Terry in 2006. Terry has also been diagnosed with a pervasive developmental disorder that reflects his severe and pervasive impairments in several areas of development, including reciprocal social interactions, communication skills, and the presence of stereotypical behaviors and activities. Superimposed on these innate conditions are several additional mental disorders, including a disruptive behavioral disorder, an attention-deficit hyperactivity disorder, and a phonological disorder, reflecting the difficulties that he has with the articulation of certain oral sounds. For the past couple of years, Terry has also been diagnosed with a mood disorder, which reflects his feeling of sadness and suicidal ideation and might encompass the more psychotic-like symptoms (for example, visual hallucinations and voices telling him to be violent) that he reported while residing at the Grafton School and Liberty Point. This combination of disorders and their associated symptoms has made it difficult if not impossible for Terry to live at home with his mother, to develop ongoing peer relationships, to accomplish what he might be capable of at school, and to navigate through any demanding social situation without becoming violent and threatening. Given one report of his father suffering from a psychotic disorder, it is not possible to rule out the possibility that these behaviors might be associated with an incipient psychotic disorder, these generally becoming more apparent in early adulthood. They might also reflect a genetic disorder that is associated with his small stature, unusual facial features, below-average IQ, and possibly his violent tendencies.

The intermingled nature of these disorders impacts Terry's current level of adjudicative competency. He has developed an accurate and fairly sophisticated understanding of the role of his defense attorney and was able to convey her role in arguing that he did not mean to commit the crime for which he is charged. He also gave a rudimentary demonstration of his understanding of the privileged nature of the relationship when telling me that he knew what he had done to be charged with assault but would tell his attorney and not me. Terry was able to articulate the nature of his charge and the possible sentences that might accrue from them, including the likelihood that he would be sent to "juvie." He understood the function of the judge and the role that he or she would play in determining if he would be confined in some way or allowed to "go free."

His chronically irritable mood appears to be influencing his current thinking about his plea options, as he asserted that he planned to plead guilty because he was "mad." His understanding of his role in the courtroom was similarly limited and reflected the need to be polite and say "yes, ma'am and yes, sir" with no understanding of the collaborative role with his attorney that might best represent his legal interests. He did not understand the meaning of a right and the protections that derived from them, and in line with his provocative behavior, he thought that the right to remain silent meant that he was to not "cuss" or "try to get back." It can be anticipated that his disruptive behavior will make it difficult for him to participate thoughtfully while in the courtroom, with the entire process becoming a power struggle that he can seek to control through threatening and possibly violent behavior. This behavior is present both when he is scared and when he thinks a situation is not unfolding as he expects or wishes.

Based upon these observations, it is my opinion that Terry is currently impaired in his capacity to achieve a rational understanding of the proceeding against him, including an understanding of his participation in the court process and making decisions in his own best interests. While he demonstrates a rudimentary but adequate factual understanding of the role of his attorney and other personnel in the court, he is limited in his understanding of how he might contribute to and use this structure to further his best interests. It appears that he does have the capacity to rationally consult with his attorney. Although Terry might at times be resistant, there are no indications that he would not be able to involve himself in restoration services and be restored in a relatively short period of time.

Should the court find Terry competent to stand trial, it will be important to have his mother and a trusted staff person in the courtroom in clear view to help temper his provocative and possibly violent behavior. If he chooses to testify, he will also need the help of his mother to interpret his comments, as they are difficult to understand without considerable experience in talking to and listening to Terry. Because of Terry's reduced attention span and ability to focus, it can also be anticipated that he will not be able to follow the nature of any proceeding for an extended period of time and may require a time-out should he become confused or agitated.

Should the court determine Terry to be incompetent to stand trial, a number of interventions might help to structure the restoration process and promote his successful remediation. It does not appear that Terry has ever received a comprehensive genetic workup, despite characteristics that are suggestive of a genetic abnormality. It would be of benefit to everyone working with Terry for this type of study to be completed and consultation obtained with experts who are knowledgeable about any condition that might be identified. I would also recommend a telephone consultation with the researchers at the Child Psychiatry Unit of the National Institute of Mental Health. They are conducting cutting-edge research on both childhood schizophrenia and the neurology of the developing brain, two areas that might inform the treatment interventions that might best help Terry. More practically, any restoration counselor assigned to the case will need to have in place a thoughtful and consistently implemented safety plan to protect them while seeking to establish a relationship with Terry. Without a relationship, Terry is likely to use each restoration session as another opportunity to demonstrate his will through domination and violence. With a relationship, Terry is likely to engage with the interesting new interactive tools that are available in Virginia, and in so doing, learn a great deal about his participation in the court process and his legal rights and options.

Regardless of the outcome concerning his competency, it will be important for anyone working with Terry in the future to remain cognizant of his biological age and the fact that he will be turning 18 years old within three years. His appearance as a prepubescent boy is compelling and tends to camouflage his teenage status, the many developmental issues that are at play during this period, and the importance of beginning to help prepare him for some type of independent living when he reaches adulthood. He is in need of vocational training, help in understanding and being involved with his medications, and assistance in beginning to develop reasonable and pro-social peer relationships. There are no indications that he will be successful living with his mother, and there are indications that this type of situation could prove dangerous in the future.

Respectfully submitted,
Janet I. Warren, DSW
Professor of Psychiatry and Neurobehavioral Sciences
Institute of Law, Psychiatry and Public Policy
University of Virginia

TEACHING POINT:
IDENTIFYING AND IMPLEMENTING STRATEGIES FOR IMPROVING INADEQUATE CONDITIONS

Forensic clinicians conduct evaluations in a variety of settings. The important considerations identified earlier (Heilbrun, Marczyk, & DeMatteo, 2002) with respect to evaluation conditions are privacy, quiet, and freedom from distraction. The content of the verbal exchanges between evaluator and evaluee should not be overheard by anyone else, for privacy reasons. The surrounding noise should be such that it is not clearly a distraction to the attention, concentration, and focus needed for meaningful participation in FMHA. Finally, other distractions (e.g., other residents waving; observing those in the visiting area) should also be minimized.

Because FMHA is often conducted in secure settings, there can be no reasonable expectation that evaluation conditions will be comparable to those in a hospital or private office. But when conditions move from *marginal* (problems in one or more of these areas, not sufficient to render the evaluation impossible, but enough to make it difficult and in need of some description in the report) to *unacceptable* (sufficient problems in one or more areas to grossly interfere with a meaningful evaluation), then the forensic clinician must take two steps. First, the problem must be acknowledged and the evaluation stopped; second, some solution must be sought. This solution may be as simple as requesting a move to a different room, or something else that can be implemented in the short term. But if this does not succeed, then the evaluation must be discontinued and a more acceptable solution sought. Typically this would begin with the referring attorney, who might contact the director of the facility to seek a better alternative for evaluation conditions. Even if the forensic clinician contacts the facility directly, the attorney should be notified in case his or her intervention becomes needed—and for an update on the progress of the evaluation. If the evaluator needs to seek a court order to facilitate such conditions, the retaining attorney would be responsible for obtaining it.

21

Juvenile Commitment

This chapter will focus on the legal question of the disposition of juvenile cases. It is called "commitment" because the commitment to a state department of juvenile justice for residential placement is one of the options before the juvenile court if there is an adjudication of delinquency. Other options typically include community placement or some form of probation, whether intensive or standard. The principle for the first case involves accepting referrals within one's area of expertise, and the teaching point addresses the training and experience needed for expertise in juvenile forensic assessment. The principle for the second case describes the importance of providing appropriate notification and obtaining authorization, and highlights considerations specific to juvenile populations. The teaching point more specifically addresses procedures for obtaining authorization when evaluating minors who cannot yet legally provide consent.

can affect cognitive and emotional functioning is important when evaluating juveniles. Similarly, it is important to have knowledge of psychological assessments and forensic assessment instruments designed specifically for use with juvenile populations (Hoge, 2012).

The evaluator in the present case has extensive expertise with offending and non-offending adolescents in both treatment and forensic capacities. These experiences provided him with a sufficient knowledge base of developmental considerations, and how those considerations might be relevant in this particular forensic context. Thus the evaluator was able to conduct a comprehensive evaluation—taking into account appropriate development considerations—that addressed the forensic issue.

FORENSIC EVALUATION
August 27, 2012
Re: John Doe
PP#: 123456

CASE ONE

PRINCIPLE: ACCEPT REFERRALS ONLY WITHIN AREA OF EXPERTISE (*PRINCIPLE 9*)

This principle was discussed in some detail in Chapter 8. Therefore, we will move directly to how the present report can illustrate its application in FMHA. When conducting evaluations with juveniles, it is important to have expertise not only within the realm of forensic psychology, but also human development and the way that developmental considerations may relate to the legal question (Heilbrun & DeMatteo, 2012). As noted by Hoge (2012), "It is important to recognize that youth are going through a developmental process and that the functioning of youth in many areas is less advanced than that of adults" (p. 1256). Therefore, an understanding of the ways that development

REFERRAL

John Doe is a 16-year-old African-American male (DOB: X/X/X) who is currently charged with robbery, aggravated assault, criminal conspiracy, theft, possession of an instrument of crime, recklessly endangering another person, and simple assault. A request for a mental health evaluation to provide the defense with information relevant to John's treatment needs and amenability in the context of public safety, pursuant to Pennsylvania Code, was made by John's attorney (Robert Smith, Esq.).

PROCEDURES

John was evaluated for approximately 5.25 hours on August 24, 2012, at the Philadelphia County Jail, where he is currently incarcerated. In addition to a psychosocial interview, John was administered a structured screening instrument for adolescent symptoms of mental and emotional disorders (the Massachusetts Youth Screening Inventory, 2nd ed. [MAYSI-2]), two subtests from a standard test of current functioning in academic areas (the Wide Range Achievement Test, 4th ed. [WRAT-4]), a standard measure of overall intellectual functioning (the Wechsler Abbreviated Scale of Intelligence, 2nd ed. [WASI-II]), and a standard objective test of mental and emotional functioning among adolescents (the Minnesota Multiphasic Personality Inventory–Adolescent [MMPI-A]). In addition, John's mother, Rhonda Doe, was interviewed for approximately 45 minutes (via telephone on 9/27/12) regarding John's past and current functioning. The following documents, obtained from John's attorney, were reviewed as part of this evaluation:

(1) Psycho-Social Summary (dated 7/13/12);
(2) Arrest Report (dated 5/15/12);
(3) Arrest Records (dated 5/15/12);
(4) Criminal Complaint (dated 5/14/12);
(5) Investigation Report (dated 5/14/12);
(6) Investigation Interview Records (dated 5/14/12);
(7) Pretrial Service Division, Investigation Report (dated 6/1/12);
(8) Preliminary Hearing Transcript (dated 7/1/12);
(9) Hospital Records;
(10) Academic Records.

Prior to the evaluation, John was notified about the purpose of the evaluation and associated limits on confidentiality. He appeared to understand the basic purpose of the evaluation, reporting back his understanding that he would be evaluated and that a written report would be submitted to his attorney. He further understood that the report could be used in his de-certification hearing and, if it were, copies would be provided to the prosecution and court. A similar notification of purpose was provided to Ms. Doe prior to the collateral interview, and she appeared to understand the information provided to her.

RELEVANT HISTORY

Historical information was obtained from John and the collateral sources noted above. The consistency of the information provided by John was assessed through the use of multiple sources whenever possible. An amended report will be filed if additional collateral information that materially changes the results of this evaluation is obtained prior to John's court date.

Family History

John Doe was born on [xx/xx/xx] in Pennsylvania to Rhonda Doe and Tom Doe. John reported that his parents were not married, but maintained a long-term relationship. He reported having two maternal half-sisters and four paternal half-brothers, noting that he is the second oldest. John reported being raised primarily by his mother, adding that his father lived with the family until John was age 11. He reported that his father occasionally took an active role in raising him, but that they had little contact once his father moved out. When asked about his relationship with his father, John stated, "We never really liked each other." He noted, however, that they have had substantially more contact since John has been incarcerated. John stated that his father is "now trying to play his part" and that they are on a "good path." John's mother, Ms. Doe, believes that John and his father are developing a healthy relationship. John described having a "good" relationship with his mother, stating that he can "talk to her about anything" and she "points me in the right direction." Ms. Doe reported that she is currently unemployed due to medical problems, including hypertension and diabetes, and that her family is supported through public assistance.

John described his childhood as "good most of the time," and he reported that his basic needs (food, clothing, shelter) were met. He described himself as a "mama's boy" who spent most of his time with his mother and grandmother. John noted that he would occasionally go outside and play sports with kids from the neighborhood. He denied any history of abuse (sexual, physical, or emotional) or neglect, although he reported that his father often demeaned him. John reported experiencing several losses. He reported that his cousin was killed in a shooting incident when John was age 12, and he described being severely affected by this event. Ms. Doe reported that John "got an 'I don't care' attitude" after his cousin died. John also reported that his grandmother died of stomach cancer in 2006, his grandfather died of cancer a short time later, and his great grandmother died last year. John reported being in an intimate relationship with his girlfriend, Gianna, for two years. He reported that Gianna gave birth to their son, Steven, in late 2011, and that she is currently pregnant with another child. John reported that he was an active father prior to his incarceration, and that he plans to support his family through gainful employment once he is released. Ms. Doe reported that John was a "pretty good" father prior to his incarceration, and she anticipates that he will be an active father once he is released.

Educational History

John reported attending Smith Elementary School for kindergarten through part of second grade before transferring to Jones Elementary School for the remainder of the second grade. He reported completing third through fifth grade at Jones. John reported attending sixth through eighth grade at Thompson Middle School, and ninth grade at Peterson High School. All of this information is consistent with John's academic records. John reported that he started tenth grade at Peterson, but that the "truancy court" sent him to Sunny Valley School because of his excessive absences from Peterson. John reported that he was in tenth grade at the time of his current arrest, but that he was planning to take General Equivalency Diploma (GED) classes.

When asked about his attendance, John described having "good" attendance through sixth grade. He reported that his attendance declined in seventh grade because he became more interested in "girls and hanging out." John reported that his attendance at Peterson was not good because he relied on public transportation. His academic records reflect high numbers of unexcused absences since 2006–2007: 2006–2007 (31); 2007–2008 (24); 2008–2009 (42); 2009–2010 (38); 2010–2011 (75). When asked about his academic performance, John reported earning mostly "Cs and Ds." Ms. Doe reported that John's academic performance declined because "he didn't care anymore." John reported being suspended "over 20 times," and his academic records reflect 26 out-of-school suspensions dating back to 2002. Ms. Doe reported that John was "always in trouble in school because of his anger." John denied participating in any sports or activities in school, although he reported that he "read to kindergarteners" when he was in fourth or fifth

grade. John reported that his educational goal is to earn his GED and attend college to study "cooking or construction."

Medical and Psychiatric History

John denied any history of serious injuries or illnesses. He reported breaking his right leg at age 12 playing basketball, and breaking his left hand in a street fight at age 14. He denied ever receiving stitches or being hospitalized. He denied any history of head injuries or loss of consciousness. John reported that he has asthma, which he treats with an inhaler.

John reported receiving therapy for "a bad temper" when he was age seven. He stated that his school referred him for therapy because "little things made me mad," adding that he attended therapy for two months and was prescribed Ritalin (a medication for attentional/behavioral disorders). Ms. Doe reported that John took Ritalin for less than a month. John reported receiving treatment for "depression" (after the death of his cousin) at a local community mental health center when he was age 13. He reported attending treatment twice per week for about two months and being prescribed "some medication that knocked me out." Despite repeated requests, his treatment records from the community mental health center were not available at the time this report was written. John reported that he was involuntarily committed at age 15 after he tried to kill himself. He reported being unsure if he actually attempted suicide, noting that he "blacked out" and has no memory of the event. He reported being prescribed two medications, but discontinuing them shortly after discharge. Ms. Doe reported that John attended outpatient therapy at the Johnson Foundation after he was discharged from the hospital, but "got kicked out because of his anger problems."

When asked about his current mental health, John reported that he refused to take psychotropic medications when he arrived at the Philadelphia County Jail because he believes he no longer needs medication. He reported being "a little depressed" because he is incarcerated and away from his girlfriend and son. He denied any recent changes in his appetite, but reported having difficulty sleeping. He denied any current suicidal ideation. Ms. Doe reported that John still needs medication because "he still has anger problems...and he used to punch holes in the walls." Ms. Doe reported a family history of bipolar disorder, schizophrenia, and ADHD.

Substance Use History

John reported first trying marijuana at age eight, but not using it regularly use until he was 14. He reported using marijuana two times per week at age 14, and then using it ten times per day for a little over a year when he was age 15. He reported using marijuana with such frequency because it "kept me calm." John reported that he stopped using marijuana in December 2011 because it exacerbated his asthma. When asked about other drugs, John reported experimenting with Valium (once) and alcohol (a few times). He denied ever selling drugs.

Social History

John reported having no friends, but spending time "with people" playing basketball, watching television, and talking to girls. He reported spending most of his spare time with his son. He denied being negatively influenced by his peers. He denied any significant history of fighting, and he denied ever being part of a gang or carrying a weapon. Ms. Doe reported that she did not care for John's friends "because they looked like trouble."

Occupational History

John denied any history of formal employment, but noted that he made side money by cleaning houses. As previously noted, John reported that his occupational goal is to get involved with construction or cooking.

Offense History

According to John's arrest records, he has one juvenile arrest. Specifically, he was arrested on October 14, 2011, and charged with conspiracy, unauthorized use of an auto, and theft–receiving stolen property. He was placed on in-home detention and then on a consent decree. In January 2012, John's consent decree was revoked because he violated the terms of the decree by not attending school. As a result, he was adjudicated delinquent and placed on probation.

CURRENT CLINICAL CONDITION

John presented as an African-American male of average height and thin build who appeared his stated age. He was dressed in jail garb and well-groomed when evaluated on August 24, 2012, at the Philadelphia County Jail, where he is currently incarcerated. He was cooperative and polite throughout the evaluation. His speech was clear, coherent, and relevant, and he appeared to give reasonable effort to the evaluation tasks. His capacity for attention and concentration appeared adequate, and he was able to focus reasonably well on a series of tasks during the entire evaluation without becoming visibly distracted or fatigued. Therefore, it appears that this evaluation provides a reasonably good estimate of John's current functioning.

John's mood during the evaluation was largely neutral, but he showed appropriate emotional variability. He was correctly oriented to time, place, and person. He denied experiencing any perceptual disturbances (auditory or visual hallucinations) or delusions (bizarre ideas with no possible basis in reality), and his train of thought was clear and logical.

Wechsler Abbreviated Scale of Intelligence (WASI)

John's intellectual functioning was formally measured with the WASI. He obtained a full scale IQ score of 87, which places him within the Low Average range of intellectual functioning and at the 19th percentile relative to others his age (meaning he obtained an IQ score equal to or higher than 19% of similarly aged individuals). Given the measurement error on the WASI, there is a 95% likelihood that John's full scale IQ score falls between 82 and 92. His Verbal IQ score was 85 (16th percentile; Low Average range) and his Performance IQ score was 92 (30th percentile; Average range).

Wide Range Achievement Test, 4th ed. (WRAT-4)

John's basic academic skills, as measured by the WRAT-4, showed deficits in both areas measured (as reflected by his grade equivalency scores): Spelling (grade 3.9 equivalent) and Word Reading (grade 2.6 equivalent). Both areas should be considered in need of remediation.

Massachusetts Youth Screening Inventory, 2nd ed. (MAYSI-2)

On a structured inventory of currently experienced symptoms of mental and emotional disorders designed for use with adolescents (the MAYSI-2), John endorsed 13 of the 52 items. Some of the items

John endorsed included having trouble falling asleep or staying asleep (since being incarcerated), having nervous or worried feelings that keep him from doing what he wants to do (because he thinks about his son and girlfriend), being easily upset (because he was not with his mother when she gave birth to his step-sister), feeling too tired to have a good time (due to poor sleeping), feeling lonely too much of the time (since being incarcerated), using drugs to help him feel better (noting he used marijuana to "keep calm"), feeling angry a lot (due to his incarceration), being high at school (one time), difficulty feeling close to people outside of his family (because he "can't trust people"), breaking something on purpose because he was mad (noting he punched a hole in a wall), having something bad/terrifying happen to him (being incarcerated).

Minnesota Multiphasic Personality Inventory-Adolescent (MMPI-A)

John was administered the MMPI-A to measure his current personality functioning. Each item was read to him to help facilitate item comprehension. He responded to the items in an inconsistent and apparently random manner, which could indicate that he did not fully understand the items' meaning or did not provide sufficient attention to the items. Although his resulting MMPI-A profile is valid, it should be interpreted with caution. John's clinical scales were within normal limits, which suggests he is not experiencing significant psychological distress at the present time. This is somewhat unusual for an adolescent in a correctional setting, but consistent with his self-report. John's profile suggests that he finds it difficult to be around other people and prefers to be alone, which is also consistent with his self-report. His MMPI-A profile suggests that he has some personality characteristics associated with the presence or development of a substance use problem, although he did not acknowledge any substance use problems on the MMPI.

TREATMENT NEEDS AND AMENABILITY

There are five areas in which John has treatment/rehabilitation needs which, if addressed, should reduce his risk for antisocial behavior. These areas are:

(1) continued education and/or vocational training, with vocational counseling;

(2) substance abuse treatment, with a particular focus on relapse prevention;

(3) skills-based training in anger management and decision-making/problem-solving;

(4) the development of a pro-social peer group; and

(5) further evaluation of his mental health functioning.

First, John would benefit from continued education and/or vocational training with vocational counseling. John's academic history is marked by several school changes, poor attendance, uneven academic performance, and many suspensions. Although John's full scale IQ score of 87 suggests he is functioning in the Low Average range, his basic academic skills are considerably underdeveloped. Earning a GED may be a reasonable goal, but in light of his age and present situation, John may also benefit from training in specific job skills and functional academic areas related to his areas of interest. He would also benefit from vocational counseling. John identified two potentially realistic goals—cooking and construction—and vocational counseling would help him identify other occupational goals that are consistent with his education/training and aptitude. This area is indirectly relevant to public safety and John's risk for future antisocial behavior, to the extent that it enhances his ability to obtain and keep a job, which would serve to provide him with income from a legitimate source and take up his free time. John acknowledged that obtaining employment is critical to his personal development and the well-being of his children, and he recognized the risk-reducing value of being employed. Ms. Doe emphasized that John would benefit from "having something to occupy his time."

Second, John would benefit from substance abuse treatment, with a particular focus on relapse prevention. John reported first trying marijuana at age eight and then using marijuana on a daily basis for a little over a year when he was age 15. Although he has reportedly not used marijuana since December 2011, his level of prior marijuana use suggests that he would benefit from substance abuse treatment to prevent further drug use. A treatment plan that includes relapse-prevention strategies would be particularly helpful. Preventing the future use of marijuana should reduce the likelihood that he will engage in antisocial behavior.

Third, John would benefit from skills-based training in anger management and decision-making/problem-solving. John reported that he is "a little" better at controlling his anger, but that he still loses his temper. Ms. Doe reported that John "still has anger problems" and is need of treatment for it. As such, John would benefit from skills-based training to teach him how to better manage his anger. Moreover, although John reported that he generally makes good decisions, his history suggests that some of his troubles are due to poor decisions. Therefore, he would benefit from skills training designed to improve his decision-making/problem-solving skills. Training in these areas is directly relevant to John's risk for future antisocial behavior, and participating in such interventions should decrease his risk for future offending.

Fourth, John would benefit from the development of a pro-social peer group. John denied having any close friends or a pro-social peer network, noting that he spent most of his time with his son. Ms. Doe denied having firsthand of knowledge of whether John's friends are a negative influence, but stated that John would benefit from spending time "with better peers." The absence of a pro-social social support network deprives John of a valuable protective factor that could reduce his likelihood of engaging in future antisocial behavior. The time that John spends with his girlfriend and son should not be undervalued, but spending leisure time with pro-social peers is important in the development of a 17-year-old. As such, he would benefit from developing pro-social friendships, perhaps structured around an appropriate leisure activity. If John spends his time with pro-social peers, his risk for becoming involved in future offending should be reduced.

Finally, John would benefit from a more in-depth evaluation of his mental health functioning. Although he did not describe experiencing any significant mental health symptoms during the present evaluation, and his MMPI-A suggests that he is not currently experiencing significant psychological distress, he reported a history of mental health treatment involving outpatient counseling, inpatient commitment, and several psychotropic medications. Moreover, his mother noted that severe mental illness runs in the family. Given John's self-reported history of experiencing depressive symptoms, and the numerous losses he has experienced (through deaths of loved ones), he would benefit from a more thorough evaluation of his current mental health functioning. Such an evaluation would provide important information on his current functioning and identify appropriate targets of treatment, if any. If the results of a mental health evaluation suggest that psychotropic medications are indicated, then an evaluation by a professional with prescriptive authority is recommended.

CONCLUSION

In the opinion of the undersigned, based on all of the above, John has treatment/rehabilitation needs in the following areas:

(1) Continued education and/or vocational training with vocational counseling;
(2) Substance abuse treatment, with a particular focus on relapse prevention;
(3) Skills-based training in anger management and decision-making/problem-solving;
(4) Development of a pro-social peer group; and
(5) Further evaluation of his mental health functioning.

John has several risk factors for future offending, including a prior arrest, uneven academic performance, truancy, numerous school suspensions, heavy marijuana use, underdeveloped basic academic skills, and the relative absence of a positive adult male role model. However, he also has some protective factors that may lessen his risk for future offending, including intellectual functioning in the Low Average range, no recent reported substance use, potentially realistic employment goals, religious beliefs that reportedly provide him with a sense of purpose and responsibility, and a desire to obtain employment. Based on a consideration of risk and protective factors, John presents as a moderate risk for reoffending. His amenability to the interventions described in the previous section appears somewhat mixed, given his previous inability to comply with terms of his consent decree and his reluctance to take responsibility for his actions. However, John's willingness to discuss treatment needs and his desire to participate in interventions that target his treatment needs suggest that he may be amenable to treatment. He would be likely to respond favorably to a skills-based training program, focusing on the treatment needs identified above, delivered in an intensive treatment program followed by case management in the community. Given his mental health history, the provision of psychiatric interventions should be considered. The development of an aftercare plan would be important to ensure that John maintains the gains he makes in treatment.

Thank you for the opportunity to evaluate John Doe.

David DeMatteo, J.D., Ph.D.
Licensed Psychologist

Heidi Strohmaier, BA
Drexel University
Graduate Student

TEACHING POINT:
WHAT TRAINING AND EXPERIENCE IN FORENSIC, DEVELOPMENTAL, AND MENTAL HEALTH AREAS ARE NEEDED FOR JUVENILE FORENSIC EXPERTISE?
(contributed by Dewey G. Cornell)

A forensic examiner for a juvenile should be a mental health professional who is experienced in clinical work with adolescents and has knowledge of the forensic issues germane to juvenile proceedings. Forensic examiners cannot assume that extensive experience with adults adequately prepares them to work with juveniles. Such examiners may conduct a superficially complete evaluation, but fail to obtain the data necessary to construct a comprehensive picture of the developmental and familial context for the youth's clinical presentation and delinquent behavior. There are some common pitfalls to avoid in establishing rapport, gathering information, and formulating the case.

Many adolescent defendants are defensive and mistrustful of authority. The clinician who maintains a wooden demeanor and steadfastly adheres to a standard interview format can elicit oppositional behavior and derision. At the same time, overly friendly overtures may backfire and trigger scorn and rejection. Juvenile forensic examiners must be prepared to maintain their objectivity in the face of resistant, and sometimes provocative and defiant, behavior. A clinician cannot be so invested in establishing rapport and gaining the adolescent's positive regard that he or she compromises objectivity or allows himself or herself to be manipulated; nevertheless, good-humored patience, persistence, and

ample display of respect and tolerance are important keys to rapport.

It can be challenging to obtain comprehensive information about an adolescent that includes a complete account of the alleged offense as well as the background circumstances leading up to it. Whereas many adults will provide an account of the offense that minimizes their blameworthiness, some adolescents will intentionally or unintentionally do the opposite. Adolescent egocentrism, sensitivity to shame, or intense counter-dependency may lead some youths to refuse to disclose information important to their defense, such as a history of physical or sexual abuse. They may refuse to provide information that casts a family member or friend in a negative light. Moreover, many adolescent defendants have such difficulty in tolerating painful feelings of shame and guilt that their minimal responsiveness to questions makes them appear cold and remorseless when the opposite may be true. In general, adolescents are not as willing as adults to engage in clinical interviews and often lack the self-knowledge and verbal skills to adequately express their thoughts and feelings. Accordingly, the adult clinician must broaden the scope of the evaluation to include information from parents and schools, and must use psychological tests and measures appropriate to this age group (Hoge & Andrews, 2010).

There are multiple challenges to assessing the presence of both mental disorder and delinquency among juvenile offenders. The prevalence of mental disorders in delinquent populations is relatively high, yet serious psychopathology may be overlooked in children and adolescents, since the symptoms and signs of disorder may be clouded by developmental limitations and variations in clinical presentation not commonly seen among adults. Youthful impulsivity and experimentation, moodiness and emotional outbursts, transient family conflicts, and negative peer influences may or may not account for seemingly disturbed reasoning and behavior. In other words, juvenile psychopathology is not simply the psychopathology of younger adults.

A further complication is that delinquent behaviors are commonplace in the general adolescent population, so it is difficult to assess the likelihood that an adolescent's offense is indicative of an established antisocial trajectory. Grisso (1998) pointed out that many clinicians misunderstand the relationship between conduct disorder and antisocial personality disorder, and often fail to recognize that most youth who engage in delinquent behavior, including those who meet criteria for conduct disorder, will desist in this behavior as adults.

The mental health professional must be cautious about conducting a forensic evaluation without specialized knowledge of juvenile forensic issues and delinquency research. Juvenile forensic issues include waiver of *Miranda* rights, adjudicative competence, transfer to adult court, rehabilitative potential, and risk of harm to others (Benedek, Ash, & Scott, 2010; Grisso, 1998). Although many of these issues are familiar to forensic clinicians who evaluate adults, legal standards for juveniles are less well defined, and the weight to be given to developmental immaturity remains largely unspecified. Moreover, even mental health clinicians experienced in treating youth may not be familiar with the large, multidisciplinary body of literature on juvenile delinquency or the specialized literatures on topics such as juvenile sex offenders, fire-setting (arson), and youth gangs.

Finally, clinicians must consider the role of cultural and socioeconomic context, especially in light of the disproportionate numbers of juvenile offenders with racial or ethnic minority backgrounds. There may be complicating issues of family immigration status and cultural identity. In any case, the forensic examiner may need some familiarity with the myriad variations of adolescent subculture, with its changing idioms, expressive styles, musical genres, and evolving use of technology for social and recreational purposes.

CASE TWO
PRINCIPLE: PROVIDE APPROPRIATE NOTIFICATION OF PURPOSE AND OBTAIN APPROPRIATE AUTHORIZATION BEFORE BEGINNING (*PRINCIPLE 23*)

This principle was discussed in Chapter 5. Therefore, the discussion will focus on the ways that the present case illustrates its application. There are some considerations that are unique to the evaluation of juveniles under the age of 18. As noted by Heilbrun and DeMatteo (2012), "A court order provides sufficient authorization for both adult and adolescent defendants who are the subject of forensic assessment" (p. 152). When the evaluation is requested by the juvenile's attorney,

however, the situation may be more complex. Although the attorney may typically provide authorization for the juvenile to be evaluated, "in cases where legal custody is shared by more than one parent or guardian, it could be important to clarify the implications of different views on retaining the attorney who would then provide such permission via proxy" (p. 152). It is also important to consider a juvenile's ability to consent to an evaluation. For court-ordered evaluations, it is not necessary to obtain the juvenile's consent, although the nature of the evaluation and limits to confidentiality should still be explained in developmentally appropriate terms. In contrast, if an evaluation is requested by a youth's attorney, the juvenile has a legal right to refuse participation (Hoge, 2012).

More specific to evaluations of juvenile commitment, state statutes guiding commitment criteria may further complicate the question of appropriate authorization. In *Parham v. J. R.* (1979), the United States Supreme Court held that when parents or guardians seek to civilly commit their children, the only due process due a child in such a situation is a review of the child's need for hospital treatment by the admitting physician acting as a neutral fact-finder. Therefore, children do not have the same due process rights as adults in civil commitment contexts. However, specific criteria may vary from state to state, and some states require more procedural protections (Melton, Petrila, Poythress, & Slobogin, 2007).

In the present case, the evaluation was requested by the public defender's office as part of a juvenile commitment proceeding. This request included authorization to proceed and was accompanied by the usual assistance with logistical arrangements and provision of relevant documents. Juan was being held in a local juvenile detention center, so permission to enter that facility was also arranged through the attorney. Juan was first told about the evaluation's purpose, who had requested it, and the limits of confidentiality. Then he was asked if he was willing to participate, and agreed to do so.

FORENSIC EVALUATION
February 21, 2012
Re: Juan Sandoval
Case Number: 2011-xxx

REFERRAL INFORMATION

Juan Sandoval is a 13-year-old Hispanic male (D.O.B. 3/29/1998) who is currently charged with aggravated battery and possessing a weapon on school property. Juan's attorney (Leigh Anderson, Esq.) requested a mental health evaluation to provide the defense with information, pursuant to Pennsylvania Code, relevant to Juan's treatment needs and amenability in the context of public safety.

PROCEDURES

Juan Sandoval was interviewed for approximately 6.5 hours on February 6, 2012, at the Juvenile Detention Center (JDC). In addition to a clinical interview, Juan was administered a risk assessment tool for use with adolescents (the Structured Assessment of Risk Violence in Youth, or SAVRY), a structured inventory of symptoms of mental and emotional disorders for use with adolescents (MAYSI-2), a standard test of current functioning in relevant academic areas (the Wide Range Achievement Test, 4th Edition, or WRAT-4), a standard test of current intellectual functioning (the Weschler Adult Intelligence Scale, 4th Edition, WAIS-IV), and a standard objective test of mental and emotional functioning for adolescents (the Minnesota Multiphasic Personality Inventory–Adolescent, or MMPI-A).

A collateral interview was conducted with Juan's foster mother, Donna Young, and his sister, Karen Forth on January 13, 2012. Ms. Young and Ms. Forth were each interviewed for approximately thirty minutes.

The following documents, obtained from Ms. Anderson's office, were reviewed as part of the evaluation:

(1) Discovery (dated 11/18/2011 through 12/2/2011),
(2) Delaware County Court Delinquent Petitions (dated 11/18/2011, 11/30/2011),
(3) Student History Profile (dated 12/4/2011),
(4) The Kennedy Clinic Records (dated 2/5/2011 through 3/4/2011),
(5) Forensic Evaluation by Samuel Collins, Ph.D. (dated 10/12/2011),
(6) Detailed School Records, including IEP evaluations and functional behavior analysis (dated 4/16/2011 through 11/28/2011), and

(7) Delaware County Department of Human Services (DHS) Records (dates 9/10/2010 through 10/6/2011).

Prior to the beginning of the evaluation, Juan was notified about the purpose of the evaluation and the associated limits of confidentiality. He was able to report back his understanding that he would be evaluated "for court" and that a written report would be submitted to his attorney. Juan further understood that the report could be used by his attorney, and, if it were, copies would be provided to the prosecution and the court. He agreed to be evaluated. In addition, Ms. Young and Ms. Forth were notified of the purpose of the evaluation and agreed to be interviewed.

RELEVANT HISTORY

Historical information was obtained from the collateral sources described above as well as from Juan. Whenever possible, we have assessed the consistency of self-reported information with that obtained from collateral sources. If additional information is obtained prior to Juan's hearing, a supplemental report will be filed.

Family History

Juan was born on March 29, 1998. Juan reported that his mother is deceased. He stated that he was the youngest of the children in his family, and had seven older sisters and six older brothers. He was unable to recall all of their names and described relationships with only a few of them. His sister reported that there were only 11 brothers and sisters.

Regarding his parents, Juan stated, "My mother died when I was six. Then I lived with my sister. She took care of me while my dad was in prison. Then when he got out, I went back to live with him because he wanted me back." Consistent with Juan's report, Ms. Forth recalled that she took care of Juan for about three years after their mother died. Juan recalled that his family "kind of broke apart when my mother died," and Ms. Forth reported that it was very difficult for the family. She also stated that the death of their mother was very hard on Juan. Juan frequently spoke very fondly of his mother, stating that he loved her a lot and misses her.

According to Ms. Young, Juan's father has been "in and out of prison for drug charges." Juan also reported that his father was arrested for drugs.

Department of Human Services (DHS) records note that Juan's father has "problems with drugs and alcohol." According to Kennedy Clinic records, Juan did not attend school for three years while he was living with his father. Instead, Juan stated, he would sell drugs "to get money so I didn't have to ask my dad [for it]." Kennedy Clinic records note that Juan came to the attention of DHS when he asked his brother's social worker for help and that he was placed in foster care has remained in foster care since that time. However, DHS records note that Juan's "family was receiving services for some time," and a social worker noticed during a home visit that Juan was not attending school.

Juan reported that his family moved four times when he was growing up. He recounted these times as going to live with his sister when his mother died, then moving into a larger house once with his sister's family, then moving to live with his father, and finally moving into foster care. It appears that Juan has had numerous homes throughout his life. According to DHS records, Juan resided with his father after the death of his mother. DHS records further indicate that he was first placed in foster care on 9/12/2010, then resided at Jackson Hospital from 10/19/2010 until 1/27/2011, then was placed in another foster family until 6/25/2011, and finally was placed with Ms. Young, his current foster parent. He described his most recent home with his foster mother, Ms. Young, as "the only place where I actually feel safe and comfortable. I've learned a lot from them and don't get into fights at home." Regarding discipline, Juan said that "my brother would try to fight me." He was unclear when answering this question and seemed to state that one of his brothers would try to "fight" him when Juan did not attend school.

When asked about the strengths and challenges of his family, Juan asked, "What's that?" After receiving an explanation, Juan identified when "my sister took me in and made sure I was going to school" as a strength. Regarding challenges, he stated, "when my mom died, my whole family broke up." Juan also reported that his father was incarcerated shortly after the death of his mother.

Juan denied witnessing anyone fighting in the home, although he did report that he fought with his brother. He also denied abuse, exposure to domestic violence, and neglect. Ms. Forth denied a history of abuse in the household, and Ms. Young reported that she was unaware of any abuse. Despite denials of abuse and neglect, Juan was placed in the foster care system when he was living with his father and not attending school. The Kennedy Clinic Records state that Juan "was placed into foster care secondary to neglect." Additionally, these records indicate that there were "accusations of physical abuse by foster family that [were] reported and being investigated." DHS records also indicate that there were allegations of physical abuse against Juan's first foster family.

Medical and Psychiatric History

Medically, Juan denied a history of serious medical illnesses. However, Juan and Ms. Forth reported that Juan has asthma. Regarding psychiatric history, Ms. Young reported that Juan received treatment from Jackson Behavioral Health and the Kennedy Clinic. She recalled, "He has a diagnosis of Mental Retardation." Kennedy Clinic Records also indicate that he has a history of previous hospitalizations, "possibly at Friends. He was at Jackson from 10/2010–1/2011." The Kennedy Clinic records indicate that he participated in individual therapy, group therapy, educational services, and was prescribed medications (i.e., Abilify and Benadryl at time of discharge). Ms. Forth also reported that Juan participated in therapy when he lived with her. She stated, "We used to all go to therapy. It was a family thing after the death of my mother." DHS records note that Juan lived with an uncle who "had schizophrenia/depression," and that he has "multiple siblings with borderline intellectual functioning and low IQs."

At the time of his discharge from the partial program at Kennedy Clinic (3/2/2011), Kennedy Clinic records diagnosed Juan with mood disorder, not otherwise specified; oppositional defiant disorder; rule out post-traumatic stress disorder, chronic; and borderline intellectual functioning. Other diagnoses during the time he spent at the Kennedy Clinic include anxiety disorder and learning disorder. The forensic evaluation by Dr. Collins (10/12/2011) diagnosed Juan with adjustment disorder with mixed disturbance of emotions and conduct; neglect of a child, focus on victim, and rule out learning disorder, not otherwise specified. Along with appropriate psychiatric medications and individual therapy, the forensic evaluation recommended that Juan receive "outpatient therapy with a clinician experienced in working with adolescents who engage in sexually inappropriate behaviors. The focus of therapy should be on help-ing Juan develop an understanding of healthy, age-appropriate behaviors, as well as internal and external controls for his behavior." Jackson Behavior Health records diagnosed Juan with intermittent explosive disorder; reading disorder, not otherwise specified; and rule out mood disor-der, not otherwise specified.

Educational History

Juan reported that he attended two elementary schools and that he switched schools because his family moved. His student history profile indicates that Juan attended Washington, Adams, Jefferson, and Lincoln schools. Regarding his attendance, he stated, "I was on time every day." He reported that his performance was "low." His student his-tory profile notes that Juan had many unexcused absences during this time: 46 during first grade, 14 during second, 23 during third, (no information provided for fourth), and 21 during the 2008–2009 fifth-grade year. Additionally, the Kennedy Clinic records note that Juan stopped attending school during the third grade and did not resume atten-dance until 2009–2010, when he was placed in the sixth grade due to his age. Juan reported that he was suspended approximately four times a year for fighting and that he was "expelled from Willard for fighting, cursing, and throwing desks." His stu-dent history profile reports that he was suspended seven times during the 2006–2007 school year (i.e., third grade), four times during the 2005–2006 school year (i.e., second grade). He was unable to recall if he had an IEP or if he was enrolled in spe-cial education classes during elementary school. According to Juan's most recent IEP reevaluation report (4/16/2011), Juan had been evaluated for an IEP beginning in April 2006, but these forms appeared incomplete and were not signed, result-ing in the "supposition...Juan was never placed." He reported that he was involved in an after-school program "to do my homework and get my grades up. My sister put me in it."

Juan reported that he had attended three middle schools. He stated that his foster mother removed him from one of the schools because of multiple problems and that he "stopped going" to the second school. His student history profile indi-cates that Juan currently attends seventh grade at Roosevelt and that he was originally enrolled at Martin Luther King High School and then transferred to Delaware Charter at Birney before attending Roosevelt during the 2011–2012 school year. Additionally, the student profiles notes that Juan attended two schools during his sixth-grade year, Grant School and Thomas Hardy School. The student history profiles indicate that Juan had five unexcused absences during sixth and seventh grade. He was unsure if he had been expelled but reported that he currently has an IEP and that he repeated seventh grade "because my grades was very low." The student history profile notes that Juan receives supplemental learning services due to an emotional disturbance. According to the functional behavior assessment (11/28/2011) included as part of Juan's IEP, Juan had difficulty in school regulating his emotions, de-escalating peer confrontations, and refraining from outbursts. School records for this time report that Juan was suspended once during the 2011–2012 school year (i.e., his seventh-grade year).

Ms. Young reported that Juan had difficulties with peers at school. She stated, "He had problems with the kids—jealousy and stuff like that. They would pick on him and tried to jump him a few times." Ms. Forth reported that Juan was "really bad at school. He had a hard time with classes." Although she denied that he had problems with other students, she also stated that "they would expel him a lot."

Substance Abuse History

Juan reported that he "used to drink Hennessy and Grey Goose....I stopped when I got into foster care." He denied using drugs but reported that he sold them beginning when he was about eight or nine years old. However, the forensic evaluation notes that Juan reported having "smoked weed" while he was living with his father.

Social History

Juan reported that he used to spend time with friends who were older than him. Ms. Forth also reported that his friends were generally older than he was when he lived with her. Ms. Young reported that Juan's friends were generally members of her family. She stated that he spent time with "my chil-dren and grandchildren. They were older, younger, male, and female. He got along well with all of them. He really looked up to my son even though he is 14—Juan is about his age." Regarding the activi-ties he enjoys, Juan said he likes to "play basketball;

play football; go on the computer; or go shopping, to the mall, or movies." He said that the friends he used to hang out with had been arrested for drugs. Ms. Young reported that he "spent his time with the family. He wasn't in the streets when he lived with us."

Juan reported that, when making decisions, he likes to "talk about it. If my foster dad is around, I talk to him or my foster mom or brother," and he depends on his foster brother and foster dad for advice. Ms. Young stated that Juan views her boyfriend as his foster father and "really looks up to him." Consistent with Juan's report, Ms. Young said that Juan always talks to the family when he makes decisions. She said that he will either ask her or her boyfriend for advice, and he also really looks up to her son, Juan's foster brother. This past year Juan has experienced a number of stressors, including his first arrest, leaving a foster home where "I felt I was safe," and being placed in juvenile detention.

When asked or expected to do something, Juan reported, "Sometimes I always do what I'm asked in school, unless I don't want to do it. If I don't want to do it, I would get demerits." Ms. Young stated, "Juan always does what he is told. He does his chores, his work, he'll eat, clean. Whatever you ask him to do, he'll do it." He stated that he is closest to his sister, brother, foster mom, foster brother, and foster dad, and that he most admires his foster brother and foster dad.

Juan reported that he has no formal employment history. He reported that he would like to be an "engineer or a home builder." He reported that after being placed with his most recent foster family, he now believes in the value of an education and that he would like to obtain a two-year degree after high school. However, he was concerned that being unable to read would create problems for his future.

Offense History

Juan denied having any charges prior to the current two. He recalled that the first time he was arrested was when he was 13 for "the school grounds case and this one." Consistent with Juan's report, the delinquency petition notes that Juan does not have any prior arrests or charges.

CURRENT CLINICAL CONDITION

Juan presented as a 13-year-old Hispanic male of average height and medium to heavy build who appeared his stated age. He wore casual attire (sweatpants and a T-shirt) and appeared appropriately groomed. He reported that he has a scar on his left hand "from a dog bite when I was eight years old." He stated that he does not have tattoos or piercings.

Although Juan's speech was slurred and slow, it was relevant and clear. Juan was cooperative and polite throughout the evaluation. He appeared open and talkative, often providing extensive responses to questions or spontaneously offering information. He exhibited good effort. Over the course of the testing portion of the evaluation, Juan's attention and concentration varied. It was clear that he was trying to focus on the tasks, but towards the end of testing, individuals and noises outside the testing room were distracting to him. When this occurred, Juan was generally easily redirected to the task, but often needed to have the questions repeated. There was no evidence of bizarre thinking. Therefore, it appears that the present evaluation provides a valid reflection of Juan's current functioning.

Juan's basic academic skills, as measured by the WRAT-4, showed significant deficits in Word Reading (grade equivalent = 1.7), Sentence Comprehension (grade equivalent = 1.9), Spelling (grade equivalent < K.0), and deficits in Arithmetic skills (grade equivalent = 3.5). All of his academic skills are below his current grade level and should be considered in need of remediation. His reading and spelling skills are extremely low for his grade and serve as a source of concern for him. Throughout the evaluation, he frequently referenced his difficulty with reading and his embarrassment at being unable to read.

Juan completed a standard test of current intellectual functioning (WISC-IV) as part of the current evaluation. On the WISC-IV, Juan was measured as performing in the Borderline range (full scale IQ = 70), placing him in the 2nd percentile relative to his peers. On the Verbal Comprehension Index, which measures verbal reasoning, he achieved a score of 67 (Extremely Low range, 1st percentile). He achieved a score of 56 (Extremely Low range, 0.2nd percentile) on the Working Memory Index, which measures short-term memory. On the Processing Speed Index, which measures cognitive processing efficiency, he achieved a score of 73 (Borderline range, 4th percentile). On the Perceptual Reasoning Index, which measures spatial processing and perceptual reasoning, he achieved a score of 98 (Average range, 45th percentile). Juan's perceptual reasoning skills are a relative strength, while his other verbal, working memory, and processing skills are consistently much lower.

On a structured inventory of symptoms of mental and emotional disorders specifically designed for use with adolescents (MAYSI-2), Juan reported some symptoms. Out of a total of 52 items, Juan endorsed 27 items. Specifically, he reported having trouble falling asleep, having lost his temper easily, having nervous or worried feelings that keep him from doing things he wants to, having difficulty paying attention or concentrating, having enjoyed fighting, being easily upset, having thought a lot about getting back at someone he was angry at, being really jumpy or hyper, having too many bad moods, having felt like life was not worth living, feeling like some part of his body always hurts, having a bad feeling that things don't seem real (i.e., like he is in a dream), feeling nervous and being shaky, feeling nervous and having his heart beat fast, feeling nervous and short of breath, feeling nervous and having an upset stomach, feeling angry a lot, getting frustrated a lot, having a hard time feeling close to people outside his family, staying mad for a long time once mad, having bad headaches, having people talk about him a lot when he's not there, having something very bad or terrifying happen to him, having been badly hurt or in danger of getting badly hurt or killed, and having seen someone be severely injured or killed.

When asked to elaborate on these symptoms, Juan's responses suggested that many of his symptoms were related to his difficulties with peers and academics in school, the loss of his mother, the possibility that he will not be placed back with his most recent foster family, and his charges. Specifically, he stated that he has had trouble falling asleep "for a couple days now. I just start singing." He reported that he loses his temper easily, that "I start punching stuff. Not a lot at home...at school sometimes. It's when people talk about my mom or that I won't be something." He stated that he has nervous or worried feelings that keep him from doing things he wants to "when I go to court." He reported that he has problems concentrating or paying attention "in school...that's the most." He said that he enjoyed fighting and explained, "I get excited when I win the fight, but I'm not the fighting type no more." He said that he has been easily upset "when people bother me...laugh at me. It happens a lot."

He indicated that he thinks a lot about getting even with "a kid that jumped me in school." He stated that he has been really jumpy or hyper, specifically, "I was hyper yesterday at court in the holding room because a kid pushed the sheriff and ran and I know that kid." He reported experiencing too many bad moods and explained, "like after a fight, in school, get to school. Morning time is not for me." Juan said that it felt like life was not worth living "when I'm locked up." He said that his head felt like it always hurt him, particularly "when I think too hard or about something that can't happen at the moment." He reported that has had a bad feeling that things do not seem real "when I was in a cell, locked up." He reported that he felt shaky, his heart beats very fast, he feels short of breath, and his stomach gets upset when he is nervous, and stated, "It's all when I feel nervous. On my way to court I start getting worked when I think about things that can happen to my real brothers." He stated that he felt angry a lot "when I'm in here." Additionally, Juan reported that he feels like he doesn't want to go to school anymore and explained, "I feel like that when I can't do the work." He stated that he felt like he couldn't do anything right "when I do the work at school." He also stated that he has gotten frustrated a lot with "schoolwork and when I'm thinking about stuff." Juan reported that it has been hard for him to feel close to people outside his family, "like when I know you but at the same time I don't know you like that. I can't really say you're my friend." He stated that he has gotten mad and stayed mad for a long time when "my mom passed away." He reported having bad headaches "when I know I can't go nowhere." He also reported that people talk about him a lot when he's not there because "friends talk behind my back." Juan reported having had a very bad or terrifying event happen to him and described it as "when my mom passed away. I missed her a lot. That's the worst thing." He also reported feeling in danger of getting badly hurt or killed "when I took drugs from somebody." Finally, Juan stated that he saw someone severely injured, explaining, "I saw someone severely injured when they were riding a dirt bike and fell off and their body was messed up. I also saw someone get shot. They had like four holes in them."

Juan completed the MMPI-A as part of the current evaluation to measure his current mental and emotional functioning. His clinical profile (Welsh Code 9*"1678'204+-3/5: F-/L:K#) may reflect a tendency to endorse extreme symptoms or problems. Additionally, he had serious difficulty understanding the questions. Since he was unable to read the questions, the MMPI-A was read aloud to him. During its administration, Juan frequently asked for definitions of words and had difficulty understanding the questions. It became apparent that he was answering questions in a manner that did not account for negatives in the question. He was answering questions such that he replied "true" if he had experienced a symptom, regardless of whether the question was framed in the negative. When this became apparent, the assessor framed questions to provide the options for a true response and a false response. In light of his high endorsement of symptoms on the MAYSI-2 and his limited verbal capacities, it is likely that Juan's score on the MMPI-A reflects both his tendency to endorse items and his intellectual limitations. Despite these limitations, Juan's profile reflects a high number of somatic complaints; symptoms of anxiety, worry, and tension; behavioral problems; difficulty controlling anger; and an energetic, active, and fast-paced tempo. Individuals with this type of profile may come across as clingy, self-critical, impulsive, prone to excessive worry, and may have a tendency to develop difficulties with alcohol or other drugs. It is likely that Juan is experiencing a number of these symptoms due to his lack of a stable family life, his current placement, and his pending charges. The symptoms Juan endorsed on the MMPI-A are consistent with his report on the MAYSI-2, where he endorsed a high number symptoms that included difficulties with anger and impulsivity and somatic complaints of headaches related to his tendency to ruminate about his situation.

The SAVRY was completed based on information obtained from Juan and collateral sources as part of the current evaluation. The SAVRY is a structured risk-assessment tool for use with adolescents that aids in determining an adolescent's future risk for violence. Based on the presence and absence of various risk and protective factors, it appears Juan is at high risk for future violence relative to other delinquent youth. Juan presents a high risk based on his history of violence, as suggested by the presence of certain risk factors: numerous fights in school, first known violent act occurred before he was 11 years old, his father's criminal involvement, significant discontinuity of care, significant difficulties in school achievement, significant peer rejection, his moderate stress and poor coping ability, inconsistent parenting due to multiple caregivers and placements, impulsivity, past substance use problems, significant difficulty controlling his anger, moderate difficulties with concentration, and the community disorganization present in Juan's neighborhood. However, Juan also reported a recently obtained conviction in and strong commitment to education (i.e., he is extremely worried and embarrassed about his inability to read, is aware of the importance of being able to read, wants to improve his school performance, aspires to graduate from high school and pursue a two-year degree); having strong social support from his most recent foster family; having a strong relationship with his foster mother, foster father, and foster brother; was open and receptive to remediation and authority; and exhibited resilient personality traits (i.e., despite past and current negative life events, Juan is still hopeful about his future; he is able to form close relationships to a mother and father figure). These factors suggest that if he responds well to intervention and receives consistent treatment, his current risk estimate may be lowered despite his previously negative, chaotic life experiences.

TREATMENT NEEDS AND AMENABILITY

There are four areas in which Juan has treatment/rehabilitation needs, which, if addressed, may reduce his risk for future offending. These areas include:

(1) Training and counseling in decision-making, problem-solving, establishing appropriate boundaries, and anger management skills;

(2) Further evaluation and treatment of mental health needs to address his poor coping skills and psychological distress;

(3) A continued emphasis on positive and appropriate peer relationships and involvement in structured activities; and

(4) Continued education and training in both academic and vocational areas.

First, Juan has treatment needs in the areas of decision-making, problem-solving, establishing appropriate boundaries, and anger management skills. When asked how he handles making a decision, Juan replied, "I talk with someone." Although

Juan and his foster mother reported that he often talks about decisions with his foster family, it appears that Juan is likely to act impulsively. His limited working memory and processing skills probably impact his ability to think through difficult situations, consider long-term consequences, and mentally manipulate possible options and outcomes. Therefore, it is likely that Juan may talk a lot about a decision but may be more likely to act in the moment. During the evaluation, Juan appeared somewhat impulsive and easily frustrated. He seemed to talk about whatever came to mind, whenever it came to mind. Additionally, once frustrated, Juan had difficulty managing his distress and quickly became angry. He acknowledged that he is easily upset and frustrated by his peers, particularly when someone says something about his mother or makes fun of him. During these times, he is likely to act on impulses and may physically lash out at peers, rather than employ anger management techniques or consider the longer-term consequences of his actions. Additionally, the functional behavior assessment conducted as part of Juan's IEP indicates that Juan has difficulty regulating his emotions. He engages in verbal confrontations and quickly escalates them, becoming aggressive and unable to calm down.

Assisting Juan in identifying triggers for his anger, identifying more appropriate methods to resolve these feelings, and effectively regulating his emotions would be likely to reduce conflict with his peers and disruption in the classroom setting. In addition to his individual impulsivity and reactiveness, it appears that Juan's decisions may be dependent on the group of peers he is around at the time. For example, Juan reported that he began selling drugs when he was around older peers who were involved in this activity. In contrast, when he was provided with a set of pro-social peers in the context of Ms. Young's family, he quickly adapted and "got along" with this peer group, avoiding antisocial and criminal behaviors. Juan fondly recalled his time with Ms. Young's family as a point in his life when he felt "part of a family," and Ms. Young denied that Juan had any behavioral problems at home or any problems with the children in the family. His decisions, therefore, may be more reflective of the group rather than of his independent evaluation of choices. Given his chaotic family life, it is highly likely that Juan had inconsistent discipline and experienced a variety of family structures and

rules. It appears that Juan has had difficulty identifying and establishing appropriate boundaries with others. Given adequate structure, it seems as though Juan is able to adjust and act appropriately within boundaries. Ms. Young described how Juan was able to conform his behavior to the rules and structures of the foster family. Helping Juan learn how to identify and establish boundaries may reduce his likelihood of crossing individual boundaries that are not concretely established for him. Additionally, counseling in decision-making, problem-solving, and anger management skills may allow Juan to find additional ways to meet his needs in ways that are positive and legal when he is confronted with stressful situations and problems. If Juan responds favorably to such interventions with an experienced clinician, this should serve to reduce his risk for future criminal offending.

Second, Juan would benefit from further evaluation of his mental health needs. Ms. Forth reported that the family sought and received counseling following the death of their mother. However, Juan still seems to be grieving this loss and may need individual counseling to express his feelings about and process the death of his mother. In addition to processing this loss, counseling may serve as a venue for Juan to process the neglect and absence of a stable family life that he has experienced. The Kennedy Clinic records note that Juan had previously been hospitalized for mental health treatment at Kennedy, Jackson, and possibly Friends. He received individual counseling, group counseling, educational services, and psychiatric medications. Progress notes from the Kennedy Clinic note that Juan was able to adjust to new settings and peers but often required assurance and one-to-one support to do so. Dealing with adjustment issues in therapy may ease transitions for Juan, reducing the level of anxiety and frustration he experiences. Juan reported numerous symptoms related to depression, anxiety, and somatic complaints. Although these may be related to his current environment and circumstances, further assessment and treatment outside of this setting may be warranted. It is possible that his high symptom endorsement may be an attempt to call attention to the psychological distress he is experiencing. Previous psychological evaluations and Juan's self-report have noted that Juan has had much difficulty with peers at school, and this has resulted in a number of suspensions. It appears that Juan has difficulty handling these situations with his peers and will often act aggressively in response. In additional to anger management, Juan may benefit from coping skills, frustration tolerance, and problem-solving training to help him deal with stressors in his life. Juan's records indicate that he was previously diagnosed with mood disorder, oppositional defiant disorder, borderline intellectual functioning, anxiety disorder, learning disorder, and possibly post-traumatic stress disorder. Juan's current mental health should be further evaluated to determine a current clinical picture. Based on a more in-depth evaluation, treatment can be tailored to address his specific needs.

Third, Juan would benefit from interacting in more positive peer relationships. Juan reported engaging in antisocial activities when he spent time with peers who engaged in such activities. However, both Juan and Ms. Young reported that he engaged in pro-social activities and "did not spend time on the streets" when he spent time with children from Ms. Young's extended family. Because he is able to adjust to different peer groups, Juan would probably benefit from spending additional time with positive peers who participate in pro-social behaviors. For example, Juan's activities during the time he spent with Ms. Young's family including playing with other children, going to the movies, playing sports, playing video games, and going shopping. In contrast, when he was involved with antisocial peers, his time was spent selling drugs and using alcohol. It appears that Juan's behavior may be highly dependent on the activities of the individuals he spends his time with. Identifying structured activities for Juan to participate in would probably increase his access to appropriate mentors, provide a goal for Juan to focus on, and reduce the time available for him to participate in activities with antisocial peers. Juan reported that his foster family, particularly his foster mother, foster brother, and foster father, along with his biological brother and sister, are his main sources of social support. Additionally, Juan has had difficulties at school with other students "picking on him," resulting in fights. Identifying other sources of social support and structured activities outside of school may reduce the effects of the peer rejection Juan has experienced at school. Interacting with positive mentors and pro-social peers in structured activities would reduce Juan's risk of interacting with future antisocial peers.

Fourth, Juan would benefit from continued education and training in both academic and vocational areas. His performance on the WRAT-4 indicates he has significant deficits in word reading, sentence comprehension, spelling, and arithmetic. Specifically, his reading, spelling, and sentence comprehension skills are extremely low and serve as a source of stress and embarrassment for Juan. Juan repeatedly reported anxiety over his inability to read and expressed a strong desire to be able read like his peers. He is interested in furthering his education but is aware that this may not be possible if he cannot read. Because he missed approximately three years of schooling, Juan would need compensatory education to develop his skills to an adequate level. Continued education, even with supplemental assistance, at his current grade level (i.e., seventh) would probably not address the deficits he has. Although he is enrolled in seventh grade, he is functioning at or below a first-grade level in spelling, word reading, and sentence comprehension, and at a third-grade level in arithmetic. Due to his strong motivation, additional education that provides Juan with basic reading skills could provide a structured, engaging activity for Juan to participate in. Although he may easily become frustrated, working in a small classroom setting or one-to-one would provide Juan with more individualized assistance and structure so he could remain on-task and focused. It would also reduce that likelihood that Juan would experience embarrassment or harassment from peers. His student history profile notes that Juan currently has an IEP. Juan's school records indicate that he received one A in science, one B in Social Studies, a C in Visual Arts, and two Ds in Reading and Mathematics for the first quarter of the 2011–2012 school year. Additionally, he received satisfactory grades in behavior and effort for the majority of these classes. Juan reported that he is interested in pursuing a career as an engineer or, alternatively, building houses. Continued educational and vocational training would serve to keep Juan occupied in positive activities.

CONCLUSIONS

In the opinion of the undersigned, based on all of the above, Juan has treatment/rehabilitation needs in the following areas:

1. Training and counseling in
   decision-making, problem-solving skills,

establishing appropriate boundaries, and anger management skills;

2. Further evaluation and treatment of mental health needs regarding his poor coping skills, and distress;

3. Continued participation with positive and appropriate peer relationships and involvement in structured activities; and

4. Continued vocational training and academic skills remediation and further training, particularly in the areas of spelling and reading.

Juan does not have a history of prior arrests, and his two current charges are his first contact with the juvenile justice system. He has treatment needs related to his poor coping, anger management, and boundary setting skills and further development of problem-solving and decision-making skills. Juan's academic achievement indicates that his reading, sentence comprehension, spelling, and arithmetic require remediation. Additionally, he has had limited success in school, has missed three years of schooling, and has required an IEP. Beyond his academic difficulties, Juan has also experienced social rejection by his peers. Ms. Young reported that he is often picked on at school, while Juan reported that he often feels embarrassed when he can't read. He has a history of fighting with his peers at school, often in response to a remark about his mother or his reading ability. Juan possesses strengths that may positively influence his continued development, including having a supportive foster mother and foster family, being able to develop relationships with peers who do not engage in criminal activities, and other active protective factors (e.g., positive attitude toward intervention, interest in schooling and academic achievement, hopefulness about the future). Based on the presence of numerous historical factors (e.g., parental criminal activity, multiple/inconsistent caregivers, involvement in antisocial activities before the age of 12), Juan appears to be at high risk for future violence relative to other delinquent youth. However, a number of factors that increase his risk for future offending are targets for intervention (e.g., his academic difficulties, peer rejection, involvement in more structured activities with pro-social peers, addressing mental health needs, training in decision-making and coping skills). Additionally, his amenability to the interventions described above appears possible,

based on his openness to intervention and his interest in pursuing a more positive future. Therefore, if these interventions can be made successfully, with monitoring to ensure compliance, Juan's risk of future offending should be further reduced.

It is our opinion that his needs could be met in an intense intervention program that addresses his unique set of needs related to education, psychotherapy, psycho-education, vocational training, and structured activities.

Thank you for the opportunity to evaluate Juan Sandoval.

Kirk Heilbrun, Ph.D.
Consulting Psychologist
Lindsey Peterson, M.S.
Psychology Graduate Student

TEACHING POINT:
OBTAINING AUTHORIZATION FOR EVALUATING MINORS WHO CANNOT YET LEGALLY CONSENT

When FMHA is court-ordered, it is not necessary to obtain informed consent from an evaluee—although the forensic clinician should provide a notification of purpose describing the basis for the evaluation, purposes for which it might be used, and associated limits on confidentiality. In contrast, an evaluation that is requested by the defense attorney or plaintiff's attorney is subject to the individual's declining to participate, and accordingly does require informed consent.

This is complicated when the individual being evaluated is under the age of 18 and thus not yet able to give informed consent for most legal purposes. When informed consent would be needed for an adult, an adolescent must assent—basically agree to participate in light of the available information—but the question is whether an additional level of authorization is needed. Such additional authorization would usually be requested from the parent or guardian of the minor.

If the forensic clinician wishes to obtain the permission of a parent or guardian in addition to the adolescent's assent and the attorney's referral (with associated permission to conduct the evaluation), then this might seem prudent. However, there are two considerations suggesting that this is rarely necessary. The primary consideration involves the importance of allowing the defense attorney to provide effective representation. If the attorney determines that a juvenile FMHA is important in defending the client, then that attorney should have the authority to request that such (non-invasive, minimal risk) procedures be conducted as part of the defense. If a parent or guardian objected to this request, then a reasonable response might involve the forensic clinician's seeking clarification through the attorney in the form of a court order. But such a parental objection is unlikely and rare. The second consideration is practical. Some adolescents do not have a parent or guardian who is readily available to provide permission. In such cases, it is important that the juvenile's attorney be able to request a procedure that may be an important aspect of the defense without unduly delaying the process.

22

Juvenile Transfer and Decertification

The two reports in this chapter focus on the questions that can arise when juvenile offenders are charged in the adult criminal justice system. In many jurisdictions, juvenile defendants in criminal courts can attempt to have their cases *decertified* or *transferred back* to the juvenile justice system for disposition. Decisions regarding juvenile transfer have the potential to greatly affect the lives of those being evaluated, given the vastly different sentencing practices within the adult and juvenile justice systems, and usually incorporate FMHA regarding treatment needs and amenability to interventions in the context of public safety.

The principle applied to the first case concerns assessing legally relevant behavior, and how this information can be used to aid the court in accurate decision-making. The teaching point in the first case will highlight the importance of translating legal criteria into forensic capacities, and the value of providing data and reasoning that are directly relevant to forensic capacities and the corresponding legal question. The principle associated with the second case discusses how a variety of collateral sources can be used to assess the accuracy of self-report information provided in an evaluation. The teaching point in the second case addresses how to balance the results of psychological testing, self-report, and third party collateral information as they relate to response style.

a juvenile who has been initially charged in criminal court. Pennsylvania is fairly representative of many of the jurisdictions and their laws pertaining to transfer and decertification. Under applicable Pennsylvania law (42 Pa. C.S.A. § 6355), a juvenile who is between the ages of 14 and 17 (inclusive) can be automatically charged in the adult criminal system if arrested for a certain (i.e., very serious) kind of offense. Section 6355 allows the court to consider the following factors in deciding whether a juvenile initially charged as an adult should be decertified:

(1) the impact of the offense on the victim or victims,
(2) the impact of the offense on the community,
(3) the threat to safety of the public or any individual posed by the child,
(4) the nature and circumstances of the offense allegedly committed by the child,
(5) the degree of the child's culpability,
(6) the adequacy and duration of dispositional alternatives available under Pennsylvania law applicable to juveniles and in the adult criminal justice system, and
(7) whether the child is amenable to treatment, supervision, or rehabilitation as a juvenile.

In weighing the last factor (7), the court may further consider:

(a) the individual's age;
(b) the individual's mental capacity;
(c) the individual's maturity;
(d) the degree of criminal sophistication exhibited by the child;
(e) previous records, if any;
(f) the nature and extent of any prior delinquent history, including the success or

---

CASE ONE

PRINCIPLE: ASSESS LEGALLY RELEVANT BEHAVIOR (*PRINCIPLE 21*)
This principle was discussed in some detail in Chapter 15 (this volume), and another example was provided in Chapter 18 (this volume), so we will move directly to how the present report illustrates its application in FMHA. In the present case, the legal question is *decertification* (reverse waiver) of

failure of any previous attempts by the juvenile court to rehabilitate the child;

(g) whether the child can be rehabilitated prior to the expiration of the juvenile court jurisdiction;

(h) probation or institutional reports, if any,

(i) any other relevant factors; and

(j) whether there are reasonable grounds to believe that the child is not committable to an institution for the mentally retarded or mentally ill.

The forensic evaluation in such cases is conducted to provide the court with information and guidance on the factors that are not issues of fact or judgments beyond the scope of clinical forensic expertise. Many of the factors just described are issues of fact (e.g., age) or questions beyond the scope of clinical forensic expertise (e.g., the impact of the offense on the community), and therefore are not an appropriate focus when conducting a decertification FMHA. Although these factors are not "assessed" in a decertification FMHA, information in these areas is important for the assessment of legally relevant capacities and behavior that are addressed by the evaluation.

In the present case, the relevant legal behaviors and capacities are first sought in the relevant statute. In Texas, juvenile transfer proceedings can be ordered by the court if, "because of the seriousness of the offense alleged or the background of the child, the welfare of the community requires criminal proceedings" (Texas Family Code Section 54.02(a)). Specifically, it is indicated that the court shall consider, among other matters:

(1) whether the alleged offense was against person or property, with greater weight in favor of transfer given to offenses against the person;

(2) the sophistication and maturity of the child;

(3) the record and previous history of the child; and

(4) the prospects of adequate protection of the public and the likelihood of the rehabilitation of the child by use of procedures, services, and facilities currently available to the juvenile court (Texas Family Code Section 54.02 (f)).

A "diagnostic study" is used to assist the court in this determination (Kurlycheck & Johnson, 2010). The evaluator then uses this statutory guidance to specify criteria for assessment. In this report, the evaluators do this by framing the referral question as follows: "to assist in the determination of appropriateness for juvenile certification and waiver of juvenile court jurisdiction." The legally relevant forensic issues were identified later in the report as seriousness of the offense (deferred entirely to the court's discretion), risk for dangerousness, sophistication/maturity, and treatment amenability. Note that the record and history of the evaluee are also described in the history sections of the report.

FORENSIC EVALUATION
JUVENILE CERTIFICATION

Name of Respondent:	Bryan Morgan
County:	Redwood
Cause:	JUV 00000
Date of Evaluation:	11/30/2012
Date of Birth:	00/00/1995
Date of Report:	12/7/2012

SPECIFIC ISSUES REFERRED FOR EVALUATION

Bryan Morgan, a 17-year-old Caucasian male, was referred for a psychological evaluation to assist in the determination of appropriateness for juvenile certification and waiver of juvenile court jurisdiction regarding one charge of aggravated sexual assault of a child (his 10-year-old sister).

DISCLOSURES

The respondent was evaluated at the Psychological Services Center. Prior to beginning the interview, the purpose of the evaluation, procedures involved, and limits of confidentiality were explained to the respondent, and he agreed to participate. The respondent's mother, Laura Morgan, was also present and agreed to participate. Bryan and Ms. Morgan were interviewed separately for a total of approximately 3.5 hours, including a mental status examination and administration of the Wechsler Abbreviated Scale of Intelligence–Second Edition (WASI-II) and the Wide Range Achievement Test–Fourth Edition (WRAT-4).

PROCEDURES, TECHNIQUES, TESTS, AND COLLATERAL INFORMATION REVIEWED

Interviews:

Interviews with Bryan and Karen Morgan: 11/30/2012

Assessment Instruments:

Wechsler Abbreviated Scale of Intelligence–Second Edition: 11/30/2012
Wide Range Achievement Test–Fourth Edition: 11/30/2012

Records reviewed:

- Order for Psychological Examination, dated 11/15/2012
- Redwood County Sheriff's Office Incident Report, dated 8/6/2012
- Sexual Assault Examination Forensic Report Form, dated 8/6/2012
- Magistrate's Verification and Certification for Admissibility of Voluntary Statement of a Juvenile, State Family Code Section 51.095, dated 8/7/2012
- Exhibit "A" Case#: S000000 Aggravated Sexual Assault Child, dated 8/7/2012
- MAYSI-2 Questionnaire Completed by Bryan Morgan, dated 8/13/2012
- Juvenile Probation Risk and Needs Assessment, dated 8/14/2012
- Letter from Redwood County Special Services Cooperative to Jane Wilson, dated 8/14/2012
- Redwood County Juvenile Probation Department Report, dated 11/26/2012
- Lakeville Jr./Sr. High School Report Card for Bryan Morgan, undated

No additional records were made available for this evaluation.

CLINICAL OBSERVATIONS AND FINDINGS

Mental Status

The Morgans arrived on time for the appointment. Bryan was casually dressed and presented with a slightly unkempt appearance. He appeared alert and oriented to time, place, person, and situation. Eye contact was appropriate. His speech was consistently within normal limits for rate, volume, and tone. He frequently offered information spontaneously or with little prompting, but declined to comment on issues directly related to the case at hand. His responses to evaluators' questions were appropriate, and his thought processes appeared logical and goal-directed. His level of motor activity and ability to remain attentive, follow examiners' questions, and engage in structured conversation for an extended period were all age-appropriate. He was able to provide a coherent timeline of his major life events with no indications of memory impairment. Mood appeared euthymic, with affect that was notably relaxed given his present circumstances. Bryan was cooperative throughout the interview but appeared to engage in attempts to present himself favorably and ingratiate himself to the interviewers. Rapport adequate to conducting the evaluation was established and maintained.

There were no indications Bryan was experiencing visual or auditory hallucinations either during the evaluation or at any point prior to the evaluation. There was also no evidence of psychotic thought processes or bizarre ideation that might suggest a thought disorder. There was no evidence of clinical depression, and Bryan denied any history of self-injurious behavior or suicidal ideation.

Background/Social History

Bryan was born to an intact family. He has an older half-brother and two younger sisters who were adopted as young children. Both Bryan and Ms. Morgan reported mainly positive familial relationships, with the exception of Bryan's relationship with his father. Following his parents' recent separation, Bryan's negative feelings toward his father appear to have increased. Bryan perceives his father as unsupportive, uncaring, and abusive, and reportedly contacted CPS himself on several occasions as a result of his father's behavior. However, these contacts did not result in a substantiated finding of abuse in the single CPS investigation that resulted, according to Ms. Morgan. Records from the Juvenile Probation Department indicated Bryan previously reported sexual abuse by a cousin at age seven. However, he did not report this during the present evaluation.

Ms. Morgan denied any history of significant behavioral problems or assaultive behavior at home. However, she reported that Bryan frequently displaces responsibility for behaviors for which he is punished. While he had very few responsibilities within the home prior to his arrest, he was often charged with supervising his sisters while Ms. Morgan worked. Probation records indicate the Morgans provided generally adequate parental supervision. As a result of the current charge, Bryan's sisters are living with his father, while Bryan resides with his mother. As a result of their home entering foreclosure, Bryan and Ms. Morgan are preparing to move.

Although Bryan described himself as having many friends, including two best friends, this report is somewhat suspect. For example, Bryan admitted to not remaining in regular contact with one of the individuals whom he identified as a best friend. He also reported that he has been the target of bullying at school and, according to his mother, he spends much of his time outside of school alone. Bryan denied associating with delinquent peers, and Ms. Morgan reported knowing and approving of many of Bryan's friends. The respondent characterized his role in many of his friendships as that of "big brother" or "therapist," indicating he had even singlehandedly talked one friend out of committing suicide. Ms. Morgan described Bryan as more immature than his peers and indicated that many of his friends are three to four years his junior. In spite of this, she said he is not likely to assume leadership roles in group social activities. Ms. Morgan indicated that much of Bryan's time is consumed with video games; however, Bryan reported engaging in highly intellectual pursuits during his free time, such as studying history, physics, and philosophy. While he presents with some conversational knowledge on these topics, the depth of his understanding is unclear.

The extent of Bryan's dating history appears exceedingly limited. He reported two previous romantic relationships; however, one of these may have been limited to one date. Ms. Morgan reported knowledge of one prior girlfriend but indicated the relationship consisted largely of phone conversations. Ms. Morgan also reported that while Bryan had engaged in sexual intercourse on one prior occasion, the behavior was initiated by the female and was overall a negative experience for Bryan. Bryan denied any interest in sexual activity to examiners.

The respondent was most recently enrolled in twelfth grade at Lakeville High School but is transferring due to his pending relocation. Reports from the Juvenile Probation Department indicated his attendance is reportedly regular, and he has no history of special education services or grade retention. A recent report card indicated grades ranging from 62 to 100. As a result of his grades, Bryan is precluded from participating in extracurricular activities. However, he would like to become involved in the theater club at his new school. When asked what steps he might take to ensure this was possible, he indicated he would "talk my way into it."

Both Ms. Morgan and Bryan denied significant behavioral problems at school. Although Bryan has been the target of bullying, he indicated he does not retaliate against his own bullies but will often intervene when he sees others, even those whom he is not close to, being bullied. Although Bryan reported having positive relationships with several teachers, these relationships appear to lack significant depth and longevity. Furthermore, Bryan described several teachers whom he perceives as "abusing their authority." On at least one occasion, he elected to approach one such teacher to discuss appropriately respectful behavior.

Bryan denied any history of employment. He indicated he would like to obtain a job at a video game store but has not done so because he does not have a driver's license, a deficit he attributed to laziness. The respondent has early enlisted in the Air Force and is set to begin training after graduation. He plans to spend 20 years in the Air Force before retiring and seeking employment at a video game production company. He indicated some awareness of the credentials necessary for this type of job (i.e., a degree, particularly one from a university recognized in the field) and has reportedly read the employee handbook of the desired company, however, he did not appear to recognize the potential difficulties he might encounter attempting to obtain such a position.

Prior to his current arrest, Bryan had had no history of legal contact. He denied engaging in any behaviors that could have resulted in arrest, such as theft or vandalism.

Bryan denied any history of substance use, save one instance occurring at age 10 when he unknowingly consumed a marijuana brownie. He denied any further alcohol or substance use. Neither his mother nor the probation department was aware of any substance usage.

Medical Health History

Bryan began psychiatric treatment for attention-deficit hyperactivity disorder (ADHD) in kindergarten. He discontinued treatment in eighth grade and denied ongoing hyperactivity or inattentiveness since that time. He said that he was seen by a counselor on one occasion at age seven because "[my dad] thought I wanted to kill everyone." He also reportedly "visited with" a school counselor during elementary school. Bryan completed the Massachusetts Youth Screening Instrument (MAYSI), a psychological screening measure, following his arrest in August 2012. His responses did not indicate significant distress at that time. According to Ms. Morgan, Bryan displays no indications of anger control problems or emotional instability.

Wechsler Abbreviated Scale of Intelligence Scale–Second Edition (WASI-II)

The WASI-II, a brief measure of cognitive abilities, was administered to assess Bryan's intellectual functioning and gain additional information regarding his cognitive maturity. The WASI-II yields a full scale IQ equivalent and two index scores. Throughout the testing session, Bryan was cooperative and appeared to enjoy the testing procedures. The WASI-II was administered according to standard procedures.

This evaluation assessed Bryan's full scale IQ equivalent to be 104, which is in the Average range. Index scores assessing his verbal comprehension and perceptual reasoning skills were 99 and 107 respectively, also falling in the Average range. Bryan's performance across tasks was reasonably consistent and did not indicate any relative or normative cognitive weaknesses.

Wide Range Achievement Test–Fourth Education (WRAT-4)

The WRAT-4, a brief measure of academic skills, was administered to obtain information regarding Bryan's level of academic achievement. The WRAT-4 assesses phonemic awareness, reading comprehension, spelling, and mathematical skills. Bryan's scores of 105, 112, 133, and 90, respectively, fell in the Average to Very Superior ranges. His Reading Composite score of 109 also fell into the Average range. These scores suggest he is functioning at a grade level consistent with his current enrollment status in all areas except for mathematical computation. However, his score on this subtest is still normatively average.

Case Formulation

Bryan denied any symptoms that would indicate the presence of any significant mental illness at the time of the interview. Although he had received treatment for ADHD symptoms as a child, there are no indications of ongoing concerns related to hyperactivity or inattentiveness. While he reported some minimal level of distress associated with his recent arrest, it does not appear to be in excess of what would be reasonably expected from others in his situation.

Much of the respondent's presentation and self-description suggest he may be evidencing the early stages of a personality disorder (i.e., a number of aberrant personality traits that tend to be socially maladaptive). However, given his age and the dearth of available records, no definitive diagnosis of this type can be made.

Diagnostic Impressions

Axis I: V71.09: No Diagnosis
Axis II: 799.9: Diagnosis Deferred

FACTORS RELEVANT TO THE WAIVER DECISION

Seriousness of the Crime(s)

Decisions related to the seriousness of the charges are deferred to the jurisdiction of the court.

Risk for Dangerousness

While it is not possible to predict *whether* an adolescent will engage in future criminal activity, research has identified many factors related to elevated risk for future dangerousness in this population. Before providing an explanation of those factors observed in Bryan, it should be noted that any juvenile risk assessment is subject to a number of caveats. First, the accuracy of such assessments is inherently limited by the transient and evolving nature of adolescence. Although psychological science has identified factors that may aggravate or mitigate risk, short-term risk judgments are often more accurate than estimates of long-term risk. Secondly, while we know that some level of antisocial behavior in adolescence is typical, and certain factors are related to the continuation of

such behavior in adulthood, it is extremely difficult to accurately identify which youth are at risk
for engaging in antisocial behavior into adulthood.
In fact, data indicate that a significant majority of
juvenile offenders (including those who commit
serious or violent offenses) do not continue criminal careers as adults. Therefore, the discussion
below should be interpreted with these caveats in
mind, as Bryan's risk could change as he matures
and amasses more life experiences.

Research indicates that a history of violent behavior is perhaps the strongest predictor of future violent
behavior. Prior to his recent charges, Bryan has no
criminal record nor are there any indications of a pattern of aggressive or assaultive behavior in any setting. In fact, Bryan has no known history of any kind
of antisocial behavior and does not appear to associate with peers who might increase his risk of engaging
in such behavior. Substance use is also known to significantly increase risk; however, there is no evidence
Bryan engages in even occasional use of drugs or
alcohol. The single factor with the largest correlation
with continued adult criminality is early onset of such
activity. Prior to the age of 16, Bryan had never been
charged with any criminal offense. It should be noted
that he has not yet been convicted of any charge,
and it would be grossly inappropriate for a mental
health professional to determine his guilt. However,
even should the charges be sustained, data suggest
that adolescents who engage in sexually assaultive
behavior typically do not continue to engage in such
behavior as adults. Therefore, even if it were unequiv-
ocally determined that Bryan committed the alleged
offense, the fact that the current charge is of a sexual
nature and that the alleged behavior occurred at a relatively advanced age collectively suggest he is at low
risk for future violent behavior.

In addition to the factors discussed above,
there are several less strongly predictive risk factors for violence that are absent in Bryan. He has
no history of impulsive or risk-taking behavior.
Although Ms. Morgan reported a limited history of
defiant behavior at school, this was entirely verbal
in nature, is not at all atypical for adolescents, and
does not indicate an increased risk for adulthood
antisocial behavior. Furthermore, the respondent
does not evidence deficits in anger or stress management, nor does he present with any symptoms
of an active mental illness.

In addition to the factors named above that
elevate a juvenile's risk for future dangerousness,

Bryan evidences several factors which may serve
to mitigate any risk that is present. These include
attachments to seemingly prosocial adults, including his mother, his grandmother, and a neighbor.
Ms. Morgan also appears to be supportive of Bryan,
a factor known to decrease risk. Additionally,
Bryan continues to engage in school, is considering attending college, and has a serious and feasible career plan in place. Based on all available
evidence, it appears that, without treatment, legal
consequences, or time to mature, Bryan would still
present a low risk for future dangerousness.

Sophistication/Maturity

Assessments of sophistication for the purpose of
juvenile certification generally focus on criminal sophistication. "Maturity" refers to the
age-appropriateness of a juvenile's behavior in light
of what is known about typical adolescent development. Bryan evidences a number of factors that
indicate a low level of sophistication and maturity.
Prior to his current charges, there are no records
of Bryan engaging in, or attempting to engage in,
any type of sophisticated schemes of an antisocial
nature. The only alleged crime with which he is
charged does not require an advanced level of planning, significant manipulation of others or the environment, or any demonstration of leadership skills.
In discussing outcomes for his case, it appears
Bryan genuinely believes his physical appearance
would be a key element in proving his innocence, as
he repeatedly made statements to the effect of "Do
I look like a bad guy?" In terms of overall maturity
relative to persons of his age, both the respondent
and Ms. Morgan indicated Bryan is heavily reliant
on his mother to meet his daily needs, as well as for
transportation, entertainment, emotional support,
and significant assistance with decision making.
The respondent himself even indicated he is heavily reliant upon others to assist him in arriving at
decisions regarding issues of more than trivial
importance. Bryan has also not displayed levels of
autonomy that are typical for his age. He has not
assumed any significant responsibilities within the
home, sought employment or a driver's license, and
has not engaged in any notable romantic relationships. He did not express the interest in sexuality
typical of late adolescence. His social maturity
also appears to lag behind that of his peers, given
Ms. Morgan's report that many of Bryan's friends are
several years younger than he. She further reported

that, in spite of this age gap, Bryan is unlikely to assume a leadership role in social situations. When interacting with the examiners, Bryan's attempts to ingratiate himself and present himself favorably were somewhat unsophisticated and transparent. Although the respondent described himself as an intellectual and the "therapist" and "defender" to his friends, Ms. Morgan's description of her son presents an image of a somewhat socially immature and inept teenager who has yet to definitively individuate from his mother.

Alternatively, there are several factors that indicate a more age-appropriate level of maturity. Ms. Morgan denied any behavioral issues at home and indicated she often receives positive comments from others regarding Bryan's behavior. This indicates that Bryan is able to recognize socially appropriate behavioral standards and conform his behavior as needed. During the interview, he demonstrated an understanding that forced sexual activity is unacceptable and illegal. He also discussed a relatively mature moral rationale for not engaging in criminal behavior, demonstrating recognition of the societal level consequences of such behavior. Although his reasoning is at times egocentric, Bryan appears able to engage in logical cost–benefit analyses and anticipate potential outcomes. He appears to have developed the ability to cognitively project into the future and understand the consequences of yet-to-occur events, an ability that is indicative of higher level thinking skills. He has also taken steps toward developing a realistic career plan over the past year. Finally, he demonstrated cognitive abilities that are normatively average and levels of academic achievement that are commensurate with or exceed those of his typical peer.

Treatment Amenability

During this evaluation, Bryan evidenced several tendencies that could serve to impair his ability to either participate in or benefit fully from treatment. For instance, it does not appear that Bryan is experiencing any symptoms consistent with mental illness. His presentation during the evaluation also suggested he may have a tendency to present himself in a favorable light and deny even minor flaws. Furthermore, Bryan perceives no need for mental health treatment or significant personal change, factors that would be likely to impair his motivation for treatment, should attempts at intervention be initiated. Generally, past response to treatment is a key indicator of treatment amenability; however, as the respondent has an extremely limited history of intervention, it is difficult to anticipate his response to treatment. However, his history suggests he may experience difficulty with establishing substantial relationships with adults outside of his family, which may create problems in establishing an appropriate therapeutic relationship with a treatment provider. For therapeutic intervention to succeed, it is essential that the person be experiencing some level of discomfort or distress to motivate change. During the current evaluation, the respondent gave the impression of complete equanimity and lack of concern regarding his legal outcomes. However, his mother indicated her impression that Bryan is actually highly anxious and distressed regarding his future. Although it is possible that Bryan is evidencing the early stages of a personality disorder, the features he displays most prominently (e.g., grandiosity and egocentricity) are not particularly amendable to treatment. While Bryan possesses the requisite cognitive and verbal abilities required to participate in treatment, overall it is uncertain whether he would be amenable to psychological intervention at the present time.

Amy L. Wevodau, MA
Student Clinician

Mary Alice Conroy, PhD, ABPP
Board Certified in Forensic Psychology

TEACHING POINT:
TRANSLATING LEGAL CRITERIA INTO FORENSIC CAPACITIES

Forensic clinicians conducting FMHA begin by reviewing the legal standard that guides the evaluation and provides the functional-legal criteria on which the evaluator can focus. This is a straightforward process when the legal standard is *elaborated* and includes a detailed set of criteria that can be used to define the functional-legal criteria. Two good examples of elaborated legal standards are competence to stand trial and capital sentencing. Both include a number of components that can be used to provide a framework for the evaluation. But they also include some criteria that are not appropriate for the forensic clinician to consider. How should this distinction be made?

The primary consideration in whether the criterion should be considered appropriate for FMHA is whether the forensic clinician has genuine expertise in that area. Some are simply factual (e.g., the age of the defendant at the time of the offense). Others call for some judgment (e.g., the seriousness of the offense), but such judgment is not within the expertise that is specific to mental health professionals. Both of these would most appropriately be excluded by the forensic clinician interested in limiting his or her contribution to areas of genuine expertise. The remaining criteria are those calling for evaluation and judgment in areas requiring genuine mental health expertise. These are the criteria that should most appropriately be employed as functional-legal domains in the evaluation. The Texas statute used for guidance in this case is reasonably well elaborated.

There are other times, however, when the forensic clinician must conduct an evaluation that is guided by an *unelaborated* legal standard. When the applicable legal standard does not offer any detail suitable for guiding the operationalization of functional-legal criteria, the evaluator must use a different approach. One that has been used with some success involves reviewing the legal, scientific, and professional literatures to identify functional-legal criteria that are used in other jurisdictions and have been identified by researchers and professionals as frequently applicable. When that is done for the legal proceeding of juvenile transfer, there are three criteria that are frequently cited: public safety, treatment needs and amenability, and sophistication and maturity. These are very close to the criteria set forth in the applicable Texas statute, and applied to the evaluation in this case.

But identifying frequently cited criteria through a survey of other jurisdictions provides no assurance that a court in that jurisdiction would find these applicable in a juvenile transfer proceeding. So the second consideration in using this approach involves evaluating these criteria separately, and communicating the results of each in a distinct section of the report. A judge finding that all were relevant could simply review and consider each of these subsections. If the same judge decided that only some of these criteria were applicable, then the information from the other section(s) could be ignored. Evaluators using this approach should clearly refrain from answering the ultimate legal question, as they would not be certain which of the criteria they evaluated would be considered by the court.

CASE TWO
PRINCIPLE: USE THIRD PARTY INFORMATION IN ASSESSING RESPONSE STYLE (*PRINCIPLE 25*)

This principle was discussed in some detail in Chapter 10 (this volume), so we will move directly to how the present report can illustrate its application in FMHA. This report provides a good example of using third party information to assess response style in the context of juvenile decertification. It should be noted that the evaluation of Shawn did not provide particular evidence that he was exaggerating deficits or symptoms, which might have provided some reason to administer an objective psychological test with validity scales (i.e., the MMPI-A). If anything, Shawn might have under-reported possible deficits. Third party information was obtained through interviews with Shawn's mother and his caseworker, and through reviewing the delinquent petition, probable cause affidavit, and the written allegation and deposition of the arresting officer. As a routine matter, this third party information was integrated with self-report by assessing the "consistency of self-reported information with that obtained from collateral sources" (language used in all reports of evaluations conducted by the contributor, Kirk Heilbrun). When there are significant discrepancies between self-report and third party information, this may suggest the need for more specialized measures of response style.

Juvenile Forensic Evaluation
January 14, 2013
Re: Shawn Johnson

REFERRAL INFORMATION

Shawn Johnson is a 17-year-old African American male (DOB: 4/7/1985) who is currently charged with possession with intent to deliver, possession of a firearm, and criminal conspiracy related to his arrest on November 15, 2012. The Philadelphia County Public Defender's Office (David Bunker, Esq.) requested a mental health evaluation to provide the defense with information relevant to Shawn's treatment needs and amenability in the context of public safety.

PROCEDURES

Shawn was evaluated for approximately four hours on Friday, January 4, 2013, at the Philadelphia County Youth Center. In addition to a clinical interview, Shawn was administered a standard test of current functioning in relevant academic areas (the Wide Range Achievement Test, 4th Edition, or WRAT-4), a structured inventory of symptoms of mental and emotional disorders specifically designed for use with adolescents, (the Massachusetts Youth Screening Instrument, 2nd Edition, or MAYSI-2), and a risk-assessment tool for use with adolescents (the Structured Assessment of Risk Violence in Youth, or SAVRY).

Collateral interviews were conducted by telephone with Shawn's mother, Andrea Baker, for approximately 30 minutes on January 11, 2013, and with Shawn's assigned caseworker at the Philadelphia County Youth Center, Jason Day, for approximately 15 minutes on January 11, 2013.

The following documents, obtained from David Bunker, Esq., were also reviewed as part of the evaluation:

1. Delinquent Petition, Juvenile Division, Family Court of Philadelphia County (dated 2/9/08, 5/21/08, 2/2/11);
2. Delinquent Court Hearing List, Philadelphia Juvenile Court (dated 2/25/08, 5/30/08, 7/17/08, 10/12/08, 2/5/09, 6/3/09);
3. Adjudicatory Hearing Orders, Juvenile Division, Family Court of Philadelphia County (dated 2/26/11, 3/7/11, 3/18/11, 4/2/11, 4/16/11, 4/16/11);
4. Order of Disposition, Juvenile Division, Family Court of Philadelphia County (dated 5/4/11, 5/15/11);
5. Master's Recommendations, Juvenile Division, Family Court of Philadelphia County (dated 2/3/11, 6/5/11, 10/13/11, 12/8/11, 2/10/12, 2/12/12, 4/6/12, 4/30/12, 7/28/12);
6. Bench Warrant, Family Court of Philadelphia County (dated 7/28/12);
7. Affidavit of Probable Cause, Court of Common Pleas of Philadelphia County (dated 12/1/12).

Additional records that were reviewed but are not part of the current evaluation are the Deposition of Sgt. Frank Mitchell (dated 11/31/12), Written Allegation of Sgt. Frank Mitchell (dated 12/1/12), Order from the Court of Common Pleas of Philadelphia County (undated), Certification Hearing Order from the Court of Common Pleas of Philadelphia County (undated), the Commonwealth's Petition to Transfer Juvenile to Adult Court (undated), and Certificate of Service (undated).

Prior to the beginning of the evaluation, Shawn was notified about the purpose of the evaluation and the associated limits of confidentiality. He was able to report back his understanding that he was being evaluated regarding his current charges and his treatment needs. After further questioning, Shawn stated that he understood that a report would be written and submitted to his attorney, who could then use it at his hearing; and if it were used, that copies would be provided to the prosecution and the court. In addition, Ms. Baker and Mr. Day were notified about the purpose of the evaluation and agreed to be interviewed.

COMMENT

Often when records are provided as part of FMHA, they include documents that are not relevant to the evaluation. This can't be judged without reviewing them, and the forensic clinician should do this review personally rather than leaving it to the person providing the records. But when records are reviewed and are judged as not relevant to the evaluation, the previous paragraph provides a brief way of indicating what has been reviewed and why it will not be cited in the report.

RELEVANT HISTORY

Historical information was obtained from Shawn and from the collateral sources described above. Whenever possible, we have assessed the consistency of self-report information with that obtained from collateral sources.

Family History

Shawn reported that he was born to his biological parents on April 7, 1985, in Germantown, Pennsylvania. He indicated that his biological parents were together at the time of his birth, but they are not together currently. He reported that his father has started another family in the Philadelphia area, and that his mother had had several relationships while he was growing up, most significantly with Joseph Abbo, who lived with the family for approximately three or four years. Shawn indicated that he had considered Mr. Abbo to be his stepfather. Andrea Baker, Shawn's mother (DOB: 9/1/74), reported that Shawn was born on April 7, 1985, to her and his father, Michael Young (DOB: 9/16/74). She described Shawn as "my youngest son...my baby" and indicated that they had a "good relationship." Ms. Baker also added that "he just grew up, he wanted to do what he wants to do...got a little rough there."

Shawn indicated that when growing up he primarily lived with his mother in the West Philadelphia and Germantown areas. He noted that the family moved approximately four times while he was growing up, although he did not know why. Shawn indicated that he was "sort of" living with his mother in Germantown at the time of his arrest. He also reported living with his father at one point, but did not state for how long. Shawn noted that his father has lived in the same house for as long as he can remember. He indicated that at the time of his arrest he was living in an apartment in Philadelphia County: "Yeah...you could say I was living there." According to Ms. Baker, Shawn and his family lived in the West Philadelphia and Germantown areas. She stated that the family moved approximately five times when Shawn was younger, explaining that each time the family "moved into something better...better houses." She reported that the family last moved four years ago to Germantown, and has lived in the same house since. She indicated that Shawn was living there with the family, but that he was "on the streets" for the three to four months prior to his arrest in November 2012. She said that Shawn didn't want to go to school or "do the things he was supposed to do" (e.g., obey curfew), and that he was given the choice to stay or leave the house. She stated that her reasoning was to allow him to make that choice "if you think you're that grown and can make your own decisions."

Shawn reported having a total of nine siblings, including four sisters and five brothers. He indicated that two of his sisters (approximately ages 14 and 21) are the children of Ms. Baker and Mr. Johnson, and his half-sister (6) is the child of Ms. Baker and Mr. Abbo; he also reported having a step-sister (16) through his father's current relationship. He said that two of his brothers (19 and 20) are the children of Ms. Baker and Mr. Johnson, and two half-brothers (6 and 8) are from his father's current relationship. He also reported having one step-brother through his father's current relationship. He noted that he lived at home with his mother, "godmother," sister, half-sister, and two brothers; his oldest sister previously lived with the family but is currently living independently. He noted that his father lives with his half-brothers, step-sister, and step-brother. When asked about his relationship with his siblings, Shawn responded, "We get along good."

When asked about the strengths of his family, Shawn indicated, "they don't give up on you." When asked about the challenges his family has faced, he indicated "my mom seeing her kids locked up." When asked how his mother would discipline him and his siblings, Shawn reported that "when we were bad we were put on punishment," and that the level of punishment would "depend on the act." For example, Shawn said that when he was suspended from school, his mother would make him stay home and take away his phone and computer. He also indicated that if he or his siblings continued to do the "same small thing," the punishment would get "bigger," and if they did something "big" that the punishment was "big." He reported that his mother would lock the removed items in her room to prevent him and his siblings from accessing them, as she was frequently working and not in the home. Ms. Baker indicated that she "tried to" discipline her children—specifically, "they got beatings like any kid" and she would "take things away, cell phone and computer, that kind of stuff." She added that when her children would do things that were particularly serious, she would "take things away they really liked...that's how kids understand."

Shawn denied witnessing or experiencing any physical violence, neglect, or abuse when growing up—including physical, sexual, or emotional abuse. He reported that neither his mother nor his father has ever been arrested "that I recall," and that neither had ever committed any acts that might have resulted in their arrest.

Educational and Vocational History

Shawn reported that he attended two elementary schools. He noted that he attended multiple schools because of his family moving to another area. Shawn stated that he went to elementary school "every day" and that his grades were in the A and B range: "I think good, I can't remember back that far." He stated that he had no behavioral reports, suspensions, or expulsions in elementary school, and that he did not receive special education or repeat grades. Shawn reported that he did not participate in any after-school activities or programs. Ms. Baker reported that Shawn did well in school but began receiving special education (called "emotional support") around the fourth grade because "he wasn't learning at the right level." She indicated that she thinks his difficulties in school are "probably nearer to him not being able to see…he went years without glasses and couldn't learn."

Shawn reported that he attended three middle schools. He again noted that he attended multiple schools because his family had moved to another area. Shawn said that his attendance began to decline in middle school, because he "just wouldn't go; be 'sick' or play hooky." When asked what he would do with his time, Shawn replied that he would "probably chill in the park." He reported that his grades in middle school were in the B and C range, and that he had an individualized education plan (IEP) beginning around eighth grade. He stated that he didn't know what this was for, but noted that he was placed in "emotional support" (i.e., special education) because he needed help with his schoolwork, particularly "focusing…reading." Shawn also described getting into fights in middle school, specifically in seventh and eighth grade. He described getting into fights approximately one to three times per year, and said that he would sometimes be suspended for fighting. He stated that he was never expelled from middle school.

Shawn reported not participating in any after-school activities or programs. Ms. Baker reported that Shawn's grades growing up were "okay, some

good and some bad," and that when he received low grades "he would bring them up with me." Ms. Baker also reported that Shawn received "emotional support" in school for learning difficulties, but that she thinks these difficulties resulted from his poor vision beginning in elementary school, "so he had always been behind." She related that she thought he "started shutting down" when experiencing academic difficulties as he got older, and that Shawn had "emotional issues, depression and stuff, related to school stuff." She added that his special education made him feel "out of place, it made him shut down and not want to do work because he was embarrassed." She also indicated that Shawn might have been teased because of his difficulties in school, which led to his fighting "because kids were picking on him." She reported that Shawn was suspended "quite a few times" for these fights. Ms. Baker said that, around this time, his peer group "got worse," which she thinks made it even harder for Shawn to deal with his academic difficulties: "You wouldn't talk to those kids about problems in school, it just wasn't something they talked about." She also noted that when Shawn began "hanging out with this group of friends" he "stopped going more" to school.

Shawn reported that he attended two formal high schools, including Thomas Jefferson High School and the Germantown Charter Academy. He indicated that he had attended multiple high schools because he was "locked up" around this time, and that he attained additional educational instruction during these placements. He described his attendance as "all right" and added that "I would go but I wasn't there long…when I was home I was going." Shawn reported that his grades in high school were in the B, C, and D range. He indicated that he may have repeated the tenth grade due to his disrupted school schedule, and that he currently has enough credits to be in the twelfth grade. Shawn said that he continues to receive educational instruction in the Philadelphia County Youth Center, and that he is "doing well." According to Jason Day, the assigned caseworker at the Philadelphia County Youth Center, Shawn's reports from the school section indicate "he's doing well here, and does what he needs to do."

When asked generally about his schoolwork, Shawn reported, "I always wait to the last minute to do my homework" but that his assignments "would always be complete." He added that when his mother was home he would have to complete his schoolwork "immediately."

Shawn reported that he has not yet held a job. When asked about his career goals, he responded, "What do I want to be? I don't know...I haven't started thinking about that yet."

Social and Avocational History

Shawn reported having associates and friends who are "my same age and older." When asked to elaborate, he indicated that his oldest friend was "probably 20." He stated that his friends "smoke a lot...weed and cigarettes," and also that they play basketball. He indicated that some of his friends have been arrested—specifically for assault—and that they have committed several acts that may get them arrested (e.g., fighting in school and smoking). He denied being involved in more serious antisocial activities such as selling drugs or stealing cars. Shawn also noted that the events leading to his arrest for assault when he was age 15 or 16 occurred with three other individuals, and that at the time of the instant offenses he was living with "my man" (age 18) in the apartment in Philadelphia County.

Ms. Baker reported knowing some of Shawn's friends, but added that, with her three sons, it was hard to "remember everyone they were around with." She also indicated that Shawn was friends with his older brothers' friends, which she noted was "not a good choice...different ages do different things." She noted that some of Shawn's friends were "okay" but "not many...some kids were out too late." She reported that some of Shawn's friends were arrested or in juvenile placements, but that for the most part she thought Shawn and his friends "were just hanging out." When asked if she believed Shawn was involved in gang activity, Ms. Baker responded she "heard of gangs" but was "not positive if he was in it."

Shawn indicated that his hobbies include video games—particularly *Call of Duty* "right now." When asked about how much time he thinks he spent on prosocial versus antisocial activities in the community, Shawn responded that he doesn't consider what he and his friends do as antisocial: "We don't go around looking for trouble," and "We go around looking for girls...play a lot of cards, card games." Ms. Baker reported that Shawn enjoyed playing soccer around ages seven to nine, including playing on community soccer teams and attending soccer camps. She said that as he became older he seemed to lose interest, possibly related to his friends' "not [being] into it."

Medical and Mental Health History

Shawn's medical history is significant for a diagnosis of Crohn's disease, a form of inflammatory bowel disease. Ms. Baker reported that Shawn was diagnosed with Crohn's Disease approximately three to four years ago when he was in a prior placement. She also reported that Shawn fell approximately nine feet from a stairway when he was around two or three years old, for which he was hospitalized. She reported that he briefly lost his eyesight as a result of this fall.

When asked if he had ever received counseling or therapy, Shawn reported that he attended family therapy for one visit with his mother, following his release from his first placement. He also reported receiving counseling during his placements. Shawn reported that this treatment was "not really helpful" but did not provide any further details; he also reported that he found "some stress relief helpful." Shawn also reported being prescribed "Seroquil" (Seroquel) for sleeping troubles for approximately two years between ages 14 and 16. He indicated that he has "trouble sleeping when not home...it's just not home." Shawn reported that there is no family history of mental illness. Shawn denied any current or previous suicidal ideation or intent. Ms. Baker also indicated that Shawn received counseling in his prior placements, and also in school through "emotional support" (i.e., special education). The Adjudicatory Hearing Order (dated 3/16/11) indicated that Shawn was ordered to undergo a Behavioral Health Evaluation for reading and IQ assessment, but no records of this evaluation were available for review.

Substance Abuse History

Shawn reported that he has previously used marijuana and smoked cigarettes. He estimated his marijuana usage to be three "blunts" per day. He reported that he did not drink alcohol, and denied using any other substances. Ms. Baker reported that she did not think Shawn drank alcohol but had heard that he was using marijuana. She stated that she had never seen him high and that he never used any substances at the house.

Offense History

Shawn reported three previous arrests, resulting in two prior placements. He said that his first arrest occurred when he was approximately age 13 in 2007, for robbery. Shawn indicated that he was placed at

Xavier House for approximately 1.5 years as a result of his adjudication on this charge. According to the Delinquent Petition (dated 2/9/08), on 2/5/08, Shawn (in concert with another unnamed individual) entered the home belonging to his father by breaking a window, ransacked the house, and stole $80. He was charged with burglary, criminal conspiracy, theft, criminal trespassing, and criminal mischief.

Shawn reported that he was next arrested around age 15 or 16 for assault. Shawn indicated that he received six months' probation with a stipulation of house arrest and reporting. A Delinquent Petition (dated 6/21/08) indicates that on or about 6/20/08, Shawn was charged with disorderly conduct, terroristic threats, and harassment/stalking for an incident in which he yelled insults to another individual on the street, including threats to kill the individual. The Delinquent Court Hearing List (dated 6/30/08) indicates that Shawn accepted deferred adjudication and was placed on intensive supervision until placement, with orders of random drug screens, anger management counseling, and electronic monitoring. Delinquent Court Hearing Lists indicate that Shawn was placed at Xavier House (dated 8/17/08) and held there through at least July 2009 (dated 11/12/08, 3/5/09, 7/3/09).

He reported that he violated this probation as a result of his third arrest when he was approximately age 15 or 16, again for assault. He indicated that he was placed at Jackson for approximately 11 months. According to the Delinquent Petitions (both dated 2/2/11) on or around 2/1/11, Shawn, in concert with other individuals, took a cell phone from two separate complainants at two different times, causing both of them bodily injury by hitting and kicking them multiple times. The Adjudicatory Hearing Orders) indicate that Shawn was adjudicated delinquent on the charges of aggravated assault, robbery, and conspiracy, and that he was ordered to undergo a Behavioral Health Evaluation for reading and IQ assessment, pay restitution, and be placed at Jackson Academy at Franklin. According to the Order of Disposition, he was formally placed in Jackson on 5/15/11, and this placement was continued based on Master's Recommendations dated 6/5/11, 10/13/11, 12/8/11, 2/10/12, 2/12/12, and 4/6/12. The Master's Recommendation dated 4/30/12 indicates Shawn was then placed on aftercare probation with orders to attend case management, undergo random drug testing, undergo DNA

testing, and have a set curfew; he was to attend a review hearing on July 28, 2012.

When asked about the instant offenses, Shawn indicated that he was at the apartment "because I had a bench warrant in Philadelphia and didn't want to go to court." He indicated that this bench warrant was issued "for not showing up at court." The Master's Recommendation (dated 7/28/12) and a Bench Warrant (dated 7/28/12) indicates a bench warrant was issued by the Family Court of Philadelphia County for Shawn on 7/28/12 for failing to appear for his review hearing. When asked if he was living at the apartment, Shawn responded, "Yeah…you could say I was living there." He indicated that he was living there with "my man" (age 18), adding, "I just knew he had a place where I could stay." Ms. Baker indicated that she was "shocked as hell" when she was called after Shawn's arrest, and that "all I know is about the charges…he wasn't at home for months." The Affidavit of Probable Cause (dated 12/1/12) indicates that Shawn was observed in the apartment in November 2012, and that during a search of the apartment in December 2012, Shawn was found sleeping on a mattress in the living room.

Currently, Shawn is placed at the Philadelphia County Youth Center. He indicated that he "was just doing what I gotta do and get out of here," and that he had attained the highest level of the Youth Center's privileges system. He indicated "it took me not that long, no trouble" gaining these privileges, and that "I watch my behavior here…I don't want to lose what I got." According to Mr. Day, Shawn has earned the highest level of their privilege system, has done "exceptionally well," and has had "no behavioral concerns his entire time." Specifically, he noted that Shawn has earned the most privileges allowed at the placement and additionally that he was chosen to be a Representative, meaning he has added responsibilities such as chores, making sure the other individuals in the placement are "doing what they should do," and "looking after the new kids." Mr. Day indicated that Shawn "does tend to be more mature than the other kids" and that he tends to be by himself, but added that Shawn does interact with other individuals in the placement: "He will interact but prefers to lay back and let things go on around him." He also noted that Shawn is "not teased by the other kids," "stays out of the petty stuff some of the kids try and do," and that he interacts appropriately with the staff.

Mr. Day reported that because of his Crohn's disease, Shawn has issues with eating and "appears sickly from time to time." He also said that while there is a mental health counselor on staff, Shawn "hasn't needed that" and has not received any formal counseling. Mr. Day indicated that Shawn "says the right things, knows what to do...he's an intelligent kid, and says he wants to change but it's not sure how serious he is." Overall Mr. Day described Shawn as the "best-behaved kid we got here."

CURRENT CLINICAL CONDITION

Shawn Johnson presented as a 17-year-old African American male of below-average height and slender build who appeared younger than his stated age. He was dressed in casual attire and appeared appropriately groomed. Identifying marks include several scars, including one on his forehead from stitches resulting from a fall when he was approximately age four, and another on his hand from stitches results from his trying to climb a fence when he was approximately age 15 or 16. Additionally, Shawn has one tattoo—"WP"—on his left forearm, which he stated stands for "West Philly." Shawn reported problems with his vision, specifically that he required glasses for seeing things "up close." Shawn reported no difficulties with his hearing or movement, and denied any history of seizures. Shawn said that his dominant language is English, and that this is the only language spoken in his home. Shawn's speech was clear and relevant, and he appeared to understand the questions asked of him. It was noted that Shawn spoke in a low voice during the evaluation, frequently responded to questions by asking for additional information, and generally appeared guarded—he was particularly reluctant to discuss topics that appeared to upset him (e.g., health concerns in his family).

Shawn reported symptoms related to a diagnosis of attention-deficit hyperactivity disorder—specifically, trouble concentrating and "always moving around"—and also indicated that a prior teacher had reported these symptoms. A screening of ADHD symptoms indicated that Shawn probably does not meet the clinical criteria for a diagnosis of ADHD. Shawn reported no problems with his memory, adding, "I got a good memory...I only forget stuff I don't want to remember." There was no evidence of bizarre thinking. Therefore, it appears that the present evaluation provides a valid reflection of Shawn's current functioning.

Shawn's basic academic skills, as measured by the WRAT-4, are significantly below grade level in Word Reading (5th percentile compared to individuals of the same age, equivalent to grade 4.4), Sentence Comprehension (19th percentile, grade equivalent 7.7), Spelling (5th percentile, grade equivalent 4.7), and Math Computation (8th percentile, grade equivalent 5.1). During Word Reading, Shawn was reluctant to continue past the words he knew immediately, and frequently verbalized this reluctance. When additional effort was requested, it was observed that Shawn frequently asked about specific letters (e.g., "Is that a p?") and had difficulty sounding out words. Importantly, Shawn's errors on the Word Reading subtest were frequently whole words, usually similar to the target words (e.g., "horizontal" for horizon) but not always (e.g., "stomped" for triumph). Shawn's difficulty or inability to sound out words was also observed during the Spelling subtest. During Sentence Comprehension, Shawn would frequently say that he did not know the response, but when asked for additional effort, he responded with the correct answer on the less difficult items; he would ultimately give up on the more challenging items. This subtest was eventually discontinued, as Shawn stated that he could no longer read the words because they were blurring. He reported that that he still could not read the words even after a short break. As the subtest was discontinued after three consecutive incorrect responses, it is unlikely that this discontinuation significantly affected the results. Finally, it was observed on the Math Computation subtest that Shawn wanted to give up after 6 minutes (participants are given 15 minutes), stating, "I just don't want to do them anymore." After additional effort was requested, Shawn worked for an additional 3 minutes before stopping.

On a structured inventory of symptoms of mental and emotional disorders specifically designed for use with adolescents (MAYSI-2), Shawn endorsed 10 of 52 possible symptoms. He did not score within the clinical range on any of the scales included in this measure. Shawn responded to two items on the Angry-Irritable scale, specifically, that he has been easily upset ("things on the outside...brother being locked up, Mom going through a lot, people sick") and has gotten frustrated a lot ("kids here be talking, asking questions [to staff] they know the answers to, not acting their age"). He also responded to two items on the Depressed-Anxious scale, specifically that he has felt lonely too much of the time ("in here") and feeling like some part of his body is always hurting him ("sometimes my legs hurt...after I wake up"). He responded to two items on the Somatic Complaints scale, specifically, that he feels his heart racing when he gets nervous or anxious ("I just know [I am nervous]") and having bad headaches ("because I'm not wearing my glasses...migraines...during the day and when I wake up"). (Shawn also responded on the Somatic Complaints scale to having his stomach being upset, but this is probably due to Shawn's history of Crohn's disease.) Finally, Shawn responded to two items on the Traumatic Experiences scale, specifically, being in a situation where he could have been badly hurt ("long time ago, three or four years ago...somebody started shooting on the street") and has seen someone severely injured or killed ("people getting shot...a couple times"). Shawn also reported having a lot of trouble falling asleep despite "doing everything" he could, which he attributed to not being at home. Shawn did not respond to any of the items on the Alcohol/Drug Use scale, Suicide Ideation scale, or Thought Disturbance scale.

The SAVRY was completed based on information obtained from Shawn and collateral sources as part of the current evaluation. The SAVRY is a structured risk-assessment tool for use with adolescents that aids in determining an adolescent's future risk of violence. Based on the presence and absence of various risk and protective factors, it appears that Shawn is at a moderate–high risk for future violence relative to other youth his age. Shawn presents a moderate–high risk based on the presence of certain historical, social/contextual, and individual/clinical risk factors.

Historical risk factors are those based on Shawn's past behavior and experiences. Shawn's historical risk factors are significant for two acts of prior violence (assault charges); prior acts of nonviolent offending (burglary, conspiracy, substance use); failing to comply with prior court orders, supervision, or treatment (violation of probation, bench warrant for not reporting to court, self-reported breaching of curfews); some discontinuity of care during childhood (frequent moves, including before the age of 12 years, and a period of living with Mr. Johnson); and significant difficulties in school achievement (special education

required to assist with school performance). However, Shawn does not appear to have historical risk factors related to early initiation of violence; history of self-harm or suicide attempts; exposure to violence in the home; childhood history of maltreatment; or parental/caregiver criminality.

Social/contextual risk factors are those based on Shawn's interpersonal relationships and environment. Shawn's social/contextual risk factors are significant for his frequently associating with criminal or antisocial peers (several friends arrested for, or involved in, antisocial behaviors like drug use, drug sales, fighting, and theft); past peer rejection (particularly related to being picked on or "messed with" in school or by friends for low achievement in school, leading to fighting); moderate to significant stress, with poor coping ability (stressors include being incarcerated, safety concerns for his brother, and health concerns for family members, which Shawn is reluctant to discuss and copes with by not thinking about it: "don't think about nothing...just blank"); somewhat inconsistent parental management (particularly related to supervision by Shawn's mother due to her work schedule); few or no sources of emotional support or guidance (Shawn reporting self-reliance and having "nobody" to look to for advice); and having crime and disorganization in his community (based on data from Southwest Philadelphia and Germantown communities). Additionally, Shawn presently appears to lack some protective factors related to his relationships and environment, particularly prosocial involvement, strong social support, and strong attachments or bonds.

Individual/clinical risk factors are those based on Shawn's attitudes and psychological and behavioral functioning. Shawn's individual/clinical risk factors are significant for attitudes that condone crime and/or violence (particularly an inability to develop non-criminal alternatives and a lack of understanding of the costs/benefits associated with criminal behaviors). They also include significant risk taking or impulsivity (lack of consideration in decision making, cutting in line "if there's something good up there," making some decisions "right when I think it" [e.g., breaking up with a girlfriend] while others would "depend on if I have things lined up" [e.g., quitting a job]); and moderate difficulty controlling his expressions of anger (relying on "showing the same emotion" to avoid losing his temper, self-reported holding grudges and difficulty holding back from fighting if provoked). In addition, they include moderate impairment in age-appropriate capacity for empathy and remorse (he does not recognize times he has hurt or caused problems for others; reported that he would "not worry about" doing something wrong to someone, but also understanding challenges his mother faces in "seeing [her] kids locked up"); moderate difficulties with restlessness, hyperactivity, or concentration (difficulty concentrating on items that do not interest him, frequent leg-shaking and movements); occasionally negative attitude toward intervention or treatment (reported complying with orders but appearing to lack appreciation and motivation for intervention—for example, indicating that he would be home on curfew to report with his probation officer but then leave the house again); and low interest in and commitment to school—although he is presently attending in placement and completing school work.

Shawn presently appears to lack some protective factors related to his attitudes and psychological functioning, specifically, having a strong commitment to school and having resilient personality traits (e.g., ability to develop alternatives to antisocial behavior, positive response to challenges, adaptability). However, Shawn does appear to have a somewhat positive attitude toward intervention and authority, as exemplified by his positive behavior and performance within his current placement, based on self-report and collateral information.

TREATMENT NEEDS AND AMENABILITY

Together, these factors suggest that Shawn appears to be functioning well in his current setting (i.e., institutional placement), but that he may be behaving without an appreciation of the benefits of intervention or a motivation to change. In the community, his lack of social supports and guidance, lack of commitment to school, negative attitude toward compliance with intervention efforts, frequent association with antisocial peers, stated impulsivity, and lack of resiliency and ability to control his anger represent significant risk factors for future offending. These also represent opportunities for intervention to decrease this risk.

There are four areas in which Shawn has treatment needs that, if addressed, may reduce his risk of future offending. These areas are: (1) specialized education and learning-disability evaluation;

(2) counseling focused on his understanding of and ability to manage his risk factors; (3) mental health treatment focused on psychological distress; and (4) increased involvement in structured, prosocial activities.

First, Shawn would benefit from continued specialized training in academic areas. Despite having earned enough credits to be placed in the twelfth grade, Shawn is currently functioning below grade level in individual word reading, sentence comprehension, spelling, and math. Specialized education should focus on developing Shawn's basic academic abilities, and would be informed greatly by an independent evaluation of potential learning disability (particularly one focused on differentiating learning disability from vision problems). This is particularly important given Shawn's difficulty in school, observed difficulty in sounding out words, and reported inability to see writing after a certain length of time. Increasing Shawn's competence within the academic setting may lead to an increased interest and commitment to continued education. A reasonable goal for Shawn would be to attain his GED. Additionally, as Shawn's interests continue to develop, he may benefit from vocational training, particularly related to skill development in realistic careers of interest.

Second, Shawn would benefit from counseling focused on his understanding of his risk factors and his ability to manage these risk factors. Currently Shawn appears to have poorly developed decision-making skills, an inability to appropriately handle stress, anger management problems, and poor resiliency. Counseling focused on improving his decision-making abilities and critical thinking, recognizing and responding better to stressful events, and handling his anger would be particularly helpful for Shawn. These skills are all related to resiliency, and continued counseling around how to develop alternate solutions to conflicts and problems, respond positively to challenges, adapt to environmental changes, calm himself and be calmed by others, and develop healthy and realistic self esteem would greatly improve Shawn's interactions with others and overall psychological health. They would also help decrease Shawn's risk for committing further criminal acts.

Third, Shawn would benefit from mental health treatment focused on his psychological distress. Shawn reported significant difficulty in discussing the distress he is currently experiencing, particularly the effects of his current arrest and placement. He also found it hard to discuss how his arrest and current placement are affecting his mother and members of his family, as well as his concern about his older brother's safety and recently discovered family health problems. When asked about these stressors, Shawn refused to discuss them further and indicated that doing so "would get me mad...I don't want to do it." Shawn said that he is "dealing with a lot of stress right now" and that he isn't sure "how I'm getting rid of it." Mental health treatment would be beneficial in helping Shawn to recognize and manage his current psychological distress. This would be particularly helpful in conjunction with improving the skills noted above, which would probably increase Shawn's ability to recognize and handle challenges and decrease his risk for further offending.

Finally, Shawn would benefit from increased involvement in structured activities with prosocial peers. Increasing the amount of time he spends in structured activities will reduce the likelihood that his anger management problems and impulsivity could lead him to engage in antisocial behaviors. This may include athletic activities, community service, and youth groups. Additionally, if it is decided that juvenile placement is appropriate, Shawn may be considered for positions of responsibility over other individuals in these placements, based on his position as a Representative in his current placement and his age. Providing guidance for younger individuals may increase his understanding, appreciation, and motivation for risk-reducing interventions, with the stipulation that Shawn should only be considered for this position once he has begun to develop these skills on his own.

CONCLUSIONS

In the opinion of the undersigned, based on all of the above, Shawn has treatment/rehabilitation needs in the following areas:

1. Specialized academic and vocational training, including an evaluation of possible learning disabilities;
2. Counseling focused on decision-making, stress management, anger management, and resiliency;
3. Mental health treatment focused on recognizing and managing his psychological distress; and

4. Increased involvement in structured, prosocial activities.

Shawn presents a moderate to high risk of future offending, but appears willing to work with authority and intervention to reduce his risk of future offending. He has treatment needs related to his academic abilities, which warrant specific evaluation to better understand his stated and observed learning difficulties. Shawn currently lacks a strong support network and has few prosocial outlets, and would therefore benefit from increased involvement in structured activities with prosocial peers. Shawn's ability to handle adversity is currently underdeveloped and represents an important treatment need. Developing these resiliency skills could be assisted by mental health treatment focused on his current stressors. Shawn's amenability to the interventions described above appears probable, based on his current institutional compliance and stated motivation to avoid future incarceration. Therefore, if these interventions can be made successfully, with monitoring to ensure compliance, Shawn's risk of future offending should be further reduced.

The interventions described above would probably take about 12 to 18 months to implement. Given Shawn's history of prior interventions and his current risk factors, the interventions would best be implemented in a secure residential placement, followed by intensive case-management when he returns to the community. It is our opinion that these needs could be met in the juvenile system if the court could retain jurisdiction over Shawn beyond his eighteenth birthday.

Thank you for the opportunity to evaluate Shawn.

Kirk Heilbrun, Ph.D.
Consulting Psychologist

Casey LaDuke, M.S.
Clinical Psychology Graduate Student

TEACHING POINT:
ADDRESSING CONFLICTING INFORMATION FROM THE INTERVIEW, TESTING, AND THIRD PARTY SOURCES

The simplest way to determine whether information from different sources is conflicting is to bring each of these sources together on a point-by-point basis. For example, on the important matter of prior juvenile placements, there are questions about such placements: how many, where they were, whether they were residential or outpatient, what rehabilitative services were provided, and how the youth responded to such interventions. When these questions are addressed by self-report, collateral interviews, and records, it is possible to gauge the consistency of the information across different sources. Such consistency becomes even clearer when the information from each source is included within the discussion of each question; the reader can immediately detect the presence of meaningful differences across sources.

Once these different accounts are provided, it may be that there are only minor differences between sources. Such consistency is not synonymous with accuracy—but it does make it more likely that the information provided is accurate.

When there is a lack of consistency, however, the forensic evaluator must make sense of this discrepancy. One possibility is that the self-report is deliberately being distorted. Another possibility is that inaccurate information is being disseminated across records, with later records incorporating the inaccurate information from earlier records. Yet another possibility is that a collateral interviewee is distorting information by either exaggerating or minimizing problems. Considering influences such as (a) bias/motivation; (b) inaccurate memory due to the passage of time, limited exposure, or other influences; and (c) error, the forensic clinician must evaluate the credibility of each source and weigh it accordingly. It may be that a larger pattern (e.g., the defendant consistently under-reports symptoms; two family members who are collateral interviewees consistently over-report symptoms) becomes clearer when the various points of information are considered in the aggregate.

23

Military

This chapter focuses on evaluations conducted in a military setting, and includes considerations relevant to the evaluation of military veterans. The first two cases are unique because they were conducted under the jurisdiction of the military court-martial system. The principle associated with the first report is described in the context specific to military courts-martial and the sources of military legal authority, with a teaching point that compares civilian and military law relevant to the referral question. The second report illustrates the principle of obtaining appropriate authorization, with an emphasis on considerations specific to military courts-martial. This report is supplemented by two teaching points: the first discusses how evaluators may *address the question of "severe mental disease or defect"* within FMHA in military contexts, and the second compares the process of obtaining authorization in military versus civilian FMHA. The final case report involves the evaluation of a military veteran and illustrates the utility of using nomothetic evidence; the teaching point describes the integration of nomothetic and idiographic information.

CASE ONE

PRINCIPLE: IDENTIFY RELEVANT FORENSIC ISSUES (*PRINCIPLE 8*)

This principle was discussed in some detail in Chapter 9 (this volume). Therefore, we will move directly to how the present report can illustrate its application in FMHA.[1] Forensic evaluators may be presented with the opportunity to perform evaluations in a military context and testify in courts-martial at military installations across the globe. Military courts-martial are federal courts

governed by the U.S. Supreme Court, the military appellate court system, the Military Rules of Evidence (MRE), the Rules for Courts-Martial (RCM), and the Uniform Code of Military Justice (UCMJ). The MRE, RCM, and UCMJ are all contained within the *Manual for Courts-Martial, United States* ("MCM"; Joint Service Committee on Military Justice, 2012). The highest military court is the Court of Appeals for the Armed Forces (CAAF). There are three military appellate courts beneath CAAF: the Army Court of Criminal Appeals, the Air Force Court of Criminal Appeals, and the Navy-Marine Corps Court of Criminal Appeals.

Forensic evaluators approaching military cases will need to be familiar with the distinct legal precedents, psycholegal tests, rules of evidence, and rules of procedure operative in this context. Although there are many similarities between federal and military trial courts, there are nevertheless distinctions in how forensic evaluators will function. The MRE allow forensic evaluators to give an ultimate opinion on the issue of affirmative *mens rea* defenses. In addition, forensic evaluators can opine on the ultimate issue of partial mental responsibility; that is, the existence of mental states that negate elements of offenses where the issue of specific intent is involved. In military courts-martial, the issue of criminal responsibility (i.e., lack of mental responsibility) is typically assessed by forensic evaluators at the same time as the competency to stand trial of the accused individual, in what is called an "RCM 706 evaluation" or "Sanity Board." This evaluation can be ordered either before or after the Article 32 hearing, which is the military equivalent of a grand jury.

Military courts will also frequently appoint forensic mental health consultants who operate under a cloak of attorney privilege. However, if consultants are subsequently listed as witnesses, the privilege is waived, and they may then be

---

[1] This discussion is contributed by Michael Sweda, Ph.D., who also conducted the evaluation for the first case.

questioned regarding their expected testimony in advance of providing it in open court. In sentencing cases, because military courts go directly from the trial/merits phase to the sentencing phase, forensic evaluators will need to prepare their mitigation reports in advance of the actual trial. Hence, mitigation reports are prepared without knowledge of the outcomes regarding particular charged offenses, which requires forensic evaluators to foresee a range of possible outcomes and adjust their evaluation and report accordingly. In addition to traditional sentencing considerations on the issues of punishment, deterrence, incapacitation, and treatment/rehabilitation, military juries (which are called *panels*) may consider the issue of how the behavior of the individual accused may have impacted good order and discipline in the military.

In the present case, the evaluators identified the relevant forensic issue early in the report. Under "Reason for Referral," Drs. Sweda and Benesh indicate that the evaluation is being conducted on the issues of mental responsibility, general mitigation, and violence risk and rehabilitative potential. Later in the report, the evaluators identify the governing legal standard: "[D]efendants lack mental responsibility for a charged offense if, at the time of the offense, they suffered from a severe mental disease or defect and the severe mental disease or defect interfered with their ability to appreciate the nature and quality or wrongfulness of their actions." The evaluators also clarify how the legal standard is conceptualized: "Thus, there is a threshold criterion (whether the defendant has a severe mental disease or defect), a linkage criterion (whether the mental illness is linked to the offense), and a functional test derivative of the linkage (the person was unable to appreciate the nature and quality or wrongfulness of his/her behavior)." As discussed in Chapter 9 (this volume), clearly stating the relevant forensic issue clarifies the purpose of the evaluation, enables the evaluator to conduct an evaluation that is focused and relevant, and helps the evaluator structure the content of the evaluation.

FORENSIC PSYCHOLOGICAL
EVALUATION
September 1, 2012

IDENTIFYING INFORMATION

Master at Arms Second Class (MA2) Martin P is a 41-year-old Caucasian married male. He is an activated Navy Reservist policeman (rank of Enlisted-4), who is presently in pretrial confinement at a Naval Brig awaiting trial for several specifications of the charge of Violation of the UCMJ, Article 128; that is, "did commit an assault upon Operations Specialist First Class William Smythe by pointing at him with a dangerous weapon likely to produce death or grievous bodily harm, to wit: a loaded firearm."

REASON FOR REFERRAL

MA2 P was referred by Captain (CPT) Brian Crest for forensic psychological evaluation on the issues of mental responsibility, general mitigation, and violence risk/rehabilitative potential. MA2 P's referral for a second evaluation of mental responsibility occurred in the wake of a prior Sanity Board that did not offer a definitive opinion either as to diagnosis (but did indicate that Psychotic Disorder NOS should be ruled out) or lack of mental responsibility, but did conclude that MA2 P was presently competent to stand trial.

SOURCES OF INFORMATION

a. Expert Appointment Letter for Dr. Michael Sweda and CPT Samantha Benesh;
b. Charging Documents;
c. RCM 706 Sanity Board Conducted on 18 February 2012, with Report Dated 07 May 2012;
d. Psychological Testing of the Accused on 12 and 19 August 2012 by Dr. Benesh;
e. Interview of the Accused for 6.5 hours by Dr. Benesh and Dr. Sweda;
f. US Naval Criminal Investigative Service (NCIS) Interim Report of Investigation Dated 18 February 2012 and Component Subparts;
g. Article 32 Investigation and Component Subparts;
h. Sworn Statement of MA2 P made 21 January 2012;
i. Electronic Military Medical Records;

j. Interview with Laverne P, Mother of the Accused, on 23 August 2012 for 28 Minutes;

k. Interview with Pearl P, Wife of the Accused, on 23 August 2012 for 35 Minutes;

l. Interview with Jill J, Former Work Supervisor, on 23 August, 2012, for 25 Minutes.

GOVERNMENT'S VERSION OF THE OFFENSES

The NCIS Interim Report of Investigation indicates that on January 21, 2012, MA2 P was asked to surrender his service weapon by members of his chain of command after MA2 P's wife notified them of her concern that her husband intended to commit suicide. MA2 P refused to surrender his firearm, and when he was subsequently brought to the Command Duty Office (CDO) at his base in Afghanistan, he pulled his service weapon on his fellow military police officers and command members and held them hostage. MA2 P later relinquished his weapon and was escorted to the NCIS office for investigative action.

On January 21, 2012, NCIS agents conducted an interrogation of MA2 P. Upon waiving his UCMJ Article 31b (Miranda) rights, MA2 P admitted to removing his service weapon from its holster, loading a magazine into the weapon, and chambering a round. MA2 P said he then took the ammunition from his fellow service members who were in the room. When one of the service members requested to leave, MA2 P said he could not. MA2 P added that he took these actions at the CDO because he was afraid he was going to be sexually assaulted by a fellow service member, and he would do anything to not have to return to the barracks: to include committing suicide with his service weapon. MA2 P said that during this incident he was on the telephone with his wife apologizing to her because he was planning to commit suicide in the CDO. MA2 P opined that this was probably the reason that his Chief [Petty Officer] wanted him to turn in his weapon. MA2 P explained he did not feel comfortable turning in his weapon because of the possible sexual threats against him. When questioned about these threats, MA2 P was unable to provide any specific details about potential perpetrators or why this attack was going to occur.

On January 22, 2012, MA2 P was interrogated a second time. During this interrogation, MA2 P's wife was contacted telephonically at the request of MA2 P. During the telephonic contact, Mrs. P said MA2 P had told her somebody in the command wanted to "rape" him and, as a result, he wanted to take his own life. Mrs. P further stated that when she asked MA2 P why somebody wanted to rape him, MA2 P responded by saying, "That's what they do here." Mrs. P also reported that her husband said if he were to be raped, he would "not be a man" and he wouldn't be able face his children anymore.

Review of the Military Police Investigations (MPI) statements of the service members involved in this incident revealed that according to victim L. R., MA2 P asked him for his duty firearm, and when victim L. R. questioned why, MA2 P advised that he was "locked and loaded." Review of victim E. S.'s statement revealed E. S. witnessed MA2 P put a magazine in his duty firearm and chamber a round. According to E. S., MA2 P did this after being asked to turn over his duty firearm at the request of the command. E. S. further said that in his opinion he was being held against his will.

BACKGROUND DATA PERTINENT TO THE ALLEGED OFFENSE

MA2 P indicated that at the age of 12 he was sexually assaulted by the brother of one of his best friends. MA2 P said this significantly affected him emotionally and behaviorally, and that he has taken enhanced steps to protect his own children against sexual assault and abuse. He stated during a sleep-over event at his friend's house, he awoke and discovered that his friend's brother was "fondling" and "playing with my penis. We were all asleep. He was playing with my penis. I was waking up and I thought what the freak was going on? He put his hand over my mouth and offered me money to not say anything. I started screaming and he said I had a dream. I was scared of him."

MA2 P was traumatized and embarrassed about being victimized at the age of 12. When asked if he was ever able to discuss the incident with anyone, he replied, "No. I did tell my wife, but it took a long time before I did it. I grew up in a public housing project and she didn't. I don't trust a lot of people. I don't underestimate no one. I don't want to put my kids in that sort of position. No matter how deep I try to bury it, it is still there. It don't go away." When asked to elaborate further how the sexual assault has affected him, he replied, "It makes me not trust. It makes me cautious of my surroundings. If I'm placed in a position like that I get very defensive." MA2 P stated he was "terrified" at the time of the sexual assault and that his feelings of being terrified were intensified because the assailant "was a grown muscular man."

He also described another incident from his youth involving being exposed to sexual behavior that was disturbing and fear-inducing. He stated:

> In high school, I played JV [junior varsity] football. One night I was with two guys from the senior team who played football. They wanted to go out. I thought we would go out and chase girls. They wanted to go to High Street where the prostitutes and crackheads are. I was getting weird feelings. They were playing around with homosexuals. I wasn't having fun at all. One guy said he wanted his penis sucked. There were men who were dressed like women. I didn't find it funny or humorous. I was trying to get them to go, and they started talking about whose penis was the biggest. They started talking about penises and started taking their penises out and I wanted to get out of the car and they wouldn't let me get out. The next thing I know I was getting upset, angry, and ready to fight. I asked them to pull over. I said I know a girl who stays right there. I knocked on the lady's door and said this car is following me. She let me in. I went out the back door and ran all the way home with my heart beating so fast.

ACCUSED'S ACCOUNT OF ALLEGED OFFENSES

MA2 P stated that soon after his arrival in Afghanistan, the Commander

> said there were a lot of rape cases taking place. He advised us of being on a buddy system. I thought it was women [who were mostly being victimized], but no. He said more men than women. He said a lot of military people were being assaulted. The way it was communicated was this was a tolerated behavior. I was baffled. I didn't come all this way for this. I came here to provide protection for my country.

MA2 P also stated the Commander informed newly arrived service members "Don't give your weapon to anyone. Be aware."

As a result of his perception that he could be a victim of rape, MA2 P "rarely used the bathroom. I didn't want to wake anyone. I took a watch. Nobody was watching me, so I watched myself. It was brought to my attention that I would wake up and scream, so I went to the recreation center to sleep. I felt comfortable there because there were a lot of people there. I didn't get much sleep at all." MA2 P stated, "I asked if I could go be reassigned to another base. I couldn't sleep. I thought this is not what I signed up for. I thought guys were plotting on me, saying derogatory things. I took it as threats."

MA2 P stated that shortly after he arrived in Afghanistan, he was approached by a service member who had been on the base for a while, and this service member "gave me all types of information. He said watch out for Thursday. It was a 'man night' that the locals had. It was a gay day. He pointed out a couple [of] people and said to watch out for them." MA2 P also indicated he began hearing people talking about "weird stuff" that made him uncomfortable. We inquired whether these communications were directed toward him specifically, and he replied,

> Not directly to me. It was said in my company." MA2 P stated the general theme of the commentary involved "comments and references to who they thought was cute, men. They weren't talking about girls. They were talking about guys." MA2 P further explained, "One comment was made directly to my face. I got off work late at night and a guy said, 'I notice you don't even go to your rack. You are scared to go to your rack.' I said, 'No, I just want to talk to my wife.' He said, 'They make it really easy to get raped because at night the outside lights are out.'"

MA2 P continued by saying,

> I think he was making a threat. I took that as a personal threat. I took it to mean he was saying "watch your back." They were working on a plan to take me, pull me to the side, I don't know. But to get me out of sight, take turns raping me, sticking their penis in my butt, and I can't do that. There was no way that I was going to participate or try that. But no matter how manly you are, you might not be able

to stop it. I was trying to keep myself out of the line of sight. During the day I didn't have a problem; it was at night that I had a problem.

MA2 P also came to believe that a group of service members was following him or "patrolling" him. He stated, "I thought that was strange, but then I thought this is a small base and there were not too many places to go. I kind of passed it off. But when I started to sleep at the recreation center, I kept seeing the same people popping up around me." MA2 P stated he also perceived that these individuals were intruding on his personal space by coming close to him in his rack [sleeping area]. He stated, "That was going one step too far. They would be near my rack. I could hear them talking, saying 'Yeah he has to go to the head. He has to take a shower.'" When asked why these individuals would be coming in and out of his sleeping bay, MA2 P responded that "They were mocking me, making noises with their hands like patting here. I took that they were saying someone was going to get fucked tonight."

MA2 P stated as his fears mounted he began calling his wife every night. MA2 P said that on the day of the alleged offenses, "I was talking to my wife on Skype. I told her what happened that day. I didn't have any evidence to support that they wanted to do anything, just what I had heard. I was not sleeping well, staying at the rec center, talking to wife every night. I felt my heart beating like crazy. I had that fear. I felt paranoid. People were constantly looking up at me, laughing." MA2 P said later that same night he was asked by a member of his command to inspect some trucks.

> I was out there inspecting the truck, and the Chief Petty Officer said, "Give me your weapon." I said, "Chief, you need my weapon, why?" He said he didn't know, so I asked him did I do anything wrong. I am looking around the room and thinking "Is this a drill?" I said to myself I am not supposed to give up my weapon per the Commander's orders. In my mind, the other group of people had convinced the Chief to take my weapon away so I would be more defenseless. For a moment I felt overwhelmed. I felt defenseless. I didn't give up my gun because I didn't know what was going on. It sounded crazy that they wanted my weapon. I had a whole lot of mixed thoughts. I thought I was not supposed to give

up my weapon. I refused to get my weapon. I was thinking there is no way I am going to let these guys rape me. I thought what is going on? I couldn't make logic of it. I only could think these guys were figuring out a way to get my weapon from me. I refused to get my weapon. It made it uncomfortable. It was the only thing I decided to do. I said I would rather commit suicide than get raped.

In retrospect, MA2 P said, "I was panicking and freaked out. Now, it is easier for me to rethink it. At the time I was thinking things were moving faster they were being a little more forward and I felt that something was going to happen. I asked to speak to my wife. I was getting my weapon in my hand." When asked if he locked and loaded, MA2 P replied, "I recall being locked, but I can't recall if I had racked." He stated he locked the weapon because "I got scared. I started to feel that something wasn't right. I felt like I was being set up. I didn't even see the Chief, all I was seeing was fear. I felt threatened. I felt like something was going to happen. I didn't want to go back to base and have something happen."

In response to the question of whether he felt he would have shot someone on the day of the alleged offenses, MA2 P replied,

> In my mind I felt if I had to come to that point—do or die—I don't know. If you ask me can I take another life, I don't think so. I felt like if it came to that, I would shoot myself. I couldn't live with the thought of taking a life. This wasn't like TV where you would go shooting other people. I thought I might shoot myself. My head was spinning. I had different voices going through my mind telling me what to do. I never felt that level of fear.

In reply to a query for further clarification about these voices, MA2 P said,

> Voices saying you have to protect yourself. The easy thing is to shoot yourself, but that would not be the best thing in God's eyes. My wife's voice [on the phone]: She said calm down, breathe, and please give up your guns. She said she needs me, we'll get through this. I thought I can't let them take my manhood.

I can't look my kids in the face. She was crying and everything. I tried to make sense. I started crying. The Master Chief showed up. I had holstered my weapon. Things calmed down.

When asked directly if, at the time of the alleged criminal conduct, he knew what he was doing was wrong, MS2 P replied, "My mind was on me. I was scared. The Chief wasn't thinking about this. I was thinking about me. I felt something was to take place. You can never be prepared until it's happening, until it's going down." When asked if he was surprised when he was handcuffed, he replied, "I really wasn't thinking. The Master Chief said they are going to transfer you to a facility and said 'I am going to take care of you.' I didn't think that was odd." He stated he first realized he might be in trouble when he was being fingerprinted at the facility.

MA2 P stated he had consumed no alcohol in the 24 hours prior to the alleged offenses. The only medication he had taken was two aspirins because he was experiencing headaches. He acknowledged smoking a "few puffs" from a synthetic marijuana cigarette several days before the alleged offenses. He stated that the individual who gave him the synthetic marijuana may have been part of the plan to "set me up." As a result of the incident, MA2 P was placed in confinement. He stated that when this occurred, "I was really scared of being raped in prison. It was kind of like I had to go through withdrawal. After a day or two I started seeing things in a different perspective. I started thinking 'should have, would have, could have.' I calmed down after three days in confinement." He further stated, "The first two or three weeks (of confinement) were rough. When I was in a single cell, I felt fine that way. In the general population, I have a heightened sense I have to protect against sexual assault."

SOCIAL AND DEVELOPMENTAL HISTORY

MA2 P stated he was one of three children was raised by his mother in Pennsylvania. He was the oldest, with a sister two years younger and a brother three years younger. He and his mother resided in a public housing project. He stated his biological father was a bus driver for daycare patients, and his mother worked occasionally but usually stayed at home. MA2 P stated his mother had a boyfriend who was "more of a father figure" than his biological father. The boyfriend passed away when MA2 P was 10, and his biological father died when MA2 P was 24. MA2 P indicated that as a child he was "very athletic, popular with the in crowd, and played football and basketball." He did not report any form of physical abuse as a child, though his mother did use corporal punishment in the form of strapping him with a belt on occasion. As indicated previously, he stated he was sexually assaulted at the age of 12 and experienced a frightening sexual incident when he was approximately 16 or 17.

PSYCHIATRIC HISTORY

MA2 P did not report a personal history of prior behavioral health treatment. Electronic military medical records show no evidence of prior mental health treatment. He stated he has never been prescribed any psychiatric medications. An RCM 706 Sanity Board dated May 7, 2012, indicates that at the time of the alleged offenses, the Board diagnosed MA2 P with "rule out psychotic disorder not otherwise specified."

LEGAL HISTORY

MA2 P did not report a history of prior arrest as a juvenile or adult. He stated he has had three speeding tickets, with a maximum of 15–20 miles an hour over the speed limit. An official criminal records check revealed no evidence of prior offenses.

ALCOHOL AND SUBSTANCE ABUSE HISTORY

MA2 P said he first drank alcohol at the age of 15 or 16, and that he "drank very rarely as a teenager." He stated as an adult he usually drinks one or two alcoholic beverages a week on a weekend night while socializing with his wife and friends. He did not endorse ever having any alcohol-related social or occupational problems, legal problems, blackouts, or medical problems. He stated he first used marijuana at the age of 16 or 17, and stopped using prior to entering the military. He has reportedly used marijuana four or five times his entire life. He did not endorse use of other illicit substances or abuse of prescription medications. MA2 P indicated he has been attending AA and NA during his pretrial confinement.

SOCIAL AND RELATIONSHIP HISTORY

MA2 P began dating his wife when he was in the tenth grade at the age of 17. The couple married when MA2 P was 24 or 25 years old. The couple has two children, including a 17-year-old daughter and a 4-year-old daughter. MA2 P describes his marriage as "good" and without significant problems.

EDUCATION AND OCCUPATIONAL HISTORY

MA2 P stated he is a high school graduate with no further formal education. He said he was a "C" student and generally "did enough to get by" while in school. He usually abided by rules, but acknowledged skipping school enough in the seventh grade to be held back a grade. He skipped school because "I got into girls and was messing with the eighth graders." MA2 P stated he had worked for electronic retail stores in shipping and receiving for a total of five years before enlisting with the Navy 18 years ago as a Reservist.

MILITARY HISTORY

MA2 P stated he entered the Navy Reserves on the delayed entry program. Based on his Armed Services Vocational Aptitude Battery (ASVAB) test results, he was reportedly offered positions as a military policeman, radioman, signalman, and operations specialist. He stated he had three major deployments prior to the current deployment. He reported having nearly 19 years in the Navy and that he had planned on completing this deployment so he could retire after 20 years of service with a feeling that he had contributed to the country's defense. MA2 P reported enjoying his military service and stated his experience was "great. In the Navy I went to different countries. I had the best of both worlds. I got to see places like Denmark, Russia, and Brazil."

MA2 P reported one prior incident of non-judicial punishment. He stated, "One time I was on watch. It was a weekend watch and I was asleep. They sent me to Captain's Mast [disciplinary hearing]. I was on suspension for three months, and they said I would lose rank if it happened again. They called it Dereliction of Duty."

Current Medications
None.

RELEVANT MENTAL STATUS FINDINGS

MA2 P continues to voice paranoid thinking about the alleged instant offenses, and also described having "paranoid" thinking about the possibility of being sexually assaulted in the brig, where he has been confined since his arrest. He stated that while confined, "I sometimes seem to be hearing things like someone talking over there and then I go over and I don't see anyone." He feels comfortable when he is in a cell by himself, but said once he is out of the cell, he tries to have his back against a wall. He was "open" to the idea that he may have a mental illness and need medications. He did not endorse current suicidal and homicidal ideation.

Psychological Testing

MA2 P completed the Minnesota Multiphasic Personality Inventory–2 (MMPI-2), the Structured Interview of Reported Symptoms–2nd Edition (SIRS-2), the Wechsler Adult Intelligence Scale–IV (WAIS-IV), Trail Making Test (TMT) A and B, Test of Memory Malingering (TOMM), and the Booklet Category Test (BCT) on 12 and 19 August 2012. There is no evidence of feigning on any of the test protocols, to include the MMPI-2, SIRS-2, and the TOMM. He has Low Average range intelligence, and there is no evidence of significant neuropsychological deficit.

Diagnostic Assessment

In our opinion, MA2 P did have severe mental disorders at the time of the instant offenses, namely delusional disorder, persecutory type; and anxiety disorder not otherwise specified (NOS). The hallmark of delusional disorder, persecutory type is the presence of non-bizarre delusions that persist for one month. A *non-bizarre delusion* is a false belief concerning things that can happen in real life, such as others plotting to harm or rape an individual. In MA2 P's case, the onset of the delusional thinking occurred in mid-January 2010, and he persists in believing that a plot was made to rape him. There was also considerable referential thinking present at the time of the alleged offense (e.g., believing others were talking about him, interpretation of nonverbal behaviors as pertaining to the plot to sexually assault him) and possible auditory hallucinations. However, the delusions were the central and most prominent feature of his presentation at the time of the alleged criminal conduct. Individuals afflicted with delusional disorder, persecutory type typically have unimpaired functioning apart from the direct impact of the delusions. The persecutory type of delusional disorder that MA2 P suffers from is superimposed on the psychologically traumatic event of being sexually molested when he was 12 years old.

FORENSIC OPINION AND CRIMINAL RESPONSIBILITY

According to RCM 916k, defendants lack mental responsibility for a charged offense if, at the time of the offense, they suffered from a severe mental disease or defect, and the severe mental disease or defect interfered with their ability to appreciate the nature and quality or wrongfulness of their actions. Thus, there is a threshold criterion (whether the defendant has a severe mental disease or defect), a linkage criterion (whether the mental illness is linked to the offense), and a functional test derivative from the linkage (the person was unable to appreciate the nature and quality or wrongfulness of his/her behavior).

It is our opinion, to a reasonable degree of psychological certainty, that at the time of the alleged offenses, MA2 P suffered from a combination of mental disorders, and that the mental disorders were severe. Although the definition of "severe" is not specifically clarified by the *Manual for Courts-Martial*, he was one step short of committing suicide derivative of his mental and emotional impairments, and this is a very clear indicator of how severe his mental disorders were at the time of the alleged offenses.

It is also our opinion that MA2 P's mental disorders were clearly linked to the alleged offense behaviors. The reason he did not relinquish his weapon was primarily because he believed there was a plot to rape him. Coincident to the event were indications of impaired reasoning, psychotic or psychotic-like phenomena (referential thinking and possible auditory hallucinations), and impaired judgment. Indeed, his suicidality (the result and manifestation of his mental disorders) was the reason he was brought to the attention of command. Command response to his plan to kill himself was something that he had not planned for, nor was he able to reason at the time of the alleged offenses that this was why he was being commanded to relinquish his weapons by superior non-commissioned officers (NCOs).

The final matter to consider is whether MA2 P was unable to appreciate the nature and quality or wrongfulness of his conduct at the time of the offenses, due to his severe mental disorders. It is our opinion, to a reasonable degree of psychological certainty, that he was unable to appreciate both the nature and quality and wrongfulness of his behavior at the time of the alleged offenses. An individual who was able to appreciate the nature and quality of the alleged criminal conduct would clearly perceive that he was being given a lawful order to surrender his weapon. In MA2 P's mind, at the time of the alleged offenses, this was far from clear. Instead of perceiving that he was being given a lawful order, his mental appraisal of the situation was that he was under threat of rape. The order to relinquish his weapon came at the very point when his thoughts were irrationally dominated by delusions of a rape plot. The senior NCOs approached him requesting he turn in his weapon at the very height of his acute psychotic state, and MA2 P could not think of anything he had done wrong that would spur the request for him to surrender his weapon, nor did the NCOs offer any reason why the weapon needed to be relinquished. He irrationally concluded that the NCOs were taking an action consistent with a plot wherein he would be left defenseless to be raped by others, and he made a decision that he would not allow this to happen. Thus, he was not accurately appraising the nature and quality of the circumstances due to his mental disorders.

Furthermore, it is our opinion that MA2 P, as a direct result of his mental disorders, was unable to appreciate the wrongfulness of his actions at the time of the alleged criminal conduct. Appreciation of wrongfulness involves an objective and a subjective component. At a strict and very limited objective level of analysis, MA2 P knew that if a senior NCO ordered a junior NCO to relinquish his weapon, the junior NCO would need to comply with such a lawful order. In the particular circumstance that MA2 P found himself, however, his mental disorders were impairing his ability to perceive that he was being given a lawful order. His thoughts were dominated by the plot of rape that he believed to be occurring. He also, in his impaired state, reported that he began thinking of the commanding officer's words about not relinquishing one's weapon to *anyone*. Thus, the facts of this case strongly support an opinion that he was unable to appreciate wrongfulness both from an objective and from a subjective, individualized, personal, or moral standpoint. Subjectively, and as a direct result of his severe mental disorders, MA2 P could

RISK FACTOR	CURRENT STATUS	SUGGESTED INTERVENTION
Mental Illness (Anxiety Disorder NOS and Delusional Disorder, Persecutory Type)	MA2 P continues to believe he was the prior target of a plan to be raped. He remains hypervigilant, sleeping poorly and focusing on homosexually oriented comments he reports hearing.	MA2 P should be evaluated for possible medication therapy. He should receive individual psychotherapy for his mental illness diagnoses.
Recent Use of Marijuana	MA2 P reports using marijuana once since becoming a reservist.	Although this is not a significant problem, it should be monitored via random toxicology screening.
Possible Exposure to Stressors	Confined environments pose higher actual and perceived risks of homosexual assault.	Stress and violence risk would be decreased by community-based treatment.

not reason, appreciate, or understand that it would be anything but wrong to relinquish his weapon. In his psychotic state, he believed he would lose his manhood, be terrorized and tormented, be unable to face his children, and would be violating his commanding officer's order by complying with an order that to him was incomprehensible as a result of psychosis.

RISK ASSESSMENT AND REHABILITATIVE POTENTIAL

We utilized the Psychopathy Checklist–Revised (PCL-R), the Violence Risk Assessment Guide (VRAG), and HCR-20 (Historical, Clinical, Risk—20 items) to assess risk for future violence. MA2 P had a very low score on the PCL-R (score of two (2)). MA2 P's HCR-20 results suggest he would pose a moderate risk of violence toward others if confined or hospitalized. He would pose a lower risk if treated in the community. This is because the major clinical factor driving risk in MA2 P's case is fear of homosexual assault, which would be much higher in confinement in institutional environments.

Overall, the results from the HCR-20 and VRAG suggest MA2 P poses a low to low-moderate risk of violence, with the risk increasing if he is in environments where there is a higher perceived risk of homosexual assault. Given his relatively low risk rating, history of otherwise stable behavior over his lifetime, and openness to exploring treatment for a mental illness, it is believed that he has a good potential to be rehabilitated and to live in the community as a productive member of society free of violence. This is contingent on MA2 P's adherence to an appropriate treatment plan.

Risk Management Plan

A plan to identify, monitor, and manage risk factors should be specified to contain and mitigate risk. A summary of identified risk factors and risk mitigation strategies is contained in the table below.

Michael Sweda, PhD, ABPP (Forensic)
Chief, Forensic Psychology Service: CPT, MS, USA

Samantha M. Benesh, PsyD
Forensic Psychologist: Forensic Psychology Fellow

TEACHING POINT:
FORENSIC ISSUES IN THIS KIND OF EVALUATION THAT IS CONDUCTED IN A MILITARY CONTEXT, AND COMPARABILITY WITH AND DISTINCTIONS FROM CIVILIAN LAW

Many forensic clinicians conduct FMHA in different jurisdictions. Consider the distinctions between federal law, criminal law, and civil law across different states, and juvenile and family law across different states. In some states, there are also noteworthy differences between different jurisdictions (e.g., counties or districts) within the same state.

The important distinctions may be encapsulated in the domains of *standards* and *procedures*. Moving into the system of military law is perhaps associated with a greater number of differences in standards and procedures than moving across evaluation types and jurisdictions within the civilian world, but the same principle applies: a good working familiarity with applicable legal standards and procedures is essential for conducting FMHA that will be useful to the legal decision-maker.

In the present case, the legal standard for criminal responsibility is comparable to the *M'Naghten* standard that applies in many U.S. jurisdictions. According to RCM 916k, the evaluators note, defendants lack mental responsibility if, at the time of the offense, they suffered from a severe mental disease or defect, and the severe mental disease or defect interfered with their ability to appreciate the nature and quality or wrongfulness of their actions. This standard has a threshold criterion (severe mental disease or defect), a relationship component (whether the mental illness is linked to the offense), and a functional-legal aspect (appreciation of the nature and quality or wrongfulness of his/her behavior). In many respects, therefore, the evaluation for this case is similar to FMHA addressing sanity in a civilian criminal context.

Certain military-civilian procedural differences are evident from reading this case and the next. Such differences are also discussed in some detail in the next section.

CASE TWO
PRINCIPLE: OBTAIN APPROPRIATE AUTHORIZATION (*PRINCIPLE 13*)

This principle was discussed previously in Chapter 21 (this volume), so we will not repeat this general discussion. However, keep in mind that, when conducting an evaluation in a military setting, it is essential to be familiar with the guidelines governing the performance of forensic evaluations.[2]

The legal framework for assessing pretrial inquiries of competency to stand trial and criminal responsibility is outlined in the MCM (Joint Service Committee on Military Justice, 2012). The MCM contains five parts and various appendices. Part II explains the Rules for Courts-Martial (RCM). Part III describes the Military Rules of Evidence (MRE), and Part IV contains the Putative Articles. RCM 706 explicates the procedures for performing a Sanity Board evaluation or 706 Inquiry. The 706 Inquiry is a complex task requiring the performance of various tasks often differentiated in other settings. The evaluator is

typically tasked with answering four questions that inquire about competency to stand trial, criminal responsibility, diagnosis, and whether a severe mental disease or defect was present at the time of the alleged offense. RCM 706 directs the examiner to "make separate and distinct findings" for each of these questions. The Sanity Board evaluation therefore demands a complex and wide-ranging inquiry from the examiner that assesses both current mental state and mental state at the time of the alleged offense.

Consistent with most pretrial forensic evaluations, there is a relatively low bar for ordering 706 evaluations, which can be summarized as a reasonable concern about the mental state of the accused individual, such that it is affecting either his or her ability to proceed or his or her responsibility at the time of the alleged offense. (Note that within the military justice system, the defendant is called "the accused.") The inquiry can be initiated by various parties to the legal proceeding, including defense or prosecuting attorneys, the judge, or the investigating officer. The basis for the concern is communicated in writing to the individual authorized to order the inquiry, such as the convening authority or military judge. The military does not have standing trial courts, so a court-martial is assembled by a convening authority (CA). The individual requesting the exam often submits a common template of an order for the 706. This template, called Forms for Court-Martial Orders, is printed as Appendix 17 in the MCM (2012). This inquiry may be ordered before or after charges have been referred. In military court, per RCM 601(a), "Referral is the order of a convening authority that charges against an accused will be tried by a specified court-martial." The *Military Judges' Benchbook* (Department of the Army, 2010) recommends that "any question of mental capacity should be determined as early in the trial as possible" (p. 933).

An order for a 706 Inquiry is signed by the convening authority or judge, and the usual point of contact (POC) for locating a qualified mental health professional to perform the inquiry is trial counsel or the prosecuting attorney. According to RCM 706, the Sanity Board is usually broadly defined to consist of "one or more persons" and typically stipulates that "each member of the board shall be either a physician or a clinical psychologist"; also, "normally, at least one member of the board shall be either a psychiatrist or a clinical psychologist"

(p. II-70). Once qualified professionals have been located, the POC will provide the evaluator(s) with relevant documents, arrange travel if required, and procure funding. The POC may arrange to have the board member(s) officially appointed by the Court or CA, but often the appointment is done by correspondence such as email. The official appointment therefore consists of an order for a 706 and notice of appointment, either by an additional order or by official notification.

It is important to inform the accused of the relevant limitations of confidentiality and privilege. Per RCM 706, the examiner is required to generate two reports, often referred to as the "short form" or abbreviated report, and the "long form" or full report. The short form contains "a statement consisting only of the board's ultimate conclusions as to all questions specified in the order" (p. II-70). To guard against self-incrimination and protect privilege, the long form is sent only to defense counsel. In contrast, both defense and trial counsel receive a copy of the short form. The order stipulates the parties receiving each report. In answering the four questions, the "ultimate conclusions as to all questions specified in the order" are transmitted to defense and trial counsel (p. II-70). Only if and when a mental health defense is raised can the government gain access to the information contained in the full report, if authorized by the judge. The accused should be further informed about the consequences of not participating in the evaluation. According to MRE 302(d), a potential consequence for noncompliance is that the military judge may prohibit the accused from presenting mental health evidence. In addition, since diagnoses are forwarded to all involved parties, the accused should be informed that this information may be used as the basis for military administrative action. This action may include separation from service, a medical evaluation board (MEB), or a bar to reenlistment.

In the present report, Dr. Montalbano clearly describes the source of the authorization to conduct the evaluation. Under "Identifying Information," he states that the evaluation was conducted in accordance with RCM 706, which outlines the procedures for performing a Sanity Board evaluation or 706 Inquiry. Then, under "Reason for Referral," he notes that defense counsel requested the evaluation, and that the request was approved and signed by Major General Conley. These statements

provide sufficient and detailed information about the source of the authorization to conduct the evaluation.

MEMORANDUM FOR Defense Counsel, U.S. Army Trial Defense Service
SUBJECT: Sanity Board Evaluation of Specialist Michael P.

IDENTIFYING INFORMATION

Specialist (SPC) Michael P is a 22-year-old, single, African-American male with one year of active duty service in the United States Army. He is referred for the purpose of conducting a Sanity Board in accordance with RCM 706. His military occupational specialty (MOS) is 11B (Infantryman).

REASON FOR REFERRAL

According to the Sanity Board order, Defense Counsel requested an evaluation under RCM 706 due to SPC P's report that he had been treated on an inpatient basis for Bipolar I disorder. This request of the 706 was approved and signed by Major General Conley.

RCM 706 stipulates that the following four questions be addressed by the Board:

a. At the time of the alleged criminal conduct, did the accused have a severe mental disease or defect? (The term "severe mental disease of defect" does not include an abnormality manifested only by repeated criminal or otherwise antisocial conduct, or minor disorders such as nonpsychotic disorders and personality defects.)

b. What is the clinical psychiatric diagnosis?

c. Was the accused, at the time of the alleged criminal conduct and as a result of such severe mental disease or defect, unable to appreciate the nature and quality or wrongfulness of his or her conduct?

d. Is the accused presently suffering from mental disease or defect rendering the accused unable to understand the nature of the proceedings against the accused or to conduct or cooperate intelligently in the defense?

LIST OF CHARGES

Charge I: Violation of UCMJ, Article 86 (Absence Without Leave)

Specification 1: In that Specialist (E-4) Michael P, US Army, did, on or about 10 August 2011, without authority, absent himself from his unit, to wit, 4th Brigade Combat Team, 101st Airborne Division, Fort Campbell, Kentucky, and did remain so absent until he was apprehended on or about 20 December 2011.

Charge II: Violation of UCMJ, Article 112a (Wrongful Use, Possession, etc., of Controlled Substances)

Specification 1: In that Specialist (E-4) Michael P, US Army, did, at or near Fort Campbell, Kentucky, on divers occasions between on or about 20 December and 28 December 2011, wrongfully use methamphetamine, a Schedule II controlled substance.

NOTIFICATION

SPC P was informed of the nonconfidential nature of the evaluation. He was informed that a full report of the evaluation would be sent to defense counsel, and that a summarized report consisting only of the Board's answers to the court's four questions would be sent to the trial counsel. SPC P was notified that if the full report was presented in open court, that any self-incriminating information provided by him would be redacted from the full report in accordance with MRE 302. He was informed that, if he were called to testify, the information obtained from this evaluation, as well as the conclusions, could be made public. He was further informed that the results of the report such as diagnostic formulations could be used at the sentencing phase of the trial or as a basis for military administrative action. Such actions might include separation from service, a medical evaluation board (MEB), or a bar to reenlistment. He voiced an understanding of these warnings and agreed to participate in the evaluation.

SOURCES OF INFORMATION

Legal Orders

1. Request for R.C.M. 706 Inquiry by Trial Counsel (27 Mar 2011)
2. Order to Conduct an R.C.M. 706 Inquiry into the Mental Capacity or Mental Responsibility Specialist Michael P by MG Conley, Commanding (29 Mar 2011)
3. Email from MAJ Thomas, Assistant Staff Judge Advocate, Trial Counsel, Fort Campbell, confirming appointment of Dr. Montalbano to perform Sanity Board on SPC P (2 Apr 2011)

Legal and Criminal Investigative Records

1. Charge Sheet (9 Feb 2011)
2. Search and Seizure Authorizations (28 Dec 2011)
3. Drug Testing Report (6 Jan 2012)
4. Article 32 Investigation—Report of Proceedings (5 Mar 2011)
5. Agent's Investigation Reports (28 Dec 2011, 30 Dec 2011, 3 Jan 2012, 18 Jan 2012, 31 Jan 2012, and 2 Feb 2012)
6. Investigative Documents (December 2011 to February 2012)
7. Sworn Statement by SPC P (29 Dec 2011)
8. Sworn Statements by Witnesses (28 Dec 2011, 29 Dec 2011, 3 Jan 2012, 31 Jan 2012)
9. Criminal Background Check—Defense Central Investigative Index (5 Jan 2012)
10. Norfolk Police Arrest Report (12/14/11)

Military Records

1. Enlisted Record Brief (ERB) (29 Dec 2011)
2. Counseling Statement (21 July 2011)

Medical Records

1. Norfolk Psychiatric Center (7–12 Jul 2008 & 4–9 Mar 2009)
2. Cumberland Hall Hospital Medical Records (28 Jan–8 Feb 2012)
3. AHLTA (Armed Forces Health Longitudinal Technology Application) Medical Records (12 Feb 2011—25 Feb 2012)

Collateral Interviews

1. Telephone Interview with Samuel G (Father of Accused) on 10 Apr 12 for Approximately 45 Minutes
2. Telephone Interview with Dr. H on 11 Apr 12 for Approximately 15 Minutes
3. Telephone Interview with SPC J on 11 Apr 12 for Approximately 30 Minutes
4. Telephone Interview with Johns S, Verizon Supervisor, on 12 Apr 12 for Approximately 15 Minutes

Evaluation Procedures

1. Interview and Testing on 14 April 2012 for Approximately 5.5 hours and on 15 April 2012 for Approximately 5 Hours
2. Telephone Interview of SPC P on 20 April for Approximately 20 Minutes

SOURCES OF INFORMATION NOT AVAILABLE

I was unable to contact James P, brother of the accused, or Scott M (friend of the accused). Several attempts were made to contact these individuals by telephone.

GOVERNMENT'S VERSION OF THE OFFENSES

After only a few months at his first duty station, SPC P was declared to be Absent Without Leave (AWOL) on 10 August 2011. Repeated attempts were made to contact him and encourage him to return to his duty station. According to the investigative report, while on AWOL status and living back in Virginia, he was able to maintain employment with a local employer. He was brought back to his duty station when his whereabouts were discovered following an arrest on 14 December 2011.

According to his own sworn statement, shortly after returning to Fort Campbell on 20 December 2012, he went to a Western Union store in Nashville, Tennessee, and took out some money. He stated that he was "depressed and upset and just wanted to escape reality for a little while." He then bought methamphetamine. After returning to Fort Campbell, he stated, he injected the substance in his barracks room. His roommate, SPC J, suspected illegal drug use and notified command. When his room was searched on 28 December 2011, methamphetamine was discovered. A command-directed urine drug screen later came back positive for methamphetamine.

ACCUSED'S VERSION OF THE ALLEGED OFFENSES

SPC P reported that after being sent to Fort Campbell in May 2011 to prepare for deployment, he "hated almost everyone in my command." He was stressed as his mother had grown ill, and his sister was also "falling in with the wrong crowd." He decided to leave Fort Campbell and go home to help his family. He reported that at the time of his decision, he knew what he was doing was against the rules, "so I didn't tell anybody" and "just left." He stated he "caught a good time to leave because I didn't want to be chased." He did not inform anyone of his intentions "because I didn't want to get anyone else in trouble, I guess." He denied symptoms consistent with a manic episode and stated he "just wanted to go home and be with my family and friends." When asked if he thought about the consequences of going AWOL, he stated "I just didn't give a fuck."

While AWOL, he obtained a job with Verizon and worked there regularly and was able to support himself financially. He began to hang out with friends, drink alcohol, and abuse various substances. He and his father began to argue frequently. He stated that the family was under a great deal of stress after his sister was murdered in July 2011, and his mother passed away shortly thereafter. In November 2011, SPC P began arguing with his father. His brother got involved, and SPC P reported punching his brother in the face and breaking his nose. His brother pressed charges. After this arrest, SPC P was located and brought back to Fort Campbell.

After returning to Fort Campbell, he reported, he was upset with everything and decided to "get high." He reported going to Nashville and purchasing methamphetamine. He then took the drugs back to his room on base and injected the substance intravenously. He stated that "before I could finish off the meth, people were already knocking on my door." He reported that command searched his room, where they found the remaining methamphetamine and drug paraphernalia, which he had placed in his boot. When asked if he knew that methamphetamine was illegal and against military policy, he stated "of course." He was subsequently placed in pretrial confinement.

LEGAL HISTORY

A criminal history check was performed through the Defense Central Investigative Index and revealed one prior assault charge in Norfolk. Records from the Norfolk police confirmed this charge. SPC P reports that he first interfaced with legal authorities at age sixteen, when he was arrested for trespassing. He believed that "nothing happened." Around age eighteen, he reported that he was arrested for driving without a license but "the police knew me just let me go."

PSYCHOSOCIAL AND FAMILY HISTORY

According to Michael P and his father, he was born and raised in Norfolk, Virginia. He was the second oldest child, with an older brother and younger sister. His father worked as cook and later owned a small restaurant. His mother worked off and on in a hair salon. He described his early upbringing and childhood in negative terms, noting that there was not always "enough money," and there was frequent verbal abuse. He denied any history of sexual abuse but endorsed a history of physical abuse. He stated that his mother "hit me with hangers" and his father frequently slapped him or punched him in the leg or stomach. He and his brother often fought. He reported a history of fighting, truancy, and stealing, but denied any history of animal cruelty, fire setting, bullying, or destruction of property. This was corroborated by his father. His sister was murdered for unknown reasons, and his mother recently died of coronary heart disease.

INTERPERSONAL AND SEXUAL HISTORY

SPC reported that he made friends easily as a child and adolescent. In high school, he skipped school to "hang out with friends." He reported that he began dating around age 15 and had his first sexual experience around age 16 with a same-aged peer. He described one long-term relationship that has been "on again off again" for four years. He reported that she regularly abused cocaine, alcohol, and methamphetamine. He stated that their relationship was marked by frequent arguments and separations. He estimated having had a total of "around 15" sexual partners. He reported that he has never been married and has no children.

FAMILY MEDICAL AND PSYCHIATRIC HISTORY

SPC P reported that his mother was diabetic and suffered from high blood pressure and coronary heart disease. She died from heart disease in July 2011. According to SPC P and his father, his family has a significant history of mental illness. His father stated that he has been diagnosed with bipolar disorder and has struggled with substance abuse. His brother was diagnosed with ADHD (Attention-Deficit/Hyperactivity Disorder). He and his father reported that his maternal grandmother suffered from schizophrenia, and an uncle on his father's side committed suicide.

EDUCATIONAL HISTORY

SPC P attended public schools in Norfolk, Virginia. He reported that he performed well in elementary school but became increasingly disenchanted and bored in middle school. After his parents moved, he was transferred to another school district and did not like the school or his classmates. He reported that his grades began to suffer because "I didn't give a fuck, I guess," and he grew more disobedient. He reported getting into trouble in high school but performing well enough to pass, despite being suspended multiple times fighting, truancy, and drinking during school hours. He was able to successfully graduate from high school. His father largely corroborated his educational history.

OCCUPATIONAL HISTORY

SPC P reported that he began working various jobs, as a waiter, a construction worker, and a cashier in high school. After high school, he worked at his father's restaurant. He reported that he was fired from several jobs for missing work or arguing, but overall reported a generally successful work history. He stated that after his father's restaurant went under, he enlisted in the Army as a way to help finance a college education. After going AWOL, he worked as a contractor for Verizon for several months. An interview with John S, his Verizon supervisor, confirmed his employment during this time frame and stated he was a "good worker," who was occasionally late for work.

MILITARY HISTORY

SPC P enlisted in the Army in February 2011. He successfully completed boot camp and his Advanced Individualized Training (AIT) at Fort Benning, Georgia. His first assignment in May was to Fort Campbell, Kentucky, to prepare for deployment. On 21 July 2011, he was counseled about professionalism and timeliness. He was declared to be AWOL on or about 10 August 2011 until being apprehended on or about 20 December 2011. On 28 December 2011, methamphetamine and drug paraphernalia were discovered in his room. He was subsequently placed on barracks restriction. Drug test results came back positive for methamphetamine. On 27 January 2012, he was found skinny-dipping in the base pool and taken to a local psychiatric hospital. He is currently on pretrial confinement awaiting trial. SPC J, who roomed with SPC J at Fort Campbell, described him as "easy going" and "not really focused" and as "more irritable" when he returned from AWOL.

PSYCHIATRIC HISTORY

Medical records indicate that SPC P was diagnosed with Bipolar I disorder at the age of eighteen at a psychiatric center in Norfolk, Virginia. Records describe symptoms of intense irritability, impulsivity, insomnia, and racing thoughts. He also reported smoking crack cocaine and consuming substantial amounts of alcohol before admission. He was subsequently readmitted to the same facility in March 2009 after yelling at the police, when arrested for driving without a license. During this admission, records indicate that he was diagnosed with Bipolar I disorder, cocaine abuse, alcohol abuse, and cannabis abuse. SPC P reported that he refused to stay on medication and continued to drink alcohol and use various illicit substances once discharged. He reported that he did not follow up with outpatient treatment recommendations.

After his arrest in December 2011, he was admitted on an emergency basis to the medical facility at Cumberland Hall Hospital after appearing manic and stating that he wanted to hurt another soldier. The night before this admission, he had been taken in custody for skinny-dipping at night in the base pool. He presented with symptoms of elevated mood, racing thoughts, decreased sleep, pressured speech, and extreme irritability. He was diagnosed with Bipolar I disorder and medicated with Atarax (anti-anxiety medication and sleep aid) and lithium carbonate (mood stabilizer). Dr. H, his treating physician at Walter Reed Hospital, stated that SPC P displayed a number of symptoms consistent with mania, including rapid speech, insomnia, racing thoughts, and agitation. Dr. H also characterized him as a "management problem," stating that he was caught smoking cigarettes and sneaking cigarettes onto the ward. During this evaluation, SPC P stated that he has been taking his medication and he feels "a little better" and "more in control."

MEDICAL HISTORY

SPC P reportedly suffered from mild asthma as a child but has not required medication or treatment in many years. In general he is in good physical health.

ALCOHOL AND SUBSTANCE ABUSE HISTORY

SPC P reported a significant history of abusing drugs and alcohol. He reported that he started drinking in high school. He bragged about how he and his friends "always got wasted," and that he once "drank 80 beers in one night." He reported frequent blackouts from drinking. According to inpatient records from Virginia, SPC P stated that in high school he was drinking up to three 750-milliliter bottles of vodka daily.

SPC P reported using marijuana "pretty much on a daily basis" beginning in the ninth grade. He endorsed regular cannabis use for nine years, stating that he quit upon enlisting but then starting using again periodically after going AWOL. In 2009, he reported, he began using cocaine. He stated that he used an "8-ball" (roughly 3.5 grams) of cocaine a week. He stated that he used cocaine off and on from 2009 to 2010. He reported that he began using methamphetamine around October or November 2009. Within a month, he stated, he began injecting it. He said that he progressed from around 0.2 grams daily to 0.7 grams daily, staying up for days at a time. Due to reported tolerance, he increased the amount and switched from smoking to intravenous injection to achieve the desired effect. He reported that "uppers" and methamphetamine in particular were his preferred substances, because "uppers just make me happy." He reported that he also used heroin sporadically and tried psychedelic mushrooms several times. He stated that he stopped using all illicit substances when he enlisted but relapsed after returning from being AWOL.

Current Medications

Lithium Carbonate 900 mg in the morning and 1350 mg in the evening

Atarax 50 mg every night as needed, only for sleep

MENTAL STATUS EXAMINATION

SPC P presented as a 5'11" 22-year-old African-American male who weighs approximately 190 pounds. During each of the two sessions, he was evaluated in an office at the Chesapeake Detention Facility. He was adequately groomed, with appropriate hygiene. He was alert and oriented to person, place, and time. He appeared motivated to perform well and generally able to sustain attention. He was cooperative with the interview but easily irritated. He demonstrated some psychomotor agitation, with his restlessness increasing toward the end of the day. Speech was generally goal-directed but tended to be expansive. At times he had to be redirected back to the topic. Rate of speech was mildly pressured and more accelerated when irritated. His thought patterns were clear and logical. He did not appear to be responding to internal stimuli. No delusions were elicited. There was no evidence of auditory or visual hallucinations. Overall, his reality testing appeared intact.

He reported that his mood was "less than normal" and he was "trying to forget everything." He reported that he struggled with feelings of hopelessness. During the sessions he expressed a full range of affect, from becoming sad and emotional to joking with the examiner. He endorsed a long history of sleep disturbance. He estimated currently sleeping around three hours at night but sleeping again during the day. He endorsed many symptoms consistent with mania (elevated mood state), including talkativeness, decreased need for sleep, flight of ideas (a nearly continuous flow of thoughts that jump from topic to topic), distractibility, and excessive involvement in pleasurable activities. He reported stress secondary to his pending legal charges and his separation from his family. He denied any history of suicide attempts or of any suicidal ideation. He denied current or past homicidal ideation.

PSYCHOLOGICAL TESTING AND OTHER PROCEDURES

Tests and Procedures Administered

1) Booklet Category Test (BCT)
2) Trail Making Test (TMT)
3) Validity Indicator Profile (VIP)
4) Wechsler Adult Intelligence Scale–IV (WAIS-IV)
5) Structured Interview of Reported Symptoms–2 (SIRS-2)
6) Minnesota Multiphasic Personality Inventory–2 (MMPI-2)
7) Evaluation of Competency to Stand Trial–Revised (ECST-R)

Test Results
Interpretative Framework for Psychological Test Results

The interpretative formulations produced by many psychological tests produce hypotheses based on scores and scale interpretations that have been developed on diverse groups of individuals. Psychological test scores should not be interpreted in isolation. The hypotheses that are generated are probabilistic in nature but have been identified as being more likely to occur in individuals obtaining similar scores. The application of these hypotheses to any given individual requires corroboration. By considering other sources and by integrating the information with as many other sources as possible, including clinical interview, mental status examination, interviews of collateral sources, and independent records, the hypotheses gain or lose support. Without independent corroboration, it is not possible to determine whether the individual tested matches the prototype described by the test results.

Validity and Analysis of Response Style

In a forensic evaluation, it is important to assess response style to place the self-report and testing of the subject in proper evaluative context. In order to rule in or rule out feigning as well as random responding, or minimization or denial, various procedures were performed. In order to assess the response validity to cognitive testing, the Validity Indicator Profile (VIP) was administered. A valid assessment is possible only when the subject intends to answer correctly and exerts sufficient effort. On the Nonverbal and Verbal sections of the test, he appeared to exert consistent effort and to attend correctly to the item content. Overall, the results suggest that SPC P intended to perform well, consistently exerted effort, and did not feign cognitive impairment. The results suggest valid test results on measures of cognitive ability.

The SIRS-2 was administered as a means of directly assessing the presence of feigned psychiatric symptoms. His results were not suggestive of feigned symptoms. Another method of assessing response style was by administration of the MMPI-2, which has multiple validity indices. Scales to assess response consistency were acceptable. Scales assessing usual responses were mixed. His Infrequency scale (F) (T = 75) was elevated; however, his Infrequency Psychopathology scale (Fp) (T = 56) was within normal limits. Given his psychiatric history, this combination of scores suggests that he is endorsing problems consistent with a psychiatric condition and not grossly exaggerating the extent and severity of psychiatric problems. Overall, the profile appears valid.

During the sessions, SPC P was attentive and did not appear overly fatigued or distracted. He reported some difficulty with sustained attention but with periodic breaks was able to complete the testing without significant difficulty. An integration of behavioral observations, clinical interviews, collateral reports, mental health records, and psychological testing data does not show any significant evidence of feigned psychiatric symptomatology or of feigned cognitive impairment. Overall, the test results appear valid and interpretively useful.

Cognitive/Neuropsychological Functioning

The Trail Making Test (TMT) from the Halstead-Reitan Battery (HRB) was administered. The TMT provides information on visual search, processing speed, mental flexibility, and executive functions (higher-level cognitive functions that control and manage other process). His performance on Trails A (T = 46) and Trails B (T = 49) placed him in the average range. The Booklet Category Test (BCT) from the Halstead-Reitan Battery (HRB) was also administered. The BCT is test of abstract reasoning, problem solving, and executive functioning. The BCT is a screening test for neuropsychological impairment, and scores have been found to have the highest correlation with overall Impairment Index scores on the HRB. His performance (T = 66) placed him in the Above Average range.

SPC P was administered the Wechsler Adult Intelligence Scale–IV (WAIS-IV), which is a standardized test of intellectual functioning. On the WAIS-IV he achieved a full scale IQ of 94. In terms of more specific domains, he achieved a Verbal Comprehension index score of 93, a Perceptual Reasoning index score of 86, a Working Memory index score of 108, and a Processing Speed index score of 97. He consistently demonstrated scores in the Low Average to Average range. No significant cognitive impairment was noted. Overall his scores on the TMT, BCT, and WAIS-IV suggest that his neuropsychological functioning is grossly intact and that his cognitive abilities fall in the Low Average to Average range.

Clinical Syndromes and Personality Functioning

The MMPI-2 is a 567-item, True-False, objectively scored personality test. As noted, the results were considered valid and interpretively useful. SPC P generated a profile with significant elevations for Scale 4 (T = 69) and Scale 9 (T = 72). The elevation on Scale 9 is consistent with manic-like symptoms. Individuals with these two highest scale elevations may display irritability, impulsivity, irresponsibility, and immaturity. Such individuals may have poor social adjustment and interpersonal problems. Often such individuals do not adhere to societal standards, do not accept responsibility for their behavior, blame others, and rationalize their shortcomings. They may lack the ability to postpone gratification and pursue a pleasure-seeking and self-indulgent lifestyle. A low frustration tolerance and need for emotional stimulation may result in a restless and overactive behavioral pattern. The results are consistent with a diagnosis of a bipolar disorder.

DSM-IV-TR DIAGNOSIS (AT THE TIME OF THE ALLEGED OFFENSES)

Axis I: 296.42 Bipolar I Disorder, Most Recent Episode Manic, Moderate, Without Psychotic Features

  304.80 Polysubstance Dependence

Axis II: V71.09 No Diagnosis, Antisocial Personality Traits

Axis III: None

Axis IV: Pending UCMJ Charges, Financial Stress, Problematic Relations with Family Members

Axis V: Global Assessment of Functioning (GAF) = 50

DSM-IV-TR DIAGNOSIS (CURRENT)

Axis I: 296.42 Bipolar I Disorder, Most Recent Episode Manic, Moderate, Without Psychotic Features

  304.80 Polysubstance Dependence, In a Controlled Environment

Axis II: V71.09 No Diagnosis, Antisocial Personality Traits

Axis III: None

Axis IV: Pending UCMJ Charges, Financial Stress, Problematic Relations with Family Members

Axis V: Global Assessment of Functioning (GAF) = 60

FORENSIC OPINION AND COMPETENCY TO STAND TRIAL

RCM 706(c)(2)(D) asks:

Is the accused presently suffering from mental disease or defect rendering the accused unable to understand the nature of the proceedings against the accused or to conduct or cooperate intelligently in the defense?

In the United States military, according to RCM 909, "no accused may be brought to trial by court-martial if that person is suffering from a mental disease or defect rendering him or her mentally incompetent to the extent that he or she is unable to understand the nature of the proceedings against them or to conduct or cooperate intelligently in the defense of the case." The Supreme Court held in *Dusky v. U.S.* (1960) that the standard for competency to stand trial was that a defendant has a "sufficient present ability to consult with his lawyer with a reasonable degree of rational understanding" and a "rational as well as factual understanding of the proceedings against him." The U.S. Court of Military Appeals in *U.S. v. Proctor* (1993) affirmed that the *Dusky* standard applied in military court.

As part of assessing his competency to stand trial, SPC P was administered the Evaluation of Competency to Stand Trial–Revised (ECST-R), a semi-structured interview designed to assess competency to stand trial as exemplified by the *Dusky* standard. The ECST-R yields scores for four scales: Factual Understanding of Courtroom Proceedings (FAC), Rational Understanding of Courtroom Proceedings (RAC), Consult with Counsel (CWC), and overall Rational Ability (Rational). The ECST-R also contains a screen for feigned incompetence. The results did not indicate SPC P was striving to feign incompetence.

Factual Understanding of the Proceedings

The interview with SPC P indicated no significant impairment regarding his understanding of his charges or his expected role in the process. On the ECST-R, his FAC score indicated no significant impairment. He understood the charges against him and the severity of the alleged crimes. He displayed an adequate knowledge of the various aspects of the trial process, including the respective roles and responsibilities of the various trial participants. He stated that the judge is "the boss" and "referees between defense and prosecution to make sure it is a fair trial." He described the role of defense counsel as to "put out the best defense and in my case since they probably got me to get the least punishment." He understood that it was his choice after discussion with his attorney to select either a bench trial or trial with a military panel. He grasped the two-thirds rule once it was explained to him. In military courts a conviction requires a vote of two-thirds or more of the panel members.

Ability to Consult with Counsel

SPC P identified his attorney and indicated that they had a good working relationship. He did not display any irrational beliefs about his attorney or irrational reasoning about his attorney's motivations. He described realistic expectations of his attorney and demonstrated no significant impairment in his ability to communicate with his attorney. On the ECST-R, his CWC score indicated no significant impairment.

Rational Understanding of the Proceedings

SPC P did not evidence any psychotic thought process. He demonstrated no significant impairment in decision-making regarding potential plea agreements. He stated that the best outcome in this case would be for the government to drop the charges and agree to administratively separate him in light of his bipolar disorder. He stated, "I probably had this bipolar thing when I joined and was gonna screw up sooner or later." He has been to court previously and demonstrated no inappropriate behavior, nor did he demonstrate any inappropriate behavior during the two days of this evaluation. He said that he would "behave myself" when he returned to court. His RAC score indicated no significant impairment.

The results of the clinical interview and ECST-R, in combination with all the other information reviewed, indicated that SPC P had a factual and rational understanding of the charges pending against him and was able to consult intelligently with counsel. Overall, it is my opinion that SPC P is presently not suffering from a mental disease or defect that renders him unable to understand the nature of the proceedings or to conduct or cooperate intelligently in his defense.

25. FORENSIC OPINION/ CLINICAL DIAGNOSIS:

As noted, RCM 706(c)(2)(B) asks:

What is the clinical psychiatric diagnosis?

The reasoning for the diagnostic formulations was explained in the previous section. The diagnoses are also listed there.

26. FORENSIC OPINION/ CRIMINAL RESPONSIBILITY:

RCM 706(c)(2)(A) asks:

At the time of the alleged criminal conduct, did the accused have a severe mental disease or defect? (The term "severe mental disease or defect" does not include an abnormality manifested only by repeated criminal or otherwise antisocial conduct, or minor disorders such as non-psychotic disorders and personality defects.)

RMC 706(c)(2)(C) asks:

Was the accused, at the time of the alleged criminal conduct and as a result of such severe mental disease or defect, unable to appreciate the nature and quality or wrongfulness of his or her conduct?

According to RCM 916(k), a defendant is not criminally responsible for a charged offense if, at the time of the offense, the accused suffered from a severe mental disease or defect, *and* the severe mental disease or defect rendered the accused unable to appreciate the nature and quality or wrongfulness of their actions. Thus, there is a threshold criterion (whether the defendant has a severe mental disease or defect), a linkage criterion (whether the mental illness is linked to the offense), and a functional test derivative of the linkage (the person was unable to appreciate the nature and quality or wrongfulness of their behavior due to the severe mental disease or defect).

I believe that the accused, at the time of the alleged offenses, had the following mental disorders: Bipolar I disorder, moderate, without psychotic features; polysubstance dependence, and antisocial traits. Whether at the time of the alleged offense, any of these disorders should be classified as a severe mental disease or defect is more difficult

to answer, especially with regard to bipolar disorder. According to the *Military Judges' Benchbook,* "The term *severe mental disease or defect* can be no better defined in the law than by the use of the term itself. However, a severe mental disease or defect does not, in the legal sense, include an abnormality manifested only by repeated criminal or otherwise antisocial conduct or by nonpsychotic behavior disorders and personality disorders."

It may reasonable to assert that a disorder such as bipolar disorder may be severe at a given point in time, especially if in a manic episode with psychotic features. However, I do not find this to be the case. The history gathered through interview as well as the collateral information gathered from multitude sources do not support the notion that the accused was acutely psychotic, or significantly impaired in his reality testing at the time of the alleged offenses. While he has a history of manic episodes, the data suggest that he was not in the throes of a manic episode when he chose to go AWOL or to use or possess drugs. According to DSM-IV-TR, many mental disorders may be classified as mild, moderate, or severe. "Severe" is defined as "many symptoms in excess of those required to make a diagnosis, or several symptoms that are particularly severe, are present, or the symptoms result in marked impairment in social or occupational functioning." In my view, his bipolar disorder should be classified as moderate.

Furthermore, although substance disorders can be severe mental diseases, substance intoxication is specifically excluded from forming the basis of an active defense for lacking mental responsibility. According to military law, voluntary intoxication is not a defense, and intoxication is not a mental disease or defect that would qualify for an insanity defense. According to RCM 916(1)(2), "Voluntary intoxication, whether caused by alcohol or drugs, is not a defense." In addition, as noted in the *Military Judges' Benchbook* definition of "severe mental disease or defect," "repeated criminal or otherwise antisocial conduct" is also excluded from consideration as for an insanity defense. The exclusionary criteria tend to rule out "antisocial traits" from consideration. To the extent that his conduct is viewed as stemming from antisocial traits, he does not qualify for an insanity defense.

Since SPC does not meet the threshold criteria of qualifying for a severe mental disease or defect at the time of the alleged offenses, I do not believe he lacked mental responsibility. Furthermore, records and clinical interview indicate that at the time of each of the alleged offenses, he was aware of the nature and quality and wrongfulness of his actions. He stated that he knew that the use and possession of drugs was clearly illegal and he knew there would be negative consequences, including potential UCMJ action, if he went AWOL. Regarding his AWOL in order to avoid detection he stated that he "caught a good time to leave because I didn't want to be caught." He chose not to inform anyone on base of his intentions because he did not want to get anyone else in trouble. His actions and statements suggest awareness of the wrongfulness of his behavior at the time of alleged offenses.

LIMITS ON CONCLUSIONS REACHED AND INTERPRETATION OF DATA

This report is based on a large amount of information obtained from multiple sources. I believe that the data are accurate and provide an adequate basis to form clinical and forensic opinions. However, if any information is substantially inaccurate, I would appreciate it if this were immediately called to my attention. In addition, should I learn of any additional new information which casts substantial doubt upon any of my clinical or forensic opinions, I will immediately notify the offices of Trial Counsel and Defense Counsel, and write an addendum to this report.

Questions regarding this case can be directed to Dr. Paul Montalbano.

Paul Montalbano, Ph.D., ABPP (Forensic)
Deputy Chief
Forensic Psychology Services and Postdoctoral Program in Forensic Psychology

TEACHING POINT: HOW DOES THE EVALUATOR ADDRESS THE QUESTION OF "SEVERE MENTAL DISEASE OR DEFECT?"

(contributed by Paul Montalbano)

Some guidance on the meaning of this term is included in the criteria, to the effect that the term "does not include an abnormality manifested only by repeated criminal conduct or otherwise antisocial conduct, or minor disorders such as nonpsychotic behavior disorders and personality defects." This would appear to argue strongly against including antisocial personality disorder and perhaps against personality disorders in general. As to what constitutes nonpsychotic behavior disorders, there is probably even more room for debate. The origin of the modifying adjective "severe," which first appeared in the federal insanity standard after the Insanity Defense Reform Act (1984), may be rooted in the recommendations made by various groups to reform the insanity standard. The American Psychiatric Association workgroup (1983) suggested that "any revision of insanity defense standards should indicate that mental disorders potentially leading to exculpation must be serious," adding that "such disorders should usually be of the severity (if not always the quality) of conditions that psychiatrists diagnose as psychoses" (p. 685). The workgroup cited the work of Richard Bonnie (1983), who stated, "As used in this section, the terms mental disease or mental retardation include only those severely abnormal mental conditions that grossly and demonstrably impair a person's perception or understanding of reality and that are not attributable primarily to the voluntary ingestion of alcohol or other psychoactive substances."

The Court of Military Appeals (COMA), the forerunner to the Court of Appeals for the Armed Forces (CAAF), in *U.S. v. Benedict* (1988) addressed the issue of what constituted a "mental disease or defect." This court noted that "military law has never recognized as an absolute rule that an accused must suffer from a psychosis in order to merit acquittal by reason of insanity." In *U.S. v. Proctor* (1993), the Court of Military Appeals found that personality disorders may qualify for consideration of the broader concept of "mental disease or defect." The *Military Judge's Benchbook* (Department of the Army, 2010) offers advice that is not particularly illuminating when it states: "The term severe mental disease or defect can be no better defined in the law than by the use of the term itself." DSM-IV-TR (American Psychiatric Association, 2000) strives to refine diagnoses by adding subtypes and specifiers. Severity specifiers include *mild, moderate* or *severe*. DSM-IV-TR advises that when the clinician is deciding which of these specifiers to apply, he or she "should take into account the number and intensity of the signs and symptoms of the disorder and any resulting impairment in occupational or social functioning." "Severe" is defined in DSM-IV-TR as "many symptoms in excess of those required to make a diagnosis, or several symptoms that are particularly severe, are present, or the symptoms result in marked impairment in social or occupational functioning." The guidelines in DSM-IV-TR for use of the word "severe" were not specifically designed to address the legal issue of whether the accused has a severe mental disease or defect in a Sanity Board evaluation, but they may be worth considering.

To reiterate the first question: "At the time of the alleged criminal conduct, did the accused have a severe mental disease or defect?" The evaluator should be clear whether he or she is answering this question in terms of whether the mental disorder in general should be classified as severe—or whether this individual's mental disorder at a particular time should be classified as severe. I interpret the question as asking the evaluator to ascertain, in the context of a disorder that fluctuates over time, whether there is significant impairment in reality testing at the time of the alleged offense. For example, for a soldier diagnosed with PTSD, I have suggested that PTSD (for the purpose of a Sanity Board) should be classified as severe only when there is significant impairment in reality-testing at the time of the alleged offense (due to dissociation, for example). There appears to be no uniform agreement on how to interpret the word "severe," and there also seems to be room for variability in clinical judgment in answering this question. I have reviewed some reports that summarily conclude that in the absence of a psychotic disorder, there is no severe mental disease or defect. In my view this is not advisable, and each question should be addressed. Furthermore, the question of criminal responsibility specifically focuses on impairment in appreciation of "nature and quality" or "wrongfulness." It is worth noting that a given individual may be impaired in many domains but not those specifically. Conversely, an individual may be relatively unimpaired in many domains but possess an encapsulated delusion that specifically impairs appreciation of wrongfulness.

This last point underscores the importance of fully addressing each of the four questions. RCM 706 directs the examiner to "make separate and distinct findings" for each of the questions. Consider the hypothetical case of a relatively high-functioning individual with encapsulated delusions who qualified for a diagnosis of delusional disorder. Suppose the evaluator concluded that the individual did not have a severe mental disease or defect and did not meet the threshold criteria—and, without further analysis, concluded that the defendant was responsible. A more careful analysis might demonstrate that the encapsulated delusion was directly linked to his criminal behavior and to the capacity to appreciate wrongfulness. In my view, it is important to answer the question of severe mental disease and defect carefully, with an eye focused on how the disorder may impair our understanding of its "nature and quality" or "wrongfulness." The finder of fact may disagree with your answer to the question about severe mental disease or defect, and an explanation of how the symptoms affected the functional-legal criterion of appreciating wrongfulness will reinforce your reasoning as to why the disorder was or was not severe at the time.

TEACHING POINT:
OBTAINING APPROPRIATE AUTHORIZATION IN MILITARY FMHA, AND SIMILARITIES WITH AND DIFFERENCES FROM CIVILIAN PARAMETERS
(contributed by Paul Montalbano)

Official appointment is necessary to ensure the confidentiality and privilege of the inquiry. In *United States v. Toledo* (1987), a psychologist was approached by the defense and asked to assess the accused for an insanity defense. The psychologist spent over 10 hours assessing the accused but was never appointed. Defense counsel was taken aback when the psychologist was called by trial counsel to testify. One question on appeal was whether the testimony violated the rights against self-incrimination for the accused individual. Article 31(b) of the Uniform Code of Military Justice (UCMJ) prohibits compulsory self-incrimination. The US Court of Military Appeals ruled that since the psychologist was evaluating the accused at the behest of the defense, Article 31(b) did not apply. On a petition for reconsideration (*United States v. Toledo*, 1988), the Court of Military Appeals affirmed its previous decision that an accused or their counsel may not simply annex professionals into attorney–client relationships, but must obtain authorization through proper channels.

CASE THREE
PRINCIPLE: USE NOMOTHETIC EVIDENCE OF CLINICAL CONDITION, FUNCTIONAL ABILITIES, AND CAUSAL CONNECTION
(PRINCIPLE 28)

This principle was discussed in detail in Chapter 2, and was also illustrated in Chapter 19 (this volume). Therefore, the following discussion will focus on the ways that this report provides a good example of this principle. The current evaluation—a violence risk assessment—was conducted to assist the treatment team with discharge planning of a 35-year-old male veteran with depressive disorder, post-traumatic stress disorder, and alcohol abuse who was involuntarily hospitalized pursuant to meeting commitment criteria. Mr. Smith was found running into traffic in an apparent suicide attempt, after which police brought him into the emergency room. Reportedly, Mr. Smith had also been having homicidal thoughts involving plans to kill an ex-girlfriend. His history includes alcohol abuse, unemployment, and homelessness.

After three months of hospitalization, his depression resolved, and he no longer reported homicidal or suicidal thoughts. Mental health, housing, and employment resources in the community were put into place by the treatment team. Staff was concerned about the potential long-term threat to others Mr. Smith posed in the community after discharge, so they requested a violence risk assessment.

PSYCHOLOGICAL EVALUATION: VIOLENCE RISK ASSESSMENT
Reason for Referral

Mr. Joseph Smith is a 35-year-old male veteran with depressive disorder, post-traumatic stress disorder, and alcohol abuse who was involuntarily admitted to Main State Hospital (MSH) after a two week inpatient stay at the Fort Jefferson VA Medical Center, where police originally brought Mr. Smith

after he was discovered lying on railroad tracks in an apparent suicide attempt. He had been having homicidal ideation and plans toward killing his former girlfriend. There were allegations that the veteran was physically violent with his former girlfriend last August, and she reported that Mr. Smith broke her arm in a fight a few months ago. In the current MSH hospitalization, there was an incident in which Mr. Smith apparently threatened to hurt another veteran with a pencil, and Mr. Smith was found with half a pencil on his person; he was subsequently transferred to the high-management unit at MSH.

After two months of inpatient treatment, the veteran's depressive symptoms have largely abated, and the treatment team is considering the possibility that the veteran no longer meets inpatient commitment criteria. Given his history, staff requested the current evaluation to help determine if Mr. Smith meets criteria for continued hospitalization or outpatient commitment, to provide the treatment team with a psychological assessment of Mr. Smith's risk of violence, and to make recommendations on how to optimally manage this risk when Mr. Smith is discharged to the community. Prior to the current assessment, its nature and purpose were explained to Mr. Smith. Mr. Smith stated that he knew the results from the assessment would be used by the treatment team for discharge planning, adding that the reason for this was "so I can get out of here."

Sources of Information

- Clinical Interview and Evaluation of Mr. Smith
- Review of Medical Records from Fort Jefferson VA Medical Center
- Review of Psychiatric Measures Data from Fort Jefferson VA Medical Center, Including Beck Depression Inventory (BDI), Michigan Alcohol Screening Test (MAST), PTSD Checklist (PCL), and the Mini-Mental Status Exam (MMSE)
- Review of Nursing Assessment from Main State Hospital
- Review of Psychiatric Assessment from Main State Hospital, Including Information Gathered from Mr. Smith's Ex-Girlfriend
- Review of Psychological Assessment from Main State Hospital, Including Personality Assessment Inventory (PAI) and Repeatable

Battery for the Assessment of Neuropsychological Status (RBANS)

- Review of Neurology Report from Main State Hospital
- Review of All Inpatient Medical Records from Main State Hospital Including Progress Notes, Medication Orders, and Other Clinical Staff Assessments
- Arrest Record Search of Department of Corrections Database
- Administration of the Psychopathy Checklist–Revised (PCL-R)
- Administration of the HCR-20 Violence Risk Assessment Guide

SOCIAL HISTORY

Mr. Smith grew up and lived his whole life in Johnson County. He was the oldest of five children; he has three brothers and one sister. When asked about his upbringing, he said it was "great, wish I could do it again." The veteran denied history of physical or sexual abuse, although he said he would get "bad whoopin' from my dad." He denied that his parents were alcoholic or had mental illness. This was corroborated by the veteran's former girlfriend. Mr. Smith reported he made it to the twelfth grade but was never in any special education classes or diagnosed with a learning disability. Still, he said, "I hated school, I liked to stay on the farm of my granddaddy running tractors, on the tobacco or wheat fields." Mr. Smith said that he often didn't go to school and would hide in the fields at his grandfather's. Because of this, he said, he failed first and third grades. He said he was a troublemaker as a kid ("I smacked girls in their ass") and said he and his friends were disruptive. He indicated that he did get in some fights in school but never used weapons, was called a bully, hurt anyone badly, or saw a doctor or counselor for behavioral problems. He said that he was suspended from high school several times for reasons "like chewing gum."

Mr. Smith stated he eventually quit high school so he could work. Mr. Smith reported driving trucks, working in factories or mills, and working as a car mechanic on auto transmissions. In his mid-twenties, he obtained a GED and joined the U.S. Army, where he served three years before honorable discharge.

Since returning from service six years ago, the veteran has held several odd jobs as a mechanic,

but has not been able to maintain steady work. The veteran said that since last November, he has been on unemployment and has been having difficulty finding a new job. He indicated that he has quit jobs but denied ever being fired. This is in contrast to the report of Mr. Smith's former girlfriend, who said that she was the one who maintained steady employment in the household, whereas Mr. Smith was fired from many jobs, had a problem holding jobs, and quit many jobs due to a negative attitude.

Mr. Smith says he has "lots of friends" but can't see them because they are friends of his former girlfriend. When asked about how many different sexual partners he said, he said a "shitload of 'em." Leisure activities include going to church and fishing. With respect to finances, Mr. Smith says he's never had any debts, doesn't have any credit cards, has never owed people money or failed to pay bills like rent, telephone, and gas. He said he never had a bank loan and never depended on family or friends for money. However, his former girlfriend said that she was the one who provided financial stability for the family, not Mr. Smith. Furthermore, after she broke up with him, Mr. Smith went to live with his brother in a house that is owned by the family. Apparently, the family let Mr. Smith live there, but he tried to sell the property, cursed the family, and failed to pay electricity or other bills; they eventually kicked him out.

MILITARY HISTORY

Mr. Smith is a U.S. Army veteran who served in Operational Iraqi Freedom (OIF) from 2004–2007. After receiving basic training at Fort Bradley, Mr. Smith was deployed to Kuwait, where he drove vehicles carrying weaponry, eventually traveling into Iraq. Although he was trained in combat, he served mainly in this role throughout his deployment in region of conflict. After a few months, Mr. Smith was transferred to Fallujah. In Iraq, "transport was pretty stressful," and he described driving but constantly wondering if he was "going to blow" from an IED: "I was constantly in fear." According to Mr. Smith, when he did work in a combat zone, there were several times his company was shot at—but he himself never fired a weapon. Veterans Affairs records indicate that Mr. Smith reported several infractions, including returning to the base late and once failing a urine test for alcohol (Mr. Smith himself denied infractions during the clinical interview). He indicated that eight months into his deployment, he was driving a truck near the outskirts of Bagdad and when an improvised explosive device (IED) detonated about 100 feet away. He was not injured, but he felt a shockwave from the blast. After that, he began to experience symptoms of acute stress (e.g., unable to sleep, difficulty concentrating) and was flown to an Army base in Germany to receive mental health care. He received an honorable discharge after two years of service. According to VA records, Mr. Smith is "70% service connected" for post-traumatic stress disorder.

SUBSTANCE USE HISTORY

Mr. Smith denied ever using any illegal drugs and stated, "I don't get drunk and I don't do drugs. You go to prison if you mess with drugs." According to records, however, the veteran has a significant history for alcohol dependence, and he drank heavily for most of his life. He stated that he started drinking when he was eleven years old, but says he only began drinking daily since returning from Iraq. The nursing assessment indicates heavy drinking since age 13 outside of his time during military service. In most interactions with clinical staff, he appears to minimize his alcohol use, even when describing multiple driving under the influence (DUI) convictions. His former girlfriend also reported that she believes that the veteran was using speed and cocaine at some point, and she described increased PTSD hypervigilance symptoms after cocaine use.

LEGAL HISTORY

When asked if he's ever been arrested, Mr. Smith stated in the interview, "My record is clean—I have no felonies." After additional questions, he said, "There was a DUI or three." He said that he was on probation for five years but did not violate it. He was required to attend AA meetings, according to Fort Jefferson VA Medical Center notes, which also indicate that Mr. Smith stated that he has had 13 DUIs, the most recent being 15 years ago. The veteran does indicate that AA was helpful and that he would consider attending again. Outside of these, were no charges or arrests for other violent or nonviolent crimes listed in the Department of Corrections online arrest record search. However, the Fort Jefferson VA Medical Center report indicates that Mr. Smith was arrested for drunk and disorderly conduct and assault five years ago and

arrested for public drunkenness three years ago; Mr. Smith denies any charges outside of his DUIs. Give these somewhat conflicting reports from different sources, the most reliable charges appear to be the multiple DUIs; other criminal arrests or charges could not be corroborated at the time of this evaluation. Still, the current restraining order against Mr. Smith is corroborated by the veteran, the veteran's former girlfriend, and medical records.

MEDICAL HISTORY

The veteran denied history of any medical illnesses or neurological disorders such as stroke or seizures. He stated he had never had any head injuries, although he acknowledged being in the vicinity of improvised explosive device (IED) blast explosions in Fallujah, Iraq: "I didn't get hurt or see stars or anything." Medical records confirm no evidence of major medical problems. A neurology report indicated that Mr. Smith has complained of an acutely weak left leg but was unable to make any reliable conclusions about this weakness because of overtly poor effort on the part of Mr. Smith. Otherwise, the neurology report said his language is fluent, cranial nerves were normal, motor exam was normal, and his strength was normal. The veteran has no known allergies to medications, and is currently prescribed Zoloft and Abilify.

Psychiatric History and Current Admission

According to Mr. Smith's former girlfriend, he has a history of psychiatric difficulties beginning two years ago. He had apparently never been hospitalized psychiatrically until last year. He indicated that he had not seen a mental health counselor or received psychiatric treatment until then. According to the information received from Fort Jefferson VA Medical Center, the veteran has had two recent admissions. The first hospitalization at Fort Jefferson was reportedly precipitated by depression, PTSD symptoms, and suicidal ideation; he was discharged with a prescription for Prozac but did not follow through with care at the VA. The veteran's second hospitalization this year occurred before the current admission, when he was picked up by police while running into traffic in an apparent suicide attempt. The veteran denied this and denied ever having had a plan to kill himself. He had also been having homicidal ideation and plans of violently attacking a former neighbor with a shovel. Records indicate a long history of alcohol abuse and recent homicidal ideation toward members of his family. He carries diagnoses of post-traumatic stress disorder, depressive disorder NOS, alcohol dependence, and personality disorder NOS with antisocial traits. Current medical records indicate reduction of depressive symptoms, anger and agitation, and suicidal ideation in the past two to three weeks.

BEHAVIORAL OBSERVATIONS

Mr. Smith was cooperative, casually dressed, and appeared his stated age. The veteran was oriented to person, time, place, and situation. He denied suicidal or homicidal ideation and denied auditory and visual hallucinations. He said that he has never had a plan to commit suicide and has no plan to hurt his former girlfriend. His affect fluctuated between casual calmness and mild anger and irritability, and he did not seem at all depressed. He made minimal eye contact throughout the interview. He denied current PTSD symptoms, including re-experiencing, avoidance, or hyperarousal. His mood was, "I'd be good if I'd be out of here." The veteran's thought process was organized and linear, and his thought content focused both on being discharged from the hospital and on his being angry about being hospitalized.

The veteran did not appear to have any delusional beliefs, and the vast majority of his responses were reality-based. On a few occasions he did make somewhat odd statements. For example, during the interview, Mr. Smith was asked about what his plans were, and he stated, "Ain't gonna play with vipers." When asked to elaborate, he said, "I ain't going to do nothing stupid, not going to try to commit suicide or kill anyone." A psychological assessment is noted to also show that Mr. Smith believes that his house was haunted by the ghosts of people who died in the house.

When asked about his anger problems, the veteran did acknowledge that sometimes he curses and that his girlfriend has told him he has a bad temper "just like your daddy." Mr. Smith denied ever having abused alcohol and significantly minimized his drinking habits. When asked about his future plans, Mr. Smith did say he needed to find a job and place to live but was not able to state how exactly he was achieve these goals. He said that to keep out of trouble in future, he would "keep my mouth shut

and behave and follow the program like they tell me." When asked to elaborate, he repeated himself.

During both this interview and the interview for a psychological assessment, Mr. Smith had no trouble recalling facts about his life, but he did have difficulty describing his emotional experience. For example in both interviews, he was unable to describe what feeling sad was like. The only indication or self-reported symptom of depression he gave was, "Sometimes I feel lonely." When prompted, however, he did report sleep disturbance, fluctuating appetite, reduced interest in things he used to enjoy, irritability, and thoughts of helplessness. In a psychological assessment, he reported previously having symptoms of mania, including reduced need for sleep and high levels of goal-directed behavior such as cleaning his truck. He said he's not had manic symptoms since his girlfriend broke up with him, and that the only symptoms he has had since are depressive symptoms.

HISTORY OF VIOLENCE

When initially asked about history of violence and aggression, Mr. Smith said he never hurt anyone seriously to the point where they needed to go to the hospital. He said he's never threatened anyone with a weapon, knife, or gun: "I've never even owned a gun, and I grew up on a farm." He did report that when he was 18 years old, a policeman grabbed his arm and "I hit the cop on the head with a beer bottle but did no time." He also reported that when he was 18 years old, he and his friends were driving and "I threw a bottle while we're driving; it hit a black kid on his head." When asked if he felt bad about this, he said, "Nope, didn't bother me." On the Michigan Alcohol Screening Test, he endorsed having gotten into fights when drinking and that drinking has created problems for him and his significant others. With respect to family violence, the veteran denied ever hurting his former girlfriend and denied any thoughts or plans to do so right now: "God is going to take care of her; I don't care about her anymore. The only thing I'd want is to get the money to go to court to sue her for slander." With respect to his use of the term "slander," the veteran stated he was referring to how she was able to get a restraining order against him by "lying to the judge that I beat her unconscious." He did also say he wouldn't hurt her because "I don't want to go to jail."

The veteran's former girlfriend reports a long history of domestic violence and physical abuse of her children. She reported that she stayed with him because she was in fear of his violence and also because she wanted to raise her children. She reported that he has had a bad temper and can become very physically aggressive, indicating that he broke her finger several months ago. As a result, she filed a restraining order against Mr. Smith and had the police pick him up and take him away from the house. Since that time, records from previous hospitalizations indicate that Mr. Smith has had "death wishes" toward his former girlfriend since last August and homicidal ideation with some plan. In the psychological evaluation, the veteran stated that he had a friend in Fort Bradley who was willing to get him assault rifles and shoot out his old house with his girlfriend in it. However, Mr. Smith quickly stated that he would never do this because he does not want to go to jail. Mr. Smith is reported also to have voiced homicidal ideation toward his son in the past few months because he maintains that he believes that his son is not his biological child.

Behavioral observations at Main State Hospital corroborate that the veteran has difficulty managing his anger and has acted aggressively as a result. Records indicate that Mr. Smith was apparently upset with another veteran on the ward and said he is going to hurt this veteran with a pencil. Shortly after this threat, staff did in fact find a pencil on Mr. Smith's person, transferring him to the high-management unit as a result. When asked about this incident, the veteran said nothing about the pencil but instead said that the reason they transferred him to the high-management unit was because he "kicked the door real hard because I wanted privacy to go to the bathroom." It should be noted, however, that the veteran has had no incident of violence at MSH for the past month.

Previous Testing

At Bennett Regional Medical Center, Mr. Smith received a score of 30/30 on the MMSE, showing good orientation, registration, attention and calculation, recall, and language abilities. On the PTSD checklist, he scored a 64, above the cutoff for this disorder. On the MAST, Mr. Smith indicated that he felt he was a normal drinker and that his family and friends perceived him as such, though he did endorse that drinking did lead to problems in his relationships and that his family has complained about his drinking. He denied that he had problems stopping drinking after one or two drinks and

denied that he ever blacked out while drinking or got into trouble at work because of drinking. On the Patient Health Questionnaire-9 (PHQ-9), the veteran's global severity score was in the normal range and did not indicate severe depression.

At Main State Hospital, the veteran's performance on the RBANS showed impaired immediate memory and attention, borderline visual abilities and language abilities, and low-average delayed memory. The report noted that the low scores reflected poor initial learning but that his retention was 100% for a list of words, 75% for a story, and 85% for visual information. Overall, the veteran showed scores somewhat lower than would be expected for someone with his level of education and work (as well as someone scoring perfectly on the MMSE), but it is unclear what level of effort Mr. Smith put forth, and results need to be interpreted cautiously.

Mr. Smith provided a valid PAI profile. His responses on the PAI were consistent with those of someone experiencing symptoms of depression. He endorsed sadness, hopelessness, feelings of worthlessness and personal failure, low self-esteem, and diminished expectancies from life. In addition, he expressed somatic concerns. Also elevated were scales indicative of traumatic stress; in particular, anger symptoms were more prominent. At the same time, the PAI showed the presence of more long-standing characterological traits. Specifically, the profile suggests a history of volatile relationships and fears of abandonment, as well the tendency toward impulsivity and acting out. These traits are associated with Cluster B personality disorders and are consistent with Mr. Smith's apparent suicide attempt and history of antisocial acts.

The veteran was readministered the PTSD checklist during the current interview and scored 32, below the cutoff for PTSD. Mainly, he endorsed high frequency of anger and irritability, difficulty concentrating, and emotional numbing. As such, it appears that the veteran's PTSD symptoms were less acute than upon admission.

STRUCTURED RISK ASSESSMENT

Psychopathy

The Psychopathy Checklist–Short Version (PCL-SV) is a standardized rating scale of psychopathic personality traits that is reliably associated with risk for future violence. The PCL-SV was completed in the context of the current assessment based on a review of Mr. Smith's records and clinical and collateral interviews. The veteran obtained a raw score of 10 on the PCL-SV, indicating that the veteran does not meet the cutoff score for psychopathic personality. The veteran's total score on the PCL-SV was average (38th percentile) relative to others in a civil psychiatric population. Thus, based on the single risk factor of psychopathy, Mr. Smith is at *moderate risk* of general violence.

On PCL Factor 1, which designates a "callous interpersonal style," the veteran's score was average (33rd percentile) relative to a civil psychiatric population. Specifically, the PCL Factor 1 score reflects Mr. Smith's difficulty taking responsibility for his own actions (including past violence, DUIs, alcohol abuse), glibness and superficiality talking about these behaviors, and his lack of guilt or remorse for any of these acts. On PCL Factor 2, which designates a persistent pattern of antisocial behavior, the veteran's score was average (48th percentile) relative to a civil psychiatric population. In particular, the PCL Factor 2 score reflects Mr. Smith's lack of realistic and long-term goals for how he would find a home or job, irresponsibility as evidenced by a pervasive pattern of drinking and driving, and early behavior problems, including getting suspended from school and reported juvenile antisocial and violent acts.

Using the HCR-20, among Historical (H) variables empirically shown to be associated with violence risk, Mr. Smith's scores indicate: (1) Increased risk as evidenced by age of first violent incident, history of substance abuse, employment problems, early maladjustment, relationship instability, major mental illness, and previous violence, as described above; (2) Potential increased risk as evidenced by scores on the PCL and personality disorder.

Among Clinical (C) variables empirically shown to be associated with violence risk, the veteran's scores indicate: (1) Increased risk as evidenced by low level of insight, active symptoms of major mental illness, and negative attitudes, as described above; (2) Possible increased risk as evidenced by mixed responsiveness to treatment.

Risk Management (R) variables depend in part on the nature of the veteran's discharge plan, and the following are all relevant to Mr. Smith's violence risk in the community: developing feasible plans, limiting exposure to destabilizers, personal support, compliance with treatment, and reducing stress. As a result, review of Mr. Smith's

background, psychological testing, and the clinical interview using the HCR-20 indicated *moderate to high risk* of future violence, depending on the presence or absence of risk management items.

It is important to note that both PCL-SV and the HCR-20 have not been validated in veteran populations. This is important, as is directly bears on scoring both measures. For example, PTSD is not considered a "major mental illness" on the HCR-20, and PTSD numbing symptoms arguably meet criteria for certain items on the PCL such as "'lacking empathy." With this caveat in mind, it is also critical to note that these are among the best tools that we have, given the current science of violence risk assessment. At the very least, risk assessment instrument use helps structure the current evaluation in examining factors that have been shown to be empirically related to future violence.

VETERAN-SPECIFIC RISK FACTORS

To address this, we supplement the structured risk assessment by examining risk factors that have specifically been shown to empirically relate to aggression and violence in military veterans. Mr. Smith does show evidence of some veteran-specific risk factors for general violence, including: younger age (under 40), PTSD, depression, substance abuse, higher levels of anger, combat exposure, and financial strain. At the same time, it should be noted that Mr. Smith does not show evidence of other veteran-specific risk factors for general violence, including: lower education level, witnessing violence growing up, abuse or maltreatment as a child, severe PTSD symptoms, or traumatic brain injury. Overall, Mr. Smith appears to have many, though not all, of the factors that have been most consistently associated in the scientific literature with general interpersonal violence among veterans and need to be considered with respect to conceptualizing his risk of violence in the community and developing an effective safety plan.

SUMMARY AND RECOMMENDATIONS

Mr. Joseph Smith is a 35-year-old white male with a history of PTSD, depression, and alcohol abuse who was admitted to Main State Hospital, after a two-week inpatient stay at Fort Jefferson VA Medical Center. He was referred for an assessment of his risk of violence in order to make recommendations on how this risk should be optimally managed after discharge to the community. Information about violence risk was incorporated into structured instruments to provide an empirically derived assessment about Mr. Smith's risk of violence. It is important to note that, although some of the data come from the veteran, who may be unreliable, information was also gathered from online arrest registries, behavioral observations at MSH, structured clinical interviews, and medical records from previous inpatient care. Combining these sources, it was found:

- The veteran's pattern of aggression appears to be linked to his difficulty managing anger, experiencing depressive symptoms, and frequently abusing alcohol. Mr. Smith himself acknowledges having a bad temper and having gotten into fights while drinking alcohol.
- Situational factors further exacerbate Mr. Smith's risk of violence. The recent breakup with his long-time girlfriend appears to be the main precipitant for recent homicidal ideation and violent fantasies. Mr. Smith's unemployment and homelessness also seem to have led to increased stress and possibly increased depressive symptoms.
- With respect formal assessment findings, the veteran's score on the PCL-R did not meet criteria for psychopathy but was average compared to the civil psychiatric veterans, suggesting moderate to high level of risk of violent behavior.
- Moreover, the HCR-20 indicates Mr. Smith is at moderate to high risk of violence in the future, though this depends, in part, on the extent to which a discharge plan incorporates strategies to target dynamic factors that lower violence risk.

Given his past history, Mr. Smith is most likely to be violent in the future if he is abusing alcohol, becomes depressed, has an increase in PTSD hyperarousal symptoms (particularly anger), is unemployed, and continues not living in a stable environment. These latter two situational factors not only inherently increase stress, but also potentially increase the probability of Mr. Smith's coping by drinking alcohol, which itself could further impair his ability to manage anger. In terms of

potential victims of violence, the veteran's violence history—and his admission of fantasies to shoot his old house with his ex-girlfriend in it—point to elevated risk of domestic and/or family violence toward his ex-girlfriend. Individuals with a history of domestic violence who, like Mr. Smith, (a) have difficulty with depression and anger, (b) score moderate to high on the PCL, and (c) abuse substances have been found in empirical studies to be more likely to perpetrate violence against family than against strangers, and also more likely to drop out of treatment compared to domestic violence perpetrators without significant psychopathology.

Taken together, Mr. Smith's history and clinical characteristics suggest moderate to high risk of targeted violence (as opposed to general violence), a risk that could be further elevated in the context of situational stressors and treatment noncompliance. Given the above findings, if the veteran continues to abuse alcohol in the community and have an unstable living situation, then there is a reasonable probability that Mr. Smith will repeat some type of aggressive conduct and therefore still present a risk to others, especially his ex-girlfriend. Without proper community supports and additional treatment, the data in this assessment indicate that it seems likely this scenario could recur.

However, Mr. Smith appears able to live in the community without need for inpatient commitment if treatment is available. He is service-connected at the VA and can obtain services there. He is currently stabilized on medication, is no longer exhibiting depressive symptoms, is motivated to work, denies suicidal or homicidal ideation, and states he wants to attend services. Discharge plans include substance abuse and mental health services and employment and housing resources. If Mr. Smith stays sober, engages consistently in his psychiatric treatment at VA, and attains a stable living and working environment, he appears able at this point to be able to live independently in the community and will be at lower risk of committing violence in the community.

As a result, a safety plan is developed below, which consists of recommendations to help lower the veteran's risk of violence guided by (1) the above conceptualization of Mr. Smith's violence risk; (2) risk management items from the HCR-20, and (3) empirical literature on variables associated with reduced violence risk among people with severe mental illness. Effective efforts to manage violence risk would involve a safety plan in which Mr. Smith:

(1) *Participates in substance abuse treatment.* The veteran's alcohol abuse appears possibly linked to family violence, and the veteran minimizes alcohol being a problem for him even though he has multiple DUIs and long history of alcohol abuse. Research confirms that substance abusers are significantly more likely to be violent than non-substance abusers, with alcohol use being among the most strongly linked to aggressive acts. As a result, it will be important to for Mr. Smith to participate in formal substance abuse treatment services at Fort Jefferson VA Medical Center following discharge to help Mr. Smith better acknowledge his problem-drinking patterns. Also, given his history of attending AA meetings and apparently having good conduct at the time and not violating probation in the process, providing Mr. Smith with local AA meetings that he can attend in Bennett County is warranted, may help reduce chances of alcohol abuse, and would provide another venue to address alcohol use problems.

(2) *Manages PTSD anger and depressive symptoms.* PTSD and depression elevate violence risk significantly in veterans. Moreover, in the case of Mr. Smith, his PTSD symptoms and depression may increase his level and frequency of drinking, which in turn would increase risk of violent behavior. As a result, given his link between PTSD hyperarousal, depression, agitation, and violence potential, efforts to help reduce psychiatric symptoms through medications, psychotherapy, and case management at Fort Jefferson VA Medical Center should help reduce the chances Mr. Smith will engage in violent behavior. Also, any specialized counseling to help teach Mr. Smith better ways to cope with stress and anger in a more adaptive way and help treat any depressive symptoms he may be experiencing with respect to the ending of his long-term relationship.

(3) *Develops feasible plans for employment.* The assessment showed that Mr. Smith has a good history of finding employment, whether full time or part time, but that currently he has had trouble obtaining a job. Unemployment has been linked with risk of violence for Mr. Smith, and lack of activity and financial stress can exacerbate psychiatric symptoms or increase the risk of drinking alcohol. Although the RBANS showed some cognitive impairment, which may relate to difficulties with work, it is unclear what his level of effort was in testing and behavioral observations—and the MMSE did not reveal significant attention, memory, or executive-functioning deficits. Furthermore, Mr. Smith was employed for many years until this past year, seems motivated to work, and has said he has been looking for employment. If Mr. Smith receives VA vocational rehabilitation, this can assist him in the process of finding work.

(4) *Obtains stable housing.* The veteran's history of homelessness is apparently recent, but as with unemployment, unstable living can be associated with increased stress and possible increased use of alcohol as a coping strategy. It is strongly recommended that the veteran be discharged to a structured living environment such as a group home or halfway house. If these are not available, the VA homeless programs may have housing options available. An application for Section 8 housing before the veteran is discharged is also recommended. Outpatient mental health and community support services would also be useful for attaining this goal, if he is able to obtain these in a reasonable period of time following discharge.

(5) *Increases adherence to treatment.* Given the recent history of treatment noncompliance after his hospitalization, efforts to specifically enhance adherence are recommended. Furthermore, research shows that domestic violence perpetrators who have moderate to high PCL scores and show depression, substance abuse, and anger (like Mr. Smith) are less likely to complete treatment than domestic violence perpetrators who have less psychopathological symptoms. Outpatient commitment would

not only provide a less restrictive alternative for care of Mr. Smith's mental illness, but it would address Mr. Smith's risk of non-adherence. Outpatient commitment has been shown in studies to improve treatment adherence with psychiatric services, which in turn has been shown to reduce risk of violent behavior among people with severe mental disorders such as depression. It is also strongly recommended that the treatment team place Mr. Smith on a waitlist for OEF (Operation Enduring Freedom)/OIF case management services. In the case of Mr. Smith, OEF/OIF case management would be helpful to coordinate housing, employment, and treatment, each of which factors into effectively managing Mr. Smith's risk of violence in the community.

When preparing Mr. Smith for discharge, staff should review these recommendations with the veteran and obtain his input into a safety plan to help gauge how receptive he is to the goals in the plan. In other words, staff should help Mr. Smith engage in his own treatment. Research has shown that when veterans with psychiatric disorders feel more engaged in their treatment, they are more likely to adhere to treatment and less likely to be violent. Indeed, to the extent that the veteran actively strives to achieve each of the risk management goals listed above, he will be working to reduce his risk of perpetrating violent behavior. Thus, it is also strongly recommended that each safety plan goal be monitored by the veteran himself as well as by mental health treatment providers in the future.

Thank you for referring Mr. Smith. If I can be of further assistance, please do not hesitate to contact me.

Eric B. Elbogen, Ph.D.
Clinical-Forensic Psychologist

TEACHING POINT:
COMBINING NOMOTHETIC DATA WITH CASE-SPECIFIC IDIOGRAPHIC INFORMATION

Nomothetic data—scientific data gathered on groups—can be applied to the assessment of several domains that are relevant in FMHA. Using psychological measures with established psychometric properties, validated for the purpose for which they are being used, puts evaluators on firm ground when choosing instruments to be used in an evaluation. Moreover, scientific data provide evaluators with an estimate of the base rates of relevant behavior, such as violence. It also allows the comparison of the individual being evaluated to "known groups," so that individual can be described as functioning around a certain percentile of the attribute being measured. In the context of a violence risk assessment (as illustrated by the preceding case), there are several measures that have strong scientific support and can serve as a valuable source of data in the evaluation.

Despite the value of risk assessment tools and other nomothetically derived data, however, an evaluator should not rely exclusively on such measures. Rather, best practices suggest that evaluators combine nomothetic data with case-specific idiographic information, which will lead to a more comprehensive and accurate assessment of the relevant forensic issue. Using case-specific information, which can be obtained through an interview of the examinee and review of relevant records, the evaluator is in a better position to generate and test hypotheses regarding the relationship between characteristics of the examinee and the outcome of interest. Case-specific information also allows an individualized description of the person being evaluated, consistent with the broad legal priority on individualized justice.

24

Release Decision-Making

The release decision-making process as it relates to the adult criminal justice system is the focus of the two reports in this chapter. In both of these cases, the evaluees had previously been found not guilty by reason of insanity and committed for mental health treatment. The present evaluations for release therefore focused largely on violence risk assessment and recommendations for risk management. Furthermore, the included reports consider the least restrictive setting that meets the evaluee's ongoing treatment needs while still mitigating future risk to public safety. The principle associated with the first case underscores the importance of obtaining historical information relevant to the evaluation, and the teaching point describes the integration of information from both hospitalization and pre-hospitalization in release decision-making. The second case highlights the importance of using multiple sources of information, while the teaching point outlines specific sources of information that may be informative about the individual's pre-hospitalization status and current hospitalization. Finally, the principle and teaching point associated with the third case describe the importance of reporting findings in a balanced and accurate manner.

CASE ONE
PRINCIPLE: OBTAIN RELEVANT HISTORICAL INFORMATION
(PRINCIPLE 19)

This principle is discussed in Chapter 7 (this volume), so we turn to the question of how the present report illustrates this principle. The current report provides a good example of what constitutes relevant historical information and how to obtain it in the context of an evaluation for release decision-making. The evaluators reviewed a range of documents that provided historical information relating to Mr. McKay's legal history, medical history, psychiatric history, and his previous adjustment to living in the community. All sources of information relied upon by the evaluators are clearly identified early in the report ("Sources of Information"), and there is a detailed section of the report titled "Historic Considerations" that provides specific information about Mr. McKay's psychiatric history, criminal history (juvenile and adult), history of institutional adjustment, and substance use history. The historical information was essential in terms of informing the evaluators' opinions and recommendations. Specifically, in reaching their conclusions about Mr. McKay's ability to live in the community—which involves an assessment of his risk—the evaluators cited Mr. McKay's history of violence, extensive mental health history, and his performance on prior conditional releases, among other factors.

FORENSIC PSYCHOLOGICAL REPORT
Risk Assessment

McKay, Daryll   Reg. No. 11111-111
Date of Birth: July 20, 1966
Dates of Evaluation: April 25, 2005, to August 17, 2005
Date of Report: August 17, 2005

REFERRAL

Daryll McKay is a 39-year-old African American male. In January 1997, Mr. McKay was found not guilty by reason of insanity for threatening the President of the United States. He was subsequently committed for mental health treatment, but was granted a conditional release after stabilizing on medication.

On April 23, 2005, a petition was filed with the court indicating that Mr. McKay had violated the conditions of his release. Following an initial court hearing, the United States District Judge ordered that Mr. McKay be committed for a 45-day evaluation to determine if he was currently dangerous to others (or the property of others) due to a mental illness.

Mr. McKay arrived at this facility on April 25, 2005. This writer met with Mr. McKay on April 26, 2005. At that time, this writer reviewed the nature and purpose of the evaluation with him. This writer explained that any information provided by Mr. McKay would not be confidential, could be included in this report, and would be provided to the risk assessment panel. He was also informed that a copy of the final risk assessment report would be presented to the court and would be seen by any judge, lawyers, and any outside mental health experts who may be involved in the case. Mr. McKay indicated that he understood this information and demonstrated this understanding in subsequent discussions. He indicated that he was willing to cooperate with the evaluation and agreed to proceed.

A risk assessment panel was convened to review Mr. McKay's assessment, interview him, and render an initial opinion concerning whether his release would present a substantial risk of bodily injury to others or serious damage to the property of others due to a mental illness. The panel was composed of the Chief of Psychology; the Chief of Psychiatry; and the Supervisory Social Worker. Also present was Mr. McKay's primary clinician, the writer of this report.

The Risk Assessment Panel considered a variety of factors relevant to their predictive effort. These factors are divided into two broad categories of historical issues (static risk factors) and treatment issues (dynamic risk factors). These factors were assessed both by clinical review and via the use of four formalized measures that have been found to be helpful in the assessment of future risk: the Psychopathy Checklist Revised (PCL-R), the Violence Risk Appraisal Guide (VRAG), the History-Clinical-Risk-20 (HCR-20), and the Static-99.

Future violence is difficult to accurately predict. Therefore, this report will focus on identifying factors that may place Mr. McKay at increased risk for engaging in future violence and protective factors that may help him refrain from future criminal acts. This report will also provide some recommendations for possible ways to manage the identified risk factors.

SOURCES OF INFORMATION

The evaluation was conducted in the Mental Health Unit from April 25, 2005, to August 17, 2005. This writer made use of several different sources to obtain the information required to complete the present risk assessment. Mr. McKay's day-to-day functioning on his unit of residence was routinely observed by several staff members, including correctional officers, nurses, psychiatrists, and psychologists during daily rounds. This writer completed three specific risk assessment interviews in addition to several brief contacts with him. A routine admission medical history and physical examination were completed. Several documents were reviewed, including: court orders; prior forensic evaluations; notes, reports, and medical records from an outpatient treatment center where Mr. McKay was treated during his conditional release; memorandums from the United States Probation Office regarding Mr. McKay's adjustment in the community; letters written by Mr. McKay while he was in the community; available psychological and medical records from prior incarcerations and hospitalizations; and a phone interview with staff from the outpatient treatment center.

HISTORICAL CONSIDERATIONS

Prior Psychiatric History

Mr. McKay reported that he first saw a mental health professional at age 13. He said he was initially seen because of behavioral problems. He indicated that his primary problem at that time was difficulty coping with emotions related to his father's alcohol use, physical abuse, and the divorce of his parents.

Mr. McKay stated that his first adult contact with a psychologist occurred in 1988 after he was convicted of raping a woman at knife-point. He reported that he was actively engaged in devil worship at that time. He originally claimed he viewed the rape victim as a sacrifice for the devil despite the fact that he did not cut or stab her.

Mr. McKay said he engaged in several unusual behaviors during the time of the rape. For example, he said he would cut himself and drink blood. While incarcerated for this offense in the state prison, he experienced auditory hallucinations that told him to break things and kill himself. He reported having attempted suicide by hanging on two occasions.

Mr. McKay completed eight years of a ten-year sentence for rape in 1996. He said that during his incarceration in the state prison, he completed sex offender treatment. No collateral information was available to confirm this, however, or describe the content of any treatment he might have completed.

Mr. McKay's grandmother noted that after he was released from prison he was as "crazy as a bat." She reported that he often talked "crazy," saying, "He's gonna kill this somebody or that somebody, and somebody's always trying to take his money." His grandmother noted that he often discussed moving to Europe to be in the military. An aunt indicated that he repeatedly told his grandmother, "I wish you were dead," and "When you die, I will spit on your grave."

In 1989, Mr. McKay wrote a letter predicting world events. He claimed that he was angry with his grandmother because she gave the letter to the government. On several occasions, he expressed the belief that the government was conspiring against him because he had special powers (which included the ability to end the world if he read his letter).

Mr. McKay worked at a "wood plant shop" for several months. While in this job, he severed one of his fingers and received a workmen's compensation settlement. He took the money and flew to Europe, planning to join the Foreign Legion. Prior to his departure, some of his neighbors noted that he made unusual comments about wanting to leave the country and renounce his citizenship.

While in Europe, Mr. McKay stayed in a hotel, where the staff observed bizarre behavior. He frequently called the hotel switchboard and requested to be put through to the President of the United States. Two fire extinguishers were thrown from an upper-story window at the hotel, and Mr. McKay was observed throwing one of these. He failed to gain acceptance into the Foreign Legion, started drinking heavily, and ultimately left a letter at the United States Consulate stating that he wanted to renounce his U.S. citizenship so that he could travel to Iraq. Additionally, Mr. McKay left letters threatening to kill the President of the United States.

Mr. McKay was apprehended by European authorities and was hospitalized for psychiatric care. He was initially placed in a European mental hospital, where he took medication willingly. He was eventually returned to the United States and sent to this facility for an evaluation to determine his competency and mental responsibility. The forensic staff concluded that Mr. McKay was marginally competent and able to assist in his defense. They also opined that he was legally insane at the time of writing the threatening letters in Europe.

Mr. McKay was returned to this facility for treatment after being found not guilty by reason of insanity. At that time, he was described as a model patient throughout his hospitalization. He had only one incident of violence during his initial commitment—he struck another inmate who had changed a television channel and pulled Mr. McKay's hand away when he went to change it back. Shortly after that incident, he said to a nurse, "Ms. S, I don't want any trouble, I'm trying to go home. Dr. G is going to be mad at me but I couldn't let him hit me." Mr. McKay completed a brief period of disciplinary segregation without incident. He eventually stabilized on psychiatric medication and was approved for conditional release to the community.

Between 2000 and 2005, Mr. McKay had repeated difficulties with adjusting well in community placements. He was placed in group homes on multiple occasions, but invariably had conflicts with peers or staff. On numerous occasions, Mr. McKay accused others of sexually harassing him, watching him in the shower, and trying to poison his food. Records indicate that Mr. McKay displayed these unusual beliefs even though he continued to take psychiatric medication. He engaged in several behaviors that resulted in a series of supervision violations. These included: "jumping on" a peer who, he believed, had made sexual advances toward him; staff discovering a homemade knife in his room at a group home; an altercation with an inmate while he was being held in a county jail; and a fight with a peer in a group home. Upon being readmitted to a hospital, Mr. McKay was consistently able to stabilize on psychiatric medication and earn approval for placement back in the community on a conditional release.

Records indicate that Mr. McKay was compliant with psychiatric medication and routinely attended outpatient therapy sessions during his most recent conditional release. They also noted, however, that he had difficulties getting along with peers. In particular, Mr. McKay apparently was accused by multiple residents of being threatening, and staff had concerns that he was bullying other residents. One peer accused Mr. McKay of threatening to stab him. Records indicate that Mr. McKay agreed to sign a "no harm" contract, but continued to have episodes of agitation and irritability. The clinic director noted that Mr. McKay was overtly polite and appropriate with staff but had difficulty accepting the rules of the facility. She noted that he was not overtly violent or defiant of the rules but observed that he did not like being told what to do. Mr. McKay was eventually recommended for a violation of supervised release due to his inability to maintain residence in the group home.

Antisocial Behavior and Characteristics
Juvenile History

Mr. McKay reported that he has had problems from a young age. He admitted getting into trouble for fighting before he turned 12. He noted, however, that his first serious problems began at the age of 13 after his parents divorced. He said his father was often drunk and physically abusive. Mr. McKay reported that he burned the family house down to get back at his father for beating him.

Mr. McKay said that he had problems following his parents' rules and became more difficult as he entered his teen years. He admitted to running away from home and various other placements at least six times. He said he began skipping school at age 15. He stated he joined the Gangster Disciples gang at that time but claimed he gave up being an active member several years ago. He said he was taken out of his home in 1982 and placed in a group home because he was uncontrollable. He denied, however, having any official juvenile criminal records.

Criminal History

Mr. McKay has only three charges on his adult criminal record. He was convicted of aggravated rape in 1986. He served eight years in a state prison for this offense and is currently required to register as a sex offender.

As noted previously, Mr. McKay was charged with making threats to the President of the United States in 1996 while he was visiting France. He was initially committed to a French mental hospital before being extradited back to the United States. He was eventually found not guilty by reason of insanity and he has been under a court order for mental health treatment since that time.

Mr. McKay's final adult offense was for falsification of a Sex Offender Registration Form in 2001.

No further information regarding this offense was available at the time this report was prepared. Mr. McKay has had no further criminal charges since that time, although he has had notable problems while on supervised release in community placements.

Prior Institutional Adjustment

Collateral information noted that Mr. McKay had several incident reports while he was incarcerated in the State Department of Corrections. During the eight years he served in the State, he was charged with possession of contraband, making threats to employees, assaulting a staff member, starting fires, and flooding a cell. During his prior commitments to this facility, Mr. McKay received three incident reports. He was charged with fighting with another (inmate) on two occasions (1999 and 2004). He was also charged with giving or accepting money without authority in 2001 after he was found in possession of another inmate's property.

Substance Abuse

Mr. McKay said he first began drinking alcohol at age 9 or 10. He said he used to drink a six-pack of beer on weekends. He admitted that he previously had problems in school due to his drinking. He was intoxicated during both his violent offenses (aggravated rape and threatening the President of the United States). He has, however, denied having an alcohol problem. Despite this denial, Mr. McKay has participated in Alcoholics Anonymous sessions during prior incarcerations and he claims he no longer drinks. There is no evidence he was intoxicated during his most recent period of supervised release.

In terms of illegal drugs, Mr. McKay said he began smoking marijuana at age 11 or 12. He noted that he began using Ecstasy at age 15. He described his drug use as primarily social. He denied having a drug use problem. There is no evidence that he was using drugs during his most recent period of supervised release.

EVALUATION AND TREATMENT REVIEW
Hospital Course

Mr. McKay was admitted to the Mental Health Evaluation Unit at the Medical Center on April 25, 2005. This was his sixth admission to this facility. His initial mental health assessment was conducted on April 26, 2005. At that time he showed some signs of residual thought disorder (i.e. unusual affect, stilted speech), but his symptoms appeared to be well managed by psychiatric medication. Mr. McKay reported that he was "doing okay" and explicitly denied having any current suicidal or homicidal ideation or intention.

As per standard procedure, Mr. McKay was initially placed under close monitoring on a locked ward until staff could observe him and gain more information. Correctional staff described him as cooperative and quiet. He was quickly able to transfer from a locked unit to general population.

Mr. McKay was able to remain in the open population from May to August of 2005. During that time, the correctional staff assigned to his housing unit initially reported no remarkable behavior. In June, the nursing staff overheard Mr. McKay saying "The end of the world will be about me." Despite this unusual comment, however, he appeared to be doing well on a day-to-day basis in the open population.

During this period, Mr. McKay was observed socializing with peers in the laundry room and recreation yard. He routinely attended recreation and took his meals in the inmate dining room. He was observed in the halls seeking out contacts with staff members he has known from prior commitments to this facility. He consistently presented as polite and appropriate.

On June 13, 2005, Mr. McKay approached this writer and complained that a male nurse had grabbed his buttocks during the morning medication pass. Although he has a history of delusional ideation about being sexually harassed by males, he was insistent that this really happened. His complaint was investigated, but no support was found for Mr. McKay's story. Mr. McKay handled the situation by avoiding the nurse whenever possible, but he did not become aggressive or assaultive at that time. By June 31, 2005, Mr. McKay claimed he no longer had any concerns about being harassed at this facility.

On July 3, 2005, Mr. McKay was involved in a physical conflict with a peer on his unit and was temporarily moved to a locked unit pending investigation of the incident. The fight apparently started when Mr. McKay attacked the other patient with a pen. Mr. McKay claimed that the other patient had been hired by his social worker to sexually harass him in the shower and assault him in his room. He said he knew this was true because he had

seen his social worker talking with the other patient in her office. He also claimed that he felt the other patient tried to poison him because he developed a rash after eating chocolates provided to him by the peer. He reported that he was only defending himself during the incident.

Mr. McKay was given incident reports for assault and fighting. When he was initially placed in a locked unit, Mr. McKay was irritable, agitated, and disorganized. He had some minor conflicts with staff. For example, he refused to receive medications from the nurse whom he had previously accused of sexually harassing him.

On July 23 of 2005, Mr. McKay handed this writer an unusual letter. The text of the letter was as follows: "I Daryll-McKay agree to suck a dick on video and make babies with NP [a staff member from the group home he was in while on supervised release] whenever I leave prison of Prisoners back into society." When asked about the letter, Mr. McKay reported that he had been getting "colds" from women since he was initially incarcerated in Federal Bureau of Prisons (FBOP) custody. He said the Chief Social Worker had, in fact, instructed his social worker to give Mr. McKay "colds." He went on to explain that he and everyone else knew about his blood and understood that his sperm could cure the AIDS virus. He was insistent that this belief was not irrational and that he knew it to be true because he had "a feeling." He said that several women have pursued him because his sperm can cure AIDS, but he is only interested in NP.

A psychiatric consult was requested to determine if Mr. McKay's antipsychotic medication was still effective. After interviewing him and reviewing his history, psychiatry staff recommended increasing his Geodon dose. Mr. McKay agreed to cooperate with the medication changes. He took the increased dose consistently, and his mental status appeared to improve over time. He once again began presenting as calm, polite, and cooperative with staff.

Mr. McKay was moved to the transitional unit on August 11, 2005. Shortly after moving, however, he became involved in a verbal conflict with the unit officer when she attempted to limit his property to the amount specified by policy. He became verbally aggressive and received a disciplinary report for insolence. Mr. McKay was returned to a locked unit on August 12, 2005.

While on the locked unit, Mr. McKay maintained a good attitude. He was consistently appropriate with staff. He was selected to act as a unit orderly and received good work reviews from the officers. After his sanctions were completed, the officers recommend Mr. McKay return to the transitional unit, and he was moved to that unit on August 25 of 2005 without incident. He subsequently returned to an open unit where he has remained without incident.

Mr. McKay spontaneously enrolled himself in an anger management group being run by the Social Work Department during the evaluation period here. Staff indicated that he participated regularly in group and his comments were good. They noted, however, that his answers seemed "rehearsed" and noted it was difficult to tell how invested he was in the group, given his current legal status.

During the evaluation, Mr. McKay reported that his three warning signs for future violent behavior would be becoming upset, hearing voices, and stopping his psychiatric medications. He noted that he has been taking his psychiatric medications routinely since he returned from France, and this is consistent with collateral information. He noted that he has not experienced auditory hallucinations since 2003. Mr. McKay reported that he used to have a temper problem, but he believes it is now under control. He said he used to be reactive and would react violently when angry rather than rationalizing. He said he now feels capable of containing his anger by isolating himself from others until he can discuss his problems with a counselor, family member, or mental health expert. He said the thing that is most likely to make him angry now is feeling as if others are sexually harassing him or watching him shower.

At the time of this report, Mr. McKay was taking the following psychiatric medications: Geodon (80 mg twice daily for psychosis) and Doxepin (50 mg as needed for agitation, not to exceed 150 mg in 24 hours). As noted previously, he was compliant with his Geodon prescription throughout the evaluation. Records indicate he has rarely taken any of his "as needed" Doxepin medication during his time at this facility.

Community Impressions and Resources
Family
Mr. McKay was born on July 20, 1966, in Jackson, Mississippi. He said his parents argued frequently. He described his father as alcoholic and abusive. He stated his parents divorced in 1974, and it was very hard on him. He said he tried to deal with these problems by keeping to himself, playing basketball, and joining the Gangster Disciples gang. He admitted to playing with matches at age 13 and setting the house on fire to get back at his father for beating him. He said he ran away from home numerous times after age 13 and admitted he was generally hard to manage.

Mr. McKay indicated that his mother and grandmother took care of him between 1974 and 1976. He was then transferred to his father's care from 1976 until 1982. In 1982, his father placed him in a group home because his behavior had become problematic. He remained in the group home for several months.

Mr. McKay has two brothers and four sisters. He said he got along well with them when he was growing up but lost contact with most of his family members after he was convicted of aggravated rape in 1986. He admitted that his incarceration has been hard on his family, particularly his father. As noted previously, collateral information indicates Mr. McKay made several harsh comments to family members in the past.

Mr. McKay said he resumed contact with his father and his oldest sister when he was last housed in Mississippi. He claimed they have been supportive but acknowledged he had no contact with them while he was in his last group home placement. He said his oldest brother is currently serving a life sentence in the state of Wisconsin for murder and rape.

Relationship
Mr. McKay has never been married and he has no children. He claimed to have two or three close friends but did not identify who they were. He said the longest friendship he has ever had has been two years and noted that he trusts his family more than anyone else.

Community Placement
At the time of his 2003 risk assessment, a social worker contacted Mr. McKay's case manager from the Mental Health Center. The case manager stated that the group home would not be willing to take Mr. McKay back, due to the nature of his violation.

During the evaluation, Mr. McKay reported that his ideal release plan would be to live in Jackson. He said he would accept living with family, in a group home, or in a homeless shelter. He said he wanted to be in Jackson because he would have family support in that city. He also reported that he would have the support of "the Muslim community." He indicated that he knew the city well, which would make getting a job easier. He said he was also aware of community mental health resources in Jackson he could utilize. He was able to recognize that the major obstacle to getting him placed in a group home in Jackson would be his history of violence, threats, and rape.

RISK ASSESSMENT MEASURES

This writer administered four formalized assessment measures to help evaluate Mr. McKay's relative risk for recidivism if he were to be released to the community. These measures are the Psychopathy Checklist–Revised Second Edition (PCL-R; Hare, 2003), the Violence Risk Appraisal Guide (VRAG; Quinsey, Harris, Rice, & Cormier, 1998), the HCR-20 (Webster, Douglas, Eaves, & Hart, 1997), and the Static-99 (Hanson & Thornton, 2000). The first two instruments are measures of static risk factors for general violent recidivism that are unlikely to change over time. As such, they can provide only a baseline estimate of an individual's risk for future violence. The HCR-20 measures both static and dynamic risk factors for general violent recidivism. As such, it is capable of identifying both protective factors and risk factors that may be targets for change. The Static-99 is a measure of static risk factors for future sexual offenses. This measure was included in the present assessment because Mr. McKay has a prior conviction for aggravated rape. Therefore, it seemed prudent to evaluate his risk for engaging in future sexual violence using a measure designed specifically for that purpose.

Psychopathy Checklist Revised, Second Edition (PCL-R)

The PCL-R is a 20-item instrument designed to measure negative interpersonal style, limited affect, deviant lifestyle, and antisocial behavior. PCL-R scores are determined based on information obtained from both clinical interviews and review of collateral file information. PCL-R scores range from 0 to 40. Scores below 20 are generally considered indicative of a distinct lack of psychopathic traits. Scores of 30 or more are generally considered indicative of the presence of significant psychopathic traits. Higher scores on this instrument have been found to be associated with higher

risk for revocation of parole, revocation of mandatory supervision, being unlawfully at large, and general recidivism. There are also studies linking higher PCL-R scores to higher risk for acting violently when released from prison. Published data have shown that PCL-R scores provide significant improvement in the prediction of violent recidivism over simple chance or the use of historical risk variables by themselves. Research has demonstrated that both inter-rater reliability and test-retest reliability of the PCL-R are excellent.

Mr. McKay's total PCL-R score was 25. Once error rates have been considered, his true score is probably between 22 and 28. Research with this instrument has found that individuals with similar scores are at moderate risk for recidivism compared to people with higher and lower scores. For example, one study found that 40% of individuals with mid-range PCL-R scores have violated conditional release (as opposed to 10% with low PCL-R scores and 60% with high PCL-R scores).

The PCL-R has four facets that make up two larger factors. The first factor is made up of interpersonal and affective facets that measure selfish, callous, remorseless use of others. Research has shown that individuals with higher Factor One scores are more likely to be disruptive in treatment settings and drop out of treatment prematurely. Mr. McKay's Factor One score was 12. Based on a normative sample of 5408 male prison inmates, this score is higher than those of 83% of inmates. Based on a normative sample of 1246 male forensic patients, this score is higher than those of 89% of such individuals. In other words, Mr. McKay's PCL-R Factor One score is high when compared to a sample of his peers.

The second factor is made up of lifestyle and antisocial facets that measure chronic, unstable, antisocial behavior. Research has demonstrated that individuals with higher factor two scores are at increased risk for recidivism when released to community settings. Mr. McKay's Factor Two score was 11. Based on a normative sample of 5408 male prison inmates, this score is higher than those of 43% of inmates. Based on a normative sample of 1246 male forensic patients, this score is higher than those of 40% of patients. In other words, Mr. McKay's Factor Two score is low-average compared to his peers.

Summary Scores: PCL-R Total Score: 25
PCL-R Factor One Score: 12
PCL-R Factor Two Score: 11

Violence Risk Appraisal Guide (VRAG)

The VRAG is a 12-item instrument used to assess an offender's risk to commit a violent crime within 10 years of returning to the community. Each item represents a different historical risk factor that has been demonstrated by research to predict future violent behavior. The risk factors that make up the VRAG are considered static in that each (except marital status) is highly unlikely to change over time.

Each item is weighted based on how predictive of future violence it is. VRAG scores range from –11 to +32, with higher scores indicating a higher risk of violent recidivism. Quinsey et al. (1998) divided VRAG scores into nine categories, each associated with a different risk for future violence. It has been found to be a reliable measure, with higher scores on the VRAG being associated with higher rates of violent recidivism in a variety of samples. It should be noted, however, that some researchers have questioned the validity of making risk predictions for individuals by comparing them to a standardization sample of only 600 criminal offenders. It should also be noted that static risk factors cannot account for protective factors or risk factors specific to individuals. These predictions should, therefore, be considered to be estimates with room for error.

Mr. McKay's VRAG score was +14, placing him in the seventh-highest of nine risk categories. Based on the standardization sample, inmates with scores in this category are estimated to be at moderately high risk for committing a violent offense within ten years of release (once group error estimates have been considered). Protective factors or improvement on dynamic risk factors may, however, serve to moderate Mr. McKay's offense risk.

Specific factors indicating that Mr. McKay may be at higher risk for future violence include the fact that he was raised by a single parent, has never been married, has a history of alcohol problems, has had conditional releases revoked, meets criteria for antisocial personality disorder, and has a moderate PCL-R score. Possible protective factors for Mr. McKay include having no significant problems in elementary school and his advanced age.

HCR-20

The HCR-20 is an instrument developed in Canada as way of formalizing risk assessment decisions and generating risk management plans for correctional systems. When using this instrument, the clinician's goals are (1) to render a probability statement of future risk in a specific setting for a specific time frame based on consistent and known factors related to violence, and (2) to identify problematic areas that may be targets for treatment to reduce risk of violence. The second goal is possible because, unlike the PCL-R or the VRAG, the HCR-20 makes use of items that examine dynamic risk factors that are amenable to change over time.

The HCR-20 has 10 items that measure historical, static risk factors; five items that measure current, dynamic, clinical factors; and five risk items to examine specifically how the person may react to a specific setting. The HCR-20 can be scored, and scores on the HCR-20 range from 0 to 40. The authors of the instrument recommend against using simple cutoff scores to determine if someone is at high or low risk. They emphasize that the instrument is designed as a guide for thinking about how to weight risk factors, rather than a formalized test. As such, they recommend using the instrument to make more general predictions of risk (high, moderate, or low) rather than simply relying on specific scores. Ratings of the individual risk factors identified on the HCR-20 are based on data collected during clinical interviews as well as collateral information from other data sources such as files.

Existing peer-reviewed data support the HCR-20's usefulness in risk prediction. Specifically, scores on the HCR-20 have been found to have modest but significant correlations with past violence (.44), with the VRAG (.54), and with violence observed in an inpatient setting (.30). HCR-20 scores have also been shown to be predictive of several measures of community violence, readmission to forensic hospitals, and subsequent psychiatric hospitalizations. Recent research has revealed that the HCR-20 is a better predictor of future violence than the PCL-R alone. Risk decisions made using the HCR-20 have been found to predictive of violent recidivism in prior samples.

Mr. McKay had several historical factors that may place him at risk for future violence. These include a history of previous violence beginning at a young age (as documented in file information, prior forensic reports, and by Mr. McKay himself), his history of poor juvenile adjustment, his history of schizophrenia (including paranoid delusions that have played a role in his prior acts of aggression), his prior supervision failures, his limited ability to form close relationships, his moderate PCL-R score, and his history of alcohol abuse. One possible historical protective factor for Mr. McKay is his demonstrated ability to do well in employment settings despite his mental illness.

The clinical scales suggest the presence of both risk and protective factors that might impact Mr. McKay's risk for reoffending. Mr. McKay has some insight into his problems and triggers for violence. He was able to recognize that his psychotic symptoms place him at risk, and taking medication is one means he can use to help keep himself under control. Similarly, he recognizes that he has displayed poor anger control in the past, and this is an area he needs to address. He has, however, been overly optimistic about his ability to control his temper. Even while medicated, he continues to experience paranoia—and his ability to use reality-testing skills to manage residual symptoms will be important to his ability to succeed in future placements. This is particularly true since his concerns about being "sexually harassed" by peers continue to make him irritable and aggressive.

Mr. McKay's psychotic symptoms generally appear to be well managed by antipsychotic medication. Mr. McKay has, however, had at least one recent episode of extreme paranoia and disorganization. During this episode, he became convinced that his assigned social worker had hired inmates from the unit to harass him in the shower and attack him. Mr. McKay responded by attempting to stab a peer with a pen. Mr. McKay was briefly disorganized and displayed signs of unusual ideation until his dose of antipsychotic medication was increased.

Mr. McKay has engaged in a variety of treatment programs that target his core risk factors, including anger management and Alcoholics Anonymous. He has been overtly compliant with treatment, and staff members have noted that he makes good contributions in groups. They have, however, questioned his motives for treatment or his ability to internalize the principles he needs to enact real change. To his credit, however, he seems to have remained sober on recent periods of supervised release.

Mr. McKay appears to do better in highly structured settings. Notes from a variety of treatment providers have indicated that he generally responds well to direction. They have also, however, noted that he can become irritable when challenged, and he has a habit of testing boundaries. His biggest clinical risk factor relates to antisocial attitudes. He has

a tendency to assume the worst about other people's motives, and he tends to see women in sexual terms. He seems to have embraced many attitudes that may be effective in correctional settings, but that may make adjustment in community settings more difficult (e.g., "don't trust people," "don't show signs of weakness," "don't back down from challenges," etc).

When assessing the risk management items for Mr. McKay, this writer considered how Mr. McKay would be likely to function in a community setting rather than in a secure hospital setting. Mr. McKay was well aware of the obstacles he is likely to face in transferring back to a community setting. He demonstrated a good understanding of the kinds of resources he will need in order to succeed, including mental health aftercare and psychiatric medication. He demonstrated a willingness to comply with follow-up treatment and he has followed through appropriately during prior periods of supervised release. He is also willing to be flexible about the location and placements to which he is willing to go. He suggested that he will probably do better if he can stay busy in the community; he indicated he would like to obtain a job, and he appears to have done well on job placements in the past.

Mr. McKay does, however, seem to have problems that will be difficult for most group homes to accommodate. He is a registered sex offender, which significantly limits the available placements to which he can go. His specific paranoid ideation regarding being sexually harassed by males means that he is likely to have conflicts anywhere he has a roommate. Finding a group home where he could have a single room could be difficult.

Mr. McKay is likely to experience significant destabilizing influences in the community. He is likely to have increased access to alcohol and weapons. This is of concern given his history of using a knife to threaten others, and reports from a prior community placement that he was suspected of trying to make a homemade knife. His sources of personal support are limited to family members who appear to have limited resources with which to aid him. He has also had significant conflicts with his family members in the past, and at least one of his brothers is incarcerated for serious crimes (rape and murder). He has few sources of social support, and his presentation is likely to make it difficult for him to make friends.

A potentially significant risk factor for Mr. McKay appears to be the stress he will be likely to experience in the community. Although he has responded well to antipsychotic medication, he continues to experience residual symptoms such as odd affect and paranoia. Paranoia has been a significant source of stress for Mr. McKay in the past. This stress is likely to be increased by the fact that his concerns about others "harassing" him are likely to be treated with suspicion by supervising staff and other people he wants to believe him. Being under stress is likely to increase Mr. McKay's conflict with peers and staff, thus putting him in danger of violating supervision rules in some way.

Mr. McKay's total score on the HCR-20 was 32. Based on the identified risk factors on the HCR-20, Mr. McKay appears to be at high risk to have some negative behavior within the next 12 months if he is released to a standard group home or halfway house. Based on his periods of prior supervision, these violations may be related to conflicts with peers rather than for overt criminal offenses. His recent assaultive behavior, however, suggests that he is also capable of engaging in violent behavior if his psychotic symptoms escalate.

It is worth noting that many of the factors placing Mr. McKay at risk for reoffending are static risk factors that will not change over time. He does, however, have significant dynamic risk factors that could likely be reduced through participation in specialized treatment and supervision. As noted previously, Mr. McKay has developed antisocial attitudes that may interfere with his adjustment in community settings. He may well benefit from programs that target criminal thinking. He has also admitted that he has a history of temper-control problems. Participation in further anger management programming may help him address his ongoing temper problems. He could also benefit from ongoing treatment to prevent relapse into alcohol abuse. Mr. McKay will certainly need to continue taking antipsychotic medication and will need routine follow-ups to insure that his dosages are sufficient to manage his symptoms. He may, however, also benefit from individual therapy designed to help improve his reality testing.

Based on his history, Mr. McKay appears to do better in highly supervised settings. Although he tends to test rule boundaries, he has traditionally responded well to direct orders and consistent limit setting. Due to the content of his delusional ideation, he is likely to have fewer conflicts in settings where he does not have a roommate and where he has access to a private bathroom. To the extent that Mr. McKay receives appropriate supervision, remains on medication, and chooses to make good use of mental health treatment, he will be more likely to succeed in a community placement.

The Static-99

The Static-99 was developed as an actuarial assessment to estimate risk to commit a future sexual offense within 15 years. The instrument contains ten items that have been consistently demonstrated in the research literature to be associated with higher rates of sexual reoffending in a variety of samples. Scores on this instrument range from 0–12, but scores above six do not seem to increase risk for sexual recidivism significantly. As such, scores of six or more are associated with the highest risk for sexual recidivism.

The Static-99 has been shown via peer-reviewed research to be a highly reliable measure. Higher scores on the instrument have consistently been found to be associated with higher rates of sexual recidivism in several samples. Despite this, some researchers have noted that it is difficult to predict a single individual's risk by comparing them to how groups of individuals did in the validation sample. The items making up the Static-99 are also static, unchanging risk factors. As such, the measure can not account for how protective factors or changes in dynamic risk factors may impact an individual's risk to commit a sexual offense. For these reasons, scores on the Static-99 should be treated as estimates with room for error rather than precise predictions of future sexual violence.

Mr. McKay's score on the Static-99 was 2. This score was due to Mr. McKay's history of no stable marital-like relationships and the fact that his prior victim was unrelated. Based on the sexual recidivism rates of individuals with this score in the previous samples, Mr. McKay's estimated risk for committing a sexual offense within fifteen years would low.

INTERVIEW IMPRESSIONS

Mr. McKay was interviewed by the risk assessment panel. He was oriented to person, place, time, and circumstances. He was polite, cooperative, and responsive to questions. His speech was stilted and repetitive, but coherent and on topic. He was not responsive to internal or fictional stimuli during the interview. During the interview, he displayed no overt delusional ideation. His observed affect was constricted, but anxious. He maintained appropriate eye contact. His concentration and attention appeared to be within normal limits. His memory appeared to be intact, judging by his ability to recall specific details from his prior incarcerations. No psycho-motor agitation or retardation was noted.

Mr. McKay indicated that he understood that the risk assessment panel was interviewing him to determine if he might be dangerous to others or the property of others due to a mental illness. He recognized that the risk assessment panel would make an initial determination as to whether or not he might be stable enough to return to the community.

Mr. McKay acknowledged that he had assaulted another patient recently. When asked about this, he said he did it because he was angry and upset. He admitted that he should not have hit a peer. He said he should have sought help from clinical staff instead. He noted that he has been doing better on an increased dose of anti-psychotic medication. He asserted that he would be "okay" in the future. He did, however, express an understanding of why staff may be uncomfortable discharging him to the community given his recent behavior.

DIAGNOSTIC IMPRESSION

Axis I: Schizophrenia, Paranoid Type
Axis II: Antisocial Personality Disorder

OPINIONS

It should be noted that the prediction of dangerousness is of limited accuracy at the time of formulation, and the accuracy of a prediction diminishes over time. In an effort to determine if Mr. McKay meets criteria for commitment pursuant to 18 USC 4243, the Risk Assessment Panel attempted to determine whether (1) Mr. McKay is presently suffering from a mental disease or defect, (2) his release would create a substantial risk of bodily injury to another person or serious damage to property of another, and (3) such risk would be due to a mental illness.

Does Mr. McKay presently have an identifiable disease or defect?

Mr. McKay has been diagnosed with schizophrenia (paranoid type). This diagnosis was based primarily on his history of disorganized behavior, auditory command hallucinations, flat affect, and unusual beliefs (such as the belief that he possesses supernatural powers, that others are sexually harassing him, and the like). He had a significant relapse of psychotic symptoms in July of 2005 during which he became paranoid, agitated, and violent. He has responded well to an increased dose of antipsychotic medication. He appears to be managing his symptoms better at the moment. He does, however, show some signs or residual paranoia, odd affect, and stilted speech.

Would Mr. McKay's release create a substantial risk of bodily injury to another person or serious damage to property of another?

The Risk Assessment Panel considered several factors that may impact Mr. McKay's ability to succeed upon release. Specific factors that were reviewed included his history of violence, his extensive mental health history, his current compliance with psychiatric medication, his recent institutional adjustment, his performance on prior conditional releases, his specific delusional ideation and its past impact on his behavior, his limited sources of social support, and his plans for returning to the community. The panel noted Mr. McKay's low Static-99 score, his moderate PCL-R score, his high VRAG score, and the various factors (both risk and protective) identified by the HCR-20. Mr. McKay's recent assaultive behavior was discussed at length.

Based on the available evidence, Mr. McKay's risk for sexual offending appears to be relatively low. He has only one documented sex offense in his records and there is no evidence that he has any sexually deviant interests. His score on the Static-99-R was low. He has not engaged in any sexually inappropriate behaviors in prison or hospital settings. He also has not committed any new sexual offenses during his periods of conditional release.

During the current assessment, Mr. McKay denied having any current plans or intentions to harm anyone. He presented as calm during the risk assessment interview. As such, he does not appear to be at significant risk for imminent violence. Based on the available information, however, Mr. McKay does appear to be at risk for engaging in some kind of future violence.

Mr. McKay has a well-documented history of aggression, but it has rarely risen to the point where he has been charged with a criminal offense. His two criminal offenses were, however, very serious (aggravated rape and threatening the President of the United States). A review of his records indicates that there are specific factors that appear to predict when Mr. McKay is most likely to be violent. These factors include using alcohol, not taking psychiatric medications, experiencing command hallucinations that instruct him to attack others, and having current delusional beliefs that others are trying to harm or harass him. The panel believes that Mr. McKay's risk for becoming violent and the risk for more severe violence would increase as these factors manifest. As such, the degree to which these risk factors can be explicitly addressed is likely to have a significant impact on Mr. McKay's risk for future violence.

Although Mr. McKay currently appears to be doing better, his recent assault on another patient was of great concern to the risk assessment panel. This assault was considered important because it was an episode of overt violence. It also occurred in a highly structured setting, and Mr. McKay put himself at risk for losing a conditional release by becoming violent. This suggests that Mr. McKay was unable to control his behavior or unwilling to, despite having a great deal to lose. The panel noted that Mr. McKay still has to work on controlling his impulsivity, managing his anger more effectively, having a higher tolerance for the discomfort caused by his delusional ideation, and improving his reality testing. To the extent that he can address these concerns, his ability to succeed in a community placement will increase dramatically.

Is Mr. McKay's risk for reoffense related to a mental illness?

A review of the records, as well as interviews with Mr. McKay, indicated that his behavior appears to be influenced by both antisocial attitudes and his mental illness. For example, Mr. McKay has negative attitudes towards women, he tends to test rule boundaries, and he does not back down from challenges. These kinds of attitudes do not appear to be related his mental illness, but they do make it harder for him back down from potential fights or develop empathy with others. Such beliefs appear to have played a significant role in the events leading up to Mr. McKay's aggravated rape charge.

He also, however, has mental health problems that limit his ability to manage his anger and make him prone to believe that others want to harm him. His delusional paranoid ideation clearly played a role in 1996 when he made threats against the President of the United States. It also appears to be a significant factor in his difficulties with peers whom he suspects of "harassing" him. It was

certainly a factor in the assault he committed in July of 2005. As noted previously, he appears to be at a higher risk for becoming aggressive when he is not taking medications, or when the medication he is taking is insufficient to address his psychotic symptoms. Therefore, the Risk Assessment Panel concluded that Mr. McKay's mental illness plays a role in his risk for violence, but it plays a larger role when he is untreated, undertreated, or off medications.

RECOMMENDATIONS

Mr. McKay has been diagnosed with a mental illness (schizophrenia) that has previously made him dangerous to others (or the property of others). The Risk Assessment Panel noted that Mr. McKay is currently stabilizing on medication and does not seem to be at risk for imminent violence. The panel also, however, expressed concerns about his recent relapse into paranoid delusional thinking during which he became assaultive. The panel noted that Mr. McKay has multiple risk factors that increase the risk for future problematic behaviors. They also considered his chronic difficulties in adjusting well in community placements.

After considering the relevant factors, the panel opined that Mr. McKay is not yet stable enough to release to the community. The panel expressed concern that his paranoia and delusional ideation would be likely to make him dangerous to others (or the property of others). They recommended that he be retained for inpatient treatment in a secure hospital setting for the time being. They noted that they expect his stability to improve, provided he remains compliant with treatment. Given the severity of the incident in July of 2005, however, the panel noted that they would not feel comfortable recommending a conditional release until Mr. McKay can demonstrate an extended period of behavioral and mental stability.

Chad Brinkley, Ph.D.   David F. Mrad, Ph.D.

TEACHING POINT:
INTEGRATING INFORMATION FROM HOSPITALIZATION AND PRE-HOSPITALIZATION IN RELEASE DECISION-MAKING

The influence of situation on human behavior is given insufficient attention in some assessments of hospitalization release. A hospital is an artificial environment—more structured, highly monitored, intensively resourced, and more restrictive than almost any community environment imaginable. But almost invariably, the behavior resulting in hospitalization occurred in the community, and the individual will be discharged to an environment closer to the original community setting than to the hospital from which he will be discharged. Accordingly, the focus of the anticipated interventions, stresses, and supports should be the community setting to which his discharge is proposed. Whether the individual has reached "maximum benefit of hospitalization" has little relevance in such decisions. If the evidence shows that the individual is likely to adjust favorably, and public safety considerations are addressed, then that person is a good candidate for discharge. If that is not the case, then whether they would continue to benefit from hospitalization is not the point; whether and how they can reach the status described in the previous sentence should be the focus of the discussion.

It is useful, accordingly, to combine information obtained from hospitalization with that covering the person's pre-hospitalization history. The right kind of hospital information is valuable. Among other things, being hospitalized allows the individual to be more closely observed, more intensively treated, and more fully participatory in graduated release. This is sometimes useful in ruling *out* a recommendation for release, as individuals who are significantly violent or otherwise antisocial in a secure hospital environment are not good candidates for discretionary release. But hospital information is insufficient to rule *in* a good candidate for release. For this, the forensic clinician must consider the pre-hospitalization environment and behavior as well as the proposed plan of discharge. Using a measure such as the HCR-20 facilitates this consideration—the "R" (risk management) section focuses on the environment to which the individual will return and the potentially destabilizing influences associated with it.

CASE TWO
PRINCIPLE: USE MULTIPLE SOURCES OF INFORMATION FOR EACH AREA BEING ASSESSED (*PRINCIPLE 17*)

This principle was discussed in Chapter 12 (this volume), so we will move directly to showing how the present report illustrates the application of this principle. In the present report, the evaluator relied on a wide range of information, including interview with the defendant, psychological testing (for risk assessment purposes), and a review of various records (e.g., psychiatric, neuropsychological, medical, forensic, and criminal justice). There was also a review of behavioral observations of this individual, both prior to and during hospitalization. Using multiple sources of information enables the evaluator to corroborate information, generate and test rival hypotheses relating to the relevant functional-legal criteria, and measure relevant clinical functioning in a more robust way. In this case, for example, Dr. Lareau used several measures to assess Mr. Johnson's risk of future violence—including two risk assessment measures (HCR-20 and START) and a measure of psychopathy—and effectively combined the data obtained from these measures in reaching his conclusion about Mr. Johnson's risk.

FORENSIC PSYCHOLOGY CONSULTATION

REASON FOR REFERRAL/ASSESSMENT

Mr. Darren Johnson was referred for a forensic psychology consultation by his treatment team at the current state hospital (CSH) to determine his level of violence risk and whether he is appropriate for release to a less restrictive setting through the conditional release program (CONREP). The patient has filed a writ for restoration of sanity pursuant to California Penal Code § 1026.2.[1]

IDENTIFYING INFORMATION

Darren Johnson (a.k.a. "Michael Andrews") is a 39-year-old single African-American male committed by the Superior Court of Los Angeles County. He was remanded to the California Department of Mental Health and admitted to former state hospital (FSH) on 12/12/08 pursuant to Penal Code

---

[1] The legal standard set forth in Penal Code § 1026.2 states, "whether the person…would be a danger to the health and safety of others, due to mental defect, disease, or disorder, if under supervision and treatment in the community." The term "restoration of sanity" is a legal term of art.

§ 1026 as not guilty by reason of insanity (NGRI). Mr. Johnson was transferred from FSH to CSH on 8/14/11. His maximum term of commitment is Life. Mr. Johnson's commitment offense was Penal Code § 187(a), murder. The commitment offense took place on 1/12/04. Mr. Johnson, while allegedly psychotic due to a binge on methamphetamines, stabbed his live-in girlfriend to death with a steak knife. He also attempted to kill himself using the same knife.

EVALUATION PROCEDURES AND DATES

Mr. Johnson was interviewed for this evaluation for three hours on 10/16/12. In addition to the clinical interview, the following psychological assessment instruments were administered and scored:

Hare Psychopathy Checklist–Revised-2nd Edition (PCL-R)
Historical-Clinical-Risk Management-20 (HCR-20)
Short-Term Assessment of Risk and Treatability (START)

Also, the following information was reviewed from Mr. Johnson's records:

CSH Psychiatry Monthly Progress Notes
CSH Psychosocial Assessment Update dated 10/18/12
CSH Penal Code § 1026 Court Reports dated 3/22/12 and 10/13/12
Los Angeles County CONREP Hospital Liaison Report dated 7/12/12
CSH Integrated Psychology Assessment dated 10/14/11
CSH Initial Psychosocial Assessment dated 10/13/11
FSH Neuropsychological Evaluation by Neuropsychologist, Ph.D., dated 4/25/10
Los Angeles County Jail Medical and Mental Health Records from 1/04 to 11/08
NGRI Evaluation by Psychiatrist One, M.D., dated 8/19/07
NGRI Evaluation by Psychologist One, Ph.D., dated 3/15/07
NGRI Evaluation by Psychologist Two, Ph.D., dated 2/11/07
Los Angeles County Coroner's Report by Coroner, M.D., dated 2/12/04

Los Angeles Hospital Medical Records, discharge date 1/29/04
Criminal History Report (CLETS) Generated on 1/17/04
Los Angeles County Sheriff's Department Supplemental Report by Deputy Law dated 1/13/04
Los Angeles County Sheriff's Department Supplemental Report by Deputy Justice dated 1/12/04
Los Angeles County Sheriff's Department Initial Crime Report by Deputy Law dated 1/12/04

Prior to beginning the interviews, Mr. Johnson was notified about the purpose of the evaluation and the associated limits on confidentiality. He appeared to understand the basic aspects of this notification, repeating back the essential parts that he would be evaluated, that a written report would be generated, and that the conclusions of the report could affect the decision regarding his readiness for release.

RELEVANT HISTORY

Child and Family History

Darren Johnson (a.k.a. Michael Andrews) is a 39-year-old (DOB: 7/14/73) single African-American male born in Mobile, Alabama. He is the youngest of three surviving children, with two older brothers. He had a sister pass away as an infant. Both of his parents are alive, and they have remained married. His father worked for the county as a wood shop teacher in middle school, and his mother remained at home. He described his father as the disciplinarian in the family. The family had a lower-middle-class standard of living, with adequate support. He has stated there was domestic abuse in the family home, with his father beating his mother, especially when he had been drinking. He reported also having been physically abused by his father. Mr. Johnson came to California when he was 16 years old, three years after a significant head injury in an accident. He has a brother in Los Angeles, while the rest of his family lives in Alabama.

Education History

Mr. Johnson reported that he attended school through the ninth grade in Alabama, at which time he came to California. He stated he had low average grades in his schooling, but did not attend any type of remedial or special education training. He reported problems both behaviorally and academically following his head injury at age 13, including getting expelled from two schools for fighting and disrespecting his teachers. He quit school at age 16 and moved to Los Angeles to live with his older brother. He had no other formal education.

Employment History

Mr. Johnson stated in a CSH Initial Psychosocial Assessment that before moving to California, he worked delivering newspapers. He also reported working as a gardener and in different construction jobs. He further described having worked as a limousine driver. In the interview, he stated he has worked about four years in landscaping, and he has held different construction jobs. He also stated he worked for two years in an automobile detailing business with his brother. He commented that when working in construction he made between $3,000 and $4,000 per month. Mr. Johnson said that he also made money selling illegal drugs.

Medical/Trauma History

Chart information suggests a motor vehicle accident at age 13 that resulted in a serious head injury with loss of consciousness, for which he was hospitalized for nearly two weeks. His mother has reported that he was unconscious for "six or seven days," and when he regained consciousness she noticed alterations in behavior. Initially he did not recognize family members and became confused. He demonstrated concentration and memory problems, and soon thereafter he performed very poorly in school. A number of records suggest significant alteration in his personality, with an increase in anger and aggressiveness following the head injury. He reported additional head injuries as well, including a motorcycle accident at age 18, getting hit in the head with a pipe during a fight at age 23, and another period of unconsciousness following a car accident at age 26. In the instant offense he suffered from self-inflicted, multiple stab wounds to the throat, chest, abdomen, and arms. During his medical hospitalization, he was maintained on a tracheotomy. Presently he is diagnosed with diabetes mellitus, hypertension, and hyperlipidemia.

Criminal History

According to the CSH Initial Psychosocial Assessment (10/13/11), shortly after his head injury at the age of 13, Mr. Johnson got into numerous fights at school, and he began engaging in criminal activities, including theft and destruction of property, although he was not arrested for those offenses. Due to his problems in Alabama, at the age of 16 Mr. Johnson moved to California to live with his brother. Although his juvenile history was not available for review for this evaluation, in the initial psychosocial assessment he endorsed having been found delinquent for robbery and later for DUI. Mr. Johnson's criminal history includes numerous arrests and convictions for various types of crimes. His adult history includes the following:

- NGRI for murder (offense in 2004, NGRI in 2008)
- Conviction for domestic violence (2003)
- Conviction for robbery (1999)
- Four convictions for auto theft (1992; 1994; 1997; 2001)
- Conviction for possession of stolen property (1997)
- Conviction for possession of cocaine for sale (1993)
- Conviction for possession of cocaine (1998)
- Conviction for DUI (1996)
- Conviction for false information to police (1996)
- Arrest for possession of cocaine (1994)
- Arrest for DUI (1995)
- Arrest for reckless driving (1996)
- Arrest for public intoxication (1993)

For the instant offense (described more fully below), he killed his girlfriend by stabbing her numerous times with a steak knife, and then mutilated her corpse. Four years later he was found not guilty by reason of insanity.

Substance Abuse History

During the interview for this evaluation, Mr. Johnson endorsed a history of significant substance abuse. He began alcohol abuse by age 12, drinking shots of rum and vodka, and shortly thereafter he was drinking alcohol multiple times each week to the point of intoxication. When he came to California, his alcohol abuse accelerated, with binge drinking described by late adolescence. He began marijuana abuse somewhere between ages 10 and 13, smoking about twice per week, which increased to daily abuse when he moved from Alabama. He began to abuse cocaine by age 17. He reported having stopped using marijuana around age 24, which was when he began to abuse methamphetamines, describing daily use of cocaine and methamphetamines. He admitted to binging on cocaine and methamphetamines for several days at a time. Once he began use of methamphetamines, it quickly became his drug of choice. He had multiple methamphetamine binges lasting several days. During those periods of abuse he experienced notable weight loss and increased anxiety.

Psychiatric History

There is little corroborative evidence of psychiatric history or problems prior to the instant offense, despite some records where there are reports of a vague history of prior psychiatric symptoms and treatment. For instance, during an insanity evaluation with Psychiatrist One in 2007, Mr. Johnson's family had described the presence of vague psychotic symptoms as an adolescent. The same report noted the presence of some paranoia prior to the crime, but the paranoia was most notable when he was abusing methamphetamines.

Also in that 2007 psychiatric evaluation report, Mr. Johnson endorsed having experienced years of psychotic symptoms, both before and after the crime, including auditory hallucinations, visual hallucinations, ideas of references, and paranoid delusions. Based upon his report of symptoms, he was prescribed both antidepressant and antipsychotic medications in the jail, but he did not continue to take them regularly. Notably, there was no corroboration of any psychotic symptoms reported in observations in the jail mental health records.

Despite Mr. Johnson's having described experiencing nearly constant auditory hallucinations and other psychotic symptoms in the absence of any substance abuse during his time in jail,

in a neuropsychological assessment from 2010, Mr. Johnson denied ever having any psychotic symptoms. In that report, it noted that his admission to FSH was his first psychiatric hospitalization.

In two separate insanity evaluation reports completed by psychologists in 2007, Mr. Johnson was administered intelligence tests. In both, his scores for full-scale IQ were between 60 and 65, with no appreciable differences noted between Verbal and Performance scores. In neither evaluation was there any effort testing administered; he was assumed to be putting forth a full effort. Subsequently, during his hospitalizations, there has been no evidence of significant intellectual deficits noted in the records. During a neuropsychological evaluation in 2010, the evaluator did not find evidence of any intellectual deficits.

Hospital Course

Mr. Johnson was admitted to FSH in 12/08, almost five years after his commitment offense in 1/04. What is most notable during his present course of hospitalization is the dramatic difference in Mr. Johnson's reported symptoms during his hospitalization when juxtaposed with his alleged symptoms during his years of incarceration prior to the evaluations for his NGRI defense. When Mr. Johnson was being evaluated for his NGRI defense by different evaluators, he reported experiencing ongoing psychotic symptoms that had existed prior to the murder. That is, despite not having access to illicit substances that could account for the presence of psychotic symptoms, Mr. Johnson continued to report daily psychotic symptoms, which evaluators concluded to be evidence of the presence of a psychotic disorder.

Since the start of his hospitalization, and continuing to the present time, Mr. Johnson reports to

---

COMMENT: WHY WOULDN'T MR. JOHNSON'S MENTAL HEALTH SYMPTOMS BE OBSERVED BY THE EVALUATOR OVER THE COURSE OF HIS TIME SPENT IN A FACILITY FOR THE EVALUATION?

In California, all criminal responsibility evaluations are completed by "alienists," who are psychiatrists and psychologists in the community, either court-appointed or retained by a party in the case. Defendants are not evaluated at a centralized forensic facility, such as in Michigan or in the federal prison system, where the defendants can be observed and evaluated over an extended period of time.

The honesty of his report of prior psychotic symptoms is important for two reasons: (1) it suggests that psychosis may not be a relevant consideration in his violence risk; and (2) it provides information about pathological lying and conning and being manipulative for purposes of scoring the PCL-R-2nd Edition.

not be experiencing any psychotic symptoms, and presently he is not prescribed any antipsychotic medications.

A neuropsychological assessment from 2010 described Mr. Johnson's functioning at that time. It quoted a March 2010 treatment plan that stated, "Mr. Johnson continues to report no psychiatric symptoms, such as auditory or visual hallucinations. He denies having heard voices. It appears that whatever psychotic symptoms were present were as the result of substance use. No problems with sleep or other symptoms." The report also noted recent behavioral problems, including curfew and contraband violations. On 2/1/10, he was found in possession of a cellphone, and he was under investigation for the incident. Ultimately the incident resulted in the discovery of an inappropriate relationship with a female nurse who had provided him with the cellphone. She ended up losing her job over her relationship with Mr. Johnson.

In a hospital report to the court from October 2012, it states that since Mr. Johnson's admission to CSH in September 2011, "he has been involved in strong-arming vulnerable patients (those with cognitive disabilities such as mental retardation) for their canteen [ration], as well as using patients to run errands and do his bidding in illegal trading of contraband. He was observed filling out a peer's canteen list and taking the peer's food when it came. Mr. Johnson also took quarters from that individual." Regarding other behaviors, the report continued, "A tattoo kit was found in his room. Staff suspected that he had access to black market items (contraband) and was involved in selling and controlling the distribution of contraband goods on the unit and on grounds. Although confronted and reprimanded by staff, he refused to stop engaging in these antisocial behaviors."

At the time of the October 2012 report, Mr. Johnson was denying having a mental illness, and was displaying no evidence of positive or negative symptoms of psychosis. He displayed euthymic

mood and a full range of affect. Mr. Johnson was considered a high risk for illegal substance use due to both a history of substance use disorder and antisocial personality disorder. He has undergone substance abuse treatment in the hospital, and accepted that he has a substance abuse problem. Although acknowledging an extensive history of drug use, he clarified he has not used drugs in more than eight years. He placed responsibility for his crime on his substance use.

In a psychosocial assessment update from 10/12, Mr. Johnson acknowledged that he continues to receive phone calls from the former female nurse from FSH. He speaks to her frequently, especially before and after his treatment conferences where they decide about making recommendations for release. Thus, it is important to note that he is privy to counsel from a former state hospital staff member about how to act, how to speak, and what to say to appear appropriate for release from a state hospital. He had been told that he needed to stop this relationship, but he reported not understanding why the relationship was inappropriate. He added the former FSH employee "has gotten to know his family and she has developed a relationship with them. Mr. Johnson stated that he would discontinue the relationship" (CSH Psychosocial Assessment Update, 10/18/12). However, to date he has not done so.

During his hospitalization, Mr. Johnson had not committed any acts of violence. He was described in the psychosocial update as "charming, deferential towards staff and eager to please. The veracity of his demeanor is dubious given that this behavioral style is characteristic of individuals diagnosed with Antisocial Personality Disorder" (CSH Penal Code § 1026 Court Report, 10/13/12).

COMMITMENT OFFENSE

The commitment offense occurred on 1/12/04. According to a Los Angeles County Sheriff's

Department Initial Crime Report (1/12/04), Mr. Johnson assaulted his girlfriend, stabbing her to death with dozens of stab wounds. He also mutilated her body by cutting off her thumbs (it is not known whether this occurred before or after her death). He wrote something illegible in her blood on the wall, and then he cut his own throat and abdomen. Mr. Johnson had a history of domestic violence against his girlfriend (who was the mother of his child). The victim's five-year-old daughter found the crime scene and called a maternal uncle. She reported that her mother "was asleep" and covered with blood and could not wake up. She said that her mother's hand was cut and the defendant had cuts on his throat and abdomen. The victim's mother and uncle reported to the scene, where they saw the victim lying dead in the bed. The defendant was allegedly bleeding profusely from self-inflicted wounds to his throat and abdomen. The family was able to remove the victim's daughters (one and five years old) from the crime scene.

When the police arrived they noted that the defendant was wounded but semi-coherent, presumably due to loss of blood. He was transported to a medical facility for emergency care. When police searched the apartment they found methamphetamines and a rolled dollar bill used to inhale the drug. A drug screen at the hospital was positive for methamphetamines. Police spoke with neighbors, who noted the defendant had a history of polysubstance abuse, but none observed significant drug use prior to the murder.

Mr. Johnson was hospitalized for 17 days before being cleared for admission to jail. His medical release records note he admitted stabbing both himself and his girlfriend.

According to all three insanity evaluation reports, three years after the offense, Mr. Johnson reported having no recollection of the events leading up to the victim's death. He claimed to have been very intoxicated at the time of the offense, but could recall neither which drugs he had used nor how much he had used. He described a problematic relationship with the victim. He stated she was quite jealous, and she feared he was involved in other relationships. In the report by Psychologist One (3/15/07), he admitted to many instances of domestic violence, which he considered to be "mutual combat," often initiated by the victim due to her jealousy. He admitted to two instances of incarceration prior to the instant offense, both as a result of domestic violence against his partner.

Another report (Psychologist Two, 2/11/07) indicated that Mr. Johnson was jealous of his girlfriend, believing she was cheating on him. In two instances when this occurred (February 2002 and early November 2003), he physically attacked her. By the time of the August 2007 evaluation by Psychiatrist One, Mr. Johnson had recalled a history of "disembodied voices," i.e., auditory hallucinations, which reportedly had been present for many years. He was clear that the voices did not tell him to harm anyone, but would tell him to watch for others who wanted to harm him, including believing his girlfriend wanted to harm him.

INTERVIEW BEHAVIOR AND APPEARANCE

Mr. Johnson is a 39-year-old African-American male of average height and build. He presented as exceptionally well-groomed, with a neat goatee, fashionable white Kangol hat, expensive sunglasses, clean clothes, and new sneakers. He willingly participated in the interview. Mr. Johnson appeared notably calm and relaxed throughout the interview; his posture was slouched in his chair, and his infrequent movements were smooth and deliberate. What was most noticeable during the evaluation was his level of confidence and ease, coupled with apparently average cognitive abilities (his scores on intellectual tests during his evaluations in 2007 suggested severe intellectual limitations). He also reported that he believes staff members are jealous of him, due to his looks and how "stable" he is, noting he is "respectful and athletic." He appeared proud when discussing how a female staff from FSH became attracted to him, noting she wanted him sexually.

Mental Status Examination

Mr. Johnson was alert and oriented in all spheres. Eye contact remained good throughout the interview. His speech was normal in rate, rhythm, and volume. There was no evidence of a formal thought disorder. He denied experiencing hallucinations of any type, and attributed his alleged psychotic symptoms during the crime to his drug use. He denied experiencing any beliefs of a delusional nature. He denied experiencing suicidal or homicidal ideation. His affect was full in range and appropriate to content of speech. Intellectual functioning was not formally assessed but is estimated to be in the Low Average to Average range. His memory appeared to be grossly intact, with no obvious deficits in immediate, short-term, or long-term recall. Judgment appears slightly impaired, compromised by overconfidence.

DIAGNOSIS

Mr. Johnson's current mental status and reported history of compromised psychological functioning related to methamphetamine abuse suggests the following diagnosis:

> Axis I: 292.11 Amphetamine-Induced Psychotic Disorder with Delusions, with Onset During Intoxication
> V65.2 Malingering (by history)
> 305.70 Amphetamine Abuse
> 305.00 Alcohol Abuse
> 305.60 Cocaine Abuse
> 305.20 Cannabis Abuse
> Axis II: 301.7 Antisocial Personality Disorder
> Axis III: Diabetes Mellitus; Hypertension; Hyperlipidemia
> Axis IV: Problems related to interaction with legal system/Incarceration
> Axis V: GAF (Current)—60

The Axis I diagnostic presentation of this man is problematic. The various records, reports, self-report, and present functioning require diagnostic compromise, as the available information cannot be diagnostically reconciled. According to the insanity evaluation report by Psychiatrist One (8/19/07), Mr. Johnson has endorsed significant psychotic symptoms for years prior to the offense. In all three NGRI evaluations in 2007, which took place more than three years after the offense, Mr. Johnson complained of experiencing ongoing symptoms of psychosis on a daily basis. If this were true, it would suggest either permanent psychosis secondary to methamphetamine-related brain damage, or a chronic psychotic disorder, and the ongoing symptoms would negate the possibility of a diagnosis of a transient substance-induced psychotic disorder. The following information is from the criminal responsibility evaluation from Psychiatrist One, M.D., dated 8/19/07:

> I am of the opinion that Mr. Darrin [*sic*] Johnson was experiencing psychotic symptoms during the time around the instant offense. The defendant's psychosis was associated with a Psychotic Disorder that did not primarily originate with the use of amphetamine shortly before the instant offense. Rather, the available evidence indicates that Mr. Daren [*sic*] Johnson began to experience psychotic symptoms sometime after the defendant's head injury, but before he arrived in California. The available evidence also indicates that the defendant has continued to suffer from psychotic symptoms long (i.e., several years) after the instant offense and years after discontinuing amphetamine or other illicit drugs. However, I am also of the opinion that amphetamine use had an important role in the exacerbation of the defendant's psychosis during and around the time of the instant offense. I am of the opinion that the most psychiatrically-legally relevant of the defendant's symptoms were his paranoid delusional thinking and auditory hallucinations (emphasis in original).

Despite his comments to the evaluators in 2007, in a neuropsychological evaluation from 2010, Mr. Johnson reported having experienced psychotic symptoms only associated with binging on methamphetamines during the time just prior to killing his girlfriend; this would suggest a substance-induced psychotic disorder diagnosis. Both at the time of the 2010 evaluation and continuing through this assessment, Mr. Johnson reported experiencing no ongoing psychotic symptoms, and stated that he has never experienced psychotic symptoms when not using substances, which includes the years he was in jail after the offense. These statements cannot be reconciled with his earlier reports of ongoing psychotic symptoms from prior to the crime until at least 2007. Presently Mr. Johnson is not prescribed antipsychotic medication, and he continues to report being free of any psychotic symptoms. His present functioning suggests that if Mr. Johnson has ever had psychotic symptoms, they probably were substance-induced. What is less clear is whether he experienced the psychotic symptoms he complained of at the time of the crime.

The multiple substance abuse diagnoses simply record what Mr. Johnson has described about his severe substance abuse with multiple difference substances. The information is not available to diagnose dependence on any of the substances individually or as a group.

Malingering has been diagnosed because it appears that Mr. Johnson intentionally produced the false symptoms of intellectual deficits repeatedly during psychological testing in 2007, to the point where his scores suggested mild mental retardation, which is in contrast to his average performance on similar testing in 2010. Furthermore, for years he endorsed symptoms of a psychotic illness while in jail awaiting his trial, but after the trial and hospitalization, his symptoms not only have disappeared, but also he denies having ever experienced those symptoms. For these reasons it appears probable that Mr. Johnson has malingered both psychotic and cognitive symptoms to benefit him in his legal proceedings.

Mr. Johnson's pre- and post-conviction behaviors suggest the presence of antisocial personality disorder. He had engaged in behavior consistent with evidence of conduct disorder prior to the age of 15, in that he frequently got into fights, was expelled from two schools, and admitted to both property destruction and theft. As an adult, Mr. Johnson has evidenced a pervasive disregard for and violation of the rights of others in multiple domains, including domestic violence, robbery, property crimes, and driving while intoxicated, while more recently engaging in strong-arming of low-functioning patients, repeated rules violations, and possession of contraband.

PSYCHOLOGICAL TESTING

Mr. Johnson was administered three instruments relevant to violence risk: the Psychopathy Checklist–Revised, 2nd Edition; the Historical, Clinical, Risk Management-20; and the Short-term Assessment of Risk and Treatability. Each will be discussed in turn.

Psychopathy Checklist–Revised, 2nd Edition (PCL-R)

Mr. Johnson's history and information were used to rate him on the PCL-R, a psychological testing instrument used to rate a person on the construct of psychopathy. The instrument allows for scores ranging from "0," which is the complete absence of any signs of psychopathic traits (and which virtually nobody ever scores), to "40," which is consistent with severe psychopathy. Total scores above 30 are generally consistent with "severe" psychopathy. Severe psychopaths rate high in two general areas

of pathology. The first area is defective interpersonal and affective traits, and the second is antisocial behaviors. A severe psychopath is a problematic and dangerous individual. Interpersonally, psychopaths are grandiose, egocentric, manipulative, dominant, forceful, and cold-hearted. Affectively they display shallow and labile emotions; cannot form long-lasting bonds to people, principles, or goals; and lack empathy, anxiety, and genuine guilt or remorse. Behaviorally, psychopaths are impulsive and sensation-seeking and tend to violate social norms, the most obvious expressions of which involve criminality, substance abuse, and a failure to fulfill social obligations and responsibilities. These individuals tend to victimize others without regard for the others' welfare, and are expert liars. Psychopaths are likely to recidivate with their criminal behaviors, and severe psychopathy is a robust risk factor for violence of all types.

Mr. Johnson's overall score was 33 (out of a possible 40), which places him in the very high range for the overall construct of psychopathy, and is consistent with the classification of a psychopath (which generally is given with scores over 30). His score of 33 places him in the 97th percentile when compared to other male forensic patients. The overall psychopathy score is comprised of two separate "factor" scores. Factor 1 represents deviant interpersonal and affective traits, while Factor 2 represents a deviant lifestyle and antisocial behaviors. Mr. Johnson's score on Factor 1 was 15, which places him at the 99th percentile when compared to male forensic patients. Mr. Johnson's Factor 1 score is in the very high range for deviant interpersonal and affective traits, and is suggestive of psychopathy. His score on Factor 2 was 18, which places him at the 97th percentile of male forensic patients. His Factor 2 score also is in the very high range, and is consistent with psychopathic behaviors.

In summary, Mr. Johnson's scores on the PCL-R are very high and are consistent with the personality construct of psychopathy.

Historical, Clinical, Risk Management-20 (HCR-20)

The HCR-20 is a structured professional judgment risk assessment guide that helps evaluators focus on risk-relevant factors when performing a violence risk assessment on an individual patient. The tool includes 10 historical items, 5 clinical items, and 5 risk management items to assist the evaluator who is performing the evaluation. The tool is not "scored" *per se*, but rather risk-relevant items are noted as "present," "partially present," or "absent." On the HCR-20, most historical risk items are present for Mr. Johnson, including previous violence, relationship instability, substance use problems, psychopathy, and personality disorder. Similarly, some clinical items are present, including impulsivity and unresponsiveness to treatment. As for risk management items, some items include plans lacking feasibility and likely exposure to destabilizers. Given the severity of the items that are present in Mr. Johnson, the overall "Final Risk Judgment," assuming Mr. Johnson was in the community through the conditional release program, is rated as "High."

Short-Term Assessment of Risk and Treatability (START)

The START is a newer structured professional judgment tool that looks at short-term risk for violence, self-harm, and suicide, among other things. The tool includes 20 items that can be rated as either a strength (potentially lowering risk) or a vulnerability (potentially raising risk). The purpose of the tool is to allow an individualized assessment of short-term risk while being able to capitalize on potential strengths present in the patient. Analysis of Mr. Johnson's strengths reveal potential protective factors related to: social skills, recreational activities, self-care, present mental state, and social support. Vulnerabilities include: relationships, substance use, impulse control, external triggers, material resources, attitudes, rule adherence, conduct, insight, plans, and treatability. Overall he is estimated to be at a moderate risk for short-term violence (i.e., over the next three months) towards others.

The risk formulation using the START suggests, based on Mr. Johnson's prior conduct, that he is an inherently impulsive and self-focused

individual with little tolerance for those who do not value his needs over their own. Generally in a supervised environment he can avoid overt violence, but his manipulativeness and disrespect for the needs of others result in his compromising their well-being for his own. When substance use further degrades his impulse control, he can become more openly aggressive and violent. Due to his grandiose plans and relative lack of insight, he is likely to become frustrated, but he is apt to blame his failures on others rather than accept responsibility. As this continues, he can become more volatile with an increased risk for engaging in targeted violence, especially when under the influence of substances.

VIOLENCE RISK ANALYSIS

The primary purpose of this evaluation is to assess Mr. Johnson to determine whether he would be a danger to the health and safety of others while under supervision and treatment in the community through CONREP. He has filed a writ for restoration of sanity, and if successful he would be sent to supervised release in the community. It is concluded that Mr. Johnson is not appropriate for release to a less restrictive setting; that is, he would be a danger to the health and safety of others if under supervision and treatment in the community. This conclusion is based in large part upon four factors: (1) Mr. Johnson continues to suffer from severe personality pathology; (2) he has routinely engaged in rules violations; (3) he remains dishonest with staff; and (4) he has not substantially benefitted from treatment for his primary risk issues.

Mr. Johnson Continues to Suffer from Severe Personality Pathology

Mr. Johnson has a lengthy criminal history involving acts demonstrating a pervasive disregard for the rights of others. In addition to the committing

---

COMMENT

The testing suggests somebody who is at an elevated risk for being violent. However, how does one reconcile the information that he has not been violent during his hospitalization? Considerations include: (1) the highly structured setting of the hospital limits his violent tendencies; (2) his affective violence is facilitated by substance abuse; and (3) his violence that is instrumental is within his control.

offense of murder, he has had criminal involvement in domestic violence, robbery, auto theft, reckless driving, selling cocaine, possession of cocaine, public intoxication, DUI, giving false information to a police officer, and a probation violation. His behaviors suggest that Mr. Johnson focuses only on what he wants and what is in his best interests at the time, while disregarding the welfare of others in his pursuit of those goals. This characterological deficit is seen most readily in his diagnosis of antisocial personality disorder, and his very high score on the PCL-R, suggesting severe psychopathy. In addition, Mr. Johnson's violence risk is increased through his impulsivity and affective instability, which he has demonstrated in the context of relationships. He is easily angered and can behave impulsively and violently, especially when abusing substances.

Prior to the murder of his girlfriend, Mr. Johnson had multiple arguments and disputes with her, including a recent domestic violence charge against him. He has stated that the reason that he killed her was that at the time he believed she was trying to harm him. However, the horrific nature of her injuries, coupled with his own attempted suicide, suggests that the killing probably was not in self-defense, but rather in the context of a violent and impulsive fight, most likely fueled through substance abuse and intoxication. This appears to be more a combination of uncontrolled anger, substance abuse, and a severe personality disorder than behavior affected by a psychotic thought process. That he attempted suicide after her murder not only suggests that he knew his behavior was wrong, but also that he is impulsive and emotionally labile, especially when under the influence of substances.

Since the crime, Mr. Johnson has been able to control most of his angry outbursts in the context of a highly structured and supervised setting. Clearly substance abuse reduces his ability to control his behaviors, and there is no indication he has

used substances since the crime. That notwithstanding, there continues to be evidence of a pervasive disregard for the rights of others, including how he had used the FSH nurse both for her cellphone and then for her knowledge about how to appear appropriate for conditional release. It did not matter to him that she lost her job because of how she broke rules for him, and he currently has another girlfriend at CSH while the nurse waits for his potential release. He has been known to be active with illegal contraband trading and sales on the compound; he has been seen strong-arming and manipulating lower-functioning patients; and he has been found in possession of contraband goods. If he is released, there is reason to believe that Mr. Johnson will probably continue to manipulate, deceive, and capitalize on the weaknesses of others. When those things do not work, he may use whatever force is necessary to get his needs met, especially if he returns to abusing substances.

Mr. Johnson Has Routinely Engaged in Rules Violations

Successful transition into supervised treatment in the community requires vigilance in adhering to the treatment program's requirements and rules. While at CSH and previously at FSH, Mr. Johnson has demonstrated that he will follow only those rules that he wants to follow, which are those it is in his best interest to follow. Generally speaking, Mr. Johnson realizes that he cannot cause too much trouble, lest he risk significant opposition to his petition to be released. If one truly were dedicated to successful transition into the community, it would be expected that one would scrupulously follow all rules and requirements prior to that transition. Mr. Johnson has not done so. Capitalizing on relatively lax supervision at times, he has helped himself to the benefits of illegal contraband trading and taking advantage of more vulnerable peers.

COMMENT

Violence-risk research literature has consistently shown that psychopathy can substantially increase risk for committing interpersonal violence. In this particular patient, given his domestic violence history and his pervasive disrespect for others, it appears likely that psychopathy may be a primary risk factor for violence.

With his impressive charm and interpersonally facile style, he is able to deflect most responsibility from himself so that he does not face the consequences of his rule-breaking behaviors. It is a testament to his impressive psychopathic charms that he has caused a former FSH employee to not only lose her job because of a relationship with him, but to continue to pine for him after leaving her state employment. She is useful to him. That he is able to convince staff and evaluators that he is doing well and is approaching readiness to leave suggests that he is accomplished in presenting only the façade that he wants others to see. He is quite cautious with his impression management, and he handles it artfully.

Mr. Johnson Remains Dishonest with Staff

Another positive marker for successful community transition is a willingness to be candid and truthful, even in the face of potential negative consequences. However, the available evidence regarding Mr. Johnson shows a pattern of deceitfulness over a period of many years. When he was speaking to evaluators about the crime while he was in jail, he told them about a long standing problem with psychotic symptoms that exacerbated near the time of the crime due to methamphetamine binging. However, once successful in avoiding criminal responsibility for the crime, Mr. Johnson changed his story to the point that he now variably reports never having had any psychotic symptoms, or having had symptoms due to methamphetamines only at the time of the crime. He does not account for his different story that assisted him with his NGRI defense. Also, Mr. Johnson has not been candid during psychological testing for intellectual abilities and limitations. His scores have placed him squarely in the mildly mentally retarded range of functioning, but his actual day-to-day functioning belies those scores. It appears that he believed it useful for others to think he was intellectually limited, and he perpetuated that ruse to his benefit over several years.

During the present interview for this evaluation, Mr. Johnson told implausible stories about how he came into possession of the cellphone at FSH. He stated he did nothing to encourage the female nurse, and that she essentially threw herself at him in trying to win his affections. He remarked that she had some psychological difficulties, and

he was helping her work through her wounded self-esteem, providing her with support, adding he "approved and validated her." He notes she simply was taken by his trajectory as a model patient to the present time, which "captivated her." Very little of what Mr. Johnson says can or should be taken at face value, unless it is in his best interest to be truthful at that moment. He uses both truth and lies in his attempts to get what he wants at the moment. He continues to break rules and be dishonest about it. He continues to manipulate lower-functioning patients and be dishonest about it. The cautious staff member should not assume that Mr. Johnson is telling the truth.

Mr. Johnson Has Not Substantially Benefitted from Treatment for His Primary Risk Issues

Mr. Johnson has frequently stated since his hospitalization that he became psychotic due to a methamphetamine binge, and that due to his belief that his girlfriend was going to harm him, he repeatedly stabbed and sliced her body, later removing her thumbs. It was never discussed in the forensic evaluators' reports why he felt it was legally or morally appropriate to attack his girlfriend in the manner that he did. Assuming for the sake of argument that Mr. Johnson's only mental health issue was becoming psychotic when binging on methamphetamines, his treatment focus on substance abuse issues would have been appropriate, and his attendance in such treatment would have suggested the possibility of benefit. However, Mr. Johnson's mental health functioning is strongly influenced by his severe personality disorder, and he has paid virtually no attention to how his personality functioning has caused significant problems throughout his life and has contributed to his substantial violence risk. Furthermore, the presence of his personality disorder has probably diminished the potential impact of any treatment he has received, as he does not see himself as flawed or in need of change; rather he goes through the motions necessary to affect the impression others have of him when they can have an impact on his potential for release. To benefit from treatment, one usually needs to acknowledge that one has a significant problem that must be addressed. Mr. Johnson does not see himself as flawed. He believes he can convince others that all of his problems were substance-related, and by going to substance abuse groups and being able to

---

COMMENT: HOW DOES *FOUCHA V. LOUISIANA* AFFECT THE CONCLUSION REGARDING CONTINUED INVOLUNTARY HOSPITALIZATION IN THIS CASE?

Foucha indicates that an individual must be both mentally ill and dangerous to meet the criteria for continued involuntary hospitalization as NGRI. Under California law, once a patient has been found NGRI and hospitalized as mentally ill and dangerous, the hospitalization can continue if the patient remains dangerous by reason of ANY mental disorder, not just the disorder that was instrumental in the commitment offense. Thus, personality disorders and substance abuse disorders can serve as foundational mental disorders for purposes of a violence risk analysis for continued hospitalization, even when the original commitment offense occurred by reason of the symptomatic effects of a psychotic disorder. In other words, being mentally ill and dangerous, as the basis for ongoing commitment, is not limited to the symptoms of psychotic or other severe mental illnesses.

---

repeat back some of the information, he will have addressed the issues necessary to gain his release.

However, unaddressed in his treatment are his highly dysfunctional interpersonal relationships, his proclivity towards domestic violence, his criminogenic attitudes and thinking, and his pervasive disregard for other people. Unless and until these issues are thoroughly addressed in treatment, Mr. Johnson will remain at a markedly elevated risk for future violence. These issues are known to his treatment team, and Mr. Johnson has been scheduled for treatment groups addressing several of these issues. Although Mr. Johnson regularly attends his treatment groups, he is not an active participant in these groups. Rather, in these types of groups he prefers to watch other group members participate, while occasionally making critical comments about the contributions of other patients. His level of participation is substantial enough to get "credit" for his attendance, but not enough to benefit from the content. He appears to his treatment providers to go through the motions while obtaining little or no benefit.

It is the conclusion of this evaluator that Mr. Johnson remains at an elevated risk for violence. He would be a danger to the health and safety of others, by reason of his severe personality disorder in combination with his substance abuse disorders, if under supervision and treatment in the community.

Craig R. Lareau, J.D., Ph.D., ABPP (Forensic)
Forensic Psychology Consultant,
Forensic Evaluation Department
Current State Hospital

TEACHING POINT:
USING MULTIPLE SOURCES FOR RELEVANT HOSPITALIZATION AND PRE-HOSPITALIZATION INFORMATION

Using multiple sources of information is a very basic part of FMHA. In this context, it is particularly important as the forensic clinician seeks to develop a detailed version of the individual's pre-hospitalization environment and behavior, current hospitalization, and proposed conditions of discharge. In doing this, there are two particularly important questions that arise. How similar is the environment in the proposed release to that of the individual's pre-hospitalization? What safeguards are in place to avoid recreating the risk factors that were present prior to hospitalization?

It is always useful to have the individual's perspective on each of the three domains identified earlier—pre-hospitalization, hospitalization, and release. But this account may be affected by poor self-awareness, motivation to leave the hospital, minimization of symptoms and deficits, and other considerations. Records and third party observations are a helpful antidote for these limitations. Accordingly, they are essential in the attempt to meaningfully address the relevant considerations related to hospital discharge.

Gathering this is the kind of information need not be deferred until prospective release is approaching. On the contrary, obtaining it early in hospitalization may be very helpful in identifying treatment targets and rehabilitation needs that are not clear from other kinds of assessment and staff review.

CASE THREE
PRINCIPLE: DESCRIBE FINDINGS AND LIMITS SO THAT THEY NEED CHANGE LITTLE UNDER CROSS-EXAMINATION
(*PRINCIPLE 31*)

As this principle was discussed in detail in Chapter 6 (this volume), we move directly to discussing the present report. This report provides an example of how the results of FMHA reports and testimony should be communicated in a release-decision-making evaluation. The first step in effective communication that would change little upon cross-examination is an understanding of the forensic issues and relevant legal questions. In the present case, the legal issue was whether Mr. Doe remains a mentally ill individual subject to court-ordered hospitalization. The legal issue is identified early in the report, which ensures that there is no confusion regarding the purpose of the evaluation.

This report contains several features that make it likely it would survive adversarial challenge. First, the effective communication of FMHA reasoning and conclusions is directly related to the quality and accuracy of the data gathered for the evaluation, and the reliability and validity of results can be strengthened through the use of multiple sources of information. In this case, the evaluator's conclusions relied on multiple sources of information (e.g., interview, testing, collateral interview, records), which increased the accuracy of the findings. Second, the evaluator is careful to attribute information to sources, which enables the court and attorneys to identify and confirm the source of the data. Third, the evaluator appropriately uses qualifying language to highlight limitations in the data (e.g., "Based upon the available data..."). Each of these elements strengthens the evaluator's conclusions and ensures that he will be prepared for cross-examination.

EVALUATION OF John Doe
CASE NUMBER: 03-CR-XYZ

REASON FOR EXAMINATION

Mr. John Doe is a 27-year-old African American male who was referred to the Netcare Forensic Psychiatry Center by the Honorable William Smith, Judge in the Rural County Court of Common Pleas, for a psychological evaluation pursuant to Section 2945.401 (D) of the Ohio Revised Code: the local Forensic Center shall complete a second opinion regarding a recommendation that Mr. Doe be advanced to Level 3 (Unsupervised on grounds), Level 4 (Supervised off grounds), Level 5 (Unsupervised off grounds) movement privileges, and Conditional Release. At the time of the evaluation, Mr. Doe was hospitalized at Central State Behavioral Healthcare (CSBH) pursuant to Section 2945.40 of the Ohio Revised Code and by court order.

CONFIDENTIALITY LIMITATIONS AND NOTIFICATION OF PURPOSE

Before proceeding with the interview, I provided Mr. Doe with a verbal and written explanation of the nature and general purpose of this evaluation, as well as the limitations on confidentiality. He stated that he understood the information provided to him, including the limits of confidentiality and his rights concerning the evaluation. He was informed that his CSBH treatment team has recommended Level 3, 4, 5 movement and Conditional Release and that I was asked to provide a second opinion as to whether or not he remains a mentally ill individual subject to court-ordered hospitalization, and if so, what would be the least restrictive alternative for his continuing care, balancing his needs and the safety of the community. I explained that based upon the evaluation, I would prepare a report, copies of which would be distributed to the presiding judge, and with the permission of the court, to his attorney and the prosecuting attorney. I indicated that if I were called to testify in his case, this report would also form the basis for my testimony. I also explained that the evaluation was to help answer legal questions and not to provide any counseling or psychotherapy. He indicated that he understood, and with prompting, was able to repeat this explanation back in an accurate fashion in his own words. I also reviewed his rights, as described in the Netcare Clients Rights Policy, with him. He was able to summarize these rights, then signed the disclosure and client rights forms and agreed to participate in the evaluation.

EVALUATION PROCEDURE

I, Terrance J. Kukor, Ph.D., ABPP, Diplomate in Forensic Psychology, of Netcare Forensic Center, interviewed Mr. Doe in a private office at CSBH on 08/26/04. This interview lasted approximately 1.25 hours. In addition, the following records were reviewed:

1) A review of documentation from CSBH, which included various court entries related to his commitment, a CSBH Violence Risk Factor Checklist/Progress form (dated 05/26/04), a Comprehensive Psychiatric Examination (dated 04/23/04), a History and Physical Examination (dated 4/23/04), a Psychosocial Assessment (dated 05/03/04), a Psychology Assessment (dated 04/26/04), a Substance Use Assessment (dated 04/28/04), a series of Comprehensive Treatment/Recovery Plans (the most recent dated 07/20/04), and a series of Multidisciplinary Progress Notes (the most recent dated 08/25/04);

2) A report (dated 07/12/04) pursuant to a request that Mr. Doe be advanced to Level 3, 4, and 5 privilege movement, as well as Conditional Release, completed by Melinda Blaire, M.D., his treating psychiatrist at CSBH;

3) Previous competency and sanity evaluations (both dated 02/16/04) that I performed. These evaluations were based upon the following:

a. The Court Entry and judgments ordering these evaluations;

b. A review of the information provided by the prosecuting attorney, which included but was not limited to demographic information, a transcript of Officer Barker's interview with the victim of the alleged incident, a Supplementary Investigation Report completed by Patrolman Lori Dutton; a Journal Entry dated 07/11/03 documenting Mr. Doe's plea of guilty to a prior domestic violence charge, Rural Police Department Incident Summary, and a Domestic Violence Field Report;

c. A telephone conversation with Mr. Alberto Rohos, Defense Counsel. Mr. Rohos provided a copy of Mr. Doe's records from New Hope Family Center;

d. Psychological testing consisting of the Minnesota Multiphasic Personality Inventory–2;

e. A review of the defendant's records from New Hope Family Center;

f. A review of Mr. Doe's records from Central Psychological Services, which were provided by his case manager, Mr. Francis Clarke;

g. I made several attempts to contact Mr. Doe's mother, by telephone, but was unable to reach her by the time these reports were due;

4) A telephone interview with Ms. Jasmine Beck, the defendant's probation officer;

5) A "Post Acquittal by Reason of Insanity" evaluation (dated 03/23/04) that I performed;

6) The Historical, Clinical, Risk Management–20 (HCR-20), a violence risk assessment instrument.

RELEVANT HISTORY

Note: Detailed background information and history were provided to court in previous reports regarding Mr. Doe's competency to stand trial, mental condition at the time of the alleged offense, and post-NGRI evaluations, and will not be repeated verbatim here. What follows is a brief summary of the information pertinent to this evaluation that is reported in greater detail in those earlier reports.

Concerning *family history,* Mr. Doe was born to Jane and Jonathan Doe. Mr. Doe reported that he was not certain if his biological parents were married, but indicated that he has had no contact with his biological father and does not know him. He has two half-siblings: Johnny Doe (age 21) and Janie Doe (age 17). Mr. Doe said that he was born in Indiana and that when he was approximately one year old, his family moved to Michigan, where they lived until he was about 9 or 10 years old. Reportedly, his family has lived in Ohio for approximately the last eight years. Mr. Doe previously reported that he had "a pretty good childhood" during which time he had friends and was happy. He denied having ever suffered any physical or sexual abuse as a child or adolescent. Mr. Doe previously reported that, to the best of his knowledge, no one in his family had ever had psychiatric treatment; he described his biological father as an "alcoholic," but was uncertain if he had ever received substance abuse treatment.

In terms of *educational history*, Mr. Doe previously reported that he attended public schools in Indiana, Michigan, and Ohio, where he graduated from high school. He said that he earned mostly Bs in school, and although he had some friends, he was shy and didn't like to talk to many people. He indicated that he was suspended one time in the tenth or eleventh grade when he was caught with drug paraphernalia, but did not have to repeat any grades, was never expelled, and was never truant. He denied any history of special-education classes, and indicated that he tended to get along well with teachers. He previously reported that he reads and writes well.

Concerning *employment history*, Mr. Doe reported that he had his first job in a grocery store at the age of 15. He reported that he quit this job after about six months, and then took several successive jobs at local fast food restaurants. In one such job, he reported that he got fired when he accidentally spilled hot water on a manager's leg. Typically, however, he quit these jobs. His last job was at a local light manufacturing plant, where he was working just prior to his arrest. Mr. Doe previously reported that he typically got along well with co-workers and bosses. He denied having ever received any benefits from SSI/SSD.

In terms of *interpersonal and family history*, Mr. Doe indicated that he has never married and to his knowledge has not fathered any children. He indicated that he has had girlfriends in the past, but did not characterize any of these relationships as long-term or serious to him. He has been sexually active. He reported that as an adolescent, he occasionally socialized with peers, but tended to be somewhat of a passive and shy loner. With the exception of his eighth-grade football team, he never belonged to any clubs, teams, or organizations. He denied having ever been a member of a gang. Concerning early antisocial behavioral patterns, Mr. Doe denied that he ever forced sexual activity on another, was cruel to animals, or engaged in vandalism, fire setting, truancy, runaway behavior, stealing, or excessive lying; he acknowledged starting one fight in school and one fight in jail, and acknowledged one incident of shoplifting.

Concerning *medical history*, Mr. Doe previously denied any childhood or adolescent history of severe or chronic illness, accidents, or surgeries. He indicated he has never suffered any head injuries, and has never been knocked unconscious. When asked about seizures, Mr. Doe previously reported that a maternal aunt has epilepsy, and described several episodes in which his body "phases out." During these episodes, he described diminished control of his body, but denied having ever fallen to the ground or losing consciousness. When previously asked about the reference to Wilson's disease in the police report, Mr. Doe said that he'd heard of it but was not certain if he had it or not.

In terms of *mental health history*, Mr. Doe previously reported that in February of 2002 he had his first psychiatric hospitalization. He was unclear about the reason for the hospitalization, which he said had been prompted by his telling a teacher that he did not feel safe around him. Mr. Doe was at a loss to explain this, saying that he had previously got along well with this teacher. Mr. Doe was somewhat unclear about the chronology of his post-discharge follow-up with mental health services. Mr. Doe explained that he received outpatient psychiatric treatment at one mental health center and management services from another. Mr. Doe reported that as a result of his arrest, his case was closed and that since early 2004, he has not had any of his antipsychotic medication.

In terms of *drug and alcohol history*, Mr. Doe reported that he has used alcohol only three or four times, the first use being at age 16, when he and a friend drank some hard liquor. He reported that he has been intoxicated on alcohol only one time. In terms of drugs, Mr. Doe's drug of choice appears to be cannabis, which he began using at the age of 14 or 15. Mr. Doe reported that his heaviest use of cannabis was approximately a quarter-ounce per week. Mr. Doe also indicated that he has used LSD on three occasions at the age of 16 or 17. He indicated that he stopped using LSD because it was "too dangerous to use on a regular basis." His mother thought that this self-report was accurate. When specifically asked, he denied any and all use of amphetamines, sedatives-anxiolytics, cocaine, opiates, PCP, or inhalants. He indicated that he smoked tobacco for approximately one month at age 15 or 16, and quit because he did "not want to get addicted."

Concerning *criminal history*, Mr. Doe previously reported no arrests as a juvenile. As an adult, he indicated that he had been arrested a total of four times, each time for domestic violence. He reported that after his third domestic violence charge, all three were combined into one case, for which he received 18 days' time served and one year "intensive supervised probation" in late 2003. He successfully completed this probation without further incident. Mr. Doe indicated that the prior domestic violence charges were attributable to getting into physical altercations with his mother, his mother's boyfriend, and his half-brother. According to information provided by the prosecuting attorney, Mr. Doe entered a guilty plea to a charge of domestic violence on 07/11/03. Interestingly, the Journal Entry from that date indicates the following additional term: "take medications as prescribed."

Concerning *employment history*, Mr. Doe reported that he has had a series of jobs at local fast food restaurants, all of which he quit, citing difficulty in keeping up with the required pace. His most recent job was at a local factory, where he was working just prior to his arrest. Mr. Doe indicated that he typically did not have disciplinary issues, and got along reasonably well with co-workers and supervisors despite his preference to keep to himself. He recently began receiving benefits from SSI/SSD.

In terms of *military history*, Mr. Doe has never served in the armed services. He reported that at one time he had spoken with a Navy recruiter about enlisting, but was not able to do so since he was on probation at the time.

In terms of his *post-NGRI commitment to the Ohio Department of Mental Health*, the instant offense took place on 12/04/03, when police received a call that John Doe had assaulted his brother (Johnny Doe) in a residence that they were sharing at the time. He was subsequently charged with domestic violence, a felony of the fifth degree. In a court hearing dated 02/27/04, Mr. Doe was found not guilty by reason of insanity on the charge of domestic violence. In a court hearing dated 04/05/04, Mr. Doe was ordered to be admitted to Central State Behavioral Healthcare, where he has remained since that time.

CURRENT MENTAL STATUS
Mr. Doe, a 27-year-old left-handed African American male, was wearing casual clothing that was neat and clean. He is approximately 5'9" and 165 pounds with a medium build. His hair was worn short and he was clean-shaven, giving him a reasonably neat appearance. He did not exhibit any noticeable problems with respect to his personal hygiene or grooming. There were no observable scars, piercings, or tattoos.

Mr. Doe was eager to speak with me, and presented in a much more engaging fashion than in previous evaluation meetings. Although he made few spontaneous comments, he was responsive to my questions, speaking without undue latency. He read the notification and rights forms carefully, but not with the suspiciousness he had previously exhibited. He established and maintained consistent eye contact, which lacked the fixed, staring quality he exhibited in previous evaluations. Mr. Doe appeared relaxed and at ease, and did not display any behavioral agitation or other signs of acute distress. He did not appear to be confused, and was fully oriented to person, place, time, and situation. There were no problems noted with his immediate memory or recent memory; since it was not necessary to take a history, remote memory was not formally assessed. His speech was typically normal in tone, rate, and rhythm, and no articulation difficulties were evident.

Mr. Doe did not appear to have any difficulty understanding my questions. His vocabulary, fund of general information, and verbal abstraction were suggestive of at least average intellectual functioning. Answers to questions regarding interpersonal problem-solving were free of any bizarre or idiosyncratic elements, and not characterized by antisocial or self-serving themes. His attention and concentration were within normal limits, as evidenced by his ability to track and keep up with the give and take of a conversation. He expressed a much fuller range of emotion than in previous evaluations. At no time was his affect (i.e., expressed emotion) inconsistent with the content of his thinking. He did not appear to have any difficulty modulating emotion. His mood appeared to be euthymic—that is, neither unduly elevated nor depressed. In terms of current affective symptoms, he either denied or did not exhibit the following symptoms commonly seen in depression: low mood/loss of interest, sleep disturbance, diminished appetite, diminished energy, and feelings of worthlessness. He specifically denied any current suicidal ideation, plan, or intent. He also expressed some future orientation, describing his hopes to one day go to college. He did acknowledge some difficulty in concentration. He denied any current or past homicidal thoughts, plans, and intentions. He neither exhibited nor acknowledged symptoms typically associated with mania, including periods of persistent euphoria and irritability that have been associated with decreased needs for sleep, pressured speech, racing thoughts, and increased energy.

Mr. Doe's thought process, as reflected in his speech, was logical, sequential, and goal-directed. Furthermore, he did not display symptoms of a formal thought disorder such as tangentiality (i.e., responses that veer off topic), circumstantial speech (taking a circuitous route to reach a point), or loose associations (responses that are not logically connected to conversation or questions asked). Mr. Doe described past experiences with auditory hallucinations (sensory perception in the absence of an external stimulus), and both the form and content of his descriptions were highly consistent with the known phenomenology of authentic auditory hallucinations. He also acknowledged apparent tactile hallucinations, which appear to be a rather long standing and treatment-refractory psychotic symptom. When given the opportunity to do so, he did not endorse any persecutory, somatic, referential, or grandiose delusions (i.e., fixed false beliefs that respectively involve thoughts that one is being persecuted; that one's body injured or altered; that ordinary events, objects, or behaviors of others have particular and unusual meanings for one; or that one is person of great importance, power, or knowledge). He indicated that he no longer believes that family members are responsible for the uncanny experience that his mind is "crowded" with someone else's thoughts or that someone is mysteriously touching his head. Although the progress notes clearly indicate that Mr. Doe's expressed acceptance that he has a mental illness was quite recent (i.e., the day before this evaluation), Mr. Doe asserted that he has believed this since pleading NGRI and being admitted to the hospital. It was my impression that Mr. Doe was likely exaggerating both the duration and depth of his conviction about accepting his psychiatric diagnosis. That said, he did impress me as having made progress in terms of insight, which proved to be rather resilient to mild interpersonal challenges that I made. There was no evidence of compulsions (i.e., rigid behavioral rituals), obsessional thinking (i.e., repeated unwanted thoughts), or phobias (i.e., specific fears). His judgment and his insight into his current legal situation were thought to be good; his judgment about and insight into his clinical situation were thought to be improved.

COLLATERAL INFORMATION

In my *previous competency report*, I noted that there was an abundance of evidence that Mr. Doe's mental disease (paranoid schizophrenia) and mental defect (Wilson's disease) had historically impaired his occupational and interpersonal functioning in a significant manner. However, at the time of the evaluation, he was reasonably stable, such that he had an accurate understanding of the nature and objective of the legal proceedings against him. In terms of his capacity to assist in his own defense, he did not express any undue mistrust or unrealistic expectations towards his lawyer. He expressed an appreciation for the need to tell his lawyer the truth, and based upon the behaviors exhibited during this evaluation, it was my opinion that he was capable of providing his lawyer with details related to the alleged offense in a rational fashion, capable of challenging prosecution witnesses, and could testify relevantly. His then-present mental condition was such that he had the capacity to comprehend instructions and evaluate legal advice, and that he was capable of meaningfully participating in the legal proceedings and behaving in an appropriate fashion while doing so.

According to my *previous sanity report*, based upon all the available information, including his own account of the alleged offense, Mr. Doe was confused, disoriented, and laboring under auditory hallucinations and paranoid thinking at the time of the alleged offense. There were multiple indicators that suggested the defendant's thinking and perception were impaired by symptoms of active psychosis. Specifically, the entire behavioral sequence exhibited by the defendant (i.e., assaulting his brother for no apparent reason; following his brother out of the house while staring at him in a menacing fashion; calling the police and reporting that he was the victim of a sexual assault, then taking it back and reporting that perhaps he had dreamed it), was bizarre and pointed to cognitive disorganization, an inability to guide and direct his behavior in a meaningful, goal-directed fashion, and severely compromised cognitive functioning. It was my opinion that his severe mental disease and mental defect resulted in his not knowing the wrongfulness of the act he was charged with committing.

According to my *previous post-NGRI evaluation*, at that time, Mr. Doe exhibited poor insight into his mental illness. He was questioned in great detail about mental disorder and associated symptoms, and he acknowledged only that he has had past difficulty concentrating and developed some unwarranted suspiciousness. He minimized the behavioral aggression associated with past auditory hallucinations and persecutory ideation, and from his point of view, could not think of a single reason to continue taking psychiatric medication. Furthermore, he had a poorly articulated plan for avoiding future behavioral aggression and potential legal trouble, indicating that he was "older now" and more likely to think before acting. He did not express any appreciation for the connection between symptoms of an active mental illness and past behavioral aggression. Due to his history of noncompliance with treatment in the community, along with his then-current poor degree of insight, it was my opinion that continued stabilization should take place in a secured treatment facility. This would allow for gradual transition back into the community, with a full spectrum of supports in place and a realistic aftercare plan that would enhance his chances for success when returned to the community. It was my opinion, therefore, that the least restrictive commitment alternative available that is consistent with his therapeutic treatment needs and the safety of community was the Central State Behavioral Healthcare–Civil Unit.

SUMMARY OF THE NGRI OFFENSE

According to the police reports, on 12/04/03, police received a call from the defendant's step-brother, who reported that he had been assaulted by the defendant in his residence. While the victim was on the phone with the police, the defendant called police from a pay phone via 911; the police dispatcher had difficulty understanding him, as the defendant was "real slow with his speech." The defendant reported that someone had broken into his house and had sexually assaulted him. When police officers arrived at the scene, they were flagged down by the victim, who told them that he and the defendant were in the process of moving into the residence together. A large number of boxes and items were stacked about the house, and the victim reported that the defendant approached him from behind when he was leaning over the boxes organizing items, and pushed him into the boxes and over some furniture. The victim told police that as he was lying on the floor and trying to get up, the defendant was standing over him, just staring at him. The victim was reportedly concerned for his safety; the police report noted that the defendant has had three prior domestic violence arrests, and one conviction, on his record. The victim reported that as he got up, the defendant never said anything to him and just stared at him. The victim said that he then walked out of the house toward a restaurant and that the defendant followed him all the way to the restaurant and then turned around and went back to the residence. Police subsequently found the defendant sitting in his vehicle in the parking lot of another nearby restaurant. According to the police report, the defendant "apparently did not remember what had happened," and when he was asked why he had called the police department, he said that he "just wanted to see how things were going." He reportedly made no mention of any kind of domestic violence, burglary, or sexual assault. When he was subsequently questioned about the alleged burglary and sexual assault that he had reported earlier on a 911 call, he "stated that he thought that maybe it had happened but apparently it hadn't. He was very lethargic. He acted like a zombie as we were talking to him. There was no emotion of any sort at all. He was very deliberate in his movements."

The victim then told police that his brother had been on medication for psychosis and that he had not been taking the medication. When questioned at the police department, the defendant reported that he and his brother had been arguing, but did not know what they were arguing about. He indicated that there had been no physical contact, and he didn't understand why he was under arrest. Police noted that the defendant could still not provide them any information on the alleged burglary or sexual assault, and defendant indicated that he "probably was dreaming the incident had happened."

COURSE OF TREATMENT DURING THE CURRENT HOSPITALIZATION

According to *records from Central State Behavioral Healthcare*, Mr. Doe was adjudicated not guilty by reason of insanity on charges of domestic violence, in violation of Section 2919.25 (A) of the

Ohio Revised Code, a felony of the fifth degree. He subsequently was admitted to CSBH on 04/05/04, where he has remained throughout the course of his treatment.

Since the time of his admission, Mr. Doe has not presented any behavioral aggression, and has routinely been described as pleasant, behaviorally appropriate, and medication compliant. He has been involved in a wide variety of therapies, though his participation in groups was often described as passive. Earlier notes from individual psychotherapy tend to depict him as having difficulty accepting that he had a mental illness. By the end of June, it was noted that he continued to experience tactile hallucinations, in which he felt that someone had been touching his head. Reportedly, in the past he had attributed this to family members, but had come to appreciate that such an attribution was illogical. In July, it was noted that he was using his movement privileges (Level 2, Supervised on grounds) without any problems, and was exhibiting good skills related to activities of daily living. Although he was described as medication compliant, it was noted that he did not feel the antipsychotic medication had made any significant difference in his mood or behavior, and that he was taking medication because it had been ordered and he wanted to be compliant. Tactile hallucinations diminished in intensity but remained present. He participated in an ongoing anger management group, and continued to exhibit friendly, non-aggressive behavior with staff and peers. His individual therapist noted that when provided with diagnostic criteria for psychotic disorders, he acknowledged auditory hallucinations as well as delusions of persecution, reference, somatization, and grandiosity, but was reluctant to endorse the idea that he had a mental illness. By mid-July, he was described as "stable" on his antipsychotic medication, with no delusions of control, but continued tactile hallucinations that interfered with his focus and concentration. His participation in a group on substance abuse was described as "passive." His individual therapist noted that although he was willing to acknowledge psychiatric symptomatology, he did not want to attribute such symptoms to a mental illness. By early August, it was noted that he was not overtly delusional, had not exhibited any violence, and that the intensity of the tactile hallucinations had diminished. At the same time, however, it was also noted that his "continued lack of insight was readily apparent." On 08/11/04, his individual therapist noted that he continued to exhibit poor insight, and expressed concern about the potential long-term consequences in terms of the likelihood of future clinical decompensation. On 08/25/04, his individual therapist noted that Mr. Doe continued to report tactile hallucinations, which were apparently linked to past delusional thinking. For example, he would experience a sensation that someone had touched his head, then have the experience that a delusional thought (e.g., that his brother had raped him) had been inserted into his mind. It was on this same date that Mr. Doe, for the first time, indicated that he believed he had a mental illness for which he had to take medication, and had to abstain from alcohol and drugs. Interestingly, this assertion was the day before I saw him for this evaluation.

CLINICAL FORMULATION/ RISK ASSESSMENT

The available information, as well as the clinical interview, indicates that Mr. Doe does have a serious mental illness, most likely in the psychotic spectrum, that is complicated by a mental defect (Wilson's disease). In the past he has been diagnosed by his outpatient psychiatrist with paranoid schizophrenia. More recently, he has been diagnosed by his inpatient psychiatrist at CSBH with psychosis not otherwise specified. There is no evidence that indicates that Mr. Doe is intellectually disabled.

For the court's information, according to the *Diagnostic and Statistical Manual, Fourth Edition, Text Revision* (DSM-IV-TR) published by the American Psychiatric Association, the essential feature of the *paranoid type of schizophrenia* is the presence of prominent delusions or auditory hallucinations in the context of a relative preservation of cognitive functioning and affect. Delusions are typically persecutory or grandiose, or both, but delusions with other themes (e.g., jealousy, religiosity, and somatization) may also occur. The delusions may be multiple, but are usually organized around a coherent theme. Hallucinations are also typically related to content of the delusional theme. Associated features may include anxiety, anger, aloofness, and argumentativeness. The individual may have a superior and patronizing manner and either a stilted, formal quality or extreme intensity in interpersonal interactions. Persecutory delusions are typically organized around a central theme in which the individual believes he or she is being attacked, harassed, cheated, persecuted, or conspired against. The persecutory themes may predispose the individual to suicidal behavior, and the combination of persecutory and grandiose delusions with anger may predispose the individual to violence.

According to information from the National Institute of Neurological Disorders and Stroke, *Wilson's disease* is an inherited disorder in which excessive amounts of copper accumulate in the body. Although the accumulation of copper begins at birth, symptoms of the disorder appear later in life, between the ages of 6 and 40. The primary consequence for approximately 40% of patients with Wilson's is liver disease. In other patients, the first symptoms are either neurological or psychiatric or both, and include tremor, rigidity, drooling, difficulty with speech, abrupt personality change, grossly inappropriate behavior and inexplicable deterioration of schoolwork, and neurosis or psychosis.

The essential feature of a *psychotic disorder not otherwise specified* is psychotic symptomatology (i.e., delusions, hallucinations, disorganized speech, grossly disorganized or catatonic behavior) about which there is inadequate information to make a specific diagnosis or about which there is contradictory information. This diagnosis is also used for disorders with psychotic symptoms that do not meet the criteria for any specific psychotic disorder.

The *HCR-20* was administered to assist in assessing Mr. Doe's risk of future violence. This instrument consists of 20 items, organized around ten past (historical) factors, five present (clinical) variables, and five future (risk management) issues. All items are coded on a three-point scale according to the certainty that the risk factors are present. A rating of 0 indicates that, according to the assessment information gathered, the risk factor is absent (or, put another way, there is no information to suggest that the risk factor is present). A rating of 1 indicates that the risk factor is possibly or partially present: that is, the assessment information indicates there is some, but not conclusive, evidence for its presence. A rating of 2 indicates that the risk factor is definitely or clearly present. If no information is available concerning a given item or if the information is considered unreliable, an item may be omitted. Research on the HCR-20 in a forensic

psychiatric setting indicates that HCR-20 scores predicted readmission to a forensic hospital and subsequent psychiatric hospitalizations. Although the historical item called "Psychopathy" on the HCR-20 could not be scored, Dr. Kevin Douglas, one of the authors of the instrument, suggests that the HCR-20 can be scored and interpreted without utilizing this item.[2]

HCR-20 Historical Items
Previous Violence

Historically, Mr. Doe does have a history of violent behavior. As an adult, Mr. Doe has been arrested a total of four times, each time for domestic violence. His most recent arrest was considered a felony in light of the number of previous domestic violence incidents. Mr. Doe has not exhibited any behavioral aggression since the index offense. He has not been violent towards peers or staff since his most recent admission to CSBH. His hospital records indicate that he has no episodes of seclusion or restraint in the current inpatient hospitalization. Taken as a whole, his history of violence increases risk.

Young Age at First Violent Incident

A history of serious aggressive behavior during adolescence, particularly with early onset (below age 12) would be a primary concern in terms of increased violence risk. In Mr. Doe's case, there is no such known history. However, due to his current age, he is still considered a younger individual—which increases his risk.

Relationship Instability

"Relationship instability" applies only to romantic or intimate, non-platonic partnerships and excludes relationships with friends and family. Of concern is whether the individual can maintain stable long-term relationships and engage in these when given the opportunity. Mr. Doe indicated that he has never married and to his knowledge has not fathered any children. He indicated that he has had girlfriends in the past, but did not characterize any of these relationships as long-term or serious to him. He has been sexually active. He reported that as an adolescent, he occasionally socialized

[2] Douglas, K., & Guy, L. (2008, December), *Violence risk assessment and management using structured professional judgment and the HCR-20.* Presented for the Ohio Department of Mental Health, Columbus, OH.

with peers, but tended to be somewhat of a passive and shy loner. He denied having ever forced sexual activity on another. He indicated that he is not particularly interested in developing a long-term romantic relationship at this time. In response to direct inquiry, Mr. Doe has not considered the role his mental illness has had in his ability to establish a lasting romantic relationships. Thus, the protective factor of a long-term relationship is not present in this case, and his relationship history raises risk.

Employment Problems

Mr. Doe has had various short-term employments. Mr. Doe reported seeking jobs for short-term instrumental reasons. For example, he said that he often he sought employment to earn enough money to purchase video games, which for him were solitary activities. On multiple occasions he quit the jobs because he had difficulty keeping up, and he has always done so without having previously lined up another job. He acknowledged that on one occasion, he quit a job as he was becoming suspicious that his work peers were plotting against him to get him fired. His case manager indicated that he recently became a recipient of Social Security benefits, adding that he has expressed an interest in pursuing vocational rehabilitation and possibly employment. Overall, his lack of steady employment in the past moderately increases risk.

Substance Abuse Problems

In this domain the focus is on whether there is impairment in functioning in the areas of health, employment, recreation, and interpersonal relationships attributable to substances. Mr. Doe acknowledged past use of alcohol, cannabis, and LSD. He denied experiencing any problems related to drinking or drug use. His use of alcohol and drugs has not been of sufficient severity or chronicity that it would meet diagnostic criteria for substance dependency. He has never been court-ordered into substance abuse treatment, nor has he been mandated to participate in Alcoholics Anonymous or Narcotics Anonymous meetings. Records from prior mental health treatment do not offer formal diagnoses related to his use of drugs or alcohol, and do not note such as areas of concern. At the present time, Mr. Doe expressed an understanding that indulging in either alcohol or drugs of any kind "might cause problems with my medication." Although substance use problems do not appear to represent a significant risk factor for Mr. Doe at this time, any future use of alcohol and cannabis would reasonably be expected to erode behavioral controls and increase the risk of future violence.

Major Mental Illness

The empirical literature suggests an increased risk of violence for individuals with certain serious psychiatric diagnoses, particularly when they are complicated by drug or alcohol abuse. In this case, Mr. Doe's behavioral history and mental status, as described above, suggest that he has a serious mental illness (in the psychotic spectrum) complicated by a mental defect (Wilson's disease). There is no evidence for intellectual disability. Past violence appears to have been associated with active psychotic symptoms (e.g., hallucinations and persecutory delusions). In Mr. Doe's case, hallucinations and delusions have responded reasonably well to antipsychotic medication, such that his risk for future violence associated with psychotic symptoms decreases with his medication compliance. At the present time, there is no evidence to suggest current delusional thinking or auditory hallucinations. There is evidence for current tactile hallucinations that have been reduced in intensity. Importantly, Mr. Doe appears to have abandoned the persecutory delusion that family members were somehow responsible for these tactile hallucinations. Records indicate that Mr. Doe has been medication-compliant for some time. Mr. Doe expresses an understanding of the importance of medication compliance. When queried in detail about medication compliance, Mr. Doe did not complain about any unwanted side effects, and when directly asked, indicated that if for any reason he stopped taking this medication, "the delusional thoughts would come back." When asked how long he would have to take this medication, Mr. Doe said, "I hear for the rest my life," and when challenged on this, said, "The reason I'm feeling so good now is because I'm taking the medication." Overall, the defendant has a serious major mental illness, which increases his risk.

Psychopathy

This item calls for the Hare Psychopathy Checklist–Revised (PCL-R) to be administered. The PCL-R is a tool that assesses psychopathy, which refers to a specific constellation of deviant traits and behaviors that constitute a particular personality pattern identified by research as being associated with violence, criminality, and aggression. This item was not scored due to the unavailability of a PCL-R rating by a trained psychopathy assessor.

Early Maladjustment

This item is concerned with maladjustment at home, at school, or in the community before the age of 17. There is no known history of early neglect or abuse in Mr. Doe's background, and Mr. Doe did not report any specific traumatic events from childhood. He has no juvenile legal history, and his early school history is without evidence of significant maladjustment. There is no evidence that he has been a member of a gang. A history of serious aggressive behavior during adolescence, particularly with early onset (below age 12) would be a primary concern. In Mr. Doe's case, there is no such known history. There does not appear to be significant risk associated with this factor.

Personality Disorder

It has been found that antisocial and borderline personality disorders have predictive links of violence. The key clinical factors associated with these diagnoses are anger, impulsivity, and hostility, all of which can elevate the risk for general and violent criminal behavior. Individuals with a history of antisocial behavior, including impulsivity, delinquency, and adult criminal behavior are at greater risk for violent criminal behavior. In this case, based upon the collateral information and Mr. Doe's self-report, a history of adolescent delinquent activity does not appear to be present. Per his self-report, there was some evidence of adolescent impulsivity, but this does not appear to have become a pervasive pattern of developmentally inappropriate impulsivity or inappropriate risk taking that extended into interpersonal, occupational, or cognitive domains. There is some evidence of adult antisocial activity, but his past episodes of domestic violence appear to be related to the onset of symptoms of mental illness. Mr. Doe has not been diagnosed with a specific personality disorder, which decreases risk.

Prior Supervision Failure

Since the time of his admission, Mr. Doe has not presented any behavioral aggression, and has routinely been described as pleasant, behaviorally appropriate, and medication compliant. There have been no elopement attempts. He has a history of successfully completing probation, and his probation officer reported that he did not present problems while on probation. His overall success while under formal supervision decreases risk.

CLINICAL RISK FACTORS
Lack of insight

This item concerns the degree to which an individual believes he or she has a mental disorder and/or substance abuse problem and has awareness of the effect of medication on the mental condition, and appreciates the social consequences of having a mental disorder or a substance abuse problem and the possible violence potential that the individual may have. Mr. Doe has made therapeutic gains in this area. However, the progress notes from CSBH clearly do not support his assertion that acceptance of his diagnosis and need to remain medication compliant are as long-standing as he would have one believe.

Negative Attitudes

This area relates to prosocial versus antisocial attitudes. Mr. Doe did not express any attitudes that support and/or rationalize crime or violence, and there is no evidence in the collateral information that suggests he has espoused such attitudes in the past. He does not appear callous or lacking in empathy. No sadistic, paranoid, or homicidal attitudes were apparent. No grudges were identified. Overall, the lack of negative attitudes decreases risk.

Active Symptoms of Mental Illness

At the present time, Mr. Doe is exhibiting a significant reduction in active signs or symptoms of mental illness. In Mr. Doe's case, hallucinations and delusions have responded reasonably well to antipsychotic medication, which means that his risk for future violence associated with psychotic symptoms decreases with his continued medication compliance. At the present time, there is no evidence to suggest current delusional thinking or auditory hallucinations. There is evidence for current tactile hallucinations that have been reduced in intensity. Importantly, Mr. Doe appears to have abandoned the persecutory delusion that family members were somehow responsible for these tactile hallucinations. Overall, his mental condition is rather stable at this point in time. He has no known history of malingering, and malingering is not suspected at this point in time. Since there is minimal evidence for *current* active symptoms of mental illness, risk associated with this factor is low.

Impulsivity

This refers to behavioral and affective instability such as emotional instability. "Impulsivity" basically refers to an inability to remain composed and directed when under pressure to act. Currently, Mr. Doe is not presenting as hot tempered, emotionally unstable, quick to overreact, reckless, impulsive, or affectively unstable. Rather, his current behavioral presentation is relatively stable. Of note, when he is not taking antipsychotic medication, his reality testing (i.e., his ability to accurately perceive reality and reason about it) is significantly impaired. At such times in the past, he has exhibited behavioral and affective instability and has acted without due regard for likely consequences. Per his case manager, when he is medication complaint, Mr. Doe is emotionally and behaviorally stable.

Unresponsive to Treatment

This refers to whether or not the individual has sought help and accepted it, rejected it out of hand, or agreed to it in order to be viewed in a positive light by the court, review board or authority. According to his report and collateral information, at this time, Mr. Doe is symptom-free but for occasional tactile hallucinations. Since his most recent admission to the hospital, Mr. Doe has not required recent emergency medications or placement in seclusion or restraint. Nor has he exhibited recent outbursts of poorly modulated anger. By all accounts, his response to treatment while in the hospital has been very positive. He does not exhibit attitudes that could be characterized as pro-criminal or pro-substance use. Importantly, he has recently expressed an interest in receiving vocational rehabilitation services and seeking employment post-discharge. His motivation for continued outpatient psychiatric treatment post-discharge is difficult to gauge with any precision at this point. Although he indicates that he is willing to continue with prescribed medication, as noted elsewhere, his insight is neither deep nor long standing. In this regard, his appreciation for the impact acute symptoms of mental illness have had on his functioning is minimal.

RISK MANAGEMENT RISK FACTORS

This section considered factors related to developing an estimate of how an individual will adjust to future circumstances. It is recognized that future risk depends heavily upon the context in which the individual will live or can be expected to live.

Plans Lack Feasibility

At this point, it has not been formally determined where Mr. Doe will begin his period of supervision as an insanity acquittee. Prior to the index offense, Mr. Doe lived with his step-brother (the victim of the index offense), who has indicated some willingness to have him return post-discharge. His step-brother has been invited to participate in discharge planning meetings, but of the three scheduled, he has attended only one. Although Mr. Does has expressed a willingness to return to New Hope for continued outpatient mental health care, hospital records indicate that his involvement in discharge planning has been passive; at times indifferent. In this regard, I had difficulty engaging him in a problem-solving discussion about how he might manage various contingencies in the implementation of the details of his discharge plan. His conditional release plan is thorough and appropriately focused on management of dynamic risk factors for violence, and proposes outpatient treatment at a clinically appropriate level of intensity to manage the estimated level of risk. Mr. Doe has no known learning style or abilities that would constitute a barrier to his ability to understand his discharge plan. He expresses a positive regard for his proposed treatment providers at New Hope, who are willing and able to provide the proposed behavioral health interventions on the discharge plan. Considering all the available factors, there is a moderate to high probability that the plan will succeed.

Exposure to Destabilizers

This item assesses for situations in which an individual is exposed to the hazardous conditions to which he is vulnerable or that may trigger violent episodes. Hazardous conditions are unique to specific individuals but include such concerns as the presence of weapons, substances, or certain individuals or victim groups. The discharge location being proposed—Mr. Doe's step-brother's residence—is not known to have any available weapons. In this regard it should be noted that Mr. Doe's past acts of discrete violence have never involved weapons, but have been focused exclusively upon family members as victims. His step-brother has expressed a willingness to have Mr. Doe again live with him; he does not harbor any grudge or enduring resentment about the index offense. His step-brother has said, however, that he is reluctant to remove alcohol from his residence. In this regard, Mr. Doe does not currently express any concern about exposure to alcohol. In terms of peer support, as previously noted, Mr. Doe has no known gang involvement, and per his step-brother and probation officer, there is no shared concern that individuals with whom Mr. Doe would like to reforge relationships are antisocial. Basic life skills (e.g., leisure skills, ability to cook, clean, etc.) are intact. As previously noted, his case manager indicated that he recently became a recipient of Social Security benefits. Hospital progress notes indicate that he has recently expressed an interest in pursuing vocational rehabilitation and possibly employment. This is important in that Mr. Doe expressed concern about the financial costs about associated with meeting his deductible payment for his medications. Lastly, Mr. Doe has the benefit of positive and trusting relationships with an interdisciplinary team at New Hope Mental Health Center. There is low to moderate risk associated with exposure to destabilizers at this time.

Lack of Personal Support

Networks of available social support can serve as an effective interpersonal buffer against life stressors, thereby aiding in positive adjustment and constructive coping. In this case, Mr. Doe's perceived social support centers primarily around family members. In addition to his step-brother, his mother has been strongly supportive of his consistent involvement in mental health treatment. Importantly, Mr. Doe is willing to accept such interpersonal encouragement and support from his family. It should also be noted that Mr. Doe had some difficulty articulating a realistic and meaningful coping plan for dealing with unexpected conflict with family members.

Likewise, he expressed a limited understanding of the relationship between medication compliance and his ability to remain nonviolent. Mr. Doe's personal support systems could be enhanced via participation in mental health support groups at New Hope and formal participation in the Bureau of Vocational Rehabilitation. These venues would afford him the opportunity to expand his social network by meeting and interacting with other people in the community who share similar interests, and with others who could assist him with job training, placement, and linkage to other resources. There is low risk associated with lack of personal support at this time.

Noncompliance with Remediation Attempts

Since being admitted to CSBH as not guilty by reason of insanity, Mr. Doe has been an active participant in treatment. Importantly, hospital records indicate that he has participated in groups on both anger management as well as recovery skills training, which indicates that he has been exposed to a variety of methods and techniques for managing stress and successfully coping with potentially provocative situations, which mitigates the overall risk associated with this factor. Even though Mr. Doe has only partial insight into the importance of medication compliance, hospital records do not indicate any episodes in which he has refused prescribed psychiatric medication. There is low risk associated with noncompliance with remediation attempts at this time.

Stress

It is important to understand the sources of stress Mr. Doe is likely to encounter and how he may react or cope with that stress. At this time, he is moderately anxious about the possibility of being granted a conditional release. Hospital progress notes indicate that he discloses such concerns to his treatment team, and has been willing to practice—with moderate success—cognitive-behavioral techniques for symptom management that he has learned while in the hospital. In this regard, Mr. Doe has exhibited the ability to seek out and utilize the support systems readily available to him. There is low risk associated with foreseeable sources of stress at this time.

OTHER RISK CONSIDERATIONS

A higher risk of violence is associated with multiple assaults on a narrow class of victims who remain readily available (e.g., significant others) or a broad range of victims. In this case, the primary concern appears to be Mr. Doe's family, who continue to be readily available, which increases the overall risk level. A related factor is concerned with the individual's current thoughts, feelings, and attitudes (including fantasies) regarding others, particularly in terms of resolving perceived conflicts. In this case, Mr. Doe denied any current intentions or fantasies about harming others, including his family members who have been involved in past episodes of domestic violence. He also denied any brooding resentment or grudge towards his family members, and denied any angry or aggressive feelings towards them. This is consistent with the results of the mental status examination, during which there was no evidence of irritability or underlying edginess. There was no evidence of minimization of victim impact.

Additionally, risk tends to be enhanced, particularly for more lethal forms of violence, when weapons are readily available. In this case, Mr. Doe denied any history of owning or using firearms or other weapons, and weapon use does not appear to have played a part in past episodes of domestic violence, which also mitigates risk.

In summary, concerning the questions asked by the Court in terms of overall risk assessment, it is my opinion, with a reasonable degree of psychological certainty, that although the risk of future violence cannot be ruled out, the probable risk of future behavioral aggression is relatively low, in the minimal to moderate range. There is some *concern about risk* associated with the following risk factors: history of previous violence, relationship instability, employment problems, a major mental illness complicated by Wilson's disease, and passive involvement in discharge planning. Additional risk is associated with a history of alcohol and cannabis abuse, a history of impulsivity, and victim availability.

However, significant *mitigating roles* are played by: no violence at a young age, lack of substance use problems, lack of early maladjustment, lack of personality disorder, lack of prior supervision failure, lack of negative attitudes, improvement in active symptoms of mental illness, lack of current impulsivity, responsiveness to treatment, feasible discharge plan, personal support, compliance with remediation attempts, and lack of significant current stress. Additional protection is afforded by lack of minimization of victim impact or any brooding resentment towards the victim of the index offense.

There is *equivocal evidence* about potential exposure to destabilizers and insight. With respect to the latter, it should be noted that Mr. Doe expressed at least a superficial understanding of the need to be compliant with psychiatric medication, which in the past has been problematic for him. Historically, his medication non-compliance has led to the development of acute psychotic symptoms that appear to have been directly related to subsequent interpersonal violence. Psychopathy was not formally assessed.

To the extent that Mr. Doe is fully compliant with prescribed medication, and openly works with professional treatment staff and family members in constructing, maintaining, and refining a realistic and meaningful coping plan, the probable risk of unprovoked behavioral aggression will be acceptably low, and Level 3 (Unsupervised on grounds) and Level 4 (Supervised off grounds) movement could be granted without undue risk to public safety. Naturally, should there be significant changes in risk factors, the overall risk assessment could change as well. This risk assessment should be carefully reevaluated if Mr. Doe experiences break-through psychotic symptoms, becomes behaviorally aggressive to others, or experiences a significant change in his support system. The risk of behavioral aggression taking place would be accelerated by medication non-compliance and the development of openly paranoid attributions towards others. Therefore, this examiner is in agreement with Mr. Doe's treatment team that he should be granted Level 3 (Unsupervised on grounds) and Level 4 (Supervised off grounds) movement privileges to be used in the manner and for the purpose prescribed by his treatment team and any other conditions added by the Court.

I do *not* concur that Mr. Doe is ready for Unsupervised off grounds movement privileges (Level 5) or Conditional Release at this time. Although he has made progress, the progress notes clearly do not support his assertion that acceptance of his diagnosis and need to remain medication compliant are as long standing as he would have one believe. Additionally, there is concern about Mr. Doe's: 1) passive involvement in the discharge process, 2) difficulty describing how he might constructively manage challenges in the full implementation of the discharge plan, and 3) indifference to being in the presence of a destabilizer such as alcohol. Additional therapeutic focus on these issues would be of risk-reduction benefit to Mr. Doe.

In light of these concerns, it would seem only prudent to provide an additional period of inpatient services, and to carefully evaluate how successfully Mr. Doe deals with increasing degrees of movement privileges prior to consideration of his clinical suitability for Conditional Release. Should he successfully complete several months of these privileges with no significant clinical deterioration while maintaining the clinical progress he has made, he would be an appropriate candidate for Conditional Release.

FORENSIC CONCLUSION

Pursuant to Section 2945.401 (D) of the Ohio Revised Code, it is my opinion, with a reasonable degree of psychological certainty, that Mr. Doe does have a serious mental illness, which continues to render him subject to hospitalization by court order, with the least restrictive setting consistent with his need for treatment and safety of community being inpatient hospitalization at Central State Behavioral Healthcare. It is also my opinion that Mr. Doe is ready to be granted Level 3 (Unsupervised on grounds) and Level 4 (Supervised off grounds) movement privileges.

Should he successfully complete several months of these privileges with no significant clinical deterioration while maintaining the clinical progress he has made, he would be appropriate for Level 5 (Unsupervised off grounds) movement privileges. Conditional Release can be considered should he consistently manage Level 5 privileges without incident or evidence of any clinical deterioration for a sustained period of time. The use of any increased movement privileges granted by the Court should be suspended at any sign that he has ceased complying with treatment recommendations or that his mental condition has deteriorated.

Respectfully submitted
Terrance J. Kukor, Ph.D., ABPP
Psychologist
Board Certified in Forensic Psychology
American Board of Professional Psychology
Director, Netcare Forensic Services

TEACHING POINT:
ACHIEVING BALANCE AND FACILITATING ACCURACY IN REPORTING FINDINGS

A fundamental goal in FMHA is to describe findings from the evaluation in a way that allows them to be considered, interpreted, and weighed in a transparent fashion—and then combined to reach conclusions that serve as the evaluator's opinions regarding the referral questions. Recognizing and prioritizing this goal is an important first step in achieving the necessary balance to facilitate accurate reporting of findings and impartial reasoning about their meaning.

There is sometimes the temptation to write reports in a way that is affected by two well-known social science phenomena: the "halo effect" and the "reverse halo effect." That is, if the evaluator concludes that an individual does not appear to have the necessary capacities to waive *Miranda* rights, or stand trial, or be conditionally released (for example), there is some implicit pressure to describe various findings as consistent with this conclusion. Competence to stand trial is composed of functioning in the domains of understanding the legal system and assisting counsel. Some defendants who have a reasonable understanding but are impaired in their capacity to assist might nonetheless be described as also impaired in the former area.

Beyond cultivating an awareness of this kind of potential influence, there are three steps that can be taken to manage it. First, the evaluator should be committed to describing findings that are, simply, what they are—without striving to make them consistent with an eventual conclusion. Second, the evaluator should avoid drawing any conclusions prematurely. If data are truly to drive conclusions, then the evaluator must collect and weigh the data before meaningful conclusions can be drawn. Finally, the evaluator can avoid answering the ultimate legal question whenever possible. Legal questions are "either-or," while describing data can often be more effectively captured on a continuum.

25

Threat/Risk Assessment

Risk assessment—also referred to as "violence risk assessment" or "threat assessment"—is not a legal question *per se*, but rather is incorporated into a variety of FMHA across criminal and civil forensic contexts. The role of risk assessment in a given evaluation ranges from paramount (e.g., assessing the credibility of direct or implied threats, the civil commitment of sexually violent predators) to comparably important with other questions (e.g., juvenile decertification, release decision making, capital sentencing, child custody), to nonexistent (e.g., *Atkins* evaluations, assessments of *Miranda* understanding, evaluation of civil and criminal competencies). Additionally, risk assessment is prospective; where most FMHA focuses on past thoughts and behaviors (e.g., mental state at the time of the offense, or criminal responsibility) or current functioning (e.g., current understanding of legal process, as in competence to stand trial), risk assessment involves appraising the propensity for future behavior. This can incorporate a variety of outcome periods, from long-term predictions of behavior (i.e., "traditional" risk assessment) to the shorter-term assessment of specific circumstances, such as the assessment of specific threats (see below for further discussion).

Due to the increasing prominence of risk assessment in FMHA, it will be addressed through four case reports in this chapter. The principle applied to the first case addresses the importance of identifying forensic issues as they apply to both the broad and the specific aspects of the legal question in a given case. The teaching point associated with the first case describes the role played in risk assessment of a specific model of risk assessment and management (i.e., the Risk/Need/Responsivity model; Andrews & Bonta, 1998). Second, a case report is provided that exemplifies the importance of conducting these evaluations under proper conditions, with a teaching point that addresses how to determine whether conditions are "good enough." The third case report

discusses the use of nomothetic data, which is derived from groups and applied through general laws to forensic assessment. The teaching point makes distinctions between idiographic data and nomothetic data, elaborating further on combining these types of data in FMHA. A second teaching point is included from the contributor of this report regarding how different approaches to risk assessment can inform the evaluation. Finally, the principle preceding the fourth case report concerns relevant historical information in FMHA, while the teaching point is focused on how limited access to historical information can restrict the measures available to evaluators in FMHA generally, and risk assessment specifically.

CASE ONE
PRINCIPLE: IDENTIFY RELEVANT FORENSIC ISSUES (*PRINCIPLE 8*)

This principle is discussed in more detail in Chapter 9 (this volume), so we move directly to a discussion of how the present report illustrates this principle.[1] By definition, every forensic mental health report is relevant to one or more legal issues, and a fundamental principle of forensic mental health assessment is that evaluators should understand the law as it relates to the assessments they conduct. In this case, we conducted a workplace violence risk assessment. The primary legal issue here was related to occupational health and safety law. In the jurisdiction where the evaluation was conducted, the employer had a specific statutory duty to take reasonable steps to assess and manage risk for violence in the workplace. Even if there was not an explicit statutory duty, the employer had a more general duty to stop employees from

---

[1] The discussion for this principle is provided by Stephen Hart, PhD, and Kelly Watt, PhD, who also conducted the evaluation for this case.

perpetrating violence under the doctrine of *respondeat superior*, according to common law in the jurisdiction. Finally, case law with respect to employment in the jurisdiction held that the employer had a general duty to investigate and report suspected criminal activity.

Clearly, employers in the jurisdiction had not only the legal authority to consider their employees' risk for workplace violence—they also had the responsibility to do so. But case law with respect to employment in the jurisdiction also noted that workplace violence risk assessments should not be undertaken unless there are reasonable grounds to do so. Workplace violence risk assessment is an inherently intrusive process, insofar as it involves invasion of privacy (e.g., gathering information about the employee's psychosocial functioning that might not otherwise be required for the purpose of employment). Also, workplace violence risk assessment may be coercive (e.g., participation may be required as a condition of continued employment) and can have serious consequences (e.g., up to and including dismissal or police involvement). Accordingly, the first thing we did when the employer contacted us was to determine whether such an assessment was reasonably necessary. This preliminary evaluation (or *triage*) involved reviewing the nature of complaints. The outcome was that we concurred with the employer that there were reasonable grounds to be concerned the employee might pose a risk to health and safety through perpetration of violence.

Statutory and case law with respect to employment in the jurisdiction also guided the nature and process of workplace violence risk assessment. For example, according to statutory law, employers had a duty to accommodate mental disorder. This duty was limited, however, as employers were only required to take reasonable steps to accommodate it (i.e., "reasonable" in light of the prospects for effective treatment of the mental disorder and the severity of the violence the employee might perpetrate). For this reason, we used procedures that allowed us to consider the possible role of mental disorder, develop a formulation of violence risk, consider scenarios of future violence, and identify potentially effective management strategies. Another example is that case law with respect to employment held that mental disorder should be assessed by an independent mental health professional—not someone hired by the employer to do a workplace violence risk assessment. For this reason, we were careful to base our findings and opinion with respect to

mental disorder on information provided by the employee and by an independent mental health professional. We also noted that the employee (and the union, representing the employee) declined further assessment by an independent mental health professional, and that we did not observe obvious signs of acute or serious mental disorder.

March 31, 2014
Ms. Kendra Kesler
Transportation Safety Enforcement Branch
Department of Public Safety
Re: Mr. Darcy Webb
Dear Ms. Kesler,

Per your request, we have completed a workplace violence risk assessment of Transportation Safety Enforcement Branch (TSEB) employee Mr. Darcy Webb, due to concerns he may pose a risk to the health and safety of other employees at the TSEB. Our findings and opinions are summarized below.

The assessment was based on the following sources of information:

Records pertaining to Mr. Webb, including a copy of Mr. Webb's résumé; correspondence to and from Mr. Webb; complaints made by and about Mr. Webb; photographs of Mr. Webb's office; a TSEB Workplace Assessment Report dated October 23, 2007; notes of a meeting related to concerns about Mr. Webb's behavior, dated December 23, 2013; a Request for Fitness for Duty Evaluation of Mr. Webb, dated January 8, 2014; and the outcome of the Fitness for Duty Evaluation, dated March 15, 2014.

A telephone interview with Mr. Webb, Transportation Safety Enforcement Officer, lasting about two hours, on March 24, 2014 (summarized in Attachment A [following this Case Report]).

Telephone interviews with five TSEB employees (see Attachment B [also following this Case Report]):

Employee #1, lasting 2 hours 15 minutes, on March 11, 2014.
Employee #2, lasting 1 hour, on March 14, 2014.
Employee #3, lasting 1 hour 30 minutes, on March 15, 2014.
Employee #4, lasting 1 hour 30 minutes, on March 16, 2014.
Employee #5, lasting 1 hour, on March 17, 2014.

Interviews did not take place with the majority of current employees because they did not wish to go on record with respect to Mr. Webb's conduct.

With respect to our qualifications....[2]

METHOD

For the purpose of this report, *violence* is defined as actual, attempted, or threatened physical harm of another person, including intimidation or fear-inducing behavior such as stalking. *Workplace violence* is violence that occurs in the workplace or is targeted at people due to their association with the workplace. These definitions encompass acts that would constitute criminal offences against persons, as well as other offences that are committed to further violence. These definitions are also consistent with state occupational health and safety legislation.

Workplace violence risk assessment is the process of evaluating people to characterize the risks that they will commit workplace violence in the future (e.g., the nature, severity, imminence, frequency, and likelihood of future workplace violence), as well as the steps that could be taken to minimize these risks.

There are two basic methods of conducting workplace violence risk assessments. First, the *discretionary approach* involves consideration of the totality of circumstances in the case at hand. This approach may involve reference to professional guidelines. It is used in virtually all workplace violence risk assessments. Second, the *non-discretionary approach*, sometimes referred to as *actuarial risk assessment*, involves consideration of a limited number of factors that are combined according to a fixed and explicit algorithm. It creates a statistical profile of the person that may be compared to known groups of recidivistic and non-recidivistic violent offenders. It is most often used as an adjunct to discretionary approaches. For the purpose of preparing this report, we used the discretionary method, conducting a comprehensive violence risk assessment according to the professional guidelines outlined in Version 2 of the Historical-Clinical-Risk Management Guide or HCR-20 (Webster, Douglas, Eaves, & Hart, 1997). (Below, we present general finding and opinions;

details of findings and opinions specifically with respect the HCR-20 are presented in Attachment C [following this Case Report]).

FINDINGS

For the purpose of forming opinions, we have assumed the following facts to be true, based on the information we reviewed. Most of the findings reflect reports corroborated by multiple sources, or reports by Mr. Webb that were undisputed and whose credibility we had no reason to question. When findings reflect disputed reports, we present the reports and discuss their credibility.

Mr. Webb was born on August 26, 1968, and is currently about 45 years old.

Mr. Webb has good work skills. He was described as intelligent, a good writer, and a skilled artist. He was employed as a retail sales clerk, freelance artist, and firefighter prior to commencing work at the TSEB in 2002.

The work unit at the TSEB in which Mr. Webb was employed since 2002 had some systemic (i.e., chronic and widespread) difficulties with conflict, which adversely affected him and others.

There is no indication that the systemic difficulties and conflict accounted for Mr. Webb's problems with respect to employment outlined below.

Mr. Webb has some serious problems with respect to his employment at the TSEB, apparently unrelated to or distinct from the systemic conflict discussed previously. Records and interviews indicated these included but were not limited to the following:

- Problems related to attendance: He avoided attending mandatory staff meetings, was absent for several days without explanation, failed to call in sick by an acceptable time, and took flex time without permission. He had received verbal warnings about these problems in the past (e.g., in 2007 and 2013).
- Problems getting along with supervisors: He refused to comply with their direct orders (e.g., signing a performance evaluation, opening his office door and blinds, carrying out assigned tasks), challenged their authority to give directions (e.g., "What gives you the right to tell me what to do?"), walked out of meetings with them, and spoke in a disrespectful way to and about them (e.g., calling them "lazy shits"). He complained that they

---

[2] In the original report, we provided a one-paragraph biosketch of each evaluator. This paragraph is redacted here to save space.

treated him differently from others and failed to recognize his positive contributions.

- Problems getting along with other co-workers: He was unable or unwilling to work with many other co-workers as part of investigative teams, which contributed to his productivity problems. Specifically, he worked on a limited number of files over the past five years, all of which have been discontinued, and has no active investigations. He made both formal complaints (e.g., in 2008 and 2012) and informal complaints (e.g., in 2005, 2007, 2008, and 2010) of mistreatment by co-workers. For example, he complained about co-workers' harassing or bullying him by eavesdropping on personal conversations, making insulting and discriminatory statements about him, speaking to him in a disrespectful manner, tampering with or damaging his office property, making vexatious or false complaints against him, and physically assaulting him.

- Had a pattern of conduct that might reasonably be perceived by supervisors and co-workers as intimidating and fear-inducing: This pattern of conduct continued despite repeated requests from and warnings by supervisors to desist during at least the past year and a half, although no formal disciplinary actions were taken in response. Co-workers and supervisors expressed serious concern for their safety stemming from the pattern of conduct. They took protective actions such as un-listing their phone numbers, changing their work clothes, and re-arranging office furniture to facilitate escape in the event he were to attempt to attack them; avoiding working alone with him; and seriously contemplating taking more serious security measures of a life-changing nature.

The pattern of conduct included incidents such as the following:

- He posted pictures on his office walls, placed objects on his office desk, and showed drawings to co-workers and supervisors with violent themes. For example, one of the posters in his office made reference to skulls being split; one of the objects on his desk

was a human figure labeled "Team Work" hanging from gallows by a noose; and some of the drawings he has shown co-workers and supervisors have involved skulls, skeletons, weapons, and violent acts. He also talked about resolving conflicts in a way that others interpreted as supporting or condoning the use of violence. For instance, he stated, "Violence is grossly underrated as a conflict resolution tactic."

- He behaved in an angry and aggressive manner. He swore at, made disrespectful statements about, and spoke in a raised voice to co-workers and supervisors, and was observed doing the same to others during telephone calls. He glared, stared, gritted his teeth, clenched his fists, flexed his arm muscles, and pointed fingers at co-workers and supervisors.

- He made statements that were interpreted by others as vague, indirect, or conditional threats. For example, on April 20, 2012, while taking part in the execution of a search warrant, he perceived the comments of a co-worker as harassing and challenged him to a physical fight, raising his fists and stating, "If you know me, you should know what I am capable of," and "If you have a problem with me, let's resolve it right here, man to man." This incident was reported by the co-worker at the time and subsequently discussed with Mr. Webb in a meeting with a supervisor on July 28, 2013. On March 4, 2013, when speaking with a supervisor about working with others, he stated, "If someone gets hurt, it won't be me." On August 28, 2013, when speaking with a supervisor about taking part in a team-building exercise he stated, "I will slap down anyone who gets in my face in the workplace," and "If I win the lottery, heads will start rolling."

Mr. Webb has problems with awareness or, alternatively, with self-justification in respect to conflict with supervisors and co-workers. On one hand, there are many reports of conflict involving his relations with supervisors and co-workers, as outlined above, that resulted in his making numerous complaints. He also reported experiencing significant distress (e.g., "pain and suffering") as a result of this conflict, was observed by supervisors to be experiencing stress, and was referred to interventions to assist him in coping with stress (e.g., to seek assistance from his general practitioner or the Employee Assistance Program and to take part in "Workplace Stress Management Course" on April 30, 2013). On the other hand, he characterized his problems getting along with supervisors and co-workers as limited in nature or seriousness. He acknowledged problems with only two supervisors, and placed the responsibility for the problems entirely on them. He referred to them as "liars" for whom he had no respect and who he believed might be colluding to convince him to leave his job. He reported only normal or ordinary problems with co-workers. Although he acknowledged filing grievances against "a couple" of co-workers in the past and sending emails of complaints about others, he denied this constituted a pattern of conflict. He flatly rejected the possibility that he ever engaged in behavior that might reasonably have caused others to fear for their safety, and dismissed the reports and concerns of others as lies, insinuations, or unsubstantiated claims.

Mr. Webb reported he does not have problems with physical health, mental health, or substance use. His self-report is consistent with the findings of the recent Fitness for Duty Evaluation, which concluded he did not suffer from a mental disorder that might affect his job performance. He declined the offer to undergo further assessment of his mental health, as he believed it was unnecessary in light of the findings of the recent Fitness for Duty Evaluation. He refused to answer detailed questions in this area, as he believed they were inappropriate or irrelevant.

Mr. Webb reported that he does not have problems with personal or social functioning that might be relevant to understanding his employment situation, past or present. He refused to answer detailed questions in this area, as he believed they were inappropriate or irrelevant.

Mr. Webb reported he does not expect to return to his current work unit but rather to be transferred to another position. He has filed multiple grievances related to his current absence from the workplace and referrals for assessment, and expects to receive written apologies from supervisors and monetary compensation for the pain and suffering he has experienced. He does not expect any conflict with supervisors after he is transferred. He refused to answer detailed questions in this area, including how he would react if he returned to his current work unit, as he believed they were inappropriate or irrelevant.

OPINIONS

Based on the facts outlined above, it is our opinion that Mr. Webb has a history of workplace violence in the form of a pattern of conduct that reasonably caused others to experience concern for their safety. He has for some years and on an intermittent basis engaged in intimidating and fear-inducing behavior. It is important to point out, however, that although he was requested and directed to desist from this behavior during at least the past year and half, no disciplinary action was taken. Also, it is important to point out that that although this behavior caused some significant or moderate psychological harm, it did not escalate to explicit threats of harm or to attempted or actual physical harm.

The causes of Mr. Webb's workplace violence are unclear. This is in part because he did not acknowledge any history of workplace violence or, indeed, any history of significant conflict with co-workers, other than supervisors. Also, he declined to provide information about his past and current functioning that might have helped us understand the reasons for his employment problems, and we were unable to obtain this information from other sources. Although mental health problems may play a causal role with respect to workplace violence in some cases, in this case there is no good evidence that it does: Mr. Webb denied any history of mental disorder, and the recent Fitness for Duty Evaluation concluded he does not suffer from any mental disorder that might affect his work performance. This suggests the causes of his workplace violence may include some combination of interpersonal conflicts, situational stresses, and attitude and personality problems that are not symptomatic of mental disorder.

If Mr. Webb commits workplace violence in the future, the most plausible scenario is a continuation of his past intimidating and fear-inducing behavior. In this scenario, Mr. Webb returns to work, continues to experience conflict with supervisors and co-workers, and then yells or swears at them, possibly even approaching them in an aggressive manner or making vague, indirect, or conditional threats. Such behavior would probably cause others to experience reasonable concern for their safety, but is unlikely to escalate to attempted or actual physical harm unless there is a major exacerbation of his conflict with supervisors and co-workers. Overall, if he returns to his current work unit, the likelihood of this scenario appears to be high due to the continuing conflict with supervisors and co-workers and the frequent and persistent nature of his conduct problems in the past; if he is transferred to another position and any future conflict with supervisors and co-workers is appropriately addressed and managed, the likelihood of problematic conduct would probably be lower. This would be an important management strategy to mitigate his risk towards current co-workers and supervisors.

In light of the opinions outlined above, we are not optimistic about the possibility of effective management of the workplace violence risk posed by Mr. Webb if he returns to his current work unit. That is, we do not believe there are any reasonable steps that could be taken by the TSEB to help Mr. Webb return to work in a manner that protects the health and safety of people in the workplace. First, because the causes of his past workplace violence are unclear, it is also unclear what could be done to prevent future workplace violence. Second, because he has serious problems getting along with supervisors, he is unlikely to heed their suggestions and follow their directions, even when appropriate or potentially helpful.

Finally, in light of the opinions outlined above, we are somewhat more optimistic about the possibility of effective management of the workplace violence risk posed by Mr. Webb if he is transferred to another position. If his workplace violence was simply the result of interpersonal conflicts and situational stresses, the risk should be lower in a new position. But if his workplace violence was due in part to dispositional characteristics such as attitude and personality problems, then the risk may be the same as if he returned to his current work unit. For this reason, we recommend the following management strategies to help mitigate any risk he poses if transferred to another position:

1. Directing him to have no further direct or indirect contact with his current co-workers or supervisors.
2. Entering into a behavioral contract to desist from problematic workplace conduct in the future. This behavioral contract should include a number of specific management strategies, including, but not limited to,

direction to have no further direct or indirect contact with his current co-workers or supervisors, and direction to not attend the building where the TSEB is located.
3. Developing a plan for regular monitoring of his workplace conflict and conduct by supervisors, as well as regular assessment.
4. Respectful workplace coaching or training to help him deal more effectively with conflict with supervisors and co-workers.

LIMITATIONS

A workplace violence risk assessment is only as good as the information on which it is based. In this case, missing information may have adversely affected the reliability of our findings and opinions; in general, missing information is likely to result in the failure to detect risk factors that are actually present and, subsequently, an underestimation of any risks posed.

Also, workplace violence risk is dynamic. Please contact us if new and potentially relevant information comes to light, and we can advise whether this would lead to any substantive change in our findings or opinions. In particular, please contact us if information comes to light indicating there was a major exacerbation of his conflict with supervisors and co-workers or if he continues to engage in workplace violence.

We invite you to contact us once a decision has been made regarding Mr. Webb's future at the TSEB, so we have the opportunity to discuss further with you strategies to mitigate his workplace violence risk.

Thank you for the opportunity to assist in this matter. Please contact us if you have any questions.

Sincerely,
Stephen D. Hart, PhD, and Kelly A. Watt, PhD

Attachments:

    A: Summary of Interview with Mr. Webb
    B: Employees Who Participated in Personal
       Interviews
    C: Summary of Findings With Respect to
       the HCR-20

Attachment A
Summary of Interview with Mr. Webb
Mr. Webb took part in a telephone interview with Dr. Stephen Hart and Dr. Kelly Watt on March 24,

2014. He was accompanied by his union representative, Ms. Minny Malhotra. The interview lasted about two hours in total. We briefly explained the nature and purpose of the interview, including the facts that he was not obliged to answer any questions that he was not comfortable answering, and that the interview was limited with respect to confidentiality. Mr. Webb stated he understood this information and gave his consent to proceed.

Mr. Webb refused to answer detailed questions or provide other information related to personal or social functioning; physical health, mental health, and substance use problems; and future plans. His explanation for refusal was that he believed these questions were inappropriate or irrelevant. When discussing problems related to his employment, he blamed others for any problems he experienced, claimed to have no recollection of making complaints, and denied any pattern of conflictual relations. He denied ever engaging in any previous violence or fear-inducing behavior and dismissed reports and concerns others had for their safety as lies, insinuations, and unsubstantiated claims.

Attachment B
Employees Who Participated in Personal Interviews
[REDACT PRIOR TO DISTRIBUTION]

Employee #1 Mr. Andrew A., Assistant Deputy Commissioner

Employee #2 Ms. Katy B., Deputy Commissioner

Employee #3 Ms. Christine H., Deputy Commissioner

Employee #4 Mr. Kristoff T., Senior Transportation Safety Enforcement Officer

Employee #5 Mr. Daniel H., Assistant Deputy Commissioner

Attachment C
Summary of Findings With Respect to the HCR-20

The HCR-20 is a set of structured professional guidelines for assessing risk for general violence. Evaluators use the guidelines to identify the presence and relevance of 20 basic risk factors for general violence reflecting characteristics of the perpetrator: 10 are *historical* factors, reflecting criminal history and psychosocial adjustment; 5 are *clinical* factors, reflecting recent or current functioning; and 5 are *risk management* factors, reflecting anticipated adjustment in light of plans for the future. Ratings are based on interview and case history materials. The factors in the HCR-20 are listed below. We are familiar with the development and use of the HCR-20: Dr. Hart is one of its developers, and Dr. Watt has been trained in the use of the HCR-20, both Drs. Hart and Watt have conducted research evaluating its usefulness and have trained professionals in its use, and Dr. Hart has given expert testimony about it and based on it.

With respect to presence ratings based on Mr. Webb's history, we rated 2 historical factors (H1 and H4), 2 clinical factors (C1 and C2), and 2 risk management factors (R1 and R5) as definitely present. We rated 1 clinical factor (C4) and 2 risk management factors (R2, R4) as possibly or partially present. We rated the remaining risk factors as not present either in the past or recently.

FACTORS IN THE HCR-20

Historical Factors	Clinical Factors	Risk Management Factors
Previous violence	Lack of insight	Plans lack feasibility
Young age at first violent incident	Negative attitudes	Exposure to destabilizers
Relationship instability	Active symptoms of a major mental illness	Lack of personal support
Employment problems		Noncompliance with remediation attempts
Substance use problems	Impulsivity	Stress
Major Mental Illness	Unresponsive to treatment	
Psychopathy		
Early Maladjustment		
Personality Disorder		
Prior Supervision Failure		

As the HCR-20 is an *aide mémoire* or checklist designed to assist clinical evaluations; it cannot be used to make quantitative estimates (i.e., probabilistic predictions) of risk for general violence.

Information provided in each of the three RNR-type areas can be valuable in conceptualizing and structuring the evaluation. This approach can also help in effective communication with organizations regarding their alternatives.

TEACHING POINT:
THE ROLE OF RISK-NEED-RESPONSIVITY IN CONTEMPORARY THREAT/RISK ASSESSMENT

Contemporary threat and risk assessment (see the next teaching point for a distinction between the two) is typically concerned with three questions.

- How serious is the threat? (This takes into account both the likelihood that it will be carried out and the nature of the harm that would occur if it were.)
- What needs does the person have that are related to the threat's occurrence?
- What interventions are available and appropriate to address these needs and otherwise manage the threat?

These questions closely parallel the three areas of *risk, need,* and *responsivity* that are the constituents of RNR (Andrews & Bonta, 1998). In a workplace threat assessment like that in the current case, the answers to these questions can help inform the recommendations made to the organization requesting the evaluation. That organization has three major options in such cases. They can:

1. Retain the individual in the workplace while implementing relatively minor interventions (e.g., clarifying misunderstandings, advising employee and perhaps supervisors about interactions, perhaps adjusting work shifts);
2. Retain the individual in the workplace with major interventions (e.g., counseling and possibly medical evaluation for employee; time away from work) with the possibility of dismissal if those interventions are not effective; or
3. Dismiss the employee while taking appropriate steps to be humane and respectful to that employee while also ensuring the safety of the organization's other employees.

CASE TWO
PRINCIPLE: ENSURE THAT CONDITIONS FOR EVALUATION ARE QUIET, PRIVATE, AND DISTRACTION-FREE (*PRINCIPLE 22*)

This principle is addressed in more detail in Chapter 20 (this volume), so we focus on how the present report illustrates the principle. The report indicates that the evaluation took place at the Psychological Clinic. Such a clinic would be set up to ensure that evaluations could be conducted without undue distraction, and with attention to privacy and noise considerations. Conducting an evaluation under ideal (or relatively ideal) circumstances helps alleviate concerns about the impact of the evaluation setting on the validity of the test results. Such a setting would also presumably be structured to ensure the safety of the evaluator and examinee.

Evaluators performing FMHA in secure hospitals, detention centers, jails, and prisons often encounter conditions that are far from ideal. This principle prompts the forensic clinician to consider whether any of the needs for privacy, quiet, or freedom from distraction are addressed so poorly that the results of the evaluation could be compromised. In addition, there are some matters discussed during certain evaluations that could put the evaluee at risk of harm by others if privacy were compromised and the discussion overheard. When one of these conditions is unacceptably poor, the evaluator must take steps to ensure either a more acceptable setting in which to move the evaluation at present—or return on another day, when alternative evaluation conditions have been approved.

Confidential
Psychological Evaluation
Name: Johnny Williams
Birthdate: January 2, 1999
Examiner: Dewey Cornell, Ph.D.
Report Date: April 1, 2012

PURPOSE OF EVALUATION

Johnny is a 13-year-old student at Apple Middle School who was referred for a threat assessment by the school principal because he threatened to shoot the assistant principal and a teacher. Johnny has been suspended from school, but the school board is willing to reconsider the length of his suspension pending the outcome of a psychological evaluation.

CONSENT

This evaluation was undertaken at the request of the school principal. Johnny and his mother were interviewed at the Psychological Clinic on March 5, 2012. I informed them of the purpose of the evaluation and that a report would be submitted to them and to the school principal. Both agreed to participate and signed the permission form as well as release forms to obtain additional information.

SOURCES OF INFORMATION

1. Interview and psychological testing with Johnny Williams on March 5, 2012; 5 hours
2. Interview with Johnny's mother on March 5, 2012; 90 minutes
3. Telephone interview with school principal on March 7, 2012; 45 minutes
4. Telephone interview with assistant principal on March 8, 2012; 30 minutes
5. Telephone interview with therapist at Community Counseling Center on March 8; 30 minutes
6. Behavior Assessment System for Children (BASC) Parent Rating Scales (BASC-PRS) completed collaboratively by Mr. and Mrs. Williams; Self-Report of Personality–Adolescent (BASC-SRP-A) completed by Johnny
7. Millon Adolescent Clinical Inventory (MACI) completed by Johnny
8. Spielberger State Trait Anger Expression Inventory–2 (STAXI-2) completed by Johnny
9. School records, including prior records from elementary school (42 pages)
10. Community Counseling Center records (8 pages)

BACKGROUND INFORMATION

Family History

Johnny is the younger of two children born to Father, 38, and Mother, 35. Mr. Williams works for a construction company, and Mrs. Williams is an administrative assistant. According to the Williamses, Johnny's early development was unremarkable. They described him as a very active child who tends to be impulsive and somewhat clumsy. They reported no serious misbehavior at home.

Johnny has a close relationship with his older brother and looks up to him. Notably, Johnny was quite distressed when his brother left home to join the military earlier this year. As a parting gift, his brother gave Johnny the hand-held video game that was confiscated at school. His parents feel that Johnny reacted so strongly to school authorities who confiscated the video game because of his attachment to his older brother.

According to his parents, Johnny spends much of his free time playing video games on a computer at home. Most of the games he plays are first-person shooter or quest games with a violent theme. Johnny has no history of fighting or similar aggressive or destructive behavior. His father has a hunting rifle at home. Johnny has fired it at a rifle range with his father, but has never handled it with his father's supervision. He enjoys reading about military weapons on websites and hopes to follow his brother in joining the military when he is 18.

School History

When Johnny started elementary school, his teachers reported that he did not sit still and was often out of his seat or talking when he should be quiet. Johnny's family moved after second grade and then again after fourth grade, so that he attended three different schools. In the sixth grade, Johnny was referred for a psychological evaluation due to poor grades, concerns about his organizational skills, difficulty remaining on task, and frequent absences from school. The school psychologist found that Johnny's cognitive abilities were in the high average range, and his achievement scores were commensurate with his abilities, although his grades were not. She noted no social or emotional problems in her evaluation, and attributed his academic difficulties to poor attendance, lack of motivation, and weak study skills. Johnny was found to be ineligible for special education services.

During the seventh grade, Johnny's parents took him to the Community Counseling Center where he was diagnosed with attention deficit disorder, inattentive type. According to Mrs. Williams, a physician prescribed medication to treat Johnny's attention problems. It appeared to help him in his schoolwork, but caused him to have difficulty sleeping at night. The medication was changed, but he continued to have sleep difficulties, so his parents stopped the medication.

During the eighth grade, Johnny's grades began to drop from Bs and Cs to Cs and Ds. In addition, Johnny missed approximately one day per week of school and often failed to turn in his homework.

Johnny's discipline record showed no problems with fighting, threatening, or disruptive behavior prior to the present incident. He has not previously been suspended from school or sent to the principal's office.

Since being suspended from school, Johnny has been seeing a therapist at Community Counseling Center and has attended three sessions. His therapist reports that Johnny is upset that he was suspended from school and wants to return to school. He feels that his punishment was "not fair," but denies any intention to shoot the assistant principal or teacher. He has told his therapist, "I was mad and I didn't mean it."

Threat Information

According to school reports and interviews with the principal and assistant principal, Johnny was observed playing a hand-held video game in the school cafeteria during lunchtime. Because video games are not permitted at school, a teacher reprimanded Johnny and sent him to the assistant principal, who confiscated the game. Later that day, two students reported to a teacher that Johnny was talking about "killing Mr. X (the assistant principal) and Mrs. Y (the teacher)." A third student said that Johnny was crying in class and that when the student asked Johnny what was wrong, Johnny replied, "I already told everybody what was wrong and I told everybody what I was going to do about it. I've got bullets for both of them." The principal notified Johnny's parents and told them to keep him at home until the school determined how to respond to the threat. The following week, the County School Board imposed a 365-day school suspension. Subsequently, the Williams were told that the school board would reconsider the length of the suspension if Johnny were to undergo a psychological evaluation.

MENTAL STATUS EXAM AND DIAGNOSTIC FINDINGS

Johnny was interviewed at the Psychological Clinic for approximately five hours. He is a thin,

Caucasian 13-year-old boy who wears glasses and appears younger than his actual age. Johnny was friendly and articulate during initial introductions. He easily engaged in conversation about computer games and the military. Johnny seemed to enjoy telling stories about his experiences playing computer games and describing what he knew about military firearms, grenades, and tanks.

Contrary to reports that Johnny has difficulty staying on task and concentrating, he was focused and engaged throughout the day. He followed directions without needing them repeated and showed no signs of fidgeting or distractibility. He remained on task in completing a series of self-report inventories with several hundred questions.

Johnny completed the Millon Adolescent Clinical Inventory (MACI), an objectively scored personality test. His personality profile was notable for symptoms of anxiety and depression. He identified "fearful/worrying" and "schoolwork" as the problems that are troubling him the most. In addition, he endorsed items on the MACI such as "It is not unusual to feel lonely and unwanted," and "I feel lonely and empty most of the time." When asked about these items, Johnny replied, "Well, I don't have a whole lot of friends because we have moved a lot, but now that I don't go to school, I don't have any friends." His endorsement of questions on the State Trait Anger Expression Inventory–2 showed no unusual degree of anger.

Johnny's parents completed the Behavior Assessment System for Children (BASC). The BASC is a questionnaire designed to identify and differentiate a variety of emotional and behavioral difficulties. Mr. and Mrs. Williams's ratings of Johnny's behavior indicated problems with attention, somatization (complaints about health), and withdrawal. Johnny's self-report on the BASC did not identify any problem areas outside of the normal range.

Threat Assessment Findings

This evaluation makes use of the Virginia Student Threat Assessment Guidelines (Cornell & Sheras, 2006), which is a threat assessment model based in part on the conclusions and recommendations of the Federal Bureau of Investigation (FBI) and U.S. Secret Service studies of school shootings (Fein et al., 2002; O'Toole, 2000; Vossekuil, 2002). These studies make a critical distinction between *making a threat* and *posing a threat*. Many persons will make a threatening statement but not necessarily pose a threat to others. It is critical to determine whether the person is engaging in behaviors that indicate he or she is planning and preparing to carry out the threat.

Johnny was initially reluctant to talk about the threat incident. However, when I read statements from other students about the threat incident that quoted Johnny as saying he was going to kill the assistant principal and a teacher with a gun and had bullets for them, Johnny replied, "Yeah, I said something like that."

When asked how he would have killed the principal, he replied, "I'm not sure, I didn't have any plan, I just said it." When asked why he wanted to kill the principal, Johnny responded, "I never *wanted* to kill him." He then explained that he did not *want* to kill anyone, but that he was upset because he had lost the video game. He claimed that a teacher had confiscated a military magazine from him in sixth grade and never returned it, and he was afraid the same thing was going to happen with his video game.

Johnny said that he could not bear to lose the video game because his brother had given it to him as a going-away present when his brother joined the Army. He stated that since the principal had returned the game to his parents, he had no reason to kill anyone at school. His parents have not returned the game to him as punishment for taking it to school, but he is willing to accept this punishment because he knows he will get the game back eventually.

When asked whether there is a better way to have handled the confiscation of his video game, Johnny stated, "I know, I know, I shouldn't have said I was gonna kill someone. Everyone gets freaked out and I'm sorry. I was just upset." He related that his parents have told him that he should apologize to the assistant principal and the teacher he threatened. He said he is planning to write an apology with his therapist.

The most important consideration in conducting a student threat assessment is to consider whether the individual continues to pose a threat to carry out an act of violence. This evaluation uncovered no indication that Johnny continues to harbor angry feelings or desire to harm the persons he threatened. There is no indication that Johnny has undertaken any planning or preparation to harm the persons he threatened. Moreover, Johnny does not have a history of violent behavior.

The Virginia Student Threat Assessment Guidelines makes a distinction between transient threats and substantive threats. Transient threats are expressions of anger or frustration that do not convey a sustained intent to carry out the threat, whereas a substantive threat reflects a sustained intent to harm someone. Based on the information considered in this evaluation, Johnny's threat is transient rather than substantive. His threat expresses his anger and frustration over losing his video game, but not a sustained intent to harm the persons he threatened.

Recommendations

In conclusion, Johnny does not appear to pose a threat of violence to the assistant principal or teacher at this school. He acknowledges making a threatening statement in a state of anger and frustration, but denies any intent to carry out the threat. There is no evidence of his engaging in any planning or preparation to carry out the threat. Several weeks have passed, and Johnny realizes that his threatening statement was inappropriate, and he is planning an apology. The video game has been returned, but his parents have withheld it from him because of his misbehavior, and Johnny has accepted this disciplinary consequence. Furthermore, Johnny's parents have taken him for counseling. Under these circumstances, it is feasible to plan Johnny's return to school. If the school board decides to permit Johnny to return to school, we recommend that Johnny and his parents agree to a plan for his return to school with the following components:

1. Johnny should make amends for his threatening statements by apologizing and explaining his behavior to the persons he threatened. Johnny should promise not to use threatening language in the future. Johnny should also acknowledge that he broke school rules by taking the video game to school.

2. Johnny should meet with the school resource officer and the principal to review the legal and disciplinary consequences of making threats against others in order to reinforce his understanding of the seriousness of his behavior and commitment to appropriate behavior in the future.

3. It is possible that other students and parents will have questions about Johnny's return to school. Johnny's parents should give school authorities permission to share a general statement to assure them that Johnny has apologized for his misbehavior and that it is considered safe and appropriate for him to return to school.

4. The school guidance counselor should meet with Johnny and talk through how he might react if other students were to ask him questions or to tease him about his suspension. The guidance counselor should plan to check in with Johnny each day for the first week he returns to school and then less frequently as the counselor judges appropriate to monitor his adjustment. They should agree on a plan for him to contact the guidance counselor if there is an incident or problem that makes him angry or distressed.

5. Johnny's parents should give permission for school authorities to release appropriate information to the persons who were threatened and other school staff. This information should include the plan for Johnny's return to school, including information that he has apologized for his threatening statements, he has been disciplined by his parents, he has seen a therapist, and he has been evaluated by a psychologist who concluded that he did not pose a threat.

6. Johnny's parents should agree to contact the school guidance counselor to keep the counselor informed on how Johnny is doing and to notify the counselor immediately if there are any problems with Johnny's peers.

7. The school district should consider training threat assessment teams for its schools. Use of the Virginia Student Threat Assessment Guidelines will permit school-based teams to resolve most student threats in a safe and expeditious manner and make use of disciplinary consequences that do not require long-term suspensions.

Respectfully submitted,
Dewey G. Cornell, PhD
Licensed Clinical Psychologist

TEACHING POINT:
HOW CAN THREAT ASSESSMENT BE DISTINGUISHED AS A FORM OF RISK ASSESSMENT?
(contributed by Dewey G. Cornell)

Historically, "threat assessment" has been used to describe activities ranging from an examination of a threatening letter to evaluation of an organization's vulnerability to attack (Dietz, 2012). In the forensic mental health field, threat assessment has emerged as a systematic approach to evaluating and responding to someone's threatening communications or behavior.

Threat assessment can be distinguished from other forms of risk assessment (Reddy et al., 2001). Threat assessments are concerned with the investigation of an immediate situation, such as a student who has threatened a classmate or an employee who has threatened a co-worker, whereas risk assessments typically are more open-ended and consider someone's risk of violence directed at anyone at any time. As the field matures, the global terms "threat assessment" and "risk assessment" may be replaced by terminology categorizing more specialized kinds of assessments.

Another important distinction is that risk assessments often rely on instruments designed to sum some combination of risk factors into a risk score. Such scores are problematic for threat assessment purposes. Much of the research on risk factors is concerned with *general* risk for violence at any time, which may not be useful in assessing the *immediate* risk to carry out a specific threat. The most important risk factors considered in a threat assessment may be much more situational and fluid in nature, such as an individual's willingness to resolve a conflict or dispute in a nonviolent manner and whether a targeted individual engages in conciliatory versus provocative behavior. A single factor such as recent acquisition of a firearm or evidence of planning or preparation to carry out an attack can have overriding significance, no matter what score the individual has on a lifetime-risk instrument.

Because threat assessment is more concerned with prevention than prediction, the process does not stop with the assignment of a fixed score, but leads to interventions and ongoing reassessments of risk until the threat is ended. Ideally a threat assessment concludes when the problem or conflict that was the basis for the threat is resolved.

Threat assessment in school settings must consider that students frequently threaten one another, although most of these threats are not taken seriously and few are carried out (Nekvasil & Cornell, 2012). Complicating matters further, some school authorities may overreact to student threats and make use of "zero tolerance" policies to suspend or expel students for relatively benign misbehavior (American Psychological Association Zero Tolerance Task Force, 2008). As a result, student threat assessment must provide school authorities with a flexible and efficient means of discriminating the most serious cases from a multitude of less serious ones (Cornell & Sheras, 2006). A series of field-tests and controlled studies (Cornell, Allen, & Fan, 2012) found that school-based teams using the Virginia Student Threat Assessment Guidelines could quickly resolve the most common forms of transient student threats while focusing more attention and taking protective action in the more serious, substantive cases. Schools using the Virginia Guidelines had lower rates of school suspensions, less bullying, and more positive school climates than comparison schools. The Virginia Guidelines are the first form of risk assessment to be recognized as an evidence-based practice in the National Registry of Evidence-based Programs and Practices (NREPP; http://www.nrepp.samhsa.gov/ViewIntervention.aspx?id=263).

CASE THREE
PRINCIPLE: USE NOMOTHETIC EVIDENCE IN ASSESSING CLINICAL CONDITION, FUNCTIONAL ABILITIES, AND CAUSAL CONNECTION (*PRINCIPLE 28*)

This principle was discussed in detail in Chapter 2 (this volume), so we will move directly to the case report. The purpose of the evaluation was to (1) assess Mr. Starkey's current emotional, behavioral, and cognitive functioning, (2) identify his current and future risk for violence; and (3) identify any treatment and habilitation needs. Consistent with this principle, the evaluator used several measures that have established levels of reliability and validity: Personality Assessment Inventory

(PAI), Psychopathy Checklist–Revised (PCL-R), and Historical-Clinical-Risk Management–20 (HCR-20). Moreover, the measures used by the evaluator have an empirical relationship to the forensic issues being assessed: the Montreal Cognitive Assessment (MoCA) is a screening measure for cognitive functioning; the PAI assesses emotional and behavioral functioning, which speaks to Mr. Starkey's current clinical condition; and the PCL-R and HCR-20 were used to assess violence risk. In addition, an assessment of response style was administered (Paulhus Deception Scale, or PDS), which provides the evaluator with important information about the interpretability of the results of other testing.

FORENSIC PSYCHOLOGICAL EVALUATION

Name: John Starkey   Dates of Evaluation: 11/29/10, 12/1/10

Age: 43   Date of Report: 12/11/10

Date of Birth: 1/15/67
Education: High School Diploma
Marital Status: Married
Occupation: Receiving Clerk

REFERRAL QUESTION/ NOTIFICATION

Mr. Starkey is a 43-year-old white male who was ordered by Judge Johnson to undergo a psychological evaluation. Documents provided by Mr. Starkey's attorney indicate that he had been charged with criminal mischief, unlawful discharge of a firearm, and aggravated assault on a law enforcement officer based on allegations that—on October 1, 2010—he checked into a hotel, vandalized the room, and threatened a law enforcement officer who was called to the scene.

Mr. Starkey's attorney reported that his client entered guilty pleas to all charges and was to undergo a psychological evaluation that was to (1) assess his current emotional, behavioral, and cognitive functioning; (2) identify his current and future risk for violence; and (3) identify any treatment and habilitation needs. His attorney further explained that treatment and habilitation recommendations would probably be incorporated in a probation supervision plan that would be put in place by the court and the Florida Department of Corrections.

SOURCES OF INFORMATION

Mr. Starkey was evaluated at the Falkenburg Road Jail on November 29 and December 1, 2010. Upon our meeting, Mr. Starkey indicated that he had been told about the evaluation by his attorney. He was informed that the assessment was being conducted in anticipation of a sentencing hearing, and any information he provided might be included in a report that would be submitted to his attorney, the prosecutor, and the judge. Mr. Starkey indicated his understanding of the notification, agreed to participate in the evaluation, and signed a consent form noting this.

The following sources of information were considered when conducting the evaluation:

- Clinical interviews with the examinee (11/29/10, 1.0 hours; 12/1/10, 2.0 hours)
- Telephone interview with the examinee's mother, Delores Starkey (12/3/10, 0.8 hours)
- Telephone interview with the examinee's wife, Ceil Starkey (12/3/10, 0.75 hours)
- Telephone interview with examinee's co-worker and friend, Jeff Travis (12/3/12, 0.33 hours)
- Arrest reports and supporting documents (11/20/10)
- Court order authorizing forensic evaluation (11/20/10)
- Records of examinee's medical treatment (11/29/10, 12/15/10)
- Paulhus Deception Scale (PDS, 11/29/10)
- Montreal Cognitive Assessment (MoCA, 12/1/10)
- Personality Assessment Inventory (PAI, 11/29/10)
- Psychopathy Checklist–Revised (PCL-R, 12/1/10)
- Historical, Clinical, Risk Management–20 (HCR-20, 12/1/10)

CURRENT CLINICAL FUNCTIONING

John Starkey is a 43-year-old muscular white male who appears his stated age and has the appearance of a body builder. When evaluated at the jail, Mr. Starkey was well-groomed and dressed in prison attire; his hair was cut short, and he wore glasses.

Mr. Starkey expressed himself well; his speech was well-paced, logical, and goal-directed; and there were no indications that the logic or form of his thought process was impaired by a mental disorder. Similarly, Mr. Starkey did not evidence any unusual ideas or beliefs indicative of delusional thinking (i.e., fixed, false beliefs attributable to a mental disorder), nor did he report any history of such beliefs. Mr. Starkey also reported no history suggestive of hallucinations (i.e., hearing or seeing things in the absence of external stimuli).

Mr. Starkey displayed a range of emotion during the evaluation, and his expressed emotion was always appropriate to and consistent with the content of his speech. He sometimes laughed (at appropriate times) and also adopted a more serious demeanor when appropriate. His attention and concentration appeared unimpaired, as did his memory for remote and recent events.

Mr. Starkey described himself as functioning well at and around the time of the evaluation. More specifically, he acknowledged experiencing symptoms of depression in the months preceding his arrest and thoughts of suicide immediately before he was jailed. He did, however, describe himself as feeling much better at the time of the evaluation and relayed no problems with mood, sleep, energy, or appetite. He also reported having no thoughts of harming himself or others at or around the time of the interview.

RESULTS OF PSYCHOLOGICAL TESTING

Mr. Starkey was administered a number of psychological tests, including the Paulhus Deception Scale (PDS), Montreal Cognitive Assessment (MoCA), Personality Assessment Inventory (PAI), Psychopathy Checklist–Revised (PCL-R), and the Historical-Clinical-Risk Management–20 (HCR-20).

Findings from the PDS, a structured self-report measure designed to assess an examinee's response style and approach to the evaluation, indicated an attempt on Mr. Starkey's part to portray himself in a positive light, along with overconfidence in his abilities and a lack of insight into his shortcomings and limitations. His performance on the MoCA—a screening measure of cognitive functioning—revealed no gross problems with attention, concentration, receptive language, expressive language, or memory.

Mr. Starkey was also administered the PAI, a structured self-report measure of emotional and behavioral functioning. Response style scales of the PAI indicated that Mr. Starkey was involved in the testing and responded to the items in a consistent manner, but there was evidence he made some attempt to portray himself in a positive light and deny shortcomings or problems (consistent with results of the PDS). Thus, although the PAI profile is interpreted, it may underestimate the degree of difficulties experienced by Mr. Starkey at the time of testing.

Mr. Starkey's PAI responses suggest that, at the time of testing, he was experiencing no difficulties with anxiety, depression, confused thinking, anger/irritability, paranoid or suspicious thinking, emotional lability, substance abuse, or health concerns. However, in his responses, Mr. Starkey did acknowledge some contemplation of suicide and self-injurious behavior.

Using data from collateral records and interviews with Mr. Starkey and his mother, the PCL-R—a measure designed to identify persons high in psychopathic traits—was scored. A total score of 7 places Mr. Starkey at the 4th percentile when compared to a sample of prison inmates and does not indicate the presence of a psychopathic personality style.

The HCR-20, a structured professional judgment tool, was used to ensure a comprehensive consideration of factors associated with violence. Risk factors that are present in Mr. Starkey's case (see discussion of these factors below) and that suggest a heightened risk for violence include a history of aggressive behavior, relationship instability, employment problems, substance abuse, depression, a lack of insight into the nature and extent of his emotional and substance abuse problems, negative attitudes toward treatment, marital discord, health concerns, financial problems, and employment concerns.

RELEVANT HISTORY

Family and Marital History

Mr. Starkey stated that he was born in and has always lived in Florida. He reported growing up in a middle-class neighborhood with his parents and brother, who is four years older than he. He described both parents in positive terms and stated that his mother was a homemaker and his father worked as a mechanic at an auto dealership. Although he acknowledged being subjected to corporal punishment when younger, Mr. Starkey did not believe that this constituted abuse or inappropriate treatment, and neither he nor his mother indicated any family contact with child protective services.

Mr. Starkey reported marrying at the age of 37 and having no children. He acknowledged a one-year history of marital discord revolving around financial concerns, his wife's unfounded suspicions of infidelity on his part, and their mutual alcohol abuse. He noted, however, that his wife had not used any alcohol in the preceding year, and that he had decided that he would no longer consume alcohol as result of his most recent arrest. Mr. Starkey explained that his wife owned and managed a gym that was a financial liability insofar as she had earned less than $10,000 annually for the preceding two years.

Educational History

Mr. Starkey reported graduating from high school and never having been retained, placed in special classes, or identified as having a learning disability. Mr. Starkey indicated he was never expelled but did describe once having been suspended in the eleventh grade for repeated tardiness. He described himself as an average student throughout school and opined that he probably could have obtained better grades if he had applied himself more. This history of academic performance and behavioral adjustment was largely corroborated by Mr. Starkey's mother in a phone interview.

Employment History

Mr. Starkey reported working in a variety of unskilled positions between the ages of 18 (when he graduated from high school) and 23. For the past 20 years, explained Mr. Starkey, he has worked at a gutter manufacturer (as a trailer-loader for the first eight years and as a shipping clerk since then). Mr. Starkey described his job as "good…excellent," and reported no history of workplace difficulties or sanctions. He expressed concerns, however, about whether he would continue to be employed given his recent arrest and contact he'd had with a work supervisor immediately before his arrest. Mr. Starkey explained that this supervisor, whom he considered a friend, had visited him while in jail and explained that he would be placed on administrative leave until a decision could be made about a possible return to work.

Medical History

Mr. Starkey described an unremarkable medical history with the exception of a year-long history of chronic pain he experienced since injuring himself while lifting weights. He reported that he had been diagnosed with a herniated disc and was contemplating surgery that had been recommended. Mr. Starkey indicated that his prescribed medication (Oxycodone) was helpful with controlling the pain, and indicated that he only took this medication as prescribed. Records provided by Mr. Starkey's family physician and physiatrist corroborated his reported medical history, but also indicated a recent and current prescription for anti-anxiety medication (Ativan) for "general distress and poor sleep."

Psychiatric History

Review of jail medical records indicated that the defendant had been diagnosed with alcohol abuse and depressive disorder not otherwise specified upon entering the jail after his October arrest and has been prescribed antidepressant medication since that time. In a phone interview, the examinee's work supervisor and friend, Jeff Travis, expressed concerns about Mr. Starkey's increasingly depressed behavior in the months preceding his arrest.

Mr. Starkey described the antidepressant medication he has taken since his arrest as having improved his mood and outlook, and he indicated his intention to continue taking it upon returning to the community. In contrast, Mr. Starkey did not see himself as needing to participate in individual psychotherapy focused on his problems. Rather, Mr. Starkey seemed assured that these problems would remit as a result of him and his wife "making big changes" and having a newfound commitment to each other.

Mr. Starkey acknowledged experiencing some symptoms of depression in the months preceding his recent arrest, including subjective feelings of sadness, diminished energy, impaired sleep, low self-esteem, increased irritability, anhedonia, and a lack of self-confidence. He indicated that these symptoms increased in severity in the months before his arrest and, in combination with marital discord and disinhibition via alcohol intoxication, resulted in his contemplating suicide on the night of his arrest. However, Mr. Starkey remained adamant that he had never contemplated suicide other than the evening of his arrest. Mr. Starkey

described himself as "feeling much better" subsequent to his arrest, abstinence from alcohol, and newfound motivation to make significant changes in his life. However, he acknowledged that he and his wife were at risk of foreclosure due to missing mortgage payments, and he felt added financial pressure given concerns he could lose his job.

In a phone interview, Mr. Starkey's wife expressed concern about his depression, alcohol consumption, and use of pain and anxiety medications in the months preceding his arrest. Ms. Starkey described her husband as "self-medicating" and "in denial," and she noted that while she had urged him to get treatment for these problems, he had consistently refused to do so by minimizing their severity and extent. Ms. Starkey also described marital problems, which she attributed to her unfounded suspicions of her husband's infidelity, her and her husband's substance abuse, his "bullying" of her, chronic pain he experienced from a back injury, and financial problems that she attributed, in part, to her struggling business and his gambling. Ms. Starkey expressed her hope that her husband's arrest on the current charges was "the wakeup call he needed" and expressed her intention to remain in the marriage, contingent upon his getting treatment for his depression, substance abuse, and gambling problems.

Substance Use History

Mr. Starkey reported never using illegal drugs. He stated that that he first used alcohol at the age of 16 years, when he began drinking beer on weekends to the point of intoxication (typically 4 to 6 cans of beer, 1 to 2 times per week). He noted that this pattern of use continued until 12 months before the evaluation, when he began drinking more frequently (6 to 8 cans of beer, 3 to 4 times per week) in response to marital discord. Mr. Starkey acknowledged that his alcohol use had "probably" caused problems in his marriage and was related to his only two contacts with the criminal justice system, but he offered that he did not need substance abuse treatment since he had vowed to abstain from alcohol. Mr. Starkey reported never using steroids or other illegal substances in connection with his body-building regimen.

Gambling History

Although Mr. Starkey acknowledged regularly gambling at a local casino, he reported that he had no concerns about this behavior. Mr. Starkey maintained that the losses he endured were "insignificant" insofar as they constituted no more than $8,000 during the preceding 12 months, and he had won between $8,000 and $10,000 during the prior two years. In separate phone interviews, Ms. Starkey expressed her suspicions that her husband's gambling losses were more significant than he relayed to her. Mr. Travis reported that gambling losses at a local casino combined with a pattern of alcohol abuse resulted in significant financial stress and marital discord for the examinee and his wife.

Criminal Justice History

Other than his current contact with the criminal justice system, Mr. Starkey reported that his only other arrest was for driving under the influence of alcohol in 2008, in response to which he pleaded no contest and was placed on probation, which he completed successfully. Mr. Starkey explained that this incident occurred when, after an argument with his wife, he left their home and was stopped by an officer when he failed to yield at a traffic light. Arrest reports provided for review indicated that the examinee was arrested after failing field sobriety tests; a Breathalyzer analysis revealed a blood alcohol level of 0.10. These documents further indicated that Mr. Starkey was placed on and successfully completed probation after pleading no contest to a charge of misdemeanor driving under the influence of alcohol.

CIRCUMSTANCES SURROUNDING THE INDEX OFFENSES

Mr. Starkey indicated that, in the hours preceding his arrest, he had been drinking alcohol and gambling at a local casino with friends and, upon returning home, he got into an argument with his wife about their finances. He explained that his wife kicked him, and, in response, he slapped her. After his wife threatened to report the incident to law enforcement, he reported leaving their home, buying a fifth of rum, checking into a hotel, drinking, and taking prescribed pain medication. Mr. Starkey noted that, as he became intoxicated, he became increasingly despondent about his financial and marital problems, and he contemplated suicide as a result. He acknowledged that he shot the television and mirror in his room with a handgun that he typically used at a gun range (and kept in the glove compartment

of his car), and then he communicated his intent to harm himself via text messages to his wife and Mr. Travis. When police arrived at the scene and called his room, Mr. Starkey threatened to shoot them and then himself. He then reported surrendering to police.

Ms. Starkey corroborated much of the account offered by her husband. She acknowledged that he came home intoxicated and, during an argument over finances, she kicked him and he hit her in response. She indicated that, a few hours after he left their home, she began to get text messages from him in which he identified where he was staying and his intention to harm himself. In response, she called local law enforcement.

The arrest report indicated that the police responded to the hotel after receiving a call from Mr. Starkey's wife indicating that he was intoxicated, staying at the hotel, and intended to commit suicide. Officers noted that, in a phone call with them, Mr. Starkey threatened to shoot them and himself. The report detailed that he eventually surrendered without incident, after which he was examined at the local hospital and eventually transported to the county jail.

SUMMARY AND RECOMMENDATIONS

John Starkey is a 43-year-old white male who, upon pleading guilty to charges of criminal mischief, aggravated assault on a law enforcement officer, and unlawful discharge of a firearm, was ordered to undergo a psychological evaluation to (1) assess his current emotional, behavioral, and cognitive functioning; (2) identify his current and future risk for violence; and (3) identify any treatment and habilitation needs.

Mr. Starkey is currently experiencing significant problems with depression, excessive gambling, marital discord, chronic pain, alcohol abuse, and possible prescription medication abuse. When interviewed, he acknowledged only some of these problems, and was motivated to portray himself in a positive light. Thus, Mr. Starkey is not considered to have good insight into the nature and severity of his problems or be highly motivated for some of the treatment he needs.

Although not at imminent risk, Mr. Starkey is considered to be at increased risk for both self-injurious behavior (i.e., suicidal ideation and acts) and aggressive behavior directed towards

---

COMMENT: EPILOGUE

Mr. Starkey was eventually released to the community on probation, failed to participate in recommended treatment, separated from his wife, and lost his job. Approximately 12 months after the evaluation, Mr. Starkey was arrested for attempted murder in connection with a shooting that occurred during a traffic dispute (a "road rage" incident). When out on bail on this charge, Mr. Starkey was informed by his attorney that a prolonged period of imprisonment was likely since he had used a firearm during the index offense. In an apparent attempt to obtain money to flee the jurisdiction, Mr. Starkey was involved in a foiled armed robbery during which he took hostages, and eventually shot and killed himself in a standoff with law enforcement officers called to the scene.

---

others at the current time, given a number of factors, including:

- A history of substance abuse that has gone untreated
- Lack of insight into the nature and severity of problems with substance abuse and gambling, and associated needs for treatment more generally
- A recent history of domestic violence
- Poorly controlled anger
- Recent suicidal ideation
- Access to and interest in weapons
- Significant stressors that include relationship instability, financial problems, health problems, and employment concerns

Actions that can be taken to decrease Mr. Starkey's risk for self-injurious behavior and aggressive behavior directed towards others, which could be incorporated into probationary supervision, include the following:

- Abstinence from all substances (i.e., alcohol and street drugs)
- Participation in psychotherapy focused on his substance abuse, marital discord, gambling, depression, and poor management of anger
- Reconsideration of currently prescribed pain and anxiety medications as well as continued treatment with antidepressant and other medications *as determined by one physician who coordinates all of his medications*
- Consultation with a credit counseling program designed to facilitate debt management
- Removal of and diminished access to guns and other weapons

Thank you for this evaluation opportunity. If you have any questions about this report or evaluation, please do not hesitate to contact me.

Randy K. Otto, PhD   Jay Singh, PhD
Licensed Psychologist
Board Certified in Clinical Psychology
Board Certified in Forensic Psychology
American Board of Professional Psychology

TEACHING POINT:
COMBINING NOMOTHETIC DATA WITH CASE-SPECIFIC, IDIOGRAPHIC INFORMATION

The combining of nomothetic data obtained by validated psychological tests and specialized measures with individualized information is a recurring theme in FMHA. It has some distinctive aspects in risk and threat assessment. The availability of a number of good, well-validated risk assessment measures means that nomothetic data can be obtained by using such measures in the assessments of many populations. However, their combination with case-specific information differs somewhat in broader risk assessment versus more specific threat assessment.

As Dr. Cornell indicated in the previous teaching point, threat assessment currently can be considered a more specific form of risk assessment in which the forensic clinician is evaluating the seriousness of a particular threat and the likelihood of the subject's behaving in a specific way. Rather than appraising the likelihood of violence or threats more generally and over a longer period, threat assessment focuses on the short term, and on implementing interventions to prevent the behavior. Typically the threatened harm would be very serious—another way in which threat assessment differs from the broader risk assessment, which focuses on harm to others of different severities.

So individualized, case-specific information is quite important in threat assessment. Nomothetic, specialized measures are not well suited for gauging the probability of rare events such as homicide. Even if they were used in a threat assessment, it is of limited value to simply conclude (for example) that an individual has a "10% probability" of acting on homicidal threats. If the threats are genuine and the means for acting on them present, then *whatever* the probability, a threat assessment prioritizes identifying risk factors and intervening to prevent the behavior from occurring. Individualized information is useful in risk assessment. It is crucial in threat assessment.

SECOND TEACHING POINT:
HOW CAN DIFFERENT APPROACHES TO RISK ASSESSMENT BE USED TO INFORM THE EVALUATION AND THE CASE OUTCOME?
(contributed by Randy K. Otto)

This report highlights the use of a violence risk assessment instrument, which demonstrates the way that nomothetic evidence can be incorporated into a FMHA. Risk assessment instruments have undergone an evolution over the past several years. Historically, mental health professionals' assessments of violence risk were conducted using unstructured clinical judgment. However, concerns about the reliability and validity of assessments that employed this approach have resulted in alternative approaches being used with more frequency—primarily structured professional judgment and actuarial assessment (Heilbrun, Yasuhara, & Shah, 2010; Viljoen, McLachlan, & Vincent, 2010).

The risk assessment approach employed in this evaluation was that of structured professional judgment, using the Historical-Clinical-Risk–20 (Webster, Douglas, Eaves, & Hart, 1997). As reflected above, the HCR-20 was used to (1) inform an overall judgment about the examinee's violence risk and (2) identify targets for treatment and other

interventions. For purposes of contrast, although it was not employed in this evaluation, we went back and scored the Violence Risk Appraisal Guide (VRAG; Quinsey, Harris, Rice, & Cormier, 2006), an actuarial instrument designed to mechanically estimate violence risk that was developed using a sample of violent offenders with mental disorders. Although the VRAG provides precise probabilistic estimates of risk for violence, because of its focus on static (as opposed to dynamic) risk factors, it is of limited utility compared to tools such as the HCR-20 with respect to informing judgments about treatment and other interventions designed to reduce violence risk. According to the VRAG, risk factors present in Mr. Starkey's case associated with a heightened risk for violence included a history of alcohol problems, evidence of a DSM-IV-TR (APA, 2000) personality disorder, and a lack of evidence supporting a DSM-IV-TR diagnosis of schizophrenia. Mr. Starkey's score on the VRAG placed him in a group of individuals, 17% of whom went on to violently offend within seven years and 31% of whom went on to violently offend within 10 years.

The use of the Personality Assessment Inventory (Morey, 2007) in this evaluation demonstrates the use of another type of nomothetic data, as it was employed to inform judgments about the examinee's emotional and behavioral functioning. Of course, the PAI and similar measures were not designed to inform judgments about violence risk. Nonetheless, to the degree that they provide information about clinical phenomena that are related to violent behavior (e.g., substance abuse, interpersonal hostility, paranoid thinking, emotional lability, acknowledgement of violent behaviors), these instruments can be helpful in informing judgments about violence risk and identifying potential targets for risk management.

CASE FOUR
PRINCIPLE: OBTAIN RELEVANT HISTORICAL INFORMATION
(PRINCIPLE 28)

The importance of obtaining relevant historical information in FMHA is discussed in detail in Chapter 7 (this volume). The case report for this principle demonstrates how to manage an assessment when relevant historical information is not available. Because this case involved a risk assessment of a current employee of the client, the evaluator and client deemed discretion necessary when completing the report, resulting in their having to rely on the scant historical information the client had available and preventing them from speaking directly to the individual being assessed. This is not uncommon in violence risk assessment, or indeed any other FMHA when information may be limited (e.g., workplace harassment and discrimination, criminal responsibility, psychological injury). The evaluator for this case thus included specific and consistent reference to the limits imposed these restrictions on his ultimate conclusions and recommendation, and language to allow for the modification of these in the case of more information's becoming available in the future. One major limitation due to the lack of historical information is the inability to utilize a standardized violence risk measure, which is discussed further in the teaching point following the case.

WORKPLACE VIOLENCE RISK
ASSESSMENT

From: Joel A. Dvoskin, PhD
Client: Big Country Corporation
Attention: Chester Atkins, Senior Vice-President
for Human Resources
Date: January 14, 2013
Subject: Conway Jones

CAVEATS AND LIMITATIONS TO THIS CONSULTATIVE REPORT

As we discussed, the opinions and recommendations contained in this report are entirely dependent upon the information that was provided to me by you and your colleagues on the Big Country Corporation's Response Team. In this case, the information was quite limited, for reasons that are discussed in this report. As a result, I have erred on the side of caution in my recommendations.

To the extent that the information provided to me proves to be inaccurate, please let me know as soon as possible so I can adjust my findings and recommendations accordingly. To the extent that new information becomes available, I reserve the right to amend my findings and recommendations to comport with the newly acquired information.

INTRODUCTION

I was contacted by Chester Atkins, Senior VP for Human Resources (HR) at the Big Country Corporation, who requested consultation regarding a risk assessment of Conway Jones (subject). Mr. Jones is a 49-year-old white male who has been employed at the Big Country Corporation for 31 years. He began his career in 1982 as a stock boy at the age of 18, while attending community college at night. He received several promotions during that time, eventually becoming a first-line supervisor in the warehouse. He was eventually entered into the company's management intern program after he received his bachelor's degree in business in 1988. He received several more promotions, and since 2000 he has functioned as manager of the company's main warehouse in East Mule Shoe.

For the first 25 years of his employment with the Big Country Corporation, Mr. Jones received generally positive work evaluations. He was described by former supervisors as hard-working, efficient, and serious. Several supervisors described him as "gruff"; however, at no time was he disciplined for any behavior at work. To the contrary, it appears that Mr. Jones was regarded as a valuable employee because "he could bully people into getting the work done."

In 2008, according to his then-supervisor (R. Acuff), Mr. Jones began to become vocal about his political beliefs, specifically in regard to his belief that the election of Barack Obama was a tragic mistake, and signaled a very negative turning point in the history of the United States. Over time, his rhetoric became more and more vehement. Several African-American employees filed grievances, interpreting his loud and frequent political statements as "racist." There is no record of any response to these grievances.

In 2009, an agent of the United States Secret Service requested information about Mr. Jones, but provided the company with no information about the reason for the inquiries. There was no follow-up or further contact with the agent or the Secret Service.

According to Mr. Acuff, Mr. Jones was informally asked to refrain from making political statements at work, but there is no record of any formal discipline of any kind. Several African-American employees requested transfers, which Mr. Jones denied, after which the employees reportedly resigned.

One employee, after resigning, filed a lawsuit claiming that Mr. Jones had created a racially hostile working environment. According to General Counsel Loretta Wynette, the suit was reportedly settled "for nuisance value."

The situation continued to deteriorate until October of 2012, when Mr. Jones' behavior reportedly became much more aggressive and threatening, reportedly exclusively toward African-American employees. He was alleged to have made the following statements:

> "We are going to de-thug this place."
> "You people may think that President Ebonics [*sic*] will protect you, but you're going to have to deal with me."
> "I've had just about enough of this kind of talk (reportedly referring to street slang). From now on it's English or you keep your punk mouths shut."

At this time, the office of the CEO received an anonymous petition complaining about the allegedly racist behavior of Mr. Jones, and alleging that a hostile work environment had been created. The petition vaguely hinted at some sort of action if Mr. Jones were not removed from his position. Specifically, the petition read (in part): "We are trying to deal with this in a reasonable manner, but if you don't remove this racist from his position, we will be forced to take action of a more direct type. We are afraid of this racist man and his guns, and hope that you will do the right thing. Please do not force us to handle this ourselves." Because the petition was anonymous, there was no way for the company to inquire as to the meaning of this vague and contingent threat.

In response to the petition, an investigation was launched by the company's ethics office, which is responsible for Equal Opportunity Employment and human rights issues within the corporation. The investigation was conducted by Senior HR consultant Roy Autry.

During his investigation, Mr. Autry discovered that Mr. Jones had been bragging about his extensive collection of firearms, and referring to his "boys" (i.e., firearms) in a hostile and threatening manner. For example, when someone threatened to go to senior management to complain, Mr. Jones reportedly responded: "How about you complain to my friend Mr. Glock instead?"

In November of 2012, Mr. Jones confronted his supervisor, Edward Arnold, Vice President for Operations. Mr. Jones told Mr. Arnold that Mr. Jones's performance review was overdue, that he expected to receive a merit pay increase, and added, "But first, I'd love to show you my collection of hunting rifles and shotguns. It's pretty impressive. If you have time, come out to the parking lot so I can show them to you." Mr. Arnold told Mr. Autry that the conversation frightened him, and that he avoided completing Mr. Jones' performance evaluation because he was afraid of him.

Mr. Arnold told Mr. Autry that Mr. Jones had commented on several occasions about mass homicides that were highly publicized. According to Mr. Arnold's recollection, Mr. Jones laughed and said, "I don't think anybody would ever want to fire me. It would not be a smart thing to do." Again, his comments were vague, but Mr. Arnold deemed them to be threatening.

Because of the intimidating references to firearms, and the reports that various employees, including Mr. Jones's own supervisor, were "very frightened" by Mr. Jones, Mr. Autry referred the matter to the company's Response Team. After a brief discussion of this case, the Response Team contacted me for consultation to assess and mitigate any risk of interpersonal violence involving Mr. Jones. Initially, the request dealt solely with Mr. Jones as a potential perpetrator of violence.

COMMENT

At the time this occurred, the company did not have a policy against bringing guns onto company property. Indeed, because hunting is a favored sport of many employees, there was significant sentiment against such a policy among Response Team members. However, at my strong suggestion, there is now a policy in place.

However, at my suggestion, the consultation also addressed the possibility of violence aimed against Mr. Jones by unnamed others.

FURTHER INVESTIGATION REGARDING MR. JONES

Because of fears of Mr. Jones, the Response Team decided against interviewing him unless further investigation warranted it. At my suggestion, great care was taken to conduct the investigation with complete discretion, until more information had been gathered, in order to avoid placing key informants or complainants at any additional risk. We also wanted to avoid inflaming an already difficult situation in the workplace.

At the time Mr. Jones was hired, the corporation did not conduct background checks or criminal history checks of new employees, nor was any such check conducted about Mr. Jones during his entire career. Because previous violent behavior is a risk factor, the company investigated through publicly available sources, and was unable to find any history of arrest or conviction for any violent or nonviolent crime by Mr. Jones. This of course did not preclude undetected acts of violence; however, while there were numerous reports of vague, ambiguous threats, there were no reports, formal or otherwise, of acts of physical violence. Further, Mr. Jones' employment record was devoid of any long, unexplained absences that might have reflected a period of detention or incarceration.

Another risk factor for violence is relationship instability. But almost nothing was known about Mr. Jones's social or familial relationships outside of work. No other employees were known to have associated with him, and he was known as a "loner" by his co-workers. He typically ate lunch alone at his desk, and listed his father as his emergency contact. (However, a review of public records revealed that his father had died in 2005.) Mr. Jones was believed to be single and childless.

Another known risk factor is "employment problems." In this regard, the Response Team reported strong evidence in both directions. On one hand, Mr. Jones had maintained stable employment with the same company for 31 years, without ever having received any negative disciplinary actions or negative performance reviews. On the other hand, he was apparently feared by many employees (including his own supervisor) and disliked by many others.

The investigator was able to uncover no evidence of any substance abuse problems, and Mr. Jones was not known to have sought or received services either from the company's employee assistance program or through his health insurance. Because such records are confidential, there is no way to know for certain if Mr. Jones received treatment for any mental illness or substance use problem, but none was rumored or reported.

While there was no known history of mental illness, there was some significant evidence that raised questions regarding the presence of a personality disorder. (*Note*—Without conducting a formal evaluation of Mr. Jones and significantly more collateral information, I cannot diagnose the presence of a mental condition.) Mr. Jones was quoted by numerous sources as making statements suggestive of possible paranoia. For example, he was reported to have frequently alleged that a "socialist plot" was responsible for President Obama's election and re-election. He was reported to have alleged that the "Black Mafia" had targeted him as a "true American" for harm. However, because these beliefs are shared by others with similar political views, it is difficult to distinguish between unpopular, even abhorrent beliefs on one hand and a true personality disorder or mental illness on the other.

While he was frequently described as gruff, unpleasant, and mean, there were no reports of other signs of personality disorder or psychopathy. For example, Mr. Jones was consistently described as honest and trustworthy, and prior to 2008, there were no reports of any personality problems that affected his work—although he was described as "gruff" and a "bully."

Another risk factor involves early maladjustment. However, Mr. Jones had never discussed his life prior to joining the company, and refused to discuss any personal information with any of his co-workers. Therefore, almost nothing was known about Mr. Jones's early life.

Mr. Jones did not claim to be a veteran when he first applied for employment with the Big Country Corporation, nor is he known to have mentioned military service.

As noted above, Mr. Jones was not known to suffer from a serious mental illness, although it is possible that he had a personality disorder. However, there was no indication that Mr. Jones had any insight into the way in which he was perceived by his subordinates and co-workers, nor that he would have cared. In fact, the investigation revealed various statements attributed to Mr. Jones suggesting that he wanted people to fear him, as it is a way of getting what he wanted. For example, he was quoted as frequently saying, "I don't care if you scumbags like me or not. But you damned well better fear me, and do your damned jobs."

Mr. Jones's threats were at all times ambiguous, although they were quite effective in scaring his co-workers. Generally, his threats were contingent in nature. For example, he was able to convince people to avoid filing formal complaints against him or providing him with negative performance evaluations by using ambiguous, contingent threats.

Unfortunately, because of management's consistent failure to respond to Mr. Jones's inappropriate behavior in the workplace, there is no way to assess his responsiveness to competent managerial efforts to change his behavior. Nor is there any evidence that he has ever received mental health treatment, which precludes an assessment of his responsiveness to treatment.

FURTHER ASSESSMENT REGARDING UNNAMED OTHERS

The anonymous petition vaguely referred to "taking action" if Mr. Jones were not removed from his managerial position. Because the typed petition was anonymous, it was not possible to query its author(s) about the explicit meaning of "action," which could refer to mass resignations, legal action such as lawsuits or EEOC complaints, or, in the extreme, interpersonal violence against Mr. Jones. Furthermore, the petition contained no explicit threats of violence, and Corporate Counsel opined that the petition did not constitute a crime of any type.

It should be noted that the majority of staff in the warehouse are paid at or slightly above minimum wage. Many of the employees freely acknowledged histories of arrest and conviction prior to their employment at the company. However, because of the low wages, the company has for some time been forced to hire almost anyone who wants to work there, their criminal histories notwithstanding.

The company is located in a rural area, with little or no known activity involving organized crime or street gangs; however, the payroll office reported that "most of the paychecks are cashed at bars and liquor stores." East Mule Shoe is a small town

of fewer than 5,000 residents, and Big Country Corporation is by far its largest employer. As a result, it is very likely that Mr. Jones would at some point run into various employees of the warehouse.

ASSESSMENT

In this case, no risk assessment instrument will assist in assessing Mr. Jones's risk of interpersonal violence, mainly due to a lack of data. Furthermore, because the company understandably wishes to avoid making the situation worse by conducting a thorough (and therefore indiscreet) investigation, it would be difficult or impossible to gather all of the data necessary for the use of various risk assessment instruments.

On the other hand, there are enough data to make some important inferences about Mr. Jones as a potential perpetrator and/or victim of violence. First, it is clear that informal requests to stop making inflammatory political statements at work were not effective. Thus, it is likely that Mr. Jones will continue to communicate in a racially inflammatory way unless much stronger steps are taken. Specifically, Mr. Jones has never received any negative consequences for his workplace behavior; indeed he has never received a direct order to change his behavior in any way.

If Mr. Jones continues to utter racially provocative statements at work, Corporate Counsel has advised that the company is likely to experience negative legal consequences as a result of allegations of a racially hostile environment. Moreover, it is not unlikely that these statements will cause one or more of his subordinates to respond with violence to what they regard as racially insulting remarks.

Thus, if Mr. Jones is allowed to remain employed in his current position, he should receive a strongly worded, "last chance" warning letter forbidding such communications in the workplace, and promising severe disciplinary consequences up to and including termination if they recur. However, there is some reason to believe that Mr. Jones would respond poorly to such direct supervision at this late stage in his career. Note, for example, his utter disrespect for his supervisor, who was ambiguously and contingently threatened by Mr. Jones regarding Mr. Jones' performance review. Furthermore, the lack of consequences for Mr. Jones' inappropriate workplace behavior has persisted over a long period of time, and has probably caused him to believe that no real consequences will occur, even if he is threatened with discipline.

Mr. Jones is not known to have a history of violent crime, nor is he known to have a current substance use disorder. (However, the absence of data does not allow one to rule out the presence of either of these important risk factors.)

Despite his unpleasant demeanor at work, Mr. Jones is not known to have any other interests, suggesting the likelihood that his job is very important to him. Thus, if he is separated from his employment, he will be likely to respond with anger. The absence of family or outside interests suggests the absence of any known protective factors except for his employment.

In our experience, if a subject is known to be expressing suicidal thoughts or plans, it dramatically raises the risk of violence toward others, as it would suggest the absence of virtually all protective factors. In this case, there have been no such reports of suicidal behavior or intention by Mr. Jones; however, if he expresses such thoughts, it should be regarded as seriously raising his perceived level of risk as a possible perpetrator of violence.

Even more concerning are Mr. Jones's intimidating references to guns or firearms, and the fact that he reports keeping firearms in his trunk, suggesting that they are always close at hand. Even when the likelihood of violence is deemed to be low, the use of firearms creates the presumption of a high level of severity.

The combination of repeated, racially provocative statements and his frequent and intimidating reference to guns suggest that Mr. Jones's presence in the workplace would cause his subordinates and co-workers to live in continued fear of him. The only exception to this assessment would involve a very radical and unlikely change in Mr. Jones's behavior.

If Mr. Jones is retained in his current position, it is likely that either he or the company will experience some sort of serious negative consequences, although the nature of these consequences (e.g., legal action or physical violence) is impossible to predict. Thus, the safest course of action is to remove Mr. Jones from his position.

One option is to demote Mr. Jones. However, any position that he would be likely to accept would keep him in a supervisory role over the same employees. Mr. Jones was described by his supervisor as "a very proud man who would never accept a demotion."

According to HR staff and the General Counsel, Mr. Jones' behavior has been so inappropriate that termination is legally justified. However, company officials are frightened that Mr. Jones will respond with lethal violence if he is terminated. Assessing the risk of lethal violence in this case is difficult if not impossible, for several reasons. First, we note that Mr. Jones already communicated to his supervisor an ambiguous, contingent threat aimed specifically at the possibility of his own termination.

While threats of violence are not uncommon, the actual perpetration of mass homicide is an exceptionally rare event, and rare events are very difficult to predict. Thus, likelihood of such an event must be assumed to be low. However, the severity and costs of lethal violence in the workplace are so extreme that caution is warranted in separating Mr. Jones from the company, even if the likelihood of such an event is deemed to be low, especially in light of his threatening references to firearms.

Recommended action steps:

1. I recommend that Mr. Jones be separated from the Big Country Corporation.
2. I do not recommend the termination of Mr. Jones, for several reasons. First, his ambiguous threats of firearm violence, however unlikely, represent a severity of risk that should be avoided. Second, if he is terminated, it may be perceived as rewarding the ambiguous, contingent threats contained in the anonymous petition. Third, because East Mule Shoe is a small town, if Mr. Jones leaves the company on bad terms, his is very likely to encounter his former employees or supervisors after he leaves the company.
3. If possible, Mr. Jones should be allowed to leave the company under terms that he regards as fair and respectful. He should be offered the opportunity to resign under a separation agreement crafted by Corporate Counsel, citing his many years of productive service to the company. Terms may include benefits, such as severance pay, extended health insurance benefits, and outplacement assistance to which

he would not be entitled as a terminated employee.

4. Severance benefits can be offered either as a lump sum, or in the form of a continuing periodic paycheck after he leaves the company. There are advantages and disadvantages to each form of payment:

   a. If Mr. Jones is offered severance pay in a lump sum, it would avoid continuing his association with the Big Country Corporation. However, it would also remove any influence over his post-discharge behavior.

   b. If Mr. Jones is provided bi-weekly severance checks, it provides the company with some influence over his future behavior, and contingencies that will require him to abide by the terms of his separation agreement. It may also make it easier to provide him with benefits such as health insurance, employee assistance, etc. However, this continued association with Mr. Jones increases the risk that his political statements might be viewed as representing the company, causing public and employee relations difficulties.

5. If Mr. Jones is unwilling to consider resigning, he should be informed that his threatening and racist behavior constitutes grounds for termination, and that if terminated, he would probably receive few or none of the benefits described above.

6. Once Mr. Jones has been safely and successfully separated from the company, I recommend a complete review of all policies and procedures related to workplace violence, firearms, racism, and related topics.

7. Once Mr. Jones has been safely and successfully separated from the company, I recommend extensive training for executives and managers on how to manage a safe and respectful workplace, including training on how to safely handle difficult employees, including managerial employees.

Based upon the positive manner in which the Response Team received these recommendations in our recent conference call, I believe that the Big Country Corporation is in general agreement with them. I appreciate your trust, and the opportunity to provide you with this consultative assistance. As always, please do not hesitate to call me if you have any questions or if circumstances change in any way.

Sincerely,
Joel A. Dvoskin, PhD

TEACHING POINT:
WHEN SPECIALIZED MEASURES CANNOT BE USED
(contributed by Joel A. Dvoskin)

It is important to understand not only when to use risk assessment instruments, but also when they should not be used. In this case, there are two general sets of reason arguing against the use of actuarial risk assessment instruments or structured professional judgment instruments in assessing the risks posed by Mr. Jones.

First, the vast majority of studies on risk assessment instruments have been conducted in two contexts: (1) people with histories of serious mental illness; and/or (2) people under criminal or juvenile justice supervision or with criminal or delinquent histories. In this case, the subject (Mr. Jones) did not fall into either of these categories. Consequently, there are few if any risk assessment instruments available that have been normed on people sufficiently like him in ways that are known to be related to violence risk.

Second, all risk assessment schemes rely on a sufficient quality and quantity of accurate and relevant information. In this case, very little was known about the subject, which would make it difficult to confidently rely on the data points required under actuarial or structured professional judgment risk assessment schemes.

The vast majority of risk assessment research focuses on the individual who is being assessed for violence risk. However, all human behavior is the result of an interaction between a person and a situation; violent behavior is no exception. In this case, much more was known about the situation than the individual, allowing sensible findings and recommendations to emerge even without accurate assessment of future violent behavior of this individual subject. Moreover, this report clearly demonstrates the importance of obtaining relevant historical information, as the evaluator had to rely in large part on reports of the individual's past behavior in this situation in determining the likelihood of future violent behavior.

Note that much of the literature on violence risk assessment focuses on the likelihood of violence. In this case, because of the very low base rate of the behavior in question, Bayes' theorem would tell us to simply opine that the subject would not engage in the feared behavior—mass homicide in the workplace. However, other aspects of risk may be even more important than likelihood; these include imminence, duration, and severity. In this case, the severity of risk justified recommendations for caution in spite of the presumptively low likelihood that can be inferred for any behavior with a low base rate.

26

Response Style

This chapter focuses on the assessment of response style as part of FMHA. "Response style" describes how an individual being evaluated responds to the assessment material, with primary response styles in forensic contexts including *reliable, defensive, exaggerating/malingering*, and *uncooperative* (see Rogers, 2008a). An individual's response style can be addressed in multiple ways, including through the use of general psychological testing, specialized measures, and third party information. The principle associated with the first case in this chapter describes the role of testing in assessment response style, and is highlighted in the context of response style in the testing of cognitive abilities. The associated teaching point provides a framework for the assessment of response style, and highlights specific tests that may be used. The principle associated with the second case pertains to the ways third party information can be used to assess response style, and the teaching point describes the ways that an evaluator can explore the level of consistency across sources of information.

CASE ONE
PRINCIPLE: USE TESTING WHEN INDICATED IN ASSESSING RESPONSE STYLE (*PRINCIPLE 26*)

This principle was addressed more generally in Chapter 3 (this volume), so this discussion will focus on the role of testing for response style in the present report.[1] Empirical research regarding response style in the testing of cognitive abilities has largely focused on malingering (Rogers, 2008a). Rogers (2008c) described two broad categories of detection strategies for cognitive

malingering. The first is the *unlikely presentations* approach, which focuses on "response patterns that are unusual and atypical for patients with genuine neuropsychological impairment" (p. 23). Within this category are three primary strategies:

1. *Magnitude of error*, which focuses on which responses are incorrect and how typical these errors are;
2. *Performance curve*, which relies on the pattern of errors as the difficulty of items increases; and
3. *Violation of learning principles*, which compares performance to what would be expected given our understanding of how learning occurs.

Specifically, Rogers (2008c) identified the *violation of learning principles* approach as "conceptually superior to most strategies in that specific testable hypotheses about learning principles are rigorously evaluated" (p. 24).

The second approach to the detection of cognitive malingering is *excessive impairment* (Rogers, 2008c). Within this category are three primary strategies:

1. *Floor effect*, which examines performance on "simple cognitive tasks that are successfully completed by most cognitively compromised populations" (p. 26);
2. *Symptom validity testing*, which compares an examinee's performance to known probabilities of such performance; and
3. *Forced-choice testing*, which assesses "below expected" performance on a forced-choice measure.

Rogers (2008c) notes that, although symptom validity testing produces a high level of confidence in the identification of malingerers, the relatively

---

[1] Chapter 3 also has a report contributed by Dr. Rogers (see Case One) that illustrates the use of specialized testing to appraise the possibility of malingering in FMHA.

stringent criteria may identify only a small proportion of malingerers. In contrast, he recommends against the use of forced-choice testing as the primary detection strategy. Examples of excessive impairment tests include the Test of Memory Malingering (TOMM; Tombaugh, 1996, 1997), which uses the floor effects approach, and the Portland Digit Recognition Test (PDRT; Binder, 1993), which is a symptom validity test.

In contrast to the detection of malingering, Rogers (2008c) describes the detection of defensiveness in cognitive testing as largely undeveloped. According to Rogers (2008c), "Cognitive defensiveness can involve either the masking of cognitive deficits or the false portrayal of cognitive strengths" (p. 29). He indicates that there is evidence that performance on cognitive testing can be improved via practice effects, and he describes some situations in which there may be motivation to respond in a defensive manner (e.g., evaluations for job-related purposes). Still, this remains an understudied area in FMHA.

Assessments of cognitive response style include both standard psychological tests with embedded measures (e.g., the Forced Choice trial of the California Verbal Learning Test–II; Reliable Digit Span of the WAIS-IV) and specialized measures. Two examples of specialized measures include the Validity Indicator Profile (Frederick, 2003a, 2003b) and the Test of Memory Malingering (TOMM; Tombaugh, 1996, 1997).

The Validity Indicator Profile, 2nd Edition (VIP; Frederick, 2003a, 2003b) utilizes a "modified" symptom validity testing detection strategy, and includes both verbal (VIP-V) and non-verbal (VIP-NV) subtests (Frederick & Crosby, 2000). Each subtest consists of forced-choice items with two options, and items are randomly ordered with respect to difficulty. Based on the results of the VIP, test-takers are classified into those with "valid" or "invalid" response patterns. By considering the examinee's intentions, his or her response style is classified into one of four categories: *compliant*, which reflects their intention to perform well and give high effort; *careless*, which includes individuals who are motivated to perform well but may put forth inconsistent effort; *irrelevant*, which includes individuals who are motivated to perform poorly and put forth inconsistent effort; and *suppressed*, which reflects both poor performance and an intention to perform poorly. The

non-verbal subtest yields 73.5% sensitivity and 5.7% specificity, whereas the verbal subtest yields 67.3% sensitivity and 83.1% specificity (Frederick & Crosby, 2000, p. 72). The authors also note the importance of identifying corroborating evidence in the interpretation of these outcomes; moreover, based on these classification statistics, it has been recommended that the VIP be considered a measure of *suboptimal effort* rather than feigning *per se* (Rogers & Bender, 2003).

The Test of Memory Malingering (TOMM; Tombaugh, 1996, 1997) is another test designed to detect cognitive feigning. Consisting of two learning trials and a delayed-recall trial, the learning trials begin by presenting 50 line drawings to the test-taker (the study phase). Then, the test-taker is shown 50 pairs of drawings and selects the drawing that appeared in the study phase (the test phase). For the delayed-recall trial, test-takers are presented with the 50 pairs of drawings and asked to select the drawings that were learned during the first two trials. On each trial, the examiner provides feedback to the test-taker on whether their response is correct, which is expected to serve as motivation for those who are putting forth good effort, and provide information that malingerers may use to adjust their performance (Tombaugh, 1997). The test was initially validated with multiple samples, including a community sample, a clinical sample (specifically, individuals with known cognitive impairments ranging from traumatic brain injury [TBI] to dementia to stroke), and a sample of college students randomly assigned to put forth good effort or feign impairment. A cutting score of 45 on Trial 2 accurately classified "95% of all nondemented patients (91% of all patients), 99.9% of the cognitively intact community volunteers, and 100% of the malingering participants" (Tombaugh, 1997, p. 268). However, when using the TOMM in a forensic setting, it is important to consider certain factors. For instance, the clinical validation sample received redirection that is not reflected in the administration instructions, which may have resulted in higher scores (Tombaugh, 1997). Additionally, some caution should also be taken when using the test with individuals with dementia (Tombaugh, 1997).

The present case highlights the importance of assessing response style in FMHA. The legal issue was competency to be sentenced, and the evaluation was ordered after the defendant began to display odd behavior. The evaluators used several measures that have considerable empirical support for assessing response style and detecting malingering, including the MMPI-2-RF, Structured Inventory of Reported Symptoms–2 (SIRS-2; Rogers, Sewell, & Gillard, 2011), and Validity Indicator Profile (VIP). The defendant's performance on these measures led the evaluators to conclude that the defendant's claims of being cognitively impaired and psychotic were feigned. The evaluators also used the Inventory of Legal Knowledge (ILK; Otto, Musick, & Sherrod, 2010) to assess his understanding of the legal system, and they concluded that he was also feigning lack of knowledge about the court system. In contexts in which the defendant is not particularly cooperative with the interview process, as in the present case, it may be necessary to rely on formal testing to assess the validity of claimed impairment.

COMPETENCY TO BE SENTENCED

The defendant was a 31-year-old white man who pleaded guilty to being a felon in possession of a firearm during a crime of violence. He was sent for an evaluation of his competency to be sentenced pursuant to 18 USC 4241 and 4247(b).

PAST HISTORY

He was raised in an intact family with three siblings. He reported he could not recall what his birth order was. He said he was unsure of his parents' occupations. He said he was not sure how many years he had gone to high school, but reported he had obtained a high school diploma online. He reported his only occupation had been as a janitor. He said he had a history of significant alcohol use and use of marijuana, cocaine, heroin, hallucinogens, and methamphetamine.

He said he did not know what his criminal history was, but acknowledged that he had been in prison before.

He said he had been receiving mental health treatment since "I was little." He said he had been prescribed antipsychotic medication, but said he could not remember the name of the medication. Prior jail and prison medical records indicated he had previously been diagnosed with schizophrenia and had been prescribed risperidone. Reported symptoms included auditory hallucinations, trouble sleeping, anxiety, and depression. Other medications had been prescribed, including antidepressants.

HOSPITAL COURSE

In clinical interviews, he presented in a contrived and rather preposterous manner, including acting as if he were talking to an unseen other. He claimed he could see the person, referred to him as "Joe," and talked with him as if he were present. He often would not interact with his evaluators, but when he did, his responses were coherent and relevant. There was no evidence of any significantly disordered form of thinking in his verbal interactions.

During the course of his inpatient evaluation, the defendant's behavior among other inmates was monitored. He was never seen to engage in strange behavior or to act as if he were hallucinating except in the company of his evaluators. Most curiously, once he was told the evaluation was ended, he stopped acting in a strange way with his evaluators.

PSYCHOLOGICAL TESTING

We administered a series of tests to evaluate the validity of his complaints. We first administered the MMPI-2-Restructured Form (MMPI-2-RF). He was administered the MMPI-2-RF by audiotape

COMMENT

Identifying information about this individual, including initials, certain demographic information, and some case characteristics have been disguised to protect his identify. These are his actual test results. Adapted by permission. The conclusions and opinions reported in this report and the teaching point that follow do not necessarily represent the opinions of the Federal Bureau of Prisons or the U.S. Department of Justice. We thank Lea Ann Preston, Ph.D., ABPP, for her assistance in this case.

after he failed to get even one item right on a simple reading test we routinely administer to determine if defendants should receive a booklet or audiotape administration.

He failed to provide a response for 65 of the items on the MMPI-2-RF. When the items were read to him, and he was asked to select an answer, he said that he could not. Consequently, the MMPI-2-RF was not scored.

We still believed, however, that the Structured Inventory of Reported Symptoms–2 (SIRS-2) would be a successful means of assessment. Given his proclivity for exaggerated and dramatic reports of psychotic experiences, we believed a face-to-face interview would be an effective means to assess the genuineness of his self-report.

On the SIRS-2, he said "I don't know" to 17 of the inquiries. Generally, this is a good basis to discontinue the examination. But, because it was obvious he was answering many of the items in a feigned manner, we completed the questionnaire, despite the rejection of 17 items. He obtained the following scores:

Rare Symptoms (RS) = 9 (Definite)
Symptom Combinations (SC) = 2 (Genuine)
Improbable and Absurd Symptoms (IA) = 10 (Definite)
Blatant Symptoms (BL) = 13 (Probable)
Subtle Symptoms (SU) = 11 (Indeterminate)
Selectivity of Symptoms (SEL) = 16 (Indeterminate)
Severity of Symptoms (SEV) = 8 (Indeterminate)
Reported versus Observed Symptoms (RO) = 3 (Genuine)
RS—Total = 8

For the SIRS-2, this results in an overall classification of Definite Feigning, which supports a conclusion that his representation of psychopathology is feigned.

We evaluated his claims about lowered cognitive capacity with the Validity Indicator Profile. The VIP has two subscales, Verbal and Nonverbal, that allow an examination of claims about diminished cognitive capacity in a broad manner.

His overall score on the VIP nonverbal subtest was 30 out of 100. The probability of obtaining such a low score by guessing at the items (*no* cognitive capacity to solve problems, some of which even toddlers can solve) is 4 in 10,000. Similarly, the probability of obtaining 25 out of 78 on the verbal subtest only by guessing is 6 out of 1,000. The probability of guessing alone and obtaining such low scores on both subtests is 1 in 5 million. Consequently, the reasonable conclusion is that he actually has the cognitive capacity to solve the problems, but suppressed his abilities when taking the test.

The performance curves drawn to demonstrate his approach to the items show that he did, indeed, suppress his ability for the items he knew the answers to (below-chance responding on the left side—or for the easier items), but when the items became so difficult that he did not know the answers, his response accuracy was at the rate of guessing, or about 50% accurate (see Figures 26.1 and 26.2). This is very compelling evidence of feigned cognitive impairment.

The VIP has the ability to make estimates of the lower range of IQ for persons who suppress their abilities when taking the test. For this individual, his minimal capacity is in the below average range of intellectual capacity, if not higher.

His performances on the VIP and the SIRS are good evidence that his claims of being cognitively impaired and psychotic are feigned.

He was not merely feigning cognitive impairment. He was also specifically feigning not understanding the legal system after having been convicted of his crime. The best evidence will deal directly with his claims of being unable to understand how the legal system works. We therefore administered the Inventory of Legal Knowledge (ILK), which is a direct forced-choice evaluation of his legal knowledge. The ILK asks 61 two-alternative questions about the legal system. He obtained a score of 22. The probability of obtaining a score of 22 or lower merely by guessing is 2 in 100. That is, of 100 individuals who merely guessed at the answers, only 2 would score this low. Consequently, based on his performance on this test, it is clear that he is also feigning lack of knowledge specifically about the court system.

DIAGNOSIS

We did not find any compelling evidence that he was psychologically impaired. His non-credible and dramatically exaggerated clinical presentation was objectively evaluated with psychometric measures. His performances on these measures clearly demonstrate that he is feigning psychopathology, cognitive impairment, and lack of knowledge

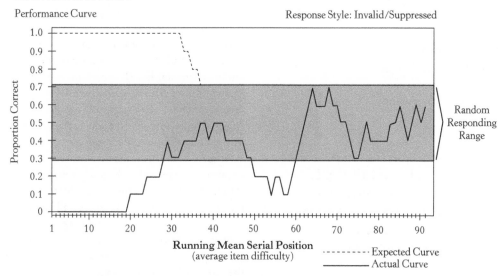

FIGURE 26.1: Nonverbal Subtest Performance Curve as a Figure.

of the legal system. Given that his motivation to feign these impairments seems obviously related to a desire to frustrate the legal process and avoid sentencing, we conclude his presentation is best explained by malingering, an intentional and willful misrepresentation of his cognitive capacities and false presentation of psychopathology.

COMPETENCY TO BE SENTENCED

Because of his non-cooperativeness in the clinical assessment, we depend on our understanding of his presentation in formal testing to conclude that he has the necessary cognitive capacity to understand the nature and potential consequences of the

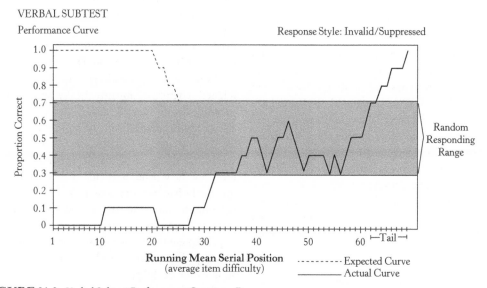

FIGURE 26.2: Verbal Subtest Performance Curve as a Figure

proceedings against him and to assist properly in his defense during the process of sentencing.

Ashley Kirk, MA[2]
Psychology Intern

Richard Frederick, PhD, ABPP[3]
Licensed Clinical Psychologist
Board Certified in Forensic Psychology

TEACHING POINT:
ASSESSING MALINGERING OF COGNITIVE DEFICITS USING TESTING
(contributed by Richard Frederick and Ashley Kirk Burgett)

This case concerns an individual who pleaded guilty to a crime and who thought he was getting a set sentence, but who was surprised to learn that the judge was not bound by any agreement reached by the prosecutor and his attorney. When he learned that he was going to get a sentence longer than he thought he had bargained for, he began to disrupt the process by claiming to see things and to act as if he did not understand anything anymore. At any time during a criminal prosecution, either party to the action (prosecutor or defense attorney) or the judge can request a competency evaluation to ensure that the defendant is competent to participate in the proceedings.

Because of the rapid initiation of the complaints of hallucinations and inability to understand things, it was pretty easy to conclude that his presentation was concocted. It was pretty obvious from conversations with attorneys that no one really believed he was ill, but it was consistent with the law to have persons with specialized knowledge evaluate his presentation and form an opinion about his ability to participate in the sentencing hearing.

The first step in evaluating feigned presentations of mental health symptoms is to make sense of the presentation. In this case, the rapid onset of symptoms, the claim of not knowing his own medical history, and the differential presentation of symptoms to other inmates and to doctors—all in the context of being unhappy about his legal circumstance—precluded serious consideration of his presentation as valid or reliable.

The second step in evaluating feigned presentations of mental health symptoms is to use tools that are designed for the task at hand. Psychological testing that has been specifically designed to assess feigning is the best way to evaluate the believability of presentation. Psychological testing effectively minimizes the idiosyncratic contributions of the examiner, and provided the test is administered in a standardized manner, the scores obtained are then interpretable according to rules validated in the research literature. Such scores make for excellent evidence in courtroom testimony, as the interpretations can be subjected to cross-examination using the research literature reports.

The MMPI-2 has excellent indicators of feigned psychopathology in the Infrequency (F), Back Infrequency (Fb), and Infrequency Psychopathology (Fp) scales, and the MMPI-2-RF has excellent revised scales of F and Fp, called F-r and Fp-r. We were hopeful that he would cooperate with the completion of the MMPI-2-RF so that we could evaluate his presentation with these scales, but he did not.

Because he would engage us in rather dramatic conversations about his experiences, the structured interview approach of the SIRS-2 was an excellent method to evaluate the believability of his presentation. Although he did say "I don't know" to a number of the inquiries, he completed the test, and we were able to score his responses. His responses were clearly designed to feign psychopathology, which is the meaning of the categorization "Definitely Feigning."

Most cognitive malingering tests evaluate feigned cognitive impairment by employing a memory-test format. The VIP directly evaluates the ability to comprehend and solve problems and word knowledge. In this case, the defendant clearly was invested in proving that he had deficits in both areas, but he was not particularly invested in proving that he had memory deficits. The below-chance responding and the suppressed areas of performance specific to easier items (with gradual improvement to chance responding on the difficult items) provides strong evidence of an intentional suppression of ability.

Because of his willingness to actively suppress his abilities, we considered it worthwhile to use the ILK to directly assess his knowledge and understanding

---

of the legal system. The forced-choice method is an effective way to directly assess the believability of such specifically claimed deficits (Frederick & Speed, 2007). Essentially, forced-choice methods allow formal testing of a null hypothesis that the person has no ability to correctly solve any of the items and is forced to guess. When scores are *worse* than can be expected for such individuals, then it is clear that they have *suppressed* their true abilities to consistently derive incorrect responses.

In this case, by using tools suited for the task, we were able to demonstrate that (1) his clinical presentation of psychosis was unbelievable, (2) he actually had much better cognitive abilities than he was willing to reveal, and (3) he actually had quite good knowledge of the legal system.

CASE TWO
PRINCIPLE: USE THIRD PARTY INFORMATION IN ASSESSING RESPONSE STYLE (*PRINCIPLE 25*)

This principle was already described in detail in Chapter 10, and illustrated by a report in Chapter 22 (this volume). Therefore, we turn to the application of this principle in the current case. The legal issue in this case was whether the defendant qualified for an insanity defense under California law. In assessing the defendant's mental state at the time of the offense, Dr. Resnick relied on multiple sources of information, including interviews and various records. He also explicitly considered whether the defendant was "faking psychiatric symptoms (malingering) to succeed with an insanity defense." To assess the defendant's response style, Dr. Resnick relied in part on third party information, and multiple sources of third party information yielded convergent evidence that the defendant was experiencing genuine mental illness at the time of the offense.

February 11, 2010
Deputy Public Defender
Small Town, CA
RE: Lisa Brent
Dear Public Defender:

At your request I performed a psychiatric evaluation of Lisa Brent to offer an opinion about whether she qualified for an insanity defense. The test for insanity in California is whether the accused "was incapable of knowing or understanding the nature and quality of her act or of distinguishing right from wrong at the time of the commission of the offense." Ms. Brent is charged with the murder of her 18-month-old son, John, on February 23, 2009. She is also charged with assault of her child by means of force that to a reasonable person would be likely to produce great bodily injury resulting in the death of the child.

Qualifications of the Examiner: I am enclosing a copy of my curriculum vitae which states my qualifications to perform this examination.

Statement of Informed Consent: Ms. Brent was informed that I was a psychiatrist employed by her public defender for the purpose of evaluating her sanity at the time of the crimes with which she is charged. She understood that what she told me was not confidential and that I may be preparing a report for the court. She agreed to proceed.

SOURCES OF INFORMATION

1. Interview of Ms. Brent on 12/19/09 for 7 hours and 40 minutes.
2. Copy of indictment.
3. Small Town Police Department reports regarding the 2/23/09 homicide of John Brent.
4. Small Town County Regional Medical Center 2/25/09–3/4/09 admission.
5. Detention Health Services records regarding Ms. Brent.
6. Medical records of Lisa Brent by Dr. Smith.
7. Medical records of Small Town Medical Clinic.
8. Letters written by Lisa Brent from jail and handwritten scroll on brown paper.
9. Copy of preliminary hearing transcript dated 10/19/09.
10. Urine drug screen dated 3/3/09. Negative for all drugs except cannabinoids, which is positive.
11. Witness statements.
12. Emails from Lisa Brent.
13. Mental Health Detention Services progress notes.
14. Medical records of Dr. Mark Jones.

BACKGROUND INFORMATION

Ms. Brent stated that she was 39 years old. She was born 4/29/70 in Detroit, Michigan, the oldest of three children. She has one brother a year and one-half younger, and a half brother ten years younger.

Ms. Brent said that her father died in 2007 at age 57 of colon cancer. She described him as an "unemployed alcoholic" who had only been in her life until she was two or three years old. Her only memories of him are of his being violent to her mother. Her parents were divorced before she was five years old.

Ms. Brent stated that her 59-year-old mother is working as a receptionist in a hotel. She described her mother as "anxious, friendly, and helpful." She added that her mother was an alcoholic with low self-esteem. She stated that she and her mother got along pretty well now, but they have had issues over her mother's alcoholism.

Ms. Brent reported that she did a great deal of moving as a child between her grandparents (mother's parents), an aunt, and her mother. She spent her four years of high school with her maternal grandparents, which she described as good years.

Educational History

Ms. Brent said that she graduated from high school in 1988 with a grade point average of 3.25. She was a pompom girl with the school band. While in the Navy she received a bachelor's degree from Southern University and a master's in education from the online University of Phoenix.

Military History

Ms. Brent reported that she was in the Navy from 12/20/89 to 3/16/98. Her highest rank was E-5, and she received an honorable discharge. She was deployed to Okinawa and Haiti. She worked in preventive medicine and public health. She reported no disciplinary actions against her in the Navy.

Employment History

Ms. Brent stated that after being discharged from the Navy she worked as an camp counselor for six months, did safety training for nine months, and then spent a year teaching computer science. Since then, she has worked at community colleges teaching and developing curriculum. Since March 2008, she has been home with her children. She and her husband opened a drive-through coffee shop, but the day-to-day operation was run by a manager.

Religious History

Ms. Brent said that she has not been involved in religion and viewed herself as an agnostic until "God showed himself" in her life on February 3, 2009.

Family Psychiatric History

Ms. Brent said that both of her parents were alcoholic. She did not know of any relatives who had significant mental illness.

Relationship History

Ms. Brent said that she started dating at age 16. She had a brief marriage to Paul in 1989. She was 18 and he was 25 when they married. Paul is the father of her daughter, Celia, who was born 6/13/89. Her second husband, Joe Piel, was in the Navy with her. She married him when she was 21 and he was 31. They were together from 1991 to 1994 and divorced in December 1995. Joe Piel is the father of her son, Mike, who was 15 years old at the time of the 2/23/09 homicide. They had shared custody of Mike.

Ms. Brent married her current husband, Al Brent in 2003. He is a professor of biology at Small Town Community College. She described her husband as "extremely kind and friendly." She said their marriage had "its ups and downs." They had been to counseling together because of her tendency to be "too aggressive." She and her husband Al had two children: Alan Brent (born 8/28/05) and John Brent (born 8/30/07), the homicide victim. Ms. Brent said, "My children are my life." She was very proud of how beautiful her children were.

Substance Use History

Ms. Brent stated that she first used alcohol at age 13 with her mother. She drank heavily for one year at age 25 after she returned from Okinawa. She did not develop tolerance or withdrawal symptoms. Her drinking did not interfere with her work in the Navy. She had no DUIs. She said she has used almost no alcohol the last four or five years because of either being pregnant or nursing.

Ms. Brent reported that she began using marijuana with friends at age 13. Sometimes she used with her mother when her mother was drunk. She used marijuana intermittently until she was 16 or 17, and then had none until using it a single time at age 25. She stopped using marijuana because it sometimes made her "nervous." She never developed any psychotic symptoms due to marijuana. She next used marijuana infrequently in 2000; one ounce lasted her for six to twelve months. She then used none until 2004. She used some again in 2006 when her father was dying. She found that marijuana "mellowed out" her angry feelings and "made me smile."

Ms. Brent said she started using marijuana again early in 2008. She obtained a medical marijuana license based on her arthritis. She believed that marijuana caused her to feel happier, not because she was depressed; marijuana made her less irritable and moody. She said that she had been "moody my whole life." From July 2008 until 2/23/09, she used a relatively constant amount of marijuana. She smoked two or three joints each day, more in the evening. The marijuana she smokes was purchased through her medical marijuana card because she had not yet harvested any of her home-grown marijuana. She said that marijuana "slowed me down." She could "listen better, do less rushing around, and feel happier." When she didn't use marijuana she returned to her "norm of irritability."

Ms. Brent reported that she used mescaline twice at age 16 and "paper acid" (LSD) once at 16. She took Darvocet intermittently once a day, about ten days a month in place of marijuana when she needed to be more accurate in working on a computer or in her coffee business. She occasionally used a Vicodin to slow her down and make her "more genial." She was prescribed Xanax .25 mgs twice or three times a day from 2000 to 2004, which she also used to slow herself down.

Legal History

Ms. Brent said that she has never been arrested. She was stopped for shoplifting at age 12, but she didn't believe she ever went to court. She has not been involved in any lawsuits. She did declare bankruptcy in 1998.

Medical History

Ms. Brent reported that she had pneumonia and a tonsillectomy at age five. She had knee surgery in 1986, 1990, 1994, and 1997. She had breast implants in 1995 and 2002. She had a vaginaplasty in 2006. She had Caesarean sections in 2005 and 2007.

Ms. Brent reported having genital herpes in 1986, followed by post-herpetic neuralgia in 2007. She found this painful and stressful. She finally concluded that she was allergic to wheat. She developed gastrointestinal reflux disease in 1995, for which she takes Tagamet. She has also been told she had some abnormality in her cervical and lumbar vertebrae.

Psychiatric History

Ms. Brent said that she has always been anxious socially and has "sweaty palms." She remained social anyway, and her anxiety diminished some as she got older. She reported that she had a single "panic attack" in 2003 during a job interview. The attack was manifested by being extremely nervous, having an elevated heart rate, shaking, rapid breathing, and "blathering" during the interview. She has also had anxiety related to public speaking, but her anxiety was extinguished by repeated teaching in the Navy. She never had anxiety attacks "out of the blue."

Ms. Brent said that she had two time periods in her life when she had some feelings of depression. One was age 12 to 14 when she was very unhappy in a middle school, and the other was for two years as an adult when she lived in overcast Bremerton, Washington. I reviewed the symptoms of a major depressive episode as delineated in the *Diagnostic and Statistical Manual of the American Psychiatric Association*, 4th Edition (DSM-IV) during each period. Ms. Brent reported that she had weight gain of 25 pounds when she was 12 to 14, and she needed to have a radio on in order to sleep, but she had no other depressive symptoms. She endorsed no symptoms of a major depression during her Bremerton period other than having a single transient suicidal thought.

I reviewed with Ms. Brent whether she had any symptoms of manic episodes as delineated in the DSM-IV. She did not endorse any periods of elevated mood. She said that she has always been confident and "cocky." She has always talked fast. The only buying spree that ever occurred in her life occurred on 2/22/09. She said that rather than that being a true buying spree, she purchased the items because she was "directed to." She reported no periods of hypersexuality.

Ms. Brent said that she initially was prescribed Prozac because of premenstrual syndrome (PMS). Although she described herself as generally irritable, she was more irritable during her premenstrual time each month. From 2002 to 2004, she elected to take Prozac throughout the month rather than only during her premenstrual days. The effect of Prozac was to reduce her irritability, make her less anxious, and keep her mood "more level."

Ms. Brent stated that throughout her life she had been moody. By "moody," she meant easily bored and irritated. She said that she always treated her peers at work and others respectfully but honestly. She said that she is not a mean person. On one occasion she woke up while camping and with no precipitant was extremely angry. She chased a man driving a pickup truck on her bicycle to "chew him out for how he was driving." Her episodes of rage and irritability are increased before her menstrual periods.

Ms. Brent said she doesn't share space with other adults well because she is a "controlling person," and sharing space threatens her control over her home. She has been controlling and very sharp-tongued with her husbands. When she lived alone, she did not have rages.

Ms. Brent said that at times in her life she's had dreams in which she could see in the future. In retrospect, she turned out to be accurate with two of her dreams when she lived in Okinawa. She said that she didn't know that her ability to prophesy was true until after her two prophetic dreams.

I asked Ms. Brent about reports from family members that she was not taking care of her house for the last few months. She confirmed that that was true and said that she had trouble focusing. She said that she was "too jittery and could only focus momentarily." She added that marijuana helped sometimes to slow her down.

MS. BRENT'S ACCOUNT OF EVENTS PRECEDING THE 2/23/09 HOMICIDE

Ms. Brent said that after she attended her first meditation class at her yoga studio involving breathing and vocalization on 2/3/09, she "started bawling afterwards." She experienced an involuntary, forced exhalation followed by a "feeling of peace." She viewed this as her "awakening." Things were great in her life, and she was very happy for the next couple of weeks. She listened to the spiritual guru Depak Chopra on CDs about seven steps to spiritual enlightenment. She had been seeking deeper meaning.

About one week before the homicide of her child on 2/23/09, she began noticing "signs."

She listened to a radio station called Jack FM 93.1. She believed that the songs and commercials were messages directing her to do things. "Dozens of songs" were directed at her. She mentioned a song by the group Lover Boy, "Everybody's Waiting for the Weekend." She took this to mean that they (God) were waiting for her to do some work. She believed that "they" needed her help.

Ms. Brent said that the music was "flirtatious" and complimentary to her. It gave her the sense that she was important to carrying out a cause and gave her a "sense of urgency." She started jotting down her impressions on a scroll. It included "symbols of infinity, lessons in opposites, black and white." She believed that if the lines of a triangle did not meet properly in the corners it would result in "madness or chaos." She carried the scroll with her.

Ms. Brent said that she believed "It will start and end with a black woman." She thought that Eve may have been black and that she was the daughter of Eve. She began to believe that she was in "the Matrix." She said that she owned all three *Matrix* movies and had watched them multiple times. She explained that in the Matrix, "persons are not in the real world." She spoke to her son, Mike, about being in the Matrix.

Ms. Brent said that one day on the way to do yoga she heard the radio referring to music "Layla Darryl," but said that she was actually listening to Eric Clapton. She took this as a "sign" that she needed "to come across a Darryl." When she got to her yoga class, she learned that a woman there needed help moving a washer and dryer to her apartment. She called her husband Al, who had a truck, and helped the woman move her appliances. She took this as a "sign" because of the perfect timing and her ability to help this woman.

Ms. Brent described multiple other examples of God's signs and intervention in her life. One day she was looking for her keys. Her four-year-old son Allan was requesting water. She kept looking for her keys and did not immediately give her son water. When she finally went to get water for her son, she found her keys. She concluded that this was a message from God to "let nature take its course—and go with the flow." She took this as an instruction on how to live her life.

Ms. Brent said that a candle burned for 20 hours, which she saw as an extraordinary length. Although she had never prayed before, she got down on her knees. She said "thank you" to God for the candlelight and then "the candle went out." She said, "I was really excited about this." She concluded that the candle going out was a personal communication from God. She explained that there could be no other explanation for it other than God.

Ms. Brent said that her husband Al had a lamp that played various recorded sounds. One night he said that he heard whale sounds on the lamp for the first time. She knew this was another sign, but her husband Al was dismissive of it.

Ms. Brent said that Thursday (2/19/09), she saw a man who was "Jesus-esque." He had his hair pulled back. She felt directed to talk to him. In her yoga class, another man she did not know appeared distressed by his manner. Since she expected to meet "a Darryl," she assumed this man was Darryl, but that was not his name. She said, "I grabbed his hand and kissed his fingers. I felt I was supposed to, compelled to." The distressed man said to her, "Are you an angel?" She replied, "Yes."

On Thursday, February 19, 2009, Ms. Brent also heard the radio station, Jack FM, direct her to go to a "Jacktivities" event, which was being held at a pizza place. A van from Jack FM was present. She took John, her 18-month-old son, with her, and she got lost. She said, "All of a sudden, I got the impression I should kill John." She was in a parking lot crying and said, "Absolutely not." This is the first time she ever had such a thought. I asked Ms. Brent why she refused to kill her child. She replied, "I would never kill my child."

Ms. Brent said she saw a bearded man in a T-shirt that said "Jack FM" at the Jacktivities event. She was waiting for her next instruction from the radio. Her son John attempted to get on the Jack FM bus. However, the bus left. On the way home she looked through her sun roof and saw a "wing in a cloud formation." She saw this as a sign that meant she had passed a test because "Angels have wings."

Ms. Brent said that on Saturday, 2/21/09, she, her husband Al, and her two sons Allan (age 4) and John (age 18 months) were directed to go Crystal Cove Beach. She knew this because a child's television show called *Blues Clues* mentioned "hands in sand."

Ms. Brent said that she became secretive because she could not talk about her special relationship to God. If she did not keep her special understanding with God a secret, the devil and evil ones would know about it. She added, "Everything had a latent meaning." She noticed that many cars had stickers with the letters NOTW that meant "Not of This World." She saw the world as being "filled with angels and demons."

Ms. Brent said that later on Saturday, 2/21/09, she felt a need to test whether God was protecting her.

John was with her in her car. She let go of the steering wheel while driving her car. She went through a red light. Her car then drifted to the right and hit a curb. Since only a small amount of damage was done to the wheels of the car, she viewed this as a "successful test" and proof that God existed and had communicated with her personally. Another evidence of God's earlier intervention was the fact that all her car radio speakers "had been blown except one." After God caused her "awakening," all of her speakers worked perfectly.

Ms. Brent said there was an "understanding" between God and her, but it was not through a voice. She described the understanding as "like you had previously been told something." She believed that through God's instruction, "you just know what you are supposed to do." She said that not all her directions came from Jack FM. "Some items you just know."

Ms. Brent said that her friend Alice had given her a six-pound brass urn (or chalice) in October 2008 that she had purchased in Saudi Arabia. Ms. Brent ordinarily kept the urn in her kitchen. However, on Sunday 2/22/09 she carried the urn and scroll in a black bag around with her because she was "directed to."

Ms. Brent said that on Sunday 2/22/09, she heard commercials on Jack FM about Ramano's Grill and a BMW car dealership. She felt directed to go to both places. Her 15-year-old son Mike went with her. She attempted to lease a BMW and take a test drive as the radio commercial had instructed her. When she was attempting to lease the BMW, she suggested to the salesman that her special urn be used for payment.

Ms. Brent said that on that Sunday she felt like she was the character Trinity in the movie *The Matrix*. When test-driving a BMW, she saw a dime on the carpet of the car. This meant to her that "Somebody dropped a dime," meaning that she was in danger.

Ms. Brent and Mike visited multiple car dealerships on that Sunday. She believed that the devil or bad demons "were on to me." She saw a newspaper that said that Chandra Levy had been killed by demons. She took this as a message to "be careful, there are enemies."

Ms. Brent said that on Sunday, 2/22/09, there were "latent meanings everywhere" conveying threats of danger to her. Nonetheless, she still had to follow her directions. She expected to meet

God. She saw a man by a Volkswagen Bug who was a "Jesus-like" character whom she perceived to be God.

Ms. Brent said that she next saw a Brinks' truck. She took this as a sign that she would "pick up a bag of cash." At that point she was convinced that she was going to win the lottery. She told Mike that if she won the lottery, she would buy him a Lamborghini. She added that now it doesn't make sense to her.

Ms. Brent said that on Sunday, 2/22/09, she told Mike to get whatever he wanted at a skateboard shop. She knew she could not afford the items, but she thought that if her credit card went through successfully "it would be a sign." She felt directed to buy clothes and a skateboard for herself. It was totally out of character for her to own a skateboard. She attempted to purchase $7000 worth of sports equipment and clothing for Mike and herself. However, her credit card did not go through. The clerk in the store was distressed.

Ms. Brent said that she asked in the skateboard store about where Ramano's restaurant was. She was told that there was an Italian restaurant nearby named Rustica's. She and Mike went to that restaurant for dinner. Based on the "instruction" from Jack FM, she attempted to order "a penne rustica" dish, but it was not on the menu. When she ordered it, the waiter raised his eyebrows. She took this as a sign that "they were communicating in code."

Ms. Brent said that she knew from God that Mike was going to die from smoking crack that Sunday. She feared that Mike would die of an overdose. She thus believed that she and Mike were having a "last supper." She left a $100 tip on her credit card for their dinner at Rustica's. When the credit card went through, she viewed this as "another sign." Most of her extraordinary buying that Sunday was simply "following directions from God." However, the decision to leave the $100 tip at the restaurant was her own.

Ms. Brent said that she then took an exit ramp and found herself going in the opposite direction from what she expected. She viewed this as further proof that she was in *The Matrix*. When it rained on her that Sunday, and she believed that "God was crying."

MS. BRENT'S ACCOUNT OF THE 2/23/09 HOMICIDE

Ms. Brent said that on Monday morning, 2/23/09, she awakened about 3:30 or 4:00 a.m. She turned the radio on for additional instructions from God.

She went into the living room and saw a change on the television set from benign programming to "demons growling." She picked up her son John, the 18-month-old victim, and took him back to bed with her, and they went to sleep.

Ms. Brent said that she awoke later in the morning, and "I knew I would kill both my boys" (Allan and John). She added, "I felt nothing." She "understood what I needed to do." She explained that any natural response she had as a mother was suppressed. "It all seemed fine without ramifications." She had no thoughts of the future.

Ms. Brent said that when her husband awakened around 6:30 a.m., he took their son Allan to school. She said she was relieved because that meant there was only one child left for her to kill. In her home Ms. Brent had a wall hanging that included an upside-down triangle, a white horse, and some actual arrows. She knew, "I would kill them with the arrows."

Ms. Brent said that she listened to Jack FM on the radio and heard a song about riding a white horse. She got down the wall hanging and straddled the white horse as she was instructed to do. She was having a heavy menstrual period and bleeding through her pad. She believed that she was supposed to get menstrual blood on the white horse.

Ms. Brent was then "directed" by the radio to go to a commercial website. On the website there was information about booking shipboard passage. She interpreted this to mean that she was to get her entire family "out of harm's way." She felt a sense of urgency because the website required the booking within five minutes to get a special price. The website did not accept her credit card to buy ship's passage for her family.

Ms. Brent said that John woke up and "toddled to Mike on the couch." Ms. Brent was bleeding and walking around naked. She put on a T-shirt. She believed that since she was in *The Matrix* "things were not real." (In the movie *The Matrix*, people falsely believe in a reality that is a digital illusion). Her menstrual blood caused a stain "the shape of angel wings" on her bed sheet.

Ms. Brent said that Mike said to her, "Mom, you're dripping blood." She replied that she knew it. She was waiting for God's directions for when she should kill John. A former neighbor, Phil, called. She believed that Phil was a demon and that the call was a diversion to stop her from killing her son. She saw a bird outside of her window looking agitated and "spying" on her. She believed that the bird was a "bad guy" who would tell the demon, so that "I needed to hurry."

Ms. Brent said that there was a book she had read to her children called, *Ten Apples Up on Top*. In the book, a tiger and a dog compete about how many apples they can put on their heads. In the book, a bear chases the tiger and dog. When she looked at the book that Monday morning, "the pages had changed." Instead of competing, all the animals had "ten apples on top." The book "showed her" that killing John was the right thing to do because she was helping God. Between the forces of evil (manifested by demons) and God, she knew she "was on the right side."

Ms. Brent said that because of her belief that she was in *The Matrix* she thought that "John was not real, Mike and I were not real, and the blood was not real." She believed that what she was doing did not matter because of the "changes" that had occurred. The changes included the "growling demons" on television that morning and "how the direction of the road had changed the previous day."

Ms. Brent said that John came over and laid his head between her legs. She didn't want to hurt him but she had "an understanding from God and a sense of urgency." She believed that she "was helping the world at large. Killing John was not hard to do" because she knew that she "was doing what was right" and she did it without hurting John at all.

Ms. Brent had no discomfort or upset when killing her son but she still felt a need to keep her conduct a secret. She trusted her directions "because I was already being led and I was in *The Matrix*." I asked Ms. Brent why on Thursday she refused to kill her son but on Sunday she did not refuse. She said that she didn't know, except that on Sunday she believed she was in *The Matrix*.

Ms. Brent said that she struck John's head with the special urn about five times. She did not want to cause her son any pain, and "he was not awake for any of it." After she struck John's head, "he was still breathing." She was then "directed by God" to the arrows in the wall hanging and a location on John's abdomen to put in an arrow. She broke an arrow from the wall hanging and inserted it in John's abdomen. John continued to breathe.

Ms. Brent said that she then "leaned my hands on his chest so he could not breathe." Based on God's directions, she next put her finger in the abdominal arrow wound and took out the twine that was wound around the arrow. She picked up John, who had stopped breathing, and placed him in the "angel wings" bloodstain and covered him with a blanket. She placed John in the "angel wings" because God wanted her "to make John an angel."

Ms. Brent then went into the shower, turned it on, and remained there for nine hours. She did this due to the fact that in the movie *The Matrix* pods grew on human beings. She believed that in the shower her "pod connections" were "popping off." She added, "I was expecting to go down the drain and get to the real world." (In the movie *The Matrix*, the character Trinity does come out of a drain.)

Ms. Brent said that her 15-year-old son Mike came in to the bathroom and cried, "Mom, Mommy!" but she ignored him. Mike then asked "Why?" She replied, " Mike, it's okay. John is okay in God's hands." She told Mike not to look at John. She said, "I think I am Trinity or the daughter of Eve." She told Mike that he should let her be, because she "needed to be in the shower."

Ms. Brent said that while in the shower she thought she "had to die also." She tried to inhale the shower water but "the drowning sensation made it unbearable." She added, "My lips were blue so I thought I was dying." She believed that "I had removed myself halfway from life support."

Ms. Brent said that her husband Al came home late that evening and said, "What have you done?" She did not reply. She thought she would have disappeared by then "by going to the real world." (In *The Matrix*, people mistakenly believe they are in the real world, but it is a digital illusion.)

Ms. Brent said that later the police came and told her to step out of the shower. She told the police, "I don't think I am supposed to." She reached for the gun of one of the police officers as the character Trinity did in *The Matrix*. (In the movie, Trinity does disarm police officers.) She reported "no plan to shoot anybody." I asked Ms. Brent about her interaction with police officers. She said that she was directed by God "not to speak to them or even to look up."

Ms. Brent indicated that she was not fearful when she was taken to jail. She "felt protected, that things were not real, like it was just a program." She acknowledged that in jail she may have appeared to be talking to herself but she "was actually talking to God." She said that she never had any auditory hallucinations; she was just talking about the "directions" she was receiving.

Ms. Brent said that although she was described as being depressed in jail by mental health professionals, she did not perceive herself to be depressed at all because she was "on a mission." During her first week in jail, she had no depression and no thoughts about what she had done to John.

I asked Ms. Brent about engaging in a "lion's roar" that was described by correctional staff when she was in jail. She explained that she believed that with a lion's roar she could "call up an earthquake." She added, "I was a lamb of God. I would be killed by a demon." She believed that she would thus sacrifice herself.

Ms. Brent said that while in jail she took some of the twine left from the arrow (used in the homicide) and tied it to a menstrual pad. She believed that when this went down the drain, it would go to the ocean, be eaten by small fish, and then the small fish would be eaten by whales. Thus, she believed that the DNA in her blood would end up in a whale. This fulfilled her "instructions" from God.

Ms. Brent said that in retrospect, she now believes that the "instructions from God" led her on a "wild goose chase." She currently believed that her son's death was "for nothing." At the time of the killing, she believed that she was helping God and was directed by God. Upon inquiry, she said she would not have killed her son if she had been directed to do so by the devil rather than by God.

MENTAL STATUS EXAMINATION

Ms. Brent was interviewed through a glass partition in the Small Town County Jail. She was dressed in jail garb and adequately groomed. She was cooperative with the examination. She showed a full range of emotional expression and cried when describing the killing of her son. She described her mood as "good; sad about John."

Ms. Brent was oriented to time, place, and person. She could name the last four presidents accurately. She could correctly identify three of the five Great Lakes. She could recall three words accurately after five minutes. She accurately spelled the word "world" forward and backward, showing adequate concentration.

Ms. Brent said that she has never had any auditory or visual hallucinations. She did not believe she had any special powers other than "some prophetic dreams." She did not show current evidence of paranoid delusions. She described many delusions of reference and paranoid delusions around 2/23/09, but she reported no new delusions since. When tested with interpreting proverbs, she had the capacity for abstract thinking. She stated that the only time she had a suicidal thought was in 1995. She lacked insight into her mental illness. She still believed that God had instructed her to kill her son.

SUMMARY OF RELEVANT RECORDS

Records of Dr. Mark Wise

11/30/07: Patient says she is very irritable and angry. She denies depression. She has been to counseling, but didn't like her counselor. She'd like to try Prozac. Plan: Start Prozac 20 mgs. daily.

7/09/08: Thirty-eight-year old female who comes in today for "shingles outbreak" over her left face. She reports being very irritable and angry. Reports seeing a psychologist about this but she didn't like the psychologist. She states that she "was so angry at a truck driver that she chased him down on her bicycle recently." She follows this by laughing. She made disparaging comments about previous physicians she had seen. She seems very wound up, agitated, and somewhat confrontational. Assessment: Anger management issues and bizarre aggressive behavior. Plan: Recommend patient contact Behavioral Health regarding anger management issues. Start Amitriptyline 25 mgs. each night for one week and then two tablets each night thereafter.

7/18/08: Patient probably had tendencies toward hypomania based on her behavior.

9/8/08: She did not find Elavil to be helpful. She is requesting a trial of Lexapro. She does seem to have symptoms that may be related to depression and/ fibromyalgia. Plan: Lexapro 10 mgs. each morning.

11/03/08: She prefers the non-generic Lexapro. Is currently taking 10 mgs. but sometimes she takes as much as 20 mgs a day. Assessment: Fibromyalgia and/or depression. Doing better.

1/16/09: Patient here for follow-up regarding symptoms of Bipolar II disorder. She is currently taking Lexapro and feels she has some hypomanic organic symptoms as well. Plan: Psychiatric evaluation. On Elavil 25 mgs. half tablet each night.

Email from Lisa Brent to Alicia Dated 1/15/09

"I'm bipolar. I recently discovered through some good reading....

"Been taking Elavil for pain and I cannot recommend it highly enough. It was prescribed for post-herpetic neuralgia, but when that went away, just as a switch to a different (and on- hand) antidepressant, from Lexapro, which made me feel nothing about anything."

Police Report of J. Cole, Dated 2/23/09

He and his partner, Officer Kite, were dispatched to 212 Oak. Saw a small child identified as John Brent lying near the bottom portion of the bed. When he and his partner approached Lisa Brent in the shower, she ignored their commands to come out. Once Lisa Brent was placed in handcuffs, she appeared "to be elated that she was in custody. She showed no remorse or sadness toward the death of her son."

The suspect, Lisa Brent, pretended to reach for a bathrobe, turned her body toward Officer Kite and suddenly lunged with both of her hands toward Officer Kite's weapon that was on the right side of his body. She refused to let go of the weapon. He struck her several times with a flashlight to the upper portion of her back. The shower in the bedroom was still running. Urine was puddled on the ground next to the shower, and blood was inside the toilet.

Police Report, Dated 2/24/09, by Officer C.

Mike, the 15-year-old son of Lisa Brent, told officers he heard a "ping" noise. He said to Lisa, "What did you do?" Lisa Brent replied, "I set him free." (In the movie *The Matrix*, the protagonists set others free from the Matrix.) Lisa Brent also told him that she was dying.

Mike said that two days ago Lisa Brent accused him of using crack, and he told her that he never used crack. When he saw his mother in the shower, he noted that her lips were purple. He described the look on her face as one he had never seen before. She told him that everything was going to be fine.

Mike said that his mom had changed in the past few months. She had been to yoga a lot and talked about God. He said she "talks about the world a lot and how the world is going to end. She also said she was going to win the lottery."

Mike said that on Sunday, February 22, his mom took him on a shopping spree in Orange County. He said this was unusual. He said she spent $4000 on clothes, watches, snowboards, skateboards, and other things. He said she bought a skateboard for herself, and she never skateboards.

Mike said that his mom was carrying the same cup (chalice) on the shopping spree that he saw on the side of the bed when he found John dead.

Police Report About Crime Scene

They found a woman's black purse on the floor. Inside of it was a large folded-up piece of paper with bizarre writings on it. They found wall art that looked like an animal skin stretched between a wooden frame with a Southwestern design on it that the arrows may have been from.

Small Town Police Department Report on Materials Found at the Crime Scene

Possible marijuana cigarettes from the kitchen stove. Broken arrow piece with possible blood. Gold chalice with possible blood.

Summary of Handwritten Documents and Scroll by Lisa Brent

Various songs are referred to, with many references to Jack FM 93.1. After songs "Let It Be" and "One" by U2, the word "God" is placed in parentheses.

The scroll is on brown paper. It includes many symbols with unclear meanings, and various writings. One remark says, "Predators eat up all the little animals and their God energy is released into the big ones easing their pain, bringing balance...." There are also references to Adam and Eve and Eve being coaxed to eat the apple, "going against the laws of nature." There are references to the universe imploding.

Reference is made to the earth drowning asunder, recombining to explode again. There is also a reference to the year 2050, the end of time. "It's why the earth is mostly water, as long as we can be refreshed in the life giving water, we will survive. When the life is gone from the water, life will be gone from the earth."

Autopsy of John Brent

The autopsy showed extensive bruising on the victim's head. The weight of the chalice was 6 pounds. There was a large hole in the victim's belly button area with a four-inch-deep wound. There was a cluster of nine small puncture wounds in the victim's back. There were multiple fractures on the left portion and rear portion of the victim's skull.

Police Interview with Al Brent, Lisa Brent's Husband

Al Brent explained that Lisa's son Mike lives with his father, but stays with Al and Lisa on weekends. He said that his marriage with Lisa had been strained and they have been under financial pressure. He described Lisa as verbally abusive, but added that she had not been physically abusive. He did say that Lisa has anger issues.

Al said that for the past few months Lisa had been acting more and more strange, stating that she had not been taking care of the house or making meals. She had also become secretive and talked about some type of enlightenment. Lisa had claimed to find "God" and now had the powers of prophecy. She talked about the end of the world's circumstances. Lisa claimed to have unlocked the mysteries of the universe. Al noticed some collision damage on Lisa's car a while back and confronted her about it. Lisa said she had been involved with a collision with a pole, but the damage did not match that type of collision.

Mike told him that Lisa had been in the shower for six hours and refused to come out. He found John's body lying on the mattress. He saw some of John's intestines coming out of a large hole where his belly button should have been. John was cold to the touch.

Al said that Lisa was sitting in the shower with the water running on her. Al asked her what happened, but Lisa did not answer him. Instead she stared at him with a look Mike described as "cold, dead, evil."

Police Interview with Fran

Fran is the manager of the yoga studio. Lisa had been attending yoga classes since the summer of 2008. Lisa was seeking a deeper understanding of yoga on a more spiritual level. She only knew Lisa as a loving mother who spoke affectionately about her children all the time.

Police Interview with Alicia

Alicia described Lisa as a good person who loved her new baby very much.

Police Interview with Dee

Dee described Lisa as "sweet, kind, normal." She talked about her kids a lot. Lisa, Dee said, was not the type of person to do something like this.

Police Interview with Celia

Celia is the oldest daughter of Lisa Brent and lives in a different city. She was in the possession of pieces of paper with odd writings in Lisa's handwriting. Celia read how Lisa felt she was getting messages through the songs she was hearing on a local radio station called "Jack FM."

5/19/09 Interview Between Robert (Investigator) and Celia

Celia said, "My mother would jump in front of a bus to save her children. She lived for her kids and loves them very much."

Robert Interview with Joe Piel 10/8/09

Mr. Piel said that his former wife had always had periods where she was emotionally up and down. "She could turn on a dime." Lisa had accused Mike of doing crack. Mike told him his mother had been carrying a bag around for several days and had talked to him about *The Matrix*. He said that Lisa Brent was always a great mother.

Joe said a few months before the homicide, Lisa had really gotten into yoga. She has lost a lot of weight. For the first time, she was talking about having a relationship with God. He was very surprised because Lisa had always been agnostic. Lisa took Prozac in the past, about two or three years ago, to help her control her emotions during her menstrual cycle.

Joe stated it was inconceivable to him that Lisa would do anything to hurt any of her children for any reason. She loved being pregnant; loved bringing them up and having them around. He does not believe that she would cause any harm to them in order to hurt Al or out of revenge or retaliation.

Detention Health Services Records Regarding Ms. Brent

2/24/09 *Intake*: Refuses to speak. Hallucinations and staring down at floor mumbling. Inmate very psychotic.

3/10/09: She is able to concentrate and read to cope with situation. Guarded.

3/12/09: Patient paranoid, evasive, "I don't want and need any meds."

3/15/09: Not talking. Psychotic.

3/23/09: "I'm fine, I don't want any meds." No longer wants to take psychotropic medications.

Small Town County Regional Medical Center

2/25/09: Patient brought for psych evaluation. Patient singing loudly, but then appears completely alert and oriented, answering questions appropriately. Banging head on mattress. She stated, "I'm not trying to hurt myself, just stop the thoughts in my head."

2/25/09: With one-to-one sitter for safety. Singing, screaming at times. Patient was heard counting and reciting ABCs. Patient is non-responsive when spoken to. Patient does not follow commands.

2/27/09: Patient is mute. Disorganized, behavior unpredictable, aggressive behavior. Still incapable of caring for herself. Confused, agitated, restless.

3/1/09: Paranoid, mute and withdrawn. Still with bizarre behaviors and noises.

3/3/09: Patient more engaged, responded appropriately to questions. Much improved. Speech clear, relevant, and coherent.

Detention Discharge Summary 2/25/09–3/4/09: Discharge diagnosis: Psychotic Disorder, not otherwise specified, resolved. Rule out Mood Disorder, not otherwise specified. Rule out cannabis abuse.

Lisa Brent initially demonstrated extremely bizarre behavior such as picking the paint off of the wall and taking off the plastic molding on the wall and sweeping paint chips into the bathroom. She was making bizarre sounds and intimidating staff by sticking out her tongue with pieces of paper on it. With improved compliance (taking Zyprexa) she demonstrated improvement in cognition and apparent resolution of her psychotic condition.

Letter from Lisa Brent in Jail to Son Mike Dated 3/16/09

"I can tell you (seriously) that the TV doesn't carry messages from God at all—it's actually quite the opposite. So turn it off and leave it off. Movies included."

DIAGNOSTIC IMPRESSION

Psychosis Not Otherwise Specified, with Manic and Paranoid Features.

Ms. Brent developed frank psychotic beliefs about 20 days before her 2/23/09, homicide and they persisted for at least two weeks after she was incarcerated. She persists in the delusional belief that God gave her instructions to kill her son, and she does not believe that she suffered from a mental illness. The specifier *manic features* is added because of Ms. Brent's grandiosity and expansiveness; for example, she left a $100 tip on 2/22/09. The specifier *paranoid features* is added because of her fear of danger from demons.

Ms. Brent's psychosis included extensive delusions of reference. They included her belief that God had revealed himself to her, her belief that dozens of songs on Jack FM radio were conveying special messages to her, and perceiving multiple "signs" from God. She had the belief that a candle burning for 20 hours was a message from God; she attributed special meaning to seeing a cloud formation in the form of a wing; and she believed that her broken car radio speakers began to work again due to God's intervention. She had the belief that she should carry out God's directions given by announcers on Jack FM; the belief that a dime on the carpet of a BMW car meant that she was in danger; and the belief that seeing a Brinks' truck meant that she would collect a bag of money. She believed that a waiter raising his eyebrows meant that they were communicating in code; that her credit card being accepted in a restaurant was a sign from God; and the fact that she found herself going in an opposite direction on a freeway exit meant that she was in *The Matrix*.

Ms. Brent's grandiose delusions included her belief that she had a special relationship to God and that God was giving her instructions through Jack FM comments and songs. She believed that she would win the lottery and that she was the female character Trinity in "The Matrix."

Ms. Brent's paranoid delusions included fear for her family, seeing herself in danger, believing that a "demon" called her, and that a bird was acting as a spy for a demon.

Other evidence of Ms. Brent's mental illness was her bizarre behavior, such as carrying around a 6-pound urn for two or three days. On admission to jail, Ms. Brent was confused and disorganized. She was putting paper on her tongue, sticking out her tongue, and roaring like a lion in the belief that this would cause an earthquake.

I considered the possibility that Ms. Brent's psychosis was induced by marijuana. Most people who use marijuana do not become psychotic. Although Ms. Brent had been using the same dose of legally purchased marijuana for many months, marijuana may have contributed to the onset of her psychosis. Ms. Brent's psychosis has persisted long after the marijuana was fully metabolized. She retained the delusional belief that God had instructed her to kill her son nine months after stopping marijuana.

The length of Ms. Brent's psychosis was greater than one month, which rules out the diagnosis of brief psychotic disorder. Although Ms. Brent had long-standing rapid speech, irritability, anger outbursts, and some manic features during her psychotic episode, she did not have discreet periods of mania or depression that would qualify her for a formal diagnosis of bipolar disorder.

I considered the possibility that Ms. Brent was faking psychiatric symptoms (malingering) to succeed with an insanity defense. I concluded that she was not malingering, for the following reasons:

1. Ms. Brent was observed by multiple staff in the jail and Small Town Regional Hospital to be bizarre, psychotic, and disorganized within 24 hours of her homicide.
2. The homicide of Ms. Brent's son was carried out in a strange manner (including an arrow in his belly button) that was consistent with her "God-given instructions."
3. Ms. Brent engaged in psychotic behavior that was out of character for her on the day before the homicide. Specifically, she attempted to spend several thousand dollars for items she did not need, and she attempted to lease a BMW car that she did not need.
4. Ms. Brent's fifteen-year-old son, Mike, confirmed that Ms. Brent carried around a 6-pound urn for three days, and that she wrote bizarre material on a scroll before her homicide.
5. A scroll (in evidence) written contemporaneously by Ms. Brent confirmed that she was "getting messages" through songs that she heard on the radio station, Jack FM. The scroll contained bizarre writings and mentioned Adam and Eve.
6. Mike confirmed that Lisa Brent spoke to him about being in The Matrix before the homicide.
7. Mike heard his mother say upon John's death, "I set him free."
8. Police officers confirmed that at the time she was arrested, Ms. Brent appeared "to be elated that she was in custody. She showed no remorse or sadness toward the death of her son."

OPINION

It is my opinion with reasonable medical certainty that Lisa Brent was suffering from a severe mental disease on February 23, 2009, when she killed her son, John Brent. Her formal psychiatric diagnosis is psychotic disorder, not otherwise specified. The manifestations of her psychotic illness on 2/23/09 included delusions of reference, paranoid delusions, grandiose delusions, bizarre behavior, and an inability to distinguish whether things were real because of her belief that she was in The Matrix.

The following specific evidence shows that Ms. Brent was severely mentally ill on 2/23/09:

1. Ms. Brent had a paranoid delusion that she and her family were in danger. For example, she believed that a bird was acting as a spy for a demon.
2. Ms. Brent engaged in bizarre behavior, including walking around naked while dripping menstrual blood and staying in the shower for nine hours.
3. Ms. Brent misperceived many ordinary events (delusions of reference) as instructions from God. For example, she straddled a wall hanging that contained a white horse because of hearing a song about a white horse.
4. Ms. Brent attributed a sinister meaning to TV programming changing to "growling demons."
5. Ms. Brent believed that a former neighbor who called her on the phone was a demon.
6. Ms. Brent had a delusion that she was The Matrix character Trinity, or the daughter of Eve.
7. Ms. Brent believed that she was in The Matrix and that her sons John and Mike were "not real."

It is my opinion with reasonable medical certainty that Ms. Brent was not capable of knowing or understanding the nature and quality of taking her son's life on 2/23/09 due to her severe mental illness. Since Ms. Brent delusionally believed that she was in The Matrix, she did not believe that her son John was "real." She believed that she would go down the drain in the shower and get to "the real world."

It is my opinion with reasonable medial certainty that Ms. Brent was not able to distinguish right from wrong at the time she took John's life on 2/23/09 due to her mental disease. The following evidence supports this opinion:

1. Ms. Brent delusionally believed that she had received instructions from God to bring

about her son's death. She believed that she was doing what was morally right based on God being the ultimate giver of law and morality.

2. Ms. Brent believed that in the contest between demons and God, she was on the side of God doing what was right. For example, she believed that a demon, Phil in particular, called her to interfere with her God-given instructions to kill her son.

3. Ms. Brent believed that taking John's life was not only helping God but "helping the world at large."

4. Ms. Brent believed that God wanted her to turn her son John into an angel. She accomplished this by placing John in a bloodstain in the shape of angel wings.

5. Ms. Brent was not fearful when taken to jail because she believed that it was just part of "the program" in *The Matrix*.

6. Ms. Brent had no rational nonpsychotic motive to kill her son. Multiple friends and relatives described her as a good mother who loved her children very much. She had never physically abused her children.

In summary, it is my opinion with reasonable medical certainty that due to a severe mental disease, Ms. Lisa Brent on 2/23/09 was not capable of knowing or understanding the nature and quality of her homicidal assault on John and that she was not capable of distinguishing right from wrong at the time of the commission of the offenses.

Sincerely,
Phillip J. Resnick, MD

TEACHING POINT:
USING RECORDS AND COLLATERAL INTERVIEWS IN ASSESSING RESPONSE STYLE

There are various ways to assess whether an examinee's clinical presentation is genuine in the context of FMHA. The role of testing in making such a determination was discussed previously and, as discussed, several psychological measures have considerable empirical support when used to assess an examinee's response style (e.g., MMPI-2, SIRS-2, VIP). These measures provide evaluators with objective data regarding an examinee's response style. Importantly, because these measures are nomothetically derived, they provide normative data against which the examinee's performance can be compared.

Despite the empirical evidence supporting the use of testing in assessing response style, evaluators are advised to rely on multiple sources of information in assessing whether the examinee's presentation is genuine. As such, relevant records and collateral interviews can be useful data points in making such a determination. Records relating to an examinee's clinical history, for example, provide the evaluator with a source of data against which the examinee's current clinical presentation can be compared. Judging the consistency between past and current clinical reports and presentations can be a useful way to assess the genuineness of an examinee's claimed impairments. Similarly, collateral interviews can provide third party information regarding the examinee's clinical functioning in other settings and at other times, which would be useful in assessing response style.

27

Expert Testimony

This final chapter on expert testimony is structured somewhat differently than the previous chapters in this volume. The sole commentator in this chapter, Stan Brodsky, Ph.D., has made extraordinary contributions to our understanding of effective expert testimony, and has authored a number of seminal works addressing this area of practice (Brodsky, 1991, 1999, 2004, 2013). In this chapter, Dr. Brodsky reviews one of the reports from this book and identifies points that would be subject to questioning in cross-examination. He describes such questions and possible responses from the expert witness, then offers his own commentary on these questions and responses.

Using this framework, this chapter addresses the three of the four principles directly related to expert testimony. The first principle is "communicate effectively during testimony," and the associated teaching point is about moving from "adequate" to "effective" in presenting this testimony. The second principle involves basing testimony on the results of properly performed FMHA, with the teaching point addressing the use of the report to facilitate effective testimony. The third principle involves controlling the message—obtaining, retaining, and regaining control over the meaning and impact of what is presented in expert testimony. The teaching point discussed in connection with this principle involves the strategies that can be used to accomplish this. Additionally, the principle of preparing for expert testimony (*Principle 36*) will receive comments throughout this chapter.

CASE ONE
PRINCIPLE: COMMUNICATE EFFECTIVELY (*PRINCIPLE 37*)

This principle addresses the importance of both substance and style in effective FMHA testimony.

"Substantive strength" involves the extent to which testimony is thorough, accurate, impartial, relevant, and supported by scientific reasoning and data. We define *substantive strength* as the overall degree to which the testimony is consistent with the 38 principles of FMHA described by Heilbrun, Grisso, and Goldstein (2009) and elaborated upon in this book. *Stylistic strength* involves a combination of professional dress and demeanor; courtroom familiarity; speech that is clear, largely free of technical jargon, fluid and variable in pace, and directed toward the judge or jury and the attorney; and the capacity to handle the challenge of cross-examination (Heilbrun et al., 2009). The effectiveness of expert testimony communication can be considered in terms of both substantive and stylistic strength, with the most effective testimony—that is, testimony that is accurate, ethical, and persuasive—being high in both.

The *Specialty Guidelines for Forensic Psychology* (APA *Specialty Guidelines*; American Psychological Association, 2013b) make it reasonably clear that stylistically strong testimony is not precluded by other parts of the Specialty Guidelines:

> When providing reports and other sworn statements or testimony in any form, forensic practitioners strive to present their conclusions, evidence, opinions, or other professional products in a fair manner. Forensic practitioners do not, by either commission or omission, participate in misrepresentation of their evidence, nor do they participate in partisan attempts to avoid, deny, or subvert the presentation of evidence contrary to their own position or opinion [citation omitted]. This does not preclude forensic practitioners from forcefully presenting the data and reasoning upon which a conclusion or professional product is based. (Guideline 11.01)

The substantive aspects of communicating effectively in expert testimony are addressed in detail through the other principles described by Heilbrun and colleagues (2009) and in this volume. The key to applying these principles to the substantive aspects of expert testimony involves considering FMHA as a process composed of distinct steps. These steps culminate in the communication of FMHA results in a detailed, thorough report describing one's data, reasoning, and conclusions. When these principles are followed, the communication of results—whether in the form of the report or the testimony based on a report—is guided by the cumulative application of these substantive principles.

The stylistic aspects of effective testimony have not yet been discussed at length in this volume, and can be considered by reference to empirical research on impression management and standards of practice for expert testimony. Empirical research on the social psychology of persuasive communication generally suggests that stylistic factors may enhance one's credibility and persuasiveness. Some of these factors include knowledge and expertise, as demonstrated through training, experience, degrees, and positions; trustworthiness, or perceptions by the judge and jurors of trustworthiness; likeability, such as demonstrating respectfulness; and confidence and dynamism, such as that demonstrated through style, charisma, and nonverbal aspects of credibility (Brodsky, 2013; Brodsky, Griffin, & Cramer, 2010; Champagne, Shuman, & Whitaker, 1991; Cramer, Harris, Fletcher, DeCoster, & Brodksy, 2011; Melton, Petrila, Poythress, & Slobogin, 2007; Rosenthal, 1983; Shuman, Champagne, & Whitaker, 1994).

Other specific factors relevant to stylistic effectiveness have been noted, such as one's style of dress, familiarity with courtroom protocol, how one speaks to the jury, and one's style of speech (Brodsky, 2013; Chappelle & Rosengren, 2001; Melton et al., 2007). Generally, the style of dress should be conservative, professional, and neat; flashy and bright clothing should be avoided. The expert should also display familiarity and comfort with the courtroom. Specific examples of such familiarity and comfort include pausing before answering each question, using a clear and even tone of voice, not volunteering information, and knowing how to react when an objection is made. The expert should also speak to the

jury, particularly during cross-examination, using understandable language, and making ample eye contact. Speech should be fluid, conversational in tone, clear, and confident.

Brodsky (2013) has elaborated on a number of ways in which to enhance the effectiveness of testimony. Some of Brodsky's (2013) points that are relevant to style include:

(a) handling loaded and half-truth questions by first acknowledging the true part in a dependent clause (e.g., "Although…"), and then "strongly denying the untrue part in an independent clause" (p. 9);

(b) meeting with the attorney prior to the direct examination and helping to prepare the questions;

(c) after a "disaster" during testimony, either correcting the error as soon as possible or letting it go;

(d) neither fraternizing nor discussing the case with opposing counsel, other witnesses, clients, or jurors;

(e) speaking slowly, stressing syllables, and varying one's loudness of speech during testimony;

(f) avoiding responding in an overly defensive manner;

(g) varying the length of responses while also avoiding becoming too repetitive; and

(h) when appropriate to disagree with cross-examination questions, doing so with "strength, clarity, and conviction" (p. 136).

Effective testimony is an important part of the FMHA process. The mastery of both substantive and stylistic aspects of testimony contributes substantially to making the forensic clinician a more effective practitioner of FMHA.

TEACHING POINT:
MOVING FROM "ADEQUATE" TO "EFFECTIVE" IN PRESENTING EXPERT TESTIMONY

Mastery of the substantive aspects of the case comes from conducting a good evaluation (consistent with broad principles of FMHA) and communicating this effectively in a report similar to the ones illustrated in this book, so the report can be used as a foundation for testimony. It also involves preparing—familiarity with the case materials beyond the report, discussion with the attorney who will be presenting the testimony, and a broader familiarity with the relevant law, science, and ethical and professional standards. The material in the previous chapters has been structured to address the substantive aspects of FMHA, using case reports as both examples of such mastery and illustrations of a solid substantive foundation for expert testimony.

Yet even substantively strong testimony may be hard to understand, boring, and dense. Cross-examination may unbalance expert witnesses so they are less able to convey and defend the important components of their findings. Experts may appear arrogant, condescending, and not likeable. Outstanding expert testimony must begin with the strong substance of the previous paragraph—but it may remain less effective than it could be without attention to the stylistic aspects of testimony as well. This chapter references both, but genuine mastery of both substantive and stylistic aspects of testimony comes through paying careful attention to both. Brodsky's maxims are the best source of guidance in both domains.

PRINCIPLE:
BASE TESTIMONY ON THE RESULTS OF THE PROPERLY PERFORMED FORENSIC MENTAL HEALTH ASSESSMENT (PRINCIPLE 35)

A properly performed FMHA creates a solid foundation for expert testimony. Conversely, a poorly performed FMHA is detrimental to expert testimony, often because of problems with validity or relevance. This principle addresses the relationship between the evaluation and the expert testimony, and underscores the need to base testimony clearly and directly on the results of the FMHA. In this context, a "properly performed" FMHA should be consistent with the principles illustrated in this book. When these principles are followed, it is likely that the quality of the FMHA will be good and will provide a substantive basis for expert testimony in that case.

The *Ethical Principles of Psychologists and Code of Conduct* (APA *Ethics* Code: American Psychological Association, 2010a) notes "the importance of using appropriate methods when conducting assessments, and specifically indicates the application to forensic testimony: Psychologists base the opinions contained in their recommendations, reports, and diagnostic or evaluative statements, including forensic testimony, on information and techniques sufficient to substantiate their findings" (Standard 9.01(a)). The APA *Specialty Guidelines* also provides substantial guidance regarding this principle. For instance, the importance of considering the behavior and performance of the individual being assessed is emphasized strongly. Accordingly, personal contact with the subject of the evaluation is stressed. When this is not possible, then the impact of this absence should be noted:

> Forensic practitioners recognize their obligations to only provide written or oral evidence about the psychological characteristics of particular individuals when they have sufficient information or data to form an adequate foundation for those opinions or to substantiate their findings (citation omitted). Forensic practitioners seek to make reasonable efforts to obtain such information or data, and they document their efforts to obtain it. When it is not possible or feasible to examine individuals about whom they are offering an opinion, forensic practitioners strive to make clear the impact of such limitations on the reliability and validity of their professional products, opinions, or testimony. (Guideline 9.03)

The APA *Specialty Guidelines* also describes information that should be communicated as a part of expert testimony, including the methods and opinions that form the basis of the testimony:

> Consistent with relevant law and rules of evidence, when providing professional reports and other sworn statements or testimony, forensic practitioners strive to offer a complete statement of all relevant opinions that they formed within the scope of their work, the basis and reasoning underlying the opinions, the salient data or other information that was considered in forming the opinions, and an indication of any additional evidence

that may be used in support of the opinions to be offered. (Guideline 11.04)

The *Ethics Guidelines for the Practice of Forensic Psychiatry* (AAPL *Ethics Guidelines*; American Academy of Psychiatry and the Law, 2005) provide similar guidance on both report writing and testimony:

> Psychiatrists practicing in a forensic role enhance the honesty and objectivity of their work by basing their forensic opinions, forensic reports and forensic testimony on all available data. They communicate the honesty of their work, efforts to attain objectivity, and the soundness of their clinical opinion, by distinguishing, to the extent possible, between verified and unverified information as well as among clinical "facts," "inferences," and "impressions." (Section IV, para. 3)

The AAPL *Ethics Guidelines* also addresses personal contact with an examinee, noting that "Honesty, objectivity and the adequacy of the clinical evaluation may be called into question when an expert opinion is offered without a personal examination" (Section IV, para. 4). When this is not possible, or not required by the type of evaluation being conducted, it is emphasized that "under these circumstances, it is the responsibility of psychiatrists to make earnest efforts to ensure that their statements, opinions and any reports or testimony based on those opinions, clearly state that there was no personal examination and note any resulting limitations to their opinions" (Section IV, para. 4).

Legal authority also supports the importance of this principle. Specifically, evidentiary standards under both *Frye v. United States* (1923) and *Daubert v. Merrell Dow Pharmaceuticals* (1993) address the admissibility of evidence based on the quality of the data available. Under *Frye*, the admissibility of evidence depends upon whether the process by which the scientific evidence is deduced is sufficiently established to have gained general acceptance in the particular field to which it belongs. In the forensic context, the question of admissibility under *Frye* would be whether the testimony was based on data and techniques that were "generally accepted" in the particular field of psychology or psychiatry. The *Daubert* decision suggested several factors that might be considered in weighing the

admissibility of scientific evidence that are consistent with this principle. These factors include whether the scientific method was applied to yield the inference forming the basis for the opinion, whether the reasoning or methodology underlying the testimony is scientifically valid, and whether it can be applied to the facts of the given case.[1]

These sources of ethical and legal authority provide support for basing testimony on the results of a properly performed FMHA. Sources of ethics authority stress the importance of describing the basis for expert testimony, whiles sources of legal authority emphasize relevance and reliability for admissibility of expert testimony. Taken together, these sources of authority underscore the importance of relevance and reliability in FMHA, for both the report and the expert testimony.

TEACHING POINT:
USING THE REPORT TO FACILITATE EXPERT TESTIMONY

The FMHA report provides a summary of what the evaluator was asked to do; the sources of information used and the other procedures employed; the findings from interview, testing, and third party information; the interpretation of findings and reasoning; and the conclusions. This provides a valuable platform upon which to construct a plan for direct examination. In preparation with the attorney, the discussion should involve whether the initial aspects of the direct examination (e.g., "Did you evaluate my client?" "When?" "What did the evaluation involve?") should be followed by a broad, open-ended questions (e.g., "What did you find?"), or by a series of more specific questions regarding findings from interview, tests, records, and third-party interviews. Both attorneys and experts will have their preferences, and one goal of the preparation meeting is to resolve those differences so questions are asked in a way that elicits the most effective communication from the evaluator. Answering an open-ended question allows

---

[1] Some jurisdictions have adopted *Daubert*; others have rejected it and retained the *Frye* standard; and yet others have yet to rule on the issue (Melton et al., 2007; Slobogin, Rai, & Reisner, 2009). Forensic clinicians should be attentive to the applicable standard in their jurisdiction.

an expert witness to go through the report, summarizing and integrating relevant findings and describing her reasoning as well, finishing with the conclusions that are supported by these findings. It also permits the expert to speak directly to the jury (in a jury trial), adjusting the pace and detail of testimony in light of the facial expressions and body posture of jurors.

Some attorneys have a different preference. The scope of the direct testimony needed may be limited, so a summary of the entire report might be excessive. (The expert witness having conducted an FMHA may be only one of several witnesses being presented by an attorney; the expert must be cognizant of the attorney's goals regarding scope of testimony and the expert's role in providing it.) The judge might not be inclined to want detailed testimony. The attorney may have other witnesses who are also testifying about certain domains covered in FMHA. So whatever the expert's preference for open-ended versus structured questions throughout the testimony, there should be a preparation meeting in which both expert and attorney preferences are discussed—and the best decision made under the circumstances.

PRINCIPLE:

CONTROL THE MESSAGE. STRIVE TO OBTAIN, RETAIN, AND REGAIN CONTROL OVER THE MEANING AND IMPACT OF WHAT IS PRESENTED IN EXPERT TESTIMONY (*PRINCIPLE 38*)

When writing a forensic report, the forensic practitioner is able to take time (within the confines of the legal system's timetable) to carefully craft his or her message, carefully consider its wording, and determine the order of information and language that best explains the data and reasoning leading to his or her conclusions.

The stylistic and substantive considerations are fully at the discretion of the evaluator. However, when testifying, there are competing influences that may change the way that one's message is communicated—for example, how questions are worded on direct examination, attempts by attorneys to find weaknesses or inconsistencies in a report during cross-examination, nervousness that often accompanies the process of testifying, and the

need to explain information in a way that is understandable to lay audiences (e.g., the jury). This principle is especially applicable to cross-examination, and the expert can continue to effectively convey his or her findings while under a vigorous and multifaceted challenge (Heilbrun et al., 2009). Specific challenges that may arise under cross-examination have been detailed by Brodsky (2013). However, in spite of these challenges to clearly communicating one's message, there are strategies that forensic practitioners can implement to ensure that they effectively control their message.

Brodsky (2013) also provides guidance on the ways that an expert witness can effectively control his or her message and ensure that its meaning is not distorted. For instance, as described previously in this chapter, when asked a complex or "loaded" question during cross-examination, the witness can acknowledge the true aspect of the question in a dependent clause and follow by strongly negating the untrue aspect. When asked questions that are designed to make experts "acquiesce that their facts, methods, or conclusions were incomplete or flawed in some manner" (Brodsky, 2013, pp. 134–135) and the content of the question is incorrect, it is important for the witness to "have clarity about what they believe and the courage to speak up for that belief" (p. 135). He further underscores the importance of familiarizing oneself with recent literature on the topic of the testimony, preparing to "present the bases for generalizability of findings in your testimony" (p. 20), basing testimony and opinions on one's data, and preparing to discuss the reliability and validity of the sources used in the evaluation.

Brodsky (2013) also describes methods that enable expert witnesses to control, not only the substance of their testimony, but also their credibility. For instance, when the cross-examining attorney is controlling the testimony, the expert witness may take a deep breath before responding and attempt to regulate the pace of the questioning. If questions are asked to expose a potential weakness in the examiner's experience or procedures, the expert witness may respond with "accurate, pointed answers stated in a confident manner" (Brodsky, 2013, p. 152). When asked questions that are beyond the scope of an expert witness's expertise, Brodsky (2013) advocates admitting one's lack of expertise rather than becoming "defensive and disorganized" (p. 185); he notes that witnesses who are willing to admit when they do not know the answer to a question "can be seen as having respect for their limitations, having humility, and having the good sense not to try to know everything in every situation" (p. 185). In addition, Brodsky (2013) notes that providing a series of blunt negative assertions in response to a cross-examining attorney's question can cast an expert witness in a defensive light, and he cautions against becoming "overly involved" in negative assertions (p. 136).

TEACHING POINT:
STRATEGIES FOR MAINTAINING SOME CONTROL OVER THE MESSAGE

Brodsky's books on expert testimony (1991, 1999, 2004, 2013) offer maxims that help to guide many aspects of expert testimony. There are many such maxims, and Brodsky alludes to some in his comments in the case presented below. Although Brodsky himself does not make this distinction, it can be useful to consider his maxims as both substantive (related to what is presented in expert testimony) and stylistic (how it is presented). Strategies for maintaining and regaining control over one's testimony on cross-examination are addressed primarily by stylistic maxims.

Reading Brodsky's maxims helps capture the full range of stylistic guidance. However, some stand out as particularly important. It helps if the forensic clinician enters with the assumption that expert testimony will be a rigorous, grueling process. (It is often not as bad as one might expect, but it's *far* preferable to over-prepare than under-prepare.) A skillful and well-prepared attorney can elicit weaknesses that invariably exist in any FMHA. Indeed, we have suggested throughout this book that the forensic clinician has an affirmative obligation to balance, thoroughness, and accuracy—which means being open about non-supportive as well as supportive findings. One good way to prepare for a skilled, ethical expert is to simply read the report! Rigorous cross-examination will elicit points that, in all fairness, should be elicited. When the expert anticipates that cross-examination will be rigorous, and understands that it should be when the adversary system works as intended, the expert will be less inclined to be argumentative, unbalanced, overreactive, or otherwise shaken by cross-examination.

Sometimes cross-examination can extend beyond this "rigorous but fair" approach to include loaded or half-truth questions, distortions of one's findings or reasoning, or other techniques that are acceptable forms of advocacy but inclined to portray a less accurate account (at least from the evaluator's perspective). Expert witnesses should pay careful attention to both the wording of individual questions, and the "flow" and direction of cross-examination. A question that is sloppily worded, or deliberately asked to convey a half-truth, can be handled with techniques such as the "zang" (answering in the opposite direction expected because there was some aspect of the question's phrasing that rendered it inaccurate) or "admit-deny" (beginning the response with a dependent clause that acknowledges that there is some element of truth to the implication in the question, but concluding with an independent clause strongly affirming the accuracy of the evaluator's position). This second technique is particularly useful because it is delivered in a single sentence that cannot be politely interrupted. Anticipating the flow of questions and monitoring one's answers allows the expert witness to avoid getting into a pattern of responding "yes" repeatedly when that is obviously the correct answer, but continuing to respond "yes" when the questions subtly shift into those for which "yes" is no longer an accurate response. Pausing or asking to have the question repeated, when used occasionally, will give the evaluator time for a more thoughtful response and allow her to avoid such a quick question-followed-by-yes-answer rhythm.

The present case is the same capital sentencing evaluation that appeared earlier in Chapter 7 (Case One, this volume). This is the kind of high-visibility, high-stakes case that would receive considerable effort from both defense counsel and prosecutors if it went to trial. Assuming that Mr. Dawkins had been tried and convicted of first degree murder, he would have a separate sentencing hearing involving the presentation of aggravating and mitigating evidence. The defense would have prepared for this possibility by retaining a psychologist or psychiatrist months in advance of his trial to conduct an evaluation in case of a conviction. The report—which would be submitted as evidence in a capital sentencing hearing—is reprinted in its entirety below, along with mock transcripts of likely targets of cross-examination. Furthermore, Dr. Brodsky has included comments that are relevant to the preparation for expert testimony in such a hearing.

FORENSIC EVALUATION
October 9, 2008
Re: David Dawkins
PP#: 123456

REFERRAL INFORMATION

David Dawkins is a 49-year-old African American male (D.O.B.: 11/1/58) who is charged with two counts of murder, carrying firearms in public street/place, possession of instruments of a crime, and carrying firearms without a license. Mr. Dawkins's attorney (Darnell Baker, Esq.) requested a mental health evaluation to provide the defense with information, pursuant to 42 Pa. C.S.A. § 9711(e), relevant to capital sentencing.

PROCEDURES

Mr. Dawkins was evaluated for a total of approximately five hours on September 7, 2007, and 2.5 hours on September 12, 2007, at the City Jail. In addition to a clinical interview, Mr. Dawkins was administered a standard screening instrument for symptoms of mental and emotional disorder experienced both currently and at the time of the offense (the Brief Symptom Inventory or BSI), a standard objective measure of risks-and-needs information relevant to offender treatment-planning and assigning levels of freedom and supervision (the Level of Service Inventory–Revised, or LSI-R), a standard test of current functioning in relevant academic areas (the Wide Range Achievement Test, 4th Edition, or WRAT-4), a measure of overall intellectual functioning (the Wechsler Adult Intelligence Scale–3rd Edition, or WAIS-III), and a standard measure of adult psychopathology and personality functioning (the Minnesota Multiphasic Personality Inventory, 2nd Edition, or MMPI-2).

Testing Conditions

Q. *Doctor, would you say that standardization is important or is it essential in the administration of psychological tests, such as the tests you administered to Mr. Dawkins?*

A. *Essential.*

Q. *Are you familiar with the standardization of test administration as specified in the manuals of the BSI, LSI-R, WRAT-4, WAIS-III, and MMPI-2?*

A. *(Probably "generally, yes")*

Q. *Let us start with the WAIS-III. You do accept the WAIS-III Manual as the source of authority on administration of the WAIS-III?*

A. *Yes.*

Q. *Is there anywhere that delineates, describes, or specifies how the test should be given in jails, taking into account all of the noise, security, lighting, jail uniforms, and other environmental factors that impact on being in a jail? Isn't it true that jail administration departs from the authoritative and specified directions for the environment in which the test should be given? Furthermore, isn't it true that there is no way that you can know for certain how administration of highly standardized test in the Philadelphia City Jail in particular will affect the validity of the test results?*

Collateral interviews were conducted with Mr. Dawkins's wife, Anna Jeffers; his daughter, Mary Jackson; and his former employer, Deanna Simmons. Anna Jeffers was interviewed for approximately forty minutes on October 7, 2007. Mary Jackson was interviewed for approximately thirty minutes, and Deanna Simmons was interviewed for approximately twenty minutes on September 18, 2007. Efforts were made to contact Mr. Dawkins's long-time friend James Peters, twice on September 18, 2007. Contact was made with James Peters on the morning of October 5, 2007. He was unable to be interviewed at that time, but agreed to be interviewed that evening at 7:00 p.m. However, he did not answer the phone at 7:00 p.m. on October 5, 2007, or at 7:30 p.m., when another attempt was made to contact him.

The following documents, obtained from Mr. Baker's office, were reviewed as part of the evaluation:

(1) County presentence and mental health reports (illegible) (dated 4/26/79),
(2) State parole records (dated 8/17/88 to 4/28/08),
(3) Prison report of psychological evaluation (dated 5/10/96),
(4) Prison psychological evaluation for parole (dated 5/21/97),
(5) Prison social services records (dated 6/17/98 to 9/18/08),
(6) Pennsylvania Department of Corrections Classification Summary (dated 6/18/01),
(7) Prison State Parole Psychological Evaluation (dated 6/22/01),

COMMENT

The standardization issue is legitimate. There are times when expert witnesses need to acquiesce to such questions from prepared attorneys. My observation is that once attorneys elicit an admission of possibly compromised standardization, they do not take the path of simply saying the equivalent of Ah-HA!, and letting it go. Instead, they seek to press the ground glass into the flesh and make more of the issue. When they seek to gain further implications of compromised standardization contaminating the results of the whole assessment, the door opens for the expert to put the issue in context.

In that case, what should experts do? Skilled experts are able to comment on collateral data. They speak to their experience in jail settings. They address concurrent validity through consistency in test results. They discuss how tests are interpreted within a range of scores to allow for measurement and administration errors. If the attorney settles for the perceived small victory of agreement on the non-standardized environment, the expert is best off comfortably agreeing. However, I love it when greedy attorneys engage in efforts at overkill, because it gives me a chance to run with it. When I see such overkill unfolding, I do my very best to avoid letting a slight smile of anticipation become visible.

(8) Criminal history record (dated 7/12/01),

(9) Report of psychological evaluation (dated 9/20/01),

(10) Parolee risk assessments (dated 1/18/02 to 5/28/04),

(11) Witness statement from Witness 1 (dated 1/18/06),

(12) Witness statement from Witness 2 (dated 1/18/06),

(13) Witness statement from Witness 3 (dated 1/18/06),

(14) Witness statement from Witness 4 (dated 1/18/06),

(15) Witness statement from Witness 5 (dated 1/18/06),

(16) Witness statement from Witness 6 (dated 1/18/06),

(17) Witness statement from Witness 7 (dated 1/18/06),

(18) Statement from Officer 1 (dated 1/18/06),

(19) Statement from Officer 2 (dated 1/20/06),

(20) Statement from Officer 3 (dated 1/18/06),

(21) Statement from Officer 4 (dated 1/18/06),

(22) Autopsy report of Max Charles (dated 1/18/06),

(23) Autopsy report of Norris Jenkins (dated 1/18/06),

(24) Property receipts of property taken from crime scene (dated 1/18/06),

(25) Policy activity sheets (dated 1/18/06 to 11/07/06),

(26) Crime scene log (dated 1/18/06),

(27) Crime scene investigation report (dated 1/18/06),

(28) Crime scene photographs (dated 1/18/06),

(29) Incident report (dated 1/18/06),

(30) Investigation report (dated 1/18/06),

(31) Search warrant (dated 1/18/06),

(32) Affidavit of probable cause (dated 1/18/06),

(33) Arrest warrant (dated 1/18/06),

(34) Attempt to Apprehend log (dated 1/19/06),

(35) Property receipts of property taken from Medical Examiner's Office (dated 1/19/06),

(36) Wanted poster (dated 1/19/06),

(37) Request cancellation of bolo alert on Chevrolet van (dated 4/28/06),

(38) Arrest warrant (dated 11/07/06),

(39) Arrest Biographical Information Report (dated 11/07/06),

(40) Arrest Transport Report (dated 11/07/06),

(41) County criminal docket (dated 11/8/06 to 4/24/08),

(42) County prison health records (dated 11/9/06 to 9/11/08),

(43) Department of Education GED transcript (dated 12/14/06),

(44) Court records (dated 2/12/88 to 5/11/07),

(45) Prison records (dated 11/8/06 to 9/15/08 and undated),

(46) Court history (dated 6/4/07),

(47) Ballistics reports (dated 7/28/08 and 7/29/08),

(48) Preliminary hearing transcript (dated 5/16/07),

(49) Mitigation report, Joanne Morris, MA (dated 10/10/08),

(50) Life history statement, David Dawkins (undated), and

(51) School Records.

Interviews and Records

Q. *Please answer these questions with simple Yes or No answers. Did you rely in part or in whole in the interviews with Ms. Jeffers, Ms. Jackson, and Ms. Simmons?*

A. Yes.

Q. *Do you know what "hearsay" is?*

A. Yes.

Q. *Are you aware that the rules of evidence in most circumstances do not permit hearsay testimony, because it is someone else's information?*

A. Yes.

Q. *You did speak to the defendant's wife, Ms. Jeffers, for 40 minutes on October 7th?*

A. Yes.

Q. *Are you also aware that in your report you drew on 17 separate statements by the defendants early life made by Ms. Jeffers?*

A. I did not count the number of separate statements.

Q. *Did you subsequently follow up by checking out the accuracy of all of the statements that Ms. Jeffers made to you?*

A. *It did not make any difference. I never take any single piece of third party information at face value.*

Prior to the evaluation, Mr. Dawkins was notified about its purpose and the associated limits of confidentiality. He appeared to understand the purpose, reporting back his understanding that he would be evaluated and that a written report would be submitted to his attorney. He further understood that the report could be used in the sentencing hearing and, if it were, copies would be provided to the prosecution and the court. In addition, Anna Jeffers, Mary Jackson, and Deanna Simmons were also notified of the purpose of the evaluation and agreed to be interviewed.

RELEVANT HISTORY

Historical information was obtained from the collateral sources described earlier, as well as from Mr. Dawkins himself. Whenever possible, we have assessed the consistency of self-reported information with that obtained from collateral sources. If additional information is obtained prior to Mr. Dawkins's hearing, a supplemental report will be filed.

Family History

Mr. Dawkins was born in Baltimore, and he resided there until he was two, when he moved to live with an aunt and uncle in Norristown. Mr. Dawkins's life history statement indicated that he lived with his aunt and uncle for approximately two years before his mother and siblings moved to Norristown. According to his wife, Anna Jeffers, Mr. Dawkins's

---

COMMENT

Until the last answer, the expert was allowing the attorney to begin to make the case of the unreliability of collateral data. Attorneys are entitled to such explorations. Furthermore, the expert did not battle against the call for Yes or No answers. This procedure is common and accepted in courtrooms. Sometimes experts get caught up early and excessively in a knee-jerk avoidance of giving such simple answers. It's okay. Like most well-constructed cross-examinations, this attorney demands the Yes-No answers to set up simplistic and misleading inferences. The scenario shows an expert waiting for the right moment to introduce a substantive corrective statement. The expert shows a comfortable responsiveness to the questions by giving four "yes" answers in a row with no explanation, even though there may have been an opportunity to address the exception of mental health expert witnesses to the hearsay rule. Furthermore, the expert who waits and allows the attorney to begin a tactic may ultimately be in a more powerful position once the line of cross-examination is out there and visible.

family moved to Norristown when he was between the ages of four and six. Mr. Dawkins reported in his life history statement that when his mother moved to Norristown he had some difficulty adjusting to the idea that his aunt was not his mother. According to Mr. Dawkins, he is the youngest of five children. However, his wife and his daughter both reported that he is the youngest of seven children. Ms. Jeffers stated that Mr. Dawkins's oldest two sisters have a different father than the rest of the children in the family. According to Ms. Jeffers, Mr. Dawkins's mother left her oldest two daughters in Baltimore with their father when she moved with Mr. Dawkins's father and the other children to Norristown. Ms. Jeffers reported that Mr. Dawkins's mother did not have contact with her oldest two children for many years after she left them in Baltimore. She noted that Mr. Dawkins told her that his mother used to cry about leaving her children behind.

Tangential Questions

Q. *You noted in your report that Mr. Dawkins thought his aunt was his mother until he was between four and six years old, is that right?*

A. Yes.

Q. *Would it have made any difference if he had not learned this until he was eight?*

A. There is no way of knowing that.

Q. *Does the belief that one's aunt is one's mother cause mental illness?*

A. Not by itself.

Q. *In Mr. Dawkins' case, did it cause mental illness?*

A. Not by itself.

Q. *In fact, Doctor, isn't it true that you have no idea whatsoever what this belief might have caused or not caused?*

A. *The issue of cause and effect for any childhood trauma and subsequent disorder is uncertain for everyone.*

Mr. Dawkins reported that he was raised by his parents until the age of 10, when his parents separated. In his life history statement, Mr. Dawkins reported that his father moved to Norristown when Mr. Dawkins was approximately 10 years old. Mr. Dawkins noted that his mother and father argued verbally, but not physically. Ms. Jeffers stated that Mr. Dawkins's father "just left" Ms. Dawkins and the children; after he left them he had contact with Mr. Dawkins "whenever he came around." Regarding Mr. Dawkins's reaction to his father's departure, Ms. Jeffers stated, "I think he took it hard, being the youngest in the family." In his life history statement, Mr. Dawkins reported that he did not "remember feeling one way or another" about his father leaving because "we lived without him before." Both Mr. Dawkins and Ms. Jeffers reported that Mr. Dawkins's mother began drinking after Mr. Dawkins's father left the home. Ms. Jeffers stated that his mother "drank a lot," and Mr. Dawkins reported that his mother would drink after work and then go to sleep. About Mr. Dawkins's mother's drinking, Ms. Jeffers noted, "It started when the dad left, but when he got older, it got heavier and heavier and heavier...then she lost her job, it got heavier." Ms. Jeffers stated that Mr. Dawkins's brother also drank "a lot."

According to Mr. Dawkins, he grew up in a "strict household....I couldn't venture off the block." He added that he "came home from school, cleaned, (and) did school work." He indicated that since he is the youngest, he "had four people to watch (him)." Deanna Simmons, Mr. Dawkins's former employer, stated that from what Mr. Dawkins told her, "his mother was strict...she didn't throw no punches."

COMMENT

Attorneys can nitpick a report to find pieces of information to attack. When an evaluator does a thorough case history, attorneys often have good nitpickings. The strategy for responding is to be non-defensive. Good replies acknowledge the limitations of case history data. When attorneys try to make a big fuss about the worthlessness of items in histories, witnesses are well off just moving with the flow and agreeing that not every statement in the report has major implications. There are lots of metaphors that can be employed towards the goal of describing the worth of life histories: constructing a mosaic, being thorough, and painting the whole picture.

Mr. Dawkins noted that his mother was the disciplinarian, and she used her "hands, [a] belt, [and a] broom" to discipline him. However, he added, his father never hit him or his siblings. Mr. Dawkins admitted that the way he was disciplined by his mother would probably be considered physical abuse by today's standards. His wife also stated that physical abuse "may have been possible" since his mom "worked a lot and the older kids watched him a lot." Both Mr. Dawkins and Ms. Jeffers stated that Mr. Dawkins had not suffered from any sexual abuse. Mr. Dawkins's school records from 1976, when he was in tenth grade, note that "general family conditions are extremely disoriented...parents separated and other siblings have severe problems."

Mr. Dawkins stated that he got along well with his sisters when he was growing up, but he fought with his brother, who is three years older, "all the time." Mr. Dawkins reported that his youngest sister "has some damage from LSD," and she began receiving treatment at the age of 17. Ms. Jeffers and Mr. Dawkins's daughter, Mary Jackson, both stated that Mr. Dawkins's sister suffers from paranoid schizophrenia. During his state parole psychological evaluation in June 2001, Mr. Dawkins also reported that his sister was diagnosed with paranoid schizophrenia. Ms. Jeffers added that Mr. Dawkins was a teenager when his sister first started showing signs of mental illness and had to be involuntarily admitted into a psychiatric hospital. She reported that this "really got to him." Although the family did not have contact with the two oldest siblings for many years after they were left in Baltimore, Ms. Jeffers reported that the family later regained contact with the oldest siblings when Mr. Dawkins was in his thirties. While Ms. Jeffers at first stated that Mr. Dawkins has "no contact" with his siblings, who all live in Norristown, she later noted that they see his brother "when he pops up." Regarding the sister who suffers from schizophrenia, Ms. Jeffers stated, "We see her when she sees us. We know she doesn't like pop-up visits." According to Ms. Jeffers, one of Mr. Dawkins's sisters is deceased, and another of his sisters moved—Mr. Dawkins never received her new address to keep in contact with her. Mr. Dawkins reported that he does not have much contact with his extended family (aunts, uncles, cousins).

Mr. Dawkins characterized his relationship with his mother as "good." He noted that he usually listened to what his mother had to say because "usually she was right." Mr. Dawkins's daughter noted that he was "the baby" of the family and that she "heard stories about him being spoiled, being a momma's boy." She added that she thought he tried to "fight the image (of being a momma's boy) by being rough on the street." Ms. Simmons reported that Mr. Dawkins had a "loving mother" and he "talked about his mother a lot." Ms. Simmons added, "He talked about how good she was and she raised him by herself." Mr. Dawkins reported that his mother died in February of 1997 and his father died in February 1990. Mr. Dawkins's daughter, Ms. Jackson, noted that Mr. Dawkins was incarcerated when his mother died. She noted, "I know that he was really close to his mother and the fact that she passed away when he was incarcerated really weighed on him."

Apparent Contradictions

Q. *On page 8 of your report, didn't you characterize Mr. Dawkins's mother as strict and physically abusive?*

A. *Yes.*

Q. *And on page 9 of your report, didn't you report that he had a good relationship with a loving mother?*

A. *That's what he said.*

Q. *In your best professional judgment, Doctor, can a physically abusive mother who hits a child with belts and brooms be a good mother?*

A. *A parent can love her child and also abuse the child.*

Q. *Are you trying to tell this court that Mr. Dawkins murdered Max Charles and Norris Jenkins because his mother would punish him with a belt?*

A. *What I am trying to tell this court is that how Mr. Dawkins was raised had a great deal to do with the kind of person he is today.*

Q. *Answer the question!*

A. *Of course not, not by itself.*

Q. *In fact, isn't it true that Mr. Dawkins murdered Max Charles and Norris Jenkins because he is an alcoholic druggie with a long criminal record who doesn't control himself?*

Ms. Simmons, Mr. Dawkins's former employer, reported that he had told her in the past that he was from a bad neighborhood. Mr. Dawkins stated that the high school he attended, Jefferson City High, was "not good," as there was often fighting and "a lot of gang activity." In his life history statement, Mr. Dawkins reported that while in high school he was not involved in a gang, but his brother was, and this meant Mr. Dawkins was "fair

COMMENT

An answer to the last question was not included because there are a number of ways to go with it. The witness could observe that alcohol and drugs do play a role in the troubles of Mr. Dawkins. The witness could simply say, "Yes and No." What set up the demanding question was the pursuit of a seeming contradiction in the description of the mother. If this line of questioning was anticipated, a statement might have been included about how many people recall deceased parents in overly positive ways and minimize their harm. The answer about both loving and abusing a child served that same purpose.

The reason that reports often have contradictions is the fragmentation of writing up and interpreting separate parts of the assessment data. Reports usually wait until the end to synthesize information, so it is normal for a thorough report to have elements that seem contradictory. Should assessors seek to reconcile contradictions at the end of a report? Probably. But that calls for making such reconciliations a specific task of the report. Not many assessors do so.

game." Mr. Dawkins reported that his high school was located in the opposing gang's neighborhood; he subsequently avoided going to school, which contributed to his failure to complete high school. Ms. Jeffers and Ms. Jackson both reported that Mr. Dawkins was stabbed when he was a teenager. In addition, Ms. Jeffers described a frightening incident that Mr. Dawkins encountered in the neighborhood that she believes affected Mr. Dawkins. She reported that when she and Mr. Dawkins were teenagers, they were sitting in the playground one day when "the police came to the playground and arrested every young black kid in the neighborhood for something that happened…they kind of beat up on those boys ridiculously (and) he was one who got beat up." She stated that she could not recall his injuries precisely, but they left the playground and found his mother immediately after this occurred. Ms. Jeffers reported that Mr. Dawkins's mother was "really upset," and she took him to the hospital. Regarding this event, Ms. Jeffers stated, "That was a really bad, nasty encounter. It was teenagers just playing in the playground and the police showed up with guns and said 'freeze'…it was crazy for a child." She stated that the police arrested the children on the playground "because something happened blocks away."

Mr. Dawkins noted that he has a common law marriage with Ms. Jeffers. He reported that they have been together since he was 14; she recalled that they have been together since they were both 15. Ms. Jeffers reported that she grew up in the same neighborhood as Mr. Dawkins. Mr. Dawkins indicated in his life history statement that Ms. Jeffers played a role in Mr. Dawkins's decision to enroll

in the Youth Corps program, through which he obtained employment after he ceased attending school. Together, Mr. Dawkins and Ms. Jeffers have four children (two daughters and two sons), according to Mr. Dawkins. Their daughter, Ms. Jackson, stated regarding her parents, "You can tell they were friends for a long time" but "they weren't very affectionate around us kids." Mr. Dawkins stated that his sons are 31 and 22 and his daughters are 28 and 23. Mr. Dawkins reported that both sons are presently incarcerated, the older for gun possession and the younger for drug possession. Ms. Jeffers reported that she and Mr. Dawkins have three grandchildren, ages 9, 6, and 5. Ms. Jackson, however, stated that he has four grandchildren, ages 8, 6, 5, and 1. Ms. Jeffers and Ms. Simmons both noted that Mr. Dawkins cares deeply about his grandchildren. Ms. Jeffers reported that Mr. Dawkins is a "softy" for the grandkids. She stated that he often told his children to bring the grandchildren over so he could take care of them. She reported that he liked to take the grandchildren to the movies. Ms. Jackson noted, "At least once a month he would take the grandchildren to Chuck E. Cheese's or just ride around with them and play with them." In addition, Ms. Simmons stated, Mr. Dawkins talks about his grandchildren "a lot and he talks about his kids, too." She added, "He used to talk about them coming over and spending the night…he missed out on his kids, so he used to talk about them a lot." Ms. Simmons also noted, "I could tell he really loved his grandkids."

Regarding her relationship with her father, Ms. Jackson stated, "When he was around, he was very playful with us." She noted that he "spent lots of weekends hanging out with us and things." She added, "He wasn't really affectionate...but he wasn't cold, either." Ms. Jackson stated, "It seems like he had a really hard time expressing his emotions, but he tried to show it." She noted that her father spent "quite a bit of time in and out of prison" when she was growing up, although she never knew why he was incarcerated. She reported that when her father was incarcerated, her mother would visit him every week, and she would take the children to visit him every month. Regarding Mr. Dawkins's criminal behavior, Ms. Jackson stated, "Whatever he did on the street, he kept from his family... there was nothing going on in our home...we were really sheltered from whatever was happening." Ms. Jeffers reported that when Mr. Dawkins was employed, he supported his children. Regarding Mr. Dawkins's parenting, Ms. Jeffers stated, "My children never been punished by him a day in their life. He was a softy towards punishing them or correcting them." She added, "They knew they could always count on him or depend on him for things."

Educational History

According to Mr. Dawkins's school records, he did not attend any kindergarten or preschool classes prior to entering first grade at the age of five. Mr. Dawkins stated that he attended one school from first grade to eighth grade. He noted that his attendance was "good" during these grades, as he lived across the street from the school. He reported that his behavior was "great," but added that he was suspended once or twice for fighting. Mr. Dawkins reported his performance was "excellent" and he had a B average. He denied repeating any grades, being placed in special education classes, or having an Individualized Educational Plan. Ms. Jeffers reported that her husband was "really good" when he was in elementary school, but she noted, "He really changed...grew life experiences when his mother started drinking."

Mr. Dawkins's first report card from first grade reflects that he received Cs, Ds, and Es in most of his classes, although he received Bs in handwriting. His teacher noted on the report card, "David is friendly and enjoys working with the other children, but he must learn to be quiet during work time. He needs help at home in every area...please come to school Tuesday evening to see how you can help him." All of his report cards from first grade request assistance from his mother in teaching Mr. Dawkins.

For instance, his third-quarter report card stated, "He needs more reading practice at home...please get him a homework book, and come to see me so we can talk about his playful behavior at home." His final report card also requests more parental involvement in his education, as it states, "Please help him at home so he can make a good start in the fall." Mr. Dawkins's final report card reports that he was absent from school three times in first grade.

According to his school records, Mr. Dawkins received Bs and Cs in second grade. His report card notes that his mother had been working with him at home, as it stated, "David has improved with the help you have given at home. Thank you for this most needed and valued assistance." According to his school records, he missed two days of school in second grade.

Mr. Dawkins's school records indicate that throughout elementary school he exhibited disruptive classroom behavior, although his records also reflect that Mr. Dawkins had potential to do well in school. According to his school records, he received Bs and Cs in all of his third-grade classes. His teacher reported on his report card that "he works well but lacks self-control," but noted that he was a hard worker. His report card from fourth grade states, "David can do good work when he shows self control in class." According to his fourth-grade report card, he received Bs, Cs, and one D in his classes. Mr. Dawkins's IQ was measured at 109 in fourth grade, according to his school records. In fifth grade, Mr. Dawkins's teacher also noted that his classroom behavior needed improvement; however, his second report card noted that he had done a "remarkable job improving his behavior in the classroom." Mr. Dawkins's report card from fifth grade indicates that he received Bs and Cs in most of his classes, although he received As in Art, Spelling, and Music. His school records note that he did not miss any days of school in the fifth grade.

According to Mr. Dawkins's sixth-grade report card, he received Bs in Arithmetic, Art, Health Education, Language Arts, Physical Education, Science, and Social Studies; he received Cs in Reading, Written Expression, Spelling, Handwriting, and Music, and he received Ds in citizenship practices and work habits. His teacher noted in his sixth-grade report card that Mr. Dawkins had a "very immature attitude" and "is capable of more than he produces." His attendance, however, was excellent, as he missed two days of school out of 184 school days. Mr. Dawkins's report card from seventh grade also notes that he missed just two days of school. According to his school records from seventh grade, he received Bs in Art, Health Education, Mathematics, and Science; received Cs in English, French, Music, Physical Education, and Shop Class; and received Es in Reading and Social Studies. His report card for the first quarter notes that Mr. Dawkins needed to improve his work habits, as he "has the ability to do much better work." His final report card indicates that Mr. Dawkins's work "improved in most areas."

According to Mr. Dawkins's school records, he had no unexcused absences during the 1971–1972 school year, when he was in the eighth grade. He received the following "end of year" grades in eighth grade: a C in Art, an E in English, a D in French, a D in Health Education, a C in Mathematics, a C in Music, a C in Physical Education, a D in Reading, a E in Science, an A in Shop, and a B in History. Mr. Dawkins's grades appeared to decline as the school year progressed, as his grades fell one grade level in three of the aforementioned classes from the mid-year report to the end of the year report, according to his school records. His school records reflect that Mr. Dawkins's scores on the Iowa Tests of Basic Skills were in the Low Average range for Reading; in the Average range for Vocabulary, Total Language, and Composite; and were in the High Average Range for Total Work-Study and Total Arithmetic. His eighth-grade report card notes, "David has a lot of talent in art. However, he does not work at achieving."

Mr. Dawkins attended high school at Jefferson High School. He reported that his grades were "excellent" in ninth grade, but he began having problems in tenth grade. Ms. Jeffers also noted that Mr. Dawkins received "good grades…especially if it was a subject he liked." Mr. Dawkins's school records reflect that he did receive good grades in ninth grade, as he received an 80 in English, a 75 in Social Studies, a 92 in Math, a 90 in Music, an 80 in "Shop—electric," a 90 in Physical Education, and a 90 in Health Education. According to his school records, he was present 179 days, was absent 8 days, and was late 41 days.

Mr. Dawkins's school records reflect that he was enrolled in tenth grade at Jefferson High School during the 1973–1974 school year. Regarding high school, Mr. Dawkins stated that it was "not conducive to my health." He reported that there was a lot of gang activity at the school, and there were tensions between students from different parts of town. He reported that he was involved in the fighting, and that his attendance was "sporadic." However, Ms. Jeffers reported that he went to school every day. Mr. Dawkins's school records for the 1973–1974 school year (tenth grade) indicate that he was suspended three times. There were no school records from the 1973–1974 school year regarding his grades. There are school records indicating that Mr. Dawkins was again enrolled in tenth grade at Jefferson High for the 1974–1975 school year. It appears based on his school records that he only attended school from September to November of the 1974–1975 school year, and his grades were poor, as he was received Es in English, Social Studies, and Science, and he received a D in Math.

Mr. Dawkins reported that he was placed in Jackson Alternative School because of his fighting behavior and was required to repeat the tenth grade because of his sporadic attendance. According to Mr. Dawkins, he was expelled from Jackson in tenth grade for "fighting the teacher." However, he stated, "If I would have went, I would have passed." He also reported, "I was always good at math." Mr. Dawkins's school records indicate that he was enrolled in tenth-grade classes in Jackson Academy's "disruptive pupil program" from September 1975 to January 1976. According to the school records, he exhibited "constant disruptive behavior" at Jackson and "was observed…causing disruptions when he should have been with the Jackson group." While at Jackson, his school records indicate, he attended counseling and met with a social worker to address his behavioral problems. However, the school records report that in February 1976, Mr. Dawkins "led [an] attack on a teacher" at Jackson Academy. He was subsequently transferred to the George Washington Disciplinary School in April of 1976, according to his school records. There are no records regarding his performance at George Washington Disciplinary School.

Ms. Jeffers reported that Mr. Dawkins did not graduate from high school, but obtained his GED when he was incarcerated. The Department of Education official transcript indicated that Mr. Dawkins withdrew from school in 1976, that his last grade completed was the ninth grade, and that he successfully tested for his GED in September 1980. Mr. Dawkins, Ms. Jeffers, and Ms. Jackson all reported that Mr. Dawkins took electrician classes when he was incarcerated. The Prison psychological evaluation report (dated 5/10/96) indicated Mr. Dawkins had been enrolled in the Electronics School program since 1991, and that Mr. Dawkins was a "Teacher's Aide" in the program at the time of the report. Ms. Jackson noted about her father, "He's very intelligent and very perceptive."

Employment History

Mr. Dawkins stated that his first job was at Norristown General Hospital, where he worked in the mailroom. He stated that he worked for the Youth Corp for one year and for ACME for three years. In his life history statement, Mr. Dawkins reported that he was placed on probation at this job after he was caught "not ringing up items" so that he could take the money paid for the items. He reported that he stopped taking money but was later fired when he accidentally missed scanning an item. According to Mr. Dawkins, he also worked as a parking lot attendant for three years, as a supervisor for after-school and summer workers for the City of Norristown for one year, and as a laborer for one year. In his life history statement, Mr. Dawkins indicated that he lost his job at the parking lot after leaving with patrons' cars during his shift (12:00 p.m. to 8:00 a.m.) in order to attend parties and clubs. He indicated that he was fired when a car went missing and he was viewed as a car thief. Mr. Dawkins reported that he was unable to retain his job with Norristown after he was incarcerated in 1985. In his life history statement, Mr. Dawkins reported that he was let go from his job as a laborer because the electrical technician he worked under would drink and not "make it to work," resulting in the company's firing both Mr. Dawkins and the technician. State parole records for Mr. Dawkins also indicate inconsistent employment. Based on Mr. Dawkins's chronology of jobs, he has not had stable employment since 1979, when he was first incarcerated. He reported that he was incarcerated from 1979–1982, 1985–1987, and 1989–1998. According to Mr. Dawkins, he worked for maintenance and electrical while he was incarcerated. He stated that since 1998, he has been self-employed, doing carpentry and remodeling homes. He added, "I do a lot of subcontracting." About his job, he reported, "I love my job—I'm real good at it." He noted that he had "a lot of customers" and "worked 5–7 days a week." Mr. Dawkins reported that he is currently employed in the kitchen of the City Jail.

Ms. Jeffers reported that Mr. Dawkins has "been steadily employed in the time he's not incarcerated." Ms. Jackson also noted that he has been "employed regularly" in the past few years. Ms. Jackson reported that in addition to doing carpentry or electrical jobs with his construction company, Mr. Dawkins "also did jobs outside of that to establish his own clientele." Ms. Jackson added, "His goal was to become a certified electrician and maintain his own business."

Ms. Simmons stated that she hired Mr. Dawkins to complete several remodeling projects at her home. She reported that he was working for her at the time he was arrested. Ms. Simmons indicated that she was pleased with the work that Mr. Dawkins had done in her home. She noted that if there were things Mr. Dawkins knew he could not do, "he wouldn't just slop it together, we would let me know that there were things he couldn't do." She added, "He would say he wouldn't even take on the plumbing job because it wouldn't work right." Ms. Simmons reported that Mr. Dawkins helped her when she was in need. According to Ms. Simmons, after her son was shot, she "didn't have much money" and Mr. Dawkins installed a floor, bathtub, and door in her bathroom for less than $300. She reported that sometimes Mr. Dawkins would tell her, "I'll do the job and you can pay me when you get the money." Ms. Simmons stated that Mr. Dawkins was proud of his job. Not only was she happy with the work that he was doing, but she reported that her husband was "very happy" with the job that Mr. Dawkins did when he fixed their door.

Records from the Social Security Administration indicate that in the period from January 2003 to December 2007, Mr. Dawkins reported earnings in 2003 and 2004. He reported earning $1,862.00 in 2003 at ABC Management Company and $532.63 in 2004 at Jamestown Hospital.

School and Employment History

Q. *You have written that Mr. Dawkins had excellent school attendance through the ninth grade and excellent skills in remodeling work for Ms. Simmons, is that right?*

A. *That is right.*

Q. *Isn't motivation important in such positive behaviors?*

A. *Sure.*

Q. *Don't these kinds of success stories point to Mr. Dawkins' being able to do well, behave*

COMMENT

One of the decisions that expert witnesses have to make is when to dig in their heels. I made the case earlier for waiting for the right moment. In this example, the expert digs in early. Note, though, that it is set up by two easy and full agreements. Sometimes a series of cross-examination questions begins with, "Do you think you can give me a simple yes or no answer?" I always reply yes to that initial inquiry, regardless of what may follow.

---

appropriately, and be a good citizen when he actually wanted to?

A. *That is not a simple question and does not lend itself to a simple yes or no answer.*

MEDICAL AND PSYCHIATRIC HISTORY

Mr. Dawkins reported no present health problems and he stated that he is not presently taking any type of medication. However, he reported that he was shot in August of 1987. According to Mr. Dawkins, the injury required surgery. As a result of the surgery, Mr. Dawkins stated, he has a large scar that extends from below his belt to his sternum. He also reported that the little finger on his left hand is "deformed" because of a "bone infection." In addition, Ms. Jeffers and Ms. Jackson reported that Mr. Dawkins was stabbed multiple times in the abdomen and chest area when he was a teenager. Ms. Jeffers stated that Mr. Dawkins was hospitalized for approximately 10 days after the stabbing.

When asked about his history of mental health treatment, Mr. Dawkins reported that he received drug counseling while he was incarcerated in the past. He also reported that he went to Father James for drug treatment in 2004. Mr. Dawkins's school records indicate that he underwent psychological examinations in 1968 and 1969, but do not indicate why the examinations were necessary or what the examinations revealed.

SUBSTANCE ABUSE HISTORY

Mr. Dawkins reported that he has used alcohol, cocaine, and marijuana. He stated that he drank "too much on the weekends," which he said was "a case of beer a weekend." When asked if he ever had a drug problem, he stated, "well, no...yes." He reported that he used cocaine once every three weeks in the year prior to his incarceration. When asked if he currently has an alcohol problem, he stated, "Right before I came here it was a problem." He added, "It's all I wanted to do." He reported that his wife complains about his drinking. Mr. Dawkins said, "I don't make too good of decisions when drinking or using drugs." When asked to elaborate, he stated that he would oversleep for work because he had a hangover. In his life history statement, Mr. Dawkins cited his drinking and nightlife as the cause of poor consequences numerous times. For example, he indicated that he missed scanning an item at his job because he had been up late the night before, and that he developed a plan to steal money from parking lot patrons while drinking with a friend. He also noted that when he was younger his drinking would cause him to get into fights. The mitigation report indicates Mr. Dawkins has been in treatment for alcohol and substance use twice while incarcerated and once while on parole. Ms. Morris also concluded in the mitigation report that Mr. Dawkins's involvement with the legal system is closely tied to his drug and alcohol use. Ms. Morris noted that while incarcerated and abstaining from substance abuse, Mr. Dawkins proves to be "a non-violent, well-mannered individual with a strong work ethic and pleasant demeanor."

Ms. Jeffers stated that Mr. Dawkins has problems with drugs and alcohol. However, she reported that he knew that she "didn't like or approve of it" so he "tried to hide it." She stated that she did not know when he began using drugs, or what drugs he uses, but she suspects drug use because of his attitude and because his personality changed. Ms. Jeffers reported that he did not drink alcohol or do drugs in the home, but he drank beer "if he was watching a fight or a football game." She noted that he would never do drugs in front of his wife or his children. She stated that there were times where Mr. Dawkins would leave and not come home for a day. She added, "That's when I know he's doing something...I can hear it in his voice." Ms. Jeffers stated that she believes "there might be times when he tried to get clean—there are times when things are going good." According to her, when Mr. Dawkins "feels bad about something he's done" like feeling "bad about being drunk, he'll go home and stay in his room for three weeks." Ms. Jeffers stated that there were times when she would tell her husband, "If you can't do it by yourself, you need to get help." However, she reported that he would respond by telling her that he was all right. She said that Mr. Dawkins never admitted to her that he used drugs, but she stated, "I could tell, I could see he was fighting his own battle."

Substance Abuse

Q. So Mr. Dawkins used crack cocaine a lot, is that right?

A. At different times, yes.

Q. And he admitted that drinking and carousing repeatedly got him in trouble?

A. Yes. He was very candid about his problems.

Q. When he would use cocaine or get drunk, he knew what he was doing, didn't he?

A. Yes.

Q. He knew that cocaine was illegal, could lead to imprisonment, and had bad consequences, but he used it anyway, didn't he?

A. Yes.

Q. Would you agree that he used cocaine willingly and intentionally?

A. Of course. It is rare that anybody is ever forced into using cocaine.

Q. And Mr. Dawkins drank lots of alcoholic beverages willingly and intentionally?

A. Yes, and he has gone into treatment for his problems with substance abuse.

When Ms. Jackson was asked if her father has ever used drugs or alcohol, she responded, "I never saw it (and) he never told me...I suspected it because of some of the behaviors, (but) I don't know." Then she stated, "It could have just been anything now that I'm thinking about it...I'm still unclear." Ms. Jackson noted that there were times when her father was hanging around people that he normally did not hang around, and she knew that some of these people were drug users. When she was asked whether Mr. Dawkins was using alcohol or drugs prior to his incarceration, she stated, "I'm sure he was consuming quite a bit of alcohol before he was arrested." She added, "He didn't drink alcohol, like 'live it up,' but more to calm down."

SOCIAL HISTORY

When asked about his interests and hobbies, Mr. Dawkins stated, "I love the gym." He stated that he lifts weights five days a week, both when he is living in the community and when he is incarcerated. In addition, he reported that he enjoys playing football, and he plays basketball every Sunday. Mr. Dawkins also reported that he belongs to the Norristown Community Organization, which is a neighborhood organization that attempts to clean up the neighborhood. He stated that he also belongs to the YMCA, and he still has a membership at a local fitness club. He reported that he has "a lot of associates," and they get together to watch fights and football games. When asked if he has positive friends (friends without criminal involvement), he stated that in the past 10 years, his good friends have been friends with no criminal involvement. However, he added that he also has friends who are involved in offending.

COMMENT

This line of questioning sought to highlight in common language the cocaine use. Cocaine use is socially unacceptable to most people on juries, and emphasis on this topic may further stigmatize a defendant already found guilty of capital murder. The proposed answers to these questions place the issue in a broader context. When the attorney asked about Mr. Dawkins admitting his use, with its suggestion of a confession, the reply presented the other side of the issue, namely candor. Should experts offer a context? I prefer that approach. This way the facts are on the table but also with some rationale. While the willingness question was reasonably answered "Yes," it would have been also possible to answer "No." That is, with cocaine dependency, one can assert that free choice has been compromised because of the addictive nature of the disorder.

Regarding Mr. Dawkins's friends, Ms. Jeffers stated that she does not know all of them, but she knew the friends that "came past the house and the ones from his childhood." She stated that she approved of "some of them," but, "a few of them weren't doing anything with their lives, but for the most part, most of them were alright people, I guess." When asked if she knew how Mr. Dawkins and his friends spent their time together, she replied, "No." She added, "They would probably just go out—probably went out to the bar or the club." She reported that she did not mind that he went out to the bar or club with his friends. Ms. Jeffers reported that Mr. Dawkins likes to play pool and go to the movies. She stated that she and her husband went to the movies together "now and then," but added, "Basically, if we went out together, we might go out to the bar, but he'll have me home by 10:00 p.m." She noted that she and Mr. Dawkins also used to go visit family and friends together.

About Mr. Dawkins's leisure activities, Ms. Jackson stated, "Him and my mom always had Friday night movie dates at least a couple times a month." She reported that her father loves music and likes to read. In addition, she stated, "I know he likes beer and he likes to eat…of course, there's football Sundays at home (and) occasionally he would go out with friends." Ms. Jackson noted that Mr. Dawkins has a few friends, but "There's not a large group of friends…he has a select group of people that he communicates with and that's usually it."

Ms. Simmons, Mr. Dawkins's former employer, reported that she met Mr. Dawkins at the gym in 1999. She stated that he trained her and some other people at the gym. About this, she stated, "He was good at the gym; he had a crowd in the gym that he was training…and he didn't charge us a penny." She reported that there were other men in the gym that charged for training, but she noted that Mr. Dawkins "said if we were serious about working out, he wouldn't charge us." She stated that Mr. Dawkins is "very serious" about working out, and she added, "He had us working really hard in the gym." In addition to enjoying working in the gym, Ms. Simmons reported that Mr. Dawkins "loves putting houses together," and he loves football. She stated that he used to talk about playing football. She reported that she met some of Mr. Dawkins's friends at the gym. When asked if she knew how they usually spent their time

together, she stated, "I know he used to be at the gym all the time."

OFFENSE AND INCARCERATION HISTORY

Mr. Dawkins's reports and his criminal record reflect the following history of criminal involvement. He stated that he was first arrested at the age of 13 for auto theft. He reported that he was incarcerated from 1979–1982 for robbery, and from 1989–1998 for aggravated assault and robbery. In addition, he was convicted of conspiracy and reported that he was incarcerated from 1985–1987 for those charges. His court history documents that he has been convicted of burglary (1978); theft and unlawful taking (1979); robbery and criminal conspiracy (1979); criminal conspiracy (1985); recklessly endangering another person and simple assault (1987); aggravated assault, simple assault, and carrying firearms in a public place (1989); and possession of the instrument of a crime and robbery (1989).

Mr. Dawkins's prison records indicate he has been involved in only one altercation during his current incarceration. The records state that Mr. Dawkins ended the altercation upon the direction of a correction officer and returned to his unit when requested to do so. Prison social services records indicate Mr. Dawkins has "adjust[ed] well" to his current incarceration, is "affable," and "works hard." The state parole psychological evaluation (dated 6/22/01) indicates Mr. Dawkins was involved in two altercations during a previous incarceration: he received misconducts for assault or fighting in 1992 and an assault in 1994, during which he beat another inmate with a "sock filled with batteries." However, the report summarizing the evaluation (dated 9/20/01) was "positive in terms of institutional adjustment" and determined "it does not appear [Mr. Dawkins] will be a management problem if he is awarded an advanced status." The summary report assigned Mr. Dawkins a "Stability Rating" of "A." Similarly, the psychological evaluation for parole conducted at prison (dated 5/21/97) determined Mr. Dawkins had "maintained a satisfactory adjustment since [the 5/10/96] review." A Department of Corrections classification summary (dated 6/21/01) indicated that Mr. Dawkins had an assault charge more than 6 months prior, had no disciplinary reports in the past 12 months, had no known escape history, was active and partially compliant in programs, demonstrated average work performance, and also had above-average housing performance, resulting in a custody level classification of 2. Ms. Morris, in the mitigation report, noted that Mr. Dawkins demonstrates "[e]xtremely positive adjustment to prison and success in highly structured environments," and is a "hard working, mature inmate." Ms. Morris also noted that Mr. Dawkins is an "older inmate whose propensity for violence decreases over time."

State parole records indicate that while on parole, Mr. Dawkins was cooperative and complied in reporting to his parole office, obtaining employment, and submitting to drug testing. Parolee risk assessments (dated 1/18/02 to 5/28/04) indicate Mr. Dawkins required medium to maximum supervision. However, state parole records indicate Mr. Dawkins violated parole on at least three occasions. Mr. Dawkins was arrested for driving under the influence on 3/26/00, and found not guilty of the charge on 4/3/01. State parole records indicate Mr. Dawkins submitted drug tests positive for cocaine in April of 2003, March of 2004, and April of 2005, and was committed to the Norristown Hall Program in 2005 for the parole violation. State parole records indicate Mr. Dawkins admitted to using cocaine in March 2004 and entered the ABC program as directed by his parole officer. State parole records also indicate Mr. Dawkins was cited for owning or possessing a firearm in July of 2004 when U.S. Marshals entered his residence in an attempt to locate another individual. The U.S. Marshals found a gun during their search of the residence. The mitigation report indicated Mr. Dawkins did not know the gun was in his house, as it belonged to his son. State parole records also indicate Mr. Dawkins was declared delinquent on 1/13/06 after not reporting to his parole officer.

Current Clinical Condition

Mr. Dawkins is a 49-year-old African American male of average height who appeared his stated age. He displayed a muscular build, good posture, and normal eye contact. He wore institutional garb, and he was adequately groomed during the evaluations on September 7, 2007, and September 12, 2007. He brought glasses to the evaluation, which he used for the testing portions of the evaluation. Mr. Dawkins reported that he has a scar that extends from below his belt to under his diaphragm from surgery on a gunshot wound in August 1987. In addition, he reported that part of the bone in his left little finger has been removed, leaving the finger slightly deformed. He attributes this injury to a "cumulative effect" of injuring his finger playing football and basketball, and a bone infection. He stated that his left ear was pierced, but it has been closed up for years. Mr. Dawkins has a tattoo of "A-N-D" on his right upper arm. He stated that the "A" stands for his wife's initial, the "N" means "and" and the "D" is his initial. He also reported having a tattoo of a Chinese symbol meaning "long life" on his left upper arm. He was very polite and cooperative throughout the evaluation sessions. In addition, his mood appeared positive and his affect was appropriate. His speech was clear and coherent, and he responded openly and with relevance when questioned. He also appeared to give reasonable effort to the tasks involved, despite the duration of the evaluation and his report that he had not eaten anything the day of testing. His capacity for attention and concentration appeared adequate. He was able to focus reasonably well on a series of tasks throughout the five-hour evaluation on September 7, 2007, and the 2.5-hour evaluation on September 12, 2007, without becoming visibly distracted. Therefore, it would appear that this evaluation provides a reasonably good estimate of Mr. Dawkins's current functioning.

Mr. Dawkins's basic academic skills, as measured by the WRAT-4, showed a marked deficit in one of four areas: Word Reading (grade equivalent = 11.6), Spelling (grade equivalent = 7.2), Math Computation (grade equivalent = 11.2), and Sentence Comprehension (grade equivalent = >12.9). On a measure of overall intellectual functioning (the WAIS-III), Mr. Dawkins was measured as performing in the Average range (Full Scale IQ = 95), placing him in the 37th percentile relative to others his age. He was also measured in the Average range for both verbal tasks (VIQ = 93) and performance tasks (PIQ = 97), placing him in the 32nd and 42nd percentiles, respectively, relative to others his age. Although Mr. Dawkins appears to have a significant deficit in his spelling, he appears to be of average intellectual functioning.

Mr. Dawkins was presented two versions of a structured inventory of symptoms of mental and emotional disorders, the Brief Symptom Inventory (BSI), one concerning his present functioning (discussed here) and the second describing his thoughts and feelings around the time of the incident for which he is currently facing charges. However, Mr. Dawkins stated that he could not report how he was feeling at the time of the offense—he could only report how he was feeling when he was arrested and told of the murders. Therefore, he only completed the BSI concerning his present functioning. On the BSI, Mr. Dawkins reported currently being "extremely" distressed on one of the 53 items. He reported that he was extremely distressed with having to check and double-check what he does. When asked to elaborate on this, he stated that he has to make sure he does things correctly so he does not get into trouble with prison staff. He reported being "moderately" distressed by getting into frequent arguments. Mr. Dawkins's scores on the nine scales (somatization, obsessive-compulsive, interpersonal sensitivity, depression, anxiety, hostility, phobic anxiety, paranoid ideation, and psychoticism) were first compared to non-patient adult males. None of the scales was significantly elevated (i.e., greater than two standard deviations above the mean).

Mr. Dawkins completed the MMPI-2 in approximately two hours, and he appeared to remain focused throughout the entire test. The personality profile generated is likely to be a valid indication of his present personality functioning. However, the results indicate that Mr. Dawkins approached the items in a defensive and overly cautious manner, and he may have been evasive and unwilling to admit many personal faults. Mr. Dawkins's profile (Welsh Code 4"+18-37259/60: K-LF/) is often seen in individuals who are described as immature, impulsive, and hedonistic, and who frequently rebel against authority. These results are consistent with the results of the psychological evaluation conducted in 1996, which described Mr. Dawkins

as "impulsive" and "impatient" and tending to "not consider the consequences of his actions." Mr. Dawkins's profile is seen in 9.1% of normative men, but found in 36.8% of men in a state prison and 21.5% of men in a federal prison. His score indicates that he may have drug or alcohol problems, as many individuals with this profile develop severe addictive problems. Furthermore, over 24% of men in substance-abuse treatment programs have this pattern. This profile indicates that Mr. Dawkins may appear charming and may make a good first impression, but may also be perceived as superficial and untrustworthy in the longer term. These results are consistent with the state parole psychological evaluation conducted in 2001, which indicated Mr. Dawkins may be "egocentric, more concerned with 'image' than substance, and lacking in personal insight." The profile also suggests that he is outgoing and sociable and has a strong need to be around others, but has more difficulty forming stable, warm relationships. However, it should be noted that Mr. Dawkins has been in a relationship with his wife for over 30 years. Many individuals with this profile have marital problems that require counseling because of the individual's behavior, although this has not been reported for Mr. Dawkins. Such individuals also frequently have a history of offending and other antisocial behavior that is significant.

MMPI-2 Challenges

Q. *Doctor, I want to be sure that I have correctly read and heard your MMPI-2 results. First, this test is the gold standard for assessing personality, isn't it?*

A. Yes.

Q. *Now, didn't Mr. Dawkins come out as defensive, immature, and impulsive?*

A. Yes.

COMMENT

Report writers need to call them as they are, and conscientious evaluators do not conceal or minimize findings, no matter who has retained them. When pressed as in this cross-examination, it is possible to own the findings and to agree strongly with the pieces that are being addressed. Still, the task of the mitigation evaluator is not to make the case for character flaws. Instead, it is to provide the court with psychological information that addresses the legal issue. This examiner could have replied that Mr. Dawkins' impulsivity and immaturity account for some aspects of the crime, but hardly fully describe him.

Q. *Furthermore, he came out as superficial, untrust-worthy, and egocentric, didn't he?*

A. *Those are some traits among many, some good and some problematic, that appeared on the test. I have never called him egocentric.*

Q. *Isn't it also true that he was way way way up there on the psychopathic deviate scale?*

A. *We no longer call scale 4 the psychopathic deviate scale because the term can be so misleading in terms of what it means. The results accurately reflect the fact that he has been in trouble with the law.*

On the LSI-R, Mr. Dawkins showed particular deficits in the domains of Criminal History, Educational/Employment, Financial, Family/Marital, Accommodation, Leisure/Recreation, Companions, Alcohol/Drug Problem, Emotional/Personal, and Attitudes/Orientation. Specifically, Mr. Dawkins's responses indicate that he has a significant history of prior offenses and convictions (seven prior adult convictions and one juvenile conviction). Mr. Dawkins also reported concerns about financial matters, housing problems (including living in an unsafe areas with frequent drug and gang activity), and marital difficulties. Although he indicated that he has some positive friends who are not involved in criminal activities, he acknowledged that some of his friends have been involved in crime. Additionally, Mr. Dawkins reported a substance abuse problem, including using crack and binge drinking. He admitted that he had a problem with alcohol at the time of the arrest, and added, "It's all I wanted to do." Mr. Dawkins showed mixed evidence in the Attitudes/Orientation domain. On one hand, he expressed attitudes reflecting the absence of distress related to being arrested or the impact of his behavior on others. On the other hand, he also reported that he would like to live a life without crime, believes that education is "extremely important," and thinks having a job "is everything." The LSI-R was also completed in March of 2004 and November of 2005 by Mr. Dawkins's parole officers. The reports concluded that Mr. Dawkins fell within the high–medium risk/needs classification. The reports indicate that Criminal History, Education/Employment, Family/Marital, Leisure/Recreation, Companions, and Alcohol/Drug Problem were problematic areas for Mr. Dawkins.

Sentencing Considerations

According to 42 Pa. C.S.A. § 9711(a)(2), any evidence relating to mitigating circumstances can be presented at the sentencing hearing. The following factors, as enumerated in 42 Pa. C.S.A. § 9711(e), can be considered as mitigating factors:

(1) The defendant has no significant history of prior criminal convictions.

(2) The defendant was under the influence of extreme mental or emotional disturbance.

(3) The capacity of the defendant to appreciate the criminality of his conduct or to conform his conduct to the requirements of law was substantially impaired.

(4) The age of the defendant at the time of the crime.

(5) The defendant acted under extreme duress, although not such duress as to constitute a defense to prosecution ... or acted under the substantial domination of another person.

(6) The victim was a participant in the defendant's homicidal conduct or consented to the homicidal acts.

(7) The defendant's participation in the homicidal act was relatively minor.

(8) Any other evidence of mitigation concerning the character and record of the defendant and the circumstances of his offense.

The mitigating factors that can be addressed through forensic mental health assessment are factors 2, 3, 5, and 8. Mr. Dawkins did not report any circumstances relevant to factors 2, 3, or 5; however, information related to factor 8 is discussed in this section.

Mitigating Factors

Q. *You did write that mitigating factors 1 through 7, out of 8, did not apply to Mr. Dawkins, is that right?*

A. *Yes.*

Q. *Let us go through these one at a time. First, that means he does have a history of prior convictions, right?*

A. *Right.*

Q. *And he was not under the influence of extreme mental disturbance, right?*

A. *Yes.*

Q. *In fact, as far as you know, a full seven of the mitigating factors just did not apply to Mr. Dawkins?*

A. *No. I did not discuss or address factors 1, 4, 6, or 7. (This question also could have been answered, "That's right.")*

COMMENT

This line of questioning raises the issue of how much of statutory information should be included in reports. After all, all of the statutory information will be buried somewhere in the judge's instruction to the jury. In this instance, the expert could have chosen to reply with an admit-deny, in which the "one of out eight criteria" is affirmed, but the minimalizing of the psychological finding is strongly denied and refuted. The last question about blatant denial is difficult. It could be answered with, "He absolutely denied committing the offense."

Q. Furthermore, according to your evaluation, Mr. Dawkins was engaged in blatant denial and lying about not having done this murder of which he has been convicted, right?

A. It is always up to the court to make judgments about guilt or innocence, and not psychological evaluators.

When asked about the circumstances surrounding the offense for which he is currently charged, Mr. Dawkins stated that he was "somewhere else" at the time of the offense. Mr. Dawkins stated that he did not know the younger victim, Norris Jenkins. However, he reported that he knows "Old Head," the other victim. He stated that Old Head (Max Charles), "is a plumber (and) also a crackhead," and Mr. Dawkins noted that he "used to use him as cheap labor." He added, "Old Head never did anything to me in my life." Mr. Dawkins denied involvement in the crime.

(8) Any other evidence of mitigation concerning the character and record of the defendant and the circumstances of his offense.

Mr. Dawkins has faced a number of difficulties throughout his life, as his father left his home when he was only 10 years old, leaving his mother to care for five children on her own. As a result of his father's absence, Mr. Dawkins's mother was forced to work long hours, leaving Mr. Dawkins in the care of his older siblings. Mr. Dawkins and Ms. Jeffers both reported that Mr. Dawkins's mother began drinking after his father left the home, and according to Ms. Jeffers, her drinking became increasingly worse. In addition, Mr. Dawkins's mother reportedly beat him with her hands, a belt, and a broom. Mr. Dawkins also was raised in a rough neighborhood and attended a school with significant gang activity. Mr. Dawkins suffers from a significant substance abuse problem with cocaine and alcohol, and he may have been prone to this problem because of his family history of alcohol problems (both his mother and brother drank excessively). His wife believes that he attempts to quit using drugs and alcohol for periods of time, but ultimately ends up relapsing. She noted that he feels guilty after he has relapsed, or drunk too much, and stays in his room for weeks at a time. It appears that he is aware of the problems that his substance abuse causes, but is unable to stop using substances on his own. Mr. Dawkins has received treatment in the past, but would benefit from further substance abuse treatment.

Mr. Dawkins has important strengths, as he has several people in his life for whom he appears to care very much, including his wife, his children, and his grandchildren. He has maintained regular contact with his wife and daughter, and he was active in his grandchildren's lives. Mr. Dawkins is also a relatively intelligent and sociable man. He reported that he has had several jobs while he has been incarcerated. Prison social service records indicate Mr. Dawkins has maintained employment during his current incarceration. Furthermore, he received training to be an electrician while he was incarcerated, which he utilized after his release to start his own business. Mr. Dawkins also received his GED while he was incarcerated. In addition, Mr. Dawkins's prison records indicate he has been involved in only one altercation during his current incarceration. The records state that Mr. Dawkins ended the altercation upon the direction of a correction officer and returned to his unit when requested to do so. Based on his achievements while he was incarcerated, and the reports of his former employer, Mr. Dawkins appears to be a hard worker who would be a relatively low risk for disciplinary problems if incarcerated in prison.

Diagnoses

Q. What is Mr. Dawkins' diagnosis?

A. I did not make a diagnosis.

COMMENT

The issue of whether to make a diagnosis in a forensic report is a judgment call. Some assessors always make them, while other assessors never make them, because they are seen as not essential to the psychological-legal issue. When no diagnosis is made, or when one mostly specific to major crimes, like Dissociative Episode, is made, attorneys sometimes pounce. My professional preference is not to make a diagnosis in mitigation evaluations such as Mr. Dawkins's. However, the omission can become a topic of drawn-out inquiry during cross-examination, and for that reason, I may present a diagnosis. When pursued about a diagnosis, it may be best to play the hand of professional mastery and give one. The alternative, presented above in this scenario, is to be a bit disingenuous, and such lack of candor does not serve us well.

Q. *I know you did not write one in your report. But what is his diagnosis?*

A. *I indicated in my report and testimony the nature of his problems.*

Q. *Please answer the question. What is his diagnosis? You do know how to make diagnoses, don't you?*

A. *Only when there is a reason to do so.*

Q. *The reason is I have asked you. Now what DSM diagnosis do you give to Mr. Dawkins?*

A. *I have not made a diagnosis because diagnoses are not part of my mitigation evaluations.*

Q. *Are you familiar with the DSM criteria for a diagnosis of Substance Abuse?*

A. *Yes.*

Q. *Has Mr. Dawkins had a maladaptive pattern of cocaine abuse that led to clinical significant impairment within a 12-month period?*

A. *Yes.*

Q. *Did he fail to fulfill a major role obligation?*

A. *Yes.*

Q. *Did he ever use drugs in a situation that could have been dangerous?*

A. *Yes.*

Q. *Did he have legal problems related to substance abuse?*

A. *Yes.*

Q. *Did he continue to use drugs even though he had repeated problems from their use?*

A. *He did.*

Q. *So he is diagnosed as a Substance Abuser, isn't he?*

A. *As I indicated repeatedly in my report, Mr. Dawkins has indeed abused substances. I have not made any diagnosis.*

CONCLUSIONS

In the opinion of the undersigned, based on all of the above:

(1) Mr. Dawkins's considerations relevant to mitigation include significant substance abuse problems, his problems in his early family life, his mother's drinking problem, and his father's absence from the home. He also has positive influences in his life and reports an attachment to his children and grandchildren. He is relatively intelligent, reports that he values work, and appears at low risk for disciplinary problems if incarcerated in prison following disposition of charges. These factors can be seen as strengths, and they are consistent with a favorable response to treatment in a structured, secure prison environment.

Thank you for the opportunity to evaluate David Dawkins.

Kirk Heilbrun, PhD
Consulting Psychologist

Jacey Erickson, BA
Clinical Psychology
Graduate Student

REFERENCES

American Academy of Child and Adolescent Psychiatry (1997). *Practice parameters for child custody evaluation*. Washington, DC: Author. Retrieved January 26, 2013, from http://www.aacap.org/galleries/practiceparameters/custody.pdf.

American Academy of Psychiatry and the Law (2005). Ethics guidelines for the practice of forensic psychiatry. Bloomfield, CT: AAPL. Retrieved January 13, 2013, from http://www.aapl.org/pdf/ethicsgdlns.pdf.

American Association on Intellectual and Developmental Disabilities (2010). *Intellectual disability: Definition, classification, and systems of supports* (11th ed.). Washington, DC: AAIDD.

American Association on Intellectual and Developmental Disabilities (2012). *User's guide to intellectual disability: Definition, classification, and systems of supports* (11th ed.). Washington, DC: AAIDD.

American Association on Mental Retardation (1992). *Mental retardation: Definition, classification, and systems of supports* (9th ed.). Washington, DC: AAMR.

American Association on Mental Retardation (2002). *Mental retardation: Definition, classification, and systems of supports* (10th ed.). Washington, DC: AAMR.

American Bar Association (1989). *Criminal justice mental health standards*. Washington, DC: ABA. Retrieved January 1, 2014, from http://www.americanbar.org/publications/criminal_justice_section_archive/crimjust_standards_mentalhealth_toc.html

American Psychiatric Association (1983). *Statement on the Insanity Defense*. Washington, DC: APA.

American Psychiatric Association (2000). *Diagnostic and statistical manual of mental disorders* (4th ed., text revision). Washington, DC: APA.

American Psychiatric Association (2013a). *Diagnostic and statistical manual of mental disorders* (5th ed.). Arlington, VA: American Psychiatric Publishing.

American Psychiatric Association (2013b). *The principles of medical ethics with annotations especially applicable to psychiatry*. Arlington, VA: APA. Retrieved January 13, 2013, from http://www.psychiatry.org/practice/ethics/resources-standards.

American Psychiatric Association (2013c). *Intellectual disability fact sheet*. Arlington, VA: American Psychiatric Publishing.

American Psychological Association (2006). *APA dictionary of psychology*. Washington, DC: APA.

American Psychological Association (2010a). Ethical principles of psychologists and code of conduct. Washington, DC: APA. Retrieved January 13, 2013, from http://www.apa.org/ethics/code/principles.pdf.

American Psychological Association (2010b). Guidelines for child custody evaluations in family law proceedings. *American Psychologist, 65*, 863–867. Available at: http://dx.doi.org/10.1037/a0021250

American Psychological Association (2013a). Guidelines for psychological evaluations in child protection matters. *American Psychologist, 68*, 20–31. Available at: http://dx.doi.org/10.1037/a0029891

American Psychological Association (2013b). Specialty guidelines for forensic psychology. *American Psychologist, 68*, 7–19. Available at: http://dx.doi.org/10.1037/a0029889

American Psychological Association Zero Tolerance Task Force. (2008). Are zero tolerance policies effective in the schools? An evidentiary review and recommendations. *American Psychologist, 63*, 852–862. Available at: http://dx.doi.org/10.1037/0003-066X.63.9.852

Anastasi, A., & Urbina, S. (2007). *Psychological testing* (7th ed.). New York: Pearson.

Andrews, D., & Bonta, J. (1998). *The psychology of criminal conduct* (2nd ed.). Cincinnati, OH: Anderson.

Association of Family and Conciliation Courts. (2007). Model standards of practice for child custody evaluations. *Family Court Review, 45*, 70–91. Available at: http://dx.doi.org/10.1111/j.1744-1617.2007.129_3.x

Bagby, M. Gillis, J., Toner, B., & Goldberg, J. (1991). Detecting fake good and fake bad responding on the Millon Clinical Multiaxial Inventory–II. *Psychological Assessment, 3,* 496–498. Available at: http://dx.doi.org/10.1037/1040-3590.3.3.496

Barnum, R. (1997). A suggested framework for forensic consultation in cases of child abuse and neglect. *Journal of the American Academy of Psychiatry and the Law, 25,* 581–594.

Barnum, R. (2002). Parenting assessment in cases of neglect and abuse. In D. Shetky & E. Benedek (Eds.), *Comprehensive textbook of child and adolescent forensic psychiatry.* Washington, DC: American Psychiatric Association Press.

Baroff, G. (1999). *Mental retardation: Nature, cause, and management* (3rd ed.). Philadelphia, PA: Brunner/Mazel.

Bathurst, K., Gottfried, A., & Gottfried, A. (1997). Normative data for the MMPI-2 in child custody litigation. *Psychological Assessment, 9,* 205–211. Available at: http://dx.doi.org/10.1037/1040-3590.9.3.205

Beirne-Thompson, M., Patton, J., & Ittenbach, R. (1994). *Intellectual disability* (4th ed.). New York: Macmillan.

Bench, L., & Allen, T. (2003). Investigating the stigma of prison classification: An experimental design. *Prison Journal, 83,* 367–382. Available at: http://dx.doi.org/10.1177/0032885503260143

Benedek, E., Ash, P., & Scott, C. (Eds.). (2010). *Principles and practice of child and adolescent forensic mental health.* Washington, DC: American Psychiatric Publishing.

Bersoff, D. (2008). *Ethical conflicts in psychology* (4th ed.). Washington, DC: American Psychological Association.

Bersoff, D., Goodman-Delahunty, J., Grisso, T., Hans, V., Poythress, N., & Roesch, R. (1997). Training in law and psychology: Models from the Villanova Conference. *American Psychologist, 52,* 1301–1310. Available at: http://dx.doi.org/10.1037/0003-066X.52.12.1301

Binder, L. (1993). An abbreviated form of the Portland Digit Recognition Test. *Clinical Neuropsychologist, 7,* 104–107. Available at: http://dx.doi.org/10.1080/13854049308401892

Blume, J., Garvey, S., & Johnson, S. (2001). Future dangerousness in capital cases: Always "at issue." *Cornell Law Review, 86,* 387–399.

Bonnie, R. (1983). The moral basis of the insanity defense. *American Bar Association Journal, 69,* 194–197.

Bonnie, R. (1992). The competence of criminal defendants: A theoretical reformulation. *Behavioral Sciences and the Law, 10,* 291–316. Available at: http://dx.doi.org/10.1002/bsl.2370100303

Bonnie, R. (2004). The American Psychiatric Association's resource document on mental retardation and capital sentencing implementing *Atkins v. Virginia. Journal of the American Academy of Psychiatry and the Law, 32,* 304–308.

Bonnie, R., & Gustafson, K. (2007). The challenge of implementing *Atkins v. Virginia*: How legislatures and courts can promote accurate assessments and adjudications of mental retardation in death penalty cases. *University of Richmond Law Review, 41,* 811–860.

Borum, R., & Grisso, T. (1996). Establishing standards for criminal forensic reports: An empirical analysis. *Bulletin of the American Academy of Psychiatry and the Law, 24,* 297–317.

Brodsky, S. (1991). *Testifying in court: Guidelines and maxims for the expert witness.* Washington, DC: American Psychological Association.

Brodsky, S. (1999). *The expert expert witness: More maxims and guidelines for testifying in court.* Washington, DC: American Psychological Association.

Brodsky, S. (2004). *Coping with cross-examination and other pathways to effective testimony.* Washington, DC: American Psychological Association. Available at: http://dx.doi.org/10.1037/10748-000

Brodsky, S. (2013). *Testifying in court: Guidelines and maxims for the expert witness* (2nd ed.). Washington, DC: American Psychological Association. Available at: http://dx.doi.org/10.1037/14037-000

Brodsky, S., Griffin, M., & Cramer, R. (2010). The Witness Credibility Scale: An outcome measure for expert witness research. *Behavioral Sciences and the Law, 28,* 892–907. Available at: http://dx.doi.org/10.1002/bsl.917

Bruininks, R., Woodcock, R., Weatherman, R., & Hill, B. (1996). *Scales of Independent Behavior revised: Comprehensive manual.* Itasca, IL: Riverside Publishing.

Butcher, J. (1997). Frequency of MMPI-2 scores in forensic evaluations. *MMPI-2 News & profiles, 8*(1), 2–4.

Butcher, J., Graham, J., Ben-Porath, Y., Tellegen, A., & Dahlstrom, W. G. (2001). *MMPI-2: Manual for administration, scoring, and interpretation* (rev. ed.). Minneapolis: University of Minnesota Press.

Ceci, S., & Bruck, M. (2000). Why judges must insist on electronically preserved recording of child interviews. *Court Review, 37,* 10–12.

Champagne, A., Shuman, D., & Whitaker, E. (1991). The problem with empirical examination of the use of Court-appointed experts: A report of nonfindings. *Behavioral Sciences and the Law, 14,* 361–365. Available at: http://dx.doi.org/10.1002/(SICI)1099-0798(199622)14:3<361::AID-BSL245>3.0.CO;2-V

Chappelle, W., & Rosengren, K. (2001). Maintaining composure and credibility as an expert witness during cross-examination. *Journal of Forensic Psychology Practice, 1,* 55–72. Available at: http://dx.doi.org/10.1300/J158v01n03_03

Christy, A., Douglas, K., Otto, R., & Petrila, J. (2004). Juveniles evaluated incompetent to proceed: Characteristics and quality of mental health professionals' evaluations. *Professional Psychology: Research and Practice, 35,* 380–388. Available at: http://dx.doi.org/10.1037/0735-7028.35.4.380

Colbach, E. (1981). Integrity checks on the witness stand. *Bulletin of the American Academy of Psychiatry and the Law, 9,* 285–288.

Condie, L., & Condie, D. (2006). Termination of parental rights. In A. Goldstein (Ed.), *Forensic psychology: Emerging topics and expanding roles* (pp. 294–331). Hoboken, NJ: John Wiley & Sons, Inc.

Conroy, M. A., & Kwartner, P. (2006). Malingering. *Applied Psychology in Criminal Justice, 2,* 29–51.

Cornell, D., & Sheras, P. (2006). *Guidelines for responding to student threats of violence.* Longmont, CO: Sopris West.

Cornell, D., Allen, K., & Fan, X. (2012). A randomized controlled study of the Virginia Student Threat Assessment Guidelines in grades K–12. *School Psychology Review, 41,* 100–115.

Cramer, R., Harris, P., Fletcher, L., DeCoster, J., & Brodsky, S. (2011). A confidence-credibility model of expert witness persuasion: Mediating effects and implications for trial consultation. *Consulting Psychology Journal: Practice and Research, 63,* 129–137. Available at: http://dx.doi.org/10.1037/a0024591

Cunningham, M. (2006). Dangerousness and death: A nexus in search of science and reason. *American Psychologist, 61,* 828–839. Available at: http://dx.doi.org/10.1037/0003-066X.61.8.827

Cunningham, M. (2010). *Evaluation for capital sentencing.* New York: Oxford University Press, Inc.

Cunningham, M., & Reidy, T. (1999). Don't confuse me with the facts: Common errors in violence risk assessment at capital sentencing. *Criminal Justice and Behavior, 26,* 20–43. Available at: http://dx.doi.org/10.1177/0093854899026001002

Cunningham, M., & Reidy, T. (2001). A matter of life or death: Special considerations and heightened practice standards in capital sentencing evaluations. *Behavioral Sciences and the Law, 19,* 473–490. Available at: http://dx.doi.org/10.1002/bsl.460

Cunningham, M., & Reidy, T. (2002). Violence risk assessment at federal capital sentencing: Individualization, generalization, relevance, and scientific standards. *Criminal Justice and Behavior, 29,* 512–537. Available at: http://dx.doi.org/10.1177/009385402236731

Cunningham, M., Reidy, T., & Sorensen, J. (2005). Is death row obsolete? A decade of mainstreaming death-sentenced inmates in Missouri. *Behavioral Sciences & the Law, 23,* 307–320. Available at: http://dx.doi.org/10.1002/bsl.608

Cunningham, M., Reidy, T., & Sorensen, J. (2008). Assertions of "future dangerousness" at federal capital sentencing: Rates and correlates of subsequent prison misconduct and violence. *Law and Human Behavior, 32,* 46–63. Available at: http://dx.doi.org/10.1007/s10979-007-9107-7

Cunningham, M., & Sorensen, J. (2006a). Actuarial models for assessment of prison violence risk: Revisions and extensions of the Risk Assessment Scale for Prison (RASP). *Assessment, 13,* 253–265. Available at: http://dx.doi.org/10.1177/1073191106287791

Cunningham, M., & Sorensen, J. (2006b). Nothing to lose? A comparative examination of prison misconduct rates among life-without-parole and other long-term high security inmates. *Criminal Justice and Behavior, 33,* 683–705. Available at: http://dx.doi.org/10.1177/0093854806288273

Cunningham, M., & Sorensen, J. (2007a). Capital offenders in Texas prisons: Rates, correlates, and an actuarial analysis of violent misconduct. *Law and Human Behavior, 31,* 553–571. Available at: http://dx.doi.org/10.1007/s10979-006-9079-z

Cunningham, M., & Sorensen, J. (2007b). Predictive factors for violent misconduct in close custody. *Prison Journal, 87,* 241–253. Available at: http://dx.doi.org/10.1177/0032885507303752

Cunningham, M., Sorensen, J., & Reidy, T. (2005). An actuarial model for assessment of prison violence risk among maximum security inmates. *Assessment, 12,* 40–49. Available at: http://dx.doi.org/10.1177/1073191104272815

Cunningham, M., Sorensen, J., & Reidy, T. (2009). Capital jury decision-making: The limitations of predictions of future violence. *Psychology, Public Policy, and Law, 15,* 223–256. Available at: http://dx.doi.org/10.1037/a0017296

Cunningham, M., Sorensen, J., Vigen, M., & Woods, S. (2011a). Correlates and actuarial models of assaultive prison misconduct among violence-predicted capital offenders. *Criminal Justice and Behavior, 38,* 5–25. Available at: http://dx.doi.org/10.1177/0093854810384830

Cunningham, M., Sorensen, J., Vigen, M., & Woods, S. (2011b). Life and death in the Lone Star State: Three decades of violence predictions by capital juries. *Behavioral Sciences & the Law, 29,* 1–22. Available at: http://dx.doi.org/10.1002/bsl.963

Cunningham, M., & Tassé, M. (2010). Looking to science rather than convention in adjusting IQ scores when death is at issue. *Professional Psychology: Research and Practice, 41,* 413–419. Available at: http://dx.doi.org/10.1037/a0020226

DeMatteo, D., Marczyk, G., Krauss, D., & Burl, J. (2009). Educational and training models in forensic psychology. *Training and Education in Professional Psychology, 3,* 184–191. Available at: http://dx.doi.org/10.1037/a0014582

DeMatteo, D., Marczyk, G., & Pich, M. (2007). A national survey of state legislation defining mental retardation: Implications for policy and practice after *Atkins. Behavioral Sciences and the Law, 25,* 781–802. Available at: http://dx.doi.org/10.1002/bsl.777

DeMatteo, D., Murrie, D., Anumba, N., & Keesler, M. (2011). *Forensic mental health assessments in death penalty cases.* New York: Oxford University Press. Available at: http://dx.doi.org/10.1093/acprof:oso/9780195385809.001.0001

Department of the Army (2010). *Military judge's benchbook.* Washington, DC: United States Army Publishing Directorate.

Dietz, P. (2012). Threat assessment: Workplace. In A. Jamieson and A. A. Moenssens (Eds.), *Wiley encyclopedia of forensic science.* Chichester, UK: John Wiley & Sons. Available at: http://dx.doi.org/10.1002/9780470061589.fsa627

Douglas, K., Robbenolt, J., & Litwack, R. (2013). Assessing violence risk. In I. B. Weiner & R. K. Otto (Eds.), *Handbook of forensic psychology* (4th ed.). Hoboken, NJ: Wiley Press.

Edens, J., Buffington-Vollum, J., Keilen, A., Roskamp, P., & Anthony, C. (2005). Predictions of future dangerousness in capital murder trials: Is it time to "disinvent the wheel"? *Law and Human Behavior, 29,* 55–86. Available at: http://dx.doi.org/10.1007/s10979-005-1399-x

Eke, A. W., & Seto, M. (2008, October). *Examining the criminal history and recidivism of registered child pornography offenders.* Presented at the 27th Annual Association for the Treatment of Sexual Offenders convention, Atlanta, GA.

Emery, R., & Rogers, K. (1990). The role of behavior therapists in child custody cases. In M. Hersen & R. Eisler (Eds.), *Progress in behavior modification* (pp. 60–89). Beverly Hills: Sage.

Endrass, J., Urbaniok, F., Hammermeister, L., Benz, C., Elbert, T., Laubacher, A., & Rossegger, A. (2009). The consumption of Internet child pornography and violent and sex offending. *BMC Psychiatry, 9,* 43–67. Available at: http://dx.doi.org/10.1186/1471-244X-9-43

Endicott, J., & Spitzer, R. L. (1978). A diagnostic interview: The schedule for affective disorders and schizophrenia. *Archives of General Psychiatry, 35,* 837–844.

Everington, C., & Keyes, D. (1999). Mental retardation: Diagnosing intellectual disability in criminal proceedings: The critical importance of documenting adaptive behavior. *Forensic Examiner, July–August,* 31–34.

Everington, C., & Olley, J. (2008). Implications of *Atkins v. Virginia:* Issues in defining and diagnosing mental retardation. *Forensic Psychology Practice, 8,* 1–23. Available at: http://dx.doi.org/10.1080/15228930801947278

Fein, R., Vossekuil, B., Pollack, W., Borum, R., Modzeleski, W., & Reddy, M. (2002). *Threat assessment in schools: A guide to managing threatening situations and to creating safe school climates.* Washington,

DC: U.S. Secret Service and Department of Education.

Ferguson, G., Eidelson, R., & Witt, P. (1998). New Jersey's sex offender risk assessment scale: Preliminary validity data. *Journal of Psychiatry and Law, 26,* 327–351.

Fletcher, R., Loschen, E., Stavrakaki, C., & First, M. (Eds.). (2007). *Diagnostic manual—intellectual disability (DM-ID): A textbook of diagnosis of mental disorders in persons with intellectual disability.* Kingston, NY: NADD Press.

Flynn, J. (1984). The mean IQ of Americans: Massive gains 1932 to 1978. *Psychological Bulletin, 95,* 29–51. Available at: http://dx.doi.org/10.1037/0033-2909.95.1.29

Flynn, J. (1987). Massive IQ gains in 14 nations: What IQ tests really measure. *Psychological Bulletin, 101,* 171–191. Available at: http://dx.doi.org/10.1037/0033-2909.101.2.171

Flynn, J. (1999). Searching for justice: The discovery of IQ gains over time. *American Psychologist, 54,* 5–20. Available at: http://dx.doi.org/10.1037/0003-066X.54.1.5

Flynn, J. (2000). The hidden history of IQ and special education: Can the problems be solved? *Psychology, Public Policy and the Law, 6,* 191–198. Available at: http://dx.doi.org/10.1037/1076-8971.6.1.191

Frederick, R. (2003a). *Validity Indicator Profile manual* (2nd ed.). Minneapolis, MN: Pearson, Inc.

Frederick, R. (2003b). *Validity Indicator Profile (Enhancement and Profile Report).* Minnetonka, MN: Pearson Assessments.

Frederick, R., & Crosby, R. (2000). Development and validation of the Validity Indicator Profile. *Law and Human Behavior, 24,* 59–82. Available at: http://dx.doi.org/10.1023/A:1005426803586

Frederick, R., & Speed, F. (2007). On the interpretation of below-chance responding in forced-choice tests. *Assessment, 14,* 3–11. Available at: http://dx.doi.org/10.1177/1073191106292009

Frumkin, I. B., Lally, S., & Sexton, J. (2012). A United States forensic sample for the Gudjonsson Suggestibility Scales. *Behavioral Sciences and the Law, 30,* 749–763. Available at: http://dx.doi.org/10.1002/bsl.2032

Fuhrmann, G., & Zibbell, R. (2012). *Evaluation for child custody.* New York: Oxford University Press.

Glassman, J. (1998). Preventing and managing board complaints: The downside risk of custody evaluation. *Professional Psychology: Research and Practice, 29,* 121–124. Available at: http://dx.doi.org/10.1037/0735-7028.29.2.121

Golding, S., & Roesch, R. (1988). Competency for adjudication: An international analysis. In D. Weisstub (Ed.), *Law and mental health: International perspectives, Vol. 4* (pp. 73–109). Elmsford, NY: Pergamon Press.

Goldstein, A. (2003). *Handbook of psychology, Volume 11: Forensic psychology.* Hoboken, NJ: John Wiley & Sons, Inc.

Goldstein, A. (Ed.). (2006). *Forensic psychology: Emerging topics and expanding roles.* New York: Wiley.

Goldstein, A., Morse, S., & Shapiro, D. (2003). Evaluation of criminal responsibility. In A. Goldstein & I. Weiner (Eds.), *Handbook of Psychology: Forensic Psychology, Vol. 11* (1st ed.; pp. 381–406). Hoboken, NJ: John Wiley & Sons.

Goldstein, N. E. S., Riggs Romaine, C., Zelle, H., Kalbeitzer, R., Mesiarik, C., & Wolbransky, M. (2011). Psychometric properties of the Miranda Rights Comprehension Instruments with a juvenile justice sample. *Assessment, 18,* 428–441. Available at: http://dx.doi.org/10.1177/1073191111400280

Goldstein, N. E. S., Zelle, H., & Grisso, T. (2012). *Miranda rights comprehension instruments: MRCI.* Sarasota, FL: Professional Resource Press.

Goll, M., Schmitt, G. Ganbmann, B., & Aderjan, R. (2002). Excretion profiles of ethyl glucuronide in human urine after internal dilution. *Journal of Analytical Toxicology, 26,* 262–266. Available at: http://dx.doi.org/10.1093/jat/26.5.262

Goodman-Delahunty, J., & Foote, W. (2011). *Evaluation for workplace discrimination and harassment.* New York: Oxford University Press.

Gottfredson, L. (1997). Why "g" matters: The complexity of everyday life. *Intelligence 24,* 79–132. Available at: http://dx.doi.org/10.1016/S0160-2896(97)90014-3

Gould, J., & Bell, L. (2000). What judges need to know in determining a competent forensic work product. *Juvenile and Family Court Journal, 21*–29. Available at: http://dx.doi.org/10.1111/j.1755-6988.2000.tb00023.x

Graham, J. (2006). *MMPI-2: Assessing personality and psychopathology* (4th ed.). New York: Oxford University Press.

Green, D., Rosenfeld, B., & Belfi, B. (2013). New and improved? A comparison of the original and revised versions of the Structured Interview of Reported Symptoms. *Assessment, 20,* 210–218. Available at: http://dx.doi.org/10.1177/1073191112464389

Greenberg, S., & Shuman, D. (2007). When worlds collide: Therapeutic and forensic roles. *Professional Psychology: Research and Practice, 38,* 129–132. Available at: http://dx.doi.org/10.1037/ 0735-7028.38.2.129

Greene, R. (2012). Malingering and defensiveness on the MMPI-2. In R. Rogers (Ed.), *Clinical assessment of malingering and deception* (3rd ed.; pp. 159–181). New York: The Guilford Press.

Grisso, T. (1986). *Evaluating competencies: Forensic assessments and instruments.* New York: Plenum Publishers.

Grisso, T. (1998a). *Forensic evaluation of juveniles.* Sarasota, FL: Professional Resource Press.

Grisso, T. (1998b). *Instruments for assessing understanding and appreciation of Miranda rights.* Sarasota, FL: Professional Resource Press.

Grisso, T. (2003). *Evaluating competencies: Forensic assessments and instruments* (2nd ed.). New York: Kluwer Academic/Plenum Publishers.

Grisso, T. (2010). Guidance for improving forensic reports: A review of common errors. *Open Access Journal of Forensic Psychology, 2,* 102–115. Retrieved January 6, 2013, from http://works.bepress.com/thomas_grisso/4/.

Grisso, T. (2013). *Forensic evaluation of juveniles* (2nd ed.). Sarasota, FL: Professional Resource Press.

Grisso, T., & Appelbaum, P. S. (1998). *Assessing competence to consent to treatment: A guide for physicians and other health professionals.* New York, NY: Oxford University Press.

Guy, L., & Miller, H. (2004). Screening for malingered psychopathology in a correctional setting: Utility of the Miller-Forensic Assessment of Symptoms Test (M-FAST). *Criminal Justice and Behavior, 31,* 695–716. Available at: http://dx.doi.org/10.1177/0093854804268754

Hagan, L., Drogin, E., & Guilmette, T. (2008). Adjusting IQ scores for the "Flynn Effect": Consistent with the standard of practice? *Professional Psychology: Research and Practice, 39,* 619–625. Available at: http:// dx.doi.org/10.1037/a0012693

Hanson, R. K., & Thornton, D. (2000). Improving risk assessments for sex offenders: A comparison of three actuarial scales. *Law and Human Behavior, 24,* 119–136. Available at: http://dx.doi.org/10.1023/A:1005482921333

Hare, R. (2003). *Manual for the Revised Psychopathy Checklist* (2nd ed.). Toronto, ON: Multi-Health Systems.

Harrison, P., & Oakland T. (2003). *ABAS-II: Adaptive Behavior Assessment System* (2nd ed.). San Antonio, TX: Psychological Corporation.

Haun, J. (April, 2007). Static and dynamic predictors of institutional misconduct and violence among incarcerated adult offenders. Doctoral dissertation, Pacific University, Forest Grove, OR.

Hawkins, J., Herrenkohl, T., Farrington, D., Brewer, D., Catalano, R., Harachi, T., & Cothern, L. (2000, April). Predictors of youth violence. *Juvenile Justice Bulletin,* 1–11. Retrieved January 1, 2014, from https://www.ncjrs.gov/pdffiles1/ojjdp/179065.pdf.

Heber, R., & Dever, R. (1970). Research on education and habilitation of the mentally retarded. In H. C. Haywood (Ed.), *Social-cultural aspect of intellectual disability* (pp. 395–427). New York: Appleton-Century-Crofts.

Heilbronner, R. (2009). Malingering, mental retardation, and the death penalty. In J. E. Morgan & J. J. Sweet

(Eds.), *Neuropsychology of malingering casebook* (pp. 438–454). New York: Psychology Press.

Heilbrun, K. (1992). The role of psychological testing in forensic assessment. *Law and Human Behavior, 16,* 257–272. Available at: http://dx.doi.org/10.1007/BF01044769

Heilbrun, K. (1995). Child custody evaluation: Critically assessing mental health experts and psychological tests. *Family Law Quarterly, 29,* 63–78.

Heilbrun, K. (2001). *Principles of forensic mental health assessment.* New York: Kluwer Academic/Plenum Publishers.

Heilbrun, K., & DeMatteo, D. (2012). Toward establishing standards of practice in juvenile forensic mental health assessment. In E. L. Grigorenko (Ed.), *Handbook of juvenile forensic psychology and psychiatry* (pp. 145–156). New York: Springer. Available at: http://dx.doi.org/10.1007/978-1-4614-0905-2_10

Heilbrun, K., Grisso, T., & Goldstein, A. (2009). *Foundations of forensic mental health assessment.* New York: Oxford University Press.

Heilbrun, K., Marczyk, G., & DeMatteo, D. (2002). *Forensic mental health assessment: A casebook.* New York: Oxford University Press

Heilbrun, K., Warren, J., & Picarello, K. (2003). Third party information in forensic assessment. In A. M. Goldstein & I. B. Weiner (Eds.), *Handbook of psychology: Vol. 11, Forensic psychology* (pp. 69–87). Hoboken, NJ: John Wiley & Sons, Inc.

Heilbrun, K., Yasuhara, K., & Shah, S. (2010). Violence risk assessment tools: Overview and critical analysis. In R. K. Otto & K. Douglas (Eds.), *Handbook of violence risk assessment* (pp. 1–18). New York: Routledge.

Hickson, L., Blackman, L., & Reis, E. (1995). *Mental retardation: Foundations of educational programming.* Boston, MA: Allyn & Bacon.

Hirschi, T., & Gottfredson, M. (1989). Age and the explanation of crime. *American Journal of Sociology, 89,* 552–584. Available at: http://dx.doi.org/10.1086/227905

Hoge, R. (2012). Forensic assessments of juveniles: Practice and legal considerations. *Criminal Justice and Behavior, 39,* 1255–1270. Available at: http://dx.doi.org/10.1177/0093854812444024

Hoge, R., & Andrews, D. (2010). *Evaluation for risk of violence in juveniles.* New York: Oxford University Press.

Howell, J. (Ed.). (1995). *Guide for implementing the comprehensive strategy for serious, violent, and chronic juvenile offenders.* Washington, DC: U.S. Department of Justice. Retrieved January 2, 2014, from https://www.ncjrs.gov/pdffiles/guide.pdf.

Hurley, K., & Deal, W. (2006). Assessment instruments measuring malingering used with individuals who have mental retardation: Potential problems and issues. *Mental Retardation, 44,* 112–119. Available

at: http://dx.doi.org/10.1352/0047-6765(2006)44[112:AIMMUW]2.0.CO;2

Jacobson, J., & Mulick J. (Eds.). (1996). *Manual on diagnosis and professional practice in mental retardation.* Washington, DC: American Psychological Association.

Joint Service Committee on Military Justice (2012). *Manual for courts-martial, United States.* Washington, DC: United States Army Publishing Directorate.

Kelley, B., Thornberry, T., & Smith, C. (1997, Aug). In the wake of childhood maltreatment. *Juvenile Justice Bulletin,* 1–15. Retrieved January 2, 2014, from https://www.ncjrs.gov/pdffiles1/165257.pdf.

Keyes, D., Edwards, J., & Derning, T. (1998). Mitigating intellectual disability in capital cases: Finding the "invisible" defendant. *Mental and Physical Disability Law Reporter, 22,* 529–539.

Krauss, D., & Goldstein, A. (2006). The role of forensic mental health experts in federal sentencing proceedings. In A. Goldstein (Ed.), *Forensic psychology: Emerging topics and expanding roles* (pp. 359–384). Hoboken, NJ: John Wiley & Sons, Inc.

Kuanliang, A., Sorensen, J., & Cunningham, M. (2008). Juvenile offenders in an adult prison system: A comparative examination of rates and correlates of misconduct. *Criminal Justice and Behavior, 35*(9), 1186–1201. Available at: http://dx.doi.org/10.1177/0093854808322744

Kuehnle, K., Sparta, S., Kirkpatrick, H. D., & Epstein, M. (2013). Special issues in forensic assessment of children and adolescents. In D. H. Saklofske, C. Reynolds, & V. L. Schwean (Eds.), *The Oxford handbook of child psychological assessment* (pp. 735–749). New York: Oxford Press. Available at: http://dx.doi.org/10.1093/oxfordhb/9780199796304.013.0032

Kurlychek, M., & Johnson, B. (2010). Juvenility and punishment: Sentencing juveniles in adult criminal court. *Criminology, 48,* 725–758. Available at: http://dx.doi.org/10.1111/j.1745-9125.2010.00200.x

Lakin, K., Prouty, R., & Coucouvanis, K. (2007). HCBS recipients are increasingly likely to live with parents or other relatives. *Intellectual and Developmental Disabilities, 45,* 359–361. Available at: http://dx.doi.org/10.1352/0047-6765(2007)45[359:HRAILT]2.0.CO;2

Lally, S. (2003). What tests are acceptable for use in forensic evaluations? A survey of experts. *Professional Psychology: Research & Practice, 34,* 491–498. Available at: http://dx.doi.org/10.1037/0735-7028.34.5.491

Lamb, D., Berry, D., Wetter, M., & Baer, R. (1994). Effects of two types of information on malingering of closed head injury on the MMPI-2: An analog investigation. *Psychological Assessment, 6,* 8–11. Available at: http://dx.doi.org/10.1037/1040-3590.6.1.8

Lamb, M., Hershkowitz, I., Orbach, Y., & Esplin, P. (2008). *Tell me what happened: Structured investigative interviews of child victims and witnesses.* Chichester, UK, and Hoboken, NJ: Wiley. Available at: http://dx.doi.org/10.1002/9780470773291

Lamb, M., Orbach, Y., Hershkowitz, I., Esplin, P., & Horowitz, D. (2007). A structured forensic interview protocol improves the quality and informativeness of investigative interviews with children: A review of research using the NICHD Investigative Interview Protocol. *Child Abuse and Neglect, 31,* 1201–1231. Available at: http://dx.doi.org/10.1016/j.chiabu.2007.03.021

Lander, T., & Heilbrun, K. (2009). The content and quality of forensic mental health assessment: Validation of a principles-based approach. *International Journal of Forensic Mental Health, 8,* 115–121. Available at: http://dx.doi.org/10.1080/14999010903199324

Lee, A., Li, N., Lamade, R., Schuler, A., & Prentky, R. A. (2012). Predicting hands-on child sexual offenses among possessors of internet child pornography. *Psychology, Public Policy, and Law. 18,* 644–672. Available at: http://dx.doi.org/10.1037/a0027517

Macvaugh, G., & Cunningham, M. (2009). *Atkins v. Virginia*: Implications and recommendations for forensic practice. *Journal of Psychiatry and Law, 37,* 131–187.

Marquart, J., Ekland-Olson, S., & Sorensen, J. (1989). Gazing into the crystal ball: Can jurors accurately predict dangerousness in capital cases? *Law & Society Review, 23,* 449–468. Available at: http://dx.doi.org/10.2307/3053829

Masten, A., & Garmezy, N. (1985). Risk, vulnerability, and protective factors in developmental psychopathology. In B. Lahey (Ed.), *Advances in clinical child psychology, Vol. 8* (pp. 1–52). New York: Plenum Press. Available at: http://dx.doi.org/10.1007/978-1-4613-9820-2_1

McLaren, J., & Bryson S. (1987). Review of recent epidemiological studies of intellectual disability: Prevalence, associated disorders, and etiology. *American Journal on Intellectual Disability, 92,* 243–254.

Melton, G., Petrila, J., Poythress, N., & Slobogin, C. (2007). *Psychological evaluations for the courts: A handbook for mental health professionals and lawyers* (3rd ed.). New York: Guilford Press.

Miller, H. (2001). *Miller-Forensic Assessment of Symptoms Test (M-FAST): Professional manual.* Odessa, FL: Psychological Assessment Resources.

Miller, H. (2005). The Miller-Forensic Assessment of Symptoms Test (M-FAST): Test generalizability and utility across race, literacy, and clinical opinion. *Criminal Justice and Behavior, 32,* 591–611. Available at: http://dx.doi.org/10.1177/0093854805278805

Millon, T. (1994). *Millon Clinical Multiaxial Inventory-III manual.* Minneapolis, MN: National Computer Systems.

Monahan, J., & Steadman, H. J. (1994). *Violence and mental disorder: Developments in risk assessment.* Chicago, IL: The University of Chicago Press.

Morey, L. (1991). *Personality Assessment Inventory professional manual.* Odessa, FL: Psychological Assessment Resources.

Morey, L. (2007). *Personality Assessment Inventory professional manual* (2nd ed.). Odessa, FL: Professional Assessment Resources.

Morse, S. (1978). Crazy behavior, morals, and science: An analysis of mental health law. *Southern California Law Review, 51,* 527–654.

Morse, S. (1999). Crazy reasons. *Journal of Contemporary Legal Issues, 10,* 189–226.

Neisser, U., Boodoo, G., Bouchard, T., Boykin, A., Brody, N., Ceci, S., et al. (1996). Intelligence: Knowns and unknowns. *American Psychologist, 51,* 77–101. Available at: http://dx.doi.org/10.1037/0003-066X.51.2.77

Nekvasil, E., & Cornell, D. (2012). Student reports of peer threats of violence: Prevalence and outcomes. *Journal of School Violence, 11,* 357–375. Available at: http://dx.doi.org/10.1080/15388220.2012.706764

Nurcombe, B., & Gallagher, R. (1986). *The clinical process in psychiatry.* Cambridge, England: Cambridge University Press.

O'Toole, M. E. (2000). *The school shooter: A threat assessment perspective.* Quantico, VA: National Center for the Analysis of Violent Crime, Federal Bureau of Investigation. Retrieved January 1, 2014, from http://www.fbi.gov/stats-services/publications/school-shooter

O'Grady, R., & Talkington, L. (1977). Selected behavioral concomitants of profound retardation. In C. Cleland, J. Swartz, & L. Talkington (Eds.), *The profoundly mentally retarded, Vol. II.* Austin, TX: Western Research Conference.

Olley, J. (2010). The death penalty, the courts, and what we have learned about intellectual disability. *Psychology in Intellectual and Developmental Disabilities, 36,* 2–5.

Olley, J., & Cox, A. W. (2008). Assessment of adaptive behavior in adult forensic cases: The use of the ABAS-II. In T. Oakland & P. L. Harrison (Eds.), *Adaptive Behavior Assessment System-II: Clinical use and interpretation* (pp. 381–398). San Diego: Elsevier. Available at: http://dx.doi.org/10.1016/B978-012373586-7.00020-5

Otto, R. K. (2012). Challenges and advances in assessment of response style in forensic examination contexts. In R. Rogers (Ed.), *Clinical assessment of malingering and deception* (3rd ed.; pp. 365–375). New York: The Guilford Press.

Otto, R. K., & Goldstein, A. (2005). Juveniles' competence to confess and competence to participate in the juvenile justice process. In K. Heilbrun,

N. E. S. Goldstein, & R. E. Redding (Eds.), *Juvenile delinquency: Prevention, assessment, and intervention* (pp. 179–208). New York: Oxford University Press.

Otto, R. K., & Heilbrun, K. (2002). The practice of forensic psychology: A look toward the future in light of the past. *American Psychologist: 57*, 5–18. Available at: http://dx.doi.org/10.1037/0003-066X.57.1.5

Otto, R. K., Musick, J., & Sherrod, C. (2010). *Manual for the Inventory of Legal Knowledge.* Odessa, FL: Psychological Assessment Resources, Inc.

Otto, R. K., Slobogin, C., & Greenberg, S. (2006). Legal and ethical issues in accessing and utilizing third-party information. In A. Goldstein (Ed.), *Forensic psychology: Emerging topics and expanding roles* (pp. 190–208). Hoboken, NJ: John Wiley & Sons.

Packer, I. K., & Grisso, T. (2011). *Specialty competencies in forensic psychology.* New York: Oxford University Press.

Petrella, R., & Poythress, N. (1983). The quality of forensic evaluations: An interdisciplinary study. *Journal of Consulting and Clinical Psychology, 51,* 76–85. Available at: http://dx.doi.org/10.1037/0022-006X.51.1.76

Pfohl, B., Blum, N., & Zimmerman, M. (1997). *Structured Interview for DSM-IV Personality (SIDP-IV).* Arlington, VA: American Psychiatric Publishing.

Pickar, D. (2007). On being a child custody evaluator: Professional and personal challenges, risks, and rewards. *Family Court Review, 45,* 103–115. Available at: http://dx.doi.org/10.1111/j.1744-1617.2007.00131.x

Piechowski, L. (2011). *Evaluation of workplace disability.* New York: Oxford.

Pinals, D., & Mossman, D. (2012). *Evaluation for civil commitment.* New York: Oxford.

Quinsey, V., Harris, G., Rice, M., & Cormier, C. (1998). *Violent offenders: Appraising and managing violence risk.* Washington, DC: American Psychological Association. Available at: http://dx.doi.org/10.1037/10304-000

Quinsey, V., Harris, G., Rice, M., & Cormier, C. (2006). *Violent offenders: Appraising and managing violence risk* (2nd ed.). Washington, DC: American Psychological Association. Available at: http://dx.doi.org/10.1037/11367-000

Reddy, M., Borum, R., Berglund, J., Vossekuil, B., Fein, R., & Modzeleski, W. (2001). Evaluating risk for targeted violence in schools: Comparing risk assessment, threat assessment, and other approaches. *Psychology in the Schools, 38,* 157–172. Available at: http://dx.doi.org/10.1002/pits.1007

Reidy, T., Sorensen, J., & Cunningham, M. (2012). Community violence to prison assault: A test of the behavior continuity hypothesis. *Law and Human Behavior, 36,* 356–363. Available at: http://dx.doi.org/10.1037/h0093934

Reidy, T., Sorensen, J., & Cunningham, M. (2013). Probability of criminal acts of violence: A test of jury predictive accuracy. *Behavioral Sciences and the Law, 31,* 286–305. Available at: http://dx.doi.org/10.1002/bsl.2064

Reschly, D., Myers, T., & Hartel, C. (Eds.). (2002). *Intellectual disability.* National Academy Press: Washington, DC.

Rogers, R. (1984). Towards an empirical model of malingering and deception. *Behavioral Sciences and the Law, 2,* 93–112. Available at: http://dx.doi.org/10.1002/bsl.2370020109

Rogers, R. (1992). *Structured Interview of Reported Symptoms.* Odessa, FL: Psychological Assessment Resources.

Rogers, R. (1997). *Clinical assessment of malingering and deception* (2nd ed.). New York: The Guilford Press.

Rogers, R. (2008a). *Clinical assessment of malingering and deception* (3rd ed.). New York: The Guilford Press.

Rogers, R. (2008b). An introduction to response styles. In R. Rogers (Ed.), *Clinical assessment of malingering and deception* (3rd ed.; pp. 3–13). New York: The Guilford Press.

Rogers, R. (2008c). Detection strategies for malingering and defensiveness. In R. Rogers (Ed.), *Clinical assessment of malingering and deception* (3rd ed.; pp. 14–35). New York: The Guilford Press.

Rogers, R., Bagby, R., & Chakraborty, D. (1993). Faking schizophrenic disorders on the MMPI-2: Detection of coached simulators. *Journal of Personality Assessment, 60,* 215–226. Available at: http://dx.doi.org/10.1207/s15327752jpa6002_1

Rogers, R., & Bender, S. (2003). Evaluation of malingering and deception. In A. Goldstein & I. B. Weiner (Eds.), *Handbook of psychology: Vol. 11, Forensic psychology* (pp. 109–129). Hoboken, NJ: John Wiley & Sons.

Rogers, R., & Ewing, C. P. (1989). Ultimate opinion proscriptions: A cosmetic fix and a plea for empiricism. *Law and Human Behavior, 13,* 357–374. Available at: http://dx.doi.org/10.1007/BF01056408

Rogers, R., Sewell, K., & Gillard, N. (2011). *Structured Interview of Reported Symptoms, 2nd Edition.* Odessa, FL: Psychological Assessment Resources, Inc.

Rogers, R., Sewell, K., Drogin, E., & Fiduccia, C. (2013). *Standardized assessment of Miranda abilities.* Lutz, FL: Professional Assessment Resources.

Rogers, R., & Shuman, D. (2000). *Conducting insanity evaluations* (2nd ed.). New York: The Guilford Press.

Roid, G. H. (2003). *SB-5: Stanford-Binet Intelligence Scales–Fifth Edition.* Austin, TX: Pro-Ed.

Rosenthal, P. (1983). Nature of jury responses to expert witness. *Journal of Forensic Sciences, 28,* 528–532.

Rubenzer, S. (2010). Review of the Structured Inventory of Reported Symptoms–2 (SIRS-2). *Open Access Journal of Forensic Psychology, 2,* 273–286. Retrieved

February 10, 2013, from http://www.forensicpsychologyunbound.ws/OAJFP/Volume_2__2010_files/Rubenzer2%202010.pdf.

Salekin, K., & Doane, B. (2009). Malingering intellectual disability: The value of available measures and methods. *Applied Neuropsychology, 16*, 105–113. Available at: http://dx.doi.org/10.1080/09084280902864485

Salekin, K., & Olley, G. (2008). Intellectual disability. *Encyclopedia of forensic science*. Indianapolis, IN: Wiley Publications.

Sandys, M., Pruss, H., & Walsh, S. (2009). Aggravation and mitigation: Findings and implications. *Journal of Psychiatry and Law, 37*, 189–235.

Seto, M. (2008). *Pedophilia and sexual offending against children*. Washington, DC: American Psychological Association. Available at: http://dx.doi.org/10.1037/11639-000

Skeem, J., & Golding, S. (1998). Community examiners' evaluations of competence to stand trial: Common problems and suggestions for improvement. *Professional Psychology: Research and Practice, 29*, 357–367. Available at: http://dx.doi.org/10.1037/0735-7028.29.4.357

Sellbom, M., & Bagby, R. M. (2012). Response styles on multiscale inventories. In R. Rogers (Ed.), *Clinical assessment of malingering and deception* (3rd ed.; pp. 182–206). New York: The Guilford Press.

Shuman, D., Champagne, A., & Whitaker, E. (1996). Juror assessments of the believability of expert witnesses: A literature review. *Jurimetrics, 36*, 371–382.

Shuman, D., Greenberg, S., Heilbrun, K., & Foote, W. (1998). Special perspective, an immodest proposal: Should treating mental health professionals be barred from testifying about their patients? *Behavioral Sciences and the Law, 16*, 509–523. Available at: http://dx.doi.org/10.1002/(SICI)1099-0798(199823)16:4<509::AID-BSL324>3.0.CO;2-Y

Slobogin, C., Rai, A., & Reisner, R. (2009). *Law and the mental health system: Civil and criminal aspects* (5th ed.). St. Paul, MN: Thomson/West.

Sorensen, J., & Cunningham, M. (2009). Once a killer always a killer? Prison misconduct of former death-sentenced inmates in Arizona. *Journal of Psychiatry and Law, 37*, 237–267.

Sorensen, J., & Cunningham, M. (2010). Conviction offense and prison violence: A comparative study of murderers and other offenders. *Crime & Delinquency, 56*, 103–125. Available at: http://dx.doi.org/10.1177/0011128707307175

Sorensen, J., & Pilgrim, R. (2000). An actuarial risk assessment of violence posed by capital murder defendants. *Journal of Criminal Law and Criminology, 90*, 1251–1270. Available at: http://dx.doi.org/10.2307/1144202

Sparrow S., Balla, D., & Cicchetti, D. (2005). *Vineland Adaptive Behavior Scales–II*. Minneapolis: Pearson Assessments.

Stahl, P. (2011). *Conducting child custody evaluations: From basic to complex issues*. Thousand Oaks, CA: Sage Publications, Inc. Available at: http://dx.doi.org/10.4135/9781452275222

Strachan, A., Lund, M., & Garcia, J. (2010). Assessing children's perceptions of family relationships: An interactive instrument for use in custody disputes. *Journal of Child Custody, 7*, 192–216. Available at: http://dx.doi.org/10.1080/15379418.2010.512236

Thames, H. (1994). *Frye gone, but not forgotten in the wake of Daubert*: New standards and procedures for admissibility of scientific expert opinion. *Mississippi Law Journal, 63*, 484–485.

Thornberry, T. (1994). *Violent families and youth violence*. National Criminal Justice Resources and Statistics, U.S. Department of Justice. Retrieved January 2, 2014, from: https://www.ncjrs.gov/txtfiles/fs-9421.txt.

Thornberry, T., Smith, C., Rivera, C., Huizinga, D., & Stouthamer-Loeber, M. (1999). *Juvenile Justice Bulletin: Family disruption and delinquency*. Washington, DC: U.S. Department of Justice. Retrieved January 1, 2014, from https://www.ncjrs.gov/pdffiles1/ojjdp/178285.pdf.

Tillbrook, C., Mumley, D., & Grisso, T. (2003). Avoiding expert opinions on the ultimate legal question: The case for integrity. *Journal of Forensic Psychology Practice, 3*, 77–87. Available at: http://dx.doi.org/10.1300/J158v03n03_05

Tombaugh, T. (1997). The Test of Memory Malingering (TOMM): Normative data form cognitively intact and cognitively impaired individuals. *Psychological Assessment, 9*, 260–268. Available at: http://dx.doi.org/10.1037/1040-3590.9.3.260

Tolman, A., & Mullendore, K. (2003). Risk evaluations for the courts: Is service quality a function of specialization? *Professional Psychology: Research and Practice, 34*, 225–232. Available at: http://dx.doi.org/10.1037/0735-7028.34.3.225

Vant Zelfde, G., & Otto. R. (1997). *Directory of practicum, internship, and fellowship training opportunities in clinical-forensic psychology*. Pittsburgh, PA: American Academy o Forensic Psychology.

Varga, A., Hansson, P., Johnson, G., & Alling, C. (2000). Normalization rate and cellular localization of phosphatidyl ethanol in whole blood from chronic alcoholics. *Clinical Chimica Acta, 299*, 141–150. Available at: http://dx.doi.org/10.1016/S0009-8981(00)00291-6

Varga, A., Hansson, P., Lindqvist, C., & Alling, C. (1998). Phosphatidylethanol as a blood marker of ethanol consumption in healthy volunteers: Comparison with other markers. *Alcoholism: Clinical and Experimental Research, 22*, 1832–1837. Available

at: http://dx.doi.org/10.1111/j.1530-0277.1998.
tb03989.x

Viljoen, J., McLachlan, K., & Vincent, G. (2010). Assessing violence risk and psychopathy in juvenile and adult offenders: A survey of clinical practices. *Assessment, 17*, 377–395. Available at: http://dx.doi.org/10.1177/1073191109359587

Vitacco, M. (2008). Syndromes associated with deception. In R. Rogers (Ed.), *Clinical assessment of malingering and deception* (3rd ed.; pp. 39–50). New York: Guilford Publications.

Vossekuil, B., Fein, R., Reddy, M., Borum, R., & Modzeleski, W. (2002). *The final report and findings of the Safe School Initiative: Implications for the prevention of school attacks in the United States.* Washington, DC: U.S. Secret Service and U.S. Department of Education.

Webster, C., Douglas, K., Eaves, D., & Hart, S. (1997). *HCR-20: Assessing risk for violence, Version 2.* Burnaby, BC, Canada: Simon Fraser University.

Wechsler, D. (2003). *The Wechsler Intelligence Scale for Children—4th Edition.* San Antonio, TX: Pearson Publishing.

Wechsler, D. (2008). *The Wechsler Adult Intelligence Scale—4th Edition.* San Antonio, TX: Pearson Publishing.

Weiner, I. B., & Hess, A. K. (2006). *The handbook of forensic psychology.* Hoboken, NJ: John Wiley & Sons, Inc.

Weissman, H., & DeBow, D. (2003). Ethical principles and professional competencies. In A. M. Goldstein & I. B. Weiner (Eds.), *Handbook of psychology: Vol. 11, Forensic psychology* (pp. 33–54). Hoboken, NJ: John Wiley & Sons, Inc.

Wetter, M., Baer, R., Berry, D., Robison, L., & Sumpter, J. (1993). MMPI-2 profiles of motivated fakers given specific symptom information: A comparison to matched patients. *Psychological Assessment, 5*, 317–323. Available at: http://dx.doi.org/10.1037/1040-3590.5.3.317

Wettstein, R. (2005). Quantity and quality improvement in forensic mental health evaluations. *Journal of the American Academy of Psychiatry and the Law, 33*, 158–177.

Widom, C. (2000). Childhood victimization: Early adversity, later psychopathology. *National Institute of Justice Journal, 3–9.* Retrieved January 2, 2014, from https://www.ncjrs.gov/pdffiles1/jr000242b.pdf.

Wilkinson, G., & Robertson, G. (2006). *Wide Range Achievement Test—Fourth Edition.* Lutz, FL: Psychological Assessment Resources.

Witt, P. (2010). Assessment of risk in child pornography cases. *Sex Offender Law Report, 11*, 1, 4, 13–15.

Witt, P., & Barone, N. (2004). Sex offender risk assessment: New Jersey's methods. *Federal Sentencing Reporter, 16*, 170–175. Available at: http://dx.doi.org/10.1525/fsr.2004.16.3.170

Witt, P., DelRusso, J., Oppenheim, J., & Ferguson, G. (1996). Sex offender risk assessment and the law. *Journal of Psychiatry and Law, 24*, 343–377.

Wurst, F., Kempter, C., Seidl, S., & Alt, A. (1999). Ethyl glucuronide: A marker of alcohol consumption and a relapse marker with clinical and forensic implications. *Alcohol & Alcoholism, 34*, 71–77. Available at: http://dx.doi.org/10.1093/alcalc/34.1.71

Zapf, P. (2008). Competency for execution. In R. Jackson (Ed.), *Learning forensic assessment* (pp. 239–261). Mahwah, NJ: Lawrence Erlbaum.

Zapf, P. (2009). Elucidating the contours of competency for execution: The implications of *Ford* and *Panetti* for the assessment of CFE. *Journal of Psychiatry and Law, 37*, 269–307.

Zapf, P., Boccaccini, M., & Brodsky, S. (2003). Assessment of competency for execution: Professional guidelines and an evaluation checklist. *Behavioral Sciences and the Law, 21*, 103–120. Available at: http://dx.doi.org/10.1002/bsl.491

Zapf, P., & Roesch, R. (2009). *Evaluation of competency to stand trial.* New York: Oxford.

CASES

Abdul-Kabir v. Quarterman, 127 S. Ct. 1654 (2007).

Adam Walsh Child Protection and Safety Act of 2006, H.R. 4472, 109th Cong., 2nd Sess. (2006).

Ake v. Oklahoma, 470 U.S. 68 (1985).

Atkins v. Virginia, 536 U.S. 304 (2002).

Burger v. Kemp, 483 U.S. 776 (1987).

California v. Brown, 479 U.S. 538 (1987).

Coker v. Georgia, 433 U.S. 584 (1977).

Colorado v. Connelly, 479 U.S. 157 (1986).

Daubert v. Merrell Dow Pharmaceuticals, Inc., 509 U.S. 579 (1993).

Dusky v. United States, 362 U.S. 402 (1960).

Estelle v. Smith, 451 U.S. 454 (1981).

Federal Rules of Evidence 401, 402, 403, 702, 703, 704, 705 (2007).

Ford v. Wainwright, 477 U.S. 399 (1986).

Foucha v. Louisiana, 504 U.S. 71 (1992).

Frye v. United States, 293 F. 1013 (D.C. Cir. 1923).

General Electric Co. v. Joiner, 522 U.S. 136 (1997).

Graham v. Collins, 113 S.Ct. 892 (1993).

Green v. Johnson, 515 F.3d 290 (4th Cir. 2008).

In the Matter of Registrant PB (July 26, 2012) NJ App. Div., slip decision.

Insanity Defense Reform Act (1984). Pub. L. 98-473, 18 U.S.C. 401–406.

Jenkins v. United States, 307 F.2d 637 (1962).

Kansas v. Hendricks, 521 U.S. 346 (1997).

Kumho Tire Co. v. Carmichael, 526 U.S. 137 (1999).

Lawlor v. Commonwealth, 738 S.E.2d 847 (Va. 2013).

Lockett v. Ohio, 438 U.S. 586 (1978).

Miller v. State, 496 N.E.2d 1297 (Ind. 1986).

Miranda v. Arizona, 384 U.S. 436 (1966).

Neal v. Texas, 256 S.W.3d 264 (Tex. Crim. App. 2008).

Panetti v. Quarterman, 551 U.S. 930 (2007).

Parham v. J. R., 442 U.S. 584 (1979).

Payne v. Tennessee, 501 U.S. 808 (1991).

Penry v. Johnson, 532 U.S. 782 (2001).

Penry v. Lynaugh, 492 U.S. 302 (1989).

People v. Goldstein, 843 N.E.2d 727 (N.Y. 2005).

Rhode Island v. Innis, 446 U.S. 291 (1980).

Roper v. Simmons, 543 U.S. 551 (2005).

Skipper v. South Carolina, 476 U.S. 1 (1986).

South Carolina v. Gathers, 490 U.S. 805 (1989).

United States ex. rel. *Edney v. Smith*, 425 F.Supp. 1038 (E.D.N.Y. 1976), aff'd, 556 F.2d 556 (2d Cir. 1977)

United States v. Alvarez, 519 F.2d 1036 (3rd Cir. 1975).

United States v. Benedict, 27 M.J. 253 (C.M.A. 1988).

United States v. Booker, 543 U.S. 220 (2005).

United States v. Green, 548 F.2d 1261 (6th Cir. 1977).

United States v. Proctor, 37 M.J. 330, 336 (C.M.A. 1993).

United States v. Toledo, 25 M.J. 270, 275-76 (C.M.A. 1987).

United States v. Toledo, 26 M.J. 104, 105 (C.M.A. 1988).

United States v. Velasquez, 885 F.2d 1076 (1989).

Wiggins v. Smith, 539 U.S. 510 (2003).

Wilson v. Lynaugh, 878 F.2d 846, 850 (5th Cir. 1988).

Woodson v. North Carolina, 428 U.S. 280 (1976).

INDEX